T0322051

Research Anthology on Edge Computing Protocols, Applications, and Integration

Information Resources Management Association
USA

IGI Global
PUBLISHER of TIMELY KNOWLEDGE

Published in the United States of America by
IGI Global
Engineering Science Reference (an imprint of IGI Global)
701 E. Chocolate Avenue
Hershey PA, USA 17033
Tel: 717-533-8845
Fax: 717-533-8661
E-mail: cust@igi-global.com
Web site: http://www.igi-global.com

Library of Congress Cataloging-in-Publication Data

Names: Information Resources Management Association, editor.
Title: Research anthology on edge computing protocols, applications, and
  integration / Information Resources Management Association, editor.
Description: Hershey, PA : Engineering Science Reference, an imprint of IGI
  Global, [2022] | Includes bibliographical references and index. |
  Summary: "This book provides critical research on the current uses,
  innovations, and challenges of edge computing across disciplines,
  highlighting the history of edge computing and how it has been adapted
  over time to improve industries by covering a range of topics such as
  bandwidth, data centers, and security,"-- Provided by publisher.
Identifiers: LCCN 2022007814 (print) | LCCN 2022007815 (ebook) | ISBN
  9781668457009 (h/c) | ISBN 9781668457016 (ebook)
Subjects: LCSH: Edge computing.
Classification: LCC QA76.583 .R43 2022 (print) | LCC QA76.583 (ebook) |
  DDC 005.758--dc23/eng/20220427
LC record available at https://lccn.loc.gov/2022007814
LC ebook record available at https://lccn.loc.gov/2022007815

British Cataloguing in Publication Data
A Cataloguing in Publication record for this book is available from the British Library.

The views expressed in this book are those of the authors, but not necessarily of the publisher.

For electronic access to this publication, please contact: eresources@igi-global.com.

List of Contributors

Table of Contents

Section 1
Architectures, Infrastructures, and Frameworks

Section 2
Challenges, Security Issues, and Solutions

Section 3
Uses and Applications

Preface

Edge computing is an innovative technology that continues to expand and develop as more companies across various industries apply it to their practices. As edge computing grows in popularity, it is important to consider the benefits the technology provides as well as the future opportunities that have yet to be discovered. Further study on the challenges this technology faces as well as on potential solutions for these problems is necessary for edge computing to continue to improve and businesses to prosper.

Thus, the *Research Anthology on Edge Computing Protocols, Applications, and Integration* seeks to fill the void for an all-encompassing and comprehensive reference book covering the latest and emerging research, concepts, and theories for those hoping to utilize edge computing in their businesses. This one-volume reference collection of reprinted IGI Global book chapters and journal articles that have been handpicked by the editor and editorial team of this research anthology on this topic will empower industry professionals, computer scientists, engineers, practitioners, researchers, academicians, scholars, instructors, and students with an advanced understanding of the critical issues and advancements of edge computing across disciplines.

The *Research Anthology on Edge Computing Protocols, Applications, and Integration* is organized into three sections that provide comprehensive coverage of important topics. The sections are:

1. Architectures, Infrastructures, and Frameworks;
2. Challenges, Security Issues, and Solutions; and
3. Uses and Applications.

The following paragraphs provide a summary of what to expect from this invaluable reference tool.

Section 1, "Architectures, Infrastructures, and Frameworks," overviews edge computing while providing research on the various frameworks and structures associated with the technology. The first chapter in this section, "Overview of Edge Computing and Its Exploring Characteristics," by Prof. Sangamithra A. from VIT University, India; Prof. Margaret Mary T. of Kristu Jayanti College, India; and Prof. Clinton G. from Sambharm Institute of Technology, India, introduces the origin of the edge paradigm as well as an overview of its benefits. Another opening chapter, "A Comprehensive Survey of IoT Edge/Fog Computing Protocols," by Profs. Madhumathi R., Dharshana R., and Kalaiyarasi N. from Sri Ramakrishna Engineering College, India and Prof. Reshma Sulthana from Coimbatore Institute of Technology, India, conveys how various protocols contribute immensely to the intended success of fog computing and analytics in the days ahead. The next chapter, "Edge Architecture Integration of Technologies," by Prof. Sandhya Devi R. S. from Kumaraguru College of Technology, India; Prof. Vijaykumar V. R. of Anna University, Coimbatore, India; and Profs. Sivakumar P., Neeraja Lakshmi

A., and Vinoth Kumar B. from PSG College of Technology, India, discusses edge computing architecture along with the various components that constitute the computing platform. Another chapter in this section, "Recent Advances in Edge Computing Paradigms: Taxonomy Benchmarks and Standards for Unconventional Computing," by Prof. Sam Goundar from the British University, Vietnam and Profs. Hewan Shrestha, Sana Sodanapalli, Chandramohan Dhasarathan, and Puviyarasi T. of Madanapalle Institute of Technology and Science, India, addresses new research challenges in the IoT paradigm and the design of highly-efficient communication technology with minimum cost and effort. The following chapter, "Distributed Intelligence Platform to the Edge Computing," by Prof. Xalphonse Inbaraj from PACE Institute of Technology and Sciences, India, discusses the main differences between edge, fog, and cloud computing as well as their pros and cons and various applications. An additional chapter, "Deep Learning With Analytics on Edge," by Prof. Kavita Srivastava from the Institute of Information Technology and Management, GGSIP University, India, contains information about various deep learning frameworks, hardware, and systems for edge computing and examples of deep neural network training using the Caffe 2 framework. The next chapter, "Deep Learning on Edge: Challenges and Trends," by Prof. Mário P. Véstias from INESC-ID, ISEL, Instituto Politécnico de Lisboa, Portugal, reviews several aspects of deep learning such as applications, deep learning models, and computing platforms. Another chapter in this section, "PrEstoCloud: A Novel Framework for Data-Intensive Multi-Cloud, Fog, and Edge Function-as-a-Service Applications," by Profs. Gregoris Mentzas, Nikos Papageorgiou, Andreas Tsagkaropoulos, and Fotis Paraskevopoulos from the National Technical University of Athens, Greece; Prof. Yiannis Verginadis from Athens University of Economics and Business, Greece; Prof. Dimitris Apostolou of the University of Piraeus, Greece; Dr. Salman Taherizadeh from Joseph Stefan Institute, Slovenia; and Dr. Ioannis Ledakis of Ubitech, Greece, reviews prominent fog computing frameworks, discusses some of the challenges and requirements of FaaS-enabled applications, and proposes a novel framework able to dynamically manage multi-cloud, fog, and edge resources. The next chapter, "Edge Cloud: The Future Technology for Internet of Things," by Prof. Lucia Agnes Beena Thomas from St. Joseph's College, India, considers the features of edge cloud, the driving industries that are providing solutions, and the use cases, benefits, and the challenges of edge cloud. A closing chapter, "Innovative Concepts and Techniques of Data Analytics in Edge Computing Paradigms," by Profs. Margaret Mary T. and Soumya K. from Kristu Jayanti College, India and Prof. Clinton G. from Sambhram Institute of Technology, India, considers how cloud computing has revolutionized how people store and use their data and the areas where cloud is limited such as latency, bandwidth, security, and a lack of offline access. The next chapter, "Expounding the Edge/Fog Computing Infrastructures for Data Science," by Dr. Pethuru Raj from Reliance Jio Infocomm. Ltd., India and Prof. Pushpa J. of Jain University, India, discusses how to accomplish real-time analytics on fog devices data. Another chapter, "Game Theory for Cooperation in Multi-Access Edge Computing," by Profs. Jose Moura, Rui Neto Marinheiro, and Joao Carlos Silva from Instituto Universitário de Lisboa, Portugal, discusses relevant theoretical models that enable cooperation amongst players in distinct ways through pricing or reputation and highlights open problems, such as the lack of proper models for dynamic and incomplete information scenarios. Another closing chapter, "Lightweight Virtualization for Edge Computing," by Prof. Fabio Diniz Rossi from IFFar, Brazil and Profs. Bruno Morais Neves de Castro and Matheus Breno Batista dos Santos of IFB, Brazil, conveys current concepts, techniques, and open challenges of lightweight virtualization for edge computing. The next chapter, "Edge-of-Things Computing-Based Smart Healthcare System," by Prof. Diana Yacchirema from Escuela Politécnica Nacional, Ecuador and Profs. Carlos Palau and Manuel Esteve of the Universitat Politècnica de València, Spain, proposes an edge-of-things computing-based architecture, which illustrates the benefits of the realization of IoT under an edge computing approach. The final chapter in this section, "Opportunistic Edge Computing Architecture for Smart Healthcare Systems," by Profs. Nivethitha V. and Aghila G. from the National Institute of Technology, Puducherry, India, introduces an opportunistic edge computing architecture for smart provisioning of healthcare data.

Section 2, "Challenges, Security Issues, and Solutions," discusses the difficulties faced when implementing edge computing into industries and considers strategies to avoid and solve these issues. Furthermore, it considers security issues in edge computing. The first chapter in this section, "A Novel Approach to Location-Aware Scheduling of Workflows Over Edge Computing Resources," by Prof. Yin Li from the Institute of Software Application Technology, Guangzhou, China & Chinese Academy of Sciences, Guangzhou, China; Prof. Yuyin Ma of Chongqing University, China; and Prof. Ziyang Zeng from Chonqing University, China, proposes a novel approach to location-aware and proximity-constrained multi-workflow scheduling with edge computing resources. The next chapter, "Mobile Edge Computing: Cost-Efficient Content Delivery in Resource-Constrained Mobile Computing Environment," by Prof. Camilius A. Sanga from Sokoine University of Agriculture, Morogoro, Tanzania; Prof. Michael P. J. Mahenge of the Wuhan University of Technology, China & Sokoine University of Agriculture, Morogoro, Tanzania; and Prof. Chunlin Li from the Wuhan University of Technology, Wuhan, China, attempts to find out the cost-efficient design that maximizes resource utilization at the edge of the mobile network and proposes cooperative mobile edge computing. Another chapter, "Bridging the IoT Gap Through Edge Computing," by Prof. G. Nagarajan from Sathyabama Institute of Science and Technology, India and Prof. R. I. Minu of SRM Institute of Science and Technology, India, provides an insight into how the internet of things (IoT) connects with edge computing. The following chapter, "Edge Computing: A Review on Computation Offloading and Light Weight Virtualization for IoT Framework," by Prof. Minal Parimalbhai Patel from A. D. Patel Institute of Technology, Gujarat Technological University, Gujarat, India and Prof. Sanjay Chaudhary of Ahmedabad University, Gujarat, India, provides a discussion on computation offloading and the importance of docker-based containers, known as light-weight virtualization, to improve the performance of edge computing systems. Another chapter in this section, "Probabilistic-QoS-Aware Multi-Workflow Scheduling Upon the Edge Computing Resources," by Profs. Tao Tang, Yuyin Ma, and Wenjiang Feng from Chongqing University, China, conducts an experimental case study based on varying types of workflow process models and a real-world dataset for edge server positions. A closing chapter in this section, "Resource Allocation Scheduling Algorithm Based on Incomplete Information Dynamic Game for Edge Computing," by Prof. Bo Wang from the Dalian University of Technology, Dalian, China & School of Applied Technology, The University of Science and Technology Liaoning, Anshan, China & Key Laboratory for Ubiquitous Network and Service Software of Liaoning Province, Dalian, China and Prof. Mingchu Li of the Dalian University of Technology, Dalian, China & Key Laboratory for Ubiquitous Network and Service Software of Liaoning Province, Dalian, China, proposes a dynamic multi-winner game model based on incomplete information to solve multi-end users' task offloading and edge resource allocation. The next chapter, "Constructive Solutions for Security and Privacy Issues at the Edge: Securing Edge Framework – A Healthcare Application Use Case," by Profs. Indra Priyadharshini S. and Pradheeba Ulaganathan from R. M. K. College of Engineering and Technology, India; Prof. Vigilson Prem M. from R. M. D. Engineering College, India; and Prof. Yuvaraj B. R. of Anna University, India, explains some of the serious and non-discussed security and privacy issues available on edge and offers some solutions. The following chapter, "The Role of Edge/Fog Computing Security in IoT and Industry 4.0 Infrastructures: Edge/Fog-Based Security in Internet of Things," by Profs. Bilgin Metin and Meltem Mutluturk from Bogazici University, Turkey and Prof. Burcu Kor from

Amsterdam University of Applied Science, The Netherlands, reviews the current literature regarding edge and fog-based cybersecurity in IoT. The closing chapter in this section, "Programmable Implementation and Blockchain Security Scheme Based on Edge Computing Firework Model," by Profs. Bao Yi Qin and Zheng Hao from the College of Information Engineering, Nanjing XiaoZhuang University, China and Prof. Zhao Qiang from the Department of Information Systems, Schulich School of Business, Canada, designs a programmable and blockchain security scheme based on the edge computing firework model, realizes the programming of the internet of things (IoT) gateway firework node under the edge computing, and appreciates the safe transmission and storage of programmable data through the blockchain system.

Section 3, "Uses and Applications," provides a thorough discussion of the many uses and benefits of edge computing in numerous fields. The first chapter, "Next Generation Multi-Access Edge-Computing Fiber-Wireless-Enhanced HetNets for Low-Latency Immersive Applications," by Profs. Amin Ebrahimzadeh and Martin Maier from INRS, Canada, presents a brief overview of the related work on multi-access edge computing (MEC). The next chapter, "Edge Computing-Induced Caching Strategy for National Traditional Sports Video Resources by Considering Unusual Items," by Profs. Wenwen Pan, Bei Liu, and Zhiliang Song from Qiqihar University, China, designs a system for national traditional sports video distribution with the help of software-defined network and mobile edge computing technologies. Another chapter, "Fog Computing and Edge Computing for the Strengthening of Structural Monitoring Systems in Health and Early Warning Score Based on Internet of Things," by Profs. Leonardo Juan Ramirez Lopez and Gabriel Alberto Puerta Aponte from the Universidad Militar Nueva Granada, Colombia, intends to deploy and develop the context of the internet of things platforms in the field of health and medicine by means of the transformation of edge and fog computing. An additional chapter, "A Comprehensive Survey on Edge Computing for the IoT," by Profs. G. Nagarajan, Pravin A., and Prem Jacob from Sathyabama Institute of Science and Technology, India, considers the basics and the uses of edge computing concepts in different applications. The next chapter, "Adaptive Edge Process Migration for IoT in Heterogeneous Fog and Edge Computing Environments," by Profs. Chii Chang, Satish Narayana Srirama, and Amnir Hadachi from the University of Tartu, Estonia, proposes a resource-aware edge process migration (REM) scheme that is capable of optimizing the process migration decision. A closing chapter, "Role of Edge Computing to Leverage IoT-Assisted AAL Ecosystem," by Profs. Madhana K. and Jayashree L. S. from PSG College of Technology, India, focuses on developing smart homes, which are intelligent atmospheres for real-time monitoring to meet the needs of independent and isolated individuals. The following chapter, "Edge Computing-Based Internet of Things Framework for Indoor Occupancy Estimation," by Profs. Krati Rastogi and Divya Lohani from Shiv Nadar University, India, proposes a decentralized edge computing-based IoT framework in which the majority of the data analytics is performed on the edge, thus saving a lot of time and network bandwidth. Another chapter, "Challenges for Convergence of Cloud and IoT in Applications and Edge Computing," by Profs. Rashmi S. and Roopashree S. from Dayananda Sagar University, India and Prof. Sathiyamoorthi V. from Sona College of Technology, India, describes the challenges faced when adopting cloud computing and the internet of things. The next chapter, "The Pivotal Role of Edge Computing With Machine Learning and Its Impact on Healthcare," by Profs. Muthukumari S. M. and George Dharma Prakash E. Raj from Bharathidasan University, India, considers the benefits of edge computing within the healthcare sector. The final chapter in this section, "A Constrained Static Scheduling Strategy in Edge Computing for Industrial Cloud Systems," by Profs. Yuliang Ma, Yinghua Han, Jinkuan Wang, and Qiang Zhao from Northeastern University at Qinhuangdao, China, investigates an edge computing supported industrial cloud system.

Although the primary organization of the contents in this work is based on its three sections offering a progression of coverage of the important concepts, methodologies, technologies, applications, social issues, and emerging trends, the reader can also identify specific contents by utilizing the extensive indexing system listed at the end. As a comprehensive collection of research on the latest findings related to edge computing, the *Research Anthology on Edge Computing Protocols, Applications, and Integration* provides industry professionals, computer scientists, engineers, practitioners, researchers, academicians, scholars, instructors, students, and all audiences with a complete understanding of the challenges that face those working with edge computing. Given the need for a better understanding of the potential uses and issues of edge computing in various industries, this extensive book presents the latest research and best practices to address these challenges and provide further opportunities for improvement.

Section 1
Architectures, Infrastructures, and Frameworks

Chapter 1
Overview of Edge Computing and Its Exploring Characteristics

Sangamithra A.
VIT University, India

Margaret Mary T.
Kristu Jayanti College, India

Clinton G.
Sambharm Institute of Technology, India

EXECUTIVE SUMMARY

Edge computing is the concept of the distributed paradigm. In order to improve the response time and to save the bandwidth, it brings the computation and the storage of the data closer to the location whenever it is needed. Edge computing is one of the very famous and blooming concept in today's era. It has been used in so many applications for various purposes. Edge computing can be defined as infrastructure of physical compute which is placed between the device and the cloud to support various application and which brings the cloud closer to the end user or end devices. In this chapter, the authors discuss the origin of the edge paradigm, introduction, benefits. These are some of the criteria to be elaborated in the chapter overview of edge paradigm.

ORIGIN/HISTORY OF EDGE COMPUTING

Edge computing is one of the most popularity concepts in the IoT platform. This edge computing forms the foundation for the next generation of digital business as one of the top most technology trends.

Because of this drastic growth of the edge computing, we were wondering how this edge computing started and how it has become more popular. Within a few decades the entire it has changed to the edge computing, which started from the mainframe, client/server to the cloud and at last to the edge comput-

DOI: 10.4018/978-1-6684-5700-9.ch001

ing. The edge computing platform allows edge nodes to respond to reducing bandwidth consumption, network latency and service demand. (Wei Yu Fan Liang & William Grant Hatcher (2017) In what way these all evolutions are interconnected. Everything is discussed detail in the below paragraph.

Figure 1. Era of Edge Computing

Figure 2. Origin of Edge computing

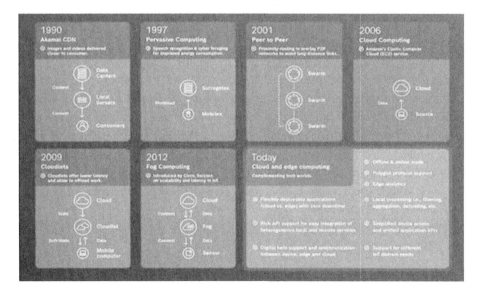

DECENTRALIZED COMPUTING

The edge computing origin can be tracked in the year 1990, when the Akamai has introduced the content delivery network. It is one of the large distributing platforms to serve the web traffic. The primary goal of the CDN is to speed up the delivery of the web content .Where the nodes will be located geographically closest to the user in order to deliver the content which is cached such as images videos documents etc..

In 1997 when nobetetol has demonstrated this agile application on different web servers, which offload the certain task in surrogates. Their surrogates fix the goal to relieve the computing resource load and also to improve the battery life of the mobile devices. In 2001, Satyanarayanan has taken this approach and generalised in the paper of the pervasive computing. (Gheorghe et.al., 2019)

Decentralized and scalable applications were used in 2001 to propose different peer to peer networks. The fault tolerant routing, object location and load balancing has enabled with these self organising overlay networks. The latency of applications is also improved with the peer to peer network. Edge Computing is a paradigm that proposes data processing and storage at the edge of the network. For the Mobile Edge Computing, the edge is represented by pervasive Radio Access Networks. Edge computing addresses a variety of applications and use cases. For instance, edge model can be used in Smart Cities, Cyber-physical infrastructures, Wireless Sensors and Actuators Networks (Gheorghe et.al., 2019)

CLOUD COMPUTING

Cloud computing is one of the powerful link to the history of the edge computing, and it has the special mention also. This cloud computing came into the market with attractive attention in the year 2006, this is the year the amazon has introduced the elastic compute cloud (Lizhe Wang & Gregor von Laszewski (2010). Which open the new opportunities in the terms of visualization, computation and capacity of the storage. Even though the cloud computing is not the solution for all the use cases. At the current stage, the Cloud computing is still evolving and there exists no widely accepted definition. Based on our experience, we propose an early definition of Cloud computing as follows: "A computing Cloud is a set of network enabled services, providing scalable, QoS guaranteed, normally personalized, inexpensive computing infrastructures on demand, which could be accessed in a simple and pervasive way" . (Lizhe Wang & Gregor von Laszewski (2010)

FOG AND CLOUDLET COMPUTING

Satyanarayanan has introduced the cloudlet in one of the paper named the case of VM based cloudlets in mobile computing in the year of 2009. In this he has focused major in the latency which is proposed with two tier architecture. Basically among the two tier the first tier indicates for the higher latency and the second indicated for the lower latency. Butmore movers this cloudlet can store only the soft state like cached copies of the data. (Satyanarayanan, M,2009)

So in 2012, fog computing was introduced by the cisco to dispread the cloud infrastructure The aim of this fog computing is to promote the scalability of the IoT. Where it can handle the large number data for real time with the low latency application.

EDGE COMPUTING FOR IOT

Now the IT technology has got a solution of various defects, with the combination of the cloud and edge computing. With the help of the edge computing the IoT generalise can make the complex ones into the simple thing in other way, we can find the solutions for the complex IoT. In any organization needs a storage, computing power to execute the various applications and visualizing the data from the different locations, at that time the cloud computing enters into the play. And in the same way when the need the low latency, with reduced backend traffic and low autonomous action for the confidential data, edge computing enters into the play(Wei Yu Fan Liang & William Grant Hatcher,2017) With the help of the combination of the cloud and edge computing so many solutions can be found for the complex IoT techniques.

With the rapid development of the technology, there are lot of IoT devices are in use in recent years. There is a chance of increase in the number of usage of IoT devices in future, because in the year 2019, there are more than 6 billion IoT devices are in use. The rise in the usage of the devices it is because there is increase in the data generation. Because of the generation of large amount of data there might be the problem to process the data; this is one of the challenging task to do that.

Figure 3. Edge Computing

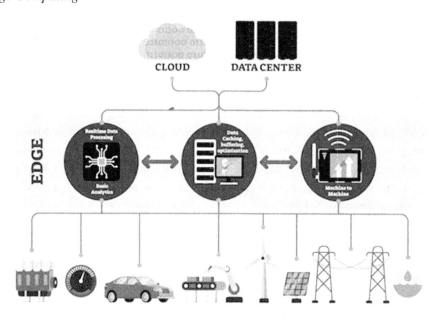

The data which is stored in the cloud can be generated with the IoTdevices, these type of data needs a faster processing and response. Because of the latency transmission increase due to the distance between the cloud and IoT, the IoT devices face some problems in the performance.

At this time the edge computing concept has been came into the play, in order to sort out this problems. Eventhough the edge computing concept similar to the content delivery network, the data generated by the IoT devices is processed by the edge server in edge computing instead of the centralized cloud. This edge server which is serve as a bridge between the user and the cloud in order to decrease the transmission latency to provide a speedy performances of the devices. Because in some area which requires the minimal transmission latency video streaming, smart devices, gaming in cloud etc. Incase if there is any delay in the data transmission, these areas will become more dangerous. Thus, the edge computing can be able to reduce the transmission latency when there is a huge data to be transmitted. (Shi W Cao, J Zhang, Q Li, Y & Xu, L. 2016).

The real time data processing without any transmission latency can be done with the help of edge computing and the network bandwidth also reduced. Edge which refers to the computing infrastructure appears closer to the data's. The edge computing is nesscessary to push from cloud service, pull from IoT and Change from data consumer to producer. So it play very significate role. It is also known as a distributed framework, where the data is processed closest to the origin. Edge computing which connects to the internet for receiving information from the cloud and to deliver back to the cloud. Which requires a effective use of resource that may not be connected to the network (Shi W Cao, J Zhang, Q Li, Y & Xu, L. 2016). The wide range of technologies like wireless sensor network, peer to peer networking cloud/ fog computing can be covered with the help of the edge computing.

Edge Computing Services

There are four types of edge computing, like how the data will be transmitted, processed and transfer back to the end user. Cloud is known as the servers, which are accessed through the internet, database and software that run on those servers. Which is located in the data centres for all over the world. Without managing the physical servers or run software applications on the machines manually can be done with the help of the cloud servers.

There are most three main categories of the cloud computing services.

- SaaS – Software as a Service

It is a cloud base service abbreviated as a Software as a Service. It is a method of delivering a software and licensing where the software can be accessed through the subscription than buying and installing in the personal compuers. Some of the example of SaaS are GooleApps, Dropbox, Zendesk, Mailchimp etc. (gudwriter,2018)

- PaaS – Platform as a Service

PaaS stands for Platform as a Service, it is also a cloud based services . According to the name it provides a platform, which includes a programming language, database, operating system etc. Some of the examples of PaaS are Heroku, Force.com, Apache, Openshift etc.

- IaaS – Infrastructure as a Service

It is a instant computing infrastructure which is termed as a Infrastructure as a Service. It is a form of a cloud based services which delivers a fundamental computing networks. Complexity of buying and managing the own physical devices and decentralized network can be avoided with the help of the IaaS. Some of the example of IaaS is Amazon Web Services, Microsoft Azure, Google Compute engine etc. (gudwriter,2018)

The cloud works through the internet service connection by enabling the acess of the user and downloading the data from any chosen devices, like smart phones,laptop, tablet etc. With the help of this cloud storage the document can be edited simultaneously along with the other user even when they are away from the working place.

Figure 4. SimpleCloudComputing

Advantages and Disadvantages

We knew that edge computing is used in many IoT devices for their advantages and it has some disadvantages too, in this content will just describe the advantages and disadvantages of edge computing.

Advantages

- Speed
- Security
- Cost
- Reliability
- Scalability

Speed

In all Company each and every seconds of a business is very much important. Because of latency issue most of the company will be cost 1000 of dollars which will make the company stock growth goes low. This edge computing which has a power like by reducing the latency it will increase the network speed. It will process the data closer to the information part so that travelling distance will b get reduced. Because of this concept of edge computing the latency can be measured in microseconds from milliseconds. Due to this the quality, speed and overall services can be increased.

Security (searchcio.techtarget)

Increasing in the technology, hacking part of the hacker also increased to steal the confidential data to hack and so on. So here whatever the information is present on the cloud, may be has the chances of getting hacked by the hacker easily. So here the edge computing plays a role, which sends only the applicable information or data to the cloud, so the hacking at the cloud can be prevented. Because sometimes the edge computing does not require a network connection. In case if the hackers manage attempt to penetrate the cloud , they cannot fetch all the information. Due to this we cannot assume that edge computing is overall free from hacking, but we can analyze that comparatively edge computing has lower risks than the cloud

Cost

IoT is one of the trending concept in today's world, because of the top trending network bandwidth, data storage and computational power the IoT devices are costly. With the help of edge computing the dta storage and bandwidth can be reduced so automatically the cost of the IoT devices also will get reduced, which is affordable to most of the users in the world. And not all the information's will sent to the cloud, only the needed data will be sent to the cloud. So obviously the infrastructure cost of IoT devices will get reduced to the affordable cost.

Reliability

Reliability part can be handled very well by the edge computing. The uninterruotible services can be given by edge computing because most of the time the edge computing will not depend on the network connections, so the user no need to worry about the internet connection interrupt or slow internet connection etc. A reliable connection is assured for the IoT devices because the data process and storage can be done locally by edge computing in microdata centres. In any remote location if there is no reliable network also the usage of edge computing is recommended.

Scalability

When we process the data in the cloud computing, the data needs to be forwarded to the centralized datacenter. Because of centralized datacenter, if any one wish to modify or expand this datacenter it will be more costly. Our own IoT network can be scaled without worrying about the storage requirements with the help of the edge,

Disadvantages

- Security
- Incomplete Data
- More Storage Space
- Investment Cost
- Maintenance

Security

Security is the main issue in all the IT technology, here also in edge distributed environment security is the challenging task. There might be risk of identity theft and security breaches in edge computing due to the concept of processing data outside of the edge network. Whenever any new IoT devices are added, there might be increase in the opportunity of the attacker to penetrate the device.

Incomplete Data

In edge computing whatever the data only the partial sets of data is analyzed,other than this data other set of data's are discarded. Because of this partial analyze most of the company has chances of losing the valuable information's. The organisation must decide what type of information they are willing to loose before using the edge computing.

More Storage Space

Comparatively edge computing takes a more storage space on any device. In order to implement the process with the hep of edge computing, we need to remember it will take more storage capacity to process the data. (searchcio.techtarget)

Investment Cost

Implementing the edge infrastructure we need additional equipments and resources because of the complexity, so the investment cost is high in edge computing. And the IoT devices also with the edge computing comes with the need of more hardware, so overall it leads to a more efficiency and substantial investment is required.

Maintenance

Edge computing is a distributed system, which means there will be so many network combinations with several nodes. Due to this edge computing requires a higher maintenance cost than any centralized infrastructure. (Gerrit Mur,IEEE)

Top 5 Benefits of Edge Computing

1. Speed and Latency

When data take much time to process then obviously the relevant of that particular data will be less. In most of the autonomous data, whatever the data it collects and requires, those data will be useless for a couple of seconds, when we take a busy roadway in that milliseconds are also matters especially. In factories milliseconds also matters, because in order to ensure data consistency the system perpetually monitor all aspects of the process manufacturing. In most of the cases there will not be no time to make a round trip of data from and to between the cloud. Latency can be eliminated by confining the data analysis to the edge and also translates into a fastest response time. Because of this the data will become more relevant, actionable and useful. Overall traffic also easily reduced with the help of the edge computing, which improvise the performance of the all enterprise applications and services. (searchcio.techtarget)

2. Security

The critical business and operating processes which rely on actionable data are highly vulnerable, when all of the data eventually feed in cloud analyzer through a single pipe. At the final result, a single DDoS attack can disturb entire operations for a multinational company. Whenever the tools of data analysis distribute across the enterprises, it will be get distributed with the risk. Because of the argues expansions of the edge computing, as a whole the organisations has been diminishes. And another truth is that when less data are transferred and there will be a less data can be intercepted. The compay issues like local compliance and privacy regulations as well as the issue of data soverginity can overcome with the help of the edge computing.

3. Cost Savings

When it comes to transporting, managing and securing how one can justify spending the same amount of money on all, since all data is not the same and does not contain the same value. Because some data are critical and some is expendable of the operation. With the help of the edge computing it is easy to categorize the data from a management perspective. With the help of the edge computing we cannot able to eliminate the cloud, it is all about optimizing the flow of the data in order to maximize the operating cost. And it also helps to reduce the redundancy in data,The data that is created at the edge is stored temporarily. Whatever the data that is sent to the cloud it should store again which creates the level of the redundancy, automatically the redundant cost will get reduced if the redundant storage is reduced.

4. Greater Reliability

When the devices of the edge store and processing the data, it automatically improves the reliability. The micro data centers which are prefabricated are built today to operate any environment. Which means that incase if there is any connection is lost to the cloud, the smart devices will not get impacted with the operation, in all the sites there will be a limitation in order to transfer the data, that is how much data can be transferred at a time. (searchcio.techtarget)

5. Scalability

Scalability is also one of the advantage of the edge computing, which seen contrary to promoted theory. In cloud computing, whatever the data is transferring, the data will be forwarded to central location datacenter in most of the cases. In that case expanding or any modifying of the data in the centralized datacenter is much expensive. In a single implementation, the IoT devices can be deployed with their processing and data management tools at the edge, instead of waiting on the multiple sites of coordinations.

Data processing speed and analysis has increased in business of edge computing. Drastically the Internet of things is expected to grow, in order to reach about $1.6 trillion USD by 2025.(Baotong Chen & Jiafu Wan, 2018)Abundant amount of data that s increased in IoT enabled devices has processed with the help of edge technology.

Immediately the data process storage analyses has informed to the user in order to get into the action, with the help of edge computing, because edge computing process the data at the location itself. One of the major benefit of edge computing compared to cloud is that the data which is analyzed and acted.

Real-Time Data Analysis

Basically the data that is analyzed in order to take a proper action is sent to a central location. Though the edge computing which analyze the data allow to take place in the area near where it is created. With the help of the edge computing the data are kept near to the origin point so that in order to make real time decision is near.

Figure 5. Benefits of Edge Computing for Business

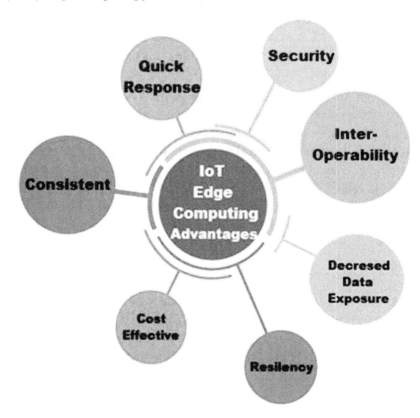

Augmented Reality

Augmented reality can be improved with the help of the edge computing. Even users can gain more realistic and augmented reality experience. By taking this as aadvantage, the technology firms is one of the first thing to provide the upgraded experience to the customer.

Smart Manufacturing

Edge computing has given more improvement in the production of the manufacturing companies. The efficiency and margins are improved with the help of the real time data analysis. The problems are identifying by analyzing the data with the help of edge computing to avoid shutdown. (searchcio.techtarget)

Security Systems

In order to keep their information and business safe the large organization needs a fast and accurate security system. In lower bandwidth operation also the edge computing makes a security system more efficient. Whatever the data processed in security camera is collected and stored in a cloud through the signal. In edge computing which will be having some device in internal computer, with this device transferring the footage to the cloud is possible when it is needed.

In some other companies it is mean for reducing the cost of organizational by using smaller deployments. One of the major key benefits of the edge computing is to meet the company needs in a customized manner. (searchcio.techtarget)

Types of Edge Computing

What exactly edge computing is, seems to be indistinct and vary depending on who you ask. This post focuses on a definition that is started using and breaks down computing into four parts, Cloud, Compute Edge, Device Edge, and Sensor, and everything outside the Cloud is considered Edge Computing.

Figure 6. Edge computing procedure

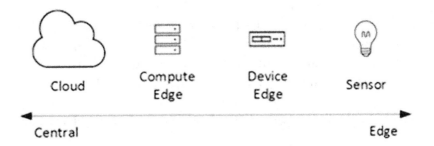

Cloud: Cloud principally alludes to gigantic server farms worked by cloud suppliers, for example, AWS, Azure, and GCP, however would likewise incorporate VMware Cloud on AWS and other cloud or facilitating suppliers. The primary qualities of the cloud are that it's brought together and work at scale. The advantage is that you have high foundation accessibility, admittance to a great deal of administrations and essentially unbounded measure of assets. The downside is that as these are unified, arrange network to sensors or gadgets at the edge can't be ensured and inactivity will be higher. System traffic to or from the cloud doubtlessly likewise causes an expense.

This is likewise alluded to as a smaller scale DC and is a little datacenter comprising of anything from a couple up to a few racks of workers. These are commonly found close or close to IoT gadgets and may likewise be fundamental for nearby consistence reasons. The key is that these server farms have cooling and so on and contain standard rack-mounted workers, (Weisong Shi & Jie Cao; Quan Zhang, 2016). You can have a considerable amount of assets situated in these server farms, however not similar scope of administrations and limit as in the cloud. An advantage is that idleness to gadgets at the edge ought to be less contrasted with the cloud, and system transmission capacity may be higher and more dependable.

Gadget Edge: This comprises of one or a couple of little workers and is additionally called a nano DC. It would just comprise of one or a couple of little workers and have insignificant figure limit. Workers in this class would likely not be rack mounted and would need to be equipped for running without cooling. They are regularly found in areas for the most part not related with a server farm, for example, in processing plants, wind turbines or vehicles and can be rough to deal with outrageous conditions. The advantage is that they could be found right close to IoT sensors and inertness, transmission capacity or network issues would be insignificant. The disadvantage is such little gadgets would just have the option to give least limit and administrations. (Baktir,et.al.,2017)

What are Edge Computing Applications

While it's not exactly accurate to define programs as specific edge computing applications, there are many ways in which edge computing infrastructure can be deployed to improve network-based services. The key factor involves pushing processing-capable hardware closer to the network edge.

This can take the form of an edge data center, which is often a multi-tenant colocation facility located in or near an emerging market with a rapidly growing consumer base. These markets are often far away from the hyper scale data centers that host the most popular cloud computing applications and streaming media platforms. (Blesson Varghese, 2016). By placing servers in an edge data center, companies can effectively create a relay station of sorts that can process essential data close to end users while passing less urgent data along to a larger facility located elsewhere. Content providers can also cache high-demand media in these data centers to allow local users to access it more easily.

Processing-capable IoT devices can perform in a similar fashion. With enough on-board computing power and storage to handle most tasks, an edge IoT device can collect and analyze local data even when disconnected from a broader network. It may not possess full functionality when running in an "offline" mode, but it can still perform a number of useful tasks. When it does reconnect to the network, it can transmit stored data and access additional processing resources. Even when connected to the network, the IoT device can still use edge computing by handling much of its data processing locally rather than relying on the servers in a cloud data center. This allows it to cut down on latency and provide much greater versatility.

The ability to capture insights from real-time data, without impacts from latency and network-related bottlenecks is changing the way many industries can operate— bringing tangible benefits to consumers and companies alike.

Grid Edge Control and Analytics

Smart Grids, as we now know them, essentially a grid which is evolved from traditional power to smarter grids. It goes on by establishing two-way communication channels between power distribution infrastructure and the recipient consumers (residential households, commercial buildings, etc.) and the efficacy head-end. Wide-area network (WAN) internet protocols plays the backbone.The implausible growth-rate the internet of things is experiencing takes gradually transferred over into the industrial side (IoT), fetching with copious technologies that can flawlessly monitor, manage and control the several functions within the electric grid's distribution infrastructure.

With the quickening development away from petroleum derivatives onto appropriated sustainable power sources (particularly sun based), current force lattices are stressed, presently entrusted with grasping demonstrated shrewd advances that are fit for incorporating and dealing with these dispersed vitality assets into existing matrices, making a blended and practical circulation arrange a brilliant matrix.

Edge grid computing technologies are aiding benefits with innovative real-time monitoring and analytics aptitudes, creating actionable and respected insights on power plant like renewables. This is something SCADA-based systems might not ever do, as they were intended well before the renewable and technological boom.

From private housetop sun oriented to business sun based homesteads, electric vehicles, wind ranches and hydroelectric dams–smart meters are creating gigantic measure of valuable information that can help utilities with investigation on vitality creation, accessibility, prerequisites and pinnacle utilization expectations. This permits utilities to all the more naturally keep away from blackouts and overcompensation lessening generally speaking expenses and vitality squander. Grid Edge Controllers are intelligent servers deployed as an interface between the edge nodes and the utility's core network.

Oil and Gas Remote Monitoring

Ongoing Safety observing is absolutely critical for basic foundation and utilities like oil and gas. In view of this wellbeing and dependability, many forefront IoT checking gadgets are as yet being created so as to shield basic apparatus and frameworks against catastrophe.

Current progressed hardware utilizes Internet of Things tactile gadgets for temperature, dampness, pressure, sound, dampness and radiation. Along with the expansive vision capacities of web convention empowered cameras (IP cameras) and different innovations, this creates a tremendous and persistent measure of information that is then joined and investigated to give key bits of knowledge that can dependably assess the soundness of any running framework.

Registering assets at the edge permit information to be investigated, handled and conveyed to end-clients progressively(Baotong Chen & Jiafu Wan,2018). Empowering control focuses with admittance to the information as it happens, anticipating and forestalling glitches in the most improved opportune way.

This is the most viable arrangement, as time is of the substance in these basic frameworks. This rings most obvious when managing basic foundation, for example, oil, gas and other vitality benefits, any disappointments inside certain will in general be cataclysmic in nature and ought to consistently be kept up with most extreme insurance and security methods.

1. Edge Video Orchestration

Edge video organization utilizes edge processing assets to actualize an exceptionally improved conveyance strategy for the broadly utilized at this point data transfer capacity substantial asset video. Rather than conveying video from a brought together center system through all the system bounces, it cleverly coordinates, stores and disseminates video records as near the gadget as could be expected under the circumstances. Think o fit as an exceptionally proficient and specific occurrence of a substance download organize (CDN) only for video, directly at the edge for end-clients.

MEC-fueled video arrangement is generally helpful for huge open settings. Sports arenas, Concerts and other restricted occasions depend intensely on live video web based and investigation to make and increment income streams. (lanner-america,2018)

Newly made video cuts and live transfers can rapidly be served to paying clients in settings through rich media preparing applications running on portable edge workers and hotspots. This brings down the administration costs and dodges numerous quality issues emerging from bottleneck circumstances with terabytes of weighty video traffic hitting the versatile systems.

This is something 5G edge figuring is intended to unravel in the coming years. As of now, arrange administrator EE is examining the potential for these sorts of administrations in a joint effort with Wembley Stadium, the public soccer arena of the UK.

2. Traffic Management

Because of the computationally costly complexities of traffic the board productivity (Read: Traveling sales rep issue), perhaps the most ideal approaches to enhance traffic the executives frameworks is by improving ongoing information. Insightful transportation frameworks utilize edge figuring advancements, particularly for traffic the executives measures

The flood of IoT gadgets and enormous measures of live information require preprocessing and sifting nearer to the gadgets, before these a great many information streams can hit the center/cloud systems.

Utilizing edge figuring the gigabytes of tangible and uncommon information is examined, separated and packed before being communicated on IoT edge Gateways to a few frameworks for additional utilization(lanner-america,2018) This edge preparing saves money on organize costs, stockpiling and working expenses for traffic the board arrangements.

3.   Autonomous Vehicles

While independent vehicles are not yet prepared for the standard, without edge figuring strategies their feasibility would be a lot more years later. With the lull of moore's law and generally advance computational force the installed PCs will currently frame a sizeable cost of self-ruling vehicles.

The hordes of complex tangible innovations associated with independent vehicles require enormous data transfer capacity and continuous equal processing abilities (Weisong Shi & Schahram Dustdar (2016). Edge and conveyed figuring methods increment wellbeing, spatial mindfulness and interoperability with current-age equipment.

With versatile edge processing, vehicles can trade on-going tangible information, substantiate and improve choices with less locally available assets bringing down the developing cost of self-governing AI frameworks.

Making the Edge Computing Business Case

As inventive gadgets like self-governing vehicles and clinical sensors become more normal, edge processing will have an inexorably huge effect on society. With edge figuring system, associations will have the option to broaden organize administrations into zones that were beforehand past the range of customary structures. On account of numerous gadgets, the capacity to improve execution could actually spare lives. Consider, for example, the effect of utilizing clinical gadgets in hard to-arrive at provincial territories with restricted medicinal services choices. Edge processing can likewise improve wellbeing for mechanical assembling by recognizing gear issues before they cause glitches that could harm laborers.

Why Edge Computing Applications Make Market Expansion Easier

The preparing capability of edge registering innovations additionally makes it simpler for organizations to grow their system administration into new business sectors without making similar framework ventures that were so important before. (Jianli Pan James Mc Elhannon (2018). That is uplifting news for districts with littler urban focuses and for provincial networks that come up short on the high-transmission capacity arranges availability normal to the Tier 1 business sectors found in and around significant urban communities.

Edge server farms are a lot littler and more affordable to fabricate and keep up than the hyper scale offices utilized by numerous endeavors and distributed computing suppliers. Building a vitality proficient edge in a little market is a generally unobtrusive venture that could give organizations a "first mover" advantage that delivers significant profits in both the short and long haul. Small scale server farms give significantly greater adaptability, permitting associations to target end clients with unmatched exactness. While an edge server farm may grow administration into a formerly underserved market, a miniaturized scale could be set in territories with more noteworthy interest to improve arrange execution or in considerably more removed regions to additionally broaden the system edge.

By and large, notwithstanding, IoT gadgets will beat these offices to the edge. Customers in generally detached zones (regarding system access) are now going to cell phones and cell systems to compensate for the absence of direct broadband access. Numerous organizations are as of now exploiting this pattern by introducing smaller scale server farms at the base of cell pinnacles to more readily encourage IoT availability. As these gadgets become more normal, imaginative systems like this will help organizations to arrive at more clients and incredibly grow their market reach.

Edge Computing and IoT

The quantity of IoT gadgets available for use today is now stunning, and there's a lot of information to propose that this figure will increment fundamentally in the coming years. With so numerous IoT gadgets associated with systems around the globe, edge registering is as of now majorly affecting how organizations structure their frameworks (Jianli Pan James Mc Elhannon,2018) The continuous interest for quicker, more proficient administrations and substance conveyance will push associations to improve their current edge systems. Organizations that neglect to put resources into edge figuring today could wind up in the unenviable situation of scrambling to make up for lost time to their rivals in the years ahead.

Gadgets associated with the web produce tremendous measures of information that gives a gigantic chance to organizations, yet in addition a similarly huge test regarding overseeing, examining, and putting away that information. Generally, these cycles were taken care of in an organization's private cloud or server farm, yet the sheer volume of information has stressed these systems to their outright cutoff points.

Edge frameworks ease this weight by pushing information handling endlessly from a unified center and dispersing it among nearby edge server farms and different gadgets closer to the source. Examining information closer to where it's gathered gives tremendous advantages regarding cost and proficiency. By using edge frameworks, organizations can likewise address issues related with low availability and the expense of moving information to a concentrated worker.

Industrial IoT

Industrial organizations remain to profit gigantically from edge processing since it permits them to change produced IoT edge gadgets (particularly modern machines) into expansions of their system foundation. Joined with present day AI and constant examination, information can be assembled, dissected, and applied quicker than at any other time, empowering IoT edge gadgets to self-control and react to changes.

5G Networks

The expansion of 5G systems, which will expand transmission capacity essentially and make it simpler to send high volumes of cell information, opens up various open doors for edge processing applications. Since G will assist with combatting inertness with its disseminated engineering, organizations will have the option to utilize these systems to extend their own system edge and move information unquestionably more effectively. As opposed to directing everything back to an incorporated worker, covering 5G systems will permit them to keep more information on the edge. These edge systems will likewise assist with conquering the inertness inciting "last mile" issue, in which communicated information bottlenecks through a progression of imperfect associations before arriving at its proposed clients. The innovation will likewise observe the development of shrewd city activities. (Gupta et., al., 2015).

Drawbacks of Edge Computing

The preparing capability of edge registering innovations additionally makes it simpler for organizations to grow their system administration into new business sectors without making similar foundation ventures that were so vital previously. That is uplifting news for districts with littler urban focuses and for country networks that come up short on the high-data transfer capacity arrange availability basic to the Tier-1 business sectors found in and around significant urban areas.

Edge server farms are a lot littler and more affordable to manufacture and keep up than the hyper scale offices utilized by numerous undertakings and distributed computing suppliers. Building a vitality effective edge in a little market is a moderately unobtrusive venture that could give organizations a "first mover" advantage that delivers significant profits in both the short and long haul. Smaller scale server farms give considerably greater adaptability, permitting associations to target end clients with unrivaled accuracy. While an edge server farm may grow administration into a formerly underserved market, a miniaturized scale could be set in territories with more prominent interest to improve organize execution or in considerably more inaccessible regions to additionally broaden the system edge.

As a rule, notwithstanding, IoT gadgets will beat these offices to the edge. Purchasers in generally secluded zones (regarding system access) are now going to cell phones and cell systems to compensate for the absence of direct broadband access. Numerous organizations are now exploiting this pattern by introducing smaller scale server farms at the base of cell pinnacles to all the more likely encourage IoT network. As these gadgets become more normal, creative systems like this will help organizations to arrive at more clients and extraordinarily grow their market reach.

The Future of Edge Computing

Moving information handling to the edge of the system can assist organizations with exploiting the developing number of IoT edge gadgets, improve arrange speeds, and upgrade client encounters. The versatile idea of edge figuring additionally makes it an ideal answer for quickly developing, light-footed organizations, particularly in the event that they're as of now utilizing colocation server farms and cloud framework. By exploiting edge figuring, organizations can enhance their systems to offer adaptable and dependable support that will reinforce their image and keep their clients cheerful.

Edge processing offers a few favorable circumstances over conventional types of system design and will doubtlessly keep on assuming a significant job for organizations going ahead. With increasingly more web associated gadgets hitting the market, inventive associations have likely just start to expose what's conceivable with edge processing.

REFERENCES

Baktir, A. C., Ozgovde, A., & Ersoy, C. (2017). How Can Edge Computing Benefit from Software-Defined Networking: A Survey, Use Cases & Future Directions. *IEEE Communications Surveys and Tutorials, 1*. Advance online publication. doi:10.1109/COMST.2017.2717482

Chen & Wan. (2018). Edge Computing in IoT-Based Manufacturing. *IEEE Communications Magazine, 56*(9). Advance online publication. doi:10.1109/MCOM.2018.1701231

Fan Liang, W. Y., He, X., & Hatcher, W. G. (2017). A Survey on the Edge Computing for the Internet of Things. IEEE Access, 6. doi:10.1109/ACCESS.2017.2778504

Gheorghe, A.-G., Crecana, C.-C., Negru, C., Pop, F., & Dobre, C. (2019). Decentralized Storage System for Edge Computing. *2019 18th International Symposium on Parallel and Distributed Computing (ISPDC)*, 41–49. doi:10.1109/ISPDC.2019.00009

Gupta, A., & Jha, R. (2015). A Survey of 5G Network: Architecture and Emerging Technologies. *IEEE Access : Practical Innovations, Open Solutions, 1*. Advance online publication. doi:10.1109/access.2015.2461602

Mur. (1994). Edge Elements, their Advantages and their Disadvantages. *IEEE Transactions on Magnetics, 30*(5).

Pan & McElhannon. (2018). Future Edge Cloud and Edge Computing for Internet of Things Applications. *IEEE Internet of Things Journal, 5*(1). Advance online publication. doi:10.1109/JIOT.2017.2767608

Satyanarayanan, M., Bahl, P., Caceres, R., & Davies, N. (2009). The Case for VM-Based Cloudlets in Mobile Computing. *IEEE Pervasive Computing, 8*(4), 14–23. doi:10.1109/MPRV.2009.82

Shi, W., Cao, J., Zhang, Q., Li, Y., & Xu, L. (2016). Edge Computing: Vision and Challenges. *IEEE Internet of Things Journal, 3*(5), 637–646. doi:10.1109/jiot.2016.2579198

Shi & Dustdar. (2016). The Promise of Edge Computing. *Computer, 49*(5). Advance online publication. doi:10.1109/MC.2016.145

Varghese, B., Wang, N., Barbhuiya, S., Kilpatrick, P., & Nikolopoulos, D. S. (2016). Challenges and Opportunities in Edge Computing. *2016 IEEE International Conference on Smart Cloud (SmartCloud)*. 10.1109/SmartCloud.2016.18

Wang, von Laszewski, Younge, He, Kunze, Tao, & Fu. (2010). *Cloud Computing: a Perspective Study*. doi:10.1007/s00354-008-0081-5

Yi, L., & Li. (2015). A Survey of Fog Computing: Concepts, Applications and Issues. *Proceedings of Workshop on Mobile Big Data*, 37-42.

This research was previously published in Cases on Edge Computing and Analytics; pages 73-94, copyright year 2021 by Engineering Science Reference (an imprint of IGI Global).

Chapter 2
A Comprehensive Survey of IoT Edge/Fog Computing Protocols

Madhumathi R.
Sri Ramakrishna Engineering College, India

Dharshana R.
Sri Ramakrishna Engineering College, India

Reshma Sulthana
Coimbatore Institute of Technology, India

Kalaiyarasi N.
Sri Ramakrishna Engineering College, India

ABSTRACT

The IoT device ecosystem is being blessed with a dazzling array of slim and sleek, trendy and handy, purpose-specific and generic, disappearing, disposable yet indispensable, resource-constrained and intensive, and embedded yet networked devices. Therefore, our personal, as well as professional, environments are increasingly being stuffed with such kinds of functionally powerful devices that are instrumented, interconnected, and intelligent. This trend and transition set a stimulating foundation for a variety of connected and smarter environments. By empowering our everyday devices to be computing, communicative, sensitive, and responsive, the newly introduced concept of edge or fog computing is to bring forth a number of innovations, disruptions, and transformations for the IT domain. This chapter conveys how the various protocols contribute immensely to the intended success of fog computing and analytics in the days ahead.

DOI: 10.4018/978-1-6684-5700-9.ch002

INTRODUCTION TO IoT EDGE/FOG COMPUTING

Edge computing refers to the processing of data nearby the IoT devices which reduces the transmission of data to be sent through long routes. Computing of data is done closer to the network which helps in the organization of data for various industries. Here, the IoT devices are used to collect massive bulks of data to send it to the cloud data center for processing. Some of the data are processed locally in order to reduce the traffic in a central repository. This can be done by transmitting all the data from IoT devices to local devices and performing the common compute storage and networking process. The edge of the network processes the data and some of the data is sent to the central repository. An example of edge computing is the 5G cellular networks. It is done by adding micro data centers to the 5G towers.

Fog refers to the interconnection between the cloud and edge devices. Edge refers to space where the processing or computing is done being closer to the edge devices.

Some of the important terms and definitions for edge computing given by (Butler, 2017):

- **Edge Devices:** These are devices that produce data. It can be sensors or any other machine which capture or produce data.
- **Edge:** The edge differs in every case. In telecommunications, the cell tower is the edge.
- **Edge Gateway:** It is the buffer between the fog network and where the processing is done. It acts like a window above the edge of the network.
- **Edge Computing Equipment:** It uses a range of devices and machines, after enabling the Internet accessibility in them. An example for this is Amazon Web Service's Snowball.

Most of the data management is done in the cloud data center. In an edge computing model, the devices transmit the data to the closest edge computing equipment, which acts as a gateway helps in the processing of data rather than sending it back to the cloud or the data centre. Therefore, edge computing helps in the processing of data on the nearest edge rather than taking the data to the cloud, which increased the transmission cost and signal strength. By 2020, most of the enterprises will make use of edge computing. It is better suited for capturing and processing using IoT devices than doing it in the cloud. All the manufacturing industries, factories, organizations can adopt this technology easily into their environment. The deployment is a difficult task but the standards could do it easily. Hence the dependency over the cloud is minimized and the management of data becomes simple.

The definition given by NIST is

Fog computing is a horizontal, physical or virtual resource paradigm that resides between smart end-devices and traditional cloud or data centers. This paradigm supports vertically-isolated, latency-sensitive applications by providing ubiquitous, scalable, layered, federated, and distributed computing, storage, and network connectivity.

Edge computing helps in improving the scalability, energy efficiency and provision of contextual information processing of cloud (Pan, Beyah, Goscinski, & Ren, 2017). It emphasizes the usage of different types of edge devices, such as smart phones, routers, etc.

Advantages

Some of the advantages of edge computing are:

- **Reduction of IoT Solution Costs:** It reduces the amount of data flowing back and forth to the cloud through the network and thus lowering the cost.
- **Security:** Edge computing address security and prevents some of the industries to use the cloud. It can filter the valuable information to process locally and sending the unprocessed data to the cloud for processing.
- **Quick Response Time:** It analyses the data instantly and lowers the possibility of the worst situation to take place, such as terminating the machines before it fails.
- **Dependable Operation:** The edge devices operate without any interference even when the connection is intermittent.
- **Interoperability:** The edge computing protocols helps in understanding the language between different devices and the cloud.
- **Preserving Privacy:** When the data is captured from one device, it is important that the data might be sensitive or insensitive and should be preserved for privacy.
- **Reducing Latency:** When the accuracy is affected, edge computing applications implement machine learning algorithms to interact with the IoT devices.

There are different modules in an edge computing applications, where each one of them runs at different levels. For instance, the data from edge gateway and devices in an analytic module runs in the cloud (Butler, 2017). Each module should clearly describe the components and communications between them.

Mobile Edge Computing (MEC) is also an extension of edge computing and it was developed to connect most of the things to the internet. This was developed because of the increased usage of smart phones today. This makes IoT scalable over a wide region and can be extended using the Software Defined Network (SDN) (Salman, Elhajj, & Kayssi, 2015).

The need for using IoT in edge computing is because the cloud models are not designed as well as IoT in managing a huge volume of data generated. Handling the data using IoT helps in minimizing the latency, address the security concerns, operate reliably, secure the data over a wide geographical area and this proves that it is the best place for processing data.

The Amazon IoT Approach

It captures all the data at once and deals with it. These data are of massive amounts i.e. it collects as much data as possible at one stroke without even caring if they are useful or not. The advantages of using this approach are:

- No data is left remained
- Big data tools for analyzing

The Dell IoT Cloud Edge Approach

Unlike Amazon which grabs all the data, Dell works with only useful and meaningful data. By analyzing the data which is nearer, it can reduce the network traffic and keeps all important information inside the network. The advantages are:

- Only useful information is taken
- Calculations are done before sending the data
- Lower bandwidth costs
- Real-time processing

SENSOR AND ACTUATOR NETWORKING

The sensors and actuators are mostly wired less and so they are called wireless sensors and actuators networks (WSANs). It is a network of sensor nodes which has the ability to change the environment. All the elements interact wirelessly and are autonomous. They are linked to a wireless medium to perform distributed sensing and actuation tasks.

Actuators are heterogeneous and have more energy. It is a device that converts an electrical signal to physical action. It has the mechanism by which the agent acts upon the environment. It is a network entity and has the capability to perform functions such as, transmit, receive, process and relay data. They control a system with various dimensions. The information flow is bidirectional between the sink and the sensors (Lee, Nam, Roh, & Kim, 2016).

Sensor hubs can be used to improve consumer services with the help of location awareness. In order to achieve this, all the devices should enable location awareness including buildings (Haughn, 2015). In these cases, combined sensors are being used. For example, a numerous range of smartphone usage can form a WSAN to control the populations.

Sensors and actuators are the central elements of control systems. They can involve more than a single actuator on a point. WSANs are made of multiple nodes ranging into thousands, with hubs and actors. When used in locations having exact measurement and control, processing of data and CPU allows for actors to change input immediately. However, WSANs and WSNs share common properties, such as connectivity, reliability, energy efficiency, some of the differences between them are:

- Sensor nodes are small inexpensive with communication and computation capabilities and actors are rich in resources which have stronger transmitting powers and long battery life.
- WSANs respond based on the environment. The sensor data must be valid at the time of acting. Therefore, real-time communication is important in WSANs.
- The number of actors is lower than the sensors because all of the actors cannot be deployed and satisfied.
- A distributed local communication between the sensors and actors is the most important.

Sensors are mainly used to gather information about the environment and send the data to actuators through single-hop or multi-hop communications. Sensor nodes are low in cost and use low power and have limited sensing capacity. WSAN can be stationary or mobile based on the target applications.

WSANs also have challenges for control applications. The wireless channels have various useful properties such as path loss, adjacent channel interference, multipath fading, etc. (Xia, Tian, Li, & Sun, 2007). They are also unreliable. Due to this, there might be a time delay and packet loss which will degrade the performance. Packet loss is merely a delay which has an impact on performance. To avoid these problems, there are several solutions, for instance, the link quality between the sensors and actuators should be good. The design and evaluation of the deployment are of major concern.

Some of the applications of WSANs are

- Advanced target tracking
- Disaster response
- Precision agriculture
- Ultra-precise chemical production

Some of the constraints on protocols are

- The transport layer is responsible for getting accurate reports of exact type, intensity, and location based on the reliability. The aggregation and dissemination should be reliable.
- The routing layer should route to sink, or coordinate.
- The MAC layer should use the mobility for connectivity between sensors and actuators.

IoT GATEWAY SOLUTIONS

IoT gateways perform functions as device connectivity, protocol translation, processing, security, updating, etc. Some latest gateways operate platforms for application code which processes data. It is the intersection of edge systems such as devices, controllers, sensors and the cloud (Figure 1)

Figure 1. IoT gateway architecture

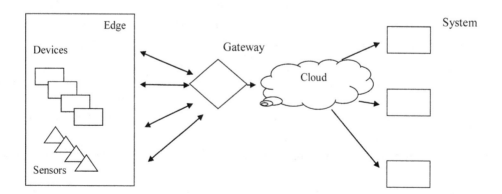

Traditional gateways could not process complex data and were not intelligent. But today's gateways are able to perform with modern operating systems. These are called intelligent gateways. These gateways can push the data closer to the edge, process them, and improve the responsiveness. It helps to filter out routine information and pass alert which are important. Recent developing companies are Wind River and Dell (Treadway, 2016). The Wind River Intelligent Device Platform XT can build its own gateway devices that can modify according to their needs. The Dell Edge Gateway 5000 series targets multiple use cases to build its own gateways. The IoT gateways should support the following functionalities:

- **Reliable Connectivity and Security:** It ensures integrity and network of the system.
- **Protocol and Data Bridge:** Can exchange data between different systems having different protocols and formats
- **Storage and Analysis:** Storage of data and intelligent decision making closer to the device.
- **Management:** It provides control access to devices with policy based permissions.

The Aricent IoT gateway is a middleware which is flexible to deal with the bottom layers of devices and the top layers of cloud platforms like, Microsoft Azure, AWS IoT, and IBM BlueMix. These solutions extend to multiple domains. For example, home automation, smart metering & smart city domains. Some of the features it provides are:

- It is designed to support various use cases across domains like home automation, Smart city, etc, using the REST API based SDK for application development.
- It uses one M2M specification to connect to cloud applications.
- The interfaces that support at the bottom layers are Zigbee, WiFi, BLE, and PLC.
- For device management such as software upgrade, OMA-DM is used.
- It is scalable to support a number of devices.
- It helps in the faster end to end realization.

SENSOR TO CLOUD COMMUNICATION

There are different ways the data can get transmitted from the sensor to the cloud (Burgess, 2015).

- **Sensor to Cloud Over Ethernet:** It is the simplest method which was developed in the 1970s before radio links were invented. The sensor has a processor to configure the data to be sent to the cloud. The Ethernet connection is a wired network service. The disadvantage is that wired connection is not possible in some places.
- **Sensor to Mobile Phone Network to Cloud:** The mobile phones were invented in the 1980s. Cellular networks use radio links for connecting sensors to the cloud. The drawback is that the sensor will need a wired connection, the uplink transmitter needs more power and the user has to pay for the service provider.
- **Sensor to Long Range Radio to Cloud:** Some of the free radio bands available are 902-928MHz and 2400-2483MHz, which are the frequencies used in IEEE 802.15.4 standard. It uses mesh network with many power radios interconnected to relay data from remote sensors. Each collected data has access to the cloud. This allows a wide area to deploy the sensors.

- **Sensor to a WiFi Router to Cloud:** The 2400-2483 MHz band and 5130-5835 MHz were the original frequency bands of the 802.11 Wi-Fi standards. Most of these routers are placed in homes, businesses, and other public places. It is the most widely used method. There are remote sensors available which could directly connect to WiFi.
- **Sensor to a Mobile Phone to Cloud:** The sensor will need a mobile phone to connect. These are served by Bluetooth standards. It can maintain its own group. Bluetooth Low Energy (BLE) is suited for sensors with low data rates

IoT COMMUNICATION PROTOCOLS

Wireless Protocols

RFID

It is a standard which enables manufacturers to differentiate between the qualities of same products from different markets (Poole, 2015). There are two different international standards:

- **ISO (International Standards Organisation):** Most of the standards fall into this category. It includes various areas, such as data content and formatting, conformance testing, etc.
- **EPCglobal (Electronics Product Code Global Incorporated):** It main aim was researching and standardizing. Majority of these activities are associated with RFID using the Auto-ID center.

RFID Standards

RFID is an air-interface protocol, depending on the type of RFID system used there are many "standards" for such protocols. Listed are the most commonly used air-interface protocol standards ratified by the International Organization for Standardization (ISO):

- **ISO 14443:** It is the high frequency (HF) standard created for the secure payment purpose. It is designed to have short read range and includes encryption and it was created for proximity cards.
- **ISO 15693:** Its development purpose is for vicinity cards. It is a longer read range than ISO 14443-based systems and no encryption is done here. It is used in many access-control systems, inventory management, and other applications.
- **ISO 18000-3:** Most of the companies use this standard for item management.
- **ISO 18000-6C:** It uses ultra-high frequency based on EPC Gen 3 air-interface and is widely used for UHF systems.
- **ISO 24730:** It monitors the communication of RFID transponders and is used in real time.

Zigbee

Zigbee wireless communication technology is a kind of newly arisen wireless network technology; the characteristic is short distance communication, low speed, low power dissipation, and low cost. It, application of Zigbee wireless communication technology, makes that inconvenient wire repeat can be avoided in the area of home, factory, hospital, etc. With the rapid development of IT industry and the strong functional expansion of SCM, Zigbee wireless communication technology will play an important role in the wireless sensor network (WSN). The basis of Zigbee is IEEE 802.15.4 standard, but it only defines the lower two layers: the physical (PHY) layer and the medium access control (MAC) sub-layer, then the Zigbee Alliance builds on this foundation by providing the network (NWK) layer and the API is standardized. It could be embedded in all kinds of devices, support Geo-location function, and be used widely in the area of industrial monitoring, safety system, smart home, etc; the protocol is realized by protocol stack (Wang, He, & Wan, 2011).

Application Layer Protocols

LoRa WAN

The LoRa physical layer establishes the communication link. Therefore, LoRaWAN defines a media access control protocol (MAC) and also the network architecture. Optimized for low-power consumption and supporting large networks with millions and millions of devices, data rates range from 0.3 kbps to 50 kbps.

- **Standard:** LoRa WAN
- **Frequency:** Various
- **Range:** 2-5km (urban environment), 15km (suburban environment)
- **Data Rates:** 0.3-50 kbps.

Some of the important terminologies of LoRaWAN are

- **Device or Node:** It is an object with the low power communication device.
- **Network:** It is the route to send and receive signals to the application back and forth.
- **Gateway:** It consists of antennas to send and receive broadcasts from nodes.
- **Application:** It is software running on the server.
- **Uplink Message:** It sends a message from device to application.
- **Downlink Message:** It sends a message from the application to device.

BLE (Bluetooth Low Energy)

It is an object code in a single library file. The latest version is 4.2 and it allows two types of wireless technologies. They are:

- Basic rate
- Bluetooth low energy

It was created to transmit small data packets using less power. It supports the following features:

- LE Secure connection
- LE Data length extension

- LE privacy 1.2

It mainly consists of a controller, host and an application (Townsend, Cufi, Akiba & Robert Davidson, 2016). The application refers to the user application with Bluetooth protocol stack. It is responsible for containing the logic and data handling. The host is present at the top layers of the Bluetooth and the controller is present at the bottom layers. Host Controller Interface (HCI) helps to communicate with the host and BLE module.

The purpose is to interface the controller with the host. The host consists of the following layers:

- Generic Access Profile (GAP)
- Generic Attribute Profile (GATT)
- Logical Link Control and Adaptation Protocol (L2CAP)
- Attribute Protocol (ATT)
- Security Manager (SM)
- Host Controller Interface (HCI), host side

The controller includes the following layers:

- Host Controller Interface (HCI), controller side
- Link Layer (LL)
- Physical Layer (PHY)

6LowPAN

It is an open IoT networking protocol. It is designed and developed in public. It is accessible to anybody without any membership. IoT makes all things aware of the internet. Hence, there is the usage of the IPv6 to make use of internet protocols. The sensors used in 6LowPAN have restricted wireless connectivity. But using IPv6 we can drive the protocols over the internet. It uses direct IP addressing of nodes. It is designed to send these packets over IEEE 802.14.4 along with some standards using the addressing nodes (Schmidt, 2016). It has a mesh network and is robust scalable. It defines encapsulation and header compression mechanisms.

CoAP

CoAP stands for Constrained Application Protocol and is an application layer protocol. It mainly focuses on document transfer. CoAP packets are much smaller than HTTP TCP flows. Bit fields and mappings from strings to integers are used extensively to save space. Generations of the packets are simple. Consumption of extra RAM space for the parsing of the packets is not required. CoAP runs over UDP, not TCP. Clients and servers communicate through connectionless datagrams. CoAP follows a client/server model. Clients make requests to servers, servers send back responses. Clients may GET, PUT, POST and DELETE resources.

The CoAP interaction model is similar to HTTP client/server model but the CoAP implementation acts as both client and server in the typical machine to machine interactions. CoAP is comprised of two layers. They are the message layer which is responsible for UDP communication and reliability and another layer is responsible for request or response interactions. CoAP also uses asynchronous message exchange between endpoints. CoAP defines four types of messages as Confirmable, Non-confirmable, Acknowledgement and Reset. The embedded Method Codes and Response Codes in some of these messages mark them as requests or responses (Joshi, & Kaur, 2015).

The four security modes defined for CoAP which are:

- **NoSec:** This alternative assumes that security is not provided in this mode or in the CoAP transmitted message.
- **PreshardKey:** This mode is enabled by sensing devices preprogrammed with symmetric cryptographic keys. This mode is suitable for applications that support devices that are unable to employ the public key cryptography. Also, applications can use one key per device or one key for a group of devices.
- **RawPublicKey:** The mandatory mode for devices that require authentication based on the public key. The devices are programmed with a pre-provisioned list of keys so that devices can initiate a DTLS session without a certificate.
- **Certificates:** Supports authentication based on public key and application that participate in certification chain. The assumption of this mode is that security infrastructure is available. Devices that include asymmetric key and have unknown X.509 certificates can be validated using the certificate mode and provisioning trusted root keys (Granjal, Monteiro, & Silva, 2015).

Applications

- Basic CoAP based System setup
- Real-Time Condition-based Monitoring in Smart Grid
- Building Automation
- Defence, Aircraft equipment, etc.

AMQP

The application layer protocol generally implied for messaging is the Advanced Message Queuing Protocol (AQMP). It creates full functional interoperability between conforming clients and messaging middleware servers. It is an openly published wire specification for asynchronous messaging. The AMQP protocol is a binary protocol with modern features: it is multi-channel, negotiated, asynchronous, secure, portable, neutral, and efficient. AMQP is usefully split into two layers:

- The functional layer defines a set of commands (grouped into logical classes of functionality) that do useful work on behalf of the application.
- The transport layer that carries these methods from application to server, and back, and which handles channel multiplexing, framing, content encoding, heart-beating, data representation, and error handling.

Applications

The programming language the developer uses determines the actual API through which applications interact with AMQP implementations. For example, you can map AMQP's capabilities such that Java applications cause them through JMS APIs. For C++, Python, and Ruby applications, however, there are no popular open messaging API standards like JMS for Java, so those languages support their own AMQP APIs, which typically reflect the AMQP application-level protocol classes and methods (Vinoski, 2006).

Communication Protocols

DDS

A distributed application can use "Data-Centric Publish-Subscribe" (DCPS) as a communication mechanism since Data Distribution Service (DDS) specification standardizes the software application programming interface (API). DDS is implemented as an "infrastructure" solution and hence it can be added to the communication interface for any software application (Gerardo, Farabaugh, & Warren, 2005). DDS is supported by Linux as well as Windows; the source code provided is complete and well supported/documented by the open DDS website. Created as a networking middleware to circumvent the disadvantages of centralized publish-subscribe architecture, DDS is a TCP-based protocol that features decentralized nodes of clients across a system and allows these nodes to identify themselves as subscribers or publishers through a localization server (Figure 2). The use of this system negates the need for users to identify where other potential nodes are or which topics they are interested in, as the DDS nodes self-discover across a network and send/receive telemetry anonymously based only on topics. After linking publishers and subscribers, the connections between these clients bypass the server and are peer-to-peer (Chen, & Kunz, 2016).

Figure 2. DDS Communication Architecture

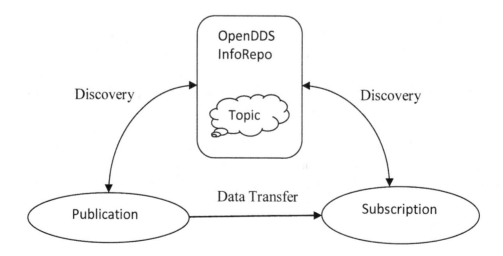

Advantages

- Based on a simple "publish-subscribe" communication paradigm.
- Flexible and adaptable architecture that supports "auto-discovery" of new or stale endpoint applications.
- **Low Overhead:** Can be used with high-performance systems.
- Deterministic data delivery.
- Dynamically scalable.
- Efficient use of transport bandwidth.
- A large number of configuration parameters that give developers complete control of each message in the system.

LTE Cat-M

The LTE Cat-M standard is a cellular standard. It has a number of benefits compared to the non-cellular technologies. One obvious benefit is the existing infrastructure for LTE, where operators around the world have been rolling out this technology since 2009. According to GSA, there are now 480 LTE networks launched in 157 countries. It supports up to up to 150Mbits/s in the downlink. LTE supports both frequency division duplex (FDD) and time division duplex (TDD) modes using a common subframe structure of 1ms. Having such a short subframe length allows for latency to be minimized, thus ensuring a good user experience. LTE-M operates on a 1.4 MHz carrier or 6 PRB. The IoT device will always listen to the center 6 PRB for control information like any normal device. When the device is scheduled for IoT traffic, it will be allocated a number of PRBs (up to 6) at any consecutive location within the spectrum of operation. This means that the device will be allocated a 1.4 MHz carrier within a, for example, 20 MHz carrier. Ignoring the legacy control information, the dedicated control and data are multiplexed in the frequency domain. This enables LTE IoT devices to be scheduled within any legacy LTE system and share the carrier capacity, antenna, radio, and hardware at the site.

NB-IoT

NB-IoT, however, is a new narrowband IoT system built from existing LTE functionalities. It can be deployed in three different operation modes.

- Stand-alone as a dedicated carrier
- In-band within the occupied bandwidth of a wideband LTE carrier
- Within the guard-band of an existing LTE carrier

In stand-alone deployment, NB-IoT can occupy one GSM channel (200 kHz) while for in-band and guard-band deployment, it will use one physical resource block (PRB) of LTE (180 kHz). The design targets of NB-IoT include low-cost devices, high coverage (a 20-dB improvement over GPRS), long device battery life (more than 10 years), and massive capacity (greater than 52K devices per channel per cell). Latency is relaxed although a delay budget of 10 seconds is the target for exception reports. Since NB-IoT is expected to adopt a design based on existing LTE functionalities, it is possible to reuse the same hardware and also to share spectrum without coexistence issues. In addition, NB-IoT can simply plug into the LTE core network. This allows all network services such as authentication, security, policy, tracking, and charging to be fully supported (Ratasuk, Vejlgaard, Mangalvedhe, & Ghosh, 2016).

Transmission Protocols

RPL

It is a distance vector and source routing protocol. The distance vector protocol manipulates the vectors of distances to other nodes in the network. It is also an intra-domain routing protocol. It has the ability to change the topology based on the requirement. It has less computational complexity (Richardson, & Robles, 2017).

Distance Vector (DV) is used to calculate the distance and direction of a link. It also finds the path which has minimum cost. It maintains a vector table to determine the shortest path. The total cost of traveling is found using routing metrics.

Source routing also known as path addressing, allows the sender of a packet to completely or partially specify the route of the packet to the network. It determines all possible routes to a host. It organizes the topology using the directed acyclic graph which is divided into one or more graphs. It uses RPL Instance ID which identifies a unique network. Since the root destines a location, the graph is also called Destination Oriented Directed Acyclic Graph (DODAG).

A grounded DODAG connects the host after satisfying the application goal. A floating DODAG doesn't satisfy the goal; rather it provides all the routes to the nodes. An RPL can have multiple instances, which can be local or global. An RPL instance field consists of control and data packets.

USB Protocol

USB, Universal Serial Bus is a polled bus for transferring data, where the nodes initiate all packet exchanges. The packet is transferred in so-called transactions. Normally, they consist of three packets:

- The token packet is the header defining the direction as well as the transmission type, the device address, and the endpoint.
- The packet is transferred in a data packet.
- The final status of the transmission is to acknowledge.

In a transmission, packets are transferred either from the Host to a Device or vice-versa. The mode of transaction is specified in the token packet that is sent from the Host. Then, a data packet indicating that it has no data to transfer is sent by the source. In general, the destination responds with a handshake packet indicating whether the transfer was successful.

MQTT

Message Queue Telemetry Transport protocol (MQTT) is based on Client-Server architecture (Ala, Guizani, & Mohammadi, 2015). This messaging protocol is introduced by an IBM developer Andy Stanford-Clark in 1993 and was internationally standardized in 2013. Embedded devices and networks are connected with the application through MQTT. MQTT provides communication facilities among connected embedded devices and application. Using MQTT, data packets can follow three routing mechanisms (one-to-one, one-to-many, many-to-many).MQTT follow the publish/subscribe pattern for communication where publisher publishes the topic and subscriber subscribes the topic. The architecture of MQTT has three main components, Subscriber, Publisher, and Broker. All three components have their independent work mechanism. Both Subscriber and Publisher are MQTT clients where Subscriber would be registered by an interesting device and subscribes to topics through Broker which acts as a server. The publisher client acts as a data generator that publishes the interesting information to a subscriber through Broker (Dhar, & Gupta, 2016). For Internet of Things and M2M, MQTT protocol proves itself an ideal messaging protocol for communication.

Applications

- Healthcare by keeping track of victims besides they go away from the clinic, upgrading the effectiveness of the consequent tests.
- In energy and utilities by making Virtual Power Plant (VPP).
- Social Networking.

XMPP

Instant Messaging (IM) service can be carried out by the standard specified by the Internet Engineering Task Force (IETF) is the eXtensible Messaging and Presence Protocol (XMPP). It is an open XML protocol for near-real-time messaging, presence, and request/response services. It is formalized by the IETF as an approved messaging and communication of structured data between two entities. Every device is identified by a unique address referred to as "bare JID" which consists of a "local part", "domain part", and "resourcepart" and represented as "<localpart@domainpart/resourcepart>". Structured data is transmitted asynchronously over the network to the global address of the given device concurrently (Valluri, 2014). Jabber open-source community was initially proposed XMPP. Later, it was formally approved and archived by the IETF in four Internet specifications (Nie, 2006).

The general procedure of a successful Transport Layer Security (TLS) + Simple Authentication and Security Protocol (SASL) negotiation is as follows:

1. The client establishes the TCP connection to the server and initiates the XML streams.
2. The server sends a STARTTLS extension to the client, including the supported authentication mechanisms.
3. The client responds to the STARTTLS command.
4. The server informs the client that it is ok to proceed.
5. The client and the server complete the TLS setup of the TCP connection.
6. Given that the success of the previous step, the client initiates a new stream to the server.
7. The response of the server can be identified by sending a stream header to client along with any available stream features.
8. The client picks up an appropriate authentication mechanism.
9. The server sends a Base64-encoded challenge to the client.
10. The client responds to the challenge with the credential.

11. The server sends another challenge to the client, as the session token.
12. The client again responds to the challenge.
13. The server informs the client of successful authentication.
14. The client triggers a new stream to the server for the application-purpose communication.

PLC (CLICK)

The communications ability of the CLICK PLC system for transmission of data between the PLC unit and other connected devices covers:

- Electrical connections used for communications
- Networking routing between the PLC and other devices,
- Setting the port communication parameters,
- Selecting the protocols and the available data addressing types to use, and
- Ladder logic program instructions that make it all work together.

Two built-in RS-232 ports are there in CLICK Basic and Standard PLCs. Both ports are 6-pin RJ12 phone type jacks. It has fixed Port 1 communication parameters and is used primarily as the programming port. Modbus RTU protocol slave device can also be used as Port 1. The Port 2 which is used for general purpose and user configurable. Modbus RTU master or slave protocol device can also be used as Port 2, or handle ASCII data in or Out (ASCII stands for American Standard Code for Information Interchange) and defines a character encoding method for text that is used in computers and other communication devices.

3-pin RS-485 port is available in Standard and Analog PLC versions. Like Port 2, Port 3 is also a general purpose port with its communication parameters being user-configurable from the programming software. Modbus RTU master or slave protocol device is used by Port 3, or handle ASCII data in or out. CLICK Ethernet Basic, Standard and Analog PLC units have one built-in Ethernet communications port and one RS-232 serial communication port. RS-485 port has Ethernet Standard and Analog PLC units. The CLICK PLC can be networked to other CLICK PLCs, data input devices, and data output devices.

CLICK PLC to other 3rd party PLCs can be networked and devices can be communicated through the Modbus RTU protocol. There are three different data addressing, CLICK addressing, Modbus 984 addressing, or Modbus HEX addressing. The CLICK addressing makes convenient to exchange of data. The other addressing choices are selected based on the Modbus protocol addressing the networked devices.

Z-Wave

Z-Wave is a low-power RF communications technology that is primarily designed for home automation for products such as lamp controllers and sensors among many others. Optimized for reliable and low-latency communication of small data packets with data rates up to 100kbit/s, it operates in the sub-1GHz band and is impervious to interference from WiFi and other wireless technologies in the 2.4-GHz range such as Bluetooth or ZigBee. It supports full mesh networks without the need for a coordinator Node and is very scalable, enabling control of up to 232 devices. Z-Wave uses a simpler protocol than some others, which can enable faster and simpler development, but the only maker of chips is Sigma Designs compared to multiple sources for other wireless technologies such as ZigBee and others.

- **Standard:** Z-Wave Alliance ZAD12837 / ITU-T G.9959
- **Frequency:** 900MHz (ISM)
- **Range:** 30m
- **Data Rates:** 9.6/40/100kbit/s

Thread

A new IP-based IPv6 protocol used for home-based automation environment is called as Thread. It is not an IoT applications protocol like Bluetooth or ZigBee and based on 6LowPAN. However, it is primarily designed to reside WiFi as it recognizes that while WiFi is good for many consumer devices that limit to a particular area.

Thread, launched in mid-2014 by the Thread Group, a free protocol is based on various standards including IEEE802.15.4 (air-interface protocol), IPv6 and 6LoWPAN, and offers an IP-based solution for the IoT. Designed to work on existing IEEE 802.15.4 wireless silicon from chip vendors such as free scale. Thread provides a mesh network using IEEE802.15.4 radio transceivers and is able of handling up to 250 nodes with high levels of authentication, encryption, and decryption. A very simple software upgrade should allow users to run a thread on existing IEEE802.15.4-enabled devices.

- **Standard:** Thread, based on IEEE802.15.4 and 6LowPAN
- **Frequency:** 2.4GHz (ISM)
- **Range:** N/A
- **Data Rates:** N/A

Cellular

Any sensor devices that need operation over long range can take advantage of GSM/3G/4G cellular communication capabilities. While cellular is capable of sending a large number of data, especially for LTE, the cost and also energy consumption will be high for many applications, but it can be the intelligent way for using sensor-based low-bandwidth-data projects that will send very low amounts of data over the web. A key product in this area is the SparqEE range of products, including the original tiny CELLv1.0 low-cost development board and a series of shield connecting boards for use with the Raspberry Pi and Arduino platforms.

- **Standard:** GSM/GPRS/EDGE (2G), UMTS/HSPA (3G), LTE (4G)
- **Frequencies:** 900/1800/1900/2100MHz
- **Range:** 35km max for GSM; 200km max for HSPA
- **Data Rates (Typical Download):** 35-170kps (GPRS), 120-384kbps (EDGE), 384Kbps-2Mbps (UMTS), 600kbps-10Mbps (HSPA), 3-10Mbps (LTE)

Sigfox

Sigfox ranges between WiFi and cellular. It uses the ISM bands, which is an open source, to communicate data over a very narrow spectrum to and from connected objects. The key factor for Sigfox is that for many M2M applications that run on a small battery and data transfer level is low, then WiFi's range is too short and cellular is too expensive and also power consumption is high. A Sigfox uses Ultra Narrow Band (UNB) which is designed to handle low data-transfer speeds of 10 to 1,000 bits per second. It consumes 50 microwatts compared to 5000 microwatts for M2M communication or can deliver a typical standby time 20 years with a 2.5Ah battery while M2M is only 0.2 years.

It is already applied for tens of thousands of connected objects, the network is currently being rolled out in major cities across Europe, for example including ten cities in the UK. The robust, ultra-low power consumption and the scalable network are offered by the network that can do its transmission over millions of battery-operated devices across the long range, making it suitable for various M2M applications such as smart meters, patient monitors, security devices, street lighting and environmental sensors. The Sigfox system contains a silicon called EZRadioPro wireless transceivers from Silicon Labs, which gives an industry-leading wireless performance, long range and very low power consumption for wireless networking applications operating in the sub-1GHz band.

- **Standard:** Sigfox
- **Frequency:** 900MHz
- **Range:** 30-50km (rural environments), 3-10km (urban environments)
- **Data Rates:** 10-1000bps

Nuel

Nuel is similar to Sigfox and rangessub-1GHz band, very small slices of the TV White Space spectrum to deliver high scalability, a large range of distance, low energy consumption and very least cost wireless networks are leveraged by Nuel. Iceni chip, which makes transmission using the white space radio to work the high-quality UHF spectrum, now available due to the analog to digital TV transition is the one system based. There are huge communications technologies which are called Weightless and is a new large area wireless networking technology designed for the sensor related things that largely challenges against existing GPRS, 3G, CDMA and LTE WAN solutions (Sethi, & Sarangi, 2017).

- **Standard:** Neul
- **Frequency:** 900MHz (ISM), 458MHz (UK), 470-790MHz (White Space)
- **Range:** 10km
- **Data Rates:** Few bps up to 100kbps

Security Protocols

Internet Protocol Security

A network protocol suite that authenticates and encrypts the packets of data sent over a network is the Internet Protocol Security (IPSec). It includes protocols for establishing mutual authentication between agents at the beginning of the session and negotiation of cryptographic keys to use during the session. IPSec is an open standard. Internet Key Exchange (IKE) Protocol, Security Association (SA) is the supporting protocols. There is two header formats namely authentication header (Figure 3) and ESP header (Figure 4).

Figure 3. Authentication Header

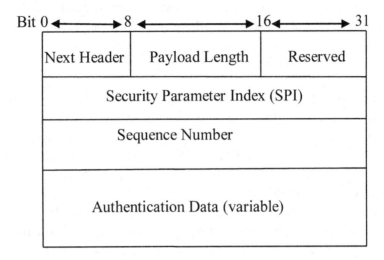

Figure 4. ESP Header

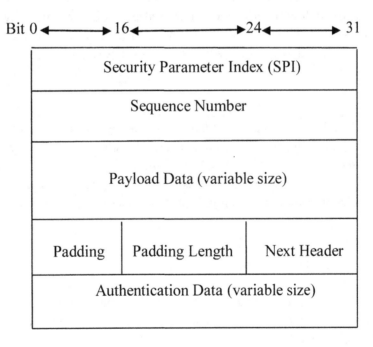

- The Authentication Header (AH) provides support for data integrity and authentication of IP packets. The data integrity service ensures that data inside IP packets is not altered during transit. The authentication service enables an end user or computer system to authenticate the user or application at other end and decide whether to accept or reject packets accordingly. Authentication is based on the use of a Message Authentication Code (MAC) which means the two parties must share a secret key.

- Encapsulating Security Payload (ESP) adds a header and trailer. ESP is based on symmetric key cryptography techniques. It can be used in isolation or can be combined with AH. It provides source authentication, integrity, and privacy (Singh, & Gahlawat, 2012).

IPsec operates in two different modes.

- The default mode for IPSec is the Transport mode. It is used for end-to-end communications. When transport mode is used, IPSec encrypts only the IP payload. Transport mode provides the protection of an IP payload through an AH or ESP header. Typical IP payloads are TCP segments, a UDP message or an ICMP message. IPSec in the transport mode does not protect the IP header; it only protects the information coming from the transport layer. This mode is normally used when we need the host-to-host protection of data.
- Tunnel mode protects the entire IP packet. The tunnel mode is normally used between two routers, between a host and a router, or between a router and a host. When IPSec tunnel mode is used, IPSec encrypts the IP header and the payload, whereas transport mode only encrypts the IP payload. The protection of an entire IP packet is provided by the Tunnel mode by treating it as an AH or ESP payload. The IP addresses of the outer IP header are the tunnel endpoints, and the IP addresses of the encapsulated IP header are the ultimate source and destination addresses. When traffic must pass through an intermediate, untrusted network, the protecting of traffic between different networks is aided by the IPSec tunnel mode. Tunnel mode can be used in the following configurations namely Gateway-to-gateway, Server-to-gateway, and Server-to-server.

Kerberos

The computer network authentication protocol that works on the basis of tickets is Kerberos protocol. The concept of tickets allows the nodes to communicate with one another and prove their identity in a secure manner. It executes client-server model and provides mutual authentication. Kerberos builds on symmetric key cryptography and requires a trusted third party and optionally may use public-key cryptography during certain phases of authentication. Kerberos uses UDP port 88 by default.

Drawbacks

The protocol weaknesses can be summarized as follows:

1. Kerberos requires continuous availability of the KDC. When the Kerberos server is down, the system will be vulnerable to the single point of failure problem. This can be mitigated by using multiple Kerberos servers.
2. The system clocks of the hosts that are involved in the protocol should be synchronized. A time availability period has been assigned to the tickets and if the host clock is not synchronized with the Kerberos server clock, the authentication will fail. In practice, Network Time Protocol daemons are usually used to keep the host clocks synchronized.
3. "Password guessing" attacks are not solved by Kerberos. A poor password must be chosen by the user. This is because it is possible for an attacker to successfully mount an offline dictionary attack

by repeatedly attempting to decrypt messages obtained which are encrypted under a key derived from the user's password (Eman, Koutlo, Kelash, & Allah, 2009).

4.   There are no standards for the administration of the Kerberos protocol. This will differ between server implementations.

Secure Shell Protocol

Secure Shell Protocol (SSH), also known as Secure Socket Shell, is a UNIX based command interface and a cryptographic network protocol used to protect data in transmission between devices providing strong authentication and establishes a secure channel over an insecure network in a client-server architecture, connecting an SSH client application with an SSH server. Secure Shell is a secure method to access the remote computer over a network, in order to execute commands in a remote machine and to move files from one machine to another. It is comprised of a suite of three utilities, Slogin, Ssh and SCP. RSA public key cryptography is used by Secure Shell protocol for connection and authentication. Working of SSH mainly relies on the exchange and verification of information, using public and private keys, to identify hosts and users. Client refers to a workstation or PC that you are already logged in to, e.g., your own personal workstation or a group workstation that provides XDM session management for several X terminals. The term server means a secondary remote workstation that you wish to log in to do some work, for example, a login session server. The client is where you type "rlogin server" or "RCP file server: newfile" and the server is where you get a new login session and shell prompt or are copying files. A user can generate an identity in the client system by running the ssh-keygen program. As a system administrator; you generate a public and private key pair for the system itself. This information contained within the system itself, greatly reduces the possibility of someone spoofing the system's identity by faking IP addresses or mugging up DNS records that associate IP addresses and domain names (Garimella, & Kumar, 2015).

Advantages
- Username and password authentication mechanisms prevent eavesdropping by attackers who would otherwise trap sensitive data.
- Using secure shell the malicious use of IP source routing can be avoided.
- As the data is encrypted, it only appears in the form of some random characters, so data manipulation at routers along the network cannot be done.
- Easy to manage a dedicated server remotely.

Disadvantage
- Port ranges & dynamic ports can't be forwarded.
- SSH server daemon problem. We cannot restrict what ports may or may not be forwarded, per user. When a user is authenticated by password, the client's RSA identity is not verified against Ssh known hosts.
- Performance is not too high on old machines.
- Licensing the original source has become very restrictive.

WiFi Protected Access Protocol (WPA)

WPA is a standard for secure communication protocol. WPA stands for WiFi Protected Access. WPA has been accepted in 2002 as a temporary solution by the WiFi Alliance, as a response to the delayed development of the IEEE 802.11i standard. The standard WPA specifies two operation manners.

1. Personal WPA or WPA-PSK (Key Pre-Shared) that use for small office and home for domestic use authentication which does not use an authentication server and the data cryptography key can go up to 256 bits. This can be any alphanumeric string and is used only to negotiate the initial session with the AP. Because both the client and the AP already possess this key, WPA provides mutual authentication, and the key is never transmitted over the air (Lashkari, & Danesh, 2009).
2. Enterprise WPA or Commercial that the authentication is made by an authentication server 802.1x, generating an excellent control and security in the users' traffic of the wireless network. This WPA uses 802.1X+EAP for authentication but again replaces WEP with the more advanced TKIP encryption. No preshared key is used here, but you will need a RADIUS server. And you get all the other benefits 802.1X+EAP provides, including integration with the Windows login process and support for EAP-TLS and PEAP authentication methods.

Advancements in WPA

-   A cryptographic message integrity code, or MIC, called Michael, to defeat forgeries.
-   A new IV sequencing discipline, to remove replay attacks from the attacker's arsenal. In order to de-correlate the public IVs from weak keys, a per-packet key mixing function.
-   A rekeying mechanism, to provide fresh encryption and integrity keys, undoing the threat of attacks stemming from key reuse.

CONCLUSION

Protocols play a very vital role in shaping up any computing and communication paradigm. For fog/edge computing, there are several protocols being bandied about widely in the literature. This chapter has listed and detailed a number of recent protocols for enabling the paradigm of fog/edge computing. The chapter is to assist the respective architects, consultants, and professionals with the sufficient knowledge on each of the popular protocols and how they fit into the scheme of things. Further on, the study on these protocols opens up fresh possibilities and opportunities for research scholars and scientists to bring forth additional capabilities for the fog world.

REFERENCES

Ala, A. F., Guizani, M., & Mohammadi, M. (2015). Internet of Things: A Survey on Enabling Technologies, Protocols, and Applications. *IEEE Communications Surveys and Tutorials*. doi:10.1109/COMST.2015.2444095

Bluetooth Low Energy Protocol Stack. (2016). Bluetooth Low Energy Software Developer's Guide. *Texas Instruments*. Retrieved November 14, 2017, from http://dev.ti.com/tirex/content/simplelink_cc2640r2_sdk_1_00_00_22/docs/blestack/html/ble-stack/index.html

Burgess, L. (2015). How Does Sensor Data Go From Device To Cloud? *readwrite*. Retrieved November 22, 2017, from https://readwrite.com/2015/10/13/sensor-data-device-to-cloud/

Butler, B. (2017). *Internet of Things. What is edge computing, how it's changing the network?* Retrieved November 1, 2017, from https://www.networkworld.com/article/3224893/internet-of-things/what-is-edge-computing-and-how-it-s-changing-the-network.html

Butler, B. (2017). *Internet of Things. What is edge computing, how it's changing the network?* Retrieved November 3, 2017, from https://www.networkworld.com/article/3224893/internet-of-things/what-is-edge-computing-and-how-it-s-changing-the-network.html

Chen, Y., & Kunz, T. (2016). Performance Evaluation of IoT Protocols under a Constrained Wireless Access Network. In *International Conference on Selected Topics in Mobile and Wireless Networking*. Cairo, Egypt. IEEE. 10.1109/MoWNet.2016.7496622

Dhar, P., Gupta, P., (2016). Intelligent Parking Cloud Services based on IoT using MQTT Protocol. *Int. J. of Engineering Research, 5*(6/12), 457-461.

Eman, E. E., Koutlo, M., Kelash, H., & Allah, O. F. (2009). A Network Authentication Protocol Based on Kerberos. Int. *J. of Computer Science and Network Security., 9*(8/12), 18–26.

Garimella, D., Kumar, R., (2015). Secure Shell-Its significance in Networking (SSH). *Int. J. of Application or Innovation in Engineering & Management, 4*(3/12), 187-196.

Gerardo, P. C., Farabaugh, B., & Warren, R. (2005). *An Introduction to DDS and Data-Centric Communications*. Real Time Innovations.

Granjal, J., Monteiro, E., & Silva, J. (2015). Security for the Internet of Things: A Survey of Existing Protocols and Open Research Issues. *IEEE Communications Surveys and Tutorials, 17*(3), 1294–1312. doi:10.1109/COMST.2015.2388550

Haughn, M. (2015). Wireless Sensor and Actuator Network. IoT Agenda. *TechTarget Network*. Retrieved November 20, 2017, from http://internetofthingsagenda.techtarget.com/definition/WSAN-wireless-sensor-and-actuator-network

Joshi, M., & Kaur, B. P. (2015). CoAP Protocol for Constrained Networks. Int. *J. of Wireless and Microwave Technologies, 6*, 1–10.

Lashkari, A. H., & Danesh, M. M. S. (2009). A Survey on Wireless Security Protocols (WEP, WPA and WPA/802.11i). 2nd *Int. Conf. on Computer Science and Information Technology (ICCSIT)*, 49-52.

Lee, W., Nam, K., Roh, H. G., & Kim, S. H. (2016). A gateway based fog computing architecture for wireless sensors and actuator networks. In *Advanced Communication Technology (ICACT). 18th Int. Conf. on Advanced Communication Technology (ICACT)*. Pyeongchang, South Korea. IEEE. doi: 10.1109/ICACT.2016.7423331

LoRaWAN. (2017). *The Things Network*. Retrieved November 11, 2017, from https://www.thethingsnetwork.org/wiki/LoRaWAN/Home

Nie, P., (2006). *A Open Standard for Instant Messaging: eXtensible Messaging and Presence Protocol*. TKK T-110.5190 Seminar on Internetworking.

Pan, Y., Beyah, R. A., Goscinski, A., & Ren, J. (2017). Edge Computing for the Internet-of-Things. *IEEE Network*. Retrieved November 3, 2017, from https://www.comsoc.org/netmag/cfp/edge-computing-internet-things

Poole, I. (2015). *RFID Standards. Radio-Electronics*. Retrieved November 11, 2017, from http://www.radio-electronics.com/info/wireless/radio-frequency-identification-rfid/iso-epcglobal-iec-standards.php

Ratasuk, R., Vejlgaard, B., Mangalvedhe, N., & Ghosh, A. (2016). NB-IoT System for M2M Communication. *Workshop on Device to Device Communications for 5G NETWORKS*.

Richardson, M., & Robles, I. (n.d.). *RPL- Routing over Low Power and Lossy Networks*. Retrieved November 21, 2017, from https://www.ietf.org/proceedings/94/slides/slides-94-rtgarea-2.pdf

Salman, O., Elhajj, I., & Kayssi, A. (2015). Edge computing enabling the Internet of Things. In *IEEE 2nd World Forum on the Internet of Things (WF-IoT)*. Milan, Italy. IEEE. 10.1109/WF-IoT.2015.7389122

Schmidt, S. (2016). 6LoWPAN: An Open IoT Networking Protocol. *Open IoT Summit*. Retrieved November 14, 2017, from http://events.linuxfoundation.org/sites/events/files/slides/6lowpan-openiot-2016.pdf

Sethi, P., & Sarangi, S.R. (2017). Internet of Things: Architectures, Protocols, and Applications. *Journal of Electrical and Computer Engineering, 17*.

Singh, A., & Gahlawat, M. (2012). Internet Protocol Security (IPSec). *International Journal of Computer Networks and Wireless Communications., 2*(6), 717–720.

Townsend, K., Cufi, C. A., & Davidson, R. (2016). Bluetooth Low Energy - Part 1: Introduction to BLE. *MikroElektronika*. Retrieved November 14, 2017 from https://learn.mikroe.com/bluetooth-low-energy-part-1-introduction-ble/

Treadway, J. (2016). Using an IoT gateway to connect the "Things" to the cloud. IoT Agenda. *TechTarget Network*. Retrieved November 21, 2017, from http://internetofthingsagenda.techtarget.com/feature/Using-an-IoT-gateway-to-connect-the-Things-to-the-cloud

Valluri, S. P. (2014). Secure Internet of Things Environment using XMPP Protocol. *International Journal of Computers and Applications, 106*(4). doi:10.5120/18511-9589

Vinoski, S., (2006). Advanced Message Queuing Protocol. *IEEE Internet Computing, 10*(6).

Wang, W., He, G., & Wan, J. (2011). Research on Zigbee Wireless Communication Technology. In *Int. Conf. on Electrical and Control Engineering (ICECE)*. Yichang, China. IEEE. doi: 10.1109/ICE-CENG.2011.6057961

Xia, F., Tian, Y. C., Li, Y., & Sun, Y. (2007). Wireless Sensor/Actuator Network Design for Mobile Control Applications. *Journal of Sensors*, *7*(10), 2157–2173. doi:10.33907102157 PMID:28903220

This research was previously published in the Handbook of Research on Cloud and Fog Computing Infrastructures for Data Science; pages 85-107, copyright year 2018 by Engineering Science Reference (an imprint of IGI Global).

Chapter 3
Edge Architecture Integration of Technologies

Sandhya Devi R. S.
 https://orcid.org/0000-0001-7021-845X
Kumaraguru College of Technology, India

Vijaykumar V. R.
Anna University, Coimbatore, India

Sivakumar P.
 https://orcid.org/0000-0002-8469-6492
PSG College of Technology, India

Neeraja Lakshmi A.
PSG College of Technology, India

Vinoth Kumar B.
PSG College of Technology, India

EXECUTIVE SUMMARY

The enormous growth of the internet of things (IoT) and cloud-based services have paved the way for edge computing, the new computing paradigm which processes the data at the edge of the network. Edge computing resolves issues related to response time, latency, battery life limitation, cost savings for bandwidth, as well as data privacy and protection. The architecture brings devices and data back to the consumer. This model of computing as a distributed IT system aims at satisfying end-user demands with faster response times by storing data closer to it. The enormous increase in individuals and locations, connected devices such as appliances, laptops, smartphones, and transport networks that communicate with each other has raised exponentially. Considering these factors in this chapter, edge computing architecture along with the various components that constitute the computing platform are discussed. The chapter also discusses resource management strategies deliberate for edge computing devices and integration of various computing technologies to support efficient IoT architecture.

DOI: 10.4018/978-1-6684-5700-9.ch003

INTRODUCTION

The IoT is a fusion of the technologies of infrastructure, applications, and networking. Data is an important aspect of an IoT device, which must be analyzed immediately. Based on the specific IoT devices that are installed under the network, an IoT framework will produce unlimited data within a second as per business needs. The data generated from IoT devices or sources are limitless and will easily absorb network bandwidth, resulting in excess data storage requirements. Aggregating and digitizing the data at the edge of the network is important, and can then be transmitted to back-end applications (Gubbi et al., 2013). Edge computing takes control of this burden and aims to reduce or automate the IT infrastructure. Such edge computing systems are positioned next to the IoT devices/data sources and therefore implement the necessary security. Edge computing has a significant benefit in reducing the response and maximizing the usage of network resources. This also aims to reduce bottlenecks in the bandwidth and the network.

Thus, IoT systems and infrastructure must be capable of serving heterogeneous devices producing vast quantities of data and events. Taking such ideas into consideration, Edge Computing improves IoT efficiency through its clustered structure where network traffic may therefore be substantially reduced and latency between the cloud's edge node and end-users may be improved. Thus, this makes IoT applications' real-time responsiveness relative to cloud and fog computing (Premsankar et al., 2018). Edge computing provides cloud services such as processing, storage, and networking closer to software, computers, and consumers. It achieves this by utilizing tiny power cell stations to facilitate high-speed transport of data without needing to drive large distances to a server or data center. The innovation of edge computing is to introduce artificial intelligence, machine learning, data analytics through the Internet of Things (IoT), the ability to operate containers, and also the ability to run entire virtual machines directly through a wide variety of computers and devices. Such devices may be as compact as a smartphone, or as large for sophisticated processing as complete computing racks. Regardless of the device's size and capacities, the information on certain computers is still connected to the cloud.

IoT-enabled systems have made cutting edge computing technologies a market requirement. Data density, speed, and new capabilities have rendered cloud computing increasingly unrealistic for devices requiring millisecond data processing. Latency is just too high (Ganz et al., 2015). Complex event processing occurs in the device or a network near to the device with edge computing architecture, which removes round-trip issues and allows activities to occur faster. For instance, vehicles with autonomous driving capability need the brakes immediately applied or will lead to the risk of crashing. With cloud computing services, the round-trip time to the cloud is too slow for this task to accommodate. If the Edge computing capabilities are equipped in a vehicle, the critical decision to stop the car will exist solely on the device of the vehicle avoiding an accident. Following this incident, the data will then be transferred to the cloud for further vehicle tracking and maintenance. Thus, edge computing is a new platform that aims to have a decrease in delays owing to its "proximity" to end-users or applications with the necessary processing and storage facilities.

The main objective of this paper is to discuss Edge computing architecture and its components. It also focusses on efficient resource management in edge computing and the Integration of various technologies to provide a flexible IoT paradigm.

BACKGROUND

Shi et al. (2016) offer a detailed overview of edge computing, with the argument that computation will occur close data sources. It lists many instances where edge computing might flourish from offloading cloud to a smart ecosystem like home and area. It also implements interactive edge, as the edge can physically and theoretically connect end-user and cloud, and not only is the traditional cloud computing model still supported, but it can also bring long-distance networks together for data exchange and coordination due to device closeness. Lastly, it overviews the problems and opportunities worth focusing on, including programmability, naming, aggregation of data, service management, privacy, and protection, as well as metrics for optimization.

The research given proposed by Sittón-Candanedo et al. (2019) is a state-of-the-art edge computing analysis and is a transformative technology powered by the growth of the Internet of Things and the environment's sensors that are constantly attached to the web. IoT applications produce the data continuously and in real-time. The huge number of sensors, connected devices, regional mobility for data storage, real-time requests responses have contributed to Edge Computing. It also improves the efficiency of IoT applications by minimizing network latency and convergence of Blockchain sequence technologies. The authors suggest the construction of an edge computing reference architecture for IoT scenarios as potential lines of study.

In the work of Asim et al. (2020), the authors analyzed the strategies of four critical Cloud (CC) and Edge (EC) computing problems: resource allocation, task offloading, joint issues, and job scheduling. The paper introduces the basic CC and EC principles along with essential problems and measurements and then concentrates on five types of Computational Intelligence (CI) methods used in CC and EC: Evolutionary Algorithms, Swarm Intelligence Algorithms, Fuzzy System, Learning-based Systems, and Edge computing. It is found Learning-Based System being used intensively in CC and EC followed by Evolutionary Algorithms and Swarm Intelligence Algorithms. The authors also highlighted some challenges and future trends in CI, CC, and EC research.

Ai et al. (2017) discuss and analyze state-of-the-art edge computing technologies. The entire paper is broadly divided into cloudlet, desktop edge computing, and fog computing to learn more intricacies of the core technologies. It provides a comprehensive overview of the theory, device design, specifications, and implementations for each of these areas. Nonetheless, despite the field's relative infancy, there are already still a variety of unresolved problems that need to be more explored from the viewpoint of core approaches and innovative solutions. In fact, with the advent of sophisticated big data mining and network slicing, the emergence of varying degrees of freedom along with the related limitations further beckons the creation and testing of the initial models in the light of edge computing.

In this survey paper proposed by Hong et al. (2019), the authors acknowledged that the technical difficulties of handling the minimal fog or edge computing tools have been tackled to a large degree. Nonetheless, there are still a few obstacles ahead to enhance resource utilization in terms of fog or edge computing technologies and efficiency. Fog and edge computing platforms also hire resource-limited machines such as WiFi APs and set-top boxes which are not ideal for operating heavyweight data analysis resources like Apache Spark and deep learning libraries. In fog or edge computing, accelerator scheduling algorithms that consider real-time characteristics are needed to reduce latency in the time-constrained workloads.

Baktir et al. (2018) discuss the computational resources required for implementing Edge computing platforms. The traditionally clustered services in Cloud data centers are being suggested to be available through Edge computing architectures at the edge of the network. Edge services should be internationally dispersed and federated with a globally open Edge layer that will meet demands from all data centers and consumer devices. This paper illustrates some of the problems facing the federating geographically dispersed Edge layer that will need to be tackled. It also deliberates the additional resource and simulation problems for a federated Edge. There is a range of relevant technical problems in networking, management, infrastructure, and modeling that need to be solved to implement innovative approaches and render the federated edge computing a reality.

The work done by Jha et al. (2019) suggests novel approaches and strategies that must be checked before the applications being introduced to the consumers. The implementation of the IoT application methods and techniques in the real environment is a complex, time-consuming process and not cost-effective, either. The application needs significant data collection and processing on autonomous end devices that require careful validation before implementation in the real world. There is a need to check the scalability of modern technologies and techniques and usability. To integrate all these unique features, the paper suggests a novel IoTSim, an Edge simulator that models various features like de-vice heterogeneity, task structure, variety of IoT connectivity protocols, system movement and agility, and battery functions. It also discusses the bottlenecks, test methods, and strategies, and their efficiency at no expense that will help to improve the reliability and performance of their proposed techniques.

MAIN FOCUS OF THE CHAPTER

Issues and Challenges in Cloud Computing:

Cloud computing (CC) is a computing technology paradigm that provides its customers with services on demand. Cloud computing's motive is to dynamically deliver processing, storage, and network services in distributed environments, connected to data centers, backhaul networks, and core networks (Zhang et al., 2010). It is an architecture that enables access to a common pool of configurable services correctly, pervasively, and on request. A large number of resources available in the central cloud can then be leveraged to deliver resource-constrained end devices with elastic computing capacity and storage capability. It has driven the rapid growth of many Internet enterprises (Bojanova & Samba, 2011). While cloud computing offers a large range of services, easy backup, and recovery, high usability as well as an environmentally safe ecosystem for consumers, it will not be able to fulfill the criteria of low latency and high-efficiency real-time applications because the central cloud is far from consumers. Some of the difficulties traditional cloud computing technology (Moghaddam et al., 2015) suffer from are,

1. **Bandwidth:** Through transferring vast volumes of data produced through edge devices to the cloud in real-time, the network bandwidth would be put under tremendous pressure. For example, a typical aircraft produces more than 5 GB per second of data, but there's inadequate bandwidth between an aircraft and satellites to sustain real-time transmission.
2. **Latency:** In the case of IoT, innovative systems have high requirements in real-time. Applications send data to the data center in the conventional cloud computing model and elicit a response, which decreases device latency. For starters, autonomous high-speed driving vehicles require millisec-

onds of response time. Serious effects will arise if latency in the device crosses expectations due to network problems.

3. **Security and Privacy:** Security has a major impact on communication systems. Data on thousands of household devices are directly related to the lives of people. Data protection and privacy issues have become more relevant for cloud computing providers with the implementation of the EU General Data Protection Regulation (GDPR).

4. **Energy:** A lot of energy consumption is used in data centers. Due to the increase in numbers of machines and communications, energy usage may become an obstacle to the growth of cloud computing centers.

5. **Availability**: Since Internet systems are gradually being built on the cloud, the provision of these services has become an important part of daily life. Smartphone owners, for example, who are used to voice-based systems may be annoyed if the app is inaccessible for a limited period. So, keeping the 24x7 promise is a big challenge for cloud service providers.

Cloud computing is not adequate when low latency is necessary for devices running the Internet of Things (IoT). High network loads, traffic congestion, and cloud-based data processing will contribute to suffering from response times. For IoT applications, edge computing can solve cloud computing challenges. Edge computing increases the performance of the IoT environment by the delivery of low latency, low energy resources.

SOLUTIONS AND RECOMMENDATIONS

Edge Computing

Edge computing refers to enabling technologies to perform computing on the edge of the network, on the cloud-based downstream data, and the upstream IoT services. Thus, Edge can be described as any device and network services along the path between data sources and data centers in the cloud. A smartphone, for instance, is the edge between body things and the cloud, a portal in a smart home is the edge between home things and the cloud, a micro data center and a server (Liu et al., 2019) is the edge between a mobile computer and server. The simple explanation for edge computing is that processing will take place close to the origins of data. Sometimes, edge computing can be interchanged with fog computing, but edge computing concentrates more on the dimension, whereas fog computing concentrates more on infrastructure. Figure 1 depicts how the data gets processed in the Edge computing platform.

Edge Computing Architecture

Figure 2 shows the overview of general Edge computing architecture. The overall edge computing architecture consists of various nodes which makes them an important component.

1. **Device Edge** The devices at the edge, such as monitors, sensors, and other physical objects, capture or connect with edge data. They collect or send data, or both, through single edge tools. The more complex edge systems can conduct more tasks. In each case, the applications on these edge

devices need to be deployed and managed (Liu et al., 2019). Different video processing, profound learning AI frameworks and basic real-time apps are examples of such technologies.

2. **Local Edge**: They are the systems running at the edge of the network or on the premises. The edge network layer and edge cluster or server may either be independent physical or virtual nodes or be merged in a hyper-converged device. This design framework comprises two main sublayers. There are all elements of the structures required for such applications to be handled in certain levels of design and equipment on the edge of computers.

3. **Cloud** It is an infrastructure commonly named as the cloud that may be run on-site or in the public domain. This design layer includes workloads which are computing tasks that cannot be managed at the other edge nodes and the management levels. Workloads require server and network workloads and use the correct orchestration levels for running them at the different edge nodes.

Figure 1. Data processing in Edge computing

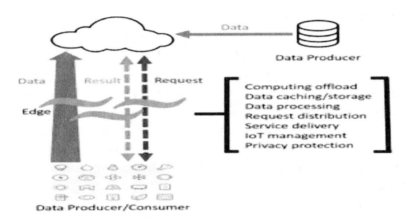

Figure 2. General Architecture of Edge Computing platform

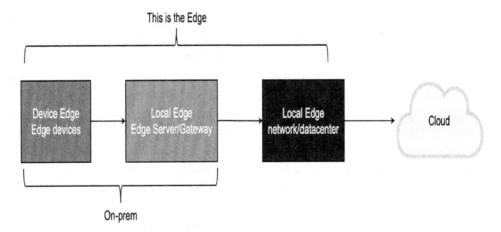

Figure 3. Edge Computing components

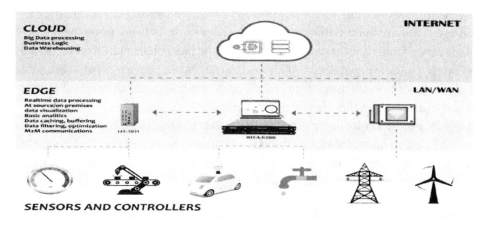

Detailed View of Edge Computing:

Figure 3 shows the components within each edge node which are significant. The key components are

1. **Edge cluster/server:** An edge cluster or server is a general-purpose IT machine situated in remote operating facilities such as a warehouse, store, hotel, or bank. An edge cluster or server is usually designed with a factor in the form of an industrial PC or a racked computer. Edge servers with 8, 16, or more cores of computing capacity, 16 GB of memory, and hundreds of GBs of local storage are commonly found. The edge cluster or server is usually used to perform workloads and shared resources for business applications.
2. **Edge gateway:** The Edge Gateway is usually an Edge Cluster or Server that offers services to perform network functions such as protocol transfer, network termination, tunneling, firewall protection, or wireless connection, in addition to application workloads and common services. While some edge devices can act as a limited gateway or host network functions, edge gateways are most commonly isolated from the edge devices.
3. **Edge Devices:** Edge computing device is meant to perform particular functions and is fitted with the programmes needed to execute these activities. One example is the use of sensors to track temperature at the unit. In this case, a sensor that can fit into the palm of your hands gathers computer temperature data and transfers the data to a data centre or an IoT server. Businesses use edge devices in various capacities. Their uses are well known in industrial processes, but their applications reach beyond the production and service provision. The use of edge computing systems in rescue efforts is an example of that. A rescue robot is a edge computing device here that can be relocated and visual data gathered autonomously in locations that are hard to access. The data collected will then be moved to a wider visual screen for decision-making purposes.
4. **Edge Software:** The Edge software increases the portability of software on edge platforms and facilitates growth and operating progress process. Sensor connections, edge hardware, and cloud connection are abstracted to provide a common API, which enables application development on the edge without the awareness of hardware resources. The applications created using the API can

be implemented on different sensors and edge devices to improve applications' portability. Figure 4 shows the hardware abstraction by Edge software.

Figure 4. Hardware abstraction by Edge Software

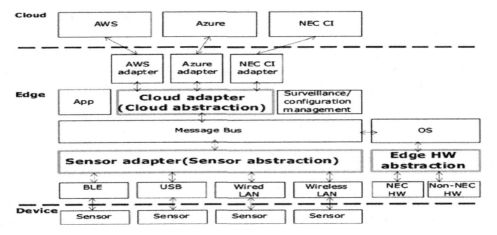

Content Caching at the Edge

Reducing backhaul, latency and growing performance consistency (QoS) are strong reasons to drive web aggregation and network security. A caching system may be as basic as a fundamental reverse-proxy or as complicated as an entire software stack that not only caches content but provides additional features, such as video transcoding using the client profile of user equipment (UE), position, and bandwidth accessible. Edge networks will use the proximity and the device load, as well as other parameters for deciding which edge data center can hold payloads to the ends. Caching networks will be used in edge settings (Tang et al., 2019). Smart caching systems are using a central cloud agent for recent prototypes that forward information demands to an excellent edge data center using metrics-based algorithms, such as the position and loading on the specified edge platform.

Edge Computing Open Platform

The intelligent distributed architecture as shown in Figure 5 allows:

Figure 5. Intelligent Distributed Architecture based on Edge computing platform

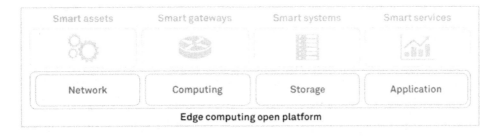

1. **Smart assets:** provide flexibility and teamwork through the incorporation of ICT technologies, such as network, computation, and storage.
2. **Smart gateways:** connect the physical and digital realms with functions like network connections and transfer protocols, provide fast communication control, data processing in real-time, and device management.
3. **Smart networks**: they are based on multiple mobile gateways or cloud partnerships and have an elastic network, processing, and storage capability.
4. **Smart Services:** include the technology service structure and the management and operational service framework, based on a single model service architecture with a range of roles including the network and maintenance staff, corporate decision-makers, systemic integrators, and program developers.

INTEGRATION OF IoT TECHNOLOGIES

IoT includes data collection along with the cloud technology Cloud providers are typically implemented throughout the main network throughout broad data centers. With a modest response time, the Core Cloud provides a strong processing capability, which satisfies the needs of distributed and intermittent providers. However, it is not a flexible long-term approach, in particular, because IoT system volume and data are supposed to burst, to collect information, and place it in a central cloud network (Mao et al., 2017). The IoT analytics deployment between the core cloud and the edge of the network (Ex first analyses on the edge of the cloud and big data processing on the core cloud) is a robust and effective solution both at the network and application level. To order to deliver IoT analytics effectively and leverage network resources, transport network controls must be built into the dispersed edge and cloud infrastructure, so that complex, effective IoT applications can be implemented.

Figure 6. Integration of various networks

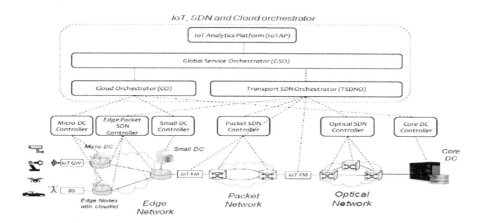

Figure 6 demonstrates the Software-Defined Networking (SDN) and cloud infrastructure for multi-layer, IoT-aware transport. It comprises multiple packets and optical transport domains, which provide links to core-DCs as well as micro and small-DCs (on the edge of the network called edge nodes). IoT Flow Monitors (IoT-FM) are implemented on the edge of packet network domains. IoT-FMs are in charge of tracking aggregate IoT traffic's maximum bandwidth.

Edge Computing Technologies

There are few edge computing technologies in the IoT, such as Mobile Edge Computing (MEC), Fog computing, Cloudlets, Mobile Edge computing, Microdata centers, and a new concept called Cloud of Things.

1.   Mobile Edge Computing

MEC incorporates information management and Cloud computing functionality within a mobile access network, which has become a standard. MEC is a modern network model. In its 2014 proposal to standardize MEC, European Telecommunications Standards Institute (ETSI) suggested that MEC provide a new ecosystem and value chain, which can use MEC to move the Mobile unit to nearby nodes for intensive calculation tasks. As the MEC is within the Radio Access Network (RAN) and similar to Mobile Users (the RAN), it has the capacity to increase service quality (QoS) and quality of experience (QoE) by lower latency. The MEC also has additional bandwidth. MEC is also a major 5G development technology (Mao et al., 2017) that contributes to meeting high 5G delay, programming, and scalability standards.

Figure 7. Mobile Edge Computing Architecture

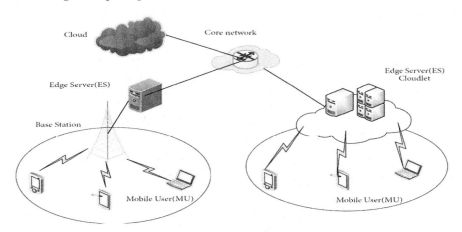

MEC can not only reduce the congestion but also effectively respond to user requests by integrating services and caching on the outskirts of the network. Edge computing (EC) is the term that is most similar to MEC. The EC refers to a modern processing mode at the edge of the network. Cloud services are represented by the edge data in the EC and interconnection service is the upstream data. The edge of the EC applies to any network measurement and boundary from the data source into the CC hub. The MEC emphasizes that the Edge Server (ES) between the Cloud computing center and the edge device is responsible for calculating MU data on the ESs, but that the MU is not computing able in the main. The Mobile User (MU) has a high computational potential in the EC model, by comparison. The MEC should therefore be considered as part of the EC scheme. The key cases in the MEC, i.e. device uploading, were checked by the customer. In specific, three sub-issues were discussed in the device offloading study: decision-making, allocating capital, and control of mobility.

The MEC architecture as illustrated in Figure 7 can be seen as the mid-range between MUs and cloud that is closer to MUs and provides services for MUs. Therefore, it is an autonomous system with two layers made up of MUs and ESs. MU applies commonly to handheld computers, phones, laptops, etc. ES often typically applies to the base station in conjunction with the server or cloudlet. MUs offload ES computing tasks, which allow MUs not only to run apps effectively but also to reduce latency due to public cloud access.

2. Fog Computing

Fog computing is a term used to describe a decentralized computing infrastructure or just a "fogging." This extends cloud infrastructure to the edge of a network while at the same time putting the most rational and productive files, processing, storage, and applications. This location takes place between the cloud and the source of the data, often called "out in the fog". The edge devices are connected to the cloud as seen in Figure 8 below called "fog nodes." Such nodes are fog computing systems that have the capability for processing and sensing. The purpose of fog computing is to extend both cloud computing and network-level service and to reduce the data transported to the cloud for processing, analysis, and storage (Naha et al., 2018).

Figure 8. Fog computing architecture

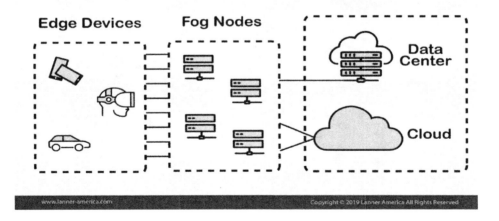

As shown in Figure 8, Fog computing fills the distance between the server and end-users, i.e. the IoT nodes, by enabler of network nodes near IoT devices processors, storage, network, and data processing. As a consequence, not just in the cloud, but also in the IoT-to-Cloud route is processing, saving, networking, evaluating, and handling data while moving over to the cloud (preferably closer IoT). In Intelligent Transport Systems (ITS), for example, GPS data can be compressed at the edge before being transmitted to the cloud. OpenFog Consortium (2017) describes Fog Computing as "the device level horizontal architecture delivering computation, storage, control and networking to the user in a cloud-to-all spectrum." Fog computing functions are spread across networks and industry by the "horizontal" model in the field of Fog Computing, while the vertical model supports Siloes.

A vertical framework can offer good support of one application category (silo), but may not take the user of device contact with other vertically oriented applications with consideration. Fog computation offers a scalable medium to satisfy the data-driven needs of operators and consumers, as well as enabling horizontal architecture. Fog computing is planned for the Internet of Things to be embraced firmly. In cloud computing, computational services are accessible at a fairly large energy usage while in fog computing, computing resources are available at a modest amount with small energy consumption (Jalali et al., 2016). The cloud uses huge storage facilities, while the fog uses tiny computers, switches, gateways, set-top boxes, or connection points. Cloud infrastructure usually requires tiny data centers. Since fog computing hardware has far fewer room than cloud computing hardware, it is more user friendly.

Connected devices from the network's edge to the network center will use Fog computing, while the network center needs cloud computing. In fact, continuing Internet access is not necessary for the operation of fog networks. This implies, programs can operate individually with minimal to no Internet access and, if the link is accessible, they can submit required notifications to the cloud. On the other hand, cloud-based computing requires the connection of devices in advance of the cloud service. Fog assists devices in the measurement, monitoring, processing, analysis, and reaction, and distributing IoT device computation, communication, storage, monitoring, and decision-making (Fatemeh et al., 2016). To their benefits, several companies may exploit fog: electricity, manufacturing, transport, education, intelligent cities, to name a few.

3. Cloudlets

Cloudlets are tiny cloud data centers at the edge of a network that are strengthened by versatility (Satyanarayanan et al., 2009). These form the second level of the hierarchy with three levels as shown in Figure 8: the IoT or edge network, Cloudlet, and Edge. Cloudlets are intended to boost smartphone applications that are resource-intensive and responsive, by offering more powerful computational services with less delay close to mobile devices. Thus, the latency delays commonly associated with WAN cloud computing can be avoided. Cloudlets will offer the required assistance to 5G networks upon their launch. To achieve the highest possible level in the network coverage, they also need to be decentralized and broadly dispersed, thus helping to leverage resources from close mobile computers. Cloudlet architecture is shown in Figure 9.

Network service owners (e.g. AT&T, Nokia, etc.) may authorize virtualized databases to be similar to their Personal devices with fewer equipment compared with large cloud data centers. The limited scale of the clouds results in less storage, resulting also lower latency and energy usage than in cloud computing. The aim of Cloudlet computing is to support local devices. Even like Mobile Adhoc Cloud Computing (MACC) varies greatly from cloud computing, it often varies drastically from desktop storage. Cloudlet requires virtualization technology in VM, while such architecture is not a prerequisite for MACC (Yousefpour et al., 2018).

Figure 9. Cloudlet Architecture

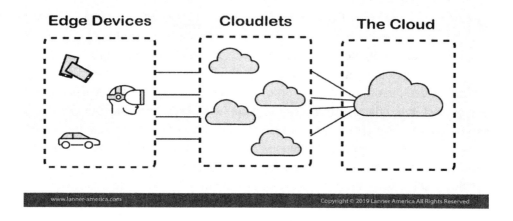

4. Multi-Access Edge Computing

Multi-Access Edge Computing is a networking architecture that allows the placement of Radio Access Network (RAN) computing and storage resources. The Multi-Access Edge Computing increases network performance and provides consumers with content (Taleb et al., 2017). To this end, it can be adjusted to the radio load to increase network performance and reduce the need for backhauling over long distances. The enhanced location, augmented reality, and the Internet of Things capabilities could be supported by mobile edge computing too. It offers these businesses a lead time until 5G networks continue to grow and respond to new technology (Mach & Becvar, 2017).

Figure 10. Multi-Access Edge Computing reference architecture

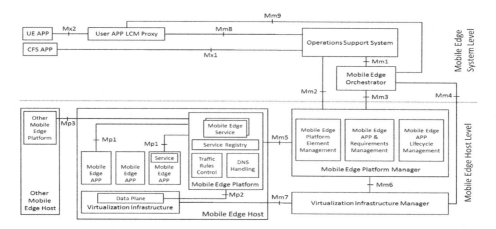

The reference architecture for Multi-Access Computing Edge is shown in Figure 10, provides a clear overview of the Multi-Access Edge Computing System features and interfaces (Taleb et al., 2017). The Reference Architecture for Multi-Access Edge Computing focuses on the level of mobile edge systems and the level of mobile edge house excluding networks. The host stage for the mobile edges is the network operator, the manager of the mobile edge framework, and the manager of the virtualization infrastructure. The Mobile Edge Host supports applications (APPs), which offer an infrastructure of virtualization that offers computing, storage, and network resources and a set of fundamental functions (mobile edge services) that are needed for mobile edge platform APPs. The mobile edge network helps apps to find, publicize, and access edge resources and provides a set of guidelines for forwarding aircraft to the virtualization system. Such communication law is focused on suggestions provided by the managers of network edge and cell networks. The mobile edge platform configures the local DSS management system that enables user traffic to access the desired mobile edge app and communicates with other peer platforms via the Mp3 interface.

Multi-access edge computing expands edge computing by connecting close low energy, low-resource handheld devices with computers, and storage space. RAN operators may connect edge computing capabilities to established base stations with a Multi-Access Edge Computing device. Small-scale virtualization power data centers may also be similarly found in multi-access cloud computing as edge computing (Taleb et al., 2017). The computing resources are moderate compared to cloud computing because of the hardware underlying MEC and edge computing.

Nevertheless, multi-access edge computing offers connectivity through WAN, DHCP, and cellular networks, while edge computing may typically decide any type of communication. MCC analysis often focuses primarily on the partnerships between Internet customers (on mobile devices) and cloud service providers, while Multi-Access Edge Computing research focuses on (RAN-based) connectivity providers. In MCC, multi-access edge computing focuses on network technology. The upcoming 5 G platform is expected to greatly benefit MEC. 5G is similarly used as an enabler for multi-access tops since it provides reduced latency and greater network app capacity and a wide variety of finest granular connected applications. MEC facilitates the use of edge computing for a wide spectrum of latency, connected computers, and more effective data core networks. MEC often requires mobile network applications that are prone to crucial delays.

5.   MicroData Centers

With the rise of the Internet of Things already encouraging the production of new smart devices and IoT sensors, a business study predicts that within the next two and half years the Microdata center solution sector could be worth an astounding 32 billion dollars. Microdata centers are expected to be more useful for small to medium-sized enterprises that do not have their own data centers, since big businesses tend to have more capital and do not require these solutions. The Microdata centers have all the core components of a conventional data center. For some edge computing applications, micro data centers, although usually much smaller for scale, are far more suited than large data centers. The size means that both within and outside conditions the microdata center can be deployed. This makes them perfect for edge computers as they can be locally distributed where the database is located and can be customized to the needs of those who wish to implement it.

6.   Cloud of Things

In a Cloud of Things (CoT), the extreme edge, the final user, takes away all processing power. While the computing power of IoT devices is still small, many modern mobiles have a high potential (Wang et al., 2018). It may be coordinated to run a cloud service on the edge. For example, a car might send warning signals to others and attempt to rearrange other routes without the user's feedback. Cloud infrastructure may be delivered at the very edge using mobile devices or IoT systems. A term related to fog computing is The Cloud of Things. A CoT is a virtualized cloud network that is used in all IoT devices.

Cloud of Things, though, is measured using the cloud created by pooled IoT sources. Edge nodes are used for identifying, virtualizing, and creating an IoT Tools (CoT) application network as near agents on the ground. Its network is an architecture that has been dispersed globally and application agents continuously discover IoT system services and pool them as server tools. CoT enables remote sensing and centralized data collection inside the network. The CoT framework can be scale-based to IoT networks, enables IoT device heterogeneity and edge computing nodes to be used, and offers a foundation for fog sensing.

Like CoT, there is a concept of PClouds (Jang et al., 2014), which are distributed as networks, both locally / personally and remotely / publicly and in machines. If remote cloud services are unavailable or hard to reach due to poor network coverage PCloud will support end-users. Cloudrone, the concept of utilizing low-cost aircraft, single-board machines, and light-weight OS systems to install ad-hoc micro-cloud infrastructures in the sky is another innovative idea, close in design to Cloud of stuff and MACCs. The drones create a cloud storage cluster in the sky that delivers the cloud resources close to the customer, often without terrestrial web connectivity networks.

Femtoclouds were also introduced to use the calculative capabilities and overall ness of under-utilized cell apps, analogous to the idea of Cloud of Things. Clusters of devices tend to be located in places such as schools, public transport, or centers, are utilized by Femtoclouds. In (Habak et al., 2017) for the control of resources and activities in Femtoclouds, a hybrid edge-cloud architecture is introduced, which will allow a low latency.

Resource Management in Edge Computing

Network services are installed on distributed cloud servers to enhance network consistency (Service quality, QoS) and gain unlimited capital. These servers will often also host data centers situated in various locations for service distribution. In the next 2020, though, the expected network interface volume would be 25 billion in the future. The networking infrastructure for the mobile network is progressed by growing the number of internet subscribers and rising the use of cellular broadband. This involves video sharing applications and software connected to computer gaming. When the Internet of Things arises, the program gathers and transfers a ton of data to the cloud. Such heavy traffic burdens the core network and QoS would impact the delivery of enhanced transmission services by the service suppliers.

Despite the rising competition in the future, telecoms service providers also face the task of providing customer access faster and growing network delivery delays. Edge Computing is a way to decentralize certain processing power into a leading network and discharge the network into the edge network so that it can spread the load on the server. Although IT companies have various edge computing concepts, edge computing may be embedded in the cloud environment. The edge network will be responsible for managing loads of data pre-processing to enable the quickest infrastructure and the application that demands a significant number of computational power or the remote storage has to be managed by the cloud. The fusion of cloud and boundary has become a phenomenon owing to the challenges of cloud computing and the benefits of edge computing. However, edge computing is less powerful than the server. Consequently, edge network resource control is a significant problem (López et al., 2015).

Three problems should be addressed. First, how edge nodes can be used for tasks (Richard & Dimitrios, 2017). The technology is commonly known as a virtual machine (VM) in the cloud computing, but the usage of a virtual computer and software upgrades is a concern for late-sensing edge networks. Second, how many cloud resources the edge node needs. It is possible to install such broad network networks with a ton of computing resources in the cloud, but a big network infrastructure with high bandwidth may be challenging at the end of the network. The extension of the infrastructure is a fatal blow to the limited-resource network. Thirdly, how edge node resources are managed. The usage of resources in the edge node is dynamically updated. The edge band node is likely to use constraints on size because of its restricted resources relative to the cloud with infinite resources. Each service has an importance and is often taken into consideration through the allocation of resources to prioritize the service.

Key Benefits of Edge Computing

Many new IoT technologies may depend on cutting edge computing, such as autonomous cars, drones, or smart grids Some of the benefits found by IoT edge computing include (Shi et al., 2016):

1. **Low latency:** The edge of the IoT system is by its definition closer to the heart of the server. This ensures a faster round trip to meet local computing capacity which accelerates network transmission which data collection dramatically.
2. **Resilience**: The edge has more connectivity possibilities than a clustered layout. The stability of data transmission is ensured by this delivery. In case of an interruption at the bottom, appropriate tools to ensure continuous service are available.
3. **Longer battery life for IoT devices:** By being able to use better latency to access communication networks for shorter periods, battery life of driven IoT devices may be enhanced. Distributed ledger or a modified open-source ledger execution such as BigchainDB may be used for gaining from a distributed ledger that offers functionality from the MongoDB NoSQL database on which it is centered.
4. **Scalability:** As communication with the edge model is decentralized, less load can be applied to the network in the end. In particular, when the application and control airplane is situated on the edge next to the results, scaling IoT devices will have less resource effect on the network
5. **Access to data analytics and AI:** The capacity of edge computing, data collection, and analysis and AIs, which allow very fast response times to handle massive 'real-time' data sets that can't be submitted to centralized networks, can all be integrated.
6. **Efficient data management:** The edge data processing enhances easy control of data content, such as extraction and prioritization. When the data storage is performed at the bottom, simpler data sets may be provided for more review for cloud-based computing.

Use Cases of Edge Computing in IoT

1. Device Management:

There are several system characteristics and settings that can be managed at the edge, with many application management systems expanding their capabilities to handle devices connecting to edge networks (Li et al., 2018). Below are descriptions of four specific characteristics that system control at the edge would need to support:

a. Device configuration updates: Edge systems must be set up locally when networks improve. When networks shift. This can be controlled remotely from the ground.
b. Distributed firmware updates: the usage of the edge gateway to locally deliver software changes, through the edge node control application, relative to the method that usually deals with the delivery of a firmware update centrally.
c. Edge node or gateway management: device management systems may be used to handle the operator 's edge network as well as the IoT system.
d. Diagnostics of devices: Using edge analytics, deep learning, or pattern detection may aid in detecting particular issues with field tools.

2. Security:

The IoT itself is a centralized, dynamic computer network. For successful IoT service, edge computing brings most of the logic and data storage closer to end-users and the edge deployment of protection systems often presents the ability to expand security capacities, as well as to provide native security for modern applications with low latency.

In data protection, the edge has a big role to play. Many specialized tools and strategies can be deployed to make sure the edge contributes to the overall IoT delivery efficiency (Ni et al., 2017). The IoT edge protection will be handled in the same manner as every other protected setting, but modern technologies are available which can guarantee security at different edge and system rates. For example, with good ID management for devices on the edge, the security becomes simpler and the concept of edge processes rigorously to ensure that they stay protected.

3. Priority Messaging:

Most of the IoT data is low in importance – irregular status changes and low priority data. However, other details would be very critical and attention will be provided to ensuring that action is taken rapidly. The essential data is possibly quite small but is the most significant percentage of the overall volume generated. To facilitate a cascade of acts through multiple platforms and computers, the reach of the priority messages extends beyond just specific applications (Grewe et al., 2017). The edge helps the production, storage, processing, and execution of high-value data rather than transferring the data to the cloud.

As part of the overall architecture of IoT devices, networks, and data processing facilities, priority communications would need to be addressed. Various forms of priority communication are open. Priority communications, for example, a fire alarm, are mainly in the established format as a contribution from a known procedure. Often, the message cannot be recognized by the system as a high priority, but it may also be detected through processing at the bottom. For example, voltage variations in a smart grid that allow data collection from multiple devices to prioritize. IoT edge is allowed for high-priority communications and more behavior. Faster answers can only be ensured by interacting with local IoT windows, clouds, and preserving the effect of local priority messages.

For more distribution and decision-making, details that have a greater influence outside the local region will, for instance, be uploaded to the central cloud for feeding into bigger databases for computational purposes, instantly or after addressing local scenarios. For fast transmission of high-priority messages, data processing is needed in near-real-time. As tagged data is obtained, if the appropriate classifications are established inside edge gateway programs, then it can quickly be detected and prioritized. Further, sorting may be used for the detection of data from many applications and computers to allow for the same priority. The program on the edge of the gateway or node will determine automatedly what to do about a high-priority message. It could well be necessary for established data types from known applications or devices to start a pre-defined procedure.

4.   Data Aggregation:

Related data will overload a network if transmitted at once, e.g. if each intelligent meter sends a message concurrently with a power failure. In such situations, the function of the application running on top is to recognize and aggregate a few related messages (Lu et al., 2017). This can be achieved in a variety of ways:

a.   Aggregated data generation: If a new edge node receives several messages within a brief period of time, such messages may be inserted and the original messages replaced. If several messages are sent, the edge does not submit any messages or info. There is also a new dataset that analyses the obtained results. It will provide a summary of all incoming communications, likely daily alerts until a shift in status happens.
b.   Sampling: A second choice is to perform sampling of systems. If a significant number of identical messages are sent, the edge may opt to only track a handful of affected units, rather than the entire fleet before the status of these shifts. When vehicles enter traffic queues, data can only be taken from each tenth car before they start moving again instead of getting status reports from an automobile in the crowd.

5.   Cloud Enablement:

It is anticipated that the edge would be desirable for cloud companies as it provides them with the opportunity to efficiently manage data loading and computing capacity to help low-latency applications, increase the efficiency of infrastructure and minimize the burden at their current data centers (Yousefpour et al., 2018). There will be a mutually profitable partnership between cloud providers and mobile operators where operators provide local ability to encourage cloud providers to use IoT edges, and cloud providers provide networks to deliver a wide spectrum of services on the operator's leading network. Some IoT consumers, whether factories or smart cities, may also insist on local storage and management of their results.

IoT edge systems never run entirely independently from a business point of view. For power, tracking, and upgrading purposes at the very least, a link to a centralized server is always important, and hence the relationship between edges and servers is complex. The great thing for both realms is a mixed edge and cloud design.

APPLICATION OF EDGE COMPUTING IN SMART AGRICULTURE

Edge computing has now started to label a number of sectors around the world. There seem to be few areas in which the presence of any sort of edge computing can't be sensed from processing and logistics to healthcare and retail. Farming and Agriculture are one of the fields in which edge computing continues to change the landscape (Li et al., 2020).

1. Environmental Monitoring:

The ability to track various facets of agricultural activities from a farmer is one of the main benefits of Edge computing on agriculture and farming in the last couple of years. Sensor networks that range from several intermittent sensors to thousands of integrated instruments measuring soil, wind, humidity and temperature conditions and acidity and pH levels. Edge computing makes it possible to produce and capture data nearer to source in order to provide these applications while still allowing some data processing operations in the edge devices themselves to be carried out.

2. Automation:

In the fourth industrial revolution, the use of virtualization, robotics, and big data have become main factors and robotics is therefore no longer playing a growing role in so many intelligent farming and agricultural enterprises. As stated, autonomous robot systems can all be used with the use of edge computing and automation systems as well as injections of soil, heaters and lighting. Automation will become a valuable tool for farmers in combination with numerous remote-control apps and tools now provided to smart farms and farmers.

3. Vertical Farming:

Vertical Farming requires the use of data from an IoT sensor and computer network to maximise food and plant production without cultivating soils. In vertical farms, for example, a network of sensors tracks humidity levels continuously around the plant (O'Grady et al., 2019). Most of the analysis of data involved in such tasks, using edge computing, can be performed on the edge devices without needing to be sent to the cloud and thereby contribute more to the importance of such systems in the agricultural environment.

4. Robotics:

Robotics has been an integral part of many industries for decades now, but automotive production, for instance, is also steadily gaining momentum elsewhere. This is no longer the case with the help of edge computing and IoT computer networks. Within agriculture, the introduction of smart farming technologies has enabled the use of sophisticated edge computing devices and the Internet of Things (IoT) programmes. These devices may be planned for automatic tasks such as plant picking and spraying plants and seeds, and further implementations are under development.

CHALLENGES IN EDGE COMPUTING

1. **Accessibility and Resource constraints:** Sometimes, Edge technologies face technical challenges to handle human IT resources and do not permit large user costs. In order to track and manage any Edge spot, businesses should provide the dedicated admin. This operator constraints – due to size, system scale, geographical connectivity and other costs/ROI requirements, Edge implementations are obliged to be very low not only on the machine footprint but also in terms of overhead technological IT. They must be "plug & play" from the perspective of installation and continued operation (Shi et al., 2016).

2. **Compute and hardware constraints:** From the point of view of technical computing, many edge environments are limited. For example, it is difficult accommodate as much hardware as a full-scale data center in the case of embedded devices.

3. **Connectivity:** The infrastructure provider's capacity to cope with latency and jitter problems of all kinds is also important.

4. **Remote management:** Skilled workers cannot routinely install and maintain the system in certain settings. An unqualified operator can have to make easy deployments for plugs and play. This covers stable edge technology upgrades, debug-ability for bugs and extra system implementation (Shi et al., 2016). Edge systems need to be extremely specialised and should provide a variety of capabilities to provide: network cache with missing links, data stream processing, appropriate data analysis, event-based message broking, system control, fault tolerance, etc.

5. **Security:** This is a critical problem. This involves protected communication between the data centre and Edge to protect data protection, whether in rest or in movement – anonymization of Edge-specified confidential consumer data. Other specifications for safety include mutual trust between the central data center and Edge devices, the ability to find and avoid rogue devices while attacking and secure communication via the WAN.

6. **Support for Air-gapped deployments**: A crucial advantage of edge computing is the ability to handle distant, air-locked devices of compute-controlled locations without the need for manual interference (Shi et al., 2016). Strong cloud latency can lead to delays and can interfere with the application's service. This also implies that expectations from the "Standard operating mode" of networking in data centers frequently tend to be valid in edge environments.

DISCUSSION

Since cloud, fog, and edge computing are designed and each is established to transcend those limits in the preceding paradigm, some of its properties are identical. The variations and needs, however, identify each model and promote the resources and applications that are expected. The design differs, but they both have the same goal of supplying devices and data. Any non-functional specifications accomplish the features of these paradigms. In terms of model protection, this can be extended in cloud computing to the service provider or framework created The first is the application creator, like configuration and control of the device, from the viewpoint of a SaaS vendor, is a manufacturer, is subject to protection controls of providers such as the network separation protocols or physical infrastructure access policies. This means that the contractor is liable for designing the software that monitors the utilization and frequency of the program. On the other side, fog computing privacy is maintained by minimizing data transmission across the network and managing data locally, thus decreasing protection vulnerabilities and growing data privacy.

Data was stored globally but closer to the device for the edge network than fog computing, to help ensure privacy. The bandwidth and reaction time metrics have proved their leading both in terms of efficiency and in terms of fog paradigms. To obtain smaller data parts that enable the achievement of low end-to-end latency, large bandwidth, and low jitter operation, Edge computing nodes have to be near to the end devices (Yousefpour et al., 2018). In comparison, fewer data in the fog computing network are transported to the data centers: local data pre-processing, and direct communication with wired computer queries that minimize the bandwidth required. Although latency is even better in cloud storage, data is still sent to the cloud and the cloud addiction is very high. But customers demand a fast operating system for cloud storage with SaaS applications. The theoretical performance constraint during design must also be taken into account and projects that utilize principles such as distributed execution, the architecture of microsystems, the functionality of multi-data, and more must be incorporated. Besides, flexibility is highly essential as SaaS models manage vital business solutions. Unforeseen downtime can lead to losses of SaaS clients, so the plan doesn't go wrong. Factors contributing to the Recovery Tune Objective (RTO) and the Recovery Point Objective (RPO) need to be taken into account.

Some other popular aspects of fog and edge computing endorse complexity as the nodes may be multiple types without a defined norm. This is extremely relevant as numerous products from different manufacturers and vendors should be associated with the recent production of IoT. Their storage and measuring output vary from the end devices and the fog or edge nodes. In contrast with cloud networks, the edge and fog nodes are significantly less computable and maintained. In addition, terminal machines and fog nodes can dynamically switch and connect to promote IoT system computing functionality. Location perception in fog-based models is another key aspect because end devices need sensing and positioning capacity to decide where the data needs to be processed. In fact, it will allow it easy to pre-process, search, and store in multiple ways, and often helps minimize latency. The existence of the design restricts this property in cloud computing (Yuyi Mao et al., 2017).

CONCLUSION

The IoT is a combination of infrastructure, applications, and networking capabilities. The development of IoT implementations both in customers and industrial use cases would result in innovations and IoT products. For an efficient and integrated IoT approach, edge computing is necessary. In the IoT domain, there are various open-source platforms. Cloud service providers provide very rich IoT and edge computing capabilities. IoT software requirements include loosely linked flexible, platform-independent, and open standards-based guidance. This paper focusses on the general architecture for the Edge computing paradigm and various components involved in the platform. The integration of various Edge technologies to provide an efficient IoT system is also discussed. Now that many businesses and development providers shifting towards the Edge environment, new architectures, a different ecosystem, and a different kind of latency constraint may emerge as a need for distributed applications.

REFERENCES

Ai, Y., Peng, M., & Zhang, K. (2017). Edge cloud computing technologies for Internet of things: A primer. *Digital Communications and Networks*, *4*(2), 77–86. doi:10.1016/j.dcan.2017.07.001

Asim, M., Wang, Y., Wang, K., & Huang, P. (2020). *A Review on Computational Intelligence Techniques in Cloud and Edge Computing.* ArXiv, abs/2007.14215.

Baktir, A. C., Sonmez, C., Ersoy, C., Ozgovde, A., & Varghese, B. (2019). *Addressing the Challenges in Federating Edge Resources.* Fog and Edge Computing. doi:10.1002/9781119525080.ch2

Bojanova, I., & Samba, A. (2011). Analysis of Cloud Computing Delivery Architecture Models. *2011 IEEE Workshops of International Conference on Advanced Information Networking and Applications*, 453-458.

Cziva, R., & Pezaros, D. P. (2017, June). Container Network Functions: Bringing NFV to the Network Edge. *IEEE Communications Magazine*, *55*(6), 24–31. doi:10.1109/MCOM.2017.1601039

Fatemeh, T., Samdanis, K., Mada, B., Flinck, H., Dutta, S., & Sabella, D. (2017). On Multi-Access Edge Computing: A Survey of the Emerging 5G Network Edge Cloud Architecture and Orchestration. *IEEE Communications Surveys and Tutorials*, *19*(3), 1657–1681. doi:10.1109/COMST.2017.2705720

Ganz, F., Puschmann, D., Barnaghi, P. M., & Carrez, F. (2015). A Practical Evaluation of Information Processing and Abstraction Techniques for the Internet of Things. *IEEE Internet of Things Journal*, *2*(4), 340–354. doi:10.1109/JIOT.2015.2411227

Grewe, D., Wagner, M., Arumaithurai, M., Psaras, I., & Kutscher, D. (2017). Information-Centric Mobile Edge Computing for Connected Vehicle Environments: Challenges and Research Directions. *Proceedings of the Workshop on Mobile Edge Communication*, 7-12. 10.1145/3098208.3098210

Gubbi, J., Buyya, R., Marusic, S., & Palaniswami, M. (2013). Internet of Things (IoT): A vision, architectural elements, and future directions. *Future Generation Computer Systems*, *29*(7), 1645–1660. doi:10.1016/j.future.2013.01.010

Habak, K., Zegura, E., Ammar, M., & Harras, K. A. (2017). Workload management for dynamic mobile device clusters in edge Femtoclouds. *Proceedings of the Second ACM/IEEE Symposium on Edge Computing*, 1-14. 10.1145/3132211.3134455

Hong, C., & Varghese, B. (2019). Resource Management in Fog/Edge Computing: A Survey on Architectures, Infrastructure, and Algorithms. *ACM Comput. Surv., 52*, 97:1-97:37.

Jalali, F., Hinton, K., Ayre, R., Alpcan, T., & Tucker, R. (2016). Fog Computing May Help to Save Energy in Cloud Computing. *IEEE Journal on Selected Areas in Communications*, *34*(5), 1728–1739. doi:10.1109/JSAC.2016.2545559

Jang, M., Schwan, K., Bhardwaj, K., Gavrilovska, A., & Avasthi, A. (2014). Personal clouds: Sharing and integrating networked resources to enhance end-user experiences. *IEEE INFOCOM 2014 - IEEE Conference on Computer Communications*, 2220-2228.

Jha, D. N., Alwasel, K., Alshoshan, A., Huang, X., Naha, R. K., Battula, S. K., Garg, S., Puthal, D., James, P., Zomaya, A. Y., Dustdar, S., & Ranjan, R. (2020). IoTSim-Edge: A simulation framework for modeling the behavior of Internet of Things and edge computing environments. *Software, Practice & Experience*, *50*(6), 844–867. doi:10.1002pe.2787

Li, C., Xue, Y., Wang, J., Zhang, W., & Li, T. (2018, April). Edge-oriented computing paradigms: A survey on architecture design and system management. *ACM Computing Surveys*, *51*(2), 1–34. doi:10.1145/3154815

Li, X., Zhu, L., Chu, X., & Fu, H. (2020). Edge Computing-Enabled Wireless Sensor Networks for Multiple Data Collection Tasks in Smart Agriculture. *J. Sensors, 2020*, 4398061:1-4398061:9.

López, P., Montresor, A., Epema, D., Datta, A., Higashino, T., Iamnitchi, A., Barcellos, M. P., Felber, P., & Rivière, E. (2015). Edge-centric Computing: Vision and Challenges. *Computer Communication Review*, *45*(5), 37–42. doi:10.1145/2831347.2831354

Lu, R., Heung, K., Lashkari, A., & Ghorbani, A. (2017). A Lightweight Privacy-Preserving Data Aggregation Scheme for Fog Computing-Enhanced IoT. *IEEE Access: Practical Innovations, Open Solutions*, *5*, 3302–3312. doi:10.1109/ACCESS.2017.2677520

Mach, P., & Becvar, Z. (2017). Mobile Edge Computing: A Survey on Architecture and Computation Offloading. *IEEE Communications Surveys and Tutorials*, *19*(3), 1628–1656. doi:10.1109/COMST.2017.2682318

Mao, Y., You, C., Zhang, J., Huang, K., & Letaief, K. (2017). A Survey on Mobile Edge Computing: The Communication Perspective. *IEEE Communications Surveys and Tutorials*, *19*(4), 2322–2358. doi:10.1109/COMST.2017.2745201

Mirkhanzadeh, B., Shakeri, A., Shao, C., Razo, M., Tacca, M., Galimberti, G., Martinelli, G., Cardani, M., & Fumagalli, A. (2018). An SDN-enabled multi-layer protection and restoration mechanism. *Optical Switching and Networking*, *30*, 23–32. doi:10.1016/j.osn.2018.05.005

Moghaddam, F. F., Ahmadi, M., Sarvari, S., Eslami, M., & Golkar, A. (2015). Cloud computing challenges and opportunities: A survey. *2015 1st International Conference on Telematics and Future Generation Networks (TAFGEN)*, 34-38.

Naha, R. K., Garg, S., Georgakopoulos, D., Jayaraman, P., Gao, L., Xiang, Y., & Ranjan, R. (2018). Fog computing: Survey of trends, architectures, requirements, and research directions. *IEEE Access: Practical Innovations, Open Solutions*, *6*(47), 980–009. doi:10.1109/ACCESS.2018.2866491

Ni, J., Zhang, A., Lin, X., & Shen, X. (2017). Security, Privacy, and Fairness in Fog-Based Vehicular Crowdsensing. *IEEE Communications Magazine*, *55*(6), 146–152. doi:10.1109/MCOM.2017.1600679

O'Grady, M., Langton, D., & O'Hare, G. (2019). *Edge computing: A tractable model for smart agriculture?* Academic Press.

OpenFogConsortium. (2017). *Openfog reference architecture for fog computing*. https://www.openfog-consortium.org/ra/

Premsankar, G., Francesco, M. D., & Taleb, T. (2018). Edge Computing for the Internet of Things: A Case Study. *IEEE Internet of Things Journal*, *5*(2), 1275–1284. doi:10.1109/JIOT.2018.2805263

Satyanarayanan, M., Bahl, P., Cáceres, R., & Davies, N. (2009). The Case for VM-Based Cloudlets in Mobile Computing. *IEEE Pervasive Computing*, *8*(4), 14–23. doi:10.1109/MPRV.2009.82

Shi, F., Tang, G., Li, Y., Cai, Z., Zhang, X., & Zhou, T. (2019). A Survey on Edge Computing Systems and Tools. *Proceedings of the IEEE*, *107*(8), 1537–1562. doi:10.1109/JPROC.2019.2920341

Shi, W., Cao, J., Zhang, Q., Li, Y., & Xu, L. (2016). Edge Computing: Vision and Challenges. *IEEE Internet of Things Journal*, *3*(5), 637–646. doi:10.1109/JIOT.2016.2579198

Sittón-Candanedo, I. & Corchado Rodríguez, J. (2019). An Edge Computing Tutorial. *Oriental Journal of Computer Science and Technology*, *12*, 34-38. . doi:10.13005/ojcst12.02.02

Tang, L., Tang, B., Kang, L., & Zhang, L. (2019). A Novel Task Caching and Migration Strategy in Multi-Access Edge Computing Based on the Genetic Algorithm. *Future Internet*, *11*(8), 1–14. doi:10.3390/fi11080181

Wang, J., Pan, J., Esposito, F., Calyam, P., Yang, Z., & Mohapatra, P. (2018). *Edge Cloud Offloading Algorithms: Issues, Methods, and Perspectives*. Networking and Internet Architecture.

Yousefpour, A., Fung, C., Nguyen, T., Kadiyala, K.P., Jalali, F., Niakanlahiji, A., Kong, J., & Jue, J. (2019). *All One Needs to Know about Fog Computing and Related Edge Computing Paradigms: A Complete Survey*. ArXiv, abs/1808.05283.

Zhang, Q., Cheng, L., & Boutaba, R. (2010). Cloud computing: State-of-the-art and research challenges. *Journal of Internet Services and Applications*, *1*(1), 7–18. doi:10.100713174-010-0007-6

This research was previously published in Cases on Edge Computing and Analytics; pages 1-30, copyright year 2021 by Engineering Science Reference (an imprint of IGI Global).

Chapter 4
Recent Advances in Edge Computing Paradigms:
Taxonomy Benchmarks and Standards for Unconventional Computing

Sana Sodanapalli
Madanapalle Institute of Technology and Science, Madanapalle, India

Hewan Shrestha
https://orcid.org/0000-0003-3901-2212
Madanapalle Institute of Technology and Science, Madanapalle, India

Chandramohan Dhasarathan
https://orcid.org/0000-0002-5279-950X
Madanapalle Institute of Technology and Science, Madanapalle, India

Puviyarasi T.
Madanapalle Institute of Technology and Science, Madanapalle, India

Sam Goundar
https://orcid.org/0000-0001-6465-1097
British University, Vietnam

ABSTRACT

Edge computing is an exciting new approach to network architecture that helps organizations break beyond the limitations imposed by traditional cloud-based networks. It has emerged as a viable and important architecture that supports distributed computing to deploy compute and storage resources closer to the data source. Edge and fog computing addresses three principles of network limitations of bandwidth, latency, congestion, and reliability. The research community sees edge computing at manufacturing, farming, network optimization, workplace safety, improved healthcare, transportation, etc. The promise of this technology will be realized through addressing new research challenges in the IoT paradigm and the design of highly-efficient communication technology with minimum cost and effort.

DOI: 10.4018/978-1-6684-5700-9.ch004

1. INTRODUCTION

Edge computing is the upcoming enhancement and advancement in technology. Edge computing brings the decentralization of networks. Edge computing is a distributed computing system that allows bringing computation of data, storage too close to the source, and minimizing the bandwidth, improving response time. Edge computing is faster than cloud computing and IoT. This is a process that exploits network gateways or smart objects for performing tasks and provide services on behalf of the cloud. Edge computing also enables data stream acceleration that includes real-time processing of data without latency use. It can use different programming languages on different platforms, each having different runtime.

2. LITERATURE STUDY

Shaoyong Guoa (2021), the edge computing environment providing includes Base Station with server cluster and many kinds of computational access points close to the devices. All of these edge computing nodes can provide service execution for the container cluster. It is challenging to achieve an optimal real-time resource allocation scheme for the container cluster in the edge environment. Delay reduction is an important performance indicator for delay-sensitive applications. The end-to-end delay analysis in the existing work often focuses on the sum of all data packet delays in the service flow. Then a delay-sensitive resource allocation algorithm based on A3C (Asynchronous Advantage Actor-Critic) is proposed to solve this problem. Finally, we utilize the ESN (Echo state network) to improve the traditional A3C algorithm.

Kyuchang Lee (2021), Deep learning is one of the AI technologies that can analyze large-scale data effectively. Edge computing is another promising technology that improves the service provision of modern smart cities. The deep learning process is suitable for Edge computing environments as some processing layers can be shifted to the edges. Subsequently, the remaining data to be processed can be transferred to the cloud to be processed by residual layers. Once DL layers are distributed by the EC system, the edge nodes reduce the data size by processing certain data portions at the edges. Therefore, the network delay and computational overhead of the cloud server can be reduced. There is a Deep learning Layer Assignment in Edge Computing (DLAEC) algorithm. Here, a task means a unit of software that improves the quality of life (QoL), utilizes data from several devices and allows usage by multiple devices independently.

Yaser Mansouri(2020), Cloud computing is the delivery of centralized and virtualized computing, storage, services, and application resources over the Internet. However, cloud computing is not able to serve real-time IoT applications, as they require ultra-low latency, low jitter, high-demand bandwidth, mobility services, etc; The extension of computing services from centralized cloud-based paradigms to the edge of the network is called edge computing that boosts the overall efficiency of infrastructures by achieving ultra-low latency, reducing backhaul load, supporting mobility services, and increasing service resilience. These paradigms consist of connected resource-constrained devices such as smartphones, wearable gadgets, and so on. The fundamental technology of edge computing paradigms is resource virtualization that decouples hardware resources from software in order to run multiple tenants on the same hardware. Application requirements are the primary factors for the selection of virtualization types in IoT frameworks. As a result, there is a need for prioritizing the requirements, integrating different virtualization techniques, and exploiting hierarchical edge-cloud architecture.

Junyou Yang (2020), Adaptive dynamic programming belongs to the reinforcement learning field, which is an important branch of artificial intelligence. Policy iteration (PI) and value iteration (VI) are mainstream iterative model-based offline ADP methods. However, in practice, system mathematical models are generally unavailable. To realize the model-free purpose without using the identification schemes, an online dual-network-based action-dependent heuristic dynamic programming method and a critic-only Q-learning approach is presented. Researchers integrate the optimal control theory and artificial-intelligence-based algorithms to search for the optimal solution, which will be shown in the numerical simulation results. Finally, these optimal control strategies are applied to a benchmark microgrid system to demonstrate the effectiveness of performance optimization.

Carine Souveyet (2020), Edge computing advocates for the deployment at the network edge of services traditionally placed on cloud platforms. These edge and fog computing are seen as the alternative for "pure cloud" solutions when it comes to telecommunications and IoT applications. Data transfers between IoT devices and cloud platforms may be subject to considerable latency, which may negatively affect application behavior. Edge platforms should ensure that the services are deployed close to the end devices and that the computing resources are assigned according to their capabilities at run time. Hence, Edge computing is a paradigm in which substantial computing and storage resources are placed at the Internet's edge in close proximity to mobile devices or sensors. we explore the two concerns: low communication latency and data caching through a comprehensive set of benchmarks and illustrate their importance with the help of two elements that should be part of any edge computing toolkit data locality and context awareness.

Shan Huang (2020), Organic agricultural supply chains have focused both in academic and agricultural fields. They are quite complex systems that are in charge of the whole process of production, storage, transportation, marketing, and consumption. The rapid popularization of computer technologies enables data acquisition and processing better among each link in OASCs. Despite all, they still fall into the predicament of information sharing and transparency which results in a severe trust crisis of consumers. Fortunately, the emerging blockchain and edge computing technology probably raise an opportunity to improve this issue. The immutability of blockchain and the paradigm of edge computing to construct an OASC's trust framework, which has a much better trade-off between cost and efficiency. Stakeholders are into four roles, proposing a novel consensus mechanism to manage the information flow. This framework will make traceable solutions for those in developing countries at a low cost in the future.

Wanting Jib (2021), in the context of the growing popularity of the IoT, some applications need lower latency, such as self-driving cars, and it is becoming more important to shift computing power closer to the edge of the network to reduce costs. Edge computing solves the problems of poor cloud computing mobility, weak geographic information awareness, and high cloud computing latency. Blockchain is a distributed architecture with the characteristics of decentralization, transparency, and openness, and cannot be tampered with. Due to the slow transaction speed in the blockchain, there is a large delay in the edge computing system based on the blockchain, and the block is connected to the node, making the nodes in the BMEC face a series of security challenges, such as clone block attack. Specifically, a neural-network-based clone block identification (NCBI) method is proposed to prevent clone block attacks. Experimental results this method can achieve block validation effectively in BMEC, and our construction of blockchain delay is lower than conventional edge computing methods.

Amritpal Singh (2020), Cloud computing sector has been one of the most affected technologies as they are responsible for handling the situation during the novel coronavirus or COVID-19 global pandemic, the delivery of online services with the huge dependence of the end-user domain. A Stackelberg game is formulated for a two-period resource allocation between end-user/IoT devices. Software-defined edge computing has emerged as a viable solution to resolve these latency-sensitive workload issues but not the energy consumption so choose the container-as-a-service (CaaS) approach which would resolve our issues. The proposed approach is validated through a simulated environment with respect to CPU serve time, the network serves time, overall delay, lastly energy consumption. The results obtained show the superiority of the proposed in comparison to the existing variants.

Ibrahim Alghamdi (2020), Mobile Edge Computing refers to a computing paradigm that moves computing resources closer to the user at the edge of the network. The problem is the offloading decision by which the mobile node selects an edge server to offload the computing task. An Optimal stopping theory problem is about deciding when to carry out an action on the basis of a random variable observed in sequence for the purpose of increasing the expected payoff or reducing the expected cost. A performance evaluation is provided using a simulation approach and real-world data sets together with the use of baseline deterministic and stochastic offloading models the results show that the proposed OST models can significantly minimize the expected processing time for analytics task execution and can be implemented in the mobile nodes efficiently.

Jian Zhanga(2020), IoT, big data, and artificial intelligence play a significant role in Cyber-Physical Systems. One of their purposes is to bring the next generation of information and communication technology to achieve mapping between physical space and virtual space. Cyber-physical machine tools will have a machine tool digital space as a digital twin with computing and networking capabilities, allowing real-time feedback loops to be established where machining process and calculation results can feedback control via digital twin. CPMT based on edge computing and digital twin techniques are developed to realize remote sensing, real-time monitoring, and scalable high-performance digital twin application, and the importance of this gap also has been analyzed and evaluated. However, the data generated would affect by network bandwidth and cloud. Furthermore, a novel edge computing algorithm is proposed to detect the abnormality of the edge data from two aspects: the unary outliers of the edge data itself and the multivariate parameter correlation among edge devices.

Ayush Goyal (2020), Increased visibility into industrial machinery and assets offers the first step towards realizing smart manufacturing. Weiss et al. have provided a cost-benefit analysis of manufacturing machinery maintenance, underscoring the vast potential and opportunity. Vibration monitoring is the most important and commonly used method in machinery condition monitoring. Both, signal processing and deep learning-based approaches are available and are being proposed for machinery vibration monitoring and other similar applications. We present an edge cloud performance evaluation for IoT-based machinery vibration monitoring, to foster deployment for the contexts considered.

Tong Zhang (2020), with a wide range of terminals connected to the Industrial Internet, data that needs processing has grown exponentially in the meantime, bringing challenges to techniques of data storage, caching, transmission and computation. However, the traditional paradigm of cloud computing, which is proposed around 2005, is not enough to support the development of the Industrial Internet. Edge computing extends the connotation of the Industrial Internet, in which things change their roles from data consumers to data providers and consumers. It saves the time of data communication and transmission, significantly reducing the latency of data processing, which is quite important to real-time applications. The shallow network algorithms such as the broad learning system (BLS), which have achieved great improvement in computing efficiency, show an optimistic outlook in this area.

Gaofei sun (2020), as the amount of IoT devices and also data produced by these devices soared in recent years; the centralized cloud computing structures become inefficient and overburdened. Nevertheless, more attention should be drawn to the privacy of user-sensitive information collected by IoT devices. By maliciously attacked the sensitive information when IoT devices upload data to multi-access edge computing, the personal data statistics would be inferred by using machine learning methods. In multi-user and multi-edge node computation offloading problem is proposed, which aimed to solve the edge computing server selection problem among multiple users distributively. The Nash equilibrium strategies for the best offloading mechanism are derived. A time average computation rate maximization (TACRM) algorithm aims at a joint allocation of spectrum and computation resources. we formulate the computing task allocation problem for IoT devices with edge computing servers, by a trade-off between three metrics, that is delay tolerance, energy consumption, and also data privacy protections.

Abdul Razaque (2020), The science of computer forensics is complex, and several criminal parties are known to use artificial and intelligent tools, not to mention protecting user's sensitive information. Evidence of a crime is different from than traditional crime act and requires specific crime detection frameworks and tools. Detection of these cases requires edge computing and network forensics to search for and confirm the identity of the criminals and the evidence, and to bring charges against the perpetrators accordingly. Existing forensic approaches using cloud computing solve the problems of privacy, data storage, and scalability. However, these are not adequate for edge resources and do not address forensic efficiency and reliability issues. An ERFF is proposed to increase the efficiency and reliability of industrial forensics. The proposed ERFF consists of a detective module and validation model, with the detective module responsible for detecting the interaction between the client terminal and the edge resource, which means the investigator, is capable of gathering the evidence securely.

Qi Wang (2020), Edge computing has been used in different areas, such as the Internet of vehicles, healthcare, and virtualization. However, the limitation in the processing ability of processors and battery run time of edge devices hinders their broad applications. Technology such as power over ethernet (POE) switches transport energy in a similar way as transferring data. We use the clustering method only once in the first time slot if the network is stable, which would give the preferred location of migration VMs, there is no need to change the migrated target node in subsequent time slots, reducing the scheduling complexity. They used an online task offloading and frequency scaling for energy efficiency (TOFFEE) algorithm to find the optimal result of these subproblems. The simulation result shows that our proposed method reduces both the total energy consumption and the energy consumption from outside of the system.

Guoan Zhang (2020), the limited computing capacity of onboard computing units has become an inescapable fact, which facilitates the development of cloud-based vehicular networking technology. Thus, the efficiency of computation offloading will be degraded. To resolve this issue, multi-access computing, pushing cloud services to wireless access networks has been proposed as an iterative solution. In vehicular edge computing networks (VECN), vehicles moving on the road can access computational and storage resources of MEC servers through vehicular-to-infrastructure (V2I) communication links. An energy-efficiency cost minimization problem is formulated to make a tradeoff between latency and energy consumption, for completing computational tasks in an effective manner.

Junjuan Xia (2021), The rise of IoT is driving the technology development of the fifth-generation (5G) cellular networks. the battery energy and storage space of smart mobile devices are limited, which not only restricts mobile devices from processing large-scale data in time but also affects the quality of user experience. The emergence of the mobile cloud computing (MCC) technique provides a way to solve these problems. A multi-objective optimization strategy based on the DQN algorithm in order to reduce latency and energy consumption. The related research on the MEC computation offloading decision can be divided into two parts. One part is binary computation offloading and the other is partial computation offloading. Finally, simulation results confirm that the proposed DQN algorithm is able to reduce the system cost in process of the secure transmission.

M. Abbasi (2021), Internet of Things (IoT) is overgrowing as a new paradigm of wireless communication. Due to the limited battery life and computing capability of the terminal devices, the cloud server usually displays the role that receives and processes the data offloaded from all kinds of terminals in traditional IoT networks. The use of fog computing in the architecture of the IoT with the aim of improving power consumption and QoS has turned into a significant field of research. Workload allocation in the cloud and the fog was formulated as an optimization problem. The aim was to minimize power consumption in the face of delay limitations. This proposes an approximate algorithm that divides the problem into three subproblems total processing delay and total power consumption of fog devices, total processing delay and total power consumption of the cloud, and delay of transmission between fog devices and the cloud. A Genetic Algorithm (GA) is used for handling a large number of requests and the corresponding quality and security limitations.

Filipe Cerqueira (2020), there is wide adoption of smartphones and tablets for performing the most diverse activities, from leisure to work-related tasks. Swift and spontaneous data storage and dissemination among neighboring mobile devices can be of great usefulness. Sometimes the devices often experience poor or intermittent connectivity, leading to availability issues if application storage and logic are fully delegated to a remote cloud infrastructure. To resolve these issues Thyme is proposed which is a novel time-aware reactive storage system for networks of mobile devices that exploits synergies between the storage substrate and the P/S communication paradigm. This is able to achieve robust, efficient, and timely data storage, dissemination, and querying. There are two different approaches to Thyme, the first one, Thyme-LS, follows a lightweight, yet effective, an unstructured approach using local storage and query flooding, and the second more intricate one, Thyme-DCS, is inspired by the fact that geographical positions have a close relation to the topology in wireless networks and follows a data-centric storage approach whereby we build a storage substrate over a geographic hash table.

Youlong Luo (2020), With the popularity of various smart mobile devices, users' demands for ultra-low latency and high-quality services are increasing. One possible solution to overcome these limitations is to use mobile edge computing but not mobility, security. To allocate cache resources to serve as many user requests as possible, and reduce latency and energy consumption, the edge cooperative caching method based on latency and energy balance in SDN-based mobile edge computing is proposed then the branch and bound algorithm is used to solve the optimal edge caching strategy. In order to effectively migrate ongoing edge services to ensure service continuity, the dynamic service migration method based on deep Q learning is proposed. In the proposed method, firstly, the service migration problem is expressed as a Markov decision process. Secondly, the service migration reward function is constructed. Finally, deep Q learning is used to further obtain the optimal service migration strategy. The proposed service migration algorithm can effectively reduce the number of service migrations and transmission costs; improve the success rate of service migration.

Xiaowen Huang (2020), To address the computational capability issue, Mobile Cloud Computing can augment the capabilities of mobile devices by offloading portion or total energy-consuming tasks of the applications to the cloud server for execution. Resource allocation for computation offloading in Mobile Edge Computing (MEC) a network has been attracted a lot of attention from researchers in order to minimize the energy consumption, offloading delay, and total cost. To tackle this problem, MEC is proposed, which allows the mobile users to offload their computational tasks to the edge cloud server is deployed at the edge of networks covering it. It analyses the competition among edge cloud servers by a no cooperative game and proposes an iteration algorithm to obtain Nash equilibrium to attract more mobile users.

Chunlin Li (2020), the network video service has become one of the fastest-growing businesses in the Internet industry. The traditional centralized cloud computing architecture cannot meet the needs of streaming media service users. There are three different edge computing schemes: Multi-access Edge Computing, fog computing, and cloudlet. Fog computing extends cloud-based network architecture by adding a fog server layer between the cloud and the mobile device and cooperative edge-cloud computing architecture, the streaming media service providers can deploy the streaming media contents in the edge servers. The popularity of content is one of the important bases for cache strategy to implement the content caching decision. In this strategy, the Markov process is used to model user mobility, and the multiple linear regression model is used to predict content popularity. Then a data placement algorithm is proposed by analyzing the marginal gain brought by placing content on edge servers to solve the data placement problem. Finally, a content replacement algorithm based on marginal gain and content popularity is proposed to perform a passive content replacement.

Yanli Li (2020), an individual IoT device has a restrained field of vision and limited sensing, computing, and caching resources, so it is significant to overcome these resource restraint issues and achieve efficient data communications. Scholars are motivated to integrate IoT with Edge computing and clustering to overcome resource limitations and achieve efficient IOTE-based data communication. As a promising data communication paradigm, the Named Data Networking uses Forwarding Interest Base to forward Interest towards any potential provider and employs Pending Interest Table to send Data back to consumers. we propose an NDN-based IOTE (NIOTE) framework to reduce data retrieval delays and Future Generation Computer Systems. The main idea behind NIOTE is that IoT devices employ clustering to regularly collect and upload sensed and captured data to edge devices for rapid processing and caching. NIOTE effectively decreases data communication latency and costs.

Thomas Rausch (2020), Serverless edge computing has emerged as a compelling model for dealing with many of these challenges associated with edge infrastructure. With the idea of serverless cloud functions, we imagine that edge functions can significantly simplify the development and operation of certain edge computing applications. Skippy, a container scheduling system that facilitates the efficient placement of serverless edge functions on distributed and heterogeneous clusters. Skippy is an online scheduler, modeled after the Kubernetes scheduler, implements a greedy multi-criteria decision-making (MCDM) algorithm. The scheduler and optimization technique work in tandem to enable serverless platforms to be used in a wide range of edge computing scenarios.

Ming Xia (2020), convolutional neural network algorithms exhibit computation-intense and memory-intense characteristics when implemented, thereby hindering their smooth deployment in numerous resource-limited devices. An emerging market is developing for running CNN inference in mobile edge computing scenarios e.g., self-driving vehicles. There are two solution ns have been highlighted to enhance the processing performance. One is to simplify the algorithmic complexity of the CNN model, and the other is to adopt hardware accelerators exhibiting less power consumption and better computing performance. Field-programmable gate array, dependent on flexibility, customizability, and energy-efficiency, refers to an optimal acceleration solution for CNN models exhibiting a large degree of parallelism. To address this challenge, the present study develops a lightweight neural network architecture termed Spark Net, capable of significantly reducing the weight parameters and computation demands. The feasibility of the Spark Net is verified on four datasets, i.e., MINIST, CIFAR-10, CIFAR-100, and SVHN.

Table 1. Artificial-intelligence and Physical communication of Edge computing

S.No.	AUTHOR	TECHNIQUES PROPOSED	APPLICABILITY
1.	Yaser Mansouri(2020)	A review of edge computing: Features and resource virtualization	Features and resource virtualization
2.	Junyou Yang (2020)	Artificial-intelligence-based algorithms in multi-access edge computing for the performance optimization control of a benchmark microgrid	Optimization control of a benchmark microgrid
3.	Shan Huang (2020)	Blockchain and edge computing technology enabling organic agricultural supply chain	A framework solution to trust crisis
4.	Wanting Jib(2021)	Blockchain-based mobile edge computing system	Information sciences
5.	Amritpal Singh	Container-based load balancing for energy efficiency in software-defined EC environment	Online delivery services
6.	Ibrahim Alghamdi(2020)	Data quality-aware task offloading in Mobile Edge Computing: An Optimal Stopping Theory approach	OST approach in MEC environment
7.	Jian Zhanga (2020)	Development of an edge computing-based cyber-physical machine tool	Robotics
8.	Ayush Goyal (2020)	Edge-cloud computing performance benchmarking for IoT based machinery vibration monitoring	Machine manufacturing
9.	Tong Zhang(2020)	Edge computing and its role in Industrial Internet: Methodologies, applications, and future directions	Information sciences
10.	Abdul Razaque (2020)	Efficient and reliable forensics using intelligent edge computing	Future generation computer system
11.	Qi Wang (2020)	Energy-aware scheduling in edge computing with a clustering method	Future generation computer system
12.	Filipe Cerqueira (2020)	It's about Thyme: On the design and implementation of a time-aware reactive storage system for pervasive edge computing environments	Mobile devices
13.	Youlong Luo (2020)	Joint edge caching and dynamic service migration in SDN based mobile edge computing	Mobile computing
14.	Thomas Rausch (2020)	Optimized container scheduling for data-intensive serverless edge computing	Scheduling
15.	Ming Xia(2020)	An energy-efficiency FPGA-based accelerator using optimized lightweight CNN for edge computing.	Artificial intelligence

3. ARTIFICIAL-INTELLIGENCE AND PHYSICAL COMMUNICATION OF EDGE COMPUTING

Edge computing paradigm for effective resource sharing would be tested under various physical communication mediums. Artificial intelligent is a contemporary research for intelligent computing and it is illustrated in table 1.

In distributed system information sharing can be handled in the form of network availability and reachability of resource sharing nodes which are participating in the edge computing process. Various research incorporations is shown in the table 2 with respect to network adaptability.

Table 2. Network Based Resource Collaboration of Edge computing

S.No.	AUTHOR	TECHNIQUES PROPOSED	APPLICABILITY
1.	Shaoyong Guoa (2021)	A delay sensitive resource allocation algorithm for container cluster in edge computing	Computer communications
2.	Kyuchang Lee(2021)	Algorithmic implementation of deep learning layer assignment in edge computing based smart city environment	Deep learning and edge computing for a smart city
3.	Carine Souveyet(2020)	Assessing the impact of unbalanced resources and communications in edge computing	communication and data caching
4.	Gaofei sun (2020)	Edge computing assisted privacy-preserving data computation for IoT devices	Computer communications
5.	Guoan Zhang (2020)	Energy-efficient computation offloading for vehicular edge computing networks	Computer communications
6.	Junjuan Xia (2021)	Intelligent Secure Mobile Edge Computing for Beyond 5G Wireless Networks	Physical communications
7.	M. Abbasi (2021)	Intelligent workload allocation in IoT–Fog–cloud architecture towards mobile edge computing	Computer communications
8.	Xiaowen Huang (2020)	Market-based dynamic resource allocation in Mobile Edge Computing systems with multi-server and multi-user	Computer communications
9.	Chunlin Li(2020)	Mobility and marginal gain based content caching and placement for cooperative edge-cloud computing.	Communication
10.	Yanli Li (2020)	NDN-based IoT with Edge computing	IoT networks

4. DISCUSSIONS

Edge computing has changed the way data is accessed and computed rationally. As per the research, the IoT base worldwide is expected to reach 75.4 billion devices. This estimate is sufficient to understand how they have been incorporated across sectors. Edge computing architecture is expected to reach the peak earlier than expected with the research and developments in artificial intelligence and connectivity technologies with the increase in demand for smart IoT applications. Edge computing facilities the delivery of some of today's new applications by bringing real-time processing closer to the customer devices. It also emphasizes that computation should be executed in the proximity of data sources to provide services with lower latency and higher quality.

5. CONCLUSION

In recent times, edge computing has evolved as a part of cloud computing with the function of operating at the edge of networking architecture. As an evolving technology, IoT with its inherent sophisticated devices and communication on technology has enormous scope to expand its applications. A systematic mapping study is aimed to identify the quality attributes and metrics used to evaluate IoT systems using an edge-computing architecture. Lucidly, edge computing technology does not only provide the necessary technical assistance, relevant notifications, security, and safety functionalities to the stakeholders but also helps grow the economy by creating business through innovative use cases. By analyzing the papers, we identified the current trends and research gaps about quality attributes. Harmonizing future research efforts would be a key step going forward to realize the promises which IoT technology has bought upon.

REFERENCES

Abbasi, Mohammadi-Pasand, & Khosravi. (2020). *Intelligent workload allocation in IoT–Fog–cloud architecture towards mobile edge computing*. . doi:10.1016/j.comcom.2021.01.022

Alghamdi & Anagnostopoulos. (2020). *Data quality-aware task offloading in Mobile Edge Computing: An Optimal Stopping Theory approach*. . doi:10.1016/j.future.2020.12.017

Zhanga, Dengb, Zhengd, & Xuc. (2020). *Development of an edge computing-based cyber-physical machine tool*. . doi:10.1016/j.rcim.2020.102042

Gu. (2020). *Energy-efficient computation offloading for vehicular edge computing networks*. . doi:10.1016/j.comcom.2020.12.010

Guo, S., Zhang, K., Gong, B., He, W., & Qiu, X. (2021). A delay-sensitive resource allocation algorithm for container cluster in edge computing environment. *Computer Communications*, *170*, 144–150. Advance online publication. doi:10.1016/j.comcom.2021.01.020

Hao, Cao, & Wang. (2020). *Energy-aware scheduling in edge computing with a clustering method.* . doi:10.1016/j.future.2020.11.029

Hu, Huang, & Huang. (2020). *Blockchain and edge computing technology enabling organic agricultural supply chain: A framework solution to trust crisis.* . doi:10.1016/j.cie.2020.107079

Huang, Zhang, Yang, Yang, & Yeo. (2020). *Market-based dynamic resource allocation in Mobile Edge Computing systems with multi-server and multi-user.* . doi:10.1016/j.comcom.2020.11.001

Lai, S., Zhao, R., Tang, S., Xia, J., Zhou, F., & Fan, L. (2021). Intelligent secure mobile edge computing for beyond 5G wireless networks. *Physical Communication, 45*, 101283. Advance online publication. doi:10.1016/j.phycom.2021.101283

Lee, Silva, & Han. (2021). *Algorithmic implementation of deep learning layer assignment in edge computing based smart city environment.* doi:10.1016/j.compeleceng.2020.106909

Li, Song, Yu, & Luo. (2020). *Mobility and marginal gain-based content caching and placement for cooperative edge-cloud computing.* . doi:10.1016/j.ins.2020.09.016

Li & Yang. (2020). *Artificial-intelligence-based algorithms in multi-access edge computing for the performance optimization control of a benchmark microgrid.* . doi:10.1016/j.phycom.2020.101240

Li, Zhu, Li, & Luo. (2020). *Joint edge caching and dynamic service migration in SDN based mobile edge computing.* . doi:10.1016/j.jnca.2020.102966

Li, G., Ren, X., Wu, J., Ji, W., Yu, H., Cao, J., & Wang, R. (2021). Blockchain-based mobile edge computing system. *Information Sciences, 561*, 70–80. Advance online publication. doi:10.1016/j.ins.2021.01.050

Mansouri. (2020). *A review of edge computing: Features and resource virtualization.* . doi:10.1016/j.jpdc.2020.12.015

Rausch, Rashed, & Dustdar. (2020). *Optimized container scheduling for data-intensive serverless edge computing.* . doi:10.1016/j.future.2020.07.017

Razaque, Aloqaily, & Almiani. (2020). *Efficient and reliable forensics using intelligent edge computing.* . doi:10.1016/j.future.2021.01.012

Silva, Cerqueira, Paulino, Lourenço, Leitão, & Preguiça. (2020). *It's about Thyme: On the design and implementation of a time-aware reactive storage system for pervasive edge computing environments.* . doi:10.1016/j.future.2020.12.008

Singh & Aujla. (2020). *Container-based load balancing for energy efficiency in software-defined edge computing environment.* . doi:10.1016/j.suscom.2020.100463

Steffenel & Pinheiro. (2020). *Assessing the impact of unbalanced resources and communications in edge computing.* . doi:10.1016/j.pmcj.2020.101321

Sun, Xing, & Qian. (2020). *Edge computing assisted privacy-preserving data computation for IoT devices.* . doi:10.1016/j.comcom.2020.11.018

Verma, Goyal, & Kumara. (2020). *Edge-cloud computing performance benchmarking for IoT based machinery vibration monitoring.* . doi:10.1016/j.mfglet.2020.12.004

Wang, Wang, & Li. (2020). *NDN-based IoT with Edge computing.* . doi:10.1016/j.future.2020.09.018

Xia, Huang, Tian, Wang, Victor, Zhu, & Feng. (2021). *SparkNoC: An energy-efficiency FPGA-based accelerator using optimized lightweight CNN for edge computing.* . doi:10.1016/j.sysarc.2021.101991

Zhang & Li. (2020). *Edge computing and its role in Industrial Internet: Methodologies, applications, and future directions.* . doi:10.1016/j.ins.2020.12.021

This research was previously published in the International Journal of Fog Computing (IJFC), 4(1); pages 37-51, copyright year 2021 by IGI Publishing (an imprint of IGI Global).

Chapter 5
Distributed Intelligence Platform to the Edge Computing

Xalphonse Inbaraj

PACE Institute of Technology and Sciences, India

ABSTRACT

With the explosion of information, devices, and interactions, cloud design on its own cannot handle the flow of data. While the cloud provides us access to compute, storage, and even connectivity that we can access easily and cost-effectively, these centralized resources can create delays and performance issues for devices and information that are far from a centralized public cloud or information center source. Internet of things-connected devices are a transparent use for edge computing architecture. In this chapter, the author discusses the main differences between edge, fog, and cloud computing; pros and cons; and various applications, namely, smart cars and traffic control in transportation scenario, visual and surveillance security, connected vehicle, and smart ID card.

INTRODUCTION

Cloud computing frees the enterprise and also the user from the specification of the many details. This blissfulness becomes a retardant for latency-sensitive applications, which need nodes within the neighborhood to satisfy their delay necessities. An rising wave of web deployments, most notably the web of Things (WoTs), requires mobility support and geo-distribution in addition to location aware-ness and low latency. We argue that a replacement platform is required to satisfy these requirements; a platform we have a tendency to decision Fog Computing, or, briefly, Fog could be a cloud close to the ground (Bonomi, Milito & Natarajan, 2014). With the explosion of data, devices and interactions, cloud architecture on its own can't handle the influx of information. While the cloud gives us access to compute, storage and even connectivity that we can access easily and cost-effectively, these centralized resources can create delays and performance issues for devices and data that are far from a centralized public cloud or data center source.

DOI: 10.4018/978-1-6684-5700-9.ch005

Copyright © 2022, IGI Global. Copying or distributing in print or electronic forms without written permission of IGI Global is prohibited.

Edge computing—also known as just "edge"—brings processing close to the data source, and it does not need to be sent to a remote cloud or other centralized systems for processing. By eliminating the distance and time it takes to send data to centralized sources, we can improve the speed and performance of data transport, as well as devices and applications on the edge.

Fog computing is a standard that defines how edge computing should work, and it facilitates the operation of compute, storage and networking services between end devices and cloud computing data centers. Additionally, many use fog as a jumping-off point for edge computing.

Therefore we can define some characteristics to define Fog Computing such that a) Low latency and location awareness; b) Wide-spread geographical distribution; c) Mobility; d) Very large number of nodes, e) Predominant role of wireless access, f) robust presence of streaming and real time applications, g) Heterogeneity.

Both fog computing and edge computing provide the same functionalities in terms of pushing both data and intelligence to analytic platforms that are situated either on, or close to where the data originated from, whether that's screens, speakers, motors, pumps or sensors.

Fog computing is projected to alter computing directly at the sting of the network, which might deliver new applications and services (Forman, 2003). For example, industrial edge routers are advertising processor speed, number of cores and built-in network storage. Those routers have the potential to become new servers and also its facilities the services at the edge of the network which are known as fog nodes. They can be resource-poor devices such as set-top boxes, access points, routers (Willis, Dasgupta & Banerjee, 2014), switches, base stations, and end devices, or resource-rich machines such as Cloudlet. Obviously, edge and fog computing architecture is all about Internet of Things (IoT)that deal with remote sensors or devices are typically where edge computing and fog computing architectures manifest in the real world. In this chapter, how Fog Computing was emerged and its various applications through its edge nods was discussed. For example, in the Fog Transportation System, the fog nodes perform some native analysis for native action, like alerting the vehicle concerning poor road conditions, triggering autonomous response to slow down, and perform some autonomous functions, although connections to higher layers are inaccessible and according to surveillance scenario, video analytics algorithms are often settled on fog nodes near to the cameras, and take advantage of the heterogeneous processor capability of fog, running parts of the video analytics algorithm on conventional processors or accelerators.

Both technologies can help organizations reduce their reliance on cloud-based platforms to analyze data, which often leads to latency issues, and instead be able to make data-driven decisions faster. The main difference between edge computing and fog computing comes down to where the processing of that data takes place.

Fully automated driving will be enabled in future by communication between vehicles and information based services increase road safety, improve more comfort. For the automotive industry, by providing advanced remote monitoring and diagnostics via over-the-air fleet management is becoming an urgent priority that will done by Low Power Wide Area (LPWA) connectivity and it can be done by allocating higher bandwidth that is best provided by technologies such as Wi-Fi and/or mobile broadband in shape of LTE and in Bitcoin, removing Electronic notecase after transaction was completed in order to ensure user anonymity and privacy protection (Tavel, 2007). Smart Id systems using Fog Computing providing e –attendance to various fields like schools, colleges and industry managements.

EMERGE OF EDGE AND FOG COMPUTING

Fog Computing is a highly virtualized platform that provides compute, storage, and networking services between end devices and traditional Cloud Computing Data Centers, typically, but not exclusively located at the edge of network. Compute, storage, and networking resources are the building blocks of Fog. "Edge of the Network", however, implies variety of characteristics that create the Fog a non-trivial extension of the Cloud.

The implementation of the edge layer can be classified into three types,

1. Mobile Edge Computing (MEC)
2. Fog Computing (FC)
3. Cloudlet Computing (CC).

Fog Computing presents a computing layer leveraging devices like M2M gateways and wireless routers. These are called Fog Computing Nodes (FCNs) and are used to compute and store data from end devices locally before forwarding to the Cloud. On the other hand, MEC proposes deployment of intermediate nodes with storage and processing capabilities in the base stations of cellular networks thus offering Cloud Computing capabilities inside the Radio Area Network (RAN). The Cloudlets are based on dedicated devices with capacities similar to a data center but on a lower scale present in logical vicinity to the consumers allows end devices to offload Computing to the Cloudlet devices with resource provisioning similar to that of a data center.

Fog computing has its benefits thanks to its edge location, and thus is in a position to support applications (e.g. gaming, increased reality, real time video stream processing) with low latency necessities. This edge location can also provide rich network context information, such as local network condition, traffic statistics and client status information, which can be used by fog applications to offer context-aware optimization. One of the character of Fog is location-awareness; not only can the geo-distributed fog node infer its own location but also the fog node can track end user devices to support quality, which can be a game ever-changing issue for location-based services and applications. Furthermore, the interplays between fog and fog, fog and cloud become necessary since fog will simply gets native summary whereas the world coverage will solely be achieved at a higher layer that is shown in Figure.1.The omnipresence of sensible devices and fast development of normal virtualization and cloud technology create many fog node implementation offered. Obviously, edge and fog computing architecture is all about Internet of Things (IoT). Generally that will deal with remote sensors or devices are typically where edge computing and fog computing architectures manifest in the real world

MCC refers to associate infrastructure within which each the info storage and also the processing happen outside of the mobile devices (Das, Chakraborty & Roy-Chowdhury, 2014). MEC specialize in resource-rich fog servers like cloudlets running at the sting of mobile networks (Zhang, Zhu & Roy-Chowdhury, 2015). Fog computing distinguishes itself as a more generalized computing paradigm especially in the context of Internet of Things. The following definition will express about emerge of Fog and Edge computing

- **Fog computing** pushes intelligence down to the local area network (LAN) level of network architecture, processing data in a fog node or IoT gateway.

- **Edge computing** pushes the intelligence, processing power, and communication capabilities of an edge gateway or appliance directly into devices like PACs (programmable automation controllers).

Figure 1. Fog computing that extends the services of cloud service to the edge of the network

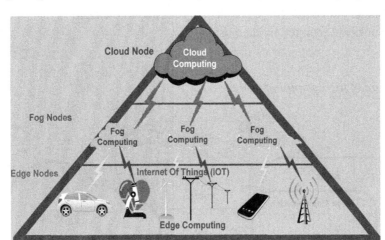

ARCHITECTURE OF FOG COMPUTING

The fog extends the cloud to be nearer to the items that manufacture and act on IoT information (Figure 2). These devices, called fog nodes, can be deployed anywhere with a network connection: on a factory floor, on top of a power pole, alongside a railway track, in a vehicle, or on an oil rig. Any device with computing, storage, and network connectivity can be a fog node. Examples embody industrial controllers, switches, routers, embedded servers, and video surveillance cameras. There is good reason: analyzing IoT data on the point of wherever it's collected minimizes latency. It offloads gigabytes of network traffic from the core network, and it keeps sensitive data inside the network. Analyzing IoT information on the point of wherever it's collected minimizes latency. It offloads the gigabytes of network traffic from the core network. And it keeps sensitive data inside the network.

The fog architecture is an intermediate layer between field applications (sensors, actuators, UI...) and the cloud. The principle of fog is to complement the cloud (centralized architecture) by a distributed set of autonomous micro systems, allowing the repatriation of intelligence at the edge of the network.

The fog node is designed based on architecture of fog .According to that, this is elaborated into two sections,

1. Architecture
2. Networking

The following procedure are used to describe the Fog Computing Service

1. The data is first partitioned into chunks.
2. The chunks are allocated to participating nodes.

3. The chunks are queued before transmission.
4. Based on the queue, the channels are allocated, which makes some chunks occupy the idle channels in the first batch and rest
5. of them wait for the next released channel.
6. After the distributed processing, the processed chunks are sorted by their finishing time.
7. Also using channel allocation, these chunks are returned to the host.
8. Finally, the chunks are reunited by the host.

Figure 2. Architecture of fog computing

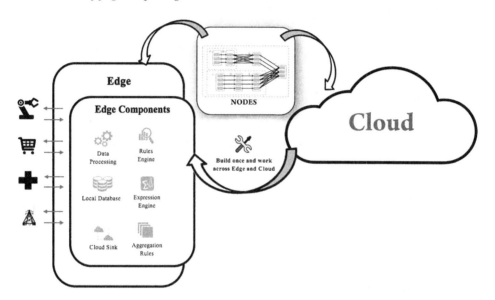

NETWORKING ARCHITECTURE

Due to set at the sting of net, fog network is heterogeneous. The duty of fog network is to attach each element of the fog. However, managing such a network, maintaining property and providing services upon that, especially in the scenarios of the Internet of Things (IoT) at large scale, is not easy. Emerging techniques, like software-defined networking (SDN) and network perform virtualization (NFV), are proposed to create flexible and easy maintaining network environment. The employment of SDN and NFV will ease the implementation and management, increase network quantifiability and scale back prices, in many aspects of fog computing, such as resource allocation, VM migration, traffic monitoring, application-aware control and programmable interfaces.

SDN

SDN "When SDN conception is enforced with physically (not simply logically) centralized management, it resembles the fog computing ideas, with fog device acting as the centralized controller" (Stejmenovic, 2014). In the fog, every node ought to be able to act as a router for near nodes and resilient to node quality and churn, which suggests controller can even be put on the end nodes in fog network. The challenges of desegregation SDN into fog network is to accommodate dynamic conditions as quality and unreliable wireless link (Bhushan & Reddy, 2016).

NFV

NFV replaces the network functions with virtual machine instances. Since the key enabler of fog computing is virtualization and people VMs may be dynamically created, destroyed and offloaded, NFV will benefit fog computing in many aspects by virtualizing gateways, switches, load balancers, firewalls and intrusion detection devices and putting those instances on fog nodes.

Capacity

Capacity has 2 folds:

1. Network Information measure,
2. Storage Capability.

In order to attain high information measure and economical storage utilization, it is important to investigate how data are placed in fog network since data locality for computation is very important. There are similar works in the context of cloud (Agarwal et al., 2010) and sensor network (Sheng, Li & Mao, 2006). However, this downside faces new challenges in fog computing. For example, a fog node may need to compute on data that is distributed in several nearby nodes. The computation cannot begin before the end of information aggregation, which definitely adds delay to services. To solve this, we may leverage user mobility pattern and service request pattern to place data on suitable fog nodes to either minimize the cost of operation, the latency or to maximize the throughput.

FOG COMPUTING WORK SCENARIO AND ITS COMPARISON WITH CLOUD COMPUTING

Fog applications are as diverse as the Internet of Things itself. What they have in common is monitoring or analyzing real-time data from network-connected things and then initiating an action. The action can involve machine-to-machine (M2M) communications or human-machine interaction (HMI). Examples include locking a door, changing equipment settings, applying the brakes on a train, zooming a video camera, opening a valve in response to a pressure reading, creating a bar chart, or sending an alert to a technician to make a preventive repair. The possibilities are unlimited.

Production of fog applications area unit quickly proliferating in producing, oil and gas, utilities, transportation, mining, and the public sector. When to Consider Fog Computing:

1. Information is collected at the acute edge: vehicles, ships, factory floors, roadways, railways, etc.
2. Thousands or scores of things across an outsized are generating information.
3. It's necessary to research and act on the information in but a second.

The fog nodes closest to the network edge consume the information from IoT devices. Then—and this is often essential—the fog IoT application directs differing types of information to the optimum place for analysis, as shown in Table 1:

1. The foremost time-sensitive information is analyzed on the fog node closest to the items generating the information. In a Cisco good Grid distribution network, for instance, the most time-sensitive requirement is to verify that protection and control loops are operating properly. Therefore, the fog nodes closest to the grid sensors will rummage around for signs of issues so forestall them by causation management commands to actuators.
2. Information (data)that may wait seconds or minutes for action is passed on to associate degree aggregation node for analysis and action. In the good Grid example, every station may need its own aggregation node that reports the operational standing of every downstream feeder and lateral.
3. Information(data) that's less time sensitive is distributed to the cloud for historical analysis, huge information analytics, and long-term storage (see sidebar). For example, each of thousands or hundreds of thousands of fog nodes might send periodic summaries of grid data to the cloud for historical analysis and storage.

Table 1. Fog nodes extend the cloud to network edge for analysis

	Fog Nodes Closest to IoT Devices	**Fog Aggregation Nodes**	**Cloud**
Response time	Milliseconds to subsecond	Seconds to minutes	Minutes, days, weeks
Application examples	M2M communication, including telemedicine and training	Visualization Simple analytics	Big data analytics Graphical dashboards
How long IoT data is stored	Transient	Short duration: perhaps hours, days, or weeks	Months or years
Geographic coverage	Very local: for example, one city block	Wider	Global
	Fog nodes are geographically distributed, scattered all over the edges of Internet, and logically decentralized in that they are maintained by different organizations		Cloud servers are usually rack-mounted, high-end servers located in large, warehouse-like data centers. Centralized cloud servers allow for replication, load balancing, failure recovery, power management, and easy access to failed hardware for repairing and replacement
Cost Analysis	fog nodes aren't as reliable as cloud servers, and physically locating a failed fog node and repairing it is more difficult and costly.		Many financial and time costs, such as those related to power and system configuration, can't be amortized as they would be with cloud computing

There are several key differences between fog and cloud computing. .Various difference can find between Fog and Cloud Computing that was discussed in Table 2 and Pros and Cons for Edge and Fog Ccomputing was explained in Table 3

Table 2. Comparison between fog and cloud computing

Cloud Computing	Fog Computing
Cloud servers are usually rack-mounted, high-end servers located in large, warehouse-like data centers. Centralized cloud servers allow for replication, load balancing, failure recovery, power management, and easy access to failed hardware for repairing and replacement. For this reason, the reliability of cloud services can be held at a high standard. But not at all time.	Fog nodes are geographically distributed, scattered all over the edges of Internet, and logically decentralized in that they are maintained by different organizations.
Cloud Servers and its nodes aren't reliable .	Consequently, fog nodes are reliable and physically locating a failed fog node and repairing it is not more difficult. Many financial and time costs, such as those related to power and system configuration, can't be amortized as they would be with cloud computing.
The network connectivity cant be guaranteed.	The network connectivity to fog nodes can be guaranteed.
An unreachable path or network can fulfill any request even if its computational hardware is fully functional. But may or might not be guarantee.	An unreachable fog node can't fulfill any request even if its computational hardware is fully functional.
In this Cloud Computing, schedule for computational task cant be predictable but not much more complex .because it is maintained by centralized service.	A fog computing application is typically spread over the client's mobile device, one of potentially many fog nodes, and occasionally a back-end cloud server. Therefore, deciding where to schedule computational tasks in fog computing is more difficult.
Deciding the scheduling task is not possible	In short, in fog computing, more factors must be considered in deciding where and when to schedule tasks to provide the best user experience.
This is not maintained by different organizations. Because of centralized server will distribute overall services.	Fog nodes, owned and maintained by different organizations, usually have vastly different RAM capacity, CPU performance, storage space, and network bandwidth.
In this cloud computing, applications are deployed in only one cloud at a time, unless the need for scaling is beyond the capacity of a single cloud provider.	Mobility is a key feature of the fog computing paradigm, and applications deployed on fog infrastructure need to always take this into account.

Advantages of both Technologies:

1. Real-time data analysis: Since, the data is processed at the source of data generation, it can be analyzed in real-time or near real-time.
2. Reduced costs: These technologies lower the costs as companies need less data bandwidth management solutions for local devices, as compared to the cloud or data center.
3. Lower bandwidth consumption: Companies wouldn't need high bandwidth to handle data, because processing will happen at the edge itself.
4. Lower latency levels: This is the main benefit of edge computing and fog computing. They lower the latency compared to a faraway cloud or data center by eliminating the time involved in sending data back and forth.

Table 3. Pros and Cons of Edge and Fog Computing

Pros of Edge Computing	Cons of Edge Computing	Pros Fog Computing	Cons of Fog Computing
one major benefit to edge computing is that data isn't transferred, and is more secure.	It can become a complex issue for brands to handle, as data sets that require more sophisticated algorithms are better handled in the cloud, whereas simpler analytical processes are best kept at the edge.	This is also providing better security (Rayani, Bhushan & Thakare, 2018)	Handling methods does not issue major problem .
Edge computing maintains all data and processing on the device that initially created it. This keeps the data discrete and contained within the source of truth, the originating device	This is striking the balance between keeping data at the edge and bringing it into a central cloud when necessary.	In a fog computing architecture, it enables organizations to, aggregate data from multi-devices into regional stores. That's in contrast to collecting data from a single touch point or device, or a single set of devices that are connected to the cloud.	More infrastructure [and thus more investment] is needed [for fog computing] and must rely on data consistency across a large network.
In edge computing, the data is processed right on the devices, or gateway devices closest to the sensors. So, the compute and storage systems are located at the edge, close to device, application, or component producing the data.		In fog computing, the edge computing happenings are moved to processors linked to a local area network or into the hardware of LAN. Therefore, the data in fog computing is processed within an IoT gateway or fog node in LAN.	
Applications		**Applications**	
1.Oil and Gas industry 2.Intelligent transportation and Traffic management 3.self –Driving vehicles and etc.,		1.Smart Cities 2.Smrt Building 3.Visual Security and etc.,	

BUSINESS BENEFITS AS FaaS AND ITS APPLICATIONS

Platform as a service (PaaS) could be a class of cloud computing services that gives a platform permitting customers to develop, run, and manage net applications while not the complexness of building and maintaining the infrastructure generally related to developing and launching an application. Some consortium defines the required infrastructure to enable building Fog as a Service (FaaS) to address certain classes of business challenges. FaaS includes Infrastructure as a Service (IaaS), Platform as a Service (PaaS), Software as a Service (SaaS), and many service constructs specific to fog. The infrastructure and design building blocks below show however FaaS is also enabled and can be enlarged upon within the reference design that shown in Figure.3 and QoS-aware service composition is building of new-valued services by combining it with the set of current existing services. Due to rapid increase in the number of services in the cloud it becomes very difficult to select an appropriate service that satisfies the user requirements. As the number of services offered by the service providers increases exponentially, the users may find difficulty in choosing the right service provider that fulfills his/her requirements. There are various techniques or methods to find the services with respect to the users expectations. One of research classifies and gives the taxonomy of approaches in QoS-aware service compositions (Bhushan & Reddy, 2016, 2018)

Figure 3. Applications benefitting from fog computing

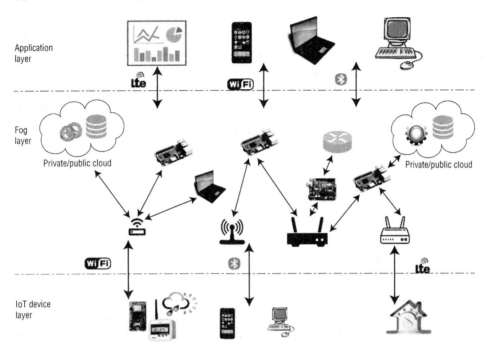

Business Benefits of Fog Computing (Ahmed & Ahmed, 2016)

Extending the cloud nearer to the items that generate and act on knowledge edges the business within the following ways:

1. **Larger Business Agility**: With the proper tools, developers will quickly develop fog applications and deploy them wherever needed. Machine manufacturers can offer MaaS to their customers. Fog applications program the machine to operate in the way each customer needs.
2. **Higher Security:** Defend your fog nodes exploitation a similar policy, controls, and procedures you utilize in alternative components of your IT environment. Use the same physical security and cyber security solutions.
3. **Deeper Insights, With Privacy Control:** Analyze sensitive knowledge domestically rather than causing it to the cloud for analysis. Your IT team will monitor and management the devices that collect, analyze, and store knowledge.
4. **Lower Operative Expense:** Conserve network information measure by process chosen knowledge domestically rather than causing it to the cloud foranalysis.

Fog computing targets cross-cutting considerations just like the management of performance, latency and efficiency are also key to the success of fog networks. Cloud and fog computing are on a mutually beneficial, interdependent continuum. The traditional backend cloud can still stay a crucial a part of computing systems as fog computing emerges. The segmentation of what tasks move to fog and what goes to the backend cloud area unit application specific. This segmentation could be planned, but also change dynamically if the network state changes in areas like processor loads, link bandwidths, storage capacities, fault events, security threats, cost targets, etc.

The vicinity unit many issues with this scenario: The information measure to move the sensing element and mechanism information to and from the cloud might price several thousands of bucks per month; those connections could be susceptible to hackers; Now, consider placing a hierarchy of local fog nodes near the pipeline. They can connect with sensors and actuators with cheap native networking facilities. Fog nodes may be extremely secure, alteration the hacker threat. Fog nodes can react to abnormal conditions in milliseconds, quickly closing valves to greatly reduce the severity.

The Transportation in Fog

The Transportation Fog Network is comprised of a three-level hierarchy of fog nodes. The first level of the hierarchy is that the infrastructure fog nodes, or roadside fog nodes. At this level, the margin fog sensors collect knowledge from different devices like edge cameras. The fog nodes perform some native analysis for native action, like alerting the vehicle concerning poor road conditions, triggering autonomous response to slow down, and perform some autonomous functions, although connections to higher layers are inaccessible.

Data from the first level of interactions is aggregated and sent up the fog hierarchy to the second and third levels of the hierarchy— neighborhood and regional fog nodes—for further analysis and distribution. Some of the info may additionally be distributed east-west to different infrastructure nodes for his or her use. Typically, every fog layer within the hierarchy can give extra process, storage, and network capabilities in service of the vertical application at their level of the hierarchy. For example, higher level layers provide additional processing to provide data analytics or large storage capacities.

Traffic Control System

Traffic control fog nodes could receive input from different sources, like sensible light systems, municipal managers, and cloud-based systems. Data flows between the traffic control system and sensors (Bowman, Debray & Peterson, 1993), infrastructure fog nodes and vehicles in all directions, insuring all levels of the hierarchy have the data and control capabilities they need that are shown in Figure.4.

Visual Security and Surveilance Scenario

Smart cities, smart homes, retail stores, public transportation, manufacturing and enterprises increasingly rely on camera sensors to secure people, identify unauthorized access, and increase safety, reliability and efficiency. The sheer information measure of visual (and different sensor) knowledge being collected over a large-scale network makes it impractical to move all the info to the cloud to get period insights. City-scale deployments that embrace putting cameras on traffic lights and different camera deployments in remote areas haven't got high-bandwidth property to the cloud to transfer the collected video, even if the video may work over the network infrastructure.

Additionally, privacy concerns must be addressed when using a camera as a sensor that collects image data so that the images do not reveal a person's identity or reveal confidential contextual information (e.g. intellectual property in a manufacturing plant) to any unauthorized parties.Fog Computing issuing deployments that provide the opportunity to build real-time, latency-sensitive distributed surveillance systems that maintain privacy. It leverages fog nodes to intelligently partition video processing between fog nodes colocated with cameras and the cloud so as to enable real-time tracking, anomaly detection, and insights from data collected over long time intervals. Video analytics algorithms are often settled on fog nodes near to the cameras, and take advantage of the heterogeneous processor capability of fog, running parts of the video analytics algorithm on conventional processors or accelerators.

Figure 4. Smart car and traffic control system

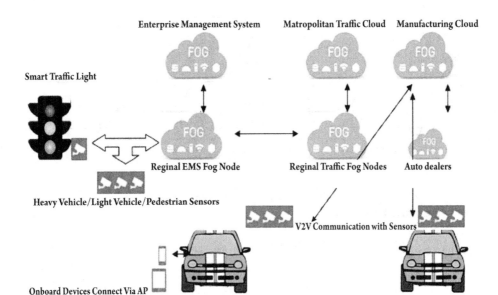

Connected Cars Towards Fully Automated Driving

Connected cars, or Vehicle-to-Everything (V2X) communication, involves communication between vehicles and between vehicles and roadside infrastructure (Frohlich & Plate, 2000). Real-time communication allows vehicles to manage things that neither the driving force nor the vehicle's sensors may otherwise determine, enabling additional prognostic driving. In-vehicle information-based services increase road safety, improve driver comfort and enable fully automated driving in the future. When augmented with Multi-access Edge Computing (MEC), LTE advanced, NB IoT and LTE V2X, LTE can provide a viable and cost-effective solution that can accelerate the adoption of V2X communications by transport authorities and the automotive industry (Sannella, 2007). The hybrid use of the LTE portfolio will meet automotive industry needs on the way to 5G (Peng, Aved & Hua, 2012). It provides support for automated driving, increased comfort and improved infotainment and increases road safety and traffic efficiency that are shown in Figure 5.

Figure 5. High level architecture of the connected cars ecosystem

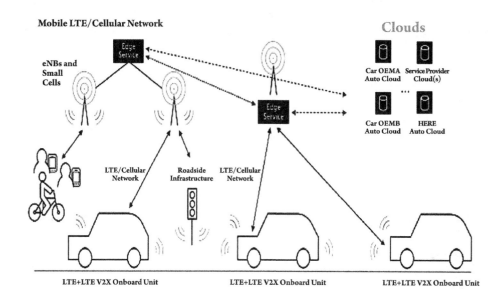

Automative Fleet Management

In 2015, more than 51 million vehicles were recalled in the US.

1.   However, some 30 percent of these recalled cars are not repaired because the owners are not aware of a recall
2.   These issues can be resolved by over-the-air software management that can remotely update in-car electronic control units (ECU)(Figure 6).

Providing advanced remote monitoring and diagnostics via over-the-air fleet management is becoming an urgent priority for the automotive industry. While Low Power Wide Area (LPWA) connectivity can support some basic fleet management monitoring apps, the need to deliver software updates will call for higher bandwidth that is best provided (Tavel, 2007) by technologies such as Wi-Fi and/or mobile broadband in shape of LTE.

Connectivity for IoT

*   Mobile radio for the IoT unleashes the IoT potential of 4G networks by optimizing LTE and TD-LTE cell capacity and the smart phone user experience. The portfolio supports normal cellular protocols (EC-GSM, NB-IOT, eMTC) as well as Wi-Fi, LoRa and MuLTEfire. Plus, our LTE technologies support mission-critical public safety and initial respondent services.
*   Support for all three 3GPP IoT radio technologies addresses the connection requirements of different applications with low-cost connectivity and improved indoor and rural coverage. It extends device battery life beyond 10 years for remote sensors and meters.

Figure 6. Secure and control IoT devices for the Automotive Fleet Management

Virtualized MEC

- MEC platform evolution to commercial off-the-shelf (COTS) servers Virtualized Multi-access Edge Computing (vMEC) could be a software-only resolution that may be deployed on industrial ready-to-wear (COTS) servers, creating it simple to integrate with existing IT infrastructure.
- MEC processes information about to wherever it's generated and consumed. This enables the network to deliver the ultra-low latency needed by business-critical applications and to support interactive user experiences in busy venues. By processing data locally, MEC applications can also significantly reduce data transfer costs[7]. vMEC software package parts are often purchased by subscription to greatly scale back your direct investment and business risk.

MEC Multi-Radio Connectivity

- MEC implements computing at the network edge. Nokia MEC multi-radio connectivity takes computing to the enterprise site, for example by making the current enterprise Wi-Fi and operator LTE work together for the benefit of both.
- MEC multi-radio connectivity enhances the capabilities of the Nokia MEC platform by providing an overlay approach for multi-operator and multi-access network integration that is truly independent of the radio access and core networks. This flexible framework mixes and matches different technologies to improve capacity and is not coupled to the capacity of underlying networks. Any access for uplink/downlink can be chosen by the framework according to application need.

Bitcoin in Cloud Computing

- There are lot of method uses a block chain-based electronic wallet in the cloud computing environment. The block chain method is used to remove the information of the user who uses cloud computing. This technique installs and uses an electronic case and removes it ordinarily.
- The electronic notecase is firmly removed by causing the finished message. Leak of user info are often prevented only if the electronic notecase is totally removed. Even though many existing studies have been performed on the block chain protocol, a method for removing the electronic wallet completely is presented to ensure user anonymity and privacy protection .

Smart ID Card for Management

Figure 7. Block diagram of smart ID card implementation

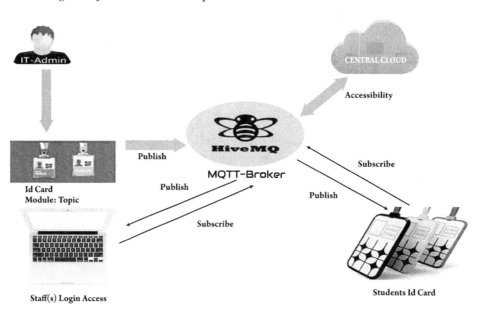

Smart ID card using IoT is very essential application for college, school and all types of industry management. here we are using MDTT protocol for publish and subscribe the topic. Here topic is generating the message which will transmit to corresponding staffs and students through MQTTBroker protocol. These information are stored in central cloud for accessibility purpose that are shown in Figure 7

EVALUATIONS AND RESULT DISCUSSIONS

According to smart card using IoT, the following result revealed that between various total number of students and timing. How many numbers of student received the topic which is generated message within the range. That is shown in Figure 8.

Figure 8. Timing vs number of students connected

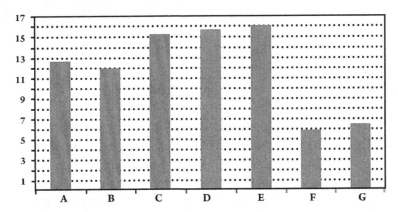

Where A,B,C,D,E,F and G are various total number of students such that 65, 80,110,120,130,50 and 45 respectively.

Figure 9. Memory usage while connecting number of students within range

	Storage (KB)	RAM (KB)
Free	3200	512
Used	83	4
% used	2.59%	0.78%

While connecting to total number of students, need to analyze and finalize the speed and capability of RAM usage and storage also. The Above shown in Figure 9 that storage and RAM usage while connect to the 120 students simultaneously.

Figure 10. Responding time vs distance place

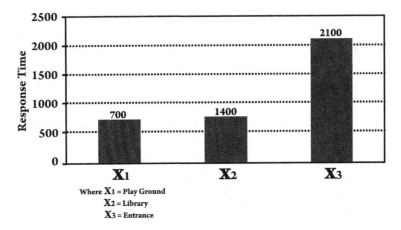

Here response time is referred to as smart card activation time calculation .Where X1,X2 and X3 are various place such that play ground, Library and entrance respectively. The above Figure 10 shows that .Note: 700mt between each place.

RESULT ANALYSIS

While Fog nodes provide localization, therefore enabling low latency and context awareness, the Cloud provides global centralization. Many applications need each Fog localization, and Cloud globalization, particularly for analytics and Big Data. With all the elements connected and the network deployed, several time measurements were obtained: startup time of the network elements, service response time, and Memory usage while connecting number of students within range. Also, the quantity of memory employed in the nodes to run the applications was measured.

As a results of this the Fog should support many sorts of storage, from passing at very cheap tier to semi-permanent at the best tier. Comparative analysis employs different parameters such as such as system performance, network performance, overhead of deployment and system migration overhead to measure the degree of effectiveness of different approaches (Cortes et al., 2015). Based on our thorough investigation, it can be asserted that MEC is a way forward for achieving 1 ms latency dream.

CONCLUSION

Fog computing accelerates awareness and response to events by eliminating a trip to the cloud for analysis. It avoids the requirement for pricey information measure additions by offloading gigabytes of network traffic from the core network.

It conjointly protects sensitive IoT knowledge by analyzing it within company walls. Ultimately, organizations that adopt fog computing gain deeper and quicker insights, leading to increased business agility, higher service levels, and improved safety.

We also note that the higher the tier, the wider the geographical coverage, and the longer the time scale. The final, global coverage is provided by the Cloud, which is used as repository for data that that has a permanence of months and years.

Edge-centric Computing could be a novel paradigm that moves the locus of management of Cloud Computing applications and services to the sides of the network. An edge could also be a mobile device, a wearable device but also a nano-data center or a user-controlled device.

While the basic reason is privacy, since Edge-centric Computing permits users to retake management of their data, leverage user's resources and even reducing response times build edge-centric computing appealing to novel personal and social online services (Starzyk & Quereshi, 2011; Poluru et al., 2019).

MQTT is proposed and experimented as a communication proposal between these layers .Some platform used to deliver different service by means an API .In this context, experts and professional in each subsystem are required to design and develop the effective services to offer the solution in real time .This will lead in AI services in future and then specific optimization and improvement will be developed. In addition, some of new control rules, model and analysis approach using Machine Learning platforms and AI paradigms will ensure that new smart services can be formed.

Edge and fog are transforming the digitally connected world. Without these technologies, the IoT couldn't be that effective. By breaking the silos of centralized cloud servers, these are making IoT a more flexible and distributed technology.

If the meaning of fog computing and edge computing is understood well, these technologies can bring limitless value to any domain.

REFERENCES

Agarwal, S., Dunagan, J., Jain, N., Saroiu, S., Wolman, A., & Bhogan, H. (2010). Volley: Automated data placement for geo-distributed cloud services. NSDI.

Ahmed, A., & Ahmed, E. (2016). A survey on mobile edge computing. Intelligent systems and control (ISCO), 2016 10th. doi:10.1109/ISCO.2016.7727082

Bhushan, S. B., & Reddy, P. (2016). A four-level linear discriminant analysis based service selection in the cloud environment. *International Journal of Technology*, *5*, 859–870. doi:10.14716/ijtech.v7i5.3546

Bhushan, S. B., & Reddy, P. C. (2018). A hybrid meta-heuristic approach for QoS-aware cloud service composition. *International Journal of Web Services Research*, *15*(2), 1–20. doi:10.4018/IJWSR.2018040101

Bonomi, F., Milito, R., & Natarajan, P. (2014). *Fog computing – A platform For Internet Of Things And Analytics*. San Jose, CA: Enterprise Networking Labs, Cisco Systems Inc. doi:10.1007/978-3-319-05029-4_7

BowmanDebray, & Peterson. (1993). Reasoning about naming systems. *ACM Trans. Program. Lang. Syst.*, *15*(5), 795-825.

Cortés, R., Bonnaire, X., Marin, O., & Sens, P. (2015). Stream Processing of Healthcare Sensor Data: Studying User Traces to Identify Challenges from a Big Data Perspective. *Procedia Computer Science*, *52*, 1004–1009. doi:10.1016/j.procs.2015.05.093

Das, A. (2014). Consistent reidentification in a camera network. In *Computer Vision–ECCV 2014* (pp. 330–345). Springer.

Forman, G. (2003, March). An extensive empirical study of feature selection metrics for text classification. *Journal of Machine Learning Research*, *3*, 1289–1305.

Frohlich, B., & Plate, J. (2000). The cubic mouse: a new device for three-dimensional input. In *Proceedings of the SIGCHI conference on Human factors in computing systems, CHI '00*, (pp. 526-531). New York, NY: ACM. 10.1145/332040.332491

Luan, Gao, & Xiang. (n.d.). *Fog Computing: Focusing on Mobile Users at the Edge*. School of Information Technology Deakin University.

Peng, R., & Alex, J. (2012). *Real-time query processing on live videos in networks of distributed cameras*. Research, Practice, and Educational Advancements in Telecommunications and Networking.

Poluru, R. K., Bhushan, B., Muzamil, B. S., Rayani, P. K., & Reddy, P. K. (2019). Applications of Domain-Specific Predictive Analytics Applied to Big Data. In *Sentiment Analysis and Knowledge Discovery in Contemporary Business* (pp. 289–306). IGI Global. doi:10.4018/978-1-5225-4999-4.ch016

Rayani, P. K., Bhushan, B., & Thakare, V. R. (2018). Multi-Layer Token Based Authentication Through Honey Password in Fog Computing. *International Journal of Fog Computing, 1*(1), 50–62. doi:10.4018/IJFC.2018010104

Sannella. (2003). *Constraint satisfaction and debugging for interactive user interfaces.* Academic Press.

Sheng, B., Li, Q., & Mao, W. (2006). Data storage placement in sensor networks. In *Mobihoc*. ACM. doi:10.1145/1132905.1132943

Starzyk & Qureshi. (2011). Learning proactive control strategies for ptz cameras. In *Distributed Smart Cameras (ICDSC), 2011 Fifth ACM/IEEE International Conference on*, (pp. 1–6). IEEE.

Stojmenovic, I. (2014). Fog computing: A cloud to the ground support for smart things and machine-to-machine networks. In *ATNAC*. IEEE. doi:10.1109/ATNAC.2014.7020884

Tavel. (2007). *Modeling and simulation design.* Academic Press.

Willis, D. F., Dasgupta, A., & Banerjee, S. (2014). Paradrop: a multi-tenant platform for dynamically installed third partyservices on home gateways. In *SIGCOMM workshop on Distributed cloud computing*. ACM. 10.1145/2627566.2627583

Zhang, S., Zhu, Y., & Roy-Chowdhury, A. (2015). Trackingmultiple interacting targets in a camera network. *Computer Vision and Image Understanding, 134*(C), 64–73. doi:10.1016/j.cviu.2015.01.002

This research was previously published in Architecture and Security Issues in Fog Computing Applications; pages 108-130, copyright year 2020 by Engineering Science Reference (an imprint of IGI Global).

Chapter 6
Deep Learning With Analytics on Edge

Kavita Srivastava

Institute of Information Technology and Management, GGSIP University, India

EXECUTIVE SUMMARY

The steep rise in autonomous systems and the internet of things in recent years has influenced the way in which computation has performed. With built-in AI (artificial intelligence) in IoT and cyber-physical systems, the need for high-performance computing has emerged. Cloud computing is no longer sufficient for the sensor-driven systems which continuously keep on collecting data from the environment. The sensor-based systems such as autonomous vehicles require analysis of data and predictions in real-time which is not possible only with the centralized cloud. This scenario has given rise to a new computing paradigm called edge computing. Edge computing requires the storage of data, analysis, and prediction performed on the network edge as opposed to a cloud server thereby enabling quick response and less storage overhead. The intelligence at the edge can be obtained through deep learning. This chapter contains information about various deep learning frameworks, hardware, and systems for edge computing and examples of deep neural network training using the Caffe 2 framework.

INTRODUCTION

Deep Learning is a subset of Machine Learning which is being used widely in many applications related to Computer Vision (CV) and Speech Processing. There are several techniques that belong to Deep Learning. These techniques include Deep Neural Network (DNN), Convolution Neural Network (CNN), Recurrent Neural Networks (RNN), Long Short Term Memory (LSTM) and Transfer Learning.

All of the deep learning methods have similar characteristics. That is, these methods are data hungry. They perform better with more data. These methods require high computation power and need longer time for training and inferences.

Since deep learning methods are resource intensive in terms of both computing power and storage requirement they often need high performance of cloud server. However, the enabling applications of deep learning such as autonomous vehicles and self-driving cars, home automation and security systems,

DOI: 10.4018/978-1-6684-5700-9.ch006

face detection applications and speech recognition systems require quick response which is not possible when the analysis is done on the cloud server because of latency inherent with cloud processing. Another problem associated with the analysis done on cloud server is that network connectivity is not available all the time.

Addressing of all these issues require the analysis and computation part to be done locally at the network edge. With data analysis and predictions done near the location of data collection, the response time can be reduced substantially. This scenario leads to the emergence of a new computing paradigm called Edge Computing.

Edge computing is distributed in nature as opposed to the Cloud Computing which makes use of a centralized cloud server. Edge computing is mostly applicable to Autonomous Systems (AS), Cyber-Physical Systems and Internet of Things (IoT) applications.

IoT applications comprise of an embedded system, communication system and several sensors. Sensor nodes don't either need extensive computing power offered by the cloud server or the storage space offered by cloud. The concept of Edge Computing refers that the computation is performed in close proximity to the end user. It means the computation is either performed locally on the sensor nodes or on a server near to these nodes, that is, at the network edge.

Edge computing offers a number of benefits to the end user. Edge computing preserves the privacy of personal data of users. The user data need not be sent to the cloud server for training of model. Only the model information is transferred to the cloud server. Since bulk data is not transferred, less number of network resources are required. The edge computing provides scalability as more edge devices can be added easily. As shown in Figure 1 intelligent IoT and other applications can utilize Edge Intelligence. The pre-trained Neural Network Model is deployed at the network edge whereas the model training is performed at the backend cloud server.

Figure 1. Intelligent Applications with Edge-Cloud Computing

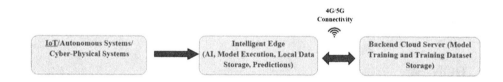

In the rest of this chapter, state-of-the-art literature survey is provided in section 2. Section 3 describes several application use cases which require the usage of deep learning along with computation on an edge device. Section 4 describes hardware systems and platforms that run deep learning applications. Section 5 provides a comprehensive discussion on various Deep Learning Frameworks both for training and deployment of Deep Neural Network Model. Section 6 presents the strategies for making inferences on edge device with pre-trained model. Section 7 describes how the training of a Deep Neural Network (DNN) takes place using a well-known framework. Section 8 provides some optimization techniques for edge computing. Section 9 provides the real-life examples of using Deep Learning techniques with Edge Computing. Section 10 presents several issues and challenges where further research is required. Finally, the chapter is concluded in section 11.

Literature Survey

When the computing task has to be done at cloud server, it the only decision need to be taken. But in case of fog computing, there are several choices for offloading. Josilo et al. (2018) proposed an offloading approach that works on minimizing the computation time. This technique is decentralized in nature and is based on a game theoretical model.

Li et al. (2018) presented a survey on design and management of Edge Computing Architecture. Their survey highlighted the key differences between existing Fog architectures and presented the detailed architecture for fog-edge computing paradigm. This survey also discussed the various resource management methods and provided various optimization solutions.

Merlino et al. (2019) proposed an OpenStack based middleware for enabling the edge computing. This paper highlighted that the raw data is first pre-processed at the edge server before being offloaded to Fog or Cloud server. Here the horizontal offloading is described for clustering of nearby devices and how the horizontal and vertical offloading can be combined. The architecture of a middleware platform is also presented.

Peng et al. (2018) presented a survey on Mobile Edge Computing (MEC). The survey highlighted the research on service adoption and service provisioning. Mobile Edge Computing (MEC) not only addresses the latency issues but also provides scalability in architecture of IoT applications.

Sodhro et al. (2019) proposed an approach for Industrial IoT (IIoT) platforms for edge computing which are AI enabled. The proposed approach promises to enhance the battery life of the sensor nodes. The Forward Central Dynamic and Available Approach (FCDAA) focuses on controlling the processing time of data sensing and data transmission functions. This approach is applied on AI based IIoT applications. In this paper a system level battery life model is also proposed for edge computing based AI systems. A data reliability model is also provided. The theoretical analysis and MATLAB simulation of these models is provided in this paper.

Sonmez et al. (2019) proposed a workload orchestration approach for edge infrastructure. In this approach the execution location for incoming tasks has been determined with a fuzzy logic based technique. The computation and network resources are taken into consideration and the off loaded tasks are examined by their properties. Edge computing provides the computational offloading service. The dynamic execution of tasks are handled such that user expectations are fulfilled. The significance of edge orchestration and various schemes of edge orchestration are provided. The workload orchestration involves considerable uncertainty in allocating network resources. The number of users and bandwidth utilization may fluctuate. Moreover, CPU utilization is dependent on the specific application. A fuzzy logic based workload orchestration scheme (Sonmez et al., 2019) may be appropriate for handling uncertainty and imprecision.

Wu et al. (2019) proposed hybrid edge-cloud IoT Base Station System. The edge nodes are implemented as embedded programmable logic controllers. The integration between edge nodes and cloud servers is established with dynamic programming method. It has been emphasized that if the cloud service is used, it is not practically possible to respond every alarm or even the most critical alarms. Therefore urgent and time-critical tasks should be delegated to edge servers. An architecture of base station management is proposed that combines the edge and cloud computing with the aim of minimizing false arms thereby increasing the system reliability, scalability, and empowering the edge nodes with increased capability. The choice of ePLC as edge nodes increases the system reliability. Use of Extensible Markup Language

(XML) increases the scalability. The response time by employing edge nodes is reduced to 0.1s and number of alarms generated is reduced to 60%.

Yousefpour et al. (2019) presented a thorough discussion on fog computing and other computing paradigms. The similarities and differences among fog computing, edge computing, cloud computing, mobile computing, mist computing and other hybrid configuration is provided in this paper. This paper also presents the fog computing taxonomy through a detailed survey. The survey highlighted the research work under several aspects of fog computing. The survey on foundation of fog computing along with its definition and standardization is provided. The survey on existing surveys pertaining to edge computing applications, research areas, industrial efforts, application use-case, challenges, architecture and design goals, fog computing models and key technologies is provided. The survey on fog computing architecture includes general architecture, resource model, ICN (Information Centric Networking) based architecture and resource allocation framework is provided. The programming models surveyed include vehicular fog computing, fog for transport computing, volunteer edge computing, path computing, fog software stack for android, service modelling, PaaS and so on. Survey on infrastructure design comprised of virtualization-based infrastructure, capacity planning etc. The survey on resource planning involves resource pricing, energy and resource estimation and load and resource time estimation. The survey on resource management and provisioning involves service provisioning, placement and control and monitoring. In this context the studies on service provisioning and migration, orchestration frameworks, virtualization technologies, IoT devices provisioning, handover, service placement, virtual machine placement, caching and other related work are described in detail. The survey on operations include scheduling, offloading, load balancing, and applications is provided. The survey on software and tools involve simulation and emulation tools, edge computing middleware, data analytics tools and so on. The survey on test-beds and experiments is also provided. The survey on security and privacy involves location and data privacy, intrusion detection and so on. This paper also highlighted various challenges and research directions on fog computing including the fog design schemes, monitoring, and green fog computing, offloading, security, trust and authentication, standardization and hardware technologies.

Han et al. (2019) proposed an Industrial IoT (IIoT) based architecture. This architecture is based on big data analytics. The architecture is applied on a smart factory which is 5G enabled. The requirement and design aspects of the proposed architecture are described. The requirements suggested the use of fog nodes that reduces the delay for real time analysis. The use of tools for handling high volume of data is also indicated. Integration involves for handling data obtained from different devices. The requirement of application specific visualization is also highlighted.

Crăciunescu et al. (2019) proposed a gateway for IIoT applications. This gateway is based on edge computing. A model for Mist Edge Gateway (MEC) is proposed which makes use of Access Edge and Aggregation Edge. The three case studies on the MEC architecture namely Hydroponic Greenhouse, Power Microgrid and Multi- Camera Surveillance System are provided.

Stojanovic (2019) proposed the intelligence at edge level processing for self-healing manufacturing. It helps in early prediction of equipment conditions. This system also provides recommendations for maintenance. This paper also highlighted the use of semantic technologies for handling unstructured, semi-structured and structured data so that integration of data from many sources can be achieved. The proposed scheme makes use of four layers. The Plug-In/Out Management layer allows enabling and disabling of sensor nodes easily. The knowledge extraction layer employs a number of data extraction methods to retrieve the desired data from sensor nodes. The data obtained from sensors is usually structured data since it is retrieved in predefined format except the videos obtained from camera sensors which is a form of unstructured data. Whereas the data coming from logs and error reports is unstructured data. The Smart Integration Layer provides the data fusion capability. This layer is responsible for integrating data from diverse sources and computing the unique result. The Intelligent Service Layer allows for applying predictive models on data and works on improving edge analytics. Several industrial strength smart applications are described which make use of the proposed model.

With this background on edge computing, the next section presents several application use cases which requires the computation to be done on the network edge rather than on a cloud server. The applications presented here also makes use of Deep Learning techniques in order to incorporate intelligence.

Deep Learning Applications on Edge Computing (DL on Edge)

The applications which are most appropriate to utilize the deep learning technique are computer vision and natural language processing. Examples of computer vision applications are given below.

Edge Computing in Computer Vision

Edge computing can offer solutions when there is limited or no connectivity to the Internet so that communication with cloud servers becomes impossible. Apart from this edge computing is also useful when data becomes too large to be financially viable to transfer on the cloud.

Edge Camera Processing

CCTV Camera is used to capture video clips in a surveillance system. An Edge computing based solution can perform video analysis and sends only analytics results and the alerts on a cloud server. This approach can substantially reduce the volume of data transferred and saved on the cloud server.

Local Processing

In a manufacturing production line the processing can be done locally so that any fault can be detected early. It can improve Quality Assurance (QA) process.

Video Analysis

Video Analysis has a number of applications ranging from surveillance systems, attendance system using face recognition and road safety. Edge computing solutions to these applications makes them fast, more efficient and cosy effective.

Smart Living Room and Smart Devices

Smart living room has many smart devices that monitors the environment continuously. The processing required to control these devices can be performed at network edge for immediate response and action. Also the unnecessary data transfer to the cloud server can be avoided. Machine learning techniques can be applied on the network edge. This forms the Smart Edge AI.

Voice Identification

Smart speakers and other smart home devices use voice assistants which can be integrated on the edge computing servers. Smart TV can recognize the voice of a person and can present the smart content. All this can be done in the privacy of the home with all learning and computation done on the edge device. This enables the protection of privacy for a person and quick response therefore achieving the improved user experience.

Face Identification

Camera and Computer vision Intelligence can be used in face recognition which has a number of applications. Above mentioned smart TV application can also utilize face recognition technique so that as soon as a person comes in front of the TV, the personalized content is presented to him or her. All the computation and machine learning tasks can be done on the edge.

Logo Detection

The Smart Edge AI technology can be used to detect what is playing on the smart TV. Based on the user's preference the appropriate advertisements can be delivered.

Event Detection

User's preference for watching specific event can be recognized and learned by Smart Edge AI. The next time user watches his favourite sports, the specific event can be identified and the user can be alerted.

Automated Packaging

The camera can be used as a sensor. It has several use cases. The packaging person will hold the packaging box in front of the camera. Using the Smart Edge AI technique automated bin packaging can be done. It also helps in creating smart conveyer belt and used to identify the missing inventory.

Event Management

The distributed AI vision can be leveraged in event management. We must do as much as possible computing on the edge. It will reduce the cost greatly and increase the speed. Most important use case of edge computing is the computer vision. We can get instant results. If we need to do real time video stream analysis, it should be done on edge only. In this scenario the cloud computing will not work due to latency.

Neural Compute Stick 2 (NCS 2) is a device manufactured by Intel that helps in creating AI algorithms at the network edge. We can also build computer vision algorithms. This device also enables deep neural network testing.

With the potential deep learning applications identified, the next section provides a detailed description of hardware systems which are specifically designed for implementing deep learning on the network edge.

Deep Learning with Edge Computing

Ubiquitous computing and smart factories are on the rise day by day. The sensors collect massive data every moment. This data need to be analysed for smart operation. This gives rise the need of computing at the network edge. In recent years Edge intelligence has emerged that facilitates machine learning and deep learning services at the network edge thereby enabling the distributed computing. There are four significant enablers for adaptation of edge computing nearly in every smart and intelligent application. These enablers are cost, latency, reliability and privacy.

Deep learning at the edge makes it intelligent edge. However, it demands significant change in hardware resources in order to execute deep learning algorithms. In recent years there have been significant development in edge computing hardware and systems. Several AI chips for edge devices have been manufactured. There are GPU based chips such as NVIDIA, Customized chips based on FPGA and ASIC based chips such as Google's TPU (Tensor Processing Unit).

The edge nodes are required to have both computing capabilities as well as the caching capabilities. For instance in case of Smart Transportation System, safety in the current state of the vehicle also depends on its past state such as driver's behaviour and road condition. Therefore, the caching capability must be there in order to store data of the recent past.

There are several Deep Learning (DL) Frameworks that support edge computing. These frameworks include TensorFlow from Google, MxNet from Apache Incubator, PyTorch from Facebook, CoreML from Apple, SNPE from Qualcomm, NCNN from Tencent, MNN from Alibaba and so on. Figure 2 gives the layered architecture for software stack that enables intelligence on the edge. The topmost layer of the architecture represents deep learning applications in several domains. The next layer describes the Deep Learning Frameworks which contain libraries for various deep neural network architectures. Since the training of deep neural network takes place on a cloud server, a software container runtime is required. Whenever the model training takes place a new instance of cloud service is created. Each new instance requires all the framework libraries to be installed from scratch. The Docker Software Container provides an instance of containerized application with no need of installing the libraries again. The bottom-most layer consists of hardware systems such as CPU and GPU available at the cloud server.

The application specific hardware systems which can be used to train the network model at cloud server and to deploy the trained model at mobile edge device are described in the next section.

Hardware Specific to Deep Learning at Network Edge

This section describes few hardware chips and systems specific to support Deep Learning (DL) on Edge devices.

Huawei Atlas AI Computing Platform is built on Huawei Ascend Series processors and other components. It provides a complete AI-Infrastructure solutions for computation on device-edge-cloud and enables edge computing for smart city, safe transportation, smart-healthcare. The in-built processors speed up AI inference and real-time video analytics. The chip supports 16 TeraOPS (TOPS) on INT8 with very low power consumption.

Figure 2. Software Stack for Intelligent Edge Computing

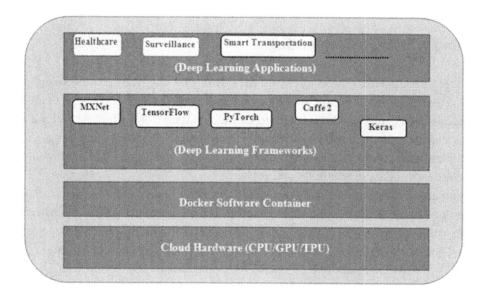

Kirin 990 5G is world's first flagship 5G System on Chip (SoC) for mobile edge devices that supports 5G connectivity and AI processing. The chip is desined for ultra-low power consumption. Kirin 810 has system level AI capabilities built on it. Kirin 980 had improved performance and energy efficiency. This chip makes use of GPU powered with dual NPU and i8 sensor coprocessor. It is the fastest and most intelligent chipset in the market with very high performance, energy efficiency and low-power consumption. The kirin series chips enable the AI powered scene recognition for photography.

MediaTek Helio P60 makes use of MediaTek NeuroPilot AI technology to enable smart imaging, video analytics and face recognition on the smart phone. The chip has Edge AI processing capability that enables machine learning on the device. The chip also has multi-core AI processing Unit (Mobile APU) that allows for AI and Augmented Reality (AR) application enhancements. The built-in APUs support common AI platforms such as TensorFlow, TensorFlow Lite, Caffe etc.

Tensor Processing Unit (TPU) is a hardware AI platform developed by Google. Google TPU is cloud based platform implemented with machine learning ASIC which are custom-designed. Google products like Search Engine, Google Assistant, Google Drive and Gmail, Google Assistant and Translate are powered by the TPU. The chip supports common AI and Deep Learning platforms like TensorFlow and supports AI application development.

Next section describes in detail the common software frameworks for Deep Learning (DL).

Deep Learning Frameworks

This section describes various Deep Learning Frameworks that enable AI and deep learning on edge devices.

CNTK or The Microsoft Cognitive Toolkit allows the users to easily realize complex neural networks such as feed-forward Deep Neural Network (DNN), Convolution Neural Networks (CNN), Recurrent

Neural Network (RNN), Long-Short Term Memory (LSTM). CNTK implements SGD (Stochastic Gradient Descent) learning. The parallelization is automatically performed by multiple GPUs. SNTK is available as python, C# and C++ libraries. CNTK also supports ONNX (Open Neural Network Exchange) format for interoperability and optimization.

Chainer is a python based framework for neural networks. This framework also makes use of multiple GPUs for parallelization and fast processing. This framework also supports different neural network architectures such as DNN, CNN and RNN. It has functions defined for both forward propagation and back propagation. In Chainer framework the neural network is dynamically defined.

TensorFlow is the Google's framework for machine learning. It is implemented in all products of Google to provide AI experience to users. TensorFlow can run on multiple CPUs and GPUs. It is available as a library in python, C++ and Java. TensorFlow performs preprocessing of the data, builds the model, train and evaluates the model. The input data is accepted as multidimensional arrays called tensors. Then, a number of operations are performed on the tensors. Training of model can be done on desktop or laptop whereas the run can be performed on cloud or mobile devices or on a PC. TensorBoard is another component that allows us to visualize what the TensorFlow is doing. TensorFlow has APIs available for common deep learning architectures such as DNN, CNN or RNN. The TensorFlow libraries can be deployed easily at scale.

DL4J or Deep Learning for Java is a deep learning framework which is based on vectors and tensor. The library used by DL4J framework is ND4J. Loading data is separate process from training data in DL4J framework. Deep Neural Network model is built in DL4J using layers. DL4J also has separate process for optimization and updating of neural network.

TensorFlow Lite

Machine learned models can be run on mobile devices with low latency using TensorFlow Lite framework. It is supported as API for both Android and iOS devices. The runtime is available which allows pre-trained models to run on mobile devices. However training of model is not supported. This framework is still evolving.

MXNet is a deep learning neural network framework that allows users to define the model, train it and deploy the trained model. MXNet has several features that makes it a better framework compared to other frameworks. These features are programmability, portability and scalability. MXNet is available in several languages such as Python, R, Julia, C++ etc. The model can be trained on a cloud platform with multiple GPUs and can be deployed on a smartphone or any other connected device.

PyTorch

PyTorch is a simple and flexible deep learning library. It allows building the neural network from scratch. It is a python based library. The paradigm followed by PyTorch is imperative/eager. Each line of code for building the graph defines a part of the graph. PyTorch framework also works with tensors. The main elements in PyTorch framework are tensors for input data, mathematical operations, Autograd module for computing differentiation automatically for computing gradients, an optimization module and nn module for implementing neural network layers. PyTorch libraries outperform several other deep learning librraies. However, PyTorch should not be used to deploy a model. In order to deploy the trained model, it should be converted to some other model such as Caffe 2.

SNPE or Snapdragon Neural Processing Engine is a deep learning framework for executing an arbitrary deep neural network on Snapdragon CPU, Ardeno GPU or the Hexagon DSP. The models from other frameworks like Caffe 2, TensorFlow or ONNX can be converted to SNPE Deep Learning Container (DLC) file. SNPE runtime is used to execute models trained on other frameworks like TensorFlow.

NCNN is a neural network computing framework optimized for mobile platforms. NCNN gives high performance in nearly all mobile phone CPUs. Deep learning models can be easily deployed on NCNN and developers can build intelligent mobile apps.

MNN or Mobile Neural Networks is another framework developed for deploying neural network models on a mobile device. MNN has also been used on devices other than mobile phones such as IoT devices. MNN is lightweight and can easily deploy a trained model. MNN supports trained models from common frameworks such as Caffe, Caffe 2 and TensorFlow. MNN allows common neural networks such as CNN, RNN and GAN to be deployed on mobile device. It is applicable for both Android and iOS.

Paddle Lite is a deep learning framework for performing inference on mobile devices, embedded systems and IoT devices. It is a lightweight framework.

The trained Deep Neural Network can be deployed on an edge device for performing the inferences. However, it is a time consuming task which can effect the application response time. This issue need to be addressed. The next section provides few strategies to speed-up the inference process.

Deep Learning Inference in Edge (DL in Edge)

As already mentioned deep learning model can be trained by a framework like TensorFlow before going into the production environment where the trained model can be used to perform inferences. In the production environment there are a number of issues that need to be addressed so that the application can perform efficiently. The latency is the most significant factor that effects the performance of an application. The deep learning framework which is used to train a model gives the trained model in the form of a collection of weights. These weights are often real numbers such as double or float. Since the computation has shifted to network edge rather than being performed on cloud server, there are few constraints in terms of speed, memory and computing power. The trained model must be fast enough to produce the prediction results in reasonable time to enhance the user experience. There are several strategies that can contribute in speeding up the computation that need to be performed for providing the prediction. These strategies are discussed below

(1)   Cropping /Pruning Insignificant Neurons

This strategy identifies which neurons have little or no impact on the final output. Once those neurons are identified, their weight can be made zero so that these neurons don't contribute the computation which leads to final output. By making the weights of insignificant neurons to zero, the weight matrix may have substantial number of zeros. Therefore the weight matrix becomes sparse and it can be easily compressed. This process speeds up the computation with slight reduction in performance. However, the latency can be reduced as the number of effective neurons are reduced to several times.

(2)   Quantization

The trained model can be optimized for the available hardware on which it is going to run. For a CPU, 8-bit integer representation is required and for a GPU, 16-bit floating point representation is required. If the trained models consists of weights in terms of 32-bit floating point values, they can be converted in appropriate format according to the available hardware. It would speed up the multiplication and activation operations since the hardware latency is reduced. The model size will decrease with slight reduction in accuracy. The quantization technique also results in low power consumption thus making the application energy-efficient.

(3)   Weight Clustering

The interconnections in a neural network that connect its different layers have weights which can be shared. The weights can be clustered together with the help of any clustering technique such as K-Means clustering. This strategy creates the clusters of neuron weights by determining the cluster centroid. The cluster centroid is that weight tht can be shared by all members of the cluster. This technique also results in substantial reduction in the size of neural network model. Therefor it will lead to fast execution of the application.

Once the trained model is optimized, inference can be made with Google Accelerator. The trained model can be compiled in a format appropriate for target environment. The converted model can be loaded to the edge device such as Raspberry Pi where it can execute. Figure 3 shows the complete process of execution of a deep learning application on the edge device. The training dataset is loaded on a cloud server for building the initial model of deep neural network. After the initial model is trained, cross-validation and testing of the model takes place by using the test dataset. These steps are performed on a cloud server. The output of this process is a model file containing the static weight matrix and biases. The weights represent the trained model. This model is now ready for deployment on the edge device. Since for deployment the frameworks being used are different from the frameworks used for training, model conversion is required. This is followed by model optimization, quantization and compression. These steps are required to make the inference and predictions fast. The deployed application now can be used by intelligent applications running on the edge device.

Next section presents the training of neural network model.

Deep Learning Training at Edge (DL at Edge)

In this section training of a deep neural network model has been demonstrated using Caffe 2 Framework.

Caffe 2 (Convolution Architecture for Fast Feature Embedding) can be used for both deep neural network learning or training the model as well as it can be used for performing inferences. Caffe 2 is cross-platform. Caffe 2 supports training Deep Neural Networks (DNN) in a distributed manner. It can utilize several GPUs for training.

The environment setup can be done as follows. First of all, download the Google Cloud SDK and unzip the tar file and then install it. Then install the NVIDIA Graphics Driver and CUDA toolkit. Then install the Caffe 2 dependencies as well as the Caffe 2. Now you can open the Jupyter Notebook and import the library.

Figure 3. Execution of Deep Learning Application.

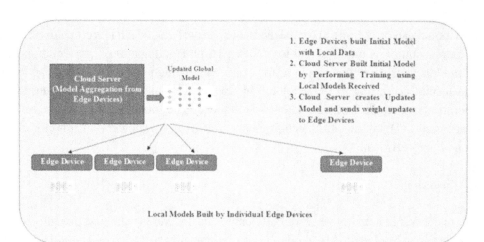

For Example,

```
Import caffe2
Import caffe2.python
```

We don't want to install Caffe 2 and Caffe 2 dependencies each time we install our application in Google Cloud. Hence we need to install Docker container. Whenever we start a new cloud instance to train our model we need Caffe 2 and Caffe 2 dependencies installed on that instance. Since each cloud instance is independent of each other, every time we need to install all libraries. Docker container provides virtualization on operating system level. Docker is basically a virtual environment for running a software.

Next the dataset for training can be read and prepared for processing. The dataset may be converted to an appropriate format. Now define the layers of neural network and start training till the network converges. The trained model can be optimized for the edge.

Deep Learning for Optimizing Edge (DL for Edge)

Deep Learning can also be used to perform optimization on the edge. Federated Learning is one such approach that enables optimization.

Federated Learning is an approach for training deep neural networks specifically on edge devices. This technique was developed by the Google. Training of a neural network model is heavily dependent on the data available. The data is fetched from various devices essentially from the edge devices. Therefore the issue of data privacy arises. The users are often reluctant in sharing their personal data. Federated learning approach aims to preserve the privacy of the user data at the same time makes it available on a centralized location where model training takes place. The data is collected and stored at the edge devices and need not be transferred to cloud server for training. Instead, only the model related updates are sent.

The Federated Learning algorithm works by computing the global model at the server. The participating clients which collect data at the edge device are sent this global model. The clients compute the updated model using the local data. These model updates are sent to the server. The improved model is constructed at the server with the help of the updated model received from the clients.

One improvement of the Federated Learning algorithm requires only gradient updates to be sent to the server instead of sending the actual weights. Figure 4 shows the optimization done by Federated Learning. The initial model is constructed at the cloud. The individual edge devices construct the local model with the help of data available locally at that device. These locally build network models are transferred to the cloud server in the form of weights. Therefore, there is no need of sharing the actual data. The cloud server receives the local model from edge devices and creates the updated model which in turn is sent to each edge device which participates in the training process.

Figure 4. Federated Learning for Edge Optimization

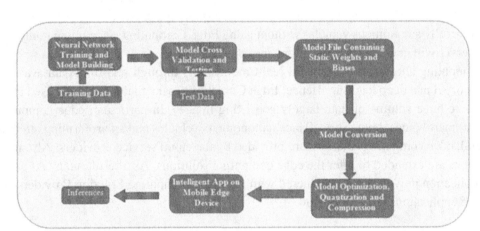

Federated Learning also has several challenges related to the security and privacy. These challenges are discussed below.

(1)   Inference Attack

Since training a neural network model require large number of iterations, the continuous sending of model weights may reveal the properties of individual client. The personal information of clients can be obtained from this auxiliary information. A solution of this kind of attack is to use differential privacy where a random noise is mixed with the data. It makes it difficult for adversary to breach the privacy, since whatever the adversary receives appears noisy and imprecise to him.

(2)   Model Poisoning

Adversary can mount a Sybil to poison the global model. Therefore additional overhead of overcoming the Sybil attack is also required.

Deep Reinforcement Learning based Online Offloading Framework is proposed in earlier research work. With this approach all computations have been performed either locally or on a MEC (Mobile-Edge-Computing) server.

In recent years the focus of AI research has been shifted to Deep Learning. As a result numerous frameworks and hardware and software platforms have been developed. This also gives rise to the possibility of several new kinds of security breaches and attacks. There are several open challenges and issues that require further research. Some of these issues and challenges are discussed in the next section.

Real Life Examples of Deep Learning in Edge Computing

This section presents several scenarios of real-life application making use of deep learning techniques and are empowered by the Edge computing Technology. As a matter of fact, the Edge Computing has become essential in implementing the solutions for many smart applications. For instance, it is not possible to realize fully autonomous vehicles without using Edge Computing since relying only on centralized cloud server will make these applications ineffective.

Edge Computing allows users to obtain real-time insights through real-time data availability and applications of AI and deep learning. Hence, Edge Computing is an enabler for IoT based applications which generate huge volume of data largely consisting images. In particular, edge computing based solutions for smart homes, home surveillance, autonomous vehicles and smart farming are in demand.

In general, edge computing solutions are provided by the cloud service providers. Also many cloud based solutions are extended to offer the edge computing solutions. As a result, many AI and machine learning application providers have partnered with the Edge Computing Solution Providers. Some use cases of such applications are given below.

Autonomous Vehicle Solution by Renovo and EdgeConnX

Connected Autonomous Vehicles require real-time analytics to operate. The data these vehicles generate is mostly in the form of images. **Renovo** is a platform for commercial deployment of fully autonomous vehicles. A single vehicle could generate up to 50TB of data per day. Most of this data is in the form of image files. Mostly, the data is required only when the vehicle is running. However, some data is also required after that, when the journey is over for further analysis.

As most of this data is generated by car's cameras, if we process this data on vehicle itself it would result in reduction of the cost and delay associated with uploading data on the cloud server. However, it will drain out or deplete the power of vehicle. Therefore, it doesn't make much sense to perform this kind of data analysis on the vehicle itself. **EdgeConnX** is a Data Centre Solution Provider company that brings together Deep Learning with Edge Computing. It provides Edge Computing solutions for the Service Provider customers. EdgeConnX deploys its computing nodes where the cars are parked at charging points. It gives enough time to transfer the data and it is done far faster than it could be uploaded on a cloud server.

AI-Powered Smart Home Camera - SimCam

The AI-powered home security cameras can also make effective use of Edge Computing. For instance, **SimShine** has developed an AI-powered smart home camera system called **SimCam**. The SimCam is featured by its ability of running AI on the local device using edge Computing. The SimCam provides double benefits to the customers by reducing the latency in uploading the data on the cloud server as well as protecting their privacy by retaining the data on local devices. Also, the Simcam makes use of latest deep learning algorithms. SimCam can recognize the faces of family members and trusted ones. The SimCam can also track other objects that are selected in the camera view. It makes SimCam a good real-life example of using Deep Learning with Edge Computing.

Edge Computing Solutions for Smart Farming by AeroFarm

Another real-life example where Edge Computing has been used is the Smart farming. A New Jersey based company, **AeroFarm** has been using edge computing for managing vertical farming and sustainable agriculture. In order to apply edge computing, AeroFarm creates its edge-to-core-to-cloud infrastructure with the help of Dell EMC IoT Technology. One application, in which this technology has been applied is about the improvement in the tracking of seeds to package through each distinct stage of farming – seeding, germination, growing, harvesting and packaging. Another application, in which edge computing has been applied to leverage the deep learning tasks is for improving real-time quality control through multi-spectral imaging of grow trays. In this application, the images are analysed using machine learning techniques.

The other applications of Edge Computing Technology with Deep Learning consists of applications in industrial control, IoT, Drones, Robotics and smart cities. Following is a list of some of the companies which offer edge computing solutions for AI and Deep Learning.

- **Omron** uses edge devices for industrial control, in particular, for controlling of production equipment with a robust, low-latency connectivity.
- **Mutable** is a microservices provider offering Platform as a Service (PaaS) solutions with Edge Technology.
- **SWIM.AI** provides edge-based solutions for the execution of real-time analytics and machine learning for enterprises in the field of equipment manufacturing, Smart Cities and IoT.
- **Affirmed Network** provides a fully virtualized Cloud Edge Solution as well as Mobile Edge Connectivity (MEC) for Content Delivery Networks (CDN), Augmented Reality and Virtual Reality, IoT, drones, autonomous vehicles etc.
- **Hanger** provides Robotics-as-a-Service (RaaS) for enabling drones without human intervention and also provides services for real-time data analysis. The combination of hardware, software and services in a single platform enables delivery of 4D Visual Insights.
- German Edge Cloud has developed an industrial edge cloud appliance called ONCITE. It enables users to find information from their production data using AI, Machine Learning and Deep Learning as the real-time data becomes available.
- AlefEdge is a 5G applications provider through open APIs at the edge for AI, Smart Cities, IoT, AR/VR etc. It provides the services through edge gateways and edge cloud and can be used in Smart Cities, Industry 4.0, IoT etc.

Future Research Directions

- **Innovation in Edge Technology**

The applications running on network edge are leveraged by several enabling technologies such as Cloudlets, Cloud of Things, Fog Computing, Mobile Edge Computing and Edge Specific Hardware. Future research in this direction will lead to faster application deployment and greater user experience.

- **Application-Specific Processing**

Application Specific Mobile Edge Computing architecture has been discussed in several research papers in recent years. There are many more application specific optimization use cases that can be explored in further research.

- **General Purpose Edge Computing Infrastructure**

Currently the development in edge computing is application specific. There is a need to develop an edge computing infrastructure that serves large number of applications.

- **Offloading the Computing Tasks**

Edge computing enables distributed processing. Therefore both horizontal and vertical offloading of tasks is required. In this direction, future research is required to develop more efficient algorithms that perform offloading tasks.

- **Security and Privacy**

There are several security and privacy related concerns related to edge computing. For instance in a healthcare application, data may be required from several unrelated places. The users may show their reluctance in sharing their personal data.

Apart from this there are a number of new kind of security breaches such as model poisoning and inference attack that need to be addressed.

- **Energy Conservation**

Mobile Edge device deploy the trained model for performing inferences and predictions. This process may be time consuming and resource intensive. Therefore future research will involve determining the new techniques for model optimization and therefore reducing the size of model.

CONCLUSION

This chapter gives insight into a very important technique for imparting intelligence at network edge – the Deep Learning technique. Deep Learning (DL) is a subset of a broader component of AI (Artificial

Intelligence) called Machine Learning. The chapter describes several aspects of Deep Learning which are applicable for Edge Computing.

The chapter starts with introduction of Edge Computing and Deep Learning. How the Deep Learning can leverage Intelligent Edge Applications is described. It is followed by Literature Review section. Literature Review presents state-of-the-art research work done in recent few years on edge computing.

The next section describes Deep Learning on the Edge where several edge computing applications are highlighted that can be benefitted by using Deep Learning Techniques. This section emphasized that computer vision is the most prominent application area which requires deep learning for inferences and predictions.

The next section describes Deep Learning with Edge Computing. In this section a number of hardware systems and chips are discussed which can make training a Deep Neural Network fast. These hardware systems can be the part of cloud infrastructure where training of neural network model takes place.

Several Deep Learning Frameworks are described next. The frameworks described in this section can be used for either performing training at cloud server or deployment at the edge device or both.

The next section discusses how inferences are obtained by the deployed model at the edge device. This section provides several strategies such as neuron cropping/pruning, quantization and weight clustering so that the deployed model can be executed faster.

How to train a DNN is described in the next section. Here an example of usage of Caffe 2 and PyTorch framework is described.

The next section discusses the optimization techniques for edge computing. This section provides an important scheme called Federated Learning that can be used for the optimization of the computation performed on the Edge.

Finally, few real-life applications of the usage of Deep Learning with Edge Computing are presented.

The last section provides future research direction in the field of deep learning with edge computing.

REFERENCES

Crăciunescu, M., Chenaru, O., Dobrescu, R., Florea, G., & Mocanu, Ş. (2020). IIoT Gateway for Edge Computing Applications. In T. Borangiu, D. Trentesaux, P. Leitão, A. Giret Boggino, & V. Botti (Eds.), *Service Oriented, Holonic and Multi-agent Manufacturing Systems for Industry of the Future. SOHOMA 2019. Studies in Computational Intelligence* (Vol. 853). Springer.

Han, Y., Park, B., & Jeong, J. (2019). Fog Based IIoT Architecture Based on Big Data Analytics for 5G-networked Smart Factory. In Lecture Notes in Computer Science: Vol. 11620. *Computational Science and Its Applications – ICCSA 2019. ICCSA 2019.* Springer. doi:10.1007/978-3-030-24296-1_5

Jošilo, S., & Dán, G. (2018). Decentralized algorithm for randomized task allocation in fog computing systems. *IEEE/ACM Transactions on Networking, 27*(1), 85–97. doi:10.1109/TNET.2018.2880874

Li, C., Xue, Y., Wang, J., Zhang, W., & Li, T. (2018). Edge-oriented computing paradigms: A survey on architecture design and system management. *ACM Computing Surveys, 51*(2), 39. doi:10.1145/3154815

Merlino, G., Dautov, R., Distefano, S., & Bruneo, D. (2019). Enabling Workload Engineering in Edge, Fog, and Cloud Computing through OpenStack-based Middleware. *ACM Transactions on Internet Technology, 19*(2), 28. doi:10.1145/3309705

Peng, K., Leung, V., Xu, X., Zheng, L., Wang, J., & Huang, Q. (2018). A Survey on Mobile Edge Computing: Focusing on Service Adoption and Provision. *Wireless Communications and Mobile Computing, 2018*, 2018. doi:10.1155/2018/8267838

Sodhro, A. H., Pirbhulal, S., & de Albuquerque, V. H. C. (2019). Artificial intelligence driven mechanism for edge computing based industrial applications. *IEEE Transactions on Industrial Informatics, 15*(7), 4235–4243. doi:10.1109/TII.2019.2902878

Sonmez, C., Ozgovde, A., & Ersoy, C. (2019). Fuzzy Workload Orchestration for Edge Computing. *IEEE eTransactions on Network and Service Management, 16*(2), 769–782. doi:10.1109/TNSM.2019.2901346

Stojanovic, L. (2020). Intelligent edge processing. In Machine Learning for Cyber Physical Systems. Technologien für die intelligente Automation (Technologies for Intelligent Automation) (vol. 11). Springer Vieweg. doi:10.1007/978-3-662-59084-3_5

Wu, H., Hu, J., Sun, J., & Sun, D. (2019). Edge Computing in an IoT Base Station System: Reprogramming and Real-Time Tasks. *Complexity, 2019*, 2019. doi:10.1155/2019/4027638

Yousefpour, A., Fung, C., Nguyen, T., Kadiyala, K., Jalali, F., Niakanlahiji, A., Kong, J., & Jue, J. P. (2019). All One Needs to Know about Fog Computing and Related Edge Computing Paradigms. *Journal of Systems Architecture, 98*, 289–330. doi:10.1016/j.sysarc.2019.02.009

Chapter 7
Deep Learning on Edge:
Challenges and Trends

Mário P. Véstias

 https://orcid.org/0000-0001-8556-4507

INESC-ID, ISEL, Instituto Politécnico de Lisboa, Portugal

ABSTRACT

Deep learning on edge has been attracting the attention of researchers and companies looking to provide solutions for the deployment of machine learning computing at the edge. A clear understanding of the design challenges and the application requirements are fundamental to understand the requirements of the next generation of edge devices to run machine learning inference. This chapter reviews several aspects of deep learning: applications, deep learning models, and computing platforms. The way deep learning is being applied to edge devices is described. A perspective of the models and computing devices being used for deep learning on edge are given, as well as what challenges face the hardware designers to guarantee the vast set of tight constraints like performance, power consumption, flexibility, etc. of edge computing platforms. Finally, a trends overview of deep learning models and architectures is discussed.

INTRODUCTION

Machine learning algorithms and, in particular, deep learning brought Artificial Intelligence to many application domains. In a deep learning workflow data is gathered and prepared for training the machine learning model. In the training step, deep learning models are trained with a large set of known instances so that they can classify new inputs not used during the training step. These trained models are then deployed for inference. Inference is when the trained model is used to classify new and unknown data instances.

Training is computationally heavy and requires high-performance computing platforms that still take hours or even days to train large deep learning models. Inference is orders of magnitude less demanding in terms of computation and can also be deployed in the same computing platform used for training. The common process is to use the high-performance computing platform for both training and inference. In many cases, data to be processed by the deep neural model is received from an edge device (any

DOI: 10.4018/978-1-6684-5700-9.ch007

hardware device that serves as an entry point of data and may store, process and/or send the data to a central server) and the inference result is sent back to the edge device. However, in a vast set of applications (security, surveillance, facial recognition, autonomous car driving, industrial, etc.) this round-trip method of doing inference is inefficient or unfeasible. Running the inference near the source of data is advantageous and in some cases necessary so that important information can be extracted in site and if necessary at real-time instead of sending data to the cloud and wait for the inference classification. Whenever the communication latency and data security violations are undesirable, like autonomous vehicles, local processing at the sensor is a requirement. In these cases, inference is done at the edge avoiding long data communications and high computing latencies. For these reasons, many deep learning tasks are migrating from the cloud of high-performance computing platforms to the low cost, low density embedded devices at the edge.

This brings new problems and open issues to the design of machine learning models at edge devices since running deep learning on edge is subject to different performance, memory and cost requirements then those considered by cloud computing design processes. Cloud inference is focused on delivering high performance inference with the highest model accuracy. Edge inference benefits from high accuracy models but achieving the highest accuracy is not the main metric. Cost, performance, energy, real-time, size are some of the most important design parameters considered when implementing computing platforms for edge inference on edge.

Deep learning on edge has been attracting the attention of researchers and companies looking to provide solutions for the deployment of machine learning computing at the edge. A clear understanding of the design challenges and the application requirements are fundamental to understand the requirements of the next generation of edge devices to run machine learning inference.

In this chapter several aspects of deep learning: applications, deep learning models and computing platforms, will be reviewed. Then the way deep learning is being applied to edge devices will be describes. A perspective of the models and computing devices that are being used for deep learning on edge will be given, what challenges are facing the hardware designers to guarantee the vast set of tight constraints like performance, power consumption, flexibility, etc. of edge computing platforms. Finally, a trends overview of deep learning models and architectures will be discussed.

BACKGROUND

Machine learning is a subfield of artificial intelligence whose objective is to give systems the capacity to learn and improve by its own without being explicitly programmed to do it. Machine learning algorithms extract features from data and build models from it so that new decisions and new outcomes are produced without being programmed a priori with these models and rules.

There are many types of machine learning algorithms with different approaches and application targets: Bayesian (Barber, 2012), clustering (Bouveyron et al., 2019), instance-based (Keogh, 2011), ensemble (Zhang, 2012), artificial neural network (Haykin, 2008), deep learning network (Patterson & Gibson, 2017), decision tree (Quinlan, 1992), association rule learning (Zhang & Zhang, 2002), regularization (Goodfellow et al., 2016), regression (Matloff, 2017), support-vector machine (Christmann & Steinwart, 2008) and others.

Different problems require different models and algorithms and so each of these algorithms apply to different types of data sets and applications. All these algorithms can be broadly classified according to the learning style: supervised, unsupervised and semi-supervised. Supervised machine learning algorithms (e.g., regression, artificial neural network and deep learning network) train the model of the algorithm with training data. Each instance of the training data has an associated label that identifies the expected result for each particular input. In the training process, the model is corrected and adjusted according to the expected outcomes. In the unsupervised class of algorithms (e.g., dimensionality reduction, k-means clustering, etc.), the training data do not have an expected outcome. The algorithms in this class try to extract features from the input data and cluster input data according to these features without any previous knowledge of the input data characteristics. The semi-supervised algorithms mixes both previous classes, that is, there is a desired outcome but the model must learn features to classify data.

Among the many machine algorithms this chapter is concerned with deep learning algorithms whose ground are artificial neural networks (ANN). ANNs are inspired by the structure of the human brain consisting of interconnected neurons. Theoretically, an ANN is a universal model capable to learn any function (Hornik et al., 1989). Deep learning is basically deep artificial neural networks with several and more complex layers designated deep neural networks. Since the introduction of deep learning that several models have been proposed, like convolutional neural network, recurrent neural network, deep belief network, deep Boltzmann machine, Kohonen self-organizing neural network, modular neural network and stacked auto-encoder.

Deep Learning

The grounds of deep learning models are artificial neural networks. Before proceeding with a description of deep neural networks the following section describes the fundamentals of ANNs

Artificial Neural Network

An artificial neural network (Haykin, 2008) consists of a basic structure known as perceptron or neuron organized in a series of layers. The first layer is the input layer, the last one is the output layer and all the other layers between the input and the output layer are known as hidden layers (see figure 1).

Neurons in the input layer receive input data and generate outcomes for the neurons of the first hidden layer, while the output layer receives the outcomes from the last hidden layer and produces the classification associated with the input data. These are feedforward networks which the underlying graph contains no feedback connections or cycles and are the focus of this chapter. Each neuron of an artificial neural network generate an output which is a function of all its inputs and sends it to all nodes of the next layer, except the output layer that does not have a next layer and so the outcomes of the neuron are the output results. The first artificial neural networks had only one hidden layer. Recently, this number has increased considerably and according to (Bengio, 2009) when a neural network has more than three layers is referred to as deep neural network.

A perceptron encodes n inputs, $\{x_1, x_2, x_3, ..., x_n\}$, from neurons of the previous layer using a vector of weights or parameters $\{w_1, w_2, w_3, ..., w_n\}$ associated with the connections between previous perceptrons and the target perceptron that determines the importance of the corresponding input to the perceptron being calculated. Each perceptron still has an additional bias value that is used to shift the output to better fit the data (see figure 2).

Figure 1. Artificial neural network

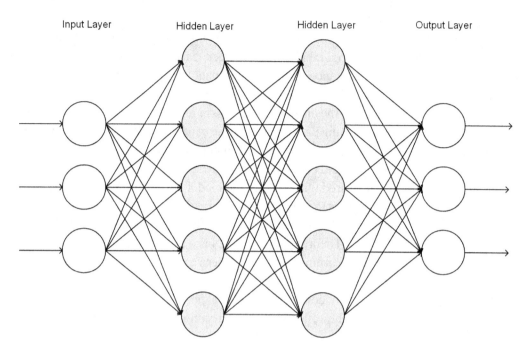

Figure 2. Perceptron or neuron

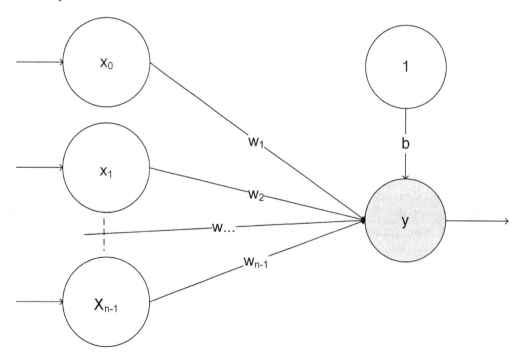

The output of a perceptron, y, its prediction value, is computed as a function of the weights and the bias:

$$y = f\left(b + \sum_{k=0}^{n-1} w_k x_k \right)$$

Function $f(.)$ referred to as activation function determines the output of the neuron. In its simplest form the activation function is binary, that is, the output is inactive, '0', or active, '1'. While simple, requires that many neurons are used for a non-linear separation of classes. A linear function can be used instead that linearly rates the output between two values. These functions exhibit similar problems of a binary function and since the output is unbounded, it leads to an unstable convergence. Instead, normalized functions are used with better properties for classification and learning stability (Nwankpa et al, 2018).

One of the first activation functions was the sigmoid given by $\frac{1}{1+e^{-z}}$ that predicts the probability of the output with values between 0 and 1, and the hyperbolic tangent, $(e^x - e^{-x})/(e^x + e^{-x})$ that increases the output range to $]-1, 1[$. Many other activation functions were proposed during the last decades but one of the most recently used is the ReLU (Rectified Linear Unit) that is 0 if the output is less or equal than 0, and 1 otherwise. In (Glorot et al., 2011) it was shown that ReLU leads to better training of deep neural networks. Previous activation functions apply to a single set. In many models, the output layer provides outputs for multiple classes. To associate values to multiple classes the softmax function is used. This function takes as input a vector of k values and normalizes it into a probability distribution of k probabilities as follows:

$$f_i(x) = \frac{e^{x_i}}{\sum_{j=1}^{K} e^{x_j}}$$

The weights of a neural network model must be adjusted for each specific problem and for the best network accuracy. Determining all weights of the network for best accuracy is known as the training step. Training can be supervised, unsupervised or semi-supervised. In the supervised training the set of weights, W, is found with the help of an objective function that quantifies the error, E, between the measured outputs for a particular set of weights, y_m, and the expected outputs, t_m, through all N data inputs, x_n. The error is calculated as the sum of the squared error:

$$E(W) = \sum_{n=1}^{N} \sum_{m=1}^{M} \left(y_m(x_n, W) - t_m \right)^2$$

The training algorithm iteratively runs the forward propagation and the backpropagation steps. Starting with an initial set of weights, an input is applied at the input layer of the network and propagated until the output layer to find an output classification. The loss function, E(W), is then applied to determine the mean squared error between the obtained output and the required output. This finishes the forward propagation step.

Then the backpropagation step starts with the objective to adjust the weights to minimize the error function. This is achieved by propagating backwards the value of the loss function to all neurons that contribute to each output neuron. Neurons with a higher contribution to the loss function value of an output neuron receive a higher fraction of this value. When all neurons have received its loss fraction, weights are adjusted to reduce the loss. The adjustment of weights is done with the *gradient descent* (Ruder, 2016) technique as follows:

$$\Delta W[i] = -^3 \left(\frac{\partial E_n}{\partial w[i]} \right)$$

In gradient descendent, weights are incrementally changed based on the derivative of the loss function and a learning rate, γ. It means that the loss function must be differentiable.

Unless the network is very simple, the model do not achieve 100% accuracy. Therefore, a criteria must be used to stop the training process. Normally the process stops when the accuracy improvement between two training iterations is below a certain threshold.

Gradient descent is an heuristic method and so it does not guarantee the global minimum. Finding a good local minimum depends on weight initialization. Some works have shown that better results can be achieved if the initial weights are randomly chosen within specific ranges (Glorot & Bengio, 2010).

Unsupervised training follows a different process since there are no expected outputs. The model is trained using extracted features from the input data. Semi-supervised training is a mix of both techniques where training is done with some labeled data and some unlabeled data.

Deep Neural Network

Deep neural networks (DNN) are an extension of the traditional artificial neural networks with more layers and different types of layers. Therefore in DNN each layer is trained with the output features extracted by the previous layer. So as the data progress through the network model more features are aggregated that represent more complex representations, like a hierarchy of features.

Unlike most traditional machine learning algorithms, deep learning is able to extract features from the input data without being explicitly programmed to do it. An important fact about deep learning is that the more data is used to train the network the better the accuracy, contrary to other machine learning algorithms. Since the size of the DNN can be freely increased it means that it can be applied to any complex classification problem with a high dimensionality of features.

The concept of a DNN with multiple layers is not new but its feasibility is recent. A neural network with many layers requires intensive computations to be trained. The required computational power is now possible with the recent high-performance computing platforms. To achieve high accuracy DNN also need a large set of data instances to train the network and it is a fact that today designers and developers have access to huge amounts of data to do it.

So, the accuracy of deep neural networks gets better with larger models and when trained with more data. The consequence is that both training and inference of DNN requires high memory size to store weights and feature maps and computational capacity to train it in reasonable times.

Since its introduction as a machine learning model, several types of deep neural networks were proposed differing mainly on how neurons are interconnected. In the following the most important types of DNNs will be briefly explained.

Types of Deep Neural Networks

Feed-Forward Neural Network is the traditional neural network model as explained in the previous section. All layers are dense and have the same structure. Dense layers means that all neurons of a layer connect to all neurons of the previous layer, except the first layer that receives inputs. Theoretically these networks can model any relationship between inputs and outputs with enough hidden neurons but this may lead to impractical implementations and so different neural networks models are adopted.

Convolutional neural networks (CNN) were introduced in (LeCun et al., 1989) to image classification.

A feed-forward neural network can be naturally applied to classify image. The problem is that input pixels are modeled with input neurons and so, for reasonably sized images the number of neurons of the input layer is large which requires many parameters from the input to the first hidden layer. Considering images of size 128×128, the first layer would have 2^{14} neurons. Assuming the next layer with the same number of nodes, the first hidden layer would require 2^{28} weights. Since a deep neural networks is being used, this number easily increases to an order that turns the training process too hard.

Instead of using a neural network with dense layers, the interconnections between layers take into consideration the type of input data (LeCun, 1989). CNNs takes advantage of the spatial correlation between neighbor pixels to establish dependencies between neurons of different layers, that is, the output of a neuron is the result of the convolution between a small window of weights and the respective output of neurons of the input map. These layers are therefore designated convolutional layers. A CNN contains one or more convolutional layers. Each convolutional layer identify features of the image which are then correlated by the next convolutional layer to learn complex features.

The set of convolutional layers may be followed by one or more fully connected layers which are dense layers identical to those used in feed-forward layers. Since these layers interconnect all neurons of previous layers the complex features extracted so far are globally correlated.

Recurrent neural networks (RNN) were introduced in (Elman, 1990) and are basically dense networks with state. RNNs have a hidden state distributed through all neurons that allows them to store information of previous data. State information is updated in a non-linear way which permits the model to follow complex state sequences. This type of networks is very powerful but must be carefully designed to avoid the vanishing problem where weights converge to extreme values loosing previous information. RNNs have a vast set of applications including also those without an explicit association with a sequence of events. A picture, for example, can be processed as a sequence of pixels. A common application of RNNs is autocompletion where the information of a sequence is automatically determined.

The vanishing problem of RNNs happens because the state of the network is hard to keep for a long time. The **long-short term memory network** – LSTM - (Hochreiter, 1998; Hochreiter & Schmidhuber, 1997) reduces the vanishing problem of RNNs with the introduction of gates and an explicit memory to store states. The memory stores the state until a gate cell tells the memory to forget a state. LSTMs add a cell layer to remember information from a previous iteration of the model. With these improvements LSTM networks were able to execute complex tasks, like music composition.

RNN and LSTM networks may have an unpredictable behavior by following a non-deterministic path or oscillating. To overcome this instability problems the **Hopfield network** (HN) introduced in (Hopfield, 1982) can be used. The HN is the densest neural network since all neurons connect to all other neurons. The network is trained for a set of patterns and only these can be identified by the network, that is, for a particular input the network will converge to one of the stable patterns learned during training. The HN has been shown to be very limited in the number of patterns (15% of the number of neurons) it can learn because of the spurious minima. This limitation is associated with the fact that if two local minima correspondent to two training patterns are too close it may create a single local minima for both and therefore none of the two patterns will be memorized.

The **Boltzmann Machine** (BM) network is an unsupervised model that was introduced in (Hinton & Sejnowski, 1986). His model is similar to the Hopfield network but only considers input and hidden neurons. After a network update during training the input neurons become output neurons. During the learning process, the BM maximizes the product of probabilities assigned to the elements of the training set. BM are used for dimensionality reduction, classification, feature learning, among others.

Deep Belief Network (DBN) introduced in (Bengio et al., 2006) are probabilistic generative models with multiple layers of the so called latent variables. The first two layers have undirected connections while the next layers have directed connections between layers. This type of networks is used recognize and generate images and videos.

The **autoencoder** (AE) network model was designed for unsupervised learning and is used to encode an input with a representation with less number of dimensions (Bourlard & Kamp, 1988). A decoder is then used to decode the data and obtain the original data. So they are basically used to reduce the size of the inputs into a compact representation.

Deep Neural Networks in Practice

From among the many different neural network models, CNNs have gained most of the attention due to its good image classification results better than other deep neural networks and because there has been an exponential increase of applications requiring image classification. In the following, some of the most known CNN for its results and novelty will be described.

LeNet (LeCun et al., 1995) proposed one of the first convolutional neural network for hand digit classification with high accuracy. The model accepts and classifies grayscale images of size 32×32 according to ten different classes representing the ten possible digits. The network has a total of 60K weights and an overall accuracy above 99%.

AlexNet was the first large CNN (Krizhevsky, 2012) with very good results for image classification. Compared to LeNet, AlexNet is deeper and has $1000\times$ more weights than LeNet. The input images are also larger ($227\times227\times3$). AlexNet has top-5 error rates around 17.0% and a top-1 error rate of 37.5% when used to classify images from ImageNet.

In 2013 a multiplayer deconvolutional neural network – ZefNet - was proposed in (Zeiler & Fergus, 2013). The authors propose a methodology to help in the design of the network based on a process to observe the network activity of neurons (Erhan, 2009; Le, 2013). Following the methodology, they were able to improve AlexNet to a top-5 error rate of 11.2%.

One year later the VGG neural network (Simonyan & Zisserman, 2014) increased the size of CNNs published so far with 138 million parameters. VGG improved previous year top-5 error rate to 7.3%. In spite of several filter size improvements to reduce the number of parameters, VGG still have a huge number of parameters requiring long training times and high inference times.

In the same year, a new CNN - GoogleNet (Szegedy et al., 2014; Szegedy, 2016) - introduced a new layer that has groups of convolutions running in parallel within a module designated Inception. In the inception module, several convolutional layers run in parallel like a small neural network inside a larger model. With 6.8 million parameters GoogleNet achieved a top-5 error rate of 6.7% for ImageNet.

A very deep neural network - ResNet (He et al., 2015) - has increased the number of layers to 152 and achieved a top-5 error rate of 3.6% in the ImageNet contest. Similar to GoogleNet, ResNet includes a new block named *Residual Block* where the output map of a series of two convolutional layers are added to the input of the block. An optimization of ResNet was proposed in (Xie et al., 2017) with the ResNeXt CNN with a top-5 error of 3.03%. Another improvement of ResNet was proposed in (Huang, 2018) - DenseNet - with a similar accuracy but with about half of the parameters. This was possible with a modification of the residual block where a layer has dependencies with all previous layers.

Recently, SENet (Hu, Shen & Sun, 2018) introduced a new network block based on the residual block – squeeze-and-excitation that emphasizes important features and cancel less useful ones. SENet won the ILSVRC competition in 2017 with a top-5 error rate of 2.25%.

Deep Learning on Edge

Deep learning algorithms are very demanding in terms of memory resources to store weights and computing power for training and inference. For these reasons, deep learning networks run of high-performance computing platforms. Data collected from edge sensors are sent to high-performance computing centers to be processed and when required the result is sent back to the edge to be presented or to help taking decisions.

Today edge devices are almost everywhere in a large set of applications in industrial environments, automotive, surveillance and security cameras, drones, satellites, medical equipment and new applications appear every day. All these devices collect an enormous amount of data to be processed by the central high-performance computing platform. This reduces the complexity and the energy required for edge devices. However, for an increasing set of applications, the processing of collected data to take decisions has to be done near the sensor for several reasons: unreliable channel transmission, large communication round-trip delay, real-time processing, security and privacy of data.

Hence, data processing algorithms and decision taking is migrating from the cloud to the edge, in particular deep learning models. The problem is that to run an inference of a deep learning network requires high computing and memory resources, scarce resources on an edge computing device. Even with the increasing capacity of edge and mobile devices, it is still a challenge to run deep neural networks within the embedded constraints of the device.

Until recently, the main concern of DNN designers was to achieve the best accuracy. With the advent of deep learning on edge, in the design and development of DNN accuracy is traded-off by energy, cost, computing resources and several other metrics associated with edge computing devices.

Two lines of research are being followed for the optimization of deep neural networks on edge: model optimization and optimized computing platforms for edge deep learning.

Model Optimization

As became evident from the neural networks describe above, the trend is to consider more layers and more weights. Sometimes, a new neural network is proposed that optimizes a previous one with the reduction of parameters but without ever reducing accuracy. DNN for edge and mobile processing reduces the number of computations and weights with eventually a slight reduction in accuracy. MobileNet (Howard et al, 2017) is a CNN for mobile devices that reduces the number of parameters by manipulating the kernels. It applies a single kernel to each input map and then combines the convolution outputs with a pointwise convolution. This leads to a reduction in the number of parameters and consequently the number of computations. Other optimizations were considered, like reducing the number of input and output maps and the image resolution. Different networks with different trade-offs were implemented achieving accuracies from 50% to 70%, a number of parameters from 0.5 to 4.2 millions and a number of multiply-accumulate (MAC) operations ranging from 41 to 559 millions. MobileNetv2 (Sandler et al., 2018) is an optimization of MobileNet that introduced some optimizations that reduce the number of parameters about 30% and the number of operations about 50% and still achieving higher accuracy.

ShuffleNet (Zhang et al., 2018) is another CNN proposed for mobile devices. Different convolutions are applied to separate parts of the input maps to reduce the number of operations. The output of convolutions are then shuffled so that the information from different groups can be mixed. The model has a complexity similar to MobileNetV2 but with better accuracy.

The optimizations proposed in the previous neural network models somehow changes the deep learning algorithm by considering different number and types of layers trying to reduce the number of parameters while keeping the accuracy. A different approach consists of reducing the complexity of the model at a lower level. In this approach, two types of techniques have been considered: data quantization and data reduction. Data quantization consists of techniques to reduce the arithmetic complexity and the number of bits used to represent parameters and activations. Data reduction is the set of techniques used to reduce the number of parameters or the volume of data transferred to the computing platform.

A commonly used data quantization technique is the conversion from single-precision floating-point representations to half-precision floating-point (Micikevicius et al., 2017) or 8-bit floating-point (Wang et al., 2018), fixed-point or integer representation. One advantage of this conversion is that the new representations are easier to implement and calculate than single-precision floating-point arithmetic. Also, with data represented with less bits the arithmetic operators are also less complex and so many operators can be implemented with the same silicon area.

Several works have shown that neural network models can use weights and activations represented with only 16 or even 8 bits and still keep accuracies close to the accuracy obtained with data represented with single-precision floating-point (Gysel et al., 2016), (Gupta et al., 2015), (Anwar et al., 2015), (Lin et al., 2016). Neural network models with weights and activations represented with a single bit have also been proposed - BNN (Binary Neural Networks) (Courbariaux et al., 2016; Umuroglu et al., 2016). BNN reduce considerably the bitwidth of data at the cost of some accuracy degradation. To reduce the impact of binarization over the network accuracy the number of weights must be considerably increased. Also, instead of using a binary representation, some works consider 2-bits to reduce the impact of the representation over the accuracy (Ubara et al., 2016).

A different approach to reduce the data volume of the network is to remove and compress data. In (Han et al., 2015) a DNN is compressed with punning and Huffman coding. Pruning is a process that removes some connections between neurons. For example, a reduction of about 90% of the weights belonging to the dense layers have a very small impact over accuracy. The disadvantage of pruning is that it introduces sparsity in the matrix of weights which complicates its implementation in hardware. When applied to dense layers, pruning is more efficient then when applied to convolutional layers, because the number of weights in dense layers is generally much higher than the set of all remaining weights.

Another technique to reduce the effects of large transfers of weights in fully connected layers is batching (Zhang et al., 2016). The batching technique stores several output feature maps of the last non-dense layers before being executed. It permits to reuse the same kernel for different input images.

Computing Platforms for Edge Deep Learning

Different technologies are available to deploy deep learning algorithms on edge devices. The right device depends on the design requirements, including delay, latency, area, energy, cost, flexibility, etc. Chips or devices for artificial intelligence at the edge try to optimize energy and performance efficiencies, that is, get the lowest energy consumption and enough performance to run a DNN model within design constraints.

General-purpose processors (CPU) can run any deep learning model and their programmability permits them to run any new DNN model without any modifications to the computing platform. The problem with CPUs is that they have a low energy and performance efficiency. GPUs (Graphics Processing Unit) are one of the most used platforms for training DNN because they are a many-core architecture with massive computing parallelism offering high-performance computing and at the same time offer a high level of programmability. They are energy and performance efficient but have high energy consumption which is infeasible for most edge platforms due to their restrictions on available energy. The highest performance and best energy efficiency is achieved with ASICs (Applications Specific Integrated Circuit). ASICs have limited programmability because the algorithm implementation is hardwired in silicon. Some hardware programmability can be considered at the cost of extra silicon to implement extra computing modules that are chosen according to the target algorithm to be implemented. FPGAs (Field-Programmable Gate Array) are more flexible than ASICs since the hardware can be reconfigured for new and different functions but are harder to reprogram than CPUs or GPUs. SoCs (Sytem-on-Chip) FPGAs are an attractive option to run deep learning models since they contain a general-purpose processor tightly connected to reprogrammable logic. The reprogrammable logic is used to design and implement the most time-consuming operations of DNNs, while the CPU is used to control the system, to run the less frequent operations and allowing the implementation of new functions whose hardware implementation is inefficient.

Most commercial solutions are based on ASICs since they provide the best solutions in terms of performance and energy consumption. Some companies provide IP (Intellectual Property) cores as DNN accelerators to be integrated in a computing system, while others provide full SoC solutions implemented on chip.

High-performance IP processors are common approaches to run machine learning algorithms. DesignWare EV6x (Synopsis, 2017) is an IP processor for vision processing on embedded devices. It consists of a 32-bit processor, a vector DSP and a dedicated accelerator for CNNs. The accelerator supports many CNN models, including regular and irregular CNNs, like GoogleNet, and supports 8 and 12 bits data quantization. The whole core has a peak performance of 4.5 TMACs with 2 TMACs/W.

DNA (Cadence, 2017) is another IP SoC processor from Cadence designed for the acceleration of deep neural networks on edge devices. The core integrates a Tensilica DSP, and the DNN accelerator. The architectures optimize the execution of the algorithm using techniques like zero-skipping (multiplications with zero are not computed), pruning, data compression and decompression. The core can be configured with different number of MACs and each MAC can be configured with different data representations (8 or 16 bits integer or 16-bits floating-point). The configuration with the highest performance has a peak performance of 12 TMACs with 3.7 TMACs/W.

NeuPro (Linley Group., 2018) is also an IP core for machine learning to be deployed in embedded devices for advanced driver-assistance systems, surveillance systems, among others. The core is a SoC with an accelerator that can execute any layer of a CNN and a vector processing unit and to control the accelerator and to run other functions not supported by the accelerator. The IP core is configurable in terms of number of MACs. MACs are configurable for the execution of MACs with different data sizes (8 or 16). The smallest configuration of the IP has a performance of 2 TOPs and the larger one has a performance of 12.5 TOPs.

In (Gyrfalcon Technology - 2018) a many core architecture with 168 processing units, each with local memory and a MAC unit, was proposed for audio and video processing, including deep learning networks. The core element of the architecture is an engine to speed-up matrix processing. With an operation frequency of 300 MHz the chip delivers 16.8 TOPs with a consumption of 700 mW corresponding to a power efficiency of 24 TOPs/W.

Movidius Myriad X processor (Intel, 2017) is a SoC vector processor with an accelerator for DNN inference at the edge. The MAC units support 16-bit fixed- and floating-point operations and 8-bit fixed-point. The accelerator has a peak performance of 1 TOPs and the whole processor has a total peak performance of 4 TOPs.

ASIC offer the best solutions but with a reduced flexibility. Deep learning networks are still in its infancy and therefore are constantly being modified and improved. Therefore, deploying an ASIC solution for deep learning is always a risk. Turning the ASIC architecture more flexibility reduces its silicon efficiency which reduces performance and increases energy consumption. These aspects open the set of available platforms for edge computing to reconfigurable devices. Coarse and fine-grained solutions were already proposed to run inference in low cost devices.

Eyeriss (Chen et al., 2017) is a coarse-grained reconfigurable accelerator for CNNs. It contains 168 processing elements connected with a network-on-chip (NoC). The NoC is configurable to adapt the dataflow of the architecture to the dataflow of the model to run. The architectures uses compression and decompression to reduce the data volume between the chip and external memory. With an operating frequency, the accelerator was tested with the inference of AlexNet with data quantized to 16-bits fixed-point has an energy efficiency of 166 GOPs/W with a measured average power of 278 mW.

DNPU is another coarse-grained reconfigurable processor (Shin et al., 2017) for CNNs and RNNs. The chip has dedicated units to the execution of convolutional layers. Pooling and activation function are executed by a centralized module shared by all convolution modules. Dense layers are implemented with a dedicated unit for matrix multiplications and multipliers can be configured (4, 8 or 16 bits fixed-point). The architecture with 4-bit multipliers has a peak performance of 1.2 TOPs with an energy efficiency of 3.9 TOPs/W.

DRP is a dynamically coarse-grained reconfigurable core to accelerate embedded machine learning algorithms (Fujii et al., 2018). The core has an array of dynamically reconfigurable processing elements. Both 16-bit fixed- and floating-point and binary precisions are supported. Dynamic reconfigurability is used to support large networks by reconfiguring the architecture for different layers at execution time. The chip achieved a performance near 1 TOPs.

Fine-grained reconfigurable devices, FPGAs, permit to optimize the hardware architecture for each particular deep learning model (Sze et al., 2017). The first FPGA implementations had the sole objective of improving performance and therefore considered high density FPGA devices (Shawahna et al., 2019). Now, with the necessity to deploy DNNs on edge devices, small to medium density FPGAs are also considered (Guo et al., 2018; Venieris et al., 2018). Recently, a solution was proposed to execute large CNNs in low density FPGAs (ZYNQ XC7Z020) with a peak performance of 400 GOPs (Véstias et al., 2018). With 8-bit fixed-point quantization, the architecture explores several levels of parallelism and proposes a method to run convolutions independently of the size of the convolution window. With all these optimizations, the architecture has a peak performance around 400 GOPs and an energy efficiency near 50 GOPs/W.

FUTURE RESEARCH DIRECTIONS

Deep learning models have improved during the last years. Typically, good accuracies are only achieved with large models. However, the evolution of DNN models have shown that with appropriate techniques it is possible to reduce the complexity of the models with a negligible accuracy loss. New models are needed that emphasize performance and energy efficiency. Binary neural networks are promising solutions with a great impact over hardware complexity and memory storage but still requires a lot of improvements to avoid large accuracy degradations.

Training and inference are still two separated steps. Training is done in high-performance computing platforms and the results are used by the same platform or by an edge device. Considering that an edge device is constantly receiving new data, these could be used to dynamically train the network to keep improving accuracy. Incremental training is executed on high-performance platforms, but the process could be also implemented in the edge device for the same reasons enumerated before.

Designing neural network models for specific problems is still an empirical process that leads to oversized networks with redundant parameters. It is important to better understand how particular layers and neurons influence the final accuracy and how to redesign the model so that the best accuracy is achieved. This will help to tailor models for specific applications, which is particularly important for edge devices.

Concerning the computing platforms, its design is somehow influenced by the fact that DNNs are still under constant research and evolution. Several ASIC solutions already exist but the risk is high since the architectures are optimized for particular neural networks. Any improvements or changes to the original network model reduces the efficiency of the ASIC solution since new functions or modules have to be executed by general purpose processors.

Reconfigurable architectures help us to overcome some of the limitations of ASICs since the hardware architecture can be upgraded on-board with new modules and/or operations. It is the only platform whose hardware can follow the constant evolution of DNNs. FPGAs allow optimized implementations of binary neural networks contrary to architectural solutions based only on CPUs or GPUs. A major problem of FPGA devices is that it is difficult to design them compared to implementations based on software only. Specific frameworks to automatically map neural networks on FPGA already exist but the results suffer some degradation compared to a hand-made design. The proliferation of reconfigurable devices as solutions for deep learning on edge depends on the availability of tools to automatically map neural network models on FPGA.

Given the heterogeneity of layers in high accuracy neural network models, it is important to consider flexible architectures with dedicated accelerators for the common operations requiring massive parallelism integrated with a high-performance processor that can execute the remaining operations or functions whose execution cannot be done by the accelerator. SoCs with a processor and dedicated hardware are the most appropriate solutions for these cases. Many of the ASIC architectures for deep learning proposed so far consider a SoC architecture. An example of this trend is the recently announced FPGA for deep learning (Xilinx, 2018) with software programmable processors, fine-grained reconfigurable hardware and an intelligent device for tasks associated with deep learning. The new FPGA upgrades previous devices with a new engine for deep learning inference.

Inference is still the only operation executed in deep learning platforms in the edge. However, the possibility to train or retrain a network in the edge opens the possibility of constant learning whenever new data is collected. Training still requires full precision and its computational complexity is much higher than that of inference. This mixed precision requires new architectures that can perform both training and inference with different data representations.

CONCLUSION

Deep learning algorithms have successfully improved the accuracy results of many machine learning algorithms. The set of applications that take advantage of these algorithmic improvements is increasing. Many of these applications are associated with edge devices and therefore running deep learning models on edge devices is now a major challenge.

This article describes the fundamentals of deep learning and known deep learning models proposed in the literature. Most of these models are only concerned with accuracy and only a few are optimized for mobile and edge computing. Neural network models for edge devices must be optimized even if this implies some accuracy degradation traded-off by lower energy consumption and improved execution times. Two main classes of optimizations have been applied so far: data quantization and data reduction. These reduce memory and computing requirements and in some cases without accuracy degradation.

ASICs and FPGAs are the most appropriate technologies for edge inference since they offer good energy and performance efficiencies. These metrics are better with ASICs, but FPGAs offer hardware flexibility to optimize the implementation of new neural network models. A brief description of recent commercial chips and published FPGA implementations were also given in this chapter.

REFERENCES

Anwar, S., Hwang, K., & Sung, W. (2015). Fixed point optimization of deep convolutional neural networks for object recognition. In *IEEE International Conference on Acoustics, Speech, and Signal Processing* (pp. 1131–1135). 10.1109/ICASSP.2015.7178146

Barber, D. (2012). *Bayesian Reasoning and Machine Learning*. Cambridge University Press.

Bengio, Y. (2009). Learning deep architectures for AI. *Foundations and Trends in Machine Learning*, 2(1), 1–127. doi:10.1561/2200000006

Bengio, Y., Lamblin, P., Popovici, D., & Larochelle, H. (2006). Greedy layer-wise training of deep networks. In B. Schölkopf, J. C. Platt, & T. Hoffman (Eds.). In *Proceedings of the 19th International Conference on Neural Information Processing Systems* (153-160). Cambridge, MA.

Bourlard, H., & Kamp, Y. (1988). Auto-association by multilayer perceptrons and singular value decomposition. *Biological Cybernetics*, *59*(4-5), 291–294. doi:10.1007/BF00332918 PMID:3196773

Bouveyron, C., Celeux, G., Murphy, T., & Raftery, A. (2019). *Model-Based Clustering and Classification for Data Science: With Applications in R (Cambridge Series in Statistical and Probabilistic Mathematics)*. Cambridge, UK: Cambridge University Press. doi:10.1017/9781108644181

Cadence: Tensilica. (2017). DNA Processor IP For AI Inference.

Chen, Y., Krishna, T., Emer, J. S., & Sze, V. (2016). Eyeriss: An Energy-Efficient Reconfigurable Accelerator for Deep Convolutional Neural Networks. *IEEE Journal of Solid-State Circuits*, *52*(1), 127–138. doi:10.1109/JSSC.2016.2616357

Christmann, A., & Steinwart, I. (2008). *Support Vector Machines*. Springer-Verlag.

Courbariaux, M., & Bengio, Y. (2016) BinaryNet: Training Deep Neural Networks with Weights and Activations Constrained to +1 or -1. In CoRR, abs/1602.02830.

Elman, J. L. (1990). Finding Structure in Time. *Cognitive Science*, *14*(2), 179–211. doi:10.120715516709cog1402_1

Erhan, D., Bengio, Y., Courville, A., & Vincent, P. (2009). Visualizing higher-layer features of a deep network. *Univ. Montr.*, *1341*, 1.

Fujii, T., Toi, T., Tanaka, T., Togawa, K., Kitaoka, T., Nishino, K., ... Motomura, M. (2018). New generation dynamically reconfigurable processor technology for accelerating embedded AI applications. In *Symposium on VLSI Circuits* (41-42). 10.1109/VLSIC.2018.8502438

Glorot, X., & Bengio, Y. (2010). Understanding the difficulty of training deep feedforward neural networks. In *International Conference on Artificial Intelligence and Statistics* (249–256).

Glorot, X., Bordes, A., & Bengio, Y. (2011). Deep Sparse Rectifier Neural Networks. In *Proceedings of the Fourteenth International Conference on Artificial Intelligence and Statistics* (315-323).

Goodfellow, I., Bengio, Y., & Courville, A. (2016). *Deep Learning*. MIT Press.

Guo, K., Sui, L., Qiu, J., Yu, J., Wang, J., Yao, S., ... Yang, H. (2018). Angel-Eye: A Complete Design Flow for Mapping CNN Onto Embedded FPGA. *IEEE Transactions on Computer-Aided Design of Integrated Circuits and Systems*, *37*(1), 35–47. doi:10.1109/TCAD.2017.2705069

Gupta, S., Agrawal, A., Gopalakrishnan, K., & Narayanan, P. (2015) Deep Learning with Limited Numerical Precision. In *Proceedings of the 32nd International Conference on International Conference on Machine Learning:* Vol. 37. (1737–1746).

Gysel, P., Motamedi, M., & Ghiasi, S. (2016). Hardware-oriented Approximation of Convolutional Neural Networks. In *Proceedings of the 4th International Conference on Learning Representations*.

Han, S., Mao, H., & Dally, W. J. (2015). "Deep Compression: Compressing Deep Neural Network with Pruning, Trained Quantization and Huffman Coding". *CoRR*, abs/1510.00149.

Haykin, S. (2008). *Neural Networks and Learning Machines* (3rd ed.). Pearson.

He, K., Zhang, X., Ren, S., & Sun, J. (2015). Deep Residual Learning for Image Recognition. *Multimedia Tools and Applications*, 77, 10437–10453.

Hinton, G. E., & Sejnowski, T. J. (1986). Learning and relearning in Boltzmann machines. In D. E. Rumelhart, J. L. McClelland, & CORPORATE PDP Research Group (Eds.), Parallel distributed processing: explorations in the microstructure of cognition. Vol. 1, MIT Press (282-317).

Hochreiter, S. (1998). The vanishing gradient problem during learning recurrent neural nets and problem solutions. *International Journal of Uncertainty, Fuzziness and Knowledge-based Systems*, 6(02), 107–116. doi:10.1142/S0218488598000094

Hochreiter, S., & Schmidhuber, J. (1997). Long Short-Term Memory. *Neural Computation*, 8(8), 1735–1780. doi:10.1162/neco.1997.9.8.1735 PMID:9377276

Hopfield, J. (1982). Neural networks and physical systems with emergent collective computational abilities. *Proceedings of the National Academy of Sciences of the United States of America*, 79(8), 2554–2558. doi:10.1073/pnas.79.8.2554 PMID:6953413

Hornik, K., Stinchcombe, M., & White, H. (1989). Multilayer feedforward networks are universal approximators. *Neural Networks*, 2(5), 359–366. doi:10.1016/0893-6080(89)90020-8

Howard, A. G., Zhu, M., Chen, B., Kalenichenko, D., Wang, W., Weyand, T., Andreetto, M., & Adam, H. (2017). MobileNets: Efficient Convolutional Neural Networks for Mobile Vision Applications. *CoRR*, abs/1704.04861.

Hu, J., Shen, L., & Sun, G. (2018). Squeeze-and-Excitation Networks, In *Proceedings IEEE Conference on Computer Vision and Pattern Recognition* (7132-7141). IEEE.

Huang, G., Liu, Z., Maaten, L., & Weinberger, K. (2018). Densely Connected Convolutional Networks. In *IEEE Conference on Computer Vision and Pattern Recognition*.

Hubara, I., Courbariaux, M., Soudry, D., El-Yaniv, R., & Bengio, Y. (2016). Binarized Neural Networks. In D. D. Lee, M. Sugiyama, I. Guyon, & R. Garnett (Ed.), Advances in Neural Information Processing Systems: Vol. 4107–4115. *Curran Associates, Inc*.

Intel. (2017). Movidius Myriad X VPU.

Keogh, E. (2011). Instance-Based Learning. In C. Sammut, & G. I. Webb (Eds.), *Encyclopedia of Machine Learning*. Boston, MA: Springer.

Krizhevsky, A., Sutskever, I., & Hinton, G. E. (2012). ImageNet Classification with Deep Convolutional Neural Networks. In Adv. Neural Inf. Process. Syst. 1–9.

Le, Q. V. (2013). Building high-level features using large scale unsupervised learning. In *IEEE International Conference on Acoustics, Speech and Signal Processing* (8595–8598). 10.1109/ICASSP.2013.6639343

LeCun, Y. (1989). Generalization and network design strategies. In Connectionism in Perspective.

LeCun, Y., Boser, B., Denker, J. S., Henderson, D., Howard, R. E., Hubbard, W., & Jackel, L. D. (1989). Backpropagation applied to handwritten zip code recognition. *Neural Computation, 1*(4), 541–551. doi:10.1162/neco.1989.1.4.541

LeCun, Y., Jackel, L. D., Bottou, L., Cortes, C., Denker, J. S., Drucker, H., ... & Vapnik, V. (1995). Learning algorithms for classification: A comparison on handwritten digit recognition. In Neural networks: the statistical mechanics perspective, 261-276. Mech. Perspect.

Lin, D. D., Talathi, S. S., & Annapureddy, V. S. (2016). Fixed Point Quantization of Deep Convolutional Networks. In *Proceedings of the 33rd International Conference on International Conference on Machine Learning.* Vol. 48. (pp. 2849–2858).

Linley Group. (2018). Ceva NeuPro Accelerates Neural Nets.

Matloff, N. (2017). *Statistical Regression and Classification: from Linear Models to Regression* (1st ed.). Chapman and Hall. doi:10.1201/9781315119588

Micikevicius, P., Narang, S., Alben, J., Diamos, G. F., Elsen, E., García, D., ... Wu, H. (2017). Mixed Precision Training. *CoRR*, abs/1710.03740.

Nwankpa, C., Ijomah, W., Gachagan, A. & Marshall, S. (2018). Activation Functions: Comparison of trends in Practice and Research for Deep Learning. *Corr*. abs/1811.03378.

Patterson, J., & Gibson, A. (2017). Deep Learning: A Practitioner's Approach. O'Reilley Media, 1st ed.

Quinlan, R. (1992). *C4.5: Programs for Machine Learning* (1st ed.). Morgan Kaufmann.

Ruder, S. (2016). An overview of gradient descent optimization algorithms. In CoRR.

Sandler, M. B., Howard, A. G., Zhu, M., Zhmoginov, A., & Chen, L. (2018). MobileNetV2: Inverted Residuals and Linear Bottlenecks. In *IEEE/CVF Conference on Computer Vision and Pattern Recognition* (4510-4520). 10.1109/CVPR.2018.00474

Shawahna, A., Sait, S. M., & El-Maleh, A. H. (2018). FPGA-Based Accelerators of Deep Learning Networks for Learning and Classification: A Review. *IEEE Access: Practical Innovations, Open Solutions, 7*, 7823–7859. doi:10.1109/ACCESS.2018.2890150

Shin, D., Lee, J., Lee, J., & Yoo, H. (2017). 14.2 DNPU: An 8.1TOPS/W reconfigurable CNN-RNN processor for general-purpose deep neural networks. In *IEEE International Solid-State Circuits Conference* (240-241). 10.1109/ISSCC.2017.7870350

Simonyan, K., & Zisserman, A. (2014). Very deep convolutional networks for large-scale image recognition. In *arXiv preprint arXiv:1409.1556.*

Synopsys DesignWare. (2017). EV6x Vision Processors.

Sze, V., Chen, Y., Yang, T., & Emer, J. S. (2017). Efficient processing of deep neural networks: A tutorial and survey. *Proceedings of the IEEE, 105*(12), 2295–2329. doi:10.1109/JPROC.2017.2761740

Szegedy, C., Vanhoucke, V., Ioffe, S., Shlens, J., & Wojna, Z. (2016). Rethinking the Inception Architecture for Computer Vision. In *IEEE Conference on Computer Vision and Pattern Recognition*, (2818-2826). 10.1109/CVPR.2016.308

Szegedy, C., Liu, W., Jia, Y., Sermanet, P., Reed, S., Anguelov, D., ... & Rabinovich, A. (2014). Going Deeper with Convolutions. *arXiv:1409.4842*.

Gyrfalcon Technology. (2018). Lightspeeur 2803S Neural Accelerator.

Umuroglu, Y., Fraser, N. J., Gambardella, G., Blott, M., Leong, P. H. W., Jahre, M., & Vissers, K. A. (2016). FINN: A Framework for Fast, Scalable Binarized Neural Network Inference. In CoRR, abs/1612.07119.

Venieris, S. I., & Bouganis, C. (2018). fpgaConvNet: Mapping Regular and Irregular Convolutional Neural Networks on FPGAs. *IEEE Transactions on Neural Networks and Learning Systems, 30*(2), 326–342. doi:10.1109/TNNLS.2018.2844093 PMID:29994725

Véstias, M. P., Duarte, R. P., Sousa, J. T., & Neto, H. C. (2018). Lite-CNN: A High-Performance Architecture to Execute CNNs in Low Density FPGAs. In *28th International Conference on Field Programmable Logic and Applications* (pp. 393-399). 10.1109/FPL.2018.00075

Wang, N., Choi, J., Brand, D., Chen, C., & Gopalakrishnan, K. (2018). Training Deep Neural Networks with 8-bit Floating Point Numbers. *CoRR* abs/1812.08011.

Xilinx, V. (2018). The first adaptive compute acceleration platform (acap).

Zeiler, M. D., & Fergus, R. (2013). Visualizing and Understanding Convolutional Networks. arXiv. vol. 30 (pp. 225–231).

Zhang, C., & Ma, Y. (2012). *Ensemble Machine Learning*. New York: Springer-Verlag. doi:10.1007/978-1-4419-9326-7

Zhang, C., Wu, D., Sun, J., Sun, G., Luo, G., & Cong, J. (2016). Energy-Efficient CNN Implementation on a Deeply Pipelined FPGA Cluster. In *Proceedings of the International Symposium on Low Power Electronics and Design* (pp. 326–331). 10.1145/2934583.2934644

Zhang, C., & Zhang, S. (2002). Association Rule Mining. In *Lecture Notes in Artificial Intelligence*. Springer-Verlag.

Zhang, X., Zhou, X., Lin, M., & Sun, J. (2018) ShuffleNet: An Extremely Efficient Convolutional Neural Network for Mobile Devices. In *IEEE/CVF Conference on Computer Vision and Pattern Recognition* (pp. 6848–6856). 10.1109/CVPR.2018.00716

ADDITIONAL READINGS

Bishop, C. (2006). *Pattern Recognition and Machine Learning*. New York: Springer Verlag.

Erhan, D., Bengio, Y., Courville, A., Manzagol, P.-A., Vincent, P., & Bengio, S. (2010). Why does unsupervised pre-training help deep learning? *Journal of Machine Learning Research, 11*, 625–660.

Erhan, D., Manzagol, P.-A., Bengio, Y., Bengio, S., & Vincent, P. (2009). The difficulty of training deep architectures and the effect of unsupervised pre-training. *In International Conference on Artificial Intelligence and Statistics* (153–160).

He, K., Gkioxari, G., Dollár, P., & Girshick, R. (2017). Mask R-CNN. In *International Conference on Computer Vision*.

Hinton, G. E., Osindero, S., & Teh, Y.-W. (2006). A fast learning algorithm for deep belief nets. *Neural Computation, 18*(7), 1527–1554. doi:10.1162/neco.2006.18.7.1527 PMID:16764513

Jarrett, K., Kavukcuogl, K., Ranzato, M., & LeCun, Y. (2009). What is the best multi-stage architecture for object recognition? In *International Conference on Computer Vision* (2146–2153). 10.1109/ICCV.2009.5459469

Kalinowski, I., & Spitsyn, V. (2015). Compact Convolutional Neural Network Cascade for Face Detection. *CoRR*, abs/1508.01292.

Lawrence, S., & Giles, C. Lee, Tsoi, Ah C. & Back, A. (1997). Face Recognition: A Convolutional Neural Network Approach. In IEEE Transactions on Neural Networks. 8 (1): 98–113.

LeCun, Y., Kavukvuoglu, K., & Farabet, C. (2010). Convolutional networks and applications in vision. In *International Symposium on Circuits and Systems* (253–256).

Lei, T., Barziley, R., & Jaakkola, T. (2016). Rationalizing Neural Predictions. In *Proceedings of the Conference on Empirical Methods in Natural Language Processing* (107-117). 10.18653/v1/D16-1011

Matsugu, M., Mori, K., Mitari, Y., & Kaneda, Y. (2003). Subject independent facial expression recognition with robust face detection using a convolutional neural network. *Neural Networks, 16*(5–6), 555–559. doi:10.1016/S0893-6080(03)00115-1 PMID:12850007

Pengcheng, Y., & Neubig, G. (2017). A Syntactic Neural Model for General-Purpose Code Generation, In *Proceedings of the 55th Annual Meeting of the Association for Computational Linguistics*, Vol. 1 (440-450).

Redmon, J., & Farhadi, A. (2017). YOLO9000: Better, Faster, Stronger. In *IEEE Conference on Computer Vision and Pattern Recognition* (6517-6525).

Scherer, D., Müller, A., & Behnke, S. (2010). Evaluation of pooling operations in convolutional architectures for object recognition". In *International Conference on Artificial Neural Networks* (92–101). 10.1007/978-3-642-15825-4_10

Xie, S., Girshick, R., Dollár, P., Tu, Z., & He, K. (2017). Aggregated Residual Transformations for Deep Neural Networks. In *IEEE Conference on Computer Vision and Pattern Recognition*. 10.1109/CVPR.2017.634

Zeiler, M. D. & Fergus, R.. (2013). Visualizing and understanding convolutional networks. *Computing Research Repository*, abs/1311.2901.

KEY TERMS AND DEFINITIONS

Activation Function: The activation function defines the output of a neuron given a set of inputs from the previous layer or data input.

Artificial Neural Network (ANN): It is a computing model based on the structure of the human brain with many interconnected processing nodes that model input-output relationships. The model is organized in layers of nodes that interconnect to each other.

Autoencoder: An unsupervised learning network and is used to encode an input with a representation with fewer dimensions.

Boltzman Machine: An unsupervised network that maximizes the product of probabilities assigned to the elements of the training set.

Convolutional Layer: A network layer that applies a series of convolutions to a block of input feature maps.

Convolutional Neural Network (CNN): A class of deep neural networks applied to image processing where some of the layers apply convolutions to input data.

Deep Belief Network: A probabilistic generative model with multiple layers of the so called latent variables tha keep the state of the network.

Deep Learning (DL): A class of machine learning algorithms for automation of predictive analytics.

Deep Neural Network (DNN): An artificial neural network with multiple hidden layers.

Edge Device: any hardware device that serves as an entry point of data and may store, process and/ or send the data to a central server.

Feature Map: A feature map is a 2D matrix of neurons. A convolutional layer receives a block of input feature maps and generates a block of output feature maps.

Fully Connected Layer: A network layer where all neurons of the layer are connected to all neurons of the previous layer.

Hopfield Network: A dense neural network where all neurons connect to all other neurons.

Long-short Term Memory Network: A variation of recurrent neural networks to reduce the vanishing problem.

Machine Learning: A subfield of artificial intelligence whose objective is to give systems the ability to learn and improve by its own without being explicitly programmed to do it.

Network Layer: A set of neurons that define the network of a CNN. Neurons in a network layer are connected to the previous and to the next layer.

Perceptron: The basic unit of a neural network that encodes inputs from neurons of the previous layer using a vector of weights or parameters associated with the connections between perceptrons.

Pooling Layer: A network layer that determines the average pooling or max pooling of a window of neurons. The pooling layer subsamples the input feature maps to achieve translation invariance and reduce over-fitting.

Pruning: An optimization technique for deep neural networks that removes some connections between neurons to reduce the complexity of the network.

Recurrent Neural Network (RNN): A class of deep neural networks consisting of dense networks with state.

Semi-Supervised: A training process of neural networks that mixes supervised and unsupervised training.

Softmax Function: A function that takes as input a vector of k values and normalizes it into a probability distribution of k probabilities.

Supervised Training: A training process of neural networks where the outcome for each input is known.

Unsupervised Training: A training process of neural networks where the training set does not have the associated outputs.

This research was previously published in Smart Systems Design, Applications, and Challenges; pages 23-42, copyright year 2020 by Engineering Science Reference (an imprint of IGI Global).

Chapter 8

PrEstoCloud:
A Novel Framework for Data-Intensive Multi-Cloud, Fog, and Edge Function-as-a-Service Applications

Yiannis Verginadis
Athens University of Economics and Business, Greece

Dimitris Apostolou
University of Piraeus, Greece

Salman Taherizadeh
Joseph Stefan Institute, Slovenia

Ioannis Ledakis
Ubitech, Greece

Gregoris Mentzas
https://orcid.org/0000-0002-3305-3796
National Technical University of Athens, Greece

Andreas Tsagkaropoulos
National Technical University of Athens, Greece

Nikos Papageorgiou
National Technical University of Athens, Greece

Fotis Paraskevopoulos
National Technical University of Athens, Greece

ABSTRACT

Fog computing extends multi-cloud computing by enabling services or application functions to be hosted close to their data sources. To take advantage of the capabilities of fog computing, serverless and the function-as-a-service (FaaS) software engineering paradigms allow for the flexible deployment of applications on multi-cloud, fog, and edge resources. This article reviews prominent fog computing frameworks and discusses some of the challenges and requirements of FaaS-enabled applications. Moreover, it proposes a novel framework able to dynamically manage multi-cloud, fog, and edge resources and to deploy data-intensive applications developed using the FaaS paradigm. The proposed framework leverages the FaaS paradigm in a way that improves the average service response time of data-intensive applications by a factor of three regardless of the underlying multi-cloud, fog, and edge resource infrastructure.

DOI: 10.4018/978-1-6684-5700-9.ch008

1. INTRODUCTION

Fog computing extends multi-cloud computing by enabling services or application functions to be hosted close to their data sources, which are typically Internet of Things (IoT) sensors. Hosting functions close to data sources can reduce the latency and cost of delivering sensor-generated data to a remote cloud and can improve the Quality of Service (QoS; Hao et al. 2017). A key challenge for fog computing is auto-scaling, i.e. the autonomous capacity for continuous adaptation and control of the computing infrastructure through the recognition of insights and knowledge in the data. Insights from the analysis of sensor-generated data can adapt the computing resources to meet current or predicted computing needs, save cost, increase performance and reliability, and meet environmental concerns.

To realize the deployment of applications and services and take advantage of the adaptive capabilities of fog computing, two new software engineering paradigms have emerged: Serverless and Function-as-a-Service (FaaS), which are seen as two enabling technologies for next-generation fog computing (Van Eyk et al. 2018). The serverless paradigm exploits functions or microservices as the unit of deployment and is hence more efficient than using a virtual machine (VM) or a container since their inherent complexity becomes transparent to the application owner (Castro et al., 2019; Trihinas et al., 2018). FaaS is a facet of serverless computing where applications can run server-side logic in stateless compute containers that can be event-triggered, ephemeral (may only last for one invocation), and fully manageable by a third party. Such a serverless paradigm is desirable for many event-based IoT applications, especially mission-intensive applications, as well as applications requiring energy efficiency and data delivery reliability (Gusev et al., 2019). The increased complexity of heterogeneous fog computing infrastructures poses management challenges to the DevOps of IoT applications, however (Chiang et al., 2016). In response, advanced cloud management tools and methods have started to emerge in an effort to automate infrastructure performance tuning and anomaly detection (Di Martino et al., 2019; Mahesh et al., 2011).

This paper reviews prominent fog frameworks that deploy and monitor applications that span over multiple clouds, fog and edge resources. It discusses associated challenges and proposes a novel fog architecture and framework for managing dynamically multi-cloud and edge resources in order to cope with the requirements of FaaS-enabled applications. Our research objective focuses on the development and evaluation of a framework to support the seamless deployment of fog computing applications on heterogeneous cloud, fog, and edge resources independently of underlying infrastructures while supporting the FaaS paradigm and providing auto-scaling capabilities.

2. FOG COMPUTING FRAMEWORKS

2.1. State of Play

Cloud, edge and fog computing is a vibrant and continuously evolving area of distributed computing (Liu et al., 2017; Carroll 2015). The US National Institute of Standards and Technology (NIST) predicts that the fog computing market is likely to emerge as a viable vertical niche, as fog computing deployment needs to adapt to particular physical devices, networks and market needs (Iorga et al. 2018). We analyzed the current snapshot of available offerings and tested prominent frameworks from leading vendors to identify the current state of the art in this domain. We evaluated if existing frameworks support the eight characteristics defined by NIST, six of them defined as essential for distinguishing fog computing from other computing paradigms while two of them are considered optional. The essential ones are a) the contextual location awareness, with the goal of low latency, b) the geographical distribution in contrast to the centralized cloud, and (c) the heterogeneity of the deployment along with (d) the interoperability and federation e) the support for real-time interactions rather than batch processing and finally, (f) the microservice scalability and agility of the federated, fog-node clusters that make fog computing adaptive. The two optional characteristics are (g) the usage of wireless networking and (h) the mobility of devices.

Since our research focuses on the enabling FaaS on heterogeneous cloud, fog, and edge resources, we augmented the eight NIST characteristics with seven additional ones that we consider relevant for supporting FaaS-enabled applications. Specifically, the vendor-specific cloud characteristic refers to whether the framework in question is bound to the use of only certain providers for virtualized computing resources. Support for FaaS characteristic indicates the ability of a framework to cope with functions deployed following the serverless paradigm; the deployment optimization characteristic refers to the capability to consider contradicting business goals and solving constraint programming problems for detecting the most optimal use of available resources. The offline device communication characteristic highlights the capability of a framework to cope with run-time situations in fog deployments in which the communication fails unexpectedly for a short period of time. The support deployment and management of application on fog and cloud resources characteristic refers to the ability to orchestrate the deployment of applications on both cloud and edge resources. The fog resources asset management characteristic refers to fog resource registration and supervision capabilities and the event-based alerting corresponds to seamless capabilities for aggregating monitoring information from the dispersed topology and detecting situations that call for adaptation.

Our analysis presented in Table 1 indicates that AWS Greengrass (2020), AWS Wavelength (2020), Azure IoT Edge (2020) and Google Cloud IoT Core (2020) are better suited to support fog computing than OpenWhiskLean (2020) because the latter does not support context awareness with respect to latency reduction, cannot cope with intermittent edge connectivity and the support for wireless communication is limited. AWS Greengrass introduces an architecture comprised of three essential components: the Greengrass Core, the Greengrass Group, and the IoT Device SDK. AWS Greengrass Core is a compute node hosted on a local device that bears the appropriate software to enable the use of local device resources like cameras, serial ports, or GPUs. IoT devices, along with Greengrass Cores and Lambda functions, are organized into Greengrass Groups that correspond to collections of inter-communicating entities. AWS Greengrass supports serverless code (i.e., AWS Lambda functions) deployable to both cloud and edge. AWS Wavelength was recently announced and a roll out of the service is expected in 2020. It enables developers to build applications that deliver single-digit millisecond latencies to mobile devices and end-users. While it doesn't support FaaS, it allows containerized applications to be deployed on Wavelength Zones. These zones embed AWS compute and storage services within the telecommunications providers' datacenters at the edge of the 5G networks and seamlessly access other AWS services in the region. Microsoft Azure IoT Edge allows the execution of Azure Functions, which refer to C# precompiled versions of application functions. The framework can be deployed on Linux and Microsoft Windows operating systems and can run on a resource-constrained device such as a Raspberry Pi Zero. The Azure IoT Edge Agent bootstraps itself each time an edge device is activated in order to connect it to the Azure IoT Edge Runtime.

Table 1. Overview of Fog Computing Framework Characteristics

	AWS Greengrass	AWS Wavelength	Azure IoT Edge	Google Cloud IoT Core	OpenWhisk Lean	Nebbiolo	Cloudify
Context awareness	Yes, location only	Yes, predefined	Yes, location only	Yes, location only	No	Yes, location only	Yes, predefined
Geographical distribution	Yes	Yes	Yes	Yes	Yes	Yes	Yes
Heterogeneity	Yes	Yes	Yes	Yes	Yes	Yes	Yes
Interoperability and federation	Yes	Yes	Yes	Yes	Federation is not supported	Yes	Yes
Real-time interactions	Yes	Yes	Yes	Yes	Yes	Yes	Yes
Microservice scalability and agility of federated, fog-node clusters	Yes	Yes	Yes	Yes	Yes	Yes	Yes
Predominance of wireless access	Yes	Yes	Yes	Yes	No	Yes	Yes
Support for mobility	No	Yes within same Wavelength Zone	No	No	No	Yes	No
Cloud Vendor Specific	Yes	Yes	Yes	Yes	No	No, AWS/ Azure	No
Support for FaaS	Yes	No	Yes	Yes	Yes	No	Yes, AWS Lambda
Deployment optimization of microservices on the edge	No	No	No	No	No	No	No
Intermittent edge connectivity support	Yes, Device Shadows	n/a	Yes	No	No	No	No
Support on Deployment and Management of application on fog/cloud resources	Partially, predefined deployment at the edge	Partially, predefined deployment at the edge of 5G networks	Yes	No	either Cloud or Edge	Yes	Yes
Fog resources Asset Management	Yes	n/a	Yes	No	Yes	Yes	Yes
Event-based alerting	Yes	Yes	Yes	Yes	No	No	Yes

Google Cloud IoT Core runs on Google's serverless infrastructure, which scales automatically in response to real-time changes and its main focus is on digesting data from edge devices in a secure way. Google advertises this technology as anti-vendor lock-in as the supported environments include Cloud Functions, local development environment, on-premises, Cloud Run for Anthos, and other Knative-based serverless environments. Nevertheless, the main functionalities are built around vendor specific products that are cannot easily accommodate applications deployed over Google Cloud IoT to be executed in an open environment like OpenWhisk Lean. Moreover, Nebiolo (2020) is hybrid platform for supporting industrial IoT applications. It introduces its own rich operating system stack (FogOS) that enables the distributed real-time processing. Although it offers an advanced management system doesn't support FaaS functionalities and optimized placement. Finally, Cloudify (2020) also known as multi-cloud everything-as-a-service (EaaS) supports both cloud and edge deployments without optimized placement. The cloud support is vendor independent while the serverless capabilities are considered only through AWS Lambda functions.

Summarizing this analysis, we found that none of the existing prominent fog computing frameworks offers an integrated solution capable of addressing the full list of the fundamental challenges of server-less data-intensive applications. Therefore, we propose a novel framework called PrEstoCloud, which can fully support these aforementioned essential characteristics of such services.

2.2. Challenges and Requirements

To investigate the challenges and requirements associated with the deployment of FaaS applications on fog infrastructures, we focus on an intelligent logistics IoT application that collects and analyzes video streams from cameras installed on and inside vehicles. The application performs real-time anomaly detections, triggering runtime alerts to the fleet manager, and observes driving dynamics for situations such as sudden acceleration and aggressive turning, where possible accidents may occur. Decomposing the application into loosely coupled functions packaged into microservices distributes computational workloads among three processing layers (Figure 1):

- *Embedded systems*: In this layer, microservices deployed on embedded systems collect video streams, process a large volume of data and store them temporarily.
- *Regional processing units (RPUs)*: This layer resides in the proximity of vehicles and is aimed at data reduction operations such as data aggregation and filtering.
- *Centralized public cloud:* This layer provides central storage and powerful processing capabilities. It also supports management functions to control IoT devices installed in vehicles remotely.

Figure 1. Intelligent logistics IoT application

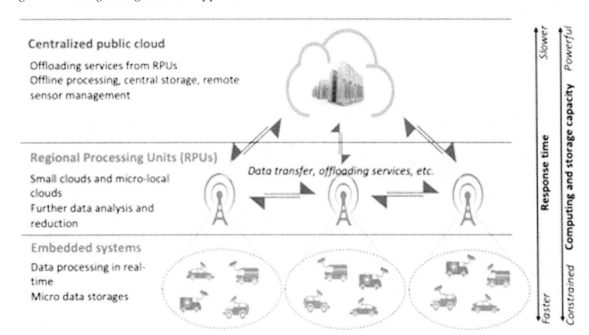

Dynamic IoT applications such as the intelligent logistics one puts forward the following challenges and requirements for the fog computing framework with respect to its auto-scaling capabilities: multi-resource allocation including edge, fog and cloud; optimal microservice deployment; and context-aware microservice offloading.

2.2.1. Multi-Resource Allocation

One of the main benefits of the cloud computing model is the elasticity of the infrastructure that allows the user to manage the size and configuration of their computing fleet finely. This adaptation can be driven by indications, coming either from the user, or from an automated system. One great challenge of cloud computing has been to build such an automated resource allocator/de-allocator, that will make it possible to accurately match the actual usage in order to avoid under-provisioning or over-provisioning. Under-provisioning leads to performance issues and additional latency, and over-provisioning uselessly increases a user's bill and poorly exploits the cloud resources. As an alternative to allocating and de-allocating, an option to optimize resource usage is to reconfigure the resources allocated to the application (Kokkinos et al., 2013). It also requires being able to accurately model variations in the workload, which is not an easy task, particularly for public clouds, where trace data is scarce. Reiss et al. (2012) paved the way to model a workload dynamicity that is experienced in (public and private) heterogeneous cloud computing platforms.

Duplyakin et al. (2013) propose a multi-cloud environment to process user requests. In this system, users specify the percentage of the resources to be used in each cloud computing environment. If user specifications are not satisfied due to a lack of resources, the system will balance the load progressively on already-deployed instances until the user requirements are met. This approach allows the best possible use of hybrid clouds, but requires an intrusive solution installed inside a VM. Kailasam et al. (2013) consider the optimization of the execution time in a hybrid cloud context. They propose three heuristic-based scheduling methods that adapt themselves to the evolution of the resources of the workload and the availability of the clouds. This approach allows the use of hybrid clouds in the context of HPC but requires modifications to the application, or, more specifically, to the application's task scheduler. Leitner et al. (2013) propose a model that enables running applications to burst into a different cloud infrastructure. The authors propose a framework for the creation of elastic cloud applications. This framework enables the monitoring of the performance and decides when to burst to a public cloud and, in the other direction, where to consolidate into the private cloud, but this approach needs the re-writing of the applications.

Other research works have been achieved on the hybrid cloud, but focusing on economic aspects, e.g., Guo et al., (2012) and Tordsson et al., (2012). In a fog environment, multi-resource allocation should not only facilitate the selection of the best resource on the grounds of cost minimization but also ensure application reliability and QoS and avoid vendor lock-in. This ability allows the selection of the best resource to run microservice-based on end-user requirements, which is considered an important challenge in fog computing.

2.2.2. Optimal Deployment

Microservices orchestration should balance various criteria, such as making the best utilization of computing resources, increasing response time while decreasing network traffic load over the Internet. There are also QoS-specific trade-offs that must be considered, particularly in situations when vehicles are dynamically changing their geographic positions. For example, some processing may need to be moved from one RPU to another in the proximity of vehicles. Reliable execution of the application as a whole requires coordination of execution flows. Fog computing requires orchestration capabilities to manage both the application and the data flow between available resources. Lorido-Botran et al. (2014) identify five categories of approaches for realizing auto-scaling: Threshold-based rules, Reinforcement learning (RL), Queuing theory (QT), Control theory (CT), and Time series analysis (TS). Gandhi et al. (2014) identify five similar auto-scaling approach categories: prediction models, control theoretic techniques, queuing-based models, and black-box and grey-box approaches. Black-box models use machine learning or statistical methods for decision making in order to overcome the problem of modeling the cloud application using expert knowledge. Grey-box models are hybrid approaches that use models in combination with machine learning. Qu et al. (2018) reason that resource estimation in horizontal or vertical auto-scaling can be performed using rules, fuzzy-inference, application-profiling, analytical modeling, machine learning or hybrid methods. Analytical modeling includes queuing theory and markov chains. Machine learning includes reinforcement learning and regression. Regression is applied in auto-scaling techniques that use time-series analysis or control theory.

Due to its highly networked nature, serverless computing challenges the ways in which auto-scaling approaches can be applied. There is a need for well-defined event protocols and methods, for example, for message queues (Abowd et al. 1999) to continuously monitor the state of serverless applications and the infrastructure to ensure that the latter always has enough capacity to handle the current workload. Resilience to failure is another essential requirement of a FaaS application because each application request is divided and translated to different service calls. A bottleneck in a specific service operation should not bring the entire system down.

2.2.3. Context-Aware Offloading

Typically, microservices offload persistence to the host or use highly available cloud data stores to provide a persistence layer. Offloading to the host makes it difficult to port containers from one host to another. Technologies like the Flocker and Docker volume plugins address this problem by creating a separate persistence layer that is not host-dependent. Other technologies such as JPPF (Java Parallel Processing Framework, JPPF, https://www.jppf.org/.), CloneCloud (Chun et al., 2011), MACS (Kovachev et al., 2012), and JADE (Qian & Andresen, 2014) enable the partitioning of cloud application processing tasks to multiple processing nodes at source-code level. JPPF, for instance, supports the allocation of processing tasks on any operating system capable of running a JVM (also on Android despite running its own JVM).

In a fog environment, offloading should span all three processing layers: embedded systems, RPUs, and centralized public clouds. For example, when instructed by the data processing performed in the embedded systems layer, video streams and other measured data should be sent to fragments deployed on the RPUs of the second layer for content analysis. Other fragments with higher processing requirements, such as driver behavior profiling can only run on the cloud. Deployment constraints should be clearly defined and interpreted by the fog framework so that fragments are deployed on capable resources. Furthermore, there is a need to manage offloading and onloading of microservices intelligently, e.g., if the processing requires to exceed the capabilities of RPUs, new processing modes should be spawned in the cloud. According to RPU mobility, location, and network condition, the system may need to dynamically select a new RPU, re-deploy the service, and hence support the application through context-aware offloading capabilities.

3. PRESTOCLOUD FRAMEWORK

In PrEstoCloud (2020), we focused our research efforts on developing capabilities that address the aforementioned challenges and requirements. The PrEstoCloud framework allows not only the execution of microservices with cloud, fog, and edge devices but also decides, at run-time, the shifting of processing tasks from edge devices to multi-cloud or fog resources and vice-versa. To facilitate this, PrEstoCloud allows DevOps to define constraints and execution preferences about microservices that can be executed either on cloud, fog, or edge resources. PrEstoCloud decides during run-time to offload/onload processing tasks on specific types or instances of edge resources to/from multi-cloud resources. Such decisions are based on the current context of the resources used, the microservices status with respect to QoS and the present and estimated workload.

3.1. Five-Layered Architecture

PrEstoCloud follows a five-layer architecture (Figure 2):

- The *meta-management layer* provides decision logic capabilities required for enhancing the control layer. Components of this layer use as input the situation details, the variation of the data streams and the context of the mobile devices at the extreme edge of the network. This layer recognizes the situations when it is required to recommend, at the appropriate time, the necessary adaptations, such as scaling of functions and on/offloading of microservices.
- The *control layer* contains components responsible for the optimized scheduling of function execution over available resources. The control layer detects available edge resources and selects target resources for deployment and plans fragment scheduling according to the recommendation of the meta-management layer. Optimization involves the examination of a big variability space to find those resources that satisfy certain business goals (e.g., reduce cloud costs while maintaining an adequate response time).

Figure 2. PrEstoCloud architecture

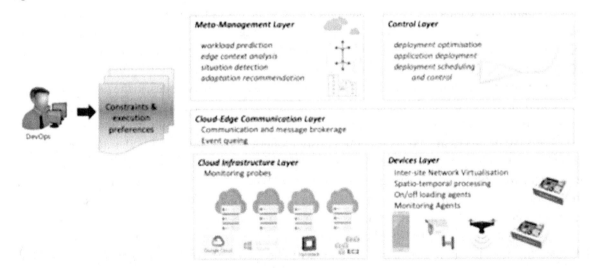

- The *cloud infrastructure layer* realizes the dynamic deployment and scheduling capabilities, according to the instructions of the control layer. The deployment of microservices is handled based on deployment constraints related to different properties like response time, security constraints or any other preferences of the DevOps.

- The *cloud–edge communication layer* contains the inter-site network virtualization technology for coping with the need for connecting resources situated in multi-cloud environments and managing their orchestration and provisioning across different and heterogeneous providers. This layer is also responsible for relaying data streams securely on and off the PrEstoCloud platform and for providing publish and subscribe event brokering capabilities.

- The *devices layer* contains edge devices that can be used as processing nodes. The appropriate agents are installed in each device for (a) network virtualization, (b) spatio-temporal processing in poor connectivity cases in which the communication to the cloud layer is maintained even if only one edge device maintains adequate connection, (c) shifting processing jobs in our out of the edge device, and (d) monitoring agents for aggregating infrastructure and application-level metrics that reveal the status of each edge device.

The framework that was developed based on this architecture provides the capability to run functions by using microservices, specifically, with the deployment of Docker images. Therefore, PrEstoCloud supports the deployment of applications built using the microservice and FaaS paradigms through the use of lambda functions, as well as the deployment of any applications capable of exploiting the distributed deployment paradigm. Deployment blueprints are expressed in an extended topology and orchestration specification for cloud applications specification (TOSCA 2020) that considers edge and FaaS-related constructs. These blueprints are exploited in processing workflows that enable the deployment of microservices.

The microservices added by the DevOps through a UI are deployed on FaaS processing nodes. Processing nodes can be further specified with the use of affinity and anti-affinity constraints, as well as the precedence of deployment of some nodes before others. Affinity constraints indicate that some nodes should be placed in the same geographical region, and if possible, in the same datacenter or rack. Similarly, anti-affinity constraints indicate that nodes should be placed in different geographic areas. Precedence-of-deployment constraints force a particular order in the deployment, enabling nodes that provide programmatic interfaces to be instantiated before the nodes that require them. New processing nodes may be added or removed from the current processing topology without affecting the overall processing structure. This enables PrEstoCloud to timely use of horizontal scaling to optimize the performance of the processing topology according to the processing specifications of the DevOps.

In addition to processing nodes, PrEstoCloud makes use of coordinator nodes, in the form of a Lambda proxy component (i.e., a Traefik instance https://traefik.io/). A coordination node acts as a gateway to access the functionality of microservices and can transmit metrics related to the running processing tasks. The state of processing nodes is continuously monitored by coordinator nodes and control layer components. If a change in the topology is detected, e.g., a node does not respond within a timeout, the platform will still be operational using short-term and medium-term measures. In the short term, a coordinator node will redirect incoming processing tasks to other nodes processing the same task—a necessary prerequisite for the effectiveness of short-term measures is the availability of such nodes. In turn, this implies that the DevOps should require a minimum number of instances for this function, balancing the need for short-term fault-tolerance with the increased cost. In the meantime, the control layer will initiate remedy actions, e.g., the instantiation of a new processing node, aiming to reinstate the balance in the processing topology in the medium term.

3.2. Deployment Lifecycle

Figure 3 illustrates the deployment cycle for the intelligent logistics application scenario. These four steps shown are fully supported by the PrEstoCloud framework to allow the DevOps to respond to business requirements.

Figure 3. PrEstoCloud deployment lifecycle

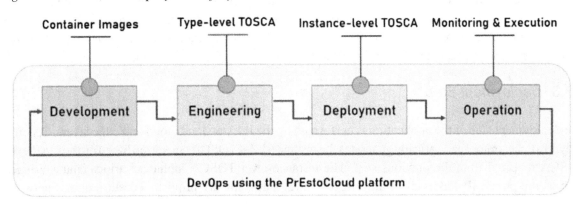

The cycle begins with the input of the developer and the DevOps and resulting in the actual deployment of the application. We focus and describe how the reconfiguration cycle is realized. Reconfiguration is based on the available VM flavors and edge devices as well as the qualitative and quantitative preferences of the DevOp. Based on this information, the system generates a type-level TOSCA specification of the fragmentation along with a recommended deployment without specific VM and edge instances. The specification takes into consideration constraints such as security constraints or other quantitative or qualitative constraints, e.g., cost, response time, and data sanitization support. The recommendation is forwarded to the control layer for optimization, instantiation of the TOSCA specification and deployment.

3.2.1. Development step

In the development step, system requirements are refined into a complete product design including the hardware and software architecture and detailed descriptions of the system, data and interfaces. Software developers know that the application includes small, self-contained deployable containers, each one acting as an individual function application, working together through APIs, which are not dependent on a particular language, library or framework. In this way, decomposing the whole logistics application into small containers enables us to distribute the computational workload of services among various resources. Besides this, each of the services can be easily developed and operated by different software engineering teams, and hence, this container-based architecture affects both organizational forms of cooperation as well as technological decisions which can be made locally by each team. Resilience to failure is another characteristic of the microservice approach because each application request is divided and translated to different service calls in this software architecture. Therefore, a bottleneck in a specific service operation will not bring the entire system down and it only affects that service. In such a situation, other services are able to carry on processing their requests as usual.

3.2.2. Engineering step

The main output in the engineering step is a type-level TOSCA file by parsing code-level annotations, as well as DevOps preferences and requirements (e.g. cloud provider requirements) expressed in a policy file (not shown for brevity). These requirements are then grouped, and a type-level TOSCA file is produced. The type-level TOSCA includes generic specifications, for example the application topology, relations among all application components, deployment order of application components, constraints such as required resource features for each application component, etc. Afterwards, the type-level TOSCA file of the logistics application is pushed to the PrEstoCloud repository, whence it is retrieved by the Control Layer in order to calculate the optimal configuration for the application deployment.

3.2.3. *Deployment Step*

The deployment step of the application is performed by the PrEstoCloud cloud and edge layers. Specifically, an orchestrator automatically generates the instance-level TOSCA converted based on the type-level TOSCA received from the previous step. The instance-level TOSCA includes various characteristics such as the public IP addresses of all host machines automatically provisioned, all required network configurations, inbound and outbound rules for VMs, security policies, components start-up sequence, and similar. When the deployment step is accomplished, VMs are automatically allocated to instantiate all containers running the application. The orchestrator automatically provisions public clouds and edge resources, which provides a wide selection of instance types optimized to fit the logistics use case. Instance types comprise varying combinations of CPU, memory, storage, and networking capacity and give the orchestrator the flexibility to choose the appropriate mix of resources for the application. Each of microservice is packaged in Docker containers is deployed on an individual host machine.

3.2.4. Operation Step

This step manages cloud and edge resources. To this end, the operation step exploits available capabilities to monitor and control cloud-based resources, which can be also extended to the edge of the network. This step is responsible for the optimal scheduling of services deployed for the application over all available resources according to the recommendation of Meta-Management Layer. The selection of cloud-based infrastructures is followed by an optimization step, which is necessary for finding the most appropriate alternatives which can satisfy certain business goals such as cloud infrastructure cost reduction while maintaining a satisfactory response time.

The monitoring system provided by the PrEstoCloud framework plays a key role to track the execution environment. The Monitoring Agent is able to continuously measure a set of necessary metrics related to both infrastructure and application performance. Infrastructure-specific metrics are CPU, memory, disk, network, etc. Furthermore, application-related metrics represent the information about the status of the application such as service response time.

4. EVALUATION

4.1. Use Case

To illustrate PrEstoCloud's capability to support auto-scaling in deployments of microservices, we use as a case study the microservice-based logistics application, which is divided into four fragments: driver dynamics service, notification server, DB server, and GUI server (Figure 4). The driver dynamics service running on the unit installed in the vehicle (edge) receives data from sensors and recognizes unexpected driving dynamics, e.g., sudden acceleration, hard braking, and aggressive turns. If there is such an occurrence, the service will instantly send a run-time message to the notification server, which is running on the RPU. Moreover, the driver dynamics service transmits some sensor data periodically to the notification server, such as the vehicle's speed and GPS information, which is helpful in knowing where the vehicle is located. All information is available for the logistic center end user via web-based GUI. The GUI server is a web server that processes all incoming requests over HTTP sent from end users (e.g., logistic center end users using web browsers) and delivers web page contents to them.

The notification server running on the RPU receives all telematics messages sent by driver dynamics services. Messages are stored in the DB server, a database used to store the time-series data, e.g., the routes where vehicles are moving, the places where driving dynamics happened. The GUI server, which is deployed on a different cloud (Google Cloud), shows end users all information stored in the DB server. Facilitating multi-cloud resource allocation, PrEstoCloud allows the DB server to be deployed on one cloud, for example, Amazon EC2, which guarantees favorable service-level agreement (SLA) terms for the DB server and web-based GUI server on another cloud, e.g., Google Cloud Platform, which offers optimal pricing.

Figure 4. Logistics application microservices

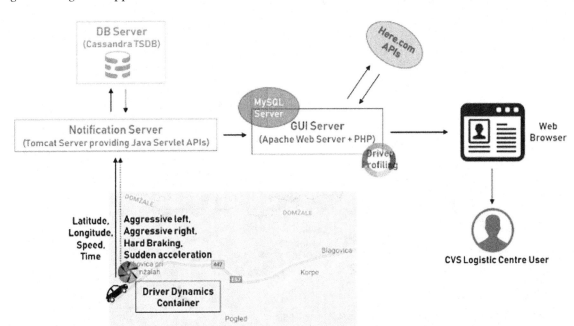

Each RPU receives messages from vehicles within its transmission range. According to the number of vehicles in every geographic region, heterogeneous RPUs with different computing capacity may be allocated. The optimized microservice deployment of Notification functions for each area, avoids resource under-provisioning and over-provisioning while adhering to the processing and functional requirements of the fragment, e.g., that the DriverDynamics fragment needs to be deployed before the Notification Server. Then, the cheapest VM having at least one CPU, 4 GB of RAM, and 4 GB of disk space is requested. According to a DevOps-configured rule, e.g., whenever the CPU load is increased by more than 70% or decreased to less than 30% over two minutes, the framework tries to add or remove notification server instances, respectively.

In some cases, a new RPU should be allocated because of a movement of the vehicle from a geographic location to a new place. In this case, the notification server running on the current RPU, which provides the service is not able to offer favorable QoS required for the intelligent logistics application. Therefore, the Notification Server needs to be migrated from the current RPU to another RPU near the vehicle. A different reason for violations of QoS constraints may also be the situation where the RPU is overloaded due to an increasing workload. In such a case, offloading the notification server from the current RPU to the cloud or vice versa is also necessary.

4.2. Deployment Using PrEstoCloud

Figure 5 shows the PrEstoCloud UI dashboard through which, the DevOps specifies the application microservices. Once specified, the DevOps can start an instance of the application which will be automatically deployed on resources already defined on the dashboard. For the specific application, four types of containerised components as specified: cvs_db_server, cvs_notification_server, cvs_gui_server, cvs_driver_dynamics_arm / cvs_driver_dynamics_x86.

Figure 5. Logistics application specification on PrEstoCloud GUI

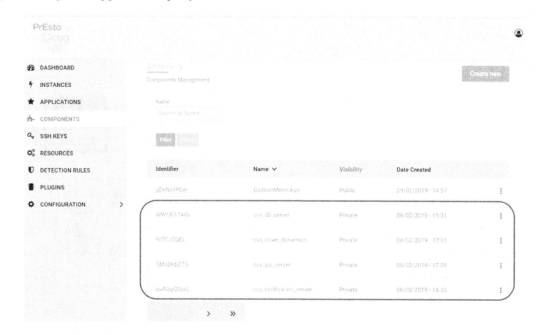

In order to specify each microservice, various parameters need to be completed, such as name of component, architecture (X86 or ARM), name of Docker registry, name of Docker image, minimum execution of hardware requirements (e.g. vCPUs, RAM, storage, etc.), health check API, environmental variables, exposed interfaces (port numbers, etc.) and required interfaces from other components (Figure 6).

Figure 6. Microservice parameters

To complete the application deployment specification, the architecture should be defined. To this end, the connections among all components are required to be precisely described through exposed interfaces and required interfaces. As mentioned before, such interfaces are already defined when we created each component. Figure 7 depicts a graph which is automatically generated via the PrEstoCloud UI based on the connections defined for each component.

Figure 7. Microservice deployment graph

Upon the successful deployment, the Cloud–edge communication layer of PrEstoCloud makes the DB Server accessible only from the Notification Server in the network, not from other hosts on the Internet. These security concerns, also for other components, are automatically addressed by the packet filtering service. For the deployment of the logistics application, three cloud providers have been used: Amazon, Azure and ARNES (Academic and Research Network of Slovenia). The DB Server is deployed on the Amazon cloud infrastructure, the Notification Server is deployed on the Azure cloud infrastructure, and the GUI Server is deployed on the ARNES cloud infrastructure.

Figure 8 shows the scenario how the Devices layer of PrEstoCloud performs at runtime a typical example of auto-scaling: off-loading. Because the Driver Dynamics Container is running on the edge, it is useful for analyzing the telematics data very fast. In this case, the container image named cvs_driver_dynamics_arm is exploited since the edge nodes use ARM processor architecture. If the limited-resource edge node is not able to provide the service (e.g., any of the monitoring metrics may show that an abnormal situation is going to happen, for example the free disk capacity or computation power on the edge node is not available anymore), the PrEstoCloud solution offloads the service from the edge node to the cloud infrastructure.

Figure 8. Microservice on/offloading

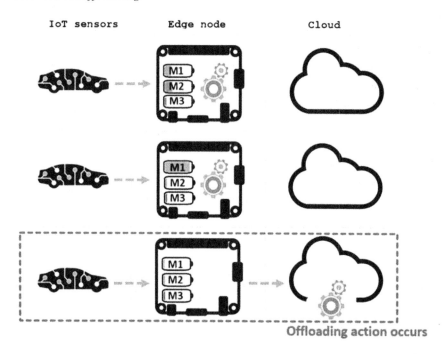

Monitoring data are communication through the Cloud-edge communication layer of PreStoCloud, which uses the MQTT protocol. MQTT is an IoT connectivity protocol, designed as an extremely lightweight publish/subscribe messaging transport. It is useful for connections with remote locations where a small code footprint is required or network bandwidth needs to be considered so it has been used in sensors communicating to the Broker.

In order to have a zero-failure rate, the start time of the Driver Dynamics Container needs to be taken into consideration when it should be offloaded from one resource to another one. In essence, any container termination on the source node before the time when the new container instance on the destination node would be ready to offer its own service means the death of this specific service for a while. Therefore, either success or failure status of start and stop requests should be observed to reach a fortunate on/offloading operation. In this regard, a numerical value will be returned by the developed On/Offloading Server that implies if the request (whether start or stop) has been successfully executed or not.

4.3. Results

To evaluate PrEstoCould's auto-scaling capabilities, we measured the average, 99th percentile, and standard deviation of application response time during an offloading action. Here, the response time is the time period from sensor data acquisition to the time when driver dynamics microservice, a function of the intelligent logistics app, detects if an unexpected event happens or not. Three different types of infrastructures were exploited to host the driver dynamics microservice to evaluate the importance of its placement, including embedded system, RPU, and centralized cloud. The custom embedded system called MACH (Motorhome AI Communication Hardware; Taherizadeh et al., 2018) developed by the Jožef Stefan Institute (JSI) is installed in the vehicle at the edge of the network. The MACH has a 4-core 1.4 GHz CPU, VideoCore-IV GPU, 1 GB of RAM, and 20 GB of storage. The RPU as a fog computing resource belonged to the Academic and Research Network of Slovenia (ARNES) with a 1-core 2397 MHz CPU, 4 GB of RAM, 10 GB of storage, and 1000 MBps bandwidth. The cloud server also had a 4-core 2659 MHz CPU, 16 GB of RAM, 80 GB of storage, and 1000 MBps bandwidth. Each experiment was repeated five times to obtain verified results.

A 25 km trip, which took 13 minutes and 16 seconds, was selected to gather sensor data from an ordinary vehicle. The vehicle's sensor measurements were sampled at the rate of 10 Hz, so each sample was recorded every 100 ms. Therefore, there were nearly 8,000 samples from the whole trip.

Figure 9. Intelligent logistics application

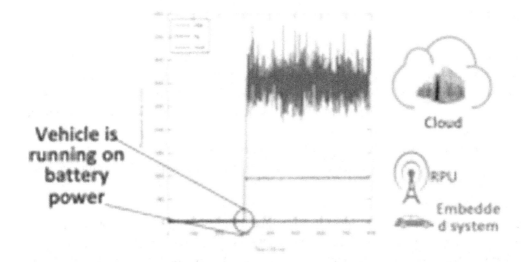

We evaluated the extent to which fog and cloud computing can help the logistics application improve the response time when PrEstoCloud handles an auto-scaling action (Figure 9). This action was performed to re-deploy the driver dynamics microservice from the edge node to either the fog or the cloud at time = 3,000 ms when the electric vehicle is running out of battery power, and hence the embedded system is not able to provide computing operations on the edge. Re-deploying the driver dynamics microservice from the edge resource to the fog or cloud helps save the battery as much as possible. Table 2 shows the response time provided in three different experiments, including edge, fog, and cloud. In the second and third experiments, the driver dynamics microservice was running respectively on the fog and cloud after the time when it was offloaded from the edge node.

Table 2. Response time offered by the Driver Dynamics Service on edge, fog and cloud resources

Time (ms)	Edge	Fog	Cloud
Average response time	35.64	948.33	3013.23
99th percentile of the response time	42.5	954.60	3901.52
Standard deviation of response time	3.52	2.62	364.50

When the driver dynamics microservice was offloaded from the edge node, the average and 99th percentile of response times for the fog test 948.33 ms and 954.60 ms, respectively, whereas these parameters were 3,013.23 ms and 3,901.52 ms in the cloud test. This means that the difference in average response times between fog and cloud is almost two seconds, while the difference in the 99th percentile of response times between fog and cloud is nearly three seconds. Moreover, the response time offered by the fog infrastructure was appropriately steady during the experiment since the standard deviation of response time was less than 3 ms, whereas the standard deviation of response time with the cloud was more than 364ms. Therefore, the fog node provided a more stable quality of computing resource in comparison to the cloud.

5. DISCUSSION

To avoid vendor lock-in and increase the choices available to DevOps, some of the available fog computing frameworks allow cross-cloud deployments as well as orchestration of deployments on fog resources using open standards such as TOSCA. Although some work has been done to extend TOSCA to support deployment on edge resources, the standard is mostly still restricted to deployments in conventional cloud resources. To facilitate the adoption of fog computing implementations, the availability of up-to-date standards supporting widely adopted deployment technologies, such as Docker containers, is essential. Further efforts should be put in extending these standards to address fog computing requirements and concerns.

Fog computing frameworks are increasingly more capable of dealing with the dynamicity of fog-deployed applications and services. Specifically, adjusting and adapting the computing infrastructure to changing data flows and producing automatically optimal orchestrations of cloud and fog-resources is a prominent trend, which ameliorates the need for the DevOps to monitor the deployment continuously and make the necessary changes manually. Still, further work is needed to fully support multi-cloud and cross-resource optimization of deployments of data-intensive applications. In this direction, PrEstoCloud allows extending the deployment and networking capabilities to the extreme edge of the network, enabling efficient processing of the data produced at the edge. Depending on the current situation, PrEstoCloud foresees to make an optimized placement of the application as well as of parts of an application, to find the right balance between edge and cloud usage. Moreover, PrEstoCloud allows for scaling and adapting the deployed applications in real-time, based on the existing and also on the anticipated processing load. Still, further research is needed to support the self-adaptivity of fog infrastructures fully. To this end, new methods and tools are needed that can detect ahead of time needed for changes by analyzing all available contextual information, generating the most efficient reconfiguration and defining the optimal redeployment of the running processing tasks. Such methods and tools will become more and more useful as their placement is feasible closer to edge nodes.

The edge-processing capability of fog computing frameworks is challenged by the serverless computing trend. PrEstoCloud combines edge computing and serverless paradigms to provide an innovative solution for FaaS-enabled applications. For example, it enables IoT applications that perform analytics to host machine learning models within an edge network, so that applications can exploit the model close or at the edge. Every edge location deploys the machine learning model as a serverless function. The edge layer simplifies the deployment experience, while serverless streamline the developer experience. Functions can be provided faster, leading to increased flexibility and greater availability of the deployed application components.

Continuous monitoring and analysis of the status of fog resources and deployed applications or application parts is a challenging task. Monitoring probes need to be capable of distributed deployment. Moreover, analysis of probed data needs to be done at or close to the edge due to network latency and throughput limitation issues. For example, instead of having a security camera stream its video and audio feed up to the cloud to be analyzed for certain situations, that analysis can be done within the camera itself. Clearly, a more advanced, cloud-based analysis may still be needed, but it is likely to be on a much smaller segment of the camera data. To analyze monitoring data on edge resources, efficient machine learning methods are needed, with minimal computing and memory requirements. Such a distributed monitoring and analysis capability can have a minimal footprint on the network traffic while leveraging effective decision making for the overall adaptation and optimization of the fog infrastructure as well as help in maintaining high QoS.

The traditional centralized cloud computing continues to remain a significant part of fog computing frameworks. Function and data portability, infrastructure monitoring as well as orchestration methods employed in the centralized cloud environment cannot be useful in the context of interconnected, heterogeneous fog computing resources, in which decision spaces become larger, increasingly complex and more dynamic. Next-generation fog computing frameworks will enable the smart deployment of applications on a combination of cloud, edge, and extreme edge resources and are expected to employ advanced methods for dealing with the dynamicity of FaaS applications and fog infrastructures.

6. CONCLUSION

In this paper, we described the details of the PrEstoCloud framework that introduces advanced methods that deal with the dynamicity of FaaS applications and fog infrastructures. The main three distinctions among the surveyed fog frameworks and PrEstocloud are the following. First, PrEstoCloud enables the use of multi-private or public clouds by considering which is the most efficient cloud resource to use in each case. Second is computation at the extreme edge on a per-device level; further, benefiting from the computational resources of cameras and mobile devices (wherever possible) is something that PrEstoCloud aspires to deliver which is not available in similar solutions like AWS Greengrass. Finally, PrEstoCloud allows the application developer and the DevOps to define their constraints properly but also provide hints about application fragments that can be executed either on cloud resources, edge resources, or both. From that point on, PrEstoCloud can decide during run-time to offload/onload processing tasks on edge resources to/from cloud resources based on the current state of the resources used, the application fragments status, and the current and predicted workload.

ACKNOWLEDGMENT

We would like to thank all partners of the PrEstoCloud project who have contributed with ideas towards the development of the PrEstoCloud framework.

Funding: This research was funded by the European Commission, grant number 732339.

REFERENCES

Abowd, G. D., Dey, A. K., Brown, P. J., Davies, N., Smith, M., & Steggles, P. (1999). Towards a better understanding of context and context-awareness. In *Proceedings of the 1st International Symposium on Handheld and Ubiquitous Computing, ser. HUC '99*. Springer. 10.1007/3-540-48157-5_29

AWS Greengrass. (n.d.). https://aws.amazon.com/greengrass/

AWS Wavelength. (n.d.). https://aws.amazon.com/wavelength

Azure IoT Edge. (n.d.). https://azure.microsoft.com/en-us/services/iot-edge/

Carroll, N. (2015). Modelling the dynamics of trust across a cloud brokerage environment. *Information Resources Management Journal, 28*(1), 17–37. doi:10.4018/irmj.2015010102

Castro, P., Ishakian, V., Muthusamy, V., & Slominski, A. (2019). The Rise of Serverless Computing. *Communications of the ACM, 62*(12), 44–54. doi:10.1145/3368454

Chiang, M., & Zhang, T. (2016). Fog and IoT: An overview of research opportunities. *IEEE Internet of Things Journal, 3*(6), 854–864. doi:10.1109/JIOT.2016.2584538

Chun, B.-G., Ihm, S., Maniatis, P., Naik, M., & Patti, A. (2011). Clonecloud: Elastic execution between mobile device and cloud. In *Proceedings of the Sixth Conference on Computer Systems, ser. EuroSys '11*. Salzburg, Austria: ACM. 10.1145/1966445.1966473

Cloudify. (n.d.). https://cloudify.co/

Di Martino, B., Esposito, A., & Damiani, E. (2019). Towards AI-Powered Multiple Cloud Management. *IEEE Internet Computing, 23*(1), 64–71. doi:10.1109/MIC.2018.2883839

Duplyakin, D., Marshall, P., Keahey, K., Tufo, H., & Alzabarah, A. (2013). Rebalancing in a multi-cloud environment. In *Proceedings of the 4th ACM Workshop on Scientific Cloud Computing*. ACM. 10.1145/2465848.2465854

Gandhi, A., Dube, P., Karve, A., Kochut, A., & Zhang, L. (2014). Adaptive, model-driven autoscaling for cloud applications. *11th International Conference on Autonomic Computing (ICAC 14), USENIX, 2014*, 57–64.

Google Cloud IoT Core. (n.d.). https://cloud.google.com/iot-core

Guo, T., Sharma, U., Wood, T., Sahu, S., & Shenoy, P. (2012). Seagull: Intelligent cloud bursting for enterprise applications. *Proceedings of the 2012 USENIX Annual Technical Conference, ser. ATC'12*.

Gusev, M., Koteska, B., Kostoska, M., Jakimovski, B., Dustdar, S., Scekic, O., Rausch, R., Nastic, S., Ristov, S., & Fahringer, T. (2019). A Deviceless Edge Computing Approach for Streaming IoT Applications. *IEEE Internet Computing, 23*(1), 37–45. doi:10.1109/MIC.2019.2892219

Hao, Z., Novak, E., Yi, S., & Li, Q. (2017). Challenges and software architecture for fog computing. *IEEE Internet Computing, 21*(2), 44–53. doi:10.1109/MIC.2017.26

Iorga, M., Feldman, L., Barton, R., Martin, M. J., Goren, N., & Mahmoudi, C. (2018). *The NIST Definition of Fog Computing*. NIST Special Publication 800-191.

Kailasam, S., Gnanasambandam, N., Dharanipragada, J., & Sharma, N. (2013, November). Optimizing ordered throughput using autonomic cloud bursting schedulers. *Transactions on Software Engineering, 39*(11), 1564–1581. doi:10.1109/TSE.2013.26

Kokkinos, P., Varvarigou, T. A., Kretsis, A., Soumplis, P., & Varvarigos, E. A. (2013). Cost and utilization optimization of amazon ec2 instances. *2013 IEEE Sixth International Conference on Cloud Computing*, 518–525. 10.1109/CLOUD.2013.52

Kovachev, D., Yu, T., & Klamma, R. (2012). Adaptive computation offloading from mobile devices into the cloud. *2012 IEEE 10th International Symposium on Parallel and Distributed Processing with Applications*, 784–791. 10.1109/ISPA.2012.115

Leitner, P., Rostyslav, Z., Gambi, A., & Dustdar, S. (2013). A framework and middleware for application-level cloud bursting on top of infrastructure-as-a-service clouds. *Proceedings of the 6th IEEE/ACM International Conference on Utility and Cloud Computing*. 10.1109/UCC.2013.39

Liu, Y., Fieldsend, J. E., & Min, G. (2017). A framework of fog computing: Architecture, challenges, and optimization. *IEEE Access: Practical Innovations, Open Solutions*, 5, 25445–25454. doi:10.1109/ACCESS.2017.2766923

Lorido-Botran, T., Miguel-Alonso, J., & Lozano, J. A. (2014, December). A review of auto-scaling techniques for elastic applications in cloud environments. *Journal of Grid Computing*, 12(4), 559–592. doi:10.100710723-014-9314-7

Mahesh, S., Landry, B. J., Sridhar, T., & Walsh, K. R. (2011). A decision table for the cloud computing decision in small business. *Information Resources Management Journal*, 24(3), 9–25. doi:10.4018/irmj.2011070102

Nebiolo. (n.d.). https://www.nebbiolo.tech/

OpenWhiskLean. (n.d.). https://github.com/kpavel/incubator-openwhisk/tree/lean

Papageorgiou, N., Apostolou, D., Verginadis, Y., & Mentzas, G. (2019). Fog Context Analytics. *IEEE Instrumentation & Measurement Magazine*.

PreStoCloud. (n.d.). https://gitlab.com/prestocloud-project

Qian, H., & Andresen, D. (2014). Jade: An efficient energy-aware computation offloading system with heterogeneous network interface bonding for ad-hoc networked mobile devices. *15th IEEE/ACIS International Conference on Software Engineering, Artificial Intelligence, Networking and Parallel/Distributed Computing (SNPD)*. 10.1109/SNPD.2014.6888703

Qu, C., Calheiros, R. N., & Buyya, R. (2018). Auto-scaling web applications in clouds: A taxonomy and survey. *ACM Computing Surveys*, 51(4), 73. doi:10.1145/3148149

Reiss, C., Tumanov, A., Ganger, G. R., Katz, R. H., & Kozuch, M. A. (2012). Heterogeneity and dynamicity of clouds at scale: Google trace analysis. In *Proceedings of the Third Symposium on Cloud Computing, ser. SoCC '12*. ACM. 10.1145/2391229.2391236

Taher, C., Mallat, I., Agoulmine, N., & El-Mawass, N. (2019). An IoT-Cloud Based Solution for Real-Time and Batch Processing of Big Data: Application in Healthcare. In *2019 3rd International Conference on Bio-engineering for Smart Technologies (BioSMART)*, (pp. 1-8). IEEE.

Taherizadeh, S., Stankovski, V., & Grobelnik, M. (2018). A Capillary Computing Architecture for Dynamic Internet of Things: Orchestration of Microservices from Edge Devices to Fog and Cloud Providers. *Sensors (Basel)*, 18(9), 2938. doi:10.339018092938 PMID:30181454

Tamrakar, K., Yazidi, A., & Haugerud, H. (2017). Cost efficient batch processing in Amazon cloud with deadline awareness. In *2017 IEEE 31st International Conference on Advanced Information Networking and Applications (AINA)*, (pp. 963-971). IEEE. 10.1109/AINA.2017.170

Tordsson, J., Montero, R. S., Moreno-Vozmediano, R., & Llorente, I. M. (2012). *Cloud brokering mechanisms for optimized placement of virtual machines across multiple providers*. Academic Press.

TOSCA. (n.d.). https://www.oasis-open.org/committees/tosca/

Trihinas, D., Tryfonos, A., Dikaiakos, M. D., & Pallis, G. (2018). Devops as a service: Pushing the boundaries of microservice adoption. *IEEE Internet Computing, 22*(3), 65–71. doi:10.1109/MIC.2018.032501519

Van Eyk, E., Toader, L., Talluri, S., Versluis, L., Uță, A., & Iosup, A. (2018). Serverless is more: From paas to present cloud computing. *IEEE Internet Computing, 22*(5), 8–17. doi:10.1109/MIC.2018.053681358

Wang, N., Varghese, B., Matthaiou, M., & Nikolopoulos, D. (2017). ENORM: A framework for edge node resource management. *IEEE Transactions on Services Computing*.

Wen, Y., Wang, Z., Zhang, Y., Liu, J., Cao, B., & Chen, J. (2019). Energy and cost aware scheduling with batch processing for instance-intensive IoT workflows in clouds. *Future Generation Computer Systems, 101*, 39–50. doi:10.1016/j.future.2019.05.046

Zhang, F., Tang, X., Li, X., Khan, S., & Li, Z. (2019). Quantifying cloud elasticity with container-based autoscaling. *Future Generation Computer Systems, 98*, 672–681. doi:10.1016/j.future.2018.09.009

Zhang, W., Xu, L., Duan, P., Gong, W., Liu, X., & Lu, Q. (2014). Towards a high speed video cloud based on batch processing integrated with fast processing. In *2014 International Conference on Identification, Information and Knowledge in the Internet of Things*, (pp. 28-33). IEEE. 10.1109/IIKI.2014.13

This research was previously published in the Information Resources Management Journal (IRMJ), 34(1); pages 66-85, copyright year 2021 by IGI Publishing (an imprint of IGI Global).

Chapter 9
Edge Cloud:
The Future Technology for Internet of Things

Lucia Agnes Beena Thomas
St. Joseph's College, India

ABSTRACT

With the proliferation of new technologies such as augmented and virtual reality, autonomous cars, 5G networks, drones, and IOT with smart cities, consumers of cloud computing are becoming the producers of data. Large volume of data is being produced at the edge of the network. This scenario insists the need for efficient real-time processing and communication at the network edge. Cloud capabilities must be distributed across the network to form an edge cloud, which places computing resources where the traffic is at the edge of the network. Edge cloud along with 5G services could also glint the next generation of robotic manufacturing. The anticipated low latency requirement, battery life constraint, bandwidth cost saving, as well as data safety and privacy are also inscribed by edge cloud. A number of giants like Nokia, AT&T, and Microsoft have emerged in the market to support edge cloud. This chapter wraps the features of edge cloud, the driving industries that are providing solutions, the use cases, benefits, and the challenges of edge cloud.

INTRODUCTION

With the rapid development of internet, provisioning of computing resources as a utility came into existence in the name of Cloud Computing. Cloud services influenced both the individual as well as the business by its cost-efficiency and scalability through centralized architecture. Since 1999, the tremendous growth of different internet connected devices give rise to a new technology called Internet of Things (IoT). Initially, IoT was applied to supply chain management and now it is adapted to health care, transport and smart home environment (Peng et al., 2018). IoT applications involve the machine to machine (M2M) interaction without the human intervention. These real time applications handle large

DOI: 10.4018/978-1-6684-5700-9.ch009

Copyright © 2022, IGI Global. Copying or distributing in print or electronic forms without written permission of IGI Global is prohibited.

amount of data that has to be analyzed critically for patterns, trends which help in better hold on problem assessment and decisions. This promising technology introduced new challenges.

The Cisco Global Cloud Index estimated that nearly 850 ZB will be generated by all people, machines, and things by 2021 (as cited in Cisco Global Cloud Index, 2018). Cloud services are to be leveraged to handle this huge data. Businesses in the utilities, oil & gas, insurance, manufacturing, transportation, infrastructure and retail sectors can reap the benefits of IoT by making more informed decisions, aided by the stream of interactional and transactional data at their disposal (as cited in happiestminds, 2018). These industrial IoT applications need high speed internet connectivity and rapid data analysis which facilitate in decisions made by autonomous or semiautonomous systems and actuators. The traditional network find it difficult to face the challenge of sending bulk data from a remote place to cloud for processing and to deliver a quick decision in a short time span to the appropriate device. Also the cost of data transfer through the satellite communication is elevated. Gartner the world's leading research and advisory company's October 2018 blog, reports that currently around 10% of enterprise-generated data is created and processed outside a traditional centralized data center or cloud. By 2022, Gartner predicts this figure will reach 75% (as cited in gartner, 2018). These challenges can be tackled by Edge Computing. For instance, in medical internet of things, wireless diabetes devices such as blood glucose monitors, continuous glucose monitors, insulin pens, insulin pumps, and closed-loop systems are used. The Cloud data centers are unable to store and analyze the data generated by these devices. The processing has to be pushed out to the edge (IoT device) of the network where the data is being generated. This give rise to a new paradigm called Edge computing. Edge computing architecture can relieve the Cloud from processing an outsized data but to store vital information. The data generated by the medical IoT devices can be processed by the device themselves nearby the patient, and transmit information machine-to-machine or machine-to-human in milliseconds or seconds (Klonoff & David, 2017). The increase in the use of IoT devices, swift data transmission speed, the necessity for faster processing and reduced latency in response time drive the Edge computing.

EDGE COMPUTING AT A GLANCE

Modern industries need innovations in products, services, and trade model. The technologies like IoT, Cloud help the industries in digital transformation in every aspect of its operations in an efficient way. For a smart IoT application, that offer real time services require heterogeneous connections, data optimization techniques and security. The term IoT was first articulated by Kevin Ashton at Procter & Gamble (P&G) in 1999 (Ashton, 2009). Days are gone where the data is created and processed by Human being with computers. Today any electronic device that is capable of accessing an internet becomes a data producer. Starting from the wearable device in the health care, tablets, game controllers and smart phones referred as edge devices, use the Cloud data centers, increase the communication between the user and the Cloud. But the Cloud applications could not satisfy its users by rapid response. This elevates the need for the processing at the edge of the network. Only the optimized data are sent to the Cloud rather than forwarding the raw data produced from the edge devices.

To promote the processing at the edge, various initiatives were taken by industries and few consortiums were formed. In 2012, Cisco (Bonomi et al., 2012) introduced a new platform named Fog Computing to meet the challenges faced by the Cloud with respect to the IoT applications. They proposed Fog (close to the Ground) computing with the connotation computing close to the edge devices. Fog computing, the data gets processed in a fog node or in an IoT gateway at the local area network level and the device or thing level (as cited in i-Scoop, 2018). Nokia Solutions and Networks designed an innovative network technology Mobile Edge Computing(MEC) through Liquid applications in 2013, at the base-station level. The application developers used the real-time network data to create innovative services, such as connecting mobile subscribers with local points-of-interest, businesses and events (as cited in Nokia Solutions and Networks, 2013). In 2014, Edge Computing Consortium (ECC) (as cited in iotaustralia, 2017) formed by six industries such as Huawei Technologies Co., Ltd., Shenyang Institute of Automation of the Chinese Academy of Sciences, China Academy of Information and Communications Technology (CAICT), Intel Corporation, ARM Holdings, and iSoftStone Information Technology (Group) Co., Ltd with the motive of promoting the development of the edge computing industry. The ECC's White Paper released at the 2016 Edge Computing Industrial Summit, during the ECC's launch ceremony, emphasis on the ECC's future development.

Different edge computing solutions for IoT are being proposed. The emerging solutions are Cloudlet, Mobile Edge Computing, Fog Computing and Edge Cloud. Figure 1 illustrates the edge computing paradigm. Based on the IoT applications, the data can be processed at the device or at the gateway level. For the applications that are sensitive to latency can apply Cloudlet or Edge cloud solutions. Mobile Edge Computing (Hu et al., 2015) unlocks services to consumers and enterprise customers as well as to adjacent industries that are engrossed in mission-critical applications over the mobile network. It facilitates a new value chain, fresh business opportunities and a countless applications across multiple sectors. Fog computing is useful for new paradigms in medical data analysis and remote health monitoring, where there is a requirement for immediate analysis of data (Klonoff & David, 2017).

Figure 1. Edge computing paradigm

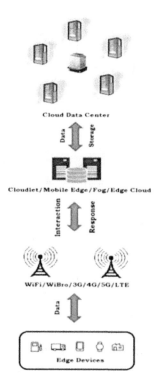

The edge cloud places compute capabilities at the edge of the network, to decrease latency and to optimize the use of network resources. Edge cloud resources serve new applications, such as virtual reality, augmented reality and autonomous driving. This chapter opens up the opportunities, benefits and challenges of Edge Cloud.

VISION OF EDGE CLOUD

The current industries demand, efficient computing to be performed in smaller devices using less expensive and powerful processors. Small data analytics has to be performed at the device level for the improved machine intelligence (as cited in ge, n.d). Edge cloud moves analytics and custom business logic to devices so that the organization can focus on business insights instead of data management. The IoT device can detect the anomaly and respond to emergencies as quickly as possible (as cited in Microsoft, 2018). In the same way data cleaning and aggregation can be performed locally to avoid terabytes of raw data being transferred to cloud. Thus reducing the bandwidth cost and only important insights can be forwarded to cloud. Irrespective of the applications, whether it is health care, economic models, business processes, Media and Broadcasters, Software and Device Manufacturers, Retail and Ecommerce, Gaming, warning of events or failures must be identified and resolved. The energy and cost are to be optimized and the future opportunities have to be forecasted. Here the edge cloud come into the picture to Monitor or analyze and perform the necessary actions. The role of Edge Cloud is depicted in Figure 2. The inspiration behind the Edge Cloud is to place the resources such as computing power, storage and network devices in the environs of the end users which serve the real time applications. For example,

1. The traffic monitoring and navigation system can report traffic data for route maintenance of a specific region in a smart city.
2. The content & data filtering and aggregation can be performed at edge before sending it to cloud to reduce the data volume being transferred to Cloud.
3. In time sensitive applications like augmented reality and health monitoring systems, faster responses can be produced using edge nodes, thereby user experience for time-sensitive applications can be improved (Bilal et al., 2018).

Figure 2. Role of edge computing paradigm

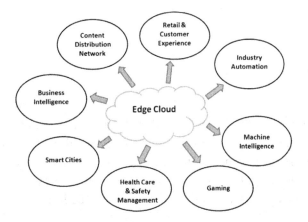

Definition

Edge computing is an emerging field. Various definitions were given by different researchers. Nokia (as cited in Nokia,2018), Fastly (as cited in Fastly, 2018a), Apigee (as cited in apigee, n.d), Infradata (as cited in infradata, 2018), Ciena (as cited in ciena, 2018) and Limelight (as cited in limelight, 2018) the current leading edge cloud platform expresses *Edge Computing* as *Edge Cloud*. In this chapter, Edge cloud and Edge computing are used interchangeably. Santhosh Rao of Gartner (as cited in gartner, 2018) said that Organizations that have embarked on a digital business journey have realized that a more decentralized approach is required to address digital business infrastructure requirements. This perspective of Rao is reflected in the following *definition of edge computing*:

Edge computing is a set of solutions that facilitate data processing at or near the source of data generation. For example, in the context of the Internet of Things (IoT), the sources of data generation are usually things with sensors or embedded devices. Edge computing serves as the decentralized extension of the campus networks, cellular networks, data center networks or the cloud.

In the perspective of IoT, Edge Cloud can gather the available computing power near the edge devices and form micro data centers where local computing needs are fulfilled. With this idea, is highlighted in the definition of edge cloud by ECC (as cited in iotaustralia, 2017) in 2014.

Edge computing is performed on an open platform at the network edge near "things" or data sources, integrating network, computing, storage, and application core capabilities, and providing edge intelligent services. Edge computing meets the key requirements of agile connection, real-time services, data optimization, smart application, security, and privacy protection.

An Edge Cloud is used to decentralize processing power to the edges (clients/devices) of your networks (as cited in infradata, 2018). The data processing power of devices in the distributed systems reduce the burden of the cloud. The data is processed and analyzed at edges and then forwarded to the cloud. Thus, the influence of cloud and edge are fused to form Edge Cloud. For example, the connected cares are able to analyze data themselves instead of using a server's processing power. In Edge Cloud, the goal is to get higher performance and lower cost. For which location becomes a critical issue. Techniques such as Geo-analytics are used to place Edge Cloud Data Centers near the clusters of end-users or devices. Thus achieving Fast, reliable and secure edge cloud services for time-sensitive applications. Edge Cloud will not replace cloud rather it extend Cloud to the edges of the real time applications.

EDGE CLOUD SERVICES

Edge Cloud will have a greater impact in the ICT field in this decade. It can also influence the human life in all perspectives. Unlike Cloud Computing, edge cloud drives the intelligence, processing power and communication capabilities of an edge gateway or appliance directly into devices (as cited in ge, 2018), which stress on some specific needs like latency reduction, effective bandwidth, fast response time, less storage, near to the ground network congestion and low energy consumption. Based on these characteristics the Edge Cloud offers various services are depicted in Figure 3. The major services are

Application as a Service (AaaS), Network as a Service (NaaS) and Infrastructure as a Service (IaaS) (El-Sayed et al., 2018).

Different types of wireless networks like mobile ad-hoc networks (MANETs), vehicular ad-hoc networks (VANETs), the Internet of Things (IoT) and intelligent transport systems (ITSs) are currently being used by the user. Edge Cloud can incorporate these networks to mitigate network-related and computational problems at the edges. Sayed et. al. discussed the taxonomy shown in Figure 3 with this perspective.

Figure 3. Taxonomy of edge cloud services

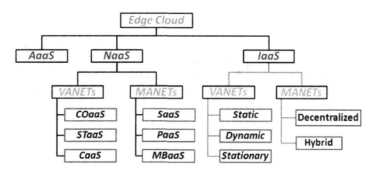

Application as a Service (AaaS)

This service helps the users for better interaction in real-time applications thus offering better Quality of Experience (QoE).

Network as Service (NaaS)

In many time-critical applications, the integration of VANETs and MANETs with Edge Cloud is crucial. This assimilation yields energy efficiency and avoids congestion in the transportation network. Thus, the services offered in NaaS, depend on the type of the network being used by the User. In VANETs, Computing as a Service (COaaS), Storage as a Service (STaaS) and Cooperation as a Service (CaaS) are feasible. Software as a Service (SaaS), Platform as a Service (PaaS) and Mobile backend as a Service (MBaaS) are viable under MANETs. STaaS Service is for small business applications that store cached data during transient time. Huge data storage is not possible and only temporary data can be used. Cooperation as a Service (CaaS)/ Collaborative edge can combine geographically distributed data by creating virtualized data views for the users, to reduce operational cost and to improve profitability (shi et al., 2016).

Infrastructure as a Service (IaaS)

VANETs are able to provide all three (Static, Dynamic & Stationary) services. In case of MANETs, dynamic IaaS is offered via decentralized, Stationary IaaS by means of Hybrid approach. But static IaaS is not applicable for Edge Cloud.

The various Edge Cloud Services are listed in Table 1.

Table 1. Edge cloud services

Type of Service	Edge Cloud Provider	Description
COaaS	Azure IoT Edge (as cited in Microsoft, 2018)	• Allow to deploy complex Artificial Intelligence activities like event processing, machine learning and image recognition using the Azure IoT edge.
	Predix Edge (GE Digital) (as cited in ge, 2018)	• It is an IIoT computing platform positioned at the intersection of industrial control systems and the enterprise. • The user can Collect data from assets and Information & communication Technology (IT) / Operational Technology(OT) sources, apply local machine learning analytics, Execute container-based applications, Securely and reliably forward data to Predix Cloud. • It has a secured stack with embedded OS and easily configurable and manageable edge devices and workloads
	Limelight Edge (as cited in limelight, 2018)	• Provides Flexible compute options where user can either rent compute resources as with cloud-based models or they can use their own hardware as with co-location models. • Organizations can easily focus building their business rather than building out a network by using the benefits of a private, high performance Limelight Edge Cloud
	Nebula (Ryden et al., 2014)	• This lightweight architecture enables the distributed data intensive computing services by optimizing location-aware data, computation placement, replication, and recovery.
	Nokia & Intel (as cited in Nokia Solutions and Networks, 2013, 2018)	• Helps in driving the implementation of Cloud RAN and Multi-access Edge Computing (MEC) using the distributing computing capacity in the network.
SaaS	Ciena (as cited in ciena, 2018)	• Blue Planet software of Ciena enables AI-enabled analytics for real-time resource sharing environments. • Orchestrates services and virtualization functions that facilitate the enhancement for real time applications.
NaaS	Infradata (as cited in infradata, 2018)	• Provides advanced container networking, security, and service chaining to users by extending their network capabilities. • The user can deploy, manage, and monetise new low-latency services such as IoT and connected cars closer to their end users. • It also provides an important foundation for 5G network.
	Fastly Edge Cloud platform (as cited in Wikipedia, 2014)	• Offers a content delivery network, Internet security services, load balancing, and video & streaming services.
PaaS	Apigee Edge (as cited in apigee, n.d)	• platform for developing and managing API proxies. • Provides value-added features like security, rate limiting, quotas, analytics, and more.
	Azure IoT Edge (as cited in Microsoft, 2018)	• offers services both for Linux and Windows • supports Java, .NET Core 2.0, Node.js, C, and Python • The developers can code in a known language and use existing business logic without writing it from scratch.

EDGE CLOUD REFERENCE MODEL

The key technologies like Big Data, machine learning, and deep learning are used in applications such as speech recognition, image recognition, and user profiling, and they progressed in terms of algorithms, models, and architectures. Engineering sectors such as manufacturing, power, healthcare, agriculture and transportation have begun to adapt these technologies, which has created new requirements and challenges. This epoch will be an industry intelligence era. It requires four important key industry transformations. They are:

- Integrated collaboration of the physical world and the digital world
- Renovation from vague experience-based decision-making to scientific decision-making based on digitalization and modeling
- Conversion from process separation to full-process collaboration
- Transformation from independent innovation of enterprises to multiparty open innovation in an industry environment.

Over the past decade, the computing, storage and network domains grew exponentially in terms of technical and economic viability. With the influence of these domains, Edge Cloud enables the industry needs by means of Smart gateways, Smart systems, Smart services and Smart assets. Hence, the Edge cloud development service framework must closely collaborate with the deployment and operation service framework to support efficient development, automatic deployment, and centralized operation of solutions. The ECC (as cited in ecconsortium, 2017) discussed that Edge Cloud must provide a "CROSS" value i.e. Mass and Heterogeneous Connection, Real-Time Services, Data Optimization, Smart Applications, Security and Privacy Protection. Based on the above concepts, the ECC proposed a Edge Computing Reference Architecture 2.0 shown in Figure 4. The different layers in Edge computing reference architecture 2.0 are Smart Service, Service Fabric, Connectivity and Computing Fabric(CCF) and Edge Computing Node (ECN).

Figure 4. Edge computing reference architecture 2.0

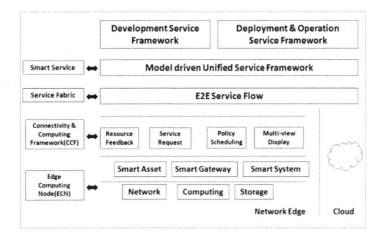

Smart Services

This layer is based on the model-driven unified service framework. The development service framework yields smart coordination between service development and deployment and deployment & operation service framework. These frameworks enable reliable software development interfaces and automatic deployment and operations.

Service Fabric

This orchestration defines the Edge to Edge (E2E) service flow through the service fabric (SF) to realize service agility.

Connectivity and Computing Fabric (CCF)

The CCF enables a simplified architecture. The CCF also enables automatic and visualized deployment and operations of the OT & IT infrastructure, supporting coordination between edge computing resource services and service needs of industries.

Edge Computing Node (ECN)

ECNs support real-time processing, response & deliver, integrated hardware and software security with a variety of heterogeneous connections.

This Edge Computing Reference Architecture 2.0 is framed based on the Guide lines given by international standards defined by ISO/IEC/IEEE 42010:2011. Edge Computing Reference Architecture 2.0 can be explained using the following views:

Concept View

The Concept view provides ICT resources such as networks, computing, and storage, and can be logically abstracted as Edge Computing Nodes (ECNs). This architecture defines four types of ECN development frameworks for different application scenarios of ECNs. Each framework comprises of an operating system, functional modules, and integrated development environment which satisfy the requirements of various scenarios. Suitable combination of ECN development frameworks with the specific hardware platform required by ECNs, six types of products are proposed. They are Embedded controller, Independent controller, Terminal perception, Smart gateway, Edge distributed gateway and Edge distributed server.

Function View

This view describes the functions and design concepts in three different layers, namely, deployment and operation framework Service Fabric (SF), Connection and Computing Fabric (CCF), and ECN based physical architecture. Through these layers, Resource awareness, Edge Virtualization Function (EVF) awareness, workload scheduling, data collaboration and multi-view display functionalities can be achieved. This view also provides cross-layer open services, management services, lifecycle data services, and security services.

Deployment View

The Deployment view portrays two types of models, three-layer deployment model and four-layer deployment model. The three-layer model is relevant to situations where the volume of traffic is low and services are deployed in one or more scattered areas in decentralized manner. The areas such as smart street lamps, smart elevators, and smart environmental protection can adopt this model. In case of the four-layer model, the services are deployed centrally and the traffic volume is high. Smart video analysis, distributed grid, and smart manufacturing are some of the sites where the four-layer model can be deployed.

CHARACTERISTICS AND BENEFITS

When the goal is on the spot analysis of data followed by instantaneous generation of a rules-based command (Klonoff & David, 2017), Edge computing could potentially be preferable to fog computing due to fewer potential failure points. Each sensor or device in the network would be independently programmed to decide the type of information that should be stored locally and the data that need to be sent to the cloud for further use. The following characteristics of Edge Cloud have made it possible (El-Sayed et al., 2018).

- **Low Latency:** Aids in time critical events occur in Healthcare applications
- **Very Low Bandwidth Utilization:** Support multiple devices to access the edge at the same time.
- **Low Response Time:** Improves the data analytics and there by the overall performance of real-time applications.
- **Less Storage:** Less storage allows only the needed data is to be kept in the edge and other data are pushed to the cloud.
- **Very Low Service Overhead:** The decentralized processing and distributed computing lessen the service overhead.
- **Low Energy Consumption:** The low bandwidth usage ensures the low energy consumption.
- **Low Network Congestion:** By using backhaul links, and distributed computing the network traffic is alleviated.
- **High Scalability:** By increasing virtualization, the scalability is improved.
- **High Quality of Service (QoS) and Quality of Experience (QoE):** By minimizing the data transfer distance the QoS and QoE are enhanced.

Edge computing saves time and money by streamlining IoT communication, reducing system and network architecture complexity, and decreasing the number of potential failure points in an IoT application. Reducing system architecture complexity is key to the success of IIoT applications.

CHALLENGES AHEAD

Edge Cloud Computational Offloading

It is reported that during a period of one minute, YouTube users upload 43,33,560 videos, Amazon ships 1,111 packages, Twitter users share 4,73,400 photos, Instagram users post 49, 380 new photos, and Vine users share 8333 videos (as cited in domo, n.d). Usually, when a video or photo is uploaded, it is subjected to lossy compression to reduce the media size. Uploading the high resolution photos and videos from user devices need lots of bandwidth and it degrades the Edge performance in the poor internet connectivity areas. Similar concerns arise in live health monitoring applications, or smart city applications where live streams of data from surveillance cameras and other sensors needs to be uploaded to cloud (Bilal et al., 2018). Owing to the flooding of data, big data mining / Hierarchical data mining techniques (Peng et al., 2018) can be applied at the edge devices, to lessen the burden on the fronthaul / backhaul while transmitting large volume of data to the Cloud. But the characteristics of Edge like less storage and quick response time compel for advanced data mining algorithms that are to be proposed.

Empowered Distributed System

The massive rise of personal computing devices introduces human-centered applications that reduce the boundaries between man and machine. For example, in the applications like crowd sensing, humen are introduced in the data-analysis loop. This brings in the challenge of designing an innovative socially-informed architecture where the information provided by the users must be hold in a secure way (Lopez, 2015). In healthcare applications, users act as a sensor and become an important source of data, which can be applied in learning algorithms and visualization tools. The Edge Cloud architecture must apply adaptive distributed systems to analysis the user behaviors depending on their location or context. It will also handle the interaction with other humans through their available connected devices. This poses serious challenges to the distributed systems. Edge cloud is based on a decentralized model that interconnects heterogeneous cloud resources controlled by a variety of entities. A fresh combination of overlay technologies with cloud resources may create another challenge.

Resource Management

Resource management is a key challenge in time critical and real-time systems. Edge cloud has to dynamically allocate resources for delay sensitive tasks. Hence priority-aware computation is required in Edge cloud (Bilal et al., 2018). As Edge cloud is an emerging arena, simple architectures are proposed for resource management. Based on the number of users and their demands, provisioning of the resources is to be made by the edge node. The Edge cloud has to choose an appropriate edge node depending on certain parameters. They are node's capacity and the proximity of the node from the user and the communication & computation resources among competing users. These parameters must also focus in energy conservation and quality of service. This state of affairs necessitates novel optimizing algorithms to address efficient resource management.

Energy Efficiency

Generally, the end devices and IoT nodes involved in the Edge Cloud are constrained by computing capabilities, battery life, and heat dissipation. Energy consuming application running in the user devices are to be offloaded to the Edge Cloud for energy consumption (Mahmud et al., 2018). While concentrating on energy consumption, the computation delay due to offload has to be tolerated. The factors that influence the energy consumptions are (i) end user device accessing the service (ii) energy consumed by internal network, storage, and servers (iii) the volume of traffic exchanged between the user and cloud (iv) the computational complexity of the task to be performed and (v) factors such as the number of users sharing a computer source (Bilal et al., 2018). However, energy can be saved by employing intelligent client-side caching techniques, and optimizing the synchronization frequency of contents between Edge Cloud and IoT devices. The optimization algorithms that minimize the additional energy wastage and Green edge cloud architecture can be applied to address this key issue.

Security and Privacy

The enabling technologies of Edge Cloud, namely, wireless networks, distributed systems, IoT and virtualization platform enforce the security and privacy issues. These technologies must provide secure communication during integration and interoperation of the devices. As the IoT devices are lightweight, Edge cloud must provide a middleware to secure data that is send out to the internet or Cloud. Also most of the end users are not aware of privacy and security issues. So an automatic mechanism ensuring security and privacy of the user data must be imposed (Bilal et al., 2018). Generally, end to end encryption is followed in Edge Cloud. For more secure communication, re-encryption, quality based encryption or attribute based encryption can also be exploited. The Edge Cloud has to identify the malicious nodes and trusted nodes while data is transmitted between nodes. Secure routing, redundant routing and trusted topologies (Lopez, 2015) are utilized to maintain integrity. Sensitive data protection is ensured by applying fragmentation of information with encryption joined with decentralized overlay technologies. Another solution for privacy protection is that the owner of the data must be given full control over the data that is used by the service providers (shi et al., 2016). Security in Edge Cloud not only comprise of data security, it also includes device security, network security and application security.

Data Abstraction

The IoT devices connected to the Edge Cloud generated huge amount of data. Handling the huge data by the devices or transmitting the raw data directly to the Cloud is the challenging process. Hence, Data abstraction (preprocessing, filtering and restructuring the raw data) (Bilal et al., 2018) can be performed at the Edge. There are a number of challenges in this process. First, the data collected from different devices are in diverse format. The privacy and security concerns may affect the applications accessing the raw data. Consequently increases the complexity level of entire data abstraction. Secondly, too much of data filtering may not provide useful knowledge, at the same time, less filtering challenge for storage. Thirdly, data collected from low precision sensor, hazard environment and unreliable connections may produce unreliable data (shi et al., 2016).

Fault Tolerance and Quality of Service

Another significant confront is QoS and Fault tolerance. The Edge Cloud is primarily utilized by the real time applications. So, automatic fault recovery may improve the QoS of the Edge Cloud. Therefore, in peak hours efficient task partitioning and scheduling mechanism are to be employed (Bilal et al., 2018). In Collaborative edge, the user data has to be cached in multiple edge nodes for better service. This amplifies the traffic among the participating nodes. Thus, best possible data placement, replication guidelines are to be designed to reduce the traffic and for better QoS.

EDGE COMPUTING PARADIGMS

Different architectures have been proposed to appreciate edge computing platforms. Currently there are four paradigms in Edge computing that serve the IoT applications. They are Cloudlet (Peng et al., 2018), Mobile Edge Computing (MEC)(Hu et al., 2015), Fog Computing (Dastjerdi et al., 2016) and

Edge Cloud (Chang et al., 2014). Based on the applications and the service request of the users, any one of the four models can be used by the edge computing ecosystem.

Cloudlet

The term Cloudlet is coined by a team at Carnegie Mellon University (CMU). A cloudlet is a trusted, resource-rich computer or cluster of computers that are well-connected to the internet and available for use by nearby mobile devices (Peng et al., 2018). The cloudlets provide powerful computing resources to mobile devices that are needed by the resource-intensive and interactive mobile applications. The mobile devices involved in the edge computing can access the cloudlet for computing resources through wireless local area network. The three layers in this architecture are mobile device layer, cloudlet layer and the cloud layer. Cloudlets are more responsive and dynamic in its provisioning as it is the needed for any mobile devices. The mobile devices have to discover, select, and associate with the appropriate cloudlet among multiple candidates before it starts provisioning. To support user mobility from one location to another, Virtual Machine(VM) handoff technology are to be used for offloading the services from one cloudlet to the another cloudlet.

Figure 5. Dynamic VM synthesis

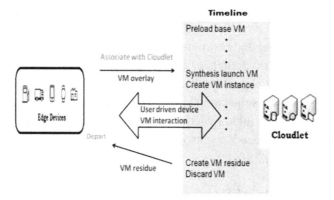

The edge devices communicate to the cloudlet for the service. The customized VM called VM overlay is received from the devices. The cloudlet has to convert the basic VM to custom VM to satisfy the user request. The process of using VM overlays to provisioning cloudlets is called VM synthesis. This procedure (Peng et al., 2018) is explained in Figure 5. The mobile devices at the edge send the VM overlay. The cloudlet decompresses the overlay, applies it to the base VM to derive the launched VM, and then creates a VM instance from it. The mobile device performs the offload operations at this instance. At the end of the session, the instance is destroyed, but the launched VM image can be retained in a persistent cache for future sessions. To retain some training data for future offload sessions, the cloudlet generates a VM residue that can be sent back to the mobile device and incorporated into its overlay. This is a potential technique for enabling user mobility with low end-to-end latency application. The Cloudlets support and enables many exciting mobile applications that are both compute-intensive and latency-sensitive (Satyanarayanan et al., 2015a). In wearable cognitive assistance, to improve the end-to-end latency and real-time interaction Cloudlet is implemented (Ha et al., 2014). Cloudlets act as a cloud during its unavailability due to failure or cyber attacks to improve the reliability (Satyanarayanan et al., 2013, 2015b). Remote access of desktop window-based applications is also feasible with Cloudlets.

Mobile Edge Computing (MEC)

The ETSI Industry Specification Group (ISG) on Mobile Edge Computing (MEC) launched in December 2014, is a new emerging technology designed to push resources closer to the radio access networks in 4G and 5G (Hu et al., 2015). The "Mobile Edge Computing" is renamed as "Multi-Access Edge Computing" in 2017 by the ETSI MEC industry group to reflect the significance of MEC. The Mobile Edge Computing is characterized by low latency, proximity, high bandwidth, and real-time insight into radio network information and location awareness (Hu et al., 2015). MEC offer services to consumers and enterprise customers in delivering their mission-critical applications at a location considered to be a rewarding point over the mobile network (Beck et al., 2014) . MEC is used in Video acceleration, augmented reality, connected vehicles, IoT analytics, enterprise services, network performance and utilization optimization, retail, and eHealth.

Figure 6. RACs architecture

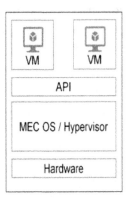

MEC servers are deployed next to base stations: they are co-hosted with base stations and are directly linked to them. MEC servers are equipped with commodity hardware, i.e. usual server CPUs, memory, and communication interfaces. In 2014, Nokia Networks introduced a very first real-world MEC platform Radio Applications Cloud Servers (RACS) represent real manifestation of MEC servers shown in Figure 6 (Beck et al., 2014). MEC servers are co-hosted with base stations and are directly linked to them. MEC servers are equipped with server CPUs, memory, and communication interfaces. Cloud technology and virtualization enable the application deployment. RACS also have a VM hypervisor for the deployment of VM images running MEC applications. VMs and RACS platform communicate with each other by means of a message bus. VMs send heartbeat messages to the RACS system as a self-monitoring service. If heartbeat messages are not sent by the VM, the hypervisor will reboot the VM, ensuring that the VM is automatically reinitialized after some applications crashed. To secure the VMs from malicious offenders, before deployment VMs have to be signed and it is verified by the operator. VMs communicate mobile devices with a specific destination address or port number. Based on the application type, additional header information is included to HTTP requests consisting of network-specific information, which is not accessible to ASP services in traditional cellular networks. The forwarding and filtering rulesets for traffic routed through MEC servers are defined by Mobile network operators. Based on both privacy concerns and application providers' demands, these rulesets specify which data are sent to which type of application. In accordance with the subscriptions, mobile traffic is routed through the VMs. Some of the applications of MEC include content scaling, edge content delivery, augmentation, aggregation, local connectivity and offloading (Beck et al., 2014).

Fog Computing

Fog computing as a distributed computing paradigm that fundamentally extends the services provided by the cloud to the edge of the network (Dastjerdi et al., 2016). Bonomi et. al. define Fog Computing as a highly virtualized platform that provides compute, storage, and networking services between end devices and traditional Cloud Computing Data Centers, typically, but not exclusively located at the edge of network (Bonomi et al., 2012). The characteristics of Fog computing are scaling computing resources, support for user mobility, communication protocols, interface heterogeneity, cloud integration, and distributed data analytics to addresses requirements of low latency applications that are geographically distributed. The application of Fog computing is preferred when reduction in network traffic, low latency requirement and scalability are the users' concern. At the same time, it is also more suitable for IoT tasks and queries processing. The Fog architecture (Dastjerdi et al, 2016) is shown in Figure 7.

Figure 7. Fog architecture

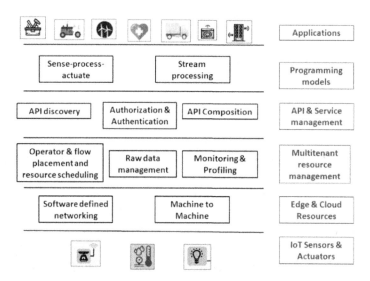

The data from the sensors and actuators in a heterogeneous network is managed by efficient Software defined network. Edge and cloud resources communicate using machine-to-machine standards such as MQTT (formerly MQ Telemetry Transport) and the Constrained Application Protocol. The tasks from different users are prioritized by resource management layer in multitenant applications. The monitoring component in the resource management layer tracks the state of the fog resources and chooses the best resource for the incoming task. In the API service management layer, APIs needed for the complex functionalities are decided dynamically. Applications running on the fog devices obtain insights from the stream data of the devices and the action to be taken are translated & sent to the actuators. This process is performed with the help of the sense-process-actuate and stream processing programming model in the fog architecture. Fog computing is more suitable for Healthcare and activity tracking, Smart utility services, Augmented reality, cognitive systems, and gaming.

Edge Cloud

A compute or storage node attached to the edge network and associated to the data center cloud is called Edge node. Edge Zone is formed by grouping together the Edge nodes in the same edge network. The Edge Cloud (Chang et al., 2014) is the association of the data center nodes along with all the edge zones. The Edge Cloud operator can extend the traditional cloud's IaaS capabilities to install applications in the Edge cloud with the pre-existing cloud functionalities. The Edge Cloud architecture (Chang et al., 2014) is shown in Figure 8.

Figure 8. Edge cloud architecture

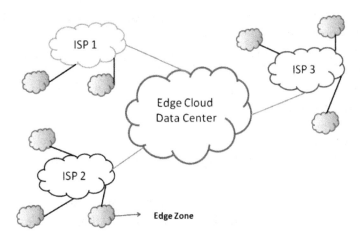

The Edge Cloud services are offered through Edge Apps for mobile devices and smart IoT devices. An Edge app is a package of IaaS images designed to initiate and work together in agreement with data centers and edge nodes. It consists of two types of compute instances. One type of compute instances run in the data center and other type in the edge zone of the edge owner. There are different form of IaaS images in each type of compute instance, which can be replicated. In virtual networks, there are two types. They are App-Private network and Edge-Local network. The App-Private network is instantiated to interconnect all instances of each Edge App at the launch. The Edge-Local network establishes the communication of the Edge App with end users and resources in the edge network. Chang (2014) discussed two Edge apps, 3D indoor Localization Application and Video Surveillance Application.

ENABLING TECHNOLOGIES OF EDGE CLOUD

Edge Cloud is realized with the existing as well as emerging technologies. They are Virtualization, Network Function Virtualization (NFV), Software Defined Networking (SDN), Network Slicing and Computation offloading (Taleb et al., 2017a, Premsankar et al., 2018). These technologies play a key role in the development of edge computing platforms.

Virtualization

Virtualization is a key technology for Cloud computing. Using virtualization multiple independent software instances can run on a single physical server. All these instances access the underlying physical resources without interfering with other instances (isolation) running on the same server. The software abstraction layer called hypervisor, the intermediate between the VMs and physical hardware directs the VMs to use the underlying CPU, storage and network resources. On top of the host server OS, the VM runs its own guest operating system. This technique is best suited for mult-tenancy but the presence of hypervisor invites non-negligible overhead. To overcome this overhead, Container-based virtualization has been proposed as a light-weight alternative.

In case of Container-based virtualization, the virtualized instances use the underlying host OS, instead of using their own guest OS. To guarantee isolation between containers, modifications are made to the OS. The container-based virtualization reduces instance start time and hence results in better performance. To support mobility, an important characteristic for the Edge Cloud, migration techniques are applied. Moving computing resources from one physical server to the other is called migration. The migration technique helps in energy consumption also. Live migration is a practice that reduces the time during which a virtual instance is not accessible as it is being moved from one server to another, which is vital in case of IoT applications. The virtualization forms the basis for Network Function Virtualization and Software Defined Networking.

Network Function Virtualization

NFV (Premsankar et al., 2018) involves the implementation of network functions as software modules that can run on general purpose hardware. NFV utilize the virtualization technologies and establishes Virtualized Network Functions (VNF). The NFV architecture has three domains (Taleb et al., 2017a):

1. VNF
2. NFV Infrastructure (NFVI)
3. NFV Management and Orchestration (NFV MANO)

NFVI is a package of the hardware and software components (CPU, storage, virtualization layer) that offer the network environment where VNFs can be installed. VNFs are software implementation of network functions. NFV MANO organizes and manages the physical and virtual resources of the NFVI and is responsible for the lifecycle management of VNFs. In MEC, VNFs enable the mobility, scalability and migration. With this technique, no dedicated hardware is needed. Hence, it is suited for efficient delivery of mobile applications and services. Portability, Network slicing, Federation support and on-demand access of pooled resources are other benefits of employing NFV in Edge Cloud.

Software Defined Networking

SDN is a technology that supports network programmability and multi-tenancy for fast deployment of innovative services at the edge of the network. By utilizing common APIs, SDNs have a logical centralized control which separates data plane from control plane and offer virtual network instances, by abstracting the underlying network infrastructure. By linking VNFs and MEC services, SDN offer a dynamic service provisioning. This satisfies the performance demand of the users at the edge by exploiting the network infrastructure. Using the concept of re-routing or changing the codec scheme of wireless microwave links, SDN overcome the routing challenges connected with IP address translation, large volume of control signaling, tunneling overhead and dynamic resource management. SDN converts the proprietary firmware-based network switches and routers forming a simple data plane, which can be controlled at the opening and outlet points of the network.

Network Slicing

Network slicing (NS) is dividing one network into multiple instances, each architected and optimized for a specific requirement of specific application or service (Taleb et al., 2017a). The network hypervisor in NS allocates the shared resources such as bandwidth, network functions, storage and access to big data or RAN analytics necessary for the tenant. The resource isolation and customization support the operation of Mobile Edge computing. It is utilized by the Personalized Mobile Telecom (Taleb et al., 2017b) and grabbing the attention of Mobile Network Alliance (NGMN), Third Generation Partnership Project (3GPP), and International Telecommunication Union — Telecommunication Standardization Sector (ITU-T). The potential benefits of NS fetch fully personalized and scalable end-to-end mobile connection service and easy, efficient access to advanced mobile services.

Computation Offloading

Computation offloading (Taleb et al., 2017) is a process where a resource constrained mobile device offloads a computation-intensive task to a resource-sufficient cloud environment. Computation offloading is carried out to save energy, battery lifetime or in case where the end device is unable to process a computation-heavy application. The computation offloading methods used by the mobile cloud computing environment are Cyber foraging (Balan et al. 2002) and CloneCloud (Chun et al., 2011). In video services, the compute-intensive encoding part can be offloaded. In the same way, in M2M, wearables and other IoT devices, splitting the compute-intensive application and offloading only the data-intensive part to the edge can be performed. In mobile gaming, by offloading the rendering part from mobile devices, gaming becomes more interactive with quick responses.

EDGE CLOUD ENVIRONMENT

Apigee Edge

Apigee Edge is a platform for developing and managing API proxies. The app developers who need backend services are the primary consumers (as cited in apigee, n.d). A company that want to expose services that provide product pricing and availability information, sales and ordering services, order tracking services, and any other services required by client apps can adopt Apigee Edge. Apigee Edge is built on Java. It enables a secure access to the services with a well-defned API that is consistent across all services, regardless of service implementation. A consistent API provides the following benefits:

- Makes it easy for app developers to consume company services.
- Provision to change the backend service implementation without affecting the public API.
- Provides additional features like analytics, monetization and developer portal that are built into Edge.

The Apigee Edge forms a layer between the client apps and backend service provider. To consume the backend services, the app developers, access an API proxy created on Edge. Thus the Edge handle the security and authorization tasks required to protect the services, as well as to analyze, monitor and monetize those services.

Limelight Networks' Edge Cloud Services

Limelight Networks' edge cloud services (as cited in limelight, 2018) offer networking solutions that allow organizations to concentrate on scaling their businesses instead of extending the underlying infrastructure. The services provided by Limelight are

- **Private managed network backbone:** Limelight's private network is one of the world's largest network that allows data to bypass the public internet and travel at high speed across the globe securely and reliably. Limelight's components ensure industry leading performance consistently, throughput the world.
- **Connections to all the last-mile providers:** Limelight provides businesses with one-hop connectivity to more than 900 global ISPs by leveraging over greater than 80 Points of Presence(PoPs). Irrespective of the users' connectivity (fixed broadband, wireless, or even emerging 5G connections) Limelight brings computing as close as possible to reduce latency.
- **Data centers at the edge:** Compute services offered by Limelight allows the customers to either rent compute resources in Limelight's data centers or deploy their own hardware. In addition to managing all aspects of data center operations for customers, Limelight ensures fulfillment of regional data autonomy regulations.

Nokia AirFrame Open Edge Infrastructure

In April 2018, Nokia has launched the industry's first Edge Cloud data center solution "Nokia AriFrame" (as cited in Nokia, 2018) to meet the diverse low latency data processing demands of Cloud RAN and advanced applications for consumers and industries. The Nokia AirFrame open edge cloud infrastructure is designed to deliver a layered network architecture that optimizes performance and operator costs for 5G era, the next generation wireless technology. This open edge infrastructure offers

- A Cloud data center solution, based on x86, designed to support edge cloud deployments.

- An edge server with the dimension 133.5 x 444 x 430mm (HWD), can be installed at existing base station sites.
- The hardware acceleration capabilities for 4G and 5G functions and applications are also offered by the AirFrame open edge server combined with Nokia ReefShark. It includes Cloud RAN and artificial intelligence (AI).
- The edge cloud with low latency along with AirFrame supports the acceleration of key machine learning and AI workloads.
- Nokia's real-time Open platform for NFV (OPNFV) which is compatible with cloud infrastructure software delivers high-performance demands of operators and applications in an edge environment.

Fastly

In 2017, Fastly edge cloud platform (as cited in Fastly, 2018b) delivers three new services Web Application Firewall (WAF), Image Optimizer and Load Balancer.

- **Web Application Firewall:** Fastly's web application firewall protects customers' applications from malicious attacks. It also protects against injection attacks, cross site scripting and HTTP protocol violations. WAF is continuously updated to address ongoing threats using multiple rule-sets. Rules can be configured in real time via Fastly's API, and can run in active blocking mode or passive logging mode only
- **Image Optimizer:** The Fastly Image Optimizer, manipulates and delivers real-time images to on-line users irrespective of their geographic location. It images dispensed by the optimizer are pixel-perfect, bandwidth-efficient and device-specific images. The Fastly's network, avoids manual optimization by adopting the offloading optimization logic at the edge and offers pre-processed images across varying devices, browsers and resolutions.
- **Load Balancer:** Today, Service providers have to plan ahead to deliver consistently exceptional, scalable experiences. Hence they use multiple active data centers, a multi-cloud strategy or a combination of both. Fastly's cloud-based Load Balancer optimizes traffic distribution across a powerful network for scalability and high availability.

StreetSmart Edge

StreetSmart Edge (as cited in StreetSmart, 2012) is "Inspired Trading, By Design." The platform focuses on the trader's workflow. It provides a robust trading experience in a user friendly way. With the StreetSmart customer can keep track of their gains and losses, and monitor their balances real-time. Additionally, there is a provision to access streaming quotes and real-time charting. User can specify Market Limit, Stop Limit, Trailing Stop and Trailing Stop Limit orders. It also allows the user to add a bracket to the primary order or filled order and option orders, depending on the option approval level.

Chart pattern recognition in StreetSmart Edge with a third party program from Recognia, support user in decision making by automating pattern recognition of more than 60 chart patterns, indicators and standard oscillators. Users can set up custom screens and email alerts, and monitor realtime technical analysis.

Azure IoT Edge

Azure IoT Edge (as cited in Microsoft, 2018) shifts cloud analytics and custom business logic to IoT devices. It helps the user to configure their IoT software and deploy it to devices using standard containers and monitor it all from the cloud. Azure IoT Edge is made up of three components:

- Azure services, 3rd party services, or customer own code are executed in IoT Edge modules using container technique. They are installed in IoT Edge devices and executed locally on those devices.
- The modules deployed in each IoT device is managed by the IoT Edge runtime environment.
- Remote monitoring and management of IoT Edge devices is performed by a cloud-based interface.

SUMMARY

Due to the innovation of various gadgets, more and more IoT devices are used in the area of public safety, transport, and healthcare. With the aim of providing better solution, new technologies, standards and policies are being proposed by leading industries. IoT applications generate large volume of data and they need rapid response. Owing to the characteristics such as less storage, short battery life, the IoT devices are not suited for storing and processing the huge data produced at the edge. The conventional cloud computing is unable to face the challenge. The enabling technologies like virtualization, software defined networks, computational offloading realized the existence of Edge Cloud Computing. Thus allowing the computational process to happen at the proximity of the edge and reduce the workload of the Cloud. Based on the requirement of the IoT applications, the edge computing technologies like, Cloudlet, Fog, Mobile Edge Computing and Edge Cloud can be adopted. The vision and services provided by Edge computing are elaborated in this chapter. The benefits of implementing edge cloud and the challenges faced are enlightened. The solutions like Limelight Network's Edge Cloud, Apigee Edge, Nokia AirFrame Open edge infrastructure and Azure IoT Edge magnetize the IoT applications as well as open new research challenges.

REFERENCES

Ai, Y., Peng, M., & Zhang, K. (2018). Edge computing technologies for Internet of Things: A primer. *Digital Communications and Networks, 4*(2), 77–86. doi:10.1016/j.dcan.2017.07.001

Ashton, K. (2009). That 'Internet of Things' thing: In the real world, things matter more than ideas. *RFID Journal.* Retrieved from http://www.rfidjournal.com/articles/view?4986

Balan, R., Flinn, J., Satyanarayanan, M., Sinnamohideen, S., & Hen-I., Y. (2002). The case for cyber foraging. *Proceedings of the 10th workshop on ACM SIGOPS European workshop*, 87-92. 10.1145/1133373.1133390

Beck, M. T., Werner, M., Feld, S., & Schimper, S. (2014). Mobile edge computing: A taxonomy. *Proc. of the Sixth International Conference on Advances in Future Internet*, 48-55.

Bilal, K., Khalid, O., Erbad, A., & Khan, S. U. (2018). Potentials, trends, and prospects in edge technologies: Fog, cloudlet, mobile edge, and micro data centers. *Computer Networks*, *130*, 94–120. doi:10.1016/j.comnet.2017.10.002

Bonomi, F., Milito, R., Zhu, J., & Addepalli, S. (2012). *Fog Computing and its Role in the Internet of Things*. MCC Work. Mob. Cloud Comput.

Chang, H., Hari, A., Mukherjee, S., & Lakshman, T. V. (2014). Bringing the cloud to the edge. *Computer Communications Workshops (INFOCOM WKSHPS), 2014 IEEE Conference*, 346-351.

Chun, B.-G., Ihm, S., Maniatis, P., Naik, M., & Patti, A. (2011). Clonecloud: elastic execution between mobile device and cloud. *Proceedings of the sixth conference on Computer systems*, 301-314. 10.1145/1966445.1966473

Ciena. (2018). Retrieved from https://www.ciena.com/insights/what-is/What-is-Edge-Cloud.html

Cisco G. C. I. Forecast and Methodology 2016–2021. (2018). Retrieved from https://www.cisco.com/c/en/us/solutions/collateral/service-provider/global-cloud-index-gci/white-paper-c11-738085.html

Dastjerdi, Gupta, Calheiros, Ghosh, & Buyya. (2016). Fog computing: Principles, architectures, and applications. *Internet of Things*, 61-75.

Dastjerdi, A. V., & Buyya, R. (2016). Fog computing: Helping the Internet of Things realize its potential. *IEEE Computer Society*, *49*(8), 112–116. doi:10.1109/MC.2016.245

Data never sleeps 6.0. (2018). Retrieved from https://www.domo.com/assets/downloads/18_domo_data-never-sleeps-6+verticals.pdf

Edge A. (2018). Retrieved from https://docs.apigee.com/api-platform/get-started/what-apigee-edge#make-avail-web

Edge C. R. A. 2.0. (2017). Retrieved from http://en.ecconsortium.net/Uploads/file/20180328/1522232376480704.pdf

Edge Computing Driving New Outcomes from Intelligent Industrial Machines. (2018). Retrieved from https://www.ge.com/digital/sites/default/files/download_assets/Edge-Computing-Driving-New-Outcomes.pdf

Edge computing and IoT 2018 – when intelligence moves to the edge. (2018). Retrieved from https://www.i-scoop.eu/internet-of-things-guide/edge-computing-iot

Edge computing consortium. (2017). Retrieved from https://www.iotaustralia.org.au/wp-content/uploads/2017/01/White-Paper-of-Edge-Computing-Consortium.pdf

El-Sayed, H., Sankar, S., Prasad, M., Puthal, D., Gupta, A., Mohanty, M., & Lin, C.-T. (2018). Edge of things: The big picture on the integration of edge, IoT and the cloud in a distributed computing environment. *IEEE Access: Practical Innovations, Open Solutions*, *6*, 1706–1717. doi:10.1109/ACCESS.2017.2780087

Fastly. (2018). Retrieved from https://www.fastly.com/press/press-releases/fastly-builds-content-delivery-network-heritage-unveils-edge-cloud-platform

Fastly. (2018a). Retrieved from https://www.fastly.com/edge-cloud-platform

Fastly. (2018b). Retrieved from https://en.wikipedia.org/wiki/Fastly

Ha, K., Chen, Z., Hu, W., Richter, W., Pillai, P., & Satyanarayanan, M. (2014). Towards wearable cognitive assistance. *Proceedings of the 12th annual international conference on Mobile systems, applications, and services*, 68-81.

Hu, Y. C., Patel, M., Sabella, D., Sprecher, N., & Young, V. (2015). Mobile edge computing—A key technology towards 5G. *ETSI White Paper, 11*, 1-16.

Infradata. (2018). Retrieved from https://www.infradata.com/resources/what-is-edge-cloud

Klonoff, D. C. (2017). Fog computing and edge computing architectures for processing data from diabetes devices connected to the medical Internet of things. *Journal of Diabetes Science and Technology, 11*(4), 647–652. doi:10.1177/1932296817717007 PMID:28745086

Limelight. (2018). Retrieved from https://www.limelight.com/resources/data-sheet/edge-analytics

Lopez, G., Pedro, A. M., Epema, D., Datta, A., Higashino, T., Iamnitchi, A., ... Riviere, E. (2015). Edge-centric computing: Vision and challenges. *Computer Communication Review, 45*(5), 37–42. doi:10.1145/2831347.2831354

Mahmud, R., Kotagiri, R., & Buyya, R. (2018). Fog computing: A taxonomy, survey and future directions. In *Internet of everything*. Springer.

Microsoft Azure IoT Reference Architecture. (2018). Retrieved from http://download.microsoft.com/download/A/4/D/A4DAD253-BC21-41D3-B9D9-87D2AE6F0719/Microsoft_Azure_IoT_Reference_Architecture.pdf

Nokia. (2018). *The edge cloud: an agile foundation to support advanced new services*. Nokia White paper. Retrieved from https://onestore.nokia.com/asset/202184

Nokia launches industry-first Edge Cloud data center solution for the 5G era, supporting industry automation and consumer applications. (2018). Retrieved from https://www.nokia.com/about-us/news/releases/2018/04/25/nokia-launches-industry-first-edge-cloud-data-center-solution-for-the-5g-era-supporting-industry-automation-and-consumer-applications

Nokia Solutions and Networks, Increasing Mobile Operators' Value Proposition with Edge Computing. (2013). Retrieved from http://nsn.com/portfolio/liquid-net/intelligent-broadband-management/liquid-applications

Predix Edge – GE Digital. (2018). Retrieved from https://www.ge.com/digital/asset/predix-edge-ge-digital

Premsankar, G., Di Francesco, M., & Taleb, T. (2018). Edge computing for the Internet of Things: A case study. *IEEE Internet of Things Journal, 5*(2), 1275–1284. doi:10.1109/JIOT.2018.2805263

Ryden, M., Oh, K., Chandra, A., & Weissman, J. (2014). Nebula: Distributed edge cloud for data-intensive computing. *IEEE 2014 International Conference on "In Collaboration Technologies and Systems (CTS)"*, 491-492.

Satyanarayanan, M. (2017). The emergence of edge computing. *Computers & Society*, *50*(1), 30–39. doi:10.1109/MC.2017.9

Satyanarayanan, M., Lewis, G., Morris, E., Simanta, S., Boleng, J., & Ha, K. (2013). The role of cloudlets in hostile environments. *IEEE Pervasive Computing*, *12*(4), 40–49. doi:10.1109/MPRV.2013.77

Satyanarayanan, M., Schuster, R., Ebling, M., Fettweis, G., Flinck, H., Joshi, K., & Sabnani, K. (2015a). An open ecosystem for mobile-cloud convergence. *IEEE Communications Magazine*, *53*(3), 63–70. doi:10.1109/MCOM.2015.7060484

Satyanarayanan, M., Simoens, P., Xiao, Y., Pillai, P., Chen, Z., Ha, K., ... Amos, B. (2015b). Edge analytics in the internet of things. *IEEE Pervasive Computing*, *2*(2), 24–31. doi:10.1109/MPRV.2015.32

Shi, W., Cao, J., Zhang, Q., Li, Y., & Xu, L. (2016). Edge computing: Vision and challenges. *IEEE Internet of Things Journal*, *3*(5), 637–646. doi:10.1109/JIOT.2016.2579198

StreetSmart. (2018). Retrieved from http://help.streetsmart.schwab.com/edge/printablemanuals/Edge-Manual.pdf

Taleb, T., Mada, B., Corici, M.-I., Nakao, A., & Flinck, H. (2017b). PERMIT: Network slicing for personalized 5G mobile telecommunications. *IEEE Communications Magazine*, *55*(5), 88–93. doi:10.1109/MCOM.2017.1600947

Taleb, T., Samdanis, K., Mada, B., Flinck, H., Dutta, S., & Sabella, D. (2017a). On multi-access edge computing: A survey of the emerging 5G network edge cloud architecture and orchestration. *IEEE Communications Surveys and Tutorials*, *19*(3), 1657–1681. doi:10.1109/COMST.2017.2705720

The lifeline for a data driven world. (2018). Retrieved from https://www.happiestminds.com/Insights/internet-of-things

What Edge Computing Means for Infrastructure and Operations Leaders. (2018). Retrieved from https://www.gartner.com/smarterwithgartner/what-edge-computing-means-for-infrastructure-and-operations-leaders

Chapter 10
Innovative Concepts and Techniques of Data Analytics in Edge Computing Paradigms

Soumya K.
Kristu Jayanti College, India

Margaret Mary T.
 https://orcid.org/0000-0001-5756-266X
Kristu Jayanti College, India

Clinton G.
Sambhram Institute of Technology, India

EXECUTIVE SUMMARY

Edge analytics is an approach to data collection and analysis in which an automated analytical computation is performed on data at a sensor, network switch, or other device instead of waiting for the data to be sent back to a centralized data store. Cloud computing has revolutionized how people store and use their data; however, there are some areas where cloud is limited; latency, bandwidth, security, and a lack of offline access can be problematic. To solve this problem, users need robust, secure, and intelligent on-premise infrastructure for edge computing. When data is physically located closer to the users who connected to it, information can be shared quickly, securely, and without latency. In financial services, gaming, healthcare, and retail, low levels of latency are vital for a great digital customer experience. To improve reliability and faster response times, combing cloud with edge infrastructure from APC by Schneider electrical is proposed.

Edge analytics is a technique of information assortment and analysis during which an automatic analytical computation is performed on the information on a detector, network adapter, or different device instead of looking forward to knowledge/the info/the information to be came back to a central data store(Keithshaw,2019). Cloud computing has revolutionized however individuals store and use their

DOI: 10.4018/978-1-6684-5700-9.ch010

knowledge, however there square measure some areas wherever the cloud is proscribed, bandwidth, security, and latency, and lack of offline access is a haul. to unravel this drawback, the user desires a strong, secure and intelligent high-end computing infrastructure. Once knowledge is physically placed in shut proximity to the users connected to that, the knowledge is shared quickly, firmly and at once in money services, play aid and low-latency retail square measure very important to a good digital client expertise. To boost irresponsibleness and quicker response times, sweep the cloud with advanced infrastructure from APC by Schneider(electrical).Edge analytics is that the assortment, processing, and analysis of information at the sting of a network at or close to a detector, network switch, or different connected device. Edge computing directs computational data, applications, and services away from Cloud servers to the network edge. The substance suppliers and application designers can utilize the Edge figuring frameworks by offering the clients benefits nearer to them. Edge computing is portrayed regarding high data transfer capacity, super low inactivity, and ongoing admittance to the organization data that can be utilized by a few applications (WazirZada Khan et al.,2019). Edge analysis is descriptive or diagnostic or prophetical analytics.

WHY EDGE ANALYTICS?

Is edge analysis another fun term coined to complicate our lives? Not really. Associations are quickly sending a huge amount of sensors or other shrewd gadgets at their organization edge, and the operational information they gather at this scale could be a significant administration issue. Edge Analytics offers several important benefits:

The first is to minimize data analysis latency. In many environments like oil platforms, airplanes, and CCTV cameras. In far off assembling conditions, there may not be adequate opportunity to send information to the focal information investigation climate and trust that the outcomes will impact choices to be made nearby in an ideal way. As mentioned in the drilling rig example, analyzing the data on the defective devices there and closing the valve immediately can be more efficient if needed.

Secondly the scalability of the analysis. As per increasing sensors and network devices, the volume of data they collect increases exponentially, and the burden on central data analytics resources to process this massive amounts of data increases. Edge computing can satisfy the developing need of applications with privacy, strict latency, and bandwidth requirements (AshkanYousefpour et al.,2019).

Third, edge analytics helps to overcome the problem of low-bandwidth environments. The bandwidth required to send all the information gathered by a great many these fringe gadgets will also increase exponentially as the count of these devices increases. What's more, a significant number of these far off destinations might not have the transmission capacity to push information and examination to and from. Edge Analytics mitigates this issue by providing analytics capabilities in these remote sites.

Recently, edge scanning has the potential to condense overall costs by minimizing bandwidth, scaling operations, and reducing latency for critical decisions. It can also solve the issue of extreme energy utilization in cloud computing, reduce costs, and reduce the pressure of network bandwidth. Edge computing is applied in many fields such as production, energy, smart home, and transportation.(Keyan Cao et al.,2020)

When Should Edge Analytics be Considered?

While edge analytics is an interesting area, it should not be considered as a possible alternative to fundamental data analytics. Both can complement each other to provide data insights, and both models have a place in organizations. One tradeoff foredge analysis is that only a subset of data can be prepared and dissected at theat the edge and results can only be transmitted over the network to HQ. This will output in the "loss" of raw data that may never be stored or processed. Therefore, edge analysis is a good thing if this "data loss" is acceptable.Compared with traditional cloud computing, edge computing has advantages in response speed and real-time. Edge computing is closer to the data source, data storage and computing tasks can be carried out in the edge computing node, which reduces the intermediate data transmission process. (KEYAN CAO et al.,2020)

Who are the Players in Edge Analytics?

Notwithstanding shrewd smart sensors and connected devices to collect data, edge analysis requires hardware and software platforms to data, prepare data, train algorithms, and process algorithms. Most of these features are increasingly being provided on server and client, generic software platforms. Intel, Cisco, IBM, HP and Dell are some of the leading companies in advanced analytics.

Where is Edge Analytics Conveyed the Most?

Since perimeter analysis is beneficial for organizations where data insight is needed, the vertical segments of Retail, Manufacturing, Energy, Smart Cities, Transportation and Logistics are at the forefront of implementing scope analysis. Some use cases are: analysis of retail customer behavior, remote checking and support as well as maintenance of energy operations, fraud detection in financial places (ATMs, etc.) and production monitoring. Web based shopping could profit by edge registering. For instance, a client may make continuous shopping basket changes. Authorities could get help from Edge analytics to find missing kids. Today, cameras conveyed in open territories in urban communities—just as cameras in certain vehicles—could catch a missing youngster's picture (Weisong Shi&Schahram Dustdar,2016).

Delivering Edge Analytics

Reaching edge analysis is not an immediate task. Usually, the analysis model is built, the model is deployed, and the model runs on the edge. In every one of these regions, decisions need to be made about how to collect data, how to prepare data, how to choose algorithms, how to consistently train algorithms, how to publish / republish models, etc. Processing / memory capacity at the edge also plays a major role. Some of the built-in publishing models include decentralized publishing models and peer-to-peer publishing models with pros and cons for each model.

How Edge Analytics Work for all Industries

Edge analytics is beneficial for establishments where data intuitions are mandatory at the edge. The assembling, retail, brilliant urban communities, energy, utilities, transportation and coordinations sections are driving the path in executing edge examination.

Retail: Brick-and-mortar businesses are rich in edge devices like beacons, cameras, sensors, Wi-Fi networks, etc. They are searching for upper hands that can help them defeat online business organizations, and edge analytics in Real-time can give you simply that.Edge Analytics is utilized to make deals information, pictures, coupons utilized, traffic examples and recordings to give remarkable experiences into customer conduct. You have the perfect infrastructure and equipment to explore edge analytics. Additionally, customers' mobile devices and the data produced by store apps add to this number. Real-time insights are paramount as retail stores need to know their customers' needs as soon as they walk in to keep them in business. A recommendation or offer that comes after the customer has left the store cannot be of any use. Identifying customer behavioral data requires high processing power in the cloud. It can be a good idea to take privilegeof some processing features like tracking items viewed, picked, and purchased. Otherwise, metadata can be sent to the Cloud Lake for recommendations, offers, etc. so that the whole process stays near real-time. A distributed edge computing architecture can further improve this.The increasing video data traffic year by year will occupy more Internet bandwidth resources. When a user sends out a video playing request, the video resource can achieve the effect of loading from the local, thus not only saving bandwidth, but also greatly falls down the waiting time of the user. Thus network efficiency is achieved(K. Cao et al.,2020).

2)   Manufacturing:

Manufacturing is associate business that needs analytics and computing at the sting. Take associate example, a median offshore oil rig has nearly thirty,000 sensors. They live gas emission, pressure, temperature, etc., unceasingly. Connecting these to cloud lake and derivation analysis are going to be too expensive and long. A majority of this knowledge is really not needed for analytics; hardly 1-3% of information is employed for analysis once cleansing the information. It will bring tremendous blessings if these edge devices knew what analysis has to be performed and what knowledge has to be sent to the cloud, therefore saving ample information measure. Embedding computing capability within the kind of advanced event process (CPE), edge devices will separate out howling knowledge and collect solely info that's deemed helpful. Within the absence of cloud, the distributed edge computing will method this knowledge for analysis, take essential actions, and may later advise the cloud regarding the updates.

Smart industry has stringent requirements in terms of reliability and real-time accessibility that cannot be fulfilled by cloud computing alone. FOG Computing has been used to meet these necessities in applications, for example, shrewd support the executives, Efficient Manufacture Inspection System and energy-consumption management and scheduling (Anderson Carvalho et al.,2019).Another example is that the good assembly line. We all know that in an exceedingly assembly line, every method is time-bound. Each action should be taken in line with production processes. Hence, it becomes vital to derive analysis at the sting. Remarking producing defects or anomalies, badly written stickers, packaging, etc., in time period will be achieved mistreatment edge analytics.

3)   Healthcare:

Healthcare is another domain wherever we tend to are seeing an enormous surge within the variety of connected devices. Within the close to future, a room on a median can have fifteen to twenty medical devices, a majority of which can be networked. An outsized hospital will have as several as eighty-five, connected medical and IoT devices, swing a colossal strain on the cloud network. Edge computing and analytics will cut back this burden to a good extent. Here again, time period analytics can carry a lot of importance than delayed analytics. For instance, a clinician's mobile device is that the edge between the patient UN agency is that the information supply and therefore the cloud. Arctician treating a patient with a pill are going to be able to enter patient information into the analytics platform at the sting wherever it's processed and displayed in close to time period. Patients not ought to watch for analytics results, which can cut back theirvarietyofvisits.

In addition, edge computing in care offers another thought referred to as cooperative edge. in a very cooperative edge, geographically spread information may be amalgamated by making virtual shared views. This shared information is exposed to the users through some pre-defined interfaces thatedge devices will directly consume.

To add this up, with edge computing practitioners and patients will get the most effective response times from the info that's generated and picked up by care facilities. Because the care sector is exploitation a lot of and a lot of medical devices that are connected to a typical network, edge computing is near to become a customary in health IT infrastructure.A medical application can include a check-up, a special-ist examination, bio-signal or genomic measurement. By utilizing Grid computing, all the assessments and estimations can be connected utilizing geologically disseminated using geographically-distributed computing resources, intelligent analysis software and algorithms, and databases via secure and reliable wired or wirelessnetworks.(FlaviaDonno&ElisabettaRonchieri,2009)

What is the Difference between Edge Analytics and Edge Computing?

Edge analyticsis a way to do contextual data analysis on sensing devices (sensors, actuators, con-trollers, concentrators), network switches or other devices instead of sending the whole data to a centralized computing environment/Cloud(Satyanarayanan M et al.,2015).Edge computing and edge analysis are not mutually exclusive, according to Bernhardy, but are two phases of the same wall. "Edge computing uses devices only to behave like computers, to record events and to track communications between devices and the site. Edge analysis takes the same device or devices and uses them to process the calculated data and turn it into actionable information right on that device, "said Bernhardy. While edge analysis can perform some analysis functions, analysis requires edge analysis on the edge computing next level, as Paul Butterworth, co-founder and CTO of Walnut Creek, CA, Vantiq explains, "Edge analytics takes edge computing to the next level by collecting more data on the edge and applying more complex analyt-ics to it," said Butterworth. He went on to give an example of a machine tension sensor that uses edge analysis. "Edge computing can apply an algorithm that shuts down a machine when a sensor indicates that the power supply is not providing the required voltage based on the last two or three sensor readings. Similarly, edge analysis could do a long-term analysis of the voltages accumulated over the past month trying to predict [possible] voltage anomalies in the near future.

Edge vs Cloud: Which Is Better for Data Analytics

Edge Computing and Cloud Computing technologies are similar regarding the methods of storing and processing data. However, the differences between these technologies are related to the physical loca-tions of storing and processing, the amount of analysed data, processing speed and so on(BojanaBajic et al.,2019).When the premise of stories for fiction films, computerized reasoning (AI) presently has valuable applications that are changing the manner in which organizations are run.Designers are looking at approaches to combine AI with regular gadgets to help organizations maintain their organizations. In this scenario, cloud computing plays an important role in making the best possible decisions.

A cloud-based platform enables developers to quickly create, deploy, and manage their applications, such as serving as a data platform for applications, building an application to scale and support millions of users and interactions, and more. You can analyze bulk amounts of data and perform analysis, create powerful visualizations, and more. Then there's state-of-the- computing, which meansservices, applications and analytical data processing are done outside of a centralized data center and closer to end clients.

Edge computing closely aligns the IoT. It's a level back from the modern cloud computing model, where all the cool bits happen in data centers. Rather than using local resources to collect data and send it to the cloud, some of the processing is done on the local resources themselves.

Latency Problems in Cloud vs Edge

We all know the value of data analytics cloud computing, and how widely it is used across businesses. On the other hand, companies may sometimes encounter the problem of having to collect transportation and analyze all that data.

Despite the fact that the computing has the incredible potential torelieve the pressure on core networks, its fundamental bottle neck is the restricted calculation and communications limits as compared with the cloud computing. Therefore, in the cloudand edge coexistence system, hierarchical computing can berealized in which tasks can be opportunistically processedby both the edge node and the cloud server(JinkeRen et al.,2019)

Suppose you have some internet-connected sensors in your repository, and they send a lot of data back to some servers. When data is transferred to a remote cloud server, you can implement complex machine learning algorithms to try to predict the maintenance needs of the warehouse. All of these helpful analyzes are then sent to a dashboard on your personal computer where you can decide what actions to take next, all from the comfort of your office or home.

This is the intensity of distributed computing; notwithstanding, as you scale up activities at the stockroom, you may begin to run into actual impediments in your organization transfer speed, and idleness issues.

Figure 1. Cloud Latency(Mitch,2019)

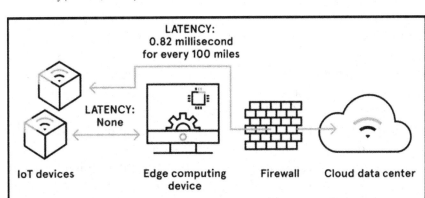

Rather than communicating your information the nation over when you transfer to the cloud, you can likewise do information handling at the edge, similar to a brilliant camera with facial acknowledgment where sending huge loads of information to an Amazon server farm probably won't be so helpful.

Edge computing attempts to bridge the gap by having that server more local, sometimes even on the device itself (Zai,2020). This takes care of the issue of inactivity to the detriment of the sheer preparing power you get by means of the cloud. Additionally, with the data collection and processing capacity now available at the edge, companies can significantly reduce the amount of data that must be uploaded and stored in the cloud, saving time and money in the process.

While edge applications don't need correspondence with the cloud, they can at present speak with online applications and workers. Huge numbers of the average edge gadgets have actual sensors, for example, temperature, lights, speakers, and information handling abilities running nearer to these sensors in the actual climate. It is this edge computing capability that is transformative and used to run intelligent artificial intelligence algorithms and real-time data processing on autonomous driving, drones and smart devices.

Edge computing may not be as strongest as remote servers,be that as it may, it can help mitigate a portion of the transmission capacity prerequisites. These edge servers can collect, organize and perform some basic analysis of the data before sending it to the remote server.

The Cloud Trend for Data Processing Will Continue Except In Special Edge Cases

It will be more interesting when we run machine learning algorithms on the edge devices, as long as the processing power allows us to do some core data analysis and retention before sending it to our servers. If you're looking for a more familiar Edge example, you can take a look at the nearest smart speaker that has a preprogrammed pattern waiting for a wake-up word or phrase. Once that word is heard, your voice is broadcast over the internet to a server where the entire request is handled remotely.

On cloud platforms like Amazon Web Services (AWS), Microsoft Azure, Google Cloud Platform, and other cloud service providers, most of the data from connected devices in the IoT network is collected and sent to the cloud for processing and analysis(Von et al.,2020). In the processing and storage capacity of the cloud data center, data is aggregated and AI-compatible models are created to make valuable decisions.

Whereas this approach is still sturdy, the time it takes for data to move in and out of the cloud generates potential issues that can impact the real-time decision-making processes required by many autonomous systems. The further geologically from a cloud data center, the more latency is added. For every 100 miles of data transfer, the speed will lose about 0.82 milliseconds. Cloud computing is agile, but it cannot meet the increasing demands of large workloads that IoT applications require for industries such as healthcare, manufacturing and transportation.

As the amount and practicality of AI-enabledIoT solutions keeps on developing, distributed computing will be a fundamental piece of the IoT biological system for intricate and recorded processing. In order to be able to make decisions in real time, edge computing is a good and more agile way of providing end devices with computer and analysis functions for many applications.Empowered by the emerging technologies such as NFV and SDN, edge cloud and edge computing technologies are privileged to address different challenges with the current cloud computing model facing with the future IoTworld(Jianli Pan& James McElhannon,2017).

IoT Edge Analytics

Edge Computing / Edge Analytics is a relatively new approach for many businesses. Most architecture is used to send all data to the Cloud / Lake. But in high-tech computing, that doesn't happen. That is to say. The data can be processed close to the source and not all the data is sent back to the cloud. For large-scale IoT deployments, this functionality is critical due to the volumes of data generated.

Figure 2. Iot Edge Analytics Factors

The importance and evolution of IoT edge analytics is that hardware capabilities will converge with major vendors (Cisco, Dell, HPE, Intel, IBM, etc.). Hence, IoT analytics will be the main distinguishing factor, as companies like Cisco, Intel, and other early computing backers have positioned their portals as Edge devices**(Aji,2016)**.

Historically, gates served the function of aggregating and directing traffic. In the advanced computing paradigm, the basic gateway functions have evolved. Portals not only route data but also store data and perform mathematical operations on the data as well. Edge Analytics allows us to do some preprocessing or filter data near where the data is created(Newman,2020). Thus, data that falls within normal parameters can be discarded or stored in low-cost storage and abnormal readings can be sent to Lake or the in-memory database. Now, a new segment of the market is being developed that is led by resellers like Dell, HPE and others. These vendors position their servers as Edge devices by adding additional storage, computing, and analytics capabilities. This has implications for Edge Analytics for IoT.

Edge Analytics typically applies to oil platforms, mines, and plants operating in low-bandwidth and low-latency environments. Edge Analytics can be applied not only to sensor data but also to richer forms of data such as video analytics. IoT datasets are huge. The Formula One concept car has 150-300 sensors.

An airline, for example, the current Airbus A350 model contains nearly 6,000 sensors and generates 2.5 terabytes of data per day. The smart cities have a network of more than 25,000 sensors. To avoid the situation of constantly testing your cloud connection, it is necessary to do interim processing. Hence, need to address the edge in IoT analytics. We can consider Edge devices from two perspectives: the evolution of traditional portal vendors and the evolution of traditional server vendors.

Evolution of the Gateway

Both Intel and Cisco have long collaborated with IoT Edge analytics and Cisco incubated / acquired a company called Parstream(Agb et al,2020). ParStream has created a lightweight database platform (less than 50MB) mainly for use in IoT platforms such as wind turbines etc. Cisco also includes IoT analytics products for specific verticals such as: Cisco Connected Analytics for Events, Retail, Service Providers, IT, Network Deployment, Mobility, Collaboration, Contact Center, etc. More recently, Cisco and IBM have begun working together to bring Watson's capabilities to the Edge.

The Intel product suite is based on a number of acquisitions such as mashery (API), MacAfee (security) etc. through the IoT Developer Kits, the end to end platform includes: The Wind River Edge Management System, IoT Gateway, Cloud Analytics, McAfee Security for IoT Gateways, Privacy Identity (EPID) modules, API and Traffic Management (based on Mashery) and possibly with synergies with Cloudera, where Intel is an investor. Of course, there are other players on the Edge who can incorporate Edge analysis as well. For example: The Access netfrontbrowser, widely used in set top boxes and automotive applications, could also perform edge analysis functions.

This offers the ability to implement IoT analytics using web technology, such as node.js or PhantomJS based JavaScript engines. Similarly, SAP has implemented functionality in HANA (in-memory database), which enables data synchronization between the company and remote locations at the edge of the network.

Evolution of the Server

More recently, we've been seeing traditional server providers deploy their servers as edge devices. On the hardware side, devices such as the Dell Edge Gateway 5000 series are specially developed for building and industrial automation. The HPE Edgeline series is also in the same room. The analysis strategy is much more interesting - for example, the use of Statistica by Dell. Dell uses Dell Statistica. As a middleware solution to provide peripheral analyzes. In this way, Dell can use a hardware / software solution for analysis (particularly relevant for IoT analysis). In particular, this enables an analysis model to be created at one location (e.g. in the cloud) and provisioned in other parts of the ecosystem (e.g. on the edge device or at the actual sensor location itself - e.g. a windmill) using technologies such as PMML (e.g. in a windmill). More on this below). Impact on IoT Analysis

So, the real question is: What does it mean for IoT Analytics?

An adaptable and proficient arrangement, both at the organization and cloud level, is to convey the IoT examination between the center cloud and the edge of the organization . For an efficient distribution of IoT analytics and use of network resources, it requires to integrate the control of the transport networks with the distributed edge and cloud resources in order to deploy dynamic and efficient IoT services(Raül Muñoz et al.,2018).

- First, we must distinguish between two stages: creating the analysis model and running the analysis model. Building the analytical model involves: collecting data, storing data, preparing the data for analysis (some ETL functions), choosing the analytical algorithm, training the algorithms, validating the analytical goodness of fit, etc. The result of this trained model will be rules, recommendations, scores, etc. Only then can we implement this model. So when we say that we are implementing analytics at the "edge", what exactly are we doing? If you follow the examples above, for example from Dell, the most general case is: build the model at one location and potentially deploy the model at multiple points (e.g. cloud to gateway, server, factory, etc.)

- PMML becomes important for the ability to distribute models in multiple locations: PMML (Predictive Model Markup Language) PMML is an XML-based predictive model interchange format. PMML permits scientific applications to depict and trade prescient models created by information mining and AI calculations. It supports ordinary models such as logistic regression and feedforward neural networks.

- Reorganizeddispensation is inherently intricate: when you decentralize processing, some innately complex situations arise - e.g. For example, master data regulation and replication, security, storage, and so on. You must also create the analysis model on a computer and deploy it on a computer another machine is new.

- Peer-to-peer node communication can be a real leeway over time: Today, IoT is implemented in silos. Edge networks offer the ability for peer-to-peer communication using edge devices if they have enough processing power.

Figure 3. Iot Analytics Server(Aji,2016)

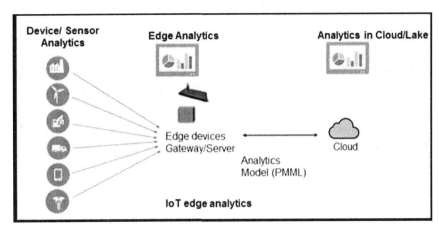

4 Emerging Use Cases for IoT Data Analytics

Use Case #1: Consumer Product Usage Analysis for Marketing

IoT solutions have the probable to entirely rewrite the way industries think about their consumers.

This is already trendy by analyzing information about how consumers use a company's internet-connected products. As an example, take the following dashboard from Birst, a developer of self-service and guided analytics solutions:

FarnazIrfan, Birst's Senior Product Strategy Manager, explains how IoT-related espresso makers transmit records to the producer approximately what number of espresso pots a purchaser brews in step with day, and that records can then be related to social media records to decide if customers are Brew greater espresso than probable to actively speak the emblem on social media. In addition, the vendor

Figure 4. Marketing Analysis

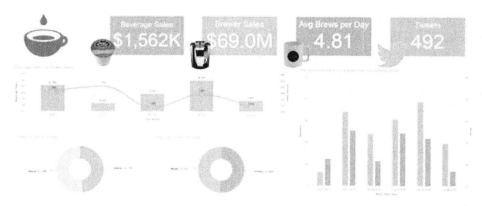

can see if the variations in the quantity of espresso brewed through the customers in shape the quantity of espresso pills that the vendor additionally sells**(Man,2020)**.

Use Case #2: Serving Consumers and Business Users with the Same Analytics

One of the great aspects of Irfan'sIoT data analytics is that the analyzes can be both business and consumer oriented, for example, Irfan mentions a Birst distribution to an accompanying customer selling smart energy meters that don't require a meter. Readers: "They sell to state and county governments as well as private energy suppliers, so organizations can conduct fraud detection on meter data and revenue projections(Ana,2020)." "However, the other channel is consumer oriented," he says, "where the analyzes allow consumers to manage their energy consumption, see what's up and down other households in the neighborhood, turn appliances on and off to determine how they affect energy consumption, etc."

"In this case, the company generates value from the same analysis in two ways:

1. Traditional data mining to identifydeceit
2. Permitting a new amenity for its customers, which appeals both prudent patrons than natural ones?

Use Case #3: Sensors and Cameras Enable Connected Events

One of the most interesting domains of IoT analysis is the emerging field of social analysis. Social data analytics uses sensor data, video data, social media data, etc. To provide useful information's on the personalities, behaviors of individuals and of other groups. Facial recognition and motion detection are crucial areas for enabling social analytics through video. In the case of fashion shows, we can use motion detection to determine where the audience is actually trying to detect events that grab the group's attention. We measure this by looking at their faces and using the position of their eyes and mouth to understand the person's focus and level of interest. Today, social analytics is creating business value by supporting video capture of important moments during events. By analyzing a crowd's emotions, behaviors, and focal points to identify event highlights, you can create video clips that naturally relate to the interests of the crowd (and, by extension, online viewers too).

Use Case #4: Video Analytics for Surveillance and Safety

Video analytics is the use of software algorithms to identify, classify, and track objects or people. The scrutiny is carried out in the form of software or hardware. It is either integrated into the camera (on the edge - which provides entry points into central corporate or service provider networks) or centrally in video processing systems such as DVRs and NVRs or the servers, video security systems smarter and more efficient than ever. From telling individuals to checking and overseeing traffic, to investigating movement by season of day and different factors, video examination has carried business security to a more significant level of sagacity.Advantages of Edge Analytics

In edge analytics, however, the devices or the gateways can handle the analysis. Advantages in doing so include:

- **Reducing network bottlenecks:** Low latency examination on geologically conveyed datasets (across datacenters, edge bunches) is a forthcoming and progressively significant test.The dominant approach of aggregating all the data to a single datacenter significantly inflates the timeliness of analytics(QifanPu et al.,2015).Some data, for example video used in smart city submissions like traffic running, is so large that it can devastate the network. A network with a 100 Gbps bandwidth, for example, can support 1080p upload from 12,000 users with a YouTube recommended upload speed of 8.5 Mbps, bestowing to a recent article in Mainstream Computing. 1 million simultaneous downloads will require 8.5 terabytes per second.

Rapid Response Times: Tenders such as spawning power from wind or solar power plants and watching sick patients require response times of one minute or less. When this data is sent to a central location for analysis, it loses its value.

Data Filter: Consents studies to be performed on actionable data; only the necessary data is analyzed or sent for further analysis. "What happens is that the [analytical] model may be produced in the cloud and then instantiated in an edge or gateway device. However, where the analysis is to be performed depends on the working condition and the effectiveness of the terminal device or gate. Certain types of edge gravity analyzes cannot be performed. Sometimes an edge device, such as a smart meter, is not sufficiently capable of running analyzes. For example, in the case of power consumption, John Thompson, General Manager of Advanced Analytics at Dell, said: "Usually smart meters in homes are not capable enough to run analytical models." Smart meter data can be sent to a gateway that filters the data, and then it is sent Data to a server running at the city or district level. "We don't really need 10 million data points to say the smart bulb is on.

The Pros—

- Too much "connection" has created, for many organizations, a clogged data transmission pipeline that can be not only cumbersome but also expensive to manage. By running data through an analytics algorithm as it is created, at the edge of a corporate network, companies can set parameters on what information is worth sending to a local cloud or data warehouse for later use, and which is not.
- Better and more Effective decision making is a direct result of edge analytics. Reducing latency due to the ability to interpret data at the edge of the network is key to making smarter and more productive decisions than ever before. taken with all subsequent analysis in a central location.

- Edge analysis diminishes the expense of information stockpiling and the executives. It likewise decreases working expenses, limits fundamental transfer speed, and lessens assets spent on information examination. All of these factors combine to provide significant financial savings. "

The Cons –

- Executing a well-thought-out edge computing policy is complex and can be expensive given the additional scheduling, resources, and apparatus required to deploy analytics at the edge. The result, of course, is to improve proficiency and hopefully lower costs. But be aware that a significant initial investment will often be necessary.
- "Not all edge analysis is good; the efficiency they bring at a cost. Only a subset of the data will be processed and analyzed, the results being sent over the network," explains Zhang. "In effect, this means that the raw data is deleted, which inevitably results in the loss of some information it might have provided. Device type and data usage must be considered - data loss is it a critical issue or a necessary aspect to increase efficiency?"
- "There is a borderline skills gap. Quite simply, many organizations are still learning to make full use of the data from which they acquire or distribute edge locations. And there is a dearth of developers who can write new applications for emerging use cases, including the "killer" applications that many companies hope to develop for true business transformation.

What Are The Limitations of Edge Analytics?

Edge analysis is a relatively new technology. Bernhardy stated that currently not all hardware "is able to your data or perform complex processing and analysis". However, we can assume that hardware manufacturers will change this fact in the months and years to come. Califano also says that while the architecture of edge computing is not "inherently bad", there are two questions to consider before investing in edge analytics(Blesson Varghese et al,2016). "The first question to be checked is whether it makes sense to invest in edge analysis for a particular application. In general, it's best for scenarios that need to be optimized for a combination of speed, efficiency, and security," Califano said. "The second question is how an IoT application can be built that includes an element of edge intelligence. Since we are relatively early in the lifecycle of adopting edge computing architectures, there are many practical hurdles that engineers (of all kinds) must overcome in this way to successfully implement an IoT application of this kind.

CONCLUSION

edge analysis is an exciting area, with organizations in the Industrial Internet of Things (IIOT) field increasing their investments year on year. Major vendors are investing broadly in this rapidly developing area in specific segments such as manufacturing, energy and logistics, retail, edge analytics delivers quantifiable business benefits by reducing decision latency, increasing scan resources, solving bandwidth issues and potentially reducing expenses.

REFERENCES

Agbehadji, I. E., Frimpong, S. O., Millham, R. C., Fong, S. J., & Jung, J. J. (2020). Intelligent energy optimization for advanced IoT analytics edge computing on wireless sensor networks. *International Journal of Distributed Sensor Networks*, *16*(7), 1550147720908772.

Amos, B. (2015). Edge analytics in the internet of things. *IEEE Pervasive Computing*, *14*(2), 24–31.

Anagnostopoulos, C. (2020). Edge-centric inferential modeling & analytics. *Journal of Network and Computer Applications*.

Carvalho, & O' Mahony, Krpalkova, Campbell, Walsh, & Doody (2019). Edge Computing Applied to Industrial Machines. *Procedia Manufacturing, 38*, 178–185.

Donno & Ronchieri. (2009). *The Impact of Grid on Health Care Digital Repositories.* Doi:10.1109/ HICSS.2009.435

Gracie, M. (2019). *The Case for Computing at the Edge.* Retrieved, 2 Nov 2020 https://www.kdnuggets. com/2016/09/evolution-iot-edge-analytics.html

Khan. (2019). Edge computing. *Survey.*

Manish. (2020). *IoT Analytics – 3 Major Uses Cases of Internet of Things Analytics.* Retrieved, 2 Nov 2020 from https://data-flair.training/blogs/iot-analytics

Muñoz, Vilalta, Yoshikane, Casellas, Martínez, Tsuritani, & Morita. (2018). *Integration of IoT, Transport SDN, and Edge/Cloud Computing for Dynamic Distribution of IoT Analytics and Efficient Use of Network Resources.* Academic Press.

Newman, D. M. (2020). *Bayesian edge analytics of machine process and health status in an IoT framework* (Doctoral dissertation). Georgia Institute of Technology.

Pan & McElhannon. (n.d.). *Future Edge Cloud and Edge Computing for Internet of Things Applications.* doi:10.1109/JIOT.2017.2767608

Pu. (n.d.). *Low Latency Geo-distributed Data Analytics.* doi:10.1145/2829988.2787505

Ren. (2019). *Collaborative Cloud and Edge Computing for Latency Minimization.* doi:10.1109/ TVT.2019.2904244

Ren, Bajic, Cosic, Katalinic, Moraca, Lazarevic, & Rikalovic. (n.d.). *Edge computing vs. cloud computing: Challenges and opportunities in Industry 4.0.* Doi:10.2507/30th.daaam.proceedings.120

Shaw, K. (2019). *What is edge computing and why it matters.* Retrieved, 14 Nov 2020 from https://www. networkworld.com/article/3224893/what-is-edge-computing-and-how-it-s-changing-the-network.html

Shi & Dustdar. (2016). The Promise of Edge Computing. *Computer, 49*(5), 78–81. doi:10.1109/ MC.2016.145

Varghese, B. (2016). Challenges and Opportunities in Edge Computing. Academic Press.

vonStietencron, M., Lewandowski, M., Lepenioti, K., Bousdekis, A., Hribernik, K., Apostolou, D., & Mentzas, G. (2020, August). Streaming Analytics in Edge-Cloud Environment for Logistics Processes.In *IFIP International Conference on Advances in Production Management Systems* (pp. 245-253).Springer.

Yousefpour, Fung, Nguyen, Kadiyala, Jalali, Niakanlahiji, … Jue. (2019). *All one needs to know about fog computing and related edge computing paradigms: A complete survey.* Academic Press.

ZAID, M. A., Faizal, M., Maheswar, R., & Abdullaziz, O. I. (2020). Toward Smart Urban Development Through Intelligent Edge Analytics. In *Integration of WSN and IoT for Smart Cities* (pp. 129–150). Springer. doi:10.1007/978-3-030-38516-3_8

This research was previously published in Cases on Edge Computing and Analytics; pages 134-152, copyright year 2021 by Engineering Science Reference (an imprint of IGI Global).

Chapter 11
Expounding the Edge/Fog Computing Infrastructures for Data Science

Pethuru Raj

ⓘ https://orcid.org/0000-0001-5220-0408

Reliance Jio Infocomm. Ltd., India

Pushpa J.

Jain University, India

ABSTRACT

Data is the new fuel for any system to deliver smart and sophisticated services. Data is being touted as the strategic asset for any organization to plan ahead and provide next-generation capabilities with all the clarity and confidence. Whether data is internally sourced or aggregated from different and distributed source, it is essential for all kinds of data to be continuously and consciously collected, transmitted, cleansed, and hosted on storage systems. There are several types of analytical methods and machines to do deeper and decisive analytics on those curated and consolidated data to extract actionable insights in real-time. Precise and concise analytics guarantee perfect decision-making and action. We need competent and highly integrated analytics platform for speeding up, simplifying and streamlining data analytics, which is becoming a hard nut to crack due to the multi-structured and massive quantities of data. On the infrastructure front, we need highly optimized compute, storage and network infrastructure for achieving data analytics with ease. Another noteworthy point is that there are batch, real-time, and interactive processing of data. Most of the personal and professional applications need real-time insights in order to produce real-time applications. That is, real-time capture, processing, and decision-making are being insisted and hence the edge or fog computing concept has become very popular. This chapter is exclusively designed in order to tell all on how to accomplish real-time analytics on fog devices data.

DOI: 10.4018/978-1-6684-5700-9.ch011

INTRODUCTION

The faster maturity and stability of edge technologies (Raj and Deka, 2014) has blossomed into a big factor in realizing scores of digitized elements / smart objects/sentient materials out of common, cheap and casual items in our midst. These empowered entities are data-generating and capturing, buffering, transmitting, etc. That is, tangible things are peppered with and prepared for the future. These are mostly resource-constrained and this phenomenon is called the Internet of Things (IoT). Further on, a wider variety of gadgets and gizmos in our working, walking and wandering locations are futuristically instrumented to be spontaneously interconnected and exceptionally intelligent in their behaviours. Thus, we hear, read and even feel connected and cognitive devices and machines in our everyday life. Once upon of a time, all our personal computers were connected via networks (LAN and WAN) and nowadays our personal and professional devices (fixed, portables, mobiles, wearables, implantables, handhelds, phablets, etc.) are increasingly interconnected (BAN, PAN, CAN, LAN. MAN and WAN) to exhibit a kind of intelligent behavior. This extreme connectivity and service-enablement of our everyday devices go to the level of getting seamlessly integrated with off-premise, online, and on-demand cloud-based applications, services, data sources, and content. This cloud-enablement is capable of making ordinary devices into extraordinary ones. However, most of the well-known and widely used embedded devices individually do not have sufficient computation power, battery, storage and I/O bandwidth to host and manage IoT applications and services. Hence performing data analytics on individual devices is a bit difficult.

As we all know, smart sensors and actuators are being randomly deployed in any significant environments such as homes, hospitals, hotels, etc. in order to minutely monitor, precisely measure, and insightfully manage the various parameters of the environments. Further on, powerful sensors are embedded and etched on different physical, mechanical, electrical and electronics systems in our everyday environments in order to empower them to join in the mainstream computing. Thus, not only environments but also all tangible things in those environments are also smartly sensor-enabled with a tactic as well as the strategic goal of making them distinctly sensitive and responsive in their operations, offerings, and outputs. Sensors are sweetly turning out to be the inseparable eyes and ears of any important thing in near future. This systematic sensor-enablement of ordinary things not only make them extraordinary but also lay out a stimulating and sparkling foundation for generating a lot of usable and time-critical data. Typically sensors and sensors-attached assets capture or generate and transmit all kinds of data to the faraway cloud environments (public, private and hybrid) through a host of standards-compliant sensor gateway devices. Precisely speaking, clouds represent the dynamic combination of several powerful server machines, storage appliances, and network solutions and are capable of processing tremendous amounts of multi-structured data to spit out actionable insights.

However, there is another side to this remote integration and data processing. For certain requirements, the local or proximate processing of data is mandated. That is, instead of capturing sensor and device data and transmitting them to the faraway cloud environments is not going to be beneficial for time-critical applications. Thereby the concept of edge or fog computing has emerged and is evolving fast these days with the concerted efforts of academic as well as corporate people. The reasonably powerful devices such as smartphones, sensor and IoT gateways, consumer electronics, set-top boxes, smart TVs, Web-enabled refrigerators, Wi-Fi routers, etc. are classified as fog or edge devices to form edge or fog clouds to do the much-needed local processing quickly and easily to arrive and articulate any hidden knowledge. Thus, fog or edge computing is termed and tuned as the serious subject of study and research for producing people-centric and real-time applications and services.

BRIEFING FOG / EDGE COMPUTING

Traditional networks, which feed data from devices or transactions to a central storage hub (data warehouses and data marts) can't keep up with the data volume and velocity created by IoT devices. Nor can the data warehouse model meet the low latency response times that users demand. The Hadoop platform in the cloud was supposed to be an answer. But sending the data to the cloud for analysis also poses a risk of data bottlenecks as well as security concerns. New business models, however, need data analytics in a minute or less. The problem of data congestion will only get worse as IoT applications and devices continue to proliferate.

There are certain interesting use cases such as rich connectivity and interactions among vehicles (V2V) and infrastructures (V2I). This emerging domain of IoT requires services like entertainment, education, and information, public safety, real-time traffic analysis and information, support for high mobility, context awareness and so forth. Such things see the light only if the infotainment systems within vehicles have to identify and interact with one another dynamically and also with wireless communication (Wang et al, 2011) infrastructures made available on the road, with remote traffic servers and FM stations, etc. The infotainment system is emerging as the highly synchronized gateway for vehicles on the road. Local devices need to interact themselves to collect data from vehicles and roads/expressways/ tunnels/bridges to process them instantaneously to spit out useful intelligence. This is the salivating and sparkling foundation for fog/edge computing.

The value of the data decreases as the time goes. That is, the timeliness and the trustworthiness of data are very important for extracting actionable insights. The moment the data gets generated and captured, it has to be subjected to processing. That is, it is all about real-time capture. Also, it is all about gaining real-time insights through rule / policy-based data filtering, enrichment, pattern searching, aggregation, knowledge discovery, etc. to take a real-time decision and to build real-time applications. The picture below clearly articulates how the delay in capturing and analyzing data costs a lot in terms of business, technical and user values.

The latest trend of computing paradigm is to push the storage, networking, and computation to edge/ fog devices for availing certain critical services. As devices are interconnected and integrated with the Internet, their computational capabilities and competencies are uniquely being leveraged in order to lessen the increasing load on cloud infrastructures. Edge devices are adequately instrumented at the design stage itself to interconnect with nearby devices automatically so that multiple devices dynamically can be found, bound, and composed for creating powerful and special-purpose edge clouds. Thus, the concept of fog or edge computing is blooming and booming these days.

The essence and gist of fog computing (Pan et al, 2017; Salman et al, 2015; Raj, 2015) are to keep data and computation close to end-users at the edge of the network and this arrangement has the added tendency of producing a new class of applications and services to end-users with low latency, high bandwidth, and context-awareness. Fog is invariably closer to humans rather than clouds and hence the name 'fog computing' is overwhelmingly accepted across. As indicated and illustrated above, fog devices are typically resource-intensive edge devices. Fog computing is usually touted as the supplement and complement to the popular cloud computing. Students, scholars, and scientists are keen towards unearthing a number of convincing and sellable business and technical cases for fog computing. Being closer to people, the revitalized fog or edge computing is to be extremely fruitful and fabulous in conceptualizing and concretizing a litany of people-centric software applications. Finally, in the era of big, fast, streaming and IoT data, fog/edge computing can facilitate edge analytics. Edge devices can filter out redundant, repetitive and routine data to reduce the precious network bandwidth and the data loads on clouds. Figure 1 vividly illustrates the fast-emerging three-tier architecture for futuristic computing.

Figure 1. The End-to-end Fog – Cloud Integration Architecture

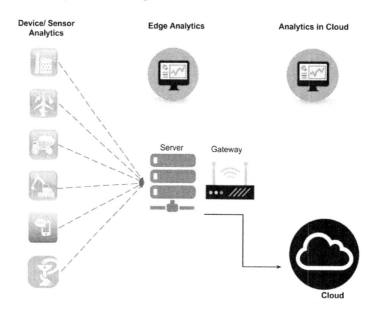

The digitized objects (sensors, beacons, etc.) at the lowest level are generating and capturing poly-structured data in big quantities. The fog devices (gateways, controllers, etc.) at the second level are reasonably blessed with computational, communication and storage power in order to mix, mingle and merge with other fog devices in the environment to ingest and accomplish the local or proximate data processing to emit viable and value-adding insights in time. The third and final level is the faraway cloud centres. This introduction of fog devices in between clouds and digitized elements is the new twist brought in towards the ensuing era of knowledge-filled services. Fog devices act as intelligent intermediaries between cloud-based cyber/virtual applications and sensor/actuator (Lee et al, 2016; Tredway et al, 2016; Poole et al, 2015) data at the ground level. Here is another representation of fog computing as articulated in Figure 2.

ILLUSTRATING THE EPOCH-MAKING IOT JOURNEY

The mesmerizing number of smart sensors and actuators being deployed in specific environments ultimately produces massive volumes of data and currently, the collected data is faithfully transmitted over the Internet or any private network to faraway cloud infrastructures in order to be concertedly and calculatedly crunched to extract exceptional insights. As we all know, clouds are the best bet for doing the batch or historical processing through the renowned Hadoop framework. That is, cloud-based analytics is the overwhelming practice. However, the emerging trend is to come with micro-scale clouds in between the ground-level sensors and the cyber-level cloud applications towards fog analytics. This specialized cloud, which is being formed out of networked and resource-intensive devices in that environment, takes out the constricting stress on the traditional clouds. The proximate processing gets accomplished through these micro-clouds whereas the device data security and privacy is maintained. This kind of cloud-in-the-middle approach is capable of unearthing fresh IoT use cases. As any micro-cloud is very near the data-emitting sensors and sensors-attached assets, the faster processing and response are being achieved in an affordable fashion.

Figure 2. The Fog as the Intermediary between the Physical and the Cyber Worlds

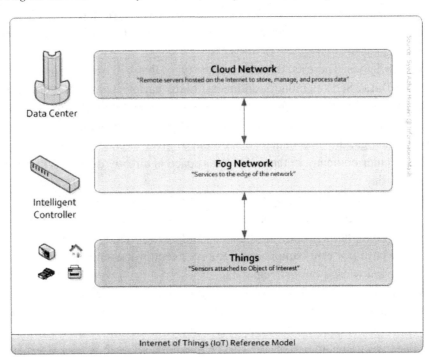

- **It Is All About the Extreme and Deeper Connectivity:** As the inventive paradigm of networked embedded devices expands into multiple business domains and industry verticals such as manufacturing facilities and floors, healthcare centers, retail stores, luxury hotels, spacious homes, energy grids and transportation systems, there is a greater scope for deriving sophisticated applications not only for businesses but also for commoners. The world is tending towards the connected world. Recent devices come with the connectivity feature and there are a vast number of hitherto unconnected legacy devices. Further on, there are resource-constrained devices such as heart rate monitors to temperature & humidity sensors, in plenty and enabling them to be integrated with other devices and web applications is definitely a big challenge. Thus, connectivity solutions and platforms are being brought in to enable every tangible device to be connected. The connectivity is not only with adjacent devices in the vicinity but also with the remotely held applications and data sources on the web/cloud.

- **The Humongous Volumes of IoT Data:** We have been fiddling with transaction systems extensively. The IT infrastructures, platforms, and applications are designed to be appropriate for streamlining and speeding up transactions. However, with the faster penetration of devices and digitized entities, there is a relook. That is, operational systems are becoming more prevalent and prominent. In the impending IoT era, a sensor or smart device that is monitoring temperature, humidity, vibration, acceleration or numerous other variables could potentially generate data that needs to be handled by back-end systems in some way every millisecond. For example, a typical Formula One car already carries 150-300 sensors and more controllers, sensors, and actuators are being continuously incorporated to bring in more automation. Today, these hundred sensors already capture data in milliseconds. The racecars generate 100-200 KBs of data per second, amounting to several terabytes in a racing season. There are twin challenges for back-end systems. Not only the storage concern but also the real-time processing of data is also equally important. That is, missing a few seconds of sensor data or being unable to analyze it efficiently and rapidly, can lead to risks and in some cases, to disasters.

- **Major IoT Data Types:** There are three major data types that will be common to most IoT projects:

- **Measurement Data:** Sensors monitor and measure the various parameters of the environment as well as the states of physical, mechanical, electrical and electronics systems. Heterogeneous and multiple sensors read and transmit data very frequently and hence with a larger number of sensors and frequent readings, the total data size is bound to grow exponentially. This is the crux of the IoT era. A particular company in the oil and gas space is already dealing with more than 100TB of such data per day.

- **Event Data:** Any status change, any break-in of the threshold value, any noteworthy incident or untoward accident, and any decision-enabling data are simply categorized event data. With devices assisting people in their daily assignments and engagements, the number of events is likely to shoot up. We have powerful simple and complex event processing engines in order to discover and disseminate knowledge out of event data.

- **Interaction and Transaction Data:** With the extreme and deeper connectivity amongst devices, the quality and quantity of purpose-specific interactions between devices are going to be greater. Several devices with unique functionality can connect and collaborate for achieving composite functions. The transaction operations are also enabled in devices. Not only inter-device communication but also human-device communication is fairly happening.

- **Diagnostics Data:** The delectable advancements in the IoT domain has led to millions of networked embedded devices and smart objects, information, transactional, analytical and operational systems. There are online, off-premise, and on-demand applications, data sources, and services in plenty. The application portfolio is consistently on the rise for worldwide enterprises. There are software infrastructure solutions, middleware, databases, data virtualization and knowledge visualization platforms, and scores of automation tool. The health of each of these systems is very important for the intended success of any business transaction. Diagnostics is the type of data that gives an insight into the overall health of a machine, system or process. Diagnostic data might not only show the overall health of a system but also show whether the monitoring of that system is also working effectively.

Precisely speaking, the IoT data is going to be big and we have techniques and platforms for big data processing. However, the intriguing challenge is to do real-time processing of IoT big data. Researchers are on the job to unearth path-breaking algorithms to extract timely insights out of big data. Fog computing is one such concept prescribed as a viable and venerable answer for the impending data-driven challenges.

The IoT is turning out to be a primary enabler of the digital transformation of any kind of enterprising businesses. Companies are eagerly looking towards pioneering digital technologies to create and sustain their business competitiveness. The IoT and other digital technologies are helping companies to facilitate process enhancement, create newer business models, optimize the IT infrastructures, bring forth competent architectures, empower workforce efficiency and innovation, etc. The IoT closes down the gap between the physical and cyber worlds. helps connect physical and digital environments. Data collected from connected devices are subjected to a variety of investigations to extract dependable insights.

THE USE CASES OF FOG / EDGE COMPUTING

The rapid growth of personal, social and professional devices in our daily environments has seeded this inimitable computing style. The communication becomes wireless, sensors and devices are heterogeneous and large in number, geo-distribution becomes the new normal, the interconnectivity and interactions among various participants emit a lot of data, etc. The amount of data getting generated and gathered at the edge of the network is really massive in volumes.

Usually, this data is transported back to the cloud for storage and processing, which incidentally requires high bandwidth connectivity. In order to save network bandwidth, there is a valid proposition of using a moderately sized platform in between to do a kind of pre-processing in order to filter out the flabs. Differently enabled cameras, for example, generate images and videos that would aggregate easily in the range of terabytes. Instead of clogging expensive and scarce network bandwidths, a kind of fog/edge processing can be initiated to ease networks. That is, reasonably powerful devices in the environment under monitoring can be individually or collectively leveraged to process cameras-emitted files in real-time. That is, the data gleaned can be subsequently segmented and shared to different devices in the vicinity in order to do the distributed processing quickly. As we all know, with more devices joining in the mainstream computing and the amount of data getting stocked is growing exponentially, the distributed computing concept has soared in the recent past and is being touted as the mandated way forward for the data-centric world.

There are a number of convincing use cases for fog/edge computing. Fog devices locally collect, cleanse, store, process, and even analyze data in order to facilitate real-time analytics towards informed decisions. There are research papers describing how connected vehicles, smart grids, wireless sensor and actuator networks, etc. are more right and relevant for people with the fast-moving fog computing paradigm. Smart building, manufacturing floors, smart traffic and retail, and smart cities are some of the often-cited domains wherein the raging fog idea chips in with real benefits. Augmented reality (AR), content delivery and mobile data analytics are also very well documented as the direct beneficiaries of fog computing. One use case for fog computing is a smart traffic light system, which can change its signals based on surveillance of incoming traffic to prevent accidents or reduce congestion. Data could also be sent to the cloud for longer-term analytics. Other use cases include rail safety; power restoration from a smart grid network; and cybersecurity. There are connected cars (for vehicle-to-vehicle and vehicle-to-cloud communication); and in smart city applications, such as intelligent lighting and smart parking meters.

- **Smart Homes:** There is a home security application profoundly discussed in a research paper. As we all know, there is a myriad of home security products (smart lock, video/audio recorder, security sensors and monitors (alarm, presence, occupancy, motion sensors etc.). These are stand-alone solutions and due to disparate data transport protocols and data formats, these products do not interoperate with one another. However, the emergence and emancipation of fog computing have simplified the process of dynamically integrating these diverse security products in order to enhance the timeliness and trustworthiness of any security information. The uniqueness of fog computing platform is that it can be flexibly deployed on a virtual machine or in a Docker container. Existing and new sensors and actuators register and get connected with the fog platform, which ensures a seamless and spontaneous interoperation between different and distributed devices and machines towards the goal. This ad-hoc collaboration capability senses any kind of security threats and immediately stimulates the necessary countermeasures through connected actuators. Energy management, device clustering and coordination, ambient assisted living (AAL), activity recognition / context-awareness for formulating and firming up people-centric services, etc. are getting streamlined with the fog computing nuances.

- **Smart Grids:** Smart electric grid is an electricity distribution network with smart meters deployed at various locations to measure the real-time power consumption level. A centrally hosted SCADA server frequently gathers and analyzes status data to send out appropriate information to power grids to adapt accordingly. If there is any palpable increment in power usage or any kind of emergency, it will be instantaneously conveyed to the power grid to act upon. Now with the fog idea, the centralized SCADA server can be supplemented by one or more decentralized microgrids. This salient setup improves scalability, cost-efficiency, security and rapid response of the power system. This also helps to integrate distributed and different power generators (solar panels, wind farms, etc.) with the main power grid. Energy load balancing applications may run on edge devices such as smart meters and microgrids. Based on energy demand, availability, and the lowest price, these devices automatically switch to alternative energies like solar and wind.

- **Smart Vehicles:** The fog concept can be extended to vehicular networks also. The fog nodes can be deployed along the roadside. The fog nodes can send to and receive information from vehicles. Vehicles through their in-vehicle infotainment systems can interact with the roadside fog systems as well as with other vehicles on the road. Thus, this kind of ad hoc networks leads to a variety of applications such as traffic light scheduling, congestion mitigation, precaution sharing, parking facility management, traffic information sharing, etc. A video camera that senses an ambulance flashing lights can automatically change streetlights to open lanes for the vehicle to pass through traffic. Smart streetlights interact locally with sensors and detect the presence of pedestrian and bikers, and measure the distance and speed of approaching vehicles.

- **Smarter Security:** Security and surveillance cameras are being fitted in different important junctions such as airports, nuclear installations, government offices, retail stores, etc. Further on, nowadays smartphones are embedded with powerful cameras to click selfies as well as produce photos of others. Still, as well as running images can be captured and communicated to nearby fog nodes as well as to faraway cloud nodes in order to readily process the photos and compare them with the face images of radicals, extremists, fundamentalists, terrorists, arsonists, trouble-makers, etc. in the already stored databases. Further on, through image processing and analytics, it is possible to extract useful information in the form unusual gestures, movements, etc. All these empower security and police officials to proceed in their investigations with clarity and confidence. The Figure 3 pictorially conveys how the fog cloud facilitates real-time sensor data processing and historical sensor data processing at nearby or faraway clouds (public, private and hybrid).

Figure 3. The Fog ensures zero latency towards Real-time Applications

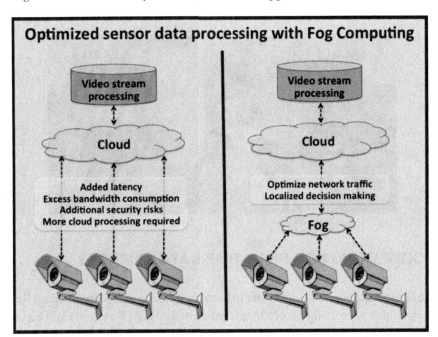

- **Smart Buildings:** Like homes, office and corporate buildings are stuffed with a number of sensors for minute monitoring, precise measurement, and management. There is a school of thought that multiple sensor values, when blended, throw more accurate value. There are advanced sensor data fusion algorithms and hence, smart sensors and actuators work in tandem towards automating and accelerating several manual tasks. For providing a seamless and smart experience to employees and visitors, the building automation domain is on the fast trajectory with a series of innovations and improvisations in the IT space. That is, computing becomes pervasive, communication is ambient, sensing is ubiquitous, actuation is intelligently accomplished, etc. The computer vision and perception topics gather momentum, knowledge engineering and enhancement are becoming common and cheap and decision-enablement becomes perfect. The edge devices participating in and contributing to the edge cloud facilitate multiple things intelligently so that the strategic goal of building automation through networking and integration is getting accomplished.

Today, a medium-sized office building could have hundreds of sensors on its equipment. A great example is chillers, a product needed to cool a building. The product manufacturer (http://www.johnson-controls.com/) monitors chillers remotely using predictive diagnostics to identify and solve issues before they become problems. The company uses internal operational data and historical records to better plan machine maintenance, leading to better operational efficiency and decreasing energy usage, in addition to increase reliability and equipment lifespan. Even better, the company has external data resources like weather patterns and grid demand costs to drive greater operational savings.

There are several other industry verticals and business domains yearning to get immensely benefited out of all the decisive and delectable advancements in the field of fog computing.

Figure 4.

WHY EDGE COMPUTING FOR REAL-TIME DATA SCIENCE?

For producing real-time applications, real-time information and insights are needed. Real-time analytics is the way forward for generating timely inputs for empowering IT systems and business workloads accordingly to exhibit adaptive behaviour. Data science covers everything that supports the transition of data to information and to knowledge. There are proven algorithms in the field of data science. There are cloud-based cognitive platforms and applications utilizing those algorithms in a progressive and positive way. Now the time for embedding data science algorithms and applications into edge appliances and clouds to supply real-time intelligence for the increasingly connected world has come. A kind of edge analytics inside vehicles goes a long way in identifying and automating a myriad of vehicle needs. Vehicles' drivers and occupants get a lot of benefits. A variety of spatial and temporal applications are being worked out. In this section, let us discuss why the fog paradigm is right and relevant to the intended success of data science.

- **Weeding out Irrelevant Data at the Source:** The IoT represents trillions of digitized objects, billions of connected devices and millions of software applications. The direct offshoot is that the amount of data getting generated, captured and transmitted is really voluminous. However, most of the data are repetitive, redundant and routine. The edge computing facilitates filtering out the inconsequential data at the edge of the network so that useful and usable data can be communicated to cloud environments in order to have speedy and sagacious analytics. There is very minimal wastage of network bandwidth with this pre-processing at the edges.

- **Real-Time IoT Data Analytics:** For certain scenarios such as historical, comprehensive and posterior processing, the traditional clouds are insisted. Faraway clouds are typically for batch processing or at the most near real-time processing. But the faster maturity and stability of edge computing readily enables real-time processing of device data. That is, there are scenarios craving for real-time data capture and analysis in order to emit out real-time insights. We have discussed the fog/edge analytics in below sections.

- **Instantaneous Response:** There are many use cases wherein faster responses are not needed. Turning on the lights, closing the garage door, or checking the vending machine status, etc. come under this category. However, there are use cases expecting a faster response. For example, vehicles on the road or any moving object has to respond immediately to surrounding situations. Thus, it is indispensable to have fog compute infrastructure in place in order to accomplish actions with very low latency.

- **Resource-Constrained Sensors Behind Fog Devices:** Many sensors do not have enough compute, memory and storage power in order to have their own IPv6 address. Hence, they can hide behind an edge device, which has the power to have its own IPv6 address. It is, therefore, pertinent to configure ground-level and resource-constrained sensors and actuators behind the edge device. The arrival of edge computing has henceforth solidified the sensors to be slimmer, purpose-specific and cheaper.

- **IoT Data Security:** Any external attack on sensors can be stopped at the edge device, which acts as a shelter, strength, stronghold, and saviour for feeble sensors. The idea is to prolong the livelihood of sensors. Also, the sensor data are transmitted to edge devices to be stocked and subjected to specific investigations over any local network only. That is, the sensor data is kept away from the public and porous Internet. Sharing sensor data to public cloud environments is beset with challenges. There can be further advancements on the security front in the days to unfurl.

- **The Formation of Edge Clouds:** All kinds of powerful edge devices can be clubbed together dynamically to form device clusters. Having such edge clouds is an important precursor for doing edge data analytics to emit out real-time intelligent to act upon with all the confidence and clarity. Thus, fog devices with the capability of realizing ad hoc clouds are the real trendsetters for doing local or proximate processing of device and sensor data.

- **Building Composite Applications:** Devices and equipment being deployed in a specific environment (say, a restaurant) communicate to their vendors directly in order to push a variety of data. Specifically, the lighting data would go to the lighting vendor, the kitchen equipment data to the kitchen equipment vendor, and so forth However there is very little for the environment occupants and owners. Now with the surging popularity of fog computing, all kinds of sensor and equipment data get aggregated at the restaurant fog device. Edge device messages are getting accentuated, enriched, secured, and directed to their proper destination through a fog middleware. The messages also can be combined with other relevant messages from other internal as well as external sources to supply viable and venerable insights to decision-making, recommender and expert systems. That is, street traffic data, weather report, demographic information, etc. can be cleansed and enriched to be a stimulant for a range of path-breaking applications including corporate, in-restaurant operational optimization, supply chain, and perhaps a variety of applications for third-party constituents, such as government regulators, suppliers, etc.

- **Policy-Based Fog Devices:** With fog devices being positioned as the most crucial component for the proclaimed success of the IoT idea, it becomes paramount for fog devices to be enabled policy-aware. The brewing idea is to establish and enforce security, governance, role-based access, activation, and configuration policies. Different policies can be inserted in fog devices to have a firm grip and control on all the sensors and actuators attached.

Precisely speaking, the unprecedented and phenomenal acceptance and adoption of the edge computing is a breakthrough for sustaining the strategic journey of the IoT concept. There is this new paradigm of fog or edge computing vigorously and rigorously capturing the imagination of IoT professionals these days. That is, the real-time and relatively small-scale processing is shifted to edge devices instead of aggregating and transmitting device data to faraway cloud servers to squeeze out insights. Localized and personalized decisions are essential in certain scenarios and hence the fast-evolving concept of fog computing is being gleefully received. The edge devices are dynamically discovered and linked through body, personal and local area networks to form ad-hoc edge clouds to accelerate and accentuate edge analytics. With the rapid explosion of connected things, devices, and services, it is understandable that the decentralized networking is the best way forward as it has the inherent potential to reduce infrastructure and maintenance costs. Decentralization guarantees increased robustness by removing single points of failure. By shifting from centralized to decentralized processing, devices at the edges gain greater autonomy to become the core and central point of transactions towards enhanced productivity and value for owners and users.

With the unprecedented success of the pioneering digitization and edge computing technologies and tools, every tangible thing in our daily environments is becoming a digitized / smart/sentient object. It is foreseen that everyone in this world will have one or more smartphones / personal digital assistants/ wearables soon. Every unique asset and artefact (physical, mechanical, electrical, and electronics) participating in our daily deals and deeds is systematically and sagaciously enabled through edge/fog technologies and cloud applications to be computational, communicative, sensitive, perceptive, responsive and cognitive. Ultimately our everyday environments are to be bedecked with a variety of smart sensors and actuators to fulfil the prime goals of precision-centric context-awareness and activity recognition. Further on, cloud-based cyber applications will have a salivating and scintillating role in empowering physical items on the ground. In short, the ensuing era is all about producing and providing knowledge-filled services that are people-centric, situation-aware, and event-driven.

In today's digitally connected society, there will be deeper and decisive affinity among enabled objects, connected devices, and humans in the days ahead. The result is that large volumes of multi-structured data are getting generated at different speeds, sizes, scopes, and schemas through the interactions and collaborations of heterogeneous digital elements, smartphones, technical experiments, social media, healthcare instruments, machines, satellite telemetry, and imagery. These data lead to formulating and firm up various new analytical competencies such as social media analytics, sentiment analytics, predictive, prognostic, prescriptive, personalized analytics etc. for people empowerment. The prickling challenge is how efficiently and effectively subjects the captured and cleansed data to various specific investigations to readily extract real-time intelligence to make right inferences. In this section, we will dig deep and describe at length about the uniqueness of edge analytics.

- **The Greatness of Edge Data:** It is a known fact that the unprecedented rise in data sources has led to the emergence of the strategically sound big data discipline and its allied technologies. The big data landscape is therefore relentlessly and rightly growing. Besides the enormity of the data being produced by knowledge workers and social animals, the growing size of machine-generated data is to get prime importance in the impending big data era. Machine data especially of edge devices is progressively playing a very pivotal role in shaping up the crucial aspect of data-driven insights and insights-driven decisions. The story thus far is that firstly there are a voluminous production and extensive deployment of smart sensors and actuators in a variety of environments (home, industrial, social, entertainment, education, etc.) for different purposes. The much-discussed connectivity, which is constantly becoming deeper and extreme, connects them via different modes: wireless, wireline and the mix of them. That is, there are millions of devices at the edges of networks and it is projected that the number of devices will turn out to be in the range of billions in the years to unfurl.

All these are being intensively deciphered and deliberated these days because of the unparalleled advancements in the embedded and connectivity domains. Both resource-rich and constrained devices are systematically hooked together in an ad hoc fashion to interchange their data and share their unique capabilities. Further on, edge devices are grandly integrated with cyber applications and services hosted at distant cloud environments. These direct, as well as indirect integrations and interactions, have laid a strong and stimulating foundation for a sharp hike in edge data generation. Data is being collected by an enormous variety of equipment, such as smart utility meters, surveillance and security cameras, actuators, robots, RFID readers, biometrics, factory-line sensors, mobile phones, fitness machines, defence equipment and weapons, launchers and satellites, avionics and automobiles, information appliances, household utensils and wares, electronic gadgets and gizmos, lab-experimentation devices, and medical instruments.

The ubiquitous connectivity and the mass production of modern sensors and actuators have opened up a whole new powerhouse for valuable information. It is clear that edge data can bring forth significant value and a rich set of sophisticated services to all stakeholders including end-users. The careful and cognitive capture, processing, and analysis of edge data in time can go a long way in empowering organizations to respond to both positive as well as negative events pre-emptively and solve many problems that were previously out of reach.

The point here is that this untapped resource of edge data has the inherent potential to deliver dependable insights that can transform the operations and strategic initiatives of public and private sector organizations. Incidentally, the edge data is becoming larger, speedier and trickier but the hidden value is definitely greater. And hence, distinct research endeavours on making sense out of edge data are drawing phenomenal attention. On the other hand, there are standards-compliant big data analytics platforms (open source as well as commercial-grade), data ingestion and crunching toolsets, data virtualization and visualization tools, knowledge engineering techniques, high-performance multicore processors, gigabits Ethernet solutions, and inexpensive storage options including object storage to extract and extrapolate knowledge.

In summary, as the size of edge data is growing significantly, there is a bigger challenge to information management professionals to evolve a pragmatic strategy for effectively leveraging all sorts of edge data for the well-being of their organizations. With the faster maturity and stability of data analytics platforms, knowledge systems and services are bound to grow and glow.

THE EDGE ANALYTICS: THE PROMINENT USE CASES

Edge data is carefully captured and crunched using fog devices for generating intelligent immediately. Here are a few interesting use cases for edge analytics.

- **IoT Sensor Data Monitoring and Analysis:** It is clear that the massive deployment of heterogeneous sensors leads to the tremendous amount of sensor data. Moving sensor data analytics to the edge with a platform that can analyze batch, fast and streaming data simultaneously enables organizations to speed and simplify analytics to get the insights they need, right where they need them.

- **Remote Monitoring and Analysis of Oil and Gas Operations:** Edge analytics is a boon for companies in oil and gas exploration, refinement, storage, and distribution. Any kind of delay in sensing and responding to such kinds of rough and risky environments paves for disaster. Cloud-based analytics is time-consuming and it is not possible to expect real-time responses from far-away cloud environments. Having near-instant analysis at the site as the data is being created can help these organizations see the signs of a disaster and take measures to prevent a catastrophe before it starts.

- **Predictive Asset Management:** This capability sharply improves the overall availability and operational performance of physical assets while reducing their total cost of ownership (TCO). Edge analytics enable organizations to move from scheduled maintenance models to predictive ones. That is, it is all about predictive and preventive maintenance giving product managers to gain the expert control over their equipment and maintenance resources. These capabilities help avoid catastrophic failures by identifying critical issues that occur inside the normally scheduled maintenance window, lower costs by eliminating unnecessary maintenance tasks and make more effective use of scarce and expensive resources (both human and capital).

- **Smarter Cities:** Intel defines that the smart city concept mandates the use of smart-grid infrastructures to improve environmental sustainability, manage energy consumption, better coordinate public resources, and protect the quality of life for urban and metropolitan citizens and plan for sustainable growth. The edge data here plays a very incredible role. For example, utility companies and governments are using data from the smart grid to understand the complex relationships between generation, transmission, distribution, and consumption with the goal of delivering reliable energy and reducing operating costs. Consumers are also empowered with insights from the smart grid to better manage their personal energy requirements. For example, a "not home" state might turn off lights, shut down unused equipment and adjust the home temperature. Utility meter readings and grid data are brought into centralized analytical systems to bring forth timely insights.

Thus, edge devices collaboratively contribute immensely to arriving at better decisions than only at a centralized control centre. Communication between devices helps determine when, where, and how much energy should be produced and consumers can use home management tools to monitor and adjust energy consumption accordingly.

- **Smart Retailers:** It is a well-known thing that supermarkets and hypermarkets across the globe duly collect a lot of data every day. If they are properly collected, cleansed, and categorized, worldwide retailers can substantially enhance their grip on their customers and their buying patterns. This incredible knowledge on customers prepares retail stores to think big and to bring forth scores of premium services in time to retain and delight their loyal customers as well as to attract new customers. The enduring challenges thrown by the hugeness in the data being captured and processed is being tackled through highly versatile Hadoop framework / Spark that can totally change the retail economics by radically lowering the cost of data storage and processing, bringing in new flexibilities to gain new insights, automated replenishment and more accurately market to individuals rather than a demographic.

Retailers are using a variety of intelligent systems that gather data and provide immediate feedback to help them to engage shoppers fruitfully. The well-known data-generation systems include digital signage, PoS systems, vending machines, transaction, in-store cameras, dispensing kiosks, etc. The ability to gain reliable insights from the data shared by these systems makes it possible to provide customer-centric "connected stores". Context-awareness is the main theme of these connected machines to precisely and perfectly understand the customer situation. The context information then greatly differentiates in showering customers with a host of unique services. In short, the insights-driven shopping experience is enabling customers immensely in getting items for the best price. Based on the edge data, retailers can integrate their supply chain activities intelligently. Further on, retailers can provide their customers with opportunities to engage with their preferred brands in more meaningful ways to cement customer loyalty.

- **Smart Automobiles:** The number of digital electronics and other automation elements in a vehicle is steadily on the climb for providing different kinds of services to drivers and the occupants. The convenience, care, choice, and comfort induced by these connected devices are definitely awesome. Sensors are being attached to every critical component in a car to pre-emptively get to know the component's status and this reading provides some leeway for drivers to ponder about the next course of action. Another interesting and involving module is the in-vehicle infotainment system, which is emerging as the core and central gateway for securing and strengthening the connectivity outside for a range of use cases. All kinds of communication, computing, and entertainment systems inside vehicles will have a seamless connection with the outside world through the well-defined in-vehicle system so that the occupants can enjoy their trip in a fruitful manner. GPS devices and smart meters of cars throw a lot of data to be captured and analyzed.

Sensors provide information to automated parking systems to substantially lessen the driver's workload. There are sensors-enabled driver assistance systems for automobiles. Location data could be combined with road work and other traffic information to help commuters avoid congestion or take a faster route. Digital signage, cameras and other infrastructures on the roadsides in synchronization with the in-vehicle infotainment module (V2I) aid drivers to give a pleasant travel experience to all. Vehicles today talk to other vehicles (V2V) on the road and interact with remote cloud services and applications (V2C). Vehicles share their data to the remotely held databases in order to facilitate the different aspects of vehicle analytics. Maps are the other salivating tool for reaching out the destination in a cool and controlled manner. Detecting real-time traffic flow from each direction and automatically changing traffic signals are to improve flow.

Autonomous vehicles are tending towards the reality with the realization of the advanced and accurate machine and deep learning algorithms. Further on, there are breakthrough technologies enabling transmission of real-time vehicle telematics, GPS tracking, and geofencing data. These noteworthy improvisations lead to improved safety, mobility, and efficiency and pave the way for new business models such as pay-as-you-go auto insurance. Proactive maintenance decreases costs and reduces vehicle downtime.

Edge data further enable automated, intelligent, and real-time decisions to optimize travel across the transportation infrastructure as cars become capable of connecting to the roadway, safety systems, and one another.

- **Smart Manufacturing:** Every tangible machine and tool in manufacturing floors and production facilities is being stuffed with a manifold of smart sensors, communication modules, etc. That is, today's devices are instrumented to interoperate and be intelligent in their operations and obligations. Machines are not only networked with others in the neighbourhood but also with remote cloud environments. Today all the production-related data are being shared with the centralized systems in the form of excel sheets at the end of the day through emails. But new-generation machines are capable of integrating with cloud-enabled software applications and cloud storages instantly and insightfully. That is, machines transfer all the ground-level information to the cyber-level transaction and analytical systems then and there. This technology-inspired real-time connectivity facilitates a number of fresh possibilities and opportunities for corporates in visualizing hitherto unforeseen competencies. In addition, chief executives and other decision-makers, who are on the move in a far away land, can be provided with decision-enabling productivity details through a real-time notification capability in order to ensure any course correction if necessary, commit something solid to their customers with all the confidence and clarity, ponder about new offerings, bring operational efficiencies, explore newer avenues for fresh revenues, etc.

That is, smart factories connect the boardroom, the factory floor and the supply chain for higher levels of manufacturing control and efficiency. Sensors and actuators in devices such as cameras, robotic machines, and motion-control equipment generate and use data to provide real-time diagnosis and predictive maintenance, increased process visibility and improved factory uptime and flexibility. Thus, edge data lays a sparkling foundation for smart manufacturing.

- **Facilities and Asset Management:** The big data generated by increasingly instrumented, interconnected and intelligent facilities and assets are useful only if transactional systems could extract applicable information and act upon it as needed. The appropriate and real-time usage of this big data is to help improve decisions or generate corrective actions that can create measurable benefits for an organization. Big data analytics can help generate revenue by providing a contextual understanding of information that the business can then employ to its fullest advantage. For example, geographic information systems (GIS) can help location-sensitive organizations such as retailers, telecommunications, and energy companies determine the most advantageous geographies for their business operations. A world's largest wind energy producer has achieved success using a big data modelling solution to harvest insights from an expanded set of location-dependent factors including historical and actual weather to help optimize wind turbine placement and performance. Exact pinpointing the optimal locations for wind turbines enables energy producers to maximize power generation and reduce energy costs as well as to provide its customers with greater business case certainty, quicker results, and increased predictability and reliability in wind power generation.

Effective facilities and asset management solution have to leverage big data analytics to enable organizations to proactively maintain facilities equipment, identify emerging problems to prevent breakdowns, lower maintenance, and operations costs and extend asset life through condition-based maintenance and automated issue-notification. To help mitigate risks to facilities and assets, predictive analytics can detect even minor anomalies and failure patterns to determine the assets that are at the greatest risk of failure. Predictive maintenance analytics can access multiple data sources in real time to predict equipment failure which helps organizations avoid costly downtime and reduce maintenance costs. Sensors could capture the operating conditions of critical equipment such as vibrations from ship engines and communicate the captured data in real time to company's command centre for proceeding with failure analysis and predictive maintenance. Similarly, the careful analysis of environmental and weather-pattern data in real time is another way of mitigating any kind of visible or invisible risks. Organizations can receive alerts of potential weather impacts in time to shut down facilities operations or pre-locate emergency response teams to minimize business disruption in case of any advancing storms.

Big data is admirably advantageous when applied to the management of facilities and assets (everything from office buildings to oil-drilling platforms to fleets of the ship). This is due to the increased instrumentation of facilities and assets, where the digital and physical worlds have synchronized to generate massive volumes of data. Therefore considering the mammoth volume of data, tool-supported analysis of big data can lead to bountiful benefits such as increased revenue, lowered operating expenses, enhanced service availability and reduced risk. In a nutshell, edge data is a ground-breaking phenomenon for all kinds of industrial sectors to zoom ahead with all the required conviction.

IoT Data Edge Analytics for Next-Gen Data Science

Embedded cognitive IoT will become a key focus area for software engineers, experts, and evangelists. One of the key ingredients will be an open source platform for building, tuning, and deploying cognitive applications into edge devices. The ideal development platform for open, embedded, and cognitive IoT applications have to have the following features.

The platform has to facilitate embedding of cognitive analytics capabilities so that IoT devices and services can adapt continuously and react locally to their environments and, as needed, to metrics and commands from neighbouring devices. This has to enable developers to access, configure, and tweak any cognitive computing algorithm that is suited to the IoT analytics requirements. Further on, it has to execute cognitive algorithms on any size IoT device. It also has to present flexible and familiar programming models for IoT development, including Python, Java, and C. The platform has the wherewithal to analyze data as it streams at the device level and thereby eliminates the need to store it persistently. The platform also ought to support the execution of all or most cognitive IoT processing locally, reducing or eliminating the need to round-trip many capabilities back to cloud-based computing clusters. The platform has to accelerate memory-speed local drill down into growing streams of locally acquired and cached sensor data. It also has the connectors, adapters, and drivers to access data from any streaming data platform, as well as from any RDBMS, hub, repository, file system, or another store in any cloud, on-premise, or off-premise.

AD HOC EDGE CLOUDS FOR EDGE ANALYTICS

The ultimate aim of edge clouds is to deliver low-latency, bandwidth-efficient, and resilient applications. Edge clouds are being formed out of connected and resource-intensive fog devices in order to do certain functionalities locally. Edge clouds stand in between faraway clouds in the cyber world and scores of sensors/actuators in the physical world. Edge clouds store every machine and sensor data, subject them to specific investigations and spit out actionable insights that can be given directly to fog devices and to resource-constrained actuators at the ground level. This level of extreme and deeper connectivity and process integration leads to the consistent eruption of path-breaking and people-centric applications. Similarly, the insights emitted out by edge clouds can be readily integrated with cloud-based applications in order to build sophisticated applications.

The edge cloud facilitates a kind of new-generation architecture for seamlessly integrating local edge networks and cloud networks. This is to keep latency-sensitive computation and user interaction components close to end-users at the edge nodes while hosting additional heavy-duty processing and database components in cloud center nodes. Another perceptible benefit is the bandwidth gets conserved by doing the initial activities at the edge so that only highly compressed and compact data get transmitted to cloud environments over the Internet communication infrastructure. The edge cloud is able to access various physical assets, mechanical and electrical devices, consumer electronics, etc. and receives their data. Edge clouds contribute to the application and system resilience. If edge cloud or one of its components fails for any reason, then the traditional cloud environment takes care of the processing. On the reverse side, when something happens to the cloud center due to network failure, natural calamities, or power outage, etc., then the edge cloud takes care of the processing. Thus, edge cloud comes as a complementary cloud environment for faster sensing and responding.

Edge computing is pushing computing applications, data, and services away from centralized cloud data centers to the edges of the underlying network. The objective is to perform data analytics near the source of data to quickly raise right alerts and indulge inappropriate actions immediately. Finally, edge clouds enable end-users getting empowered with knowledge-filled services. In short, edge clouds are for local data processing. Traditional clouds are being realized through a set of homogeneous server machines, storage appliances, and network solutions. Edge clouds are, on the other hand, is formed through clubbing together of decentralized and heterogeneous devices. Edge clouds are generally ad hoc.

The public cloud idea typically represents the online, off-premise and on-demand computing whereas the fog computing is for proximity computing. Of course, there are private and hybrid clouds that use dynamically changing clusters of commodity server machines for data processing and logic execution. The fog computing paradigm extends the computing to the network of edge devices. The fog vision was conceived and aptly concretized in order to comprehensively attend some specific use cases for the smarter computing era. There are specific applications such as gaming, video conferencing, etc. mandating very low and predictable latency. Then there are geo-distributed applications (smarter traffic, grid, etc., pipeline monitoring, environmental monitoring and management through the sensor and actuator networks, etc.). Further on, mobility applications such as connected cars and transports are pitching for the fog paradigm. The next logical step is to have hybrid environments by seamlessly and spontaneously integrating edge and traditional cloud environments for availing advanced and aggregated analytics.

In summary, clouds have been the prominent and dominant infrastructures to develop, debug, deploy, and deliver pioneering business and IT applications. However, cloud computing cannot solve all problems due to its own drawbacks. Applications, such as real-time gaming, augmented reality, and data streaming, are too latency-sensitive to be deployed in the cloud. The networks are clogged due to the growth in data transmission. Sharing sensor and device data over any network is beset with security and privacy challenges and concerns. Real-time analytics is being positioned as the most important requirements for generating real-time insights and making timely decision-making. Since cloud centers are geographically distributed, those applications and services will suffer unacceptable round-trip latency, when data are transmitted from/to end devices to/from the cloud data center through multiple gateways. Cloud-based data analytics sometimes misses the real-time mandate and hence there are efforts in order to craft ad hoc clouds out of devices in the local environment. Multiple and heterogeneous devices in the vicinity are readily identified and connected with one another to form edge or fog clouds to tackle the rising volume of device and sensor data to make sense out of it. The Figure 5 clearly depicts how edge clouds come handy in fulfilling the real-time data capture, processing, decision-making, and actuation requirements.

Figure 5. The Edge Clouds is the Next-Gen Real-time Clouds

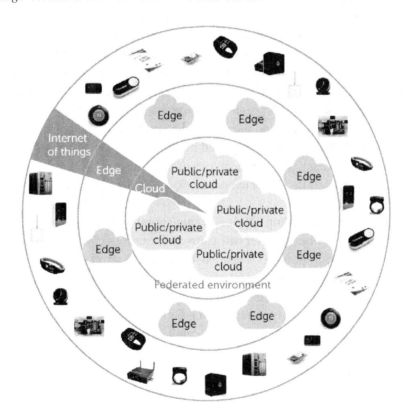

EDGE APPLICATION AND ANALYTICS PLATFORMS

Fog devices individually cannot do much. They need to be integrated and empowered through a pioneering platform. In other words, we need highly efficient and elegant platform for accomplishing and acquiring the originally envisaged benefits of fog computing and analytics. The traditional enterprise, cloud, and web-based platforms are not suitable for fog computing, as fog devices are not resource-intensive. We need highly modular and extremely adaptive platforms to activate and accentuate the fog computing ideals and ideas. Any fog computing platforms need to be fully synchronized for performing IoT data ingestion, processing, analytics, decision-making, and actuation. The platform has to have the device management and gateway capabilities. This is due to the fact that devices are typically dynamic and nomadic and can come, join and even go out of the network. In this section, we are to discuss the breakthrough techniques in building competitive fog platforms that in turn lead to highly competitive IoT gateways (Raj and Raman, 2016).

The typical fog or edge devices include reasonably powerful controllers, communication gateways, Wi-Fi routers, smartphones, consumer electronics, robots, etc. On the other side, these fog devices interact with a variety of resource-constrained sensors, actuators, digitized objects, sensors-attached physical assets, etc. with the intention of getting, cleansing, curating, translating, and transforming the IoT data. Further on, fog devices crunch the data to discover actionable insights to perform many things intelligently. Fog devices, based on the inputs and insights obtained through the stringent analytics process, activate IoT devices to do many things. Fog devices contribute as a well-intended broker and bus to enable fruitful interactions between IoT entities at the ground with cloud-based applications.

As technology continuously advances, the product vendors are steadily incorporating advanced operational as well as management capabilities into IoT elements, especially in fog devices. These capabilities vary ranging from the simple ability to turn a device on and off to more complex actions such as updating software, managing Wi-Fi connections, configuring security policies, or changing data parameters. Now the next major requirement is to have an intelligent and policy-aware platform to emphatically empower and manage fog/edge devices and the ground-level IoT devices. Raspberry Pi controllers and Arduino boards are the well-known and widely used intermediaries and gateways at this point in time for gathering data from sensors and passing them to centralized control systems. The issue here is that these microcontroller-based solutions do not exhibit any kind of sophisticated management capabilities.

- **The OSGi Standard for Building Device Management Frameworks:** Many times, we have experienced the power of the open service gateway initiative (OSGi) solutions towards having modular applications. OSGi provides a vendor-independent, standards-based approach to modularizing Java software applications, and its proven services model allows software components to communicate locally and across a distributed network. The OSGi specification defines modular based software management and its execution. OSGi makes software management and its execution simpler by making large application into a small bunch of pieces (called as modules). These modules are working independent way so that when we need them, we can start and stop modules. As for OSGi, a module is termed as Bundle or Plugin-in. OSGi provides execution environment enabling modul6.

Java-based applications or components come as an OSGi deployment bundle and can be remotely installed, started, discovered, stopped, updated, and uninstalled. OSGi inherently offers advanced remote management capabilities of embedded devices. An OSGi-based device application framework brings forth a layer between the OS and the business application on the OSGi platform. This growing collection of cohesive software components lets customers modify, reconfigure, and maintain their application over time as per the changes mandated. That is, application evolves with the changes happening around. Furthermore, the adaptability and flexibility of the OSGi application architecture provide competitive advantages. The ability to easily modify functionality is a must-have for device application frameworks

Figure 6. The OSGi Stack Model

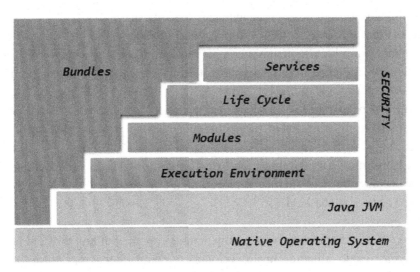

today. A device application framework built on open standards enables communication with multiple management systems, and any platform based on the Java/OSGi deployment model can manage various parts of the device from an application standpoint. The OSGi model can be ingeniously extended to develop an IoT device management framework to build powerful IoT gateways and scores of next-generation IoT applications that are generally dynamic.

- **The Eclipse Kura - An IoT Device Management & Analytics Platform:** The Eclipse Kura framework is being developed on the proven and potential OSGi idea to build next-generation IoT gateways/fog devices with device management capabilities. This Kura framework has been fitted with innovative device management features. For example, the Kura solution is exceptional here. Consider a vending machine company with machines distributed worldwide. Parameters change frequently to reflect inventory, price, and preference, and operators can benefit from remote management in order to fix the broken machine, update software, add new product lines or services, and more. That is, the Kura-empowered fog device monitors and manages different and distributed vending machines at the ground. There can be one or multiple fog devices interacting with one another. That is, fog devices are locally distributed and clubbed together on a need basis to tackle compute and data-intensive needs. In other words, fog or edge devices form an ad hoc compute and data cluster, which is touted as the fog or edge cloud. The Kura framework facilitates the formation and deployment of edge clouds.

Eclipse Kura is an open-source project that provides a platform for building IoT gateways through the use of a smart application container that enables remote management and provides a wide range of developer APIs. The goals of the Eclipse Kura project can be summarized as:

- **Provide an OSGi-Based Container for IoT Applications Running in Service Gateways:** Kura complements the Java and OSGi platforms with APIs and services covering the most common requirements of IoT applications. These extensions include I/O access, data services, watchdog, network configuration, and remote management.

- **Kura Adopts Existing Javax.* APIs When Available:** When possible, Kura will select an open-source implementation of APIs that are compatible with the Eclipse license and package it in an OSGi bundle to be included in the Kura default build (for example, javax.comm, javax.usb, and javax.bluetooth).
- **Design a Build Environment:** The Kura build environment isolates native code components and makes it simple to add ports of these components for new platforms in the Kura build and distribution.
- **Provide an Emulation Environment for IoT Applications Within the Eclipse IDE:** From the Eclipse IDE, applications can then be deployed on a target gateway and remotely provisioned to Kura-enabled devices in the field.

Eclipse Kura provides a foundation on top of which other contributions for field bus protocols and sensor integration can reside, allowing Java developers to control behaviour at the edge. The built-in functionalities include turning the serial port on or off, Wi-Fi management, remote data processing, and more. These remote management services also allow IoT applications installed in Kura to be continuously configured, upgraded, and deployed.

- **Everyware Software Framework (ESF):** ESF is a commercial and enterprise-ready edition of Eclipse Kura, the open source Java/OSGi middleware for IoT gateways. Distributed and supported by Eurotech, ESF adds advanced security, diagnostics, provisioning, remote access and full integration with Everyware Cloud, Eurotech's IoT Integration Platform. ESF is a smart application container that enables remote management of IoT gateways and provides a wide range of APIs allowing you to write and deploy your own IoT application. ESF runs on top of the Java Virtual Machine (JVM) and leverages OSGi, a dynamic component system for Java, to simplify the process of writing reusable software building blocks. ESF APIs offer easy access to the underlying hardware including serial ports, GPS, watchdog, USB, GPIOs, I2C, etc. They also offer OSGi bundles to simplify the management of network configurations, the communication with IoT servers, and the remote management of the gateway.

ESF components are designed as configurable OSGi Declarative Services exposing the service API and raising events. While several ESF components are pure Java, others are invoked through Java Native Interface (JNI) and depend on the Linux operating system. The Eurotech Everyware Software Framework (ESF) provides extensions in the areas of security, field protocol support, and native integration with the Everyware Cloud IoT service and application enablement platform. Through ESF, Eurotech provides a set of the common device, network, and service abstraction tools for Java developers building IoT applications, including I/O access, data services, network configuration, and remote management.

- **Apache Edgent Edge Analytics Platform:** Edgent is a new edge analytics platform and can be used at the edge of any networks. That is, every kind of edge devices, machines, engines, vehicles, robots, drones, rigs, equipment, wares, utensils, consumer electronics, wearables, portables, implantables, sensors-attached physical assets, etc. can be empowered to be intelligent in their operations, offerings, and outputs. Edgent could be hosted on the device itself or a gateway device collecting data from local and resource-constrained devices. It is possible to write an edge application on Edgent and connect it to an IoT application and analytics platform at cloud environments (public and private). Edgent can also be used for enterprise data collection and analysis. Applications are developed using a functional flow API to define operations on data streams that are executed as a graph of "oplets" in a lightweight embeddable runtime. The Edgent SDK provides capabilities like windowing, aggregation, and connectors with an extensible model for the community to expand its capabilities.

Edgent supports connectors for MQTT, HTTP, JDBC, File, Apache Kafka and IBM Watson IoT Platform. Edgent is extensible. It is possible to add any connector. Edgent supports open source technologies and tools such as Apache Spark, Apache Storm, Flink and samza, IBM Streams (on-premises or IBM Streaming Analytics on Bluemix), or any custom application. Edgent is designed for the edge, rather than a more centralized system. It has a small footprint, suitable for running on devices. Edgent provides simple analytics, allowing a device to analyze data locally and to only send to the centralized system if there is a need, reducing communication costs.

- **The IBM Watson IoT Platform Edge Analytics:** This capability enables running Watson IoT Platform Analytics on a gateway device. It leverages a streaming engine which is optimized for edge processing. In the Watson IoT Platform, edge analytics is defined and managed in the cloud but distributed out into the IoT network to collect, analyze and respond to conditions at the source with very low latency and without the need to send data to the cloud. Device data can also be forwarded to Watson IoT Platform for a) additional analytic processing, b) dashboard visualization, c) as input to other analytics and d) storage in a cloud-based historian repository.
- **Watson IoT Edge Analytics on a Dell Edge Gateway 3000:** The IBM Watson IoT Platform Edge Analytics Agent (EAA) enables analytics to be run at the edge of devices and gateways. The Edge Analytics Agent (EAA) is available as an SDK for devices that support Java. The SDK supports a number of different types of connectors between the gateway, IoT devices, and the Edge Analytics Agent, including MQTT, Kafka and file connectors. It is possible to configure the EAA on the Dell gateway to communicate and manage our Raspberry Pi using an MQTT connector. Here is a simplified view of the architecture with the Raspberry Pi and Dell gateway.

Figure 7.

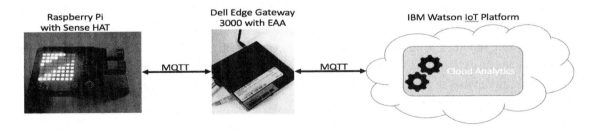

- **Microsoft Azure Stream Analytics (ASA):** on edge devices is a freshly incorporated feature of Azure IoT edge analytics. This enables customers to deploy analytical intelligence closer to the IoT devices and unlock the full value of the device-generated data. Azure Stream Analytics on edge devices extends all the benefits of the Azure's unique streaming technology from the cloud down to devices. With ASA on edge devices, Microsoft Azure is offering the power of the Complex Event Processing (CEP) solution on edge devices to easily develop and run real-time analytics on multiple streams of data. One of the key benefits of this feature is the seamless integration with the cloud: Users can develop, test, and deploy their analytics from the cloud, using the same SQL-like language for both cloud and edge analytics jobs. Like in the cloud, this SQL language notably enables temporal-based joins, windowed aggregates, temporal filters, and other common operations such as aggregates, projections, and filters. Users can also seamlessly integrate custom code in JavaScript for advanced scenarios. The reference architecture of IoT edge analytics is given below.

Figure 8.

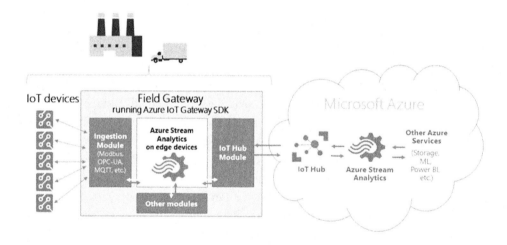

Azure IoT edge analytics lets you build different IoT solutions. It facilitates to connect new or existing devices, regardless of protocol, process the data in an on-premises gateway using many programming and script languages before sending it to the cloud.

In the image below, an existing device has been connected to the cloud using edge intelligence. The on-premises gateway not only performs protocol adaptation which allows the device to send data to the cloud, it also filters the data so that only the most important information is uploaded.

Using existing modules from the Azure IoT Edge ecosystem significantly reduces the development and maintenance costs. Running the gateway on-premises opens up all kinds of scenarios like communicating between devices in real time, operating IoT solution with an intermittent cloud connection, or enforcing additional security requirements.

- **Predixion Software:** According to ABI Research, 90% of machine data never makes it to the cloud. Predixion Software helps to capture and use this data and analyze and act on it at the edge. Predixion Software is the only advanced analytics technology that enables real-time analytics on the device, on the gateway, and in the cloud. Predixion Software has solved big problems in healthcare, fleet, telecommunications, energy, and manufacturing. With Predixion Software, various analytic models can be embedded on the device, can gather real-time data from devices and push it to the gateway, and can aggregate all this information in the cloud. This flexibility, combined with an advanced predictive model, leads to predict when a failure will occur and prescribes what action to be taken when.

Figure 9.

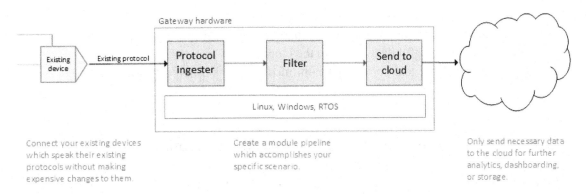

With predictive maintenance, real-time predictive insights are delivered to the point of action – whether that's into the hands of a front-lines operator, the dashboard of a project manager, or back onto the device for emergency protocols. All the empowered assets will send alert signals when they are likely to fail. The prediction capability at the edge removes the delays and expenses that result from unplanned downtime Businesses today collect and crunch historical data to gain workable intelligence. That is not sufficient anymore. All kinds of IoT device data need to be combined with historical data in order to activate comprehensive analysis to extract both tactical as well as strategic insights in time to initiate appropriate actions at different levels with all the clarity and confidence. Predixion Software's unique PredixionIQ technology allows analytic models to be deployed on the device, on the gateway, and in the cloud, so actionable insights are delivered at the point of decision. With Predixion, hospitalists know which interventions to apply to high-risk patients, technicians know where to focus their resources, productivity goes up, and costs plummet.

- **ClearBlade IoT Platform:** ClearBlade enables companies to build IoT solutions that make streaming data actionable by combining business rules and machine learning with powerful visualizations and integrations to existing business systems. Built from an enterprise-first perspective, the ClearBlade Platform runs securely in any cloud, on-premise, and at the edge.
- **The ClearBlade IoT EDGE:** This is extremely performant, small and scalable enabling companies to synchronize, configure, manage state and deploy IoT systems with one common software stack. The reference architecture of this platform is pictorially represented below.

ClearBlade IoT Edge powers activities at the edge of any IoT solutions including real-time business rules, filtering, online/offline modes and messaging. This platform carries several distinct advantages and the corporate website (https://clearblade.com/clearblade-iot-edge.html) has more interesting and inspiring details.

The Solair Smart Gateway

The Solair smart gateway is an industrial grade smart device that provides communications, computation power and a lightweight, flexible application framework for the IoT platform integration. It is designed to streamline safe and secure bidirectional communication

- Collect, store and process sensor data at the edge of the network.
- Streamline safe bidirectional communication between the field and the cloud.
- Ensure that only meaningful data is sent to the cloud.
- Enable local intelligence and performance optimization. The Solair gateway technology is based on Kura.

The Solair Platform – IoT Devices: The Integration Options

- **Direct Collection:** A common industrial scenario is when data is transmitted directly from the machine to the Solair platform by using its own internal connectivity, for example, Wi-Fi, Ethernet or 3G/4G.
- **Mobile Bridge:** The data exchange between objects and the Solair cloud is typically managed through mobile phones, via Wi-Fi or Bluetooth.
- **Smart Gateway:** The gateway collects data from machines or equipment through a series of possible protocols - most frequently field protocols such as Modbus - and submits them to the platform while optimizing a number of processes at the edge. Different sensors-attached physical assets and devices get connected to the Solair platform through a bevy of protocols. The Solair smart gateway supports communications through multiple interfaces and multiple protocols, enabling various types of devices and sensors to interact and exchange encrypted data and commands seamlessly.

With edge analytics, it is all about moving the data capture, processing, and analytics processes from the traditional cloud to edge analytics gateway that might dramatically reduce the amount of device data traffic to the cloud by doing the analytics processing close to the device. Edge devices and digitized objects send their data to an edge analytics gateway, which aggregates, segregates, slices, processes and produce actionable insights quickly. There are rules/policies and other knowledge bases being attached to enable the gateway to take right decisions.

- **Cisco Streaming Analytics (CSA):** CSA is an embeddable, horizontal and hierarchically scalable distributed in-memory streaming database designed and built for analytics at the edge. CSA runs in routers, switches, small compute and commercial servers. The streaming engine enables multi-stream, concurrent processing of "raw streams" and the generation of multiple "derived streams" from simple aggregates to advanced machine learning algorithms. CSA applies predicates, aggregates and joins with metadata tables and contextual data to identify anomalies and detect trends.

- **Cisco ParStream:** Cisco ParStream is a distributed massively parallel processing columnar database designed and built for the IoT. The small footprint of ParStream enables implementation at network edges and inside the network, as well as in data centers. Its innovative compression and bit-mapped indexing technologies enable Cisco ParStream to meet IoT historian and buffering requirements such as providing sub-second response times on billions of data records and thousands of columns, while continuously importing new data.

- **Altiux Innovations:** GWStax, a part of Altiux's IoTStax product portfolio, is a comprehensive framework of modular components that enables seamless connectivity, interoperability, security, remote management, edge analytics, and application enablement in IoT gateways. It enables OEMs to quickly develop and deploy gateway products for IoT that essentially connect end nodes to the cloud. This is built on industry standards and technologies such as 6LoWPAN (Lorwan, 2017) IPv6, Thread, CoAP, LWM2M, etc. and scalable to support application layer protocols such as OIC, AllJoyn etc. GWStax is suitable for applications such as smart home gateways, building automation, smart parking and lighting, industrial automation etc.

NodeStax is a comprehensive framework of modular components that enables seamless connectivity, security, remote management, and application enablement in constrained IoT devices. End node devices in IoT deployments are typically constrained in terms of processing power, memory availability, power availability, communication bandwidth supported, cost considerations etc. Addressing the needs of such devices, NodeStax enables OEMs to quickly develop and deploy constrained end node products for IoT. This is built on industry standards and technologies such as 6LoWPAN, IPv6, Thread, CoAP, LWM2M, etc. and is scalable to support proprietary protocols, NodeStax is suitable for constrained devices in smart homes, building automation, smart appliances, industrial automation, smart cities use cases.

- **Dell Edge Gateway:** It is all about collecting, analyzing, relaying and acting on IoT data at the edge of the network with this IoT gateway, which is purpose-built for building and industrial automation applications. The Dell Edge Gateway is designed to aggregate, secure and relay data from diverse sensors and equipment. The Intel processor provides the capacity to perform local analytics so only meaningful information is sent to the next tier, which could be another gateway, the data center or the cloud. This minimizes consumption of expensive network bandwidth and reduces overall solution latency. The Dell Edge Gateway is designed to attach to a wall or DIN rail in commercial and industrial environments. This is engineered with an industrial-grade form factor and fanless, solid-state design. The Dell gateway can reliably run 24x7 with long life at extended temperatures, in addition to withstanding the higher levels of humidity and dust typical of industrial environments.

On summary, remote management saves time and money by enabling updates, configuration, and troubleshooting without physically reaching out the device. In the medical field, the remote management capability impacts a network of thousands of devices. That is, end-user devices can be updated remotely at once, so patients can access the most up-to-date care available. In the industrial market, managing devices remotely save money by eliminating the need for technicians to service devices in the field. Advanced Java-based device application frameworks that abstract the complexity of hardware and networking subsystems simplify the development, reuse, and remote management of cross-platform IoT applications. The emergence of an Internet of Things (IoT) service gateway model, running modern software stacks and operating on the edge of an IoT deployment as an aggregator and controller, has opened up the possibility of enabling enterprise-level technologies to IoT gateways.

NoSQL Database for IoT Data Edge Analytics

Time series data is any data that has a timestamp, like IoT device data, stocks, commodity prices, tide measurements, solar are tracking, and health information. Collecting, storing, accessing, and analyzing the massive amount of sensor and actuator data with traditional databases is often not possible. Applications need to scale out, up, and down predictably and linearly as the data grows. The challenge of time series data is that reads and writes to the database must be fast, reliable, and scalable. Riak TS is a key/value store that easily scales using commodity hardware. It supports rapid ingestion of time series data from connected devices through extremely fast reads and writes. Riak TS enables application processing of this data to generate actionable information. It is designed to scale horizontally with commodity hardware, making it easy for administrators to add capacity without creating complex sharding

Traditionally, data is analyzed at the core of your network, but with the growth of IoT sensors and devices, data must be analyzed closer to its source and aggregated for core analysis. From cruise ships to health monitoring to system utilization, edge analytics create a better user experience and faster response times. Riak TS requires fewer hardware resources for the same computational power, making it an ideal choice for edge analytics, plus Riak TS makes it easy to do analysis using SQL range queries.

CONCLUSION

Fog or edge computing is gaining a lot of traction these days due to the wider articulation of various business, technical and user cases. Especially for performing and providing real-time data analytics, the role of fog or edge clouds is on the rise. There are edge appliances from different product vendors accelerating the rollout of edge analytics. There are integrated platforms for producing ad hoc fog clouds quickly to accomplish edge data capture, storage, and analytics. The deployment of digitized entities in any environment is made easier. Devices are expertly instrumented and interconnected to be intelligent. Software applications and services are finding their new rewarding residence in cloud infrastructures. Data science is a hugely popular subject of intense study and research in order to make sense out of IoT data. There are a machine and deep learning algorithms to automate the process of doing data analytics. The goal of real-time and automated analytics can be casually accomplished through fog analytics platforms and infrastructures. In this chapter, we have vividly depicted the concept of fog computing, which is the need of the hour for real-time data analytics.

REFERENCES

Lee, W., Nam, K., Roh, H. G., & Kim, S. H. (2016). A gateway based fog computing architecture for wireless sensors and actuator networks. In *Advanced Communication Technology (ICACT). 18th Int. Conf. on Advanced Communication Technology (ICACT)*. Pyeongchang, South Korea: IEEE. doi: 10.1109/ICACT.2016.7423331

LoRaWAN. (2017). *The Things Network.* Retrieved November 11, 2017, from https://www.thethingsnetwork.org/wiki/LoRaWAN/Home

Pan, Y., Beyah, R. A., Goscinski, A., & Ren, J. (2017). Edge Computing for the Internet-of-Things. *IEEE Network.* Retrieved November 3, 2017, from https://www.comsoc.org/netmag/cfp/edge-computing-internet-things

Poole, I. (2015). *RFID Standards. Radio-Electronics.* Retrieved November 11, 2017, from http://www.radio-electronics.com/info/wireless/radio-frequency-identification-rfid/iso-epcglobal-iec-standards.php

Raj. (2015). *High-Performance Big Data Analytics: the Solution Approaches and Systems.* Springer-Verlag, UK. Retrieved from http://www.springer.com/in/book/9783319207438

Raj & Deka. (2014). *Cloud Infrastructures for Big Data Analytics.* IGI Global. Retrieved from http://www.igi-global.com/book/cloud-infrastructures-big-data-analytics/95028

Raj & Raman. (2016). *The Internet of Things (IoT): the Technologies and Tools.* CRC Press. Retrieved from https://www.crcpress.com/The-Internet-of-Things-Enabling-Technologies-Platforms-and-Use-Cases/Raj-Raman/p/book/9781498761284

Salman, O., Elhajj, I., & Kayssi, A. (2015). Edge computing enabling the Internet of Things. In *IEEE 2nd World Forum on the Internet of Things (WF-IoT).* Milan, Italy. IEEE. 10.1109/WF-IoT.2015.7389122

Schmidt, S. (2016). *6LoWPAN: An Open IoT Networking Protocol.* Open IoT Summit. Retrieved November 14, 2017, from http://events.linuxfoundation.org/sites/events/files/slides/6lowpan-openiot-2016.pdf

Treadway, J. (2016). Using an IoT gateway to connect the "Things" to the cloud. IoT Agenda. *TechTarget Network.* Retrieved November 21, 2017, from http://internetofthingsagenda.techtarget.com/feature/Using-an-IoT-gateway-to-connect-the-Things-to-the-cloud

Wang, W., He, G., & Wan, J. (2011). Research on Zigbee Wireless Communication Technology. In *Int. Conf. on Electrical and Control Engineering (ICECE).* Yichang, China: IEEE. doi: 10.1109/ICECENG.2011.6057961

This research was previously published in the Handbook of Research on Cloud and Fog Computing Infrastructures for Data Science; pages 1-32, copyright year 2018 by Engineering Science Reference (an imprint of IGI Global).

APPENDIX

The Prominent Fog-Like Approaches

There are multiple trends emanating and evolving in the information and communication technologies (ICT) spaces. The number of smartphones across the globe is already more than 3 billion empowering people to do both communication and computation seamlessly on a single device. Similarly every specific environment such as homes, luxury cars, and heavy vehicles, manufacturing floors, shopping malls, eating joints and junctions, entertainment and edutainment centers, nuclear installations, research labs, business parks, etc. are being stuffed and sandwiched by a number of purpose-specific as well as generic sensors and actuators. Thus, the prediction that there will be trillions of digitized objects, billions of connected devices and millions of software services in near future is all set to become true sooner than later. There are different approaches and articulations in order to pointedly focus on this fog/edge computing concept. There are myriad of nomenclatures and buzzwords. Figure 10 clearly tells the various options for localized and nearby data processing in real-time.

- **Local / Proximate Clouds:** We have public, private and hybrid clouds in order to cater different requirements. There are specific clouds such as mobile, storage, knowledge, science, data, device, and sensor clouds. Specific communities even have their own clouds. Now with the accumulation of sensors and sensor-attached physical assets, there is a demand for localized and nearby cloud environments for performing proximate processing. Local clouds, a kind of dedicated IT environments, can interoperate with other traditional clouds (private, public, hybrid, and community) for doing comprehensive and historical data processing.

Figure 10.

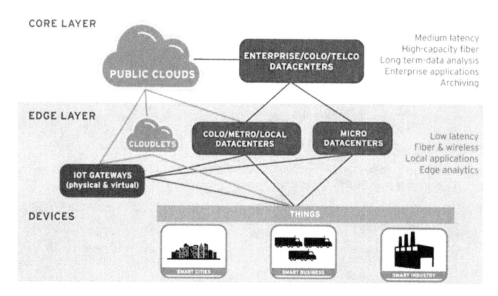

There is literature eulogizing and expressing local clouds as micro or nano clouds considering their slim and sleek nature. As it turns out, there will be thousands of local clouds in the near future. That is, every noteworthy environment has its own local cloud. The various computation and communication devices apart from consumer electronics in the neighbourhood come together to collaboratively form local clouds.

- **Cloudlet Facilities:** There are highly reliable and resilient cloud appliances and hyper-converged clouds in the form of bars and boxes these days. Instead of using commodity servers, powerful, integrated and turnkey appliances are also being used in specific contexts. Cloudlet is "a cloud in a box", which follows the same cloud paradigm but relies on high-end server machines. Cloudlets are very easy and quick to setup and activate and are being recommended to provide delay-sensitive and bandwidth-limited applications. A cloudlet is a new architectural element that arises from the convergence of mobile computing and cloud computing. It represents the middle of a three-tier hierarchy: mobile device, cloudlet, and cloud.

The following use cases for crowdsourced videos insist the need for cloudlet facilities.

The aspect of crowdsourcing has seen a phenomenal growth these days with the widespread deployment of security and surveillance cameras in important junctions. There are sellable and workable use cases being unearthed for sustaining its surging popularity. Here are a few.

- **Marketing and Advertising:** Crowd-sourced videos can provide a lot of real-time and decision-enabling insights based on observational data. For example, which billboards attract the most user attention? How successful is a new store window display in attracting interest? Which clothing colours and patterns attract the most interest? etc.
- **Capturing Theme Parks' Visit:** Visitors to places like Disneyworld can capture and share their delectable experiences, including rides, throughout the entire day. With video, audio, and accelerometer capture, the recreation of rides can be quite realistic and mesmerizing.
- **Locating People, Pets, and Things:** A missing child was last seen walking home from school. A search of crowd-sourced videos from the area shows that the child was near a particular spot an hour ago. The parent remembers that the child has a friend close to that location. She calls the friend's home and locates the child. When a dog owner reports that his dog is missing, a search of crowd-sourced videos captured in the last few hours may help locate the dog before it strays too far.
- **Fraud Detection:** A driver reports that his car was hit while it was parked at a restaurant. However, his insurance claims adjuster finds a crowdsourced video in which the car is intact when leaving the restaurant.
- **Why is Cloudlet-Like Arrangement Mandated?:** Video footages from a mobile device only travel up to its currently associated cloudlet. Computer vision analytics are run on the cloudlet platform in near real time. Only the results (recognized objects, recognized faces, and so on), along with metadata (such as the owner, capture location, and timestamp) are then sent to the remote cloud. The tags and metadata can guide deeper and more customized searches of the content of a video segment during its (finite) retention period on a cloudlet. Automated modification of video streams to preserve its privacy is done at cloudlet level.

Mobile Edge Computing (MEC)

We have mobile base stations in many locations in order to fail-safe relay mobile communication. These facilities are being recommended for doing the edge data processing and analytics. The utilization rates of those base stations go up significantly with this extra flavour. Base stations act as an intelligent intermediary between smartphones and the faraway cloud environments.

Mobile Cloud Computing (MCC)

As we all know, smartphones do not have sufficient processing, memory and storage capabilities as a typical and traditional cloud does (Off course, as per newspaper reports, there are smartphones empowered with 6 GB memory). Therefore, there are research works initiated in order to bring in an appropriate partition of software applications into a set of easily manageable modules. The specific and smaller modules are kept within smartphones whereas the common and reusable service modules are being taken to cloud environments. The data sources are being kept in cloud environments and smartphones can access the data on a need basis. Now with cloudlets and MEC models are maturing fast, there will be a consolidation and MCC will slowly disappear from the scene altogether.

Thus having understood the need for pioneering intermediaries between devices, machines, equipment, instruments, sensors, robots, actuators, etc. at the ground level and a bevy of software applications and data sources at the cyber level, researchers have proposed several propositions as described above. With the overwhelming acceptance of fog computing, all these diverging concepts are bound to converge to fulfill all the originally envisaged benefits of fog or edge computing.

It is all shifting from the "connected device" to the "intelligent device" through the computing on the edge. Making a connected device adaptive, autonomic and articulate is the important goal. This strategically sound transformation comes handy in realizing people-centric and situation-aware services.

Chapter 12
Game Theory for Cooperation in Multi-Access Edge Computing

Jose Moura
Instituto Universitário de Lisboa, Portugal

Rui Neto Marinheiro
Instituto Universitário de Lisboa, Portugal

Joao Carlos Silva
Instituto Universitário de Lisboa, Portugal

ABSTRACT

Cooperative strategies amongst network players can improve network performance and spectrum utilization in future networking environments. Game Theory is very suitable for these emerging scenarios, since it models high-complex interactions among distributed decision makers. It also finds the more convenient management policies for the diverse players (e.g., content providers, cloud providers, edge providers, brokers, network providers, or users). These management policies optimize the performance of the overall network infrastructure with a fair utilization of their resources. This chapter discusses relevant theoretical models that enable cooperation amongst the players in distinct ways through, namely, pricing or reputation. In addition, the authors highlight open problems, such as the lack of proper models for dynamic and incomplete information scenarios. These upcoming scenarios are associated to computing and storage at the network edge, as well as, the deployment of large-scale IoT systems. The chapter finalizes by discussing a business model for future networks.

1. INTRODUCTION

Game Theory (GT) techniques have recently emerged in many engineering applications, notably in communications and networking. With the emergence of cooperation as a new communication paradigm, alongside the need for self-organizing, decentralized, and autonomic networks, it has become imperative to seek suitable GT tools to analyze and study the behavior and interactions of nodes in Future Networks

DOI: 10.4018/978-1-6684-5700-9.ch012

(FNs). The final goal is to find low-complexity distributed algorithms that can efficiently manage the high-complexity future network environment formed by heterogeneous technologies, enhancing collaboration among players and punish selfish or misbehaving nodes. In addition, the new management solutions should reduce the unwanted effects of stale information (e.g. oscillation around a specific network status) by choosing the proper values, namely, for both sampling rate of network status and delay associated to the dissemination of status information amongst the network nodes. This chapter fills a hole in existing communications literature, by providing a comprehensive review about GT models/concepts that are highly relevant for enabling collaboration in FNs environments.

In FNs, distributed and intelligent management algorithms can manage (control) the network infrastructure. These algorithms create incentive mechanisms that force the players to cooperate instead of pursuing their own interest. This novel player's behavior enables the efficient usage of available (sometimes-constrained) network resources, satisfying the heterogeneous requirements of data flows. Broadly speaking, the current literature highlights two different ways to encourage cooperation (collaboration) among the players: one with a short-term control effect and the other with a long-term control effect. The first approach uses virtual payments (credit-based games) to relieve costs for relaying traffic, and the second approach enforces the creation of communities (or groups, clusters) to establish long-term relationships among the nodes (reputation-based games). The reputation-based games sustain cooperation among the players because defection against a specific node causes personal retaliation or sanction by others. In the limit, nodes that do not cooperate will not be able to use the network themselves. Effective corrective actions against cheating nodes are also required with either permanent or temporary measures. Other interesting perspective to investigate is the deployment of hybrid solutions combining credit-based and reputation-based methods to enhance collaboration amongst players.

There is a relatively new and a very interesting set of games designated by evolutionary coalitional games that can enable more intelligent, self-adjustable, and robust algorithms for the management of FNs. In addition, the social networks, like Facebook or Flickr, can rapidly disseminate the positive impact of collaborative actions among the users of FNs (Apicella, Marlowe, Fowler, & Christakis, 2012) (Bond et al., 2012). Furthermore, the deployment in large scale of vehicular and sensor networks supported by the convergent (Moura & Edwards, 2015) and heterogeneous (Moura & Edwards, 2016) wireless access can enable some collaborative behavior amongst players.

The current chapter reviews the literature to discuss the more promising GT proposals that can incentivize the collaboration among the diverse players, aiming to use more intelligently and efficiently the available resources of FNs. This chapter has the following structure. Section 2 introduces and discusses important GT aspects for FNs. Section 3 gives the background and highlights collaborative strategies in FNs. It also presents our vision about FNs. Then, section 4 describes how GT can enable and enhance collaboration in FNs. Section 5 offers a broad GT literature survey in wireless networking. Section 6 discusses some relevant research work about how GT addresses the more significant functional aspects we expect to be present in FN environments. In addition, Section 7 discusses the business perspective for FNs. Finally, Section 8 concludes with relevant GT open problems to support collaboration in FNs.

2. DISCUSSING GAME THEORY

The current section introduces and discusses relevant aspects of GT, which can be very useful to model the emergent network environments of FNs.

2.1. Roots and Scope

The earliest predecessors of GT are economic analysis of imperfectly competitive markets of the French economist Augustin Cournot in 1838 (Dutta, 1999). The next great advance is due to John Nash who, in 1950, introduced the Nash equilibrium (NE) which is the most widely used concept in modern GT. The NE consists on a game status where no rational actor playing that game has enough incentives to deviate from its current strategy. In fact, as any player would decide to use a different strategy from the one associated to the NE state then that player would be punished in the sense that his (her) reward is reduced. Nash´s initial work created a new branch in GT grouping all non-cooperative games. Further GT historical evolution is available in (Dutta, 1999).

GT is the study of multi-person decision problems (which differentiates it from the classical decision theory) in applications drawn from industrial organization, labor economics, macroeconomics, financial economics, and international economics (Gibbons, 1992). Alongside with previous applications in Economics and Finance, GT could be applied to other completely different real world cases (Dutta, 1999).

Classical GT essentially requires that all the specified players of a specific game make rational choices among a pre-defined set of static strategies. Therefore, it is fundamental in GT that each player must consider the strategic analysis that the players' opponents are making in determining that his (her) own static strategic choice is appropriate to receive the best payoff (reward) as possible. Otherwise, if other players do not influence a player's reward, then GT is not a proper tool. In this case, it is more convenient to use constrained optimization in the place of GT. Following, we discuss how GT can create a mathematical model (e.g. matrix form) that mimics real-life scenarios with conflict situations among the players, trying to solve those conflict situations.

2.2. Matrix Games

Matrix games are those in which the payoff to a player can be determined from a matrix of payoffs. The payoffs are assigned to each element of the matrix assuming that interactions among players are pairwise. One player chooses a row of the matrix and the other chooses a column of the matrix. The intersection between the row and the column points out a unique element of the matrix. As an example, if player A's strategy is to choose the third row and player B's strategy is to choose the first column, the resultant payoff to player A is the value in the third row and first column of the matrix. A consequence of this is that the number of strategies available to the players is finite and discrete.

The matrix games can be asymmetric or symmetric. On one hand, a game is asymmetric if players have different set of strategies and/or if players are distinctively rewarded from choosing a given strategy against an opponent with a particular strategy. A classic example of an asymmetric game is the battle of sexes that is modelled by two distinct payoff matrixes. On the other hand, a game is symmetric if players have the same set of strategies and experience the same reward of using a given strategy against an opponent with a particular strategy. A classic example of a symmetric game is the prisoner's dilemma, which can be modelled with a single matrix. Following, we discuss with further detail the prisoner's dilemma because is the classical GT approach to solve the dilemma of an individual choice between cooperate or defect (not cooperate) with others, which is the focus of the current chapter.

The prisoner's dilemma can be formulated in terms of a single payoff matrix with two players, each one with two possible strategies, as shown in Table 1. Suppose that two individuals are being held in a prison in isolated cells. In this game, regardless of what the other prisoner decides, each prisoner gets a higher pay-off by betraying the other ("defecting"). The reasoning involves an argument by dilemma: B will either cooperate or defect. If B cooperates, A should defect, since going free is better than serving 1 year. If B defects, A should also defect, since serving 2 years is better than serving 3. Therefore, either way, A should defect. Parallel reasoning shows that B should also defect. As both players choose to defect, they will be serving 2 years. Yet both players choosing to cooperate obtain a higher payoff (serving only 1 year) than both players defecting! In this way, GT results in both players being worse off than if each chose to lessen the sentence of his accomplice at the cost of spending more time in jail himself. Later, in the current chapter, we use this game to show that the cooperation among network operators is very useful to all of them. In the following text, we discuss evolutionary game theory.

Table 1. Payoff matrix of prisoner's dilemma

		Prisoner B	
		Cooperate (Silent)	Defect (Betray)
Prisoner A	Cooperate (Silent)	1, 1	3, free
	Defect (Betray)	free, 3	2, 2

2.3. Evolutionary Game Theory

In opposition to the classical GT, Evolutionary GT (EGT), states that the players aren´t completely rational. The players have limited information about available choices and consequences and their strategies are not static. In fact, the players have a preferred strategy that continuously compare with other strategies, checking if they need to change their current strategy to get a better reward (fitness). The decision to change the preferred strategy can be also influenced by other neighboring players belonging to the same population (by observation and leaning). In this way, the strategy with the highest selection score inside a group of individuals forming a community will become the predominant strategy for that generation of individuals. Then, this strategy is transferred to the next generation of individuals (evolutionary aspect). Following, we discuss how EGT can model the upcoming scenarios of FNs. These future scenarios will be more complex and dynamic than current networking scenarios. Table 2 briefly compares traditional GT with EGT.

Table 2. Comparison between traditional GT and EGT

Game Characteristic	Traditional GT	EGT
Pure strategies	Yes	No
Strategy adaption over time	No	Yes
Hyper rational behavior	Yes	No
Equilibria is always possible	No (in some scenarios due to restrictions on the strategy options)	Yes (i.e. at least it discovers an asymptotic equilibrium due to unrestricted strategy space)
Model dynamic and high complex game	No	Yes

EGT has been developed as a mathematical framework to study the interaction among rational biological agents in a population. In evolutionary games, the agent revolves the chosen strategy based on its payoff. In this way, both static and dynamic behavior of the game can be analyzed (Han, Niyato, Saad, Baar, & Hjrungnes, 2012). In this way, on one hand, evolutionary stable strategies (ESS) are used to study a static evolutionary game. On the other hand, replicator dynamics is used to study a dynamic evolutionary game.

EGT usually considers a set of players that interact within a game and then die, giving birth to a new player generation that fully inherits its ancestor's knowledge. The new player strategy is evaluated against the one of its ancestors and its current environmental context. Also, through mutation, a slightly distinct strategy may be selected by a set of players belonging to a specific generation, probably offering better payoffs. Next, each player competes with the other players within the evolutionary game using a strategy that increases its payoff. In this way, strategies with high payoffs will survive inside the system as more players will tend to choose them, while weak strategies will eventually disappear. Following, we present a tutorial in how EGT can be applied to wireless networks (Y. Zhang & Guizani, 2011).

Formally, we should consider within an evolutionary game an infinite population of individuals that react to changes of their environmental surroundings using a finite set of n pure strategies $S = \{s_1, s_2, ..., s_n\}$. There is also a population profile, i.e. $x = \{x_1, x_2, ..., x_n\}$, which denotes the popularity of each strategy $s_i \in S$ among the individuals. This means that x_i is the probability that a strategy s_i is played by the individuals. By this reason, x is also designated by the set of mixed strategies.

Consider an individual in a population with profile x. Its expected payoff when choosing to play strategy s_i is given by f (s_i, x). In a two-player game, if an individual chooses strategy s_i and its opponent responds with strategy s_j, the payoff of the former player is given by f (s_i, s_j). In a more generic way, the expected payoff of strategy s_i is evaluated by (1) $f_i = \sum_{j=1}^{n} x_j . f\left(s_i, s_j\right)$. whereas the average payoff is given by (2) $f_x = \sum_{i=1}^{n} x_i . f_i$.

The replicator dynamics is a differential equation that describes the dynamics of an evolutionary game without mutation (Y. Zhang & Guizani, 2011) (Taylor & Jonker, 1978). According to this differential equation, the rate of growth of a specific strategy is proportional to the difference between the expected payoff of that strategy and the overall average payoff of the population, as stated in (3) $\dot{x} = x_i . \left(f_i - f_x\right)$. Using this equation, if a strategy has a much better payoff than the average, the number of individuals from the population that tend to choose it increases. On the contrary, a strategy with a lower payoff than the average is preferred less and eventually is eliminated from the system set of strategies.

Considering now the mutation issue, suppose that a small group of mutants $m \in [0,1]$ with a profile $x' \neq x$ invades the previous population. The profile of the newly formed population is given by (4) $x_{final} = m.x' + \left(1 - m\right) .x$. Hence, the average payoff of non-mutants will be

$$f_{x_{final}}^{non-mutant} = f\left(x, x_{final}\right) = \sum_{j=1}^{n} x_j . f\left(j, x_{final}\right)$$

given by (5) and the average payoff of mutants will be given by (6)

$$f_{x_{final}}^{mutant} = f\left(x', x_{final}\right) = \sum_{j=1}^{n} x'_j . f\left(j, x_{final}\right).$$

In this context, a strategy x is called evolutionary stable strategy (ESS) if for any $x' \neq x, m_{mut} \in [0,1]$ exists such that for all $m \in [0, m_{mut}]$, then equation (7) holds true. $f_{x_{final}}^{non-mutant} > f_{x_{final}}^{mutant}$. In this way, when an ESS is reached, the population is immune from being invaded by other groups with different population profiles. By other words, in this context the population is not affected by mutation issues.

$$f_i = \sum_{j=1}^{n} x_j . f\left(s_i, s_j\right) \tag{1}$$

$$f_x = \sum_{i=1}^{n} x_i . f_i \tag{2}$$

$$\dot{x} = x_i . \left(f_i - f_x\right) \tag{3}$$

$$x_{final} = m.x' + \left(1 - m\right).x \tag{4}$$

$$f_{x_{final}}^{non-mutant} = f\left(x, x_{final}\right) = \sum_{j=1}^{n} x_j . f\left(j, x_{final}\right) \tag{5}$$

$$f_{x_{final}}^{mutant} = f\left(x', x_{final}\right) = \sum_{j=1}^{n} x'_j . f\left(j, x_{final}\right) \tag{6}$$

$$f_{x_{final}}^{non-mutant} > f_{x_{final}}^{mutant}. \tag{7}$$

EGT may be successfully applied to model a variety of network problems. The authors of (Y. Zhang & Guizani, 2011) review the literature concerning the applications of EGT to distinct network types such as wireless sensor networks, delay tolerant networks, peer-to-peer networks and wireless networks in general, including heterogeneous 4G networks and cloud environments. In addition, (Han et al., 2012) discusses selected applications of EGT in wireless communications and networking, including congestion control, contention-based (i.e. Aloha) protocol adaptation, power control in CDMA, routing, cooperative sensing in cognitive radio, TCP throughput adaptation, and service-provider network selection. By service-provider network selection, (Han et al., 2012) suggests EGT to study different scenarios:

- User churning behavior that impacts the revenue of service providers;

- User choice among candidate service providers of the access network that maximizes the perceived QoS for a service type.

In (Nazir, Bennis, Ghaboosi, MacKenzie, & Latva-aho, 2010), an evolutionary game based on replicator dynamics is formulated to model the dynamic competition in network selection among users. Each user can choose a service class from a certain service provider (i.e. available access network). They present two algorithms, namely, population evolution and reinforcement-learning for network selection. Although the network-selection algorithm based on population evolution can reach the evolutionary equilibrium faster, it requires a centralized controller to gather, process, and broadcast information about the users within the corresponding service area. In contrast, with reinforcement learning, a user can gradually learn (by interacting with the service provider) and adapt the decision on network selection (through a trial-and-error learning method) to reach evolutionary equilibrium without any interaction with other users.

Some work (Nazir et al., 2010) (Bennis, Guruacharya, & Niyato, 2011) investigated and compared the convergence behavior of Q-learning with EGT to enable a satisfactory performance of cellular networks with femtocells. The authors of (Nazir et al., 2010) introduce two mechanisms for interference mitigation supported by EGT and machine learning. In the first mechanism, stand-alone femtocells choose their strategies, observe the behavior of other players, and make the best decision based on their instantaneous payoff, as well as the average payoff of all other femtocells. They also formulate the interactions among selfish femtocells using evolutionary games and demonstrate how the system converges to equilibrium. By contrast, using the second mechanism (i.e. reinforcement learning), the information exchange among femtocells is no longer possible and hence each femtocell adapts its strategy and gradually learns by interacting with its environment (i.e., neighboring interferers). The femtocells can self-organize by relying only on local information, while mitigating interference inside the macrocell. In this way, the macrocell user can meet its Quality of Service requirements. They have concluded that the biologically inspired evolutionary approach converges more rapidly to the desired equilibrium as compared to the reinforcement learning and random approach. Nevertheless, this faster convergence requires more context information at the femtocells. The authors of (Bennis et al., 2011) reached equivalent results as (Nazir et al., 2010).

Further references that address EGT applications to the networking area are available for wireless (M. A. Khan, Tembine, & Vasilakos, 2012a) (M. A. Khan, Tembine, & Vasilakos, 2012b) and wireline (Eitan Altman, El-Azouzi, Hayel, & Tembine, 2009) networks. The impact of evolutionary games in future wireless networks is analyzed in (Tembine, Altman, El-Azouzi, & Hayel, 2010). Evolutionary models have been also proposed for hierarchical mobile (Semasinghe, Hossain, & Zhu, 2015) (Lin, Ni, Tian, & Liu, 2015) and vehicular (Shivshankar & Jamalipour, 2015) networks. In the text below, we discuss the Stackelberg game, which it is like a NC repeated game.

2.4. Stackelberg Game

Figure 1 shows the model of a Stackelberg game (SG). This game is like a Non-Cooperative (NC) game but instead of the players playing a single shot as a typical NC game, the players execute the SG game via a step-by-step way. In addition, a SG has a player, designated by a leader that has the highest priority to take the first action. However, before doing that, the leader observes other players' strategies. Then, the leader announces its preferred strategy to the remaining players, also designated by followers. The followers perceive the leader's action and adjust their strategies to minimize their own cost. After, the followers reveal their strategies again to the leader. In summary, the SG model is a sequential one with hierarchical decision-making that analyses the interaction between a leader (or leaders) and a set of followers to achieve a specific set of model goals. The final aim of a SG model is to discover the Stackelberg Equilibrium (SE), i.e. (Strategy_leader, Strategy_follower). We conclude that SE is an evolution from a NC game, where the former model adds two novel aspects: action observation and stage repetition.

Figure 1. Steps of a Stackelberg Game Theory

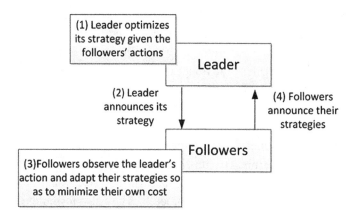

Some applications of SE games are: Software Defined Networking (SDN) scenarios, where the SDN controller is the Leader; Femtocell power control (Han et al., 2012) in hierarchized mobile networks; and device-to-device (D2D) communication (Zhu & Hossain, 2015). The main advantage of using a SG model is to optimize diverse virtualized resources (e.g. computation, storage, and networking) of very complex topologies at the network edge under users' Quality of Experience. The main challenges the network designer should be aware of are as follows: i) implement a robust mechanism to ensure the correct and synchronous shift among leaders and followers; ii) the Stackelberg Equilibrium (SE) could give a worst result than NE due to the hierarchical decision-making process among leaders and followers (Han et al., 2012); and iii) a SE game requires complete and perfect information about other strategies and payoffs. In this situation, communication jitter among a leader and followers of a SG could disrupt the right control sequence and create instabilities on the control loop, affecting the obtained results from that model. In the next section, we discuss a model game that deals with a real problem that each player could have. It is related with the player uncertainty (full or partial) about the other players decisions. In this way, the players hardly predict how the pool of network resources shared among all them will be used.

2.5. Bayesian Game

In a Bayesian game (BG) the players have incomplete information about their environment (Y. Zhang & Guizani, 2011). This can occur due to some practical physical impairments that counteract the global dissemination among the nodes of useful information about the status of the system being studied, e.g. channel gain (Duong, 2016). Following Harsanyi's work (Harsanyi, 2004), a BG has a special player with random behaviour, i.e. 'Nature'. These games are called Bayesian because they require a probabilistic analysis. Players have initial beliefs about others' payoff functions. A belief is a probability distribution over the possible types for a player. Then, the initial beliefs might change based on the actions the players of the game have taken. As a game with incomplete information is repeated, the folk theorem (Fudenberg & Maskin, 1986) can find its social-optimum solution. The game also enables a distributed model to study the system. In this way, this game type can support user privacy as users do not need to disclose private data to an external centralized server or controller. However, it could be complicated to find the Bayesian NE, due to the dynamic characteristic of this game, where the players adjust their decisions based on their learning from the acquired information during the time the game is played (Han et al., 2012). The players' learning could be adversely affected also by jitter, security attacks, interference, errors, available battery energy to transmit, system unpredictability, etc. The reader could find in (Böge & Eisele, 1979) a comparison between a BG and a non-BG. In (Chawla & Sivan, 2014) a Bayesian mechanism design is also explained.

We have found in the literature some BGs for wireless networking environments. These games cover the following areas: hierarchical small cells (Bu, Yu, & Yanikomeroglu, 2015) (Z. Khan, Lehtomaki, DaSilva, Hossain, & Latva-aho, 2016) (Duong, Madhukumar, & Niyato, 2016); D2D communications (Kebriaei, Maham, & Niyato, 2015) (Xiao, Chen, Yuen, Han, & DaSilva, 2015) (Yan, Huang, & Wang, 2013)(Yan, 2013); vehicular scenarios (Duong et al., 2016) (Kumar, Misra, Rodrigues, & Obaidat, 2015) (Kumar, Zeadally, Chilamkurti, & Vinel, 2015); and wireless sensors (Kumar, Chilamkurti, & Misra, 2015) (La, Quek, Lee, Jin, & Zhu, 2016) (Zheng, Liu, & Qi, 2012).

2.6. Mechanism Design

There is a subfield of GT designated by Mechanism Design (MD) that allows a game designer to define initially the desired outcome and then specify the game rules to achieve that outcome (Han et al., 2012, 221-252). This is the opposite of game analysis, in which the game rules are predefined and then the outcome is investigated, as shown in Figure 2. That is why MD is also designated as reverse GT.

A very important result in MD is the Revelation Principle that states for any Bayesian Nash Equilibrium is associated a Bayesian game with the same equilibrium outcome but in which players truthfully report their choices (it could be a preference list), which simplifies the game analysis, eliminating the need to consider either strategic behavior or lying. So, no matter what the mechanism, a designer can confine attention to equilibrium in which players only report truthfully. To accomplish this, the model needs to consider incentives for players to truthfully cooperate among them, optimizing the game outcome.

Figure 2. Game theory (GT) vs. mechanism design (MD)

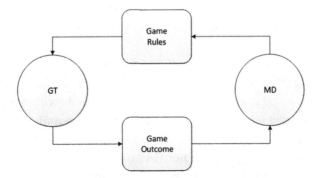

3. BACKGROUND AND TRENDS IN FUTURE NETWORKS

According to the Cisco Global Forecast (CISCO, 2016) more than three-fourths of the world's mobile data traffic will be video by 2021. From the same source, sixty percent of total mobile data traffic was offloaded onto the fixed network through Wi-Fi or femtocell in 2016. This traffic offloading occurs due to the lack of capacity in the mobile network infrastructure, originally dimensioned to support only voice and messages. The traffic offloading is one possible solution to mitigate congestion, avoiding the loss on the perceived quality by users' applications.

However, the first approach to the problem has been to perform an inter-technology handover between available technologies, with all the traffic routed through the most convenient access technology. A survey about mobility is available in (Fernandes & Karmouch, 2012). In our opinion, a better usage of available resources on the network-edge with a more fine-grained traffic management based on flows (e.g., Web traffic, VoIP) should alleviate the negative impact of network congestion, which has been reported very often essentially in the mobile broadband access. Multi-interface handheld terminals will soon have the battery autonomy and the capability to perform network access using simultaneous multi-radio access technologies (RAT). In addition, it is of particular interest the support of simultaneous data/multimedia flows through different access systems (LTE-A, WLAN, Wimax). Recent works (Yap et al., 2012) (Silva, Marinheiro, Moura, & Almeida, 2013) (Moura & Edwards, 2015) (Moura & Edwards, 2016) (Alves, Silva, Neto Marinheiro, & Moura, 2018) propose that mobile multimode terminals should use all the available connectivity options simultaneously. The mobile terminal should choose dynamically the most suitable network to each flow, obtaining faster connections by stitching flows over multiple networks, decrease the usage cost by choosing the most cost-effective network that meets application requisites, and reduce the energy consumption by selecting the technologies with the lowest energy-usage per byte. The management of the flows per network interface may not only be implemented independently by the terminal, but also be assisted transparently by the network (Alves et al., 2018).

This concept for FNs contributes to the perspective of integrating complementary access technologies with overlapping coverage to provide the expected ubiquitous coverage and to achieve the Always Best Connected (ABC) concept (Louta, Zournatzis, Kraounakis, Sarigiannidis, & Demetropoulos, 2011). This concept allows a flow to use at any time the most suitable access network/Network Attachment Point (NAP). This management of flows should be done in a distributed way with low complexity and reliable algorithms/protocols in networks formed by heterogeneous access technologies, where the most part of involved nodes should cooperate. Network brokers such as in (Moura & Edwards, 2016) follow on this idea. Brokerage systems, possibly implementing GT algorithms, can manage the network architecture, in which distributed nodes discover relevant context information to enhance the usage of local available connectivity resources (Mateus & Marinheiro, 2010). In this way, mobile operators can develop policies for IP flow mobility, and control which traffic is routed over different access technologies (Alves et al., 2018).

Another aspect to consider is that the Internet was initially designed to support communications between remote hosts. Since its early days, the Internet has evolved drastically, with a huge evolution in broadband access penetration and dissemination of mobile terminals with unforeseen capacities. This evolution has altered the Internet into a medium to connect people in multiple ways with content made available in completely new and complex modes through the entire network infrastructure. In fact, current users are more interested in searching for information over Google, watch videos on YouTube, and share files via Dropbox than to worry about connectivity to a particular host.

This content demand has catalyzed an exponential growth of Internet traffic volume and content distribution is increasingly becoming more centric in the Internet, and this is challenging and changing how the Internet is being organized.

Content delivery network (CDN) operators, content providers as well as ISPs are important players to consider in the typical content-centric cases of FNs. However, these players interact with a mix of technologies that are difficult to manage in a comprehensive and global ways.

Research efforts have been made to move the Internet away from its current reliance on purely point-to-point primitives and, to this end, have proposed detailed designs that make the Internet more data-oriented or content-centric (Jacobson et al., 2009)(L. Zhang et al., 2014). As such Information-centric networking has emerged as a new approach in the research community (Cheriton & Gritter, 2000) (Ahlgren, Dannewitz, Imbrenda, Kutscher, & Ohlman, 2012) to integrate content delivery as a native network feature and make networks natively content-aware.

Due to this, FNs most probably will sustain the next generation of the Internet infrastructure, interconnecting people and content through mobile cloud networks (as said before, the Internet is evolving from a node discovery to enable the discovery of specialized objects). These cloud networks will operate on an always best-connected scenario, where a person is allowed to choose the best available access technology (from small cells to standard base stations), access network and terminal device at any point in time. Generally, the idea is to enhance FNs to automatically interpret, process, and move content (information) independently of users' location. Additionally, the traditional approach, where resources are provided by remote clouds, is also not capable of giving adequate response to the fast-growing number of connected devises and their resource requirements. For all these reasons, new cloud architectures have been evolving, by migrating resources, such as services and data, closer to end users and devices (Figure 3).

With remote clouds, devices communicate directly with traditional distant resource-rich servers. These clouds can provide unlimited resources, but this approach does not easily scale, and long latency, bandwidth bottleneck, communication overhead, and location blindness is experienced. In face of this, it is necessary to bringing computing resources closer to end-users, to overcome the limitations of remote cloud computing (C. Li, Xue, Wang, Zhang, & Li, 2018). This is on the genesis of the edge computing paradigm, that allows more responsive cloud services, accomplished by extending the services from the core in cloud data centers to the edge of the network, by placing intermediate nodes between the cloud and the end user, which are responsible for better serving ubiquitous smart devices, fulfilling user resource requests.

Edge computing may follow different architecture implementations such as cloudlets, fog computing, or Multi-Access Edge Computing (MEC).

Cloudlets (Jararweh, Tawalbeh, Ababneh, Khreishah, & Dosari, 2014) are trusted devices or a cluster of devices with high capabilities. They are most often installed along with Access Points (AP) to allow mobile devices to access it, and in some cases both of the cloudlet and AP are integrated in one entity. Fog Computing is a term introduced by Cisco Systems (CISCO, 2015). Their rationale for coining this term is that a fog is nothing more than a cloud that is closer to the ground. Fog computing's main feature is that the fog system is deployed close to end users in a widely distributed manner (Yi, Li, & Li, 2015) (C. Li et al., 2018), in the form of fog nodes (Tordera et al., 2016), possibly at different levels and numbers (Balevi & Gitlin, 2018). The MEC paradigm (Taleb et al., 2017) was introduced by an industry lead initiative (ETSI 2014), to provide IT and cloud-computing capabilities within the Radio Access Network (RAN) in close proximity to mobile subscribers. Mobile network operators will allow the use of the access network, where low latency and high-bandwidth as well as direct access to real-time radio

Figure 3. Cloud architectures providing services to end devices

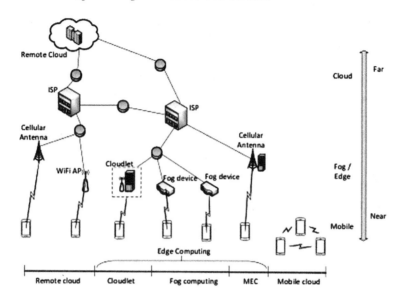

network information (such as subscriber location, cell load, etc.) is available. This can be used to allow content, services and applications to be accelerated, increasing server responsiveness from the edge. Additionally, MEC servers are context aware, as they manage information on end devices, such as their location and network information. Nevertheless, their capacity is limited, therefore deciding which and how resources can be managed at the edge can still be a trick endeavour (Gabry, Bioglio, & Land, 2016).

The clouds are migrating even closer to end users, with new computing architectures where mobile devices use their extra resources in a coordinated manner, to support cloud services. This contrasts with the previous edge implementations, where the mobile device's exclusive role in the cloud was that of a consumer. There is a myriad of proposals, either with centralised control, such as Hyrax (Marinelli, 2009) and FemtoClouds (Habak, Ammar, Harras, & Zegura, 2015), or a decentralised control, where nodes keep track of their own resources, such is the case with EECRS (Hu, Zhu, Xia, Chen, & Luo, 2012) (Lu et al., 2013), Phoenix (Panta, Jana, Cheng, Chen, & Vaishampayan, 2013), Mobile Host (Srirama & Paniagua, 2013) and (Monteiro, Silva, Lourenço, & Paulino, 2015).

This migration of clouds, to the proximity of users, in particular in the extreme case of clouds supported by autonomous mobile devices, brings new challenges regarding resource management. Once again this portrays a perfect scenario to apply game theoretic approaches, where conflicting interests have to be mediated.

Another trend gaining momentum for FNs is the Internet of Things (IoT). However, the IoT paradigm is not new (Corcoran, 2016), but building end-to-end IoT systems from scratch has always been a challenging and a risky enterprise, many times with ambiguous and uncertain business cases. To overcome this, a new trend in IoT, engaged by a surge of companies, is the building of complete solutions that encapsulate aspects of an end-to-end IoT system using building blocks that can be used in a repeatable and replicable way. These aggregated building blocks materialize many IoT platforms that allow companies to reduced development and deployment time and costs, and allow the creation of new business models, such as paying per use or fixed licensing. (Gluhak et al., 2016) provides an exhaustive review on different IoT platforms. In fact, IoT platforms have become so popular, which are present over 360 platforms on the market, with many more providers and consumers of this kind of platforms. The diversity of players at stake sometime have conflicting goals, and this challenge is an ideal use case for game theory approaches, such is the case with resource management (Semasinghe, Maghsudi, & Hossain, 2017).

But the IoT paradigm is progressing even further influencing new developments in various domains, such as the Internet of Mobile Things (IoMT), Autonomous Internet of Things (A-IoT), Autonomous System of Things (ASoT), Internet of Autonomous Things (IoAT), Internet of Things Clouds (IoT-C) and the Internet of Robotic Things (IoRT) (Vermesan et al., 2017), where new challenges are at stake. In fact, the initial tendency of centralized platforms, usually deployed at a remote cloud, following the classic centralized computing paradigm, faces several of such challenges such as high latency, low capacity and network failure. Because of these, the trend is now evolving to more distributed IoT platforms that can also, but not only, deployed at edge. This follows the same principles of fog computing to bring the cloud closer to IoT devices. The fog can provide IoT data processing and storage locally, instead of sending them to remote clouds, providing services with faster response and greater quality, enabling the IoT to provide efficient and secure services for many IoT users. (Atlam, Walters, & Wills, 2018) and (Mahmud, Kotagiri, & Buyya, 2018) reviewed pertinent state-of-the-art fog computing architectures and emerging IoT applications that will be improved by using the fog model, highlighting the benefits and implementation challenges. In these approaches, distributed resource management is usually more difficult to attain, and IoT devices are more than ever expected to act smart and resolve diverging goals. Once again, this is also a good used case for game theory approaches.

There are many applications for the IoT that include smart cities, like smart vehicles, surveillance systems, traffic monitoring, and smart parking, or homes and communities, like smart homes, wearable devices/mobile phones, healthcare, and hospitals, or the industry like business and production lines factories, or even agriculture, like automation and precision agriculture, and so on. This diversity of uses cases has also lead, regarding communication technologies, to the proliferation of a myriad of multi-radio access technologies for IoT, sometimes optimized to specific applications, to connect devices at the edge. (Vermesan et al., 2017). This has generated heterogeneous mobile networks that need complex configuration, management and maintenance, where it is important to have devices that play a more active role, at the edge of the network, making decisions and performing tasks without human intervention.

One of the major challenges for the the FN is how to achieve security in a growing networked world of distributed devices and services. To overcome this, blockchain and smart contracts have been a key technology to consider. The idea that supports blockchains, also referred to as distributed ledgers, is that distributed users maintain a public and identical dynamic digital register of all transactions that have taken place. The history of the recorded transactions alone determines the ownership, so it is imperative that transactions within this database are audited and agreed upon by consensus (Mingxiao, Xiaofeng, Zhe, Xiangwei, & Qijun, 2017). This decentralized method of keeping track of changes ensures the ledger cannot be practically controlled by any one entity. It also eliminates the possibility of single-points of failure and allows for the verification of transactions without the need for third-party intervention. The seminal paper for the Bitcoin protocol (Nakamoto, 2008) has triggered all this. With a blockchain in place, applications that could previously run only through a trusted intermediary, can now operate in a decentralized manner, without the need for a central authority, and achieve the same or better functionality with the same amount of certainty. This has prompted a new wave on security supported by blockchains and smart contracts, in several fields relevant for the FN such as the IoTs (Christidis & Devetsikiotis, 2016) and Wireless Mesh Networks (Selimi, Kabbinale, Ali, Navarro, & Sathiaseelan, 2018).

Blockchain technology can very well change and even disrupt future network (Mougayar, 2016) (Marsal-Llacuna, 2018) in several ways: it's reliable peer-to-peer communication model can lend to more effective IoT ecosystems; applications can be developed and hosted within decentralized storage environments, data bases can be connected using smart contracts; the overhead of managing and tracking large networks of devices without the need for a centralized controller could be reduced; network management could be further simplified using self-executing smart contracts, programmed to perform actions when certain requirements are met; transferring assets could be streamlined, in cloud-based architectures where edge devices are playing a greater role in networking; distributed and cooperative cloud storage environment over a peer-to-peer network could be possible.

Of course, the upcoming design of FNs (MEC/FC/IoT/Security) scheme to operate in a satisfactory way, a great number of very demanding requirements must be fulfilled, not only technical ones (e.g. autonomic self-x requisites with cognitive radios like self-learning) but also in terms of business relationships among operators and service providers, as well as, the handling of the service subscription.

The course of finding a solution that can satisfy all the involved entities in the high complex network environment of FNs, like content providers, cloud providers, home providers, brokers, network providers or users, can be found by means of GT (Moura & Hutchison, 2018). In this way, as the players define their strategies then the GT can find ways to build-up win-win situations for all of them. Cooperation between technologies and/or providers, alongside Machine to Machine (M2M) communications or Internet of Things deployment will require complex and dynamic management algorithms to maximize network efficiency, pricing, Quality of Service (QoS), Quality of Experience (QoE) and ultimately, profit.

Considering all previous facets, we foresee that FNs will have to form a network infrastructure with a collective intelligence, as shown in Figure 4. This intelligence is very pertinent in FNs to address emergent traffic requisites, the management complexity of the heterogeneous wireless access technologies, and the challenges faced by a more content and data centric network.

To enhance the network intelligence, the future network infrastructure needs to be supervised in order to enable learning processes on management algorithms when these control some network problems (e.g. congestion situation, node misbehaving behavior). In this way, the network intelligence will be enhanced, enabling the network infrastructure to manage the high complex future heterogeneous access infrastructure in a much more efficient way. As an example, the load could be balanced among the diverse wireless access technologies, reacting to a detected congestion situation to mitigate its negative effects. Alternatively, the load could be also balanced in a flash crowd scenario where a network problem is predicted and some policies are applied to the network to avoid the occurrence of that problem, e.g. offloading flows from the technology that soon could become disrupted to other available technologies with low levels of traffic load. In addition, congestion situations could be controlled by limiting the transmission rate of some users and freeing network resources to others. The one-billion-dollar question that remains to be answered is to find out the more efficient levels of aggressiveness of the algorithm that dynamically increases/decreases the rate transmission in a high complex networking scenario with diverse wireless access technologies and flow requirements.

To enable the network collective intelligence, we argue that it is important to obtain cooperation among the nodes. In this way, the network nodes need to be incentivized to cooperate, and the nodes that do not cooperate should be detected in a truthful way and be gradually penalized (e.g. their access rate is diminished). Eventually, uncooperative nodes that afterwards would change to a cooperative behavior, they could have their reputation values being restored to values that allow them to use again the network resources without any restriction on their access rate.

Figure 4. Collective intelligence in FNS to manage emergent traffic and functional requisites

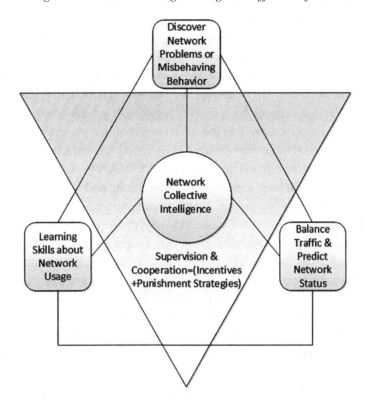

In practical terms, the FNs should require distributed management algorithms to support the network self-configuring feature. GT seems a very important area to model, analyze and decide how these distributed algorithms need to be deployed. In the following Section, we discuss some literature contributions that use theoretical games to enhance the cooperation among the diverse network players.

4. GAME THEORY CONTRIBUTIONS FOR ENHANCING NETWORK COOPERATION

FNs will be demanding for the deployment of novel management solutions aiming more efficiently and fairly usage of the available network resources. To accomplish the overall network goals, the nodes should collaborate or cooperate essentially in a multi-hop network topology, the typical scenario of future heterogeneous and high-complexity networks. For example, a terminal node should process both related and non-related traffic, whereas non-related classifies traffic not originated (not destined) from (to) that node. This new collaborative functionality will become possible at the physical layer in future multi-hop wireless networks because the network edge infrastructure will be vastly deployed by radio technologies, which allow the easy share of data messages among local terminals due to their broadcast transmission characteristic.

A very significant number of researchers have proposed GT models to encourage players (terminals and networks) to cooperate and enhance the overall network performance instead for acting selfishly to optimize their own performance. In this way, some additional incentives are required in FNs to enable collaboration among the nodes, defeating eventual misbehaving nodes like selfish or malicious ones. A selfish node may refuse to forward a non-related message to save its battery. In this way, this node needs a correct incentive to forward traffic, e.g. the network could increase the throughput of flows originated (destined) from (to) that node as a reward to previous collaboration in forwarding non-related traffic. Alternatively, a malicious node may try to disrupt the network functionality; in this case, the network could isolate that node from the network for a certain period as a punishment to that wrong procedure.

Broadly discussing, the right incentives to the nodes collaborate among them can be divided in two large groups: monetary-based and reputation-based. On one hand, the monetary-based solutions typically aim to achieve short/medium-term relationships among nodes. On the other hand, the reputation-based solutions typically aim to establish long-term relationships among nodes. This section will be highlighting some relevant work from these two groups, which is summarized in Figure 5.

The first group of contributions makes use of virtual payments for channel use and to incentive the collaboration among nodes in a multi-hop wireless network topology, as shown in Figure 6. Here, there are typically three types of nodes: the senders, the forwarders (intermediates) and the destination nodes. Some proposed credit-based systems suggest that distinct node types should be charged to cover the costs for packet forwarding. In fact, some proposals suggest that only the senders should be charged with a tariff initially specified (Zhong, Chen, & Yang, 2003) (L. Buttyan & Hubaux, 2000) (Buttyán & Hubaux, 2003) (Ileri, Siun-Chuon Mau, & Mandayam, 2005) (Shastry & Adve, 2006) (Chen, Yang, Wagener, & Nahrstedt, 2005) (T. Alpcan, Basar, Srikant, & Atman, 2001) (Saraydar, Mandayam, & Goodman, 2002) (Vassaki, Panagopoulos, Constantinou, & Vázquez-Castro, 2010). Alternatively, the destination nodes are charged (L. Buttyan & Hubaux, 2000) (Hua Liu & Krishnamachari, 2006) or destination and senders are both charged (Levente Buttyan & Hubaux, 2001) (Yanchao Zhang, Wenjing Lou, & Yuguang Fang, 2004). In addition, an incentive mechanism called bandwidth exchange was proposed in (D. Zhang, Ileri, & Mandayam, 2008), where a node can delegate a portion of its bandwidth to another node in exchange for relay cooperation. Finally, a different approach of credit-based schemes appear in (Chen & Nahrstedt, 2004) (Demir & Comaniciu, 2007), where auction-based incentive models are proposed. The basic idea of these schemes is that each intermediate node operates as a market; the users of the network put bids for their packets, the packets are accordingly scheduled to transmission and then charged after their transmission. The goals to achieve with auction models could be node truthful bidding and social network welfare maximization (Chen & Nahrstedt, 2004) or balancing residual battery energy and the current currency (credit) levels of the nodes in the network (Demir & Comaniciu, 2007).

The main advantage of credit-based approaches is that they succeed in large-scale networks to enforce a distributed cooperation mechanism among selfish nodes. Moreover, credits are useful when an action and its reward are not simultaneous. This is valid for multi-hop wireless networks: the action is packet forwarding and the reward occurs after sending their own packets. These approaches could be useful to discover the more convenient routing policies, solving very challenging dilemmas in multi-hop networks. For example, these approaches could help to choose the cheapest route between a source and a destination node either by minimizing the total number of hops (minimizing end-to-end flow delay) or by choosing the less-congested hops (increasing flow data rate). The drawbacks of credit-based proposals are extra overhead and complexity to charge users fairly and avoid cheating, turning these proposals hard to deploy.

In FNs, customers can be billed using a congestion-sensitive tariff, where prices are set in real time according to current load and taking full advantage of demand elasticity to maximize efficiency and fairness (Saraydar et al., 2002). The demand elasticity utilizes historical information about expected

Figure 5. Summary of game theory work supporting cooperation incentives

```
                    ┌─────────────────┐
                    │  Cooperation    │
                    │  Incentives     │
                    └─────────────────┘
            ┌───────────┴──────────────┐
    ┌───────────────┐          ┌────────────────┐
    │   Payment     │          │   Reputation   │
    └───────────────┘          └────────────────┘
```

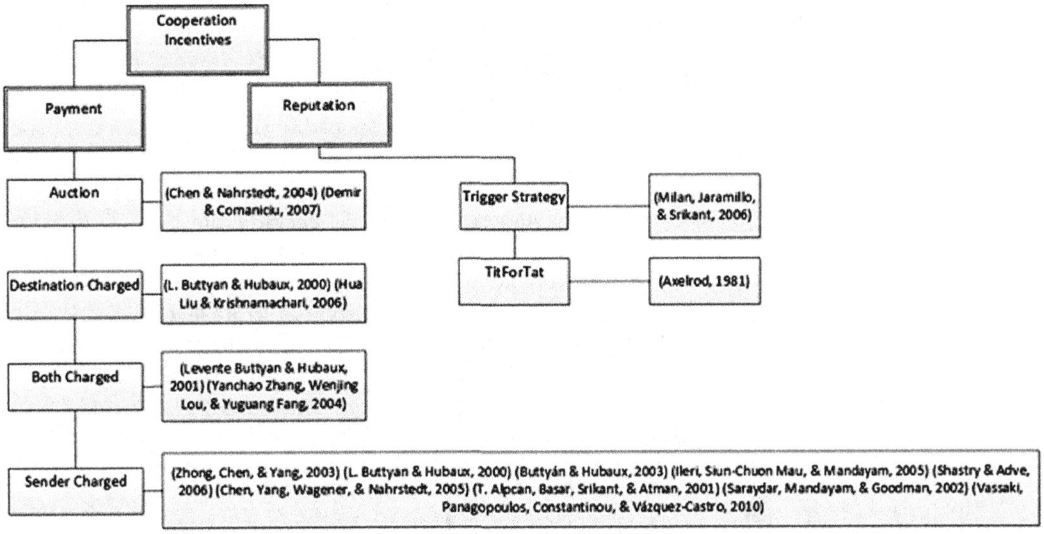

Figure 6. Credit-based incentive mechanism

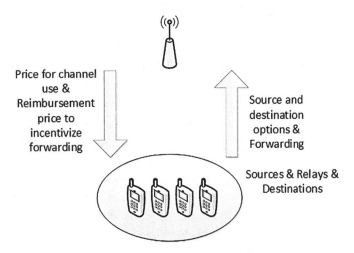

peak load periods. According to (Felegyhazi & Hubaux, 2006), an investigation area where pricing has practical relevance is service provisioning among operators (e.g., renting transmission capacity).

The second group of contributions makes use of reputation-based proposals (Trestian, Ormond, & Muntean, 2011) (Munjal & Singh, 2018) to incentivize the collaboration among nodes in a multi-hop wireless network topology. The reputation metric represents the amount of trust the network community has about a node. Figure 7 illustrates the typical phases of a reputation system to incentivize a correct node behavior.

During the initial phase, the reputation information of each node is collected to a central node connected to the wired network. After receiving the new reputation information, the central node updates a reputation matrix, which stores the reputation information from all the nodes (second phase). Then, in

Figure 7. Reputation-based incentive mechanism

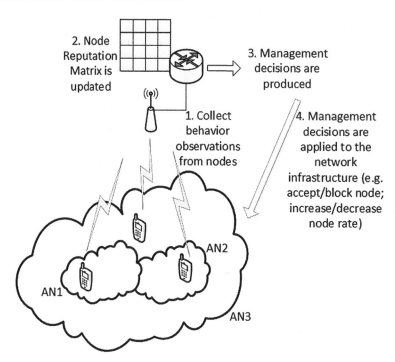

the next phase, management decisions are selected, which, during the fourth and last phase, are applied to the network infrastructure. In this way, as an example, members that have good reputation, because they helpfully contribute to the community welfare, can use the network resources; while nodes with a bad reputation, because they usually refuse to cooperate, are excluded from that community.

A very popular game-theoretic approach for reputation analysis is the repeated game because in this context it does not make sense that a game for reputation is based uniquely in its current (instantaneous) value; in fact, the reputation should be also evaluated through a historical term, normally with a higher weight than the one associated with the instantaneous value of reputation. In this way, it is possible to avoid false misbehavior detections due to temporary link communications failures. In addition, the uncertainty about the information that is available to other players and their decisions is normally modeled with Bayesian Game or Game with Incomplete Information (Harsanyi, 2004). Finally, to correctly model the robustness to changes on the behavior of the participants, auction games are preferred (Nurmi & Nurmi, 2006).

There are at least two different strategies on how the reputation could incentivize cooperation among nodes (or players). One of the ways is to develop a strategy such that the cooperation of a node is measured and if the fraction of packets it has dropped is above a threshold, it is considered selfish and is disconnected for a given amount of time. This strategy is known as a Trigger Strategy (Milan, Jaramillo, & Srikant, 2006). An alternative way is designated by Tit For Tat (TFT) (Axelrod, 1981). A player using this strategy will cooperate initially and then act regarding the opponent´s previous action: if the opponent previously was cooperative then the former player will be cooperative as well; otherwise, the former player will not cooperate. To illustrate the advantages of the TFT strategy being used by game players, a Finite Repeated Prisoner's Dilemma Game was simulated via Matlab (5000 iterations). The game is between two players. Each player tries to score the most number of points against each opponent player during each game. In this case, the player Operator1 can choose in each game's iteration between 'cooperate' or 'defect', like player Operator2. In each game's iteration, points are then awarded to both players based on the combination of their choices, following what is shown in Table 3.

Table 3. Points awarded to each player based on individual player's choices

		Operator2	
		Cooperate	Defect
Operator1	Cooperate	3, 3	0, 5
	Defect	5, 0	1, 1

The maximum number of points a player can win during a game's iteration is five. This maximum score only occurs if that player defects and the opponent cooperates. Nevertheless, the former player scores one point instead five points if both players defect. As one can easily conclude, the main difficulty imposed to each player of the current game is to choose the option that maximizes his reward because he ignores the opponent's choice, as both players, during a game's iteration, perform their choices simultaneously. The previous difficulty in a player choosing the right option to maximize the reward points won by that player is perfectly evident from the simulation results presented in Figure 8. In fact, the random strategy used by each player to make a choice gives the worst performance. In opposition, TFT strategy shows a better performance.

Figure 8. Outcomes of a finite repeated prisoner's dilemma game using two distinct strategies

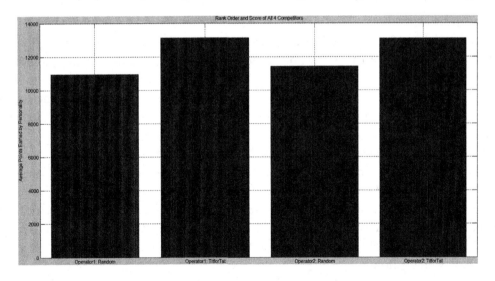

Despite the good performance of TFT, it could reveal some drawbacks in a wireless scenario. As an example, TFT does not distinguish uncooperative behavior from a transmission failure due to a collision. In this way, TFT could penalize a collaborative player that had the bad luck of suffering a collision during a data transmission tentative. Consequently, a few TFT variants have been proposed (Milan et al., 2006) (Jaramillo & Srikant, 2007) (Q. Li, Zhu, & Cao, 2010) (Vedhavathy & Manikandan, 2018) (Ntemos, Plata-Chaves, Kolokotronis, Kalouptsidis, & Moonen, 2018) to correct that problem.

For a multi-hop wireless network, there is an interesting tradeoff between the amount of available information to evaluate a node´s behavior (reputation) and the protocol overhead/complexity used to disseminate the necessary information through the network. Some proposals are more concerned with all the nodes having access to the full information about node behavior (Buchegger & Le Boudec, 2002) (Jochen & Le, 2005) (Qi He, Dapeng Wu, & Khosla, 2004) to enhance the accuracy on how the reputation is evaluated. These proposals could have problems related with fake information disseminated among the nodes that create wrong reputation values. To avoid these problems, the protocol used to disseminate the reputation values through the network must be enriched with additional authentication and trust functional features. Alternatively, to keep the protocol overhead low, each node should only disseminate the reputation values he directly measured to its neighbors (it only uses first-hand reputation changes) (Bansal & Baker, 2003).

Recent work proposed dynamic reputation-based incentives for cooperative relays present in a network topology formed by heterogeneous networks (Hwang, Shin, & Yoon, 2008) (Skraparlis, Sakarellos, Panagopoulos, & Kanellopoulos, 2009) (Z. Zhang, Long, Vasilakos, & Hanzo, 2016) (Kwon, Lim, Choi, & Hong, 2010). The incentive for cooperation among nodes can be given either by additional throughput (Hwang et al., 2008) or by additional time-slots for transmission (Skraparlis et al., 2009) (Z. Zhang et al., 2016) (Kwon et al., 2010).

Regarding strategies for penalizing misbehaving users, the research community has proposed several ways to perform it: isolate misbehaving users from the network (Buchegger & Le Boudec, 2002), reduce misbehaving users' bandwidth (Hwang et al., 2008) or reduce the transmission slots of misbehaving users (Skraparlis et al., 2009).

The main advantage of reputation-based proposals is that they rely on observations from multiple sources, turning it relatively resistant to the diffusion of false information from a small number of lying nodes. Some potential problems are the usage of additional bandwidth and battery energy to intensively monitor the behavior of each network node. In addition, some nodes could collude to cheat the reputation of other nodes by the dissemination of false information through the network about the latter nodes to the former nodes increase their benefits.

Game theory approaches have also been applied to blockchain security. The decentralized cooperative method of keeping track of blockchains, by miners, without the need for third-party intervention, is a relevant use case for many game models. (Nakamoto, 2008) already uses incentives in a simple, albeit insufficient, model. But unfortunately, distilling the essential game-theoretic properties of blockchain maintenance is far from trivial, and there have been many works that examines possible types of attacks against the blockchains and suggest adaptations of the protocol to ensure its security. A brief mention of some of these works follows.

In (Kroll, Davey, & Felten, 2013) the equilibria of the Bitcoin game are considered, and prove that any monotonic strategy is a Nash equilibrium (one of many). In (Eyal and Sirer, 2014), present a specific attack strategy called the "Selfish Mine" and examine when it is beneficial for a pool of miners. This is further exploited by (Sapirshtein, Sompolinsky, & Zohar, 2017), with a wider set of possible strategies, that includes the "Selfish-Mine" strategy, and explore this space computationally. In (Eyal, 2015) the author considers attacks performed between different pools where users are sent to infiltrate a competitive pool, giving raise to a pool game, the miner's dilemma, an instance of the iterative prisoner's dilemma. Further on, (Lewenberg, Bachrach, Sompolinsky, Zohar, & Rosenschein, 2015) has made a (cooperative) game theoretic analysis regarding pool mining. (Babaioff, Dobzinski, Oren, & Zohar, 2012) deals with Sybil attacks and propose a reward scheme which will make it in the best interest of a miner to propagate transactions. (Kiayias, Koutsoupias, Kyropoulou, & Tselekounis, 2016) have considered two simplified forms of a stochastic game, in which the miners have complete information: the Immediate-Release Game and the Strategic-Release Game.

The development of more suitable and fair schemes to incentivize cooperation in FNs is a challenging research direction. According to the authors of (Han et al., 2012) (Bouhaddi, Radjef, & Adi, 2018) (Ungureanu, 2018), hybrid schemes that combine both reputation and credit aspects are of particular interest to be further investigated. Lastly, by defining mechanisms of incentives for cooperation and disincentives against cheating or selfish behavior, and applying repeatedly both of these mechanisms, the cooperation among the players apparently becomes stronger in a distributed way without the need to sign a contract among the players (Trestian et al., 2011) (Munjal & Singh, 2018).

5. GAME THEORY FOR WIRELESS NETWORKING

In this section, we revise the literature in terms of how GT can be successfully applied to networking and wireless communications areas, including IoT.

(MacKenzie & DaSilva, 2006) describes ways in which GT can be applied to real applications in wireless communications and networking, such as: pricing, flow control, power control, medium access and interference avoidance. They also pointed out some appealing future applications of GT: cognitive networks and learning, mobility support and cooperation in wireless networks. (Y. Zhang & Guizani, 2011) explores applications of different economic approaches, including bargaining, auctions, cooperation incentives and dynamic coalition games for cooperation. (Han et al., 2012) discusses game-theoretic models in a wide range of wireless and communication applications such as cellular and broadband wireless access networks, wireless local area networks, multi-hop networks, cooperative networks, cognitive-radio networks, and Internet networks. In addition, some relevant Internet problems such as, congestion control, pricing, revenue sharing among Internet service providers, and incentive mechanisms to enable cooperation into peer-to-peer applications, are also discussed.

(Jianwei Huang & Zhu Han, 2010) presents several GT models/concepts that are highly relevant for spectrum sharing, including iterative water-filling, potential game, supermodular game, bargaining, auction, and correlated equilibrium. (Huang, 2013) outlines a taxonomy to systematically understand and tackle the issue of economic viability of cooperation in dynamic spectrum management. The framework divides the problem space according to four orthogonal dimensions, including complete/incomplete network information, loose/tight decision couplings, user/operator interactions, and static/dynamic decision processes. The vast majority of the key methodologies for each dimension involve GT. (Walid Saad, Han, & Hjørungnes, 2011) reviews coalitional GT for cooperative cellular wireless networks. (Marina, Saad, Han, & Hjørungnes, 2011) revises GT work about malicious behavior.

From the literature a significant number of surveys have been found about GT application in wireless communications and networking, as summarized in Figure 9. These surveys cover the following areas: wireless networks (Charilas & Panagopoulos, 2010) (Akkarajitsakul, Hossain, Niyato, & Kim, 2011) (Ghazvini, Movahedinia, Jamshidi, & Moghim, 2013) (Niyato & Hossain, 2007) (Trestian et al., 2011) (Larsson, Jorswieck, Lindblom, & Mochaourab, 2009) (M. A. Khan et al., 2012a); wireless Ad Hoc networks (Srivastava et al., 2005); wireless sensor networks (WSNs) (Machado & Tekinay, 2008) (Shen, Yue, Cao, & Yu, 2011) (Shi, Wang, Kwok, & Chen, 2012); MIMO systems (Scutari, Palomar, & Barbarossa, 2008); cognitive radio networks (Beibei Wang, Wu, & Liu, 2010) (B Wang, Wu, Liu, & Clancy, 2011); 4G networks (M. A. Khan et al., 2012b); smart grids (Fadlullah, Nozaki, Takeuchi, & Kato, 2011) (W Saad, Han, Poor, & Basar, 2012); telecommunications (E Altman, Boulogne, El-Azouzi, Jiménez, & Wynter, 2006); and Internet of Things (IoT) (Semasinghe et al., 2017).

Figure 9. Summary of game theory surveys

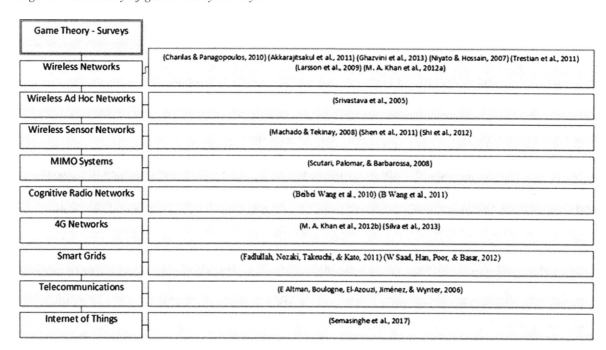

Covering the area of wireless networks where GT is applied, we can explicit the following surveys: a significant number of GT proposals are discussed in a network-layered perspective (Charilas & Panagopoulos, 2010); multiple access games are analyzed in (Akkarajitsakul et al., 2011); games of random access with Carrier Sense Multiple Access (CSMA) are covered in (Ghazvini et al., 2013); games about resource management and admission control are addressed by (Niyato & Hossain, 2007); games for network selection and resource allocation are available in (Trestian et al., 2011); games of spectrum allocation, power control, interference are covered in (Larsson et al., 2009); and finally, evolutionary coalitional games for wireless networking and communications are available in (M. A. Khan et al., 2012a).

Since the application of GT to enhance cooperation in FNs, formed by heterogeneous wireless access networks, is the main focus of the present chapter, we particularize now some surveys related to Wireless Sensor Networks (WSNs), cognitive radio networks and 4G networks. (Machado & Tekinay, 2008) reviewed the literature about the usage of game-theoretic approaches to address problems related to security and energy efficiency in WSNs. (Shen et al., 2011) main concern was to revise GT approaches towards the enhancement of WSN security. Finally, (Shi et al., 2012) offered a more comprehensive survey than previous referred ones about GT applied to WSNs.

The games for cognitive radio networks are classified by (Beibei Wang et al., 2010) into four categories: non-cooperative spectrum sharing, spectrum trading and mechanism design, cooperative spectrum sharing, and stochastic spectrum sharing games. For each category, they explained the fundamental concepts and properties, and provided a detailed discussion about the methodologies on how to apply these games in spectrum sharing protocol design. They also discussed some research challenges and future research directions related to game theoretic modeling in cognitive radio networks.

Cognitive attackers may exist in a cognitive radio network, who can adapt their attacking strategy to the time-varying spectrum opportunities and secondary users' strategy. To alleviate the damage caused by cognitive attackers, a dynamic security mechanism is investigated in (B Wang et al., 2011) by a stochastic game modeling. The state of the anti-jamming game includes the spectrum availability, channel quality, and the status of jammed channels observed at the current time slot. The action of the secondary users reflects how many channels they should reserve for transmitting control and data messages and how to switch between the different channels. Since the secondary users and attackers have opposite goals, the antijamming game can be classified as a zero-sum game.

Regarding IoT, many challenges need to be addressed in order to efficiently manage available resources. Centralised resource management is however infeasible when a large number of entities is involved, not only because of the computational complexity involved but also due to information acquisition requirements. For this reason, in IoT there has been a trend in performing distributed resource management, in particular using game theoretic approaches such as proposed by (Al-Kashoash, Hafeez, & Kemp, 2017) (Borah, Dhurandher, Woungang, & Kumar, 2017) (Kim, 2016) (Sedjelmaci, Senouci, & Al-Bahri, 2016).

However, conventional game models are not always suitable for large-scale IoT systems, due to the massive information acquisition overhead, the slow convergence to equilibrium, the inefficiency of equilibrium, the extreme computational complexity, and the complexity required to characterize the equilibrium set (Semasinghe et al., 2017). Therefore, non-conventional game theoretic models are required to match the intrinsic characteristics of future large-scale IoT systems. These are characterized by having random deployments, scalability issues, limited fronthaul/backhaul, inhomogeneity, non-guaranteed energy supply, uncertain and incomplete information. Game models will inevitably have to overcome these challenges for an efficient distributed resource management. (Semasinghe et al., 2017) discusses several promising game models for IoT such as evolutionary games, mean field games, minority games, mean field bandit games, and mean field auctions. They describe the basics of each of these game models and access the potential IoT-related resource management problems that can be solved by using these models (Table 4)

The authors of (M. A. Khan et al., 2012b) study game dynamics and learning schemes for heterogeneous 4G networks. They propose a novel learning scheme called cost-to-learn that incorporates the cost to switch, the switching delay, and the cost of changing to a new action. Considering a dynamic and uncertain environment, where the users and operators have only a numerical value of their own payoffs as information, and strategy reinforcement learning (CODIPAS-RL) is used, they show the users are able to learn their own optimal payoff and their optimal strategy simultaneously. Using evolutionary game dynamics, they prove the convergence and stability properties in specific classes of dynamic robust games. They also provide various numerical and simulation results in the context of network selection in wireless local area networks (WLAN) and Long Term Evolution (LTE). In addition, (Silva et al., 2013) clearly shows the main advantages of cooperation among wireless access technologies. The following sections justify why the collaboration aspect should be very important in FNs and how GT can help to study the best ways to deploy this new functionality in a distributed way.

Table 4. Potential IoT applications for different game models

Game Theoretic Model	Potential Use Case for IoT
Evolutionary games	Power control, spectrum/subcarrier allocation, transmission mode/network selection
Mean field games	Energy/queue/channel-aware resource allocation, resource management under mobility
Minority games	Scheduling, transmission mode/network selection, interference management
Mean field bandit games	User association, scheduling, channel allocation
Mean field dynamic auctions	User association, scheduling, channel allocation

6. GUIDELINES TO APPLY GAME THEORY ON FUTURE NETWORKS

The current section discusses some relevant research work in how GT can be used to address the more significant operational or functional expected aspects of Future Network (FN) environments. The most-part of the discussed scenarios belongs to the network edge of Internet. More specifically, these scenarios are concerned in how the heterogeneous wireless access infrastructure can be efficiently used by multi-mode terminals, as well as, to guarantee a reliable access to the Internet through wireless backhaul links. In this way, several possible functional/operational enhancements are envisioned to use efficiently the heterogeneous wireless access infrastructure in the following topics: network planning, multi-technology wireless networks, network management, Internet of Things (multi-hop reliable networks) and reliable wireless backhaul. These should be hot research areas in FNs and are summarized in Table 5 together with references for relevant work that should be initially studied in order to find innovative ways to plan, control, manage and operate FNs.

6.1. Network Planning

Imperfect network coverage, especially in indoor locations is an important problem in existing cellular networks. To overcome this problem, the concept of Femtocell Access Points (FAPs) has recently been proposed as a means to overlay, on existing mobile networks, low-power and low-cost Base Stations (BSs). FAPs are connected by an IP backhaul through a local broadband connection such as DSL, cable or fiber.

Notably, various benefits of using FAP technology have been already identified:

- Enhances indoor coverage
- Provides high data rates
- Improves Quality-of-Service (QoS) to subscribers
- Ensures longer battery life for handheld terminals
- Offloads traffic from the mobile operator's backhaul to the wired residential broadband connection, reducing the backhaul cost of the mobile operator.

Table 5. Relevant FN topics/areas where GT can be successfully applied

Topic/Area	Scenario/Game Type	Reference
Network planning	Stackelberg game to control power transmission in a network formed by macrocells and femtocells	(Guruacharya, Niyato, Hossain, & Kim, 2010)
Multi-technology wireless networks	Bayesian game to study vertical-handovers in which the users have distinct bandwidth requirements	(Zhu, Niyato, & Wang, 2010)
Network management	Evolutionary game to study rate selection for VoIP service; non-zero sum game for studying user admission control to avoid congestion	(Watanabe, Menasche, de Souza e Silva, & Leao, 2008) (Yu-Liang Kuo, Eric Hsiao-Kuang Wu, & Gen-Huey Chen, 2004)
Internet of things (multi-hop reliable networks)	Hop price-based routing game; auction theory to support truthfulness and security;	(Hua Liu & Krishnamachari, 2006) (Anderegg & Eidenbenz, 2003) (Eidenbenz, Resta, & Santi, 2008)
Reliable wireless backhaul	Evolutionary game to study traffic routing through multi-hop wireless backhaul links	(Anastasopoulos, Arapoglou, Kannan, & Cottis, 2008)
Multi-access edge computing	How game theoretical games should model wireless data communication networks to understand how to deploy in an efficient way upcoming edge technologies/ services, such as the Internet of Things, user wearables, and virtual/augmented reality applications.	(Moura & Hutchison, 2018)

When FAPs are deployed on top of an existing cellular system, and since FAPs operate on the same frequency bands as macrocell BSs, a new problem arises. This problem is related with the interference among channels that can impair the overall network performance. In such a network scenario, it is of interest to study the problem of transmit-power control in the downlink, minimizing the interference problem and ensuring an acceptable network performance.

In this section, we adopt the approach of (Guruacharya et al., 2010), also thoroughly discussed in (Han et al., 2012), for studying the transmit-power control in the downlink from a game-theory perspective. First, we model the scenario as a Stackelberg game. Then, we discuss the properties of the considered game and its solution. In the following text, we present a low-complexity algorithm to reach the desired outcome (Han et al., 2012).

6.1.1. Stackelberg Game to Control Transmission Power

In order to tackle the power-control problem using GT, a framework of a Stackelberg game has been used (Han et al., 2012). In the studied femtocell deployment model, it is considered that the macrocell BSs are the leaders and the FAPs are the followers in a Stackelberg game, as summarized in Table 6. In this multi-leader multi-follower Stackelberg game, there exists a competitive game among the leaders and a competitive game among the followers. The Stackelberg game keeps a distinct hierarchy among leaders and followers such that the leaders can anticipate, and take this into consideration, the behavior of the followers (the reciprocal is not true), before making their own decisions to maximize their data rate.

It was considered a Stackelberg game with complete and perfect information. As already mentioned, the leaders are the set of macrocell BS transceivers M, the followers are the set of FAPs N. Therefore, the total set of players in this game is $M \cup N$. The strategy space of the leaders is given by $P^{up} = \prod_{i \in M} P_i$, and any point in P^{up} is called a leader strategy. Let P_i denote the set of all feasible power vectors of transmitter i. The leaders compete with each other in a non-cooperative way to maximize their individual data rate, while always anticipating the strategic responses of the followers. This game among the leaders is referred as the upper subgame, and its equilibrium is referred as the upper subgame equilibrium. After the leaders apply their strategies, the followers make their moves in response to the leaders' strategies.

The strategy space of the followers is $P^{low} = \prod_{i \in N} P_i$, and any point in P^{low} is called a follower strategy.

The followers also compete with each other in a non-cooperative way to maximize their own data rate, and this competition among the followers is referred as the lower subgame. It is expected this game could offer an equilibrium state designated by the lower subgame equilibrium.

Table 6. Summary of relevant characteristics of femtocell deployment game

Scenario	Game Type	Player	Player's Strategy	Payoff
Femtocell deployment	Stackelberg with complete and perfect information to control power	Base-stations (leaders)/ femtocell access points (followers)	Choose the maximum transmission power constrained by power constraints	Maximize Shannon data rate that each player can achieve

(Guruacharya et al., 2010)

For any user $i \in \{M \cup N\}$, it is defined the best-response function as shown in (8).

$$p_i = \arg\max_{p_i} \left(p_i, p_{-i}\right) = b_i \left(p_{-i}, \overline{p_i}, \overline{m_i}\right) \tag{8}$$

where the notation $-i$ refers to all of the users in the set $\{M \ U \ N\}$ except user i; $\overline{p_i}$ is the total power constraint; $\overline{m_i}$ .is the individual power constraint, where $\overline{m_i}$ is chosen so as to maximize user i's capacity function subject to the power constraints.

6.1.2. Lower Subgame Equilibrium

It is defined the lower subgame equilibrium as any fixed point $p^{low^*} = \left(p_1^*, \cdots, p_N^*\right) \in P^{low}$ such that expression in (9) is satisfied.

$$p_i^* = b_i(p_{-i}^*, p^{up}, \overline{p_i m_i}) \tag{9}$$

where $p^{up} \in P^{up}$ is a fixed but arbitrary leader strategy for all the $i \in N$. Note that this definition is the same as a Nash Equilibrium (NE) of the lower subgame.

Following (Han et al., 2012), since every user participating in the lower subgame will maximize in a myopic way their individual data rate, the best response $b_i(.)$ of each user in the subgame can be given by the following water-filling game function (Lai & El Gamal, 2008), as shown in (10).

$$p_i = F\left(p_{-i}, \overline{p_i}, \overline{m_i}\right) = w_i\left(A_i\right)v_i + r_i\left(A_i, S_i\right) \tag{10}$$

where $W_i(A_i)$ is an $L_i \times L_i$ symmetric matrix which contents is explained in more detail in (Han et al., 2012); $r_i(A_i, S_i)$ is an L_i-dimensional column vector detailed in (Han et al., 2012).

The main goal of a water-filling game is to identify a set of resource allocation strategies distributed among rational and selfish users (i.e. not interested in the overall system performance), who are interested in maximizing the utilities they obtain from the network (Lai & El Gamal, 2008).

By letting $b^{low} \equiv (b_i(.))^N_{i=1}$, it is possible to express the lower subgame equilibrium as any fixed point of the system-power space $p^* \in P$ such that $p^* = b^{low}(p^*)$.

Note that the function $b^{low}(.)$ does not impact the upper subgame strategy.

6.1.3. Upper Subgame Equilibrium

It is defined the upper subgame equilibrium as any fixed point $p^{up^*} = \left(p_1^*, \cdots, p_M^*\right) \in P^{up}$ such that the expression in (11) is satisfied.

$$p_i^* = b_i\left(p_{-i}^*, p^{low^*}, \overline{p_i}, \overline{m_i}\right) \tag{11}$$

where $p^{low^*} \in P^{low}$ is an equilibrium follower strategy conditioned on the upper subgame strategy, for all $i \in M$.

Equivalently, let $b^{up} \equiv (b_i(.))^M_{i=1}$; then the upper subgame equilibrium as the fixed point $p^{up^*} \in P^{up}$ such that (12) is a valid expression.

$$p^{up^*} = b^{up}\left(p^{up^*}, b^{low}\left(p^{low^*}, p^{up^*}\right)\right) \tag{12}$$

For convenience, the notation can be further simplified by writing the upper subgame equilibrium in terms of a system-power vector, i.e. as any fixed point $p^* \in P$ such that (13) is true.

$$p^* = b^{up}(b^{low}(p^*)) \tag{13}$$

Note that although the function $b^{up}(.)$ acts only on the upper subgame strategy, the lower subgame equilibrium strategy (the reaction of the followers) associated with each upper subgame strategy needs to be computed as well, since the leaders compute their strategies given their knowledge of what the followers might play.

6.1.4. Multi-Leader Multi-Follower Stackelberg Equilibrium

A suitable solution for the formulated hierarchical game between the base stations and the FAPs is the Stackelberg equilibrium. In such a multi-leader multi-follower game, the Stackelberg equilibrium is defined as any fixed-point $\left(p^{up^*}, p^{low^*}\right) = p^* \in P$ .that satisfies both conditions as shown in (14).

$$\begin{cases} p^* = b^{low}\left(p^*\right) \\ p^* = b^{up}\left(b^{low}\left(p^*\right)\right) \end{cases} \tag{14}$$

6.1.5. Algorithm for Reaching the Stackelberg Equilibrium

Finding, iteratively, the fixed point of the lower subgame using the water-filling algorithm usually yields an unstable system for a random channel gain matrix (Han et al., 2012). Therefore, it can be used a technique designated by Mann iterative methods, which allows a weaker stability criterion but it ensures that a stable system status point can be reached. To achieve this further discussion is available in (Han et al., 2012).

6.2. Multi-Technology Wireless Networks

The FN environment will be a heterogeneous network infrastructure composed by distinct wireless access technologies and several users/terminals aiming to monitor and select the best technology/Access Point (AP)/ Base Station (BS) to connect to, depending on their Quality-of-Service (QoS) requirements. One possible QoS requirement is the best throughput as possible each user can have through each AP/BS taking in consideration the overload imposed by the other attached users. Each user (the player of this network selection/vertical handover game) after its monitoring phase about all the available AP/BS connection possibilities should choose the one that ensures the maximum throughput value among all the options. Most of the existing work on vertical handover assumes that users have complete information on one another (Han et al., 2012). In FNs, the users will lack the ability to predict the behaviors of others based on past actions. In this case, it is more convenient to utilize a game with incomplete information, i.e. a Bayesian game, like the one adopted by (Zhu et al., 2010). Since the payoff (i.e. utility) for a mobile user is composed by private information (see Table 7), each user has to make a network selection given only the distribution of the preferences of other users (Han et al., 2012). In this game, it is very interesting to investigate the impact of different system parameters on the game performance itself using a practical setting, like the one composed by three different access technologies (Wifi, Wimax and cellular). The studied system parameters have been the convergence property of the aggregate best-response dynamics for the considered network selection game, the game adaptation for different handover costs (delay or packet loss), the impact of connection price on the equilibrium distribution and the impact of learning (i.e. user strategy adjustment) rate on game dynamics. The obtained results are discussed in (Han et al., 2012).

Table 7. Summary of relevant characteristics of network selection with incomplete information game

Scenario	Game Type	Player	Player's Strategy	Payoff
Network selection with incomplete information	Bayesian game	Users in a service area with K available access networks	Represents the probability of choosing an access network K and the minimum user bandwidth requirement (only the user knows about this, which turns this game an incomplete one)	User utility combines user achieved throughput above a minimum threshold (user private information) vs. price paid for the connection

(Zhu et al., 2010)

6.3. Network Management

The support of voice service in FNs will be a challenging task due the heterogeneity of both the network infrastructure and user requirements. A very interesting starting point to this problem is available in (Watanabe et al., 2008). It is proposed an analytical model based on Evolutionary Game Theory (EGT) (see Table 8) to analyze the consequences of a situation in which all users are allowed to freely choose the transmission rate. They perform that by selecting the codec and Forward Error Correction (FEC) mode to maximize the voice quality (payoff), which can be experienced by them. They show that in a scenario where the users know only their own perceived voice quality, the system converges to a total transmission rate close to that of the effective cell's capacity. They concluded that each individual user's MOS, which is estimated by a Random Neural Network (RNN), can also be satisfied. Further, cell's congestion is avoided by local user adaptation (dynamically changing its codec/FEC to maximize its perceived quality) without any intervention from a centralized controller.

Table 8. Summary of relevant characteristics of an evolutionary game to study rate selection for VoIP service

Scenario	Game Type	Player	Player's Strategy	Payoff
Study rate selection to guarantee the QoS offered to VoIP users	Evolutionary game	VoIP users in a service area	Each user selects the transmission rate through the codec and FEC mode	Voice quality experienced by the user and measured via a Mean Opinion Score (MOS) technique

(Watanabe et al., 2008)

6.4. Internet of Things (Multi-Hop Reliable Networks)

FN environments will have a large-scale deployment of wireless networks, which consist of small, low-cost nodes with simple processing and networking capabilities. This emergent environment is commonly designated inside the research community as the Internet of Things. In order to reach the desired destination such as the data sink node, transmissions depending on multiple hops are necessary (Han et al., 2012). Because of this, the routing optimization is a pertinent problem that involves many aspects but the one more relevant for the current work is the nodes not willing to fully cooperate in the routing process through multiple wireless hops, forwarding traffic from other nodes, because relaying external traffic consumes their limited battery power. Hence, it is crucial to design a distributed –control mechanism encouraging cooperation among the nodes in the routing process (see Table 9). The literature describes two typical approaches to enforce cooperation. First, in a price-based approach, each hop has a price and the game outcome is controlled between the source-destination pair and the intermediate hops. Second, an auction-based approach is suggested to ensure that users reveal their information truthfully to others for network cooperation, because this strategy will bring them the best benefits.

Table 9. Summary of characteristics of games to incentivize cooperation among multi-hop nodes

Scenario	Game Type	Player	Player's Strategy	Payoff
Incentivize cooperation among nodes (Hua Liu & Krishnamachari, 2006)	Hop price-based reliable routing game	All the nodes except the destination one	A node to participate in this game should at least choose one next hop node in the path from the source to the destination; otherwise it is out of this game	The source's utility is the expected income (destination payment minus the payments to all of the intermediate nodes, times the probability that the packet will be delivered over the route) minus the link set-up cost for the first hop of the route; The utility for each intermediate routing node equals the expected payment that it obtains from the source node, times the ongoing route reliability minus the transmission cost per packet to its next-hop neighbor. If any node does not participate in the routing, it gains (and loses) nothing.
Incentivize cooperation among nodes (Eidenbenz et al., 2008)	Vickrey-Clarke-Groves (VCG) auction to prevent players from lying and to route messages along the most energy-efficient paths (as defined by the topology control protocol)	All the network nodes	A strategy is a combination of strategies from the following base space: 1. a node can declare any value for its type; 2. a node can drop control messages that it should forward; 3. a node can modify messages before forwarding, and 4. a node can create bogus messages.	Maximizing the node's utility. The sender's node utility is the difference between the amount of money it is willing to pay for the connection and the amount it effectively pays for that; the intermediate's node utility is the difference about the amount of money received from the sender and the total cost incurred by relaying the sender's packet.

6.5. Reliable Wireless Backhaul

In FN environments wireless multi-hop backhaul links are expected to be very popular deployments. In this case, the channel quality between relay stations can fluctuate because of fading. Therefore, the users (players) at the source node must be able to observe, learn, and change the routing strategy to achieve the most reliable path from source node to the Internet gateway, as summarized in Table 10.

Table 10. Summary of relevant characteristics of game to study traffic routing through multi-hop wireless backhaul links

Scenario	Game Type	Player	Player's Strategy	Payoff
Multi-hop Wireless Backhaul Links	Evolutionary game	Users	Users periodically and randomly sampling different wireless backhaul links to select a convenient path between a source node and an Internet gateway	Find a backhaul link that ensures the smallest number of packet errors due to rain attenuation

(Anastasopoulos et al., 2008)

6.6. Computing and Storage at the Network Edge

The paradigm of Multi-Access Edge Computing (MEC) (Yi et al., 2015) (Abbas, Zhang, Taherkordi, & Skeie, 2018) (Hang Liu et al., 2017) is finally possible to deploy because foundational technologies such as virtualization (e.g. docker, Linux Containers) and communications (e.g. 5G) are becoming a reality now more than ever. Edge computing aims to provide more compute and storage power at either Base Stations or Access Points. The potential benefits to the data traffic are: i) diminish the data access latency; ii) decrease the load on the backhaul links; iii) save users' cost because less traffic is exchanged with remote clouds. Nevertheless, this new paradigm can increase the battery consumption on mobile nodes. To overcome this potential problem, computation offloading from mobile devices to edge devices (APs or BSs) can be a viable solution.

The authors of (Nawab, Agrawal, & El Abbadi, 2018) propose extending edge computing technology with dynamic, mobile edge datacenters, which they designate as nomadic datacenters. Nomadic datacenters are small and portable edge datacenters that can be easily moved around according the traffic load needs. In this way, nomadic datacenters can replace a damaged communications infrastructure by a natural disaster. Alternatively, nomadic datacenters can temporarily extend the capacity of a mobile network in the case of a public event that concentrates several hundreds of thousands of people (e.g. musical concert within a stadium).

There is a huge number of recent literature contributions on MEC, namely covering the next topics: i) the communication perspective (Mao, You, Zhang, Huang, & Letaief, 2017); ii) computation offloading (Mach & Becvar, 2017); iii) convergence of computing, caching and communications (S. Wang et al., 2017); iv) emerging 5G network edge cloud architecture and orchestration (Taleb et al., 2017); v) software-defined networking (Kumar, Chilamkurti, et al., 2015); vi) architecture harmonization between cloud radio access networks and fog networks (Hung, Hsu, Lien, & Chen, 2015); vii) Internet of Things (Chiang & Zhang, 2016); and viii) latency control in software-defined mobile-edge vehicular networking (Deng, Lien, Lin, Hung, & Chen, 2017). None of the previous surveys comprehensively analyzes GT into MEC. Nevertheless, there is a very work (Moura & Hutchison, 2018) that tries to discuss in a comprehensive way those two pertinent areas, in the sense to understand how GT can address in a successful way the emerging requirements of MEC use cases. They also discuss GT research topics related to MEC, namely on wireless sensor networks, cognitive small cells, vehicular networks, and unmanned vehicles.

7. BUSINESS PERSPECTIVE

From a business viewpoint, collaboration may be positive or negative – if a certain company plans to take over the market, it would engage in an open competition with its competitors in the hope to conquer most of the market, but in doing so it would have to pay the price of being competitive; be it by lowering their prices or by increasing their quality. If the company would engage in collaboration with its competitors, they would assess the market needs together and become more efficient, operating at a point where all would maximize their profit. In this case, assuming a total of n companies, and taking Pm as the maximum price for the product that all the companies manufacture, we can build an inverse demand curve (the demand curve solves for Quantity, whereas the inverse for Price), where the price charged for one of those products is equal to the Pm minus the quantity Q, multiplied by a factor α (assuming a

Figure 10. Inverse demand curve, total revenue and marginal revenue

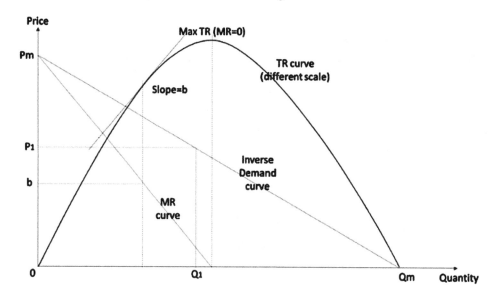

linear relationship for simplicity, as shown in (15); more detailed curves can be found in (O'Sullivan, Sheffrin, & Perez, 2003).

$$P = P_m - \alpha Q \tag{15}$$

In the case of n competing companies, we have the total quantity given by (16).

$$Q = Q_1 + Q_2 + ... + Q_n \tag{16}$$

The total revenue is given by the product price x quantity. The total revenue for all companies can thus be calculated as shown in (17).

$$TR = P \times Q = (P_m - \alpha Q) \times Q = Pm_Q - \alpha Q2 \tag{17}$$

The derivative of TR with respect to Q gives us the Marginal Revenue (MR), which in our simple linear model is given by (18).

$$MR = P_m - 2\alpha Q \tag{18}$$

In Figure 10, we have an illustration of the above formulas. Note that the MR curve represents the slope of the TR curve (which is drawn at a different scale, for practical reasons), and that maximum total revenue is obtain when MR=0.

Since the objective is to maximize profit, we must check at which point MR equals the Marginal Cost (MC), to find the ideal price and quantity to produce, as we evaluate below:

$$MR = MC \rightarrow P_m - 2\alpha Q - MC = 0$$

$$\Leftrightarrow Q = \frac{P_m - MC}{2\alpha}$$

$$\Leftrightarrow P = \frac{P_m + MC}{2}$$

The Figure 11 illustrates the trend's point in which MC=MR (point b), and the corresponding Price and Quantity (P_1 and Q_1). From the previous figure, notice also that Q_0 denotes the free market equilibrium quantity, in which the marginal cost of producing a unit equals its price – in a hyper competition setting, companies may operate close to this point, ideally a bit more to the left to obtain some (minimal) profit. The difference between quantities Q_1 and Q_0, and between prices P_1 and C_0, can be regarded as the difference between operating collaboratively (or in a monopoly) and competitively (the area of the triangle *abc* is also referred to as the deadweight loss of monopoly). It is up to each company's strategy if it should consolidate or invest/risk to (try to) conquer market (operating close to C_0 will lead many less cost-effective companies to file for bankruptcy, allowing for the bigger companies to take over their market-share).

Should the companies engage in competition, all would be losing out, operating with a higher quantity each, and subsequently lower prices and profit margins. There is a clear incentive to appeal to collaboration, although all companies want the best possible deal for themselves, which sometimes might hinder the collaboration attempts. Game theory models try to assess the best possible solution for all parties, quantifying the possible gains and losses predicted by the used model. Collaboration goes beyond revenue sharing (Bhaskaran & Krishnan, 2009); it may include the sharing of knowledge about the markets and technologies, setting the market standards, the sharing of facilities, etc. (Goyal & Joshi, 2003). To reap the full benefits of collaborating, one must analyze the collaborative conditions beforehand, hence negotiating the collaboration terms is of paramount importance. Important decisions need to be taken, such as the level of investment, profit sharing, knowledge and trust.

There has been some interesting work on the field to obtain win-win solutions for collaborative partners, and the authors would like to highlight (Arsenyan, Büyüközkan, & Feyzioğlu, 2015) for the proposed mathematical model integrating trust, coordination, co-learning and co-innovation for collaborative product development using Nash bargaining, as well as work in Hospital Information Exchange (HIE) networks that attempt to quantify the benefits and losses from the exchange of patient information both to the hospitals and patients (Martinez, Feijoo, Zayas-Castro, Levin, & Das, 2018). In the same field, Desai developed a game theoretical model to analyze the potential loss of competitive advantage due to HIE adoption (Desai, 2014).

8. CONCLUSION

8.1. Cooperation: Current Status and Open Issues

Cooperation is a revolutionary wireless communication paradigm that can achieve much higher network performance and spectrum utilization in future networking environments. Many technical challenges, however, need to be addressed to make this vision a reality. In particular, the distributed and dynamic

Figure 11. Collaboration and competition operating points

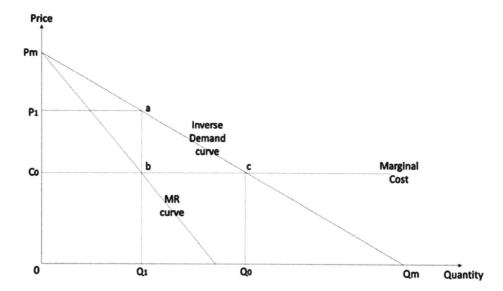

nature of the sharing of information about node cooperation requires a new design and analysis framework. GT provides a very solid solution for this challenging task. In this book chapter, we describe several GT models that have been successfully used to solve various problems associated with node cooperation.

The most part of discussed models relies on the concept of Nash Equilibrium (NE) in games with complete information and static strategies. Although mathematically convenient, this may not be the most suitable GT model in practice. For example, the complete information assumption is difficult to be satisfied in practice, due to the dynamic and uncertain environment associated to FNs (or MEC / FC) formed by heterogeneous wireless access technologies and a huge variety of flow types. A model of incomplete games will be more suitable. Moreover, NE assumes rational players and static strategies but the players in FNs aren´t completely rational; the players have limited information about available choices and consequences of others; the game strategies are not static (in fact, the strategies are highly dynamic). A recent branch of GT - Evolutionary GT (EGT) seems a very promising alternative to the traditional GT to be applied in FNs. Some preliminary work has been reported along these directions (M. A. Khan et al., 2012a) (Nazir et al., 2010) (Bennis et al., 2011) (Eitan Altman et al., 2009) and definitely much more is required. As a pertinent example, evolutionary network models can provide useful guidelines for upgrading protocols/algorithms to achieve stable infrastructure functionality around preferred status/ configuration in FNs. Other interesting models are Stackelberg and Bayesian ones. Finally, in Table 11, some relevant contributions found in the literature, which can be the foundations for new work in the FN area, are listed together with some associated open issues.

As a final conclusion, the current authors think that non-conventional game theoretic models are required to fulfill the demanding requisites of upcoming scenarios, such as: i) computing and storage at the network edge; ii) large-scale IoT systems; and iii) business models based on virtual money.

Table 11. Open issues in applying GT to future wireless networking scenarios

Scenario	Reference	Open Issue
Network planning	(Guruacharya et al., 2010)	Due to the notorious computational burden of estimating the Stackelberg equilibrium, a low complexity algorithm based on Lagrangian dual theory was chosen. However, the numerical results show that the adopted algorithm is suboptimal.
Multi-technology wireless networks	(Zhu et al., 2010)	Future work can study based on the Equilibrium distribution, how the service providers can adjust the system capacity and price accordingly to maximize the profits
Network management	(Watanabe et al., 2008)	The experiments were performed with small populations. Future work can devise more scalable experiments.
Internet of things (multi-hop reliable networks)	(Hua Liu & Krishnamachari, 2006)	Add the destination as a player; consider scenarios where the destination can choose from several source nodes for a given piece of information. This will allow for an auction to be held among the source nodes to optimize destination's payoff
Internet of things (multi-hop reliable networks)	(Eidenbenz et al., 2008)	Enhance previous protocol to be robust against malicious nodes and collusion
Reliable wireless backhaul	(Anastasopoulos et al., 2008)	Extend previous work in the direction of IEEE 802.11s (wireless mesh networking)
Computing and Storage at the Network Edge	(Moura & Hutchison, 2018)	Low data/service access latency; distributed offloading computing hierarchical mobile environments; proactive data caching at the network edge managed by data popularity, social links, and available node battery energy; low-power wireless communications and networking for IoT; fingerprinting localization technology to support indoor location-based services; and understand emerging security and privacy problems in cyberspace and potential solutions.

REFERENCES

Abbas, N., Zhang, Y., Taherkordi, A., & Skeie, T. (2018). Mobile Edge Computing: A Survey. *IEEE Internet of Things Journal, 5*(1), 450–465. doi:10.1109/JIOT.2017.2750180

Ahlgren, B., Dannewitz, C., Imbrenda, C., Kutscher, D., & Ohlman, B. (2012). A survey of information-centric networking. *IEEE Communications Magazine, 50*(7), 26–36. doi:10.1109/MCOM.2012.6231276

Akkarajitsakul, K., Hossain, E., Niyato, D., & Kim, D. I. (2011). Game Theoretic Approaches for Multiple Access in Wireless Networks: A Survey. *IEEE Communications Surveys and Tutorials, 13*(3), 372–395. doi:10.1109/SURV.2011.122310.000119

Al-Kashoash, H. A. A., Hafeez, M., & Kemp, A. H. (2017). Congestion Control for 6LoWPAN Networks: A Game Theoretic Framework. *IEEE Internet of Things Journal, 4*(3), 760–771. doi:10.1109/JIOT.2017.2666269

Alpcan, T., Basar, T., Srikant, R., & Atman, E. (2001). CDMA uplink power control as a noncooperative game. In *Proceedings of the 40th IEEE Conference on Decision and Control (Cat. No.01CH37228)* (Vol. 1, pp. 197–202). IEEE. 10.1109/CDC.2001.980097

Altman, E., Boulogne, T., El-Azouzi, R., Jiménez, T., & Wynter, L. (2006). A Survey on Networking Games in Telecommunications. *Computers & Operations Research, 33*(2), 286–311. doi:10.1016/j.cor.2004.06.005

Altman, E., El-Azouzi, R., Hayel, Y., & Tembine, H. (2009). The evolution of transport protocols: An evolutionary game perspective. *Computer Networks, 53*(10), 1751–1759. doi:10.1016/j.comnet.2008.12.023

Alves, H., Silva, L. M., Neto Marinheiro, R., & Moura, J. (2018). PMIPv6 Integrated with MIH for Flow Mobility Management: A Real Testbed with Simultaneous Multi-Access in Heterogeneous Mobile Networks. *Wireless Personal Communications, 98*(1), 1055–1082. doi:10.100711277-017-4908-6

Anastasopoulos, M., Arapoglou, P.-D., Kannan, R., & Cottis, P. (2008). Adaptive Routing Strategies in IEEE 802.16 Multi-Hop Wireless Backhaul Networks Based On Evolutionary Game Theory. *IEEE Journal on Selected Areas in Communications, 26*(7), 1218–1225. doi:10.1109/JSAC.2008.080918

Anderegg, L., & Eidenbenz, S. (2003). Ad hoc-VCG Ad hoc-VCG: a truthful and cost-efficient routing protocol for mobile ad hoc networks with selfish agents. In *Proceedings of the 9th annual international conference on Mobile computing and networking - MobiCom '03* (p. 245). New York: ACM Press. 10.1145/938985.939011

Apicella, C. L., Marlowe, F. W., Fowler, J. H., & Christakis, N. A. (2012). Social networks and cooperation in hunter-gatherers. *Nature, 481*(7382), 497–501. doi:10.1038/nature10736 PMID:22281599

Arsenyan, J., Büyüközkan, G., & Feyzioğlu, O. (2015). Modeling collaboration formation with a game theory approach. *Expert Systems with Applications, 42*(4), 2073–2085. doi:10.1016/j.eswa.2014.10.010

Atlam, H. F., Walters, R. J., & Wills, G. B. (2018). Fog Computing and the Internet of Things: A Review. *Big Data and Cognitive Computing, 2*(2).

Axelrod, R. (1981). The Emergence of Cooperation among Egoists. *The American Political Science Review, 75*(02), 306–318. doi:10.2307/1961366

Babaioff, M., Dobzinski, S., Oren, S., & Zohar, A. (2012). On bitcoin and red balloons. In *Proceedings of the 13th ACM Conference on Electronic Commerce - EC '12* (p. 56). New York: ACM Press. 10.1145/2229012.2229022

Balevi, E., & Gitlin, R. D. (2018). Optimizing the Number of Fog Nodes for Cloud-Fog-Thing Networks. *IEEE Access: Practical Innovations, Open Solutions, 6*, 11173–11183. doi:10.1109/ACCESS.2018.2808598

Bansal, S., & Baker, M. (2003). Observation-based Cooperation Enforcement in Ad Hoc Networks. *CoRR*, cs.NI/0307.

Bennis, M., Guruacharya, S., & Niyato, D. (2011). Distributed Learning Strategies for Interference Mitigation in Femtocell Networks. In *Global Telecommunications Conference (GLOBECOM 2011), 2011 IEEE* (pp. 1–5). IEEE. 10.1109/GLOCOM.2011.6134218

Bhaskaran, S. R., & Krishnan, V. (2009). Effort, Revenue, and Cost Sharing Mechanisms for Collaborative New Product Development. *Management Science, 55*(7), 1152–1169. doi:10.1287/mnsc.1090.1010

Böge, W., & Eisele, T. (1979). On solutions of Bayesian games. *International Journal of Game Theory*, *8*(4), 193–215. doi:10.1007/BF01766706

Bond, R. M., Fariss, C. J., Jones, J. J., Kramer, A. D. I., Marlow, C., Settle, J. E., & Fowler, J. H. (2012). A 61-million-person experiment in social influence and political mobilization. *Nature*, *489*(7415), 295–298. doi:10.1038/nature11421 PMID:22972300

Borah, S. J., Dhurandher, S. K., Woungang, I., & Kumar, V. (2017). A game theoretic context-based routing protocol for opportunistic networks in an IoT scenario. *Computer Networks*, *129*, 572–584. doi:10.1016/j.comnet.2017.07.005

Bouhaddi, M., Radjef, M. S., & Adi, K. (2018). An efficient intrusion detection in resource-constrained mobile ad-hoc networks. *Computers & Security*, *76*, 156–177. doi:10.1016/j.cose.2018.02.018

Bu, S., Yu, F. R., & Yanikomeroglu, H. (2015). Interference-Aware Energy-Efficient Resource Allocation for OFDMA-Based Heterogeneous Networks With Incomplete Channel State Information. *IEEE Transactions on Vehicular Technology*, *64*(3), 1036–1050. doi:10.1109/TVT.2014.2325823

Buchegger, S., & Le Boudec, J.-Y. (2002). Performance analysis of the CONFIDANT protocol. In *Proceedings of the 3rd ACM international symposium on Mobile ad hoc networking & computing - MobiHoc '02* (p. 226). New York: ACM Press. 10.1145/513800.513828

Buttyan, L., & Hubaux, J.-P. (2000). Enforcing service availability in mobile ad-hoc WANs. In *2000 First Annual Workshop on Mobile and Ad Hoc Networking and Computing. MobiHOC (Cat. No.00EX444)* (pp. 87–96). IEEE. 10.1109/MOBHOC.2000.869216

Buttyan, L., & Hubaux, J.-P. (2001). Nuglets: A Virtual Currency to Stimulate Cooperation in Self-Organized Mobile. *Ad Hoc Networks*.

Buttyán, L., & Hubaux, J.-P. (2003). Stimulating Cooperation in Self-Organizing Mobile Ad Hoc Networks. *Mobile Networks and Applications*, *8*(5), 579–592. doi:10.1023/A:1025146013151

Charilas, D. E., & Panagopoulos, A. D. (2010). A Survey on Game Theory Applications in Wireless Networks. *Computer Networks*, *54*(18), 3421–3430. doi:10.1016/j.comnet.2010.06.020

Chawla, S., & Sivan, B. (2014). Bayesian Algorithmic Mechanism Design. *SIGecom Exch.*, *13*(1), 5–49. doi:10.1145/2692375.2692378

Chen, K., & Nahrstedt, K. (2004). iPass: an incentive compatible auction scheme to enable packet forwarding service in MANET. In *24th International Conference on Distributed Computing Systems, 2004. Proceedings.* (pp. 534–542). IEEE. 10.1109/ICDCS.2004.1281620

Chen, K., Yang, Z., Wagener, C., & Nahrstedt, K. (2005). Market models and pricing mechanisms in a multihop wireless hotspot network. In *The Second Annual International Conference on Mobile and Ubiquitous Systems: Networking and Services* (pp. 73–82). IEEE. 10.1109/MOBIQUITOUS.2005.36

Cheriton, D. R., & Gritter, M. (2000). *TRIAD: A New Next-Generation Internet Architecture*. Academic Press.

Chiang, M., & Zhang, T. (2016). Fog and IoT: An Overview of Research Opportunities. *IEEE Internet of Things Journal, 3*(6), 854–864. doi:10.1109/JIOT.2016.2584538

Christidis, K., & Devetsikiotis, M. (2016). Blockchains and Smart Contracts for the Internet of Things. *IEEE Access: Practical Innovations, Open Solutions, 4,* 2292–2303. doi:10.1109/ACCESS.2016.2566339

CISCO. (2015). *Cisco Fog Computing Solutions: Unleash the Power of the Internet of Things.* Retrieved July 26, 2018, from https://www.cisco.com/c/dam/en_us/solutions/trends/iot/docs/computing-solutions.pdf

CISCO. (2016). *VNI Global Fixed and Mobile Internet Traffic Forecasts (2016-2021).* Retrieved June 2, 2018, from https://www.cisco.com/c/en/us/solutions/service-provider/visual-networking-index-vni/index.html

Corcoran, P. (2016). The Internet of Things: Why now, and what's next? *IEEE Consumer Electronics Magazine, 5*(1), 63–68. doi:10.1109/MCE.2015.2484659

Demir, C., & Comaniciu, C. (2007). An Auction based AODV Protocol for Mobile Ad Hoc Networks with Selfish Nodes. In *2007 IEEE International Conference on Communications* (pp. 3351–3356). IEEE. 10.1109/ICC.2007.555

Deng, D.-J., Lien, S.-Y., Lin, C.-C., Hung, S.-C., & Chen, W.-B. (2017). Latency Control in Software-Defined Mobile-Edge Vehicular Networking. *IEEE Communications Magazine, 55*(8), 87–93. doi:10.1109/MCOM.2017.1601165

Desai, S. (2014). *Electronic Health Information Exchange, Switching Costs, and Network Effects.* SSRN Electronic Journal. doi:10.2139srn.2525084

Duong, N. D., Madhukumar, A. S., & Niyato, D. (2016). Stackelberg Bayesian Game for Power Allocation in Two-Tier Networks. *IEEE Transactions on Vehicular Technology, 65*(4), 2341–2354. doi:10.1109/TVT.2015.2418297

Dutta, P. K. (1999). *Strategies and games: Theory and practice.* MIT Press.

Eidenbenz, S., Resta, G., & Santi, P. (2008). The COMMIT Protocol for Truthful and Cost-Efficient Routing in Ad Hoc Networks with Selfish Nodes. *IEEE Transactions on Mobile Computing, 7*(1), 19–33. doi:10.1109/TMC.2007.1069

Eyal, I. (2015). The Miner's Dilemma. In *2015 IEEE Symposium on Security and Privacy* (pp. 89–103). IEEE. 10.1109/SP.2015.13

Fadlullah, Z. M., Nozaki, Y., Takeuchi, A., & Kato, N. (2011). A survey of game theoretic approaches in smart grid. In *Wireless Communications and Signal Processing (WCSP), 2011 International Conference on* (pp. 1–4). Academic Press. 10.1109/WCSP.2011.6096962

Felegyhazi, M., & Hubaux, J.-P. (2006). *Game Theory in Wireless Networks: A Tutorial.* Academic Press.

Fernandes, S., & Karmouch, A. (2012). Vertical Mobility Management Architectures in Wireless Networks: A Comprehensive Survey and Future Directions. *IEEE Communications Surveys and Tutorials, 14*(1), 45–63. doi:10.1109/SURV.2011.082010.00099

Fudenberg, D., & Maskin, E. (1986). The Folk Theorem in Repeated Games with Discounting or with Incomplete Information. *Econometrica, 54*(3), 533–554. doi:10.2307/1911307

Gabry, F., Bioglio, V., & Land, I. (2016). On Energy-Efficient Edge Caching in Heterogeneous Networks. *IEEE Journal on Selected Areas in Communications, 34*(12), 3288–3298. doi:10.1109/JSAC.2016.2611845

Ghazvini, M., Movahedinia, N., Jamshidi, K., & Moghim, N. (2013). Game Theory Applications in CSMA Methods. *IEEE Communications Surveys and Tutorials, 15*(3), 1062–1087. doi:10.1109/SURV.2012.111412.00167

Gibbons, R. (1992). *A primer in game theory*. Harvester.

Gluhak, A., Vermesan, O., Bahr, R., Clari, F., MacchiaMaria, T., Delgado, T., … Barchetti, V. (2016). *Report on IoT platform activities*. Retrieved July 26, 2018, from http://www.internet-of-things-research.eu/pdf/D03_01_WP03_H2020_UNIFY-IoT_Final.pdf

Goyal, S., & Joshi, S. (2003). Networks of collaboration in oligopoly. *Games and Economic Behavior, 43*(1), 57–85. doi:10.1016/S0899-8256(02)00562-6

Guruacharya, S., Niyato, D., Hossain, E., & Kim, D. I. (2010). Hierarchical Competition in Femtocell-Based Cellular Networks. In *2010 IEEE Global Telecommunications Conference GLOBECOM 2010* (pp. 1–5). IEEE. 10.1109/GLOCOM.2010.5683278

Habak, K., Ammar, M., Harras, K. A., & Zegura, E. (2015). Femto Clouds: Leveraging Mobile Devices to Provide Cloud Service at the Edge. In *2015 IEEE 8th International Conference on Cloud Computing* (pp. 9–16). IEEE. Retrieved from https://www.cc.gatech.edu/%7B~%7Dkhabak3/papers/FemtoCloud-CLOUD%7B25%7D2715.pdf

Hajir, M., Langar, R., & Gagnon, F. (2016). Coalitional Games for Joint Co-Tier and Cross-Tier Cooperative Spectrum Sharing in Dense Heterogeneous Networks. *IEEE Access: Practical Innovations, Open Solutions, 4*, 2450–2464. doi:10.1109/ACCESS.2016.2562498

Han, Z., Niyato, D., Saad, W., Baar, T., & Hjrungnes, A. (2012). *Game Theory in Wireless and Communication Networks: Theory, Models, and Applications*. Cambridge University Press.

Harsanyi, J. C. (2004). Games with Incomplete Information Played by "Bayesian" Players, I–III: Part I. The Basic Model. *Management Science, 50*(12S), 1804–1817. doi:10.1287/mnsc.1040.0270

He, Q., Wu, D., & Khosla, P. (2004). SORI: a secure and objective reputation-based incentive scheme for ad-hoc networks. In 2004 IEEE Wireless Communications and Networking Conference (IEEE Cat. No.04TH8733) (p. 825–830 Vol.2). IEEE. doi:10.1109/WCNC.2004.1311293

Hu, Y., Zhu, M., Xia, Y., Chen, K., & Luo, Y. (2012). GARDEN: Generic Addressing and Routing for Data Center Networks. In *Cloud Computing (CLOUD), 2012 IEEE 5th International Conference on* (pp. 107–114). IEEE. 10.1109/CLOUD.2012.9

Huang, J. (2013). Economic viability of dynamic spectrum management. In T. Alpcan, H. Boche, M. L. Honig, & H. V. Poor (Eds.), *Mechanisms and Games for Dynamic Spectrum Allocation* (pp. 396–432). Cambridge University Press; doi:10.1017/CBO9781139524421.018

Huang, J., & Han, Z. (2010). Game {Theory} for {Spectrum} {Sharing}. In Cognitive {Radio} {Networks} (pp. 291–317). CRC Press. Retrieved from doi:10.1201/EBK1420077759-c10

Hung, S.-C., Hsu, H., Lien, S.-Y., & Chen, K.-C. (2015). Architecture Harmonization Between Cloud Radio Access Networks and Fog Networks. *IEEE Access: Practical Innovations, Open Solutions*, *3*, 3019–3034. doi:10.1109/ACCESS.2015.2509638

Hwang, J., Shin, A., & Yoon, H. (2008). Dynamic Reputation-based Incentive Mechanism Considering Heterogeneous Networks. In *Proceedings of the 3Nd ACM Workshop on Performance Monitoring and Measurement of Heterogeneous Wireless and Wired Networks* (pp. 137–144). New York, NY: ACM. 10.1145/1454630.1454651

Ileri, O., Siun-Chuon Mau, & Mandayam, N. B. (2005). Pricing for enabling forwarding in self-configuring ad hoc networks. *IEEE Journal on Selected Areas in Communications*, *23*(1), 151–162. doi:10.1109/JSAC.2004.837356

Jacobson, V., Smetters, D. K., Thornton, J. D., Plass, M. F., Briggs, N. H., & Braynard, R. L. (2009). Networking Named Content. In *Proceedings of the 5th International Conference on Emerging Networking Experiments and Technologies* (pp. 1–12). New York: ACM. 10.1145/1658939.1658941

Jaramillo, J. J. & Srikant, R. (2007). DARWIN: Distributed and adaptive reputation mechanism for wireless ad-hoc networks. In *Proceedings of the 13th annual ACM international conference on Mobile computing and networking - MobiCom '07* (p. 87). New York: ACM Press. 10.1145/1287853.1287865

Jararweh, Y., Tawalbeh, L., Ababneh, F., Khreishah, A., & Dosari, F. (2014). Scalable Cloudlet-based Mobile Computing Model. *Procedia Computer Science*, *34*, 434–441. doi:10.1016/j.procs.2014.07.051

Jochen, M., & Le, B. J. (2005). Analysis of a robust reputation system for self-organised networks. *European Transactions on Telecommunications*, *16*(5), 375–384. doi:10.1002/ett.1066

Kebriaei, H., Maham, B., & Niyato, D. (2015). Double Sided Bandwidth-Auction Game for Cognitive Device-to-Device Communication in Cellular Networks. *IEEE Transactions on Vehicular Technology*, (99), 1–1. doi:10.1109/TVT.2015.2485304

Khan, M. A., Tembine, H., & Vasilakos, A. V. (2012a). Evolutionary coalitional games: Design and challenges in wireless networks. *IEEE Wireless Communications*, *19*(2), 50–56. doi:10.1109/MWC.2012.6189413

Khan, M. A., Tembine, H., & Vasilakos, A. V. (2012b). Game Dynamics and Cost of Learning in Heterogeneous 4G Networks. *IEEE Journal on Selected Areas in Communications*, *30*(1), 198–213. doi:10.1109/JSAC.2012.120118

Khan, Z., Lehtomaki, J. J., DaSilva, L. A., Hossain, E., & Latva-aho, M. (2016). Opportunistic Channel Selection by Cognitive Wireless Nodes Under Imperfect Observations and Limited Memory: A Repeated Game Model. *IEEE Transactions on Mobile Computing*, *15*(1), 173–187. doi:10.1109/TMC.2015.2412940

Kiayias, A., Koutsoupias, E., Kyropoulou, M., & Tselekounis, Y. (2016). Blockchain Mining Games. In *Proceedings of the 2016 ACM Conference on Economics and Computation - EC '16* (pp. 365–382). New York: ACM Press. 10.1145/2940716.2940773

Kim, S. (2016). Cognitive hierarchy thinking based behavioral game model for IoT power control algorithm. *Computer Networks*, *110*, 79–90. doi:10.1016/j.comnet.2016.09.020

Kroll, J. A., Davey, I. C., & Felten, E. W. (2013). The Economics of Bitcoin Mining, or Bitcoin in the Presence of Adversaries. In *Proceedings of WEIS* (p. 21). Academic Press.

Kumar, N., Chilamkurti, N., & Misra, S. (2015). Bayesian coalition game for the internet of things: An ambient intelligence-based evaluation. *IEEE Communications Magazine*, *53*(1), 48–55. doi:10.1109/MCOM.2015.7010515

Kumar, N., Misra, S., Rodrigues, J. J. P. C., & Obaidat, M. S. (2015). Coalition Games for Spatio-Temporal Big Data in Internet of Vehicles Environment: A Comparative Analysis. *IEEE Internet of Things Journal*, *2*(4), 310–320. doi:10.1109/JIOT.2015.2388588

Kumar, N., Zeadally, S., Chilamkurti, N., & Vinel, A. (2015). Performance analysis of Bayesian coalition game-based energy-aware virtual machine migration in vehicular mobile cloud. *IEEE Network*, *29*(2), 62–69. doi:10.1109/MNET.2015.7064905

Kuo, Y.-L., Wu, E. H.-K., & Chen, G.-H. (2004). Noncooperative admission control for differentiated services in IEEE 802.11 WLANs. In *IEEE Global Telecommunications Conference, 2004. GLOBECOM '04* (Vol. 5, pp. 2981–2986). IEEE. 10.1109/GLOCOM.2004.1378899

Kwon, T., Lim, S., Choi, S., & Hong, D. (2010). Optimal Duplex Mode for DF Relay in Terms of the Outage Probability. *IEEE Transactions on Vehicular Technology*, *59*(7), 3628–3634. doi:10.1109/TVT.2010.2050503

La, Q. D., Quek, T. Q. S., Lee, J., Jin, S., & Zhu, H. (2016). Deceptive Attack and Defense Game in Honeypot-Enabled Networks for the Internet of Things. *IEEE Internet of Things Journal*, *3*(6), 1025–1035. doi:10.1109/JIOT.2016.2547994

Lai, L., & El Gamal, H. (2008). The Water-Filling Game in Fading Multiple-Access Channels. *IEEE Transactions on Information Theory*, *54*(5), 2110–2122. doi:10.1109/TIT.2008.920340

Larsson, E. G., Jorswieck, E. A., Lindblom, J., & Mochaourab, R. (2009). Game theory and the flat-fading gaussian interference channel. *IEEE Signal Processing Magazine*, *26*(5), 18–27. doi:10.1109/MSP.2009.933370

Lewenberg, Y., Bachrach, Y., Sompolinsky, Y., Zohar, A., & Rosenschein, J. S. (2015). Bitcoin Mining Pools: A Cooperative Game Theoretic Analysis. In *Proceedings of the 2015 International Conference on Autonomous Agents and Multiagent Systems* (pp. 919–927). Richland, SC: International Foundation for Autonomous Agents and Multiagent Systems. Retrieved from http://dl.acm.org/citation.cfm?id=2772879.2773270

Li, C., Xue, Y., Wang, J., Zhang, W., & Li, T. (2018). Edge-Oriented Computing Paradigms: A Survey on Architecture Design and System Management. *ACM Computing Surveys*, *51*(2), 1–34. doi:10.1145/3154815

Li, Q., Zhu, S., & Cao, G. (2010). Routing in Socially Selfish Delay Tolerant Networks. In 2010 Proceedings IEEE INFOCOM (pp. 1–9). IEEE. doi:10.1109/INFCOM.2010.5462138

Lin, S., Ni, W., Tian, H., & Liu, R. P. (2015). An Evolutionary Game Theoretic Framework for Femtocell Radio Resource Management. *IEEE Transactions on Wireless Communications*, *14*(11), 6365–6376. doi:10.1109/TWC.2015.2453170

Liu, H., Eldarrat, F., Alqahtani, H., Reznik, A., de Foy, X., & Zhang, Y. (2017). Mobile Edge Cloud System: Architectures, Challenges, and Approaches. *IEEE Systems Journal*, 1–14. doi:10.1109/JSYST.2017.2654119

Liu, H., & Krishnamachari, B. (2006). A price-based reliable routing game in wireless networks. In *Proceeding from the 2006 workshop on Game theory for communications and networks - GameNets '06* (p. 7). New York: ACM Press. 10.1145/1190195.1190201

Louta, M., Zournatzis, P., Kraounakis, S., Sarigiannidis, P., & Demetropoulos, I. (2011). Towards realization of the ABC vision: A comparative survey of Access Network Selection. In *2011 IEEE Symposium on Computers and Communications (ISCC)* (pp. 472–477). IEEE. 10.1109/ISCC.2011.5983882

Lu, Y., Zhou, B., Tung, L.-C., Gerla, M., Ramesh, A., & Nagaraja, L. (2013). Energy-efficient content retrieval in mobile cloud. In *Proceedings of the second ACM SIGCOMM workshop on Mobile cloud computing - MCC '13* (p. 21). New York: ACM Press. 10.1145/2491266.2491271

Mach, P., & Becvar, Z. (2017). Mobile Edge Computing: A Survey on Architecture and Computation Offloading. *IEEE Communications Surveys and Tutorials*, *19*(3), 1628–1656. doi:10.1109/COMST.2017.2682318

Machado, R., & Tekinay, S. (2008). A survey of game-theoretic approaches in wireless sensor networks. *Computer Networks*, *52*(16), 3047–3061. doi:10.1016/j.gaceta.2008.07.003

MacKenzie, A. B., & DaSilva, L. A. (2006). Game Theory for Wireless Engineers. *Synthesis Lectures on Communications*, *1*(1), 1–86. doi:10.2200/S00014ED1V01Y200508COM001

Mahmud, R., Kotagiri, R., & Buyya, R. (2018). Fog Computing: A Taxonomy, Survey and Future Directions. In B. Di Martino, K.-C. Li, L. T. Yang, & A. Esposito (Eds.), *Internet of Everything: Algorithms, Methodologies, Technologies and Perspectives* (pp. 103–130). Singapore: Springer Singapore. doi:10.1007/978-981-10-5861-5_5

Mao, Y., You, C., Zhang, J., Huang, K., & Letaief, K. B. (2017). A Survey on Mobile Edge Computing: The Communication Perspective. *IEEE Communications Surveys and Tutorials*, *19*(4), 2322–2358. doi:10.1109/COMST.2017.2745201

Marina, N., Saad, W., Han, Z., & Hjørungnes, A. (2011). Modeling malicious behavior in cooperative cellular wireless networks. In E. Hossain, D. I. Kim, & V. K. Bhargava (Eds.), *Cooperative Cellular Wireless Networks* (pp. 382–422). Cambridge University Press. doi:10.1017/CBO9780511667008.015

Marinelli, E. E. (2009). *Hyrax: Cloud Computing on Mobile Devices using MapReduce* (MSc thesis). CMU. Retrieved from https://pdfs.semanticscholar.org/8cd2/11cc816952f036ed65a7022adba063486008.pdf

Marsal-Llacuna, M.-L. (2018). Future living framework: Is blockchain the next enabling network? *Technological Forecasting and Social Change*, *128*, 226–234. doi:10.1016/j.techfore.2017.12.005

Martinez, D. A., Feijoo, F., Zayas-Castro, J. L., Levin, S., & Das, T. K. (2018). A strategic gaming model for health information exchange markets. *Health Care Management Science, 21*(1), 119–130. doi:10.100710729-016-9382-2 PMID:27600378

Mateus, A., & Marinheiro, R. N. (2010). A Media Independent Information Service Integration Architecture for Media Independent Handover. In *2010 Ninth International Conference on Networks* (pp. 173–178). IEEE. 10.1109/ICN.2010.71

Milan, F., Jaramillo, J. J., & Srikant, R. (2006). Achieving cooperation in multihop wireless networks of selfish nodes. In *Proceeding from the 2006 workshop on Game theory for communications and networks - GameNets '06* (p. 3). New York: ACM Press. 10.1145/1190195.1190197

Mingxiao, D., Xiaofeng, M., Zhe, Z., Xiangwei, W., & Qijun, C. (2017). A review on consensus algorithm of blockchain. In *2017 IEEE International Conference on Systems, Man, and Cybernetics (SMC)* (pp. 2567–2572). IEEE. 10.1109/SMC.2017.8123011

Monteiro, R., Silva, J., Lourenço, J., & Paulino, H. (2015). Decentralized Storage for Networks of Hand-held Devices. In *Proceedings of the 12th EAI International Conference on Mobile and Ubiquitous Systems: Computing, Networking and Services* (pp. 299–300). ACM. 10.4108/eai.22-7-2015.2260263

Mougayar, W. (2016). *The Business Blockchain: Promise, Practice, and Application of the Next Internet Technology*. John Wiley & Sons, Inc.

Moura, J., & Edwards, C. (2015). Future Trends and Challenges for Mobile and Convergent Networks. In A. Yarali (Ed.), *4G & Beyond: The Convergence of Networks, Devices and Services* (pp. 35–80). Nova Science Publishers. Retrieved from https://arxiv.org/abs/1601.06202v1

Moura, J., & Edwards, C. (2016). Efficient access of mobile flows to heterogeneous networks under flash crowds. *Computer Networks, 107*(2), 163–177. doi:10.1016/j.comnet.2016.04.010

Moura, J., & Hutchison, D. (2018). Survey of Game Theory and Future Trends with Application to Emerging Wireless Data Communication Networks. *ArXiv E-Prints*, 46. Retrieved from https://arxiv.org/abs/1704.00323v1

Munjal, M., & Singh, N. P. (2018). Utility aware network selection in small cell. *Wireless Networks*, 1–14. doi:10.100711276-018-1676-5

Nakamoto, S. (2008). *Bitcoin: A peer-to-peer electronic cash system*. Retrieved July 27, 2018, from https://bitcoin.org/bitcoin.pdf

Nawab, F., Agrawal, D., & El Abbadi, A. (2018). Nomadic Datacenters at the Network Edge: Data Management Challenges for the Cloud with Mobile Infrastructure. In M. H. Böhlen, R. Pichler, N. May, E. Rahm, S.-H. Wu, & K. Hose (Eds.), *Proceedings of the 21th International Conference on Extending Database Technology, {EDBT} 2018, Vienna, Austria, March 26-29, 2018* (pp. 497–500). OpenProceedings.org. 10.5441/002/edbt.2018.56

Nazir, M., Bennis, M., Ghaboosi, K., MacKenzie, A. B., & Latva-aho, M. (2010). Learning based mechanisms for interference mitigation in self-organized femtocell networks. In *2010 Conference Record of the Forty Fourth Asilomar Conference on Signals, Systems and Computers* (pp. 1886–1890). Academic Press. 10.1109/ACSSC.2010.5757866

Niyato, D., & Hossain, E. (2007). Radio resource management games in wireless networks: An approach to bandwidth allocation and admission control for polling service in IEEE 802.16. *IEEE Wireless Communications, 14*(1), 27–35. doi:10.1109/MWC.2007.314548

Ntemos, K., Plata-Chaves, J., Kolokotronis, N., Kalouptsidis, N., & Moonen, M. (2018). Secure Information Sharing in Adversarial Adaptive Diffusion Networks. *IEEE Transactions on Signal and Information Processing over Networks, 4*(1), 111–124. doi:10.1109/TSIPN.2017.2787910

Nurmi, P., & Nurmi, P. (2006). A Bayesian framework for online reputation systems. In *Advanced International Conference on Telecommunications and International Conference on Internet and Web Applications and Services. IEEE.*

O'Sullivan, A., Sheffrin, S., & Perez, S. (2003). *Economics : principles in action*. Prentice Hall.

Panta, R. K., Jana, R., Cheng, F., Chen, Y.-F. R., & Vaishampayan, V. A. (2013). Phoenix: Storage Using an Autonomous Mobile Infrastructure. *IEEE Transactions on Parallel and Distributed Systems, 24*(9), 1863–1873. doi:10.1109/TPDS.2013.84

Saad, W., Han, Z., & Hjørungnes, A. (2011). Coalitional games for cooperative cellular wireless networks. In E. Hossain, D. I. Kim, & V. K. Bhargava (Eds.), *Cooperative Cellular Wireless Networks* (pp. 347–381). Cambridge University Press. doi:10.1017/CBO9780511667008.014

Saad, W., Han, Z., Poor, H. V., & Basar, T. (2012). Game-Theoretic Methods for the Smart Grid: An Overview of Microgrid Systems, Demand-Side Management, and Smart Grid Communications. *IEEE Signal Processing Magazine, 29*(5), 86–105. doi:10.1109/MSP.2012.2186410

Sapirshtein, A., Sompolinsky, Y., & Zohar, A. (2017). *Optimal Selfish Mining Strategies in Bitcoin*. Berlin: Springer; doi:10.1007/978-3-662-54970-4_30

Saraydar, C. U., Mandayam, N. B., & Goodman, D. J. (2002). Efficient power control via pricing in wireless data networks. *IEEE Transactions on Communications, 50*(2), 291–303. doi:10.1109/26.983324

Scutari, G., Palomar, D. P., & Barbarossa, S. (2008). Competitive Design of Multiuser MIMO Systems Based on Game Theory: A Unified View. *IEEE Journal on Selected Areas in Communications, 26*(7), 1089–1103. doi:10.1109/JSAC.2008.080907

Sedjelmaci, H., Senouci, S. M., & Al-Bahri, M. (2016). A lightweight anomaly detection technique for low-resource IoT devices: A game-theoretic methodology. In *2016 IEEE International Conference on Communications (ICC)* (pp. 1–6). IEEE. 10.1109/ICC.2016.7510811

Selimi, M., Kabbinale, A. R., Ali, A., Navarro, L., & Sathiaseelan, A. (2018). Towards Blockchain-enabled Wireless Mesh Networks. In *Proceedings of the 1st Workshop on Cryptocurrencies and Blockchains for Distributed Systems - CryBlock'18* (pp. 13–18). New York: ACM Press. 10.1145/3211933.3211936

Semasinghe, P., Hossain, E., & Zhu, K. (2015). An Evolutionary Game for Distributed Resource Allocation in Self-Organizing Small Cells. *IEEE Transactions on Mobile Computing, 14*(2), 274–287. doi:10.1109/TMC.2014.2318700

Semasinghe, P., Maghsudi, S., & Hossain, E. (2017). Game Theoretic Mechanisms for Resource Management in Massive Wireless IoT Systems. *IEEE Communications Magazine, 55*(2), 121–127. doi:10.1109/MCOM.2017.1600568CM

Shastry, N., & Adve, R. (2006). Stimulating Cooperative Diversity in Wireless Ad Hoc Networks through Pricing. In *2006 IEEE International Conference on Communications* (pp. 3747–3752). IEEE. 10.1109/ICC.2006.255655

Shen, S., Yue, G., Cao, Q., & Yu, F. (2011). A Survey of Game Theory in Wireless Sensor Networks Security. *JNW, 6*(3), 521–532. doi:10.4304/jnw.6.3.521-532

Shi, H.-Y., Wang, W.-L., Kwok, N.-M., & Chen, S.-Y. (2012). Game Theory for Wireless Sensor Networks: A Survey. *Sensors (Basel), 12*(7), 9055–9097. doi:10.3390120709055 PMID:23012533

Shivshankar, S., & Jamalipour, A. (2015). An Evolutionary Game Theory-Based Approach to Cooperation in VANETs Under Different Network Conditions. *IEEE Transactions on Vehicular Technology, 64*(5), 2015–2022. doi:10.1109/TVT.2014.2334655

Silva, J., Marinheiro, R., Moura, J., & Almeida, J. (2013). Differentiated classes of service and flow management using an hybrid broker. *ACEEE International Journal on Communication, 4*(2), 13–22.

Skraparlis, D., Sakarellos, V., Panagopoulos, A., & Kanellopoulos, J. (2009). Outage Performance Analysis of Cooperative Diversity with MRC and SC in Correlated Lognormal Channels. *EURASIP Journal on Wireless Communications and Networking, 707839*(1), 707839. doi:10.1155/2009/707839

Srirama, S., & Paniagua, C. (2013). Mobile web service provisioning and discovery in android days. In *Conference on Mobile Services* (pp. 15–22). Washington, DC: IEEE Computer Society. 10.1109/MS.2013.14

Srivastava, V., Neel, J., Mackenzie, A. B., Menon, R., Dasilva, L. A., Hicks, J. E., ... Gilles, R. P. (2005). Using game theory to analyze wireless ad hoc networks. *IEEE Communications Surveys and Tutorials, 7*(4), 46–56. doi:10.1109/COMST.2005.1593279

Taleb, T., Samdanis, K., Mada, B., Flinck, H., Dutta, S., & Sabella, D. (2017). On Multi-Access Edge Computing: A Survey of the Emerging 5G Network Edge Architecture & Orchestration. *IEEE Communications Surveys & Tutorials,* (99), 1–1. doi:10.1109/COMST.2017.2705720

Taylor, P. D., & Jonker, L. B. (1978). Evolutionary stable strategies and game dynamics. *Mathematical Biosciences, 40*(1–2), 145–156. doi:10.1016/0025-5564(78)90077-9

Tembine, H., Altman, E., El-Azouzi, R., & Hayel, Y. (2010). Evolutionary Games in Wireless Networks. *IEEE Transactions on Systems, Man, and Cybernetics. Part B, Cybernetics, 40*(3), 634–646. doi:10.1109/TSMCB.2009.2034631 PMID:19963703

Tordera, E., Masip-Bruin, X., Garcia-Almiana, J., Jukan, A., Ren, G.-J., Zhu, J., & Farre, J. (2016). *What is a Fog Node? A Tutorial on Current Concepts towards a Common Definition*. Retrieved from http://arxiv.org/abs/1611.09193

Trestian, R., Ormond, O., & Muntean, G.-M. (2011). Reputation-based network selection mechanism using game theory. *Physical Communication*, *4*(3), 156–171. doi:10.1016/j.phycom.2011.06.004

Ungureanu, V. (2018). Strategic Form Games on Digraphs. In *Pareto-Nash-Stackelberg Game and Control Theory. Smart Innovation, Systems and Technologies* (pp. 167–197). Cham: Springer; doi:10.1007/978-3-319-75151-1_8

Vassaki, S., Panagopoulos, A. D., Constantinou, P., & Vázquez-Castro, M. A. (2010). Market-Based Bandwidth Allocation for Broadband Satellite Communication Networks. In *2010 Second International Conference on Advances in Satellite and Space Communications* (pp. 110–115). IEEE. 10.1109/SPACOMM.2010.22

Vedhavathy, T. R., & Manikandan, M. S. K. (2018). Triple referee incentive mechanism for secure mobile adhoc networks. *Cluster Computing*, 1–10. doi:10.100710586-017-1631-8

Vermesan, O., Bröring, A., Tragos, E., Serrano, M., Bacciu, D., Chessa, S. … Bahr, R. (2017). Internet of robotic things : converging sensing/actuating, hypoconnectivity, artificial intelligence and IoT Platforms. In Cognitive Hyperconnected Digital Transformation : Internet of Things Intelligence Evolution (pp. 97–155). Academic Press.

Wang, B., Wu, Y., & Liu, K. J. R. (2010). Game Theory for Cognitive Radio Networks: An Overview. *Computer Networks*, *54*(14), 2537–2561. doi:10.1016/j.comnet.2010.04.004

Wang, B., Wu, Y., Liu, K. J. R., & Clancy, T. C. (2011). An anti-jamming stochastic game for cognitive radio networks. *IEEE Journal on Selected Areas in Communications*, *29*(4), 877–889. doi:10.1109/JSAC.2011.110418

Wang, S., Zhang, X., Zhang, Y., Wang, L., Yang, J., & Wang, W. (2017). A Survey on Mobile Edge Networks: Convergence of Computing, Caching and Communications. *IEEE Access: Practical Innovations, Open Solutions*, *5*, 6757–6779. doi:10.1109/ACCESS.2017.2685434

Watanabe, E. H., Menasche, D. S., de Souza e Silva, E., & Leao, R. M. M. (2008). Modeling Resource Sharing Dynamics of VoIP Users over a WLAN Using a Game-Theoretic Approach. In *IEEE INFOCOM 2008 - The 27th Conference on Computer Communications* (pp. 915–923). IEEE. 10.1109/INFOCOM.2008.144

Xiao, Y., Chen, K. C., Yuen, C., Han, Z., & DaSilva, L. A. (2015). A Bayesian Overlapping Coalition Formation Game for Device-to-Device Spectrum Sharing in Cellular Networks. *IEEE Transactions on Wireless Communications*, *14*(7), 4034–4051. doi:10.1109/TWC.2015.2416178

Yan, Y., Huang, J., & Wang, J. (2013). Dynamic Bargaining for Relay-Based Cooperative Spectrum Sharing. *IEEE Journal on Selected Areas in Communications*, *31*(8), 1480–1493. doi:10.1109/JSAC.2013.130812

Yap, K.-K., Huang, T.-Y., Kobayashi, M., Yiakoumis, Y., McKeown, N., Katti, S., & Parulkar, G. (2012). Making use of all the networks around us. In *Proceedings of the 2012 ACM SIGCOMM workshop on Cellular networks: operations, challenges, and future design - CellNet '12* (p. 19). New York: ACM Press. 10.1145/2342468.2342474

Yi, S., Li, C., & Li, Q. (2015). A Survey of Fog Computing: Concepts, Applications and Issues. In *Proceedings of the 2015 Workshop on Mobile Big Data - Mobidata '15* (pp. 37–42). New York: ACM Press. 10.1145/2757384.2757397

Zhang, D., Ileri, O., & Mandayam, N. (2008). Bandwidth exchange as an incentive for relaying. In *2008 42nd Annual Conference on Information Sciences and Systems* (pp. 749–754). IEEE. 10.1109/CISS.2008.4558621

Zhang, L., Afanasyev, A., Burke, J., Jacobson, V., Claffy, K., Crowley, P., ... Zhang, B. (2014). Named Data Networking. *Computer Communication Review, 44*(3), 66–73. doi:10.1145/2656877.2656887

Zhang, Y., & Guizani, M. (2011). *Game theory for wireless communications and networking.* CRC Press.

Zhang, Y., Lou, W., & Fang, Y. (2004). SIP: a secure incentive protocol against selfishness in mobile ad hoc networks. In 2004 IEEE Wireless Communications and Networking Conference (IEEE Cat. No.04TH8733) (pp. 1679–1684). IEEE. doi:10.1109/WCNC.2004.1311805

Zhang, Z., Long, K., Vasilakos, A. V., & Hanzo, L. (2016). Full-Duplex Wireless Communications: Challenges, Solutions, and Future Research Directions. *Proceedings of the IEEE, 104*(7), 1369–1409. doi:10.1109/JPROC.2015.2497203

Zheng, G., Liu, S., & Qi, X. (2012). Clustering routing algorithm of wireless sensor networks based on Bayesian game. *Journal of Systems Engineering and Electronics, 23*(1), 154–159. doi:10.1109/JSEE.2012.00019

Zhong, S., Chen, J., & Yang, Y. R. (2003). Sprite: a simple, cheat-proof, credit-based system for mobile ad-hoc networks. In *IEEE INFOCOM 2003. Twenty-second Annual Joint Conference of the IEEE Computer and Communications Societies (IEEE Cat. No.03CH37428)* (Vol. 3, pp. 1987–1997). IEEE. 10.1109/INFCOM.2003.1209220

Zhu, K., & Hossain, E. (2015). Joint Mode Selection and Spectrum Partitioning for Device-to-Device Communication: A Dynamic Stackelberg Game. *IEEE Transactions on Wireless Communications, 14*(3), 1406–1420. doi:10.1109/TWC.2014.2366136

Zhu, K., Niyato, D., & Wang, P. (2010). Network Selection in Heterogeneous Wireless Networks: Evolution with Incomplete Information. In 2010 IEEE Wireless Communication and Networking Conference (pp. 1–6). IEEE. doi:10.1109/WCNC.2010.5506371

ADDITIONAL READING

Ackermann, H., Briest, P., Fanghänel, A., & Vöcking, B. (2008). Who Should Pay for Forwarding Packets? *Internet Mathematics, 5*(4), 459–475. doi:10.1080/15427951.2008.10129168

Akyildiz, I. F., Lee, W.-Y., Vuran, M. C., & Mohanty, S. (2006). NeXt Generation/Dynamic Spectrum Access/Cognitive Radio Wireless Networks: A Survey. *Computer Networks*, *50*(13), 2127–2159. doi:10.1016/j.comnet.2006.05.001

Al-Manthari, B., Nasser, N., & Hassanein, H. (2011). Congestion Pricing in Wireless Cellular Networks. *IEEE Communications Surveys and Tutorials*, *13*(3), 358–371. doi:10.1109/SURV.2011.090710.00042

Alayesh, M. A., & Ghani, N. (2012). Performance of a primary-secondary user power control under rayleigh fast flat fading channel with pricing. In Telecommunications (ICT), 2012 19th International Conference on (pp. 1–5). 10.1109/ICTEL.2012.6221257

Buddhikot, M. M. (2007). Understanding Dynamic Spectrum Access: Models, Taxonomy and Challenges. In 2007 2nd IEEE International Symposium on New Frontiers in Dynamic Spectrum Access Networks (pp. 649–663). 10.1109/DYSPAN.2007.88

Buddhikot, M. M., & Ryan, K. (2005). Spectrum management in coordinated dynamic spectrum access based cellular networks. In First IEEE International Symposium on New Frontiers in Dynamic Spectrum Access Networks, 2005. DySPAN 2005. (pp. 299–307). 10.1109/DYSPAN.2005.1542646

Buttyán, L., & Hubaux, J.-P. (2008). *Security and cooperation in wireless networks : thwarting malicious and selfish behavior in the age of ubiquitous computing*. Cambridge University Press; Retrieved from http://www.cambridge.org/gb/academic/subjects/engineering/wireless-communications/security-and-cooperation-wireless-networks-thwarting-malicious-and-selfish-behavior-age-ubiquitous-computing?format=HB&isbn=9780521873710#xEQOI7PilMoKvAgD.97

Courcoubetis, C., & Weber, R. (2003). *Pricing Communication Networks*. Chichester, UK: John Wiley & Sons, Ltd.; doi:10.1002/0470867175

DaSilva, L. A. (2000). Pricing for QoS-enabled networks: A survey. *IEEE Communications Surveys and Tutorials*, *3*(2), 2–8. doi:10.1109/COMST.2000.5340797

Etkin, R., Parekh, A., & Tse, D. (2007). Spectrum sharing for unlicensed bands. *IEEE Journal on Selected Areas in Communications*, *25*(3), 517–528. doi:10.1109/JSAC.2007.070402

Felegyhazi, M., Cagalj, M., Bidokhti, S. S., & Hubaux, J. P. (2007). Non-Cooperative Multi-Radio Channel Allocation in Wireless Networks. In IEEE INFOCOM 2007 - 26th IEEE International Conference on Computer Communications (pp. 1442–1450). 10.1109/INFCOM.2007.170

Halpern, J. Y. (2007). Computer Science and Game Theory: A Brief Survey. Work, abs/cs/070, 1–17. doi:10.1145/1378704.1378721

Heikkinen, T. (2004). Distributed Scheduling and Dynamic Pricing in a Communication Network. *Wireless Networks*, *10*(3), 233–244. doi:10.1023/B:WINE.0000023858.20849.ab

Heikkinen, T. (2006). A Potential Game Approach to Distributed Power Control and Scheduling. *Computer Networks*, *50*(13), 2295–2311. doi:10.1016/j.comnet.2005.09.010

Heikkinen, T. M. (2002). On Congestion Pricing in a Wireless Network. *Wireless Networks*, *8*(4), 347–354. doi:10.1023/A:1015578321066

Huang, J., Berry, R. A., & Honig, M. L. (2006a). Auction-Based Spectrum Sharing. *Mobile Networks and Applications*, *11*(3), 405–408. doi:10.100711036-006-5192-y

Huang, J., Berry, R. A., & Honig, M. L. (2006b). Distributed interference compensation for wireless networks. *IEEE Journal on Selected Areas in Communications*, *24*(5), 1074–1084. doi:10.1109/JSAC.2006.872889

Ileri, O., Samardzija, D., Sizer, T., & Mandayam, N. B. (2005). Demand responsive pricing and competitive spectrum allocation via a spectrum server. In First IEEE International Symposium on New Frontiers in Dynamic Spectrum Access Networks, 2005. DySPAN 2005. (pp. 194–202). 10.1109/DYSPAN.2005.1542635

Inaltekin, H., Wexler, T., & Wicker, S. B. (2007). A Duopoly Pricing Game for Wireless IP Services. In 2007 4th Annual IEEE Communications Society Conference on Sensor, Mesh and Ad Hoc Communications and Networks (pp. 600–609). 10.1109/SAHCN.2007.4292872

Jia, J., & Zhang, Q. (2008). Competitions and Dynamics of Duopoly Wireless Service Providers in Dynamic Spectrum Market. In *Proceedings of the 9th ACM International Symposium on Mobile Ad Hoc Networking and Computing* (pp. 313–322). New York, NY, USA: ACM. 10.1145/1374618.1374660

Koutsopoulou, M., Kaloxylos, A., Alonistioti, A., Merakos, L., & Kawamura, K. (2004). Charging, accounting and billing management schemes in mobile telecommunication networks and the internet. *IEEE Communications Surveys and Tutorials*, *6*(1), 50–58. doi:10.1109/COMST.2004.5342234

Lee, J., Tang, A., Huang, J., Chiang, M., & Calderbank, A. R. (2007). Reverse-Engineering MAC: A Non-Cooperative Game Model. *IEEE Journal on Selected Areas in Communications*, *25*(6), 1135–1147. doi:10.1109/JSAC.2007.070808

MacKenzie, A. B., & Wicker, S. B. (2003). Stability of multipacket slotted Aloha with selfish users and perfect information. In INFOCOM 2003. Twenty-Second Annual Joint Conference of the IEEE Computer and Communications. IEEE Societies (Vol. 3, pp. 1583–1590 vol.3). 10.1109/INFCOM.2003.1209181

Maharjan, S., Zhang, Y., & Gjessing, S. (2011). Economic Approaches for Cognitive Radio Networks: A Survey. *Wireless Personal Communications*, *57*(1), 33–51. doi:10.100711277-010-0005-9

Maillé, P., & Tuffin, B. (2006). Pricing the Internet with Multibid Auctions. *IEEE/ACM Transactions on Networking*, *14*(5), 992–1004. doi:10.1109/TNET.2006.882861

Maskery, M., Krishnamurthy, V., & Zhao, Q. (2009). Decentralized dynamic spectrum access for cognitive radios: Cooperative design of a non-cooperative game. *IEEE Transactions on Communications*, *57*(2), 459–469. doi:10.1109/TCOMM.2009.02.070158

Meshkati, F., Poor, H. V., & Schwartz, S. C. (2007). Energy-Efficient Resource Allocation in Wireless Networks. *IEEE Signal Processing Magazine*, *24*(3), 58–68. doi:10.1109/MSP.2007.361602

Mingbo Xiao, M., Shroff, N. B., & Chong, E. K. P. (2003). A utility-based power-control scheme in wireless cellular systems. *IEEE/ACM Transactions on Networking*, *11*(2), 210–221. doi:10.1109/TNET.2003.810314

Nguyen, D. N., & Krunz, M. (2012). Price-Based Joint Beamforming and Spectrum Management in Multi-Antenna Cognitive Radio Networks. *IEEE Journal on Selected Areas in Communications*, *30*(11), 2295–2305. doi:10.1109/JSAC.2012.121221

Nie, N., & Comaniciu, C. (2005). Adaptive channel allocation spectrum etiquette for cognitive radio networks. In First IEEE International Symposium on New Frontiers in Dynamic Spectrum Access Networks, 2005. DySPAN 2005. (pp. 269–278). 10.1109/DYSPAN.2005.1542643

Niyato, D., & Hossain, E. (2009). Dynamics of Network Selection in Heterogeneous Wireless Networks: An Evolutionary Game Approach. *IEEE Transactions on Vehicular Technology*, *58*(4), 2008–2017. doi:10.1109/TVT.2008.2004588

Niyato, D., Hossain, E., & Han, Z. (2009). Dynamic spectrum access in IEEE 802.22- based cognitive wireless networks: A game theoretic model for competitive spectrum bidding and pricing. *IEEE Wireless Communications*, *16*(2), 16–23. doi:10.1109/MWC.2009.4907555

Novelti, P., Satya, A., & Wardana, A. (2007). Cooperation in Wireless Grids An Energy Efficient MAC Protocol for Cooperative Network with Game Theory Model Cooperation in Wireless Grids – An Energy Efficient MAC Protocol for Cooperative Network with Game Theory Model.

Rasti, M., Sharafat, A. R., & Seyfe, B. (2009). Pareto-efficient and Goal-driven Power Control in Wireless Networks: A Game-theoretic Approach with a Novel Pricing Scheme. *IEEE/ACM Transactions on Networking*, *17*(2), 556–569. doi:10.1109/TNET.2009.2014655

Ren, W., Zhao, Q., & Swami, A. (2008). Power control in spectrum overlay networks: How to cross a multi-lane highway. In *2008 IEEE International Conference on Acoustics, Speech and Signal Processing* (pp. 2773–2776). 10.1109/ICASSP.2008.4518224

Sengupta, S., Anand, S., Chatterjee, M., & Chandramouli, R. (2009). Dynamic pricing for service provisioning and network selection in heterogeneous networks. *Physical Communication*, *2*(1–2), 138–150. doi:10.1016/j.phycom.2009.02.009

Thomas, R. W., DaSilva, L. A., & MacKenzie, A. B. (2005). Cognitive networks. In First IEEE International Symposium on New Frontiers in Dynamic Spectrum Access Networks, 2005. DySPAN 2005. (pp. 352–360). IEEE. 10.1109/DYSPAN.2005.1542652

Vincent, T. L., Vincent, T. L. S., & Cohen, Y. (2011). Darwinian dynamics and evolutionary game theory. *Journal of Biological Dynamics*, *5*(3), 215–226. doi:10.1080/17513758.2010.526306

Wang, D., Comaniciu, C., & Tureli, U. (2006). A Fair and Efficient Pricing Strategy for Slotted Aloha in MPR Models. In *IEEE Vehicular Technology Conference* (pp. 1–5). 10.1109/VTCF.2006.509

Youngmi Jin, Y., & Kesidis, G. (2002). Equilibria of a noncooperative game for heterogeneous users of an ALOHA network. *IEEE Communications Letters*, *6*(7), 282–284. doi:10.1109/LCOMM.2002.801326

Zhang, J., & Zhang, Q. (2009). Stackelberg Game for Utility-based Cooperative Cognitive Radio Networks. In *Proceedings of the Tenth ACM International Symposium on Mobile Ad Hoc Networking and Computing* (pp. 23–32). New York, NY, USA: ACM. 10.1145/1530748.1530753

Zhao, L., Zhang, J., & Zhang, H. (2008). Using Incompletely Cooperative Game Theory in Wireless Mesh Networks. *IEEE Network*, *22*(1), 39–44. doi:10.1109/MNET.2008.4435901

Zhao, Q., & Sadler, B. M. (2007). A Survey of Dynamic Spectrum Access. *IEEE Signal Processing Magazine*, *24*(3), 79–89. doi:10.1109/MSP.2007.361604

Chapter 13
Lightweight Virtualization for Edge Computing

Fabio Diniz Rossi

https://orcid.org/0000-0002-2450-1024

IFFar, Brazil

Bruno Morais Neves de Castro

IFB, Brazil

Matheus Breno Batista dos Santos

IFB, Brazil

ABSTRACT

In infrastructure as a service (IaaS), the edge computing paradigm proposes the network node distribution of storage and computing resources to ensure swift access throughout a fog environment. The edge platform landscape fragmentation requires flexible and scalable approaches. Based on the above, the most recent works highlight lightweight virtualization, the process of making any hardware shares its resources with other applications without impacting on performance issues. In this sense, this chapter conveys current concepts, techniques and open challenges of lightweight virtualization for edge computing.

INTRODUCTION

Internet of Things (IoT) development technologies surrounds the world promoting massive impact on numerous industries and fields of humanity (Vaquero & Rodero-Merino, 2014). Strictly linked to sensor networks, IoT huge capacity of data collection brought new insights into the world, from connecting ordinary objects to build a vast network of sensors.

Based on the market, IoT brings meaning to the concept of ubiquitous connectivity for businesses, governments, and customers with its innate management, monitoring, and analytics. This IoT distinct, innovative potential swiftly embraced Cloud computing comprehensive services exponential growth,

DOI: 10.4018/978-1-6684-5700-9.ch013

suddenly proving its utility on automating ordinary tasks (Galante & Bona, 2012) and, consequently, generating tons of data to be interpreted in an online environment.

The exponential requisition of the cloud-based centralized gateway infrastructure prompted inefficiency to the real-time services supply chain, where delay barrier constraints the development of self-driven cars and other low-latency IoT initiatives. This new obstacle promoted scientific approaches around edge computing concept of network node distributed resources intermediate layer, where the servers reversely dispatch data processing to constrained devices deployed at the network edge, providing low-latency domain to data generators (Shi, Cao, Zhang, Li, & Xu, 2016).

Figure 1 demonstrates the entire Fog computing architecture, where we have multiple sensors distributed geographically, searching data from various sources, and sending such data in real time to be processed. On the other hand, a set of servers running cloud services must receive such a massive amount of data and turn it into information. In order to bring cloud services closer to customers (in this case represented by IoT sensors), parts of the cloud services can pre-process on intermediate network devices, known as edge devices (Shi & Dustdar, 2016).

Figure 1. Fog architecture

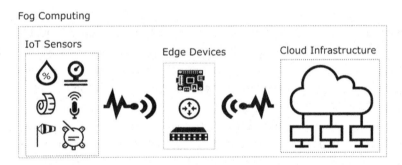

Supported by these concepts, many past works highlight the use of virtualization on top of edge devices due to its potential elasticity. Despite traditional hardware and software configuration for a dedicated server, virtualization allows running multiple OS and applications over same hardware. Being Lightweight Virtualization more adaptable and versatile than traditional Hypervisors techniques, it has the independence of OS base and works without virtualization of hardware. This somewhat disruptive technology can lead to faster initialization, lower system overhead and, lastly, excellent energy efficiency to the nodes (Xavier, Neves, Rossi, Ferreto, Lange, & De Rose, 2013).

Over the last decade, the proposal of Lightweight Virtualization implementation to edge-driven IoT has become popular as a feature to fulfill network scalability, multi-tenancy, and privacy. A direct benefit that emerges from employing Lightweight Virtualization in the IoT edge domain is avoiding the strict dependency on any given technology or use case (Morabito et al., 2018), which, in IoT heterogeneous environment can provide the flexibility to connect to any device and distribute computational and data-base services around the edge network seamlessly.

Virtualization support enables the possibility of Network Function Virtualization (NFV) over such devices. Based on this, the service provider can deploy various types of network and computing services in the form of micro clouds. Virtualization on edge devices minimizes investment as there is no need for a massive centralized infrastructure. Services are instantiated depending on consumer demand. Also, the core infrastructure does not need significant modifications to accommodate any service (Chiosi, Clarke, Willis, Reid, Feger, Bugenhagen, & Benitez, 2012; Morabito et al., 2018; Vaquero & Rodero-Merino, 2014; Chiosi, Clarke, Willis, Reid, Feger, Bugenhagen, & Benitez, 2012).

NFV over edge devices can directly offer network failover, security in the form of channel encryption with the consumer, WAN optimization where there are low link speed channels, and analysis and diagnosis based on network traffic for troubleshooting purposes or package prioritization. In the sense of micro clouds, the computing node is migrated from a centralized infrastructure to the edge device, facilitating the delivery of the service to the consumer, regarding the quality of service (Chiosi et al., 2012; Vaquero & Rodero-Merino, 2014; Chiosi et al., 2012) .

This chapter presents the following contributions:

- The integration of lightweight virtualization within edge computing.
- The importance of edge computing devices regarding the flexibility of running lightweight virtualization and sharing of physical resources.
- A discussion of the challenges, opportunities, and trends for lightweight virtualization and edge computing.

From the above, lightweight virtualization is an approach to implement applications in a very different scenario, in which a system run on top of hardware sharing processing power and storage with the operational system base and other applications in virtualization, requiring fewer devices dedicated to one specific task. Edge computing best use relies on lightweight virtualization, transforming intermediary server in a more useful machine without upgrades or top of the line hardware.

This chapter discusses the advantages offered by the many kinds of lightweight virtualization, besides the importance and simultaneously of edge computing in a Fog environment. Afterward, the authors will summarize the work, making it possible to view challenges, trends, and future research directions.

VIRTUALIZATION LANDSCAPE

First, this section introduces the virtualization and a quick history of its evolution. Virtualization consists of providing a platform that supports concurrent execution of multiple operating systems or applications in a parallel and isolated manner. Due to the speed of deploying a large number of virtual machines (VMs), this is the base technology for several other computational paradigms. The elasticity and fault tolerance of virtualized environments allow the fulfillment of customer requests in order to maintain the agreed quality of service. Therefore, virtualization is presented as a fundamental component to cloud infrastructures, offering such features.

However, more traditional virtualization technologies cause overhead on application performance (Morabito, 2017). It is mainly caused by (1) virtualization layer, which must translate all application-level instructions to the host operating system, and (2) a ring-blocking system, which controls all input and output data to be interpreted by virtualization layer. Although there is a loss of performance in this virtualization model, there are some features that still hold them as an ideal choice, such as resource isolation.

These are essential requirements when it comes to embedded platforms such as edge devices. Such devices have limited hardware regarding design, which limits them in resources as well. Also, their applications are usually time-based, which characterizes them as real-time designed equipment, operating systems, and applications.

Thus, in order to reduce the performance overhead caused by the more traditional virtualization proposals, the containers technology was proposed. Container-based virtualization runs at the operating system level, and all VMs share a single kernel, which reduces the overhead commonly caused by traditional virtualization technologies (Xavier et al., 2013). Therefore, containers offer almost native performance to the supported applications. However, there is a loss of resource isolation, since the kernel can not limit the use of slices of distributed resources between VMs. Also, since containers run on the same Kernel, that is, the entire environment must run on the same operating system.

To address environments that must maintain heterogeneous operating systems, a new virtualization proposal emerges, called microservice architecture (unikernels). This paradigm consists of small operating systems compiled for specific purposes that are staggered and managed as processes by the host operating system (Morabito, Cozzolino, Ding, & Beijar, 2018). As a result, VMs can be delivered faster due to reduced system image size, resulting in scalability improvements, ease of maintenance of applications, and reduced instantiation time of VMs.

All previous virtualization proposals allow charging based on the number of resources used versus the time. Thus, until then, the service providers had their costs tied to the number of resources required to meet the requests of customers.

A new virtualization proposal called serverless (also called Function as a Service - FaaS) allows billing only based on the code running in the cloud environment. Serverless has been widely adopted due to the recent shift from enterprise application architectures to containers and microservices. This new paradigm provides developers with a simplified programming model for creating cloud applications that abstracts most operational concerns. This way, when Serverless is adopted, the service customer has no control over the resources where part of the application is running, nor does it need to create VMs or network configurations.

Through this new paradigm, a computing model is envisaged in which all resources are effectively grouped, including hardware, operating systems, and runtime environments. Also, Serverless enables developers to deploy large applications in a variety of small roles, allowing application components to be scaled individually.

Besides, when this paradigm is adopted, collections are only performed based on the number of requests and the execution time of the functions. Therefore, this characteristic can generate significant cost reduction when compared to the traditional model of service deployment through VMs.

Several papers in the literature present serverless computing emphasize that the Serverless paradigm was presented as a means to (1) introduce more cost efficiencies, (2) reduce configuration overhead, and (3) rapidly increase an application's ability to scale over the resources of the cloud. Based on this, the authors provide an overview and feature analysis of various serverless computing platforms from multiple providers, such as AWS Lambda and Google Cloud functions (Villamizar, Garcés, Ochoa, Castro, Salamanca, Verano, & Lang, 2017).

All of these virtualization models can and do apply to fog and edge computing environments. This chapter will present each type of virtualization and its applicability on fog environments and edge computing devices individually, discussing, in the end, some open challenges.

LIGHTWEIGHT VIRTUALIZATION CONCEPTS

The idea of virtualization is not new. The IBM System 360 of the 1960s already offered to partition between operating systems. However, virtualization is a technology that has remained dormant due to the need for powerful computational resources for the satisfactory execution of several VMs (Barham, Dragovic, Fraser, Hand, Harris, Ho, & Warfield, 2003).

The increase in the potential of computing resources, especially regarding processor speed, provides an environment conducive to the emergence of Xen in 2004. It is a proposal that allows the execution of multiple guests operating systems on a para-virtualized base system, and which offers the execution of virtualized applications, although it presents a small loss of performance (Barham et al., 2003). Several other proposals followed the same path of Xen, only with modifications between virtualization or paravirtualization, as in the case of VMWare, Bochs, VirtualBox, and so on.

Due to the overhead caused by the virtualization layers of previous paradigms, newer lighter virtualization proposals are beginning to be studied. The LXC (Linux Containers) project starts in 2008, delivering virtualized application performance equal to or very close to its native environment runs. Stable versions of Containers have emerged almost ten years later and currently offer high performance, although they have a direct negative implication on other metrics, especially on the issue of resource isolation (Xavier et al., 2013).

At this point, the embedded systems community focuses their attention on the capabilities that virtualization can deliver for environments that require real-time responses but at the same time would like to run stand-alone applications in parallel or even migrate applications from one device to another.

In the same period, new proposals for virtualization arise, such as unikernels and serverless computing. The first consists of a kernel only recompiled with the minimum necessary for the application to execute correctly. It creates a small operating system and application image, which can instantiate how many replicas are needed to meet customer demand. Serverless allows part of the application code - the most massive part - to run outside the embedded device, usually having the workload sent to a function that is located in an external cloud environment.

Typically a Telco company offers services directed to its customer, as a firewall, DNS, VPN, and other services. It usually has dedicated hardware to each service spread along its network. This approach turned out to be painful to set up and to maintain considering how heterogeneous and diverse can be the devices, systems, and integration between them. Network Function Virtualization (NFV) is born as an alternative to the traditional model, suggesting generic network devices, but management over which service (and where and when it) should be deployed using lightweight virtualization (Vaquero & Rodero-Merino, 2014).

In partnership with NFV, the idea of software defined networks is really useful for NFV considering its capabilities of separate planes of control and data forwarding. Software defined networks are based on the separation of the data planes and control of the network, which refers to the set of functions, logically centralized in network controllers, which influences how the packets are routed to destinations in the network by elements that it defines to accomplish such task through a well-defined communication interface. In this way, the intelligence of the network concentrates mostly in the control plane, which can potentially harbor any network application that allows the implementation of better strategies for routing traffic by many actuators in different granularities (Chiosi et al., 2012). Consequently, software defined networks can establish efficient algorithms in the data plane to act in the load balancing in links, having as political criteria that contain any requirements that are useful to this task.

It is needed to clarify that Software Defined Networks isn't dependent on NFV and vice versa, although, approaches relying on both can have fuller exploitation of resources available and better execution. NFV benefits include, but aren't limited to:

- Reducing equipment cost and power consumption.
- Increased speed of time-to-market, reducing the innovation cycle.
- Multiple environments are running simultaneously, allowing production, testing, and reference development workspace running on the same conditions.
- An offer of services and adjustments based on geography and consumer profile.
- Open the market for new players and more innovative takes on software development.
- Multi-tenancy for secure separation of administrative domains.
- Maximize the efficiency of the network.

Building NFV applications on the hypervisor model allow orchestration software (e.g., vSphere, OpenStack, CloudStack) to select, configure, and initialize VMs and hosts according to high-level service operations for specifying application profiles with specific settings depending on your location and network service. In this way, the tasks of orchestration and management become flexible to the point of forming chains of services easily by programming elements at the edges of the network.

The major premise of NFV is the high-volume support of low-cost servers playing a variety of roles to make efficient resource allocation dynamic to different VNFs. Addressing the efficient use of virtualized resources requires that they are scalable to the dimensions of the services offered by VNFs as well as that they, defined in an extensive heterogeneity (e.g., firewall, DPI, BRAS), can use data plan applications depending on the need (Bremler-Barr, Harchol, Hay, & Koral, 2014; Technical Report, 2004).

At different geographic scales, from data centers to WANs, the capacity to adapt to current virtualization technologies, especially concerning network equipment, may have different peculiarities. For example, currently routers in large Internet domains, around thousands worldwide, have significant buffers, make use of large amounts of memory for storing their BGP tables, and thus differ from centralized data network about 100,000 in a single data center, where it prizes for small rows and routing tables due to the nature of the traffic in this environment.

In performance requirements for NFs virtualization technologies, the following parameters stand out: a VNF instance must have its performance specifications well-defined to operate according to the available resources of the shared and isolated infrastructure in which it is instantiated; and forms of collecting information on storage, network, and processing of VNFs must be well defined and consequently carried out at different levels of infrastructure (eg, hypervisors, servers, VMs). These requirements will significantly influence the continuity of NFs and the very concept of NFV. In this case, virtualization technologies will possibly have, initially, not as good behaviors as dedicated middleboxes, but will bring the flexibility needed to provide elasticity to network functions. In this case, they are much better established and guaranteed if they can be scalably monitored at various levels of operation and granularity, thus providing consistent states of NFs and their respective environments.

LIGHTWEIGHT VIRTUALIZATION PARADIGMS

Virtualization is a reasonably widespread concept for large servers, but it is a relatively new technology for embedded systems. However, it is a technology mature enough to address some of the challenges of the area, such as the increase in software complexity given new market demands. In particular, embedded systems can benefit from virtualization's ability to deal with heterogeneous and competing systems. Also, the virtualization layer makes the underlying application transparent to the application, allowing the same application to run over multi-core to migrate to single-core overhead without requiring any modification to the application code.

In the context of fog and edge computing, elasticity capabilities allow new features to be added at runtime depending on demand and released when there is no longer such a need, saving resources. Besides, the ability to migrate VMs between devices over the network makes infrastructure management more flexible. Finally, the security provided by virtualization between the base system running at the superuser level is separate from the applications, ensuring that codes in userspace will not access resources outside of their quota system.

A few years ago, virtualization began to move into the embedded systems field. At that time, virtualization was managed by hypervisors. Although some popular hypervisors used for server computing have been adapted for embedded systems, currently with the advancement of semiconductor technology and the reduction of its costs, hardware support for virtualization can be created and new hypervisors for embedded environments have been developed from scratch (Mitake, 2011).

Traditional Virtualization

One of the most used virtualization proposals on servers is Xen. Xen is an open-source hypervisor that supports the largest current cloud environments, but although it was developed for servers, it was modified for embedded environments, especially for running on ARM processors.

Xen is responsible for manipulating the CPU, memory, stopping, and scheduling the VMs. Xen is a type 1 hypervisor, so it interacts directly with the hardware and the VMs that run on it. An instance running in a VM on Xen is called the domain or guest. There is a particular domain, called Domain 0 (dom0), which is responsible for I/O.

Figure 2 shows the Xen framework, which is a traditional virtualization paradigm. On the hardware, there is a modified operating system where the hypervisor is inserted to perform the translation of the system calls coming from the VMs (dom0). On the hypervisor, each VM contains a new operating system that supports one or more applications. This operating system does not have to be the same as the underlying system and does not require any modification. For the VM, there is the impression that the slice of hardware resources destined for each VM is the real underlying hardware. This slice of resources can be reallocated between VMs when needed.

The Xen I/O system is based on a ring structure for reading and writing between the application and the underlying operating system. Therefore, there is a loss of performance of virtualized applications due to overhead in the interpretation of the signals by the hypervisor.

For its execution on embedded environments, where time happens to be a decisive factor, changes were made on the scheduler, implemented real-time concepts for specific VMs. It enabled applications to keep running over the traditional scheduler (Credit Scheduler) while an RT-Xen managed other VMs.

Figure 2. Xen, a traditional model of virtualization

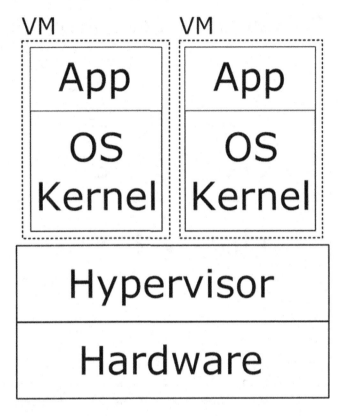

Containers

A container is a set of processes that are isolated from the rest of the system and managed directly by the kernel. These processes are run from a distinct image that provides all the files needed for its execution. By providing an image that contains all the dependencies of an application, the container is portable and consistent during all stages from development, testing, and ultimately production.

Figure 3 shows the layer structure of the Containers. Unlike traditional virtualization, Containers do not maintain a hypervisor. Process management is performed directly by the operating system kernel, very similar to Jails. The non-existence of a hypervisor enables Containers to provide applications with performance identical to a native environment.

On the other hand, the new design of management of the VMs in Containers enabled improvement in performance, but it impacted another fundamental metric: the isolation of resources. While in traditional virtualization resource management is relatively rigid in a sense and maintain the number of resources intended for each virtual machine, regardless of the need for resources of such VMs, Containers cannot preserve such limits (Xavier et al., 2013).

Because the Kernel manages containers, applications running on this paradigm must run on the same operating system. It is a fascinating proposal for embedded devices when competing applications do not compete for the same resources. In edge computing environments, Containers allow applications to migrate dynamically between devices, bringing some of the processing to the customer.

Figure 3. Containers structure and organization

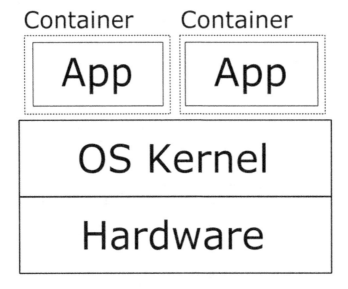

Unikernel

Unikernel is a library operating system. Although not a new idea, it was not implemented due to the inability to deal with numerous different hardware. With the advent of hypervisors, this concern to deal directly with the hardware has been overcome making it possible for an operating system with these characteristics to be executed in any computational environment.

Figure 4. Unikernel structure and organization

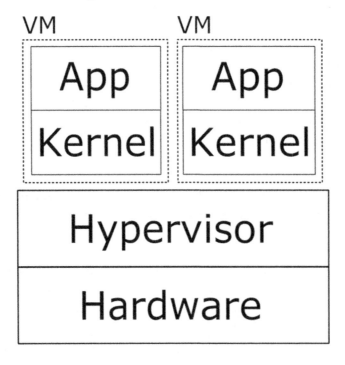

As can be seen in Figure 4, when we use Unikernel, there is no division between user space and kernel space. There is only one program running, and it contains everything from the high-level code of the application to the low-level device I/O routines, being a unique and self-contained image that does not require anything additional to be initialized.

Unikernel can be considered a sort of light virtualization, but implemented in a way different from the shared vision in the same operating system as in other paradigms of virtualization. Therefore, it is an operating system that uses a genuinely minimalist concept to create the software stack, that is, it is only concerned with the specific needs for each application. In operating system design, the libraries used to build it are the ones strictly required to run the application, thereby making it lighter than traditional VMs.

One of the advantages of Unikernel over other paradigms is that it improves security by being a tiny and specific operating system with no applications/ports that are not used by the standard application. Also, its performance is high due to its lightness, the inexistence of multiple processes with the need for management and the exclusion of changes in user contexts in its implementation (Kuenzer, Ivanov, Manco, Mendes, Volchkov, Schmidt, & Huici, 2017).

Fog and edge computing environments can benefit from this type of virtualization because the VMs created are minimalist, allowing you to put full applications in a few kilobytes. Also, since they are small, a large number of these can be instantiated on the same device, serving a large number of requests with little hardware design space.

Serverless Computing

Serverless has emerged as a new paradigm aimed at deployment of fog applications and has been boosted due to the migration of enterprise applications to new architectures through the adoption of Containers and Microservices. The term Serverless computing was defined by the industry to describe a programming model and a design in which small snippets of code run in the cloud as a function. It is important to emphasize that the Serverless paradigm uses servers, but resource management such as resource provisioning, monitoring, maintenance, scalability, and fault tolerance is the responsibility of the cloud service provider.

Serverless computing is defined as a paradigm where the customer provides the code, and the cloud provider manages the environmental life cycle of running that code. Serverless can be defined as the partial realization of an event-oriented ideal, in which applications are determined by the actions and events that trigger them (Baldini, Castro, Chang, Cheng, Fink,, Ishakian, & Suter, 2017).

Event-based systems are two entities called publisher and subscriber. This paradigm, called Publish / Subscribe, is suitable for the development of several new applications that are developed for collaborative environments or high-performance code compositions. Besides, this model is also ideal for a controlled environment which requires the immediate notification of any changes in the data to the customer. For this, the customer only needs to subscribe to a specific service and the server will register the subscriber for that service.

In serverless computing, similar to general-purpose event-based systems, users register their roles in the cloud provider that offers the option of deploying applications through the use of Serverless, and in turn, such functions are driven on a basis in events. Events can trigger functions in a variety of ways, such as through a Hypertext Transfer Protocol route, or even based on a timer or object added or removed from a database.

Serverless computing is a paradigm that must be exploited by IoT embeds, edge and fog computing, since part of the code (usually the heaviest) can be processor outside the embedded intermediate device. Therefore, the local code makes an Hypertext Transfer Protocol request to an external cloud environment, and this external function processes data directly and returns only the responses to the edge device.

Summary

Figure 5 summarizes this section on the different virtualization paradigms that can be applied to the fog computing environments. In Figure 5 we can see the difference between the paradigms regarding the responsibility of administration of part of the computational environment between the provider of the service and the customer.

Figure 5. Virtualization paradigm administration layers

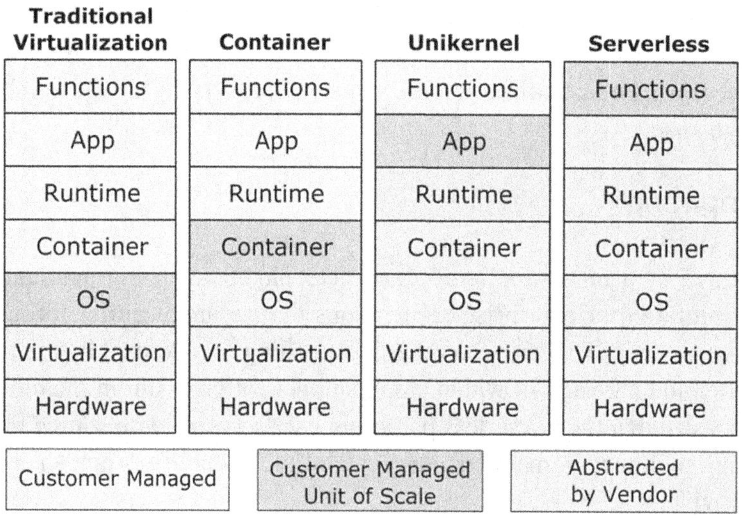

Traditional Virtualization	Container	Unikernel	Serverless
Functions	Functions	Functions	Functions
App	App	App	App
Runtime	Runtime	Runtime	Runtime
Container	Container	Container	Container
OS	OS	OS	OS
Virtualization	Virtualization	Virtualization	Virtualization
Hardware	Hardware	Hardware	Hardware

Customer Managed	Customer Managed Unit of Scale	Abstracted by Vendor

Based on the previously discussed, we can see that choosing the virtualization paradigm appropriate to each context of fog computing depends necessarily on the metrics that must be addressed. If the main issue is to maintain the isolation of resources, the ideal is still more traditional virtualization. Containers can deliver performance when that is the most critical issue. Unikernel enables high scalability to meet growing demands. Serverless can provide a response when the matter consists of resource saving or battery.

In addition to the above proposals, there are some isolated implementations of virtualizers for embedded systems that can be implemented on edge devices.

SPUMONE (Multiplexing one into two) consists of a lightweight virtualization layer that provides a hybrid operating system environment that is composed of a Real-Time Operating System that runs on a General Purpose Operating System. SPUMONE was designed with three primary goals: to enable minimal modification in the guest operating system through paravirtualization; the hypervisor should be as light as possible; operating systems should be able to reboot without interfering with the others. This proposal supports SH-4 architecture and virtualizes only the processor (Kanda, Yumura, Kinebuchi, Makijima, & Nakajima, 2008).

XtratuM was developed for RISC and ARM architectures and consists of a hypervisor specially designed for mission-critical real-time embedded systems. XtratuM was developed based on the following requirements: data structures are stationary to allow better control of the resources used; the code is not preemptive to make the system fast and straightforward; the VMs manage the peripherals.

EDGE COMPUTING INTEGRATION

Cloud computing paradigm for years provisioned effective computational power supply-chain to the market. However, due to its centralized gateway design (Fig. 6), the increasing network traffic and IoT exponential data production growth in edge side defined the need for cloud alternative solutions. In order to support this new and volatile market, the industry made an effort to find efficient ways to provide services with reduced latency and data access barriers.

Figure 6. Cloud Computing paradigm

The statement defined Edge Computing paradigm, which proposes data storage and processing in distributed servers through the network edge. This intermediate layer aims to make possible preparation, analysis and, in specific cases, the process of data generated from edge devices before its transmission to the cloud. Besides, Edge Computing is not intended to substitute the actual Cloud Computing paradigm, but complement it by offloading its heavy single gateway design and allowing the execution of real-time IoT applications, once the model mitigates the significant demand for faster communication and processing (Bonomi, Milito, Natarajan, & Zhu, 2014; Morabito, Petrolo, Loscri, & Mitton, 2018).

Therefore, Edge Computing implementation benefits include (1) privacy enhancement by the possibility of preprocessing and filter data locally (2) cloud outage mask (3) highly responsive cloud services (Satyanarayanan, Lewis, Morris, Simanta, Boleng, & Ha, 2013) . However, in IoT heterogeneous environment not only the privilege of upload and request in fast speed is needed, but also interoperability, scalability, hardware abstraction and elasticity. For those reasons, the proposal of Lightweight Virtualization application in edge-driven IoT has been discussed.

Before entering Edge Computing demands of Lightweight Virtualization, we have to comprehend its implementation challenges:

- **Programmability:** Edge Computing platform heterogeneity characterizes different runtime power along the network (Bonomi, Milito, Natarajan, & Zhu, 2014; Awadam, 2018). It raises questions about what method could resolve deployment for Edge Computing paradigm, considering the requirement of applications capable of conducting real-time requisitions by defining on what nodes in area computation should occur.

- **Standardization of Communication Protocols:** Having multiples systems and devices working together is hard to establish a network pattern between them. Some ecosystems have their protocols, difficulting integration among other devices. At the same time, how they would identify each device beyond MAC address and IP address still to be defined.

- **Data Abstraction:** Cloud current environment embeds information composition and treatment strategy, providing relevant functionalities to data analytics. However, at the same time, it turns the entire solution gamma, to a certain degree, addicted to its resources. In the Edge Computing approach, data abstraction issues comprise innovative ways to grant equivalent or higher-level analytics delivery with active data edge filtering.

- **Service Management:** It should have four fundamental features: differentiation, extensibility, isolation, and reliability. The distinction means that every device is unique and for that should be treated differently. Extensibility is the capacity to absorbing new devices under the same network and devices be replaced by others. Isolation means that located failures should not affect the whole system, as also every device on the network should be integrated with others but the private info is protected. Reliability of the system, managing as many devices as possible, for devices, presenting alerts when close to a failure, and, for data, being constant and trustable.

- **Optimization Metrics:** Due to the Edge Computing diverse computation capability, metrics have to be defined when it means management of workload distribution. The primary objective is the optimal allocation rules achievement, where latency and energy efficiency are the most relevant metrics. Latency consists of performance evaluation, considering computation time, bandwidth availability and, in a macro view, WAN delays. Energy efficiency defines the tradeoff around computation and transmission relative costs. Finally, this parameter measurement target resource usage information, which results in better cost-benefit to clients and service providers.

Edge Computing constraints observation alert to two elected Lightweight Virtualization models: unikernels and container-based virtualization. Both fulfill scalability by reducing storage and power consumption with its independence of hardware virtualization and heavy OS dependencies (Plauth, Feinbube, & Polze, 2017). However, the most significant advantage of Lightweight Virtualization for Edge Computing implementation is the defined interoperability by avoiding strict dependence on any given technology (Vashi, Ram, Modi, Verma, & Prakash, 2017).

Lightweight Virtualization comes as an Edge Computing boosting. Therefore, Edge Computing use cases are also put in higher-level. For example, Edge Computing papers often mention smart home applicability, while Lightweight Virtualization for Edge Computing impact brings to the table intelligent city discussions. Furthermore, the debate incorporates autonomous cars, augmented reality, and other higher proportion stuff.

In smart city solutions, Lightweight Virtualization for Edge Computing expands possibilities in data collected computation management domain. In particular, the proposal of a sensorial network with implemented Edge Computing and other edge elements around the city could improve real-time search for valuable data easiness, like suspects of a recent crime. The contemporary ubiquitous computing concept of interconnected processing devices is compelled as well. For example, a traditional computing architecture outage mask could concede reliability reduction to the smart traffic light scenario, once edge elements could support in case of signal unavailability or pedestrian vacancy.

The field of research and development established many concepts and directives. Those initiatives include: Internet of Vehicles - idea of a network of cars which can communicate with each other, Vehicular Cloud computing - the architectural model for Internet of Vehicles, vehicular edge computing – edge computing designed for vehicles and devices related to it, car's on-board units - hardware inside of vehicles for processing and exchange info with networks, and Vehicle-to-everything – systems for connecting with any device or node in the network that can interfere in the car, comprehends other kinds of systems as Vehicle to Vehicle.

This area can be expanded and improved by lightweight virtualization in the edge elements, allowing Vehicular Edge Computing to add functionality to vehicle to vehicle. Instead of only receive and sending info between cars, a lightweight virtualization enabled on-board unit can execute a functioning delivery by another vehicle or other edge element and vice versa. Another use of Lightweight Virtualization in Internet of Vehicles is the always perform the most recent version of an application and systems delivered over the air in the time of execution of a specific task, overcoming the complex updating process. Better management of resources can provide better autonomy for electric cars and keep some hardware dedicated to critic situations thanks to Lightweight Virtualization.

In augmented and virtual reality, high-resolution graphics help to immerse in the virtual world generated. Although, devices used for it usually don't bear the requirements to achieve the developer's desired experience. To workaround this problem, some applications use cloud computing for most heavy processing (Yu et al., 2018). The problem with cloud computing is an unwanted delay.

Therefore, the use of edge computing and lightweight virtualization can remove the need for cloud computing solutions and keep end-user hardware more simple. Not only image processing would take advantage of Lightweight Virtualization, but other elements could use the features of lightweight virtualization as multi-tenancy for multiplayer or container isolated execution for privacy.

DISCUSSION AND OPEN CHALLENGES

Edge orchestration of services is enhanced by virtualization. Services can be instantiated or released on demand, or even migrated from one device to another at runtime. It means that in times of high demand, services can maintain the quality of service agreed between provider and consumers, and in times of low demand, the services released save costs to the provider. However, there is still a research area to be explored that consists of deploying the virtualized infrastructure on the physical substrate. No specific platform allows the provider manager to instantiate a whole fog architecture from a controller.

Monitoring virtualized services is another issue that deserves attention. There are several Application Programming Interfaces that allow the management of virtualized environments that meet the requirements of edge devices. However, this heterogeneity of environments causes the provider to opt for a minimum number of solutions since most monitoring environments are designed for specific virtualizers. Also, edge devices, in general, are equipped with more limited processing and memory components than larger servers. It means that the impact of monitoring tools on such devices should be extensively studied. The most common is to define a set of few metrics to be monitored, with acceptable measurement intervals, so as not to cause device purpose overhead. It is not a trivial operation, so such monitoring characteristics should be studied and configured on a case-by-case basis.

From the point where services are moved to an environment outside the core infrastructure, such services become vulnerable to security issues such as integrity. Well-known techniques in traditional networks that culminate in a redirection of packet flow from real devices to fake devices can capture data can affect the environment of fog computing. Therefore, authentication methods between consumer and edge devices must be implemented. Also, data traffic between edge devices and the cloud is proposed to be performed through encrypted networks. These two mechanisms try to ensure reliable and fast communication between consumer and edge devices, and seamless integration between edge devices and cloud environments. However, the fog computing environment is diverse and heterogeneous, which makes it difficult to propose a single model of security and privacy.

A significant issue to be further developed when it comes to virtualization over edge devices falls on standards and regulations. Not every edge device supports any paradigm or virtualization proposal. Many processors that power devices do not offer a virtualization instruction set architecture capable of enabling and maintaining virtualizers running. While this is an architectural option for some device vendors, perhaps this is a deciding factor in choosing these devices in the coming years. For these devices, some hardware emulation tools have been developed and can be a way to keep older devices running virtualized applications.

Being a recent field in IT makes in the last years, containers technologies have emerged and become more popular because of full support by open source communities. Unikernels need mature more to competing with containers regarding development effort for portability. Containers can be adapted to carry any application, but unikernels are limited by the programming language and libraries inside of minimalistic operational system.

For its characteristics, edge devices must not store relevant data. With data stored in edge devices, you increase insecurity for them be more physical close to nodes. But dealing with a massive amount of data not stored locally can increase the time of response and consumption over broadband, and for that making it less worthwhile. Distributed data among edge devices can be impossible to reunite in one unit to process info. To solve partially, it can use volatile date locally and save reduced data centrally.

Faced with the growth prospects of the current plans for implementing NFV fundamentals in proofs of concept, some questions arise and raise resolution requirements are still not observed by telecom companies. For example, virtual customer premises equipment, where network equipment sits at the frontier between users and service providers, brings with it the properties of portability and elasticity, which will suppress costs of telecommunication companies' operational services. Network Function Virtualization comes as an alternative to that, providing the ability to dynamically deploying on-demand network services or user-services where and when needed. At the first moment it can pretend to cause an adverse impact for the telco in opening the market for more experienced players, but in the long run, it will bring them closer to users. Unikernels are more comfortable to be used than containers in this scenario for their characteristic of running on the same hypervisor as VMs with a slight impact on the infrastructure. Although, security and reliability remain as the main topic for technology questions.

When dealing with network function virtualization for edge architecture, the customization of network functions, as well as their programming in the data plane, need attention concerning the permissiveness of agents, whether these end users or network operators. Therefore, according to Network Function Virtualization portability requirements, such agents may require the installation of applications and network functions in generic devices similar to what exists in computing, in operating systems. Thus, the standardization of northbound and southbound interfaces for software defined networking need to be defined either by hardware or software in different low or high-level languages for orchestration and network management to define NFs in programming paths in wireless network cores.

Security is still a trend for embedded edge virtualization. IoT devices are going to be used in large scale in industrial and household applications. Such devices are more susceptible to hacker attacks than any other connected devices in the network. Therefore, methods to improve security must be utilized for the embedded hypervisors. For example, a secure boot process must be implemented to ensure the authenticity of the hypervisor and VMs.

When we work on server virtualization, VMs on the same host can perform various services for different users without any association among them. On the contrary, embedded systems are customized devices with a defined purpose. Consequently, VMs on an embedded hypervisor would play different services to achieve a common aim. As a result, the VMs must interact using the hypervisor interface mechanism. Consequently, more effective and secure communication services must be introduced.

Multicore processors are broadly utilized for embedded devices. Therefore, the hypervisor must be designed to work on a multicore platform. However, multicore support adds parallel execution at the hypervisor's kernel, which requires synchronization primitives. It increases the hypervisor's kernel complexity significantly, and it can impact on performance issues. Therefore, the port to multicore processors must be prudently designed (Morabito et al., 2018).

FUTURE RESEARCH DIRECTIONS

Virtualized edge computing is a deployed computing resource on the margins of the business, a recent trend of decentralization that promises many changes in how IoT will interact with the cloud, especially remote facilities away from data centers, as is the case officer, retail stores, factories, and others. Several works argue that edge computing would not be an innovation, but it would be a departure from the cloud the return of traditional models of computing distribution. However, most of them overlook the fact that with the Internet of Things and extensive device connectivity, this departure from the cloud does not mean a setback in digital transformation, but a new one. This computational model is already widely used in monitoring network security and detecting threats. When failures are detected at marginal points on the network, these network streams or devices can be quarantined, which ensures that internal systems are not compromised.

Virtualization on edge computing presents a series of critical future directions and open challenges for the IT area, including:

- Proper operation and maintenance for sensors and other mobile devices deployed at remote sites.
- Need for structured security and able to ensure that remote devices are not compromised.
- The requirement by companies that IT professionals and operators be trained to work with virtualization on IoT and edge devices.
- The importance of constant revisions in business processes that use virtualization on edge and IoT.
- Indispensability to establish adequate bandwidth so that data of concern to the business, collected by edge devices, reach the areas where they are needed.

Understanding these characteristics is essential to understanding the importance that virtualization on edge computing has for the IT market and the changes that this concept may pose to IT professionals. When we look at the growth of mobile device usage, it is impossible not to take into account that the large volume of data produced is far away from corporate headquarters at points considered to be of organizational advantage outside the core servers.

Therefore, the movement of organizations towards lightweight virtualized edge computing is a shift towards the devices that produce the most significant volume of information, ensuring faster data processing than would be possible if data were to be transported to data centers. In this way, lightweight virtualization provides the scalable and secure environment required to process such a large volume of data in real time.

The importance of IoT to the operational area is another important reason for the relevance of the virtualization on edge devices, which allow the strategic application of these platforms, turning to the automation of machines and alerts in the management of problems with the network, equipment, and infrastructure.

REFERENCES

Awada, U. (2018). CMS: Container Orchestration Across Multi-region Clouds.

Baldini, I., Castro, P., Chang, K., Cheng, P., Fink, S., Ishakian, V., & Suter, P. (2017). Serverless computing: Current trends and open problems. *Research Advances in Cloud Computing*, 1-20.

Barham, P., Dragovic, B., Fraser, K., Hand, S., Harris, T., Ho, A., & Warfield, A. (2003). Xen and the art of virtualization. *Operating Systems Review*, *37*(5), 164–177. doi:10.1145/1165389.945462

Bonomi, F., Milito, R., Natarajan, P., & Zhu, J. (2014). Fog Computing: A Platform for Internet of Things and Analytics. In *Big Data and Internet of Things: A Roadmap for Smart Environments* (pp. 169-186).

Bremler-Barr, A., Harchol, Y., Hay, D., & Koral, Y. (2014). Deep packet inspection as a service. In *Proceedings of the 10th ACM International on Conference on emerging Networking Experiments and Technologies* (pp. 271-282). New York: ACM.

Broido, A. (2001). Analysis of RouteViews BGP data: Policy atoms.

Chiosi, M., Clarke, D., Willis, P., Reid, A., Feger, J., Bugenhagen, M., & Benitez, J. (2012). Network functions virtualisation: An introduction, benefits, enablers, challenges and call for action. In *SDN and OpenFlow World Congress*.

Galante, G., & Bona, L. C. E. D. (2012). A survey on cloud computing elasticity. In *Proceedings of the 2012 IEEE/ACM Fifth International Conference on Utility and Cloud Computing* (pp. 263-270). 10.1109/UCC.2012.30

Kanda, W., Yumura, Y., Kinebuchi, Y., Makijima, K., & Nakajima, T. (2008). Spumone: Lightweight cpu virtualization layer for embedded systems. In *Proceedings of the IEEE/IFIP International Conference* on *Embedded and Ubiquitous Computing* (Vol. 1, pp. 144-151). IEEE. 10.1109/EUC.2008.157

Kuenzer, S., Ivanov, A., Manco, F., Mendes, J., Volchkov, Y., Schmidt, F., & Huici, F. (2017). Unikernels Everywhere: The Case for Elastic CDNs. *ACM SIGPLAN Notices*, *52*(7), 15–29. doi:10.1145/3140607.3050757

Masmano, M., Ripoll, I., Crespo, A., & Metge, J. (2009). Xtratum: a hypervisor for safety critical embedded systems. In *Proceedings of the 11th Real-Time Linux Workshop* (pp. 263-272).

Mitake, H., Kinebuchi, Y., Courbot, A., & Nakajima, T. (2011). Coexisting real-time OS and general purpose OS on an embedded virtualization layer for a multicore processor. In *Proceedings of the 2011 ACM Symposium on Applied Computing* (pp. 629-630). New York: ACM. 10.1145/1982185.1982322

Morabito, R. (2017). Virtualization on internet of things edge devices with container technologies: A performance evaluation. *IEEE Access*, *5*, 8835–8850. doi:10.1109/ACCESS.2017.2704444

Morabito, R., Cozzolino, V., Ding, A. Y., Beijar, N., & Ott, J. (2018). Consolidate IoT edge computing with lightweight virtualization. *IEEE Network*, *32*(1), 102–111. doi:10.1109/MNET.2018.1700175

Morabito, R., Petrolo, R., Loscrì, V., & Mitton, N. (2018). LEGIoT: A Lightweight Edge Gateway for the Internet of Things. *Future Generation Computer Systems*, *81*, 1–15. doi:10.1016/j.future.2017.10.011

Plauth, M., Feinbube, L., & Polze, A. (2017, September). A performance survey of lightweight virtualization techniques. In *Proceedings of the European Conference on Service-Oriented and Cloud Computing* (pp. 34-48). Cham: Springer.

Satyanarayanan, M. (2017). The emergence of edge computing. *Computer*, *50*(1), 30–39. doi:10.1109/MC.2017.9

Satyanarayanan, M., Lewis, G., Morris, E., Simanta, S., Boleng, J., & Ha, K. (2013). The Role of Cloudlets in Hostile Environments. *IEEE Pervasive Computing*, *12*(4), 40–49. doi:10.1109/MPRV.2013.77

Server., B.R.A. (2004). Technical Report DSL Forum TR-092.

Shi, W., Cao, J., Zhang, Q., Li, Y., & Xu, L. (2016). Edge computing: Vision and challenges. *IEEE Internet of Things Journal*, *3*(5), 637–646. doi:10.1109/JIOT.2016.2579198

Shi, W., & Dustdar, S. (2016). The Promise of Edge Computing. *Computer*, *49*(5), 78–81. doi:10.1109/MC.2016.145

Vaquero, L. M., & Rodero-Merino, L. (2014). Finding your way in the fog: Towards a comprehensive definition of fog computing. *Computer Communication Review*, *44*(5), 27–32. doi:10.1145/2677046.2677052

Vashi, S., Ram, J., Modi, J., Verma, S., & Prakash, C. (2017). Internet of Things (IoT): A vision, architectural elements, and security issues. In *Proceedings of the International Conference on I-SMAC (IoT in Social, Mobile, Analytics and Cloud)*. 10.1109/I-SMAC.2017.8058399

Villamizar, M., Garcés, O., Ochoa, L., Castro, H., Salamanca, L., Verano, M., ... Lang, M. (2017). Cost comparison of running web applications in the cloud using monolithic, microservice, and aws lambda architectures. *Service Oriented Computing and Applications*, *11*(2), 233–247. doi:10.100711761-017-0208-y

Xavier, M. G., Neves, M. V., Rossi, F. D., Ferreto, T. C., Lange, T., & De Rose, C. A. (2013). Performance evaluation of container-based virtualization for high performance computing environments. In *Proceedings of the 21st Euromicro International Conference* on *Parallel, Distributed and Network-Based Processing (PDP)* (pp. 233-240). 10.1109/PDP.2013.41

Xavier, M. G., Neves, M. V., Rossi, F. D., Ferreto, T. C., Lange, T., & De Rose, C. A. (2013). Performance evaluation of container-based virtualization for high performance computing environments. In *Proceedings of the 21st Euromicro International Conference* on *Parallel, Distributed and Network-Based Processing (PDP)* (pp. 233-240). 10.1109/PDP.2013.41

Yu, W., Liang, F., He, X., Hatcher, W., Lu, C., Lin, J., & Yang, X. (2018). A Survey on the Edge Computing for the Internet of Things. *IEEE Access*, *6*, 6900–6919. doi:10.1109/ACCESS.2017.2778504

Chapter 14
Edge–of–Things Computing–Based Smart Healthcare System

Diana Yacchirema
Escuela Politécnica Nacional, Ecuador

Carlos Palau
Universitat Politècnica de València, Spain

Manuel Esteve
Universitat Politècnica de València, Spain

ABSTRACT

Any delay introduced in healthcare applications could critically affect the health of patients. Edge computing paradigm has been introduced recently as an alternative to develop such applications, where a rapid response is necessary to ensure the immediate assistance of patients when they need help. In this chapter, the authors propose an edge-of-things computing-based architecture, which illustrates the benefits of the realization of IoT under edge computing approach. The proposed architecture offers significant advantages: 1) it reduces the latency time in the data transmission for processing and analysis; 2) it improves the response time of the delivery of notifications or emergency alerts; 3) it provides real-time processing and big data analysis in the proximity of data sources; 4) it enables interoperability between heterogeneous devices; and 5) it provides security and QoS in the data transmission. The usefulness and relevance of the proposed architecture is evaluated through the implementation of a smart healthcare system applied to a medical case study.

INTRODUCTION

The advancement and proliferation of communication technologies and the growing presence of a variety of wearable devices with communication, identification, sensing and actuating capabilities, have enabled the Internet of things (IoT) to rapidly gain ground as a key research theme both in the academic

DOI: 10.4018/978-1-6684-5700-9.ch014

institutions and industrial organizations, notably in agriculture, logistic and healthcare fields. In this latter field, due to the fast-growing numbers of elderly persons over 65.

According to the World Health Organization (WHO), by 2050, the current elderly population (8.5%) will increase, representing 20% of the world's population (He, Goodkind, & Kowal, 2016). On the basis of these trends, many countries are adopting healthy aging policies with the aim of helping the elderly to lead independent and active lives. In particular, ensuring active and healthy aging (AHA) of the elderly is one of the greatest challenges, but also a great opportunity for society in the upcoming decades. The notion of AHA has been lately characterized as a broad concept, which seeks to improve the quality of life (QoL) of the elderly people as they age, optimizing opportunities for health, participation and security (Bousquet, Kuh, Bewick, Standberg, & Farrell et al., 2015). In healthcare, the AHA brings with it some main concerns about the growth in social demand and financial feasibility of traditional healthcare systems. Therefore, pervasive solutions that enable the delivering patient-focused services of high quality is highly desired. To achieve these ends, new computing approaches have been developed.

Over the past few years, the integration of IoT and cloud computing often simply referred to as CloudIoT, which have contributed to the implementation of various application scenarios such as smart transportation, cities and communities, homes, logistic, environment and healthcare. The adoption of the CloudIoT paradigm in healthcare scenarios offer many opportunities, particularly in simplifying healthcare processes and enhancing the quality of the medical services by enabling the collaboration between the different entities engaged (Botta, de Donato, Persico, & Pescapé, 2014).

In particular, IoT enables the sensing and processing of biomedical signals and physiological parameters through a variety of devices, which are interconnected through the Internet with a view so they can work with other connected devices and share information between them. The interconnection of devices generates a large amount of data that require scalable computing infrastructure for further processing and analysis (Dastjerdi & Buyya, 2016). In such context, the adoption of cloud computing represents a promising solution for providing healthcare sensor data on-demand and scalable storage processing and analyzing services efficiently. However, cloud computing is not especially suited for data processing in latency-sensitive solutions, as in the case of healthcare solutions.

There are issues in the traditional CloudIoT- based architectures, which can have a direct negative impact on the health of patients with urgent needs, who need to be assisted on time. For example, in emergency situations, a delay in the latency caused by the transfer of data from the sensors to the cloud may produce fatal consequences for the patient. In addition, the processing and analysis of data in a server hosted in the cloud prevents the timely detection of unusual events in the health of patients, and the report of appropriate alerts to the professionals involved in their care (i.e., caregivers, health professionals, etc). Moreover, the majority of end nodes (i.e., sensors) are resource-constrained devices, i.e., class 0 devices. Class 0 devices are characterized by constraints in memory (10KiB of RAM and 100KiB of flash) and processing capabilities (Bormann, 2014). These devices have severe constraints to communicate with the Internet and send the data directly to the cloud or store records for a very long time in local memory, so they usually connect to gateway-like devices for internet communication.

The alternative approach proposes the use of an intermediate edge layer, able to process the data at the edge of the network, to improve the efficiency of CloudIoT- based architectures. An intelligent use of this layer can lead to a sufficient performance to meet the strict requirements of health care applications, without using a technological infrastructure of great features that are currently achieved in the cloud.

In this sense, we propose, edge-IoTA, an architecture based on IoT and edge to support remote health monitoring, in order to achieve:

- Reduce the latency in the transmission of data for processing and analysis.
- Reduce the response time for the delivery of notifications or emergency alerts.
- Real–time processing and big data analysis in the proximity of data sources.
- Interoperability between heterogeneous devices in terms of protocols, communication technologies and data format.
- Security and QoS in the data transmission.

The edge-IoTA architecture designed and implemented consists mainly of three layers shown in Figure 1. The IoT layer is the basis of the entire system, responsible for collecting physiological data from patients through different sensors integrated in IoT nodes, and forwarding them to the edge layer. The edge layer is responsible for processing and analyzing health data in a timely manner. To do this, it implements several services at the edge of the network. Finally, the Cloud layer is responsible for data management (i.e., storage, visualization and creation of supervised learning models).

In order to evaluate the functionality and the real feasibility of the architecture, an intelligent health system has been implemented to support the monitoring of metabolic syndrome for patients with diabetes. Additionally, the performance of the system was evaluated in terms of the latency time introduced in the transmission of data and in the sending of notifications. The results obtained highlighted the advantages of the proposed architecture compared with traditional systems based on CloudIoT.

The rest of this document is structured as follows: Section 2 describes and analyses the related works on IoT, cloud computing and edge computing for health care systems. Section 3 describes in detail the architecture of the edge-of-things computing-based smart healthcare system, and the functionalities of each of its modules. Based on this architecture, the section 4 describes the implementation of a smart healthcare system for metabolic syndrome monitoring for patients with diabetes, as well as the results of the evaluation of the system's performance in terms of latency time. Finally, Section 5 concludes the document and describes main future research directions.

RELATED WORK

The use of IoT technologies is becoming increasingly popular, especially in the field of health care, where personalized monitoring of health and continuous monitoring have become essential to improve the QoL and the well-being of patients. In fact, IoT from an empowering perspective is a cornerstone of the digital transformation of healthcare. According to recent estimates (Aruba Networks, 2017), almost two thirds (60%) of health care organizations worldwide have started to implement IoT technology and connect IoT devices to their networks and by 2019, 87% of these organizations are expected to adopt this ubiquitous technology. The continuous monitoring of patients was identified as the most impressive use case in the health industry with 64%. In addition, the global smart health market value is expected to reach USD 169.30 billion by 2020. The IoT benefits achieved in the health industry report, an 80% increase in innovation, a 73% saving in costs and an 83% increase in commercial efficiency. These figures clearly show that healthcare is one of the most appealing areas for the development of IoT.

The computational cost, storage and analysis capabilities required by the huge data generated in the healthcare environment by IoT devices or hospital information systems, have led the way for the adoption of cloud computing in the health industry (Sanjay P. Ahuja, Sindhu Mani, 2012). Cloud Computing facilitates the storing, processing and analysis of the data collected (e.g., electronic health records, doctor's references, insurance information, test results, prescriptions, etc) through the provisioning of computing capabilities in a completely dynamic way, which is characterized by adaptability, flexibility and scalability, without the need to invest in IT infrastructure, implement or manage any software or hardware (Rolim et al., 2010).

In recent years, several solutions based on CloudIoT have been proposed to support health care services. Yang *et al.* (2016) proposed a monitoring system for electrocardiogram (ECG) signals. The ECG data is collected using a wearable monitoring node and transmitted directly to the cloud via a Wi-Fi connection. Servers hosted in the cloud are responsible for storing, processing and displaying ECG data. Hussain *et al.* (2014) proposed a system to analyze lifestyle through the extraction of sensory data from a mobile phone. Big data technologies such as Hadoop and MapReduce are used at the cloud level to provide information on the lifestyle trends of the user. Muhammad *et al.* (2017), proposed a system to monitor the pathology of the voice of the elderly. The processing of the data is done in the cloud using a learning machine classifier. Despite the multiple benefits derived from CloudIoT solutions in the connected care ecosystem, the need for context-aware knowledge, interoperability, and strong temporal requirements in data processing are the main limitations of these solutions. These problems are very critical for health care and AHA scenarios where a correct and timely response to respond immediately to certain emergency events can result in saving a life.

With the advent of edge computing, edge services (i.e., data storage, data processing and data analysis) will be mainly implemented as software components executing on edge computing devices located closest to patients, hospital and clinic facilities. Edge computing has been used in literature to refer to fog computing (Bonomi, Milito, Zhu, & Addepalli, 2012). Both computing approaches enable processing capabilities closely to the source of data. However, fog computing pushes the intelligence in the local area network while edge computing locates it inside the devices themselves (i.e., it focuses more toward the things side).

In this regard, many research works have been carried out. Shi *et al.* (2016) define edge computing as an innovative distributed cloud architecture that allows the calculation to be performed at the proximity of data sources. Under the paradigm of edge computing, some application services are handled by an edge node in the edge of the network and others are handled by a remote server in the cloud. This type of distributed analysis offers great potential to overcome the challenges of medical care, improving the effectiveness and efficiency of health monitoring.

Being motivated by this, Gia *et al.* (2015), proposed a fog computing-based ubiquitous health monitoring system for electrocardiogram (ECG) monitoring. The main goal of this system is to assist healthcare professionals in the diagnosis of cardiac diseases through processing ECG signals at the edge network. The system uses a fog node equipped with several adapters to support the connectivity of heterogeneous devices through different network technologies, such as Wi-Fi, Ethernet, BLE and 6LoWPAN, and provides other services as embedded data mining, distributed storage, location awareness and emergency notification. The result shows that the latency of transmission of ECG data from sensor to fog node via Wi-Fi, achieve a reduction of 3% to 48, 5% (depending on the size of the sample) by moving computation from cloud to the fog. However, the notifications are sent from edge network to remote cloud, where finally these messages are referred to the user's devices, it increases the communication latency and the burden in the network infrastructure. As a result, the end user may experience a poor experience while the immediate help required for the patient might not be met in emergency situations. In the same direction, Rahmani *et al.* (2018), proposed a fog-assisted system for early warning score (EWS) health monitoring. A system designed to monitor patients with acute illnesses. The authors leveraged and implemented the concept fog computing in a geo-distributed intermediary layer between sensor nodes and cloud, which is formed by smart gateways. The gateways enable the seamless communication between different sensors working on distinct networks and standards (i.e., technical interoperability), such as 6LoWPAN, Wi-Fi, Bluetooth 2.0. Moreover, these gateways provide higher-level services, such as local data processing, local storage, notification sending, mobility and security at the edge network. These results in terms of latency time are similar to Gia *et al.* (2015). Such results show that the improvement of response time is between 3.5% and 48.5% by performing the computation at the edge network. However, this solution does not support Big Data edge analysis. Moreover, the authors do not demonstrate how semantic interoperability is achieved. Dubey *et al.* (2016), proposed a service-oriented architecture based on fog computing to monitor the speech motor disorders and ECG. This system facilitates collection, storage, and analysis of healthcare data at the edge network through a smart gateway. This gateway gathers speech signals from the Android smartwatch through Bluetooth connection. The data analysis of the solution is justified by the ability to mine, filter and reduction the ECG data and speech data in order to reduce the data transmission from fog to the cloud. The results show a 98% and 99% reduction in the size of ECG data and speech data, respectively. However, this solution does not provide QoS and security mechanism in the data transmission and not support real-time big data analysis. Cao *et al.* (2015), proposed a pervasive health monitoring system known FAST to monitor fall for stroke mitigation. FAST is based on both the cloud and fog computing model. It distributes the analytics throughout the network by splitting the fall detection task between the fog devices (smartphone attached to the user) and the server in the cloud in order to improve the accuracy and reduce the false alarms. The prototype system was implemented on a smartphone and Amazon AWS. In particular, the front–end module is performed at the smartphone and it is in charge of data pre-processing by filter fall data in order to remove many false alarms, while the fall detection is performed in the cloud using Non-Linear Analyzer. This work supports one of the most features of the edge solutions, and Big Data edge analysis. Nevertheless, this solution is does not support QoS and security mechanisms in the data transmissions. Finally, Verma *et al.* (2018), proposed an IoT system for remote patient health monitoring by using fog computing paradigm. This system provides embedded data mining, distributed storage, and notification services at the edge of the network by a fog node provided by Amazon. Bayesian belief network classifier is used in the fog node to detect the unusual events in the patient's health. Additionally, the fog node enables the security of data transmission among the different entities of the system by SSL protocol. However, this solution does not provide interoperability and QoS. Additionally, the system performance has not been evaluated.

One service of edge computing that could be particularly useful for healthcare is real-time big data analysis. Instead of waiting until the patient can to go to a medical facility, every period of time to upload their health data (e.g., heart data) from their wearable devices (e.g. smart bangle) or mobile phones, waiting another additional week until the data can be analyzed and several days until the care manager can send an email when an abnormality is detected, edge nodes can locally collect, classify, and analyze the patient data, and send an alert in real time to the health care provider when an unusual pattern arises. In addition, the edge nodes can also provide context information of geographical location of sensors, patients as well as of the smart environments where the emergence took place. In this context, a health professional treating a patient with their mobile device or tablet will be able to access patient data into the analytics platform where these are displayed in near real-time. Thus, patients won't have to wait anymore for analytic results; this can significantly reduce the hospital re-admissions or the emergency department visit rate. In addition, these data can be merged with other data geographically distributed and belonging to multiple providers involved in a patient's care (hospitals, specialized medical institutions, duty pharmacies, emergency centers, ambulatory centers) by creating virtual views of shared data (Shi et al., 2016). Which can be exposed to the end users through a common interface, upon which several complex services can be built to support the comprehensive care of patients' health. These services can be provided by collaborative level participants in ways that can help patient care, however, the calculation is only done locally in the participant's edge nodes, so that the privacy and integrity of the data can be guaranteed. Relative to this context, big data provides advanced techniques and technologies to enable the analysis of the health data. Big data goes even further size and volume to embrace such characteristics as variety, velocity, and, with respect specifically to health care, value. Unarguably, value is the most important V or dimension of Big Data. The value generated from big data analysis provides intelligent insight, and perform informed and calculated decisions for healthcare professionals, in turn this derives in high benefits for patients.

In this chapter, we address the shortcomings of the previous works on interoperability, local processing, real-time big data analysis, security and QoS through intelligent use of edge devices. We present an innovative three-layer architecture for smart healthcare monitoring.

EDGE-OF-THINGS COMPUTING-BASED SMART HEALTHCARE SYSTEM ARCHITECTURE

In this section, we describe edge-IoTA, a computing architecture designed for IoT systems that takes advantage of the edge computing paradigm for remote monitoring of health in indoor environments. The main motivation for developing such architecture is real-time processing and analysis of health data, in which the requirements such as low latency, security, QoS are acquiring greater significance. Therefore, the integration and prudent use of an edge device can play a key role in addressing some limitations of traditional CloudIoT-based architectures as noted in the previous section. Figure 1 illustrates the use of the edge-IoTA architecture proposed in health care scenarios applied in smart cities, in which users can be patients of a hospital, elderly people in their homes, or emergency centers. The edge resources can locally collect, process and analyse in a timely manner the data coming from several sensor nodes. In these scenarios, because the data is processed at the edge of the network, based on the results, rapid control loops such as emergency notifications in real time to professionals involved in patient care or actions on the environment are feasible using the edge computing model.

In particular, as shown in Figure 1, the proposed architecture consists of three functional layers (IoT/Edge/Cloud). The IoT layer obtains and aggregates data from multiple heterogeneous IoT devices that employ different communication technologies, such as ZigBee, 6LoWPAN, WiFi or LoRa, and transfers them to the edge layer. The edge layer represents the connection between the cloud layer and IoT physical devices. This layer is responsible for providing connectivity and interoperability, local storage, processing, real-time big data analysis, emergency notification, QoS and security services through an edge node. Finally, the cloud layer is responsible for the storage of the processed data, as well as the visualization of them through a web application via a graphical user interface (GUI), which converts the processed information into rich content to support the medical decision making. In addition, this layer is responsible for sharing data with other applications or environments.

Figure 1. Three-layer edge-IoTA architecture

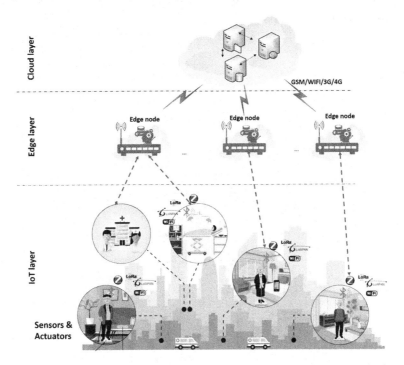

IoT Layer

The IoT layer is the basis of the entire system, since it acquires data from different heterogeneous sources; environment sensors strategically placed in the patient's home, wearable sensors located over the patient's skin or sensors embedded in mobile devices worn by the patient. These sensors acquire data of multiple physiological and context parameters (such as heart rate, blood pressure, blood sugar, glucose, respiratory rate, air pollution, weight, GPS location, etc) and transmit them to edge nodes through various network technologies and protocols, such as: Wi-Fi, BLE, 6LowPAN, ZigBee and LoRA.

Edge Layer

As edge computing drives intelligence to the edge of the network, smart devices located in local area networks play a predominant role in this modern architecture. These devices are often used as smart IoT gateways (Yacchirema, Palau, & Esteve, 2016) or to support the interoperability of heterogeneous IoT devices in ubiquitous environments (Yacchirema, Palau, & Esteve, 2016). In our opinion, this interoperability between heterogeneous devices can be expanded to allow several services at the edge of the network, in order to reduce the latency time in the data transmission and the response time required for sending emergency notifications. The edge layer, which is represented by an IoT edge gateway has a double objective. On one hand, it abstracts the heterogeneity of the data format, communication technologies and protocols used by the devices in the IoT layer for integrating them and making them interoperable. On the other hand, it performs real-time processing and analysis of data, and transmits the result to the cloud layer. Figure 2 shows the functional blocks and the constituent components of the IoT edge gateway architecture.

Figure 2. IoT edge gateway architecture

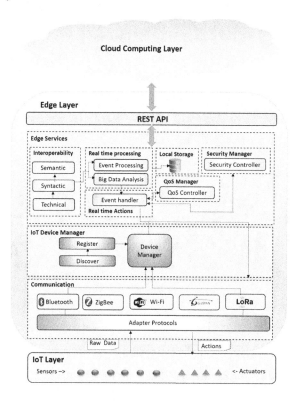

REST API Interface

Through this northbound interface, the IoT edge gateway can directly communicate with the cloud layer services, in particular, this interface translates the execution requirements of the IoT edge gateway.

IoT Device Manager Block

It is able to provide the dynamic search of IoT devices (sensors and actuators) registered in the architecture, as well as register capabilities, and retrieve information about them to be used by other architecture's components. Two distinct functional sub-modules are implemented by the IoT Device Manager.

- **Discovery:** It allows access to features of the IoT devices connected to the IoT edge gateway and returns a list of discovered active IoT devices and of new and unknown devices that request to connect with the IoT edge gateway.
- **Register:** It enables the register of the IoT devices towards the IoT edge gateway prior to sending or receiving any data or commands. The register includes the Device-ID, type and attributes

related to each sensor and actuator (such as the communication protocol used and the device's physical address).

Edge Services Block

Edge Services block has the capability to provide various services at the edge network (i.e., Communication and interoperability, data processing, Big Data analysis, data storage, security and privacy protection of data transmission and management of quality of service) depending on the requirements of specific application context.

Communication and Interoperability Module (CIM)

As the number of IoT devices grows in modern medical care, one of the main challenges for the adoption of IoT in the health industry has to do with communication and interoperability. IoT devices from different manufacturers can not necessarily talk to each other or focus on a specific purpose and are isolated from the rest of the world. In this context, this module allows seamless interoperability between heterogeneous underlying devices and communication technologies, from communication and transparent integration of devices to the exchange of data generated by them, in order to facilitate the medical decision making of a faster and more efficient way. In this work, the edge IoT edge gateway facilitates three levels of interoperability.

- **Technical interoperability:** In our implementation of the IoT edge gateway, technical interoperability is achieved through an adaptation layer that i) coordinates the communication tasks through the different adapters incorporated in it, and ii) resolves the incompatibility problem of different protocols and the conflict of messages between different networks through the encapsulation of the data sent by the origin protocol in a format compatible with the destination communication protocol.
- **Syntactic interoperability:** Given that heterogeneity is also present in the different data formats supported by IoT devices. According to the type of data collected, the IoT edge gateway maps the data structure of the IoT devices to a common data standard defined by the system architecture and vice versa; using high-level transfer syntax such as JSON and XML, among others.
- **Semantic interoperability:** Ensuring the understanding of information and knowledge, in a readable and interpretative manner, is of vital importance to facilitate the exchange and automatic reuse of information. In this sense, ontologies can facilitate the semantic notation of the collected data, manage access and extract knowledge of this information. The IoT edge gateway maps the structure of the processed data to a contextualized information model compatible with an ontological vocabulary to define the types and the relationship between them. At the same time, it enables the use and sharing of data with other systems or external health applications.

Data Storage Module (DSM)

Health data plays a vital role in the diagnosis and support of the treatment of diseases. Therefore, data from the IoT layer is needed to be stored temporarily for processing and analysis. The data includes the time and value of the parameter monitored. Once the data is processed, they are sent to the cloud layer and removed from the edge layer. The storage temporarily ensures continuous service even when the connectivity between edge layer and cloud layer is unavailable.

Data Processing Module (DPM)

This module performs local processing of acquired data according to a set of previously defined rules in order to detect potential events in the monitored data, which could worsen the patient's health, such as high glucose, overweight, etc, so that the patient can receive immediate help or notifications to improve their health status.

Big Data Analysis Module (BDAM)

Since the monitored parameters can shed a lot of information about the patient's health, in addition to data processing, the analysis of this information is very useful to extract valuable insight from the collected data in order to support medical decision. In this context, Big Data algorithms and predictive analysis have great potential to support better and more efficient care in the healthcare industry. This module performs a real-time predictive analysis of the collected data using different machine learning approaches according to the application scenario. For example, a decision trees algorithm can be established to fall detection in elderly people (Yacchirema, Suárez de Puga, Palau, & Esteve, 2018). By successfully applying predictive analytics, the healthcare professionals can effectively make informed decisions, which impacts on a better health service for patients. Indeed, according to recent International Data Corporation forecasts by 2018 that up to 40% of IoT data will be analyzed at the edge of the network.

Event Handler Module (ECM)

Several risk factors can seriously threaten the health of patients, especially when patients are alone. Therefore, timely notifications and the sending of alert messages is of vital importance. Based on the results of data processing and analysis, this module triggers immediate actions with a reduced response time and latency, sending emergency notifications to the groups responsible for patient care by using a publish/subscribe architecture. Depending on the application scenario, this module also sends control commands to the actuator devices in the IoT layer.

Security Management Module (SMM)

Owing to the sensitivity and potential consequences of unauthorized access and improper handling of patient data, the security requirement in healthcare industry are of the utmost importance. In this sense, this module provides end-to-end secured communication and reliability based on SSL (Secure Socket Layer) and private key and certificates for the sending of emergency notifications and for transferring patient data to the cloud Layer, respectively.

Quality of Service Management Module (QoSMM)

Despite that health applications are sensitive to delay, each healthcare application has their own Quality of service (QoS) requirements. In this sense, this module provides several QoS levels to confirm the delivery of messages, from a non-optimal minimum level (QoS0) to a double-recognition level (QoS2), depending on network traffic class: delay sensitive traffic (e.g., delivery of a fall event) or delay tolerant traffic (e.g., delivery of the temperature measurement of the patient's home environment). In the first type of traffic, the QoS manager shall establish a QoS2 level in order to reduce the bit-error rate over the communication media and improve the packet delivery probability.

Cloud Layer

This layer is responsible for storing the processed data in order to allow its availability, visualization and the creation of Big Data models. This layer consists of three modules: Data Management, Big Data analysis Model and Graphical User Interface.

Data Management Module (DMM)

This module acts as a central repository and is responsible for managing and providing access to information from the edge layer. The DMM handles the context information as "entities" that consist of elements and attributes. In particular, it allows the creation, storage, updating and elimination of these entities, as well as the publication of these contextual information to any authorized party in the consumption of this information as external health services or applications, through operations of Publication / Subscription. In this architecture, the Big data analysis model and Graphical user interface modules (described below) subscribe to the DMM to obtain the context information of the results of the predictive analysis and of the detected events.

Big Data Analysis Model Module (BDAM)

The BDAM provides a data analysis platform to allow the creation and training of big data models. Specific machine learning approaches can be applied for this purpose. Based on the big data model, the edge layer is able to instance this model locally for the effective prediction and / or discovery of significant relationships in the monitored health data.

Graphical User Interface Module (GUIM)

The GUIM is responsible for converting the received data into rich content and displaying it. The GUIM provides easy access to data in the cloud. Health professionals and caregivers can log onto cloud to visualize the statistics and results of the processed data in real time.

CASE STUDY: IMPLEMENTATION OF AN EDGE-OF-THINGS-BASED SMART HEALTHCARE SYSTEM FOR METABOLIC SYNDROME MONITORING

In this section, in order to evaluate the functionality and robustness of the proposed architecture, an edge-based smart IoT system for metabolic syndrome monitoring is implemented using open platforms, IoT protocols and sensing technologies. First we describe the application scenario and then we detail the implementation of the system, including all its components.

Application Scenario

As people get older they run a greater risk of developing serious diseases such as diabetes and cardiovascular problems. In this context, the monitoring of the metabolic syndrome is one of the main factors that can help detect and prevent these diseases. Metabolic syndrome describes a constellation of cardiovascular risk factors and type 2 diabetes, which can occur when 3 or more than 5 factors (obesity, blood pressure, glucose, triglycerides and HDL cholesterol) exceed the allowed standard values (U.S. Department of Health and Human Services, 2004). This severity that is conferred in clinical terms to the metabolic syndrome is largely due to the fact that it is capable of increasing the risk of developing diabetes by more than 10 times and the risk of death due to cardiovascular causes by 3.5 times. Table 1 shows the inclusion criteria of the metabolic syndrome, which are considered in this system.

Table 1. Risk factors of metabolic syndrome

Risk Factors		Normal	Pre-stage	Stage 1
Blood Pressure (mm/Hg)	DBP	< 80	80-89	90-99
Glucose (mg/dl)	2h-PG	<140	140-199	>200
BMI (kg/m²)		18.5-24.9	25.0-29.9	30.0-34.9
Waist Circumference (cm)		≤ 90, ≤ 80	> 90, > 80	

To better understand, we describe to the metabolic syndrome monitoring according the following scenario.

Valentina Torres is 70 years old and she lives in Valencia City, she is slightly overweight and has been diagnosed with prediabetes. For some time she has felt a little tired and therefore went to the family doctor for a check-up. The doctor prescribes her control tests. The test results reveals that she has high a risk state for developing diabetes. As a result, the doctor suggests that she changes her lifestyle to prevent deterioration in her current health condition and the emergence of new diseases such as cardiovascular illness, which is directly related to overweight. In particular, the doctor advised her to enter a chronic disease prevention program, which is focused on remote monitoring the main risk factors associated with the metabolic syndrome through a Smart Care system. The doctor provides a set of behavioural and dietary recommendations, proposes to Valentina to undergo a period of continuous monitoring until her health status has improved. Valentina agrees that such a system will be suitable for her. The doctor registers current records for Valentina's personal data as well as BMI (weight and height), waist circumference, diastolic blood pressure (DBP) and glucose (2h-PG) measures in the system, with the aim of assessing Valentina's health status and the efficacy of treatment in the future. Moreover, the doctor provides her the devices to make periodic measurements and tells her how to use them.

System Implementation

We have implemented the architecture of the system using open standards, avoiding the technological dependence of patented solutions and favoring the personalization and development of new functionalities. In addition, our architecture advocates the use of commercial-off-the-self (COTS) devices. The system consists of four components: IoT devices, a Mobile application, IoT edge gateway and a private cloud server. Figure 3 illustrates the hardware and software components used in the system, which are described in detail as follows.

Figure 3. Hardware and software components of the implemented system

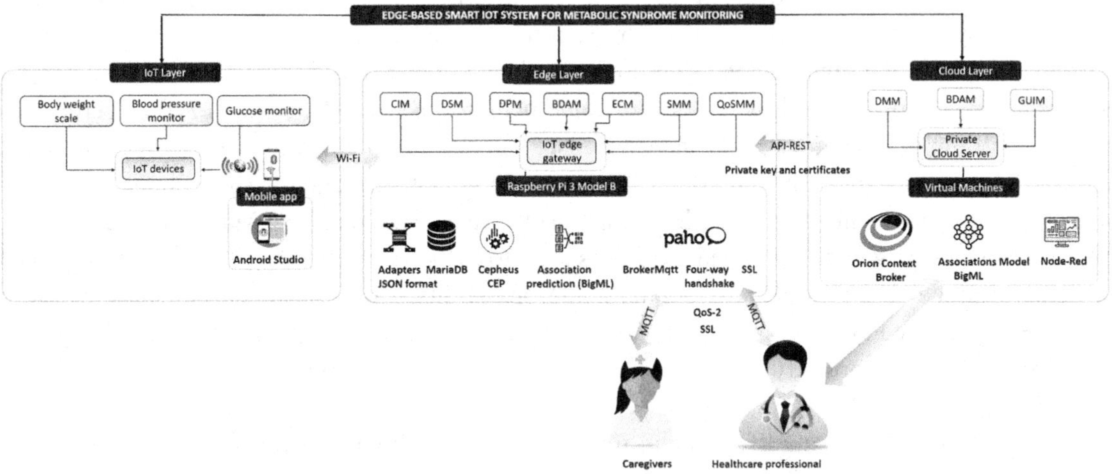

IoT Devices

IoT devices are the basis of the monitoring system. Three types of sensors were used for the monitoring of metabolic syndrome factors; a medical precision body weight scale (A & D UC-411PBT-C), a blood pressure monitor (A & D UA-851PBT-C) and a glucose monitor (iHealth Glucose). All devices are connected using the low power BLE protocol. Due to the communication limits of BLE, a smartphone was used to receive data from the sensor devices and to transmit them to the edge layer. The smartphone plays a key role as an interface between the IoT nodes and the IoT edge gateway. It also acts as an access terminal allowing patients to interact with the system.

Mobile Application

We developed a mobile application, which was installed on a Samsung S7 Edge with Exynos 8890 processor running at 2.3 GHz and 4 GB of RAM, and which supports the Android 6.0 operating system. This mobile application consists of several classes, which have been developed using Android Studio. A class called *Obesity* was implemented to treat the weight, height and waist circumference readings and calculate the BMI value. The circumference readings are entered by the patient through the application. Two other classes were used: *BloodPressure* for the administration of diastolic blood pressure (DBP) readings and *Glucose*, which treats the 2-hour (2h-PG) plasma glucose concentration readings. Finally, a class called *Broker* was implemented to subscribe to the notifications sent by the gateway and display the notifications on the screen.

IoT Edge Gateway

IoT edge gateway consists of a set of modular components written in the Python programming language, which have been implemented in a Raspberry Pi3 (RPI3) model B. RPi3 is widely used for developing IoT applications due to its powerful hardware, e.g., the 64-bits Broadcom BCM2837 Quad core (ARM Cortex-A53) SoC operating at 1.2 Ghz with 512kB shared L2 cache, a range of interfaces integrated, i.e., 802.11n wireless LAN, Bluetooth 4 and Ethernet. The RPI3 is equipped with additional communication modules to allow the seamless technical interoperability of heterogeneous devices that employ different wireless connections communication technologies such as ZigBee, Wi-Fi, 6lowPAN and Bluetooth. In this work, two networks of wireless sensors are implemented; a Bluetooth network to connect the smartphone with all the devices involved in the used case, and a Wi-Fi network formed by the smartphone and the RPI3. Once the gateway obtains the data from the sensors through the smartphone, a quick and convenient way to store this data is needed temporarily, the NoSQL database MariaDB is used for this purpose. Prior to storage, the JSON language was used to map the original format of the acquired data to a standard model and thus achieve syntactic interoperability. JSON has been the standard used to format the system data due to its simplicity and compatibility with multiple programming languages. The definition of a common structure before processing directly contributes to the lower consumption of resources and bandwidth.

To carry out the processing of the data, the generic Cepheus CEP enabler provided by the open Fiware platform (Fiware, 2017) is adopted in this system. The Fiware platform is composed of a set of components known as generic enablers (GEs) that offer reusable and commonly shared functionalities to facilitate the development of intelligent applications and services based on the open OpenStack standard. The CEP receives the data in JSON format and processes this data according to the rules defined in the system (Table 1) with the aim of detecting unusual events that affect the health of the monitored patients. The system detects an unusual event when the monitored parameters exceed the threshold defined in the pre-status or status 1 stage. The CEP verifies that the conditions for each measurement value are met. This direct processing of data at the edge of the network improves the efficiency of the system while contributing to the rapid delivery of notifications that are necessary for the immediate assistance of patients

In this case study, to perform the data analysis, the BDAM uses a Big Data model based on an unsupervised automatic learning algorithm of associations. The algorithms of associations seek possible relationships between the different values of the fields that occur with a higher frequency than the random case. It is important to point out that the associations that are sought are not correlations, but concurrences, that is, that "field 1" takes the "value 1" happens frequently when the "field 2" takes the "value 2". In these cases, we say that association rules can be established, which reveal facts that happen in common within a certain set of data. Therefore, the type of rules expressed by associations have the following format:

{Antecedent} => {Consequent}

The association discovery model is used to identify statistically significant relationships between different risk factors, with the aim of supporting the medical decision-making in an efficient manner. This model has been selected because it is one of the most used techniques in decision support processes. In addition, the construction of an association model has, in general, low computational cost (Joel Pinho Lucas, 2010). Note that the choice of model will depend on the application scenario.

The BDAM creates a local instance of the model to predict the associations (antecedent-consequent), so these predictions can be made independently in the edge network without having to send the data to the cloud layer for analysis. The Big data model is created and trained in the cloud (as described below). Figure 4 graphically illustrates three instances of the associations discovered from the monitored data. Instance C indicates that if the patient has a BMI> 32, blood pressure (DBP)> 93 and glucose (2 h-PG)> 211 (antecedent), the patient is likely to suffer from diabetes (Stage-1) (consequential).

Figure 4. Associations discovered among the risk factors

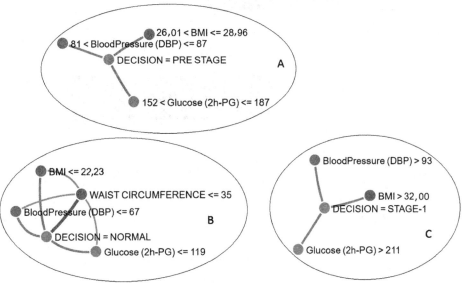

If the result of the prediction is a previous stage or stage 1 or the values of the parameters established in the CEP activate at least one rule, the ECM sends emergency messages in real time, including the GPS location of the patient's house. The latter is gathered from an MT3339 GPS module with a patch antenna 15.0 *15.0 *4.0 mm, which connects to RPi3 through the USB port. ECM uses a broker based on the MQTT (Message Queue Telemetry Transport) protocol to send emergency notifications to the responsibles for the care of the patient's health. MQTT has been selected because it is a lightweight and secure protocol designed especially for devices with limited resources and suitable for IoT applications. Its implementation follows a publication/subscription architecture based on '' topics '', which are messages sent by publishers to the broker and received by subscribers. The ECM is designed to assume the role of broker; for this, it creates specific topics based on the different rules of the CEP and discovered associations. The ECM publishes the messages to health professionals, caregivers and patients, who are previously subscribed to one or several topics of interest as shown in Figure 5. This information, also is sent to DMM in the cloud. These messages are published using secure and reliable communication based on hash algorithm that employs the SSL protocol, enabled in the MQTT protocol. Additionally, MQTT incorporates several QoS levels to confirm the delivery of messages, from a non-optimal minimum level

(QoS0) to a double recognition level (QoS2) using a four-way handshake mechanism. Since our system is closely tied to medical care, the level of QoS2 has been configured to ensure the reliability of the delivery of notifications. The MQTT broker is implemented using the paho-mqtt Python library. The events and associations data are also sent to cloud layer using the API REST provided by Fiware platform, as further described. Private keys and certificates are used to guarantee security in the transmission of data.

Figure 5. Example of the notification messages for healthcare professionals and caregivers (back) and location of patient's house (front)

Private Cloud Server

A private server based on virtual machines was implemented in the vSphere platform to provide the function of the cloud layer. The server consists of three virtual machines, each of which has the same hardware configuration.

The virtual machine assigned to the DMM contains the generic Context Broker Orion enabler, also provided by the Fiware platform, this enabler supports context management specifications to create, update or delete entities by using operation NGSI standard via REST API. For example *update Context* operation with *APPEND* action type is employed for creating the entities. The MongoDB data manager is used to store the entities. In this scenario, the entities representing the events and associations detected by the DPM and by the BDAM, respectively. The entities have been previously mapped by the CIM to a NGSI format (i.e., contextualized information model) compatible with the ontological vocabulary. NGSI doesn't provide native the semantic representation of information. However, it enables the option to user references to ontology concepts, so it can be used to represent semantic information needed for sharing the information with others systems and applications. Therefore, our system is interoperable.

The virtual machine assigned to the BDAM contains the Big data model, which is created by using the BigML platform (BigML, 2016), which is a scalable and programmable SaaS platform designed to create predictive models that can be integrated into software applications through RESTful APIs. The Big Data model was initially created and trained, based on a public access data set provided by the Pima Indians Diabetes Database (PIDD) (Pima Indians Diabetes Database, 2016) that contains historical knowledge of the metabolic risk factors of patients diagnosed with and without diabetes. Before creating the model, the data set was mined in order to eliminate irrelevant, incomplete and unnecessary data. For this, tasks of cleaning, extraction, transformation and fusion of data are carried out on the dataset.

The efficiency and effectiveness of the model was evaluated with the data coming from the IoT devices. Each time the decision of a discovered association is pre-stage or stage -1, the model is retrained and created using previous historical knowledge plus the new knowledge generated by the newly discovered associations. Later this model is locally instantiated by the BDAM of the gateway to make future predictions.

Finally, the virtual machine destined to the graphical user interface implements a web server based on Node-RED, which handles the information received from the DMM and serves as a front-end, Node-RED is an open tool designed for the development of applications IoT. The front-end includes the history data of the last discovered associations, the detected events regarding to the risk factor, and the location of the detection environment, as shown in Figure. 6

Figure 6. Web application showing in real-time the measurement of each factors risk and context-aware information

Performance Evaluation of the Proposed System

In this section, numerical results are provided of the evaluation of the performance of the proposed system. We evaluated edge-IoTA according to the latency time. In particular, we evaluate the response time of the system to alert users in case of an emergency. To do this, we split the latency time in data transmission time (DTT), and notifications transmission time (NTT). Table 2 summarizes the results of the average latency measurements achieved by sending 1000 measurements from each of the sensors. These results show a 63-66% lower latency time compared with the CloudIoT- based traditional approach. The latency comes from the time taken to send the data from the sensors to the gateway and the time for sending the notifications from the gateway to the patients (i,e., the patient's smartphone). Compared to the latency time consumed when sending the data from the IoT devices directly to the cloud, and notifications from the cloud layer to patients, our system is more efficient. The results validate the suitability of our system for latency-sensitive applications and open the way to its real-world implementation in the healthcare industry.

The data processing and analysis at the edge of the network also reduces the amount of data sent to the cloud layer due that only events and associations detected are sent to this layer.

Table 2. Measurements of latency time

System	DTT (ms)	NTT (ms)
edge-IoTA	18	22
CloudIoT traditional	53	60

CONCLUSION

In this chapter, we present an IoT system architecture that takes advantage of edge computing to support the creation of patient-centered healthcare solutions and services. The architecture takes advantage of the communication capabilities provided by an IoT edge gateway, which could be strategically located in smart homes or medical facilities. Interoperability (technical, syntactic and semantic), local storage, data processing, and big data analysis, emergency notification, security, and QoS services are provided thanks to intelligent use of IoT edge gateway. The efficiency and suitability of the system are demonstrated through a complete implementation of a smart health system applied to the monitoring of the metabolic syndrome. From a latency time point of view, the results of system performance reveals that the data processing and analysis at the edge layer is more efficient than CloudIoT-based traditional approach due to a remarkable reduction in the latency time of data transmission from the IoT devices to the edge layer (66%), while reducing the amount of data sent to the cloud layer. As a result, the delivery of emergency notifications from the edge of the network to end users has also been reduced by 63%. Future work may focus on the integration of this interoperable architecture with others medical solutions to enable the achievement of interoperable ecosystems in the health industry that improve patient care.

ACKNOWLEDGMENT

This research was supported by Research and Innovation programme- European Union's Horizon 2020 under the framework of INTER-IoT, Grant Agreement #687283; ACTIVAGE project under grant agreement 732679; the SENESCYT fellowship program, Ecuador; and the National Polytechnic School, Ecuador.

REFERENCES

Ahuja & Mani. (2012). A survey of the state of cloud computing in healthcare. *Network and Communication Technologies, 1*(2).

Aruba Networks. (2017). *IoT Heading for Mass Adoption by 2019 Driven by Better-Than-Expected Business Results.* Retrieved June 5, 2018, from https://goo.gl/22UZ8e

Big, M. L. (2016). Retrieved August 12, 2018, from https://bigml.com/

Bonomi, F., Milito, R., Zhu, J., & Addepalli, S. (2012). Fog Computing and Its Role in the Internet of Things. In *Proceedings of the First Edition of the MCC Workshop on Mobile Cloud Computing* (pp. 13–16). New York: ACM. 10.1145/2342509.2342513

Bormann, C. M. E. A. K. (2014). *Terminology for Constrained-Node Networks RFC 7228.* Retrieved August 12, 2016, from https://tools.ietf.org/html/rfc7228#section-2.3.2

Botta, A., de Donato, W., Persico, V., & Pescapé, A. (2014). Integration of Cloud computing and Internet of Things: A survey. *Future Generation Computer Systems, 56*, 684–700. doi:10.1016/j.future.2015.09.021

Bousquet, J., Kuh, D., Bewick, M., Standberg, T., & Farrell, J. (2015). Operational definition of Active and Healthy Ageing (AHA): A conceptual framework. *The Journal of Nutrition, Health & Aging, 19*(9), 955–960. doi:10.1007/s12603-015-0589-6

Cao, Y., Chen, S., Hou, P., & Brown, D. (2015). FAST: A fog computing assisted distributed analytics system to monitor fall for stroke mitigation. In *2015 IEEE International Conference on Networking, Architecture and Storage (NAS)* (pp. 2–11). IEEE. 10.1109/NAS.2015.7255196

Dastjerdi, A. V., & Buyya, R. (2016). Fog Computing: Helping the Internet of Things Realize Its Potential. *Computer, 49*(8), 112–116. doi:10.1109/MC.2016.245

Dubey, H., Yang, J., Constant, N., Amiri, A. M., Yang, Q., & Mankodiya, K. (2016). *Fog Data: Enhancing Telehealth Big Data Through Fog Computing.* Retrieved from http://arxiv.org/abs/1605.09437

Fiware. (2017). *Fiware-Cepheus CEP.* Retrieved August 12, 2017, from http://fiware-cepheus.readthedocs.io/en/latest/cep/index.html

Gia, T. N., Jiang, M., Rahmani, A. M., Westerlund, T., Liljeberg, P., & Tenhunen, H. (2015). Fog Computing in Healthcare Internet of Things: A Case Study on ECG Feature Extraction. In *2015 IEEE International Conference on Computer and Information Technology; Ubiquitous Computing and Communications; Dependable, Autonomic and Secure Computing; Pervasive Intelligence and Computing* (pp. 356–363). IEEE. 10.1109/CIT/IUCC/DASC/PICOM.2015.51

He, W., Goodkind, D., & Kowal, P. (2016). *An Aging World: 2015 International Population Reports. Aging*. Academic Press.

Hussain, S., Bang, H. J., Han, M., Ahmed, I. M., Amin, B. M., & Lee, S., … Parr, G. (2014). Behavior Life Style Analysis for Mobile Sensory Data in Cloud Computing through MapReduce. *Sensors (Basel)*. doi:10.3390141122001

Lucas, J. P. (2010). *Métodos De Clasificación Basados En Asociación Aplicados A Sistemas De Recomendación*. Academic Press.

Muhammad, G., Rahman, S. M. M., Alelaiwi, A., & Alamri, A. (2017). Smart Health Solution Integrating IoT and Cloud: A Case Study of Voice Pathology Monitoring. *IEEE Communications Magazine*, *55*(1), 69–73. doi:10.1109/MCOM.2017.1600425CM

Pima Indians Diabetes Database. (n.d.). Retrieved August 12, 2018, from https://www.kaggle.com/uciml/pima-indians-diabetes-database

Rahmani, A. M., Gia, T. N., Negash, B., Anzanpour, A., Azimi, I., Jiang, M., & Liljeberg, P. (2018). Exploiting smart e-Health gateways at the edge of healthcare Internet-of-Things: A fog computing approach. *Future Generation Computer Systems*, *78*, 641–658. doi:10.1016/j.future.2017.02.014

Rolim, C. O., Koch, F. L., Westphall, C. B., Werner, J., Fracalossi, A., & Salvador, G. S. (2010). A cloud computing solution for patient's data collection in health care institutions. In *eHealth, Telemedicine, and Social Medicine, 2010. ETELEMED'10. Second International Conference on* (pp. 95–99). IEEE.

Shi, W., Cao, J., Zhang, Q., Li, Y., & Xu, L. (2016). Edge computing: Vision and challenges. *IEEE Internet of Things Journal*, *3*(5), 637–646. doi:10.1109/JIOT.2016.2579198

U.S. Department of Health and Human Services. (2004). *The Seventh Report of the Joint National Committee on Prevention, Detection, Evaluation, and Treatment of High Blood Pressure*. Retrieved from https://www.nhlbi.nih.gov/files/docs/guidelines/jnc7full.pdf

Verma, P., & Sood, S. K. (2018). Fog Assisted-IoT Enabled Patient Health Monitoring in Smart Homes. *IEEE Internet of Things Journal*, *5*(3), 1789–1796. doi:10.1109/JIOT.2018.2803201

Yacchirema, D., Palau, C., & Esteve, M. (2016a). Design and Implementation of a Gateway for Pervasive Smart Environments. In *IEEE International Conference on Systems, Man, and Cybernetics* (pp. 4454–4459). Budapest, Hungary: IEEE. 10.1109/SMC.2016.7844933

Yacchirema, D., Palau, C., & Esteve, M. (2016b). Smart IoT Gateway For Heterogeneous Devices Interoperability. *IEEE Latin America Transactions, 14*(8), 3900–3906.

Yacchirema, D., Suárez de Puga, J., Palau, C., & Esteve, M. (2018). Fall detection system for elderly people using IoT and Big Data. *Procedia Computer Science*, *130*, 603–610.

Yang, Z., Zhou, Q., Lei, L., Zheng, K., & Xiang, W. (2016). An IoT-cloud Based Wearable ECG Monitoring System for Smart Healthcare. *Journal of Medical Systems*, *40*(12), 286. doi:10.100710916-016-0644-9 PMID:27796840

ADDITIONAL READING

Ahuja, S. P., & Deval, N. (2018). From Cloud Computing to Fog Computing: Platforms for the Internet of Things (IoT). [*International Journal of Fog Computing*, *1*(1), 1–14. doi:10.4018/IJFC.2018010101

Ai, Y., Peng, M., & Zhang, K. (2018). Edge computing technologies for Internet of Things: a primer. *Digital Communications and Networks*, *4*(2), 77–86.

Akmandor, A. O., & Jha, N. K. (2018). Smart Health Care: An Edge-Side Computing Perspective. *IEEE Consumer Electronics Magazine*, *7*(1), 29–37. doi:10.1109/MCE.2017.2746096

Alageswaran, R., & Amali, S. M. J. (2018). Evolution of Fog Computing and Its Role in IoT Applications. In P. Raj & A. Raman (Eds.), *Handbook of Research on Cloud and Fog Computing Infrastructures for Data Science* (pp. 33–52). Hershey, PA, USA: IGI Global; doi:10.4018/978-1-5225-5972-6.ch002

Hassan, N., Gillani, S., Ahmed, E., Yaqoob, I., & Imran, M. (2018). The Role of Edge Computing in Internet of Things. *IEEE Communications Magazine*, 1–6. doi:10.1109/MCOM.2018.1700906

Premsankar, G., Di Francesco, M., & Taleb, T. (2018). Edge Computing for the Internet of Things: A Case Study. *IEEE Internet of Things Journal*, *5*(2), 1275–1284. doi:10.1109/JIOT.2018.2805263

Suresh, P., Koteeswaran, S., Malarvizhi, N., & Aswathy, R. H. (2018). Internet of Things (IoT): A Study on Key Elements, Protocols, Application, Research Challenges, and Fog Computing. In P. Raj & A. Raman (Eds.), *Handbook of Research on Cloud and Fog Computing Infrastructures for Data Science* (pp. 124–148). Hershey, PA, USA: IGI Global; doi:10.4018/978-1-5225-5972-6.ch007

Tekeste Habte, T., Saleh, H., & Mohammad, B. I. M. (2019). IoT for Healthcare. In Ultra Low Power ECG Processing System for IoT Devices. Analog Circuits and Signal Processing. Springer, Cham.

KEY TERMS AND DEFINITIONS

Cloud IoT: Refers a set of tools to connect, process, store, and analyze data coming from IoT devices in the cloud.

Constrained Device: Is a device with sensing capabilities, which presents limited CPU, energy resources, and memory.

Interoperability: Is the ability to exchange data and use the information across devices, systems, applications, or system components.

IoT: Refers to a network of things (which includes physical and virtual devices) interconnected over the internet.

Ontology: Is a vocabulary that contains the formal naming of concepts and the definition of their types, properties, and interrelations. It enables a common interpretation of semantic metadata, which allows systems to understand the actual meaning and context of exchanged data.

Smart City: City that employs digital technology to enhance the quality and performance of urban services (such as transportation, energy, environment, etc.) through the leverage of modern technologies such as IoT.

Smart Health: Is defined by the technology that enables to better treatment for patients and improve their QoL.

SoC (System on Chip): Refers to an integrated circuit that encompasses all components of an electronic system.

Things: In the context of the IoT, refers to a physical and/or virtual device connected within an IoT system, which has a unique identifier and the ability to transfer data over a network.

This research was previously published in the Handbook of Research on the IoT, Cloud Computing, and Wireless Network Optimization; pages 1-22, copyright year 2019 by Engineering Science Reference (an imprint of IGI Global).

Chapter 15
Opportunistic Edge Computing Architecture for Smart Healthcare Systems

Nivethitha V.
National Institute of Technology, Puducherry, India

Aghila G.
National Institute of Technology, Puducherry, India

ABSTRACT

Some of the largest global industries that is driving smart city environments are anywhere and anytime health monitoring applications. Smart healthcare systems need to be more preventive and responsive as they deal with sensitive data. Even though cloud computing provides solutions to the smart healthcare applications, the major challenge imposed on cloud computing is how could the centralized traditional cloud computing handle voluminous data. The existing models may encounter problems related to network resource utilization, overheads in network response time, and communication latency. As a solution to these problems, edge-oriented computing has emerged as a new computing paradigm through localized computing. Edge computing expands the compute, storage, and networking capabilities to the edge of the network which will respond to the above-mentioned issues. Based on cloud computing and edge computing, in this chapter an opportunistic edge computing architecture is introduced for smart provisioning of healthcare data.

1. INTRODUCTION

The evolution of the Internet of Things and technology has led to the unbelievable growth in the deployment of smart sensors, actuators, and low power consuming hardware chips, smart devices in various fields like telecommunication, manufacturing, aerospace, smart homes, smart city etc .Smart health care systems are one of the important fields that are witnessing this change (Sodhro, Pirbhulal, & Sangaiah, 2018). This development of smart environment creates a great burden on the network due to the enor-

DOI: 10.4018/978-1-6684-5700-9.ch015

mous data transmission. This creates a challenge for the existing cloud infrastructure to provide timely service to the end users(Zhang et al., 2015). The burden that is put on the data processing and analytics on the cloud computing paved the way for the development of new computing paradigm that brings the compute, storage, and processing to the edge of the network that are closer to the user premises. The method of computing at the edge of the network is called "Edge Computing" (Yu et al., 2017).

According to the predictions that are made by (Koop et al., 2008), the present hospital-based health care systems will take a drift to hospital and home balanced by the year of 2020 and will eventually lead to home-based by the year 2030. To make this happen new architectures, technologies and new computing paradigms should be developed specifically to health care domain. Sending the data for computation to the cloud involves latency delay and health care applications are not tolerant of this delay. Hence Edge computing will provide solutions to this data intensive health monitoring system by reducing the network communication for data transfer, storage issues and latency. This chapter demonstrates the use of Edge computing wherein, the real-time data can be monitored, stored and later can be sent to other storages or clouds if required

Contribution of Edge Computing To Data Science and Analytics

Data science and analytics uses various methods, algorithms, and machine learning models to gain knowledge about the data that are analysed. Edge Computing has evolved to overcome many challenges and issues of cloud computing. They provide a way to make analysis and computation at the IOT domain level and at a level that are one step next to the IOT plane. Edge computing enables different stake holders and systems to perform analytics near to the users with the available resources. Developing various analytics and machine learning models at the edge level may reduce the computation time, response time, latency, bandwidth consumption and improve the quality of service.

Role of Edge Computing in Health Care Domain

The technology advancement in today world has created a need for anywhere and anytime responsive service to the end users. The health care monitoring systems are in no way less and be the most needed of the hour. Now a days the health care monitoring systems enable the humans to wear smart watches and trackers that are in charge of continuously monitoring the human health in terms of heart beat, blood pressure, diabetic, body temperature, footsteps covered, calories of food consumed etc. These data are continuously streamed to the cloud storage where data analytics and processing are done to make inferences and predict the health conditions of the individuals. These health care data are data intensive and they are sensitive in nature.

(i)The health care monitoring systems should be quick, responsive as they deal with intensive data. Any delayed response to the end users of these services might lead to fatal situations. For example, a delayed alert generated for a patient whose heart beats are abnormal might give a delayed assistance to the patient and increase the complexity.

(ii) Data gathered and analysed from e-health records, sensor equipment's, medical sensors, devices, and smartphones are analysed over the edge computing. This analysis enhances the decision-making power of healthcare professionals, and helps patients have an active role in managing their personal health. The health care monitoring systems should be reliable and trustworthy to handle the data

(iii) The health care monitoring systems should provide a secure means of analysis, processing and storage. They should preserve the user's privacy and integrity of the data by providing secure mechanisms. Edge computing provides a secure localized computing and preserves the user data

(iv) The health care monitoring systems should be cost effective and be affordable by the end users who can use them for wellbeing of one's life. The edge computing can reduce the cost of transmission of data, bandwidth consumption and network resources. Thus providing a cost effective provisioning of data.

Bringing the Computation and Analytics to the Edge

The edge computing is a new concept in the evolution of computing paradigm. It brings the service and utilities of cloud computing closer to the end user and enables fast processing and less response time (Khan, Ahmed, Hakak, Yaqoob, & Ahmed, 2019). The developing Health care industry that are connected to internet requires a delay resistant and quick response time. Edge computing gives promising solutions as they support mobility of the users, location aware, low latency and close proximity to the users.

The terminology that are used in Edge computing are:

Table 1. Terminology used in edge computing

Terms	Definition
Edge (Khan et al., 2019)	Any device or entity closer to the user, sensors having a computing capacity.
Edge device (Shi, Cao, Zhang, Li, & Xu, 2016)	Any device that produce /consume data
Edge gateway(Yousefpour et al., 2019)	It is the window that separates the edge computing processing and the large network environment
Edge Server (Yousefpour et al., 2019)	Edge server is a computer that exists at the logical extreme or "edge" of a network. Edge servers will connect with multiple different networks.

Edge Computing Architecture

Edge computing moves the data processing and analytics, applications, and services from the far end cloud servers to the edge of a network. The service providers and application developers, end users can use the Edge computing systems for better quality of service and optimal usage of resources. Edge computing is characterized in terms of less energy consumption, less communication latency, high bandwidth, and real-time access to the network data that can be used by several applications.

Edge computing architecture can be devised into three planes

(i) **IOT Device Plane**: This plane has all the smart IOT devices like the mobile phones, smart sensors and actuators, smart wearables, embedded systems, vehicles and any Edge device that produce data and consume data. These edge devices stream data continuously to the cloud for analysis and storage.

(ii) **Edge Server Plane**: This part of the edge computing architecture comprises the gateways, switches edge servers and small data centres that has some constrained memory and processing capability.

(iii) **Cloud Plane:** The cloud plane possess the cloud computing data centres and servers that are able to perform large big analytics, processing and storage.

The Edge computing allows the application developers and service providers to make the computing possible at the edge server plane and thus reducing the burden imposed on the existing cloud architectures.

Characteristics of Edge Computing

Bandwidth Utilization

Bandwidth describes the maximum data transfer rate of a network or Internet connection. Bringing the computational and storage to the edge of the network can reduce the bandwidth consumption and thus reduce the data transfer rates(Hassan, Gillani, Ahmed, Yaqoob, & Imran, 2018). Optimal use of the bandwidth resources led to the cost effective provisioning of the data.

Latency

Latency refers to delays that is incurred during transmitting or processing data, which can be caused by varied reasons. Edge computing addresses this issue for many data intensive applications and provide a quicker service delivery to the end users.

Response Time

As the computation, analytics, data mining, data pre-processing and some decision making are done at the edge level of the network that are in close proximity to the user, the response time of any service or data access is very less(Hassan et al., 2018) . When compared to the centralized cloud computing, the quality of service in terms of response time is much better.

Energy Consumption

The transmission of the data from the user devices to the far end cloud servers incurs a lot of bandwidth energy(Zhang et al., 2015), thus edge computing develops new architectural models and solutions that reduces the usage and consumption of network resources like bandwidth and thus reduce the server overheads by reducing the load of the central cloud servers.

Storage

Storage at the edge is the methods capture and keep information at the edge of the network, as close to the originating source as possible(Jalali, Hinton, Ayre, Alpcan, & Tucker, 2016). The storage capacity of the edge is minimal when compared to storage capacity of the central data centres. Thus all data cannot be stored near to the sources. Storage at the end aims to provide intermittent and fast connectivity access to data that are needed for computing. Thus data that are needed indefinitely are archived at the edge of the network.

Server Overhead

In Edge computing, the server overhead is relatively low when compared with the overhead that is caused to the servers of the central cloud(Jalali et al., 2016). In edge computing the load is distributed among the servers and they have parallel processing of data unlike cloud servers where all the client request are addressed. Communication overhead is also reduced as the data originating from the source can be processed at the edge instead of communicating them to the central cloud.

2. LITERATURE REVIEW

In this research(Ray, Dash, & De, 2019), the authors presents a taxonomical classification of edge computing and the industrial use cases of edge computing paradigm. A novel edge-IoT based architecture for e-healthcare named as EH-IoT and developed a demo test-bed. EH-IoT architecture encompasses three key modules such as, (i) Apache Edgent engine, (ii) embedded hardware-based sensing unit and (iii) IoT-based cloud repository. The experimental results showed results towards reducing the dependency over IoT cloud for processing, analytics and storage facility.

Md. Golam Rabiul Alam et al., proposed an Edge-of-Things (EoT)-based healthcare services(Dubey et al., 2015). In this paper an optimized selection of virtual machines (VMs) of edge and cloud computing that are offered by service providers is proposed. A dynamic pricing model for an EoT health service is considered by the EoT broker for optimal usage of VM in an EoT environment.

Considering the emergency situations of patients,(Chen, Li, Hao, Qian, & Humar, 2018)an Edge-Cognitive-Computing-based (ECC-based) smart-healthcare system is proposed. This system monitors the physical health of the end users by the use of cognitive computing. Based on the health risk grade of each user, the system uses an optimal resource allocation in the edge computing network. The experimental results show cased that ECC-based healthcare system enhances the user experience and optimizes the computing resources.

To enable awareness and prevention of Chikungunya disease a new paradigm in Smart Health is devised in (Rani, Ahmed, & Shah, 2019). Information about causes of growth of mosquitoes is collected and transmitted to the cloud. This approach is validated at the bottom layer of the network and data is transmitted to the cloud with the help of edge nodes. In this framework, edge servers are deployed at the predefined locations in the city. They are responsible for collecting the data from the users and pre-processing it before communicating to the cloud. They trace the location and will send it for further analysis at cloud.

A wearable sensor-based activity prediction system (Uddin, 2019)was developed to facilitate edge computing in smart healthcare system. In this work, the activity prediction is enabled by Recurrent Neural Network (RNN) on an edge device (personal computer or laptop). GPU of the edge device has been utilized to accelerate the computational speed. Healthcare services are enhanced by using the RNN for real-time analysing and predicting human activities combined with newest technologies IOT, Edge of Things, and Cloud of Things.

The research (Subahi, 2019)work presents a conceptual architectural design, for the IoT Edge based healthcare management system. The nodes located closer to the user are called edges. In this architecture these edge nodes are responsible for getting data from smart sensors and IoT devices. This data is been processed and analysed at local premises, to infer an make decisions on unusual health patterns and also reports to the health service providers in the network to respond.

Prabal Verma et al., (Verma & Sood, 2018) proposed the remote patient health monitoring in smart homes by using the concept of fog computing at the smart gateway . The proposed model uses advanced techniques and services, such as embedded data mining, distributed storage, and notification services at the edge of the network. Event triggering-based data transmission methodology is adopted to process the patient's real-time data at fog layer.

In this Paper(Rahmani et al., 2018), the authors determine the feasible positions of the gateways at the edge of the network and these gateways offer high –level services for the data that are transferred to the cloud. Thus Smart e-Health Gateway is proposed which offers a local data processing, local storage and real- time data processing. The Smart Health Gateway called UT-GATE is implemented in an IoT-based Early Warning health monitoring to show the competence and significance of the system in addressing medical situations.

The authors (Lin, Pankaj, & Wang, 2018)proposed an edge computing framework for health care systems. They developed an efficient task offloading and resource allocation schemes for edge of thing. A fruit fly optimization algorithm is proposed to leverage the data analytics at the edge level for further processing and analysis. The novel FOTO algorithm that is proposed reduces the energy consumption, minimizes the task completion time and optimal cost for the data centre when unloading the jobs from smart devices to the cloudlet. This algorithm has been applied in smart health care systems using Edge-of-things computing.

In (Greco, Ritrovato, & Xhafa, 2019) an architectural solution, based on big data technologies to perform real-time analysis of streaming data that are obtained from the wearable sensors. The proposed architecture is defined by four abstract layers: a sensing layer, a pre-processing layer (Raspberry Pi), a cluster processing layer and a persistence layer. The proposed architecture taking into account of Medical Things situation, the data collected from sensing devices make it possible for the system to rise alarms or initiate automatic reactions whenever an emergency medical situation arises.

Thus the recent related works of edge computing in the health care domain depicts the advantages of localized computing in latency intensive applications. Even though edge computing provides solution to many problems faced by cloud. Scalability, energy consumption of edge servers, dynamic adaptation as per the needs of the health care services is challenging and still there is a need for resource aware and cost effective computing model.

3. NEED FOR OPPORTUNISTIC EDGE COMPUTING

Unlike edge computing, opportunistic are centrally managed networks which provide better quality of services to the applications. OEC architectures allows the dynamic creation of resource pools at the user end as per the need and requirement of the application(Casadei et al., 2019). The need of opportunistic edge computing in smart health care domain are as follows

1. The health monitoring systems are smart systems that deal with sensitive data and the applications should be delay resistant and be responsive. Processing and analysing the data at distributed environment may be a tedious method as the data has to collected and send to the distributed data

centres. This acquires a lot of network resources like bandwidth that may lead to communication latency, delayed responses and the end user may not be benefitted with the available resources.

2. To overcome the challenges of analysing data at the remote cloud, edge computing a hyper distributed computing paradigm came into existence. But there are many challenges that edge computing paradigm faces with respect to the health care domain. As the health care applications require continuous monitoring of patients, the static placement of edge servers and resources at the user end may not support the dynamically changing nature of the health care applications and addition to this the system has to be scalable also.

3. Due to the increasing demands of quick response and optimal use of resources, the analysis and processing of health care monitoring systems data will be deployed at edge level. Without a proper framework for amalgamating, orchestrating and allocation of the distributed resources a lot of available compute and storage resources may go in vain.

4. The health care applications need 24*7 services for which the data servers at the edge layer should be fully dedicated and available. The energy and the resource consumption in terms power backup, battery for the edge servers is a challenging problem. Thus scaling of the edge servers to meet the emergency needs of the health monitoring systems can be difficult. Alternate solutions like peering the neighbour resources and using opportunistic resources can be used.

4. OPPORTUNISTIC EDGE COMPUTING(OEC) IN SMART HEALTH CARE DOMAIN

The opportunistic edge computing tries to push the computing capability to the edge of the network unlike edge computing which locates the available resource pools at static pre-determined edge locations(Casadei et al., 2019). It tries to provide an instant access to the resources which are on demand by using the available resources and infrastructures. The main participants of the OEC models in figure 2 are (i) Resource owners (ii) Broker (iii) Service Providers (iv)End-users. The OEC broker is responsible for creating resource pools at the edge of the network using the resources contributed by the end user's. The resources pooled are not permanent. The broker module is responsible for managing the resources in the pool by leasing the resources for certain duration based on the demand and correspondingly incentives will be computed. If resources are withdrawn by resource owners before the completion of the leased duration then they are considered as less trust worthy and faulty resources. OEC based architectures benefits the health care applications in a major way as they can be deployed very close to the end users. The latency and communication, response time are reduced. They are auto scalable where the resources that are pooled is proportionally equivalent to the participating end users.

OEC Model

The OEC Model has 4 major participants

(i) *Resource Owners*: They are the ones who own the physical computing and storage resources for example the desktops, laptops, LAN's Mobiles. The broker leases the resources from the owners.

(ii) *Broker*: Brokers are responsible for managing the resource pools. They are responsible for making contracts with the resource owners and offers them to the service providers.

(iii) *Service Providers*: The Service providers lease the resources from the brokers and runs their application or services. The clients may also run their applications on the opportunistic edge clouds.

(iv) *End Users*: End users are those who the consumers of the services offered by the service providers.

Figure 1 gives a diagrammatic representation of the participants involved in OEC Model

Figure 1. Opportunistic edge computing Model

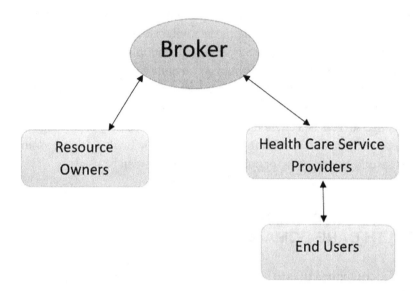

The development of health care monitoring systems and provisioning of the health care data is a challenging area. Many approaches have been proposed to efficiently process and provision the data. In this proposal, an Opportunistic Edge Computing is introduced for health care domain that gives a better response and efficient use of network resources. Considering the dynamic demands of the health care domain a new opportunistic edge architectural model for the smart provisioning of health care application data is proposed that overcomes the challenges of the traditional computing and edge computing models. The proposed architecture model provides an opportunity for processing and analysing data at the edge level by dynamically pooling the available resources thus overcoming the drawbacks of the traditional computing methods.

OEC Architectural Model for Health Care Monitoring

The main architectural elements of the OEC framework are the resource management module of the broker that is responsible for creating the pool of resources at the user end using the resources contributed by the participants. The service providers make use of the broker to run their health care applications that aims to provide fast and quick response to the requests made by the clients for health care services.

Figure 2 show cases the arrangement of OEC framework for health care monitoring of the systems into three layers

Figure 2. OEC Architecture for smart Health care Domain

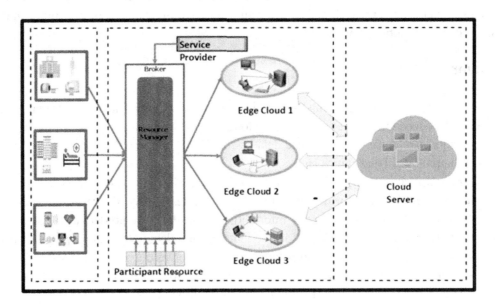

The opportunistic edge computing frame work proposed in this chapter gives to the broker the effort of building and managing the opportunistic edge cloud. In this architecture, the resources are contributed to the broker for computation by the participants and registered with the resource managers.

The OEC framework determines the characteristics of the resources and correspondingly create the virtualized resource units that can be allocated to the service providers to deploy the application. In OEC based health care systems a novel trust management scheme guarantees the broker-to-participant trust and determine how far the broker can rely on resources and infrastructures that are offered by the participants .This scheme allows the participants to take more informed and proper decisions taking into account expectations in terms of reliability, performance and availability

The three layered architecture can be detailed as follows

Medical Sensors Unit

This module is responsible for sensing and recording the health data like temperature, blood pressure, heart rate, sleep pattern from the end users. This data is communicated to the next level through the gateways by WIFI, ZigBee or Bluetooth for further analysis.

Edge Cloud Layer

The broker and its resource manager in the edge layer is responsible for handling the client requests. Based on the demand the resources are pooled and processing of the data is done. Edge clouds are constructed based on the availability of the resources. In this, each contributed and available resource OEC broker module is responsible for analysis of the type, availability, cost of usage, location and reliability The OEC broker also determines the demand for the resources and determine their incentives and pricing models for the resource owners and the service providers respectively. The service providers lend the resources from the brokers and run the application that provide inference on the sensed data. This layer provides higher level services like Data filtering, aggregation, Data pre-processing, Data mining, Decision making, local notifications.

Cloud Layer

The cloud layer is responsible for holding the details of the patients/ individual records that are updated periodically by the edge clouds. They possess the cloud data centres and takes care of the data storage, data analytics, data warehouse. The collected data is stored and represents the big data that are further involved in epidemiological and statics analysis

The OEC framework is in charge for resource monitoring which continuously observe the contributed resources and provide relevant information to the other modules. Lastly, the resource database keeps track of all the statistics, along with relevant information about the stake holders involved in this computing like the participants, the service providers /clients, request description and the allotted resources.

The proposed OEC architecture for health care monitoring solves the problem of static placement of edge servers and make it scalable as per the needs of the application. The resource that are available and contributed by the participants are also considered for the creation of resource pools. The architecture is cost efficient by reducing the needs for providing a continuous power backup and infrastructure needs. Though the opportunistic computing model is efficient in various aspects there are many challenges that has to be explored.

5. RESEARCH SCOPE

The opportunistic edge computing model enables to bring the cloud computing to the edge of the network. The dynamic nature of the edge cloud enables to scale as per the demands of the application but there are many challenges that has to be addressed. The research challenges that are associated with OEC framework are

Resource Management in Opportunistic Edge Computing

OEC resource management is a very challenging area as the resources that are involved in computation are not stable resources. They are dynamic in nature and are not permanent. They are not homogeneous and differ with processing capacity, duration of availability, speed and memory. So the major resource management challenges in this area are

- Resource Orchestration and Monitoring

The health care domain application requires continuous monitoring and availability of resources for computation thus presenting reliable resources is the burden of the OEC resource management. The OEC architecture delegates the process of managing the resources and analysing the characteristics of the resources to the broker. The broker creates the virtualized resource units for processing of health care data based on the needs of the end user and service provider. The dynamic creation of resource pool and organizing the pools is very difficult as the resource availability vary with time. Thus new orchestration techniques that could share the work of the broker making it a distributed approach should be developed.

- **Data Placement**

Data placement is the technique of placing the needed or frequently accessed data near to the edge of the network for better response time and fast access of data. In health care applications, the main requirement is a delay resistant system as they deal with emergency situations. The resource pools are not stagnant and they are opportunistically created based on the needs of the service. The data placement approaches that are designed for the edge computing scenario (Li, Tang, Tang, & Luo, 2019) may not be efficient for the OEC framework. Thus data-placement algorithms with respect OEC framework has to be developed to enhance the users experience.

- **Resource Allocation and Scheduling**

There are number of smart devices that are involved in monitoring the individual's health and they continuously stream data to the cloud for processing. With OEC framework, the data can be filtered and processed at the edge of the network. Scheduling the resources on unchanging topology is relatively easy when compared to resource allocation in a dynamic environment. The scheduling should consider more parameters like the device lifetime, availability, reliability, speed and time duration along with network parameters. Thus new scheduling and allocation schemes should be proposed that ensure the accessibility of the resources by the service providers.

Service Management

The research challenges that are associated with OEC architecture are

- **Building opportunistic edge clouds**

As per changing needs of the health care application the OEC framework should be scalable to process the requests of the end users and improve the quality of service. To create resource pools resource and the characteristics of the resource should be analysed. The designing schemes should be able to discover the appropriate and available resources to involve in edge computing. As the health care application deal with sensitive data the resource should be carefully selected. New resource discovery schemes should be proposed for dynamically selecting the resources and devices for participation

- **Incentives**

The participants who contribute the resources for service should be incentivized. Incentives can be either be budgetary or simple services to be offered to the participants who offer their resources. The incentives should be based on the demands for the particular services. A resource in high demand should be incentivized with higher prices and that with low demand with low pricing. More attractive incentive mechanism should be designed by the broker components of the OEC architecture to make more participants contribute resources.

- **Pricing Model**

Pricing models determine the prices that are to be charged by the brokers for lending their resources to the service providers. The widely used pricing model 'Pay as you go' in cloud computing infrastructure may not be supportive for edge scenarios as the resources are limited and in high demand. Thus novel model for pricing has to be devised taking into consideration the OEC parameters of resource. They should consider the type of resource, reliability and availability over time.

Security and Privacy

Security concerns are the ones that have direct impact on the system performance. OEC resources has many challenging security issues as they deal with shared resources contributed by the participants. OEC framework should earn the trust of all the stake holders including the end user, resource owners and the service providers. The failure or withdrawal of any resource should not hamper the privacy of the user data. New security mechanisms has to be carefully designed to overcome the drawbacks of the issues that arise with OEC model.

Machine Learning in Edge Computing

Machine learning is currently widely used in a variety of applications. With the growing advancements in technology and Internet of things large amount of data are generated at the network edge. Machine Learning models are developed on this gathered data for classification, analysis, and forecast the future events. In OEC, machine learning models can be built on the edge cloud layer where some machine learning algorithms can be run on resource constrained environments to perform data filtering and data processing.

Federated Learning in Resource Constrained Edge Computing Systems

To analyse large amounts of data and gain useful facts for classification, and prediction, machine learning techniques are often applied. The machine learning model has the ability to learn or train the machine using the large set of data. The training is usually done on centralized environment. New machine learning models have been proposed that gathers data from different systems and train based on distributed approach. The main challenging part is to perform machine learning on resource constrained edge computing systems. To enable the distributed learning, the concept of federated learning came into existence.

Federated learning makes it possible to train the machine learning models while not transferring probably sensitive user data from devices or native deployments to a central server. The trained model can further be used to predict and discover new inference. This federated machine learning approach can be used or deployed on the OEC models for creating the resource pools by making appropriate classification based on the type of resources.

In addition they can be used to determine the user's preference or the content popularity for placing the needed content (data) at the edge of the network and improve the data access in OEC models.

This Machine learning approaches can further be improved to run on resource constrained edge devices for various application.

6. APPLICATION OF OEC MODEL IN REAL WORLD SCENARIOS

The various scenario of health care domain are as follows

Scenario A: Smart Health Care System Considering the Emergency Situation in Hospitals / Home

In hospitals/homes consider a scenario where patients/ individuals are monitored continuously. Various parameters such as heartbeat, blood pressure, heart rate etc. are sensed by different sensors and the sensed data are streamed. Any difference or unusual patterns observed in the readings of the patients/ individuals has to be immediately responded and taken action to save the patients/ individuals from critical situations.

i)   Using the cloud computing models

The data are sensed and streamed to the far end cloud servers through different layers of the network. In cloud data centres, decision making and unusual patterns are identified by running different algorithms. Consider an emergency situation where a patients readings of heart rate are unusual. The heart rate sensed are sent to the cloud, the intelligent algorithms determine the unusual patterns and notify to the health care service providers/ Emergency units/ local care takers to give immediate first aids to the patients/ individuals.

Figure 3. Smart health care system using cloud computing models

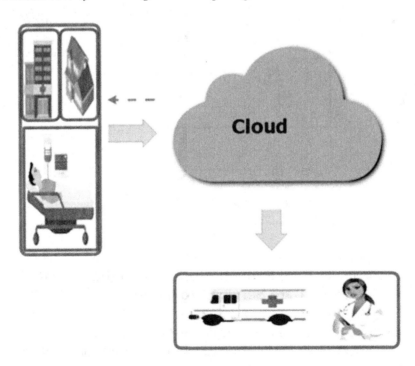

During this process, in cloud computing as depicted in figure 4, the data are routed to multiple layers and then the unusual patterns of the readings are identified. The notification to the care takers/ medical practitioners may be delayed due to the existence of communication latency. Apart from this, the streaming of the data also incurs cost because of bandwidth consumption and network resources. This delay might lead the individuals/ patients to a critical condition.

ii)   Using opportunistic edge computing models

While using opportunistic edge computing model in considered emergency situations instead of cloud computing, any difference in health patterns are determined near to the edge of the network, and they can quickly respond to the patients/ individuals who suffer from disorders.

In this model, the data is processed near to the user premises as shown in figure 5, computation time will be relatively low than the cloud computing model which has to stream the data to far end data centres. The cost of the computation and service are low as the computation and analysis is done using the resources that are available and contributed by the users. The servers need not be dedicated to this application and can be scalable to various needs of the application.

Figure 4. Smart health care system using opportunistic edge computing models

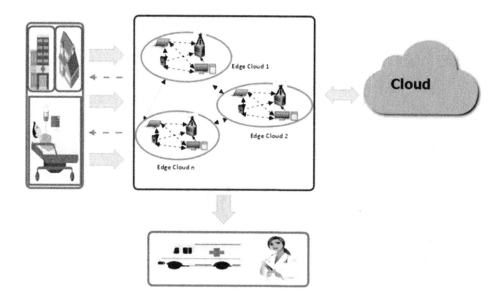

Scenario B: Smart Health Care System, Considering the Availability and Location of the Health Care Service Providers

Consider a scenario where the availability of the doctors/ health care units are scarce. The available services has to be optimally allocated to intensive care units where the patients need immediate attention. In this situation, hence a location aware scheduling to the individuals who need service is required

i)   Using the cloud computing models

The cloud computing provides a location aware service but still there are many challenges that has to be addressed. Consider a situation where a patient who is located in a place where there is no hospitals/ emergency care units and the patient is in a critical condition. Determining the location of medical professionals / emergency care units and then intimating them is long process. This involves tracking and location detection which is difficult and time consuming for the cloud environment.

ii)   Using Opportunistic Edge Computing Model

When a patient is in critical condition, in place where there are no care takers in nearby premises, it would be easy for the opportunistic models to scale as per the needs, process and determine the location of the nearby emergency units and respond quickly. As the OEC models supports the mobility feature, this location aware service delivery will be consuming less time and leading to a cost effective system too.

Scenario C: Edge Computing as a First aid

i)   Using cloud computing Models

Consider a critical condition of a patient/ individual who is under monitoring at home and needs a first aids immediately, For example a need for oxygen immediately. For the considered scenario the data is streamed and decision making will be done at the cloud and the first aid will be given to the patients by opening the oxygen mask. This response may be delayed if there is traffic and congestion at the network. There is a possibility of a failure where the cloud fails to communicate to the devices that are responsible for providing the first aid which will eventually lead the patient to more critical conditions.

ii)   Using opportunistic edge computing Models

For the considered case, the intelligence of decision making will be given to the equipment's sensing and the home computers, laptops that are not in use at present can be contributed. So there will be quick determination of the critical condition and first aid will be given to the patients with no delay which could save them from fatal conditions.

CONCLUSION

In this work, an OEC architecture for healthcare service provisioning which enables personalized and smart-healthcare systems by leveraging healthcare data processing at the edge of the networks is proposed. It clearly shows that OEC architecture succeeds to lower the latency and consumption of the bandwidth. The chapter gives an insight about the emerging edge computing paradigm in health care services and their characteristics. The OEC architecture proposed overcomes the main challenges that are imposed by the cloud computing in health care domain. The proposed architecture aims to reduce request time for the health care services that are requested by the users. They give more appropriate and quick decisions to the stake holders involved in the smart health care systems. This work also explores the possible research challenges that has to be developed to improve the Opportunistic model of edge computing (Amir Ahmad Dara,2017). Various application scenario are also discussed which gives an understanding about the advantages of the opportunistic edge computing than traditional cloud computing models. The cost-effective health-care system is the demand in need which has to be further developed. The chapter can be explored to improve and the model could be implemented.

REFERENCES

Casadei, R., Fortino, G., Pianini, D., Russo, W., Savaglio, C., & Viroli, M. (2019). A development approach for collective opportunistic Edge-of-Things services. *Information Sciences*, *498*, 154–169. doi:10.1016/j.ins.2019.05.058

Chen, M., Li, W., Hao, Y., Qian, Y., & Humar, I. (2018). Edge cognitive computing based smart healthcare system. *Future Generation Computer Systems*, *86*, 403–411. doi:10.1016/j.future.2018.03.054

Dara & Anuradhab. (2017). *Use of orthogonal arrays and design of experiment via Taguchi L9 method in probability of default*. Growing Science Ltd., doi:10.5267/j.ac.2017.11.001

Dubey, H., Yang, J., Constant, N., Amiri, A. M., Yang, Q., & Makodiya, K. (2015). Fog Data: Enhancing Telehealth Big Data Through Fog Computing (#4). Proceedings of the ASE BigData & SocialInformatics 2015, 14:1-14:6. 10.1145/2818869.2818889

Greco, L., Ritrovato, P., & Xhafa, F. (2019). An edge-stream computing infrastructure for real-time analysis of wearable sensors data. *Future Generation Computer Systems*, *93*, 515–528. doi:10.1016/j.future.2018.10.058

Hassan, N., Gillani, S., Ahmed, E., Yaqoob, I., & Imran, M. (2018). The Role of Edge Computing in Internet of Things. *IEEE Communications Magazine*, *56*(11), 110–115. doi:10.1109/MCOM.2018.1700906

Jalali, F., Hinton, K., Ayre, R., Alpcan, T., & Tucker, R. S. (2016). Fog computing may help to save energy in cloud computing. *IEEE Journal on Selected Areas in Communications*, *34*(5), 1728–1739. doi:10.1109/JSAC.2016.2545559

Khan, W. Z., Ahmed, E., Hakak, S., Yaqoob, I., & Ahmed, A. (2019). Edge computing: A survey. *Future Generation Computer Systems*, *97*, 219–235. doi:10.1016/j.future.2019.02.050

Koop, C., Mosher, R., Kun, L., Geiling, J., Grigg, E., Long, S., Macedonia, C., Merrell, R., Satava, R., & Rosen, J. (2008). Future delivery of health care: Cybercare. *IEEE Engineering in Medicine and Biology Magazine*, *27*(6), 29–38. doi:10.1109/MEMB.2008.929888 PubMed

Li, C., Tang, J., Tang, H., & Luo, Y. (2019). Collaborative cache allocation and task scheduling for data-intensive applications in edge computing environment. *Future Generation Computer Systems*, *95*, 249–264. doi:10.1016/j.future.2019.01.007

Lin, K., Pankaj, S., & Wang, D. (2018). Task offloading and resource allocation for edge-of-things computing on smart healthcare systems. *Computers & Electrical Engineering*, *72*, 348–360. doi:10.1016/j.compeleceng.2018.10.003

Rahmani, A. M., Gia, T. N., Negash, B., Anzanpour, A., Azimi, I., Jiang, M., & Liljeberg, P. (2018). Exploiting smart e-Health gateways at the edge of healthcare Internet-of-Things: A fog computing approach. *Future Generation Computer Systems*, *78*, 641–658. doi:10.1016/j.future.2017.02.014

Rani, S., Ahmed, S. H., & Shah, S. C. (2019). Smart health: A novel paradigm to control the chickungunya virus. IEEE Internet of Things Journal, 6(2), 1306–1311. doi:10.1109/JIOT.2018.2802898

Ray, P. P., Dash, D., & De, D. (2019). Edge computing for Internet of Things: A survey, e-healthcare case study and future direction. *Journal of Network and Computer Applications*, *140*(December), 1–22. doi:10.1016/j.jnca.2019.05.005

Shi, W., Cao, J., Zhang, Q., Li, Y., & Xu, L. (2016). Edge Computing: Vision and Challenges. IEEE Internet of Things Journal, 3(5), 637–646. doi:10.1109/JIOT.2016.2579198

Sodhro, A. H., Pirbhulal, S., & Sangaiah, A. K. (2018). Convergence of IoT and product lifecycle management in medical health care. *Future Generation Computer Systems*, *86*, 380–391. doi:10.1016/j.future.2018.03.052

Subahi, A. F. (2019). Edge-Based IoT Medical Record System: Requirements, Recommendations and Conceptual Design. *IEEE Access : Practical Innovations, Open Solutions*, *7*, 94150–94159. doi:10.1109/ACCESS.2019.2927958

Uddin, M. Z. (2019). A wearable sensor-based activity prediction system to facilitate edge computing in smart healthcare system. *Journal of Parallel and Distributed Computing*, *123*, 46–53. doi:10.1016/j.jpdc.2018.08.010

Verma, P., & Sood, S. K. (2018). Fog assisted-IoT enabled patient health monitoring in smart homes. IEEE Internet of Things Journal, 5(3), 1789–1796. doi:10.1109/JIOT.2018.2803201

Yousefpour, A., Fung, C., Nguyen, T., Kadiyala, K., Jalali, F., Niakanlahiji, A., Kong, J., & Jue, J. P. (2019). All one needs to know about fog computing and related edge computing paradigms: A complete survey. *Journal of Systems Architecture*, *98*(February), 289–330. doi:10.1016/j.sysarc.2019.02.009

Yu, W., Liang, F., He, X., Hatcher, W. G., Lu, C., Lin, J., & Yang, X. (2017). A Survey on the Edge Computing for the Internet of Things. *IEEE Access : Practical Innovations, Open Solutions*, *3536*(c), 1–1. doi:10.1109/ACCESS.2017.2674687

Zhang, B., Mor, N., Kolb, J., Chan, D. S., Lutz, K., Allman, E., Wawrzyne, J., Lee, E., & Kubiatowicz, J. (2015). The Cloud is Not Enough: Saving IoT from the Cloud. 7th USENIX Workshop on Hot Topics in Cloud Computing, HotCloud'15. Retrieved from https://dl.acm.org/citation.cfm?id=2827740%0Ahttps://www.usenix.org/conference/hotcloud15/workshop-program/presentation/zhang

KEY TERMS AND DEFINITIONS

Bandwidth: Bandwidth describes the maximum data transfer rate of a network or Internet connection.
Broker: The intermediate layer that are responsible for managing the resource pools.

Communication Latency: Latency refers to delays that is incurred during transmitting or processing data, which can be caused by varied reasons.

Edge Computing: It is a distributed computing paradigm which brings computation and data storage closer to the needed location and near to the users, in order to improve response times, bandwidth consumptions.

Machine Learning: Machine Learning models are scientific and statistical model that are developed on gathered data for classification, analysis, and forecast the future events.

Opportunistic Computing: Opportunistic computing use the resources, services, applications, and computing resources, contributed by the devices connected in an opportunistic network, for performing the execution of distributed computing tasks.

Service Providers: A service provider is a vendor that provides IT solutions and/or services to end users and organizations.

This research was previously published in the Handbook of Research on Engineering, Business, and Healthcare Applications of Data Science and Analytics; pages 289-306, copyright year 2021 by Engineering Science Reference (an imprint of IGI Global).

Section 2
Challenges, Security Issues, and Solutions

Chapter 16
A Novel Approach to Location–Aware Scheduling of Workflows Over Edge Computing Resources

Yin Li

Institute of Software Application Technology, Guangzhou, China & Chinese Academy of Sciences, Guangzhou, China

Yuyin Ma

Chongqing University, China

Ziyang Zeng

Chonqing University, China

ABSTRACT

Edge computing is pushing the frontier of computing applications, data, and services away from centralized nodes to the logical extremes of a network. A major technological challenge for workflow scheduling in the edge computing environment is cost reduction with service-level-agreement (SLA) constraints in terms of performance and quality-of-service requirements because real-world workflow applications are constantly subject to negative impacts (e.g., network congestions, unexpected long message delays, shrinking coverage, range of edge servers due to battery depletion. To address the above concern, we propose a novel approach to location-aware and proximity-constrained multi-workflow scheduling with edge computing resources). The proposed approach is capable of minimizing monetary costs with user-required workflow completion deadlines. It employs an evolutionary algorithm (i.e., the discrete firefly algorithm) for the generation of near-optimal scheduling decisions. For the validation purpose, the authors show that our proposed approach outperforms traditional peers in terms multiple metrics based on a real-world dataset of edge resource locations and multiple well-known scientific workflow templates.

DOI: 10.4018/978-1-6684-5700-9.ch016

INTRODUCTION

In the past decades, the cloud computing paradigm has evolved as a major force to provide computing, storage and network services, which have been applied in various fields, e.g., scientific workflow execution (Li, 2018; Peng, 2018; Wang 2019; Guo 2019). However, the cloud computing paradigm can be ineffective in supporting IoT-based and time-critical applications due to the fact traditional cloud (Xia 2015) infrastructures far away from the edge while smart IoT devices are usually located at the edge of network. To address the above challenge, the edge computing paradigm (Li 2019; Chen 2020; Xiang 2020) is derived to satisfy the demanding requirements of low-latency, location-awareness, and mobility. This novel paradigm can be seen as a network edge cloud, which effectively compensates for the disadvantages of cloud computing such as communication latency. Edge resources are usually located close to end-user applications to better serve delay-sensitive and time-critical tasks. Due to the improvement of resource-user proximity, power consumption, network traffic, operating expenses, and fault tolerance of edge-oriented applications are improved as well.

Figure 1. Edge computing deployment example

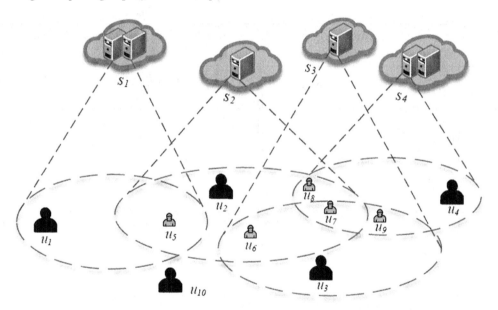

Although extensive research efforts were paid to the problem of scheduling workflows over cloud infrastructures with multiple objectives and constraints, which is known to be NP-hard. Scheduling workflows upon edge infrastructures can be intrinsically different and it remains a challenge how to optimize the cost of workflow execution with the proximity constraint, i.e., every edge service can only support users within its communication range. Figure 1 illustrates a good example of deploying and offloading tasks among edge nodes. It's assumed that there are four edge servers in a particular area and each server covers a specific area. A user can offload computing tasks to any server within the coverage. User u_6 can offload computing tasks to servers s_2 and s_3, and u_7 can offload tasks to s_2, s_3, and s_4. u_1 can only offload tasks to s_1. Since user u_{10} is out of the coverage of any server, the task cannot be offloaded to the server. Each user initiates a workflow with multiple tasks to be offloaded. Tasks belonging to the same user can be offloaded to different edge servers. For instance, tasks belonging to u_5 can be offloaded to both s_1 and s_2.

In this paper, we study the problem of location-aware and proximity-constrained cost-efficient multi-workflow scheduling in the edge computing environment. We consider a multi-edge-user, multi-workflow, cost-reduction, and completion-time-constrained formulation and employ a discrete firefly algorithm (DFA) for solution. To validate our proposed approach, we conduct simulative case studies and show that our proposed method beats its peers in terms of cost and workflow completion time.

Table 1. Variables and symbols used in this paper

Notation	Description	Notation	Description
n	The total number of workflows	n_i	The total number of tasks in workflow
m	The total number of edge servers	M	The total number of tasks in all workflow
m_p	The total number of virtual machines in server p	T_i	The set of tasks in workflow i, $T_i = \{t_{i1}, t_{i1}, \ldots, t_{in_i}\}$
t_{ij}	The jth task of workflow i	VM_{pk}	The kth virtual machine of server p
t_{ijpk}	The execute time of t_{ij} on VM_{pk}	$pred(t_{ij})$	All predecessor node tasks of t_{ij}
x_{ijpk}	A boolean variable indicating whether VM_{pk} is selected for t_{ij}	c_{pk}	The unit-price-time of VM_{pk}
G	The directed acyclic graph(DAG)	E	The set of dependencies in a workflow
$D(W_i)$	User defined deadline of the workflow i	$T(W_i)$	The finish time of the workflow i
d_{ip}	The distance between server p and workflow i	cov_p	The coverage area of server p
$ST(t_{ijpk})$	The start time of t_{ij} on VM_{pk}	$FT(t_{ijpk})$	The completion time of t_{ij} on VM_{pk}

RELATED WORK

It is widely known that scheduling multi-task workflows on distributed platforms, e.g., clouds or edge nodes, is NP-hard. It is thus extremely time-consuming to decide optimal schedules by using traversal-based procedures. Fortunately, heuristic and meta-heuristic algorithms with polynomial complexity are able to yield approximate or near-optimal solutions at the cost of acceptable optimality loss. For example, (Habak 2015) proposed and designed the FEMTO system, which provides cloud services through mobile devices at the edge of network. They developed an optimization framework that generates scalable heuristic solutions to the problem. (Mao 2016) proposed a multi-users mobile devices resource management method. Its objective is minimizing the power consumption and its constraint is task buffer stability.

For utilization optimization of cloud resources, (Liang 2016) proposed a workload placement strategy that decides the destination edge server and assigned computational capacity for a given task. Their basic idea is to opportunistically aggregate and serve at the peak loads that exceed the capacities of lower tiers of edge cloud servers to other servers at higher tiers in the edge cloud hierarchy. (Zhang 2018) considered the cost optimization of the task scheduling problem over the edge computing infrastructure and proposed the TTSCO (Two-stage Task Scheduling Cost Optimization) algorithm. (Zhao 2017) considered the offloading of delay-bounded tasks over heterogeneous cloud infrastructure and aimed at maximizing the probability that tasks meet delay requirements. (Sahni 2018) developed a deadline-constrained scientific workflow scheduling method. It takes into account virtual machine (VM) performance variability and heterogeneous nature of cloud resources. Their proposed optimization formulation aims at minimizing cost-efficiency.

FIREFLY ALGORITHM

(Yang 2010) proposed the Firefly algorithm (FA) and showed its high potency in dealing with complex combinatorial optimization problems and versatile types of engineering and industrial optimization scenarios. It's a swarm-based meta-heuristic algorithm inspired by the flashing of fireflies. (Sanaei 2013) gave a typical example of using FA in solving Resource Constrained Project Scheduling Problem (RCPSP). The algorithm starts by generating a set of random schedules. After that, the initial schedules are improved iteratively using the FA-based flying approach. By termination of algorithm, the best schedule found by the method is returned as the final result. (Marichelvam 2014) proposed a discrete firefly algorithm to minimize makespan for an M-stage hybrid flowshop scheduling problems.

FA usually contains two elements, namely brightness and attractiveness, which are being repeatedly updated. Brightness refers to the position of the firefly and decides its moving direction. Attractiveness determines the distance that the firefly moves through. It's usually assumed that: 1) A firefly will be attracted to each other regardless of their sex because they are unisexual; 2) Attractiveness is proportional to their brightness whereas the less bright firefly will be attracted to the brighter firefly. However, the attractiveness decreases when the distance between the two fireflies increases; and 3) If the brightness of both fireflies is the same, they will move randomly. The generations of new solutions are by a random-walk manner. The brightness of the fireflies should be associated with the objective function of the related problem. Their attractiveness makes them capable of subdividing themselves into smaller groups and each subgroup swarms around the local models.

The relative brightness of fireflies can be calculated as:

$$I(r) = I_0 \cdot e - \gamma r ij \tag{1}$$

where, I_0 represents the fluorescent brightness of the firefly, i.e., the fluorescence brightness when $r=0$. The higher the objective function value is, the higher the brightness is. γ is the light intensity absorption coefficient, r_{ij} is the distance between the fireflies i and j.

The attraction of fireflies can be calculated as:

$$\beta(r) = \beta_0 \cdot e^{-\gamma r_{ij}^2} \tag{2}$$

where β_0 is the maximum attraction when r=0.

Firefly location is updated according to:

$$x_i = x_i + B(r) \cdot (x_j - x_i) + \propto (rand - 1/2) \tag{3}$$

where x_i and x_j are the spatial locations of fireflies *i* and *j*. α is the step factor, *rand* is a random factor that is uniformly distributed over *(0,1)*. *rand-1/2* is a random disturbance to avoid prematurely falling into local optimum during the position update process.

According to the calculation, the firefly with low brightness moves to that with high brightness. The moving distance is decided according to (2) and (3).

SYSTEM MODEL AND PROBLEM FORMULATION

The edge computing system is composed of an edge computing agent (ECA) and multiple edge servers. The edge computing agent manages all resources. An edge server owns several VMs and each of which can handle a workflow task that a user offloads at a time. An edge server usually has limited capacity for storage and computation. For the energy saving purpose, offloading and execution of workflow tasks are subject to the proximity constraint, i.e., an edge server can only support tasks of its nearby edge users that fall in with its communication range.

As an example given in Figure 2, an edge user organizes its tasks in the form of a workflow. Therefore, there exist multiple workflows in the edge environment to be handled and executed.

Figure 2. Multiple workflows to be executed in the edge environment

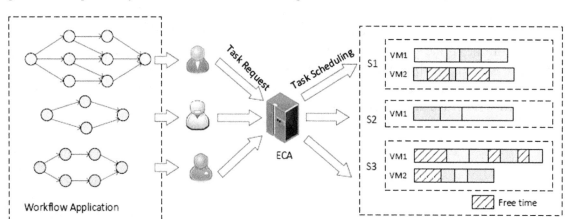

A workflow refers to a directed acyclic graph DAG, $G=(T,E)$. T denotes the task set $T=\{t_1,t_2...t_n\}$, E the set of edges between tasks, and $e_{ij}=(t_i, t_j)$ is a priority constraint indicating that t_i is the precedent task of t_j.

Based on the described system configuration, the problem that we are interested in is thus, for given proximity constraints of server-user communications, how to schedule workflows with as low as possible cost and completion time. The resulting formulation is thus:

$$Min\ f = Cost = \sum_{p=1}^{m}\sum_{k=1}^{m_p}\sum_{i=1}^{n}\sum_{j=1}^{n_i} C_{pk} \cdot x_{ijpk} \cdot \left[FT\left(T_{ijpk}\right) - ST\left(T_{ijpk}\right)\right] \tag{4}$$

subject to:

$$ST\left(T_{ij}\right) \geq max\left[FT(T_{il} \in pred\left(T_{ij}\right) and\ l \in \left\{1,...,n_i\right\}\right] \tag{5}$$

$$T(W_i) \leq D(W_i) \tag{6}$$

$$d_{ij} \leq cov_p \tag{7}$$

$$x_{ijpk} \leq 1 \tag{8}$$

where:

$$x_{ijpk} = \begin{cases} 1, if\ VM_{pk}\ is\ selected\ for\ task\ T_{ij} \\ \qquad 0, otherwise \end{cases} \tag{9}$$

DISCRETE FIREFLY ALGORITHM FOR MULTI-WORKFLOW SCHEDULING

In this section, we present novel schemes of coding rules, decoding rules, and updating rules that deal with the location-aware and proximity-constrained multi-workflows scheduling problem.

The encoding scheme includes two parts:

- **Virtual Machine Assignment:** The encoding of the VM selection part comprises a set of integer values. The encoding length is the same as the number of tasks of all workflows. We use a **VM-string** to represent its encoding. An example of such encoding scheme is shown in Figure 3, where it is assumed that there are three workflows w_1, w_2, and w_3. w_1 can be assigned to s_2 and s_3, w_2 can be assigned to s_2, s_3, and s_2, s_3, s_4 cover w_3;
- **Task Scheduling:** Tasks are scheduled according to the topological constraints of workflows. The encoding of the task scheduling part is similarly composed of a set of integer values in terms of **Task-string**. Figure 4 shows an example of its encoding. As can be seen, from left to right, the task-string shows the first task of the third workflow, the first task of the second workflow, etc.

Figure 3. VM-string representations

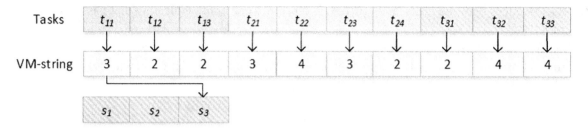

Firefly population initialization consists of two parts: the **VM-string** initialization and the **Task-string** one. The former is related to proximity constraint, while the latter is related to the topological structure of the workflow. Populations generated follow the proximity and topological constraints to avoid the existence of infeasible solutions.

Figure 4. Task-string representations

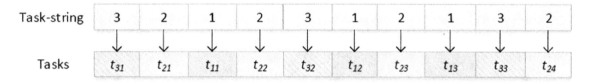

The fitness value of firefly is closely related to the light intensity. In this paper, we employ (10) represent the fitness, in terms of the light intensity of individuals:

$$F = \begin{cases} f + \propto \sum_{i=1}^{n} \left[T\left(W_i\right) - D\left(W_i\right) \right]^m, T\left(W_i\right) > D\left(W_i\right) \, and \; m \geq 1 \\ f, T\left(W_i\right) \leq D\left(W_i\right) \end{cases} \tag{10}$$

The direction of movement of fireflies is determined by the light intensity and the fitness value. For any two fireflies, the darker one will move to the brighter one. The movement of fireflies is realized through discrete steps described below:

1. **Distance Calculation:** In a VM-string, the distance between any two fireflies p and p_{best} is measured by its corresponding hamming distance:

$$r\left(x_i, x_j\right) = x_{id} \oplus x_{jd}, d \in \left\{1, 2, ..., M\right\} \tag{11}$$

where an exclusive *OR* operations is employed to decide the hamming distance (Lunardi 2018). The distance between two fireflies in the **Task-string** is decided by the swap distance, which is the minimum number of exchanges required to exchange one string to another. As shown by an example in Table 2 the swap distance between p and p_{best} is 4:

2. **β–setp update:** The firefly position update requires two consecutive steps: β-step and α-step. β-step is a process of moving fireflies towards brighter fireflies according to the following steps: (1) Calculate the hamming distance of the VM-**string and** the swap distance of the Task-**string as** r_1 and r_2; (2) Calculate the attractiveness, $\beta(r)$, according to (12); (3) Generate $|r_1|$ and $|r_2|$ random numbers between 0 and 1. If the random number is lower than $\beta(r)$, th*e* element of the p is replaced by the corresponding element of the brightest firefly; and (4) Fireflies move to the brightest one:

$$\beta(r) = \frac{\beta_0}{\left(1 + \gamma r^2\right)} \tag{12}$$

$$X_i = x_i + \alpha(rand_{int}) \tag{13}$$

Table 2. Solution update

Updation	VM-string	Task-string
Current firefly p	$\{2, 3, 2, 2, 3, 3, 4, 2, 2, 4\}$	$\{2, 3, 1, 1, 3, 2, 1, 3, 2, 2\}$
Best firefly p_{best}	$\{3, 2, 2, 3, 4, 3, 2, 2, 4, 4\}$	$\{3, 2, 1, 2, 3, 1, 2, 1, 3, 2\}$
Distance r_1 and r_2	6	4
Attractiveness $\beta(r)$	0.22	0.38
$rand(\ )between(0, 1)$	$\{\boxed{0.17}, 0.59, 0.83, \boxed{0.06}, \boxed{0.11}, 0.51\}$	$\{\boxed{0.29}, 0.75, \boxed{0.33}, 0.42\}$
Update position after β-step	$\{3, 3, 2, 2, 4, 3, 2, 2, 2, 4\}$	$\{3, 2, 1, 1, 3, 2, 2, 1, 3, 2\}$
Update position after α-step	$\{3, 3, 2, \boxed{4}, \boxed{2}, 3, 2, 2, 2, 4\}$	$\{3, 2, 1, \boxed{3}, \boxed{1}, 2, 2, 1, 3, 2\}$

3. **α-step update:** It carries out random disturbance to avoid local optimum. Its details can be found in (Mariappan 2014) and thus are not elaborated due to the page limit.

Algorithm 1: Firefly Algorithm

Objective function $F(x)$ Algorithm related parameters: α, β_0, γ, $iter_{max}$
Generate initial population of fireflies: $X_1, X_2, \ldots, X_n$
Light intensity I_i and x_i is determined by $F(X_i)$
while $t < iter_{max}$ do
    for $i = 1{:}n$ do
        for $j = 1{:}i$ do
            if $F(x_i) > F(x_j)$ then
            | move firefly i towards firefly j;
            else
            | move firefly j towards firefly i;
            end
            Update the attractiveness of all fireflies;
            Evaluate new solution and update light intensity;
        end
        Rank the fireflies and find the current best;
    end
end

Based on the designs described above, the overall algorithm is illustrated as Algorithm 1.

PERFORMANCE EVALUATION

In this section, we evaluate the performance of our proposed method by comparing it with three existing methods, namely, MinMin+ (Tabak 2014), GAMEC (Wu 2018), and WaterDrop (Mainak 2019). All experiments were performed on a Windows PC with an Intel Core i5-4210U processor and 12 GB RAM. The proposed algorithm is implemented in Matlab and the performance of the algorithm is evaluated by two indexes, cost and workflow completion time.

Figure 5. The case templates of workflow

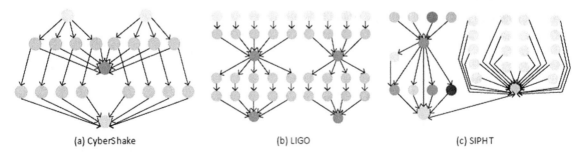

(a) CyberShake   (b) LIGO   (c) SIPHT

We used three well-known scientific workflow templates (juve 2013), namely, *CyberShake*, *LIGO* and *SIPHT* as shown in Figure 5: (a) *CyberShake: CyberShake* workflow is used by the Southern California Earthquake Center to characterize earthquake hazards in a region; (b) *LIGO: LIGO*'s Inspiral Analysis workflow is used to generate and analyze gravitational waveforms from data collected during the coalescing of compact binary systems; and (c) *SIPHT*: The *SIPHT* workflow, from the bioinformatics project at Harvard, is used to automate the search for un-translated RNAs(sRNAs) for bacterial replicons in the NCBI database.

Figure 6. Edge server deployment

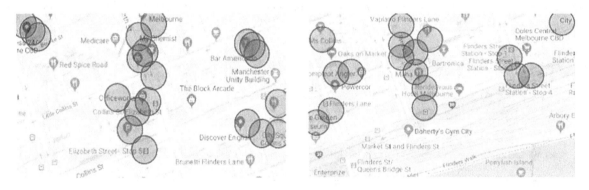

Table 3. The unit price of heterogeneous VMs from three edge service providers

Edge service provider	VType	VCPU	Memory	Unit-price/hour
EP1	s3.small	1	1	0.0612$
	s3.medium	1	2	0.0757$
	s3.medium	1	4	0.1005$
	s3.large	2	8	0.1500$
EP2	s2.standard	1	1	0.0335$
	s2.standard	1	2	0.0509$
	s2.standard	1	4	0.08$
	s2.standard	2	4	0.1019$
EP3	t3.nano	2	0.5	0.0052$
	t3.small	2	2	0.0208$
	t3.medium	2	4	0.0416$
	t3.large	2	8	0.0832$

We consider that there are three edge service providers with different resource configurations and charging plans as shown by Table 3. We assume as well that edge servers and users are located according to the position dataset of (Lai 2019), and the edge server deployment diagram is shown in Figure 6.

Figure 7 shows the comparison of cost and workflow completion time of different methods with varying numbers of edge servers and tasks. As can be seen, the average cost of our proposed method is lower than that of its peers. Similarly, the averaged workflow completion time of our method is lower as well than those of its peers, because our algorithm considers a new encoding method that takes into account the proximity constraint between servers and users.

Figure 7. Performance comparison of different algorithms with varying numbers of edge servers

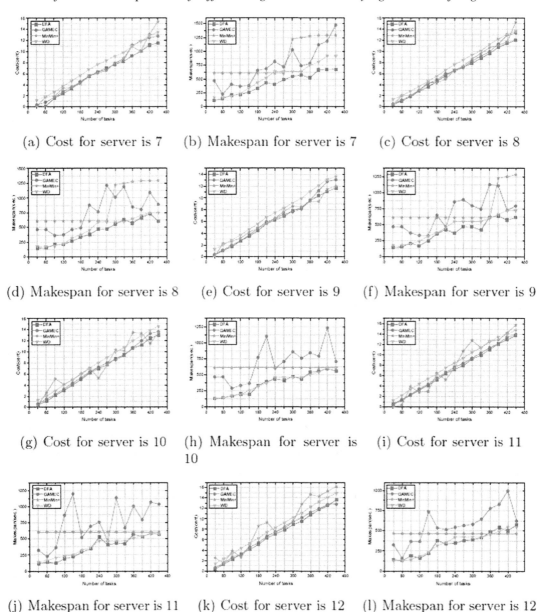

(a) Cost for server is 7   (b) Makespan for server is 7   (c) Cost for server is 8

(d) Makespan for server is 8   (e) Cost for server is 9   (f) Makespan for server is 9

(g) Cost for server is 10   (h) Makespan for server is 10   (i) Cost for server is 11

(j) Makespan for server is 11   (k) Cost for server is 12   (l) Makespan for server is 12

CONCLUSION

In this paper, we address the cost optimization of the multi-user multi-workflow scheduling environment over edge service infrastructure. We propose a discrete firefly algorithm to optimize the cost-effectiveness, while satisfy the proximity and workflow deadline constraints. Experimental results based on multiple well-known workflow templates and a real-world position dataset for edge service providers show that our proposed method clearly outperform traditional ones in terms of cost and completion time.

ACKNOWLEDGMENT

This work is in part supported by Fundamental Research Funds for the Central Universities under project Nos.106112014CDJZR185503 and CDJZR12180012; Guangzhou Science and Technology Projects (Grant Nos. 201807010052);Nansha Science and Technology Projects (Grant No. 2017GJ001);Science foundation of Chongqing Nos.cstc2014jcyjA40010 and cstc2014jcyjA90027; Chongqing Social Undertakings and Livelihood Security Science and Technology Innovation Project Special Program No.cstc2016shms-zx90002; China Postdoctoral Science Foundation No.2015M570770; Chongqing Postdoctoral Science special Foundation No.Xm2015078; Universities Sci-tech Achievements Transformation Project of Chongqing No.KJZH17104.

REFERENCES

Adhikari, M., & Amgoth, T. (2019). An intelligent water drops-based workflow scheduling for iaas cloud. *Applied Soft Computing*, 77, 547–566. doi:10.1016/j.asoc.2019.02.004

Chen, Y., Zhang, N., Zhang, Y., Chen, X., Wu, W., & Shen, X. (2020). (accepted). TOFFEE.(2020) Task Offloading and Frequency Scaling for Energy Efficiency of Mobile Devices in Mobile Edge Computing. *IEEE Transactions on Cloud Computing*. doi:10.1109/TCC.2019.2923692

Guo, X., Wang, S., You, D., Li, Z., & Jiang, X. (2019). A Siphon-Based Deadlock Prevention Strategy for S3PR. *IEEE Access : Practical Innovations, Open Solutions*, 7, 86863–86873. doi:10.1109/ACCESS.2019.2920677

Habak, K., Ammar, M., Harras, K. A., & Zegura, E. (2015). Femtoclouds: Leveraging mobile devices to provide cloud service at the edge. *8th IEEE International Conference on Cloud Computing*, 9-16.

Juve, G., Chervenak, A., Deelman, E., Bharathi, S., Mehta, G., & Vahi, K. (2013). Characterizing and profiling scientic work ows. *Future Generation Computer Systems*, 29(3), 682–692. doi:10.1016/j.future.2012.08.015

Lai, P., He, Q., Abdelrazek, M., Chen, F., Hosking, J. G., Grundy, J. C., & Yang, Y. (2019) Optimal edge user allocation in edge computing with variable sized vector binpacking. *Service-Oriented Computing, 16th International Conference*, 230-245.

Li, W. L., Xia, Y. N., Zhou, M. C., Sun, X. N., & Zhu, Q. S. (2008). Fluctuation-Aware and Predictive Workflow Scheduling in Cost-Effective Infrastructure-as-a-Service Clouds. *IEEE Access : Practical Innovations, Open Solutions*, 6, 61488–61502. doi:10.1109/ACCESS.2018.2869827

Li, W., Liao, K., He, Q., & Xia, Y. (2019) Performance-aware Cost-effective Resource Provisioning for Future Grid IoT-Cloud System. *Journal of Energy Engineering.* Doi:10.1061/(ASCE)EY.1943-7897.0000611

Liang, T., Yong, L., & Wei, G. (2016) A hierarchical edge cloud architecture for mobile computing. *35th Annual IEEE International Conference on Computer Communications*, 1-9.

Lunardi, W. T., & Voos, H. (2018). An extended exible job shop scheduling problem with parallel operations. *Applied Computing Review*, 18(2), 46–56. doi:10.1145/3243064.3243068

Mao, Y., Zhang, J., & Letaief, K. B. (2016). Dynamic computation ooading for mobile-edge computing with energy harvesting devices. *IEEE Journal on Selected Areas in Communications*, 34(12), 3590–3605. doi:10.1109/JSAC.2016.2611964

Marichelvam, M. K., Prabaharan, T., & Yang, X. (2014). A discrete rey algorithm for the multi-objective hybrid owshop scheduling problems. *IEEE Transactions on Evolutionary Computation*, 18(2), 301–305. doi:10.1109/TEVC.2013.2240304

Peng, Q. L., Zhou, M. C., He, Q., Xia, Y. N., Wu, C. R., & Deng, S. G. (2018). Multi Objective Optimization for Location Prediction of Mobile Devices in Sensor-Based Applications. *IEEE Access : Practical Innovations, Open Solutions*, 6, 77123–77132. doi:10.1109/ACCESS.2018.2869897

Sahni, J., & Vidyarthi, D. (2018). A cost-ective deadline-constrained dynamic scheduling algorithm for scienic workflows in a cloud environment. *IEEE Transactions on Cloud Computing*, 6(1), 2–18. doi:10.1109/TCC.2015.2451649

Sanaei, P., Akbari, R., Zeighami, V., & Shams, S. (2013). Using Firefly Algorithm to Solve Resource Constrained Project Scheduling Problem. *BIC-TA*, 2012(1), 417-428.

Tabak, E. K., Cambazoglu, B. B., & Aykanat, C. (2014). Improving the performance of in-dependent task assignment heuristics minmin, maxmin and sufferage. *IEEE Transactions on Parallel and Distributed Systems*, 25(5), 1244–1256. doi:10.1109/TPDS.2013.107

Wang, Y. D., Liu, H., Zheng, W. B., Xia, Y. N., Li, Y. W., Chen, P., ... Xie, H. (2019). Multi-Objective Workflow Scheduling With Deep-Q-Network-Based Multi-Agent Reinforcement Learning. *IEEE Access : Practical Innovations, Open Solutions*, 7, 39974–39982. doi:10.1109/ACCESS.2019.2902846

Wu, H. Y., Deng, S. G., Li, W., Fu, M., Yin, J., & Zomaya, A. Y. (2018). Service selection for composition in mobile edge computing systems. In *IEEE International Conference on Web Services,* (pp. 355-358). IEEE. 10.1109/ICWS.2018.00060

Xia, Y. N., Zhou, M. C., Luo, X., Pang, S. C., & Zhu, Q. S. (2015). Stochastic Modeling and Quality Evaluation of Infrastructure-as-a-Service Clouds. *IEEE Transactions on Automation Science and Engineering*, 12(1), 162–170. doi:10.1109/TASE.2013.2276477

Xiang, Z., & Deng, S. (2020). Dynamical Service Deploy Replacement in Resource-constrained Edges. *Mobile Networks and Applications*. doi:10.100711036-019-01449-7

Yang, X. S. (2010). Firefly algorithm, stochastic test functions and design optimisation. *International Journal of Bio-inspired Computation*, 2(2), 78–84. doi:10.1504/IJBIC.2010.032124

Zhang, Y., Chen, X., Chen, Y., Li, Z., & Huang, J. (2018). Cost efficient scheduling for delay-sensitive tasks in edge computing system. *2018 IEEE International Conference on Services Computing*, 73-80. 10.1109/SCC.2018.00017

Zhao, T., Sheng, Z., Guo, X., & Niu, Z. (2017). Tasks scheduling and resource allocation in heterogeneous cloud for delay-bounded mobile edge computing. *IEEE International Conference on Communications*, 1-7. 10.1109/ICC.2017.7996858

This research was previously published in the International Journal of Web Services Research (IJWSR), 17(3); pages 56-68, copyright year 2020 by IGI Publishing (an imprint of IGI Global).

Chapter 17
Mobile Edge Computing:
Cost–Efficient Content Delivery in Resource–Constrained Mobile Computing Environment

Michael P. J. Mahenge
Wuhan University of Technology, China & Sokoine University of Agriculture, Morogoro, Tanzania

Chunlin Li
Wuhan University of Technology, Wuhan, China

Camilius A. Sanga
Sokoine University of Agriculture, Morogoro, Tanzania

ABSTRACT

The overwhelming growth of resource-intensive and latency-sensitive applications trigger challenges in legacy systems of mobile cloud computing (MCC) architecture. Such challenges include congestion in the backhaul link, high latency, inefficient bandwidth usage, insufficient performance, and quality of service (QoS) metrics. The objective of this study was to find out the cost-efficient design that maximizes resource utilization at the edge of the mobile network which in return minimizes the task processing costs. Thus, this study proposes a cooperative mobile edge computing (coopMEC) to address the afore-mentioned challenges in MCC architecture. Also, in the proposed approach, resource-intensive jobs can be unloaded from users' equipment to MEC layer which is potential for enhancing performance in resource-constrained mobile devices. The simulation results demonstrate the potential gain from the proposed approach in terms of reducing response delay and resource consumption. This, in turn, improves performance, QoS, and guarantees cost-effectiveness in meeting users' demands.

DOI: 10.4018/978-1-6684-5700-9.ch017

INTRODUCTION

Mobile Cloud Computing (MCC) is considered to be important in this era of technological advancement in order to improve performance in resource-constrained mobile devices through unloading resource-intensive loads to the cloud for processing and storage. However, the overwhelming growth of big data and latency-sensitive applications bring challenges that require innovative approaches to meet users' and systems requirements (Hashem et al., 2015; Skourlelopoulos et al., 2017). For example, big data produced by sensors and multimedia require intensive resources for computing, storage and bandwidth. Therefore, innovative approaches which merge the capability of Mobile Edge Computing (MEC) and cloud computing are needed to provide cost-effective content delivery and improve Quality of Experience (QoE) in resource-constrained computing devices (Holzinger et al., 2015). Innovative approaches use Information and Communication Technologies (ICTs) especially MCC, MEC, and Internet of Things (IoTs) to enhance performance and wellbeing, improve Quality of Service (QoS) and QoE, lower costs and resource consumption, and improve participation of stakeholders in service delivery (Mahenge & Mwangoka, 2014).

The innovation in the IoTs (e.g. smart mobile devices and sensors) and cloud computing enable data to be acquired anywhere and anytime as well as processed on time with wireless distribution using IoTs (Sundmacker et al., 2016). IoTs devices such as sensor nodes are used to gather patients' raw data which pass through gateway for aggregation and control in mobile-based cloud E-healthcare application (Figure1). The patients' data are uploaded into the cloud for processing, analysis and storage. The analyzed data are sent wirelessly to the health provider for further analysis, review and interpretation of the results. The health provider can take the required action for healthcare service delivery by consulting the patients online or physically. Furthermore, the rapid advancement of mobile computing devices such as smartphones, laptops, notebooks and tablets facilitate easy access to health services anywhere and anytime. Also, it enables materialization of emerging highly demanding services and applications. However, these mobile computing devices are limited in terms of battery life, storage and capability to handle applications demanding massive processing within a short period of time. Moreover, uploading data into the cloud for processing might be costly in terms of bandwidth and resource consumption (Shi et al., 2016). Also, data transportation and centralized processing can cause response delay which has impact on QoE.

Motivations and Contributions

Mobile data traffic has grown rapidly and will grow more in the coming years (Cisco, 2017) due to increased demands of big data (Skourlelopoulos et al., 2017) and latency-sensitive applications (Carlini, 2016). Such growth triggers challenges to legacy systems in MCC architecture. For mobile devices, problems originate from limited energy sources and resource such as low processing capacity, storage, and bandwidth. For cloud-based mobile applications, problems originate from network latency, processing time, data transportation from the device to the cloud as well as data processing and responding back to the service consumer. These problems, in return, become barriers for attaining the demands for low latency, QoE, cost-effectiveness, and location awareness (Siddiga et al., 2016; Soo et al., 2017).

To address such challenges, the MEC architecture deployed closer to end-users at the Base Station (BS) of cellular networks has been proposed to boost cloud computing (Patel et al., 2014). According to Patel et al. (2014), such proposed architecture has unique features to guarantee low latency, geo-distribution,

Figure 1. Example of mobile-based cloud E-healthcare

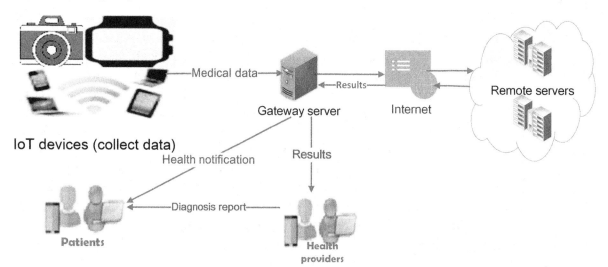

location awareness, mobility support and security. However, deploying MEC alone is not sufficient to guarantee enhanced performance in resource-constrained environments as many studies assume that MEC has abundant resources, while in fact resources at the MEC are limited in terms of power, bandwidth and processing capability compared to cloud computing (Shi et al., 2016). Therefore, this study proposes a cost-efficient approach that maximizes resource utilization at the MEC through collaboration between MEC servers to enhance performance and reduce cost and resource consumption by leveraging the capability of cloud computing architecture. The contributions of this paper include the following:

1. A proposed cost-efficient MEC-based architecture that exploits cooperative capabilities between MEC servers for task processing. MEC provides services to end-users through shorter distance compared to the cloud computing which minimizes resource consumption and response delay;
2. The proposed approach employs cooperative task unloading and resource assignment based on First-Come-First-Served (FCFS) and weighted-proportional distribution policies for task scheduling and processing;
3. Extensive simulations were conducted to demonstrate the effectiveness of the proposed architecture with various parameters.

The rest of the paper is structured as follows: Section "related works" presents state-of-the-art review of literature related to this study, section "mobile edge computing framework" describes the building blocks of MEC, and section "components of the proposed architecture" presents the building blocks of the proposed approach. Furthermore, section "system models" presents models of the proposed approach, and section "simulation results and discussion" presents the discussion of simulation results. Final section gives conclusion and proposes future works.

RELATED WORKS

Previous studies have been conducted on MCC and MEC which investigated unloading architectures focusing on energy and delay efficient approaches. However, only few studies have been done on collaborative approaches between MEC servers, and by considering the advanced capability of cloud computing architecture. Satyanarayanan et al. (2009) proposed cloudlet which is small-scale data center located close to mobile users and which offers both computation resources and storage. It is accessed by mobile devices through WiFi connection configured locally within a strategic location. However, some challenges reported in the literature includes: first, user devices shift amongst mobile network and WiFi each time the cloudlet services are requested; and second, limited coverage of WiFi since it is configured only locally to support a specific location range. According to Nkansah-Gyekye (2010), hand off management using intelligent algorithm is necessity in such a scenario. Nangyala and Kim (2016) proposed an IoTs based system applied in healthcare by leveraging the fog and cloud computing architecture. Furthermore, fog computing which is potential for improving performance of mobile applications is referred to as the key implementer of IoT and big data applications (Zhu et al., 2013). Moreover, in view of fog architecture, edges are part of core networks and data centers (Chiang, 2016), therefore one of the challenges reported in the literature is difficult to guarantee QoE especially for users of mobile applications because computations are not integrated in the mobile network architecture. Khan et al. (2014) surveyed on MCC application models which integrate the cloud computing into the mobile environment to overcome the obstacles related to the performance. They found that the integrated approach improved performance of mobile devices in terms of extending battery life span and allowing massive storage of data in the cloud. However, it was further reported that the MCC architecture still face challenges related to latency, inefficient QoS and QoE, bandwidth utilization and cost of data transportation because the data must be sent to the cloud for processing and storage. Also, Oludele and Oluwabukola (2016) surveyed on MCC applications and highlighted communication challenges related to low bandwidth, service availability and heterogeneity of the networks. The study reported that unloading is not always effective in saving energy. Therefore, it was proposed to find out whether to unload some part of the services in order to improve performance. Mach and Becvar (2017) surveyed MEC focusing on architecture and computation unloading. In their study, they found that unloading is highly demanding computations to the edge of network which is potential for improving performance on mobile applications especially on reducing latency and energy consumption at the mobile device. Yang et al. (2016) proposed an architecture based on the IoTs and the cloud. The proposed architecture applied in healthcare whereby the data gathered from the human body is transmitted directly to the cloud using Wi-Fi. Ndikumana et al. (2017) proposed collaborative model in which MEC servers cooperate in performing computation tasks and data caching. The proposed approach integrates allocation of cache and task offloading in MEC environments. Furthermore, Pham et al. (2018) proposed architecture for computation offloading decisions focusing on the heterogeneous networks with MEC which uses the game theory for user assignments and channel allocations.

Many previous studies have focused on offloading tasks from mobile devices to the MEC servers to enhance performance of mobile applications and improve users' QoE. However, many studies assume that MEC servers have abundant resources, while in fact resources at the MEC servers are limited in terms of power, bandwidth and processing capability. Only few studies considered either horizontal collaboration (between MECs) or vertical collaboration (MEC and cloud). Thus, this study proposes a collaborative MEC architecture which integrates horizontal and vertical collaboration. The performance evaluation of a proposed architecture is validated using a simulation approach which differs from previous studies (Ndume et al., 2014). Through collaborative edges and cloud computing, it is possible to establish efficient, usable, sustainable and cost-effective solution for content delivery in many domains such as E-healthcare especially for developing countries where scarcity of resources is a major problem.

MOBILE EDGE COMPUTING FRAMEWORK

According to European Telecommunications Standards Institute ([ETSI], 2016), MEC refers to the distributed mobile cloud computing system which provides computing resources at the proximity of the users' equipment. The cloud offers virtually limitless computing capability to supplement the limited processing ability of mobile devices. However, due to increasing of IoT applications demand which lead to the increase of the amount and volume of data, the communication between clients and the remote cloud in the traditional MCC approach become inefficient, thereby lowering the QoE. The MEC servers which are located closest to the user equipment provides potential opportunities in improving QoE by bringing compute and storage services at the edge of the network (Shi et al., 2016). These services and resources can be accessed by clients in a virtualized and distributed manner from local servers through mobile network or wireless access points. Also, MEC architecture possesses unique features to eliminate the shortcoming of the centralized cloud computing approach such as low latency, location awareness, geo-distribution, support for mobility, security and big data analytics (Patel et al., 2014; ETSI, 2016).

For this study, a conceptual framework was established to provide a logical organization of building blocks and concepts for achieving cost-efficiency in content delivery particularly in resource-poverty computing devices. The MEC framework (Figure 2) offers extremely distributed computing environment which facilitates deployment of mobile applications and services. It also provides storage and processing capability near to clients (Borcoci, 2016; Mohammed & Ahmed, 2017). The MEC framework (ETSI, 2016) comprises of four major building blocks, namely: mobile edge system, mobile edge host, mobile edge host level management and networks. The *mobile edge system level* comprising of user equipment (UE) and third part services has an overall management role to the whole mobile edge system. The *mobile edge host level* comprises a collection of vital functionalities which are essential to run mobile edge applications on a specific virtualization setup and enable such applications to deliver and use mobile edge services. The *mobile edge host* is further divided into mobile edge platform, the mobile edge applications and the virtualization infrastructure. The *networks level* comprises of cellular network, the local networks and the external networks. The *network level* has an overall role on the connectivity to local area networks, cellular networks and to external networks such as Internet.

The framework which was originally established by ESTI was adapted and extended to allow cooperation between various components and infrastructures in the mobile-edge-cloud computing architecture. In this framework, *the mobile edge system level* focuses on improving management, delivery and accessibility of services. Therefore, it is split into mobile edge orchestrator, UE applications, QoE improvement services, and operators and third-party services.

The *mobile edge orchestrator* handles core functionalities of the system. It not only interacts with the virtualization infrastructure to manage the available resources and services but also coordinates the resources between the UEs, the mobile edge hosts, and the network operator.

Figure 2. Mobile edge computing framework

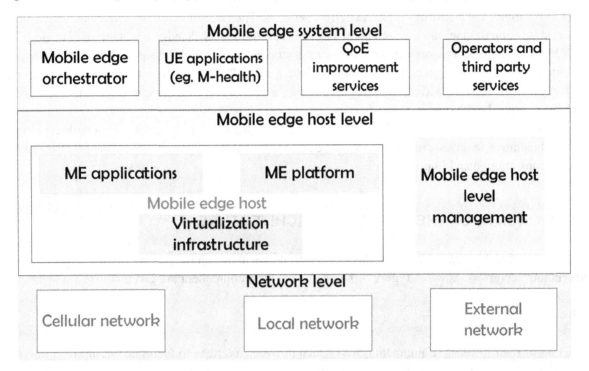

The *UE applications* refer to the mobile applications for example M-health that run or accessed through mobile devices. MEC bring advantages to users through unloading user-oriented services for example web browsing tasks to the MEC and allowing running of applications at the mobile devices. This is potential for extending battery lifespan and improving performance of mobile applications.

The *QoE improvement services* focus on improving users' QoE and network performance through synchronizing, caching and storing contents locally in the edge servers related to particular geographical location. Therefore, contents available in a local cache can be accessed by a user without forwarding requests to the data centers in the distant cloud. This is potential for reducing data transfer cost between user and data center over network, improve QoE and QoS.

The *operators and third-party services* focus on the gathering of data from users or IoTs (e.g. sensors and smart mobile devices) and use the data to improve decision making. The gathered data can be pre-processed and analyzed at the MEC, thereafter forwarded to the main servers in the distant cloud for more analysis and long-term storage. Considering M-health applications, healthcare providers can view patients' records from the data transferred automatically by the IoT devices and give feedback to the patient remotely.

The *mobile edge host* consists of mobile edge platform, mobile edge application and virtualization infrastructure. The *mobile edge platform* comprises of collection of vital functionalities which are essential to run mobile edge applications on a specific virtualization setup and enable them to deliver and use mobile edge services. Examples of mobile edge services include location-aware for tracking mobile user equipment, bandwidth management service to facilitate efficient utilization of available bandwidth by allocating bandwidth based on priority of traffic on the mobile edge applications, and ability to delivery services remotely. The *mobile edge applications* operate as virtual machines (VMs) supported by virtualization infrastructure delivered by the mobile edge host. Furthermore, it can interact with the mobile edge platform to use and deliver services. The *virtualization infrastructure* offers VMs to facilitate computation, storage, and network resources for the mobile edge applications. The purpose of VMs is to enhance resource sharing by many users and improve system performance in terms of resource utilization and application flexibility (Hwang et al., 2012). This is vital in enhancing service delivery in environments with limited resource setting especially developing countries where resources have been proved to be scarce.

In conclusion, the conceptual framework shows a comprehensive and organized set of building blocks for establishment of architecture that meet the demand for low latency, cost-effectiveness, efficient resource consumption and improved QoE.

COMPONENTS OF THE PROPOSED ARCHITECTURE

The proposed architecture consists of three major components which include clients, MEC servers and the remote servers as shown in Figure 3. The details of each component are given below.

The Clients

The *clients* refer to Users' Equipment (UEs) which provides interface to facilitate end-users to interact with the system. The UEs can include smart mobile devices such as smart phones, sensors, wearable devices, actuators, scanners and others. In this study, the clients (mobile users) are randomly and uniformly distributed in the base stations/access points. Also, owing to limited capacity of UEs, the data gathered by clients can be sent to the nearby MEC server for processing and returned to the clients after completion. The user interface also provides opportunities for users with preference and intentions to synchronize data between MEC servers and mobile devices depending on the device's storage capacity. Smartphones have reasonable computing and storage capacity which can facilitate processing locally in mobile devices for tasks that are not resource intensive. Synchronizing data locally on mobile devices is potential for minimizing bandwidth utilization, network overloading and hence improving QoE (Mahenge, 2017).

MEC Servers

The *MEC servers* refer to the servers installed at the cellular network Base Stations (BS) or local wireless access points located close to the clients (ESTI, 2017). The MEC servers have resources for computation and storage whereby in this case the total capacity for computational resources are denoted as K. Also, the manager server (powerful machine or server cluster) at each BS controls MEC nodes to guarantee efficient job reception, scheduling, resource allocation, data retrieval, and job processing. To ensure efficiency in job processing and content retrieval, MEC servers in the same cooperative domain can collaborate (horizontal collaboration). Nevertheless, if within the cooperative domain there are no requested content/resources, the BS will forward the request to the cloud (vertical collaboration) through the Internet. Also, the nearby server can respond directly to users' requests if it contains the requested data/services, otherwise it forwards the request to the Data Centers (DCs) in the cloud and the content distribution networks (CDNs) (ETSI, 2015; Shi et al., 2016). Furthermore, MEC provides

Figure 3. Components of the proposed coopMEC architecture

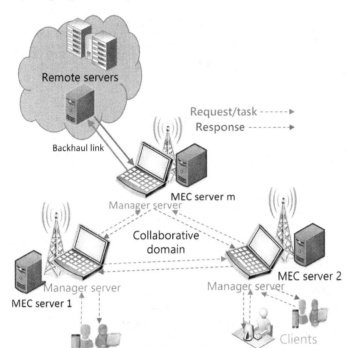

functionalities for task unloading, caching and data processing, thereby reducing resource consumption, response delay and improving QoE. The proposed design follows the specifications developed by ETSI Industry Specification Group (ISG) which supports hosting of third-party innovative applications on MEC servers placed nearness user equipment (Hu et al., 2015). Moreover, Dastjerdi and Buyya (2016) proved that a system using edge computing (fog) approach responds quicker and more energy efficient than using an approach whereby cloud is connected directly to UEs. In view of fog computing, nodes are greatly distributed over wide area whereas the edge is part of core networks and DCs (Chiang, 2016). In contrast, MEC is part of the mobile network with the computations integrated in the mobile network architecture, thus promising to enhance QoE and reduce the computation cost (Mahenge et al, 2019).

The Remote Servers

The remote servers refer to the traditional centralized computing data centers in the cloud. Cloud computing provides infrastructure, platforms and software (applications) as services (Sanga & Kibirige, 2016). Consumers (cloud users and end users) can subscribe on the required service and pay based on the use of such service. The cloud computing services usually are categorized in three service delivery models known as Infrastructure as a service (IaaS), Platform as a service (PaaS), and Software as a service (SaaS) (Figure 4). In *IaaS* service delivery model, users can utilize resources for compute, storage and network to deploy and run their applications (Figure 4(a)). However, the user does not have ability to manage or control the core cloud computing infrastructure. The *PaaS* model provides required resources to develop, deploy and manage execution of applications and services without installing the software in the computer used by a user (client) (Figure 4(b)). Also, it includes platform such as operating systems

Figure 4. Cloud computing actors and service models

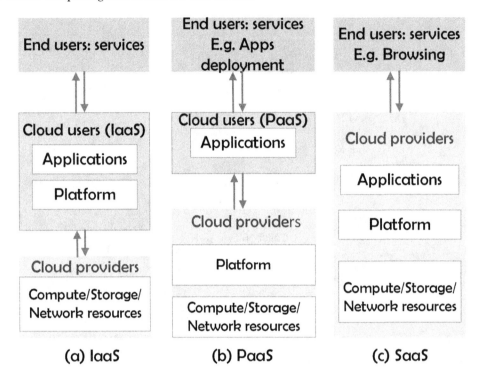

(a) IaaS   (b) PaaS   (c) SaaS

and runtime library support. Furthermore, it provides services such as application design, development, testing, deployment, management and hosting (Vetle et al., 2010). The *SaaS* model offers software applications as a service to a large number of cloud customers. These services are browser-initiated applications which are accessed via the Internet (Figure 4(c)).

Cloud computing comprises of several actors playing different roles in provision of cloud services. These actors include cloud provider, cloud user and end-users (Figure 4). *Cloud providers* are responsible for the management of compute, storage and network resources in the context of public cloud offering either IaaS or PaaS to the cloud users. They are also responsible for managing the resources necessary to deliver SaaS to end users. Furthermore, the cloud provider plays vital roles in allocating cloud resources based on Service Level Agreement (SLAs) contracted with cloud users or end-users. *Cloud user* utilizes the cloud resources to host applications that are offered as a service to the end-user based on the SLAs. The *end-user* can be an individual or organization that requests to use applications or services managed by the cloud users or cloud provider. Also, based on the requirements, it can make requests to utilize the applications housed on virtualized resources which includes computations, storage, and connectivity. However, end-users cannot be involved directly in cloud resource management, but their requirements are used as significant inputs for cloud resource management by cloud users and cloud providers.

The innovation in the cloud technology creates an opportunity to use virtual machines with high capacity universal servers to the locations like BS and gateways (Wang et al., 2017). Also, cloud computing provides powerful processing and storage capabilities. As such, it has potential for big data analysis and long-term storage. Table 1 summarizes the data processing chain, tools offered by cloud and key challenges in big data.

Table 1. Big data processing chain, technologies and key challenges

Data Processing Chain	Tools/Technologies	Key Challenges
Data collection	Sensors, open data, websites, smart mobile devices	Data availability, size, format and quality of data
Data storage	Cloud-based platform, Hadoop Distributed File System(HDFS), Cloud based data warehouse, NoSQL	Efficiency in data accessibility, privacy, security and cost
Data transmission	Wireless, Cloud based applications	Cost, Security, privacy and reliability
Data representation	Data mining algorithms, Machine learning, Visualization techniques	Data sources heterogeneity, data extraction and cleaning
Data Analysis	Big data analytics software	Real-time analytics, scalability, heterogeneity
Interpretation/ Communication	Data visualization techniques	Ownership, privacy, share ability

Furthermore, cloud computing provides Big Data-as-a-service (BDaaS) feature that allows storage and management of big data sets through service-oriented applications in the cloud. However, huge volume and fastness of data streams (from IoTs applications) increase network traffic and transportation cost of data to the cloud for processing (Siddiga et al., 2016), consequently lower QoE. Another critical challenge reported in the literatures includes inefficient big data and service delivery through the cloud-based applications (Drolia et al., 2013; Luan et al., 2015). Also, due to their characteristics, efficient processing of big data demands combination of both the data and data analytic tools to be housed closely to minimize congestion to the network, bandwidth utilization and augment performance. Therefore, leveraging the cooperative benefits between the MEC and the cloud is the promising solution to address the existing challenges in cloud computing.

To this end, a cost-efficient cooperative MEC-based architecture is proposed to minimize resource consumption and enhance QoE. MEC offers two-fold functionality. First, by providing services to clients through single-hop communication which guarantees low energy consumption and fast response time thereby improve QoE (Shi et al., 2016). Second, by forwarding resource intensive loads to the cloud to utilize its advanced resources and functionalities (Borylo et al., 2016) can improve service delivery (Botta et al., 2014). Also, by categorizing latency-sensitive loads to run at the mobile edge and forward resource intensive to the data centers on the cloud may minimize energy requirement and enhance performance (Kaur et al., 2018; Miettinen & Nurminen, 2010).

SYSTEM MODEL

In this section, the system models are presented, it is referred to $\phi=\{1,2,3,\ldots,\tau\}$ as the set of clients, and $S_m=\{1,2,3,\ldots,m\}$ as the set of MEC servers respectively. Also, it is considered that MEC servers with necessary processing resources are deployed in BS located in different places (Figure 5). In the next sub-sections, the detailed models for local and remote execution are presented.

Figure 5. System models for the proposed coopMEC architecture

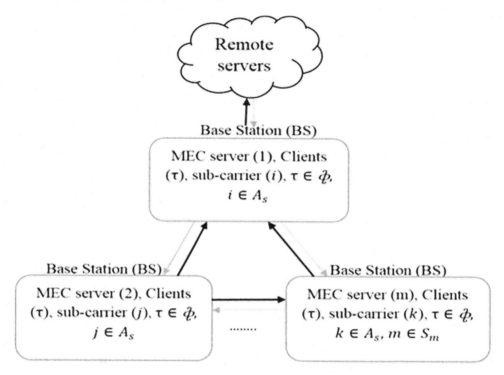

Local Computation

Let J_τ represents the job to be executed, W_r [CPU cycles] denotes the processing capacity (workload) required to complete the job and W_d denotes the processing capacity [CPU cycles per second] of users' equipment. The time to accomplish the job (t_{loc}) when computed locally in mobile device can be found by:

$$t_{loc} = \frac{W_r}{W_d} \text{ [Seconds]} \tag{1}$$

Also, the energy used per execution cycle is given by $e = \gamma_d f_d^2$ (Wen et al., 2012) where, γ_d is the CPU energy constant and f is the CPU frequency of user equipment. Therefore, the energy consumption (E_{loc}) in Joules for local computation can be found by:

$$E_{loc} = \gamma_d (W_d)^2 W_r \tag{2}$$

Unloading Models

Let $A_s = \{1,2,3,\dots,s\}$ denotes the set of accessible sub-carriers for uploading job J_τ to the MEC. It is assumed that the MEC system uses orthogonal frequency-division multiplexing access scheme. Then, the proportion (P_{sb}) of each sub-carrier can be obtained by $P_{sb} = \frac{B}{A_s}$ [Hertz] where, B is the frequency band.

The unloading parameter can be expressed as $x_{\tau m}^i, i \in A_s, \tau \in \phi, m \in S_m$ where $x_{\tau m}^i = 1$ specify that the sub-carrier i is assigned to client τ whose job is unloaded to MEC m and $x_{\tau m}^i = 0$ otherwise. Consequently, the sub-carrier assignment matrix can be expressed as $W = \left\{ x_{\tau m}^i \mid i \in A_s, \tau \in \phi, m \in S_m \right\}$. Moreover, the unloading strategy can be defined as $X_p = \left\{ x_{\tau m}^i \in W \mid x_{\tau m}^i = 1 \right\}$ which must satisfy the following achievable condition:

$$\sum_{m \in S_m} \sum_{i \in A_s} x_{\tau m}^i \leq 1, \forall_{\tau \in \phi} \tag{3}$$

In this case it is considered that a single antenna is used for each client and BS during uploading task J_τ to MEC and each client can only upload data using one sub-carrier. Let P_τ [Watts] be the power for transferring a job J_τ from user equipment to MEC server and $z_{\tau m}^i$ be the sub-carrier channel gain. The sub-carrier power assignment matrix is indicated by:

$$\mathcal{F} = \left\{ p_{\tau m}^i \mid p_{\tau m}^i \in \left[0, P_\tau \right], i \in A_s, \tau \in \phi, m \in S_m \right\}$$

where $p_{\tau m}^i$ denotes the power assigned to client τ whose job is unloaded to MEC m through sub-carrier i. In the proposed architecture, clients can experience interference caused by inter-cell communication. Therefore, the Signal-to-Noise-Ratio (SINR) from client τ to base station hosting MEC server (m) on sub-carrier i *is* obtained by:

$$\delta_{\tau m}^i = \frac{P_\tau z_{\tau m}^i}{\left(\sum_{k \in \phi} x_{km}^i P_k z_{km}^i \right) + \sigma^2}, \forall_{\tau \in \phi, m \in S_m, i \in A_s} \tag{4}$$

where:

$$\left(\sum_{k \in \phi} x_{km}^i P_k z_{km}^i \right)$$

is the aggregated interference from clients connected to other base station through similar sub-band i and $\sigma 2$ is the variance related to system noise. Also, the feasible rate [bits per second] when a client τ upload data to MEC server m *is* computed as:

$$R_f = P_{sb} log2(1 + \delta_{\tau m}) \tag{5}$$

where $\delta_{\tau m} = \sum_{i \in A_s} \delta_{\tau m}^i$. Furthermore, considering one BS having s sub-bands used to serve τ clients unloading tasks to MEC server m, let $x_{\tau i} = \sum_{i \in A_s} x_{\tau m}^i$ and d_i[bits] be the quantity of input data required to upload the task to MEC server. Therefore, when a client τ transfer the task input d_i the transmission time t_{tr}^τ is obtained by:

$$t_{tr}^\tau = \sum_{i \in A_s} \frac{x_{\tau i} d_i}{R_f}, \forall_{\tau \in \phi} \tag{6}$$

Queuing and Job Execution at the MEC

This section presents the models for job processing resource assignment, execution time cost and the overhead time cost caused by queuing and scheduling for the job executed remotely. It is assumed that for each job arriving at BS, the scheduler assigns resources based on non-preemptive First-Come-First-Served (FCFS) algorithm. Furthermore, it is considered that each MEC server is installed with essential resources such as compute, storage, and connectivity. Moreover, the virtual machines (VMs) as considered in (Bruneo, 2014) are established asynchronously on similar physical machine (PM) to perform parallel computing on diverse jobs submitted. The considered approach for VMs establishment allows installation or removal of a particular VM any time based on the job processing demands. It is obvious that VMs that are able to share corporate resources from PMs such as Central-Processing Unit, storage, and buses for I/O are significant for reducing the cost of hardware especially for computing environments with limited resource setting.

Let K_i be the computational capacity of each BS. Then, the total capacity for computing resources in all BS within the cooperative domain is expressed as:

$$K = \sum_{i=1}^{m} K_i, \forall_{i \in S_m} \tag{7}$$

It is assumed that each BS can receive multiple computing inquiries, let $r_{\tau m}$ be the compute resources assigned to client τ requesting processing service at MEC server $i \in S_m$. Furthermore, a variable $\psi_{\tau i}$ denotes the inquiries for job processing submitted to a particular MEC server $i \in S_m$. Then, the total processing inquiries become $\sum_{\tau: i \in S_m} \psi_{\tau i}$. Thus, the BS allocates resources to multiple users grounded on weighted proportional distribution (Nguyen & Vojnovic, 2011) whereby every individual user obtains the portion of resource requested at MEC server $i \in S_m$ computed as:

$$r_{\tau m} = K_i \frac{\psi_{\tau i}}{\sum_{\tau: i \in S_m} \psi_{\tau i}} \tag{8}$$

where K_i is the total computing capability for MEC servers $i \in S_m$. Furthermore, when the task arrives at the MEC server, it is critical to assign resources based on the resource assignment policy. Let r_m denote the computational rate [CPU cycles per second] that quantify the vacant computational resources at individual MEC server that can be shared by multiple clients. Also, the expression $R_a = \{r_{\tau m} \mid \tau \in \phi, m \in S_m\}$ defines the resource assignment policy whereby $r_{\tau m} [cycles\,per\,second] > 0$ indicates the quantity of computing resources assigned to client $\tau \in \phi$. Furthermore, the achievable resource assignment policy must agree with the available computing resources such that:

$$\sum_{\tau \in \phi} r_{\tau m} \le r_m, \forall_{m \in S_m} \tag{9}$$

Therefore, the computing resources being assigned, the remote execution time $\left(t_e^\tau \right)$ of the unloaded job J_τ can be obtained by:

$$t_e^\tau = \sum_{i \in A_s} \frac{x_{\tau i} W_r}{r_{\tau m}}, \forall_{\tau \in \phi} \tag{10}$$

Moreover, in order to consider the overhead cost incurred during task scheduling, it is assumed that the jobs are scheduled based on non-preemptive policy whereby each job is allocated a specific time-slot until the execution is completed. Then, let the job scheduling sequence for execution in the MEC server be denoted as $X = \left\{ s_i \mid s_i \ne s_j, i, j \in \phi \right\}$. As considered by Yu et al. (2016), the overhead time $\left(t_{oh}^\tau \right)$ due to scheduling and queuing of job i from user τ when jt^h job execution is in progress is obtained by:

$$t_{oh}^\tau = \sum_{i \in A_s} \frac{x_{\tau i} W_j}{r_{\tau m}} \tag{11}$$

where W_j is the input-data size of job j.

Unloading Utility Models

With resources $(r_{\tau m}, p_\tau)$ being assigned to the task (J_τ) and the offloading strategy (X_p) being defined, the total waiting time (t_w) by a client when unloading the task from mobile device to the MEC server can be obtained by combining Expression (6) and (10) and (11) which gives:

$$t_w = \sum_{i \in A_s} x_{\tau i} \left(\frac{d_i}{R_f} + \frac{W_r}{r_{\tau m}} + \frac{W_j}{r_{\tau m}} \right) \tag{12}$$

Also, the energy $(E_{\tau p})$ in Joules required to transfer the job during unloading is obtained by:

$$E_\tau = \frac{P_\tau t_{tr}^\tau}{\varepsilon_\tau}, \forall_{\tau \in \phi}$$

where ε_τ is constant related to power amplification effectiveness which is assumed to be 1. Therefore, the required energy for uploading is given by:

$$E_{\tau p} = P_\tau d_i \sum_{i \in A_s} \frac{x_{\tau i}}{R_f}, \forall_{\tau \in \phi} \tag{13}$$

Corresponding with processing the job locally, let W_{mec} represent the processing capacity (CPU frequency) of MEC server m, the energy required for executing J_τ in $m \in S_m$ can be given by:

$$E_{proc} = \gamma_{mec}(W_{mec})^2 W_r \tag{14}$$

where γ_{mec} indicates the co-efficient associated with the MEC server CPU energy. Consequently, the total energy cost incurred for remote execution can be found by combining (13) and (14) which gives:

$$E_\tau = P_\tau d_i \sum_{i \in A_s} \frac{x_{\tau i}}{R_f} + \gamma_{mec} \left(W_{mec}\right)^2 W_r \tag{15}$$

In the proposed architecture, the cost-effectiveness and enhanced QoE can be assured in different ways. First, they are assured by allowing computation nearness to the user in the home BS where the user is currently associated; and second, through cooperation between the neighboring MEC servers. Also, for the job to be unloaded to the MEC layer, the constraints $t_{loc} - t_w > 0$ and $E_{loc} - E_\tau > 0$ must be satisfied (Kumar & Lu, 2010). Let:

$$\alpha = \left(1 - \frac{t_w}{t_{loc}}\right) \text{ and } \beta = \left(1 - \frac{E_\tau}{E_{loc}}\right)$$

denote the improvement in response time and energy consumption, respectively. Therefore, the total cost $(D_c(\alpha, \beta))$ for serving all user requests is defined as considered in (Lyu et al., 2016):

$$D_c\left(\alpha, \beta\right) = \left(\gamma_\tau^t \alpha + \gamma_\tau^e \beta\right) \sum_{k=1}^{m} x_{\tau k}, \forall_{\tau \in \phi, k \in S_m} \tag{16}$$

where $x_{\tau k}$ indicates whether task is unloaded to MEC servers. Moreover, the variables $\gamma_\tau^t, \gamma_\tau^e \in [0,1]$ where $\gamma_\tau^t + \gamma_\tau^e = 1, \forall_{\tau \in \phi}$ are indicators for client's desirability on time and energy costs. Therefore, expression (16) can be re-written as:

$$D_c\left(\alpha, \beta\right) = \left(\gamma_\tau^t \alpha + \left(1 - \gamma_\tau^t\right)\beta\right) \sum_{k=1}^{m} x_{\tau k}, \forall_{\tau \in \phi, k \in S_m} \tag{17}$$

The objective of this paper is to find out the cost-efficient design that minimizes the task processing costs subject to the capacity constraint and coverage constraint which, in return, maximizes resource utilization at the MEC. Consequently, improves performance and QoS for resource-constrained computing environments. Therefore, the objective function is expressed as:

$$\min D_c(\alpha,\beta) \tag{18}$$

subject to:

$$\sum_{\tau \in C} r_{\tau m} \leq r_m, \forall_{m \in S_m} \tag{19}$$

$$\sum_{i=1}^{s} x_{\tau m}^i \geq 1, \forall_{\tau \in \phi, m \in S_m} \tag{20}$$

In the objective function above, the variables represent response time and energy consumption. The constraints in Expression (19) guarantees that the resources can be assigned to job if are available and the allocation cannot exceed the available capacity, while the set of constraints in Expression (20) guarantees that if the unloading decision is made, then the task can either be unloaded to home BS where the user is currently associated, any other nearby BS in the cooperative domain, or forwarded to the cloud. Algorithm 1 gives the details of task unloading and allocation of resources for execution.

Algorithm 1: Task unloading and resource assignment algorithm

```
Input:   J_τ,W_r,γ_τ^t,γ_τ^e,m
Output:  Best task unloading and resource assignment scheme
1:  Initialize: x_τm^i,a_i^τ,a_j^τ,x_τk,t_loc,t_w,E_loc,E_τ
2:  For each task T_τ received at BS i ∈ S_m, do
3:     compute t_loc,t_w,E_loc,E_τ,D_c(α,β) by (1),(2),(12),(15),(17)
4:        if t_loc − t_w ≤ 0 and E_loc − E_τ ≤ 0
5:           compute J_τ locally
6:        else
7:              unload to MEC
8:        end if
9:         if a_i^τ = 1
10:            allocate < r_τm > at MEC server i ∈ S_m
11:            else if a_i^τ = 0 and a_j^τ = 1
12:               allocate < r_τm > at nearby MEC server j ∈ S_m
13:               else if ∑_{j∈S_m} a_j^τ ≥ 1
14:               v = arg min D_c(α,β)        // v relate to minimum execution cost
                       j ≠ i, j ∈ S_m
15:               allocate < r_τm > at MEC server v ∈ S_m
16:                  else
17:                     forward the request to remote servers
```

```
18:                 allocate < r_{τm} > based on least loaded policy
19:          end if
20:       end if
21:       end if
22:    update RAT
23: end for
```

Algorithm 1 represents the pseudo-code of the task unloading and resource assignment algorithm (TURAA). Essentially the algorithm can be parted into two (2) main steps: first, decision to compute locally or unload task to MEC layer (Algorithm 1 line 2-8), and second, resource assignment for task computing (Algorithm 1 line 9-22). The task can be unloaded to upper layers only if satisfies the constraints $t_{loc}-t_w>0$ and $E_{loc}-E_τ>0$ otherwise it is more beneficial to compute the task locally in users' equipment than unloading (Algorithm 1 line 4 and 5). For each task unloaded to upper layer, the BS chooses the location to perform execution by considering capacity and proximity constraints. Moreover, resource assignment assumes non-preemptive based on FCFS algorithm. If the required resources are available at MEC servers $i \in S_m$ then the BS allocates them to execute the task, otherwise the vacant resources $j \in S_m$ at the neighboring BS will be allocated (Algorithm 1 line 9-12). Similarly, if more than one vacant resource are available at nearby BS, the MEC server $v \in S_m$ related to the minimum execution cost will be selected (Algorithm 1 line 14). Finally, if the required resources are neither in $i \in S_m$ nor $j \in S_m$ the BS transfers the request to the remote servers for execution and update the Resource Allocation Table (RAT). Furthermore, the time complexity of Algorithm 1 for computing the minimum task processing cost and determining the best MEC server for each request arriving at the BS is $O(m)$ where m denotes the number of MEC servers (Algorithm 1 line 2-23). Therefore, for all tasks k the time complexity to find the lowest execution cost is $O(k \times m)$. The following section presents the simulation results.

SIMULATION RESULTS AND DISCUSSION

This section presents the simulation results to evaluate the potential benefits from the proposed architecture. The aim of the simulation was to determine the implications of the proposed architecture in terms of response time, energy usage, and bandwidth consumption on different parameters such as varying number of clients, workload, number of MEC servers and size of input data. The following metrics were considered for evaluation: (i) average energy consumption-the average energy consumed by mobile devices for both case, local and remote task processing; and (ii) average response delay-the average time a server can respond to the requesting user. The simulation results were compared with the following baselines approaches:

1. **Remote execution without collaboration:** This approach dynamically unloads tasks to the remote servers for execution in order to improve performance and save energy in resource-poverty mobile devices (Liu, Guo & Yang, 2017);
2. **Random Unloading approach (RUA):** In this approach, each client randomly and autonomously chooses a server to offload the job (Shahzad & Szymanski, 2016);
3. **Local execution:** The tasks are processed by mobile devices.

Throughout, the storage and computation capabilities for each MEC server were considered to be randomly and uniformly distributed ranging between 100 to 1000 GB for storage and 50 to 1000 MIPS for computations. Also, as considered by Cheng et al. (2018), the CPU energy coefficients γ_d and γ_{mec} are set to be 1×10^{-24} and 1×10^{-26} respectively. Other parameters are presented in Table 2. The simulation experiment was performed on computer with processor Intel(R) core i7-3770 CPU@3.40GHz, 4.00GB (RAM), x64 architecture running Ubuntu 16.04.

Table 2. Present the variables, value and description of each variable used in the simulation

Variables	Value	Variable Narration
S_m	10	Number of MEC servers
τ	50~250	Number of active users (randomly and evenly distributed)
P_τ	20dBm	Power required to transfer job from users' equipment to MEC
B	20Mbps	Network Bandwidth
$\sigma2$	-102dBm	noise variance
r_m	20Gbps	Processing capability of each edge server
W_τ	1Gbps	Processing capacity of each user device
d_i	500~1000 KB	Size of input data needed to transfer the job from device to MEC
W_r	100~1,000 MHz	Maximum Processing capacity needed to complete the job
$\gamma_\tau^t \big/ \gamma_\tau^e$	0.25~2	Users' desirability
$x_{\tau m}^i$	{0,1}	Task unloading decision variable

Impacts of Clients' Desirability on Response Time and Energy Usage

In order to investigate the impacts of clients' desirability on response time and energy consumption, the number of clients is fixed while the clients' desirability $\left(\gamma_\tau^t / \gamma_\tau^e\right)$ varies between 0.25 and 2 where $\gamma_\tau^t, \gamma_\tau^e \in [0,1]$. As shown in Figure 6, the average response time decreases while the energy consumption increases when $\gamma_\tau^t / \gamma_\tau^e$ increases. Energy usage increases with increase in clients' desirability because when desirability to time $\left(\gamma_\tau^t\right)$ increases, the desirability to energy $\left(\gamma_\tau^e\right)$ decreases since $\gamma_\tau^t + \gamma_\tau^e = 1$ resulting to increase in energy usage. Therefore, mobile users can achieve the cost-efficiency in terms of energy saving and reduced delay in different ways based on the priority. Example of application scenario includes:

1. In latency-sensitive tasks such as video streaming the clients' desirability can be set $\gamma_\tau^t > \gamma_\tau^e$ to indicate high priority on response time;
2. When the clients' priority is to save more energy in mobile devices, the clients' desirability can be set $\gamma_\tau^t < \gamma_\tau^e$;

3. If both delay and energy usage has the same priority, the clients' desirability can be set $\gamma_\tau^t = \gamma_\tau^e$ which cooperatively improves energy usage by mobile devices and achieves minimum response time.

Figure 6. Impact of clients' desirability on response time and energy usage

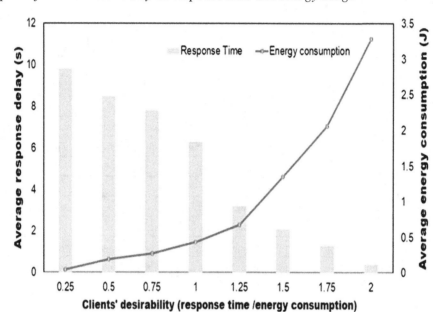

Impacts of Workload on Energy Consumption

This section presents the comparative results on the impact of workload on energy consumption for three approaches: Local execution, Remote execution without cooperation and the proposed coopMEC. As shown in Figure 7, the energy consumption increases when the workload increases in each case because more workload require more resources for processing which has an impact on energy consumption. However, the proposed coopMEC consumes less energy in each case compared to Local execution and Remote execution without cooperation approaches. This is because exploring cooperative approach between MEC maximizes resource utilization at the MEC layer which in return minimizes the transmission energy to the distant servers as many requests can be handled by MEC servers (Kaur et al., 2018; Shi et al., 2016). Therefore, the results demonstrate the potential advantage of the proposed coopMEC architecture in minimizing energy consumption, thereby improving users' QoE. However, due to constrain in bandwidth and computing resources at the MEC server, unloading a large number of huge tasks at once might reduce the QoE to clients when processing tasks at the MEC server rather than processing locally.

Figure 7. Comparison of energy consumption for Local execution, Remote execution without cooperation and the proposed coopMEC when the workload varies

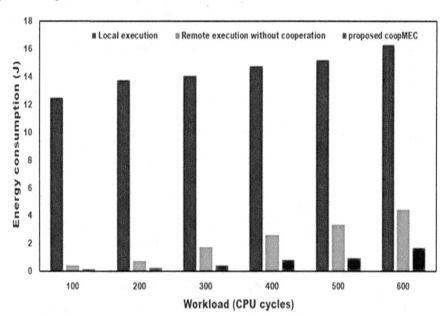

Impacts of Number of MEC Servers on Response Time

Figure 8 presents the comparison in response time when the number of MEC servers varies. In all cases it is assumed that the task has the same size. The response delay is high when the task is executed locally because of the limited processing capacity of mobile devices. Likewise, as shown in the Figure, when the number of MEC servers rise, resources for executing the tasks become plenty bringing more opportunities for resource-constrained mobile devices to unload tasks to MEC layer. Moreover, due to abundant resources in coopMEC, the tasks can be distributed and processed jointly which contribute to fast response compared to Remote execution without cooperation where tasks' queue can be long waiting for execution resources.

Impacts of Task Input Size

In Figure 9 the impact of task size on the total cost for processing user requests is presented. As the task size increases, it is obvious that the execution energy increases in a similar trend which has an impact on the total task execution cost. However, from the figure, it can be observed that the proposed approach outperforms the two baselines approaches in terms of energy saving for similar input data size. This is because, first, the offloading decision in the proposed approach must satisfy the minimum task execution cost, and second, cooperative approach between MEC which are located closer to users save more transmission and execution energy which, in return decreases the total cost as shown in Figure 9.

Figure 8. Impacts of number of MEC servers on response time

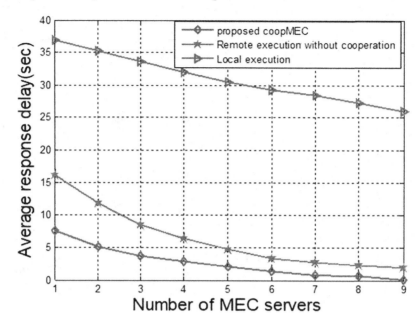

Figure 9. Comparison of total cost for four approaches when the task input size varies from 5 to 30MB

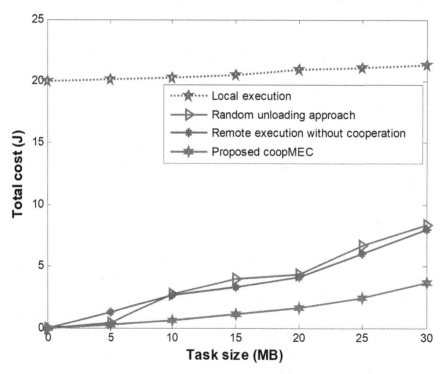

Impacts on Bandwidth Consumption

Figure 10 demonstrates the implication of the proposed approach on bandwidth consumption when users vary. From the figure, it can be observed that among all users' bandwidth consumption exhibit a similar trend when the system utility increases. Furthermore, it is observed that, the bandwidth consumption increases slightly with small difference for all users when unloading utility increases from 0 to 50 per cent. However, beyond 50 per cent, the bandwidth consumption increases with significant difference among users because when many users upload tasks to the MEC servers, they consume more bandwidth for uploading tasks. Also, when the number of users is small, the bandwidth consumption is much lower than when the number of users is larger. For example, for 50 and 100 users, the bandwidth consumption is less than 10Mbps as shown in Figure 10. This is because, when there are fewer users, most requests can be handled by the MEC servers without passing traffics through the backhaul link to the remote server which saves more bandwidth. However, when the number of service requesters becomes high, they can necessitate forwarding requests to the remote server which consumes more bandwidth. Therefore, in terms of bandwidth consumption, the proposed approach is cost-effective because more traffics can be transferred through shorter distance which frees the backhaul link from congestion and guarantee improved QoE.

Figure 10. Comparing bandwidth consumption for various concurrent users unloading tasks

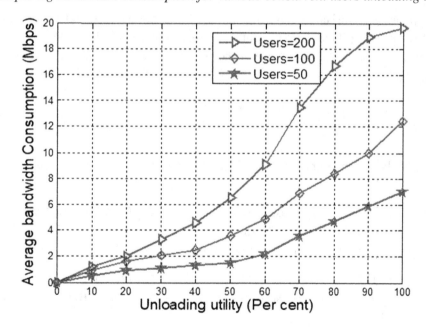

CONCLUSION AND FUTURE WORKS

In this paper, the authors study the problem of content delivery in resource-constrained mobile devices with the objective of minimizing resource consumption and response delay. Thus, a cost-efficient architecture which exploits cooperative capabilities between MECs is proposed to maximize resource utilization at the MEC layer through unloading resource-intensive tasks from mobile devices to more resourceful MEC. MEC plays potential role in providing services to clients through single-hop communication as it minimizes resource consumption and latency. Also, it exploits the advanced capability of cloud computing for tasks requiring massive processing resources which ensure efficient processing and storage. Moreover, extensive simulations were conducted to evaluate the effectiveness of the proposed architecture using various parameters. The numerical results demonstrate the advantages of the proposed approach which includes: first, minimize the computation time by distributing the workload amongst available compute resources in the cooperative space; second, lower response delay by executing job at the nearby edge servers instead of distance cloud; third, reduce congestion to the core network link by executing task at the edge servers located nearness to services consumers; fourth, cross-cut bandwidth usage cost by computing job at the edge servers located at a short distance from users compared to the distance cloud; and fifth, enhance the QoE by allowing service delivery in a single-hop edge servers. Also, improves data processing and retrieval by service consumers. Therefore, this study contributes significantly in addressing some problems identified by (Skourlelopoulos et al., 2017) related to big data in MCC. In the future, the researchers aim to perform more experiments in the field and extend the scope of the work.

ACKNOWLEDGMENT

The work was supported by the National Natural Science Foundation (NSF) under grants (No.61672397, No. 61873341), Application Foundation Frontier Project of WuHan (No. 2018010401011290). Any opinions, findings, and conclusions are those of the authors and do not necessarily reflect the views of the above agencies.

REFERENCES

Borcoci, E. (2016). Fog Computing, Mobile Edge Computing, and Cloudlets - which one? SoftNet Conference, 1-122.

Borylo, P., Lason, A., Rzasa, J., Szymanski, A., & Jajszczyk, A. (2016). Energy-Aware Fog and Cloud Interplay Supported by Wide Area Software Defined Networking. In *Proceeding of 2016 IEEE International Conference on Communications*, (pp. 1-7). Kuala Lumpur, Malaysia: IEEE. 10.1109/ICC.2016.7511451

Botta, A., Donato, W. D., Persico, V., & Pescap, A. (2014). On the integration of cloud computing and Internet of Things. In *FiCloud International Conference*, (pp. 23-30). Barcelona: Academic Press. 10.1109/FiCloud.2014.14

Bruneo, D. (2014). A stochastic model to investigate data center performance and QoS in IAAS cloud computing systems. *IEEE Transactions on Parallel and Distributed Systems, 25*(3), 560–569. doi:10.1109/TPDS.2013.67

Carlini, S. (2016). *The drivers and benefits of edge computing* (White paper 226). Schneider Electric –Data Center Science Center. Retrieved September, 22, 2018, from https://www.apc.com/salestools/VAVR-A4M867/VAVR-A4M867_R0_EN.pdf?sdirect=true

Cheng, K., Teng, Y., Sun, W., Liu, A., & Wang, X. (2018). *Energy-Efficient Joint Offloading and Wireless Resource Allocation Strategy in Multi-MEC Server Systems*. available: arXiv: 1803.07243v1

Chiang, M. (2016). *Fog networking: An overview on research opportunities*. Retrieved January, 1, 2018, from: http://arxiv.org/pdf/1601.00835

Cisco. Cisco visual networking index: Global mobile data traffic forecast update, 2016-2021 white paper. (n.d.). Retrieved July, 20, 2018, from https://www.cisco.com/c/en/us/solutions/collateral/service-provider/visual-networking-index-vni/mobile-white-paper-c11-520862.html

Dastjerdi, A. V., & Buyya, R. (2016). Fog Computing: Helping the Internet of Things Realize its Potential. *Computer*, *49*(8), 112–116. doi:10.1109/MC.2016.245

Drolia, U., Martins, R. P., Tan, J., Chheda, A., Sanghavi, M., Gandhi, R., & Narasimhan, P. (2013). The Case for Mobile Edge-Clouds. In *Proceedings of the IEEE 10th UIC/ATC*, (pp. 209–215). Vietri sul Mare, Italy: IEEE.

European Telecommunications Standards Institute. (2015). *Mobile-Edge Computing* (White Paper). Author.

European Telecommunications Standards Institute. (2016). *GS MEC 001*. Available: http://www.etsi.org/deliver/etsi gs/MEC/001 099/003/01.01.01 60/gs MEC003v010101p.pdf

Hashem, I. A. T., Yaqoob, I., Anuar, N. B., Mokhtar, S., Gani, A., & Khan, S. U. (2015). The rise of big data on cloud computing: Review and open research issues. *Information Systems*, *47*, 98–115. doi:10.1016/j.is.2014.07.006

Holzinger, A., Roecker, C., & Ziefle, M. (Eds.). (2015). *Smart Health, State-of-the-Art SOTA Lecture Notes in Computer Science, LNCS 8700* (pp. 21–40). Heidelberg, Germany: Springer.

Hu, Y. C., Patel, M., Sabella, D., Sprecher, N., & Young, V. (2015). Mobile edge computing—A key technology towards 5G. *ETSI White Paper*, *11*(11), 1-16.

Hwang, K., Fox, G. C., & Dongarra, J. J. (2012). Virtual Machines and Virtualization of clusters and data centers. In *Distributed and Cloud Computing from Parallel Processing to the Internet of Things* (pp. 129–183). Morgan Kaufmann.

Kaur, K., Garg, S., Aujla, G. S., Kumar, N., Rodrigues, J., & Guizani, M. (2018, February). Computing in the Industrial Internet of Things Environments: Software-Defined-Network-Based Edge-Cloud Interplay. *IEEE Communications Magazine*, 44–51.

Khan, A. R., Othman, M., Madani, S. A., & Khan, S. U. (2014). A Survey of Mobile Cloud Computing Application Models. *IEEE Communications Surveys and Tutorials*, *16*(1), 393–413. doi:10.1109/SURV.2013.062613.00160

Kumar, K., & Lu, Y. H. (2010). Cloud Computing for Mobile Users: Can Offloading Computation Save Energy? *Computer*, *43*(4), 51–56. doi:10.1109/MC.2010.98

Liu, X., Guo, S., & Yang, Y. (2017). Task offloading with execution cost minimization in heterogeneous mobile cloud computing. In *13th Mobile Ad-hoc and sensor network (MSN) International Conference*, (pp.509-522). Beijing, China: Academic Press.

Luan, T. H., Gao, L., Li, Z., Xiang, Y., & Sun, L. (2015). *Fog Computing: Focusing on Mobile Users at the Edge*. arXiv: 1502.01815

Lyu, X., Tian, H., Zhang, P., & Sengul, C. (2016). Multi-user joint task offloading and resources optimization in proximate clouds. *IEEE Transactions on Vehicular Technology, 99*, 1–17.

Mach, P., & Becvar, Z. (2017). *Mobile Edge Computing: A Survey on Architecture and Computation Offloading*. Retrieved December, 28, 2017, from arXiv: 1702.05309v2 [cs.IT]

Mahenge, M. P. J. (2017). Potential of Cost-Effective Mobile Learning in Resource and Bandwidth Constrained Environments. *International Journal of Information Communication Technologies and Human Development, 9*(1), 1–14. doi:10.4018/IJICTHD.2017010101

Mahenge, M. P. J., & Mwangoka, J. W. (2014). Mobile-based system for cost-effective e-learning contents delivery in resource and bandwidth constrained learning environments. *Knowledge Management and E-Learning, 6*(4), 449–463.

Mahenge, M. P. J., Sanga, C. A., & Li, C. (2019). Collaborative Mobile Edge and Cloud Computing: Tasks Unloading for Improving Users' Quality of Experience in Resource-Intensive Mobile Applications, *Proceeding of 4th IEEE International Conference on Computer and Communication Systems*, 322-326.

Miettinen, A. P., & Nurminen, J. K. (2010). Energy efficiency of mobile clients in cloud computing. In *Proceeding of 2nd USENIX Conference HotCloud*, (pp. 1-7). USENIX.

Mohammed, Z. K. A., & Ahmed, E. S. A. (2017). Internet of Things Applications, Challenges and Related Future Technologies. *World Science News, 67*(2), 126–148.

Nandyala, C.S., & Kim, H. (2016). IoT-based real time healthcare monitoring for smart homes and hospitals. *International Journal of smart Home, 10*(2), 187-196.

Ndikumana, A., Ullah, S., Leanh, T., Tran, N. H., & Hong, C. S. (2017). *Collaborative Cache Allocation and Computation Offloading in Mobile Edge Computing*. IEEE -APNOMS. doi:10.1109/APNOMS.2017.8094149

Ndume, V., Nkansah-Gyekye, Y., & Ko, J. (2014). A Novel Algorithm for Integrating E-Health Data in Distributed Low Bandwidth Environment. *Journal of Emerging Trends in Computing and Information Sciences, 5*(3), 10–21.

Nguyen, T., & Vojnovic, M. (2011). Weighted proportional allocation. Proceedings of the ACM SIGMETRICS Joint International Conference on Measurement and Modeling of Computer Systems, 173-184. doi:10.1145/1993744.1993760

Nkansah-Gyekye, Y. (2010). *An intelligent vertical handoff decision algorithm in next generation wireless networks* (Doctoral dissertation), Available from UWC Electronic Thesis and Dissertation Repository. Retrieved from http://hdl.handle.net/11394/3449

Oludele, A., & Oluwabukola, O. (2016). A Survey of Mobile Cloud Computing Applications: Perspectives and Challenges. In Proceedings of 7th IMCIC - ICSIT, (Vol. 1, pp. 238-243). Orlando, FL: Academic Press.

Patel, M., Joubert, J., Ramos, J. R., Sprecher, N., & Abeta, S. (2014). Mobile-Edge Computing. *Technical White Paper, 1*, 1-36.

Pham, Q., Leanh, T., Tran, N. H., & Hong, C. S. (2018). Decentralized Computation Offloading and Resource Allocation in Heterogeneous Networks with Mobile Edge Computing. *IEEE Transactions on Mobile Computing*, 1-17.

Sanga, C., & Kibirige, G. (2016). Applying Kolb learning experiential theory with cloud computing in higher education institutions: Tanzania. In *Web-based services: Concepts, methodologies, tools, and applications* (pp. 1968–2000). IGI Global. doi:10.4018/978-1-4666-9466-8.ch087

Satyanarayanan, M., Bahl, P., Caceres, R., & Davies, N. (2009). The Case for VM-Based Cloudlets in Mobile Computing. *IEEE Pervasive Computing, 8*(4), 14–23. doi:10.1109/MPRV.2009.82

Shahzad, H., & Szymanski, T. H. (2016). A Dynamic programming offloading algorithm for Mobile Cloud Computing. In *2016 IEEE Canadian Conference on Electrical and Computer Engineering (CCECE)*, (pp.1-5). Vancouver, BC, Canada: IEEE. 10.1109/CCECE.2016.7726790

Shi, W., Cao, J., Zhang, Q., Li, Y., & Xu, L. (2016). Edge Computing: Vision and Challenges. *IEEE Internet of Things Journal, 3*(5), 637–646. doi:10.1109/JIOT.2016.2579198

Siddiqa, A., Hashem, I. A. T., Yaqoob, I., Marjani, M., Shamshirband, S., Gani, A., & Nasaruddin, F. (2016). A Survey of big data management: Taxonomy and state-of-the-art. *Journal of Network and Computer Applications, 71*, 151–166. doi:10.1016/j.jnca.2016.04.008

Skourletopoulos, G., Mavromoustakis, C. X., Mastorakis, G., Batalla, J. M., Dobre, C., Panagiotakis, S., & Pallis, E. (2017). Big Data and Cloud Computing: A Survey of the State-of-the-Art and Research Challenges. In C.X. Mavromoustakis (Ed.), Advances in Mobile Cloud Computing and Big Data in the 5G Era, Studies in Big Data (pp. 23-41). Springer. doi:10.1007/978-3-319-45145-9_2

Soo, S., Chang, C., Loke, S. W., & Srirama, S. N. (2017). Proactive Mobile Fog Computing using Work Stealing: Data Processing at the Edge. *International Journal of Mobile Computing and Multimedia Communications, 8*(4), 1–19. doi:10.4018/IJMCMC.2017100101

Sundmaeker, H., Verdouw, C., Wolfert, S., & Freire, L. P. (2016). Internet of food and farm 2020. In O. Vermesan & P. Friess (Eds.), Digitizing the Industry - Internet of Things Connecting Physical, Digital and Virtual Worlds (pp. 129–151). River Publishers.

Velte, A. T., Velte, T. J., & Elsenpeter, R. (2010). Cloud computing technology. In Cloud computing: A practical Approach, (pp. 91-110). Chicago: McGraw Hill.

Wang, S., Zhang, X., Zhang, Y., Wang, L., Yang, J., & Wang, W. (2017). A Survey on Mobile Edge Networks: Convergence of Computing, Caching and Communications. *IEEE Special Section on Security Analytics and Intelligence for Cyber Physical Systems, 5*, 6757-6779.

Wen, Y., Zhang, W., & Luo, H. (2012). Energy-optimal mobile application execution: Taming resource-poor mobile devices with cloud clones. *Proceeding of IEEE INFOCOM*, 2716–2720. 10.1109/INFCOM.2012.6195685

Yang, Z., Zhou, Q., Lei, L., Zheng, K., & Xiang, W. (2016). An IoT-cloud Based Wearable ECG Monitoring System for Smart Healthcare. *Journal of Medical Systems*, *40*(12), 1–11. doi:10.100710916-016-0644-9 PMID:27796840

Yu, J., Zhang, J., Letaief, K. B., & Khalifa, H. B. (2016). *Joint Subcarrier and CPU Time Allocation for Mobile Edge Computing*. arXiv: 1608.06128v2 [cs.IT]

Zhu, J., Chan, D. S., Prabhu, M. S., Natarajan, P., Hu, H., & Bonomi, F. (2013). Improving Web Sites Performance Using Edge Servers in Fog Computing Architecture. *IEEE International Symposium on Service-Oriented System Engineering*, 320-323.

This research was previously published in the International Journal of Mobile Computing and Multimedia Communications (IJMCMC), 10(3); pages 23-46, copyright year 2019 by IGI Publishing (an imprint of IGI Global).

Chapter 18
Bridging the IoT Gap Through Edge Computing

R. I. Minu
SRM Institute of Science and Technology, India

G. Nagarajan
Sathyabama Institute of Science and Technology, India

ABSTRACT

In the present-day scenario, computing is migrating from the on-premises server to the cloud server and now, progressively from the cloud to Edge server where the data is gathered from the origin point. So, the clear objective is to support the execution and unwavering quality of applications and benefits, and decrease the cost of running them, by shortening the separation information needs to travel, subsequently alleviating transmission capacity and inactivity issues. This chapter provides an insight of how the internet of things (IoT) connects with edge computing.

INTRODUCTION

Electronic gadgets connected to one another and doing the magic is the key concept of Internet of Things (IOT). Mark Hung (2018), VP of Gartner sited that the magic word (IoT) had reached beyond the hype and started to operate in many phases. They insist all the major leaders to practice and provide complete insight about it. This technology was first introduced in the year 1999 as cited by Shi, Cao, Zhang, Li, and Xu (2016). At present this technology is used to many domain such as smart agriculture, smart city, smart Government, smart healthcare and the list goes on. According to the Cisco datasheet (Cisco Knowledge Network, 2014) and Evans (2011) that by 2019, more than 45% of data created, processed, analyzed would be from IoT devices. They had given a figure of 500 zettabytes of data will be generated by the IoT devices. So this much data is needed to be stored and analyzed in the Cloud.

DOI: 10.4018/978-1-6684-5700-9.ch018

BASIC STRUCTURE OF INTERNET OF THINGS

Processing of this much amount of data is one of the challenging parts. In IoT the cloud computing is one of the major backbones, but due to uncontrolled data flow it requires some intelligent service. One of the evolving technologies to speed-up the procedure is the Edge Computing. The basic differences between cloud and Edge computing is that, in cloud the processing of data done in a centralized manner. As shown in the Figure 1 the device generated data are taken directly in cloud and processed and the output is sent back to the actuator. Where is Edge computing as shown in Figure 2, the data are pushed, collected and analyzed near the IoT devices.

Figure 1. IoT basic schematic without edge

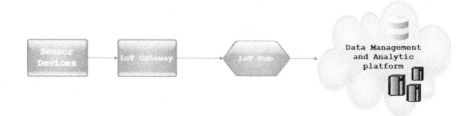

Figure 2. IoT basic schematic with edge

WHY WE NEED EDGE COMPUTING?

To answer the question of why we need again a new Edge computing is listed in Figure 3. The three main reasons of why we prefer Edge computing.

Edge figuring is ideal for IoT for three reasons. Immediately, in light of the way that the data is taken care of nearer the motivation behind root, you diminish the inactivity among devices and data getting ready layer, along these lines engaging speedier response and fundamental authority. This in like manner suggests the costs related to ingesting a considerable measure of data in the cloud are broadly lower and framework limit is opened up for various exceptional weights.

Furthermore, as edge enrolling suggests the data is limited, should any individual contraption breakdown, it doesn't have a pound on effect on others as needs be. Holding the data locally similarly gives a lift to consistence and security as there are fewer open entryways for software engineers to get to all data immediately.

Finally, by circling and securing your data into humbler data vaults, you can even more adequately section creating examination into specific sorts of gathering and geographic locale as you don't have to pull data removes from a bound together corporate database. This makes data accumulation stunningly less complex and empowers you to give progressing examination explicitly to overseers specifically locale.

Figure 3. Need for edge computing

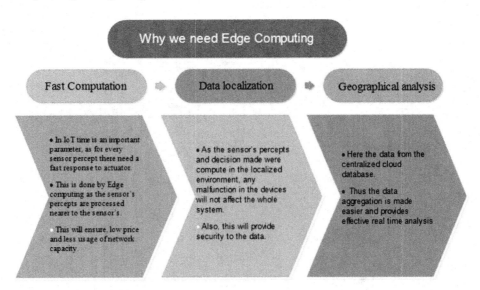

IoT BASED EDGE COMPUTING ENVIRONMENT

The list of Internet of Thing based Edge computing environment is shown in Figure 4. The considered parameters are networking technologies, computing paradigms Attributes, Computing nodes and Application. The networking technologies used by an IoT devices would be mainly wireless communication as most of the sensors would be deployed in remote areas were wired connection is impossible to connected. So the general technologies used to get connected are Bluetooth, Wi-Fi, ZigBee, 3G, 4G, 5G, and so on. Various paradigms were used in IoT to provide all kind of services. Cloud computing is used to store and retrieve data generated by an IoT devices. To reduce the latency, the Fog computing is used to provide data for the instant decision making. The other kind of computing is used to provide better computing. At different service level, different kind of management strategy were used to maintain the flow of process. The first management to be deal with latency management, with respect to IoT, the signals diverted to the actuator should be less. If the processing time is more that kind of system never help the Smart World. As in IoT, the sensors would flourish with enormous amount of data, it requires data management, network management, resource management and cost optimization management. Next comes the attributes, for different project environment various set of attributes is required, in the figure few of them are listed. For effective data transfer, it required several kinds of nodes. The major computing nodes are server, router, wireless sensor nodes, and so on. Then comes the major component application. Smart Healthcare, in this application there are various product are now available such as Fitbit, smart syringe, smart pill, smart BP controller and so on. Smart cities, this is one of the Global projects of all developed and developing countries. Under Smart cities comes the Smart Hospital, Smart Government, Smart Road management, Smart School, Smart Agriculture, and so on. Nagarajan and Minu (2018) had explained the usage of Smart IoT devices in agriculture. Smart grids are one of the answers for today's Energy management crises.

Figure 4. IoT based edge computing environment

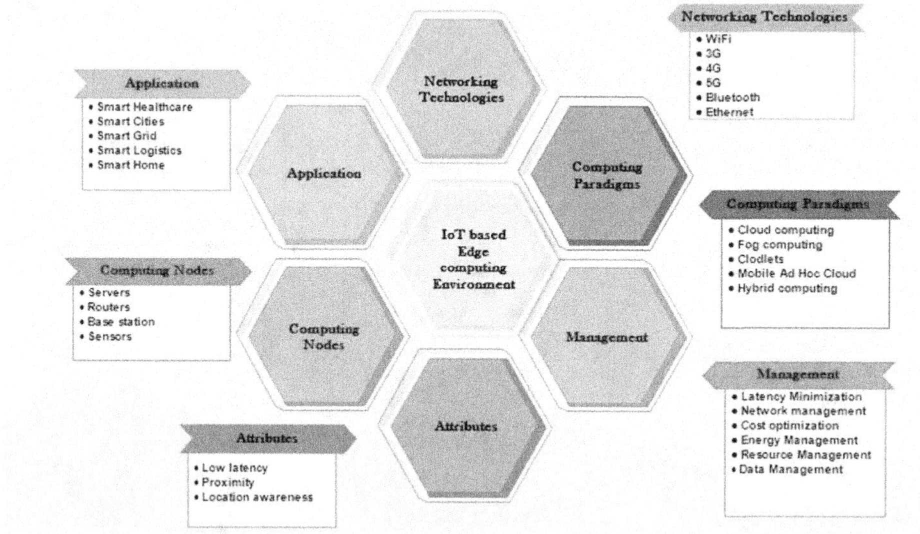

Table 1. Summary of existing technology

Model	Author	Contributions
Cloudlet	• Satyanarayanan, Bahl, Caceres, & Davies (2009) • Satyanarayanan, Schuster, Ebling, Fettweis, Flinck, Joshi, & Sabnani (2015)	• A new cloudlet-based architecture for overcoming the technical obstacles in mobile computing. • An open ecosystem based on the concept of cloudlets supporting many exciting mobile applications.
Mobile edge computing	• Mobile-edge Computing Industry Initiative-ETSI (2015) • Mao, You, Zhang, Huang, & Letaief (2017) • Mach, & Becvar (2017)	• An overview of MEC definition, architectural blueprint, requirements, and challenges of MEC as well as the objectives of the MEC initiative. • A comprehensive survey of the state-of-the-art MEC research focusing on joint radio and computational resource management. • A comprehensive survey of major use cases and reference scenarios, current advancement in standardization of MEC, and research on computation offloading.
Fog computing	• Chiang, & Zhang (2016) • OpenFog Consortium (2016)	• A summary of the opportunities and challenges of fog computing focusing primarily on the networking context of IoT. • An overview of Fog computing definition, reference architecture, use cases and challenges for fog computing as well as the future research and work.
Comprehensive Surveys	• Satyanarayanan (2017) • Klas (2015) • Hassan, Gillani, Ahmed, Yaqoob, & Imran (2018)	• An overview of edge computing definition, origin and background, challenges, and applications. Discussions of the future research directions of edge computing. • A comprehensive comparison of three approaches: fog computing, MEC and Cloudlet. Discussions of further work and research in order to get concepts like Fog, MEC and Cloudlets adopted by industry. • A comprehensive tutorial of three state-of-threat edge computing technologies, namely MEC, cloudlets, and fog computing. A comparison of standardization efforts, principles, architectures, and applications for these three technologies. The difference between mobile edge computing and fog computing from the • View point of RANs.

SUMMARY

The Edge computing is one of the budding technology which will enrich the Internet of Things. The overall summary of all the technology used in Edge computing with respect to IoT is briefed in Table 1 and Table 2

Table 2. Comparison of different computing technique

Features	FOG computing	Edge computing	Cloud computing
Availability of server nodes	Availability high range of servers	Less scalable than fog computing	Availability of few servers
Type of services	Distributed and localized limited and special for specific domain	Mostly uses in cellular mobile networks	Worldwide and global services
Location identification	Yes	Yes	NO
Mobility features	Provided and fully supported	Provided and partially supported	Limited
Node devices	Routers, Switches, Access Points, Gateways	Servers running in base stations	Data Center in a box
Node location	Varying between End Devices and Cloud	Radio Network Controller/ Macro Base Station	Local/Outdoor installation
Software Architecture	Fog Abstraction Layer based	Mobile Orchestrator based	Cloudlet Agent based
Context awareness	Medium	High	Low
Proximity	One or Multiple Hops	One Hops	One Hops
Access Mechanisms	Bluetooth, Wi-Fi, Mobile Networks	Mobile	Wi-Fi
Internode Communication	Supported	Partial	Partial
Real-time interaction	Supported	Supported	Supported
Real-time response	Highest	Highest	Lower
Big data storage & duration	Short duration and targeted to specific area	Depends on the scenario of services and applications	Life time duration as its managing for big data
Big data analytic capacity and computation quality	Life time duration as its managing for big data	Short time capacity for prioritized computing facilities	Long-time capacity only with categorization computing facilities
Working environment & positions	Streets, roadside, home, malls, field tracks (e.g., every Internet existing areas)	Deployed by the specific services provider in specific indoor areas	Indoors with massive components at cloud service provider owned place
Architectural design	Distributed	Distributed	Centralized
Number of users facilitated	Locally related fields (e.g., IIoT, STL devices)	Specific related fields (e.g., mobile users)	General Internet connected users
Major service provided	Cisco IOx, Intel	Cellular network companies	Google, Amazon, IBM, and Microsoft Azure

REFERENCES

Chiang, M., & Zhang, T. (2016). Fog and IoT: An overview of research opportunities. *IEEE Internet Things J.*, *3*(6), 854–864. doi:10.1109/JIOT.2016.2584538

Cisco Knowledge Network. (2014). Cisco global cloud index: Forecast and methodology 2014–2019 [Data file]. Retrieved from https://www.cisco.com/Cisco_GCI_Deck_2014-2019_for_CKN__10NOV2015_.pdf

Evans, D. (2011). The Internet of Things: How the next evolution of the Internet is changing everything. CISCO.

Hassan, N., Gillani, S., Ahmed, E., Yaqoob, I., & Imran, M. (2018). The Role of Edge Computing in Internet of Things. *IEEE Communications Magazine*, (99), 1–6.

Hung, M. (2018). Control your IoT Destiny: Insights of IoT. *Gartner*. Retrieved from https://www.gartner.com/en/information-technology/insights/internet-of-things

Mach, P., & Becvar, Z. (2017). Mobile edge computing: A survey on architecture and computation offloading. *IEEE Communications Surveys and Tutorials*, *19*(3), 1628–1656. doi:10.1109/COMST.2017.2682318

Mao, Y., You, C., Zhang, J., Huang, K., & Letaief, K. B. (2017). A survey on mobile edge computing: The communication perspective. *IEEE Communications Surveys and Tutorials*, *19*(4), 2322–2358. doi:10.1109/COMST.2017.2745201

Mobile-edge Computing Industry Initiative-ETSI. (2015),Mobile-edge Computing Introductory Technical White Paper [Data Sheet]. Retrieved from, https://portal.etsi.org/

Nagarajan, G., & Minu, R. I. (2018). Wireless soil monitoring sensor for sprinkler irrigation automation system. *Wireless Personal Communications*, *98*(2), 1835–1851. doi:10.100711277-017-4948-y

OpenFog Consortium. (2016). OpenFog Reference Architecture for Fog Computing [Data Sheet]. Retrieved from https://www.openfogconsortium.org

Satyanarayanan, M. (2017). The emergence of edge computing. *Computer*, *50*(1), 30–39. doi:10.1109/MC.2017.9

Satyanarayanan, M., Bahl, P., Caceres, R., & Davies, N. (2009). The case for VM-base cloudlets in mobile computing. *Pervasive Comput.*, *8*(4), 14–23. doi:10.1109/MPRV.2009.82

Satyanarayanan, M., Schuster, R., Ebling, M., Fettweis, G., Flinck, H., Joshi, K., & Sabnani, K. (2015). An open ecosystem for mobile-cloud convergence. *IEEE Communications Magazine*, *53*(3), 63–70. doi:10.1109/MCOM.2015.7060484

Shi, W., Cao, J., Zhang, Q., Li, Y., & Xu, L. (2016). Edge computing: Vision and challenges. *IEEE Internet of Things Journal*, *3*(5), 637–646. doi:10.1109/JIOT.2016.2579198

This research was previously published in Edge Computing and Computational Intelligence Paradigms for the IoT; pages 1-9, copyright year 2019 by Engineering Science Reference (an imprint of IGI Global).

Chapter 19
Edge Computing:
A Review on Computation Offloading and Light Weight Virtualization for IoT Framework

Minal Parimalbhai Patel

Computer Engineering Department, A. D. Patel Institute of Technology, Gujarat Technological University, Gujarat, India

Sanjay Chaudhary

School of Engineering and Applied Science, Ahmedabad University, Gujarat, India

ABSTRACT

In this article, the researchers have provided a discussion on computation offloading and the importance of docker-based containers, known as light weight virtualization, to improve the performance of edge computing systems. At the end, they have also proposed techniques and a case study for computation offloading and light weight virtualization.

1. INTRODUCTION

In the current trend of technology (Wang & Alexander, 2016), the emergence of IoT is considered for enabling real-world applications and it has been justified by following technologies such as sensors and embedded systems, ultra-low power based processors, Radio Frequency Identification (RFID), mobile services, cloud and fog computing, wireless communication etc. The computation off-loading is performed using cloud and fog technologies for managing large-scale data analysis and managing huge operations.

The questions raised by IoT designer is so challenging and there may be multiple solutions exist: i) trade-off between quality of service and energy consumption, ii) off-load data for computation and storage or consider on-board processing, iii) which communication technology is applied under certain requirements to bring IoT system more adequate for real-world operations? iv) requirement analysis for relevant range of IoT devices for communication, considering data-rate and low-power devices constraints

DOI: 10.4018/978-1-6684-5700-9.ch019

etc. The data generated from IoT devices including audio, video or unstructured data is processed using big-data approach. In Figure 1, the IoT edge computing layers are shown to manage the services from cloud to smart devices.

Figure 1. Fundamentals of IoT Edge Computing (Premsankar, Di Francesco, & Taleb, 2018)

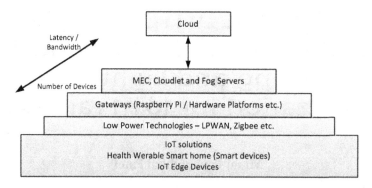

The different computing mechanism (Premsankar, Di Francesco, & Taleb, 2018) for IoT edge computing is discussed below:

- **Device level:** This mechanism is used mainly for low-power requirements and the major decision is required to perform computation on device itself or to offload it for better computation;
- **Gateway level:** It is also known as smart phone centric approach. It is used for those devices which require more computational power and useful for healthcare and engineering applications. It is able to manage the data communication through the wireless communication and the issues concern with latency is required to minimize for better performance;
- **Fog level:** This layer is able to give more computation power compared with device and gateway approaches. It is a micro cloud activity to manage the data closer to the user and it is able to solve data analysis at greater depth;
- **Compare to cloud computing:** It is used to reduce latency and bandwidth issues for different IoT applications;
- **Cloud level:** It is mainly used for server processing at cloud and big data can be processed to provide decision making in different cloud layers.

In Figure 2, three different edge computing platforms (Premsankar, Di Francesco, & Taleb, 2018) are shown and the comparison of edge system to the fog and cloud systems are shown with necessary elements.

2. IoT-ENABLE MIDDLE LAYER TECHNOLOGIES

In this section, three different IoT-enable middle layer technologies are discussed below:

Figure 2. Edge Computing platforms (Premsankar, Di Francesco, & Taleb, 2018)

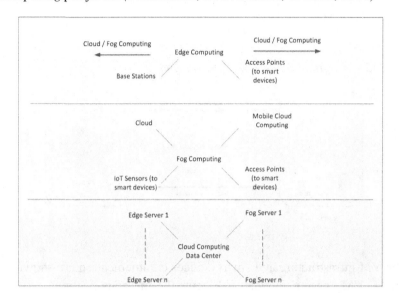

1. Fog Computing

The fog computing (Ai, Peng, & Zhang, 2018; Atlam, Walters, & Wills, 2018; Yi, Li, C., & Li, Q., 2015) is useful for variety of tasks between cloud and edge architectures for end-to-end IoT applications. The fog is used between cloud to things providing different services such as storage, computation and networking. The fog is different than the edge, as it is the concept in which services are provided among networks and between different devices that reside at the edge. The fog is extension to cloud at finer detail for service proving at closer to the user, while edge is known to work without cloud. The IoT data is very huge in amount that is generated by various applications. The fog nodes are considered as key elements for cloud-IoT solution and it is used to perform data analysis and mining of data generated by sensor devices to perform faster execution. The fog architecture is designed to provide decision making of such sensor data to manage IoT devices. The fog computing is useful for face recognition-based security and privacy issues, driver based assistance service, healthcare and emergency based latency services etc.

For example, considering vehicle-to-vehicle application, the processing is to be performed with the support of middle layer platforms, so it is mandatory to offload data at any cost. Using fog computing, fog manager can handle offloading request between fog orchestrator and fog abstraction layers. It can manage certain issues such as quality service, optimal fog node selection, load balancing etc. for better execution of data (Dolui & Datta, 2017; Yousefpour, Fung, Nguyen, Kadiyala, Jalali, Niakanlahiji, Kong & Jue, 2018).

2. Cloudlet

A cloudlet (Ai, Peng, & Zhang, 2018; Pan, Thulasiraman, & Wang, 2018), three tire hierarchy is worked nearer to the user. It is a small datacenter which can overcome the latency issue raised by cloud computing framework. The three layers of technology for IoT based systems are: i) cloud; ii) mobile device; and iii) cloudlet. The data is provided on demand using virtual machine through mobile device.

In cloudlet platform, the optimal node is chosen, and complex querying is initiated with high processing capacity of nodes (Dolui, & Datta, 2017).

Figure 3. Cloudlet and VM infrastructure (Ai, Peng, & Zhang, 2018)

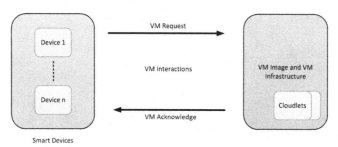

In Figure 3, the VM infrastructure and smart devices communication are shown. In this approach, the data is provided as VM image in cloudlet to execute the smart applications.

3.   Mobile Edge Computing (MEC)

In Figure 4, the architecture of MEC (Ai, Peng, & Zhang, 2018) is shown. It has two major components: i) MEC manager and ii) virtulization manager. The different applications are able to run based on these two components.

Figure 4. MEC system for IoT Edge Computing (Ai, Peng, & Zhang, 2018)

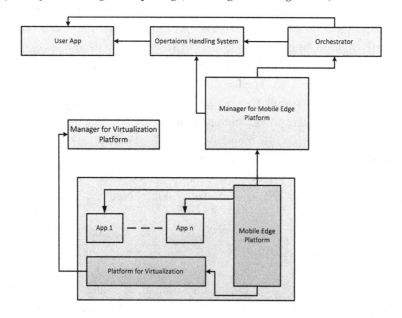

The use of MEC is to provide VM on top of infrastructure layer and it can use to manage procedure to lifecycle of application. The mobile edge platform is able to use for traffic management among applications, local networks and other parts of system. The important role of MEC is to find out whether to work data on smart device or offload it for processing to edge network based on data analytic algorithm.

2.1. Comparison of IoT-Enable Middle Layer Technologies

In this discussion, the focus is to choose the real-world implementation of fog, cloudlet or MEC based on technical parameters and its suitability for the application. The fog can be used to manage data locally using decentralized computing framework for storage and computation and after that, data are sent to cloud for further processing. MEC and cloudlet are able to provide services dynamically to manage processing and storage requirements. MEC works with base stations of cellular networks inside Radio Area Network (RAN) while cloudlet is a dedicated device like small data center which can provide data like managing data center (Yousefpour, Fung, Nguyen, Kadiyala, Jalali, Niakanlahiji, Kong, & Jue, 2018).

The taxonomy of edge computing platforms is given based on architecture, managing requests and availability of applications. The fog is used to work at protocol level, and it connects fog node and end devices with non-IP based communication while MEC and cloulet are designed to work on mobile network or Wi-Fi. The resources are allocated as per the requirement of request from end users. On the other hand, MEC has the concept to run with visualized infrastructure based on RAN to reduce latency and improving context awareness (Yousefpour, Fung, Nguyen, Kadiyala, Jalali, Niakanlahiji, Kong, & Jue, 2018). The working of cloudlet (Yousefpour, Fung, Nguyen, Kadiyala, Jalali, Niakanlahiji, Kong, & Jue, 2018; Pan, Thulasiraman, & Wang, 2018) is mainly operated on the virtulization concept, with minimum access time of applications.

The other differences are (Dolui, & Datta, 2017): i) fog computing is able to give more flexibility compare to MEC and cloudlet but at the same time, fog works at lower level devices so it can have less support for computation and storage capacities compare to MEC and cloudlet. ii) The fog nodes and cloudlet are also have context awareness issues to find location services and load of network compare to MEC. iii) It is quite complex to build MEC and cloudlet and these platforms are slower compare to fog computing.

The cloudlet is able to update data instantly at distant cloud with the working of customized resource provisioning and such scenarios are not found in fog computing and MEC. It is always considering the physical and logical proximity while working with edge computing platforms. This proximity is taken as distance from edge computing platform to end device. MEC and cloudlet are designed with high processing so both of them need to work with higher power consumption compare with fog nodes which work with access mediums. The MEC and cloudlet are used with virtualized resource management and so both technologies provide dynamic resource provisioning with less computation time compare to fog nodes (Dolui & Datta, 2017; Yousefpour, Fung, Nguyen, Kadiyala, Jalali, Niakanlahiji, Kong, & Jue, 2018).

3. RESEARCH DIRECTIONS ON COMPUTATION OFFLOADING AND LIGHT WEIGHT VIRTUALIZATION

In this section, the two research directions; i) computation offloading; and ii) light weight virtualization are discussed.

Figure 5. Computation offloading (Mach & Becvar, 2017)

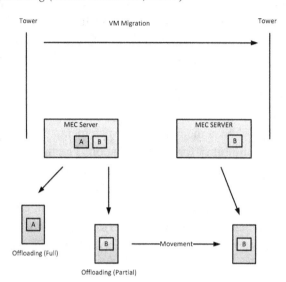

3.1. Overview of Computation Offloading

In computation offloading, it is assumed that there are total n sensors having computational task on which it is working. Now, if there are m number of cloudlets through which IoT sensors can offload the tasks. The sensors are connected to wireless access points to make the communication among them. The performance of any sensor is affected by computation and communication process (Ma, Lin, Zhang, & Liu, 2018) for making the action using computational offloading.

In (Ma, Lin, Zhang, & Liu, 2018), the process of computation offloading is formulated as computational offloading game. The tasks are offloaded by IoT sensors which act as players. The computation offloading has several advantages like battery life of end devices are extended due to unwanted local processing. The applications of computation offloading are gaming, learning, healthcare, server programming etc. It is a novel technique which incorporates to work with low power smart devices like smartphone, smartwatch, other different wearable to offload the local processing to other place where higher speed and resources provided.

In Figure 5, the computation offloading mechanism is shown. There are two types of offloading: i) full and ii) partial. In MEC based computation offloading, if the movement of user is found then the data will be transferred to nearby edge server to improve the efficiency of the system.

The data to be offloaded is required or not that is primary concern. If data is offloaded with insufficient resources for available computation, it can degrade the performance. It is necessary to understand the edge computing nodes capability to perform the computation. The final goal of offloading the computation is to reduce the processing time of data and extend the life of battery so the computation offloading is not always to be operated without measuring the communication cost.

3.2. Overview of Light Weight Virtualization

In Figure 6, the architecture of container for virtualization is shown. In this architecture, different activities can run on top of container engine in various containers to provide multiple execution on single host OS.

The Docker (Morabito, Cozzolino, Ding, Beijar, & Ott, 2018; Ismail, Goortani, Ab Karim, Tat, Setapa, Luke, & Hoe, 2015) developed by Linux containers library. It provides the isolation of different applications in OS-virtualization using containers. The container is allowed to make necessary requirement for any dependencies. It is a software-oriented process called images which can have its own registry and other information to work on OS level virtualization. It works like file system which is faster to update data and it is used as smart device platform in IoT resource management.

Figure 6. Virtualization: Container architecture (Morabito, Cozzolino, Ding, Beijar, & Ott, 2018)

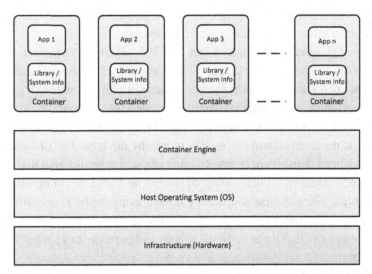

The container is configured with Linux-based resource allocation such as CPU, network, memory management and I/O for file. During computation at edge node, the same functions are executed by light weight virtualization called container technology. The container has single OS isolation and it shares the same OS kernel with host, so applications are running separately in different containers. The docker is able to manage different functions, provide resource allocation and collaboration of various applications to the containers.

The container (Morabito & Beijar, 2016; Pahl, Helmer, Miori, Sanin, & Lee, 2016) has many advantages over virtualization to work better in cloud-based system. It can have few key advantages like efficient performance on resources, accurate monitoring on system, scheduling etc. The hypervisor virtualize the hardware and device drivers and it can produce more overhead while, container is enough capable to avoid such overheads by proving process isolation at OS level.

3.3. Proposed Techniques for Computation Offloading in Edge Computing Framework

In (Liu, Xu, Zhan, Liu, Guan, Zhang, 2017), the computation offloading is performed based on incentive method which is the approach to encourage edge nodes. The Stackelberg game-based technique is used to maximize cloud utilities between cloud and edge nodes. The game-based approach is used to make tie up between cloud and edge and the cloud is able to use for accepting or rejecting request, while edge node is managed by incentive technique to offload tasks.

In paper (Meurisch, Gedeon, Nguyen, Kaup, & Muhlhauser, 2017), it is shown that the data can be offloaded with best offloading system at runtime and it uses the probing mechanism which uses the available unknown cloudlet or cloud services. The main objective of this mechanism is to offload micro tasks and then make the prediction for larger offloading tasks using regression models. In this paper, few challenges are discussed: i) how many micro tasks are evaluated for larger offloading estimation ii) considering energy consumption by taking correlation between overhead costs and micro tasks iii) tradeoff between accuracy and cost for probing micro tasks.

The Aura mechanism (Hasan, Hossain, & Khan, 2017) is able to give more than 85% prediction to offload the task or not by creating ad hoc cloud for IoT devices. The method is able to decide when to start the offloading and it can also suggest surrogate nodes with known network parameters to perform any decision. The authors have suggested that smart-phones and other smart devices are usually become idle and many times, devices found under-loaded, it could be an innovative mechanism to outsourced the computing power using computation offloading to nearby devices. The offloading is performed by incentive method considered in the form of crypto-currency and it would give high rating to participant nodes based on high performance of offloading of data. The cloud-based computations evaluated in Aura are good enough for computation and nearby device availability. It contains the reward scheme based on different tasks categories and it is designed with rating point calculation and task properties estimation with device selection. The aura cloud is also compared with mobile device and traditional cloud to get more analysis.

The fog datacenter (Fricker, Guillemin, Robert, & Thompson, 2016) based load balancing is achieved when to offload a request. The analytical model for computation offloading in data centers under heavy loads is discussed. It can possible that the present fog datacenter is overloaded so the request has to be forwarded to next fog datacenter having higher priority to receive request. The request blocking rate mechanism is used to offload the tasks in this paper. The blocking of heavy request can be identified using probability approach at small datacenter (fog node) so that it could not be forwarded to other fog node. The system can handle the heavy request by big data center and blocking that request at fog nodes.

In (Liu & Liu, 2018; Orsini, Bade, & Lamersdorf, 2015), the offloading is performed based on mobile edge and the emergence of such system is to manage latency sensitive applications to provide high speed communication which is the main issue to handle requests from cloud. The MEC is used based on computation offloading for low latency based smart systems. The authors declare the hierarchical offloading among mobile, mist, fog and cloud to give better performance.

It could be observed that in Stackelberg game approach (Liu, Xu, Zhan, Liu, Guan, & Zhang, 2017) the private information among players are revealed indirectly for certain conditions in equilibrium strategy and it is considered the drawback of this approach. This can be overcome by checking certain parameters of this approach while dynamically joining or leaving situations of edge servers. The paper (Meurisch, Gedeon, Nguyen, Kaup, & Muhlhauser, 2017) can work for larger offloading tasks and it can use regression models to predict the accuracy. It can be found that the data are always sent to cloud computing from the fog nodes, so this approach is only suitable if the offloading is needed on urgent basis for larger tasks. This paper (Hasan, Hossain, & Khan, 2017) is presented with aura cloud mechanism and it can serve response quickly as it manages the data through localized IoT based cloud. The discussion of fog and cloudlet using cloud computing as extended layer were implemented in (Liu, Xu, Zhan, Liu, Guan, Zhang, 2017; Meurisch, Gedeon, Nguyen, Kaup, & Muhlhauser, 2017). The limitation (Fricker, Guillemin, Robert, & Thompson, 2016) of such system is that the working of fog node can become idle if the request is generated from heavy loads. The approach discussed in (Liu, Xu, Zhan, Liu, Guan, & Zhang, 2017; Hasan, Hossain, & Khan, 2017) is more suitable to offload data in fog environment and the other approaches discussed in (Meurisch, Gedeon, Nguyen, Kaup, & Muhlhauser, 2017; Fricker, Guillemin, Robert, & Thompson, 2016) are used with particular situations with heavy load or cloud-based offloading.

3.4. Proposed Techniques for Light Weight Virtualization in Edge Computing Framework

The paper (Ismail, Goortani, Ab Karim, Tat, Setapa, Luke, & Hoe, 2015) evaluated docker containers to provide edge computing platform. It works with the resource management, deployment services and caching of data and it provides the efficiency to improve performance in edge computing using docker system.

In (Petrolo, Morabito, Loscr, & Mitton, 2017), it uses edge computing at gateway level. In this work, the study is discussed on interaction between IoT sensors and gateway. In (Morabito & Beijar, 2016), docker mechanism is discussed and it is suggested that docker is important for virtualization that offers many services such as software defined networking (SDN), orchestration and device management functionalities etc. The overhead of virtualization layer is overcome by synthetic analysis and application benchmarks. The container-based edge cloud PaaS architecture based on Raspberry Pi (Pahl, Helmer, Miori, Sanin & Lee, 2016) is discussed and it migrates containers towards edge cloud architectures. In (Bellavista & Zanni, 2017), the docker containers and Raspberry Pi are efficient mechanism to deploy framework for fog computing networks. It also focuses the performance of raspberry pi and cloud when making analysis of big data applications using docker containers.

The integration of docker with SDN and orchestration functionalities (Morabito & Beijar, 2016) and Raspberry Pi (Pahl, Helmer, Miori, Sanin & Lee, 2016; Bellavista & Zanni, 2017) discussed.

3.5. Case Study on Computation Offloading and Light Weight Virtualization

iFogSim simulator (Gupta, Dastjerdi, Ghosh, & Buyya, 2017; Patel & Chauhan, 2019) is designed to manage fog nodes with IoT devices for resource allocation, network congestion, cost and energy consumption. The main components of iFogSim are: FogDevice, Sensor, Tuple, Application and Resource management service. The simulation results can show that fog is more suitable compare to cloud for latency, resolving network delay, consumption of energy (Gupta, Dastjerdi, Ghosh, & Buyya, 2017).

Figure 7 shows a topology for physical layer and it contains the components such as cloud(datacenter), gateway, sensor and actuator with their connections. When connection is started from its origin (sensor/actuator) to cloud(datacenter), it can handle many intermediate devices in-between and these devices are

Figure 7. Network topology for Edge Computing framework (Gupta, Dastjerdi, Ghosh, & Buyya, 2017)

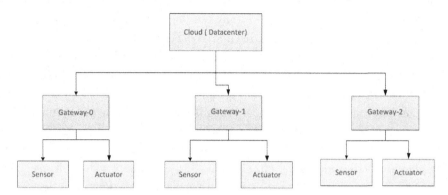

used for computation offloading. The Figure 7 represents that the computation and storage capabilities can be used for offloading.

The paper (Orsini, Bade, & Lamersdorf, 2015) is designed to provide logical infrastructure to create adhoc mobile clouds. This approach is extended to use MEC functionalities in mobile apps. CloudAware framework can facilitate MEC to work with cetneralized resources as well as nearby devices. Docker containers can be the integration part with computation offloading because it can provide the quick deployment with the mixture of code fragments and libraries of different applications for execution environment. The same mixture of components can be available for edge devices using routers and base stations for final deployment and on the other side, computation offloading can be decided by CloudAware framework.

The similar approach like CloudAware based activity is shown in Figure 7 to offload data in intermediate devices.

4. CONCLUSION

In this paper, we have discussed different architecture of recent edge computing technologies and comparison between fog computing, cloudlet and MEC is also discussed in detail. The detail study on middle layer technologies is briefly discussed to give the idea of working of each of these technologies with their advantages and disadvantages. In this paper, we have given the performance analysis for computation offloading for IoT edge computing to build smart systems. It is also discussed that the docker based container is used instead of hypervisor based virtulization to reduce the overhead of computation and the container is also able to provide pre-defined functions as per need. The container technology is widely adopted to gain the power of light weight virtulization and its usefulness to improve the efficiency in computation offloading also. The proposed techniques for computation offloading and container visualization are surveyed and compared between each other to provide the execution environment using middle layer technologies. The brief case study is able to convey the working model for computation offloading with light weight visualization as proposed combined approach. In future work, we would like to configure fog computing, cloudlet and MEC platforms using container virtualization to perform use case study on different scenarios.

REFERENCES

Ai, Y., Peng, M., & Zhang, K. (2018). Edge computing technologies for Internet of Things: A primer. *Digital Communications and Networks*, 4(2), 77–86. doi:10.1016/j.dcan.2017.07.001

Atlam, H., Walters, R., & Wills, G. (2018). Fog Computing and the Internet of Things: A Review. *Big Data and Cognitive Computing*, 2(2), 10. doi:10.3390/bdcc2020010

Bellavista, P., & Zanni, A. (2017, January). Feasibility of fog computing deployment based on docker containerization over Raspberry Pi. *Proceedings of the 18th international conference on distributed computing and networking* (p. 16). ACM.

Dolui, K., & Datta, S. K. (2017, June). Comparison of edge computing implementations: Fog computing, cloudlet and mobile edge computing. *Proceedings of the 2017 Global Internet of Things Summit (GIoTS)* (pp. 1-6). IEEE.

Fricker, C., Guillemin, F., Robert, P., & Thompson, G. (2016). Analysis of an offloading scheme for data centers in the framework of fog computing. *ACM Trans. Model. Perform. Eval. Comput. Syst.*, 1(4), 16.

Gupta, H., Dastjerdi, A., Ghosh, S., & Buyya, R. (2017). iFogSim: A Toolkit for Modeling and Simulation of Resource Management Techniques in Internet of Things, Edge and Fog Computing Environments, Software. *Practice and Experience*, 47(9), 1275–1296. doi:10.1002pe.2509

Hasan, R., Hossain, M., & Khan, R. (2017). Aura: An incentive-driven ad-hoc IoT cloud framework for proximal mobile computation offloading. *Future Generation Computer Systems*.

Ismail, B. I., Goortani, E. M., Ab Karim, M. B., Tat, W. M., Setapa, S., Luke, J. Y., & Hoe, O. H. (2015, August). Evaluation of docker as edge computing platform. *Proceedings of the 2015 IEEE Conference on Open Systems (ICOS)* (pp. 130-135). IEEE. 10.1109/ICOS.2015.7377291

Liu, M., & Liu, Y. (2018). Price-based distributed offloading for mobile-edge computing with computation capacity constraints. *IEEE Wireless Communications Letters*, 7(3), 420–423. doi:10.1109/LWC.2017.2780128

Liu, Y., Xu, C., Zhan, Y., Liu, Z., Guan, J., & Zhang, H. (2017). Incentive mechanism for computation offloading using edge computing: A Stackelberg game approach. *Computer Networks*, 129, 399409. doi:10.1016/j.comnet.2017.03.015

Ma, X., Lin, C., Zhang, H., & Liu, J. (2018). Energy-Aware Computation Offloading of IoT Sensors in Cloudlet-Based Mobile Edge Computing. *Sensors (Basel)*, 18(6), 1945. doi:10.339018061945 PMID:29914104

Mach, P., & Becvar, Z. (2017). Mobile edge computing: A survey on architecture and computation offloading. *IEEE Communications Surveys and Tutorials*, 19(3), 1628–1656. doi:10.1109/COMST.2017.2682318

Meurisch, C., Gedeon, J., Nguyen, T. A. B., Kaup, F., & Muhlhauser, M. (2017). Decision support for computational offloading by probing unknown services. *Proceedings of the 2017 26th International Conference on Computer Communication and Networks, ICCCN*. IEEE. 10.1109/ICCCN.2017.8038406

Morabito, R., & Beijar, N. (2016, June). Enabling data processing at the network edge through lightweight virtualization technologies. *Proceedings of the 2016 IEEE International Conference on Sensing, Communication and Networking (SECON Workshops)* (pp. 1-6). IEEE. 10.1109/SECONW.2016.7746807

Morabito, R., Cozzolino, V., Ding, A. Y., Beijar, N., & Ott, J. (2018). Consolidate IoT edge computing with lightweight virtualization. *IEEE Network*, *32*(1), 102–111. doi:10.1109/MNET.2018.1700175

Orsini, G., Bade, D., & Lamersdorf, W. (2015). Computing at the mobile edge: Designing elastic android applications for computation offloading. Proceedings of the *2015 8th IFIP Wireless and Mobile Networking Conference, WMNC* (p. 112119). IEEE. doi:10.1109/WMNC.2015.10

Pahl, C., Helmer, S., Miori, L., Sanin, J., & Lee, B. (2016, August). A container-based edge cloud paas architecture based on raspberry pi clusters. *Proceedings of the IEEE International Conference on Future Internet of Things and Cloud Workshops (FiCloudW)* (pp. 117-124). IEEE. 10.1109/W-FiCloud.2016.36

Pan, Y., Thulasiraman, P., & Wang, Y. (2018, October). Overview of Cloudlet, Fog Computing, Edge Computing, and Dew Computing. *Proceedings of the 3rd International Workshop on Dew Computing* (pp. 20-23). Academic Press.

Patel, M., & Chauhan, N. (2019, June). Smart Dashboard: A Novel Approach for Sustainable Development of Smart Cities using Fog Computing. *Proceedings of the 2019 3rd International conference on Electronics, Communication and Aerospace Technology (ICECA)* (pp. 632-636). IEEE. 10.1109/ICECA.2019.8821813

Petrolo, R., Morabito, R., Loscr, V., & Mitton, N. (2017). The design of the gateway for the cloud of things. *Annales des Télécommunications*, *72*(1-2), 31–40. doi:10.100712243-016-0521-z

Premsankar, G., Di Francesco, M., & Taleb, T. (2018). Edge computing for the Internet of Things: A case study. *IEEE Internet of Things Journal*, *5*(2), 1275–1284. doi:10.1109/JIOT.2018.2805263

Wang, L., & Alexander, C. A. (2016). Big Data Analytics and Cloud Computing in Internet of Things. *American Journal of Information Science and Computer Engineering*, *2*(6), 70–78.

Yi, S., Li, C., & Li, Q. (2015, June). A survey of fog computing: concepts, applications and issues. *Proceedings of the 2015 workshop on mobile big data* (pp. 37-42). ACM. 10.1145/2757384.2757397

Yousefpour, A., Fung, C., Nguyen, T., Kadiyala, K., Jalali, F., Niakanlahiji, A., Kong, J., & Jue, J. P. (2018). All One Needs to Know about Fog Computing and Related Edge Computing Paradigms.

This research was previously published in the International Journal of Fog Computing (IJFC), 3(1); pages 64-74, copyright year 2020 by IGI Publishing (an imprint of IGI Global).

Chapter 20
Probabilistic–QoS–Aware Multi–Workflow Scheduling Upon the Edge Computing Resources

Tao Tang
Chongqing University, China

Yuyin Ma
Chongqing University, China

Wenjiang Feng
Chongqing University, China

ABSTRACT

Edge computing is an evolving decentralized computing infrastructure by which end applications are situated near the computing facilities. While the edge servers leverage the close proximity to the end-users for provisioning services at reduced latency and lower energy costs, their capabilities are constrained by limitations in computational and radio resources, which calls for smart, quality-of-service (QoS) guaranteed, and efficient task scheduling methods and algorithms. For addressing the edge-environment-oriented multi-workflow scheduling problem, the authors consider a probabilistic-QoS-aware approach to multi-workflow scheduling upon edge servers and resources. It leverages a probability-mass function-based QoS aggregation model and a discrete firefly algorithm for generating the multi-workflow scheduling plans. This research conducted an experimental case study based on varying types of workflow process models and a real-world dataset for edge server positions. It can be observed the method clearly outperforms its peers in terms of workflow completion time, cost, and deadline violation rate.

DOI: 10.4018/978-1-6684-5700-9.ch020

INTRODUCTION

The edge computing paradigm is emerging as a high performance computing environment with a large-scale, heterogeneous collection of autonomous systems and flexible computational architecture. It provides the tools and technologies to build data or computational intensive parallel applications with much more affordable prices compared to traditional parallel computing techniques. Hence, there has been an increasingly growth in the number of active research work in edge computing such as scheduling, placement, energy management, privacy and policy, security, etc. Workflow scheduling in cloud and edge environment has recently drawn enormous attention thanks to its wide application in both scientific and economic areas. A workflow is usually formulized as a Directed-Acyclic-Graph (DAG) with multiple tasks that satisfy the precedent constraints. Scheduling multi-workflows upon an edge environment is referred to as matching tasks onto edge services or edge nodes.

It is widely acknowledged as well that to schedule multi-workflows on distributed platforms is an NP-hard problem. It is therefore extremely time-consuming to yield optimal schedules through traversal-based algorithms. Recently, as novel bio-inspired and genetic algorithms are becoming increasingly versatile and powerful, considerable research efforts are paid to using them in dealing with edge-environment-oriented workflow scheduling problem and yielding near-optimal scheduling solutions. Nevertheless, for simplicity, most existing contributions in this direction consider that edge servers are with static and invariable performance. However, edge and cloud servers in real-world can show unstable and time-varying performance. For example, Schad *et al* (2010) obverse that Amazon EC2 cloud services are subject to performance variations of 24%, 20% and 19% for CPU performance, I/O performance and network performance, respectively. Jakson *et al* (2010) show that the difference between the maximum and minimum runtime of servers is 7,900 seconds, or approximately 42% of the mean runtime within EC2.

As can be seen from the above analysis, existing heuristic and bio-inspired algorithms with static and time-invariant performance models can be ineffective in dealing with real-world edge-environment-oriented workflow scheduling requirements, where performance of edge servers and platform-level infrastructures themselves are with highly unstable and time-varying performance. To overcome this limitation, in this work, we propose a probabilistic-performance-aware approach to edge-environment-oriented multi-workflow scheduling. Instead of considering single-point and static performance, this article proposed method captures the dynamics of performance of edge servers by leveraging the probability mass functions (PMF) of historical performance data and utilizes a firefly algorithm for optimizing the workflow scheduling plans via maximizing the probability that the cumulative distribution of workflow completion time and cost meets the deadline constraint.

To validate this article proposed method, we conduct extensive experimental studies based on various well-known scientific workflow templates and a position dataset for real-world edge servers. Experimental results clearly suggest that the article proposed method outperforms traditional ones in terms of workflow completion time, execution cost, and deadline validation rate.

BACKGROUND

It is widely acknowledged that to schedule multi-tasks workflow on distributed platforms, e.g., clouds or edge nodes, is an NP-hard problem. It is there for extremely time-consuming to yield optimal schedule through traversal-based algorithms. Fortunately, heuristic and meta-heuristic algorithms with polynomial complexity are able to produce approximate or near optimal solutions at the cost of acceptable optimality loss.

For instance, Zhang Y. *et al.* (2018) developed a Two-stage Cost Optimization algorithm to schedule workflows on edge clouds. The algorithm first leverages a BF algorithm for obtaining the initial scheduling strategy and then further optimizes the scheduling plans by the first stage. Their algorithm aims to minimize the system cost while meeting the delay requirements of workflows. Kim *et al.* (2017) studied the trade-off between execution cost and workflow delays in the mobile computing system and proposed an intelligent-control-based algorithm for achieving near-optimal trade-offs. The trace-driven simulation showed that the algorithm can achieve 71% saving of execution cost and 82% gain of as opposed to its peers. Pandey *et al.* (2010) proposed a particle swarm optimization (PSO) algorithm for load-balancing of cloud servers, while minimizing the execution cost, i.e., communication cost plus cloud resource cost of workflows.

Kaur *et al.* (2018) leveraged a multi-objective bio-inspired procedure (MOBFOA) by augmenting the traditional BFOA with Pareto-optimal fronts. Their method deals with the reduction of on-time, completion duration, and operational cost. Zhang L. *et al.* (2017) considered a multi-objective genetic optimization (BOGA) and optimized both electricity consumption and DAG reliability. Casas *et al.* (2018) considered an augmented GA with the Efficient Tune-In (GA-ETI) mechanism for the optimization of turnaround time. Verma *et al.* (2017) employed a non-dominated-sorting-based Hybrid PSO approach and aimed at minimizing both turnaround time and cost. Zhou *et al.* (2019) introduced a fuzzy dominance sort based heterogeneous finishing time minimization approach for the optimization of both cost and turnaround time of DAG executed on IaaS clouds.

SYSTEM MODEL AND PROBLEM FORMULATION

The System Model

As shown in Figure 1, an edge computing environment can be seen as a collection of multiple edge servers usually deployed near base stations. By this way, users are allowed to offload compute-intensive and latency-sensitive applications, e.g., Augmented Reality (AR), Virtual Reality (VR), Artificial Intelligence (AI), to edge servers. Within an edge computing environment, there exist m users, denote by $U = \{u_1, u_2, ..., u_m\}$, and n edge servers stations, denote by $ES = \{e_1, e_2, ..., e_n\}$. Each user has an application, in terms of a batch of tasks organized by a workflow, to be executed, and mobile device is allowed to offload tasks to nearby edge servers.

The Probabilistic Performance Model

In this work, instead of considering static and time-invariant performance of edge servers, we consider time-varying performance of them. To be specific, we consider that the historical execution time of a certain workflow task upon an edge server, i.e., X, can be described by an empirical probabilistic distribution.

Consequently, the cumulative distribution function (CDF) of execution time and cost can be calculated as follows:

Figure 1. The system architecture

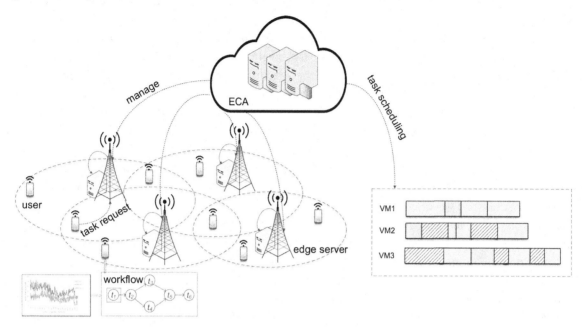

$$P(X \leq c) = P(X \leq floor(c)) + f_X(ceil(c)) \times \frac{c - floor(c)}{ceil(c) - floor(c)} \tag{1}$$

Where c is deadline value, $Min(Dom(X)) < c \leq Max(Dom(X))$, $ceil(c) = Min\{c|c \in Dom(X)$ and $c \geq x\}$ and $floor(c) = Max\{c|c \in Dom(X)$ and $c < x\}$.

Let $w_i(t_{1_{j_1}}, t_{2_{j_2}}, ..., t_{n_{j_n}})^{et}$ and $w_i(t_{1_{j_1}}, t_{2_{j_2}}, ..., t_{n_{j_n}})^{cost}$ be the execution time and cost of a workflow w_i when it select edge servers of $(j_1, j_2, ..., j_n)$. The probability that the resulting workflow completion time and cost meets the deadline constraint, can be estimated according to the following performance aggregation functions and probabilistic performance aggregation rules in Tables 1 and 2 (Hwang, 2007).

Table 1. The performance aggregation function of different workflow structural patterns

Workflow Patterns	Response Time	Cost
Sequence	$\sum_{i=1}^{n} RT(t_i)$	$\sum_{i=1}^{n} C(t_i)$
Parallel	$\max_{1 \leq i \leq n} RT(t_i)$	$\sum_{i=1}^{n} C(t_i)$
Loop	$k \times RT(t_i)$	$k \times C(t_i)$

Table 2. The Probabilistic Performance Aggregation Rules

Qos aggregation	Probability
$Z=X+Y$	$Dom(Z)=\{z_1,z_2,\ldots,z_k\}$, $Max(m,n)\leq k\leq mn^1$, Each z_i, $1\leq i\leq k$, is the sum of some $x\in Dom(X)$ and $y\in Dom(Y)$, $$f_z(z_i) = \sum_{x+y=z_i} f_X(x)f_Y(y)$$
$Z=X\cdot Y$	$Dom(Z)=\{z_1,z_2,\ldots,z_k\}$, $Max(m,n)\leq k\leq mn^1$, Each z_i, $1\leq i\leq k$, is the product of some $x\in Dom(X)$ and $y\in Dom(Y)$, $$f_z(z_i) = \sum_{x\cdot y=z_i} f_X(x)f_Y(y)$$
$Z=MAX(X,Y)$	$Dom(Z) = Dom(X) \cup Dom(Y), f_Z(z) = f_X(z)\cdot \sum_{y<z,y\in Dom(Y)} f_Y(y)$ $if\ z \in Dom(X)\ and\ z \notin Dom(Y); f_Z(z) = f_Y(z)\cdot \sum_{x<z,x\in Dom(X)} f_X(x)$ $if\ z \in Dom(Y)\ and\ z \notin Dom(X); f_Z(z) = f_X(z)\cdot \sum_{y\leq z,y\in Dom(Y)} f_Y(y)$ $+f_Y(z)\cdot \sum_{x<z,x\in Dom(X)} f_X(x)\ if\ z \in Dom(X)\ and\ z \in Dom(Y);$

Problem Description

Based on the above analysis, the problem of probabilistic-performance-aware multi-workflow scheduling can be described as follows: given multiple workflows $w_{i_{1\leq i\leq m}}$, we are interested to identify an edge server assignment plan $(t_{1_{j_1}}, t_{2_{j_2}},\ldots,t_{n_{j_n}})$ of w_i, with the highest probability that the workflow completion time and cost meets the deadline constraint.

$$\max \quad f = \prod P(w_i(t_{1_{j_1}}, t_{2_{j_2}},\ldots,t_{n_{j_n}}))^{et_i} \leq C_i^{et_i}$$
$$\times \prod P(w_i(t_{1_{j_1}}, t_{2_{j_2}},\ldots,t_{n_{j_n}}))^{\cos t_i} \leq C_i^{\cos t_i} \tag{2}$$

s.t.

$$d_{ij} \leq \text{cov}_j,\ i\in\{1,\ldots,m\}\ \text{and}\ j\in\{1,\ldots,m\} \tag{3}$$

$$x_{ij} \leq 1,\ x_{ij} = \begin{cases} 1, & \text{if } e_j \text{ is selected for task } t_i \\ 0, & \text{otherwise} \end{cases} \tag{3}$$

where $C_i^{et_i}(C_i^{\cos t_i})$ is the deadline constraint for completion time and cost of each workflow, d_{ij} is the distance between e_j and w_i, and cov_j is the coverage area of the j_{th} the server.

FIREFLY ALGORITHM

The firefly algorithm (FA), proposed by Yuan X.S.(2009, 2010), has shown its high potency in dealing with complex combinatorial optimization problems and versatile types of engineering and industrial optimization scenarios. It is a swarm-based meta-heuristic algorithm inspired by the flashing behavior of fireflies. FA is with the following assumptions: 1) A firefly will be attracted to each other regardless of their sex because they are unisexual; 2) Attractiveness is proportional to their brightness, whereas the less bright firefly will be attracted to the brighter firefly. However, the attractiveness decreased when the distance of the two fireflies increased; and 3) If the brightness of both fireflies is the same, the fireflies will move randomly. The generations of new solutions are by random walk and attraction of the fireflies. The brightness of the fireflies should be associated with the objective function of the related problem. Their attractiveness makes them capable of subdividing themselves into smaller groups, and each subgroup swarm around the local models.

In this work, we leverage the discrete derivative of FA, i.e., DFA, for solving the probabilistic-performance-aware workflow scheduling problem. The details are described as follows.

Encoding

In DFA, a schedule is an individual, described as a vector of integer values. The length of a vector is the same as the number of tasks in a workflow. The i_{th} element of the individual indicates to which server the i_{th} task of the workflow is scheduled to execute. Figure 2 shows an example of an individual coding and a given workflow deployment, assuming that the workflow consists of eight tasks and is within the coverage range of by e_2, e_3 and e_4. In this schedule, t_1, t_4, t_6 are scheduled to be executed on e_3, t_2, t_3, t_7 are scheduled on e_2, and t_5, t_8 are scheduled on e_4, respectively.

Figure 2. An example of encoding

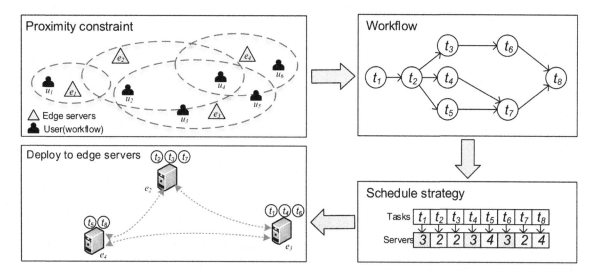

Population Initialization and Firefly Evaluation

Firefly population initialization is affected by the coverage range constraints due to the fact that, users can only offload tasks to reachable, in terms of the coverage range edge server.

As described in Section 3, this article goal is to find the highest probability that the deadline constraint is met. The constraint is interpreted as a penalty function, where the highest probability is integrated into

(5) as an evaluation of the fitness value of an individual. In case that the user is not reachable to servers, the fitness value is decided by the number of tasks that violate the deadline constraint.

$$
F = \frac{1}{m} \times \begin{cases} \sum_{i=1}^{m} f_i, & if \ d_{ij} \leq cov_j \\ \sum_{i=1}^{m} f_i \times (\sqrt[n]{f_i})^{num}, & otherwise \end{cases}
\tag{5}
$$

where n is the total number of tasks in workflow w_i, and $num \in \{1, 2, ..., n\}$, is the number of tasks that are unreachable by edge servers.

Individuals Update

The stipulation of update is that the darker firefly moves towards the brighter one. The population is updated iteratively and the scheduling strategy keeps being optimized. An example showing the update process is given in Table 3. The movement process is as follows.

Table 3. Solution updation

Update	Edge server assignment
Current firefly p	{2,3,2,2,3,3,4,2}
Best firefly p_{best}	{3,2,2,3,4,3,2,2}
Distance dis_l	5
Attractiveness $\beta(r)$	0.24
rand() between(0,1)	{*0.13*,0.29,*0.03*,*0.11*,0.67}
firefly p after β-step	{3,3,2,3,4,3,4,2}
firefly p after α-step	{3,3,2,*4*,*3*,3,4,2}

Distance Calculation

The distance between any two fireflies p and p_{best} is measured by its corresponding hamming distance.

$$
dis(x_i, x_j) = x_{id} \oplus x_{jd}, d \in \{1, 2, ..., n\}
\tag{6}
$$

where an exclusive *OR* is employed to decide the hamming distance (Lunardi, 2018).

β-Step Update

β-step is a process of moving fireflies towards brighter fireflies according to the following steps.

Step 1: Calculate the hamming distance of individuals as dis_l;

Step 2: Calculate the attractiveness, $\beta(r)$, according to (7);

Step 3: Generate $|dis_l|$ random numbers between 0 and 1. If the random number is lower than $\beta(r)$, the element of the p is replaced by the corresponding element of the brightest firefly;

Step 4: Fireflies move to the brightest one.

$$\beta(r) = \frac{\beta_0}{(1 + \gamma \times dis^2)} \tag{7}$$

α-Step Update

The α-step update must be after the β-step update, according to (8), which is a process of random disturbance to avoid the solution space falling into the local optimization. Algorithm 1 presents all the operations of the discrete firefly algorithm.

$$x_i = x_i + \alpha(rand_{int}) \tag{8}$$

Algorithm 1. Firefly Algorithm

Input: Algorithm related parameters: α, β_0, γ, $iter_{max}$
Output: Global QoS probability F_{best}, and schedule strategy S
Initial population of fireflies: $x_i, i \in \{1, 2, \ldots, n\}$;
while $t < iter_{max}$ **do**
  for $i = 1:n$ **do**
    for $j = 1:i$ **do**
      if $F(x_i) > F(x_j)$ **then**
        | move firefly j towards firefly i;
      else
        | move firefly i towards firefly j;
      end
      Update the attractiveness of all fireflies;
      Evaluate new solution and update $F(x_i)$;
    end
    Rank the fireflies and find the current Global QoS probability F_{best}, and schedule strategy S;
  end
end
return F_{best}, S;

PERFORMANCE EVALUATION

Experimental Design

To evaluate the effectiveness and correctness of this article proposed method, we conduct simulative experiments based on three well-known workflow templates (Juve, 2013), namely, ***CyberShake***, ***Inspiral***, and ***Sipht***, as shown in Figure 3.

We consider that all edge servers are with 3 different types of resource configurations and charging plans, i.e., ***tp1***, ***tp2***, and ***tp3***. We tested the completion time of tasks on three types of edge servers at different periods, i.e., (a), (b) and (c), as shown in Figure 4. As can be seen, the period of 4(a) shows the weakest performance fluctuations while 4(c) shows the greatest. The positions for edge servers and users are based on the dataset given in (Lai, 2018) and illustrated in Figure 5. For comparison, we consider **Random** (Pavithr, 2013), **pure FA** (Ma, 2019), **Greedy** (Kazakovtsev, 2020), and **GA** (Zhu, 2016) as peers.

Figure 3. The case templates of workflows

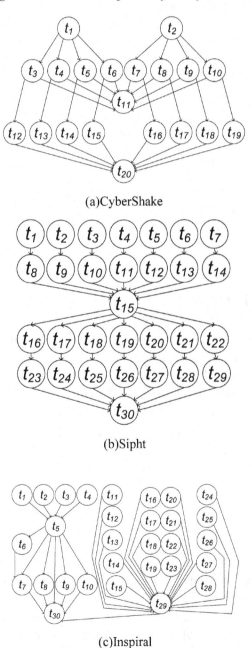

(a)CyberShake

(b)Sipht

(c)Inspiral

Figure 4. The completion time of workflow tasks at different types of edge servers in different periods

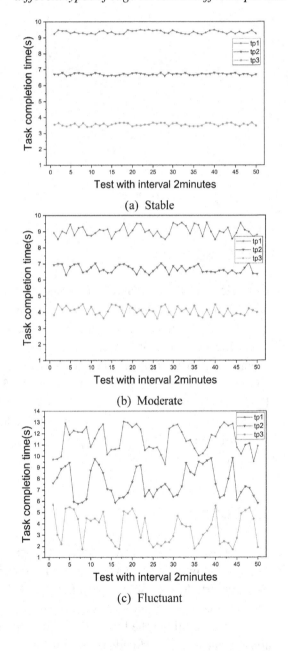

(a) Stable

(b) Moderate

(c) Fluctuant

Figure 5. Edge servers and users deployment

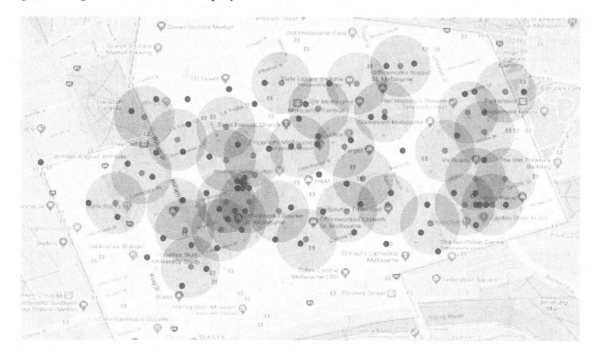

Result Analysis

At the periods of 4(a), 4(b) and 4(c), we show in Figures 6-8 the comparison of scheduling performance of different methods in terms of deadline constraint satisfaction rate, workflow completion time, and cost. As can be observed, the article method beats *Random*, *pure FA*, *Greedy* and *GA* in terms of average deadline validation rate. Moreover, this article method clearly achieves lower workflow completion time and cost. To be specific, the cost of this article method is 1.7%, 1.4%, and 3.4% lower than *pure FA* on average at three periods, respectively; 5.7%, 5.4%, and 8.4% lower than *Random*; 5.3%, 6.1%, and 5.6% lower than *Greedy*; and 2.2%, 1.4%, and 3.5% lower than *GA*. The workflow completion time of this article method is 4.5%, 45.8%, and 49.7% lower than that of *pure FA* on average; 12.8%, 26.4%, and 62.3% lower than *Random*; 4.4%, 23%, and 34.7% lower than *Greedy*; and 14.5%, 51.4%, and 37.1% lower than *GA*, respectively.

CONCLUSION

In this work, we proposed a novel probabilistic-performance-aware approach to multi-workflow scheduling in the edge computing environment. Instead of considering static and time-invariant performance of edge servers, this article approach fully exploits the real-time performance fluctuations of them and leverages a probabilistic-performance-distribution-based mechanism in feeding a discrete-FA-based optimization method for generating scheduling plans. Experimental results based on several well-known workflow templates, and a real-world edge-server-location dataset show that the article proposed method clearly outperforms traditional approaches in terms of multiple performance metrics.

Figure 6. The comparison of different methods at the period of 4(a) as the input performance data

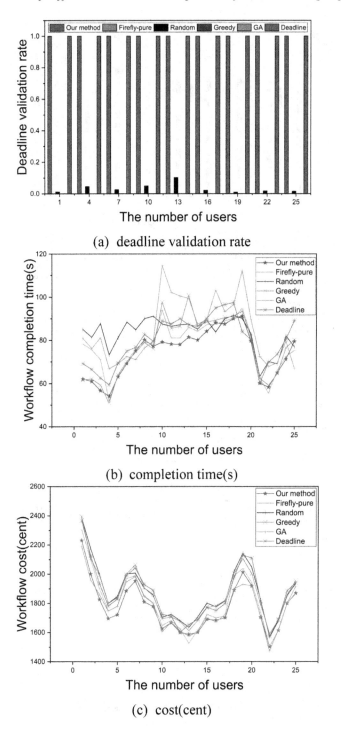

(a) deadline validation rate

(b) completion time(s)

(c) cost(cent)

Figure 7. The comparison of different methods at the period of 4(b) as the input performance data

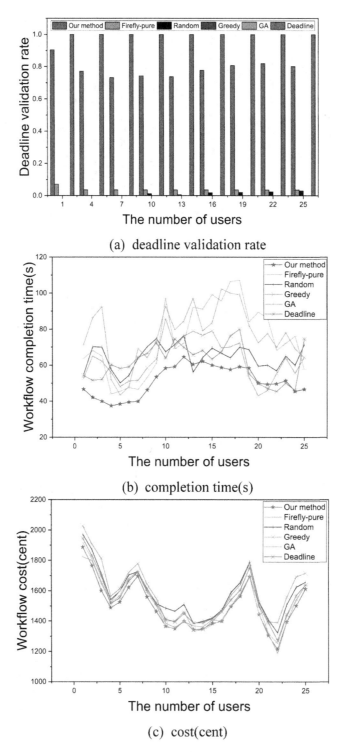

(a) deadline validation rate

(b) completion time(s)

(c) cost(cent)

Figure 8. The comparison of different methods at the period of 4(c) as the input performance data

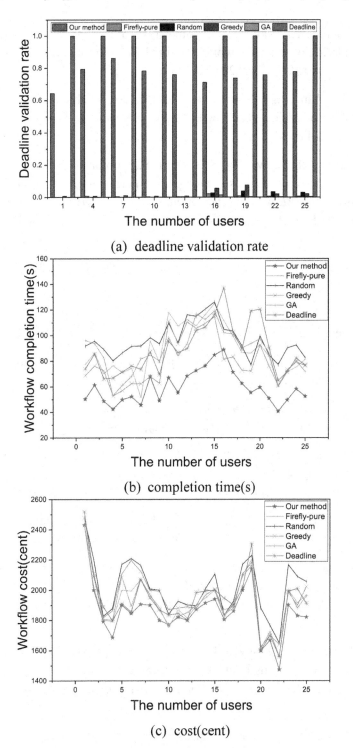

(a) deadline validation rate

(b) completion time(s)

(c) cost(cent)

REFERENCES

Casas, I., Taheri, J., Ranjan, R., Wang, L., & Zomaya, A. Y. (2018). GA-ETI: An enhanced genetic algorithm for the scheduling of scientific workflows in cloud environments. *Journal of Computational Science*, *26*, 318–331. doi:10.1016/j.jocs.2016.08.007

Hwang, S. Y., Wang, H., Tang, J., & Srivastava, J. (2007). A probabilistic approach to modeling and estimating the qos of web-services-based workflows. *Information Sciences*, *177*(23), 5484–5503. doi:10.1016/j.ins.2007.07.011

Jackson, K. R., Ramakrishnan, L., Muriki, K., Canon, S., Cholia, S., Shalf, J., Wasserman, H. J., & Wright, N. J. (2010). Performance analysis of high performance computing applications on the amazon web services cloud. In *2010 IEEE second international conference on cloud computing technology and science* (pp. 159-168). IEEE. 10.1109/CloudCom.2010.69

Juve, G., Chervenak, A., Deelman, E., Bharathi, S., Mehta, G., & Vahi, K. (2013). Characterizing and profiling scientific workflows. *Future Generation Computer Systems*, *29*(3), 682–692. doi:10.1016/j.future.2012.08.015

Kaur, M., & Kadam, S. (2018). A novel multi-objective bacteria foraging optimization algorithm (mobfoa) for multi-objective scheduling. *Applied Soft Computing*, *66*, 183–195. doi:10.1016/j.asoc.2018.02.011

Kazakovtsev, L. A., & Rozhnov, I. (2020). Application of algorithms with variable greedy heuristics for k-medoids problems. Informatica, 44(1). doi:10.31449/inf.v44i1.2737

Kim, Y., Kwak, J., & Chong, S. (2017). Dual-side optimization for cost-delay tradeoff in mobile edge computing. *IEEE Transactions on Vehicular Technology*, *67*(2), 1765–1781. doi:10.1109/TVT.2017.2762423

Lai, P., He, Q., Abdelrazek, M., Chen, F., Hosking, J., Grundy, J., & Yang, Y. (2018). Optimal edge user allocation in edge computing with variable sized vector bin packing. In *International Conference on Service-Oriented Computing* (pp. 230-245). Springer. 10.1007/978-3-030-03596-9_15

Lunardi, W. T., & Voos, H. (2018). An extended flexible job shop scheduling problem with parallel operations. *Applied Computing Review*, *18*(2), 46–56. doi:10.1145/3243064.3243068

Ma, Y., Zhang, J., Wang, S., Xia, Y., Chen, P., Wu, L., & Zheng, W. (2019). A novel approach to cost-efficient scheduling of multi-workflows in the edge computing environment with the proximity constraint. In *International Conference on Algorithms and Architectures for Parallel Processing* (pp. 655-668). Springer.

Pandey, S., Wu, L., Guru, S. M., & Buyya, R. (2010). A particle swarm optimization-based heuristic for scheduling workflow applications in cloud computing environments. In *2010 24th IEEE international conference on advanced information networking and applications* (pp. 400-407). IEEE. 10.1109/AINA.2010.31

Pavithr, R. S. (2013). Gursaran: A random search and greedy selection based genetic quantum algorithm for combinatorial optimization. In *Proceedings of the IEEE Congress on Evolutionary Computation, CEC 2013*, (pp. 2422-2427). IEEE. 10.1109/CEC.2013.6557859

Schad, J., Dittrich, J., & Quianeruiz, J. (2010). *Runtime measurements in the cloud: observing, analyzing, and reducing variance.* Academic Press.

Verma, A., & Kaushal, S. (2017). A hybrid multi-objective Particle Swarm Optimization for scientific workflow scheduling. *Parallel Computing*, *62*, 1–19. doi:10.1016/j.parco.2017.01.002

Yang, X. S. (2009). Firefly algorithms for multimodal optimization. In *International symposium on stochastic algorithms* (pp. 169-178). Springer.

Yang, X. S. (2010). *Firefly algorithm, stochastic test functions and design optimisation.* arXiv preprint arXiv:1003.1409.

Zhang, L., Li, K., Li, C., & Li, K. (2017, February). Bi-objective workflow scheduling of the energy consumption and reliability in heterogeneous computing systems. *Information Sciences*, *379*, 241–256. doi:10.1016/j.ins.2016.08.003

Zhang, Y., Chen, X., Chen, Y., Li, Z., & Huang, J. (2018). Cost efficient scheduling for delay-sensitive tasks in edge computing system. In *2018 IEEE International Conference on Services Computing (SCC)* (pp. 73-80). IEEE. 10.1109/SCC.2018.00017

Zhou, X., Zhang, G., Sun, J., Zhou, J., Wei, T., & Hu, S. (2019, April). Minimizing cost and makespan for workflow scheduling in cloud using fuzzy dominance sort based HEFT. *Future Generation Computer Systems*, *93*, 278–289. doi:10.1016/j.future.2018.10.046

Zhu, Z., Zhang, G., Li, M., & Liu, X. (2016). Evolutionary multi-objective workflow scheduling in cloud. *IEEE Transactions on Parallel and Distributed Systems*, *27*(5), 1344–1357. doi:10.1109/TPDS.2015.2446459

This research was previously published in the International Journal of Web Services Research (IJWSR), 18(2); pages 25-39, copyright year 2021 by IGI Publishing (an imprint of IGI Global).

Chapter 21
Resource Allocation Scheduling Algorithm Based on Incomplete Information Dynamic Game for Edge Computing

Bo Wang

https://orcid.org/0000-0001-9320-7534

School of Software Technology, Dalian University of Technology, Dalian, China & School of Applied Technology, University of Science and Technology Liaoning, Anshan, China & Key Laboratory for Ubiquitous Network and Service Software of Liaoning Province, Dalian, China

Mingchu Li

School of Software Technology, Dalian University of Technology, Dalian, China & Key Laboratory for Ubiquitous Network and Service Software of Liaoning Province, Dalian, China

ABSTRACT

With the advent of the 5G era, the demands for features such as low latency and high concurrency are becoming increasingly significant. These sophisticated new network applications and services require huge gaps in network transmission bandwidth, network transmission latency, and user experience, making cloud computing face many technical challenges in terms of applicability. In response to cloud computing's shortcomings, edge computing has come into its own. However, many factors affect task offloading and resource allocation in the edge computing environment, such as the task offload latency, energy consumption, smart device mobility, end-user power, and other issues. This paper proposes a dynamic multi-winner game model based on incomplete information to solve multi-end users' task offloading and edge resource allocation. First, based on the history of end-users storage in edge data centers, a hidden Markov model can predict other end-users' bid prices at time t. Based on these predicted auction prices, the model determines their bids. A dynamic multi-winner game model is used to solve the offload strategy that minimizes latency, energy consumption, cost, and to maximizes end-user satisfaction at the edge data center. Finally, the authors designed a resource allocation algorithm based on different priorities

DOI: 10.4018/978-1-6684-5700-9.ch021

and task types to implement resource allocation in edge data centers. To ensure the prediction model's accuracy, the authors also use the expectation-maximization algorithm to learn the model parameters. Comparative experimental results show that the proposed model can better results in time delay, energy consumption, and cost.

INTRODUCTION

Cloud computing technology has dramatically promoted social development and produced substantial economic benefits. Data obtained from terminal devices such as sensors, cameras, and smartphones has exploded with the advent of the Internet of Thing's era. However, a significant amount of IoT data only needs localization, and If it is transmitted back to a remote cloud computing center, it will cause tremendous pressure on network bandwidth and cloud computing center. On the other hand, with the advent of the 5G era, the demands for features such as low latency and high concurrency are becoming increasingly important. These sophisticated new network applications and services require huge gaps in network transmission bandwidth, network transmission latency, user experience, making cloud computing face many technical challenges in terms of applicability. In response to cloud computing's shortcomings, edge computing (Satyanarayanan, 2017) has come into its own. Edge computing provides services between the cloud data center and end devices, and a computing mode is provided close to the user (Shi et al., 2016). In applications requiring high concurrency, low latency, and massive bandwidth, the use of edge computing can play a role that traditional cloud computing cannot achieve (Lopez et al., 2015). Using edge data center resources efficiently and rationally to reduce latency and energy consumption is critical in edge computing. Existing researches cover two aspects: resource allocation in edge data centers and strategies for task offloading. The edge data center resource refers to allocate efficiently limited CPU, memory, storage, and other resources to meet more end-users' needs. Task offloading strategy research refers to how tasks are offloaded between end-users and edge data centers in a multi-user edge computing environment to maximize overall benefits and ensure fairness. However, with many end-users joining the IoT, the resource allocation and task offloading strategies of edge computing data centers face many challenges due to end-device power, end-device mobility, energy consumption, and time delay. How to allocate the edge computing data center's limited-service resources becomes an urgent problem to be solved. In reality, on the one hand, the edge computing data center as an edge service provider will face conflicts between energy consumption, cost, and user satisfaction when managing and allocating service resources. On the other hand, as users of edge services, end-users want to pay a certain amount of money to complete their submitted tasks and ensure high satisfaction and quality requirements. In addition to the existing research methods, game theory is a useful tool to solve resource allocation competition among multiple participants. The strategy adopted by each participant in the game will affect the competitive strategy of other participants. Participants choose strategies to maximize each other's benefits. In this paper, the conflicts between energy consumption, cost, and user satisfaction are transformed into the competition between edge data centers and end-users. The auction mechanism simulates the interaction process between them, thereby effectively solving the conflict problem. This article's research will focus on the conflict between energy consumption, cost, and user satisfaction to discuss service resources' pricing in edge data centers.

This paper proposes a dynamic multi-winner game model based on incomplete information to solve multi-end users' task offloading and edge resource allocation. First, based on the history of end-users storage in edge data centers, a hidden Markov model can predict other end-users' bid prices at time t. Based on these predicted auction prices, the model determines their bids. A dynamic multi-winner game model is used to solve the offload strategy that minimizes latency, energy consumption, cost and maximizes end-user satisfaction at the edge data center. Finally, the authors designed a resource allocation algorithm based on different priorities and task types to implement resource allocation in edge data centers. Besides, to ensure the prediction model's accuracy, the authors also use the Expectation-Maximization algorithm to learn the model parameters. This paper has the following contributions.

1. In the task offloading process, both end-user and edge data centers maximize the overall benefits and ensure fairness; We propose a dynamic multi-winner game model based on incomplete information. This model uses historical data to predict other end-users ' bids. To improve the accuracy of the predictions, we dynamically adjust the parameters for the model to improve the accuracy of the model.
2. We propose a scheduling algorithm to solve edge resource allocation. We propose a user satisfaction model based on task priority with the end-users' proximity to the edge computing data center as an influencing factor, which makes the model more realistic by considering the task type and energy consumption of the end-user offloaded the edge computing data center separately during the algorithm implementation.
3. We conducted numerous experiments and compared them with other algorithms regarding the delay, energy consumption, and cost. The experimental results show that our proposed algorithm is better than others.

The rest of this paper is organized as follows. We describe the related work in Section 2. Section 3 describes the system model and problem formulation. We present the end-users' prediction model based on the Hidden Markov model, model parameter learning model, and a scheduling algorithm for edge resource allocation in Section 4. Section 5 presents the performance evaluation results of the proposed algorithm. Finally, we conclude this paper and future work in Section 6.

RELATED WORK

Many end-users are accessing edge data centers through personal wearable devices, smartphones, and sensors to fulfill their own needs with IoT technology development. Various literature studies have solved task offloading and resource allocation in different architectures.

As (Lopez et al., 2015; Shi et al., 2016) pointed out in the paper, task offloading and resource allocation are among the most important edge computing challenges. Simultaneously, resource allocation is affected by various factors, such as the delay of offloading tasks, energy consumption, smart device mobility, and end-user power. Related researchers have also conducted much research. (Liu et al., 2016) adopted the Markov decision process method to deal with the task offloading problem, in which the calculation tasks were scheduled according to the task buffer's queue status and the execution status of the local processing unit, and the status of the transmission unit. By analyzing the average delay of each task and energy consumption of mobile devices, the power-limited delay minimization problem was formulated, and an effective one-dimensional search algorithm was proposed to find the optimal task scheduling strategy. (Mao et al., 2016) studied a dynamic computational offloading algorithm based on Lyapunov optimization and used performance cost and energy consumption in performance indicators. It also considered execution delay and task failure rate. (Zhang et al., 2013) proposed a theoretical framework for energy-optimal mobile cloud computing, which sequentially reconfigures the CPU frequency and dynamically changes the cloud's data transfer rate in response to the stochastic channel conditions. A closed-ended solution to the optimal scheduling strategy was obtained. (Zhang et al., 2016) proposed an efficient MEC computational offloading mechanism in a 5G heterogeneous network. Minimize the optimization of system energy consumption while considering the energy consumption for task calculation and file transfer. In combination with 5G heterogeneous networks' multi-access characteristics, an energy-saving computational offloading scheme was designed. The scheme jointly optimized offloading and wireless resource allocation for minimal energy consumption within latency constraints. To solve the fine-grained task offloading computing of IoT systems, (Shu et al., 2020) proposed a multi-user lightweight and efficient offloading solution, which offloaded the most suitable IoT tasks/subtasks to the edge server, thus minimizing the expected execution time. A distributed consensus algorithm is also proposed for low-power IoT devices to support offloading. To solve the resource conflict problem, (Zheng et al., 2020) proposed an extended Hungarian algorithm based on edge computing, which obtained small latency and achieved sustainable services. (Guo et al., 2016) proposed an equivalent discrete-time Markov decision process and obtained an algorithm to determine the optimal strategy. These strategies perform the distribution of tasks generated by mobile users with edge clouds in an online manner. The proposed strategy achieves the best power delay tradeoff in the system. (Jamil et al., 2020) proposed a different fog computational scheduler that supports the IoT service configuration, optimizing latency, and network usage. Requests for the IoT devices were optimally scheduled on Fog devices, considering latency and energy consumption as performance metrics, and optimizing each fog device's available resource requirements. (Li et al., 2019) proposed a computing offloading policy and resource allocation optimization scheme in MEC multi-wireless access point network to minimize system cost by providing optimal computing offloading policy, transmission power allocation, bandwidth allocation, and computing resource scheduling. Since the problem is NP-hard, the proposed solution decomposes the optimization problem into two sub-problems, offload strategy and resource allocation. The offload strategy involved the selection of the optimal access point and was analyzed through potential games. The resource allocation was obtained using Lagrange's multiplication. (W. Chen et al., 2018) proposed a green mobile edge cloud computing multi-user multitask computing offloading method, using the Lyapunov optimization method to determine energy consumption strategies, and introducing centralized and distributed performance constraint-based greedy scheduling algorithms multi-user offloading issues effectively. (M.-H. Chen et al., 2018) proposed the co-optimization of offloading decisions for all users and allocation of computing and communication resources to minimize energy consumption, the overall cost of computing, and minimize latency between users. (Cao et al., 2015) proposed an energy-optimized offloading algorithm to solve the mobile computing offloading of Heterogeneous Networks to maximize the mobile terminal's energy savings under a given application execution time requirement. (Zhao et al., 2015) studied the joint optimization of multi-user wireless resources and computing resources in mobile cloud computing to reduce terminal energy consumption. They proposed a heuristic strategy based on delay constraints and mobile application types for resource allocation with low computational complexity. (You et al., 2016) studied the resource allocation of a multi-user mobile-edge computation offloading system based on time-division multiple access and orthogonal frequency-division multiple access. A user's priority was derived based on the user's channel revenue and locally calculated energy consumption. As a result, users with a higher and lower priority than a given threshold performed full and minimum unloading. (Kuang et al., 2019) studied the joint problem of partial offload scheduling and resource allocation for a mobile edge computing system with multiple independent tasks. An issue of partial offload scheduling and power distribution in a single-user mobile edge computing system was raised. The goal was to minimize the weighted sum of execution delay and energy consumption while ensuring the task's transmission power constraints. The issue of execution latency for tasks running on mobile edge computing and mobile devices was considered. The energy consumption of the task calculation and task data transfer was also considered. (Wang et al., 2019) formulated the computational offloading problem as an energy and cost minimization problem by considering completion time and energy consumption. A distributed algorithm consisting of clock frequency configuration, transmission power distribution, channel rate schedule, and offload policy selection was proposed by solving the optimization problem. In this algorithm, the local execution's clock frequency and the transmission power in the edge cloud execution were jointly optimized. (Zhang et al., 2018) investigated the task scheduling problem of reducing the cost of edge computing systems. The task scheduling problem is an optimization problem to minimize system costs while meeting all tasks' latency requirements. A task scheduling algorithm called two-stage task scheduling cost optimization is proposed to solve this optimization problem effectively.

As a useful tool to solve competition among multiple participants for resource allocation, game theory has also been widely applied to solve task offloading and resource allocation problems. (Chen et al., 2016) proposed a multi-user computing offloading game approach to solving computing offloading for mobile edge cloud computing in a multi-channel wireless interference environment. (Jie et al., 2018) proposed a task scheduling algorithm based on the repeated Stackelberg game to map various tasks to a given relevant resource. As a short-term leader, the requesting user determines the processing task's unit price within the relevant budget to maximize the current task's total satisfaction. Then, according to different users' quotations in different rounds, the edge service provider serves as a follower to maximize users' long-term profits. (Niyato et al., 2012) proposed that service providers formed a resource alliance in a mobile computing environment and established a resource pool to support mobile applications. An alliance game model is established to obtain the optimal strategy of service providers to expand and maximize their profits.

Although the idea of game theory is applied to study task offloading and resource allocation for edge computing, the issues of minimizes energy consumption and costs, maximize user satisfaction, and the distance between end-users and edge data center on strategy has not been entirely resolved, and this is what this article needs to try to solve.

SYSTEM MODEL AND PROBLEM FORMULATION

System Model

As shown in Figure 1, the entire system consists of end-users, edge service providers, and cloud service providers. End-users can access the edge service providers through wired or wireless network access and can complete the necessary computing and storage capabilities of devices, and users can become end-users. Use set $Eu=\{Eu_1,Eu_2,Eu_3,\ldots,Eu_N\}$ to represent all end-users collections and use set

$r=\{r_1,r_2,r_3,\ldots,r_N\}$ to represent all end user's resource requirements such as CPU, memory, and storage, where N represents the number of end-users. End-users can decide which edge service provider they are connected to or switch to another edge service provider as appropriate. Since end-users select the nearest edge service provider for access, all submitted service requests will have significantly lower latency, and end-users can quickly execute them. The tasks that cannot be completed by edge service providers can be dispatched to cloud service providers, and cloud service providers and edge service providers are connected through the high-speed backbone network. Cloud service providers can monitor each edge service provider's operation status and resource usage in real-time. Cloud service providers and edge service providers collaborate to provide robust cloud computing and storage services for end-users. In reality, many end-users submit tasks to various edge service providers and are paid to meet the processing tasks' cost. Many tasks do not reach the system simultaneously due to the volume of tasks, the distance to individual Edge service providers, the power consumption of the devices, and the quality of network communication. Therefore, we assume that an end-user can commit many tasks; each task can use multiple kinds of resources, such as CPU, memory, and storage. The edge service provider has a large number of edge devices that can handle all types of tasks. It also has the function of allocation and scheduling, assigning the tasks submitted by end-users to different edge devices as far as possible, and when the resources are not enough, it can schedule the unfinished tasks to the cloud service provider for processing and pay the corresponding compensation. The scheduling algorithms for scheduling to cloud service providers and other edge service providers are beyond this article's scope and discussed in other articles.

Figure 1. Multi-user edge computing system

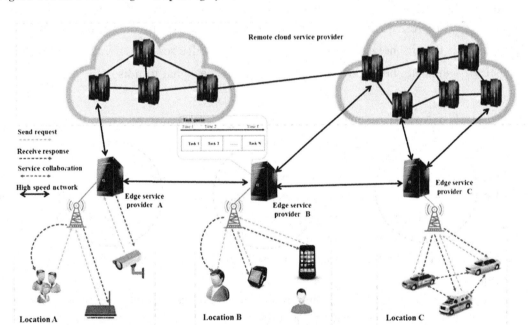

User Satisfaction Model

Quality of Experience refers to the user's subjective experience of the quality and performance of devices, networks, and systems, applications, or services. Based on (Li et al., 2014) and (Bergstra & Middelburg, 2003), in this paper, we define the satisfaction function for end-users, as shown in Equation 1.

$$US_i = \rho \, \log_\alpha \left(priority_i \left(1 - \frac{price_i^{esp}}{bid_i^{eu}} \right) \right) + 4.5 \tag{1}$$

US_i represents the user's satisfaction rating. The larger the value of US_i, the more satisfied user i is. $price_i^{esp}$ is the resource price for the edge data center. bid_i^{eu} is the bid for the smart device. α and ρ represent the correlation coefficient. $priority_i$ represents the ith task's priority submitted by the user.

Energy Consumption Model

According to Shannon's formula (Shannon, 1948; Shannon, 1949), the upload and the return data transmission rates are shown in Equations 2 and 3.

$$C_{eu,esp}^{uplink} = W_{eu,esp} \times \log_2 \left(1 + \frac{P_{eu,esp}^{uplink} \times G_{eu,esp}}{P_{noise}} \right) \tag{2}$$

$W_{eu,esp}$ represents the bandwidth of the wireless transmission channel from the end-user to the edge service provider. $P_{eu,esp}^{uplink}$ represents the transmit power of the device used by the end-user during data upload. $G_{eu,esp}$ indicates the channel gain from the end-user to the edge service provider wireless transmission channel. P_{noise} indicates noise power. $\frac{P_{eu,esp}^{uplink} G_{eu,esp}}{P_{noise}}$ is called the signal-to-noise ratio (SNR).

$$C_{esp,eu}^{downlink} = W_{esp,eu} \times \log_2 \left(1 + \frac{P_{esp,eu}^{downlink} \times G_{esp,eu}}{P_{noise}} \right) \tag{3}$$

$W_{esp,eu}$ indicates the bandwidth of the wireless backhaul data transmission channel from the edge service provider to the end-user, and $P_{esp,eu}^{downlink}$ indicates the transmit power of the edge service provider during the wireless link backhaul data process. P_{noise} indicates Gaussian white-noise power. $G_{esp,eu}$ indicates the channel gain from the edge service provider to the end-user wireless transmission channel. From reference (Ding et al., 2018), we can see $G_{esp,eu} = 103.8 + 20.9 \times \log_{10}^{dist_{eu,esp}}$, where $dist_{eu,esp}$ indicates the distance between the end-user and edge service provider.

From Equations 2 and 3, the energy consumption from the end-user to the edge service provider and the result return process's energy consumption after the task is completed expressed by Equations 4 and 5, respectively.

$$E_{eu}^{uplink} = P_{eu,esp}^{uplink} \times \frac{B_{eu,esp}}{C_{eu,esp}^{uplink}} = \frac{P_{eu,esp}^{uplink} \times B_{eu,esp}}{W_{eu,esp} \times \log_2 \left(1 + \frac{P_{eu,esp}^{uplink} \times G_{eu,esp}}{P_{noise}}\right)} \tag{4}$$

$$E_{esp}^{downlink} = P_{esp,eu}^{downlink} \times \frac{B_{esp,eu}}{C_{esp,eu}^{downlink}} = \frac{P_{esp,eu}^{downlink} \times B_{esp,eu}}{W_{esp,eu} \times \log_2 \left(1 + \frac{P_{esp,eu}^{downlink} \times G_{esp,eu}}{P_{noise}}\right)} \tag{5}$$

$B_{eu,esp}$ indicates the size of the uploaded task data, and $B_{esp,eu}$ indicates the data size of the returned task execution results' data size.

The end-users energy consumption is equal to the transfer power during upload and download plus the energy consumption during the idle time, expressed by Equation 6.

$$E_{eu}^{total} = E_{eu}^{uplink} + E_{esp}^{downlink} + E_{eu}^{idle} \tag{6}$$

In particular, since the energy consumption at the end-user idle time is much smaller than the energy consumption at the time of request and response, we ignore the energy consumption at the idle time in this paper.

The edge service provider can perform many types of tasks. In this article, we only consider the CPU-intensive tasks and storage-intensive task tasks. Energy consumption for performing computationally intensive tasks is equal to the energy consumption per CPU clock cycle multiplied by the number of CPU clock cycles for processing computationally intensive tasks and multiplied by the amount of computationally intensive tasks assigned (Kumar & Lu, 2010). It can be expressed by Equation 7.

$$E_{esp}^{computing} = \delta_{esp}^{computing} \times T_{esp}^{computing} \times B_{eu,esp}^{computing} \tag{7}$$

$T_{esp}^{computing}$ represents the number of CPU clock cycles when processing each bit of the CPU-intensive task on the edge service provider, and $\delta_{esp}^{computing}$ represents the edge service provider's energy consumption in the unit CPU clock cycle. $B_{eu,esp}^{computing}$ represents the number of allocated CPU-intensive tasks. Equation 8 comes from (Cheng et al., 2016).

$$\delta_{esp}^{computing} = c \times \left(A_{esp}^{computing}\right)^2 \tag{8}$$

$A_{esp}^{computing}$ denotes the CPU computing power provided by the edge service provider, and c denotes the average capacitance coefficient. Equation 7 can be rewritten as Equation 9.

$$E_{esp}^{computing} = c \times \left(A_{esp}^{computing}\right)^2 \times T_{esp}^{computing} \times B_{eu,esp}^{computing} \tag{9}$$

The end-user can access files stored on edge or in the remote cloud at any time but must download and edit them before sending the modified files back to the edge or cloud. The cloud service provider ensures that the cloud service and edge service have sufficient storage space and can manage data backups. From (Baliga et al., 2011), it is known that the energy consumption function for storage-intensive tasks is shown in Equation 10.

$$E_{esp}^{storage} = \sum_{\kappa=1}^{tasknum} \left[B_{\kappa}^{storage} \times \zeta_{\kappa} \times \left(E_{\kappa}^{downlink} + \frac{1.5 \times P_{\kappa}^{contentserver}}{C_{\kappa}^{contentserver}} \right) + 2 \times B_{\kappa}^{storage} \times \frac{1.5 \times P_{\kappa}^{diskarray}}{C_{\kappa}^{diskarray}} \right] \tag{10}$$

$B_{\kappa}^{storage}$ represents the size of the stored file; ζ_{κ} represents the number of downloads per unit time; $E_{\kappa}^{downlink}$ represents download energy consumption. $P_{\kappa}^{contentserver}$ and $C_{\kappa}^{contentserver}$ represent the energy consumption and capacity of the content server, respectively. $P_{\kappa}^{diskarray}$ and $C_{\kappa}^{diskarray}$ represent the energy consumption and capacity of the disk array, respectively. 1.5 represents the power requirements for cooling and other daily expenses, and 2 represents the power requirements for storage redundancy. We assume that only files that are accessed regularly will consume energy when stored. Files that are not accessed from time to time are stored in other disk drives in the low-energy mode, so energy consumption is negligible.

Cost Model

Each edge service provider provides related resources to complete various types of tasks submitted by end-users. Each edge service provider will incur costs when performing tasks. The cost of the edge service providers can be expressed as Equation 11.

$$C^{esp}\left(r^{total} \right) = \sum_{j=1}^{N} \left(p_{j}^{cpu} + p_{j}^{memory} + p_{j}^{storage} + p_{j}^{bandwidth} \right) \times \Omega_{j} \tag{11}$$

In particular, if the task is executed, Ω_j is equal to 1. Otherwise, Ω_j is equal to 0.

Problem Formulation

It can be seen from the functional description of the system model that there is a conflict of interest between the edge service provider and end-users. On the one hand, the edge service provider has many edge devices that can handle various tasks. The edge service provider determines the allocation and scheduling of tasks. The edge service provider hopes to use the least resources and energy consumption to process more tasks to obtain much profit. On the other hand, end-users are mobile. By choosing different edge service providers to accomplish the most tasks with the least cost and energy consumption, it can also satisfy the Quality of Experience of end-users.

RESOURCE ALLOCATION SCHEDULING ALGORITHM BASED ON INCOMPLETE INFORMATION DYNAMIC MULTI-WINNER GAME

End-User Resource Auction Price Prediction Based on a Hidden Markov Model

In Figure 1, end-users are independent and compete with each other in the system structure, and they all want to acquire more resources to accomplish their tasks and maximize their interests. Because relevant information is incomplete or unobservable, this paper uses a hidden Markov model (Rabiner, 1989) to predict each end-user auction price. We use the end-users historical resource request records to predict the end-users bid for the edge resource requests.

In this paper, the hidden Markov model can be composed of a 5-tuple $\langle S, O, \pi, A, B \rangle$. $S = \{s_1, s_2, \ldots, s_K\}$ is a set of actual states, that is, the set of individual end-user bids. These states are usually not directly observed. $O = \{o_1, o_2, \ldots, o_K\}$ represents a set of historical records on the resource status obtained by each end-user. It is associated with the model's hidden state, but there is no one-to-one correspondence, which can be obtained by direct observation. The bid probability distribution π for each end-user at the start time, representing the probability matrix of the hidden state at the start moment t=1. $s1$ takes the probability $p(s_1)$ of the kth state, and we can write it as Equation 12.

$$p\left(s_1 \big| \pi\right) = \prod_{k-1}^{K} \pi_k^{s_{1,k}}$$

(12)

A describes the transition probability between the hidden states. The elements in row j and column k indicate that under the condition, s_{n-1} is known to be the jth state, the conditional probability that s_n takes the kth state is $A_{j,k} = p\left(s_{n,k} = 1 \big| s_{n-1,j} = 1\right)$. Since these elements are all probability values, $0 \leq A_{j,k} \leq 1$ and $\sum_{k=1}^{K} A_{j,k} = 1$ are satisfied, and the sum of each row of matrix A is 1. The conditional distribution $p\left(s_n \big| s_{n-1}\right)$ can be written, as shown in Equation 13.

$$p\left(s_n \big| s_{n-1}, A\right) = \prod_{j=1}^{K} \prod_{k=1}^{K} A_{j,k}^{s_{n-1,j} s_{n,k}}$$

(13)

According to the above definition, all variables' joint distribution can be written, as shown in Equation 14.

$$p\left(O, S \big| \theta\right) = p\left(s_1 \big| \pi\right) \left[\prod_{n=2}^{N} p\left(s_n \big| s_{n-1}, A\right) \right] \left[\prod_{n=1}^{N} p\left(o_n \big| s_n, \phi\right) \right]$$

(14)

$O = \{o_1, \ldots, o_N\}$ represents all observed variables. $S = \{s_1, \ldots, s_N\}$ represents all hidden variables, and $\theta = \{\pi, A, \phi\}$ represents all parameters. Equation 15 can be derived from $p\left(o_{N+1} \big| s_{N+1}, O\right) = p\left(o_{N+1} \big| s_{N+1}\right)$ and $P\left(s_{N+1} \big| s_N, O\right) = p\left(s_{n+1} \big| s_n\right)$.

$$p\left(o_{N+1}|O\right) = \sum_{s_{N+1}} p\left(o_{N+1}, s_{N+1}|O\right)$$

$$= \sum_{s_{N+1}} p\left(o_{N+1}|s_{N+1}\right) \sum_{s_N} \frac{p\left(s_N, O\right)}{p(O)} p\left(s_{N+1}|s_N\right) \tag{15}$$

$$= \frac{\sum_{s_{N+1}} p\left(o_{N+1}|s_{N+1}\right) \sum_{s_N} \alpha\left(s_N\right) p\left(s_{N+1}|s_N\right)}{p(O)}$$

$\alpha(s_N)$ is first obtained by stepwise recursion using forward computation and then summed for s_N and s_{N+1}, respectively, where the result can be used as an intermediate result to calculate $\alpha\left(s_{N+1}\right)$ and thus the further predicted value. Use this analogy to derive the desired auction value.

The optimization problem can be defined as Equation 16.

$$\delta\left(s_N\right) = \max_{s_1, s_2, \cdots, s_{N-1}} p\left(o_1, o_2, \cdots, o_N, s_1, s_2, \cdots, s_N\right) = \max_{s_1, s_2, \cdots, s_{N-1}} p\left(s_1, s_2, \cdots, s_N, o_1, o_2, \cdots, o_N\right) \tag{16}$$

To solve this optimization problem, recursively find $\delta(s_N)$. We use Bayes' theorem (Nelson, 2013) and conditional independence to obtain Equation 17.

$$\delta\left(s_N\right) = \max_{s_1, s_2, \cdots, s_{N-1}} p\left(o_1, o_2, \cdots, o_N, s_1, s_2, \cdots, s_N\right)$$

$$= \max_{s_1, s_2, \cdots, s_{N-1}} p\left(o_1, o_2, \cdots, o_{N-1}, s_1, s_2, \cdots, s_{N-1}\right) p\left(s_N | o_1, o_2, \cdots, o_{N-1}, s_1, s_2, \cdots, s_{N-1}\right) p\left(o_N | s_N, o_1, o_2, \cdots, o_{N-1}, s_1, s_2, \cdots, s_{N-1}\right) \tag{17}$$

$$= \max_{s_{N-1}} p\left(o_1, o_2, \cdots, o_N | s_1, s_2, \cdots, s_N\right) p\left(s_1, s_2, \cdots, s_N | s_1, s_2, \cdots, s_{N-1}\right) \max_{s_1, s_2, \cdots, s_{N-1}} p\left(o_1, o_2, \cdots, o_{N-1}, s_1, s_2, \cdots, s_{N-1}\right)$$

The recursive formula about $\delta(s_N)$ can be obtained after the collation, as shown in Equation 18.

$$\delta\left(s_N\right) = p\left(o_N | s_N\right) \max_{s_{N-1}} p\left(s_N | s_{N-1}\right) \delta\left(s_{N-1}\right) \tag{18}$$

When we are seeking $\delta(s_{n,k})$, $\forall k=1,2,\ldots,K$, we must choose one of s_{n-1}'s K possibilities to maximize the value of $\delta(s_{n,k})$ and let the selected sequence number be $\varphi(k_n)$. Using Equation 19, the state of each hidden variable under the optimal solution can be obtained.

$$k_{n-1}^{\max} = \varphi\left(k_n^{\max}\right) \tag{19}$$

Predictive Model Parameter Learning

This paper uses the maximum likelihood method to learn the model's parameters to improve the model's accuracy. It is impossible to obtain the analytical solution of the parameters directly due to hidden variables. The Expectation-Maximization algorithm must be used to iterate until convergence to obtain the model parameters gradually. The EM algorithm is divided into two parts: The E step and the M step. In the E step, assuming known model parameters, the algorithm finds the posterior distribution $p(S|O, \theta^{old})$

of hidden variables; in the M step, the log-likelihood of the expected maximum under this a posteriori distribution is calculated. This expectation is shown in Equation 20.

$$Q\left(\theta,\theta^{old}\right) = \sum_{S} p\left(S|O,\theta^{old}\right) \ln p\left(O,S|\theta\right) \tag{20}$$

By maximizing this expectation function, θ's solution can be obtained, and then the solution is taken as a new θ^{old} into step E and iterates until the algorithm finally converges. From the definition of the model above, the log-likelihood can be expressed, as shown in Equation 21.

$$\ln p\left(O,S|\theta\right) = \ln p\left(s_1|\pi\right) \left[\sum_{n=2}^{N} \ln p\left(s_n|s_{n-1},A\right)\right] \left[\sum_{n=1}^{N} \ln p\left(o_n|s_n,\phi\right)\right]$$
$$= \sum_{k=1}^{K} s_{1,k} \ln \pi_k + \sum_{n=2}^{N}\sum_{k=1}^{K}\sum_{j=1}^{K} s_{n-1,j} s_{n,k} \ln A_{j,k} + \sum_{n=1}^{N}\sum_{k=1}^{K} s_{n,k} \ln p\left(o_n|\phi_k\right) \tag{21}$$

$\gamma(s_n)$ and $\xi\left(s_{n-1},s_n\right)$ represent the posterior distribution of z_n and the joint posterior distribution of z_{n-1} and z_n, there are Equations 22 and 23.

$$\gamma(s_n)\ni \tag{22}$$

$$\xi\left(s_{n-1},s_n\right) = p\left(s_{n-1},s_n|O,\theta^{old}\right) \tag{23}$$

Similarly, we use $s_{n,k}$ to represent the conditional probability of $z_{n,k}=1$ and $\xi\left(s_{n-1,j},s_{n,k}\right)$ to represent the conditional probability of $s_{n-1,j}=1$ and $s_{n,k}=1$. Therefore, Equations 22 and 23 can be rewritten into Equations 24 and 25, respectively.

$$\gamma\left(s_{n,k}\right) = p\left(s_{n,k}=1|O,\theta^{old}\right) = E\left[s_{n,k}\right] = \sum_{z_n} s_{n,k}\gamma\left(s_n\right) \tag{24}$$

$$\xi\left(s_{n-1,j},s_{n,k}\right) = p\left(s_{n-1,j}=1,s_n=1|O,\theta^{old}\right) = E\left[s_{n-1,j},s_{n,k}\right] = \sum_{z_{n-1}}\sum_{z_n} s_{n-1,j} s_{n,k}\xi\left(s_{n-1},s_n\right) \tag{25}$$

Because the maximum likelihood method is used, it is often necessary to observe the change in the likelihood value during the iteration process of the EM algorithm and the condition that the likelihood value does not increase as the iteration stops.

Resource Allocation Scheduling Algorithm Based on Incomplete Information Dynamic Multi-Winner Game

This paper proposes a multi-winner auction algorithm from the perspective of resource allocation in the edge data center. Unlike the previous auction mechanism, the number of end-users that the multi-winner auction algorithm ultimately wins is more than one. In the whole multi-winner auction process, due to the existence of the sealing mechanism, it can be regarded as a game process with incomplete information. Bidders compete for the edge data center resources through different bid prices without fully understanding each other's information. Eventually, the auction broker selects the winner based on the multi-winner auction algorithm and allocates resources. Table 1 summarizes the notations used in the paper.

Table 1. Summary of notations

Symbol	Description
N	Number of end-users
$cpu[i]$	Number of cpu resources required by the ith end-user's submission task
$storage[i]$	Number of storage resources required by the ith end-user 's submission task
$energy[i]$	Energy consumption of the submitted task of the ith end user
$bid[i]$	Bid of the ith end-user
b_{cpu}	The lowest transaction price of cpu resources in the edge data center
$b_{storage}$	The lowest transaction price of storage resources in the edge data center
$b_{cpu}[i]$	Unit price of the ith end user 's bidding cpu resource
$b_{storage}[i]$	Unit price of the ith end user 's bidding storage resource
$profit$	Edge data center revenue
$priority[i]$	Priority of the ith end user to submit a task
CPU	Total amount of CPU resources
$STORAGE$	Total amount of storage resources
$ENERAGE$	Maximum upper limit of energy consumption

The resource allocation algorithm based on the multi-winner auction game model is described as follows:

Step 1: The edge data center publishes resource information, including resource type, resource size, network bandwidth. Each end-user calculates the probability of winning at time t through a prediction model and then determines its bid at time t. The auction broker conducts a multi-winner sealed auction based on each end-user current bid and the resource requested.

Step 2: The edge data center submits the lowest transaction price of various resources to the auction broker.

Step 3: According to the minimum price and resource information submitted by the edge data center, the auction broker removes end-users who do not meet the conditions, such as end-users whose bid is lower than the minimum price. The auction broker will not add it to the auction process and refuse to provide services.

Step 4: The auction broker calculates the unit price of various resources required by each end-user participating in the game at time t according to the bid of the end-users and resource requirements in the list of qualified end-users.

Step 5: Sort the unit prices of each end-user participating in the game in descending order. If the unit prices are the same, sort them in descending order according to the total number of end-users' resources. In particular, if the task is a high priority or urgent, put it at the top of the list. The algorithm is shown in Algorithm 1.

Step 6: Iteratively judges from the first end-user in the sorted list at time t to calculate whether the demand and energy consumption of the tasks submitted by it for resources is higher than that of the edge data center at time t can provide the size of various resources and its energy consumption limit. If it is not higher, these resources will be allocated to the end-user to perform tasks and get paid. If higher, select the next end-user from the sorted end-user list for comparison, until a particular resource in the edge data center is 0 or the end-user list is all allocated. The end-user who gets the resource to perform the task is set as the winner. The resource allocation algorithm is shown in Algorithm 2.

Step 7: If there are any other end users' requests, repeat the above steps to initiate a new auction. Otherwise, quit.

Algorithm 1. Multi-winner auction game algorithm

```
Input: N , cpu[i] , storage[i] , bid[i] , b_cpu , b_storage , b_cpu[i] , b_storage[i]
Output: Multi-winner information
1: For i=1 to N then
2: {
3:      Through the prediction model, calculate the probability of
    winning, and then determine the bid[i];
4:    If task type is computationally intensive then
5:                b_cpu[i] = bid[i]/cpu[i];
6:    If task type is storage-intensive then
7:                b_storage[i] = bid[i]/storage[i];
8:    If  b_cpu[i] < b_cpu  or  b_storage[i] < b_storage  then
9:                Remove this end-user
10:}
11:   Sort the unit prices of each end-user participating in the game
in descending order.
12:    If the unit prices are the same, sort them in descending order
according to the total number of resources requested by end-users.
13:  For i=1 to N then
14: {
15: Find the top l end-users in the list that meet the demand for
various resources and energy consumption requirements as winners.
16:}
17: Return winner
```

Analysis of Algorithms

The model proposed in this paper is composed of three parts: auction price prediction algorithm, multi-winner algorithm, and resource allocation algorithm. Since there are n end-users in the auction price prediction algorithm, the auction price prediction algorithm's time complexity is $O(n)$. The multi-winner algorithm can be regarded as a sorting algorithm to find multiple winners, so the multi-winner algorithm's actual complexity is $O(n \log n)$. Since the resource allocation algorithm is a greedy algorithm, the resource allocation algorithm's time complexity is $O(n \log n)$. In summary, the time complexity of the model is $O(n) + O(n \log n) + O(n \log n) = O(n \log n)$.

Algorithm 2. Edge computing data center resource allocation algorithm

```
Input: N , cpu[i] , storage[i] ,   energy[i]   , profit , bid[i] , priority[i] , CPU , STORAGE ,
ENERAGE
Output:   profit[i],cpu,storage,energy;
1: cpu = 0;
2: storage = 0;
3: energy = 0;
4: profit=0;
5: For  i =1 to  N  then
6: {
7:    If  cpu[i] + cpu  ≤ CPU  and  storage[i] + storage ≤ STORAGE and  priority[i] > 0  and
energy[i] ≤ ENERAGE  then
8:        {
9:              profit+ = bid[i];
10:             cpu+ = cpu[i];
11:           storage+ = storage[i];
12:           energy+ = energy[i];
13:       }
14:      else  if   cpu[i] + cpu  ≤ CPU    and    storage[i] + storage ≤ STORAGE    and
priority[i] = 0  and  energy[i] ≤ ENERAGE  then
15:      {
16:        profit+ = bid[i];
17:        cpu+ = cpu[i];
18:        storage+ = storage[i];
19:        energy+ = energy[i];
20:      }
21:        else  if   cpu[i] + cpu  > CPU    or    storage[i] + storage > STORAGE    or
energy[i] > ENERAGE  then
22:      {
23:                 i++;
24:      }
25:    Return  profit[i],cpu,storage,energy;
26:}
```

NUMERICAL RESULTS AND DISCUSSION

Experimental Parameter Setting

We chose the Dell PowerEdge R730 as our edge server. An IntelR XeonTME5-2620 v4 processor powers with 2.1GHz CPU, 32GB of RAM, and 495W of full-state power. The experiments use smartphones such as Huawei p20 and Apple 8 as smart devices. Table 2 summarizes the simulation setting used in the experiment.

Table 2. Simulation setting

Symbol	Description	Value
$P_{eu,esp}^{uplink}$	Data transmission power	1.258 W
$P_{esp,eu}^{downlink}$	Transmit power of the backhaul data process	1.181 W
$W_{eu,esp}$	Bandwidth of the wireless transmission channel	20M bps
$W_{esp,eu}$	Bandwidth of backhaul data transmission channel	10M bps
$\eta c^{omputing}$	Profit from the unit's utility of the compute-intensive task.	40
ηs^{torage}	Profit from the unit's utility of the storage-intensive task.	20
$\alpha_i^{computing}$	Compute-intensive tasks' preference for execution time and resource requirements	0.7
$\alpha_i^{storage}$	Storage-intensive tasks' preference for execution time and resource requirements	0.3
Size	Task size	[174.4215,8153.468]
Vm	Number of virtual machines	4

Satisfaction Function Analysis

We set the experimental scenario where the bid price for the end-user to complete the task in the system ranges from 100 to 900. The lowest edge data center prices are 10, 30, 50, 70, and 90, respectively. The experimental results were obtained when $\alpha=2$ and $\rho=0.8$, as shown in Figure 2. When the range of $priority_i$ is 0.4 to 1, and the interval is 0.1, the results were obtained, as shown in Figure 3.

Figures 2 and 3 show the effect of different edge resource prices and task priorities on the satisfaction model. Figures 2 and 3 show that the satisfaction model's value increases rapidly as the value of the end-user payment to the edge service provider increases. The result indicates that end-users pay more attention to this task, and end-users want to obtain higher satisfaction. For example, when a = 2 and b = 0.8, there are two tasks task1 and task2. The bid price of task1 is 800, and task2 is 600. When the service provider's minimum bid is 90, and the task priority is 1, their satisfaction values are 4.36225522 and 4.312427797, respectively. When the priorities are all 0.6, their satisfaction values are 3.772682744 and 3.722855322, respectively. Under the same minimum bid of the service provider, (1) the higher the task's actual cost, the higher the satisfaction value obtained. (2) Tasks with high priority have higher satisfaction scores than tasks with low priority. On the other hand, it can be seen from Figure 2 that the lower the minimum bid of the service provider, the higher the value of the satisfaction model. However, if the end-user payment value is lower than the service provider's minimum price, the service provider will refuse service.

Figure 4 shows the relationship between end-user payment values to the edge service provider for different task priorities. From this, we can see that as the task priority increases, the end-user payment value to the edge service provider decreases instead. Since end-users' total cost of submitting tasks is fixed, no more spending can be provided to satisfy low-level tasks while ensuring that high-priority tasks are completed first.

Figure 2. Effect of different end-user bids on satisfaction

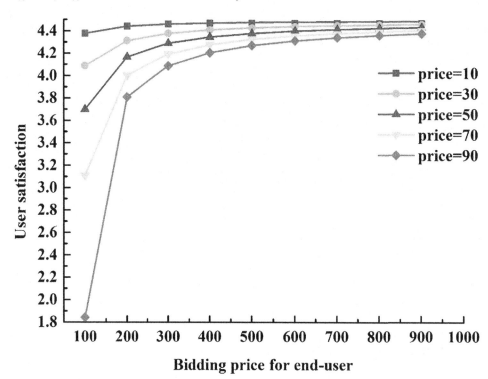

Figure 3. Effect of different priorities on satisfaction

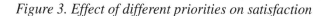

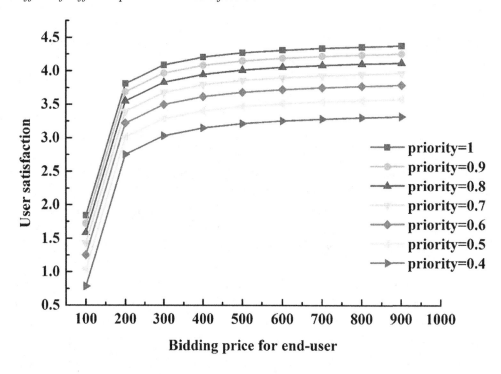

Figure 4. The impact of different satisfactions on the actual cost of tasks

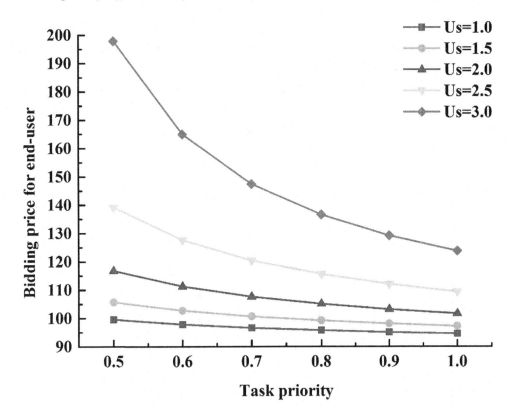

Comparison of Actual Value and Predicted Value

For 100 different end-users, they submitted CPU-intensive and storage-intensive tasks, using historical transaction data for model training. After 1000 rounds of training, the optimal parameters were substituted into the prediction model to calculate the end-user's bid. Figure 5 shows a comparison between the actual bid and the predicted value. From the results, we can see that the more abundant the historical transaction data, the closer the predicted result is to the actual value. There is a significant difference between the predicted and actual values for equipment with little historical transaction data or that has just joined the edge data center, but this difference can be gradually reduced after several rounds of transactions. Therefore, the prediction model built in this paper can reflect the actual value more accurately.

In this paper, the Cobb-Douglas utility function (Liu & Wang, 2010) is used to describe the user's simulation of the edge data center resources' actual resource price. In the resource supply and demand relationship in the edge computing environment, the higher the demand of smart terminals for edge data center resources, the higher the real bid tends to be; At the same time, each terminal hopes to obtain more resources to complete its task. The longer the terminal occupies resources, the higher the edge data center's relative cost and the final price will increase accordingly. Therefore, the actual value simulation function in this paper is shown in equations 26 and 27.

$$A_i^{cpu}\left(T_i^{cpu}, R_i^{cpu}, \alpha_i^{cpu}\right) = \eta\left(\alpha_i^{cpu} \ln T_i^{cpu} + \left(1 - \alpha_i^{cpu}\right) \ln R_i^{cpu}\right) \tag{26}$$

$$A_i^{storage}\left(T_i^{storage}, R_i^{storage}, \alpha_i^{storage}\right) = \eta^{storage}\left(\alpha_i^{storage} \ln T_i^{storage} + \left(1 - \alpha_i^{storage}\right)\ln R_i^{storage}\right) \qquad (27)$$

T_i^{cpu} and $T_i^{storage}$ respectively represent the execution time of the CPU-intensive tasks and storage-intensive tasks submitted by the end-user in the edge data center. R_i^{cpu} and $R_i^{storage}$ represent resource requirements of CPU-intensive and storage-intensive tasks submitted by the end-user. α_i^{cpu} and $\alpha_i^{storage}$ represent the preference of execution time and resource requirements for CPU-intensive tasks and storage-intensive tasks, respectively. η^{cpu} and $\eta^{storage}$ represent the benefits of the unit utility of CPU-intensive and storage-intensive tasks, respectively.

Figure 5. Comparison of the actual and projected value of smart device bids

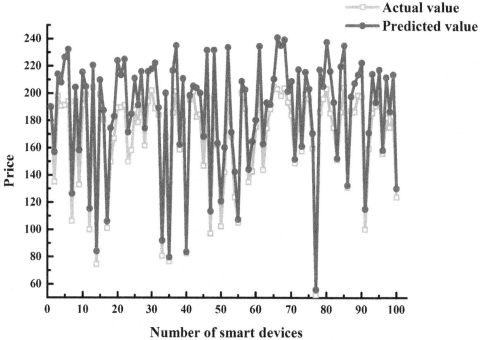

Comparison of Average Delay of Task Offloading

The algorithm proposed in this paper will be compared with the following three algorithms in performance:

FCFS: First-come, first-served is the most straightforward strategy, and it has also become FIFO. It decides which process to run first based on the arrival time of the process.

SJF: Prioritize scheduling algorithms for temporary jobs or short processes.

Round-Robin: Each time a request from a user is allocated to the edge computing data center, in turn, starting from 1 until N (the number of internal servers), and then restarting the cycle.

Double Auction: An auction procedure in which buyers and sellers submit bids and asking prices to the auctioneer simultaneously, and the auctioneer determines the transaction price.

We choose FCFS, SJF, and Round-Robin because these methods are more classic resource allocation or task scheduling methods, and these methods are also suitable for resource allocation in edge data centers. Therefore, we want to compare whether the algorithm proposed in this article has better performance than these excellent algorithms. We choose double auction because it is an algorithm based on the combined double auction principle. This algorithm is suitable for edge computing environments to achieve an acceptable and satisfactory state to both end-users and edge service providers.

After submitting tasks of different sizes through the numbers of smart devices, we use algorithms to allocate resources and compare the average delay of task execution to get the results shown in Figure 6.

Figure 6. Comparison of average delays for different numbers of tasks

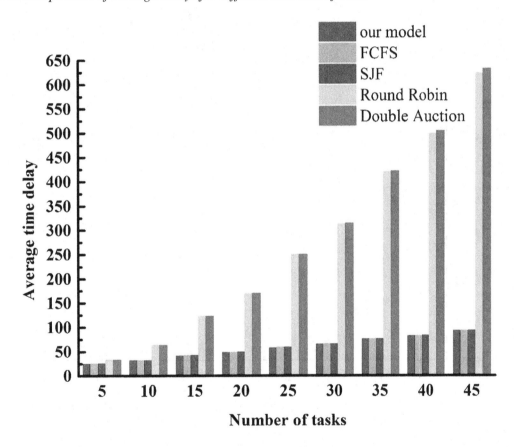

It can be seen from the results in Figure 6 that the proposed algorithm and FCFS and SJF are significantly better than Round-Robin and Double Auction algorithms. When the number of tasks is relatively small, the algorithm result proposed in this paper is 24.196 milliseconds, the FCFS algorithm result is 24.896 milliseconds, the SJF algorithm is 24.966 milliseconds, the Round-Robin is 32.416 milliseconds, and the Double Auction algorithm is 32.526 milliseconds. With the increase in the number of smart devices, when the number of submitted tasks is 45, the algorithm results presented in this paper are 92.348 milliseconds, FCFS algorithm results are 92.438 milliseconds. SJF algorithm is 92.708 milliseconds. Round-Robin is 622.98 milliseconds, and the Double Auction algorithm is 632.918 milliseconds. Experimental results show that the algorithm proposed in this paper is the shortest among these algorithms in terms of average delay.

Cost Comparison

We use devices to submit different types of tasks and compare the edge data center's cost results after allocating resources by different algorithms.

Figure 7. Comparison of edge data center costs after a different number of end-users submits tasks

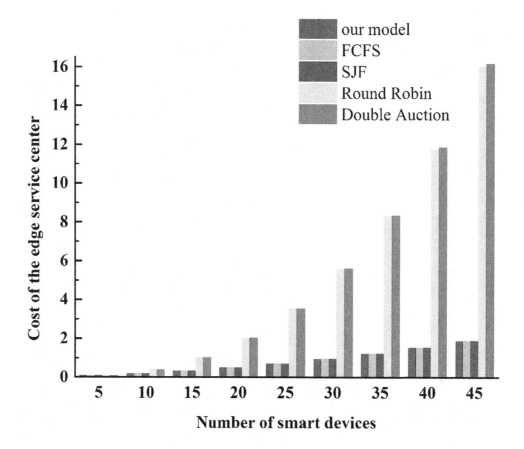

Figure 7 shows that when there are fewer end users, the cost of the edge data center is relatively small. As the number of end-users increases, and the number of tasks increases, the edge data center's cost also increases. When the number of end-users is 5, the result of the FCFS algorithm is 0.069125, the result of the SJF algorithm is 0.069267, the result of the Round-Robin algorithm is 0.081617, the result of the Double Auction algorithm is 0.081875, and the result of the algorithm proposed in this paper is 0.0675. When the number of end-users increases to 45, the result of the FCFS algorithm is 1.880333, the result of the SJF algorithm is 1.883383, the result of the Round-Robin algorithm is 16.02333, the result of the Double Auction algorithm is 16.16681, and the result of the algorithm proposed in this paper is

1.861667. Experimental results show that the algorithm proposed in this paper obtains a lower cost of an edge data center than other algorithms.

Comparison of Energy Consumption at the Same Distance

When we submit multiple tasks at the same location (500 meters from the edge data center), the energy consumption results obtained after allocating resources through different algorithms are shown in Figure 8.

Figure 8. Comparison of energy consumption for different numbers of tasks

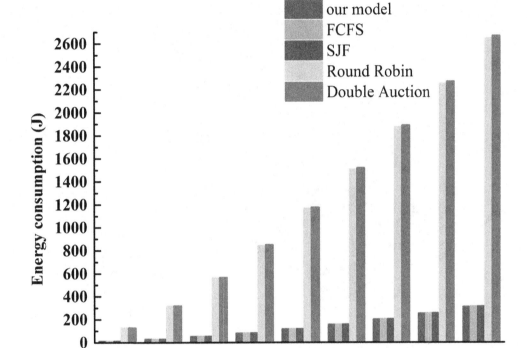

From the experimental results, when only one task is submitted, the FCFS algorithm's result is 1.029928. The result of the SJF algorithm is 1.034053. The result of the Round-Robin algorithm is 12.37368. The Double Auction algorithm results are 12.3888, and the result of the algorithm proposed in this paper is 0.962553. When the number of tasks increases to 45, the total energy consumption is 310.2706 for the FCFS algorithm, 310.7739 for the SJF algorithm, 2643.866 for the Round-Robin algorithm, and 2667.539 for the Double Auction algorithm, and the algorithm proposed in this paper's result is 307.1906. Experimental results show that as the number of tasks increases, the five algorithms' energy consumption to allocate resources to perform tasks also increases. The algorithm proposed in this paper achieves lower energy consumption than other algorithms.

Comparison of Energy Consumption at Different Distances

Due to the end-users mobility, we compare the results of energy consumption for end-users at different distances from the edge data center, as shown in Figure 9.

Figure 9. Comparison of energy consumption of different size's tasks at different locations

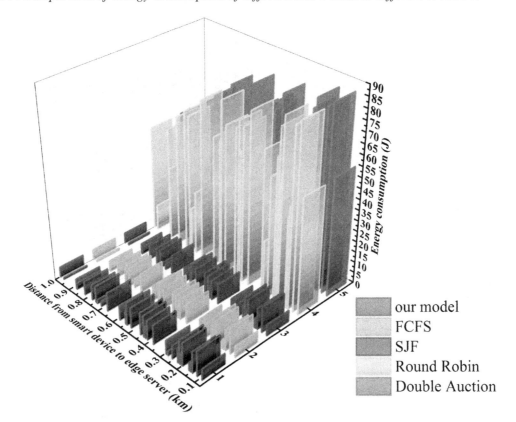

Figure 9 shows the five algorithms' total energy consumption after submitting tasks at different distances from the edge data center within the range of 1km * 1km. As shown in Figure 9, as the task size increases, the five algorithms' energy consumption is rising. Our proposed algorithm performs best and consumes the least energy (average 88.83% lower than Double Auction, average 88.73% lower than Round-Robin, average 1.2% lower than FCFS, and average 1.33% lower than SJF).

CONCLUSION AND FUTURE WORK

This paper proposes a dynamic multi-winner game model based on incomplete information to solve the edge data center's multi-end user task offloading and resource allocation problems. Since the information about other participants in the game is incomplete, we propose a model that uses historical data to predict other participants' bids. We dynamically adjust the parameters for the model to improve the accuracy of prediction. We propose a resource allocation scheduling algorithm of edge computing. In implementing the algorithm, it is more realistic to consider the task types and energy consumption of end-users offloading to the edge computing data center, and a user satisfaction model based on task priority is proposed. As an influencing factor, the model is more realistic.

Future research work includes how to offload tasks that cannot be done by the edge data center to other devices, such as other edge data centers or end-users, to meet actual needs. The securities of many devices are connected to the edge data center also needs to be considered.

ACKNOWLEDGMENT

This research was supported in part by the National Nature Science Foundation of China [grant number 61572095]; the National Nature Science Foundation of China [grant number 61877007]; and the Fund of University of Science and Technology Liaoning [grant number 2017QN03].

REFERENCES

Baliga, J., Ayre, R. W., Hinton, K., & Tucker, R. S. (2011). Green cloud computing: Balancing energy in processing, storage, and transport. *Proceedings of the IEEE*, *99*(1), 149–167. doi:10.1109/JPROC.2010.2060451

Bergstra, J. A., & Middelburg, C. (2003). *ITU-T Recommendation G. 107: The E-Model, a computational model for use in transmission planning*. Academic Press.

Cao, S., Tao, X., Hou, Y., & Cui, Q. (2015). An energy-optimal offloading algorithm of mobile computing based on HetNets. *2015 International Conference on Connected Vehicles and Expo (ICCVE)*. 10.1109/ICCVE.2015.68

Chen, M.-H., Dong, M., & Liang, B. (2018). Resource sharing of a computing access point for multi-user mobile cloud offloading with delay constraints. *IEEE Transactions on Mobile Computing*, *17*(12), 2868–2881. doi:10.1109/TMC.2018.2815533

Chen, W., Wang, D., & Li, K. (2018). Multi-user multi-task computation offloading in green mobile edge cloud computing. *IEEE Transactions on Services Computing*, *12*(5), 726–738. doi:10.1109/TSC.2018.2826544

Chen, X., Jiao, L., Li, W., & Fu, X. (2016). Efficient Multi-User Computation Offloading for Mobile-Edge Cloud Computing. *IEEE/ACM Transactions on Networking*, *24*(5), 2795–2808. doi:10.1109/TNET.2015.2487344

Cheng, J., Shi, Y., Bai, B., & Chen, W. (2016). Computation offloading in cloud-RAN based mobile cloud computing system. *2016 IEEE International Conference on Communications (ICC)*. 10.1109/ICC.2016.7511367

Ding, M., Lopez-Perez, D., Claussen, H., & Kaafar, M. A. (2018). On the fundamental characteristics of ultra-dense small cell networks. *IEEE Network*, *32*(3), 92–100. doi:10.1109/MNET.2018.1700096

Guo, X., Singh, R., Zhao, T., & Niu, Z. (2016). An index based task assignment policy for achieving optimal power-delay tradeoff in edge cloud systems. *2016 IEEE International Conference on Communications*. 10.1109/ICC.2016.7511147

Jamil, B., Shojafar, M., Ahmed, I., Ullah, A., Munir, K., & Ijaz, H. (2020). A job scheduling algorithm for delay and performance optimization in fog computing. *Concurrency and Computation*, *32*(7), 1532–0626. doi:10.1002/cpe.5581

Jie, Y., Tang, X., Raymond, K. K., Su, S., Li, M., & Guo, C. (2018). Online task scheduling for edge computing based on repeated Stackelberg game. *Journal of Parallel and Distributed Computing*, *122*, 159–172. doi:10.1016/j.jpdc.2018.07.019

Kuang, Z., Li, L., Gao, J., Zhao, L., & Liu, A. (2019). Partial offloading scheduling and power allocation for mobile edge computing systems. *IEEE Internet of Things Journal*, *6*(4), 6774–6785. doi:10.1109/JIOT.2019.2911455

Kumar, K., & Lu, Y.-H. (2010). Cloud computing for mobile users: Can offloading computation save energy? *Computer*, *43*(4), 51–56. doi:10.1109/MC.2010.98

Li, P., Wang, Y., Zhang, W., & Huang, Y. (2014). *QoE-oriented two-stage resource allocation in femtocell networks*. 2014 IEEE 80th Vehicular Technology Conference (VTC2014-Fall), Vancouver, BC.

Li, Q., Zhao, J., & Yi, G. (2019). Computation Offloading and Resource Allocation for Mobile Edge Computing with Multiple Access Points. *IET Communications*, *13*(17), 2668–2677. doi:10.1049/iet-com.2019.0446

Liu, J., Mao, Y., Zhang, J., & Letaief, K. B. (2016). Delay-Optimal Computation Task Scheduling for Mobile-Edge Computing Systems. *2016 IEEE International Symposium on Information Theory (ISIT)*. 10.1109/ISIT.2016.7541539

Liu, S., & Wang, M. (2010). Sealed-bid auctions based on Cobb–Douglas utility function. *Economics Letters*, *107*(1), 1–3. doi:10.1016/j.econlet.2009.05.019

Lopez, P. G., Montresor, A., Epema, D., Datta, A., Higashino, T., Iamnitchi, A., Barcellos, M., Felber, P., & Riviere, E. (2015). Edge-centric Computing: Vision and Challenges. *Computer Communication Review*, *45*(5), 37–42. doi:10.1145/2831347.2831354

Mao, Y., Zhang, J., & Letaief, K. B. (2016). Dynamic Computation Offloading for Mobile-Edge Computing with Energy Harvesting Devices. *IEEE Journal on Selected Areas in Communications*, *34*(12), 3590–3605. doi:10.1109/JSAC.2016.2611964

Nelson, R. (2013). *Probability, stochastic processes, and queueing theory: the mathematics of computer performance modeling*. Springer Science & Business Media.

Niyato, D., Wang, P., Hossain, E., Saad, W., & Han, Z. (2012). *Game theoretic modeling of cooperation among service providers in mobile cloud computing environments. In 2012 IEEE Wireless Communications & Networking Conference*. WCNC.

Rabiner, L. R. (1989). A tutorial on hidden Markov models and selected applications in speech recognition. *Proceedings of the IEEE*, *77*(2), 257–286. doi:10.1109/5.18626

Satyanarayanan, M. (2017). The emergence of edge computing. *Computer*, *50*(1), 30–39. doi:10.1109/MC.2017.9

Shannon, C. E. (1948). A mathematical theory of communication. *The Bell System Technical Journal*, *27*(3), 379–423. doi:10.1002/j.1538-7305.1948.tb01338.x

Shannon, C. E. (1949). Communication in the presence of noise. *Proceedings of the IRE*, *37*(1), 10–21. doi:10.1109/JRPROC.1949.232969

Shi, W., Cao, J., Zhang, Q., Li, Y., & Xu, L. (2016). Edge computing: Vision and challenges. *IEEE Internet of Things Journal*, *3*(5), 637–646. doi:10.1109/JIOT.2016.2579198

Shu, C., Zhao, Z., Han, Y., Min, G., & Duan, H. (2020). Multi-User Offloading for Edge Computing Networks: A Dependency-Aware and Latency-Optimal Approach. *IEEE Internet of Things Journal*, *7*(3), 1678–1689. doi:10.1109/JIOT.2019.2943373

Wang, Q., Guo, S., Liu, J., & Yang, Y. (2019). Energy-efficient computation offloading and resource allocation for delay-sensitive mobile edge computing. *Sustainable Computing: Informatics Systems*, *21*, 154–164. doi:10.1016/j.suscom.2019.01.007

You, C., Huang, K., Chae, H., & Kim, B.-H. (2016). Energy-efficient resource allocation for mobile-edge computation offloading. *IEEE Transactions on Wireless Communications*, *16*(3), 1397–1411. doi:10.1109/TWC.2016.2633522

Zhang, K., Mao, Y., Leng, S., Zhao, Q., Li, L., Peng, X., Pan, L., Maharjan, S., & Zhang, Y. (2016). Energy-Efficient Offloading for Mobile Edge Computing in 5G Heterogeneous Networks. *IEEE Access: Practical Innovations, Open Solutions*, *4*, 5896–5907. doi:10.1109/ACCESS.2016.2597169

Zhang, W., Wen, Y., Guan, K., Kilper, D., Luo, H., & Wu, D. O. (2013). Energy-Optimal Mobile Cloud Computing under Stochastic Wireless Channel. *IEEE Transactions on Wireless Communications*, *12*(9), 4569–4581. doi:10.1109/TWC.2013.072513.121842

Zhang, Y., Chen, X., Chen, Y., Li, Z., & Huang, J. (2018). Cost efficient scheduling for delay-sensitive tasks in edge computing system. *2018 IEEE International Conference on Services Computing (SCC)*. 10.1109/SCC.2018.00017

Zhao, Y., Zhou, S., Zhao, T., & Niu, Z. (2015). Energy-efficient task offloading for multiuser mobile cloud computing. *2015 IEEE/CIC International Conference on Communications in China (ICCC)*. 10.1109/ICCChina.2015.7448613

Zheng, X., Li, M., & Guo, J. (2020). Task scheduling using edge computing system in smart city. *International Journal of Communication Systems*, (5), e4422.

Chapter 22
Constructive Solutions for Security and Privacy Issues at the Edge:
Securing Edge Framework – A Healthcare Application Use Case

Indra Priyadharshini S.
R. M. K. College of Engineering and Technology, India

Pradheeba Ulaganathan
R. M. K. College of Engineering and Technology, India

Vigilson Prem M.
R. M. D. Engineering College, India

Yuvaraj B. R.
Anna University, India

EXECUTIVE SUMMARY

The evolution in computing strategies has shown wonders in reducing the reachability issue among different end devices. After centralized approaches, decentralized approaches started to take action, but with the latency in data pre-processing, computing very simple requests was the same as for the larger computations. Now it's time to have a simple decentralized environment called edge that is created very near to the end device. This makes edge location friendly and time friendly to different kinds of devices like smart, sensor, grid, etc. In this chapter, some of the serious and non-discussed security issues and privacy issues available on edge are explained neatly, and for a few of the problems, some solutions are also recommended. At last, a separate case study of edge computing challenges in healthcare is also explored, and solutions to those issues concerning that domain are shown.

DOI: 10.4018/978-1-6684-5700-9.ch022

INTRODUCTION

Edge is only the augmentation of the fog. Edge computing has the accompanying attributes: it ranges to contiguous physical areas; upholds online examination; the administration is given by savvy, yet not ground-breaking gadgets; underpins different interchanges arranges, and is circulated computing The objectives of the edge computing worldview are to diminish the information volume and traffic to fog workers, decline inertness, and improve nature of administration (QoS). Edge computing comprises 3 fundamental parts, (an) IoT nodes, (b) edge nodes, and (c) back-end fog. The principle parts of layer 1 are the IoT gadgets and correspondence joins between them. These gadgets are answerable for detecting and acting in the earth by producing occasions and sending them to higher layers. Layer 2 involves the switches, switches, entryways, and gadgets that encourage the associations between gadgets at the edge of the system and the Internet. This layer mirrors the great definition proposed for Edge computing. At present, the Edge infrastructure idea may likewise remember the gadgets for layer 3. Layer 3 contains the infrastructure for customary Fog computing (elite workers, and server farms with immense capacity and processing limits) (Ren et al., 2019)

Another captivating zone where the modernization has pushed its foundations is IoT. IoT is getting expanding coordinated into our everyday lives. Contemplating this IoT can be utilized to give a skilled and sorted out way to deal with and improve the healthcare of humankind. By utilizing these smart articles, they can be coordinated into healthcare to offer wise types of assistance for far off observing the wellbeing and prosperity of patients. By utilizing this it could help manage staff deficiencies and reaction times inside healthcare. As IoT has the attribute of pervasiveness the frameworks associated with healthcare (medication, apparatuses, and people) can permit the ceaseless observing and the board of these substances. Along these lines, the expense and nature of the healthcare offered can be improved via robotizing processes that were recently directed by people. How IoT and Edge go connected at the hip?

Edge computing gives calculation, stockpiling, and systems administration administrations between end gadgets (Things) and customary fog computing server farms. Edge computing stage is ordinarily situated at the edge of the system; here and there the expression "edge" is utilized reciprocally with the expression "edge". It gives low inertness, area mindfulness and improves Quality of Service (QoS) and Quality of Experience (QoE) for healthcare administrations by diminishing idleness and expanding its consistency when contrasted with the fog. Despite edge computing being a promising new turn of events, to serve IoT Things and applications effectively, there are various explorations provokes that should be thought of. Inside edge computing which can comprise of different gadgets in the system (switches, switches, and so on.) and end gadgets or potentially things (smartphones, wearable gadgets, and virtual sensor nodes that could be utilized inside healthcare frameworks)? Consequently having the option to gather, configuration, and process this heterogeneous information just as the capacity of correspondence among various gadgets is as yet an open examination challenge.

Considering that edge devices work at the edge of networks, edge faces new security also, security challenges on the head of those inherited from fog computing. Assault vectors, for example, man-in-the-middle have the potential to become an ordinary assault in Edge computing. Edge computing is a promising answer for help data fusion, filtering, and investigation in e-healthcare systems since it extends data computing from fog to the edge of a network and is more intelligent and powerful than e-healthcare devices. Without appropriate security and protection protections for underlying connected health systems, providers and patients need trust in the arrangements. News about the absence of security of IoT devices and unethical practices of some companies that gather and abuse personal data from owners of connected devices have made consumers care about the technology and more proactive in protecting personal data. Even when the IoT health care system itself isn't compromised, the care receivers can be the casualties of overzealous enterprises that have questionable use of patient data with potential legal ramifications, as medical data in numerous countries is protected by law.

In the customary edge-assisted data sharing scheme the edge node is integrated to process and re-encrypt the shared data for efficient medical examination. Privacy leakage and security threats may happen during data partaking in edge-assisted e-healthcare systems. Initially, personal privacy may be disclosed during data sharing. Unauthorized users may access the shared data collected from patients. For example, some corrupt pharmaceutical companies may analyze the health data and get patients' health status to spread advertisements and medication advancements. The shared health data might be tampered with during data transmission from data collection to storage. For instance, the blood glucose of patients might be altered when it is delivered to healthcare centers, leading to incorrect healthcare treatments. To protect the shared data against privacy leakage, unauthorized data access, and data tampering, Ciphertext-Policy Attribute-Based Encryption (CP-ABE)(Tang et al., 2019) is widely proposed for health data sharing through the fog, because it can uphold multiple data accessing standards with data confidentiality preservation. Patients define access policies to encrypt their shared data and send the ciphertext to the fog server. Data users access the shared data and decrypt the ciphertext just if their attributes fulfill access policies. But the same level of protection can't be given to the edge side, as they are different devices in nature. Some of the popular research articles give solutions to general issues like data accumulation, latency, preliminary security for transferring data, etc., However, the accompanying issues despite everything remain unaddressed. (1) How would we pre-process health data on the edge node for efficient data use? (2) How would patients be able to retrieve and decrypt their health data after the edge node encrypts them? (3) How would we be able to guarantee patient privacy when the shared data are re-encrypted? by the semi-trusted edge node? (4) How would we prevent unauthorized data access if the edge node collides with other entities for the shared plaintext?

With these brief introductions, this chapter is organized as follows: the immediate next topic briefs the reason for the evolution of edge computing from fog (along with issues in fog), then a general architecture of edge with obligatory working details, attacks &threats, Cryptographic techniques, authentication and access control policies and a case study of edge based healthcare framework with specific security issues, solutions and recommendations is explained.

NECESSITY OF EDGE COMPUTING – FROM THE PERSPECTIVE OF SECURITY AND PRIVACY

Before getting into the necessity of Edge, one ought to get into the real difference between fog and Edge. Some of the key features which make both of these computing ends differently are, Fog architecture is centralized and comprises large data centers that can be located the world over, a thousand miles from client devices. Edge architecture is distributed and comprises a large number of little nodes located as close to client devices as could be expected under the circumstances. Edge goes about as a mediator between data centers and hardware(Ren et al., 2017), and hence it is closer to end-users. On the off chance that there is no edge layer, the fog communicates with devices directly, which is time-expending. In fog computing, data processing takes place in remote data centers. Edge processing and storage are done on the edge of the network close to the source of data, which is critical for real-time control. Fog is more powerful than an edge regarding computing capabilities and storage limits. The fog comprises a few large server nodes. Edge includes a huge number of little nodes. Edge performs momentary edge examination due to moment responsiveness, while the fog focuses on long haul deep investigation due to slower responsiveness. Edge provides low latency; fog — high latency.

A fog system collapses without an Internet connection. Edge computing uses different conventions and standards, so the danger of failure is a lot of lower. Edge is a more secure system than the fog due to its distributed architecture(Dimitrievski et al., 2019). Like Fog systems, an Edge system is composed of IaaS, PaaS, and SaaS respectively, alongside the expansion of Data services. The Edge IaaS stage is created utilizing Cisco IOx API, which includes a Linux and CISCO IOS networking operating system. Any device, for example, switches, routers, servers, and even cameras can become an Edge node that has computing, storage, and network connectivity. Edge nodes collaborate among themselves with either a Peer-to-Peer network, Master-Slave architecture, or by framing a Cluster. The Cisco IOx APIs enable Edge applications(Wang et al., 2014) to communicate with IoT devices and Fog systems by any user-defined convention. It provides simplified management of utilizations, automates policy enforcement, and supports multiple development environments and programming languages. The data service decides the suitable place (Fog or Edge) for data examination identifies which data. Numerous researchers are embracing a security-centric or secure by design reasoning for creating such distributed systems. Yet, this viewpoint is still in its outset and needs a comprehensive understanding of the security threats and challenges confronting an Edge infrastructure. This chapter provides a systematic review of Edge stage applications, determines their possible security holes, analyses existing security arrangements, and then advances a rundown of comprehensive security arrangements that can eliminate numerous potential security flaws of Edge-based systems.

Fog Security Alliance(Waters & Encryption, 2011) has identified five basic security issues and these issues directly sway the distributed, shared, and on-demand nature of fog computing. Being a virtualized environment like Fog, the Edge stage can likewise be affected by the same threats however there are very solid security mechanisms that could easily get integrated with edge architecture.

1. Authentication and Trust issues
2. Privacy
3. Security
4. Fog Servers
5. Energy consumption

Details about the above sorts of threats are explained in (Curtis, 2020). However, the betterment over the fog stage can be discussed as follows. The accompanying rundown details three such technologies, including some of their key differences with Edge systems. Edge Computing performs localized processing on the device utilizing Programmable Automation Controllers (PAC), which can handle data processing, storage, and correspondence. It poses an advantage over Edge computing as it reduces the purposes of failure and makes each device more independent. However, the same feature makes it hard to manage and accumulate data on large scale networks. Foglet is a middle piece of the 3-tier hierarchy "mobile device - foglet - fog". There are four significant attributes of Foglet: entirely self-overseeing possesses enough compute power, low end-to-end latency, and expands on standard Fog technology. Foglet differs from fog computing as application virtualization isn't suitable for the environment, consumes more resources, and can't work in offline mode. A miniaturized scale data center is a little and completely useful data center containing multiple servers and is capable of provisioning numerous virtual machines. Numerous technologies, including Edge computing, can benefit from Microdata centers as it reduces latency, enhances reliability, is relatively portable, has underlying security conventions(Yang et al., 2015), saves bandwidth utilization by compression, and can accommodate numerous new services. So on the whole the accompanying attributes make the edge it gets different from the fog and makes it better than the above.

An Edge framework will have moderately small registering assets (memory, preparing, and capacity) when contrasted with a Fog framework, notwithstanding, the assets can be expanded on-request; They can process data generated from a diverse set of devices; They can be both dense and sparsely distributed based on the geographical area; They uphold Machine-to-Machine correspondence and wireless connectivity; an Edge system can be installed on low specification devices like switches and IP cameras, and One of their principal uses is currently for mobile and portable devices. On the whole, these are the main differences between fog and edge because of which edge has become flexible to most of the devices. So it's time to learn some problems that are available with edge and to know some common solutions to those problems.

GENERAL EDGE ARCHITECTURE

The physical distance to the Cloud and the available resources inside the infrastructure increases the latency and reduce the Quality of Service (QoS). One of the recent standards in this area to solve issues of Cloud Computing is Edge Computing. Even though there are several naming for Edge computing, for example, Fog Computing and Cloudlets, inside this paper, just the term Edge Computing will be used. Figure 1 shows how the layered architecture can be the plot in between Cloud, Fog, and Edge Computing. Edge Computing combines multiple technologies, for example, Cloud Computing, Grid Computing, and IoT. It includes an extra tier between the Cloud and the end-devices and moves computational power to the end-device as close as could be expected under the circumstances. This means that, in the need of more computational resources by the end-device or a system, the errand can be offloaded to an Edge Server instead of the Cloud. Edge Computing is expected to reduce the latency and increase the QoS for errands which can't be handled by these devices. These undertakings are normally computationally heavy, for example, enormous data processing, video processing, computerized reasoning, or time-sensitive. On the off chance that the calculation must be done in real-time, usage of Cloud is not feasible since Cloud and Internet offer just best-effort service and delivery. Devices with limited computing limits may likewise have basic deadlines for their essential errand. In these circumstances, the errand can be offloaded to an Edge Server utilizing the same imperatives and can be accomplished at this level. Depending on the outcome of the undertaking, the system reacts to the result, e.g., sends the data back to the end-device. The Edge Servers can likewise offload the errands to other Edge Servers by considering the available resources, network, and calculation delays. One of the principle objectives of Edge Computing is to reduce latency and to keep the QoS as high as could reasonably be expected. Edge Computing intends to solve the issues of Cloud Computing or IoT by including an extra tier between the IoT devices and back-end infrastructure for computing and correspondence purposes. As this tier additionally have intermediate components for the primary gathering, investigation, calculation of the data. These intermediate components are called Edge Servers. Edge Server is definitely not a complete replacement of the Cloud with respect to its functionalities. Even though its available resources are higher than the end-devices, they are lower than the Cloud. Instead, exceptionally repeated errands, or undertakings that require in time response are preferred to be executed in an Edge Server. The proposed architecture for Edge Computing comprises of Cloud Tier, Edge Tier, and Device Tier. In the Device Tier, there are end-user devices. The green squares in the Edge Tier are Edge Servers. These servers gather, aggregate, analyze, and process the data before offloading them to the Cloud Tier or send back to the devices. The end devices can be in the same physical area, or in different areas as depicted in the figure. When an end-device needs to communicate with the Cloud, first, the request is sent to then, if the Edge Server is capable of completing the assignment without anyone else, it naturally handles the data and responds to the end-device with the result. If not, the data is offloaded to another server in the same tier provided that it exists. Otherwise, the data is offloaded to the Cloud. Edge Computing is a worldview which uses Cloud Computing technologies and gives more responsibilities to the Edge tier. These responsibilities are namely, computing offload data reserving/storage, data processing, service appropriation, IoT management, security, and privacy protection. Edge Computing is a worldview which uses Cloud Computing technologies and gives more responsibilities to the Edge tier. These responsibilities are namely, computing offload data reserving/storage, data processing, service appropriation, IoT management, security, and privacy protection Without restricting the Cloud Computing features, Edge Computing needs to have the accompanying requirements, some of which are likewise defined for Cloud Computing: Interoperability, Scalability, Extensibility, Abstraction, Time sensitiveness, Security & Privacy, Reliability

Figure 1. Layered Architecture of Edge with Fog and Cloud Layers

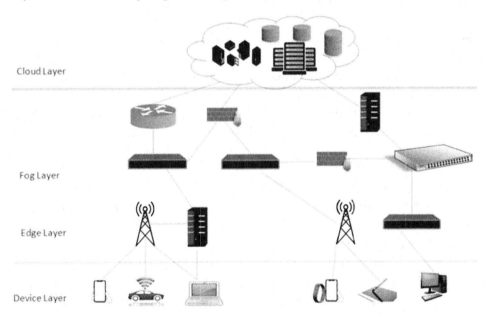

Edge arrangements are typically multi-layered disseminated models incorporating and adjusting the remaining task at hand between the Edge layer, the Edge cloud or Edge organization, and the Enterprise layer(Li et al., 2018). Moreover, when we talk about the Edge, there are the Edge gadgets and the

neighborhood Edge workers. It should be noted that Edge processing structures are an extension of IoT (Internet of Things) models and use terms like OT for operational innovation. The change and union of IT and OT advancements can convey colossal incentive throughout the following decade. Brief flow of computing in the edge environment is shown in Figure 2.

Figure 2. Edge Computing Device Hierarchy

From a systematic perspective, edge networks provide a distributed computing system with hierarchical geography. Edge networks target meeting stringent latency requirements, reducing power utilization of end devices, giving real-time data processing and control with localized computing resources, and decreasing the burden of backhaul traffic to centralized data centers. And of course, excellent network security, reliability, and accessibility must be inherent in edge networks. Edge Computing utilizes wide scope of advancements and unites them. Inside this area, Edge Computing uses numerous innovations, for example, remote sensor organizations (WSN), portable information securing, versatile mark examination, Fog/Grid Computing, disseminated information activities, distant Cloud administrations, and so forth. Also, it consolidates the accompanying conventions and terms:

1) **5G correspondence**: It is the fifth era remote framework that focuses on the higher limit, lower power utilization, and lower dormancy contrasted with the past ages. Because of the expanded measure of information between the information, 5G is required to understand traffic issues that emerged with the expanded number of associated gadgets.

2) **PLC conventions**: Object Linking and Embedding for Process Control Unified Architecture (OPC-UA) is a convention created for mechanical computerization. Because of its transparency and strength, it is broadly utilized by ventures in the region of oil and gas, drug, advanced mechanics, and assembling.

3) **Message line specialist**: MQTT and TCP/IP are famous message conventions of savvy sensors and IoT gadgets. Supporting these message intermediaries, Edge Computing expands the gadget check that it interfaces. For the issue of MQTT security, AMQP is helpful in the correspondence with Cloud Computing worker.

4) **Event processor**: After messages of IoT show up in the Edge worker, occasion processor investigations those messages and makes semantic occasions utilizing pre-characterized rules. EsperNet, Apache Spark, and Flink are a few models for this empowering influence.

5) **Virtualisation**: Cloud administrations are conveyed as virtual machines on a Cloud worker or bunches. Utilizing virtual machines permit running different examples of working frameworks (OS) on a similar worker.

6) **Hypervisor**: As well as a virtual machine, execution assessment and information dealing with are required and acknowledged by the hypervisor to control virtual machines in the host PC.

7) **OpenStack**: Managing numerous assets could be testing. OpenStack is a Cloud working framework that makes a difference control of pools of processing and capacity assets quiet through a control board and observing devices.

8) **AI stage**: Rule-based motor and Machine learning stage upholds information investigation in neighborhood level. As expressed in

Segment III-A, this is very critical to arrive at one of the objectives of Edge Computing which is to assemble, break down, and play out the first sifting of the information.

9) **Docker**: Virtual machines work with establishment of working frameworks. In contrast to virtual machines, Docker is a Container as a Service (CaaS), which can utilize a solitary shared working framework and run programming in detached condition. It just requires the libraries of the product which makes it a lightweight framework without agonizing over where the product is conveyed.

That is about the prologue to edge design with every minor detail. We should save this one as the base for comprehension for investigating the security issues and their proposals which can be application explicit.

GENERAL ISSUES IN EDGE ARCHITECTURE

Web Advancement

What's more, edge nodes can recognize users based on MAC addresses or cookies, track user requests, cache files, determine nearby network conditions. It is additionally possible to embed feedback contents inside a web page to measure the user browser's rendering speed. The feedback content reports directly to the Edge nodes and illuminates the user's graphical resolution, current area reception (if wireless), and network congestion. In another comparable paper, Edge computing altogether reduced the response time of a Fog-based temperature prediction system. Due to Edge systems, the prediction latency was decreased from 5 to 1.5 s, web-page show latency from 8 to 3 s and internet traffic throughput from 75 to 10 Kbps. Utilizing Edge stages for upgrading web-services will likewise introduce web security issues. For example, if user input isn't properly validated, the application becomes vulnerable to the code injection assaults, SQL injection, where SQL code provided by the user is consequently executed resulting in the potential for unauthorized data access and change. This could result in the compromise of the entire Edge system's database or the sending of modified data to a central server. Additionally, due to insecure web APIs, assaults like a session and cookie hijacking (acting as a legitimate user), insecure direct object references for illegal data access, pernicious re-directions, and drive-by assaults could force an Edge stage to expose itself and the attached users.

Reconnaissance Video Transfer Preparing

A video data stream generated by camera sensors is sent to the respective Edge nodes, where it is stored and processed. The privacy of the stream ought to be maintained as it contains sound and visual data, which are transmitted to heterogeneous clients. Here, not exclusively is the security of Edge node is significant, yet the network and all end-user devices involved in the transmission ought to likewise be considered, especially against APTs. On the off chance that an Edge stage or network contains any bugs due to the absence of diligence, the critical video stream may be viewed, altered, and even destroyed. It is significant that the Edge node ensures a secure connection between all imparting devices and protects multi-media content by obscurity techniques, fine-grained access control, generating a new connection for the video stream, selective encryption, and restricting the number of connections.

Sparing Energy in Edge Computing

This specific application encourages the use of Edge stages in putting away and processing specific (user-defined) sorts of the (private) data locally in the Edge nodes, reducing the correspondence cost and delay. However, the presence of such private data places the Edge stage in a sensitive position(Merlino et al., 2019). As previously mentioned there are numerous threats, which are capable of bargaining the CIA of data, for example, noxious insiders can read, alter, and delete data. These issues can be resolved using encryption, authentication (uniquely approving and verifying each user), data characterization based on sensitivity, checking, and data coverage.

Catastrophe Reaction and Antagonistic Situations

Disaster recovery is a sensitive area whereby Edge systems and connected devices are supposed to work in extreme circumstances. In this case, the integrity and accessibility of the system are more significant than confidentiality. Wireless security conventions can do checksum (detect data errors), encrypt packets with negligible resources, and arrange fine-grained access control to carefully validate users (terminating unwanted connections(Glikson et al., 2017)). Furthermore, in case of emergency and key management to prevent losing decryption keys, these mechanisms ought to be considered to retain accessibility and integrity without trading off the overall performance of the system.

SECURITY AND PRIVACY ISSUES IN EDGE COMPUTING:

Edge Computing facilitates the shift of storage and computation jobs from execution in cloud environments to the edge of the network. But this comfort comes with the confront questions in Privacy and security. The integration of emerging technologies such as Cloud or Edge computing, IoT, Artificial Intelligence, Machine Learning, Big Data Analytics is bringing enormous outcomes in various domains like Finance, Health, Education, E-commerce, etc., (Alabdulatif et al., 2019) The characteristics of Edge computing gives an easy way for lightweight devices to efficiently perform the complex processing tasks in the network edge itself. The Healthcare industry is also undergoing a huge paradigm shift from its traditional working model to digital services. The rapid advancement of this digitization of health records, IoT devices, and edge computing all together is transforming the healthcare industry.

The wide use of smart IoT devices, attached to networking technologies these days have improved less expensive and more reasonable medical systems. IoT has become a significant factor in the development of these health frameworks, giving (cheap cost) sensors to monitor the status of patient life. Health Frameworks based on Edge computing consists of sensitive patient data which has to be protected from unauthorized access (Alabdulatif et al., 2019). The electronic health records stored should be anonymous in such a way that the patient's identity should not be revealed, as the privacy of the patients has to be preserved. Sensitive patient health records should maintain the integrity and must be available with no delay. Hence security and privacy of outsourced patient's sensitive data is a challenging problem in the health frameworks built on Edge Computing.

Where to Enforce Security?

Security procedures are not confined to the basic networking level and can likewise be significant at much higher abstractions, for instance, at the service provisioning level. As services become more distributed, data such as service type and interface, device hostname, and possession might be viewed as delicate and require protection. Huge consideration has been devoted to the design of protocols for private (as in privacy-preserving) service discovery over the network (Khan et al., 2017). Unfortunately, a significant number of these conventions were proposed as of late and have not been completely investigated concerning security, performance, or simplicity of deployment, which adds up to interesting research challenges.

1) **Cloud Data Center – Top Layer**:

It is important to indicate that, all edge paradigms might be supported by many infrastructures like centralized cloud service and the administration frameworks, core infrastructures are managed by similar third party providers such as mobile network operators. This would raise tremendous difficulties, for example, privacy leakage, data altering; denial of service attacks and service control, given these core infrastructures might be semi-trusted or totally untrusted. This results in challenges of privacy disclosure and damage to data integrity.

2) Distributed Edge Nodes:

As previously mentioned, edge computing understands the interconnection of IoT devices and sensors by the combination of various communications, for example, mobile core network, wireless network, and the Internet, which raise many network security difficulties of these communication infrastructures. By utilizing the servers at the edge of the network, the conventional network attacks, such as denial of service (DOS) and distributed denial of service (DDOS) attacks, can be restricted efficiently. Such attacks will just upset the vicinity of the edge networks and have very little impact on the core network; additionally, the DOS or DDOS attacks happening in core networks may not truly interfere with the security of the edge data centers..

3) IoT Devices on the Edge:

In edge computing, the edge devices dynamically played as an active participant in the distributed edge network at different layers, so that even a small loophole in the security aspect of edge devices may lead to dangerous outcomes for the whole edge ecosystem. For example, any devices controlled by an adversary can endeavor to agitate the services with a mixture of false information or intrude the system with some malicious actions. Likewise, malicious devices can control services in some particular circumstances, where the malicious enemies have captured the control advantage of one of these devices.

ATTACKS & THREATS

The following list shows the predominant threats and attacks that are encountered by the edge computing frameworks in various application domains (Xiao et al., 2019). These types of threats are usually caused because of the weak framework design or flaws in the design, security misconfigurations and errors due to the implementation.The protective mechanisms deals with detection of such loopholes in the system which acts as an entry point for the attacks or preventing the attacks from happening through blocking the unusual activities.

1)   Distributed Denial of Service Attacks (DDoS)

DDoS is the attack which disturbs the services given by a single or set of servers by using botnets i.e. by compromising a cluster of edge devices and sending continuous requests to the server. This attack is a dangerous attack as it blocks the service of authorised users through bogus requests pretending as legitimate requests. A conventional DDos attack happens when the attacker continuously sends many request packets to the server from the compromised devices in the distributed network. The server's hardware resources gets exhausted servicing these bogus requests persistently thereby leaving the legitimate requests unserviced. DDos attacks are more troublesome in case of edge servers because they are computationally less capable to defend themselves when compared to cloud servers. These bogus requests might confuse the edge server to decide that all its communication channels and hardware resources are busy. Edge servers provide services to the edge devices connected to them. In general, these edge devices are weak with respect to security because they have limited hardware resources and multiplatform software. Attackers utilize this and attack the edge devices first and then they use these compromised edge devices to attack the edge server. A notorious example is the 'Mirai' botnet where the attacker compromised 65000 IOT devices and these devices are used to initiate a DDoS attack to attack the servers like Kerbs and Dyn.

The Figure 3 depicts an example DDoS attack on Edge Server. DDoS attacks can be categorized into flooding attacks and zero day attacks.

Figure 3. DDoS attack on Edge Server

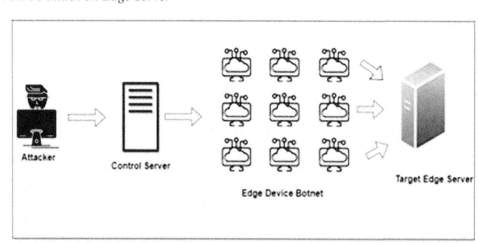

a. **Flooding Attacks:**

This attack is a common type of DDoS attack which stops or limits the service of a server by flooding huge numbers of bogus or malicious packets. The different kinds of flooding attacks are as follows,

i) UDP Flooding:
The attacker persistently floods many UDP packets to the victim edge server resulting in the failure of the victim edge server where it can't service the legitimate UDP packets and leads to disturbed UDP services from the edge server.

ii) CMP Flooding:
This attack makes use of ICMP protocol and sends a huge number of ICMP request packets continuously not even bothering about the reply messages. This makes the victim edge server suffer on the two way communication channel receiving the ICMP echo request and sending the reply messages which slowly turns the server incapable.

iii) SYN Flooding:
The three way handshake protocol of TCP is utilized by this attack. The attacker sends a lot of SYN requests with spoofed IP addresses continuously and the victim servers respond with SYN+ACK messages to the spoofed IP addresses, waiting for the reply ACK messages which would never come from the spoofed IP addresses.

iv) Ping of Death (PoD):
This attack exploits the maximum size of an IP packet which is 65535 bytes. The attacker creates an intended IP packet with malicious content which is more than the maximum number of bytes. so the IP packet is splitted into fragments. These segmented packets are again reassembled at the edge server again. If an attacker keeps on sending such large packets, the victim edge server is kept busy and all its resources are utilized in the fragmentation and reassembly process.

v) HTTP Flooding Attack:
This type of attack generates many standard requests like HTTP GET, PUT, POST and sends them as legitimate requests to the target edge server. This results in the choking of edge server as it becomes busy serving bogus requests and it runs out of computational resources to resolve the real legitimate requests.

vi) Slowloris Attack:
In this type of attack, the attacker initiates a number of incomplete HTTP connections resulting in keeping the target server maintaining these partial HTTP connections in parallel till it reaches the maximum pool size after which the server crashes. Incomplete HTTP connections are created by sending only the HTTP headers and not the subsequent messages.

b. **Zero-day DDoS attacks**:

This attack is usually launched by an experienced attacker where he finds an unknown vulnerability in the application code or operating system running on the target server. This unknown vulnerability found is called zero-day vulnerability, which is exploited and attack is made with a relevant payload causing serious damage in memory or computing ability leading to server crash. These attacks cause serious damage and it is difficult to detect and defend because it utilizes the zero-day vulnerability which is not known before.

2)   Side Channel Attacks:

The escape characters are not filtered in SQL queries when it is processed in database management systems. Attackers make use of this loophole and attempt to do SQL injection attacks resulting in loss of data confidentiality and integrity. In addition, a more serious problem is that attackers can inject malicious scripts or malwares through SQL select statements. Consider this scenario, when an edge server gets service from other cloud servers or edge servers, it visits them as a client and accesses the services. If an attacker tries to perform an XSS attack now, it is a client side attack which injects malicious javascript codes into the code executed by the target server. The client is the edge server which gets the service and the target server is the edge or cloud server which provides the service. Unlike conventional client -server systems, XSS attacks can happen in edge servers in edge computing model.

The technique of compromising security and privacy through publicly available information is called side channel attacks. This kind of public information which need not be privacy-sensitive is called side channel information.Such side channel information related to secret private data must be protected. Side channel attacks are more prevalent in edge computing systems. Because there are lot of side channels in edge computing systems like communication paths, power consumption by edge devices, /proc file system used by smartphones, sensors etc., Consider the following scenario, when an attacker compromises an edge framework by collecting particular side channel information (for example, accessing the data from /proc file of mobile phones) and the obtained information is given as input to particular machine learning models, a lot of sensitive inferences can be obtained as output.

a)   Communication Channel attacks:

Utilizing the communication channels in the edge computing system is the easiest way to initiate the attack and also an effective way to steal the sensitive information. Because the attacker need not be an edge device or an edge server to monitor the communication channel, he can be any malicious node on the network who passively sits and eavesdrops the communication channel to pull out the sensitive information from it. Communication channel attacks can be categorized into two kinds i) Analyzing the packet streams in channel and ii) Analyzing the wave signals in channel.

b)   Attacks based on Power Consumption:

Attacks based on the analysis of power consumption of various devices on the edge system reveals the information about the devices itself through the power consumption profiles.The consumption of power is based on the strength of computations of a process. so this might give a lead to explore its relationship with sensitive data. This attack can be categorized into i) attacks based on power consumption measured by meters ii) attacks based on power consumption measured by oscilloscopes.

i)   Attacks based on power consumption measured by meters:

Nowadays smart electric meters are available which precisely calculates the power consumption of households. In the era of IoT and Cloud, smart homes are implemented where everything is connected. Therefore analysing the power consumption data of smart home appliances, sensitive activities at home can be detected.

ii)   Attacks based on power consumption measured by oscilloscopes:

In embedded systems, security is achieved by implementing the cryptographic algorithms in a chip. The power consumption of a hardware device can be measured by an instrument called an oscillator. Researchers have proved that the key to break the algorithm can be guessed by analysing the power consumption of hardware. however such power analysis attacks can be done only when the attacker is able to access the target device physically or gets access to the target device through some malicious applications.

c)   Attacks based on smartphone communication channels:

Smartphones play a key role in edge based systems. In addition to IoT devices, smartphones also act as edge devices in the system. They are more advanced than IoT devices as well as more prone to attacking. Attacks on smartphones can be done in two ways.i) attacks on the /proc file system and ii) attacks on the sensors embedded in smartphones

3)   Malware Injection Attacks

The process of injecting malicious code or malwares into computers is termed as malware injection attacks. The conventional computer networks have strong attack defence systems to enforce security and maintain data integrity like firewalls, Intrusion Detection Systems etc., But edge based systems have less computational power devices and minimally configured edge servers. so they may not have strong defence mechanisms and are prone to these injection attacks. Figure 4 shows the architecture of malware injection attacks in edge computing systems.

Figure 4. Malware Injection attacks in Edge systems

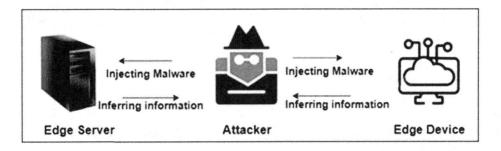

As shown in the architecture diagram above, the malwares are injected to both edge server and edge devices to steal sensitive information.

i)   Injection on Edge Server

In edge based frameworks, injection attacks primarily focus on the edge servers. Popular injection attacks which gets placed in OWASP top 10 releases include XSS - cross site scripting, CSRF- Cross-site Request Forgery and XML based attacks. SQL injection attacks utilizes the loophole of SQL's nature of not filtering the escape characters in the user constructed sql queries. Authorized users may construct sql queries with columns they are allowed to access but the attacker constructs SQL queries inserting escape characters like quotation marks and tries to access the unauthorized data.

XSS attacks tries to include malicious client side scripts in the web data content which is automatically executed by the server. CSRF is a similar attack where an edge server is tricked to execute malicious code through web applications. When edge based frameworks use Simple Object Access Protocol (SOAP) for communication, XML based attacks can be easily deployed because SOAP exchanges messages in XML format.

ii)   Injection on Edge Device

IoT devices are lightweight and heterogeneous in nature of both hardware and firmware. If any zero-day vulnerabilities are found by attackers in firmware, malwares can be injected to gain the command and control of edge devices.

CRYPTOGRAPHIC TECHNIQUES TO ENFORCE SECURITY

In the edge computing paradigm, the edge devices are more reliable and have incredible performance than cloud computing terminals, they are data owners, yet in addition they also play the job of data producers. For an edge user, the advantages from edge thing are as per the following: processing offload, caching the data, storage ability and processing, decreased maintenance cost, minimal transmission consumption and response time, and also the distributed request and service delivery from edge things, brings about a more elevated level of utilization of resources, and along these lines, forces little power cost to service providers (Alabdulatif et al., 2019). Despite the fact that the edge computing model has many advantages contrasted with conventional cloud computing model, there are still security concerns that developed as a hitch to acquisition of edge computing model.

1)   Symmetric key Encryption

Symmetric encryption algorithms can be grouped into stream ciphers and block ciphers where the plain text bits are encoded individually in stream ciphers and using blocks of bits in block ciphers. Despite the fact that block ciphers require more hardware and memory, their performance is commonly better than stream ciphers since they have a permutation stage and also a substitution stage. As recommended by Shannon, plaintext must be prepared by two primary substitution and permutation stages to achieve the confusion and diffusion properties.

2)   Public Key Encryption

Symmetric key encryption or public key encryption is utilized to solve the issue of key circulation. In Asymmetric keys, two keys are utilized; private and public keys. Public key is utilized for encryption and private key is utilized for decryption (E.g. RSA and Digital Signatures). Since users will in general utilize two keys: public key, which is known to the public and private key which is known uniquely to the user[2]. There is no requirement for conveying them preceding transmission. In any case, public key encryption depends on mathematical functions, computationally intensive and isn't exceptionally effective for small mobile devices. (Curtis, 2020). Asymmetric encryption strategies are very nearly 1000 times more slow than Symmetric methods, since they require more computational processing power.

3)   Attribute Based Encryption

Attribute-based encryption (ABE) is a basic cryptographic technique to control the decryption capacity of the data owner over the encrypted data. An attribute-based access control framework comprises two elements: 1) Trusted authority (TA) who is responsible for distributing attribute keys and dealing with users' attribute set, 2) The user incorporates the message sender and the recipient which relate to the data owner and user. The basic Attribute-Based Encryption (fuzzy IBE) as a modification of IBE scheme in which the identities are replaced with a set of attributes. In ABE algorithm, the attributes of the user is mapped as $Z*p$ by the hash functions, which the ciphertext and private keys are identified with the attributes. Two types of ABE are i) Key Policy based ABE (KP-ABE) and ii) Cipher Text based ABE (CP-ABE).

4)   Identity based Encryption

Identity-Based Encryption (IBE) is a public key encryption methodology where a public key is a random string, for example, an email address or a phone number (Patonico et al., 2019). The respective private key in the pair must be produced by a Private Key Generator (PKG) who knows about a master secret. Utilizing this development, anybody can encode messages or validated signatures without prior key distribution past the spread of public boundaries and the public key "strings." This is valuable where the arrangement of a conventional authentication authority-based PKI is badly designed or infeasible, as IBE-based frameworks don't need certificate manager, eliminating the requirement for certificate searches and complex certificate revocation schemes. The main focus of Identity-Based Cryptography is that private keys must be received from the PKG. How one safely and productively acquires this private key is essential to the security of the framework. For instance, how the PKG concludes who has to be given the private key related to an email address is pivotal to maintain the integrity of the system. Another thought is cost: key generation can be computationally costly.

5)   Proxy Re-encryption

Proxy Re-encryption (PRE) is the ciphertext switching protocol which converts the ciphertext of one key into ciphertexts of another key by using a proxy element. In other words, a proxy is made to convert the ciphertext encrypted by the data owner's public key into a ciphertext as if it is encrypted by data user's public key with the help of encryption key and also there is an assurance that the proxy may not be able to decrypt the ciphertext. So the PRE scheme is popularly used in cloud based applications for performing data forwarding, data distribution, and data exchange operation in multiuser environments.

6)   Homomorphic Encryption

Homomorphic encryption, otherwise called privacy homomorphism, is a cryptography method that permits users to work the ciphertext to perform arbitrary mathematical operations. This means, when we perform one basic mathematical operation, say addition, on the ciphertexts and, at that point when you decrypt, this decryption result is the same as the outcome that we legitimately perform addition on the plaintext. The benefit of this particular encryption form is that the user can perform any operation on the encrypted data with explicit conditions, the encryption strategies with these benefits can improve the effectiveness of data processing, guarantee the protected transmission of data, and also can get the correct decryption results. From this unique computing feature, the homomorphic encryption technique can be broadly utilized in data encryption, preserving the privacy, encrypted querying, and secure multi-party computation, The different types of Homomorphic encryption are as follows,

a.   Full Homomorphic Encryption
b.   Partial Homomorphic Encryption
c.   Somewhat Homomorphic Encryption

7)   Searchable Encryption

It is desirable to store data on data storage servers, for example, mail servers and file servers in encrypted form to decrease security and privacy dangers. In any case, this normally infers one needs to forfeit usefulness for security. For instance, if a customer wishes to recover just reports containing certain words, it was not recently realized how to let the data storage server perform the search and answer the question without loss of data classification''. The most immediate arrangements are as per the following: 1) One technique is to download all the ciphertext data to the nearby and decryption, at that point search in plaintext with keywords, however this activity will likewise download the superfluous records that don't contain the specific keywords which may cause the asset squandering of network and storage. Moreover, the decryption and searching activity of superfluous records will cost the enormous computational overhead, and this technique isn't reasonable for low broadband network situations. 2) Another outrageous arrangement is sending the private key and keywords to the storage server, at that point decode the encrypted archives and search on the server. An undeniable downside to this methodology is that the user's private data is re-presented to the server which will be a genuine danger to data security and individual privacy. Two types of searchable encryption are 1) Symmetric searchable encryption and 2) asymmetric searchable encryption.

AUTHENTICATION POLICIES AND ACCESS CONTROL SCHEMES

Access control policies identify authority, that is, power which has been authentically acquired, and to how authority is designated. Access control is related to guarantee that subjects and processes in a system access resources in a controlled and approved way (Moffett, 1994). Resources, for example, files and directories must be shielded from unapproved access and access authorization must be allocated distinctly by subjects or managers with authority to do such tasks. The Figure 5 shown below describes the entities participating in the Access Control Policies.

Figure 5. Entities in Access Control Policies

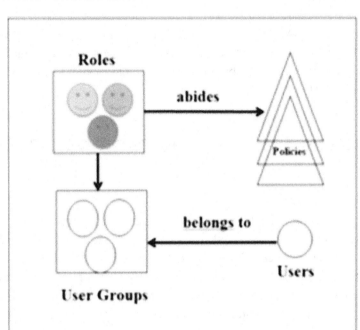

1) Attribute based Access Control

Attribute-based control policies (ABAC) is one of the transcendent innovative technologies to control information access in cloud computing, which can be all around applied to the distributed architecture and accomplished fine-grained data access control by setting up the decoding ability based on a user's attributes.

2) Role-based Access Control

Role Based Access Control (RBAC) can give an adaptable access control and privilege management by users-to-roles and roles-to-objects authority mapping mechanism which implies the RBAC can manage the access of users to resources and applications dependent on recognizing roles and actions of users in the framework(Osborn et al., 2000).

3) Discretionary Access Control

Discretionary access control policies allow users to assign rights to objects through building rules by subjects. Subjects have the control to decide who can access objects. DAC model is followed by major operating systems to implement file systems (Li & Tripunitara, 2005). For example, sample.txt rwxr-xr-x indicates the owner of sample.txt can read, write and execute the file, the other user groups can execute and read the file but could not write it.

4)   Mandatory Access Control

Mandatory access control (MAC) assigns privileges based on a tree -like structured hierarchical model (Ausanka-Crues, 2001). All users in the system are assigned with a security clearance level. All object resources are assigned with the security label in the hierarchical model. Users can access a resource in the same security level or below level in the hierarchy.

CASE STUDY: HEALTHCARE FRAMEWORK BASED ON EDGE COMPUTING

Introduction

Another use of Edge computing in healthcare includes Electrocardiogram (ECG) feature extraction to diagnose heart diseases. This involves medical sensors communicating data to an Edge layer that stores data in distributed databases, extract ECG features, and giving a graphical interface to show results in real-time.. The detection of a person having a stroke is of key importance as the speed of medical intervention is a life basic. Two fall detection systems have been implemented utilizing the Edge stage, named U-FALL and FAST. The two systems distribute computational errands between Edge and Fog stages to provide an efficient and scalable arrangement, which is essential as it considers a fast detection and notice of a patient fall. Patient health records contain sensitive data and there are multiple focuses in any Edge stage where they can be compromised, for example, by exploiting any system and application vulnerability, unauthorized data access while in storage or during transmission, malignant insiders threat, and while offering data to other systems. Medical sensors are constantly communicating data to Edge stages, through either wired or wireless connection. It is quite possible to compromise patient privacy, data integrity, and system accessibility by exploiting sensors and their underlying correspondence network. Wireless sensors for the most part work in open, unattended, and hostile environments. This ease-of-access can increase the chances of assaults like DoS, report disturbance, and selective sending assaults. What's more, if the Edge node manages sensitive data and needs access control mechanisms, it may leak the data due to account hijacking, unintended access, and other vulnerable purposes of entry. To stay away from such issues, exacting policies ought to be enforced to keep up a significant level of control utilizing multifaceted or shared authentication, private networks, and fractional (selective) encryption.

Requirements of the Edge based HealthCare Framework

The requirements (Zhang et al., 2018) of healthcare framework build using edge computing is as shown in the Figure 6 below.

1)   Confidentiality

Figure 6. Security Requirements

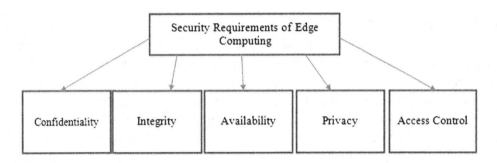

The basic need of any healthcare framework is to ensure that the EHRs of patients are only accessed by the EHR owner and authorised users, if any. EHRs must not be accessed by unauthorized users when it is being processed or stored in the edge or cloud data centers. In edge computing, the sensitive health data of patients is moved to the edge server and its ownership and control are isolated, which makes users lose their physical authority over the outsourced health data. Moreover, the sensitive health data in the edge servers are prone to data loss, breach of EHRs (Electronic Health Records), illegitimate data access or alterations (for example duplicating or removing the health records, and disclosure or distribution of health records). To address these dangers, a proper data confidentiality scheme has to be prepared to ensure the security of health data moved in the edge servers, which implies the patient's sensitive data has to be encrypted before moving it to the edge servers. At present, to maintain the confidentiality and to secure the patient data, the traditional method is to encrypt the sensitive data, and then it is outsourced to edge servers, after which it is uploaded to the data centers and can be decrypted by any legitimate user on demand.

2)   Integrity

This requirement ensures the correctness of the patient's data stored in the edge or cloud. If the integrity of the EHR is not maintained, it may lead to serious problems. Assume if the vital signs of the patient are altered by an intruder, it may result in critical issues even causing the loss of the patient's life. Data integrity is a significant issue for the security of edge computing since the patient's data is moved to the edge servers while the data integrity is questionable during this transit. This leads to the process that the data owners must check the integrity and accessibility of outsourced data to ensure that there are no undetected modifications of data by any illegitimate users or systems. With respect to edge computing, data integrity must be concentrated on the following factors, batch auditing, dynamic auditing, privacy preserving and low complexity.

3)   Availability

Health data stored in the system should be made available to the authorised users on demand for quick diagnosis. To maintain the purpose of automated healthcare services the immediate availability of EHRs is very much essential for quick diagnosis of diseases. The shorter the delay in response time and the reliable maintenance makes the automation of healthcare systems more popular.

4) Privacy

Privacy is one of the significant difficulties in other computing standards as the patients' sensitive data and personal data are moved from edge devices to the remote servers. In edge computing, privacy issues are an important issue because there are various honest but curious adversaries, for example, edge data centres, infrastructure service providers, other service providers and even some users. These attackers are generally approved entities whose main objective is to acquire sensitive data that can be utilized in different selfish manners. In this circumstance, it is unacceptable to expect to know whether a service provider is trustworthy in such an open ecosystem with various trust spaces. For instance in smart grid, a considerable amount of private data of a family can be revealed from reading the smart meters or some other IoT gadgets, it implies that regardless of the house is empty or not, if the smart meters were controlled by an adversary, the user's privacy is completely leaked. Specifically, the leakage of private data, for example, data, identification, can lead to dangerous situations.

5) Access Control

Due to the outsourcing characteristic of edge computing, if there are no proficient authentication policies in that place, any malicious user without an authorized access can misuse the resources in edge or cloud data centers. This presents a major security challenge for the protected access control framework; for instance, the virtualization asset of edge servers can be accessed, misused, and altered by edge devices if they hold any specific privileges. Furthermore, in the distributed edge computing paradigm, there are numerous trust areas by various infrastructures cohabiting in one edge ecosystem, so it is important to build up the fine-grained access control framework in each trust domain. But most of the conventional access control mechanism usually focuses on one trust domain, and not on multiple trust domains in edge computing. There are many cryptography based solutions and policies to enforce access control in edge computing paradigms.

Architecture of the Edge based HealthCare Framework

Here we are representing a sample framework for depicting Healthcare networks with computational ends. Figure 7 shows the flow of processing the healthcare data right from the sensor till the higher end.
The following scenario in a health cloud environment which uses Proxy Reencryption(PRE) scheme is explained below.

1) Doctor encrypts the EHR of a Patient or the sensor data of patients using his Public Key PU_A - Ciphertext C1 is moved to cloud
2) Re-encryption key is generated to give access to an insurance agent. Doctor generates the re-encryption key encrypting his/her Public Key PU_A with the Insurance agent's public key PU_B and the encryption key $RK_{A->B}$ is transmitted to the cloud.
3) The cloud service provider may act as a proxy and it re-encrypts the Ciphertext C1 with $RK_{A->B}$ - Ciphertext C2
4) The Insurance agent decrypts the re-encrypted ciphertext with his private key PR_B.

Figure 7. Healthcare Framework with Edge Computing

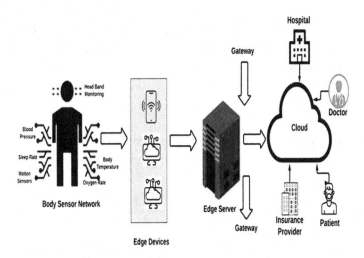

The above procedure clearly shows that the intruder or adverse enemy can't decrypt the encrypted text. The disadvantage is that the semi-trusted proxy not only transfers the ciphertext from doctor to insurance agent but also vice-versa, which means it can reversibly converts the ciphertext of insurance agent to doctor without the permission of insurance agent by exploiting the discrete logarithm properties. Another issue with the PRE scheme is that both doctor and proxy can collude and try to deduce the private key of the insurance agent. To solve these problems variants of this scheme are introduced namely Identity based PRE, Conditional PRE etc.

Security Requirements in Edge based HealthCare Framework

Even however each Edge deployment has a different set of security requirements, applications, and sensitivity, the accompanying subsections provide comprehensive, efficient, and applicable security requirements for healthcare systems. They can likewise be used as generic best practice guidelines while developing the Edge software, so the security is enabled from inside the stage. Some of the working arrangements are,

Data Encryption

The data needs to be secured before (at rest in source area), during (moving through the network) and after (at rest in destination area) correspondence among IoT devices, the Edge network, and the Fog stage.

Preventing Cache Assaults

Edge stages maintained for the Cache management system are prone to software cache-based side-channel assaults, for example, exposing cryptographic keys, which may lead toward leaking sensitive data.

Network Checking

Edge systems that are consistently handling private data (e.g. generated by IoT devices) from end-user to Fog stage and vice versa, should screen and detect abnormal action in a network through automated enforcement of correspondence security rules and policies.

Malware Protection

Edge systems ought to protect themselves against both new and existing malware-based assaults, which can happen as infection, Trojan, rootkit, spyware, and worms to keep away from unwanted infection and serious damage.

Wireless Security

The internal and external wireless interchanges of the Edge stage with end-user devices need to minimize packet sniffing, rouge access focuses, and comparative challenges by implementing both encryption and authentication procedures. In Secured vehicular networks, to increase street safety and real-time utilization of vehicular networks(Freedman, 2003), they ought to protect themselves from internal and external security threats.

Secured Multi-Tenancy

Edge computing should enable profoundly constrained access control on both data and network, alongside reasonable resource assignment mechanisms to protect confidentiality and integrity inside a multi-user environment.

Backup and Recovery

Depending upon the sort of utilization, Edge stages ought to have a data backup and recovery modules. Such a system should reflect copies of data on location, off-site, or both on a regular premise. It will benefit the two customers and friends to keep the operations running from utilizing previous backups, limiting service interruptions.

Security with Performance

A balanced trade-off between the level of usefulness and integrated security is fundamental for Edge network performance. It will enable completely featured applications meanwhile protecting the CIA of data and networks against internal and external threats.

Security Solutions Recommendations for Edge Based HealthCare Framework

Privacy Safeguarding in Edge Figuring

With regards to medical care, the primary examination gets into safeguarding protection in sensor-edge networks comprises of the accompanying summed up steps to make sure about wellbeing sensor information between end-client gadget and Edge organization: They gather sensor information and concentrate highlights. Fluffing of information by embeddings Gaussian commotion in information at a specific degree of difference to bring down the opportunity of listening in and sniffing assaults; Segregation by parting information into squares and rearranging them to maintain a strategic distance from Man-in-the-Middle (MITM) assaults; Implementing Public Key Infrastructure for encoding every information square; and Transmit isolated information to Edge hub, where information bundles are unscrambled and re-requested. The framework additionally incorporates a component decrease capacity for limiting information correspondence with Edge hubs to help limit hazard. This work is of criticalness as it focussed on safeguarding individual and basic information during transmission. A method can be improved by choosing an encryption and key administration calculation, focussing on those that assume a significant part in keeping up the security of information. Anyway, the necessary computational overheads for performing broad information control (fluffing, isolation, encryption, unscrambling and requesting, reordering) when the correspondence must be investigated before its gets into the real usage of the situation. This could be of essentialness when planning and creating an Edge framework as the necessary calculation overheads probably won't be accessible. Another significant perspective to see here is that sensors send information persistently, perhaps over longer timeframes, stickand the proposed security structure may over-burden or even accident the fundamental Edge framework. That is the place the heap adjusting calculations must be work.

Alleviating Insider Information Burglary

One path for shielding information from malignant insiders any delicate gadget organization, for example, medical services utilizing parts of Edge and Cloud figuring would consolidates conduct profiling and fake ways to deal with alleviate security dangers. On the off chance that any profile shows anomalous conduct, for example, the expansion of getting to various archives at uncommon occasions, the framework will label the entrance as dubious and square the individual client. Fake is a disinformation assault that incorporates counterfeit reports, honeyfiles, honeypots and different sorts of goading information that can be utilized to distinguish, befuddle and get the malevolent insider. This examination space is huge as it exhibits likely adjusting and alleviation strategies to shield against information burglary. All the more explicitly, One can show that the proposed strategy can accurately distinguish unusual conduct with a normal exactness more noteworthy than 90%. For instance, an examination is performed with a restricted measure of information. All the more explicitly, eighteen understudies from a solitary college over the term of four days. Consequently, the outcomes regarding exactness they guarantee may not reproducible or widespread. Their procedure can be improved by expanding the populace size and running the trial over longer stretch of time(Stolfo et al., 2012). Moreover, the computational prerequisites of such a methodology are not referenced. The paper gives no subtleties on the amount of information that is put away, just as the CPU time and memory required during investigation. Such conduct profiling methods are regularly acted in a conventional customer worker engineering where calculation assets are openly accessible. It isn't clear how this strategy can be executed on an Edge hub without having unfriendly effects on center usefulness. The method can be additionally improved through fundamentally breaking down and choosing achievable machines learning procedures and preparing information required for conduct profiling. This conveys more significance because of the presence of an enormous number of patients and records. The conduct profiling, checking and client coordinating cycle would not apply any weight on Cloud assets and forestall real information burglary without uncovering any patient touchy information. As an additional advantage, these tasks will happen on-premise and execute generally quicker because of low transmission capacity idleness.

Strategy Driven Secure Administration of Assets

The following famous issue in medical care is strategy the board system for the assets of Edge registering to upgrade secure collaboration, sharing and interoperability among client mentioned assets. The framework is separated into five significant modules:

1) Policy Decision Engine (PDE) for making a move dependent on pre-characterized strategy rules;
2) Application Administrator (AA) to oversee Edge multi-occupancy;
3) Policy Resolver (PR) for characteristic based validation;
4) Policy Repository (PRep) holding rules and approaches; and
5) Policy Enforcer (PE) to distinguish any inconsistencies in strategy execution.

AA is answerable for characterizing rules and arrangements (put away in PRep) while thinking about different occupants, applications, information sharing and correspondence administrations. At the point when a specific assistance demand is produced using a client, it is sent to a PR that recognizes the client dependent on explicit arrangement of traits and access benefits against a mentioned asset. The client ascribes and their separate authorizations are put away in an information base. PDE takes client data from the PR, separates rules from the PRep, dissect them and authorize through the PE. The eXtensible Access Control Markup Language (XACML) is utilized to make rules and the OpenAZ system for building PDE. Regardless of being in an underlying stage, this strategy structure can possibly turn into a vital piece of constant circulated frameworks in future, where there is a solid requirement for access, personality and asset the executives capacities. Notwithstanding, this structure is restricted to just those frameworks, which can distribute devoted assets inside Edge stages for the greater part of calculations required by different modules to execute the system. Edge stages ought to be fit for dealing with profoundly time-delicate applications, be that as it may, the proposed approval cycle may take more time to decide. Another imperfection in their strategy is that the arrangement itself is characteristically powerless against DoS assaults because of the intricate confirmation measure in PR and PDE. On the off chance that an aggressor sets up a lot of associations all the while, rehashes the 'approval cycle's in a similar association ceaselessly or reacts to the validation convention in a low and moderate way, the Edge assets will get depleted and delivered inaccessible for the proposed clients. In any case, these security concerns can be decreased by building an exhibition model that is gathering estimations of memory, CPU and plate use and occasionally contrasting and assessed values. In the event that the framework recognizes an oddity, the client would be diverted to the Shark Tank group, which is basically an intermediary to intently screen the client however can give full application capacities.

Verification in Edge Stage

Shaky validation conventions between Edge stages And medical care gadgets have been recognized as a fundamental security worry of Edge registering. The case is that that the IoT gadgets, particularly in keen lattices, are inclined to information altering and satirizing assaults and can be forestalled with the assistance of a Public Key Infrastructure (PKI), Diffie-Hellman key trade, Intrusion discovery strategies and observing for changed info esteems. Moreover, effect of MITM assault on Edge processing by dispatching a Stealth assault on video call among 3G and the WLAN clients inside an Edge network didn't cause any noticeable change in memory and CPU utilization of Edge hub, henceforth it is very hard to distinguish what's more, relieve. The proposal is that the danger of such assaults can be forestalled by making sure about correspondence channels between the Edge stage and the client of medical services gadgets to execute validation plans. In view of the present status of validation in wellbeing system Edge stage, they are missing thorough verification and secure correspondence conventions according to their determination and prerequisites. In an Edge stage both security and execution factors are considered related, and systems, for example, the encryption procedures known as completely homomorphic and Fan-Vercauteren to some degree homomorphic can be utilized to make sure about the information. These plans comprises of a half and half of symmetric and public-key encryption calculations, just as different variations of quality based encryption. As homomorphic encryption grants ordinary activities over the records information without decoding the information, the decrease in key dissemination will keep up the protection of information. A framework can perform information collection dependent on the homomorphicPaillier cryptosystem. As the homomorphic capacity of encryption makes it workable for neighborhood network passages to play out a procedure on figure text without decoding, it decreases the confirmation cost (regarding preparing power) while keeping up the mystery of information.

Utilizing Advance Encryption Standard (AES)

Some examination may infer that AES is a reasonable encryption calculation for a gigantic information collection in medical services where Edge stage assumes a significant job. Different measurements have been considered for the presentation assessment: client load against CPU time and document size against encryption/unscrambling time and memory usage. Our case is that, encryption time will be almost the equivalent for cell phone and PC, any sort of fitbits and other computerized screens for persistent information which collects modest quantity of information, for example, 500 Kb, 5 Mb, and 10 Mb. In spite of the fact that, AES encryption is all around acknowledged and is attainable for Edge figuring, because of low equipment particulars and littler calculations, one can't contrast AES and some other accessible encryption calculation. What's more, the size of the encryption key assumes a significant function in reinforcing the encryption. Utilizing little example size probably won't give the profound knowledge to whether AES is an appropriate calculation for Edge organizations and capacity or not. So it is suggested that, distinctive measured information must be put for AES choice. Moreover, literary information, pictures or some other information configuration can be utilized for encryption/unscrambling measures. In addition, the Edge stage comprises of heterogeneous gadgets with various details and single calculation probably won't have the option to cover every conceivable situation. Encryption is now an extra assignment for the Edge stage and furthermore devours a lot of assets. The determination of encryption calculation (regardless of whether symmetric, hilter kilter or cross breed) ought to be acted as per supplier and foundation necessities.

REFERENCES

Alabdulatif, A., Khalil, I., Yi, X., & Guizani, M. (2019). Secure Edge of Things for Smart Healthcare Surveillance Framework. *IEEE Access: Practical Innovations, Open Solutions*, *7*(c), 31010–31021. doi:10.1109/ACCESS.2019.2899323

Ausanka-Crues, R. (2001). *Methods for access control : Advances and limitations*. Harvey Mudd College.

Curtis. (2020). *What are the issues with fog computing*. https://www.yourtechdiet.com/blogs/fog-computing-issues/

Dimitrievski, A., Zdravevski, E., Lameski, P., & Trajkovik, V. (2019, September). Addressing Privacy and Security in Connected Health with Fog Computing. In *Proceedings of the 5th EAI International Conference on Smart Objects and Technologies for Social Good* (pp. 255-260). 10.1145/3342428.3342654

Freedman, A. (2003). Securing the Edge. *Queue, 1*(1), 6-9.

Glikson, A., Nastic, S., & Dustdar, S. (2017, May). Deviceless edge computing: extending serverless computing to the edge of the network. In *Proceedings of the 10th ACM International Systems and Storage Conference* (pp. 1-1). 10.1145/3078468.3078497

Khan, S., Parkinson, S., & Qin, Y. (2017). Fog computing security: A review of current applications and security solutions. *Journal of Cloud Computing, 6*(1), 19. Advance online publication. doi:10.118613677-017-0090-3

Li, C., Xue, Y., Wang, J., Zhang, W., & Li, T. (2018). Edge-oriented computing paradigms: A survey on architecture design and system management. [*ACM Computing Surveys, 51*(2), 1–34. doi:10.1145/3154815

Li, N., & Tripunitara, M. V. (2005). On safety in discretionary access control. *Proceedings - IEEE Symposium on Security and Privacy*. 10.1109/SP.2005.14

Merlino, G., Dautov, R., Distefano, S., & Bruneo, D. (2019). Enabling workload engineering in edge, fog, and cloud computing through OpenStack-based middleware. *ACM Transactions on Internet Technology, 19*(2), 1–22. doi:10.1145/3309705

Moffett, J. D. (1994). Specification of management policies and discretionary access control. *Network and Distributed Systems Management*, 455–479. http://scholar.google.com/scholar?hl=en&btnG=Search&q=intitle:The+Even+More+Irresistible+SROIQ#0%5Cnhttp://citeseerx.ist.psu.edu/viewdoc/download?doi=10.1.1.17.7145&rep=rep1&type=pdf

Osborn, S., Sandhu, R., & Munawer, Q. (2000). Configuring Role-Based Access Control to Enforce Mandatory and Discretionary Access Control Policies. *ACM Transactions on Information and System Security, 3*(2), 85–106. Advance online publication. doi:10.1145/354876.354878

Patonico, S., Braeken, A., & Steenhaut, K. (2019). Identity-based and anonymous key agreement protocol for fog computing resistant in the Canetti–Krawczyk security model. *Wireless Networks, 6*. Advance online publication. doi:10.100711276-019-02084-6

Ren, J., Guo, H., Xu, C., & Zhang, Y. (2017). Serving at the edge: A scalable IoT architecture based on transparent computing. *IEEE Network, 31*(5), 96–105. doi:10.1109/MNET.2017.1700030

Ren, J., Zhang, D., He, S., Zhang, Y., & Li, T. (2019). A Survey on End-Edge-Cloud Orchestrated Network Computing Paradigms: Transparent Computing, Mobile Edge Computing, Fog Computing, and Cloudlet. *ACM Computing Surveys*, *52*(6), 1–36. doi:10.1145/3362031

Stolfo, S. J., Salem, M. B., & Keromytis, A. D. (2012, May). Fog computing: Mitigating insider data theft attacks in the cloud. In *2012 IEEE symposium on security and privacy workshops* (pp. 125-128). IEEE.

Tang, W., Ren, J., Zhang, K., Zhang, D., Zhang, Y., & Shen, X. (2019). Efficient and privacy-preserving fog-assisted health data sharing scheme. *ACM Transactions on Intelligent Systems and Technology*, *10*(6), 1–23. doi:10.1145/3341104

Wang, X., Zhang, J., Schooler, E. M., & Ion, M. (2014, June). Performance evaluation of attribute-based encryption: Toward data privacy in the IoT. In *2014 IEEE International Conference on Communications (ICC)* (pp. 725-730). IEEE. 10.1109/ICC.2014.6883405

Waters, B., & Encryption, C. P. A. B. (2011). An Expressive, Efficient, and Provably Secure Realization. Lecture Notes in Computer Science, 6571.

Xiao, Y., Jia, Y., Liu, C., Cheng, X., Yu, J., & Lv, W. (2019). Edge Computing Security: State of the Art and Challenges. *Proceedings of the IEEE*, *107*(8), 1608–1631. Advance online publication. doi:10.1109/JPROC.2019.2918437

Yang, J. J., Li, J. Q., & Niu, Y. (2015). A hybrid solution for privacy preserving medical data sharing in the cloud environment. *Future Generation Computer Systems*, *43*, 74–86. doi:10.1016/j.future.2014.06.004

Zhang, J., Chen, B., Zhao, Y., Cheng, X., & Hu, F. (2018). Data Security and Privacy-Preserving in Edge Computing Paradigm: Survey and Open Issues. *IEEE Access*, *6*(Idc), 18209–18237. doi:10.1109/ACCESS.2018.2820162

This research was previously published in Cases on Edge Computing and Analytics; pages 235-269, copyright year 2021 by Engineering Science Reference (an imprint of IGI Global).

Chapter 23
The Role of Edge/Fog Computing Security in IoT and Industry 4.0 Infrastructures:
Edge/Fog-Based Security in Internet of Things

Meltem Mutluturk
https://orcid.org/0000-0001-5666-594X
Bogazici University, Turkey

Burcu Kor
Amsterdam University of Applied Science, The Netherlands

Bilgin Metin
https://orcid.org/0000-0002-5828-9770
Bogazici University, Turkey

ABSTRACT

The development of information and communication technologies (ICT) has led to many innovative technologies. The integration of technologies such as the internet of things (IoT), cloud computing, and machine learning concepts have given rise to Industry 4.0. Fog and edge computing have stepped in to fill the areas where cloud computing is inadequate to ensure these systems work quickly and efficiently. The number of connected devices has brought about cybersecurity issues. This study reviewed the current literature regarding edge/fog-based cybersecurity in IoT to display the current state.

DOI: 10.4018/978-1-6684-5700-9.ch023

INTRODUCTION

In an era of rapid growth in science and technology and aggressive competition, an innovative capability is associated with an advance in knowledge and the welfare of many in the population (West & Altink, 1996). Innovative capability is crucial because innovation plays essential roles in emerging technologies or new information and communication technologies (ICT). Firstly, new ideas are required to develop innovative products or technologies. The increasing use of new and innovative ICT such as mobile computing, social media, Web 2.0 networking, cloud computing, Internet of Things (IoT), and virtual collaborative environments have enabled a voluminous exchange of data, information and intellectual property (Mejias & Balthazard, 2014).

It has been forecasted that the number of devices connected over the internet will be around 50 billion by the end of this decade. By the end of 2020, the massive increase in the number of connected smart things, known as IoT, is estimated to be about six times the world's population (Boakye-Boateng et al., 2019). Alongside mobile devices, the digitalization of home devices (refrigerators, fans), smart city applications (connected cars, smart traffic lights, smart grids, smart wear utilities, etc.) and operational technologies (factory machines) across the globe are the main factors for this increase (Boakye-Boateng et al., 2019). These connected devices lead to the problem of vast masses of data being processed and applications with low latency expectancy. The huge scale adoption of IoT, and big data creation has led businesses and industries to find new methods for data processing, storage and communications. For example, cloud computing enables IT outsourcing capability with value-added services for customers (Diro, Chilamkurti & Nam, 2018).

Cloud computing architecture means uploading data through the Internet and realizing CPU and storage operations in data centers. Benefiting from the processing power of datacenters sounds good but the high latency due to Internet connection can be seen as a disadvantage. Lately, a new computing paradigm is to extend traditional data centers for the cloud to the edge of the network to decrease transmission and processing-response delays (Tsaur & Yeh, 2019). In order to decrease delays, the most straightforward approach could be handling data operations such as processing tasks, analytics, and knowledge generation closer to the data source. This is called edge computing.

Cloud computing has provided on-demand access to computing, storage infrastructure, and services for corporates and individuals at a reduced cost. The communicated IoT devices continually generated and transmitted different types of data in different amount. However, the current cloud models are not proposed to deal with the type of data generated by IoT devices, so they must consider some issues such as latency, bandwidth utilization, and throughput (Viejo & Sánchez, 2019).

This study reviews the cybersecurity issues faced within IoT with fog/edge computing. The rest of the paper is structured as follows: the next section explains the Edge and Fog Computing concepts along with their place regarding cybersecurity and IoT devices. The subsequent section presents the reviewing method of the study. The 'Findings' section reveals the results of the review based on the variables selected in the method section. Finally, the conclusion and limitations of the study are given.

INDUSTRY 4.0 TECHNOLOGIES

Industry 4.0 is transforming manufacturing by integrating manufacturing operations with ICT. There is a various amount of technologies that are utilized within Industry 4.0. Among these are cyber physical systems (CPS), cloud computing, blockchain, IoT, and big data analytics among others (Bai et al., 2020).

CPS combines information and material to increase industrial performance. IoT is seen as a complex form of CPS, integrating multiple devices that have capabilities such as sensing, communicating, and processing. An IoT system consists of machines, networks, the cloud, and terminals. The development of IoT is seen as a contributing factor to the development of Industry 4.0. By facilitating the communication between people and machines, IoT enables knowledge transfer between and within companies (Lu, 2017).

As part of an IoT system, cloud computing is an important technology utilized within Industry 4.0. This technology enables the collection of large amounts of data from other Industry 4.0 essential technologies such as sensors and also enables the communication between networked systems. Cloud computing also contributes to more data-driven decision making for service and production systems (Salkin et al., 2018).

With the cloud and IoT technologies, the industry is continuously evolving by way of the different types of information that are created and collected. There are a few important elements of IoT such as embedded sensors, image recognition, and Near Field Communication (NFC) payment. These elements of IoT contribute to the creation of information from various fields and functions. While these elements and technologies has helped improve efficiency and decreased service times increasing customer service in industries such as transportation, retail, and healthcare, they also bring about multiple issues with data security being one of the more critical (Yusof et al., 2020).

Managing and protecting the big data produced by IoT can be taxing. IoT devices generates and stores mass amounts of information regarding the behaviors and attitudes of customers and their environment. As these are sensitive data this may be a cause for concern for companies generate a large amount of sensitive data. The proper management of data along with IoT will benefit companies immensely (Yusof et al., 2020).

EDGE AND FOG COMPUTING

The concept of Edge Computing is often used interchangeably with that of Fog Computing, which was introduced by Cisco Systems in 2012. Fog computing pushes IoT data to the edge of the network to be processed without sending it to the cloud. The data can be sent to the cloud if need be to be stored for further processing. Devices called fog nodes are used to achieve this system. Analyzing data close to its connection lowers bandwidth usage and improves latency (Boakye-Boateng et al., 2019).

Since fog computing devices are serviced at the edge network, the advantages contain low service latency, high quality of services, support for mobility, awareness of location, and easier control of security measures (Pacheco & Hariri, 2018). Ferretti, Marchetti and Colajanni (2019, p. 1) emphasized that *"If the cloud service is temporarily unavailable, then even communications among local objects become impossible. In many scenarios, such as health-care, home automation, and control of industrial processes, this drawback is not acceptable. The fog computing paradigm aims to address issues related to cloud-assisted architectures by moving some operational capabilities from the cloud toward the edge of the network."*

Edge computing provides a new computing paradigm where data is processed at the nearest edge node with enough resources in order to mitigate the delay causes in delay-sensitive applications and satisfy the performance. There are two significant advantages of edge computing architecture in comparison to cloud computing. First, it leverages the available computing and storage resources on edge nodes that are close to users so that the response time can be improved. Second, since the massive data do not need to be transmitted to the cloud, the backbone bandwidth is also saved. (Li, et al., 2019).

Because of fog computing, IoT services will be a critical technology for the development of smart cities. Pacheco and Hariri (2018) indicate that technology transforms the way we do business, maintain our health, manage critical infrastructure, and conduct education and how we secure, protect, and entertain ourselves. A study undertaken by HP Fortify found that 70% of the most commonly used IoT devices contain security vulnerabilities and there is an average of 25 security concerns per device (Tankard, 2015). Accordingly, Fog computing architecture provides solutions to solve the security challenges of IoT devices by distributing computing, control, storage, and networking functions closer to end-user devices. Fog computing can be presented as a three-layer hierarchical architecture: Cloud-Fog-End Devices (Venckauskas et al., 2018). According to Barbareschi, et al. (2019, p. 247), security challenges are mainly characterized by:

- "the adoption of low-range, low-power communication technologies with heterogeneous and often resource-constrained devices (e.g., sensors, actuators, RFID-based systems, etc.),
- the typically autonomous nature of such devices and the lack of centralized control, and
- the processing of sensitive information (belonging for example to the private sphere, the daily routines, the industrial systems or the critical infrastructures)."

Additionally, fog computing facilitates smart application processes on network devices, such as routers, gateways or switches rather than sending data to cloud datacenters (Sohal, Sandhu, Sood, & Chang, 2018). However, there are also new challenges in the new edge computing architectures (Li, et al., 2019). For instance, fog nodes are more vulnerable to hackers because of the deployment of fog nodes at the edge of the network and low-traffic nodes, as well as these nodes hold a lot of privacy-sensitive user data (Zhang, Chen, Li, Wong & Li, 2017; Zhang, et al., 2018; Li, et al., 2019). In addition, when a large number of IoT device data is transmitted to fog nodes, it will affect the requirements for a real-time response of IoT, as well as cause problems such as network congestion (Zhang, et al., 2018).

CYBERSECURITY, FOG COMPUTING AND IOT DEVICES

IoT connects everyday objects in a network. IoT devices produce an abundance of information causing problems regarding bandwidth leading to processing-response lags toward the cloud. IoT devices also collect private information when engaged by the end-user. This brings about many security and privacy issues (Fedrecheski et al., 2019). Fog computing has been seen as the solution for a new architecture to address the vulnerabilities brought about by IoT (Venckauskas et al., 2018).

The philosophy of IoT technology is to extend the intelligence of nonliving entities and to support their ability to process information and make decisions without any intervention from human or living bodies (Alshahrani & Traore, 2019). The massive number of IoT devices connected to the Internet and each other and the large amounts of data being shared and processed is causing a significant problem resource-wise. Also, the limited storage and computing capacity of most devices that store and process these chunks of data has led to the necessity of cloud computing to provide a practical solution to address these capacity issues (Boakye-Boateng et al., 2019). Collecting a massive amount of sensed data from IoT devices to the cloud cause several challenges, particularly transmission and processing-response delays. Accordingly, causing delay problems in the process delay-sensitive applications, such as power control, emergency assistance, and health monitoring (Xu, Ding, Li, & Wang, 2018). In order to mitigate the burden of cloud computing, the extensions of the Fog computing architecture leads to a hierarchical infrastructure design as shown where the analysis of local information is performed at the "ground," and the coordination and global analytics are performed at the "cloud". In 2013, IBM and Nokia Siemens Network first introduced the term mobile edge computing (MEC) to describe the execution of services at the edge of the network. In their case, a platform that could run applications within a mobile base station (Tsaur & Yeh, 2019).

The number and diversity of networked devices such as wireless sensors, wearable devices, household appliances, and smart objects have been growing. However, Ferretti, Marchetti and Colajanni (2019) emphasize that these innovative technologies present new vulnerabilities and insecure scenarios. Indeed, the adoption of secure protocols over large networks of low-power objects can be impacted by the inherent limitations of storage, computational capacity, and energy consumption characterizing most devices (Ferretti, Marchetti & Colajanni, 2019).

IoT-based systems are mostly mobile devices so they may be connected to different networks and they have interaction with several IoT devices. Traditional fixed security measures are infeasible to protect such environments (Aman & Kausar, 2019). Herein, fog computing architecture allows data from IoT to be processed at the edge of the network without reaching the cloud. The data can later be sent to the cloud for storage or further processing or analytics. To minimize latency and conserve network bandwidth, the data can later be sent to the cloud for storage or further processing or analytics (Boakye-Boateng et al., 2019).

Diro, Chilamkurti and Nam (2018) emphasize the importance of distributed fog nodes for implementing and deploying security mechanisms. The implementation and deployment of security mechanisms at fog nodes may provide a protective shield for IoT, thereby creating a complete shift in premise to traditional IT perimeter security (Diro, Chilamkurti, & Nam, 2018).

METHOD

The aim of the study is to review the literature on fog/edge computing in IoT infrastructures in the context of security. To achieve this aim, the Scopus database which provides a wide range of scholarly journals as well as multiple filtering criteria was used to reach the articles necessary for the study. The search was conducted without any time restrictions. The keywords used within the search were: "fog or edge", "internet of things" or "IoT", "security". The search provided 894 articles for analysis. These articles were journal articles written in the English language.

The elimination phase consisted of reviewing the abstracts of all 894 articles and eliminating any irrelevant studies. The screening criteria was that all articles had to utilize edge or fog computing to mitigate security risks of IoT architectures or enhance the security of an existing fog based IoT system. The elimination left 155 articles for full review (see Appendix). The remaining articles were examined and their security method, security goal, and attack type information were collected.

FINDINGS

The articles reviewed within this study can be seen to have been spread out between the last five years, growing in number significantly. The reason being is that although IoT and cloud computing concepts have been around for more than five years, edge and fog computing are rather new concepts. Figure 1 shows the frequency of articles according to the years published.

Figure 1. Article frequencies according to years

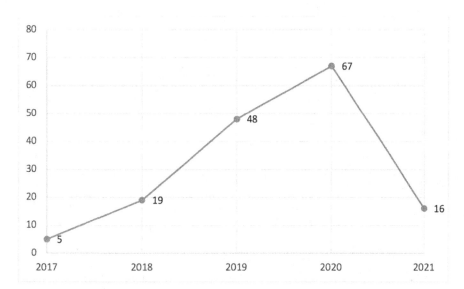

As the screening criteria for this study was that the articles to be reviewed had to either utilize edge or fog computing to mitigate the security risks of IoT architectures (edge/fog computing for security) or enhance the security of an existing fog based IoT system (edge/fog security enhancement), the percentage of each purpose was examined (Figure 2). More than half (56%) of the studies were conducted to enhance edge/fog computing security in IoT systems. This is seen to be in keeping with the literature as cloud computing comes with many security issues and as edge/fog computing also inherent some of these issues it is natural that a number of studies focus on enhancing security.

OWASP (Open Web Application Security Project) has published a list of IoT attack surfaces. The articles reviewed were analyzed according to the attack surfaces found within the list. Table 1 shows all attack types the articles addressed. Many articles aimed to address all types of attacks found in IoT systems, so they are not included in the table.

In Table 1, DoS/DDoS, Man-in-the-middle, and Replay attacks are the most frequently addressed attack types within the inspected papers. It is no coincidence that Man-in-the-middle and replay attacks are addressed the most as these attacks are used to eavesdrop on networks and intercept communication over secure networks. As IoT is based on communication of devices, this finding is consistent with the nature of the system. DoS and DDoS attack are based on flooding a server with high traffic, making a service unavailable, critical to an IoT system. Eavesdropping and flooding have been taken as separate attacks. However, they can also be seen as part of replay and DoS attacks.

Figure 2. Purpose of study

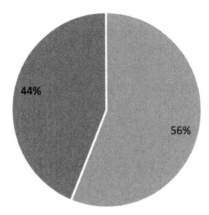

■ edge/fog security enhancement ■ edge/fog computing for security

Table 1. Attack types addressed

Attack Type	Frequency	Reference
Man-in-the-middle	24	Zhang et al. (2021), Wu et al. (2021), Singh et al. (2021), Misra et al. (2020), Kumar & Chouhan (2021), Sadique, Rahmani & Johannesson (2020), Rostampour et al. (2020), Hussein, Saleh & Mostafa (2020), Nawaz et al. (2020), Aslam et al. (2020), Rathee et al. (2020), Li et al. (2020), Akkaoui, Hei & Cheng (2020), Zahra & Chishti (2020), Saha et al. (2020), Hsu et al. (2020), Chen et al. (2020), Wazid et al. (2019), Ma et al. (2019), Rahman & Wen (2019), Alshahrani & Traore (2019), Liao et al. (2019), Sathyadevan et al. (2019), Barbareschi et al. (2019)
Tampering	3	Aujla & Jindal (2021), Ma et al. (2019), Barbareschi et al. (2019)
Replay Attack	24	Zhang et al. (2021), Li et al. (2021), Wu et al. (2021), Khan et al. (2021), Kumar & Chouhan (2021), Sadique, Rahmani & Johannesson (2020), Usman et al. (2019), Aslam et al. (2020), Puthal et al. (2020), Tian & Wang (2020), Li et al. (2020), Akkaoui, Hei & Cheng (2020), Saha et al. (2020), Hsu et al. (2020), Chen et al. (2020), De Rango et al. (2020), Wazid et al. (2019), Hao & Wang (2019), Ma et al. (2019), Lohachab (2019), Wang et al. (2018), Boakye-Boateng et al. (2019), Alshahrani & Traore (2019), Sathyadevan et al. (2019)
DoS/DDoS	33	Moustafa et al. (2021), Qureshi, Jeon & Piccialli (2021), Chen et al. (2021), Singh, Pan & Park (2021), Kumar & Chouhan (2021), Sadique, Rahmani & Johannesson (2020), Jia et al. (2020), Qureshi et al. (2020), Huang et al. (2020), Nawaz et al. (2020), Aslam et al. (2020), Puthal et al. (2020), Rathee et al. (2020), Sood (2019), Junejo, Komninos & McCann (2020), Demirpolat, Sarica, Angin (2020), Kumar et al. (2020), Chang, Feng, Duan (2020), Li et al. (2020), Akkaoui, Hei & Cheng (2020), Zahra & Chishti (2020), Hao & Wang (2019), Rathore, Kwon & Park (2019), Zhou, Guo & Deng (2019), Lohachab (2019), Wang et al. (2018), Tiburski et al. (2019), Liao et al. (2019), Mahdikhani et al. (2019), Jayasinghe et al. (2019), Yan et al. (2018), Shafi et al. (2018), Lin & Hwang (2018)
Brute Force	6	Zhaofeng et al. (2020), Maharaja, Iyer & Ye (2019), Chang, Feng & Duan (2020), Li et al. (2019), Mahdikhani et al. (2019), Koo & Hur (2018)
Collusion Attacks	13	Chen et al. (2021), Yu et al. (2020), Zhang et al. (2020), Maharaja, Iyer & Ye (2019), Zhang et al. (2020), Rathee et al. (2020), Sood (2019), Junejo, Komninos & McCann (2020), Zahra & Chishti (2020), Tiburski et al. (2019), Zhang, Bai & Wang (2019), Yaseen et al. (2018), Fan et al. (2017)
Eavesdropping	8	Zhang et al. (2021), Qureshi, Jeon & Picialli (2021), Chen, You & Ruan (2020), Zahed et al. (2020), Lohachab (2019), Sathyadevan et al. (2019), Koo & Hur (2018), Alrawais et al. (2017)
Ciphertext	2	Li et al. (2019), Zuo et al. (2018)
Sybill	4	Rathee et al. (2020), Junejo, Komninos & McCann (2020), Li et al. (2020), Liu et al. (2019)
Spoofing	4	Li et al. (2020), Zahed et al. (2020), Hao & Wang (2019), Liao et al. (2019)
Flooding	2	Pacheco et al. (2020), Rathore, Kwon & Park (2019)
Impersonation	8	Li et al. (2021), De Smet et al. (2021), Wu et al. (2021), Kumar & Chouhan (2021), Sadique, Rahmani & Johannesson (2020), Khalid et al. (2020), Aslam et al. (2020), Wazid et al. (2019)

The main goal of cybersecurity is to enable the Confidentiality, Integrity and Availability (CIA) of information. Requirements such as privacy, accessibility, authentication, and non-repudiation can also be added to the list. In the context of IoT, confidentiality requires limiting unauthorized access to certain information. For example, unauthorized access to health records may lead to undesired situations. Integrity ensures the completeness and accuracy of data and secures data so it cannot be manipulated. Availability is crucial in IoT as the applications and devices must always be available to requests made by users. Non-repudiation confirmation regarding whether an action has occurred or not. Lastly, privacy ensures that the system conforms to privacy policies and that users can control their personal information (Mosenia & Niraj, 2016). Figure 3 shows the number of studies that were conducted with the basic CIA security goals.

Figure 3. Security goal distribution

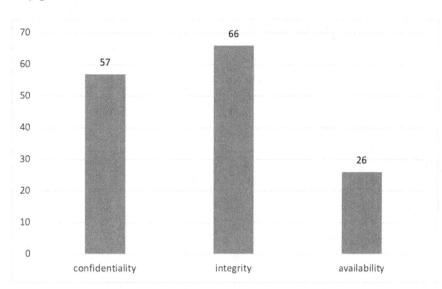

Table 2 gives the other security goals that were intended to be met within the articles reviewed.

Authentication has been found in many papers that have been inspected. This is consistent with the fact that IoT devices use authentication to ensure the security of messages and packets sent along the network.

Table 3 gives the methods used to either enhance fog computing security or ensure security using a fog-based model. As the aim of the study implies, all studies utilized some sort of fog or edge computing system. However, the articles referenced within Table 3 have given specific methods for their studies. Blockchain-based solutions can be seen to be used the most. This could be due to blockchain solutions enabling secure communication between devices among a network. This is consistent with the most common attack types and security goals all having to do with secure communication between devices.

Lastly, the evaluation techniques were examined, and all studies evaluated their proposed models using experimental techniques such as simulations and testbeds along with security analysis. The variables used to test performance mainly were response time and cost.

Table 2. Security goals

Security Goal	Frequency	Reference
Non-repudiation	6	Khalid et al. (2020), Kumar et al. (2020), Hussein, Saleh & Mostafa (2020), Zhang, Yang & Wang (2020), Abbas et al. (2019); Venčkauskas et al. (2018)
Privacy	12	Aujla & Jindal (2020), Yu et al. (2020), Usman et al. (2019), slam et al. (2020), Wang et al. (2020), Zhang, Gao & Mu (2020), Tsaur & Yeh (2018), Batalla & Gonciarz (2018), Zhang et al. (2018), Ni, Lin & Shen (2018), El-Latif et al. (2018), Rahman et al. (2018)
Authentication	45	Zhaofeng et al. (2020), De Smet (2021), Pallavi & Kumar (2021), Kumar, Gupta & Tripathi (2021), Chen et al. (2021), Wu et al. (2021), Kumar & Chouhan (2021), Khalid et al. (2020), Zhang et al. (2020), Kumar et al. (2020), Hussein, Saleh & Mostafa (2020), Viejo & Sanchez (2020), Zeng et al. (2020), Maharaja, Iyer & Ye (2019), Puthal et al. (2020), Zhang et al. (2020), Junejo, Komninos & McCann (2020), Akkaoui, Hei & Cheng (2020), Cano & Canavate-Sanchez (2020), Ram et al. (2020), De Rango et al. (2020), Wazid et al. (2019), Hao & Wang (2019), Wazid et al. (2019), Ma et al. (2019), Rahman & Wen (2019), Lohachab (2019), Wang et al. (2018), Tsaur & Ye (2018), Batalla & Gonciarz (2019), Ren et al. (2019), Lu (2018), Gu et al. (2019), Tiburski et al. (2019), Liao et al. (2019), Sathyadevan et al. (2019), Abbas et al. (2019), Aman & Kausar (2019), Guan et al. (2019), Venckauskas et al. (2018), Ni, Lin & Shen (2018), Rahman et al. (2018), Koo & Hur (2018), Diro, Chilamkurti & Kumar (2017), Huang, Yang & Wang (2017)
Anonymity	4	Singh, Pan & Park (2021), Nawaz et al. (2020), Cui et al. (2020), Akkaoui, Hei & Cheng (2020)
Access Control	2	Junejo, Komninos & McCann (2020), Zhang, Yang & Wang (2020)

Table 3. Methods used for security

Method	Frequency	Reference
Hardware authentication based on PUFs	2	Moustafa et al. (2021), Barbareschi et al. (2019)
Machine Learning Techniques	3	Sairam et al. (2019), Maharaja, Iyer & Ye (2019), Shafi et al. (2018)
Proxy re-encryption	3	Khashan (2020), Feretti, Marchetti & Colajanni (2019), Diro, Chilamkurti & Nam (2018)
Encryption	13	Shi et al. (2020), Dar et al. (2020), Zhang, Gao & Mu (2020), Khashan (2020), Li et al. (2019), Rahman & Wen (2019), Boakye-Boateng et al. (2019), Feretti, Marchetti & Colajanni (2019), Li et al. (2019), Alabdulatif et al. (2019), Zhang et al. (2018), Diro, Chilamkurti & Nam (2018), Hu et al. (2017)
Key Exchange/Key Management Scheme/Protocol	10	Chen et al. (2021), Wu et al. (2021), Shi et al. (2020), Hsu et al. (2020), Chen et al. (2020), Wazid et al. (2019), Ma et al. (2019), Alshahrani & Traore (2019), Abbas et al. (2019), Alrawais et al. (2017)
Software-Defined Network (SDN)	8	Qureshi, Jeon & Piccialli (2021), Li et al. (2020), Hermosilla et al. (2020), Rathore, Kwon & Park (2019), Molina Zarca et al. (2019), Yan et al. (2018), Shafi et al. (2018), Sharma, Chen & Park (2017)
Blockchain-based solution	25	Zhaofeng et al. (2020), Aujla & Jindal (2020), Chen et al. (2021), Singh, Pan & Park (2021), Misra et al. (2020), Yang et al. (2020), Yu et al. (2020), Huang et al. (2020), Khalid et al. (2020), Zhaofeng et al. (2019), Alam et al. (2020), George & Thampi (2020), Zhang et al. (2020), Liu, Zhang & Zhan (2020), Kumar et al. (2020), Akkaoui, Hei & Cheng (2020), Saha et al. (2020), Liu et al. (2019), Rathore, Kwon & Park (2019), Pan et al. (2018), Ren et al. (2019), Jayasinghe et al. (2019), Rahman et al. (2019), Rahman et al. (2018), Sharma, Chen & Park (2017)
Data Aggregation Scheme	6	Khan et al. (2021), Zhang et al. (2020), Zeng et al. (2020), Zhang et al. (2020), Chen, You & Ruan (2020), Zhang et al. (2018)
Elliptic Curve Cryptography	5	AlMajed & AlMogren (2020), Rostampour et al. (2020), Cano & Canavate-Sanchez (2020), De Rango et al. (2020), Lohachab (2019)
Hybrid solution	6	Lawal, Shaikh & Hassan (2020), Hussein, Saleh & Mostafa (2020), Maharaja, Iyer & Ye (2019), Akkaoui, Hei & Cheng (2020), Khashan (2020), Ram et al. (2020)

DISCUSSION AND CONCLUSION

Though fog and edge computing seem to be more secure than traditional cloud computing, they do inherit some security issues. Because the edge nodes hold a lot of sensitive data, common cloud computing security approaches cannot be employed. Although the edge environment is more complex and more secure in comparison to cloud environments, this leads to more complicated security measures. Also, with end-user devices, privileges can change frequently, and this can make for an insecure environment (Li et al., 2019).

There are already other new extensions of cloud architecture such as mist computing (Suarez et al., 2018). In such a fast-changing and multiplying industry, securing devices and systems in order to enable knowledge creation and sharing is crucial. As new solutions arise, so will attack types.

This study reviewed the existing literature for edge/fog-based cybersecurity in IoT. The current studies have utilized new and innovative technologies such as Blockchain to ensure security within IoT. Machine learning techniques along with encryption have also been used to provide more secure and efficient data processing and storage within IoT.

Overall, looking at the findings of the study, it can be said that research is moving in the direction of securing the communication of devices within a network using new technologies such as Blockchain. The increase of studies conducted using fog and edge computing to move the computational power of the cloud to the edge of a network also brings along the necessity to secure these devices without comprising said computational power and speed.

LIMITATIONS

The main limitation could be the database used within the study. A future study could incorporate multiple databases to enlarge the article sample size. This brings about the second limitation being the number of articles reviewed. This is due to the screening criteria. This could be enhanced in future studies. The last limitation may be the number of variables extracted from the articles; these could be widened in future studies. Despite the limitations, the authors believe that the study will provide insight into the security problems and current fog/edge-based security in IoT.

REFERENCES

Abd El-Latif, A. A., Abd-El-Atty, B., Hossain, M. S., Elmougy, S., & Ghoneim, A. (2018). Secure quantum steganography protocol for fog cloud internet of things. *IEEE Access: Practical Innovations, Open Solutions*, *6*, 10332–10340. doi:10.1109/ACCESS.2018.2799879

Alshahrani, M., & Traore, I. (2019). Secure mutual authentication and automated access control for IoT smart home using cumulative Keyed-hash chain. *Journal of Information Security and Applications, 45*, 156-175.

Aman, W., & Kausar, F. (2019). Towards a gateway-based context-aware and self-adaptive security management model for IoT-based eHealth systems. *International Journal of Advanced Computer Science and Applications*, *10*(1), 280–287. doi:10.14569/IJACSA.2019.0100137

Andriole, S. J. (2014). *Ready technology: Fast tracking emerging business technologies.* CRC Press. doi:10.1201/b17468

Bai, C., Dallasega, P., Orzes, G., & Sarkis, J. (2020). Industry 4.0 technologies assessment: A sustainability perspective. *International Journal of Production Economics, 229,* 107776. doi:10.1016/j.ijpe.2020.107776

Barbareschi, M., De Benedictis, A., La Montagna, E., Mazzeo, A., & Mazzocca, N. (2019). A PUF-based mutual authentication scheme for Cloud-Edges IoT systems. *Future Generation Computer Systems, 101,* 246–261. doi:10.1016/j.future.2019.06.012

Batalla, J. M., & Gonciarz, F. (2019). Deployment of smart home management system at the edge: Mechanisms and protocols. *Neural Computing & Applications, 31*(5), 1301–1315. doi:10.100700521-018-3545-7

Boakye-Boateng, K., Kuada, E., Antwi-Boasiako, E., & Djaba, E. (2019). Encryption protocol for resource-constrained devices in fog-based IoT Using one-time pads. *IEEE Internet of Things Journal, 6*(2), 3925–3933. doi:10.1109/JIOT.2019.2893172

Boudi, A., Farris, I., Bagaa, M., & Taleb, T. (2019). *Assessing lightweight virtualization for security-as-a-service at the network edge.* Academic Press.

Celesti, A., Fazio, M., Galletta, A., Carnevale, L., Wan, J., & Villari, M. (2019). An approach for the secure management of hybrid cloud–edge environments. *Future Generation Computer Systems, 90,* 1–19. doi:10.1016/j.future.2018.06.043

Diro, A., Chilamkurti, N., & Nam, Y. (2018). Analysis of Lightweight Encryption Scheme for Fog-to-Things Communication. *IEEE Access: Practical Innovations, Open Solutions, 6,* 26820–26830. doi:10.1109/ACCESS.2018.2822822

Duan, H., Zheng, Y., Wang, C., & Yuan, X. (2019). Treasure collection on foggy islands: Building secure network archives for internet of things. *IEEE Internet of Things Journal, 6*(2), 2637–2650. doi:10.1109/JIOT.2018.2872461

Fedrecheski, G., De Biase, L. C., Calcina-Ccori, P. C., & Zuffo, M. K. (2018). Attribute-Based Access Control for the Swarm with Distributed Policy Management. *IEEE Transactions on Consumer Electronics, 65*(1), 90–98. doi:10.1109/TCE.2018.2883382

Ferretti, L., Marchetti, M., & Colajanni, M. (2019). Fog-based secure communications for low-power IoT devices. *ACM Transactions on Internet Technology, 19*(2), 1–21. doi:10.1145/3284554

Li, Y., Dong, Z., Sha, K., Jiang, C., Wan, J., & Wang, Y. (2019). TMO: Time Domain Outsourcing Attribute-Based Encryption Scheme for Data Acquisition in Edge Computing. *IEEE Access: Practical Innovations, Open Solutions, 7,* 40240–40257. doi:10.1109/ACCESS.2019.2907319

Lu, Y. (2017). Industry 4.0: A survey on technologies, applications and open research issues. *Journal of Industrial Information Integration, 6,* 1–10. doi:10.1016/j.jii.2017.04.005

Mejias, R. J., & Balthazard, P. A. (2014). A model of information security awareness for assessing information security risk for emerging technologies. *Journal of Information Privacy and Security, 10*(4), 160–185. doi:10.1080/15536548.2014.974407

Pacheco, J., & Hariri, S. (2018). Anomaly behavior analysis for IoT sensors. *Transactions on Emerging Telecommunications Technologies, 29*(4), e3188. doi:10.1002/ett.3188

Salkin, C., Oner, M., Ustundag, A., & Cevikcan, E. (2018). A conceptual framework for Industry 4.0. In *Industry 4.0: Managing the Digital Transformation* (pp. 3–23). Springer. doi:10.1007/978-3-319-57870-5_1

Sohal, A., Sandhu, R., Sood, S., & Chang, V. (2018). A cybersecurity framework to identify malicious edge device in fog computing and cloud-of-things environments. *Computers & Security, 74*, 340–354. doi:10.1016/j.cose.2017.08.016

Suárez-Albela, M., Fraga-Lamas, P., & Fernández-Caramés, T. M. (2018). A practical evaluation on RSA and ECC-based cipher suites for iot high-security energy-efficient fog and mist computing devices. *Sensors (Basel), 18*(1), 3868. doi:10.339018113868 PMID:30423831

Tankard, C. (2015). The security issues of the Internet of Things. *Computer Fraud & Security, 2015*(9), 11–14. doi:10.1016/S1361-3723(15)30084-1

Tsaur, W.-J., & Yeh, L.-Y. (2019). DANS: A Secure and Efficient Driver-Abnormal Notification Scheme with IoT Devices over IoV. *IEEE Systems Journal, 13*(2), 1628–1639. doi:10.1109/JSYST.2018.2883411

Venčkauskas, A., Morkevicius, N., Bagdonas, K., Damaševičius, R., & Maskeliūnas, R. (2018). A lightweight protocol for secure video streaming. *Sensors (Basel), 18*(5), 1554. doi:10.339018051554 PMID:29757988

Viejo, A., & Sánchez, D. (2019). *Secure and privacy-preserving orchestration and delivery of fog-enabled IoT services*. Academic Press.

West, M. A., & Altink, W. M. (1996). Innovation at work: Individual, group, organizational, and socio-historical perspectives. *European Journal of Work and Organizational Psychology, 5*(1), 3–11. doi:10.1080/13594329608414834

Xu, H., Ding, J., Li, P., & Wang, R. (2018). Edge computing-based security authentication algorithm for multiple RFID tags. *International Journal of Intelligent Information and Database Systems, 11*(2-3), 132–152. doi:10.1504/IJIIDS.2018.092000

Yusof, A. M., Hussin, N., Azman, K. A., Amran, N., Daud, S. C., & Tarmuchi, N. R. (2020). The Internet of Things (IOT): Impacts on Information Management Field. *International Journal of Academic Research in Business & Social Sciences, 10*(11), 1208–1216. doi:10.6007/IJARBSS/v10-i11/8197

Zhang, Y., Chen, X., Li, J., Wong, D. S., & Li, H. (2017). Ensuring attribute privacy protection and fast decryption for outsourced data security in mobile cloud computing. *information. The Sciences, 379*, 42–61.

Zhang, Y., Zhao, J., Zheng, D., Deng, K., Ren, F., Zheng, X., & Shu, J. (2018). Privacy-preserving data aggregation against false data injection attacks in fog computing. *Sensors (Basel), 18*(8), 1–16. doi:10.339018082659 PMID:30104516

This research was previously published in the Handbook of Research on Information and Records Management in the Fourth Industrial Revolution; pages 211-222, copyright year 2021 by Information Science Reference (an imprint of IGI Global).

Chapter 24
Programmable Implementation and Blockchain Security Scheme Based on Edge Computing Firework Model

Bao Yi Qin

College of Information Engineering, Nanjing XiaoZhuang University, China

Zheng Hao

College of Information Engineering, Nanjing XiaoZhuang University, China

Zhao Qiang

Department of Information Systems, Schulich School of Business, Canada

ABSTRACT

In cloud computing, since the program runs in cloud, it can be written in programming language and maintained only in the cloud after compilation. Due to the heterogeneous nature of the edge node platform, many tasks are migrated from the cloud to the edge terminal. It is not easy to realize the programming under the edge computing, and the maintenance cost is also high. At the same time, because the programmable is a high-risk activity, it has high security requirements. In order to solve this problem, this paper designs a programmable and blockchain security scheme based on the edge computing firework model, realizes the programming of the internet of things (IoT) gateway firework node under the edge computing, and appreciates the safe transmission and storage of programmable data through the blockchain system. The experimental results show that this scheme not only facilitates the user's programming, enhances the real-time performance, and saves the data transmission cost, but also ensures the security and reliability of the system.

DOI: 10.4018/978-1-6684-5700-9.ch024

1. INTRODUCTION

The unprecedent development of the Internet of Things (IoT) and the popularization of 5G network, has significantly increased the number of network edge devices. The centralized big data processing technology with cloud computing model as the core is not able to efficiently process the data generated by edge devices. Therefore, the edge data processing with the edge computing model as the core emerges as the need of the hour. The former generates a small amount of data computing, which is consistent with the existing centralized data processing with the latter as the core, and better solves the problems existing in the era of IoT.

In the cloud computing model, users write applications and deploy them to the cloud. User programs are usually written and compiled on the target platform, run on the cloud server, save or transfer data to the cloud, and finally process in the cloud. Based on this centralized data processing model, there are batch processing (Dean et al., 2008; Isard et al., 2007; Saha al., 2015; Zaharia al., 2010; Shvachko et al., 2010) and flow processing (Qian et al.,2013; Akidau et al., 2013; Apache storm 2016; Neumeyer et al., 2010; Kulkarni et al., 2015; IBM 2016; Zaharia et al., 2013) methods, and the application program can be centralized processing on the cloud platform. However, in the edge computing model, some or all the computing tasks are migrated from the cloud to the edge nodes, but most of the edge nodes are heterogeneous platforms, and the running environment of each node may be different. Therefore, while deploying user applications under the edge computing model, programmers encounter greater difficulties. The traditional programming method MapReduce, Spark and others are not suitable, so it is necessary to study a new programming method based on edge computing (Weisong et al., 2017).

In order to realize the programmability of edge computing, Hongjie et al. (2019) proposed a state perception model of building equipment based on edge computing. Xiong et al. (2019) studied the safety risk assessment method based on edge computing in the national grid. In terms of the task migration, Jia et al. (2019) suggested a task migration model for mobile edge computing. Xin-feng et al. (2019) advocated a dynamic resource allocation strategy in mobile edge computing environment. These models lack the programmable strategy of edge computing. Edge Computing: Platforms, Applications and Challenges (Ziming et al. 2018), and Near end Cloud Computing: opportunities and challenges in the post cloud computing era (Yuezhi et al. 2019), took programmability as the challenge of edge computing and showed the importance of edge computing programmability.

Hong et al. (2013) proposed a high-level programming model for future Internet applications, which has the characteristics of on-demand expansion, large-scale geographical location distribution and delay sensitivity. The programming model cloud aware proposed by Orsimi et al. (2015) estimates the connection state of the network through a context manager and splits the application and performs the uninstall by solving the optimization problem. Quan et al. (2016) suggested a new programming model based on edge computing firework model. Firework model is a kind of object-oriented programming model and has good generality. It extends the visualization boundary of data and provides a new programming model for data processing in collaborative edge environment (CEE). However, most of the current achievements are based on theoretical research, and the realization in the real environment is still unknown.

Since programmability is carried out on the network, it is easy to attack on the network, and the whole device will be paralyzed, so programmability is a high-risk activity, the entire system will crash after being attacked hence, more reliable security solutions need to be added to the application. Lamport (1981), first proposed a password authentication scheme within secure communication to solve the security problem of communication in insecure channel. However, the scheme has some disadvantages:

(1) it cannot resist replay attack and, (2) hash has a large amount of computation. Jaewook et al. (2018) suggested an efficient and secure password authentication scheme based on the smart card, which makes the smart card more secure by using cryptography technology. Qiushi et al. (2018) presented an identity authentication scheme based on the bio fuzzy extraction technology, which effectively avoided the common network attacks such as man in the middle attack but could not avoid password guessing attack. The emergence of blockchain technology solves the security problem. Blockchain technology first appeared in "bitcoin: a peer-to-peer electronic cash system" published by Nakamotos (2019), which details the characteristics of blockchain, such as decentralization, peer-to-peer transmission consensus mechanism and cryptography technology. Raju et al. (2017) preferred to use Ethereum's anonymous account wallet to realize identity management blockchain technology of network users through public key address. Cuong et al. (2020) proposed blockchain technique is considered as one of the major security methods to ensure a transparent communication among individuals. It can be used by various applications such as industries, marketing, transportation systems, etc. Dey et al. (2018) proposed cloud technology still faces security and authenticity issues, which have created an obstacle for adapting edge computing as a widespread technology. For the programmable security in edge computing, the blockchain scheme is an effective guarantee for programmable high-risk operations.

Aiming at the programmable and security problems under the edge computing architecture, this paper designs the programmable and blockchain security scheme of firework model, realizes the programmable of IoT gateway (edge node), which has obvious effect on reducing communication data flow and system maintenance; at the same time, the blockchain security transmission and storage are adopted to ensure the safety and reliability of the system.

Section 2 introduces the firework model structure under the edge computing architecture; section 3 describes the blockchain technology and its key features; section 4 defines programmable firework model and blockchain security scheme and makes the application of the programmable strategy in the remote automatic monitoring platform system; section 5 tests and compares the systems under three different architectures; and finally, section 6 summarizes the full text.

2. FIREWORK MODEL STRUCTURE

In the era of IoT, many data production and consumption need to be transferred from the cloud to the edge devices, which increases the requirements for the distributed sharing and processing of big data. Therefore, a firework model is proposed, which can realize the distributed sharing and processing of big data, and enable private data to be processed on the devices of data stakeholders (such as firework nodes).

Firework model (Quan et al. 2016)) is a programming model based on edge computing, which mainly includes two parts: firework manager and firework node, as shown in Figure 1. Firework model promotes geographically distributed data sources by creating virtual shared data views, while data stakeholders (firework model nodes) provide a level of predefined functional interface for end users to access.

The interface form of firework model is a set of data sets and functions, as shown in Figure 1. The function is bound with the data set. The data processing of firework model is closer to the data producer, avoiding the long-distance data transmission from the network edge device to the cloud center, and reducing the subject delay. In the firework model, all the data use the relevant devices (firework model nodes), need to register their own data sets and corresponding functions to abstract into a unified data view. The registered data view is not visible to all the participants in the same firework model. Any participant can combine multiple views to realize data analysis in a specific situation. The firework model manager decomposes the service request of the combined data view. It is divided into several subtasks and sent to each participant. Each subtask performs corresponding calculation tasks on its local device.

Figure 1. Overall structure of firework model

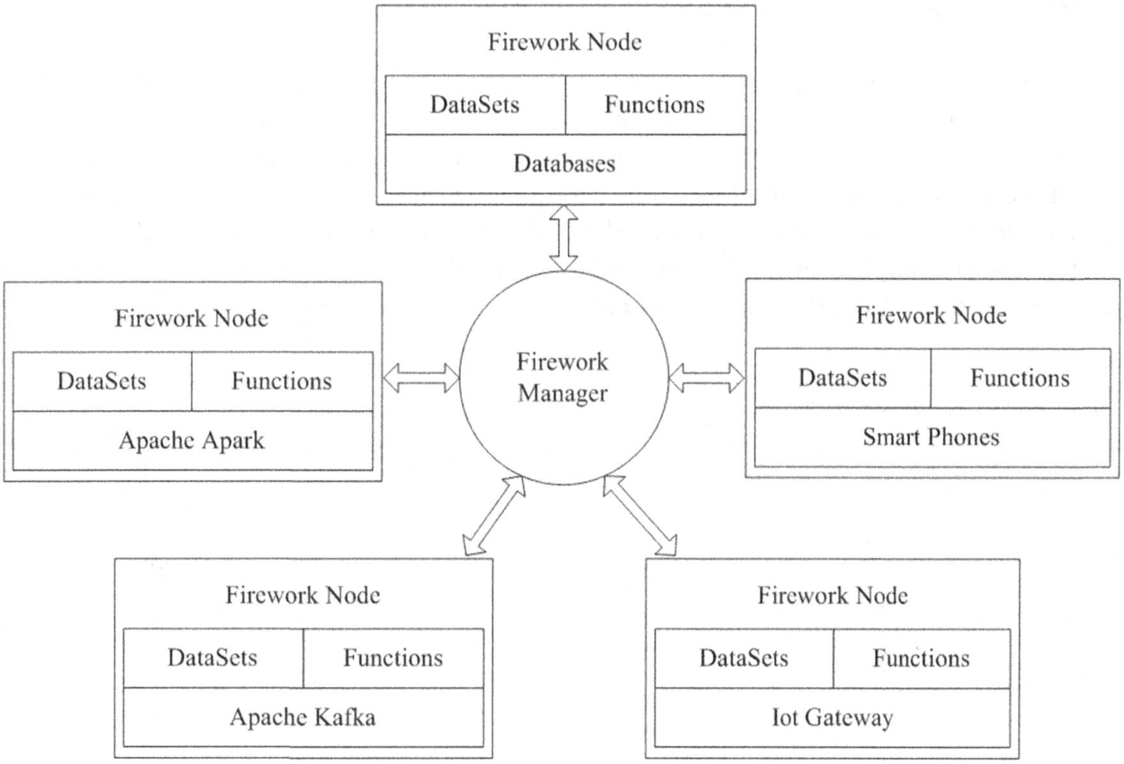

3. BLOCKCHAIN TECHNOLOGY

In essence, the blockchain is a distributed shared ledger, which is jointly maintained by all nodes currently involved in transactions and databases. It makes the transaction based on the principle of cryptography, so that any agreed parties can directly conduct the transaction without the participation of a third party(Zhaopeng et al., 2019). Blockchain has four key features.

3.1. Decentralized Network

In the network based on blockchain, there is no centralized node or management organization, and all nodes in the same position constitute a decentralized network. Each node has a record of all database information. When a node receives data from another node, the node verifies the identity information of the other node. If the verification is successful, the information it receives will be broadcast to the whole network. The verification, storage, maintenance and transmission of data in the blockchain network are all based on the distributed system structure, which uses mathematical methods rather than central institutions to establish trust between the nodes (Yong et al., 2016; Aadroul et al., 2018). Therefore, blockchain technology has a better optimization effect on the physical problem centered structure of the IoT. By using the characteristics of blockchain, decentralization can improve the existing state of data storage centralization and architecture centralization, reduce the dependence of the system on the center structure, and effectively improve the response speed and security of the whole system (Zhen et al., 2019).

3.2. Trusted Blockchain Structure

A block consists of block header and block body, as shown in Figure 2. The block header of each block contains the block hash value, the hash value of the previous block, the Merkel hash value generated by the transaction order No. TX ID, the transaction single number, the timestamp of the generated block (time, the public key of the generated block and the digital signature for signing the block header). Each block contains a policy header (Dorri et al., 2017) and several transaction orders. A blockchain is connected by blocks through "chain". The hash value of the block head links each block with the previous block to ensure the immutability of the block data and the timing of the data.

Figure 2. Block structure

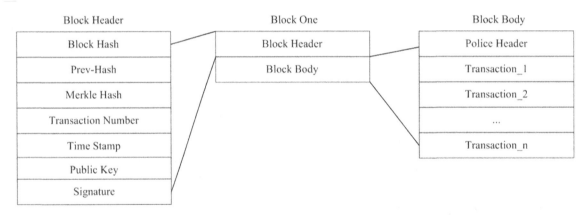

In the blockchain network, any operation identification (registration, login and data transmission) will generate a transaction and attach the transaction number (TX ID), which will be recorded in the block by consensus mechanism.

A block must contain the SHA256 hash value of the previous block head, which ensures that the file is basically impossible to tamper with. If a block is tampered, the hash value of all subsequent blocks must be changed. And each block contains the timestamp at the time of creation, which also ensures that the blocks are orderly linked in time. At the same time, in order to achieve the consensus, the blockchain adopts the workload proof mechanism. The workload is proved by the random number in the block. Through the above protocols and algorithms, the blockchain has realized a distributed, transparent and secure database(Yu et al., 2020) .

3.3. "Smart Contract" Management Mechanism

The concept of "smart contract" in blockchain was proposed by Nick Szabo, who interpreted "Smart contract" as a set of contracts defined in digital form (Buterin 2014). From the user's point of view, the "Smart contract" is usually considered as an automatic guarantee program Whereas, from technical point of view, it is considered as network servers. These servers are not set up on the Internet, but on the blockchain, so that specific contract programs can be run on these servers.

"Smart contract" is a kind of programmable contract, which can transform the contracts of the two parties that need to interact into the form of a code, store it in the blockchain, and mark it with a unique blockchain address. When the conditions of contract establishment are met, the code contract will be executed automatically. A smart contract is an important reason why blockchain is called "decentralized". They allow us to execute traceable, irreversible and secure transactions without the need for a third party.

3.4. Consensus Algorithm

The consensus algorithm adopts the practical Byzantine fault tolerance (PBFT) algorithm(Castro et al., 2002) . PBFT comes from the Byzantine general problem and is a fictitious model used to analyze the consistency problem. The practical Byzantine fault tolerant consensus mechanism was proposed by Miguel and Barbara in 1999. The specific steps are as follows:

1. Request: each node of the client sends a service operation request.
2. Pre - prepare: the master node broadcasts the request to the backup node.
3. Prepare: the replica node sends the validation result of the pre-prepared message to the primary node and other replica nodes.
4. Commit: when the master node and the replica node receive $2F + 1$ (F is the number of tolerated Byzantine nodes) consistent preparation messages, execute the request and send the results to the client.
5. Reply: after receiving $F + 1$ identical replies, the client determines that the message is acknowledged and executed by all replica nodes, so the consensus ends.

The process of PBFT algorithm(Wankai et al., 2020) is shown in Figure 3.

4. PROGRAMMABLE FIREWORK MODEL AND BLOCKCHAIN SECURITY SCHEME

4.1 Firework Model Programmable Blockchain Scheme Architecture

The firework model programmable blockchain scheme is applied in firework model blockchain system (FMBS), FMBS mainly includes four parts: firework manager, firework node, blockchain system and cloud platform. 1) Firework manager refers to the remote centralized manager unit (RCU), which mainly realizes the management of firework nodes, the realization of blockchain transactions and programmable security management functions; 2) Firework node refers to remote terminal unit (RTU), which is a high-performance measurement and control device for signal acquisition and processing, as well as the 1o

Figure 3. The PBFT algorithm process

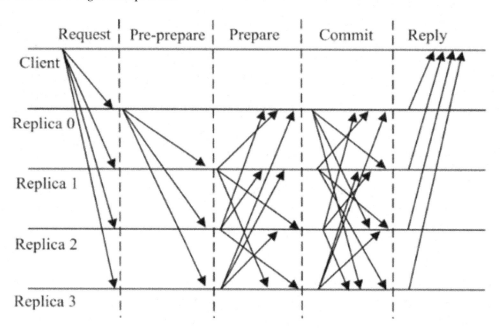

signal control of some devices; 3) Blockchain system is a blockchain platform system running on the covering network and cloud platform is the network; 4) Platform is responsible for the management and Application. The overall structure of the system is shown in Figure 4.

Blockchain technology is used in the architecture to effectively solve the security problems in traditional centralized way. The blockchain encryption scheme of firework model mainly has two stages: authentication and programming (trading), as shown in Figure 5. In the authentication stage, users input authentication information. In the decentralized network, using cryptography technology and consensus mechanism, authentication information is stored on each node of the blockchain in the form of transaction. In the programming stage, programmable data information is stored in the blockchain in the form of transaction, and the programmable data information is transmitted to the firework node through the security channel.

4.2 Firework Manager

Firework model programmable blockchain system corresponding to specific application: remote automatic monitoring system based on edge computing firework model is shown in Figure 4. Firework model is mainly composed of firework manager and firework node, one of which is IoT gateway, defined as RTU. The firework manager is a concentrator, defined as an RCU.

The management of RCU primarily includes block header and block body as shown in Figure 6. The block body includes policy header and several transaction orders. While block header is a structure used to ensure the security and integrity of blockchain information.

Figure 4. Firework model programmable blockchain system architecture

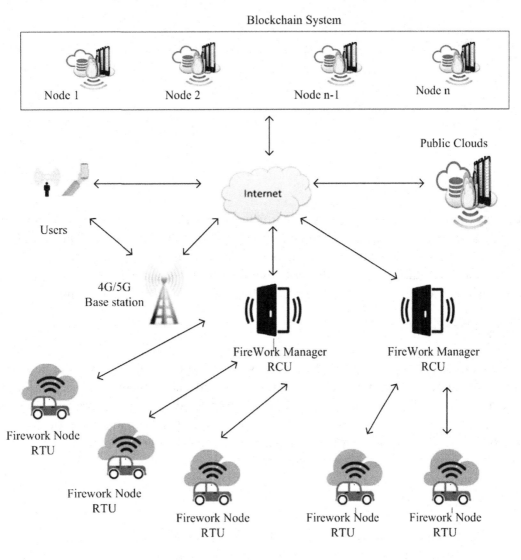

Figure 5. Data flow of firework model blockchain encryption scheme

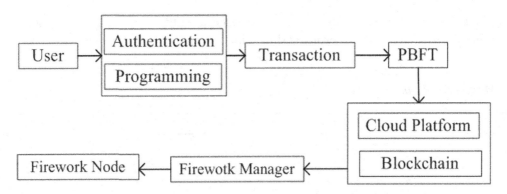

Figure 6. Composition of block

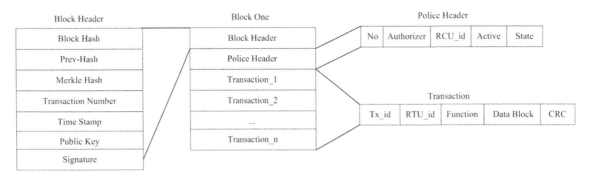

Authority control head is used to provide data structure foundation for fine-grained authority control of equipment room in dynamic environment monitoring system. The data structure includes serial number, authorizer, authorized action, authorized equipment, status and other information. Authorizer includes but is not limited to authorizing to single entity user or specific user group. Authorization actions are based on business requirements (Jianfeng et al., 2019). There are three main functions:

4.2.1. Rights Management

RCU authority management completes the authority control through authority control header, which includes record number (No), authorizer, RCU_ID, active and state. Function is a very important part of the remote automatic monitoring system. RCU is the basic equipment for managing RTU and the carrier of information collection and control. Its security is directly related to the security of the whole system. RCU authority management mainly involves two aspects: user access management authority and equipment communication authority management.

4.2.2. Storage Management

The storage management of the RCU also includes the transaction list. The transaction list stores and manages the message data of the RCU, including the transaction number (TX_ ID) and the Modbus message. The Modbus data format is the most basic component of the remote automatic monitoring system. The storage structure is illustrated in Figure 6.

RTU has the electrical characteristics of serial interface and Ethernet interface, and adopts Modbus specification. The Modbus protocol format is shown in Table 1.

Table 1. Modbus protocol format

Device Adress	Function	Data_Adress	DATA	CRC

4.2.3. Data Forwarding

RCU is a centralized manager to manage RTU, which is connected with RTU through communication interface and sends the user's command to RTU safely. Modbus protocol is adopted for specific communication protocol.

4.3 Firework Node

Firework node corresponds to IoT gateway, which is defined as RTU. RTU is connected with many signal input / output modules (such as DI-switch input, DO-switch output, AI-analog input, AO-analog output), but the internal logic relationship between them needs to be programmed according to the site conditions, and even if multiple RTUs want to achieve linkage, they need to realize PLC (programmable logic) function by means of software definition controller (programmable logic controller). Because of the high price of PLC terminal, it is difficult to master the PLC terminal, and the programming of PLC requires certain programming basis, so RTU is used as the remote terminal unit, and PLC function is realized at the same time. However, the remote automatic monitoring system based on the cloud platform cannot efficiently process the data generated by the RTU through the centralized control of the cloud platform, so it is necessary to use the RTU as the edge device to realize the programmability. As a result, a software defined strategy through HTML file is designed, and the RTU is used as a firework node (IoT gateway).

4.3.1 Interface of Firework Node

The interface form of firework model is a set of datasets and functions. The specific functions of firework node RTU are defined as five scheme types, which constitute five functions. According to the functional requirements of PLC, the following five schemes can be defined (not limited to this, expandable): 1) input scheme 2) change scheme 3) timing scheme 4) times scheme 5) conversion scheme, as shown in Figure 7.

Each scheme has a set of datasets. Each scheme is composed of scheme expression, which consists of two parts: condition expression and result expression. Condition / result expression consists of multiple linked lists or a single linked list, and multiple linked lists consist of a single linked list. Therefore, as long as a single linked list is defined, the firework node interface can be defined.

4.3.1.1. Firework Node Functions Definition

According to the internal logic function requirements of RTU, the functions of firework node can be defined by five schemes (not limited to this). The contents of five schemes are as follows: 1) input scheme: takes the defined switch input or analog input as the condition, if the condition is met, define the switch output or analog output; 2) change scheme: takes the change of switch input as the condition, If the conditions are met, the defined switch output or analog output; 3) timing scheme: the defined timer time (seconds) and signal input are used as timing and input conditions; if the conditions are met, the switch output or analog output are defined; 4) frequency scheme: the number of defined signal input is used as input conditions; if the conditions are met, the switch output is defined output or analog output; 5) conversion scheme: the maximum range MX, analog reference JZ and analog range reference MZ are defined as the input conditions. If the conditions are met, the output of analog quantity is defined as $((AI-JZ) * MX) / (MZ-JZ)$, so as to realize the conversion function.

Figure 7. IoT gateway firework node interface

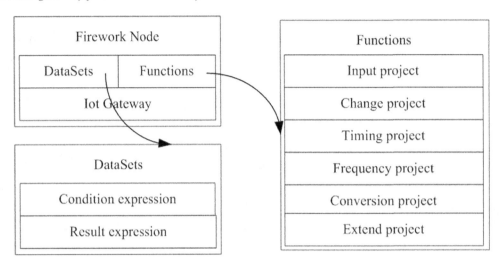

4.3.1.2. Firework Node Datasets Definition

Each function of RTU is defined by scheme expression, and the datasets of firework node corresponds to scheme expression. The scheme expression consists of condition expression and result expression. The condition / result expression consists of multiple linked lists or a single linked list, and multiple linked lists consist of a single linked list. A single linked list is defined as follows:

1. A single linked list: Register (REG), Number (NUM), Operator (OP), Register value (REV), as shown in Figure 8.

Figure 8. Condition expression and result expression

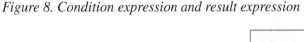

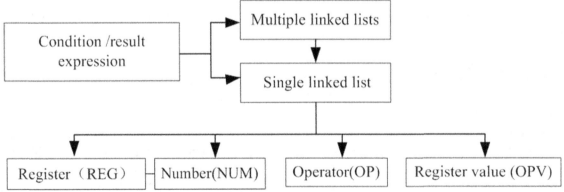

2. The single linked list has 5 bytes in total, and the number of bytes in each data field of the single chain table is shown in Table 2. The multi linked list consists of n single linked lists with a total of 5*N bytes.

Table 2. Bytes of the single linked list data field

REG	NUM	OP	REV
1	1	1	2

3. The single linked list data field definition:
   a. Register (REG) definition, as shown in Table 3.

Table 3. Definition of REG

Name	Meaning	Value
DI	Switching value input	0
AI	Analog input	1
DO	Switching value output	2
AO	Analog output	3
TM	Timer	4
CS	Switching input times	5
MX	Maximum of analog	6
JZ	Analog reference	7
MZ	Analog range reference	8

   b. Number (NUM) definition:

   The range from 0 to 255.

   c. Operator (OP) definition, as shown in Table 4.

Table 4. Definition of OP

OP	Representative	value
=	equal	0
>	greater	1
<	less	2
!	not equal	3

   d. Register value (REV) definition:

   The range is 0-0xffff, occupying 2 bytes, from low to high.

4.3.2 Software Definition of Firework Node

RTU receives the Modbus message of the master station through the network port, reads the data in the scheme data area, and translates it into the scheme condition expression and result expression in turn. RTU judges that when the condition expression is met, the result expression will be executed automatically thus, realizing the function of software definable programming. The process from data to function of RTU is shown in Figure 9.

Figure 9. Process from data to function of RTU

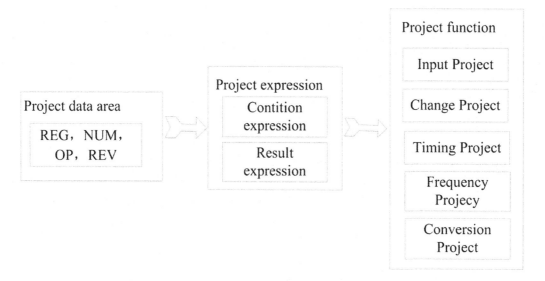

According to the requirements of the system, the software of the firework node RTU can be defined and programmed by HTML file. A complete set of specific system software can be defined and programmed steps, mainly including three parts: HTML file (responsible for defining the internal logic scheme of RTU), python software (responsible for scheme feature extraction, data packaging and downloading), RTU software (responsible for scheme saving and running logic scheme), such as Figure 10.

The implementation process includes the following 6 steps:

1. HTML file definition scheme: the scheme definition is realized by an HTML file, which can be edited by a text editor and opened and browsed by a browser. All schemes are saved in HTML file, and each scheme corresponds to table. According to the programming strategy, each table stores scheme expressions, which are composed of condition expressions and result expressions, and condition expressions and result expressions are composed of linked list expressions. Corresponding to each requirement in 4.1, five schemes are defined by HTML file as follows:

```
1) Input scheme
Condition expression:<th>DI2:=1</th>
Result expression:<td>DO4:=0,DO5:=0,DO6:=0,DO7:=0</td>
```

```
Condition expression:<th>AI2:>75</th>
Result expression:<td>DO8:=0</td>
2) Change scheme
Condition expression:<th>DI3:!0</th>
Result expression:<td>DO9:=1</td>
3) Timing scheme
Condition expression:<th>TM1:=5,AI3:>25</th>
Result expression:<td>DO10:=1,AO10:=22</td>
4) Frequency scheme
Condition expression:<th>DI0:=1,CS0:=2</th>
Result expression:<td>DO20:=0</td>
Condition expression:<th>DI0:=1,CS1:=4</th>
Result expression:<td>DO21:=0</td>
Condition expression:<th>DI0:=1,CS2:=6</th>
Result expression:<td>DO22:=0</td>
5) Conversion scheme
Condition expression:<th>MX5:=5000,JZ5:=196,MZ5:=993</th>
Result expression:<td>AO5:=1</td>
```

Figure 10. Software definition programmable steps

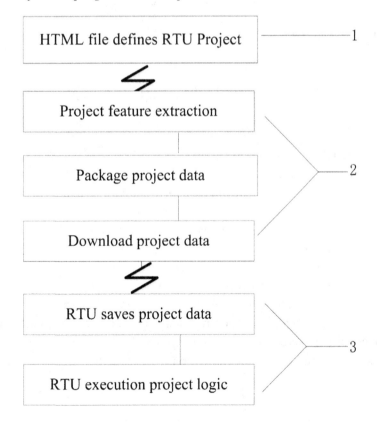

Through IE, open the HTML visualization interface, as shown in Figure 11:

Figure 11. Software definable interface example

Input scheme	
DI2:=1	DO4:=0,DO5:=0,DO6:=0,DO7:=0
AI2:>75	DO8:=0

Change scheme	
DI3:!0	DO9:=1

Timing scheme	
TM1:=5,AI3:>25	DO10:=1,AO10:=22

Frequency scheme	
DI0:=1,CS0:=2	DO20:=0
DI0:=1,CS1:=4	DO21:=0
DI0:=1,CS2:=6	DO22:=0

Conversion scheme	
MX5:=5000,JZ5:=196,MZ5:=993	AO5:=0

2. Scheme feature extraction: extract scheme name according to HTML tag table; extract condition expression according to tag th; extract result expression according to tag td.

3. Package scheme data: generate scheme data block = number of condition data + condition data + number of result data + result data. Package into Modbus message. Modbus protocol format: address + function code + number of schemes + scheme data block + CRC check code.

4. Scheme data download: RTU has the electrical characteristics of serial interface and Ethernet interface, which can download Modbus messages locally and remotely.

5. RTU scheme data saving: RTU receives Modbus message through serial port or network port. If CRC is correct, the scheme data is saved in different scheme data areas.

6. RTU execution scheme logic: RTU regularly reads the data in the scheme data area and translates it into scheme condition expression and result expression. When the condition expression is met, RTU automatically executes the result expression thus, realizing the software definable programming function.

4.4 Programmable Blockchain Security Scheme

The programmable blockchain security scheme of firework model is used to realize the safe transmission and preservation of the programmable scheme of firework model through the blockchain system, mainly involving: encryption method, blockchain authentication process, and the blockchain transmission process of the programmable scheme.

4.4.1 Encryption Method

Asymmetric encryption algorithm: Both sides disclose an integer g and a prime N. First, a private key x and y are generated respectively, and their public keys X and Y are calculated, and X and Y are exchanged with each other. Secondly, after the public key exchange, the two sides calculate the key K and G for encryption and decryption, and the result is the same. In this way, the communication parties encrypt and decrypt the message through the key K and G, so as to realize the encrypted transmission of data. The theoretical basis is: the complexity of discrete logarithm calculation, it is known that $X= g^x \bmod N$, it is not feasible to find x directly.

4.4.2 Certification Process

The user authentication flow chart in the system is shown in Figure 12.

Step 1: U initially determines two parameters g, N, randomly generates its own private key x, and calculates X = gen (g,x, n). define gen (g, x, n) = $g^x \bmod N$, and X is the public key of U.

Step 2: U sends g, N and X to cloud platform S through secure channel.

U=>S:{g,N,X}

Step 3: S randomly generates its own private key y, and calculates Y= gen (g, y, N),Y is the public key of S, Calculate encryption key G at the same time, G==gen(X, y, N)=$x^y \bmod N= g^{xy} \bmod N$.

Step 4: S transmits the public key Y to u through the secure channel.

S=>U:{Y}

Step 5: U calculates the encryption key K according to the Y transmitted from S

K= $y^x \bmod N= g^{xy} \bmod N$

Step 6: U input the user ID, password PW, and encrypt (ID, PW) by the encryption key K, C=E(ID, PW,K),U passes

ID and C to S through secure channel.

U->S:{ID,C}

Step 7: S decrypts C from U with encryption key G.

1) ID,PW=Z (C, G)

2) Find ID in database, check PW and PW in database is equal or not.

3) Calculating user ID address with hash operation, Uaddr=H (ID, PW).

4) Computing digital signature with key G, S=sign (Uaddr, G).

Step 8: S transmits the user ID address Uaddr to U through the security channel.

S=>U:{Uaddr}

Step 9: S transmits the user ID address(Uaddr),timestamp(T), public key(P), digital signature(S) and block(B_hash) to blockchain system(B).

S=>B:{Uaddr,T,T,S,B_hash}

Step 10: B form a transaction list of blockclain and save it to each blockclain node.

Figure 12. Authentication flow chart of User

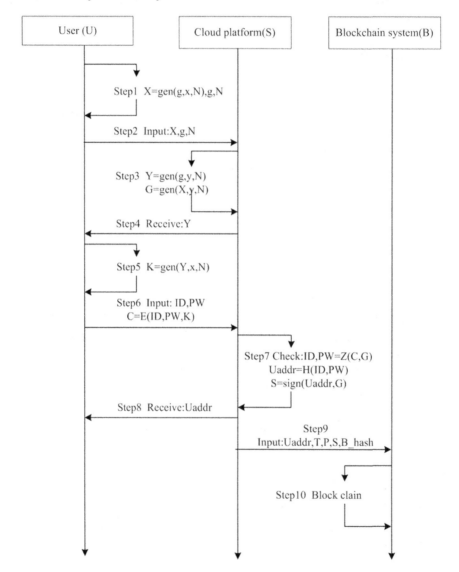

4.4.3 Programmable Data Blockchain Transmission Process

The user's programmable data transmission flow chart is shown in Figure 13.

Step 1: U input the user address (Uaddr), the firework manager address (RCU_ID), the programmable packet (P_data) of firework model, S transmit them to S.

U=>S:{Uaddr, RCU_id, P_data}

Step 2: S check if Uaddr is equal to Uaddr of database,Computing digital signature with key G, S=sign
(Uaddr,G)

Step 3: S transmit the user ID address (Uaddr),timestamp(T), public key(P), digital signature(S) and
block (B_hash) to blockchain system(B).

S=>B:{Uaddr,T,T,S,B_hash}

Step 4: B Forms a transaction list of block clain and save it to each block clain node.

Step 5: S transmit Police_head and Transaction to RCU through the security channel.

S=>RCU:{Police_head,Transaction}

Step 6: RCU check RCU_id is consistent with its own, parse the programming package(P_data) from
the transaction.

Step 7: RCU transmit the programming package(P_data) to RTU through the security channel.

Step 8: RTU checks whether CRC verification is correct and saves programmable data package (P_ data).

Step 9: RTU transmit Ack_data to RCU through the security channel.

RTU=>RCU:{Ack_data}

Step 10: RCU transmit Ack_data to S through the security channel.

RCU=>S:{Ack_data}

Step 11: S transmit Ack_data to U through the security channel.

S=>U:{Ack_data}

5. TESTING AND COMPARISON

Apply the programmable and blockchain security scheme of firework model to the system, test and compare on the remote automatic monitoring system, combined with the traditional cloud architecture system and edge computing architecture system, in the same hardware and network environment, mainly from two aspects: 1) Communication data flow; 2) Programmable, security and other performance indicators.

First, the definition is: the total number of edge node RTU is N, the number of changing RTU (indicating that he state changes) is K, the average number of changes is k1, the number of linked RTU (indicating that the state changes need to be linked) is G, and the average number of links is g1. Set the system to run for 3 days and poll once in 5 minutes, then the polling times are 24 * 12 * 3 = 864 times, the data flow of each status packet is L = 50 bytes, and the total data flow of heartbeat packet is H = 24 * 6 * 10 * 3 = 4320 (heartbeat once in 10 minutes, heartbeat six times in one hour, heartbeat message 10 bytes). The communication data flow formula of three systems running for three days is as follows:

Figure 13. Programmable blockchain flowchart of User

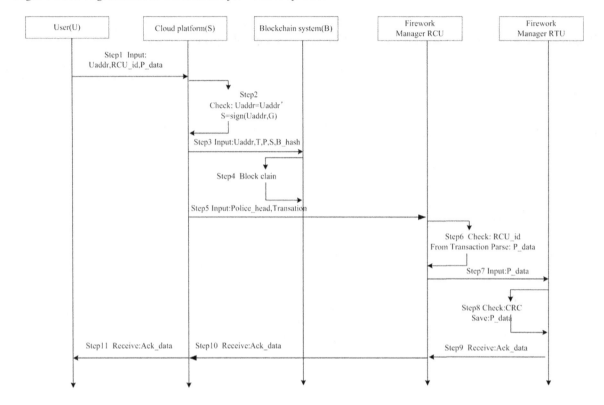

1. The communication data flow formula under the traditional cloud computing architecture (because cloud computing keeps polling, it has polled once in 5 minutes and 864 times in 3 days, so there is no need for heartbeat):

$$Z1=(N*864+G*g1)*L \tag{1}$$

2. The communication data flow formula under edge computing architecture:

$$Z2=(K*k1+G*g1)*L+H \tag{2}$$

3. The communication data flow formula of firework model is applied:

$$Z3=K*k1*L+H \tag{3}$$

From (2) and (3), Z2 is larger than Z3, and the data of G * G1 * l is larger, so Z3 is much smaller than Z2; From (1) and (2), because K is less than N (not all RTU states change), k1 is less than 864 (RTU state changes are few in 5 minutes), H value is not very large, so Z2 less than Z1. From the above, Z3 is much smaller than Z2 and Z1, under the edge computing firework model architecture, the data flow will be lesser than the traditional edge computing architecture and edge computing architecture. At the same time, since the RTU linkage of edge computing firework model architecture need not be completed through the cloud platform, it can be realized only through the definition and programming of RTU software to complete the local linkage function, which greatly increases the real-time performance; the user can define the linkage function at any time, which is easy to maintain; in addition, as the data uploaded by communication often needs to be stored in the cloud therefore, in the edge architecture, the amount of cloud data storage also gets substantially reduced as compared to the traditional ones and releases the storage pressure on the cloud platform.

In the remote automatic monitoring system test with the same hardware, software and network environment, through the upgrade and transformation of the three architectures respectively, run the test, statistics of the data transmission flow in three days results are shown in Table 5.

Table 5. Comparison of data flow test of three architectures

Residential	RTU N	Change RTU		Linkage RTU		Cloud (Mb)	Edge (Mb)	Firework (Mb)
		K	k1	G	g1			
TianRun	182	120	50	63	45	8.342	1.020	0.540
Mingfa	157	110	59	72	42	7.148	0.779	0.414
QiaoBai	95	81	56	57	51	4.371	0.534	0.268
ChuangYi	125	90	66	71	53	5.738	0.705	0.367
XinJaiKo	168	150	55	80	45	7.648	0.885	0.495
Total	727	636	323	583	316	33.247	3.923	2.084

According to the test results in Table 5, the comparison curves of the three architectures, the number of RTU in operation corresponding to the X axis and the corresponding data transmission flow corresponding to the Y axis, are depicted in Figure 14:

It is evident from the above figure that the data flow of edge computing and firework model is greatly reduced, indicating the importance of edge computing. From the summary of the statistical results in Table 5, cloud computing flow: 33.247 Mb, edge computing: 3.923Mb, firework model: 2.084Mb, edge computing system data flow is 11.8% of cloud computing system, firework model system data flow is 53.1% of edge computing system, and the firework model architecture system data flow is the lowest. The analysis results show that after the introduction of firework model into the edge calculation, the software of RTU can be defined and programmed to achieve substantial traffic reduction.

Combined with the system performance indicators: 1) data flow, 2) real-time, 3) programmability. Data flow comparison: as can be seen from Figure 14; Real-time comparison: cloud computing need to communicate back and forth, with poor real-time performance. Edge computing is controlled locally, but if there is a linkage, it needs to go through the server, with medium real-time performance. The linkage of firework model is defined locally, with the best real-time performance. Programmable comparison: cloud computing is easy to be realized in the cloud, and firework model is easy to implement by software definition method, whereas, the edge computing programmability is not easy to implement on each RTU. The performance comparison of the three architectures is shown in Table 6.

Figure 14. Data flow comparison curve of three architectures

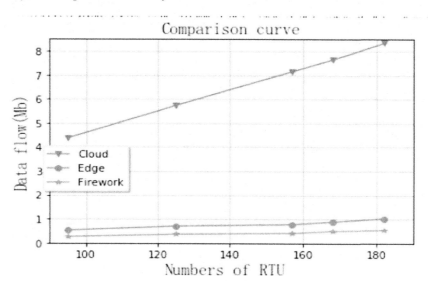

Table 6. Performance comparison of three architectures

System Performance	Cloud Computing	Edge Computing	Firework Model
Data flow	Big	Small	Small
Real-time	Bad	Medium	Good
Programmability	Easy	Not easy	Easy

In addition, due to the low data flow of the system using the firework model, the storage pressure of the cloud platform is relieved, so the storage capacity of the cloud data is greatly reduced as compared to the traditional one, and the power consumption due to data transmission is also reduced. Through the above testing and comparison, the application of firework model programmable strategy in edge computing achieves ideal results, while using the blockchain security transmission and storage it ensures the security of the system.

6. CONCLUSION

In this paper, the edge computing firework node model and blockchain security scheme are designed to solve the programming and security problems of edge computing firework nodes. The test results show that the firework model programmable blockchain security scheme not only increases the programmability of firework nodes, reduces the programming difficulty and reduces the communication flow, but also enhances the security of the system through the block chain security transmission and storage because programming is a high-risk activity. In addition to the application of the monitoring system, the scheme can also provide a good programming security idea and scheme for other edge computing systems.

In our future research, we will apply the edge computing firework node model and blockchain security scheme to other Iot fields and study a general edge computing programmable security platform to enhance security, integrity and availability.

ACKNOWLEDGMENT

This work is supported by Natural Science Foundation Project of China (61976118), Natural Science Foundation Project of Jiangsu Province (BK20180142), key topics of the '13th five-year plan' for Education Science in Jiangsu Province (B-b /2020/01/18).

REFERENCES

Aadroul Aki, E., Manevich, Y., & Muralidharan. (2018). Hyperledger fabric: a distributed operating system for pe missioned blockchains. *The Thirteenth EuroSys Conference*, 1-15.

Akidau, T., Balikov, A., Bekiroglu, K., Chernyak, S., Haberman, J., Lax, R., McVeety, S., Mills, D., Nordstrom, P., & Whittle, S. (2013). Millwheel: Fault tolerant stream processing at internet scale. *Proceedings of the VLDB Endowment International Conference on Very Large Data Bases*, 6(11), 1033–1044.

Apache Storm. (2016). Retrieved from https://storm.apache.org/

Buterin, V. (2014). *A next generation smart contract and decentralized application platform*. White Paper.

Castro, M., & Liskov, B. (2002). Practical Byzantine fault tolerance and proactive recovery. *ACM Transactions on Computer Systems*, 20(1), 398–161.

Cuong, N. H. H., Kumar, G., & Solanki, V. K. (2020). Blockchain-Based Digital Rights Management Techniques. Large-Scale Data Streaming, Processing, and Blockchain Security, 168-180.

Dean, J., & Ghemawat, S. (2008). Mapreduce: Simplifified data processing on large clusters. *Communications of the ACM*, 51(1), 107–113. doi:10.1145/1327452.1327492

Dey, S., Solanki, V. K., & Sen, S. K. (2018). SVM—A Way to Measure the Trust Ability of a Cloud Service Based on Rank. *International Conference on Communications and Cyber Physical Engineering*. 105-113.

Dorri, A., Kanhere, S., & Jurdak, R. (2017). Blockchain for IoT security and privacy: The case study of smart home. *2017 IEEE International Conference on Pervasive Computing and Communications Workshops*, 5-17.

Hong, K., Lillethun, D., & Ramachandran, U. (2013). Mobile fog: A programming model for large-scale application on the Internet of Things. *The 2nd ACM Sigcomm Workshop on Mobile Cloud Computing*, 15-20.

Hongjie, W., Huaxiang, S., Huajing, L., Qiming, F., Weizhong, L., & Baochuan, F. (2019). Construction Equipment State Perception Model and Application Based on Edge Computing. *CEA*, 55(18), 263–270.

IBM. (2016). *IBM infosphere streams*. Retrieved from www.ibm.com/software/products/en/infosphere-streams

Isard, M., Budiu, M., Yu, Y., Birrell, A., & Fetterly, D. (2007). Dryad: Distributed data-parallel programs from sequential building blocks. *Operating Systems Review*, *41*(3), 59–72. doi:10.1145/1272998.1273005

Jaewook,, J., DongHoon, L., Hakjun, L., & Dongho, W. (2018). Security Enhanced Anonymous User Authenticated Key Agreement Scheme Using Smart Card. *Journal of Electronic Science and Technology*, *16*(1), 45–19.

Jia, Y., Xin-jie, G., & Guang-wei, B. (2019). Task Offloading and Cooperative Load Balancing Mechanism Based on Mobile Edge Computing. *Computer Science*, *46*(12), 126–131.

Jianfeng, F., Yi, L., Wenyuan, W., & Yong, F. (2019). Mobile environment information monitoring system of base station based on dual blockchain. *Computer Science*, *46*(12), 155–164.

Kulkarni, S., Bhagat, N., Fu, M., Kedigehalli, V., Kellogg, C., Mittal, S., Patel, J. M., Ramasamy, K., & Taneja, S. (2015). Twitter heron: Stream processing at scale. *The 2015 ACM SIGMOD International Conference on Management of Data*, 239–250.

Lamport, L. (1981). Password authentication with in secure comnication. *Communications of the ACM*, 770–772.

Nakamotos. (2019). *Bitcoin: A Peer-to-Peer Electronic Cash System*. Retrieved from https:// bitcoin. Org/bitcoin.pdf

Neumeyer, R. B., Nair, A., & Kesari, A. (2010). S4: Distributed stream computing platform. *Data Mining Workshops (ICDMW), 2010 IEEE International Conference on*, 170–177.

Orsimi, G., Bade, D., & Lamersdorf, W. (2015). Computing at the mobile edge: designing elastic android application for computation offloading. *The IFIP Wireless and Mobile Networking Conference*, 112-119.

Qian, Z., He, Y., Su, C., Wu, Z., Zhu, H., Zhang, T., Zhou, L., Yu, Y., & Zhang, Z. (2013). Timestream: Reliable stream computation in the cloud. *The 8th ACM European Conference on Computer Systems*, 1–14.

Qiushi, Y., & Jian-hua, C. (2018). Improved Identity Authentication Protocol Based on Ell Curve Cryptography in Multi-server Environment. *Computer Science*, *45*(6), 111–116.

Quan, Z., XiaoHong, Z., & Qingyang, Z. (2016). Firework: Big data sharing and processing in collaborative edge environment. *IEEE/ACM Symp on Edge Computing (SEC2016)*, 81-82.

Raju, S., Boddepalli, S., & Aapa, S. (2017). Identity management using blokchain for cognitive cellular networks. *IEEE International Conference on Comnication*, 1-6.

Saha, B., Shah, H., Seth, S., Vijayaraghavan, G., Murthy, A., & Curino, C. (2015). Apache tez: A unifying framework for modeling and building data processing applications. *The 2015 ACM SIGMOD International Conference on Management of Data*, 1357–1369. 10.1145/2723372.2742790

Shvachko, K., Hairong Kuang, K., Radia, S., & Chansler, R. (2010). The Hadoop Distributed File System. *The 26th Symposium on Mass Storage Systems and Technologies (MSST), 3*(7), 1-10. 10.1109/MSST.2010.5496972

Wankai, Z., & Min, L. (2020). Secure transmission scheme of environmental monitoring data based on blockchain. *Computer Science, 47*(1), 315–320.

Weisong, S., Hui, S., Jie, C., Quan, Z., & Wei, L. (2017). Edge computing: A new computing model in the age of Internet of things. *Jisuanji Yanjiu Yu Fazhan, 54*(5), 907–924.

Xin-feng Z., Zhi-hao Z., & Yan-ling W. (2019). Dynamic resource allocation strategy in mobile edge computing environment. *Computer Engineering and Science, 41*(7),1184-1190.

Xiong, Z., Hao, G., Xiao-yun, H., Zhou-bin, L., Xue-jie, S., & Hong-song, C. (2019). Research on Security Risk Assessment Method of State Grid Edge Computing Information System. *Computer Science, 46*(11A), 428–432.

Yong Y., & Feiyue W. (2016). Current situation and Prospect of blockchain technology development. *Journal of Automation*, 481-49.

Yu, Q., Chi, W., Kaiyue, Q., Yao, S., Chao, L., & Zhang, C. (2020). Review of intelligent health research: System from cloud to edge. *Jisuanji Yanjiu Yu Fazhan, 57*(1), 53–73.

Yuezhi, Z., & Di, Z. (2019). Near end Cloud Computing: Opportunities and challenges in the post cloud computing era. *Journal of Computational Science, 42*(4), 677–699.

Zaharia, M., Chowdhury, M., Franklin, J., Shenker, S., & Stoica, I. (2010). Spark: cluster computing with working sets. *The 2nd USENIX conference on Hot topics in cloud computing*, 10.

Zaharia, M., Das, T., Li, H., Hunter, T., Shenker, S., & Stoica, I. (2013). Discretized streams: Fault-tolerant streaming computation at scale. *The Twenty-Fourth ACM Symposium on Operating Systems Principles*, 423–438.

Zhaopeng, H., Weiping, D., Zhan, G., Xiaohui, Z., & Jiehua, W. (2019). A multi-stage wireless security authentication scheme based on blockchain technology. *Computer Science, 46*(12), 180–185.

Zhen, W., Ying, Z., Jidong, H., & Quanqiang, M. (2019). Overview of blockchain solutions for big data applications. *Computer Science, 46*(6a), 6–10.

Ziming, Z., Fang, L., Zhiping, C., & Nong, X. (2018). Edge Computing: Platforms, Applications and Challenges. *Journal of Computer Research and Development, 55*(2), 327–337.

This research was previously published in the International Journal of Information Technology and Web Engineering (IJITWE), 16(1); pages 1-22, copyright year 2021 by IGI Publishing (an imprint of IGI Global).

Section 3
Uses and Applications

Chapter 25

Next Generation Multi-Access Edge-Computing Fiber-Wireless-Enhanced HetNets for Low-Latency Immersive Applications

Amin Ebrahimzadeh
INRS, Canada

Martin Maier
INRS, Canada

ABSTRACT

Next generation optical access networks have to cope with the contradiction between the intense computation and ultra-low latency requirements of the immersive applications and limited resources of smart mobile devices. In this chapter, after presenting a brief overview of the related work on multi-access edge computing (MEC), the authors explore the potential of full and partial decentralization of computation by leveraging mobile end-user equipment in an MEC-enabled FiWi-enhanced LTE-A HetNet, by designing a two-tier hierarchical MEC-enabled FiWi-enhanced HetNet-based architecture for computation offloading, which leverages both local (i.e., on-device) and nonlocal (i.e., MEC/cloud-assisted) computing resources to achieve low response time and energy consumption for mobile users. They also propose a simple yet efficient task offloading mechanism to achieve an improved quality of experience (QoE) for mobile users.

DOI: 10.4018/978-1-6684-5700-9.ch025

INTRODUCTION

The Internet has constantly evolved from the mobile Internet dominated by human-to-human (H2H) traffic to the emerging Internet of Things (IoT) with its underlying machine-to-machine (M2M) communications. The advent of advanced robotics, along with the emerging ultra responsive networking infrastructures, will allow for transmitting the modality of touch (also known as haptic sensation) in addition to the traditional triple-play traffic (i.e., voice, video, and data) under the commonly known term *Tactile Internet*. The term Tactile Internet was first coined by G. P. Fettweis in 2014. In his seminal paper, Fettweis (2014) defined the Tactile Internet as a new breakthrough enabling unprecedented mobile applications for tactile steering and control of real and virtual objects by requiring a round-trip latency of 1-10 milliseconds. Later in 2014, ITU-T published a Technology Watch Report (2014) on the Tactile Internet, which emphasized that scaling up research in the area of wired and wireless access networks will be essential, ushering in new ideas and concepts to boost access networks' redundancy and diversity to meet the stringent latency as well as carrier-grade reliability requirements of Tactile Internet applications.

The IoT without any human involvement in its underlying M2M communications is useful for the automation of industrial and other machine-centric processes while keeping the human largely out of the loop. In contrast, according to Maier et al. (2016) and Maier et al. (2018), the Tactile Internet, which allows for the tactile steering and control of not only virtual but also real objects via teleoperated robots, will be centered around human-to-robot/machine (H2R/M) communications, thus calling for a human-centric design approach. To give it a more 5G-centric flavor, the Tactile Internet has been more recently also referred to as the 5G-enabled Tactile Internet (see Simsek et al. (2016) and Aijaz et al. (2017)). Andrews et al. (2014) have argued that unlike the previous four generations, future 5G networks will lead to an increasing integration of cellular and WiFi technologies and standards. Furthermore, the importance of the so-called *backhaul bottleneck* needs to be recognized as well, calling for an end-to-end design approach leveraging on both wireless front-end and wired backhaul technologies. Or as once eloquently put by J. G. Andrews et al. (2013), "placing base stations all over the place is great for providing the mobile stations high-speed access, but does this not just pass the buck to the base stations, which must now somehow get this data to and from the wired core network?".

This mandatory end-to-end design approach is fully reflected in the key principles of the reference architecture within the emerging IEEE P1918.1 standards working group, which aims at defining a framework for the Tactile Internet. Among others, the key principles envision to (*i*) develop a generic Tactile Internet reference architecture, (*ii*) support local area as well as wide area connectivity through wireless (e.g., cellular, WiFi) or hybrid wireless/wired networking, and (*iii*) leverage computing resources from cloud variants at the edge of the network. The IEEE P1918.1 standards working group was approved by the IEEE Standards Association in March 2016. The group defines the Tactile Internet as follows: "*A network, or a network of networks, for remotely accessing, perceiving, manipulating or controlling real and virtual objects or processes in perceived real-time.* Some of the key use cases considered in IEEE P1918.1 include teleoperation, haptic communications, immersive augmented/virtual reality (AR/VR), and automotive control. Such applications may require the processing of large amounts of computation-intensive, delay-sensitive tasks. Mobile devices, however, are subject to limited hardware resources (e.g., battery life, CPU, and storage) and therefore may not be able to satisfy the stringent latency requirements of complex tasks.

To fill the gap between the increasing demands of computation-intensive, delay-sensitive tasks driven by emerging Tactile Internet applications and the availability of limited resources on smart mobile devices, mobile cloud computing (MCC) has emerged to reduce the computational burden of mobile devices and broaden their capabilities by extending the concept of cloud computing to the mobile environment by means of full and/or partial computation offloading. The MCC paradigm enables mobile devices to use infrastructures, platforms, and software packages offered by cloud providers at affordable costs to save battery power and accelerate task execution. We note, however, that the applicability of MCC to delay-sensitive tasks raises several technical challenges due to additional communication overhead and poor reliability that remote computation offloading may introduce. To cope with these limitations, mobile edge computing has recently emerged to provide cloud computing capabilities at the edge of access networks, leveraging the physical proximity of edge servers and mobile users to achieve reduced communication latency and increased reliability, e.g., Chen et al. (2016). As stated by Taleb et al. (2017), the European Telecommunications Standards Institute (ETSI) has recently dropped the word "mobile" and introduced the term multi-access edge computing (MEC) in order to broaden its applicability to heterogeneous networks, including WiFi and fixed access technologies (e.g., fiber).

Although a conventional (remote) cloud can provide high storage and computational resources, its applicability to immersive applications is often limited, which is due to large incurred latency, as task inputs have to travel all the way through the backhaul to reach the processing units. On the other hand, MEC may offer a reduced communication induced latency due to its proximity to end users, but it may suffer from an increased processing latency due to limited available computational resources. Therefore, MEC and remote cloud can be complementary to each other, creating a hierarchical computing paradigm to help end users experience an ultra low response time. In addition to the discussion above, we note that an important aspect of the 5G vision is decentralization. While 2G-3G-4G cellular networks were built under the design premise of having complete control at the infrastructure side, 5G systems may drop this design assumption and evolve the cell-centric architecture into a more device-centric one. Coexistence of MEC and remote cloud, along with on-device processing, gives rise to the so-called *hierarchical cooperative computing* (HCC), where the proximity of the MEC serves on one hand and strong computational capabilities of the remote cloud on the other hand may be leveraged to augment the limited on-device processing capabilities of end devices to give way to a flexible computing paradigm, which is able to satisfy different quality-of-experience (QoE) requirements of offloaded tasks generated by different types of emerging applications.

It is evident that future 5G mobile networks will lead to an increasing integration of cellular and WiFi technologies and standards, giving rise to so-called heterogenous networks (HetNets), which mandates the need for addressing the backhaul bottleneck challenge. Recently, Beyranvand et al. (2017) have explored the performance gains obtained from unifying coverage-centric 4G LTE-Advanced (LTE-A) HetNets and capacity-centric fiber-wireless (FiWi) access networks based on data-centric Ethernet technologies with resulting fiber backhaul sharing and WiFi offloading capabilities towards realizing future 5G networks. By means of probabilistic analysis and verifying simulations based on recent and comprehensive smartphone traces, Beyranvand et al. (2017) showed that an average end-to-end latency of <10 ms can be achieved for a wide range of traffic loads and that mobile users can be provided with highly fault-tolerant FiWi connectivity for reliable low-latency fiber backhaul sharing and WiFi offloading. Note, however, that Beyranvand et al. (2017) considered only data offloading without any computation offloading via MEC. Furthermore, Rimal et al. (2016) and Rimal et al. (2017) have investigated the feasibility of implementing conventional cloud and MEC in FiWi access networks, where the main objective was to design a unified resource management scheme to integrate offloading activities with the underlying FiWi operations. While much of the effort in these papers has been devoted to the management of networking resources, cooperation between mobile devices, MEC servers, the remote cloud and the problem of offloading decision making have not been investigated.

In this chapter, we examine the performance gains obtained by the decentralization of computation resources using our proposed hierarchical cooperative computation offloading in MEC enabled FiWi enhanced HetNets, which relies not only on the computational capabilities of edge/cloud servers but also on the limited local computing resources at the device side. More specifically, we aim to design a two-tier MEC enabled FiWi enhanced HetNet architecture, where the mobile devices as well as the edge servers cooperatively offload their computation tasks towards achieving a reduced average response time. In our design approach, we take into account the limitations stemming from both communications and computation via accurate modeling of the fronthaul/backhaul as well as edge/cloud servers, while paying particular attention to the offloading decision making between mobile users and edge servers as well as edge servers and the remote cloud.

The remainder of the chapter is structured as follows. In Section II, we revisit FiWi access networks in the context of conventional clouds and emerging cloudlets, thereby highlighting the limitations of centralized C-RAN in light of future 5G networks moving toward decentralization based on cloudlets and MEC. In Section III we present our proposed hierarchical cooperative computing scheme for FiWi enhanced HetNets, which leverages on a two-level non-local computing hierarchy as well as local computing to obtain a reduced response time in a cooperative manner. In Section VI, we present our analytical framework for estimating the energy-delay performance of our proposed cooperative task offloading scheme. We present the numerical results in Section V. Finally, Section VI draws conclusions.

MEC ENABLED FIWI ACCESS NETWORKS

Although a few FiWi architectural studies exist on the integration of passive optical network (PON) with LTE or WiMAX wireless front-end networks, the vast majority of studies such as Aurzada et al. (2014) have considered FiWi access networks consisting of a conventional IEEE 802.3ah Ethernet PON (EPON) fiber backhaul and an IEEE 802.11b/g/n/s wireless local area network (WLAN) mesh front-end, which may be further upgraded by leveraging NG-PONs, notably 10+ Gb/s TDM/WDM PONs, and Gigabit-class IEEE 802.11ac very high throughput (VHT) WLAN technologies. Most FiWi access architectures thus rely on low-cost data-centric optical fiber Ethernet (i.e., EPON) and wireless Ethernet (i.e., WLAN) technologies, which provide a number of important benefits, as elaborated in the following. First, economic considerations are expected to play an even more critical role in 5G networks compared to previous generations, due to an unprecedented increase of the number of mobile devices. Such economic considerations, along with the fact that today's service providers have to cope with an unprecedented growth of mobile data traffic worldwide, have spurred a great deal of interest toward complementing 4G LTE-A HetNets with already widely deployed WiFi access points. This represents a key aspect of the strategy of today's operators to offload mobile data traffic from their cellular networks, a technique also known as *WiFi offloading*. Clearly, FiWi access networks with a WLAN based front-end represent a promising approach to realize WiFi offloading in a cost-efficient manner.

We note that, unlike LTE, WLANs use a *distributed* medium access control (MAC) protocol for arbitrating access to the wireless medium among stations. Specifically, the so-called distributed coordination function (DCF) typically deployed in WLANs may suffer from a seriously deteriorated throughput performance due to the propagation delay of the fiber backhaul. These limitations of WLAN based FiWi access networks can be avoided by controlling access to the optical fiber and wireless media separately from each other, giving rise to so-called radio-and-fiber (R&F) networks. R\&F networks use in general two different MAC protocols, with protocol translation taking place at their interface. As a consequence, wireless MAC frames do not have to travel along the backhaul fiber to be processed at any central control station, but simply traverse their associated access point and remain in the WLAN. Access control is done locally inside the WLAN in a fully decentralized fashion. Note that in doing so, WLAN based FiWi access networks of extended coverage can be built without imposing stringent limits on the size of the fiber backhaul. Recall that this holds only for distributed MAC protocols such as DCF, but not for MAC protocols that deploy centralized polling and scheduling such as EPON and LTE. Thus, in a typical R&F based FiWi access network consisting of a cascaded EPON backhaul and WLAN front-end for WiFi offloading, the end-to-end coordination of both fiber and wireless network resources may be done by a co-dynamic bandwidth allocation (co-DBA) algorithm that uses the centralized IEEE 802.3ah multipoint control protocol (MPCP) for EPON and the decentralized DCF for WiFi, with MAC protocol translation taking place at the optical-wireless interface. Note that the decentralized nature of WLAN's access protocol DCF is instrumental in realizing one of the key attributes of future 5G networks, decentralization.

Maier and Rimal (2015) studied FiWi access networks in the context of both conventional clouds and emerging cloudlets, paying particular attention to the difference of R&F and traditional radio-over-fiber (RoF) networks. RoF networks have been studied for decades and were also used in China Mobile's C-RAN, which relies on a centralized cloud infrastructure and moves baseband units (BBUs) away from remote radio heads (RRHs), rendering the latter ones intentionally as simple as possible without any processing and storage capabilities. In contrast, beside MAC protocol translation, the distributed processing and storage capabilities inherently built into R&F networks may be exploited for a number of additional tasks. Therefore, Maier and Rimal (2015) argued that R&F based FiWi access networks may become the solution of choice in light of the aforementioned trends of future 5G mobile networks toward decentralization based on cloudlets and MEC. Note however that Rimal et al. (2017), Rimal et al. (2017), and Rimal (2018) have argued that R&F and RoF technologies may be also used jointly together in FiWi access networks for providing multi-tier cloud computing services.

Maier et al. (2018) have put forward the idea that the Tactile Internet may be the harbinger of human augmentation and human-machine symbiosis envisioned by contemporary and early-day Internet pioneers. More specifically, they explored the idea of treating the human as a "member" of a team of intelligent machines rather than keep viewing him as a conventional "user." In addition, they elaborated on the role of artificial intelligence (AI) enhanced agents in supporting humans in their task coordination between humans and machines. Toward achieving advanced human-machine coordination, we developed a distributed allocation algorithm of computational and physical tasks for fluidly orchestrating human-agent-robot teamwork (HART) coactivities, e.g., the shared use of user- and/or network-owned robots. In their design approach, all HART members established through communication a collective self-awareness with the objective of minimizing the task completion time.

Tan et al. (2017) proposed a scalable online algorithm for task scheduling in an edge-cloud system, which was verified by simulations using real-world traces from Google. Tong et al. presented a hierarchical MEC-based architecture with a focus on the workload placement problem. Chen et al. (2017) presented an optimization framework for solving the problem of joint offloading decision and allocation of computation and communication resources with the aim of minimizing a weighted sum of the costs of energy, cost of computation, and the delay for all users. More recently, Xiao and Krunz (2018) studied the computation offloading problem for cooperative fog computing networks and investigated the fundamental tradeoff between QoE of mobile users and power efficiency of fog nodes. Guo et al. (2018) presented a collaborative computation offloading scheme for MEC over FiWi networks. All mentioned papers, however, mainly focused on the management of computing resources without further investigating the impact of the capacity-limited backhaul.

While computation offloading for mobile computing systems has been around for almost a decade, the edge/fog computing paradigm has emerged only recently. Sun et al. (2017) proposed a novel cloudlet cellular network architecture to enable mobile users to offload their computation workload to nearby cloudlets and then designed a latency-aware workload offloading strategy to allocate the offloaded workloads to suitable cloudlets. Fan et al. (2018) extended the research done by Sun et al. (2017) by incorporating a two-tier hierarchical architecture for cloudlets. Liu et al. (2018) formulated a multiobjective optimization problem for fog computing systems with the joint objective of minimizing energy consumption, execution delay, and payment cost by finding the optimal offloading probability and transmit power of mobile devices. Note, however, that in the research done by Liu et al. (2018), the cooperation between edge servers and remote cloud is limited to the case when the edge servers are overloaded with the offloaded tasks from mobile devices, thus not fully reaping the benefits of the two-tier hierarchical edge computing architecture. Rodriguez et al. (2017) aimed to minimize the response time in a scenario with two MEC servers by focusing on both computation and communication latencies through virtual machine migration and transmission power control, respectively. Rodriguez et al. (2018) extended the research of Rodriguez et al. (2017) to further reduce the average response time of users by using a particle swarm optimization approach to balance the workload between MEC servers. Note that these studies considered only the cellular access mode without any computation offloading through WiFi. Muoz et al. (2015) jointly optimized the transmit power, precoder, and computation load distribution for femto-cloud computing systems, where the cloud server is formed by a set of femto access points. Guo et al. (2016) were one of the first to address the joint computation offloading and resource scheduling problem with task dependencies for mobile cloud computing.

Note that the placement of MEC servers on a FiWi based networking architecture may have a significant impact on the resultant user experience. Thus, the problem of MEC server placement represents one of the important design issues from a network planning viewpoint. Toward this end, Wong et al. (2017), Mondal et al. (2017), Mondal et al. (2018), and Mondal et al. (2018) have argued that proactive placement stands as a promising approach, where the network planner builds a model for placing MEC servers after analyzing the traffic and mobility history of mobile users. In this context, Xu et al. (2016) explored the exact solution of the ILP formulation of the capacitated cloudlet placement problem. Due to poor scalability of the optimal approach to the developed ILP, Xu et al. (2016) proposed an efficient solution to obtain satisfactory results in terms of reduced complexity. Jia et al. (2017) elaborated on the shortcomings of the heaviest access point-first placement method and proposed the so-called density-based clustering placement heuristic, which was shown to achieve near optimal results.

HIERARCHICAL COOPERATIVE COMPUTING

As discussed in Section I, one of the key attributes of future 5G networks is decentralization from both communications and computation viewpoints. While much attention has been devoted to designing distributed wireless access mechanisms (e.g., WLAN), decentralization of computational resources has not been explored in great depth. Contributing to this effort, we elaborate on our proposed decentralized hierarchical cooperative computing scheme for FiWi enhanced HetNets, where the entire set of available computational resources, including the remote cloud, MEC serves, and end devices' local CPUs are leveraged to allow mobile users to experience a reduced response time as well as decreased energy consumption.

Figure 1 depicts the generic architecture of the considered FiWi enhanced LTE-A HetNets. The fiber backhaul consists of a time or wavelength division multiplexing (TDM/WDM) IEEE 802.3ah/av 1/10 Gbps Ethernet PON (EPON) with a typical fiber range of 20 km between the central optical line terminal (OLT) and remote optical network units (ONUs). The EPON may comprise multiple stages, each separated by a wavelength broadcasting splitter/combiner or a wavelength multiplexer/demultiplexer. There are three different subsets of ONUs. An ONU may either serve fixed (wired) subscribers. Alternatively, it may connect to a cellular network base station (BS) or an IEEE 802.11n/ac/s WLAN mesh portal point (MPP), giving rise to a collocated ONU-BS or ONU-MPP, respectively. Depending on her trajectory, a mobile user (MU) may communicate through the cellular network and/or WLAN mesh front-end, which consists of ONU-MPPs, intermediate mesh points (MPs), and mesh access points (MAPs).

Figure 1. Generic MEC-enabled FiWi enhanced LTE-A HetNets architecture

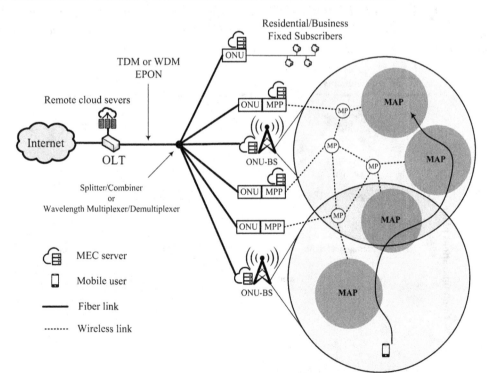

We equip selected ONU-BSs/MPPs with MEC servers (or simply called *edge servers[1]* hereafter) collocated at the optical-wireless interface. MUs may offload fully or portion of their incoming computational tasks to nearby edge servers. In addition to edge servers, the OLT is equipped with cloud computing facilities, which consist of multiple servers dedicated to processing mobile tasks. Each MU uses a task scheduler that decides whether to offload a task to an edge server or execute it locally in its local CPU. We model the task scheduler in each MU by a queuing system, as illustrated in Figure 2. We assume that in each mobile device there are two servers, namely, the CPU and the wireless interface (i.e., WiFi or LTE-A). The former server is used to model the local task execution at the MU's CPU, whereas the latter is responsible for offloading tasks to an edge server in proximity. We assume that tasks arrive at MU$_i$'s scheduler at rate λ_{MU_i}.

The task scheduler at MU$_i$ makes its decision based on the value of the so-called *offloading probability*, β_i, which is defined as the probability that an incoming task is offloaded to the edge server. Tasks generated by MU i are characterized by B_i^l and D_i^l, which denote the average size of computation input data (e.g., program codes and input parameters) and average number of CPU cycles required, respectively. Computation tasks are assumed to be atomic and thus cannot be divided into sub-tasks. We also assume that each edge server is equipped with a task scheduler, which decides whether to execute an incoming task or further offload it to the remote cloud. Similarly to MUs, a task arriving at edge server j is further offloaded to the remote cloud with probability α_j or executed locally with probability ($1 - \alpha_j$).

Figure 2. Schematic diagram of the proposed hierarchical cooperative computing scheme, leveraging local-, edge-, and remote cloud-computing. Task scheduler and queueing system of MU i includes two disjoint queues served by local CPU and WiFi/LTE-A wireless interface. Likewise, the queueing system of ONU j comprises two disjoint queues served by MEC server j and optical interface to offload the tasks to the remote cloud in the upstream direction of the backhaul EPON.

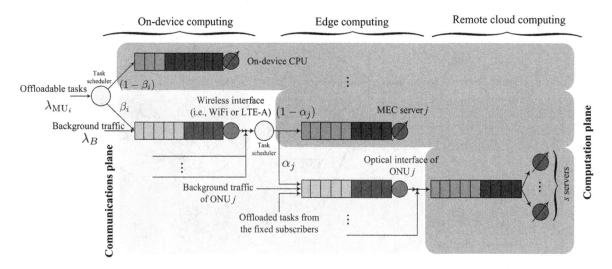

ENERGY-LATENCY ANALYSIS

In this section, we analyze the performance of our proposed cooperative MEC enabled FiWi enhanced LTE-A HetNets in terms of average response time and energy consumption for task offloading coexistent with conventional H2H traffic.

Assumptions

In the analysis, we make the following assumptions.

- We assume a Poisson task arrival model and an exponentially distributed number of required CPU cycles for task execution. Further, tasks are assumed to be computationally intensive, mutually independent, and can be executed either locally or remotely on an edge server or the remote cloud via computation offloading. According to Xiao and Krunz (2018) and Sun et al. (2017), each edge server has a limited computational capability and can serve a single task at a time. Besides, the remote cloud comprises a limited number of high-performance computing servers, each of which can serve a single task at a time.
- Similar to Chen et al. (2016), Guo et al. (2018), Liu et al. (2018), and Guo et al. (2016), we neglect the time overhead for sending the computation result back to the mobile users due to the fact that for many applications (e.g., face/object recognition) the size of the computation result is generally smaller than that of the computation input data.
- Each MU is directly associated with an ONU-AP or a cellular BS via a wireless single hop, whereby ONU-MPPs serve as ONU-APs. The WiFi connection and interconnection times of MUs are assumed to fit a truncated Pareto distribution, as validated by Beyranvand et al. (2017) via recent smartphone traces. The probability P_{temp}^{MU} that an MU is temporarily connected to an ONU-AP is estimated as $\bar{T}_{on} / \left(\bar{T}_{on} + \bar{T}_{off} \right)$, whereby $\bar{T}_{on}$ and $\bar{T}_{off}$ denote the average WiFi connection and interconnection time, respectively. In this chapter, we assume that $\bar{T}_{on}$ =28.1 minute and $\bar{T}_{off}$ =10.3 minute, which are consistent with the measurements of PhoneLab traces (see Beyranvand et al. (2017) for further details).
- In addition to the conventional MUs that generate Poisson H2H traffic at rate λ_B, background traffic coming from ONUs with attached fixed (wired) subscribers is set to $\alpha_p ON \lambda_B$, where $\alpha_p ON > 1$ is a traffic scaling factor for fixed subscribers that are directly connected to the backhaul EPON.

Average Response Time

In the proposed HCC scheme, both computation and communication induced latencies may contribute to the resultant response time experienced by MUs. Note that under the proposed HCC scheme, MUs can be either fully decentralized, partially decentralized, or fully centralized. While fully decentralized MUs rely on their local computing capabilities without offloading any task to the edge or remote cloud, fully centralized MUs rely only on the computing capabilities of the edge/remote cloud by offloading all the incoming tasks. In contrast, partially decentralized MUs rely on both local and non-local computing capabilities in a cooperative manner, as elaborated in Section III.

First, we estimate the latencies due to computation for both local and nonlocal computing. For a given MU_i, who is involved in task offloading, assuming i.i.d exponentially distributed task interarrival times and given the offloading probability β_i, the tasks arriving at the CPU queue for local computing follow a Poisson process with rate $(1 - \beta_i) \cdot \lambda_{MU_i}$, whereas the offloaded tasks arriving at the wireless interface queue follow a Poisson process with rate $\beta_i \cdot \lambda_{MU_i}$. This is because thinning a Poisson process with a fixed probability results in another Poisson process. Let D_i^l be the average number of required CPU cycles to execute a task arriving at MU i. The average local task execution time τ_i^l at MU i is given by

$$\tau_i^l = \frac{D_i^l}{f_i}, \tag{1}$$

where f_i is the clock frequency (in CPU cycles per second) of MU i. Assuming that the number of required CPU cycles per task follows an exponential distribution, we can model the local CPU server of MU i as an M/M/1 queue with mean arrival rate $(1 - \beta_i) \lambda_{MU_i}$ and mean task execution time τ_i^l. The average delay Δ_{MU_i} of local task execution (which includes both queueing and service times) at MU i's CPU is then given by

$$\Delta_{MU_i} = \frac{1}{\mu_i^l - \left(1 - \beta_i\right)\lambda_{MU_i}}, \tag{2}$$

where μ_i^l, which is equal to $1/\tau_i^l$, is the rate at which the executed tasks depart from MU i' CPU.

Let R_j denote the set of MUs that are served by edge server j. Further, let $\lambda_{o,j}^e$ be the mean arrival rate and $D_{o,j}^e$ denote the required number of CPU cycles of offloaded tasks from the fixed (wired) subscribers, if any, which may be directly connected to edge server j. Given the offloading probabilities β_i, $\forall MU_i \in R_j$, the mean arrival rate λ_{MEC_j} at the task scheduler of edge server j is computed as follows:

$$\lambda_{MEC_j} = \lambda_{0,j}^e + \sum_{MU_i \in R_j} \beta_i \lambda_{MU_i}, \tag{3}$$

Let τ_j^e denote the average task execution time at edge server j. For estimating τ_j^e, we compute the average number $D_{o,j}^e$ of CPU cycles required to execute a task at edge sever j as follows:

$$\bar{D}_j^e = \frac{\lambda_{0,j}^e D_{0,j}^e + \sum\limits_{MU_i \in R_j} \beta_i \lambda_{MU_i} D_i^l}{\lambda_{0,j}^e + \sum\limits_{MU_i \in R_j} \beta_i \lambda_{MU_i}}, \tag{4}$$

which is then used to calculate τ_j^e, which is given by

$$\tau_j^e = \frac{\bar{D}_j^e}{f_j^e}, \tag{5}$$

where f_j^e is the computational capability (in CPU cycles per second) of edge server j. Modeling edge server j as an M/M/1 queue with mean arrival rate $(1 - \alpha_j) \lambda_{\mathrm{MEC}_j}$ and mean service time τ_j^e, the average delay Δ_{MEC_j} of task execution at edge server j is calculated as follows:

$$\Delta_{\mathrm{MEC}_j} = \frac{1}{\mu_j^e - \left(1 - \alpha_j\right)\lambda_{\mathrm{MEC}_j}}, \tag{6}$$

whereby $\mu_j^e = 1 / \tau_j^e$. Substituting Equation (3) in Equation (6) provides the following expression:

$$\Delta_{\mathrm{MEC}_j} = \frac{1}{\mu_j^e - \left(1 - \alpha_j\right)\left(\lambda_{0,j}^e + \sum_{\mathrm{MU}_i \in R_j} \beta_i \lambda_{\mathrm{MU}_i}\right)}, \tag{7}$$

which is valid only if

$$\mu_j^e - \left(1 - \alpha_j\right)\left(\lambda_{0,j}^e + \sum_{\mathrm{MU}_i \in R_j} \beta_i \lambda_{\mathrm{MU}_i}\right) < 1.$$

Next, we proceed to estimate the task execution delay at the remote cloud. Let R denote the set of edge servers that are connected to the remote cloud. The mean arrival rate λ_c at the remote cloud is obtained as follows:

$$\lambda_{\mathrm{c}} = \lambda_{BKGD}^{cloud} + \sum_{\mathrm{MEC}_j \in R} \alpha_j \lambda_{\mathrm{MEC}_j}, \tag{8}$$

Let λ_{BKGD}^{cloud} and D_0^c denote the arrival rate and number of CPU cycles required to execute the background tasks at the remote cloud, respectively. Moreover, let τ_c denote the average task execution time at the remote cloud. In order to estimate τ_c, we first calculate the average number $\bar{D}_c$ of CPU cycles required to execute a task at the remote cloud, which is given by

$$\bar{D}_c = \frac{\lambda_0^c D_0^c + \sum_{\mathrm{MEC}_j \in R} \alpha_j \lambda_{\mathrm{MEC}_j} \bar{D}_j^e}{\lambda_{BKGD}^{cloud} + \sum_{\mathrm{MEC}_j \in R} \alpha_j \lambda_{\mathrm{MEC}_j}}, \tag{9}$$

which is then used to estimate τc as follows:

$$\tau_c = \frac{\bar{D}_c}{f^c}, \tag{10}$$

where f^c is the computational capability of each of the s homogeneous servers deployed at the remote cloud. We can thus model the remote cloud as an M/M/s queue with mean arrival rate λ_c (given by Equation (8)) and mean service time τ_c (given by Equation (10)). The average delay Δ_c experienced by an arbitrary task in the remote cloud is then estimated by the well-known

Erlang-C formula:

$$\Delta_c = \frac{c(s,a).\tau_c}{s-a} + \tau_c, \tag{11}$$

where a is equal to $\lambda c.\tau_c$ and $C(s,a)$ is given by:

$$C(s,a) = \frac{\dfrac{a^s.s}{s!(s-a)}}{\displaystyle\sum_{k=1}^{s-1} \frac{a^k}{k!} + \frac{a^s.s}{s!(s-a)}}, \tag{12}$$

Next, we turn our attention to calculating the communication induced latency in our cooperative task offloading scheme. Recall from above that the offloaded tasks arrive at the wireless interface of MU i with rate $\beta_i . \lambda_{\mathrm{MU}_i}$. With L_m denoting the maximum payload size of a single packet, the number of packets per task is equal to $\left\lceil \dfrac{B_i^l}{L_m} \right\rceil$. We can then estimate the rate Γ_{MU_i} at which packets arrive at the wireless interface of MU i as follows:

$$\Gamma_{\mathrm{MU}_i} = \lambda_B + \left\lceil \frac{B_i^l}{L_m} \right\rceil . \beta_i . \lambda_{\mathrm{MU}_i}, \tag{13}$$

where λ_B denotes the background H2H traffic (see also Figure 2).

In the following, we calculate the average packet delay Θ_i^{WiFi} in the uplink for MU i, who is associated with an ONU-AP through WiFi. Similar to Aurzada et al. (2014), for a given set of network model parameters, we can estimate Θ_i^{WiFi} as

$$\Theta_i^{\text{WiFi}} = \frac{1}{\dfrac{1}{\Delta_i} - \Gamma_{\text{MU}_i}}, \tag{14}$$

where Δ_i denotes the average channel access delay and Γ_{MU_i} is given by Equation (13). Note that

Equation (14) accounts for both queueing and channel access delay. We also note that the average access delay Δ_i consists of time delays due to carrier sensing, exponential back-offs, collided and erroneous (if any) attempts, successful transmission, and acknowledgement. To compute the average channel access delay, we define a two-dimensional Markov process $(s(t),b(t))$ under unsaturated conditions and estimate the average service time Δ_i in a WLAN using the IEEE 802.11 distributed coordination function (DCF) for access control, whereby $b(t)$ and $s(t)$ denote the random back-off counter and size of the contention window at time t, respectively. Due to given space constraints, we don't provide further details, but for completeness briefly note that Δ_i is obtained as follows:

$$\Delta_i = \sum_{k=0}^{\infty} p_{e,i}^k \left(1 - p_{e,i}\right) \left[\sum_{j=0}^{\infty} p_{c,i}^j \left(1 - p_{c,i}\right) \right.$$
$$\left. \left(\left(\sum_{b=0}^{k+j} \frac{2^{\min(b.m)} W_0 - 1}{2} E_s \right) + jT_{c,i} + kT_{e,i} + T_{s,i} \right) \right], \tag{15}$$

where $p_{e,i}$ is the probability of an erroneous transmission, $p_{c,i}$ is the probability of a collision, W_0 is the initial contention window size, E_s is the expected time-slot duration, and $T_{c,i}$, $T_{e,i}$, and $T_{s,i}$ denote the average duration of a collided, erroneous, successful transmission of MU i, respectively.

Next, we assume a 4G LTE-A cellular network and estimate its uplink delay. Let p_i^{tx} denote the transmission power of MU i. We use the Shannon-Hartley Theorem to estimate the uplink data rate r_i^{LTE} of MU i transmitting to BS k via 4G LTE-A cellular network as follows:

$$r_i^{\text{LTE}} = \omega \log_2 \left(1 + \frac{p_i^{tx} G_{i,k}}{\overline{\omega}_0^2 + \sum_{j \neq i} p_j^{tx} G_{j,k}} \right), \tag{16}$$

where ω and $\overline{\omega}_0^2$ are the channel bandwidth and background noise power, respectively; $G_{i,k}$ denotes the channel gain between MU i and BS k. Similar to Beyranvand et al. (2017), the uplink delay of LTE-A users can be estimated by

$$\Theta_i^{\text{LTE}} = \frac{\rho_{BS}^u}{2r_i^{\text{LTE}}\left(1 - \rho_{BS}^u\right)}\left(\frac{\varsigma_L^2}{\bar{L}} + \bar{L}\right) + \frac{\bar{L}}{r_i^{\text{LTE}}} + D_{RA}^{up} + D_{setup} + \tau_{BS}, \tag{17}$$

where D_{RA}^{up} is the initial random access delay, D_{setup} denotes the connection setup delay after passing the random access process successfully, ρ_{BS}^{up} denotes the uplink traffic intensity, τ_{BS} is the propagation delay in the cellular network, and $\bar{L}$ and ς_L^2 denote the mean and variance of the packet length, respectively.

Considering the user mobility model in the assumptions above, MU i is either connected to an ONU-AP through WiFi with probability P_{temp}^{MU} or an ONU-BS through cellular network with probability $\left(1 - P_{temp}^{\text{MU}}\right)$. The average task transmission delay Θ_i^{UL} in the uplink is then computed as follows:

$$\Theta_i^{\text{UL}} = \left(P_{temp}^{\text{MU}}.\Theta_i^{\text{WiFi}} + \left(1 - P_{temp}^{\text{MU}}\right).\Theta_i^{\text{LTE}}\right).\left\lceil\frac{B_i^l}{L_m}\right\rceil. \tag{18}$$

Next, we present the delay analysis of backhaul EPON. Let D_{PON}^u denote the average packet delay in the backhaul EPON in the upstream direction. The average task transmission delay Θ^{PON} in the backhaul is then equal to $D_{\text{PON}}^u.\left\lceil\frac{B_i^l}{L_m}\right\rceil$, where D_{PON}^u is given by Aurzada et al. (2014):

$$D_{\text{PON}}^u = \Phi\left(\rho^u, \bar{L}, \varsigma_L^2, c_{PON}\right) + \frac{\bar{L}}{c_{PON}} + 2\tau_{PON}\frac{2 - \rho^u}{1 - \rho^u} - B^u, \tag{19}$$

whereby ρ^u is the upstream traffic intensity, τ_{PON} is the propagation delay between ONUs and OLT, c_{PON} is the EPON data rate, $\Phi(.)$ denotes the well-known Pollaczek-Khintchine formula, and B^u is obtained as

$$\Phi\left(\frac{1}{\Lambda c_{PON}}\sum_{i=1}^{O}\sum_{q=1}^{O}\Gamma_{iq}^{PON}, \bar{L}, \varsigma_L^2, c_{PON}\right),$$

where O is the number of ONUs and Γ_{iq}^{PON} is the traffic coming from ONU$_i$ to ONU$_j$, and Λ denotes the number of wavelengths in the WDM PON.

After calculating the computation and communication delay components, we proceed to compute the total average response time Ψ_i of MU i as follows:

$$\Psi_i = \left(1 - \beta_i\right).\Delta_{\text{MU}_i} + \beta_i.\left(\Theta_i^{\text{UL}} + \left(1 - \alpha_j\right)\Delta_{\text{MEC}_j} + \alpha_j\left(\Theta^{\text{PON}} + \Delta_c\right)\right), \tag{20}$$

where the terms denoted by Δ and Θ represent the latency components of computation and communication, respectively. Note that the communication-induced latency terms Θ_i^{UL} and Θ_i^{PON} depend on the offloading probabilities β_i and α_i, respectively. More specifically, if MUs decide to offload a large portion of their incoming tasks to the edge servers, the average task transmission delay in the uplink as well as the waiting times in the edge server may increase significantly. On the other hand, if the edge servers also decide to further offload a large portion of their tasks arriving from MUs and fixed subscribers to the remote cloud, the backhaul upstream delay as well as waiting delay at the cloud servers may increase as a result. Therefore, in order for the MUs to benefit from the powerful computational capabilities of the edge/remote servers and experience a low response time, it is important for both device and edge-server schedulers to optimally adjust their offloading probabilities.

Average Energy Consumption

Similar to Xiao and Krunz (2018), we model the power consumption of MU i's CPU as κf_i^3, where κ is the effective switched capacitance related to the chip architecture, as argued by Wang et al. (2016). The energy consumption per CPU cycle is thus equal to κf_i^3, as f_i represents the number of CPU cycles per second. The average energy consumption E_i^l for local execution of a task at MU i is then given by

$$E_i^l = \kappa . f_i^3 . D_i^l, \tag{21}$$

Recall from above that an incoming task at MU i is either executed locally with probability $(1-\beta_i)$ or it is offloaded for nonlocal execution with probability β_i. Let E_i^o denote the average energy consumption of MU i to offload an incoming task, which is calculated as follows:

$$E_i^o = \left(k_1^{tx} + k_2^{tx} . p_i^{tx} \right) . \Theta_i^{\mathrm{UL}}, \tag{22}$$

where k_1^{kx} represents the static power consumption for having the radio frequency (RF) transmission circuitries switched on and k_1^{kx} measures the linear increase of the transmitter power consumption with radiated power p_i^{kx}. The average energy consumption E_i (for either executing a task locally or transmitting its input data to an edge server) of MU i is then estimated as

$$E_i = \left(1 - \beta_i\right) . E_i^l + \beta_i E_i^o. \tag{23}$$

By substituting Eqs. (21) and (22) into Equation (23), we have

$$E_i = \left(1 - \beta_i\right) . \left(\kappa . f_i^3 . D_i^l\right) + \beta_i \left(k_1^{tx} + k_2^{tx} . p_i^{tx} \right) . \Theta_i^{\mathrm{UL}}. \tag{24}$$

RESULTS

The following numerical results were obtained by using the LTE-A and FiWi network and traffic parameter settings listed in Table 1, which are consistent with those in the researches of Beyranvand et al. (2017), Aurzada et al. (2014), Muoz et al. (2015), Guo et al. (2016), and Wang et al. (2016). In our considered scenario, 50 MUs are scattered randomly within the range of 50 m from each ONU-BS. Besides, we consider four MUs within the coverage area of each ONU-AP. In the cellular access mode, we set the channel gain to $G_{i,k} = d_{i,k}^{-\zeta}$ between MU i and BS k, where $d_{i,k}$ is the distance between MU i and BS k, and $\zeta=4$ is the path loss factor. Further, we set $\beta_i=\beta(\forall i=1,2,\ldots)$ and $\alpha_j=\alpha(\forall j=1,2,\ldots)$. We consider Nedge=4 MEC servers, each associated with 8 end-users, whereof $1 \leq N_{PD} \leq 8$ partially decentralized end-users can flexibly control the amount of offloaded tasks by varying their computation offloading probability. The remaining 8-N_{PD} are fully centralized end-users that rely on edge computing only (i.e., their computation offloading probability equals 1).

Table 1. MEC-enabled FiWi enhanced HetNet Parameters and Default Values

Parameter	Value	Parameter	Value
Traffic Model Parameters			
L_m	1500 Bytes	λ_B	30 packets/s
α_{PON}	100	$\overline{L}$, ς^2_L	1500 Bytes, 0
Backhaul EPON			
l_{PON}	100 km	c_{PON}	10 Gbps
N_{ONU}	12	Λ	1
WiFi Parameters			
DIFS	34 µsec	SIFS	16 µsec
PHY Header	20 µsec	W_0, H	16 slots, 6
ϵ	9 µsec	RTS	20 Bytes
CTS	14 bytes	ACK	14 Bytes
r in WMN	300 Mbps	ONU-AP radius	15 m
LTE-A Parameters			
p^{rx}	100 mW	ω	5 Mhz
$\overline{\omega}^2_0$	-100 dBm	k^{tx}_1	0.4 W
k^{tx}_2	18	ONU-BS radius	50 m
p^{rx}	200 mW		
Task and Edge/Cloud Server Parameters			
λ_{MU}	25 tasks/min	f_i	185 MHz
λ^e_0	12 tasks/min	f^e_j	1.44 GHz
λ^{cloud}_{BKGD}	480 tasks/min	s	6
f^c	1.44 GHz	B^l	66 KB
D^l, D^e_0, D^c_0	400 Mcycles	κ	10^{-26}

For completeness, we first illustrate the average response time of fully decentralized MUs, who use only their local CPUs for computation, as well as the fully centralized ones, who rely on either edge- or cloud-only computing. The average response time vs. task arrival rate is depicted in Figure 3, which is helpful to compare the delay performance of local-, edge-, and cloud-computing without any hierarchical cooperation. We observe that cloud computing, among others, is a promising solution toward achieving the smallest average response time if the background task arrival rate to the cloud doesn't exceed 6. Otherwise, depending on the rate which tasks arrive at MUs, we observe that either local-, edge-, or cloud-computing can yield the smallest average response time. Our major takeaway from Figure 3 is that although cloud- or edge-computing often results in a reduced response time, MUs may be able to experience a small response time even if they rely on their local CPUs, especially when the edge and/ or cloud servers are over-utilized.

Figure 3. Performance comparison of local vs. non-local computing in terms of average response time for different values of background task arrival rate λ_{BKGD}^{cloud} (in tasks per second) to remote cloud

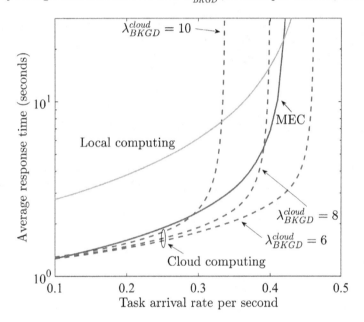

Next, we consider the cooperation between device and edge servers, which is characterized by the offloading probability β of N_{PD} partially decentralized MUs. Figures 4(a) and (b) illustrate the average response time and energy consumption vs. offloading probability β of partially decentralized MUs, respectively. We observe from Figure 4(a) that the average response time is a strictly convex function of offloading probability β, having a global optimum for a given N_{PD}. For instance, for N_{PD}=8, the MUs, on average, can experience a response time of 2.4 s when the partially distributed MUs set their offloading probability to β*=0.65, which represents a significant reduction of 89.6% compared with 23.5 s for the case where β is set to 0, i.e., local computing. Also, note that β* increases as the number N_{PD} of partially decentralized MUs increases. This happens in light of the fact that increasing N_{PD} leaves fewer fully centralized MUs that offload their entire incoming tasks, thus alleviating the burden on edge servers. This, in turn, allows other MUs to benefit from the computational resources of the edge servers by optimally adjusting their offloading probabilities, resulting in a reduced response time. More interestingly, Figures 4(a) and (b) characterize the energy-delay trade-off in our proposed device-edge cooperative computing scheme. More specifically, given an energy budget, Figure 4(b) determines the feasible set for β, which, together with Figure 4(a), can be used to find β^* that minimizes the average response time.

Figure 4. Device-edge cooperative offloading: (a) average response time of MUs vs. offloading probability β for different number of partially distributed MUs, $N_{PD}=[1,2,3,4,8]$; (b) energy consumption vs. offloading probability β ($\lambda_{MU}=25$ tasks per minute and $\alpha=0$).

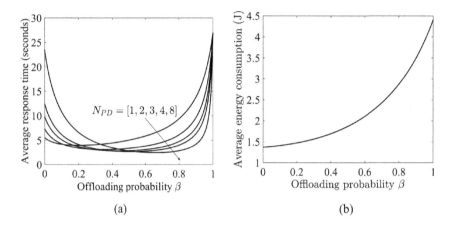

(a)   (b)

Figure 5. Device-edge-cloud cooperative computing: (a) average response time of MUs vs. offloading probability α for different number of partially distributed MUs, $N_{PD}=[1,4,8]$; (b) energy consumption vs. offloading probability α ($N_{edge}=4$ fixed and $\beta=\beta^*$).

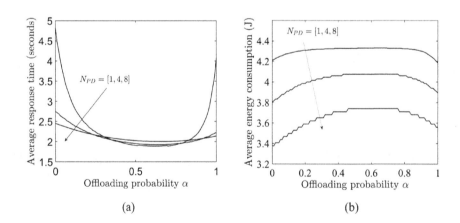

(a)   (b)

Finally, we consider the cooperation between device, edge, and cloud and investigate the average response time and energy consumption vs. α for different number N_{PD} of partially decentralized MUs in Figures 5(a) and (b), respectively. Note that for a given α and N_{PD}, each point shown on the curves in Figures 5(a)-(b) is obtained by setting the offloading probability to $\beta=\beta^*$ for a given network configuration and traffic scenario. First, we observe that the cooperation between device, edge, and cloud yields even better results in terms of average response time compared with the device-edge cooperation (see Figs 4(a) and 5(a)). Second, we observe from Figures 5(a)-(b) that increasing the number of partially decentralized MUs reduces the average response time as well as energy consumption. More interestingly, our findings demonstrate that decentralization of computation decreases the sensitivity of the average response time to the fluctuations of the offloading probability α. More specifically, when all MUs are partially decentralized, i.e., $N_{PD}=8$, a slight deviation from the optimal setting of α doesn't have a significant detrimental impact on the average response time, provided that the MUs locally set their offloading probabilities β to the optimal value β^*.

CONCLUSION

This chapter studied the hierarchical cooperative computation offloading in MEC enabled FiWi enhanced HetNets from both network architecture and offlading mechanism design perspectives. We revisited FiWi access networks in the context of conventional clouds and emerging cloudlets, thereby highlighting the limitations of centralized C-RAN in light of future 5G networks moving toward decentralization based on cloudlets and MEC. Importantly, we elaborated on which implications wireless access via WiFi has for the design of decentralized co-DBA algorithms in support of future 5G low-latency applications. After compiling and classifying the research work conducted for the MEC in the context of the Tactile Internet, we presented our simple but efficient offloading strategy that leverages trilateral cooperation among device, edge server, and remote cloud. We developed an analytical framework to estimate the average response time and energy consumption of mobile users in a FiWi based MEC enabled network infrastructure. Our results demonstrate that the proposed hierarchical cooperative computing scheme outperforms edge- or cloud-only solutions.

REFERENCES

Aijaz, A., Dohler, M., Aghvami, A. H., Friderikos, V., & Frodigh, M. (2017). Realizing the Tactile Internet: Haptic communications over next generation 5G cellular networks. *IEEE Wireless Communications*, *24*(2), 82–89. doi:10.1109/MWC.2016.1500157RP

Andrews, J. G. (2013). Seven ways that HetNets are a cellular paradigm shift. *IEEE Communications Magazine*, *51*(3), 136–144. doi:10.1109/MCOM.2013.6476878

Andrews, J. G., Buzzi, S., Choi, W., Hanly, S. V., Lozano, A., Soong, A. C., & Zhang, J. C. (2014). What will 5G be? *IEEE Journal on Selected Areas in Communications*, *32*(6), 1065–1082. doi:10.1109/JSAC.2014.2328098

Aurzada, F., Lévesque, M., Maier, M., & Reisslein, M. (2014). FiWi access networks based on next-generation PON and gigabit-class WLAN technologies: A capacity and delay analysis. *IEEE/ACM Transactions on Networking*, *22*(4), 1176–1189. doi:10.1109/TNET.2013.2270360

Beyranvand, H., Lévesque, M., Maier, M., Salehi, J. A., Verikoukis, C., & Tipper, D. (2017). Toward 5G: FiWi enhanced LTE-A HetNets with reliable low-latency fiber backhaul sharing and WiFi offloading. *IEEE/ACM Transactions on Networking*, *25*(2), 690–707. doi:10.1109/TNET.2016.2599780

Chen, M. H., Liang, B., & Dong, M. (2017, May). Joint offloading and resource allocation for computation and communication in mobile cloud with computing access point. In *INFOCOM 2017-IEEE Conference on Computer Communications, IEEE* (pp. 1-9). IEEE. doi:10.1109/INFOCOM.2016.7524340

Chen, X., Jiao, L., Li, W., & Fu, X. (2016). Efficient multi-user computation offloading for mobile-edge cloud computing. *IEEE/ACM Transactions on Networking, 24*(5), 2795–2808. doi:10.1109/TNET.2015.2487344

Fan, Q., & Ansari, N. (2018). Workload allocation in hierarchical cloudlet networks. *IEEE Communications Letters, 22*(4), 820–823. doi:10.1109/LCOMM.2018.2801866

Fettweis, G. P. (2014). The Tactile Internet: Applications and Challenges. *IEEE Vehicular Technology Magazine, 9*(1), 64–70. doi:10.1109/MVT.2013.2295069

Guo, H., & Liu, J. (2018). Collaborative computation offloading for multi-access edge computing over fiber-wireless networks. *IEEE Transactions on Vehicular Technology, 67*(5).

Guo, S., Xiao, B., Yang, Y., & Yang, Y. (2016, April). Energy-efficient dynamic offloading and resource scheduling in mobile cloud computing. In *INFOCOM 2016-The 35th Annual IEEE International Conference on Computer Communications, IEEE* (pp. 1-9). IEEE. 10.1109/INFOCOM.2016.7524497

Jia, M., Cao, J., & Liang, W. (2017). Optimal cloudlet placement and user to cloudlet allocation in wireless metropolitan area networks. *IEEE Transactions on Cloud Computing, 5*(4), 725–737. doi:10.1109/TCC.2015.2449834

Liu, L., Chang, Z., Guo, X., Mao, S., & Ristaniemi, T. (2018). Multiobjective optimization for computation offloading in fog computing. *IEEE Internet of Things Journal, 5*(1), 283–294. doi:10.1109/JIOT.2017.2780236

Maier, M., Chowdhury, M., Rimal, B. P., & Van, D. P. (2016). The Tactile Internet: Vision, recent progress, and open challenges. *IEEE Communications Magazine, 54*(5), 138–145. doi:10.1109/MCOM.2016.7470948

Maier, M., Ebrahimzadeh, A., & Chowdhury, M. (2018). The Tactile Internet: Automation or Augmentation of the Human? *IEEE Access: Practical Innovations, Open Solutions, 6*, 41607–41618. doi:10.1109/ACCESS.2018.2861768

Maier, M., & Rimal, B. P. (2015). The audacity of fiber-wireless (FiWi) networks: Revisited for clouds and cloudlets. *China Communications, 12*(8), 33–45. doi:10.1109/CC.2015.7224704

Miettinen, A. P., & Nurminen, J. K. (2010). Energy Efficiency of Mobile Clients in Cloud Computing. *HotCloud, 10*, 1–7.

Mondal, S., Das, G., & Wong, E. (2017, December). A Novel Cost Optimization Framework for Multi-Cloudlet Environment over Optical Access Networks. In *GLOBECOM 2017-2017 IEEE Global Communications Conference* (pp. 1-7). IEEE. 10.1109/GLOCOM.2017.8254251

Mondal, S., Das, G., & Wong, E. (2018, April). CCOMPASSION: A hybrid cloudlet placement framework over passive optical access networks. In *IEEE INFOCOM 2018-IEEE Conference on Computer Communications* (pp. 216-224). IEEE. 10.1109/INFOCOM.2018.8485846

Mondal, S., Das, G., & Wong, E. (2018, July). Supporting Low-Latency Applications through Hybrid Cost-Optimised Cloudlet Placement. In *2018 20th International Conference on Transparent Optical Networks (ICTON)* (pp. 1-4). IEEE. 10.1109/ICTON.2018.8473911

Munoz, O., Pascual-Iserte, A., & Vidal, J. (2015). Optimization of radio and computational resources for energy efficiency in latency-constrained application offloading. *IEEE Transactions on Vehicular Technology*, 64(10), 4738–4755. doi:10.1109/TVT.2014.2372852

Rimal, B. P., Maier, M., & Satyanarayanan, M. (2018). Experimental Testbed for Edge Computing in Fiber-Wireless Broadband Access Networks. *IEEE Communications Magazine*, 56(8), 160–167. doi:10.1109/MCOM.2018.1700793

Rimal, B. P., Van, D. P., & Maier, M. (2016, April). Mobile-edge computing vs. centralized cloud computing in fiber-wireless access networks. In *Computer Communications Workshops (INFOCOM WKSHPS), 2016 IEEE Conference on* (pp. 991-996). IEEE. 10.1109/INFCOMW.2016.7562226

Rimal, B. P., Van, D. P., & Maier, M. (2017). Mobile edge computing empowered fiber-wireless access networks in the 5G era. *IEEE Communications Magazine*, 55(2), 192–200. doi:10.1109/MCOM.2017.1600156CM

Rimal, B. P., Van, D. P., & Maier, M. (2017). Cloudlet enhanced fiber-wireless access networks for mobile-edge computing. *IEEE Transactions on Wireless Communications*, 16(6), 3601–3618. doi:10.1109/TWC.2017.2685578

Rimal, B. P., Van, D. P., & Maier, M. (2017). Mobile-edge computing versus centralized cloud computing over a converged FiWi access network. *IEEE eTransactions on Network and Service Management*, 14(3), 498–513. doi:10.1109/TNSM.2017.2706085

Rodrigues, T. G., Suto, K., Nishiyama, H., & Kato, N. (2017). Hybrid method for minimizing service delay in edge cloud computing through VM migration and transmission power control. *IEEE Transactions on Computers*, 66(5), 810–819. doi:10.1109/TC.2016.2620469

Rodrigues, T. G., Suto, K., Nishiyama, H., Kato, N., & Temma, K. (2018). Cloudlets Activation Scheme for Scalable Mobile Edge Computing with Transmission Power Control and Virtual Machine Migration. *IEEE Transactions on Computers*, 67(9), 1287–1300. doi:10.1109/TC.2018.2818144

Simsek, M., Aijaz, A., Dohler, M., Sachs, J., & Fettweis, G. (2016). 5G-enabled Tactile Internet. *IEEE Journal on Selected Areas in Communications*, 34(3), 460–473. doi:10.1109/JSAC.2016.2525398

Sun, X., & Ansari, N. (2017). Latency aware workload offloading in the cloudlet network. *IEEE Communications Letters*, 21(7), 1481–1484. doi:10.1109/LCOMM.2017.2690678

Taleb, T., Samdanis, K., Mada, B., Flinck, H., Dutta, S., & Sabella, D. (2017). On multi-access edge computing: A survey of the emerging 5G network edge cloud architecture and orchestration. *IEEE Communications Surveys and Tutorials*, 19(3), 1657–1681. doi:10.1109/COMST.2017.2705720

Tan, H., Han, Z., Li, X. Y., & Lau, F. C. (2017, May). Online job dispatching and scheduling in edge-clouds. In *INFOCOM 2017-IEEE Conference on Computer Communications, IEEE* (pp. 1-9). IEEE. 10.1109/INFOCOM.2017.8057116

ITU-T Technology Watch Report. (2014). *The Tactile Internet*. ITU-T.

Tong, L., Li, Y., & Gao, W. (2016, April). A hierarchical edge cloud architecture for mobile computing. In *INFOCOM 2016-The 35th Annual IEEE International Conference on Computer Communications, IEEE* (pp. 1-9). IEEE.

Wang, Y., Sheng, M., Wang, X., Wang, L., & Li, J. (2016). Mobile-edge computing: Partial computation offloading using dynamic voltage scaling. *IEEE Transactions on Communications*, *64*(10), 4268–4282.

Wong, E., Mondal, S., & Das, G. (2017, July). Latency-aware optimisation framework for cloudlet placement. In *Transparent Optical Networks (ICTON), 2017 19th International Conference on* (pp. 1-2). IEEE. 10.1109/ICTON.2017.8024881

Xiao, Y., & Krunz, M. (2018). Distributed Optimization for Energy-efficient Fog Computing in the Tactile Internet. *IEEE Journal on Selected Areas in Communications*.

Xu, Z., Liang, W., Xu, W., Jia, M., & Guo, S. (2016). Efficient algorithms for capacitated cloudlet placements. *IEEE Transactions on Parallel and Distributed Systems*, *27*(10), 2866–2880. doi:10.1109/TPDS.2015.2510638

ENDNOTE

[1]   A cloudlet or edge server is defined as a trusted cluster of computers that comprise resources available to use for nearby mobile devices. A cloudlet can be treated as data center in a box, running a virtual machine capable of provisioning resources to end devices in real time.

This research was previously published in Design, Implementation, and Analysis of Next Generation Optical Networks; pages 40-68, copyright year 2020 by Information Science Reference (an imprint of IGI Global).

Chapter 26
Edge Computing–Induced Caching Strategy for National Traditional Sports Video Resources by Considering Unusual Items

Wenwen Pan
Qiqihar University, China

Bei Liu
Qiqihar University, China

Zhiliang Song
Qiqihar University, China

ABSTRACT

In order to promote the development of national traditional sports to carry forward the spirit and culture of a country or nation, this paper designs a system for national traditional sports video distribution with the help of software-defined network and mobile edge computing technologies. Thus, the popular national traditional sports resources can be cached in mobile edge computing servers, which can reduce the delay time from cloud center directly. In order to improve the hit rate of the cached videos, the ant colony-stimulated annealing is used as the caching strategy. The experimental results show that the ant colony-stimulated annealing caching strategy can increase the hit rate of the contents in mobile edge computing servers as well as decrease the delay time of the request videos. The ant colony-stimulated annealing caching strategy performs better than previous caching strategies for updating contents in mobile edge computing servers.

DOI: 10.4018/978-1-6684-5700-9.ch026

1. INTRODUCTION

The national traditional sports inherit and carry forward a country's spirit and culture, and deeply root in the national culture (Li 2017). However, the development of national traditional sports is relatively slow due to the globalization. It is urgent to integrate the national traditional sports into people's daily exercises and sports. Recently, more and more videos are emerging on the internet, which include massive traditional sports teaching videos. It becomes a new way to learn national traditional sports via online videos.

The traditional video services (Wang 2018) have grown rapidly, including video on demand (VOD), live video and video surveillance, etc. All of these have greatly improved the quality of people's daily life and promoted the progress of video service-related industries, but at the same time, they have brought unprecedented pressure to video content providers and Internet service Providers (ISPs). Due to the multiple growth of the video bit rate and the rigid requirements of the video transmission business (Zeng 2018) on the quality of service (QoS) (Ning 2017) related indicators such as delay, jitter and packet loss, the video traffic in the network shows an exponential rising trend (Kassim 2017). However, the current network infrastructure cannot provide enough capacity to support the bandwidth demand of the video transmit. In order to guarantee the user service experience of video transmission (Quality of Experience, QoE) (Zhao 2016), ISPs have to spend a lot of money to update network equipment and improve hardware performance. Fortunately, the emergence of in-network caching technology (Zhou 2017) provides a new solution to this problem. By using the storage capacity of edge network node devices, it is possible to save the highly popular video files, which are frequently requested by local users, on the edge node. The requested videos are provided by the nearby nodes. Thus, the redundant traffic is eliminated, the load on the core network is alleviated, the transmission rate is increased, and transmission delay is reduced. Due to the shortcomings of traditional network structure, such as closure, functional solidification, low scalability, and poor controllability, it is necessary to use a new network architecture as network cache platform to design specific caching mechanisms and caching strategies, and support video transmission services, such as national traditional sports video.

By taking into account the importance of videos and unusual items, this paper designs an architecture for national traditional sports video distribution with the help of edge computing, and utilizes an ant colony-simulated annealing algorithm as the caching strategy for local node in the architecture. The following part of this paper is organized as follows: the architecture for national traditional sports video distribution is proposed in Section 2; the ant colony-simulated annealing algorithm is used as the caching strategy for video distribution in Section 3; the experiments are provided in Section 4; Section 5 is the conclusion and discussion.

2. ARCHITECTURE FOR NATIONAL TRADITIONAL SPORTS VIDEO DISTRIBUTION

In order to ensure that the request can be responded in time, an architecture based on edge computing is proposed for national traditional sports video distribution, which is shown in Figure 1.

In Figure 1, the software defined network (SDN) (Huang 2018) is used to manage several mobile edge computing (MEC) servers (Wang 2019) and configure the resources for mobile edge computing servers and the cloud platform. Each MEC server supports several clients which connect to the network

Figure 1. The illustration of the architecture for national traditional sports video distribution

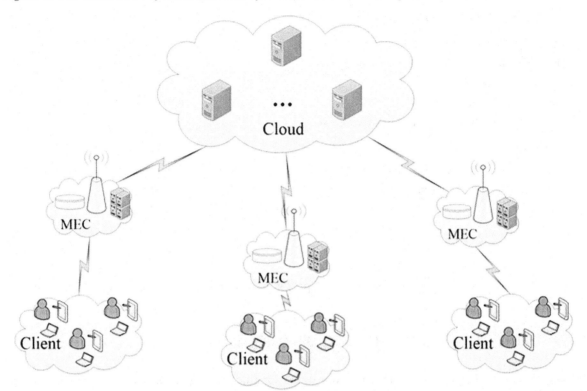

by personal computer, laptop, smart phone etc. In order to reduce the load on the backbone network, the popular videos are cached in MEC servers. First, the client sends the request to closest MEC server. If the closest MEC server has cached the requested video, the video is sent to the client; otherwise, the MEC server sends the request to the cloud and downloads the video from cloud.

Let us suppose that there are m MEC servers and n clients. The $E=\{E_1,...,E_m\}$ represents the set of MEC server, $C=\{C_1,...,C_n\}$ represents the set of clients, $U = E \cup C$, and l be the number of videos to provide for clients $V=\{v_1,...,v_l\}$.

Let p_f represent the probability of video v_f. The p_f follows Zipf distribution which is written as follows

$$p_f = \frac{f^{-\theta}}{\sum_{j=1}^{l} j^{-\theta}} \tag{1}$$

Here, θ is the factor of Zipf distribution. Let us suppose that the requests from client follow the Poisson distribution whose expectation is θ_i, then the probability of v_f during Δt is $p_{if}=p_f \bullet \theta_i$.

Let $X=\{x_{m,f}|E_m \in E, v_f \in V\}$ and $Y=\{y_{i,f}|C_i \in C, v_f \in V\}$ be the cache matrix in MEC servers and clients. The element in X is defined as follows:

$$x_{m,f} = \begin{cases} 1, & v_f \text{ is cached in MEC server} \\ 0, & v_f \text{ is cached in client} \end{cases} \tag{2}$$

The element in Y is defined as follows:

$$y_{i,f} = \begin{cases} 1, & v_f \text{ is cached in client } C_i \\ 0, & v_f \text{ is cached in client and MEC server} \end{cases} \tag{3}$$

The hit rate of cache in MEC server is defined as the ratio of the number of requests in MEC and the total requests, which is written as follows:

$$R = \frac{Q}{Z} \tag{4}$$

Here, Z represents the total requests, and Q represents the number of hit request in MEC servers.

3. CACHING STRATEGY FOR VIDEO DISTRIBUTION

In this section, we use ant colony-simulated annealing to update caching items in MEC server. Ant colony algorithm is inspired by a series of behaviors produced by ants in the process of foraging, and selects a route based on the concentration of pheromone (Liu 2017). When there is a high pheromone concentration remaining on a certain path, the path has a great possibility to be selected. The classical ant colony algorithm has parallelism. However, when using ant colony algorithm to solve cache optimization, it still exists the shortcomings: the convergence speed is slow and it is difficult to jump out of local minimum.

The simulated annealing is a stochastic optimization algorithm. The simulated annealing algorithm (Assad 2018) is only related to the initial temperature, the minimum temperature and the number of annealing. The advantage of simulated annealing is that it can effectively find a qualified solution to avoid getting stuck in local optimal area. The shortcoming of simulated annealing algorithm is that it depends on the initial temperature which is selected randomly.

In this paper, we combine ant colony algorithm with simulated annealing algorithm as the cache strategy for the videos in MEC servers. The ACSA is short for ant colony-simulated annealing cache strategy. The ACSA has the advantages of both ant colony and simulated annealing, overcomes the disadvantages. It can not only increase the annealing speed, but also avoid falling into the local optimum. By pre-caching popular content in MEC servers, the cost of transmission time can be significantly reduced and response client's request in time.

Let t_{i,y_i} represent the time delay for downloading a video from MEC server. The t_{i,y_i} is defined as follows:

$$t_{i,y_i} = \frac{v_{length}}{w_{i,y_i}} \tag{5}$$

Here, v_{length} is the length of the video, while w_{i,y_i} is the download speed.

The heuristic function $\eta_j(t)$ is defined as follows:

$$\eta_j(t) = \left(10 \frac{t_{i,v_j} - t_{avg}}{t_{i,v_j} + t_{avg}}\right)^2 \tag{6}$$

Here, t_{avg} represents the average time delay from MEC servers on best circumstance. Obviously, the more $\eta_j(t)$ is, the higher probability v_i is selected.

The path in stimulated annealing algorithm is searched by ant colony algorithm. The direction of each step is determined by the pheromone concentration $\tau_j(t)$. The transfer probability of each step is calculated according to Eq. (7).

$$p_j(t) = \begin{cases} \dfrac{[\tau_j(t)]^\alpha [\eta_j(t)]^\beta}{\sum\limits_{s \in V_k}[\tau_s(t)]^\alpha [\eta_s(t)]^\beta}, & j \in V_k \\ 0, & otherwise. \end{cases} \tag{7}$$

Here, $V_k = \{1,2,\ldots,m+n\} - tabu_k$ represents the set of MEC servers and clients, α and β indicates the importance of pheromone and heuristic factors, respectively. The $tabu_k$ represents the set of locations that the ants have walked.

The pheromone is updated according to the following rules.

Rule 1: when the task of a certain ant colony is finished, the pheromone concentration of the visited nodes is updated according to the following equation.

$$\tau_j(t + n) = (1 - \rho)\bullet\tau_j(t) + \Delta\tau_j(t) \tag{8}$$

Here, $\rho(0<\rho<1)$ represents the evaporation coefficient of the pheromone, $\Delta\tau_j(t)=1/t_j$, t_j represents the time from request to download V_j from MEC server.

Rule 2: When all ant colonies complete their tasks, the global pheromone is updated according to the following equation.

$$\tau_j(t + n) = (1 - \rho)\bullet\tau_j(t) + \Delta\tau_j(t) \tag{9}$$

Here, $\Delta\tau_j(t)=1/t_{bestj}$, t_{bestj} is the download time after obtaining the global optimal solution.

In stimulated annealing algorithm, the current temperature t is compared with previous solution. The simulated annealing algorithm is used to perturb the optimal solution through the replacement rule. For two randomly selected videos, if the response time reduces after exchanging the locations of the videos, the new solution is accepted. The new solution is accepted with the probability which is written as follows:

$$p = 1 \begin{cases} \exp\left(-\dfrac{t(L) - \overline{t(L)}}{T}\right), & t(L) - \overline{t(L)} > 0 \\ 0, & otherwise. \end{cases} \tag{10}$$

Here, $t(L)$ represents the download delay from the exchangeable location to obtaining the video during current temperature T; the $\overline{t(L)}$ represents the local minimum download delay obtained by the ant colony algorithm.

The procedure of ACSA caching strategy is summarized as following algorithm.

Algorithm 1 (ACSA caching strategy)

Step 1: initialize the parameter: the number of iterations, pheromone concentration, initial temperature and termination temperature, etc.

Step 2: use ant colony algorithm to search the paths and construct candidate solutions according to Equation (7).

Step 3: calculate the local optimal solution according to the principle of the shortest time to complete the download of all contents, and update the local pheromone according to Equation (8).

Step 4: use simulated annealing algorithm to perturb the optimal solution in the current area through permutation rules to construct a new solution, and determine the probability of the new solution to be accepted.

Step 5: determine whether the local optimal solution obtained under the current temperature T meets the sampling stability criterion. If the local optimal solution satisfies the stability criterion, the procedure goes to next step; otherwise, the procedure goes to step 4;

Step 6: update the global pheromone concentration according to Equation (9).

Step 7: if the number of tempering times reaches predefined constant or the current temperature is lower than the termination temperature, the optimal solution will be output; otherwise, the procedure goes back to step 2.

4. EXPERIMENTS AND SIMULATIONS

In order to verify the architecture for national traditional sports video distribution by using ant colony-stimulated annealing cache strategy, we compare ACSA with ant colony algorithm (AC), stimulated annealing algorithm (SA), DLC (Matsuzono 2017), and random-based caching strategy (RC). The experimental results are reported in terms of time delay and hit rate of caching items. By caching popular videos in MEC server, the delay time can be reduced. An efficient caching strategy can increase the hit rate of caching items and reduce the delay time as well. It is assumed that the popularity of videos follows Zipf distribution whose influence factor is set as 0.47. The parameters, α, β, in Eq. (7) are set as 0.25, 0.95, respectively. The initial temperature, T0, is set as 900. The minimum temperature, Tmi_n is set as 20.

First, we validate the influence of iterations on ant colony-simulated annealing caching strategy. We compare ant colony-simulated annealing caching strategy with ant colony algorithm and stimulated annealing algorithm. The number of MEC servers is set as 30, the number of national traditional sports videos is set as 2000, and the range of iteration times is set as {40,60,80,100,120,140,160}. The result

Figure 2. The influence of iterations on ant colony-stimulated annealing caching strategy

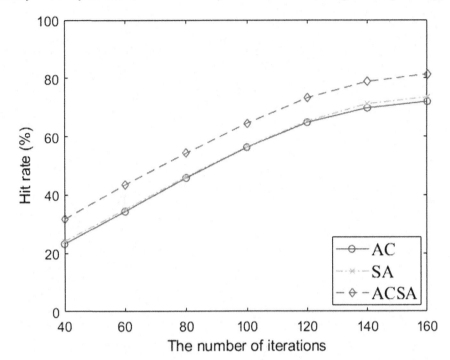

of hit rate is reported in Figure 2. The horizontal axis represents the number of iterations, while vertical axis represents the hit rate.

From Figure 2, it can be found that ant colony algorithm, stimulated annealing algorithm, and colony-stimulated annealing caching strategy all converge with the increase of iterations; ant colony-stimulated annealing caching strategy converges faster than both ant colony algorithm and stimulated annealing algorithm; ant colony-stimulated annealing caching strategy achieves higher hit rate than both ant colony algorithm and stimulated annealing algorithm.

Second, we evaluate the influence of the number of MEC servers on caching strategies. We compare the ant colony-stimulated annealing caching strategy with ant colony algorithm, stimulated annealing algorithm, DLC and random-based caching strategy. The number of national traditional sports videos is set as 2000, and the number of MEC servers is set as 10, 15, 20, 25, 30. The number of iterations is set as 150 in ant colony algorithm, stimulated annealing algorithm, and ant colony-stimulated annealing caching strategy. The curves of hit rate are reported in Figure 3. The horizontal axis represents the number of MEC servers, while vertical axis represents the hit rate.

From Figure 3, it can be found that the hit rate increases with the number of MEC servers for ant colony algorithm, stimulated annealing algorithm, DLC, random-based caching strategy, and colony-stimulated annealing caching strategy; the ant colony-stimulated annealing caching strategy performs better than other caching strategies. The result of corresponding delay time is shown in Figure 4. The horizontal axis represents the number of MEC servers, while vertical axis represents the delay time.

Figure 3. The relation between the hit rate and the number of MEC servers

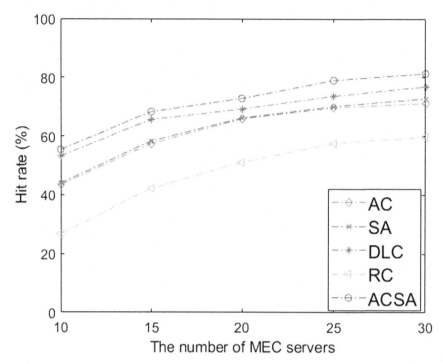

Figure 4 The relation between the delay time and the number of MEC servers

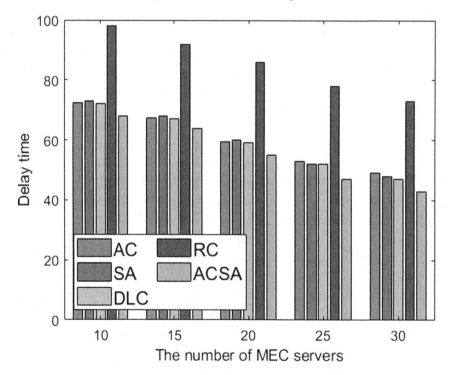

From Figure 4, it can be found that the delay time decreases with the number of MEC servers for ant colony algorithm, stimulated annealing algorithm, DLC, random-based caching strategy, and colony-stimulated annealing caching strategy; the ant colony-stimulated annealing caching strategy spends fewer delay time than other caching strategies. The reason is that a higher hit rate means fewer requests from cloud center.

Third, we evaluate the influence of the number of videos on caching strategies. Obviously, the more the videos the cloud center contains, the lower the hit rate is. We still compare the ant colony-stimulated annealing caching strategy with ant colony algorithm, stimulated annealing algorithm, DLC and random-based caching strategy. The number of MEC servers, and the number of iterations is set as 150 in ant colony algorithm, stimulated annealing algorithm, and ant colony-stimulated annealing caching strategy. The number of national traditional sports videos is set as 2000, 3000, 4000, 5000, 6000. The curves between hit rate and the number of videos are reported in Figure 5. The horizontal axis represents the number of videos in cloud center, while vertical axis represents the hit rate.

Figure 5. The relation between the hit rate and the number of videos in cloud center

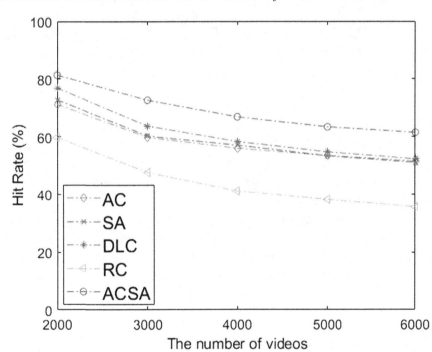

From Figure 5, it can be found that the hit rate decreases with the number of videos in cloud center for ant colony algorithm, stimulated annealing algorithm, DLC, random-based caching strategy, and colony-stimulated annealing caching strategy; the ant colony-stimulated annealing caching strategy decreases slower than other caching strategies. Thus, ant colony-stimulated annealing caching strategy performs better than other caching strategies. The result of corresponding delay time is shown in Figure 6. The horizontal axis represents the number of videos in cloud center, while vertical axis represents the delay time.

Figure 6. The relation between the delay time and the number of videos in cloud center

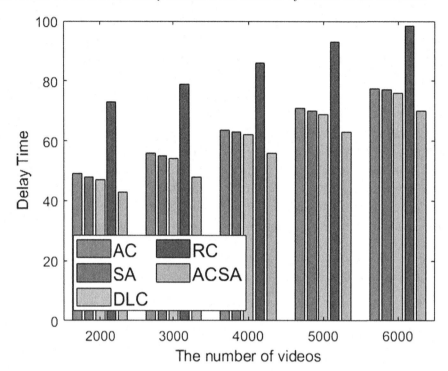

From Figure 6, it can be found that the delay time increases with the number of videos in cloud center for ant colony algorithm, stimulated annealing algorithm, DLC, random-based caching strategy, and ant colony-stimulated annealing caching strategy. However, the ant colony-stimulated annealing caching strategy still spends fewer delay time than other caching strategies and the cost of delay time increases more slowly than other caching strategies.

From above experiments, we can find that ant colony-stimulated annealing caching strategy can increase the hit rate of the videos in MEC servers and reduce the delay time. The ant colony-stimulated annealing caching strategy can solve the content distribution for national traditional sports video and is helpful to promote the development of national traditional sports.

5. CONCLUSION

The national traditional sports represent the spirit and culture of a country or nation. In order to promote the development of national traditional sports, this paper designs a distribution structure which utilizes software defined network (SDN) and mobile edge computing (MEC) technologies. In order to increase the hit rate of the caching national traditional sports videos in mobile edge computing servers, we design a novel caching strategy by combining ant colony algorithm and stimulated annealing algorithm in order to overcome the weaknesses when using ant colony algorithm or stimulated annealing algorithm lonely. In experiments, we compare ant colony-stimulated annealing caching strategy with ant colony algorithm, stimulated annealing algorithm, DLC, and random-based caching strategy. The experimental results shows that ant colony-stimulated annealing caching strategy converges faster than both ant colony algorithm and stimulated annealing algorithm, the hit rate of ant colony-stimulated annealing caching strategy is higher than other caching strategies, and the delay time of ant colony-stimulated annealing caching strategy is less than other caching strategies. However, the hit rate of ant colony-stimulated annealing still needs to be improved further. Our future work will focus on improving the hit rate of caching strategy for the contents which are stored in the MEC servers.

ACKNOWLEDGMENT

This work is supported by the research and planning project of Philosophy and Social Science Research Planning Project In Heilongjiang Province (19TYC157), University Nuring Program for Young Scholars with Creative Talents in Heilongjiang Porovince (UNPYSCT-2020077).

REFERENCES

Assad, A., & Deep, K. (2018). A hybrid harmony search and simulated annealing algorithm for continuous optimization. *Information Sciences*, *450*, 246–266. doi:10.1016/j.ins.2018.03.042

Huang, C. M., Chiang, M. S., Dao, D. T., Su, W. L., Xu, S., & Zhou, H. (2018). V2V data offloading for cellular network based on the software defined network (SDN) inside mobile edge computing (MEC) architecture. *IEEE Access : Practical Innovations, Open Solutions*, *6*, 17741–17755. doi:10.1109/ACCESS.2018.2820679

Kassim, M., Azmi, A., Rahman, R. A., Yusof, M. I., Mohamad, R., & Idris, A. (2018). Bandwidth control algorithm on youtube video traffic in broadband network. *Journal of Telecommunication Electronic and Computer Engineering*, *10*(1-5), 151–156.

Li, Z., Zhang, L., & Li, L. (2017, February). National traditional sports culture elites and the inheritance and protection of national traditional sports culture. In *2016 7th International Conference on Education, Management, Computer and Medicine (EMCM 2016)*. Atlantis Press. 10.2991/emcm-16.2017.144

Liu, J., Yang, J., Liu, H., Tian, X., & Gao, M. (2017). An improved ant colony algorithm for robot path planning. *Soft Computing*, *21*(19), 5829–5839. doi:10.100700500-016-2161-7

Matsuzono, K., Asaeda, H., & Turletti, T. (2017, May). Low latency low loss streaming using in-network coding and caching. In *IEEE INFOCOM 2017-IEEE Conference on Computer Communications* (pp. 1-9). IEEE. 10.1109/INFOCOM.2017.8057026

Ning, Z., Hu, X., Chen, Z., Zhou, M., Hu, B., Cheng, J., & Obaidat, M. S. (2017). A cooperative quality-aware service access system for social Internet of vehicles. *IEEE Internet of Things Journal*, *5*(4), 2506–2517. doi:10.1109/JIOT.2017.2764259

Wang, J., Hu, Y., Li, H., & Shou, G. (2018, August). A lightweight edge computing platform integration video services. In *2018 International Conference on Network Infrastructure and Digital Content (IC-NIDC)* (pp. 183-187). IEEE. 10.1109/ICNIDC.2018.8525808

Wang, S., Zhao, Y., Xu, J., Yuan, J., & Hsu, C. H. (2019). Edge server placement in mobile edge computing. *Journal of Parallel and Distributed Computing*, *127*, 160–168. doi:10.1016/j.jpdc.2018.06.008

Zhang, Z., Zeng, T., Yu, X., & Sun, S. (2018). Social-aware D2D pairing for cooperative video transmission using matching theory. *Mobile Networks and Applications*, *23*(3), 639–649. doi:10.100711036-017-0973-z

Zhao, T., Liu, Q., & Chen, C. W. (2016). QoE in video transmission: A user experience-driven strategy. *IEEE Communications Surveys and Tutorials*, *19*(1), 285–302. doi:10.1109/COMST.2016.2619982

Zhou, Y., Yu, F. R., Chen, J., & Kuo, Y. (2017). Resource allocation for information-centric virtualized heterogeneous networks with in-network caching and mobile edge computing. *IEEE Transactions on Vehicular Technology*, *66*(12), 11339–11351. doi:10.1109/TVT.2017.2737028

This research was previously published in the International Journal of Distributed Systems and Technologies (IJDST), 12(2); pages 1-12, copyright year 2021 by IGI Publishing (an imprint of IGI Global).

Chapter 27

Fog Computing and Edge Computing for the Strengthening of Structural Monitoring Systems in Health and Early Warning Score Based on Internet of Things

Leonardo Juan Ramirez Lopez

ⓘ https://orcid.org/0000-0002-6473-5685

Universidad Militar Nueva Granada, Colombia

Gabriel Alberto Puerta Aponte

ⓘ https://orcid.org/0000-0003-1730-170X

Universidad Militar Nueva Granada, Colombia

ABSTRACT

Currently, with the implementation of IoT, it is expected that medicine and health obtain a great benefit derived from the development of portable devices and connected sensors, which allow acquiring and communicating data on symptoms, vital signs, medicines, and activities of daily life that can affect health. Despite the possible benefits of health services assisted by IoT, there are barriers such as the storage of data in the cloud for analysis by physicians, the security and privacy of the data that are communicated, the cost of communication of the data that is collected, and the manipulation and maintenance of the sensors. This chapter intends to deploy and develop the context of the IoT platforms in the field of health and medicine by means of the transformation of edge and fog computing, as intermediate layers that provide interfaces between heterogeneous networks, networks inherited infrastructure, and servers in the cloud for the ease of data analysis and connectivity in order to implement a structural health monitoring based on IoT for application of early warning score.

DOI: 10.4018/978-1-6684-5700-9.ch027

INTRODUCTION

The new platforms, being a great collaborator and promoter of the new tools, models, instruments and appearances of the health sector (Marolla, 2018). The most implemented applications through IoT is the monitoring, monitoring and management of sector contents (Hsieh, Lee, & Chen, 2018). These applications show great problems according to the sensitive characteristic of the information that is managed. Some of the most representative issues of IoT implementation, in the e-health electronic health management systems, are due to the need for information privacy, secure communication in the media, authentication, protocols control, transport and service orchestration (Aghili, Mala, Shojafar, & Peris-Lopez, 2019). In addition to this the growth of these applications and users, can cause the growth of large volumes of data, which will require great resources or for their transport and analysis (Annamalai, Bapat, & Das, 2019).

IoT can define as a global infrastructure for the information society, which through available services enables the interconnection of physical and virtual objects based on interoperable business-to-business communication technologies (Networks, 2012).The IETF defines IoT as the Internet that considers simultaneous TCP / IP and non-TCP / IP sets and devices or items as objects "created" by single directives (Valdivieso, Peral, Barona & García, 2014). IEEE IoT in its Special Report on "Internet of Things" as defined: A device that connects devices with detection storage (Minerva, Biru, & Rotondi, 2015). Now redefine as a red that connects uniquely identifiable virtual and physical devices using new or existing communication protocols. Verify that dynamically configured devices or devices and user interfaces are accessible from a distance from the Internet (Mirón Rubio et al., 2018).

INTERNET OF THINGS

Currently, science debates about the Internet of Things (IoT) paradig, given the technological advance and the increase of application fields (Lee & Lee, 2015). Even more so when technological trends and innovation at the global level, the results for the diversification of services for society and industry in general (Vögler Matrikelnummer, 2016a). Thus, applications based on the use of content, the possibilities in the services of smart and connected homes, industries 4.0, the orange economy, specialized medical care, health self-care, environmental monitoring, adaptive logistics, the national defense, the automatic transport and the cybersecurity (O. Salman, Elhajj, Chehab, & Kayssi, 2018) .

For the implementation of IoT there are different platforms, hardware and architectures, they are used for different providers, they are given the opportunity to have heterogeneous networks of inherited technology and a variety of them, or the means of communication, the formats of the data and the means of transmission (Cha et al., 2016; S. Lee, Bae, & Kim, 2017). On the other hand, interoperability becomes the priority of the integration of communication systems, the interconnected media, not only at a physical level, but at the level of applications and services (Jabbar, Ullah, Khalid, Khan, & Han, 2017; Bhattarai & Wang, 2018). As an alternative, IoT technology designers use protocols such as: ZigBee, Z-wave, LTE, Wi-Fi, Ethernet, X10, Bluetooth, among others; However, in the standard IoT application network (Minerva et al., 2015) it can be used as an intermediate manager between the legacy data networks and the final sensors.

The International Telecommunications Union (ITU), expected before 2020, the IoT platforms are around 50,000 million network devices (ITU Corporation, 2015). Forbes publishes that the prediction of the IoT markets for the year 2021 will be approximately 521 billion dollars, more than double the year 2017 (Forbes, 2018). This is a sample that in the future. This trend shows that in the near future there will be more connected devices than people, which will have an impact on almost every aspect of our lives (Bramsen, 2017). The communication capacity will not be limited simply to mobile devices, on the contrary this capacity will expand to the things we live with every day (Atzori, Iera, & Morabito, 2017). This means that not only objects or things can communicate, but contents and other media also enter into this new scenario, which can change the paradigm of legacy technologies and networks (O. Salman, Elhajj, Chehab, & Kayssi, 2018).

IoT can be defined as a global infrastructure for the information society, which allows through advanced services the interconnection of physical and virtual objects, based on interoperable communication technologies between existing and evolving (Mehner, e.d.). The IETF defines IoT as the Internet that considers sets of TCP / IP and not TCP / IP simulate us and devices or things as "objects" identified by unique addresses. IEEE IoT in its special report on "Internet of Things", defined it as: A network that connects devices with detection capabilities (J. Wang & Li, 2018). Now it redefines it, as a network that connects identifiable virtual and physical devices in a unique way, using new or existing communication protocols. Where things or devices can be dynamically configured and have interfaces that must be accessible remotely via the Internet (Atzori, Iera & Morabito, 2017).

The concept of IoT, is related to other concepts and tools, which in turn can complement these platforms, for this, some of the connections that were considered the most relevant are described by next figure.

Figure 1. Concepts related to internet of things

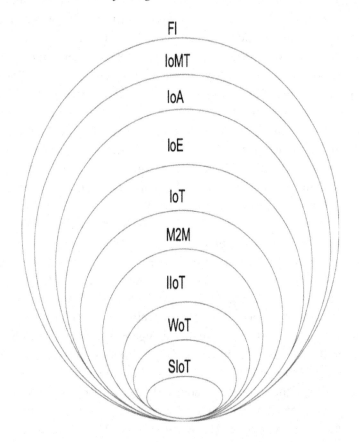

SIoT: Social Internet of Things (SIoT), is considered as the ability of objects as instruments for the establishment of social connectivity and autonomous relationship with users, for the discovery of network services and resources (Panda & Bhatnagar, 2020b). The social network of objects can find novel resources for the best domain in the implementation of user services. In social networks, physical or virtual objects are interconnected to the network to transmit the virtual dimension in decision making to the physical world (Roopa et al., 2019). The SIoT, allows objects to connect to social networks, can publish autonomous information in the owners' social loops, this for the realization of actions and activities related to the users of an automatic machine (Takiddeen & Zualkernan, 2019). The realization of activities automatically and the interaction with the social devices of the users and devices, implies that SIoT establishes and configures new rules, uses and benefits (Panda & Bhatnagar, 2020a).

WoT: The Web of Things (WoT), describes the integration of everyday objects with the web, for it requires integrated computer systems that allow communication and interoperability in the platforms and domains of the applications, that is, WoT generates mechanisms that give the possibility that the devices and services communicate with each other, and allows access and control of IoT resources and applications using conventional web technologies. Unlike IoT, WoT tries to integrate the network of objects, things, people, systems and applications, but still has several challenges of scalability and security (Médini et al., 2017; Chauhan & Babar, 2017).

IIoT: Industrial Internet of Things (IIoT), is how IoT platforms are considered, which provide interconnection and intelligence to industrial systems through the implementation of detection devices, sensors and actuators capable of belonging to ubiquitous and heterogeneous networks (Li & Wang, 2019). The IIoT platforms are positioning themselves as an effective and impacting industry 4.0, a concept of industrial development trends globally (Kabugo, Jämsä-Jounela, Schiemann, & Binder, 2020).

M2M: Machine to Machine (M2M), refers to communications and interactions between machines and devices, these interactions can occur through one or more communication networks or through a cloud computing infrastructure (Shala, Trick, Lehmann, Ghita, & Shiaeles, 2019). M2M offers the means to manage devices interactively, while collecting data from machines or sensors, facilitating communications with mechanical automation (Azad, Bag, Hao, & Salah, 2018). M2M applications cover different areas such as intelligent networks, transport systems, industrial automation, environmental monitoring and e-healthcare (R. H. Ahmad & Pathan, 2016).

IoE: The Internet of Everything (IoE), is a global dynamic information network that links any object and people on the Internet, this is how the internet of things involves, but also expands to include people, processes and data in a broader scope, that allows to make connections generating the capacity to collect large amounts of data and the analysis of them (Iannacci, 2018). The exchange of information and communications is one of the most relevant aspects, which enables the development of other applications such as monitoring biometric data in real time (Galitsky & Parnis, 2019).

IoA: Internet of Agents (IoA), can be defined as an evolutionary IoT process, where the participation of the final devices is considered as a fundamental factor for the adaptability to the behavior of the networks within the IoT platforms (Pico-Valencia, Holgado-Terriza, Herrera-Sánchez, & Sampietro, 2018). This adaptation of network resources is obtained by customizing specific agents at runtimes of the services in IoT (R. Wang et al., 2020). Other authors identify IoA, as an intelligent ecosystem of agents that can manage the resources associated with IoT objects. Resources are management can achieve a level of cognition through software agents that employ semantic techniques that are embedded within the infrastructure (R. Wang et al., 2020). In this way agents have the ability to manage context, loops or social circles, services and resources of IoT (Mostafa, Gunasekaran, Mustapha, Mohammed, & Abduallah, 2020).

IoMT: The Internet of Medical products or the Internet of Medical Things (IoMT), can be defined as the connectivity of a medical device to a health care system through an online network, such as a cloud, which often involves machine communication machine. This refers to the devices based on medical sensors that are incorporated with IoT and whose data collected with these devices are combined with the electronic medical records systems to achieve the transformation of health systems, making them more efficient and efficient. Thus, with the growing development of IoT health sensors, the collection and analysis of medical data is achieved, to reduce the annual costs of managing chronic diseases by about one third (Basatneh, Najafi, & Armstrong, 2018).

FI: Future Internet (FI), is a global network that will encompass all the above-mentioned networks (You, 2016). The FI has six fundamental principles that respond to the requirements of innovation and operation; The six basic principles are the following: Connectivity, Context, Collaboration, Cognition, Cloud and Content (Salamatian, 2011). This network will allow the connection of any type of device, which will generate large volumes of data; this data that will be handled by technologies based on cloud computing, which in turn will contribute to the analysis and transformation of behavior and the context of collaboration between devices, users, contents and things (You, 2016).

Challenges of Internet of Things

For the implementation of IoT there are different platforms and architectures, designed by different providers, which causes heterogeneous networks of inherited technology and a diverse range of physical or virtual sensor devices, communication protocols, data formats and transmission media (Farris, Taleb, Khettab, & Song, 2018). Moreover, interoperability is appropriate in the priority of integrating existing communication systems with new ones to interconnect, on the ground at the physical level, bell at the level of applications and services (Jabbar Ullah, Khalid, Khan & Han, 2017; Farris Taleb, Khettab & Song, 2018). Alternatively, IoT technology designers use protocols such as: ZigBee, Z-wave, LTE, Wi-Fi, Ethernet, X10, Bluetooth, among others; It is not possible to use some standardization protocol for IoT applications which acts as an intermediate manager between inherited data networks and final sensors (Vögler Matrikelnummer, 2016).

The Internet of things presents major challenges, due to its growth and dynamism (Bhattarai & Wang, 2018); in addition to its lack of standards, despite the spur of the moment and business and government initiatives for the development of open source code and hardware. For this reason, researchers have confronted solutions from different fields (Tayyaba, Shah, Khan, & Ahmed, 2017). Some authors define IoT architecture in ways such as internet-centric or home-centric (Almusaylim & Zaman, 2018).

Connectivity: The action of connecting thousands of millions of devices in red is not easy (Atzori Iera & Morabito, 2017). Summed up by the number of devices, it is the variety and variety of different categories and types of devices that constitute the heterogeneity of these platforms, it seems to be one of the most difficult but to achieve connectivity in these conditions (You, 2016). These major differences can break communication and expected performance metrics (Son, 2018).

Energy Consumption: The basic input for the operation of any electronic device is the energy. This input can be supplied by an electrical network, batteries or other forms of energy collection (Liu & Ansari, 2019). In any case, as a result of the scalability and size of the IoT platforms, the devices must be designed and built on the basis of low energy consumption (Ramirez Lopez, Puerta Aponte, & Rodriguez Garcia, 2019).

Interoperability and Integration: IoT implementations are based on many devices from different providers, which sometimes use different technologies (Grigoryan, Njilla, Kamhoua, & Kwiat, 2017). Successful solo integration is possible with IoT systems operating over open standards (El-Mougy, Al-Shiab, & Ibnkahla, 2019). Of any way there may be a number of standards for the same scope of application, but should be established and guaranteed interoperability between them (Soursos, Zarko, Zwickl, Gojmerac, Bianchi & Carrozzo, 2016).

Computing and Storage Capacity: The devices that can compose an IoT system generate large data chants (van Oorschot & Smith, 2019). These data can be presented in continuous form of ragages, can be structured or unstructured. For further analysis, data are transported, stored, and serviced by a large number of hardware and connectivity features (Dolui & Datta, 2017).

Security, Reliability and Privacy of Information: Establishing and penetrating IoT figures on a day-to-day basis, there is a need for generation and implementation of tailor-made secure solutions (Dolui & Datta, 2017). It should also be foreseen that the number of devices and the tendency to increase the number of devices in the design of secure IoT systems (Krishnan, Najeem, & Achuthan, 2018). For this reason, security solutions adapted to IoT must be portable, multi-device and reliable (Bull, Austin, Popov, Sharma, & Watson, 2016).

Different authors and organizations have initiated the response to the challenges of IoT implementation, from several trends, some focused on software and others focused on hardware (Atzori Iera & Morabito, 2017). From the conception of hardware and architecture, some researchers have come up with new solutions to the challenges of implementing IoT platforms, from the perspective of computing paradigms, cloud computing, fog computing and edge computing can be considered as another way to meet Iot's challenges in search of solutions (Li & Wang, 2019).

Cloud Computing: Cloud computing can be described as a paradigm that influences the form of design, development, implementation, prevention, and maintenance of applications across the network (Bull o.fl., 2016). Cloud computing is built as a utility model for the deployment of storage resources and computing capacity (Andreev, Petrov, Huang, Lema, & Dohler, 2019). This utility model is supported by network resources, which support the ability to access remote services (Dolui & Datta, 2017).

From the infrastructure in the cloud it is possible to access the sensors layer (things), where you can get, manage, store, analyze and view the data and services of users (Mourad, Nassehi, Schaefer, & Newman, 2020). Because of its storage and process capability, cloud computing allows for an important number of storage and processing service requests (K. Ahmad, Mohammad, Atieh, & Ramadan, 2019). Cloud computing is a tool for enhancing IoT platforms, where you can meet IoT implementation challenges, as long as you take care of the connectivity and network resources required over the latencies and connection times (Rayes & Salam, 2016). The Figure shows the principal features that must have a node to belong to the cloud computing paradigm.

In some IoT applications, they are considered critical to bandwidth latency and another's requirements and response times; In these circumstances, it is not practically dependent on cloud computing due to the need for small response times (Avasalcai & Dustdar, 2020). In these scenarios, where critical bandwidth resources and latencies are critical, where the fog computing paradigm nevertheless promises to

Figure 2. Features of cloud computing
Source Author

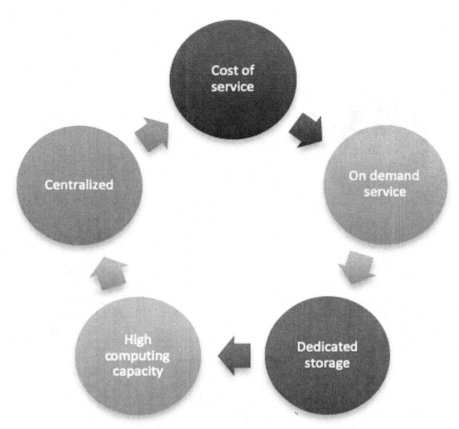

address the challenges and contribute to local and distributed solutions (Andreev, Petrov, Huang, Lema & Dohler, 2019; Yang et al., 2018).

Fog Computing: This paradigm has a main objective, this objective is ensure the inherited networks and infrastructure in the cloud, a large amount of storage, processing and connectivity requirements, performing around the end user (Avasalcai & Dustdar, 2020). The next figure shows the features of Fog computing.

The nearness of computation in the network with devices and users allows us to address problems related to bandwidth and latency requirements on a smaller scale (Casadei et al., 2019). From this location the architecture in the whole, it can improve the distributed nature of the applications, contributing to the increase of agility and efficiency (El-Mougy, Al-Shiab & Ibnkahla, 2019). However, this computing paradigm in some ways contributes to solving certain challenges of the IoT platforms, by itself, computing in its own presents its own challenges, which must be addressed so as to provide an acceptable computing framework (Naeem, Bashir, Amjad, Abbas, & Afzal, 2019). Some of the challenges of computing in the whole are given by sensitivity to delay and latencies, limitations of bandwidth, privacy, movement, and dynamism in topologies (Vilela, Rodrigues, Solic, Saleem, & Furtado, 2019).

Figure 3. Features of fog computing
Source Author

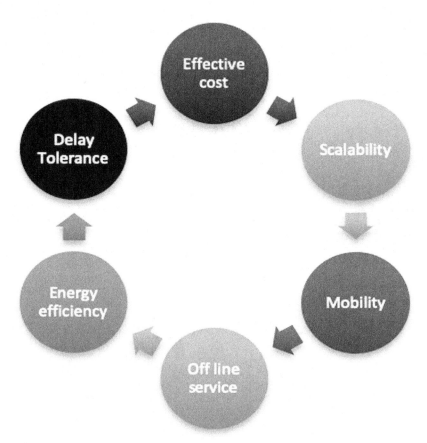

Edge Computing: There is another computing paradigm that is ubiquitous but close to users (devices and persons), this paradigm presents a distributed computing that implements services and resources in a decentralized way (Janjua, Vecchio, Antonini, & Antonelli, 2019). Decentralization allows labor to be carried out from the domains of data, devices, and applications (Galitsky & Parnis, 2019). The figure represents the main features for a node to fall into the computing paradigm at the edge.

Some researchers discuss the need Fog computing and Edge computing, as the only mechanism for meeting the requirements and overcoming the limitations of mobile devices (Cao, Zhang, & Shi, 2018). These limitations are added when mobile devices, which are immersed in personal area networks (PANs), there is a need to minimize the computing capacity that requires the areas, energy consumption, and data storage (Dolui & Datta, 2017). The next figure shows the principals and commons features of the three computations paradigms.

In an ideal scenario the constraints on the problem, as all would be without computer limitations on the infrastructure, the bandwidth would always be sufficient and redundant, the latency would be negligible and all the resources would be available for any request (Dolui & Datta, 2017). But for the implementation of applications, services and IoT platforms, in abrasive scenarios, with major restrictions on bandwidth, interoperability and connectivity, where remote discharge can be an unviable scenario;

Figure 4. Features of edge computing
Source Author

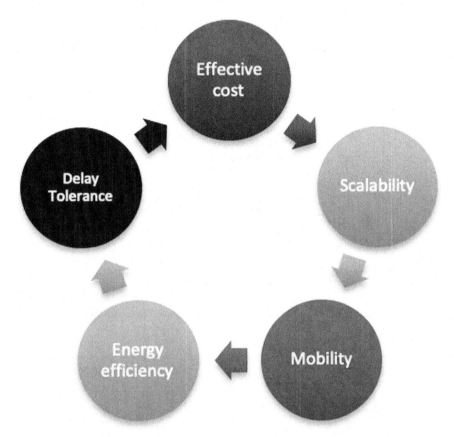

Occurring with the likelihood of what you think, in these scenarios, the computational paradigms in the field and in the border can manage resources efficiently, converting into an important tool in the search for solutions and capabilities in IoT platforms (Cao, Zhang & Shi, 2018).

Internet of Things Infrastructure and Architecture

This infrastructure, coast of an intermediate node architecture, this architecture will be the basis for the design and the way to ensure the deployment of resources and transport and connectivity services, which can enable the functioning of the applications in IoT, under critical conditions, with bandwidth finder restrictions and connectivity to the public cloud infrastructure. The solution must comply with the Service Level Agreement (SLA) parameters to achieve compliance with the maximum levels except for delays and latencies . The figure shows the general structure of IoT, with each part of the structure relating some resources and example services.

It is difficult to find a universal consensus on IoT architecture (Sethi & Sarangi, 2017a). Different architectures have been proposed from different fields between them and the field of research (Yaqoob et al., 2017). If I consider the different models of architecture proposed, the models of three and five layers (Madakam, Ramaswamy, & Tripathi, 2015). The Figure shows three and five layer architectural

Figure 5. Features of cloud computing
Source Author

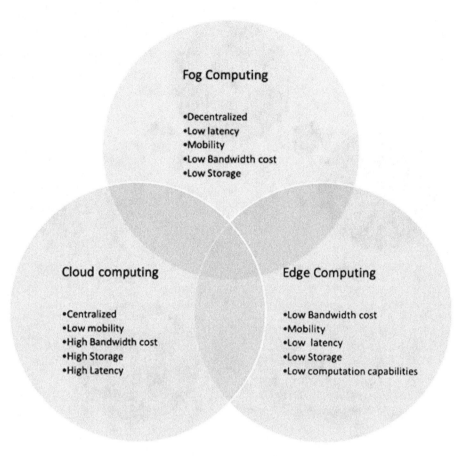

models for IoT. In these models we can see the architectural approaches, the first three-layer and resource-oriented, the second five-layer, service-oriented model.

Three-layer Internet of Things Architecture

This architecture defines the main idea of the IoT platforms, but is not sufficiently embraced for IoT deepening and research (Madakam, Ramaswamy & Tripathi, 2015). For this reason, some authors propose more architectures with more layers; but this three-layer architecture can be considered as the starting point for the implementation of other more complex and number of layers (O. Salman, Elhajj, Chehab & Kayssi, 2018).

Perception Layer: This layer is the physical layer of the architecture, in this layer if the sensors, personas the generators or collectors of information and contained (Santos, Wauters, Volckaert, & de Turck, 2018) (Poongodi, Krishnamurthi, Indrakumari, Suresh, & Balusamy, 2020). This layer detects physical parameters, recognizes their surroundings, detects objects or people around them (Tao, Zuo, Xu, & Zhang, 2014).

Figure 6. IoT Infrastructure
Source Author

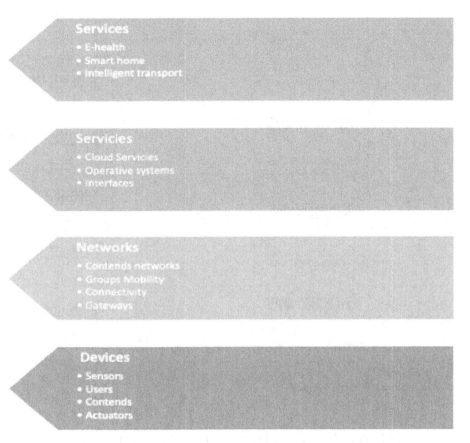

Network Layer: This layer has the responsibility to connect with other devices, users, network nodes and servers (Kulkarni & Bakal, 2019). The main features of this layer are the ability to transmit and process sensor actuator data (Hsieh, Lee & Chen, 2018).

Application Layer: The responsibility for this layer is for the purpose of delivering specific services for managed applications (Karagiannis, Chatzimisios, Vazquez-Gallego, & Alonso-Zarate, 2015) (Shang, Yu, Zhang, & Droms, 2016). If fields and applications on which IoT platforms are being implemented, some of the most popular applications are given in the fields of smart homes, smart transport, smart cities, smart farms, e-health, self-care systems and IoTM., among others (Chen et al., 2019)

Five-layer IoT Architecture

The architecture of five layers, is based on the architecture of three layers, adding the layers but called the next way; the processing layer and business layer (Kumar & Mallick, 2018) (Kumar & Mallick, 2018). Adding the layers, the model drops as follows; perception, transportation, processing, application and business. The role of the layers of perception and application varies with respect to their exposed in the model of three layers, as it is in the object of clarification in this section.

Figure 7. IoT architecture
Source Author

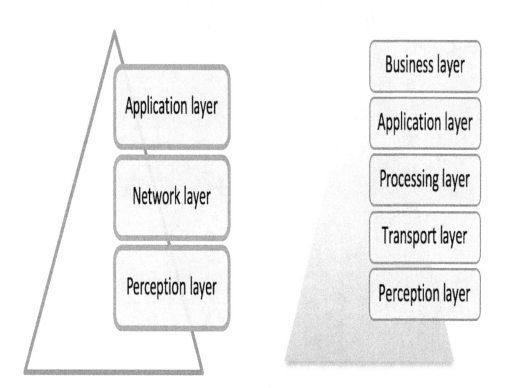

Transport Layer: This layer is charged with the transfer of data from the perception layer devices to the sense processing layer, through the use of inherited network services (Kumar & Mallick, 2018). Some examples of services and protocols networks: Zigbee, Z-wave, wifi, LTE, 3g, Bluetooth, among others.

Processor Layer: The processing layer is also called middleware. This layer analyzes and processes large data volumes, which are generated in the perception layer and transport layer (Kumar & Mallick, 2018). This layer is able to provide services to lower layers in accordance with requests and available resources (Mathew, Atif, & El-Barachi, 2017). Here you can find the full range of technologies such as data bases, processing modules and big data (Mathew, Atif, & El-Barachi, 2017).

Business Layer: Business layer is the task of managing the entire IoT platform, including all profit and commercial applications (Mathew, Atif, & El-Barachi, 2017). This layer includes efforts to protect the privacy of the user (Ikävalko, Turkama, & Smedlund, 2018a). This layer focuses on services and micro services that can be generalized from applications to users and users to IoT platforms (Ikävalko, Turkama, & Smedlund, 2018b).

Internet of Things Protocol Stack Architecture

IoT has been developed on the composition between networks, a heterogeneous network, an inherited network and a dedicated infrastructure (Soursos, Zarko, Zwickl, Gojmerac, Bianchi & Carrozzo, 2016).

For this reason the operation of the IoT platforms is supported in some cases by protocols belonging to the inherited networks (Sethi & Sarangi, 2017b). The development of proprietary protocols for operation and support on IoT platforms is given the premise of meeting the requirements for devices with low memory and process capability, but also limited bandwidth capability and high latency. (T. Salman & Jain, 2017). The next figure shows the protocol stack for IoT.

Figure 8. IoT protocols stack
Source (C.P, 2016)

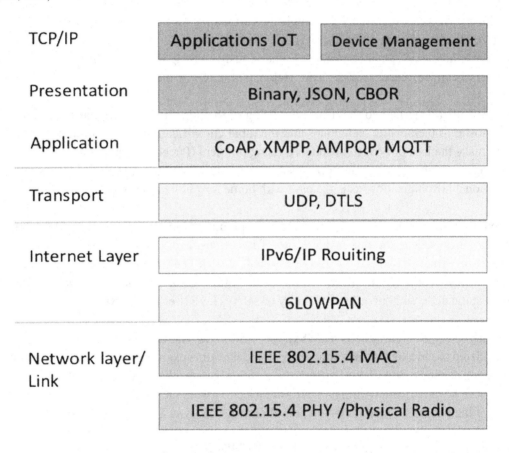

INTERNET OF THINGS HEALTH APPLICATIONS

One of the great applications and uses of IoT in health is remote monitoring systems, this systems can become an effective tool for health services, since these systems could provide several benefits in different contexts (McDaniel, Novicoff, Gunnell, & Cattell Gordon, 2018). It could provide feasible access for older people living independently in the home or people living in rural areas. In particular, it minimizes stress for health care users, such as non-critical patients at home instead of staying in hospitals (Mc-Curdy, 2012). The remote health monitoring system provides better control so that patients maintain their health at all times. The remote monitoring medical care system minimizes the cost and overcrowding of hospital beds (Bozorgchami, Member, Sodagari, & Member, e.d.).

E-health: The application of IoT technologies enables the application of electronic health, an assisted health modality that allows remote monitoring of patients in real time, creating a continuous record of record of data in the form of texts and graphics in the cloud (Journal, Engineering, & Kumar, 2019). On the other hand, the detection of variations in the signals, can be informed in real time to whom it corresponds (Kulkarni & Bakal, 2019).

The data monitored by e-health correspond to vital signs such as heart rate, which are complemented with the data record of the environment in which the individual is located, such as humidity and temperature, factors that can affect the health of people and whose knowledge allows to improve the monitoring via e-health and medical diagnosis, for example the variation of the heart rate can be presented according to the activity that the person performs, so that if this situation is known, false alerts will be avoided. In this way, the health service can be managed continuously, making the quality of medical care improve and the cost of care decreases (Zikria, Kim, Hahm, Afzal, & Aalsalem, 2019).

Home Hospitalization: Due to the increasing aging of the population, as well as the advancement in diagnostic or therapeutic techniques and the rapid chronification of noncommunicable diseases, they make the lack of beds in hospitals a rising problem (Puchi-Gómez, Paravic-Klijn, & Salazar, 2018). To weigh this, new care formulas have been developed for patient care, as an alternative to traditional hospitalization, as is the case with home hospitalization (Commonwealth, 2017).

Home hospitalization must respond to three basic premises: improve the quality of life of the patient and their families; reduce the rate and severity of infections, avoiding the onset of nosocomial infections; and reduce transfer and entry costs (Brody et al., 2019). The findings of the first randomized pilot study on the control of home health care in the United States show significantly lower costs, compared to usual hospital care, without reducing quality or safety (Levine et al., 2018).

EWSs: Early Warn Scored systems (EWSs), are built under the composition of scales, these scales considered the bio signals and vital signs of people, some examples of these are; heart rate, blood pressure, respiratory rate, body temperature, position among others (Albur, Hamilton, & MacGowan, 2016). In hospitalization settings, EWSs are used to assess the status, improvement or determination of the patient's condition over a period of time (Gerry et al., 2017).

Proposed Architecture for E-health and EWS Systems

In this architecture three intermediate layers are considered where the hardware associated with each one of the three computing paradigms is available; cloud, fog and edge computing.

This architecture have a four layers, three layers of them are the computer paradigms for IoT and the fourth layer are associated with devices and users (Naeem, Bashir, Amjad, Abbas, & Afzal, 2019). The layer of devices and users, works in principle as the layer of perception of the previous architectures, for this reason, it will not enter it in this section.

Cloud Layer: The cloud layer, as a rule, is burdened by the tasks that do not have to proceed in real time, these tasks are provided by data analysis, data storage and device management services. These services are preceded by non-access to network resources. Transmission time should not be a critical requirement for the delivery of required services, as the latency and delay time in this case is likely to be high (R. Wang et al., 2020; Cavalcante et al., 2016).

Fog Layer: The fog layer usually handles tasks, which requires a moderately high computational cost, but low latency times (Cavalcante et al., 2016). This layer is responsible for distributing tasks throughout its neighbors and storing a reduced volume of data (O. Salman, Elhajj, Chehab, & Kayssi, 2017). The hardware used in this capacity allows the process of micro analytics, analytics, storage and limited processing (Hsieh, Lee & Chen, 2018).

Edge Layer: This layer is oriented to cover particular requirements, such as basic network resources, connectivity between devices, real-time micro analytics and notification (Yu et al., 2017). This layer is the one that is closest to the devices, so it can provide cooperation between nodes and intermediation to upper and lower layers (Nunna & Ganesan, 2017).

Devices Layer: In this layer are the devices, users and things, it is in this layer where the perception or the execution of final tasks is carried out. This layer represents the heterogeneity of dispositive networks and platform protocols (O. Salman, Elhajj, Chehab, & Kayssi, 2018) .

Figure 9. IoT architecture
Source Author

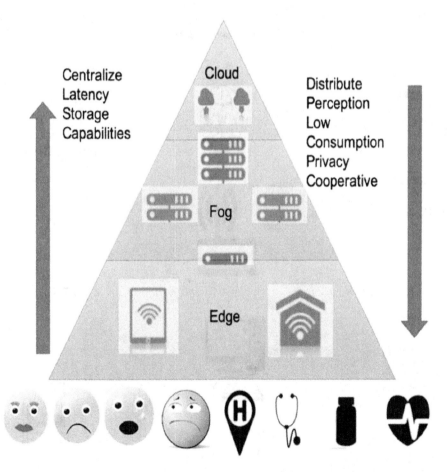

Proposed E-health and EWS Systems

The general design proposed for the implementation of e-health and EWS systems, based on two possible scenarios; The first scenario takes place with cloud connectivity and the second does not have that type of connectivity. In the case of the first scenario, the sensors are connected to an edge device, which performs data aggregation of all sensors and preprocessing them. After the data are avoided through the internet to the cloud infrastructure and replicated to the fog node. Once the data is in the cloud node, it is processed and stored; for the relationship of alerts, validations, alerts, alarms and the establishment of patterns and rules. The node in the cloud is responsible for verifying the codifications and issuing alarms when necessary.

In the second scenario, the data is collected by the edge device, then sent to the fog node, where they are temporarily stored, until connectivity to the cloud infrastructure is restored. These data are treated locally and micro analytical are performed to determine if it is necessary to measure alerts, alarms or notifications. Alerts and alarms are sent from the fog node to the other available fog nodes, local visualization is also provided for users and health professionals. Once it is determined that the connection to the cloud infrastructure is lost, it notifies the health professional of remote monitoring and the start of local services. The next figure shows de general overview of system proposed.

Figure 10. General overview E-health and EWSs work flow
Source Author

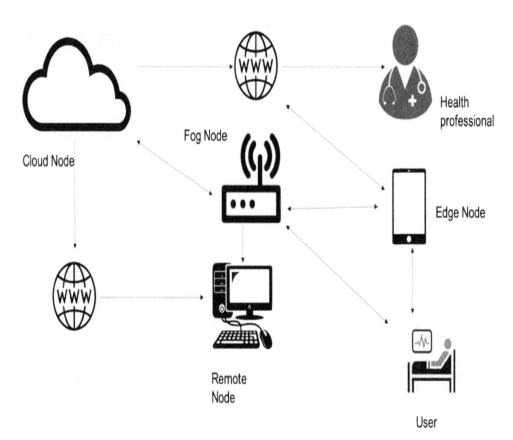

Figure 11. E-health and EWSs work flow
Source Author

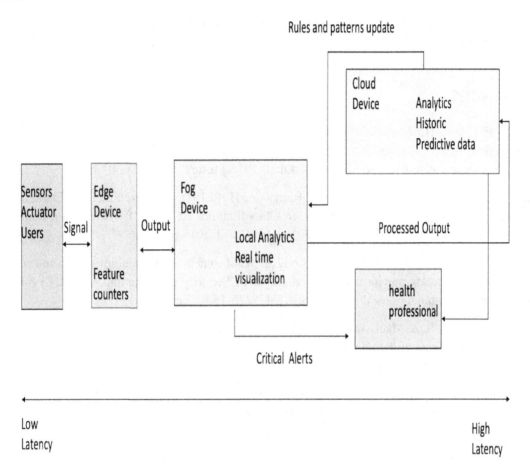

Proposed Data Flow for E-health and EWS Systems

The proposed detailed workflow can be seen in the following figure. The edge and fog nodes provide local services and support for cloud services when connectivity is not available. The fog node provides the service of visualization and local notification to the user to the health professional as the case may be. Once the data is collected, the edge or fog nodes are able to generate a corresponding alert or response for the actuators.

On the edge device the data of the sensors, devices and users are extracted, they are added and processed to be sent to the cloud or to the fog depending on the connectivity conditions. Once the data is sent, it is analyzed and stored; This data can be the object of integration or merger with other funetes of data, for the validation, comparison or verification of alerts. Once the alert is sent and processed the fog or cloud nodes send a response pattern to the edge nodes, so that in this way a preventive action is executed. Since fog devices have limited computational capabilities, data analysis and data storage activities are done in a modular manner, in the absence of cloud connectivity.

ACKNOWLEDGMENT

The authors are grateful for the support of the Universidad Militar Nueva Granada through its Research Vice-Rectory with project code IMP-ING-2660.

REFERENCES

Aghili, S. F., Mala, H., Shojafar, M., & Peris-Lopez, P. (2019). LACO: Lightweight Three-Factor Authentication, Access Control and Ownership Transfer Scheme for E-Health Systems in IoT. *Future Generation Computer Systems*, *96*, 410–424. doi:10.1016/j.future.2019.02.020

Ahmad, K., Mohammad, O., Atieh, M., & Ramadan, H. (2019). IoT: Architecture, Challenges, and Solutions Using Fog Network and Application Classification. ACIT 2018 - 19th International Arab Conference on Information Technology, 1–7. 10.1109/ACIT.2018.8672696

Ahmad, R. H., & Pathan, A.-S. K. (2016). A study on M2M (machine to machine) system and communication: Its security, threats, and intrusion detection system. Security Solutions and Applied Cryptography in Smart Grid Communications. doi:10.4018/978-1-5225-1829-7.ch010

Albur, M., Hamilton, F., & MacGowan, A. P. (2016). Early warning score: A dynamic marker of severity and prognosis in patients with Gram-negative bacteraemia and sepsis. *Annals of Clinical Microbiology and Antimicrobials*, *15*(1), 1–10. doi:10.1186/s12941-016-0139-z PubMed

Almusaylim, Z. A., & Zaman, N. (2018). A review on smart home present state and challenges: Linked to context-awareness internet of things (IoT). *Wireless Networks*, *5*, 1–12. doi:10.100711276-018-1712-5

Andreev, S., Petrov, V., Huang, K., Lema, M. A., & Dohler, M. (2019). Dense Moving Fog for Intelligent IoT: Key Challenges and Opportunities. *IEEE Communications Magazine*, *57*(5), 34–41. doi:10.1109/MCOM.2019.1800226

Annamalai, P., Bapat, J., & Das, D. (2019). Emerging Access Technologies and Open Challenges in 5G IoT: From Physical Layer Perspective. *2018 IEEE International Conference on Advanced Networks and Telecommunications Systems (ANTS)*, 1–6. 10.1109/ants.2018.8710133

Atzori, L., Iera, A., & Morabito, G. (2017). Understanding the Internet of Things: Definition, potentials, and societal role of a fast evolving paradigm. *Ad Hoc Networks*, *56*, 122–140. doi:10.1016/j.adhoc.2016.12.004

Avasalcai, C., & Dustdar, S. (2020). Latency-aware distributed resource provisioning for deploying IoT applications at the edge of the network. Lecture Notes in Networks and Systems, 69, 377–391. doi:10.1007/978-3-030-12388-8_27

Azad, M. A., Bag, S., Hao, F., & Salah, K. (2018). M2M-REP: Reputation system for machines in the internet of things. *Computers & Security*, *79*, 1–16. doi:10.1016/j.cose.2018.07.014

Basatneh, R., Najafi, B., & Armstrong, D. G. (2018). Health Sensors, Smart Home Devices, and the Internet of Medical Things: An Opportunity for Dramatic Improvement in Care for the Lower Extremity Complications of Diabetes. *Journal of Diabetes Science and Technology*, *12*(3), 577–586. doi:10.1177/1932296818768618 PubMed

Bhattarai, S., & Wang, Y. (2018). Internet of Things Security and Challenges. IEEE Computer, 78, 544–546. Retrieved from https://www.sciencedirect.com/science/article/pii/S0167739X17316667

Bozorgchami, B., Member, S., Sodagari, S., & Member, S. (n.d.). Spectrally Efficient Telemedicine and In-Hospital Patient Data Transfer. Academic Press.

Bramsen, P. (2017). Exploring a New IoT Infrastructure. University of California at Berkley. Retrieved from http://www2.eecs.berkeley.edu/Pubs/TechRpts/2017/EECS-2017-56.html

Brody, A. A., Arbaje, A. I., DeCherrie, L. V., Federman, A. D., Leff, B., & Siu, A. L. (2019). Starting Up a Hospital at Home Program: Facilitators and Barriers to Implementation. *Journal of the American Geriatrics Society*, *67*(3), 588–595. doi:10.1111/jgs.15782 PubMed

Bull, P., Austin, R., Popov, E., Sharma, M., & Watson, R. (2016). Flow based security for IoT devices using an SDN gateway. Proceedings - 2016 IEEE 4th International Conference on Future Internet of Things and Cloud, FiCloud 2016, 157–163. doi:10.1109/FiCloud.2016.30

Cao, J., Zhang, Q., & Shi, W. (2018). Challenges and opportunities in edge computing. Í. SpringerBriefs in Computer Science. doi:10.1007/978-3-030-02083-5_5

Casadei, R., Fortino, G., Pianini, D., Russo, W., Savaglio, C., & Viroli, M. (2019). A development approach for collective opportunistic Edge-of-Things services. *Information Sciences*, *498*, 154–169. doi:10.1016/j.ins.2019.05.058

Cavalcante, E., Pereira, J., Alves, M. P., Maia, P., Moura, R., & Batista, T. … Pires, P. F. (2016). On the interplay of Internet of Things and Cloud Computing: A systematic mapping study. *Computer Communications*. doi:10.1016/j.comcom.2016.03.012

Cha, S., Ruiz, M. P., Wachowicz, M., Tran, L. H., Cao, H., & Maduako, I. (2016). The role of an IoT platform in the design of real-time recommender systems. 2016 IEEE 3rd World Forum on Internet of Things (WF-IoT), 448–453. 10.1109/WF-IoT.2016.7845469

Chauhan, M. A., & Babar, M. A. (2017). Using Reference Architectures for Design and Evaluation of Web of Things Systems: A Case of Smart Homes Domain. Managing the Web of Things: Linking the Real World to the Web. doi:10.1016/B978-0-12-809764-9.00009-3

Chen, W., Zhang, Z., Hong, Z., Chen, C., Wu, J., & Maharjan, S. (2019). *Zhang, Y.* Cooperative and Distributed Computation Offloading for Blockchain-Empowered Industrial Internet of Things. IEEE Internet of Things Journal; doi:10.1109/jiot.2019.2918296

Commonwealth. (2017). Hospital at Home" Programs Improve Outcomes, Lower Costs But Face Resistance from Providers and Payers. Author.

Corporation, I. T. U. (2015). Internet of Things Global Standards Initiative. Internet of Things Global Standards Initiative. Retrieved from http://www.itu.int/en/ITU-T/gsi/iot/Pages/default.aspx

C.P., V. (2016). Security improvement in IoT based on Software Defined Networking (SDN). *International Journal of Science Engineering and Technology Research*, 5(1), 291–295.

Dolui, K., & Datta, S. K. (2017). Comparison of edge computing implementations: Fog computing, cloudlet and mobile edge computing. GIoTS 2017 - Global Internet of Things Summit Proceedings. doi:10.1109/GIOTS.2017.8016213

El-Mougy, A., Al-Shiab, I., & Ibnkahla, M. (2019). Scalable Personalized IoT Networks. *Proceedings of the IEEE*. 10.1109/JPROC.2019.2894515

Farris, I., Taleb, T., Khettab, Y., & Song, J. S. (2018). A survey on emerging SDN and NFV security mechanisms for IoT systems. *IEEE Communications Surveys and Tutorials*, (c): 1–26. doi:10.1109/COMST.2018.2862350

Forbes. (2018). IoT Market Predicted To Double By 2021, Reaching $520B. Author.

Galitsky, B., & Parnis, A. (2019). Accessing Validity of Argumentation of Agents of the Internet of Everything. Artificial Intelligence for the Internet of Everything. doi:10.1016/B978-0-12-817636-8.00011-9

Gerry, S., Birks, J., Bonnici, T., Watkinson, P. J., Kirtley, S., & Collins, G. S. (2017). Early warning scores for detecting deterioration in adult hospital patients: A systematic review protocol. *BMJ Open*, 7(12), 1–5. doi:10.1136/bmjopen-2017-019268 PubMed

Grigoryan, G., Njilla, L., Kamhoua, C., & Kwiat, K. (2017). *Enabling Cooperative IoT Security via Software Defined Networks*. SDN; doi:10.1109/ICC.2018.8423017

Hsieh, H.-C., Lee, C.-S., & Chen, J.-L. (2018). Mobile Edge Computing Platform with Container-Based Virtualization Technology for IoT Applications. *Wireless Personal Communications, 1*. doi:10.100711277-018-5856-5

Iannacci, J. (2018). Internet of things (IoT); internet of everything (IoE); tactile internet; 5G – A (not so evanescent) unifying vision empowered by EH-MEMS (energy harvesting MEMS) and RF-MEMS (radio frequency MEMS). *Sensors and Actuators. A, Physical*, 272, 187–198. doi:10.1016/j.sna.2018.01.038

Ikävalko, H., Turkama, P., & Smedlund, A. (2018a). Enabling the Mapping of Internet of Things Ecosystem Business Models Through Roles and Activities in Value Co-creation. Proceedings of the 51st Hawaii International Conference on System Sciences. doi:10.24251/HICSS.2018.620

Ikävalko, H., Turkama, P., & Smedlund, A. (2018b). *Value Creation in the Internet of Things: Mapping Business Models and Ecosystem Roles*. Technology Innovation Management Review; doi:10.22215/timreview/1142

Jabbar, S., Ullah, F., Khalid, S., Khan, M., & Han, K. (2017). Semantic {Interoperability} in {Heterogeneous} {IoT} {Infrastructure} for {Healthcare}. *Wireless Communications and Mobile Computing, 2017*, e9731806. doi:10.1155/2017/9731806

Janjua, Z. H., Vecchio, M., Antonini, M., & Antonelli, F. (2019). IRESE: An intelligent rare-event detection system using unsupervised learning on the IoT edge. *Engineering Applications of Artificial Intelligence*, 84(May), 41–50. doi:10.1016/j.engappai.2019.05.011

Journal, I., Engineering, A., & Kumar, S. (2019). An Extensive Review on Sensing as a Service Paradigm in IoT : Architecture, Research Challenges. *Lessons Learned and Future Directions, 14*(6), 1220–1243.

Kabugo, J. C., Jämsä-Jounela, S.-L., Schiemann, R., & Binder, C. (2020). Industry 4.0 based process data analytics platform: A waste-to-energy plant case study. *International Journal of Electrical Power & Energy Systems, 115*. doi:10.1016/j.ijepes.2019.105508

Karagiannis, V., Chatzimisios, P., Vazquez-Gallego, F., & Alonso-Zarate, J. (2015). *A Survey on Application Layer Protocols for the Internet of Things*. Transaction on IoT and Cloud Computing; doi:10.5281/ZENODO.51613

Krishnan, P., Najeem, J. S., & Achuthan, K. (2018). SDN framework for securing IoT networks. Lecture Notes of the Institute for Computer Sciences. *Social-Informatics and Telecommunications Engineering, LNICST, 218*, 116–129. doi:10.1007/978-3-319-73423-1_11

Kulkarni, N. J., & Bakal, J. W. (2019). E-Health: IoT Based System and Correlation of Vital Stats in Identification of Mass Disaster Event. Proceedings - 2018 4th International Conference on Computing, Communication Control and Automation, ICCUBEA 2018, 1–6. 10.1109/ICCUBEA.2018.8697529

Kumar, N. M., & Mallick, P. K. (2018). The Internet of Things: Insights into the building blocks, component interactions, and architecture layers. Í. *Procedia Computer Science.* doi:10.1016/j.procs.2018.05.170

Lee, I., & Lee, K. (2015). The Internet of Things (IoT): Applications, investments, and challenges for enterprises. *Business Horizons, 58*(4), 431–440. doi:10.1016/j.bushor.2015.03.008

Lee, S., Bae, M., & Kim, H. (2017). Future of IoT Networks: A Survey. Applied Sciences, 7(10), 1072. doi:10.3390/app7101072

Levine, D. M., Ouchi, K., Blanchfield, B., Diamond, K., Licurse, A., Pu, C. T., & Schnipper, J. L. (2018). Hospital-Level Care at Home for Acutely Ill Adults: A Pilot Randomized Controlled Trial. Journal of General Internal Medicine, 1–8. doi:10.1007/s11606-018-4307-z

Li, W., & Wang, P. (2019). Two-factor authentication in industrial Internet-of-Things: Attacks, evaluation and new construction. *Future Generation Computer Systems, 101*, 694–708. doi:10.1016/j.future.2019.06.020

Liu, X., & Ansari, N. (2019). Toward Green IoT: Energy Solutions and Key Challenges. *IEEE Communications Magazine, 57*(3), 104–110. doi:10.1109/MCOM.2019.1800175

Madakam, S., Ramaswamy, R., & Tripathi, S. (2015). Internet of Things (IoT): A Literature Review. Journal of Computer and Communications. doi:10.4236/jcc.2015.35021

Marolla, C. (2018). Information and Communication Technology for Sustainable Development. Information and Communication Technology for Sustainable Development. Springer Singapore. doi:10.1201/9781351045230

Mathew, S. S., Atif, Y., & El-Barachi, M. (2017). From the Internet of Things to the web of things-enabling by sensing as-A service. *Proceedings of the 2016 12th International Conference on Innovations in Information Technology, IIT 2016.* 10.1109/INNOVATIONS.2016.7880055

McCurdy, B. R. (2012). hospital-at-home programs for patients with acute exacerbations of chronic obstructive pulmonary disease (COPD): An evidence-based analysis. Ontario Health Technology Assessment Series.

McDaniel, N. L., Novicoff, W., Gunnell, B., & Cattell Gordon, D. (2018). Comparison of a Novel Handheld Telehealth Device with Stand-Alone Examination Tools in a Clinic Setting. Telemedicine Journal and e-Health. doi:10.1089/tmj.2018.0214

Médini, L., Mrissa, M., Khalfi, E. M., Terdjimi, M., Le Sommer, N., Capdepuy, P., … Touseau, L. (2017). Building a Web of Things with Avatars: A comprehensive approach for concern management in WoT applications. Managing the Web of Things: Linking the Real World to the Web. doi:10.1016/B978-0-12-809764-9.00007-X

Mehner, S. (n.d.). Secure and Flexible Internet of Things using Software Defined Networking. Academic Press.

Minerva, R., Biru, A., & Rotondi, D. (2015). Towards a definition of the Internet of Things (IoT). Retrieved from https://iot.ieee.org/definition.html

Mirón Rubio, M., Ceballos Fernández, R., Parras Pastor, I., Palomo Iloro, A., Fernández Félix, B. M., Medina Miralles, J., ... Alonso-Viteri, S. (2018). Telemonitoring and home hospitalization in patients with chronic obstructive pulmonary disease: Study TELEPOC. *Expert Review of Respiratory Medicine*, *12*(4), 335–343. doi:10.1080/17476348.2018.1442214 PubMed

Mostafa, S. A., Gunasekaran, S. S., Mustapha, A., Mohammed, M. A., & Abduallah, W. M. (2020). Modelling an adjustable autonomous multi-agent internet of things system for elderly smart home. Advances in Intelligent Systems and Computing, 953, 301–311. doi:10.1007/978-3-030-20473-0_29

Mourad, M. H., Nassehi, A., Schaefer, D., & Newman, S. T. (2020). Assessment of interoperability in cloud manufacturing. *Robotics and Computer-integrated Manufacturing*, *61*(June), 101832. doi:10.1016/j.rcim.2019.101832

Naeem, R. Z., Bashir, S., Amjad, M. F., Abbas, H., & Afzal, H. (2019). Fog computing in internet of things: Practical applications and future directions. *Peer-to-Peer Networking and Applications*, *12*(5), 1236–1262. doi:10.1007/s12083-019-00728-0

Nunna, S., & Ganesan, K. (2017). Mobile edge computing. Health 4.0: How Virtualization and Big Data are Revolutionizing Healthcare. doi:10.1007/978-3-319-47617-9_9

Panda, C. K., & Bhatnagar, R. (2020a). Social Internet of Things in Agriculture: An Overview and Future Scope. doi:10.1007/978-3-030-24513-9_18

Panda, C. K., & Bhatnagar, R. (2020b). Toward Social Internet of Things (SIoT): Enabling Technologies, Architectures and Applications (B. 846). doi:10.1007/978-3-030-24513-9

Pico-Valencia, P., Holgado-Terriza, J. A., Herrera-Sánchez, D., & Sampietro, J. (2018). Towards the internet of agents: An analysis of the internet of things from the intelligence and autonomy perspective. *Ingenieria e Investigacion*, *38*(1), 121–129. doi:10.15446/ing.investig.v38n1.65638

Poongodi, T., Krishnamurthi, R., Indrakumari, R., Suresh, P., & Balusamy, B. (2020). Wearable Devices and IoT. doi:10.1007/978-3-030-23983-1_10

Puchi-Gómez, C., Paravic-Klijn, T., & Salazar, A. (2018). Indicators of the quality of health care in home hospitalization: An integrative review. *Aquichan, 18*(2), 186–197. doi:10.5294/aqui.2018.18.2.6

Ramirez Lopez, L. J., Puerta Aponte, G., & Rodriguez Garcia, A. (2019). Internet of Things Applied in Healthcare Based on Open Hardware with Low-Energy Consumption. *Healthcare Informatics Research, 25*(3), 230. doi:10.4258/hir.2019.25.3.230 PubMed

Rayes, A., & Salam, S. (2016). Internet of things-from hype to reality: The road to digitization. doi:10.1007/978-3-319-44860-2

Roopa, M. S., Pattar, S., Buyya, R., Venugopal, K. R., Iyengar, S. S., & Patnaik, L. M. (2019). Social Internet of Things (SIoT): Foundations, thrust areas, systematic review and future directions. *Computer Communications, 139*, 32–57. doi:10.1016/j.comcom.2019.03.009

Salamatian, K. (2011). Toward a polymorphic future internet: A networking science approach. *IEEE Communications Magazine, 49*(10), 174–178. doi:10.1109/MCOM.2011.6035832

Salman, O., Elhajj, I., Chehab, A., & Kayssi, A. (2017). Software Defined IoT security framework. 2017 Fourth International Conference on Software Defined Systems (SDS), 75–80. doi:10.1109/SDS.2017.7939144

Salman, O., Elhajj, I., Chehab, A., & Kayssi, A. (2018). IoT survey: An SDN and fog computing perspective. *Computer Networks, 143*, 221–246. doi:10.1016/j.comnet.2018.07.020

Salman, T., & Jain, R. (2017). Networking protocols and standards for internet of things. Internet of Things and Data Analytics Handbook. doi:10.1002/9781119173601.ch13

Santos, J., Wauters, T., Volckaert, B., & de Turck, F. (2018). Fog computing: Enabling the management and orchestration of smart city applications in 5G networks. *Entropy (Basel, Switzerland), 20*(1). doi:10.3390/e20010004

Sethi, P., & Sarangi, S. R. (2017a). Internet of Things: Architectures, Protocols, and Applications. *Journal of Electrical and Computer Engineering, 2017*, 1–25. doi:10.1155/2017/9324035

Sethi, P., & Sarangi, S. R. (2017b). *Review Article Internet of Things : Architectures, Protocols, and Applications*. Academic Press.

Shala, B., Trick, U., Lehmann, A., Ghita, B., & Shiaeles, S. (2019). Novel Trust Consensus Protocol and Blockchain-based Trust Evaluation System for M2M Application Services. Internet of Things. doi:10.1016/j.iot.2019.100058

Shang, W., Yu, Y., Zhang, L., & Droms, R. (2016). Challenges in IoT Networking via TCP/IP Architecture. NDN Project, Tech. Rep. NDN-0038.

Son, J. (2018). Integrated Provisioning of Compute and Network Resources in Software-Defined Cloud Data Centers. Retrieved from https://minerva-access.unimelb.edu.au/bitstream/handle/11343/212287/thesis.pdf?sequence=1&isAllowed=y

Soursos, S., Zarko, I. P., Zwickl, P., Gojmerac, I., Bianchi, G., & Carrozzo, G. (2016). Towards the cross-domain interoperability of IoT platforms. EUCNC 2016 - European Conference on Networks and Communications, 398–402. 10.1109/EuCNC.2016.7561070

Takiddeen, N., & Zualkernan, I. (2019). Smartwatches as IoT Edge Devices: A Framework and Survey. 2019 Fourth International Conference on Fog and Mobile Edge Computing (FMEC), 216–222. doi:10.1109/FMEC.2019.8795338

Tao, F., Zuo, Y., Da Xu, L., & Zhang, L. (2014). IoT-Based intelligent perception and access of manufacturing resource toward cloud manufacturing. *IEEE Transactions on Industrial Informatics*. doi:10.1109/TII.2014.2306397

Tayyaba, S. K., Shah, M. A., Khan, O. A., & Ahmed, A. W. (2017). Software defined network (SDN) based internet of things (IoT): A road ahead. ACM International Conference Proceeding Series, Part F1305. doi:10.1145/3102304.3102319

Valdivieso, A., Peral, A., Barona, L., & García, L. (2014). Evolution and Opportunities in the Development IoT Applications. Retrieved from Http://Journals.Sagepub.Com/Doi/Full/10.1155/2014/735142

van Oorschot, P. C., & Smith, S. W. (2019). The Internet of Things: Security Challenges. *IEEE Security and Privacy*, *17*(5), 7–9. doi:10.1109/MSEC.2019.2925918

Vilela, P. H., Rodrigues, J. J. P. C., Solic, P., Saleem, K., & Furtado, V. (2019). Performance evaluation of a Fog-assisted IoT solution for e-Health applications. *Future Generation Computer Systems*, *97*, 379–386. doi:10.1016/j.future.2019.02.055

Vögler Matrikelnummer, M. (2016a). Efficient IoT Application Delivery and Management in Smart City Environments. Universität Wien. Retrieved from http://www.infosys.tuwien.ac.at/Staff/sd/papers/Diss_Voegler_Michael.pdf

Vögler Matrikelnummer, M. (2016b). *Efficient IoT Application Delivery and Management in Smart City Environments*. Academic Press.

Wang, J., & Li, D. (2018). Adaptive computing optimization in software-defined network-based industrial internet of things with fog computing. Sensors (Switzerland), 18(8), 2509. doi:10.3390/s18082509

Wang, R., Li, M., Peng, L., Hu, Y., Hassan, M. M., & Alelaiwi, A. (2020). Cognitive multi-agent empowering mobile edge computing for resource caching and collaboration. *Future Generation Computer Systems*, *102*, 66–74. doi:10.1016/j.future.2019.08.001

Yang, R., Wen, Z., Mckee, D., Lin, T., Xu, J., & Garraghan, P. (2018). *Chapter #: Fog Orchestration and Simulation for IoT Services*. Academic Press.

Yaqoob, I., Ahmed, E., Hashem, I. A. T., Ahmed, A. I. A., Gani, A., Imran, M., & Guizani, M. (2017). Internet of Things Architecture: Recent Advances, Taxonomy, Requirements, and Open Challenges. *IEEE Wireless Communications*, *24*(3), 10–16. doi:10.1109/MWC.2017.1600421

You, T. (2016). *Toward the future of Internet architecture for IoE*. Academic Press.

Yu, W., Liang, F., He, X., Hatcher, W. G., Lu, C., Lin, J., & Yang, X. (2017). A Survey on the Edge Computing for the Internet of Things. *IEEE Access : Practical Innovations, Open Solutions*. doi:10.1109/ACCESS.2017.2778504

Zikria, Y., Kim, S. W., Hahm, O., Afzal, M. K., & Aalsalem, M. Y. (2019). Internet of Things (IoT) Operating Systems Management: Opportunities, Challenges, and Solution. *Sensors (Basel)*, *19*(8), 1793. doi:10.3390/s19081793 PubMed

This research was previously published in Pattern Recognition Applications in Engineering; pages 59-83, copyright year 2020 by Engineering Science Reference (an imprint of IGI Global).

Chapter 28
A Comprehensive Survey on Edge Computing for the IoT

Pravin A.
Sathyabama Institute of Science and Technology, India

Prem Jacob
Sathyabama Institute of Science and Technology, India

G. Nagarajan
Sathyabama Institute of Science and Technology, India

ABSTRACT

The IoT concept is used in various applications and it uses different devices for collecting data and processing the data. Various sets of devices such as sensors generate a large amount of data and the data will be forwarded to the appropriate devices for processing. The devices used will range from small devices to larger devices. The edge computing becomes the major role in overcoming the difficulties in cloud computing, the nearby devices are used as servers for providing better services. Most of the issues such as power consumption, data security, and response time will be addressed. The IoT plays a major role in many real-world applications. In this chapter, the basics and the use of the Edge computing concept in different applications are discussed. Edge computing can be used to increase the overall performance of the IoT. The performance of various applications in terms of edge computing and other methodologies are analyzed.

INTRODUCTION

IoT Plays a major part in the real world due to the increase in the use of the IoT devices. In recent many IoT devices are used which will be gathering large amount of data and the data will be send to the appropriate devices for processing. The IoT devices such as sensors and other devices which will be interconnected through the network for the proper flow of data. The amount of data generated by these devices will be a huge one due to the increase in the use of these devices. In many real world application

DOI: 10.4018/978-1-6684-5700-9.ch028

such as electricity grid, Agriculture, Vehicle monitoring, Smart city and other applications are using these IoT devices. The IoT applications which will be using the Cloud concept cannot able to meet the upcoming demands. There are some difficulties which are faced by applications and that drawback can be overcome by using some new technology. The difficulties such as the delay in the transmission of the data through the network, power consumption, data security and the response time. The Edge computing plays a major role in the IoT applications. The edge computing will have multiple nodes and the user will be very near to that. Due to the Edge computing concept the performance of the IoT applications will be improved. The Edge technology will provide mechanisms for reducing the network traffic, the reducing the response time and other problems that exists in the network. The other factors are increase in the lifetime of the nodes. The major things to be focused is about the advantages of the Edge computing and comparing it with the existing technology. The major focus is towards the Integration of the IoT and the Edge computing concept.

INTERNET OF THINGS

There are many IoT applications such as smart grids, smart homes, smart city, Agriculture, smart health etc. Every application will be using the sensors for gathering information and other devices for processing. The IoT Devices which can be able to communicate with each other through Internet and can be controlled Remotely.

Sensors

The application uses large amounts of sensors for collecting the information, the sensors are used to sense the temperature, humidity, sound and other information. The information that is sensed by the sensor will depends up on the type of the sensors that will be used.

Figure 1. Different types of sensors

Figure 1 specifies different types of sensors such as the passive infrared sensor (PIR), the soil humidity sensor, the touch sensor, the ultrasonic sensor, the temperature sensor and the light sensor is represented in the Figure 1, There are many other sensors which will be used for sensing different types of data. For example, the soil humidity sensor which will be used to measure the humidity level in the soil.

IoT Applications

Figure 2. Different IoT applications

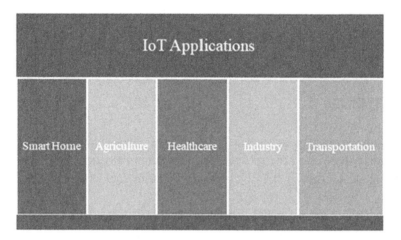

The Figure 2 specifies different IoT application such as health care, agriculture, industry, transportation and smart home, other than the listed areas IoT is used in many others such as wearables, retail, automation, security, etc. The applications use IoT devices for collecting and processing the information, for example the sensors will continuously gather the information. The information collected by the sensors will be transferred to the cloud environment and further the information will be accessed by the application and processed. If the Healthcare is considered various information from the patient will be gathered by the sensors that are attached. There are certain IoT devices we are using in our daily life such as Laptops, smartphone, television, smart meters, Setupbox, printers, connected cars and other set of devices that are connected. The usage of these devices is increasing and in future the usage of connected devices will be keep on increasing. In future most of the devices that are used in our day to day life will be connected and these devices will be generating a large amount of data. The data generated by these devices will be processed and depends upon the outcome further action will be taken.

The IoT devices that are used in our day to day life is given in the Figure 3, It is not at all limited to the devices that are given in the figure.

The entire process flow of an IoT application is given in the Figure 4, where the data gathered by the IoT devices is transferred through the network to the cloud environment and further it will be given to the particular application. The data gathered by the IoT devices will be stored in the cloud environment. The IoT gateway which will perform some set of data processing task by collecting the information from the sensors and the data will be forwarded to the cloud environment. The data will be further send to the application for further process.

Figure 3. IoT devices used in our day to day life

Figure 4. General process flow of IoT Application

EDGE COMPUTING

In the Edge computing concept, the servers will be very close to the users compared to the cloud environment. It will provide a better service and latency will also be low compared to the cloud. There will be an increase in the performance in terms of less computing power.

Architecture

At the bottom of the architecture the end devices such as sensors and other devices and the next level is the Edge nodes which will provide a better service to the end users, the computation and the storage of data is limited. The cloud environment which will provide unlimited storage and processing and the response time is slow.

Figure 5. Architecture of Edge computing Network

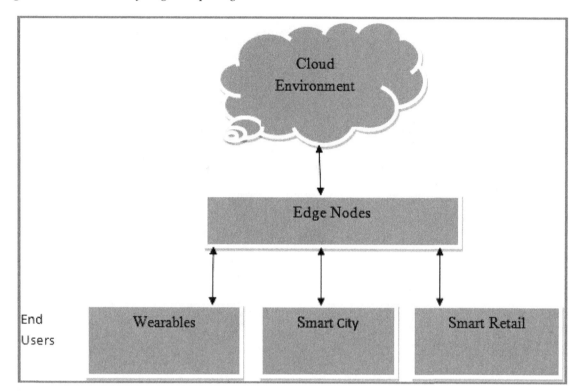

Survey

The Edge computing concept for the IoT applications is discussed by many researchers and also, they have further compared the existing methodology with the Edge computing concept. The impact and the use of Edge computing is analysed (Zhao et al., 2018) and proposed a three-phase methodology for analysing the traffic in the network. The concept of the Edge computing is discussed (Shi et al., 2016) and they have analysed different case studies and provided detail about different challenges that are faced. The Social IoT and the Edge computing concept is combined by means of an Agent approach and the effectiveness is analysed by using certain use cases (Circielli et al., 2018). The use of MEC (Multi-Access Edge Computing) in different application and various technical aspects related to that is discussed (Mach et al., 2017). Discussed about major use cases and reference categories and how the existing methods integrated with the concept (Mach et la, 2017). The comparison in terms of Edge computing and the Fog computing is performed and the Radio Access network in terms of Fog computing are also discussed (Ai et al., 2018a). The set of survey about Integrating the IoT with the cloud environment is discussed and clear clarification is given (Atlam et al., 2018). The entire concept of the Fog computing and how it can be used to improve the performance of the new set of IoT application. Fog computing related papers are discussed (Dasgupta et al., 2017) by analysing various set of research papers and also suggested what are the further advancement that can be done. Different set of use case for Fog computing is discussed and comparison is done with the existing research (Perera et al., 2017). Discussed about the steps to increase the performance of the IoT and also the Edge computing is categorized based on various factors (Yu et al., 2018). The impact of the Edge computing technologies with the IoT applications is discussed and also compared the performance by performing certain experimental analysis. Discussed about certain amount of security issues and privacy in terms of Fog computing (Premsankar et al., 2018). The overview and future work in terms of the multi access Edge computing concept is discussed (Yi et al., 2015) and comparison is performed. Main focus is on Fog computing and several surveys are made related to the security issues (Shahzadi et al., 2017).

REFERENCES

Ai, Y., Peng, M., & Zhang, K. (2018). Edge computing technologies for Internet of Things: A primer. *Digital Communications and Networks*, 4(2), 77–86. doi:10.1016/j.dcan.2017.07.001

Atlam, H., Walters, R., & Wills, G. (2018). Fog Computing and the Internet of Things: A Review. *Big Data and Cognitive Computing*, 2(2), 10.

Bhanu Sravanthi, D., & Rekha, G. (2017). Fog Computing a Survey of Integrating Cloud and IOT. *International Journal of Innovative Research in Computer and Communication Engineering*, 5(3).

Cicirelli, F., Guerrieri, A., Spezzano, G., Vinci, A., Briante, O., Iera, A., & Ruggeri, G. (2018). Edge computing and social internet of things for large-scale smart environments development. *IEEE Internet of Things Journal*, 5(4), 2557–2571.

Dasgupta, A., & Gill, A. Q. (2017). Fog Computing Challenges: A Systematic Review. In Proceedings of the *Australasian Conference on Information Systems*.

Mach, P., & Becvar, Z. (2017). Mobile Edge Computing: A Survey on Architecture and Computation Offloading. IEEE Communications Surveys & Tutorials, 19(3), 1628-1656.

Perera, C., Qin, Y., Estrella, J. C., Reiff-Marganiec, S., & Vasilakos, A. V. (2017). Fog computing for sustainable smart cities: A survey. *ACM Computing Surveys*, 50(3), 32.

Porambage, P., Okwuibe, J., Liyanage, M., Ylianttila, M., & Taleb, T. (2018). Survey on Multi-Access Edge Computing for Internet of Things Realization. IEEE Communications Surveys & Tutorials, 20(4), 2961-2991. doi:10.1109/COMST.2018.2849509

Premsankar, G., Di Francesco, M., & Taleb, T. (2018). Edge computing for the Internet of Things: A case study. *IEEE Internet of Things Journal*, 5(2), 1275–1284. doi:10.1109/JIOT.2018.2805263

Shahzadi, S., Iqbal, M., Dagiuklas, T., & Qayyum, Z. U. (2017). Multi-access edge computing: Open issues, challenges and future perspectives. *Journal of Cloud Computing*, 6(1), 30.

Shi, W., Cao, J., Zhang, Q., Li, Y., & Xu, L. (2016). Edge computing: Vision and challenges. *IEEE Internet of Things Journal*, 3(5), 637–646.

Yi, S., Qin, Z., & Li, Q. (2015). Security and privacy issues of fog computing: A survey. In *Proceedings of the International conference on wireless algorithms, systems, and applications*. Cham: Springer. 10.1007/978-3-319-21837-3_67

Yu, W., Liang, F., He, X., Hatcher, W. G., Lu, C., Lin, J., & Yang, X. (2018). A Survey on the Edge Computing for the Internet of Things. *IEEE Access*, *6*, 6900–6919. doi:10.1109/ACCESS.2017.2778504

Zhao, Z., Min, G., Gao, W., Wu, Y., Duan, H., & Ni, Q. (2018). Deploying edge computing nodes for large-scale IoT: A diversity aware approach. *IEEE Internet of Things Journal*, *5*(5), 3606–3614.

Chapter 29
Adaptive Edge Process Migration for IoT in Heterogeneous Fog and Edge Computing Environments

Chii Chang
University of Tartu, Estonia

Amnir Hadachi
https://orcid.org/0000-0001-9257-3858
University of Tartu, Estonia

Satish Narayana Srirama
University of Tartu, Estonia

ABSTRACT

To address the latency issue of the cloud-centric IoT management systems, researchers have introduced fog and edge computing (FEC) architecture, which distributes the computational tasks and decision making from the distant cloud to the edge or near the edge of IoT network. Considering the need for dynamic process migration from the mobile sensors to other resources when the mobile sensors are unable to continue their tasks, the IoT system needs to provide a flexible mechanism that allows the mobile sensors to dynamically migrate their tasks to the other FEC resources at runtime. The paper proposes a resource-aware edge process migration (REM) scheme that is capable of optimising the process migration decision. To realise such a system and to validate the REM scheme, the authors have developed a framework called edge process-enabled internet of thing (EPIoT) host. The framework and the REM scheme are implemented and evaluated. The results have shown that the REM scheme is capable of enhancing the performance of the process migration in heterogeneous FEC environment.

DOI: 10.4018/978-1-6684-5700-9.ch029

INTRODUCTION

The cloud computing paradigm has motivated various information systems moving from the local to the global Internet-based servers (Buyya et al, 2009; Buyya et al, 2017). Hence, having the management systems reside remotely have become a common practice for information systems. Unexceptionally, common Internet of Things (IoT) management systems have also followed the same architecture design (Chang et al, 2016). As the IoT front-ends continue increasing, and the involved data is getting larger, the drawback of the distant centralised system has risen, which is known as the latency issues, and it mainly derives from the fact that IoT system relies on the Internet as the main communication protocol between the front-end IoT devices and the back-end management server. Researchers discovered that there is a need to keep a certain process and decision making within or near the network where the front-ends are located in order to enhance the agility of the decision making in IoT applications. Such a paradigm is known as fog computing architecture.

A fog computing server is capable of providing storage, compute, acceleration, networking and control services by utilising virtualisation or containerisation technologies. For example, industrial integrated routers, which are capable of providing Virtual Machine (VM) or containers engine mechanisms, can support similar software deployment platform as the common cloud services. Moreover, by extending the Over-The-Air (OTA) programming mechanisms (Rossi et al, 2010), the IoT system can also distribute certain tasks to the resource constraint devices towards enabling self-managed IoT devices.

Today, fog computing architecture has become one of the main elements of IoT. Specifically, the market research has specified that the main applications of fog computing will be electricity/utilities, transportation, healthcare, industrial activities, agriculture, distributed datacenters, wearables, smart buildings, smart cities, retail and smart homes (451Research, 2017). Further, the emerged industrial standard IEEE 1934[1] and the market research report (451Research, 2017) indicate that the population of fog services will increase and it is foreseeable that fog services will not be limited in private networks but also available as public cloud today, in which different service providers can provide their fog computing servers for general public (Chang et al, 2017), which we can consider it as the public fog.

Suppose the near future smart cities encompass many local service providers who provide various public fog features, performing fog computing is no longer requiring IoT system management team to deploy their own physical fog computing servers (e.g. the high-end industrial routers), neither require them to upgrade their IoT equipment to compliant to fog computing; the management team can invoke the public fog to their system in order to distribute the tasks from their central server to the public fog in the proximity of their front-end IoT devices. Certainly, such an environment simplifies the establishment of fog computing and ideally reduces the cost from installing and maintaining physical equipment. However, it also raises a new challenge regarding the work assignment optimisation. Here, Figure 1 illustrates a Mobile Big Data acquisition (Chang et al, 2018) scenario that expresses the challenge.

In this scenario, a Big Data Service Provision (BDSP) system allows its client to request on-demand sensory data collection and pre-processing based on the customised algorithm of the client. Suppose the Big Data Service Provision Server (BDSP Server) has received a request from a Bid Data Service client (BDS Client) who intends to collect semi-real time information within the same district based on processing the collected sensory data using the client's algorithm written in the script supported by the BDSP. After BDSP Server validates the request package, it creates and dispatches the Process Deployment Package (PDP) to a Data Source Server (DSS) hosted on a mobile sensor located in the same district as the BDS Client. The request involves collecting 100 sensory data objects in a period of time and

Figure 1. Distributed processing in heterogeneous fog computing environment

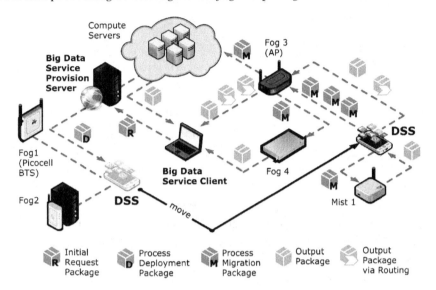

process the sensory data objects one by one using the client's algorithm. Although the distant compute servers (co-located with the BDSP Server) are always available for reducing the resource usage of DSS in performing the data processing, in order to reduce the latency, BDSP Server has commanded DSS to migrate the process to proximal fog servers managed by their partner companies whenever they are available. Initially, when DSS received the PDP from BDSP Server, it has discovered Fog1 and Fog2 servers. However, when the sensory data is ready to be processed, DSS has moved to another location where Fog1 and Fog2 are no longer connectable, and the new discovered servers are Fog3, Fog4 and Mist1. Since the fog servers may be serving the other clients, their resource states are dynamically changing all the time.

The scenario raises two questions:

- What is the optimal approach to migrate DDS's tasks to the heterogeneous fog servers?
- How to realise such dynamic process deployment and execution on DSS?

In order to answer the questions and after exploring the literature (section 2), we propose Resource-aware Edge process Migration (REM) scheme which is capable of assigning works based on runtime hardware states of the participants. Further, in order to realise such a system and to evaluate the proposed scheme, we developed Edge Process-enabled Internet of Things (EPIoT) host, which is an evolved software framework from the classic embedded Web server (Srirama et al, 2006). Further, we have implemented the proposed solution and have tested it on real-world equipment. In general, the results have shown that the proposed scheme is capable of improving the overall speed of the process distribution in the heterogeneous fog and edge computing environment.

This paper is organised as follows. Section 2 summarises the related works and specifies the differences between the proposed work and the past related works. Follow up in Section 3, the authors describe the proposed EPIoT framework and the involved components. Afterwards, in Section 4, the authors explain the proposed REM scheme and provide the details of the prototype implementation and the evaluation of the REM scheme in Section 5. Finally, this article is concluded in Section 6 together with future research directions.

RELATED WORK

The massive increase of connected ubiquitous and smart devices in our lives have been leading in the development of data streaming and cloud computing applications, such as computer vision (Zubal et al, 2016; Lopez et al, 2018), augmented reality (Alam et al, 2017), security (Levi et al, 2017), real-time monitoring (Kresimir et al, 2016) and tracking (Lucaet al, 2015). Consequently, the Internet of things (IoT) constitutes a major fabricator of big data which leads to two major issues for computing IoT-generated data. First one is related to the processing time since there are so many factors that can affect the response time such as the network delay and the performance of the available processing power. The second issue is related to the data uploading from a large number of IoT devices which can introduce network congestion and network delay. Therefore, it is important to know how to partition the data among all the available resources in the network for better performance in the processing time. Accordingly, many researchers have engaged in investigating the data partitioning and stream processing for analytics purposes. For example, Yang (Yang et al, 2017) has proposed a general model and architecture of fog data streaming based on analyzing common properties of numerous applications. Specifically, the approach took into consideration four important dimensions: system, data, human, and optimization. Correspondingly, the results were promoting the combination of network edge and stream processing. However, concerning human behavior in interacting with the devices and their movement, there is a need for developing new methods in each dimension (system, data, human, and optimization) to achieve cross-dimension optimization.

Another simple and widely spread approach is focusing on duplicating the data. Specifically, the concept is literally based on replicating the data in order to strengthen and reinforce the key characteristic of an efficient system: its availability, its increasing fault-tolerance, its low bandwidth consumption, and its enhanced scalability. Thus, many works addressed this point and proposed methods with low-cost and high data availability protocol. For example, (Deris et al, 2008) presented a box-shaped grid structure that helps to maintain the consistency of the replicated data on a networked distributed computing system. Further, the outcome of their approach demonstrated a high data availability with a low communication cost which influenced positively the fault-tolerance with respect to baseline protocols. This protocol has been analyzed with respect to distributed databases and focuses only on data partitioning without considering the processing.

With a focus on the network capacities, there is always this issue of network skew that can cause workers to struggle in completing the tasks. As a solution, Rupprecht et al. (Lukas et al, 2017) presented a *SquirreJoin* approach based on distributed join processing technique using *lazy partitioning* in which the algorithm helps in adapting to transient network skew in clusters. In detail, the process starts by maintaining lazy partitions in memory by the workers, then these partitions are assigned dynamically to other workers based on the network conditions. In general, the whole principle allows this ability to distribute the data flow and to minimize the join completion time. Particularly, the solution was capable of speeding up 2.9x times performance with only small overhead. In addition, the approach can easily create bottlenecks and it considers only the horizontal network layer for partitioning.

Yang et al. (Lei et al, 2013) have also introduced a solution for optimizing the data partitioning where the focus was on computation partitioning, which means that the optimization is done on the partitioning of the data stream. Specifically, the authors proposed a framework to provide runtime support for a dynamic partitioning of the data and sharing the computational instances in the cloud among multiple users. In addition, the framework is characterized by its flexibility to serve a large number of mobile users by leveraging the existing elastic resources. Particularly, the partitioning problem was solved by using a genetic algorithm which allowed the framework to have 2X improvement on the performance. Another example is proposed by (Fernando et al, 2013), where the solutions is based on distributing data processing tasks among devices; however, both papers they have not either considered the heterogeneity of the participative computational resources or have not included resources across different layers from the cloud to the edge.

The optimization of data partitioning can present some additional challenges when the data itself is with higher dimensions which are the case in IoT applications (Marjani et al, 2017) and also with respect to security (Wang 2019). This means that the data has to be fused in order to ensure a good quality of the information. Therefore, the researchers focused on data fusion techniques as a mean to fuse the data and facilitate the process of improving efficiency and computational performance. This aspect is clearly stated and illustrated in the work of Zhou et al. (Zhou et al, 2013), where the authors proposed a multidimensional fusion approach for IoT data based on partitioning. Specifically, the concept relies on splitting the size of the data with high attributes into small subsets for processing and then apply reduction and extraction methods to fuse the results together. Further, a simulation was executed for testing the correctness of the algorithm which has proven to be effective. However, the relationship between dimensions, number partition, and volume of objects is not reflected and how it influences the computational efficiency.

With this respect, the rise of IoT offers this possibility of producing a massive amount of data with possibilities of processing in it at different locations and levels which makes data partitioning strategy equivalent to NP-hard problem. Hence, Naas et al. (Naas et al, 2018) tried to propose a solution to the issue based on dividing the original data problem into subproblems using graph modelling and partitioning methods. The resulting heuristics makes it possible to reduce the solving time by 450 times with 5% optimality loss. At this point, the method proposed is only focusing on data partitioning among the resources without considering the availability of the computational processing.

Other papers raised the importance of mobility-awareness for example in (Soo et al, 2017), the authors proposed a mobility-aware framework for proactive Fog service provisioning. The approach is capable of being less sensitive to the unstable connectivity since it handles computational offloading with computing servers and with minimal prerequisite analysis. This is manifested by the capability of the fog node in defining the most appropriate strategy of delivering the results to the mobile delegator node via a local network worker or through the Cloud. However, there is still space for improving the technique or optimize it, which has followed in the paper proposed in (Michael et al 2019), where the authors proposed architecture based on cooperative mobile edge computing, which introduces an improvement in the efficiency and performance in resource-constrained mobile devices. However, both approaches do not make use in its process of other devices connected in the same fog network at the horizontal level and introducing preplanning for computation.

All the methods and approaches discussed in this section show that most of the methods proposed for partitioning and processing are relying on the database management for data partitioning with Cloud resources, cooperative mobile edge or IoT within their Vertical networks layer. In some cases, the computational instances are shared by multiple devices connected in the horizontal network layer when there is an offload. Nevertheless, there is no exploration of the usage of both horizontal and vertical correlation in the network for partitioning the data processing task. Therefore, in this paper, we are presenting a new design for exploring data partitioning and processing by considering all available resources both at the vertical and horizontal layers of the network.

SYSTEM DESIGN

This section describes the proposed system for dynamic process deployment and execution. Follow up, we explain the proposed REM scheme used for performing optimal process migration among heterogeneous servers.

System Architecture

In this paper, we call the activities performed to fulfil the required tasks at the front-end IoT devices as Edge Network Entities-Assigned Processes or simply Edge Processes. Here, the edge represents the network where the front end IoT devices located and near edge denotes the intermediate network between the network of the front-end and the distant backend central server (Figure 2).

Figure 2. Software architecture of EPIoT host. An EPIoT host contains two main elements - EPIoT Server, which is the manager of EPIoT host, and DCE Server, which handles EP work packages

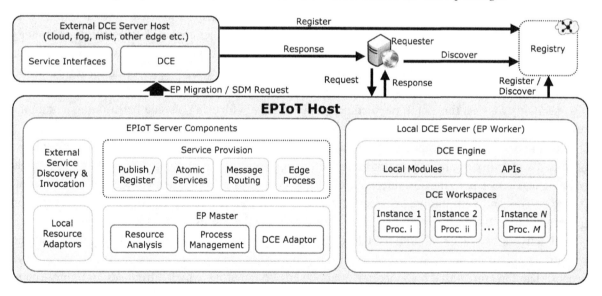

In this system, dynamic process deployment is the core enabler, it is realised by implementing a corresponding engine for Dynamic Code Execution (DCE).

DCE is a mechanism that allows a client to send the package, which may contain the configuration description file, program source code files and optional dependencies, module or library files, to the

DCE server and the DCE server is capable of executing the program on-the-fly using real-time code compiler. Note that the DCE client may require the DCE server to download the dependencies instead of sending them to the server directly.

Commonly, a system can provide DCE by utilising virtualisation or containerisation technologies. Similarly, we expect the participative servers of the dynamic fog computing environment (dynamic fog) are providing DCE mechanism. In a dynamic fog-enabled IoT system, we call a DCE-supported IoT device as Edge Process-enabled Internet of Thing (EPIoT) host. EPIoT host is discoverable via both registry servers and proximity-based wireless communication protocols (e.g. Wi-Fi or Bluetooth). It is accessible to an organisation and its partners as long as the corresponding software agent has been installed in the participants. It may have different hardware states at different period of time depending on the missions they are carried. Hence, it periodically updates its Service Description Metadata (SDM) to the registry via the Internet.

An EPIoT host contains two main parts---EPIoT Server and DCE Server. EPIoT Server contains the basic mechanisms of a service-oriented IoT device together with additional components that allow it to manage DCE tasks. EPIoT Server has following service provision related components:

- Publish/Register component monitors hardware states and manages service availability. It needs to include hardware states in the Service Description Metadata (SDM) of EPIoT Host when it publishes it to the registry. Further, Publish/Register component is capable of identifying the availability of the services based on the corresponding hardware states. For example, if EPIoT Server has received a request that requires continuous network transmission for a period of time, it may stop providing the Message Routing Service in order achieve better quality for the current task;
- Atomic Services component provides simple services such as sensory data service, which allows the requester to use EPIoT host to collect real-time sensory data, or actuating service that allows the requester to access the actuators connected with the EPIoT host. For example, a connected mobile actuator, which embeds EPIoT, allows distant control centre to use it to access a wireless light switch in the proximity of the mobile actuator;
- Message Routing service component is a service that supports the basic function of Software-Defined Networking (SDN). Specifically, an IoT system can utilise multiple EPIoT host devices to establish a dynamic re-configurable sensory data routing network. Further, internal components can also use Message Routing to route messages to external nodes. For example, if the description metadata of an edge process service request package has specified the output receiver to be a different node from the initial requester, EP Master will use Message Routing to route the output to the receiver node;
- Edge Process service component allows the requester to send a request package to EPIoT host and execute the program to fulfil the request in a secure sandbox environment. In particular, the request package should contain the source code of the program, required dependencies/library for the program (in case they are not available in the EPIoT host) and the metadata which specifies the process configuration details. For example, the metadata should describe which file contains the starting point of the program, which sensory data is needed (in case the program involves pre-processing the data collected by the EPIoT host), the receiver of the final output (in case if the requester and receiver are different nodes) etc.

External Service Discovery and Invocation component allows EPIoT host:

- To discover external servers via global federated registry and it also allows the EPIoT host to discover proximity-based servers using proximity-based wireless service discovery mechanisms such as Wi-Fi, Wi-Fi Direct, Bluetooth etc. We assume the available external servers are following an industrial standard format to describe their services and their resource availability. For example, they may follow ETSI Multi-access Edge Computing API standard[2] and discoverable using IETF RFC 6762 - Multicast DNS with IETF RFC 6763 - DNS Based Service Discovery;
- To send the process migration package to external servers such as the cloud, the fog, edge computing or mist computing servers. Similarly, the request package should include the program, dependencies, the configuration metadata and the involved data objects (if the request involves them);
- To request Service Description Metadata (SDM) from external DCE server and also managing the SDM of EPIoT host itself.

Local Resource Adaptors are the adaptors for other entities to access the basic functions of EPIoT host device (which fundamentally is an IoT device) which are accessing sensory data and interacting with actuators.

EP Master handles the request package of edge process service. Specifically, it contains the following main mechanisms:

- *Resource Analysis* function allows EP Master access the information of the underline hardware and network resource. For example, when EP Master intends to migrate the processes it received from the requester, it uses Resource Analysis function to identify the current CPU, RAM and networking states towards performing adaptive process migration mechanism;
- *Process Management* function allows EP Master:
  - To extract the content of an edge process request package and adding the required data (if the request involves sensory data collected by the EPIoT host) to create a work package. Afterwards, Work Manager sends the work package to the DCE server for execution;
  - To partition the work package and to create a number of new edge process packages when EPIoT host intends to distribute the work to external servers. Further, as mentioned previously, Work Manager can send the edge process packages to external servers via the External Service Invocation component. EP Manager partitions the work based on DIPHDA scheme, we will describe it in the next section;
- *DCE Adaptor* is a component that allows EP Master to deploy work packages to DCE Engine. A different system may use different type DCE engine, in order to deploy process packages to the DCE engine, a corresponding adaptor needs to be installed in EP Master so that the format of process/work package is compliant to the DCE engine.

Local Dynamic Code Execution (DCE) Server. In general, every node in the distributed fog computing has hosted a DCE engine and the engine is managed by an isolated server. The EPIoT host device can install DCE server to allow itself processing the work locally. This server is an independent server from the EPIoT Server because in different cases, the administrator may prefer to use a different type of DCE, such as Virtual Machine (VM) or containers engine (e.g. Docker). Hence, this part does not bound with EPIoT Server.

DCE Engine is a component that is capable of receiving process package and executing the process. Afterwards, the DCE engine will return the output to the process package sender.

Due to the security reason, DCE engine executes each process package in an isolated sandbox environment. Further, the executed program of the process package has limited accessibility to Local Resource Adaptors via the pre-installed Application Program Interface (API) of the engine. Certainly, the corresponding information about API is also included in the SDM of EPIoT host.

DCE engine may also provide a number of Local Modules (i.e. pre-installed dependencies or libraries) for the programming language it supports. Fundamentally, edge process service requester cannot expect EPIoT host to support all the dependencies they need. Hence, the edge process request packages should include the corresponding dependencies/libraries for their programs. Otherwise, the EPIoT host may need to spend extra time to download the dependencies/libraries from external sources.

Process Migration

The EPIoT host is capable of migrating the work it received to external DCE-enabled servers. In this case, the role of EPIoT host becomes Master Node or Delegator Node and the roles of external DCE servers will be Worker Nodes.

Below, we use Business Process Management Notation (BPMN) model to explain how a Master Node migrates its works to a Worker Nodes in which the Worker Node is a Fog Computing server hosted on the Wi-Fi access point connected by the Master Node.

Figure 3. The workflow of handling edge process service request. When EPIoT host receives Edge Process (EP) service request, it may handle the request using local DCE server or it may migrate the work to external DCE servers.

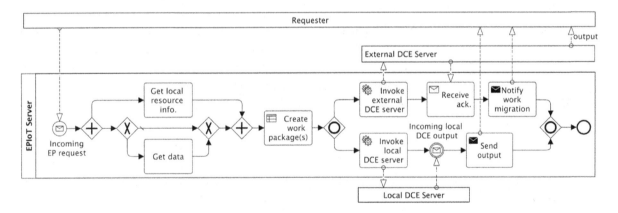

As Figure 3 shows, when the EPIoT host receives EP request, it first checks the local resource states and in parallel, if the request involves sensory data, it will get the data either by utilising adaptors to collect on-demand data or get the data from local storage, depending on the requested content. Afterwards, the EPIoT host will create process packages. Each process package contains the original files included in the request package, and the data retrieved in the previous step (if involved). Further, EPIoT host allocates the data to each process. For example, suppose the request involves 100 sequel sensory data and every 10-sequel data is the input of one process, which indicates that there will be 10 processes in total. Based on the rules set by the system admin or the manager of the EPIoT host device, there can be three cases:

1. EPIoT host creates one process package and sends it to local DCE server. Afterwards, receive the output from local DCE server and forward the output to the requester;
2. EPIoT host creates one or more process package and invokes external DCE servers to send them the process packages. When an external DCE server receives a completed process package, it will send an acknowledgement to EPIoT host. Afterwards, EPIoT host notifies the initial requester that the process has been migrated to external servers and EPIoT host also provide the information (e.g. IP address, identification etc.) about the external servers. This case is known as process migration. Based on the metadata included in the work package, the external DCE servers know the address of the initial requester. Hence, they can directly send the final outputs to the initial requester;
3. EPIoT host creates multiple process packages and sends the process packages to both local DCE server and external DCE server(s). In this hybrid case, the system intends to use all the possible resources to hasten the overall speed and in addition, reduce the burden of the EPIoT host.

The decision of how EPIoT assigns the process packages is based on the proposed resource-aware edge process migration scheme explained in the next section.

RESOURCE-AWARE EDGE PROCESS MIGRATION SCHEME

The proposed Resource-aware Edge process Migration (REM) scheme is capable of identifying the optimal partition for migrating processes from EPIoT node to heterogeneous external servers situated at the cloud and the edge network resources.

REM scheme requires four sets of parameters in order to measure the optimal partition:

1. Static resource specification of the participants. Here, the participants include the EPIoT host in which the EPIoT server of the EPIoT host is the master node or the delegator node exchangeable, and the local DCE server of EPIoT host and the external DCE servers are worker nodes. To enumerate, the information of the static resource specification includes the CPU benchmark value, RAM size, disk read and write speed;
2. Dynamic context parameters, which include the current network transmission speed between EPIoT host and the participants, current CPU usage, current RAM usage, which are the parameters that can influence the overall speed of the entire operation. Here, we consider the entire edge process migration operation encompassed deployment, which includes packing the process package and sending the package to the internal or external DCE server, process execution timespan and the timespan of sending the output to the receiver;
3. Request parameters, which include the following values:
    a. $byte_{alg}$: Bytes of the algorithm source code, which is visible when EP Master receives the EP request package;
    b. $byte_{mdl}$: Bytes of modules, which is visible when EP Master receives the EP request package;
    c. $byte_{desc}$: Bytes of the description metadata, which describes the program configuration and the address of receiver node and it is visible when EP Master receives the EP request package;
    d. $byte_{d}$: Bytes of one data object involved in the request. EPIoT knows the size of the data since it is from one of the localhost components;

4. Local process time. In order to perform the measurement, EPIoT host has to perform at least one process once locally. Specifically, one process involves:

    a. Packing the process package, which include the algorithm source code, dependencies, metadata and one of the requested data;

    b. Sending the process package to local DCE server for execution and generating output package;

    c. Sending the output package to the receiver. Afterwards, EPIoT host can obtain the values described in Table 1.

Table 1. Description of the notations involved in measuring local process time

Notation	Description
$\Delta t_{local}^{upk_{mdl}}$	Timespan to unpack modules/dependencies.
$\Delta t_{local}^{upk_{alg}}$	Timespan to unpack Algorithm/main program.
$\Delta t^{pk_{mdl}}$	Timespan to pack modules/dependencies.
$\Delta t^{pk_{alg}}$	Timespan to pack Algorithm/main program.
Δt^{pk_d}	Timespan to pack 1 data object.
$\Delta t_{local}^{upk_d}$	Timespan to unpack 1 data object.
Δt_{local}^{o1}	Timespan to pack 1 output data.
Δt_{local}^{proc1}	Timespan to process 1 data object.
$\Delta t_{local}^{npk_{o1}}$	Timespan to unpack 1 archived output. Note that this is an additional trial that EPIoT needs to perform in order to measure the timespan of the output.

REM scheme performs in the steps described below. Firstly, REM scheme scores each server based on the values described previously by using the function *getTime(i,wp$_i$)* where *i* denotes worker *i* and *wp$_i$* denotes the number of data object assigned to worker *i*.

Let *WT*={*wt$_i$*: 0≤*i*≤*N*} be a set of the total timespan of each worker *i* after assigning *wp$_i$* to it.

REM scheme uses the process assignment function (i.e. Algorithm 1) to assign works to the workers. In Algorithm 1:

- min{*wt$_i$*} is a function that returns the smallest number in *WT*;
- *getTime(i,wp$_i$)* is a function defined as follows:

$$getTime\left(i, wp_i\right) = \Delta t_i^{pk} + \Delta t_i^{req} + \Delta t_i^{upk} + \Delta t_i^{proc} + \Delta t_i^{pk_O} + \Delta t_i^{po_O} + \Delta t_r^{npk_O}$$

Algorithm 1. Process assignment function

```
 1  for i ∈ WP do
 2  │   wp_i = 0
 3  end
 4  while #D > 0 do
 5  │   for wt_i ∈ WT do
 6  │   │   if wt_i ≡ min{wt_i} then
 7  │   │   │   #D = #D - 1:
 8  │   │   │   wp_i = wo_i + 1:
 9  │   │   │   wt_i = getTime(i, wp_i):
10  │   │   end
11  │   end
12  end
```

where:

- Δt_i^{pk} is the time to pack the request package assigned to worker *i* in which:

$$\Delta t_i^{pk} = \Delta t^{pk_{mdl}} + \Delta t^{pk_{alg}} + \Delta t^{pk_d} \times wp_i$$

where:

- $\Delta t^{pk_d} \times wp_i$ is the data object packing time based on the number of assigned data objects;
- Δt_i^{req} is the time to send the request package to worker *i* in which:

$$\Delta t_i^{req} = \Delta t_i^{po_{1byte}} \times \left(byte_{mdl} + byte_{alg} + byte_d \times wp_i \right)$$

where:

- $byte_d \times wp_i$ is the size of data object in byte times number of data object assigned to the worker;
- Δt_{local}^{upk} is the timespan when the request package is handled by the delegator itself in which:

$$\Delta t_{local}^{upk} = \Delta t_{local}^{upk_{mdl}} + \Delta t_{local}^{upk_{alg}} + \Delta t_{local}^{upk_d} \times wp_i$$

- Δt_i^{upk} is the measured process package unpacking time of worker *i*, which is measured based on Read/Write speed in which:

$$\Delta t_i^{upk} = \frac{1}{\Delta t_{local}^{upk}} \times \frac{RW_i}{RW_{local}}$$

where:

- RW_{local} is the average read and write performance of the delegator in which:

$$RW_{local} = \frac{R_{local} + W_{local}}{2}$$

- RW_i is the average read and write performance of worker i in which:

$$RW_i = \frac{R_i + R_w}{2}$$

- Δt_{local}^{proc} is the timespan when the delegator executes the process by itself in which:

$$\Delta t_{local}^{proc} = \Delta t_{local}^{procl} \times wp_i$$

- Δt_i^{proc} is the measured timespan for worker i to execute the process in which:

$$\Delta t_i^{proc} = wp_i \times \frac{1}{\Delta t_{local}^{proc}} \times \frac{\dfrac{1}{\sum_{k \in |H_i|} \omega_k} \sum_{k \in |H_i|} \eta_k^i \times \omega_k}{\dfrac{1}{\sum_{k \in |H_{local}|} \omega_k} \sum_{k \in |H_{local}|} \eta_k^{local} \times \omega_k}$$

and it can be also written as:

$$\Delta t_i^{proc} = \frac{wp_i}{\Delta t_{local}^{proc}} \times \frac{\sum_{k \in |H_i|} \eta_k^i \times \omega_k}{\sum_{k \in |H_i|} \omega_k} \times \frac{\sum_{k \in |H_{local}|} \omega_k}{\sum_{k \in |H_{local}|} \eta_k^{local} \times \omega_k}$$

where:

- ωk is the weight of the computational resource k;
- η_k^{local} is the value of the computational resource k of delegator;
- η_k^i is the value of the computational resource k of worker i;
- $\Delta t_{local}^{pk_o}$ is the output packing time when the delegator is handling it, in which:

$$\Delta t_{local}^{pk_O} = \Delta t_{local}^{o1} \times wp_i$$

- $\Delta t_i^{pk_O}$ is the output packing time when worker \$i\$ is handling it. Specifically, it is based on the disk read and write speed, in which:

$$\Delta t_i^{pk_O} = \frac{1}{\Delta t_{local}^{pk_O}} \times \frac{RW_i}{RW_{local}}$$

- $\Delta t_i^{po_O}$ is the measured timespan to send result to the output receiver described in the metadata of the request package. Further, this value is based on the network speed of the worker i (described in its Service Description Metadata) and the network speed of receiver (provided in the metadata in the request package) and also the size of the output package;
- $\Delta t_r^{npk_O}$ is the timespan to unpack the output package at the receiver side and it is measured as below:

$$\Delta t_r^{upk_O} = \frac{1}{\Delta t_{local}^{upk_O}} \times \frac{RW_i}{RW_{local}}$$

Evaluation

In order to evaluate the proposed EPIoT framework and the proposed REM scheme, we have implemented a prototype software and have deployed it on real world devices. First, we explain the configuration of the test cases which is based on the scenario described in Figure 1 of Section 1.

Figure 4 illustrates the configuration used for the evaluation which include five nodes:

- Node-T, which has hosted EPIoT host, is a Nokia 8 smartphone that represents a mobile data source server and is capable of migrating processes to the other nodes;
- Node-M, which has hosted DCE server, is a Sony Xperia XZ1 Compact that represents a Wi-Fi Direct (P2P)-based fog/mist computing server and it will be one of the worker nodes of Node-T;
- Node-F, which has hosted DCE server, is a Macbook Pro model A1502 that represents the main Wi-Fi Access Point (AP) of Node-T and the main fog of Node-T;
- Node-E, which has hosted DCE server, is a Dell Latitude E5430 laptop computing that represents a fog server co-located with the Local Area Network (LAN) switch;
- Node-C, which has hosted DCE server, is a virtual machine located in the datacenter of Tallinn University of Technology and is representing the compute service cloud.

Excluding Node-C, which is located in Tallinn city, the rest of the nodes are within the same LAN as Figure 4 has illustrated. Table 2 summarises the specification of the nodes.

Note that although the CPU specifications of the nodes are 4 or more cores, we have configured a limited core to the DCE servers hosted on those nodes towards simulating the constraint resource availabilities of the nodes.

Figure 4. The configuration of the prototype evaluation where the T Node represents the EPIoT host-embedded Data Source Server device, C Node denotes the compute cloud service and E, F, M Nodes denote the heterogeneous proximal fog server

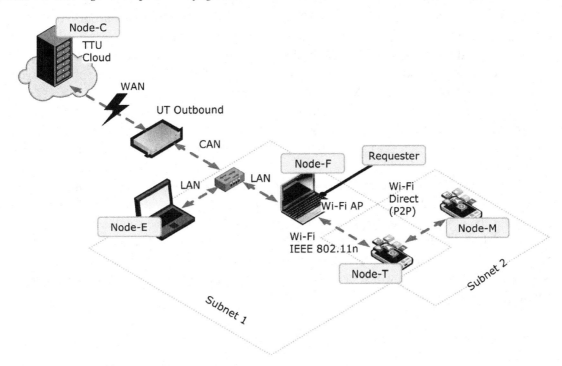

Table 2. Static specifications and configurations of the participative nodes in evaluation

	Node-T	Node-M	Node-F	Node-E	Node-C
Represented Concept	Thing	Mist	Fog	Fog	Geo-distributed Cloud
Hardware Model	Nokia 8 Smartphone	Sony Xperia XZ1 Compact Smartphone	Macbook Pro A1502	Dell Latitude E5430	VM
OS	Android	Android	Mac OS	Ubuntu	Debian
CPU	Qualcomm MSM8998 Snapdragon 835 Octa-core (4x2.5 GHz Kryo & 4x1.8 Ghz Kryo)	Qualcomm MSM8998 Snapdragon 835 Octa-core (4x2.5 GHz Kryo & 4x1.8 Ghz Kryo)	Intel Core i5 2.6GHz	Intel Core i5-3210M; 4x2.5GHz	QEMU Virtual CPU version 2.5+; 4x2.4 GHz
Available CPU core	2	2	3	3	3
RAM	4 GB	4 GB	16 GB	4 GB	8 GB
Disk speed	547 MB/s (R); 220 MB/s (W)	237 MB/s (R); 121 MB/s (W)	566 MB/s (R/W)	105 MB/s (R/W)	61 MB/s (R/W)
Communication	Localhost	Wi-Fi Direct	Wi-Fi 802.11n	Via Node-F	Via Node-F

Besides the static values, participative nodes have to collect the dynamic values such as CPU usage, RAM usage, network speed at runtime. In general, each node is collecting such information at the background and periodically update such information to their Service Description Metadata (SDM). Further, Node-T (the EPIoT host) retrieves SDM from the other nodes when it connects to the network.

Regarding the software prototype, we have implemented EPIoT host and DCE server using Node.js. Further, we installed the Node.js-based EPIoT host on Nokia 8 via Termux (Linux command prompt emulator for Android OS)[3] and all the nodes are using the same DCE server software. Similarly, we also installed DCE server on Sony Xperia XZ1 Compact via Termux.

The sensory data objects used in test cases are image files of different sizes and the algorithm program source code included in the request package is 1203 bytes. Further, the size of the modules/libraries used by the algorithm program is 14.1 megabytes and the size of the configuration metadata (in JSON format) is 226 bytes.

The following evaluation consists of three parts - the first part is the preliminary testing that focuses on the plain testing of local process and mono-process migration, which shows the performance when EPIoT handles the processes locally or when it migrates its process to one single external server; the second part of the evaluation aims to demonstrate how much the proposed REM scheme can optimise the process migration when EPIoT host considers to migrate its processes to multiple heterogeneous nodes; the final part tends to show that the proposed REM scheme can improve the speed in all the possible multi-process migration cases.

Preliminary Testing

This section describes the test cases for local processes and mono-process migrations. In particular, the involved sensory data object size was 1 megabyte and we have used a different number of data objects in different test cases.

Note that the following test results have excluded the timespan of the initial request. Specifically, the figures have only contained the timespan of Deploy, which consists of packing the process migration package, sending the package to the worker node and the unpacking time of the worker node, and the Process \& Response represents the program execution time on the worker node, output packing time and the time to send the output to the receiver node, which in our test cases is the initial requester.

Local Process

Figure 5 illustrates the test cases for local processes performed on Node-T (i.e. EPIoT host) based on 50 involved data objects per one request package and the number of available CPU core assigned to the local DCE server of the EPIoT host.

The main objective of these test cases is to show that Node-T device itself is only capable of allocating a limited number of CPU cores to the local DCE server. Explicitly, when we force the system to allocate more than 3 CPU cores to the local DCE server, DCE server could not reduce the timespan for executing the processes. Instead, it could produce the negative effect.

In the rest of the test cases, we only allocate 2 CPU core to the DCE server of Node-T and the CPU core allocations of the other nodes have followed the setting in Table 2 described previously.

Figure 5. Edge process performance on local server based on the number of allocated CPU resources with 50 of 3 megabyte data object included in the deployment package

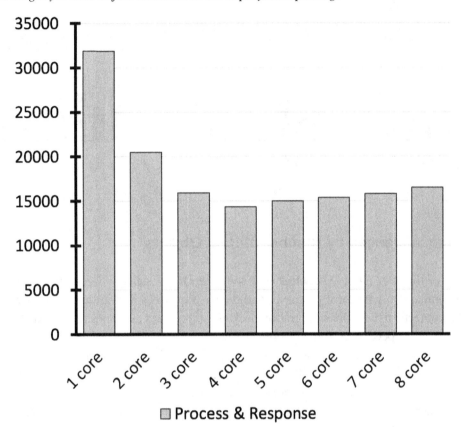

Mono-Process Migration

Figure 6 illustrates the results of the test cases for mono-process migration based on a different number of data objects included in the initial request. To enumerate, 10d denotes 10 data objects, 20d denotes 20 data objects and so forth. Further, we use a single alphabet, which corresponding to the nodes in Figure 4, to represent the node that was handling the processes. For example, T denotes Node-T, M denotes Note-M and so forth.

As the figure shows, Node-T has the lowest deployment time because EPIoT server only needs to send the process package to the local DCE server. Follow up by Node-F, which is the main Internet gateway of Node-T and is accessible via IEEE 802.11n. In comparison, Node-M has higher latency than Node-F because the performance of Wi-Fi Direct is slower than the regular Wi-Fi IEEE 802.11n connection in these test cases. Further, Node-E has higher latency than Node-F since it is co-located with the 2nd hop from Node-T and finally, Node-C, which is the cloud server located in another city, has the highest latency among all the nodes.

Regarding the computational performance, Node-F, Node-E and Node-C have quite similar results and Node-T and Node-M have very similar performance since both of them have similar CPU chip.

Figure 6. Time comparison for local processes and mono-process migration with different number of 3 megabytes data objects included in the process deployment package

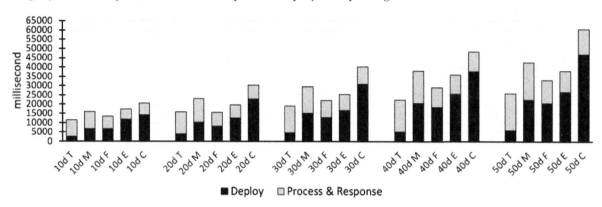

Performance Influenced by Number of Data Objects

The test cases of this part aim to show that how much the REM scheme can improve the overall performance in comparison with local processes and the naive process migration approach which equally divide the data objects to the process migration packages regardless the runtime context (e.g. CPU load, RAM usage, network speed etc.) of the worker nodes.

Figure 7 illustrates the results of the test cases that involved 25 to 100 data objects (denoted by 25d, 50d, 75d, 100d) in the request. Specifically, each set of test cases (i.e. based on the number of the involved data objects) consists of one case of mono-process migration to the cloud (denoted by C), one case of local process (denoted by T), one naive case which equally migrate the processes to all nodes including localhost (denoted by TMFEC) and the last case of a set represents the result that have applied REM scheme (denoted by Adapt).

Figure 7. Deployment, process and response timespan comparison among solo, equal and REM-based process migration using multiple worker nodes. Individual data object size is 3 megabyte.

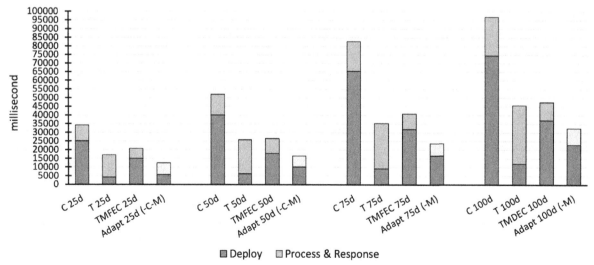

As the results have shown, naive approaches can improve the performance comparing to the mono-process migration to the cloud. However, the case that is based on the local process can outperform the naive approach. In contrast, when the system utilised REM scheme, the system has adaptively assigned the data objects to the processor package and has also excluded the nodes that cloud reduce the performance from the candidate workers. Hence, in all the sets of test cases, REM scheme-based approach has outperformed all the other approaches. Further, we have included the annotations in order to clarify which worker nodes have been excluded by the REM scheme. For example, -C denotes REM scheme has excluded Node-C and -M denotes REM scheme has excluded Node-M.

Performance Influenced by the Size of Data Objects

In contrast to the previous part of test cases, the test cases described in this section were based on the size of the data objects while the request package has involved 25 data objects (Figure 8).

Figure 8. Deployment, process and response timespan comparison among cloud-based process migration, solo processing, equal process migration and adaptive process migration. The number of requested data object is 25.

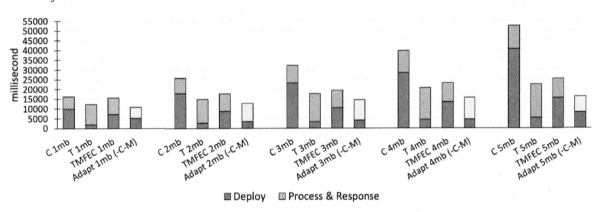

Similarly to the results of the previous section, the cloud-based mono-process migration has suffered from the network latency even though its processing performance was better than the EPIoT host device. Moreover, the naive approach (denoted by TMFEC) also did not perform well and the local process-based approach (denoted by T) has outperformed the naive approach. Explicitly, the REM scheme-based approaches have outperformed the other approaches in all the sets of test cases.

Note that REM scheme improves the performance based on all the runtime context factors. Hence, it does not always reduce one part of timespan. For example, when the data object size was 4 megabyte per each, REM scheme-based approach has reduced the network latency in order to improve the performance. In contrast, when the data object size was 5 megabyte, REM scheme-based approach produced a different option in which it results that the network latency was much higher in comparison to the case that involved 4-megabyte data. However, REM scheme's decision has reduced the timespan of processing. Hence, the overall performance has still been improved.

Applying REM Scheme in Different Computing Models

In fog and edge computing paradigms, there are many different possible approaches to selecting the nodes for process migration or process distribution. In order to further validate the REM scheme, we have conducted all the possible setting in our testing environment. Correspondingly, we use a single alphabet to represent a node in which T denotes Node-T, M denotes Node-M and so forth. Further, we use "A." to notate the cases that have applied REM scheme.

Figure 9. Deployment, process and response timespan comparison among different cases. REM scheme is capable of improving the performance of all the cases. The number of requested data object is 25 with the size of 5 megabyte per each data object.

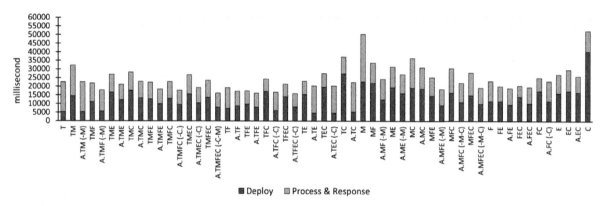

Figure 9 illustrate the results of the test cases that have 25 involved data objects in the size of 5 megabytes per each data object. Note that we have performed the test cases of each section in a different period of time. Hence, due to the context changes, the timespans of test cases can be different in different sections of this paper.

In these test cases, we can consider T as edge computing or Things Computing, M and as mist computing, C as cloud computing, F as fog computing, E as fog or edge computing and the rest test cases are the combination of different elements. For examples, TM, which utilises Node-T and Node-M, would be a common paradigm of mist computing and TFE, which utilises Node-T, Node-F and Node-E would be a common paradigm of fog computing and so forth.

As the results have shown, REM scheme can improve the performance of all the test cases that involve more than one participative process executioner. Similar to the previous sections, we have annotated the test cases in which REM scheme has excluded a number of candidate nodes.

CONCLUSION

In this paper, the authors have proposed a scheme and a framework to address two questions in the domain of the distributed process migration from mobile IoT devices (connected mobile sensors) to heterogeneous Fog and Edge Computing (FEC) resources. Specifically, in order to improve the performance of the process migration, the authors proposed Resource-aware Edge process Migration (REM) scheme. Further, the authors have developed and have implemented Edge Process-enabled Internet of Things (EPIoT) host framework, which has been utilised to evaluate the REM scheme. Overall, based on the experimental testing on real-world equipment and devices, the authors have shown that the proposed REM scheme is capable of improving the performance of different types of FEC settings that contains heterogeneous resources and dynamic runtime context factors.

For the future work, the authors plan to extend the work with the following mechanisms:

- Enabling generic Software-Defined Networking (SDN) service from the EPIoT host. Current EPIoT host supports message routing mechanism. However, it is not yet fully compliant with the mechanisms of SDN in which the nodes should be able to manage routing tables and is capable of reducing the traffic by eliminating redundant bytes of routing packages;
- Integrates the proposed EPIoT framework and REM scheme with the Intelligent Transport System (ITS) (Plangi et al, 2018) in order to enhance the speed of the real-time process management and decision making. Further, the authors plan to implement and to validate the framework based on real-world use cases.

ACKNOWLEDGMENT

The work is supported by the Estonian Centre of Excellence in IT (EXCITE), funded by the European Regional Development Fund.

REFERENCES

Alam, M. F., Katsikas, S., Beltramello, O., & Hadjiefthymiades, S. (2017). Augmented and virtual reality based monitoring and safety system: A prototype IoT platform. *Journal of Network and Computer Applications*, *89*, 109–119. doi:10.1016/j.jnca.2017.03.022

Buyya, R., Srirama, S. N., Casale, G., Calheiros, R., Simmhan, Y., Varghese, B., Gelenbe, E., Javadi, B., Vaquero, L. M., Netto, M. A. S., Toosi, A. N., Rodriguez, M. A., Llorente, I. M., Vimercati, S. D. C. D., Samarati, P., Milojicic, D., Varela, C., Bahsoon, R., Assuncao, M. D. D., ... Shen, H. (2019). A manifesto for future generation cloud computing: Research directions for the next decade. *ACM Computing Surveys*, *51*(5), 105. doi:10.1145/3241737

Buyya, R., Yeo, C. S., Venugopal, S., Broberg, J., & Brandic, I. (2009). Cloud computing and emerging IT platforms: Vision, hype, and reality for delivering computing as the 5th utility. *Future Generation Computer Systems*, *25*(6), 599–616. doi:10.1016/j.future.2008.12.001

Catarinucci, L., De Donno, D., Mainetti, L., Palano, L., Patrono, L., Stefanizzi, M. L., & Tarricone, L. (2015). An IoT-aware architecture for smart healthcare systems. *IEEE Internet of Things Journal*, *2*(6), 515–526. doi:10.1109/JIOT.2015.2417684

Chang, C., Hadachi, A., Srirama, S. N., & Min, M. (2018). Mobile Big Data: Foundations, State of the Art, and Future Directions. In S. Sakr & A. Zomaya (Eds.), *Book title: Encyclopedia of Big Data Technologies*. doi:10.1007/978-3-319-63962-8_46-1

Chang, C., Srirama, S. N., & Buyya, R. (2017). Mobile cloud business process management system for the internet of things: A survey. *ACM Computing Surveys*, *49*(4), 70. doi:10.1145/3012000

Chang, C., Srirama, S. N., & Buyya, R. (2017). Indie fog: An efficient fog-computing infrastructure for the internet of things. *IEEE Computer*, *50*(9), 92–98. doi:10.1109/MC.2017.3571049

Deris, M. M., Abawajy, J. H., & Mamat, A. (2008). An efficient replicated data access approach for large-scale distributed systems. *Future Generation Computer Systems*, *24*(1), 1–9. doi:10.1016/j.future.2007.04.010

Fernando, N., Loke, S. W., & Rahayu, W. (2013). Mobile cloud computing: A survey. *Future Generation Computer Systems*, *29*(1), 84–106. doi:10.1016/j.future.2012.05.023

Grgić, K., Špeh, I., & Heđi, I. (2016, October). A web-based IoT solution for monitoring data using MQTT protocol. In *2016 International Conference on Smart Systems and Technologies (SST)* (pp. 249-253). IEEE. 10.1109/SST.2016.7765668

Levitin, G., Xing, L., & Dai, Y. (2017). Optimal data partitioning in cloud computing system with random server assignment. *Future Generation Computer Systems*, *70*, 17–25. doi:10.1016/j.future.2016.12.025

Lopez-Castaño, C., Ferrin-Bolaños, C., & Castillo-Ossa, L. (2018, June). Computer vision and the internet of things ecosystem in the connected home. In *International Symposium on Distributed Computing and Artificial Intelligence* (pp. 213-220). Springer.

Mahenge, M. P., Li, C., & Sanga, C. A. (2019). Mobile Edge Computing: Cost-Efficient Content Delivery in Resource-Constrained Mobile Computing Environment. *International Journal of Mobile Computing and Multimedia Communications*, *10*(3), 23–46. doi:10.4018/IJMCMC.2019070102

Marjani, M., Nasaruddin, F., Gani, A., Karim, A., Hashem, I. A. T., Siddiqa, A., & Yaqoob, I. (2017). Big IoT data analytics: Architecture, opportunities, and open research challenges. *IEEE Access: Practical Innovations, Open Solutions*, *5*, 5247–5261. doi:10.1109/ACCESS.2017.2689040

Naas, M. I., Lemarchand, L., Boukhobza, J., & Raipin, P. (2018, April). A graph partitioning-based heuristic for runtime iot data placement strategies in a fog infrastructure. In *Proceedings of the 33rd Annual ACM Symposium on Applied Computing* (pp. 767-774). ACM. 10.1145/3167132.3167217

Plangi, S., Hadachi, A., Lind, A., & Bensrhair, A. (2018). Real-Time Vehicles Tracking Based on Mobile Multi-Sensor Fusion. *IEEE Sensors Journal*, *18*(24), 10077–10084. doi:10.1109/JSEN.2018.2873050

Research. (n.d.). *Size and Impact of Fog Computing Market*. https://www.openfogconsortium.org/wp-content/uploads/451-Research-report-on-5-year-Market-Sizing-of-Fog-Oct-2017.pdf

Rossi, M., Bui, N., Zanca, G., Stabellini, L., Crepaldi, R., & Zorzi, M. (2010). SYNAPSE++: Code dissemination in wireless sensor networks using fountain codes. *IEEE Transactions on Mobile Computing*, *9*(12), 1749–1765. doi:10.1109/TMC.2010.109

Rupprecht, L., Culhane, W., & Pietzuch, P. (2017). SquirrelJoin: Network-aware distributed join processing with lazy partitioning. *Proceedings of the VLDB Endowment International Conference on Very Large Data Bases*, *10*(11), 1250–1261. doi:10.14778/3137628.3137636

Soo, S., Chang, C., Loke, S. W., & Srirama, S. N. (2017). Proactive mobile fog computing using work stealing: Data processing at the edge. *International Journal of Mobile Computing and Multimedia Communications*, *8*(4), 1–19. doi:10.4018/IJMCMC.2017100101

Srirama, S. N., Jarke, M., & Prinz, W. (2006). Mobile web service provisioning. In Advanced int'l conference on telecommunications and int'l conference on internet and web applications and services (AICT-ICIW'06) (pp. 120-120). IEEE. doi:10.1109/AICT-ICIW.2006.215

Wang, X. A., Liu, Y., Sangaiah, A. K., & Zhang, J. (2019). Improved publicly verifiable group sum evaluation over outsourced data streams in IoT setting. *Computing*, *101*(7), 773–790. doi:10.100700607-018-0641-6

Yang, L., Cao, J., Yuan, Y., Li, T., Han, A., & Chan, A. (2013). A framework for partitioning and execution of data stream applications in mobile cloud computing. *Performance Evaluation Review*, *40*(4), 23–32. doi:10.1145/2479942.2479946

Yang, S. (2017). IoT stream processing and analytics in the fog. *IEEE Communications Magazine*, *55*(8), 21–27. doi:10.1109/MCOM.2017.1600840

Zhou, J., Hu, L., Wang, F., Lu, H., & Zhao, K. (2013). An efficient multidimensional fusion algorithm for IoT data based on partitioning. *Tsinghua Science and Technology*, *18*(4), 369–378. doi:10.1109/TST.2013.6574675

Zubaľ, M., Lojka, T., & Zolotová, I. (2016, January). IoT gateway and industrial safety with computer vision. In *2016 IEEE 14th International Symposium on Applied Machine Intelligence and Informatics (SAMI)* (pp. 183-186). IEEE. 10.1109/SAMI.2016.7423004

ENDNOTES

[1]   see https://standards.ieee.org/news/2018/ieee1934-standard-fog-computing.html
[2]   see https://www.etsi.org/technologies-clusters/technologies/multi-access-edge-computing
[3]   see https://termux.com/

This research was previously published in the International Journal of Mobile Computing and Multimedia Communications (IJMCMC), 11(3); pages 1-21, copyright year 2020 by IGI Publishing (an imprint of IGI Global).

Chapter 30
Role of Edge Computing to Leverage IoT–Assisted AAL Ecosystem

Madhana K.
PSG College of Technology, India

Jayashree L. S.
PSG College of Technology, India

ABSTRACT

The medical advancement in recent years is addressing challenges of the dependent people like senior citizens, physically challenged, and cognitively impaired individuals by providing technical aids to promote a healthier society. The radical improvement in the digital world is trying to make their life smoother by creating a smart living environment via ambient assisted living (AAL) rather than hospitalization. In this chapter, an Edge-based AAL-IoT ecosystem is introduced with the prime objective of delivering telehealthcare to elderly and telerehabilitation to disabled individuals. The proposed framework focuses on developing smart home, an intelligent atmosphere for real-time monitoring in regard to meet the needs of independent and isolated individuals. The supporting technologies to leverage the edge computing concept, to enable scalability and reliability are also studied. A case study on proposed architecture for quarantined patient monitoring remotely in the event of epidemic or pandemic diseases is presented.

INTRODUCTION

As claimed by WHO, the old age population above 60 years in the world will double from 12% to 22% shortly. As per 2017 report, the elder population aged above 60 years is 962 Million and is expected to reach more than twofold i.e., 2.1 Billion by 2050 dramatically (World Health Organization, February 5, 2018). For instance, if the elder people experience a better quality of life during their later years, then their value and ability will be more respected. On the other hand, if their dependency on others due to physical or mental health decline increases in these added years, then the impact will be negative.

DOI: 10.4018/978-1-6684-5700-9.ch030

As per the plan developed by WHO on aging and health, it is significant (i) To create awareness on healthy and active aging (ii) To design next-generation pervasive healthcare solutions based on elderly needs and preferences (iii) To provide long-term healthcare monitoring and (iv) To create an elder-friendly environment (World Health Organization, February 5, 2018). In addition to the age-related health risks, the surrounding also plays a major role in declining their risk of developing diseases such as improper intake of food, sleeping disorder, lack of physical activities, lack of simple exercises and so on.

According to the report issued by Market Research Future, it is indicated that the AAL market has produced 13 Billion USD over the period 2017 - 2027 and is estimated to reach 19% by 2027. One of the prime parts of the AAL market namely, the medical assistance system has achieved the highest 22% CAGR (Compound Annual Growth Rate) over the above estimated period (Market Research Future, April 2018). The advancement in the Internet of Things (IoT) technology and smart home technology, a huge growth of the elderly population, and a rapid increase in age-related chronic diseases are the driving factors for the rapid growth of the AAL market. In this regard, the role of healthcare service providers is going to be remarkable in the coming years.

In the present impending IoT era, almost every object or thing can be interrelated with each other in a large number, and it becomes an essential part of every domain of human life. With improved Internet connectivity, the proliferation of IoT enabled devices is expected to reach 75 Billion by the year 2025 (Statistica, 2016). As the booming IoT evolves, it has been adopted not only in many business sectors such as smart agriculture and farming, smart healthcare, automotive, industrial IoT, transportation but also for sophisticated applications like retail stores, luxurious hotels/inns, etc.

Similarly, cloud computing (Emeakaroha et al., 2015; Qabil et al., 2019) enables seamless integration of physical and smart devices by endorsing on-demand delivery of required computation, networking, and storage resources to analyze IoT big data, acquire deep insights and deliver intelligent value-added services to the end-users. Nevertheless, the raw data generated by the IoT devices have to traverse a long way through various intermediate networks to reach the remote cloud data center for further processing and analysis. So, cloud computing becomes unsuitable in meeting the diverse quality requirements such as low latency, limited bandwidth, intermittent connectivity and instant real-time response.

On that account, fog computing or fog networking, the term framed by Cisco (Cisco, 2015), a decentralized computing architecture is introduced to utilize the resources available at the edge of the network. The idea is extending cloud computing to make it idealized for IoT and other mission-critical or industrial applications. Edge computing (Yu et al., 2017) being a subset of Fog computing, has attracted many researchers to come up with real-time solutions. It has brought intelligence near to the end-user. When the data generation source and computation are closer by localizing data processing and storage then it will combat the latency, smoothing real-time interactions by affording instantaneous computing and immediate response.

In other words, the service requests and service consumers are one hop away distant to meet the real-time requirements of emerging services. Thus, edge computing and IoT are the significant elements of AAL, also known as welfare technology, to create a ubiquitous, assisted, and cost-effective architecture for the challenged and elderly people.

In this chapter, an edge-based system architecture for AAL is presented, involving diverse stakeholders, the user's independent atmosphere and the required elements of the edge-IoT ecosystem. The method of how the different elements of architecture are integrated to provide care and assistance to the targeted individuals is given. The role of edge computing in IoT assisted AAL systems to achieve benefits such as ultra-low latency, bandwidth, interoperability, throughput, and reliability is explored. An AAL case study that inherits edge computing technology is also described. Furthermore, the enabling technologies to implement and integrate edge computing with IoT based AAL ecosystem are presented.

BACKGROUND

In the last decade, cloud computing has provided a technological revolution and paradigm shift in the field of data transmission and smart living through Information and Communication Technology (ICT). The proliferation of mobile devices and smart things to trillions in number has leveraged the IoT era. The IoT paradigm can interrelate everyday objects such as physical devices, buildings, machines, embedded objects, sensors, actuators, even people or animals. It enables communication among them without human-computer interaction, using which the physical IoT devices can be monitored or controlled remotely to provide Quality of Service (QoS) and Quality of Experience (QoE) to the users.

Cloud Computing

Cloud computing is similar to old networking technology but when integrated with the Internet during the last decade, it has become more appropriate for broader applications. Cloud data center houses physical servers either a single server or a complex network of multiple server racks to hold computing resources to ensure services like backup, networking, data storage and management. It empowers on-demand provisioning of resources such as platform, infrastructure, storage, software, sensors, actuators, sensing, data, database, Ethernet, etc., through the network connection to the required users. Business vendors and software users do not need to possess physical devices and infrastructure to implement a vast program. Rather, the cloud ensures flexibility of allocation and de-allocation of computing resources on-demand basis using virtual infrastructure by maximizing computing power and minimizing the cost required for such resources.

Edge Computing

Edge computing, one of the middleware technologies under the umbrella of fog computing creates a new genre of the ecosystem along with IoT. It shifts cloud computing capabilities to the network edge, thus enhancing the speed of response and minimizing the network latency. The idea is to utilize the computing features of the peripheral devices to pre-process the data and send only relevant data to the cloud, thus reducing bandwidth costs. The computational resources are brought closer to the users where the actual services are consumed. Enabling real-time perception and actions makes it desirable for time-sensitive applications. Having supported the green computing revolution it decreases the network processing and maintenance cost because it reduces the data load and burden of data traversal through the network. Besides, it supports a high degree of mobility of end-users and serves emerging localized smart applications (Ray et al., 2019).

Under the sub-domains of fog computing, the related technologies have been introduced including cloudlets, mobile edge computing, and edge computing. Both fog computing and edge computing move the intelligence to the edge. As shown in Figure 1, the main difference between edge and fog computing is the place where intelligence and computing power are residing. In a fog layer, the intelligence is available at the LAN and the raw data generated from the edge devices are forwarded to the gateway for further processing. In an edge layer, the intelligence and the source of data are merely one hop away to mitigate the latency and network backbone bandwidth and to achieve more energy efficiency than the cloud (Bilal et al., 2018).

Edge computing fabric is a heterogeneous environment of edge servers, routers, switches, access points, mobile devices, or any computer-like Single Board devices. Most popular industry leading-edge applications include retail, smart manufacturing, smart city, connected cars, vehicular networks, cognitive computing, augmented and virtual reality, and similar use cases requiring real-time analytics.

Figure 1. Fog Computing and Edge Computing

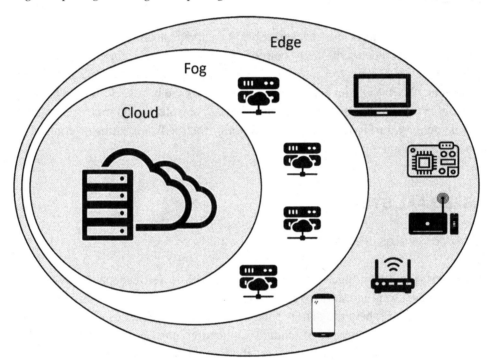

Ambient Assisted Living

With the advancement in a connected digital age, AAL attracts multiple fields including academic and industrial research communities and various public sectors. AAL based smart enhanced living place consists of (i) smart objects such as sensors, actuators and smart mobile phones (acting as a gateway for data transmission), interactive set-top boxes, modems, etc., and (ii) physical objects such as TV, lights, fans, stoves, doors, windows, mattress and so on (Haghi et al., 2019).

AAL solutions focus on the following aspects (Foko et al., 2013; Siegel et al., 2014):

- Improve the quality of life of elderly and disabled people by enhancing autonomy and emergency treatment services
- Round-the-clock assessment of an individual
- Reduce the burden on caretakers or relatives

- Improved personal care measures based on individual needs
- Reduce health care costs for the individual and society
- Advanced social interaction and participation in society
- Prevention and management of chronic conditions of the elderly
- Management of daily tasks for dependent people
- Provision of house comfort, personal safety, and edutainment.
- Ensuring physical as well as mental health by inhibiting anxiousness
- Avoid stigmatization of the elderly

Role of Assistive Technology

The role of assistive technology is one such agreeable in smart and healthy aging and living. The medical assistive devices have become increasingly comfortable for the people, for example, wearable fitness monitors (Chou et al., 2005; Zainudin et al., 2017), smartwatches (Ohtsuka et al., 2014), blood glucose monitors (Hou et al., 2019; Siddiqui et al., 2018), armbands, knee bands, etc. These health-monitoring wearables can either locally analyse the unstructured data like walking patterns, sleeping patterns, vital signs, or muscle activity during rehabilitation and notify the medicare teams or connect to the cloud directly for accurate insight analysis.

IOT ASSISTED AAL SYSTEM

Issues, Controversies, Problems

The IoT ecosystem is producing huge volumes of data that leads to a strict dependency on cloud computing platform for data analysis and storage requirements. The data generated by the sensors is forwarded to the remote cloud server where the data is filtered, processed to extract the knowledgeable insights and delivered to the end-users through a standard application interface. It then activates the actuators installed in the sensing environment. In this context, the continuous data requires extensive storage capacity which is provided by cloud computing and machine learning or deep learning models implemented in the cloud accelerate the long-term cognizance analytics.

Over recent years, the frequency of data generated by the IoT devices and sensors is vast to expose as it is, to the network to reach the centralized cloud server for data processing and analytics. For example, a remotely located oil mine produces 10TB of data per well for a single day. Another example is a commercial jet generating 5-10 TB of data per day (Cisco, 2015; Western Digital website, n.d.). When this big data is exposed as raw to get forwarded to the cloud, it not only affects the network performance but also cloud computing inhibits its suitability to serve the above-mentioned use cases.

Meanwhile, real-time and user-centric applications require faster and almost zero-latency response time. For example, across healthcare services, the unstructured data corresponding to the medical conditions of users or ambient data of users' living environments have to reach the distant cloud server. The large real-time medical data if it makes even the smallest delay in service can be a matter of life or demise. In addition, the security of personal and other sensitive data remains questionable when it traverses across multiple networks when stored in a centralized place. The different volumes of data are generated by different models at different rates, will generally be stored, analysed, visualized, and consumed by users of the IoT ecosystem. It consumes a substantial amount of network bandwidth resulting in high latency for real-time services. Moreover, it lacks mainly in three areas: 1) increased response time, 2) heavy load on the backbone network and 3) increased bandwidth costs to forward tons of data. So it makes an adverse effect on IoT tasks and thus becomes unsuitable for latency-sensitive applications such as healthcare. Though the cloud emphasizes a substantial amount of storage, computing, networking resources, services, and applications, there is a need to bring the cloud power much nearer and distributed. Therefore, a distributed network architecture named Fog computing is introduced to make IoT ideal for prominent real-time applications (Ray et al., 2019).

To solve the problems mentioned above, edge computing has been introduced in the recent past. Edge computing technology is a vast growing technology as it gives more opportunities to process data at the network boundary wherever it is most appropriate to do so. For example, in a real-time ECG monitoring system for patients affected with a cardiac problem in telehealthcare, when the measured ECG value enters the risky range of values, the service needs to quickly respond to it as soon as possible. Another example, emergency in a smart manufacturing use case, the service has to react with a low delay so that connected machines have to take measures to avoid any loss of production and safety.

On the other hand, edge computing is not intended to replace cloud computing technology as edge devices do not have much computing power, required battery life for big data processing, and storage capabilities, although the nano-technological components of mobile devices are well evolved. Thus the edge computing is observed as an extension of cloud computing to overcome innumerable problems ranging from communication delay to energy efficiency (Bilal et al., 2018).

However, the distributed nature of the edge paradigm exposes different challenges like ensuring the security of data over scattered devices, maintaining consistency over the data, discovering the service modules in dispersed devices, orchestration of edge devices and services, etc. These issues noted in edge computing grab greater research activities and contributions in the academic as well as industrial fields.

Need for AAL

Due to the expansion in IoT generation, it has evolved as a promising solution for healthcare scenarios which transformed the way healthcare services are provided to the users and other different stakeholders such as patients, relatives, medical practitioners/clinicians, etc. Healthcare becomes one of the increasingly eminent application domains in IoT. In recent years, developing geriatric care solutions for elder people and telemedicine solutions for people affected with neurological disorders or chronic diseases have become a significant element in the healthcare business to improve the quality of life by eradicating the challenges in their daily life.

AAL is one such emerging ecosystem, capable of reinforcing the independence and well-being of older adults, cognitively impaired people, and persons with chronic illness in a safe, secure and relaxed living environment, specifically where they survive or work. AAL provides a domain of wearable and ambient sensors, actuators, personal mobile devices with necessary software applications, computers, and wireless communication standards, aiming as a multi-disciplinary field to afford personal healthcare monitoring and telehealth systems for senior and independent citizens. Thus, AAL is believed to be a counterpart technology to treat the effects of the increasing aged population as a result of a gradual rise in life expectancy rate and decline in birth and mortality rate.

AAL Services

In a smart living context, AAL services, among which some examples are illustrated in Figure 2, can be the solutions for heterogeneous physical challenges experienced by senior citizens or cognitively impaired people. For instance, remainder services are deployed to remind about certain significant activities like intake of medicine, meals, balanced diet, water or health drinks, regular physical exercise, bill payment, etc., to improve physical and mental health and to enable independent living. This service could also be a better way to compensate the neuro-cognitive disabilities like Alzheimer's Disease.

As Shown in Table 1, these set of AAL services are categorized under the independent living, individual healthcare, and social and recreational services (Camarinha-Matos et al., 2015; Labonnote & Høyland, 2015).

Figure 2. Examples of AAL Services

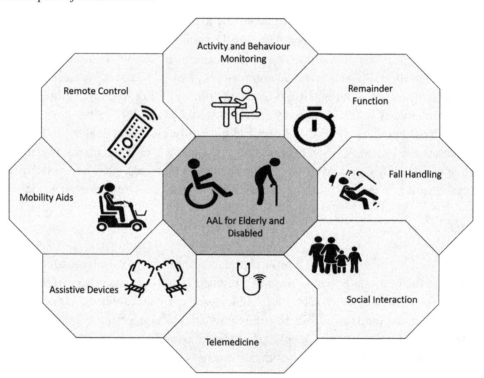

Challenges in Elders' Life

To ensure a quality life, elderly people have to be independent for their regular needs and to maintain social and physical interaction with their family members consistently. Their mental health plays a crucial role in promising healthier aging and comfort rather than their physical disabilities. If they are treated lovingly with fulfilled wishes, fun and entertainment they will be healthier and mentally stronger.

Table 1. Categorization of AAL Services

Independent Living Services	Healthcare Services	Social and Recreational Services
• Daily activity Management • Home comfort and safety • Secure Mobility • Indoor Localization	• Remote Patient Monitoring • Behaviour Monitoring • Rehabilitation Services • Fall handling • Sleep Monitoring • Emotion Recognition • Automatic Speech Recognition • Chronic disorder Management • Chronic Disease management • Cognitive Impairment services • Medication and Lifestyle Assistance	• Media Access Services • Home Mood Control services • Entertainment Services • Link with Relatives Services

The circumstances seem different in the case of older people with disorders, in the way they became dependent on caregiving staff or relatives for their daily routines - e.g. feeding, pottery, bathing, dressing, mobility, etc. It is crucial to improve their health status by treating them with the best care services.

Categories of Data

An AAL ecosystem is a collection of myriads of teleservices and thus includes a vast number of sensors deployed in its environment. Sometimes, the sensors' functionality may be redundant in regard to ensure the availability of any such services. Besides, comprehensive parameters are essential in contributing to the health of a person including vital, physiological, and environmental data (Haghi et al., 2019), which are the different types of data. In healthcare, the vital signs of a person include body temperature, heart rate, ECG, pressure, blood oxygen level, and respiratory rate. The physiological data indicate human activities such as walking, sitting, sleeping, and so on. Ambient sensors deployed in the home are involved in obtaining environmental parameters such as humidity, air pressure, temperature, CO_2, CO, NO_2, noise, etc.,

In recent years our smartphones are embedded with multiple sensors to advance personalized services. Such sensors are involved in obtaining AAL user information like their activities, behaviors, and health data in order to improve assistance and user awareness. Like in the existing work, smartphone photography with a high-resolution camera can be useful for early detection of skin-related diseases like melanoma (Vano-Galvan et al., 2015). The embedded accelerometer and gyroscopes in the smartphone with the GPS or any communication interfaces are useful to enhance the users' mobility.

The health-monitoring dedicated wearable devices available in the market sophisticates measuring specific or combined information of the patient namely body temperature, heart rate, blood pressure, oxygen saturation rate, ECG, muscle strength, muscle fatigue status, step count, moving distance, current location, breathing rate, sleep position, calories burnt, sleep tracking, sleep quality, diet, body weight, motion tracking and so on.

IoT-AAL Ecosystem

A general IoT based AAL architecture is illustrated in Figure 3 in which it comprises four layers - IoT layer, Edge Layer, Cloud Layer, and Application layer. Many existing works (Zgheib et al., 2017; Gomes et al., 2015) presented hierarchical IoT-AAL frameworks, in several contexts. An ontology framework (Zgheib et al., 2017) is presented to enable cognitive detection of events with identified changes in smart homes and surroundings using cognitive sensors (virtual sensors). A scalable IoT-based middleware infrastructure for the AAL system is described in (Gomes et al., 2015) for telehealthcare service.

IoT Layer

The first tier, IoT layer comprises of many geographically distributed intelligent devices and sensor nodes - may be in the form of activity sensors (to monitor users' physiological or behavioral activities) deployed in the smart environment or embedded in hand-held devices or medical sensors associated with dedicated wearable devices or ambient sensors, forming wireless sensor networks (WSN).

The raw data obtained by the sensors is heavy, and the generation is based on the behavior of the sensors - continuous, periodic, or event-based forwarding (Gomes et al., 2015). They are forwarded to the edge layer through short-range wireless communication standards such as Bluetooth, Bluetooth Smart (BLE), ZigBee, etc. The sensor nodes form star topology with the gateway device in transmitting the information.

Edge Layer

An edge gateway device is neither a simple sensor collecting analog signal along with sending digital data nor a collection of rack servers, rather it can be any endpoint device with inbuilt processing power and communication capabilities. Mostly, hand-held devices like smartphones, ipads, and tablets are being used as a gateway at the edge layer to transmit the sensor data to the cloud data center. Normally the peripheral devices which can be useful for data collection are any network-enabled processing elements such as notebook computers, laptops, security cameras, drones or low-cost Single Board Computers like Raspberry Pi or small computers like development boards or kits. The software applications installed in edge devices are involved in pre-processing, filtering (unstructured data may contain noise) or aggregating (sensor data may be redundant) the sensor data and forwarded using long-range connectivity standards such as 3G/4G/5G, LoRa, LWPAN, WiFi and so on.

Cloud Layer

This layer is dedicated to executing computing-intensive tasks with an abundant number of resources. The filtered sensor data is sorted out, managed, stored, and analyzed to produce remarkable understandings at the data center. The data center is administered with a deep learning algorithm that enables long-term analytics and storage. The learning model is essential to predict the pattern and behavior of the user data to afford advanced services. The cloud server can also be accessed by authorized individuals - for instance, in healthcare, the doctors are allowed authorized access to patients' medical history. The data delivery and emergency notification can be made to occur manually assigning some parameters such as time interval, priority, etc., by authorized medical professionals.

Application Layer

The users' communication devices like smartphones provide an application interface that delivers procured cognizance from the cloud, both to the service consumers and service producers, expediting personalized services.

Figure 3. AAL-IoT Architecture

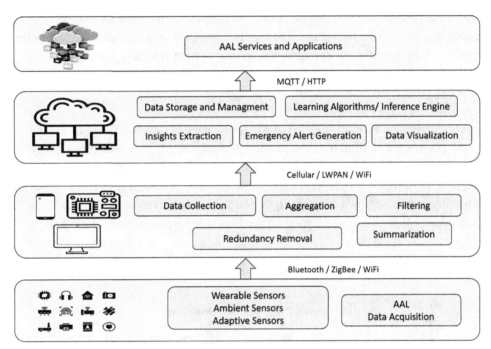

EDGE BASED AAL-IOT FRAMEWORK

With the enhanced growth of IoT devices along with its new business applications, real-time computing and processing power closer to the edge is significant. The edge revolution, a distributed computing topology is transforming massively the way big data is being handled by the server. Consider, a self-driving car is associated with 200+ sensors and capable of generating a 4 TB of data per day (Suhrid Barua, n.d.). Having hundreds, thousands or millions of such devices affects the performance of real-time applications. It results in quality degradation due to latency and increases bandwidth needs.

Nawaz et al. (2016) discussed an embedded vision-based security camera for human monitoring scenarios that employ sensor edge computing to mitigate security and privacy issues in collecting raw video data. Enterprises like NVIDIA introduced an edge platform to bring the power of Artificial Intelligence (AI) to the edge. Nvidia Jetson Nano Developer kit (Sheshadri & Franklin, 2020), one such example edge-based powerful computer, yet as small as credit cards, can run multiple AI algorithms in parallel at the edge. It deploys end-to-end AI-based applications, achieving much higher performance and energy efficiency. Healthcare experts reported that faster and local data processing using the edge paradigm is highly useful to be a life-saving one (CBINSIGHTS, April 28, 2020).

Many works related to the AAL concept blended with edge technology have been studied. Some of the fog computing architecture (Cerina et al., 2017; Nikoloudakis et al., 2016; Vora et al., 2017) for AAL concepts are also examined. A fog-based AAL framework (Vora et al., 2017) for remote patient monitoring applications is proffered in which priority gateway is used for emergency measures if any abnormal situation is found from a regression analysis. It also uses the clustering algorithm in regard to reduce the data to be forwarded to the fog gateway. Another fog-based system architecture for remote patient surveillance applications is proposed (Nikoloudakis et al., 2016) in which ubiquitous alerting service is implemented in a virtual fog layer to locate the activity-challenged individuals. The system notifies the caregivers about the patients moving into an unsafe geographic boundary. Cerina et al. (2017) discussed a multi-level fog architecture for health and AAL applications, using reconfigurable fog nodes to achieve high performance. It implements an emergency response system with low latency.

Solutions and Recommendations

In this context, an edge-based multi-tier IoT-AAL framework is proposed here as shown in Figure 4. The base of the framework is similar to the previously explained IoT architecture with enhanced edge functionalities in order to enable immediate response from the system. Comparing to the IoT based AAL architecture, the proposed system is capable of enabling reliability, security (ensuring integrity and confidentiality of the obtained user data), availability (edge level decision making easily handles intermittent network connection), and achieving zero-latency response time for an AAL individual.

Figure 4. Proposed Edge-based AAL-IoT Architecture

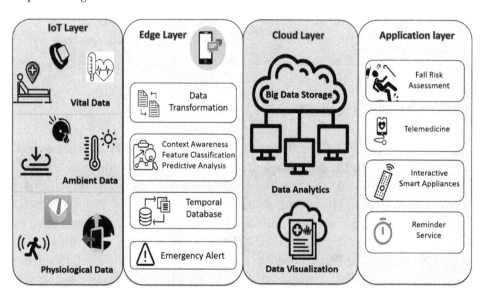

As given in the framework, the mobile edge gateway gathers all data from the IoT layer and involves data transformation operations - aggregation, filter, compression, and fusion. The near-real-time data analytics at the edge requires some extended technologies like machine learning and deep learning model (Bailas et al., 2018) to incorporate the feature of predictive analytics into the edge layer. As the AI technique plays a crucial role in the edge computing paradigm, implementing edge intelligence scenarios in the area of AAL significantly improves the QoE of the user. The added benefit of inculcating AI into the edge is not only enabling various aspects such as data analysis, feature classification, regression analysis, and clustering but also contextual classification of data and achieving reliable end service (Pazienza et al., 2019). Adopting AI techniques to describe intelligent edge architecture is carried out in some researches (Jacome et al., 2019; Keum et al., 2020; Pazienza et al., 2019). One such work is suggested in (Jacome et al., 2019) which deployed predictive analytics at the edge for the IoT-AAL ecosystem suiting healthcare scenarios. An edge intelligent architecture (Pazienza et al., 2019) is introduced to perform the real-time decision-making process in case of complex applications like the AAL concept. Establishing awareness of patients' activities of daily life, an edge-based self-organized device network (Keum et al., 2020) is proposed for real-time user activity monitoring scenarios to determine their physical ability and alert them about their incomplete or forgotten activities.

An AAL environment gathers distinct types of data from different sensors or sensing devices like environmental, medical, and physiological data. It does not mean that all the data is required all the time. Determining the real emergency data among them makes more sense and creates a great impact on life. For example, data from a fire detection sensor is more significant when smoke is detected than the normal range of medical data. Another example, heart rate sensor data is more important when its value falls within an unsafe range for a person with chronic heart disease than other safe ambient parameters. In these similar circumstances, the concept of contextual awareness (Brouwer et al., 2018; Hassan et al., 2019) helps the AAL to predict the real appropriateness for emergency care. An edge-based prediction model for the AAL framework (Hassan et al., 2019) is recommended to identify the emergency medical data with the feature of contextual awareness. An edge-based cascading reasoning framework (Brouwer et al., 2018) is presented for pervasive healthcare to combine the data streams from various medical sensors and create new deep and accurate awareness.

The edge layer is deployed with a temporal database to store processed data and results from predictive analytics for a certain period. The database stores data in JSON format and the query-based language can be used for retrieving data from it. In the event of an emergency alert, the formal stakeholders like medicare teams or caretakers or relatives will be notified with ultra-low latency with an immediate response.

Table 2. Collection of Stakeholders

Formal Stakeholders	Informal Stakeholders
• Hospitals • Medical Centers • Doctors / Medical Professionals • Clinics • Nursing Homes • Rehabilitation Centers • Police • Ambulatory Services • Telemedicine / Telehealthcare Service Providers	• Relatives/ Caretakers • Elder Care /Disabled Home Association • Social Voluntary Groups

AAL Integrated Service Platform

In addition to the AAL market service providers, an AAL ecosystem collaborates with a collection of different formal and informal stakeholders (Camarinha-Matos et al., 2015) as shown in Table 2, in addition to the user in the smart home. In (Camarinha-Matos et al., 2015), a virtual service integrator combines multiple service providers into a single platform to enable the user, a composite set of services.

An edge-based service provisioning AAL platform is employed in (Lopez-de-Ipina et al., 2010), the proposed architecture includes an AAL kit - a collection of software and hardware components and centralized service provisioning and management server. The AAL kit, like a set-top box, can be easily used in the smart home, the required services such as smart TV, emergency or alerts, remote patients' vital signs monitoring and so on can easily be installed or uninstalled whenever required.

The edge-based integrated platform emphasizes service discovery and device discovery using which the devices deployed in the smart home are automatically discovered. It is intended to build a telemedicine solution offering services such as telecare, teletreatment, teleconsultation, home care, and mobility. The dissimilar stakeholders of the AAL system will be given a standard application interface to access the common integrated platform.

ENABLING TECHNOLOGIES FOR EDGE COMPUTING AND AAL

Numerous ground-breaking technologies serve as a solution for blending edge computing and AAL paradigm by achieving even more application performance and instantaneous service response. This section describes some of the enabling technologies such as Mobile Edge Computing (MEC), 5G, virtualization, containers, and Software-Defined Networking (SDN).

MEC

Also known as Multi-access Edge Computing, it is considered another enabler of IoT applications. It brings networking, storage, and computational power to the edge of the radio access network with respect to prohibit long-distance backhauling, thus upgrading network efficiency and service delivery to the consumers. It enables cloud platforms at the network edge and facilitates low latency and high bandwidth access to radio access network resources (Porambage et al., 2018). A MEC-based solution (Pham et al., 2019) is proposed, executing an optimal selection algorithm for service placement and request scheduling placement to improve the total utility (satisfaction) of all the IoT users.

5G

The faster wireless networking technology, 5G, one of the biggest drivers for edge computing increases bandwidth significantly and depletes latency with its distributed nature. Many companies started to deploy this technology as overlapping 5G networks can keep bandwidth-intensive content closer to the edge or even on-premises to meet the ongoing demands for faster and efficient services. The evolution in 5G mobile communications becomes a major key player in AAL healthcare scenarios.

In the 5G spectrum, the expansion of frequency bands inhibits the use of full-duplex channels for data communications. To overcome this, Kaneriya et al. (2019) described an AAL system architecture with a full-duplex communication standard that acquires low delay and more communication accuracy in transmitting patients' vital data. In another work, intelligent peer-to-peer backhaul is procured by establishing a peer port at each mobile station, hence the data streams of IoT devices in a fog environment is allowed to take the optimal route dynamically for the desired speed, delay and cost in alternative radio access networks, providing AAL as a Service (Stainov et al., 2016).

Virtualizations

For intensifying network resource utilization, a virtual sensor network can be formed by connecting logical instances of underlying physical sensor nodes and serve multiple applications rather than a specific service with several numbers of sensors. Khalid et al. (2015) described a middleware architecture integrating and managing resources and communication protocols and standards in smart home and AAL service. Besides, the framework employs a multi-threading concept in order to enable manifold isolated applications to run on dissimilar sensor networks.

Network Function Virtualization (NFV) is a network architecture concept, virtualizing functions of every network element namely load balancing, traffic control, virtual routing, firewall, intrusion detection, and so on. Differing from traditional virtualization, it decouples network functions from the actual physical network hardware elements. NFV based AAL system (Nikoloudakis et al., 2017) is discussed to escalate the user's mobility with the help of assistive technology. Though the patient wearing the dedicated service is allowed to move outside, continuous monitoring is provided and the nearest caretakers will be notified if an emergency is required.

Docker Containers

Docker enables platform-as-a-service by virtualizing operating system (OS) - a set of software packages called containers containing software, system tools and libraries, configuration files to run an application regardless of actual physical infrastructure.

Due to the depletion of computing resources at the network edge, the performance of the application may degrade while executing data-intensive tasks on the endpoint devices because of resource overhead. An AAL healthcare environment contains a spectrum of IoT devices or sensors connected to a single edge gateway and if overhead occurs in the end devices then it will create a great impact on service deployment and meeting the service requirements, increasing the chance of loss of life. An efficient resource management scheme (Ahmeda et al., 2019) is recommended based on Docker container virtualization techniques by mitigating resource overhead and network failures. The virtualization technology helps greatly to enhance the application performance when the learning models are assimilated at the edge (Jacome et al., 2019). Thus it sophisticates service life cycle management and deployment in AAL systems.

In pursuance of maintaining a secured electronic patient record in healthcare service scenarios targeting the AAL domain, a fog computing architecture with blockchain functionality (Cech et al., 2019) is proposed which adopts container virtualization and SDN for dynamic resource management and orchestration. It also ensures secure data processing and retrieval.

Software-Defined Networking

SDN is a network architecture separating the data plane (forwarding behavior) from the control plane (network routing intelligence) and placing the intelligence in a central place called the SDN controller. Contrasting from the traditional networking technology, SDN makes the network programmable and controllable from the centralized controller. Silva et al. (2016) proposed an AAL architecture for managing and distributing context information from smart home to enable context-based processing of raw sensor data and transport the relevant resulting data to the cloud using SDN functionality, upgrading QoS of the presented framework.

CASE STUDY

In this section, a real-life use case study utilizing the AAL concept and its applicability is presented. Considering an AAL patient requiring constant monitoring during the COVID-19 crisis in a quarantined environment, an edge-based model is discussed.

Vital Sign Monitoring During COVID-19 Pandemic

The coronavirus disease 2019 (COVID-19) started as an epidemic, primarily spread within China since December 2019, and is declared as a global pandemic on March 11, 2020, when it started spreading outside china secondarily. It causes 1.6 million deaths and affects more than 75 million people worldwide (World Health Organization, December 22, 2020). As the disease is highly contagious, the spread occurs mostly from person-to-person through respiratory droplets from coughing and sneezing, whilst being in close contact (NPTEL, May 18, 2020). Besides, the patients are reported with acute respiratory distress syndrome and have shown varying degrees of complications, and their severity is diagnosed as mild, severe or critical (Huang et al., 2020; Lescure et al., 2020; Wang et al., 2020). Especially people with comorbidities such as lung disease, heart disease, kidney failure, diabetes, hypertension, etc., have developed severe complications resulting in increased mortality. Hence, the mortality rate of older people with a chronic illness is higher than that of other aged adults.

Due to the high risk of transmissibility of the virus by people with mild illness, the infected or suspected persons should be isolated at hospitals and continuously monitored to know the stage of the illness. This increases the risk of acquiring the symptoms to nursing staff while accomplishing regular monitoring of the patients and possibly to other people or patients who have come in contact with the staff. Furthermore, the travellers have to be quarantined for 14 days as the symptoms may appear 2 - 14 days (estimated incubation period) after exposure to the viral disease for an individual (NPTEL, May 18, 2020).

Among the globally reported cases, around 14% are healthcare people (World Health Organization, September 17, 2020). The physical and mental health of medical professionals is equally important in this pandemic crisis. They are suffering from psychological stress, anxiety, depression and insomnia due to long working hours, fear of direct disease exposure, and being virus transmitters to their family members (Pappaa et al., 2020). Immediate telemedicine technology intervention is essential in managing this crisis in several ways and has become a triage engine during this pandemic period. The people with early or mild symptoms and people with travel history can be isolated and quarantined in a smart enhanced living environment enabled with AAL services rather than being at hospitals.

The integrated AAL and telemonitoring technology reduce anxiety and prevent the probability of spreading the infection to the healthcare personnel, by accelerating services such as video consultation with medical care teams, remote monitoring, automatic medication remainders/providers, automatic ventilation control, diet monitoring, sleep monitoring, hygiene monitoring and so on. It paves a way for a massive scale and asynchronous solution to handle such a pandemic crisis. It prevents direct contact between the patient and healthcare teams, thus avoiding the risk of exposure. It enables well in time organized isolation of elderly or infected or suspected individuals. In consequence, telemedicine technology also helps to keep the morbidity level and fatality risk at a minimum.

Some related works (Sandhu et al., 2016; Watson et al., 2020) have been studied in which cloud computing has been exploited in the screening and monitoring of pandemic outbreaks. A cloud computing architecture for smart monitoring of pandemic Influenza A1(H1N1) is presented as a framework in (Sandhu et al., 2016). It calculates an index value to predict the future probability of the person spreading or catching the infection by collecting their medical reports from doctors/clinicians. A notification is sent to the respective caretakers if the patients' condition is at high risk. The remote monitoring service is advantageous in several ways (Watson et al., 2020). It enables the safe delivery of required medical equipment to the patient without direct contact. It ensures the safety of collected data from patients by storing them in a secure database.

The major symptoms of COVID-19 from which one can suspect are fever, cough, and shortness of breath. The other symptoms and associated range of values for the mild, severe, and critical stage are shown in Table 3 and Table 4, adopted from the NEWS (National Early Warning Score) scoring system (Royal College of Physicians, 2012).

Table 3. Adopted from NEWS Scoring System (Royal College of Physicians, 2012)

Parameters	0	1	2	3
Body Temperature (degree celsius)	36.1 - 38.0	35.1 - 36 or 38.1 - 39	>= 39.1	<= 35
Heart Rate (per min)	51 - 90	41 - 50 or 91 - 110	111 - 130	<= 40 or >= 131
Blood Pressure (systolic)	111 - 219	101 - 110	91 - 100	<= 90 or >= 220
Respiratory Rate (per min)	12 - 20	9 - 11	21 - 24	<= 8 or >= 25
Blood Oxygen Saturation Rate	>=96	94 - 95	92 - 93	<= 91
Supplemental oxygen	No	No	Yes	Yes
Consciousness	Yes	Yes	Yes	Drowsiness Lethargy
Age	< 65			>=65

Table 4. Adopted from NEWS Thresholds and Triggers (Royal College of Physicians, 2012)

Aggregate Score	Risk level	Warning level	Monitoring Frequency	Response	Solution
0	-	-	12 hrs once	Ward based	Monitoring
1 - 4	Mild	Yellow	6 hrs once	Urgent ward based	Monitoring / Intimate doctor
5 - 6	Severe	Orange	1-2 hrs once	Key threshold for urgent	Evaluation and Remote Consultation by Doctor
>= 7	Critical	Red	Continuous	Emergency	On-site Consultation by Doctor

The edge-based AAL model for COVID-19 telemonitoring and teleconsultation applications are shown in Figure 5. In this context, having presented the comorbidity status and travel history, the patient is assumed to be isolated in a smart living scenario deployed with vital and medical sensors or equipped with special-purpose wearable devices. It is proven that a healthy diet and personal hygiene are significant to recover soon from the disease by improving the immune system against the virus. The patient should be affirmed to follow the strict infection control protocols established nationwide, being in a safe atmosphere. Hence, the physiological parameters of the patient (diet intake, sleeping habit, hand washing, and other related activities) are also retrieved to ensure the patient is taken good care of as if they were at a hospital-related secure environment.

The edge server with a necessary software application can be useful in gathering vital data from the patient persistently. Then it involves a general pre-processing and filtering of the sensor data. The cloud server distributes the instance of the inference model to the edge device with respect to monitor the disease progression. The edge server can run the distributed instance to predict the risk level of the person and to enable them with suitable clinical responses and solutions. The emergency response will be immediately sent from the edge device to the medical practitioners if the warning level reaches the Orange or Red stage. The healthcare professional can visualize the data stored in the remote cloud for further information via authorized access. Whenever required, the patient and the doctor can have online video consultations about the medication or relevant information.

Instead of the inference analysis occurs at the remote cloud, the edge computing solution can offer low latency and immediate response with the increased number of quarantined persons accessing the same service deployed in a cloud server, supporting scalability for COVID-19 screening.

FUTURE RESEARCH DIRECTIONS

The concept of edge computing crucially relies on edge gateway devices for processing complex tasks and running AI models at the periphery of the users' personalized network. Such devices should support long-range communication standards to leverage their capabilities. The telehealthcare solutions can provide real-time medical recommendations, disease diagnosis or emergency prediction using the power of the edge with regard to control or handle chronic disorders. Furthermore, they are capable of predicting patients' disease patterns and provide customized care services.

Even though telemedicine plays a greater role in AAL business, it is equally important to integrate the AAL platform, healthcare technologies, and formal & informal telehealth stakeholders to enable scalable and sustainable telecare solutions. By including more number of users, practically implemented evidence-based studies and solutions will give direction to future research. However, the elderly or physically impaired person should be self-determined and motivated to use advanced mobile technologies.

Figure 5. Edge-based AAL Environment for COVID-19 Isolated Patient Monitoring

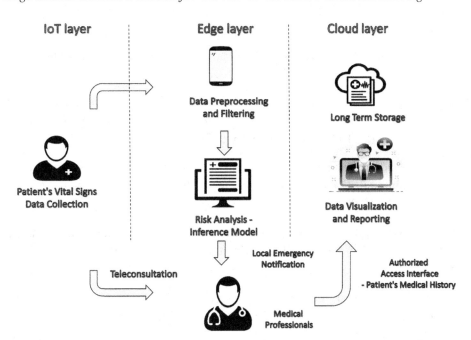

CONCLUSION

AAL is an emerging technology providing sustainable telehealthcare solutions to older adults, impaired people, or isolated individuals. The cloud-based AAL system lacks in affording real-time decision making capability to an intelligent environment, especially in healthcare services due to large data communication, processing, and management in the already hectic network. The importance of these issues led to the development of edge-based AAL systems collaborating multiple stakeholders namely medical specialists, remote care centers, caretakers, and so on. The integration of edge computing solutions into these systems helps to improve the QoS of the end-users.

In this chapter, the edge-based IoT framework for AAL scenarios is presented which inculcates AI and deep learning techniques into the endpoint devices. Signifying many edge solutions in the field of AAL, how it accelerates context-based classification and predictive learning from the pattern behaviour in order to enable cloud-like resource infrastructure at one hop away from the end-users is mentioned. In the event of having computational and storage resources at the edge to implement AI algorithms, recent technologies like virtualization, SDN, 5G to strengthen the edge computing capabilities are discussed. Thus, expediting the real-time edge-based health-related emergency response will have the biggest positive impact, improving the health of independently living individuals and the quality of their life in a smart environment.

A case study on remote vital sign monitoring of a COVID-19 patient at his living place itself more comfortable to handle the eerie happening of pandemic crisis. The edge intelligence helps in reacting immediately with the patients' health triggers and providing clinical emergency response.

REFERENCES

Ahmeda, B., Seghira, B., Al-Ostaa, M., & Abdelouahed, G. (2019). Container Based Resource Management for Data Processing on IoT Gateways. In *Proceedings of the 16th International Conference on Mobile Systems and Pervasive Computing*. Elsevier. 10.1016/j.procs.2019.08.034

Bailas, C., Marsden, M., Zhang, D., O'Connor, N. E., & Little, S. (2018). Performance of Video Processing at the Edge for Crowd-Monitoring Applications. In *Proceedings of the 4th World Forum on Internet of Things (WF-IoT)*. IEEE. 10.1109/WF-IoT.2018.8355170

Bilal, K., Khalid, O., Erbad, A., & Khan, S. U. (2018). Potentials, trends, and prospects in edge technologies: Fog, cloudlet, mobile edge, and micro data centers. *Elsevier Computer Networks*, *130*, 94–120. doi:10.1016/j.comnet.2017.10.002

Brouwer, M. D., Ongenae, F., Bonte, P., & Turck, F. D. (2018). Towards a Cascading Reasoning Framework to Support Responsive Ambient-Intelligent Healthcare Interventions. *MDPI Sensors - Wearable and Ambient Sensors for Healthcare and Wellness Applications, 18*(10), 3514.

Camarinha-Matos, L. M., Rosas, J., Oliveira, A. I., & Ferrada, F. (2015). Care services ecosystem for ambient assisted living. *Enterprise Information Systems*, *9*(5-6), 607–633.

CBINSIGHTS. (2020, April 28). *What is Edge Computing?* Retrieved from https://www.cbinsights.com/research/what-is-edge-computing/

Cech, H. L., Grobmann, M., & Krieger, U. R. (2019). A Fog Computing Architecture to Share Sensor Data by Means of Blockchain Functionality. In *Proceedings of International Conference on Fog Computing*. IEEE. 10.1109/ICFC.2019.00013

Cerina, L., Notargiacomo, S., Paccanit, M. G. L., & Santambrogio, M. D. (2017). A Fog-Computing architecture for Preventive Healthcare and Assisted Living in Smart Ambients. In *Proceedings of the 3rd International Forum on Research and Technologies for Society and Industry (RTSI)*. IEEE. 10.1109/RTSI.2017.8065939

Chou, T. C., Chiu, N. F., Liao, F. R., Lu, S. S., Ping, F., Yang, C. R., & Lin, C. W. (2005). A Multi Parameters Wearable Telemetric System for Cardio-Pulmonary Fitness of e-Health. In *Proceedings of the 27th Annual Conference on Engineering in Medicine and Biology*. IEEE. 10.1109/IEMBS.2005.1617233

Cisco. (2015). *Fog Computing and the Internet of Things: Extend the Cloud to Where the Things Are: Whitepaper*. Retrieved from https://www.cisco.com/c/dam/en_us/solutions/trends/iot/docs/computing-overview.pdf

Emeakaroha, V. C., Cafferkey, N., Healy, P., & Morrison, J. P. (2015). A Cloud-Based IoT Data Gathering and Processing Platform. In *Proceedings of the 3rd International Conference on Future Internet of Things and Cloud*. IEEE. 10.1109/FiCloud.2015.53

Foko, T., Dlodlo, N., & Montsi, L. (2013). An Integrated Smart System for Ambient-Assisted Living. *Internet of Things, Smart Spaces, and Next Generation Networking, 8121*, 128–138. doi:10.1007/978-3-642-40316-3_12

Gomes, B., Muniz, L., Silva, F. J. S., Rios, L. T. E., & Endler, M. (2015). A Comprehensive Cloud-based IoT Software Infrastructure for Ambient Assisted Living. In *Proceedings of International Conference on Cloud Technologies and Applications (CloudTech)*. IEEE. 10.1109/CloudTech.2015.7336998

Haghi, M., Geissler, A., Fleischer, H., Stoll, N., & Thurow, K. (2019). Ubiqsense: A Personal Wearable in Ambient Parameters Monitoring Based on IoT Platform. In *Proceedings of International Conference on Sensing and Instrumentation in IoT Era (ISSI)*. IEEE. 10.1109/ISSI47111.2019.9043713

Hassan, M. K., Desouky, A. I. E., Badawy, M. M., Sarhan, A. M., Elhoseny, M., & Gunasekaran, M. (2019). EoT-driven hybrid ambient assisted living framework with naive Bayes–firefly algorithm. *Springer Neural Computing and Applications, 31*(5), 1275–1300. doi:10.100700521-018-3533-y

Hou, L., Zhang, H., Wang, J., & Shi, D. (2019). Optimal Blood Glucose Prediction based on Intermittent Data from Wearable Glucose Monitoring Sensors. In *Proceedings of Chinese Control Conference (CCC)*. IEEE. 10.23919/ChiCC.2019.8866572

Huang, C., Wang, Y., Li, X., Ren, L., Zhao, J., Hu, Y., Zhang, L., Fan, G., Xu, J., Gu, X., Cheng, Z., Yu, T., Xia, J., Wei, Y., Wu, W., Xie, X., Yin, W., Li, H., Liu, M., ... Cao, B. (2020). Clinical features of patients infected with 2019 novel coronavirus in Wuhan, China. *Lancet, 395*(10223), 497–506. doi:10.1016/S0140-6736(20)30183-5 PMID:31986264

Jacome, D. S., Lacalle, I., Palau, C. E., & Esteve, M. (2019). Efficient Deployment of Predictive Analytics in Edge Gateways: Fall Detection Scenario. In *Proceedings of the 5th World Forum on Internet of Things (WF-IoT)*. IEEE.

Kaneriya, S., Vora, J., Tanwar, S., & Tyagi, S. (2019). Standardising the use of Duplex Channels in 5G-WiFi Networking for Ambient Assisted Living. In *Proceedings of International Conference on Communications Workshops*. IEEE. 10.1109/ICCW.2019.8757145

Keum, S. S., Park, Y. J., & Kang, S. J. (2020). Edge Computing-Based Self-Organized Device Network for Awareness Activities of Daily Living in the Home. *MDPI Applied Sciences - Software Approaches to Improve the Performance of IoT Systems, 10*(7), 2475.

Khalid, Z., Fisal, N., Zubair, S., Ullah, R., Safdar, H., Maqbool, W., & Khalid, U. (2015). Multi-Thread based Middleware for Sensor Network Virtualization. In *Proceedings of the 5th National Symposium on Information Technology: Towards New Smart World (NSITNSW)*. IEEE. 10.1109/NSITNSW.2015.7176421

Labonnote, N., & Høyland, K. (2015). Smart home technologies that support independent living: Challenges and opportunities for the building industry – a systematic mapping study. *Taylor & Francis Intelligent Buildings International, 9*(1), 40–63. doi:10.1080/17508975.2015.1048767

Lescure, F. X., Bouadma, L., Parisey, D. N. M., Wicky, P. H., Behillil, S., Gaymard, A., Duchamp, M. B., Donati, F., Hingrat, Q. L., Enouf, V., Houhou-Fidouh, N., Valette, M., Mailles, A., Lucet, J. C., Mentre, F., Duval, X., Descamps, D., Malvy, D., Timsit, J. F., ... Yazdanpanah, Y. (2020). Clinical and virological data of the first cases of COVID-19 in Europe: A case series. *THE LANCET Infectious Diseases*, *20*(6), 697–706. doi:10.1016/S1473-3099(20)30200-0 PMID:32224310

Lopez-de-Ipina, D., Blanco, S., Diaz-de-Sarralde, I., & Laiseca, X. (2010). A Platform for a More Widespread Adoption of AAL. *Aging Friendly Technology for Health and Independence*, *6159*, 250–253. doi:10.1007/978-3-642-13778-5_35

Market Research Future. (2018, April). *Global Ambient Assisted Living Market Research Report, by System (Entertainment, Communication, Medical Assistance, Transportation), Sensor (Temperature, Occupancy), Service (Installation & Repair) – Forecast till 2027* (ID: MRFR/SEM/0509-CR). Retrieved from https://www.marketresearchfuture.com/reports/ambient-assisted-living-market-1015

Nawaz, T., Rinner, B., & Ferryman, J. (2016). User-centric, embedded vision-based human monitoring: A concept and a healthcare use case. In *Proceedings of the 10th International Conference on Distributed Smart Camera ICDSC '16*. Association for Computing Machinery. 10.1145/2967413.2967422

Nikoloudakis, Y., Markakis, E., Mastorakis, G., Pallis, E., & Skianis, C. (2017). An NFV-Powered Emergency System for Smart Enhanced Living Environment. In *Proceedings of Conference on Network Function Virtualization and Software Defined Networks (NFV-SDN)*. IEEE.

Nikoloudakis, Y., Panagiotakis, S., Markakis, E., Pallis, E., Mastorakis, G., Mavromoustakis, C. X., & Dobre, C. (2016). A Fog-Based Emergency System for Smart Enhanced Living Environments. *IEEE Cloud Computing*, *3*(6), 54–62. doi:10.1109/MCC.2016.118

NPTEL. (2020, May 18). Live_Covid 19: A Clinician's Perspective. *NPTEL Live Streaming*. https://www.youtube.com/watch?v=8ZUXSXFYEk4&t=4431s

Ohtsuka, S., Usami, T., & Sasaki, N. (2014). A vibration watch using a smart phone for visually impaired people. In *Proceedings of the 3rd Global Conference on Consumer Electronics (GCCE)*. IEEE. 10.1109/GCCE.2014.7031094

Pappaa, S., Ntellac, V., Giannakasc, T., Giannakoulisc, V. G., Papoutsic, E., & Katsaounou, P. (2020). Prevalence of depression, anxiety, and insomnia among healthcare workers during the COVID-19 pandemic: A systematic review and meta-analysis. *Elsevier Brain, Behavior, and Immunity*, *88*, 901–907. doi:10.1016/j.bbi.2020.05.026 PMID:32437915

Pazienza, A., Mallardi, G., Fasciano, C., & Vitulano, F. (2019). Artificial Intelligence on Edge Computing: a Healthcare Scenario in Ambient Assisted Living. In *Proceedings of the Fifth Italian Workshop on Artificial Intelligence for Ambient Assisted Living (AI*AAL.it 2019), co-located with 18th International Conference of the Italian Association for Artificial Intelligence (AIxIA 2019)*. CEUR-WS.

Pham, X. Q., Nguyen, T. D., Nguyen, V. D., & Huh, E. N. (2019). Utility-Centric Service Provisioning in Multi-Access Edge Computing. *MDPI Applied Sciences - Intelligent Centralized and Distributed Secure Edge Computing for Internet of Things Applications*, *9*(18), 3776.

Porambage, P., Okwuibe, J., Liyanage, M., Ylianttila, M., & Taleb, T. (2018). Survey on Multi-Access Edge Computing for Internet of Things Realization. *IEEE Communications Surveys and Tutorials*, *20*(4), 2961–2991. doi:10.1109/COMST.2018.2849509

Qabil, S., Waheed, U., Awan, S. M., Mansoor, Y., & Khan, M. A. (2019). A Survey on Emerging Integration of Cloud Computing and Internet of Things. In *Proceedings of the International Conference on Information Science and Communication Technology (ICISCT)*. IEEE. 10.1109/CISCT.2019.8777438

Ray, P. P., Dash, D., & De, D. (2019). Edge computing for Internet of Things: A survey, e-healthcare case study and future direction. *Elsevier Journal of Network and Computer Applications*, *140*, 1–22. doi:10.1016/j.jnca.2019.05.005

Royal College of Physicians. (2012). *National Early Warning Score (NEWS): Standardising the assessment of acute illness severity in the NHS. Report of a working party*. RCP.

Sandhu, R., Gill, H. K., & Sood, S. K. (2016). Smart monitoring and controlling of pandemic influenza A (H1N1) using social network analysis and cloud computing. *Journal of Computational Science*, *12*, 11–22. doi:10.1016/j.jocs.2015.11.001 PMID:32362959

Sheshadri, S. H., & Franklin, D. (2020) *Introducing the Ultimate Starter AI Computer, the NVIDIA Jetson Nano 2GB Developer Kit*. NVIDIA Developer. Retrieved from https://developer.nvidia.com/blog/ultimate-starter-ai-computer-jetson-nano-2gb-developer-kit/

Siddiqui, S. A., Zhang, Y., Lloret, J., Song, H., & Obradovic, Z. (2018). Pain-Free Blood Glucose Monitoring Using Wearable Sensors: Recent Advancements and Future Prospects. *IEEE Reviews in Biomedical Engineering*, *11*, 21–35. doi:10.1109/RBME.2018.2822301 PMID:29993663

Siegel, C., Hochgatterer, A., & Dorne, T. E. (2014). Contributions of ambient assisted living for health and quality of life in the elderly and care services - a qualitative analysis from the experts' perspective of care service professionals. *BMC Geriatrics*, *14*(1), 112. doi:10.1186/1471-2318-14-112 PMID:25326149

Silva, M. P., Nazario, D. C., Dantas, M. A. R., Goncalves, A. L., Pinto, A. R., Manerichi, G., & Vanelli, B. (2016). An eHealth Context Management and Distribution Approach in AAL Environments. In *Proceedings of the 29th International Symposium on Computer-Based Medical Systems (CBMS)*. IEEE. 10.1109/CBMS.2016.15

Stainov, R., Mirchev, M., Goleva, R., Mirtchev, S., Atamian, D., Savov, A., & Draganov, P. (2016). AALaaS Intelligent Backhauls for P2P Communication in 5G Mobile Networks. In *Proceedings of International Black Sea Conference on Communications and Networking (BlackSeaCom)*. IEEE.

Statistica. (2016, November). *Internet of Things (IoT) connected devices installed base worldwide from 2015 to 2025*. Statista Research Department. Retrieved from https://www.statista.com/statistics/471264/iot-number-of-connected-devices-worldwide/

Suhrid Barua. (n.d.). Flood of Data Will Get Generated in Autonomous Cars. *Auto Tech Review*. Retrieved from https://autotechreview.com/features/flood-of-data-will-get-generated-in-autonomous-cars#:~:text=There%20is%20a%20great%20deal,cars%20in%20the%20automotive%20industry.&text=According%20to%20various%20industry%20experts,hour%20of%20driving%20a%20day

Vano-Galvan, S., Paoli, J., Rios-Buceta, L., & Jaen, P. (2015). Skin self- examination using smartphone photography to improve the early diagnosis of melanoma. *Actas Dermo-Sifilograficas*, *106*(1), 75–77. PMID:25173155

Vora, J., Tanwar, S., Tyagi, S., Kumar, N., & Rodrigues, J. J. P. C. (2017). FAAL: Fog Computing-based Patient Monitoring System for Ambient Assisted Living. In *Proceedings of the 19th International Conference on e-Health Networking, Applications and Services (Healthcom)*. IEEE. 10.1109/Health-Com.2017.8210825

Wang, D., Hu, B., Hu, C., Zhu, F., Liu, X., Zhang, J., Wang, B., Xiang, H., Cheng, Z., Xiong, Y., Zhao, Y., Li, Y., Wang, X., & Peng, Z. (2020). Clinical characteristics of 138 hospitalized patients with 2019 novel coronavirus-infected pneumonia in Wuhan, China. *JAMA Network*, *323*(11), 1061–1069. doi:10.1001/jama.2020.1585 PMID:32031570

Watson, A. R., Wah, R., & Thamman, R. (2020). The Value of Remote Monitoring for the COVID-19 Pandemic. *Telemedicine Journal and e-Health*, *26*(9), 1110–1112. Advance online publication. doi:10.1089/tmj.2020.0134 PMID:32384251

Western Digital Website. (n.d.). Retrieved from https://www.westerndigital.com/solutions/oil-gas

World Health Organization. (2018, February 5). *Ageing and Health*. Retrieved from https://www.who.int/news-room/fact-sheets/detail/ageing-and-health

World Health Organization. (2020, September 17). *Keep health workers safe to keep patients safe: WHO*. Retrieved from https://www.who.int/news/item/17-09-2020-keep-health-workers-safe-to-keep-patients-safe-who

World Health Organization. (2020, December 22). *COVID-19 Weekly Epidemiological Update*. Retrieved from https://www.who.int/publications/m/item/weekly-epidemiological-update---22-december-2020

Yu, W., Liang, F., He, X., Hatcher, W. G., Lu, C., Lin, J., & Yang, X. (2017). A Survey on the Edge Computing for the Internet of Things. *IEEE Access: Practical Innovations, Open Solutions*, *6*, 6900–6919. doi:10.1109/ACCESS.2017.2778504

Zainudin, M. N. S., Sulaiman, M. N., Mustapha, N., & Perumal, T. (2017). Monitoring daily fitness activity using accelerometer sensor fusion. In *Proceedings of the International Symposium on Consumer Electronics (ISCE)*. IEEE. 10.1109/ISCE.2017.8355540

Zgheib, R., Nicola, A. D., Villani, M. L., Conchon, E., & Bastide, R. (2017). A Flexible Architecture for Cognitive Sensing of Activities in Ambient Assisted Living. In *Proceedings of the 26th International Conference on Enabling Technologies: Infrastructure for Collaborative Enterprises*. IEEE. 10.1109/WETICE.2017.41

ADDITIONAL READING

Aloi, G., Fortino, G., Gravina, R., Pace, P., & Savaglio, C. (2020). E-ALPHA: Edge-based Assisted Living Platform for Home cAre. In *Proceedings of IEEE Conference on Computer Communications Workshops (INFOCOM WKSHPS)*. IEEE INFOCOM 2020. 10.1109/INFOCOMWKSHPS50562.2020.9163018

Ashraf, M. U., Hannan, A., Cheema, S. M., Ali, Z., Jambi, K. M., & Alofi, A. (2020). Detection and Tracking Contagion using IoT-Edge Technologies: Confronting COVID-19 Pandemic. In *Proceedings of International Conference on Electrical, Communication, and Computer Engineering (ICECCE)*. IEEE.

Dilibal, C. (2020). Development of Edge-IoMT Computing Architecture for Smart Healthcare Monitoring Platform. In *Proceedings of 4th International Symposium on Multidisciplinary Studies and Innovative Technologies (ISMSIT)*. IEEE. 10.1109/ISMSIT50672.2020.9254501

Dimitrievski, A., Zdravevski, E., Lameski, P., & Trajkovik, V. (2017). A survey of Ambient Assisted Living systems: challenges and opportunities. In *Proceedings of 12th International Conference on Intelligent Computer Communication and Processing (ICCP)*. IEEE.

Ksentini, A., & Brik, B. (2020). An Edge-Based Social Distancing Detection Service to Mitigate COVID-19 Propagation. *IEEE Internet of Things Magazine*, *3*(3), 35–39. doi:10.1109/IOTM.0001.2000138

Pazienza, A., Mallardi, G., Fasciano, C., & Vitulano, F. (2019). Artificial Intelligence on Edge Computing: a Healthcare Scenario in Ambient Assisted Living. In Proceedings of Artificial Intelligence for Ambient Assisted Living (Corpus ID: 211567409). Rende (CS), Italy.

Rahman, M. A., Hossain, M. S., Alrajeh, N. A., & Guizani, N. (2020). B5G and Explainable Deep Learning Assisted Healthcare Vertical at the Edge: COVID-19 Perspective. *IEEE Network*, *34*(4), 98–105. doi:10.1109/MNET.011.2000353

Stojkoska, B. R., Trivodaliev, K., & Davcev, D. (2017). *Internet of Things Framework for Home Care Systems. Wireless Communications and Mobile Computing*. Hindawi.

KEY TERMS AND DEFINITIONS

Data Aggregation/Filtering: The raw data collected from sensors is unstructured and contains noise. It has to be processed and computed to obtain structured data through a process called data aggregation or filtering.

Data Analytics: The raw data collected by the IoT environment is analyzed in a cloud/edge server to find trends, hidden patterns, and knowledgeable insights.

Edge Intelligence: The devices available at the edge layer have some limited amount of computing resources which can be utilized and incorporated with machine learning or AI algorithms to perform real-time data analytics.

QoS: Measurement of the overall service performance guaranteeing the minimal users' requirements like latency, responsiveness, reliability, throughput, etc., while consuming a service.

Response Time: The time duration between the users requesting the service and the service is actually consumed by them.

Software-Defined Networking: Different from the traditional networking infrastructure, it moves intelligence from the network hardware devices to the centralized place called SDN controller by making all the hardware devices as dummy forwarding devices. The SDN controller where intelligence is available provides global network view and makes network management easier.

Time-Critical Application: The application required real-time or almost zero delayed response is called time-critical or time-sensitive application.

Wireless Sensor Network: It is a self-configured wireless network of sensors or sensing devices to collect physical or environmental data and send the data wirelessly to a central location to get connected to the external world.

This research was previously published in Applications of Big Data in Large- and Small-Scale Systems; pages 282-306, copyright year 2021 by Engineering Science Reference (an imprint of IGI Global).

Chapter 31
Edge Computing–Based Internet of Things Framework for Indoor Occupancy Estimation

Krati Rastogi
Shiv Nadar University, India

Divya Lohani
Shiv Nadar University, India

ABSTRACT

Indoor occupancy estimation has become an important area of research in the recent past. Information about the number of people entering or leaving a building is useful in estimation of hourly sales, dynamic seat allocation, building climate control, etc. This work proposes a decentralized edge computing-based IoT framework in which the majority of the data analytics is performed on the edge, thus saving a lot of time and network bandwidth. For occupancy estimation, relative humidity and carbon dioxide concentration are used as inputs, and estimation models are developed using multiple linear regression, quantile regression, support vector regression, kernel ridge regression, and artificial neural networks. These estimations are compared using execution speed, power consumption, accuracy, root mean square error, and mean absolute percentage error.

1. INTRODUCTION

Air quality has a direct impact on human health and to the productivity and comfort of the people. As air is all around us and constantly needed for survival, it is important that the air we breathe is clean and free from hazardous pollutants. Indoor air quality (IAQ) is an important factor for human health because the present generation spends most of the time indoors- in their homes, offices, factories, schools, malls and theatres. Poor levels of indoor quality may cause allergy or asthma symptoms, sinus trouble, coughing, fatigue, eye irritation, nausea, skin rashes and other health problems. Continued poor air quality conditions may cause sick building syndrome.

DOI: 10.4018/978-1-6684-5700-9.ch031

Maintaining good levels of air quality in non-residential buildings such as factories, malls, offices and educational institutions is important to enhance the well-being, comfort and productivity of the occupants. Main factors that affect IAQ are ventilation, occupancy, and the surrounding air. Ventilation helps in maintaining proper air quality by circulating the air in and out, thus diffusing harmful pollutants and bringing in fresh air. The presence and activates of people leads to deterioration of IAQ. The number of occupants present in a building or enclosed area considerably affects the air quality as CO_2 is released with the air exhaled by individuals. The change in the number of occupants changes the ventilation and cooling/heating requirement of the enclosed space.

Occupancy of non-residential buildings is constantly fluctuating as people enter and leave shops, malls, theatres, offices, factories and schools for work purposes, communicating with others, attending lectures, delivering goods, relishing food or watching shows. Keeping a count on the number of occupants is useful in improving building security, estimating building energy demand, tracking human movement, finding if some space is occupied or not and rescuing survivors in emergencies such as fires. Occupancy estimation can thus be classified into (Akkaya et al 2015):

1. **Occupancy Detection:** This problem addresses the presence or absence of occupants. The result is zero if the space is unoccupied and one if one if occupants are present. The count of occupants is not taken care of in this problem;
2. **Occupancy Counting:** Contrary to the first problem, this problem takes into record, the number of persons a place is occupied with;
3. **Occupancy Tracking:** It is the super-set of the above problems in the sense that it not only detects occupancy of a space, but also takes into account, the occupancy count of the place;
4. **Occupancy Event/ Behaviour Recognition:** If occupants are detected at a space under study, the activity or behaviour of the occupant is analysed using this problem. Figure 1 shows the relationship between different occupancy monitoring problems discussed in the above paragraph.

Internet of Things (IoT) has revolutionized the way we monitor and analyse physical phenomenon indoors and outdoors. Small size and low cost sensors and chips relay data and communicate with each other without human involvement, enabling frequent sampling, enhancing the range of monitoring and sampling and decreasing the need of human labour. It is seen that deployment of devices, connections and communication with the Internet becomes easy with the use of IoT. The Perpetual connectivity to the internet and easy of storing high volumes of data in the cloud eliminates the requirement of large storage and communication algorithms with the sensing devices (Rathore et al 2018). An IoT system that can be used to estimate occupant count in university classrooms has been presented in this work. The proposed system uses CO_2 concentration and relative humidity (RH) values to develop a real time occupancy estimation system. An occupancy estimation system which uses CO_2 and RH sensors has been preferred over WiFi, surveillance camera, radio frequency identification (RFID), infra-red and ultraviolet sensor based occupancy estimation systems because of relatively low cost and ease of availability of these sensors (Chen, Jiang, and Xie, 2018). The proposed system is accurate, simple, low-cost, and portable and eliminates the need for building expensive, stand-alone, complex and cumbersome systems to determine occupant count.

Most IoT systems used today employ the client-server based cloud computing approach in which the sensor nodes use internet to upload data to cloud servers for storage and analysis. These cloud servers and services are distributed all over the world. Real-time systems upload large amount of data to the cloud

Figure 1. Classification of occupancy monitoring problems

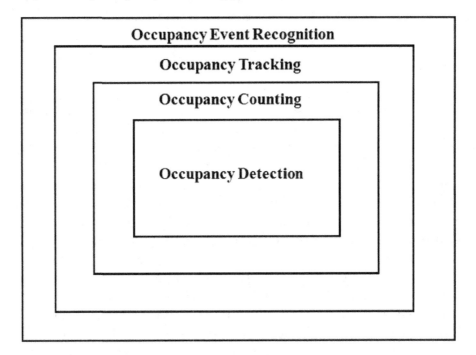

servers. The transmission, processing and analysis of this data requires high computation capability and causes high latency (Esposito et al, 2017). As there is a need for fast communication between devices and users, the distributed computing approach introduces intermediate nodes between the sensor node and the cloud, known as the smart edge. The edge nodes have high computational capability, storage and internet connectivity (Pan and McElhannon, 2018). Most of the computational tasks and data processing is performed at these intermediate nodes. As large amount of data can be processed near the source, the requirement of internet bandwidth is reduced. Processing of data near the source also decreases the traffic and network latency (Ren et al, 2019).On the other hand, the cloud computing approach ensures better security of data and increased fault-tolerance (El-Sayed et al, 2018). This work aims to build an IoT system which uses both decentralized as well as client-server approaches to generate occupancy estimates of a university classroom, so that the performance of overall occupancy estimation IoT system can be improved.

Contribution of this work: A real time, IoT occupancy estimation system for university classrooms has been developed. The performance of the decentralized edge based architecture been evaluated for occupancy estimation. The improvement in performance by adopting edge computing architecture has been measured with the help of network parameters such as latency, bandwidth, and throughput and packet loss. For occupancy estimation, multiple linear regression, quantile regression, kernel ridge regression, support vector regression and artificial neural network based estimation models have been developed. The speed, power consumption and accuracy of these estimation models has been computed to determine the most suitable model.

The rest of the paper is organized as follows: Section 2 discusses the state of art of IAQ monitoring and analysis developed for estimation of occupancy. IoT sensing system is explained in Section 3, Section 4 describes data collection. In section 5 the methodology for estimation of classroom occupancy with the help of regression based estimation models. The performance evaluation of our estimation models is discussed in Section 6. Section 7 discusses the conclusion and future work.

2. RELATED WORK

Determination of occupant count for various purposes has been reported by several authors. Candanedo et al. (2016) have predicted occupancy in an office room using data from light, temperature, humidity and CO_2 sensors. The statistical classification models evaluated in this work for prediction are CART, RF, GBM and LDA. Jiang (2016) has developed an indoor occupancy estimator for the number of real-time indoor occupants based on CO_2 measurement. The Feature Scaled Extreme Learning Machine (FS-ELM) algorithm, which is a variation of the standard Extreme Learning Machine (ELM), has been explored as occupant estimator. It greatly improves the performance of the standard ELM. Ryu et al. (2016) have developed an indoor environmental data-driven model for occupancy prediction using machine learning techniques. HMM and CART decision tree algorithms were implemented using MATLAB's Statistics and Machine Learning Toolbox. Dong (2014) has presented a methodology reduce energy consumption based on prediction of occupant behaviour patterns and local weather conditions. Adaptive Gaussian Process, Hidden Markov Model, Episode Discovery and Semi-Markov Model are modified and implemented into this study. CO_2, acoustics, motion and lighting changes have been used as input features.

Labeodan et al. (2015) have introduced and evaluated the performance of chair sensors in an office building for providing fine-grained occupancy information. This information is hence used for improving demand-driven control applications in the building. The development of a Markov chain based four-state model has been described by McKenna et al. (2015) in which the absent/present state and the active/inactive state are treated separately. This provides a distinction between sleeping and absence and so offers an improved basis for demand modeling, particularly high-resolution thermal modeling. Li and Calis (2012) have introduced an RFID based occupancy detection system to support demand-driven HVAC operations by detecting and tracking multiple stationary and mobile occupants in multiple spaces simultaneously. The proposed system estimates the thermal zone where each occupant is located, and reports the number of occupants for each thermal zone in real time.

In (2017) Delzendeha has discussed the impact of occupants' behaviour and its significance in the analysis of building energy demand. Occupants' behaviour has been analyzed to improve the calculation of energy consumption of buildings. Depatla et al. (2015) have developed a mathematical model to count the number of persons walking in an area, on the basis of WiFi received signal strength indicator (RSSI) measurements between a transmitter/receiver antenna pair.

The model uses probability distribution of the received signal amplitude to estimate the occupant countby calculating Kullback-Leibler divergence. The authors Alex and Guillaume (2013) propose a simple algorithm that uses indoor carbon dioxide concentrations to provide estimated occupancy profiles in office buildings. The authors show qualitative arguments of its reliability and usefulness for service, for lack of available validation data.

Szczurek et al. (2017) have proposed the pattern matching approach between the CO_2 and the occupant count time series. Two types of indexes were used to determine similarity between time series- correlation coefficients and distance measures. The best performance to estimate occupant count was achieved with angular distance as the similarity index. Sangoboye et al. (2016) have compared the performance of occupancy estimation models built using common sensors such as temperature, humidity and CO_2 and dedicated sensors such as 3D stereovision cameras. The authors have concluded that the use of common sensors for occupancy estimation is a satisfactory alternative to an expensive, sophisticated and stand-alone system built using dedicated sensors. Szczurek et al. (2016) and Jiang et al. (2016) have developed occupancy estimation models using CO_2 concentrations only but the estimation accuracy with a single parameter model is relatively low.

Jin et al, (2016) have developed coupled a partial differential and ordinary differential equation system to model the effect of occupants on indoor environments. Using the proposed Sensing by proxy (SbP) technique, the authors claim to have achieved an overall mean square error (RMSE) of 0.6044. A pedestrian detection system based on IR sensors is presented by Linzmeier (2004). An array of ther-mopile sensors are arranged on the front bumper of the vehicle such that sensor field of view covers the region of interest. The paper presents a reliable method for estimation of position of pedestrians using a combination of the optimized sensor arrangement and the occupancy grid technique. A prototype has been developed to capture CO_2 concentrations which is used to train four different machine learning oc-cupancy estimation models. Gradient boosting, linear discriminant analysis, k-nearest neighbours (KNN) and random forests have been investigated. The best occupancy estimation results were obtained with the KNN model with an RMSE value of 1.021.

Brennan et al, (2018) have presented an infra-red array sensor based wireless system for monitoring of occupancy states across the thermal zones of a building. The challenges faced in sensing, calibra-tion and prediction algorithms are discussed along with experimental results. Measurements from CO_2, relative humidity and passive infra-red (PIR) sensors have been used in Chiţu et al, (2017) to model the occupancy pattern using Autoregressive Hidden Markov Models (ARHMM). The results have been compared with those obtained with the classical Hidden Markov Models (HMM) and Support Vector Machines (SVM). The ARHMM estimation method out-performed the other methods, with an average estimation accuracy of 80.78%. Han, Gao and Fan (2012) have used pervasive WiFi infrastructure to estimating attendance in a dense campus environment. WiFi connectivity counts are poor estimators of room occupancy, since they are polluted by adjoining rooms, outdoor walkways, and network load balancing. New method has been proposed to distinguish and filter out WiFi users outside of the lecture room, and feed such data to a regression analyser to accurately estimate occupancy.

An approach to estimate people count in office space using distributed, strategically placed PIR sen-sors has been presented in Mohottige and Moors (2018). A floor-wide simulation of realistic occupant behaviours was performed to investigate two algorithms to estimate people count per office space. An estimation system to detect the number of persons and their directions of movement at an entrance has been proposed Wahl et al (2012). The output of IR sensor array is binaries using the background mean method and the number of persons and their directions of movement are determined by a pattern recogni-tion algorithm. General state-space models have been developed in Hashimoto et al (2017) that use IR sensor data to estimate occupancy in different rooms of a house has been presented. Actual as well as artificial data obtained by adding noise to data collected in an experimental house is used. 10% - 40% improvement in accuracy was achieved by the proposed method over conventional estimation methods in experimental results.

The dynamics of indoor occupancy i.e., location of the occupant and his motion patterns along with environmental parameters have been used in Imahara et al (2010) to develop an occupancy estimation system. The estimation system uses Location-Aware Hidden Markov Model (HMM) which dynami-cally adapts the feature space based on the occupant's location. Experiments on real data showed that the proposed could reach 10% better accuracy than Conventional HMM. An infrastructure-less, zero-configuration method to detect occupancy has been proposed in Yoshida et al (2018). It opportunistically exploits the smartphones' acoustic sensors and motion sensors. The proposed method has been evaluated in different environments- silence, conversational and mixed, in the presence of 10 domestic users. Using the proposed approach, occupancy estimation error of 0.76 was achieved in the experiments.

Data from CO_2, temperature, illumination, sound and motion sensors was used in Khan, Hossain and Roy (2015) to build supervised learning occupancy estimation models using linear discriminant analysis (LDA), support vector machine (SVM), random forest (RF) and quadratic discriminant analysis (QDA). The performance of estimation models was investigated using performance metrics such as accuracy, confusion matrix and F1 score. Experimental results demonstrated a maximum accuracy of 98.4% and a high F1 score of 0.953. An occupancy estimation method using surveillance cameras in buildings has been proposed in Jain et al (2018). Recorded videos by surveillance cameras are processed to recognize the passing occupants at the entrance. The proposed method was tested and validated in a real functioning building.

In Singh et al (2018), Wi-Fi interfaces have been used in monitoring mode so that all local packets are recorded and observed. An estimate of the number of active devices within the area is obtained using a network of such monitoring sensors. Input received signal strength indicators (RSSI) and media access control (MAC) addresses are used as estimators. Experimental results of the implementation of the proposed occupancy estimation system favour the proposed techniques. Results on application of machine learning to the detection of human presence and estimation of the number of occupants in an office have been presented in Zhang and Jia (2017). Data from CO_2, temperature, light, and humidity and PIR sensors is fed to two-layer feed forward neural network for training, validation and testing. Estimation accuracy of up to 94.6% and 91.5% for the binary (presence or absence of persons) and multi-class (no person, one person or two or more persons) problems is achieved.

The application of occupancy estimation models is discussed several recent works. Kim et al. (2018) have used building occupancy estimates to build personal comfort models (PCS) which help predict individual thermal preferences. Wang et al, (2018) used Wi-Fi to estimate building occupancy patterns, which are used to develop ventilation control strategies. Labeodan et al, (2016), occupancy information collected with the help of wireless sensors and actuators is used to regulate the use of lighting systems in office buildings.

Edge computing serves to enhance the performance of the IoT cloud architecture by bringing data storage and computation in proximity of the sensor network Shah Nirali, Bhatt Chintan and Patel Divyesh,(2018). An edge computing enabled middleware is detailed in Mukherjee T., Dey N., De D.(2020), which addresses network QoS, arbitrary resource availability and client mobility by transparently migrating MQTT clients to brokers in close proximity. It is claimed that the proposed system is able to significantly reduce end to end latencies. Higuchi Dimension (DH) Ciobotaru, A., Andronache, I., Dey, N. et al.(2019) is used for analysis of temperature humidity index (THI) and its impact on tourism activity. This information helps in promotion of tourist activity in favourable weather conditions and better management of regional tourism. Curran, Kevin and Norrby, (2009) developed a Radio Frequency Identification (RFID) prototype to determine the occupant location and movement. The prototype was found to generate inaccurate occupancy estimates due to obstacles, interference from other RF devices and short range of communication between RFID tags and readers. Algorithms that use vision based recognition of human motion Kale, Vinayak and Patil, (2016) are accurate but have issues of privacy concern, require line of sight vision and require deployment of expensive cameras.

3. SYSTEM ARCHITECTURE

In this work, edge computing based decentralized architecture is used to build an end to end occupancy estimation system. In the layered *edge computing* architecture sensor nodes transmit the sensed data to the smart edge first. As shown in Figure 2, most of the processing and analysis takes place at the edge before the data is uploaded to the IoT cloud. The processed data is stored for in the cloud for visualization. The results are conveyed to the end users via smartphone application and website. The hardware and software setup is described in details in the following paragraphs.

Figure 2. Flow-chart of the working of the proposed occupancy estimation system

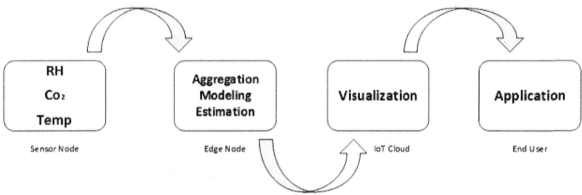

3.1. Hardware System Setup

A sensor node is placed in every classroom to collect and transmit the sensed data to IoT cloud. Each sensor node has sensors to detect relative humidity (RH), CO_2 and temperature. The sensors are connected to the Arduino Uno micro-controller. MQ135 gas sensor has been used for detection of CO_2, DHT22 sensor for temperature and humidity and IR sensor for determining the person count. The sensor type, the parameter that it measures and the unit of measurement is described in Table 1.

Table 1. Details of sensors used

Sr. No.	Parameter	Unit	Sensor
1.	Temperature	℃	DHT22
2.	Relative Humidity	%	DHT22
3.	CO_2	ppm	MQ135
4.	Person count	persons	Sharp GP2Y0A02YK0F Infrared Proximity Sensor

The Arduino Uno micro-controller is responsible for collection, calibration and transmission of the sensed data. It is based on ATmega328P 8-bit micro-controller. The sensor nodes use Wifi module *ESP 8266* to transmit the sensed RH, CO_2 and temperature values to the IoT cloud. The data sensed by the IR, DHT22 and MQ135 sensors is collected by the Arduino Uno micro-controller board. As shown in Figure 3, the micro-controller board transmits the sensed data to the edge node using the *ESP 8266* Wifi module. The edge device in our case is a credit card sized computer called Raspberry Pi 3 model B. Raspberry Pi is a single board computer with 1.2 GHz, 64-bit quad-core processor, 1 GB RAM and executes a Linux based OS. Estimation algorithms are applied to the aggregated data at the edge and the results are uploaded to the IoT cloud. The processed data is stored in the cloud for visualization and analysis. The air quality information and occupancy estimates are provided to the end users in form of plots and alerts with the help of an Android application.

Figure 3. Hardware architecture for the edge computing approach

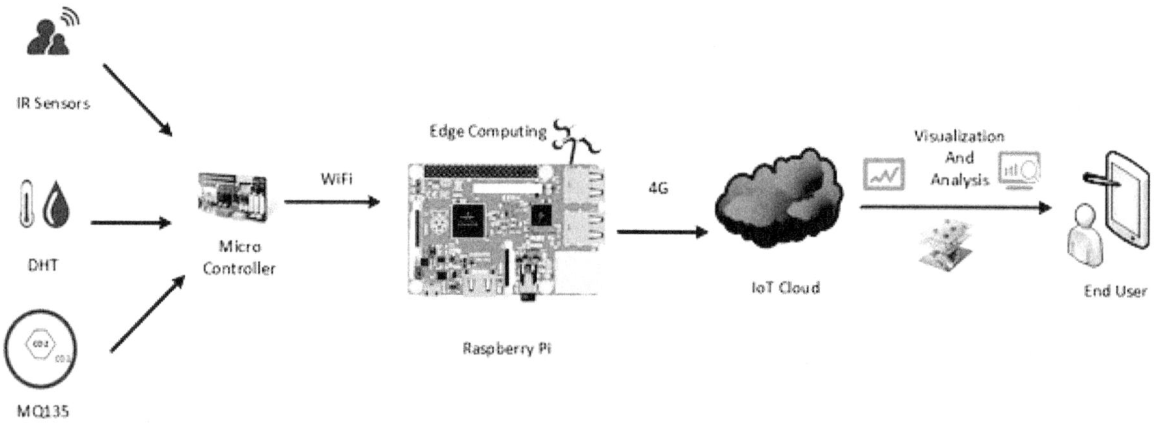

3.2. Software System Setup

The software system of the edge computing architecture has been divided into distinct layers according to the functions and services provides by the services and protocols. These layers have been discussed in details in the following paragraphs. The software system architecture for the edge computing approach consists of 3 layers (Figure 4 and Table 2):

1. **Sensor Layer:** Layer 1 is the sensor layer which is performs sensing of environmental parameters. In this layer, sensors to measure parameters like temperature, humidity and CO2 are connected to Arduino Uno which store and forward the sensed data to the intermediate layer;
2. **Data processing layer:** Layer 2 is the data processing layer which aggregates the data transmitted by sensor nodes at different locations. Analysis and processing of sensed data takes place in this layer. The real-stream processed data is used to train and test occupancy estimation algorithms that are stored in the edge node in the form of python code. It uses 4G LTE network to transmit the data to IoT cloud;

3. **Application Layer:** The third layer is the application layer which receives processed and analyzed data from the data processing layer. The analyzed and processed data is uploaded to the IoT cloud by the smart edge device and stored in cloud for visualization. The data is made available to users through cloud servers. Amazon Web Services (AWS) is an on-demand cloud computing platform. It provides a set of abstract technical infrastructure and distributed computing tools and building blocks. Amazon Elastic Compute Cloud (EC2) is a service provided by AWS which provides the users, through internet, a 24×7 virtual cluster of computers.

Figure 4. Software architecture for the edge computing approach

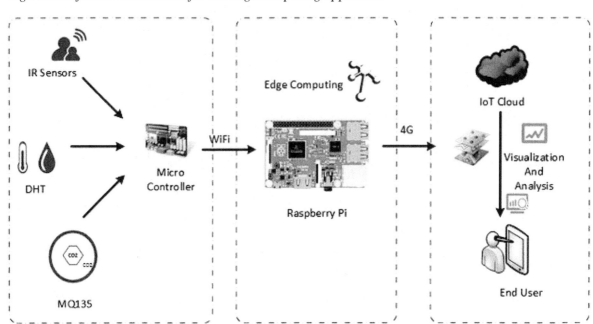

Table 2. Software requirements (edge processing approach)

Sr. No.	Application	Software
1	Arduino Uno	C++ and AVR C programming
2	Raspberry Pi	Python
2	IoT Cloud	MongodB
3	Visualization & Analytics	Amazon Web Services

4. TEST BED AND DATA COLLECTION

The study has been conducted in the classrooms of the Engineering block of the university. The rooms have centralized heating, ventilating and air conditioning (HVAC) system. The classroom windows are fully covered and the doors are closed during the experiment. The average dimensions of the classrooms under study are 144×56×15 feet. The sensor node was placed at the centre of the classroom at a height of about 2 feet above the ground. Sensor data was collected and transmitted once per minute. Relative humidity (RH), CO_2 and temperature values collected by the sensor node have been used to estimate occupancy inside the classroom during lectures.

Each experimental observation began with the commencement of the lecture and lasted for two hours. Average values of RH, CO_2 concentration and occupancy recorded using our setups during the experimental observation of 2 hours have been used to build models to estimate classroom occupancy. Figure 5 is the plot of average CO_2 concentration against indoor occupant count for 37 such periods of 2-hour observations. Temperature is kept constant during these experimental observations.

Figure 5. Plot of CO2 and occupancy count against 2-hour observations

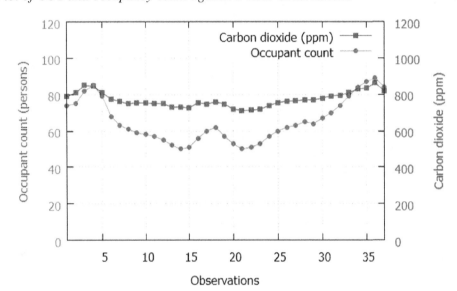

Figure 6 shows the variation in average RH values against indoor occupant count recorded at different periods of 2-hour observation from the beginning to the end of the lecture. A strong correlation between student occupancy and average RH/CO_2 values is observed in these plots.

5. OCCUPANCY ESTIMATION MODELS

In this work, occupancy estimation systems have been developed using RH and CO_2 separately, as well as both RH and CO_2 together. Regression based models tend to determine a relationship between dependent (RH and CO_2) and independent variables, the independent variable being the occupancy to be estimated. Hence, regression based estimation has been deemed to be optimal for this exercise and multiple linear regression, quantile regression, kernel ridge regression techniques have been used for this purpose. Support vector regression has been used for occupancy models as it is well suited to capture complex, non-linear relationships between dependent and independent variables, which regression based models fail to realize. ANN is a non-linear, non-parametric model which is based on black-box learning approach. It works without interpreting relationships between dependent and independent variables.

Figure 6. Plot of RH and occupancy count against 2-hour observations

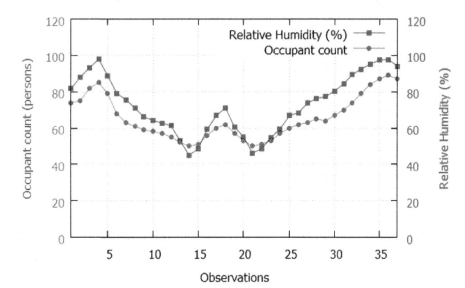

5.1. Multiple Linear Regression Model

Occupancy estimation model using MLR attempts to develop a relationship between indoor occupant count and one or more explanatory variables. The occupancy estimate (Y) depends on multiple inputs $(X_1, X_2, .., X_n)$, represented by the equation:

$$Y = aX_1X + ... + aX + c \qquad (1)$$

where:

Y = dependent variable (occupancy count)

$X_1, X_2, .., X_n$ = independent variables (RH and CO_2)

$a_1, a_2, .., a_n$ = coefficients of independent variables, and

c = intercept

Using MLR, the estimation equation that uses CO_2 as input is given as:

$$Y = -155.73 + 0.285 \times X \qquad (2)$$

The estimation equation using only RH as input is obtained as:

$$Y = 13.56 + 0.711 \times X \qquad (3)$$

MLR equation that uses both RH and CO_2 is found to be:

$$Y = -80.966 + 0.336 \times RH + 0.158 \times CO2 \tag{4}$$

Using the above model Equations (2), (3) and (4), MAPE for the MLR estimation models that use CO_2, RH and both RH and CO_2 respectively is calculated. As seen in Table 3, a MAPE of 2.47 is obtained with the (RH + CO_2) model which is not satisfactory. To further improve the estimation accuracy, quantile regression based estimation is investigated.

Table 3. MAPE for MLR and QR models

Parameters	MAPE	
	MLR	QR
RH	3.49	3.36
CO_2	3.25	3.16
RH + CO_2	2.51	2.47

5.2. Quantile Regression Model

The linear regression technique is highly sensitive to outliers. An outlier is an observation that significantly differs from other observations of the time-series. Spikes and dips in the observed time-series of occupant count is best handled using quantile regression. Quantile regression is an extension to the linear regression technique, and serves to nullify or offset the effect of outliers on the trend line or regression line. To define quantile regression model, we consider 'n' observations of relative humidity (X_1) and carbon dioxide concentration (X_2). The occupancy count Y_i is bound within a known interval y_{min} and y_{max}:

$$Y_i = X_{1i} \cdot \beta_{1i} + X_{2i} \cdot \beta_{2i} + \in_i \tag{5}$$

where, Yi is the occupancy to be estimated, X_1 is relative humidity value, X_2 is the CO_2 concentration and $\beta_i = \beta_1, \beta_2, \dots, \beta_n$ and it represents the unknown regression parameters. The 'p' quantile of the conditional distribution of the estimated occupancy y_i, given:

$$Q_y(p) = x_{1i} \cdot \beta_{1p} + x_{2i} \cdot \beta_{2p} \tag{6}$$

where, (0< p < 1) indicates the proportion of the population having scores below the quantile at p. In this way, we are able to eliminate the outliers, and get better trend-line. For any quantile p, there exists a fixed set of parameters p and the non-decreasing function 'h' from the interval (y_{min}, y_{max}) to the real line such that:

$$h\{Q_y(p)\} = x_{1i} \cdot \beta_{1i} + x_{2i} \cdot \beta_{2i} \tag{7}$$

The logistic transformation is defined as:

$$h\left(y_i\right) = \log\left(\frac{y_i - y_{\min}}{y_{\max} - y_i}\right) = \log\left(it\left(y_i\right)\right) \tag{8}$$

We get the inverse function by integrating Equations (7) and (8):

$$Q_y\left(p\right) = \frac{\exp\left(x_i \cdot \beta_p\right) \cdot y_{\max} + y_{\min}}{1 + \exp\left(x_i \cdot \beta_p\right)} \tag{9}$$

Inference on $Q_y(p)$ can be made through the inverse transform in Equation (9):

$$Q_{h\left(y_i\right)}\left(p\right) = Q \log(it(y_i))\left(p\right) = x_{1i} \cdot \beta_{1i} + x_{2i} \cdot \beta_{2i} \tag{10}$$

As compared with other regression methods for occupancy estimation, quantile regression is most suited for our problem of estimating occupancy in classrooms and laboratories. The occupancy in the University class-rooms and laboratories is sporadic. The occupancy is high during regular lectures and classes, and variable at other times. This gives rise to outliers in occupancy time-series. Quantile regression equation for our estimation model using only CO_2 as input is:

$$Y = -147.37 + 0.275 \times X \tag{11}$$

The estimation equation using only RH is given as:

$$Y = 15.36 + 0.681 \times X \tag{12}$$

Quantile regression equation that uses both RH and CO_2 is found to be:

$$Y = -87.09 + 0.302 \times RH + 0.169 \times CO2 \tag{13}$$

The MAPE for the QR estimation models using CO_2, RH and RH + CO_2 respectively is shown in Table 3. The MAPE of 2.47, which is obtained using the (RH + CO_2) models could be further improved by evaluating non-linear estimation models. Linear estimation techniques work under the assumption that the relationship between dependent and independent variables is linear. To model complex, non-linear relationships between the input and the output variables, artificial neural networks, support vector regression and kernel ridge regression are evaluated for occupancy estimation.

5.3. Artificial Neural Networks (ANNs)

ANNs are used to develop an estimation model like the human nervous system consisting of inter-connective neurons in a computing network (Figure 7). The network is trained by regulating the values of the weights between neurons which make it possible to assume output occupancy values after taking delivery of a number of instructing input occupancy data from previous experiments. Tangent sigmoid has been used as transfer function for hidden layers and linear function for output layer.

Figure 7. 2-layer artificial neural network architecture

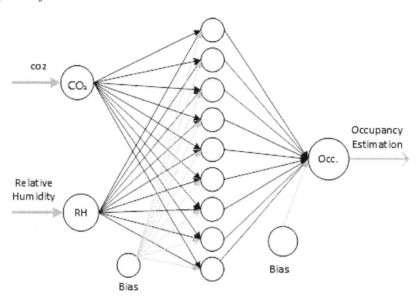

In this work, extreme learning machine algorithm (ELM) is derived from single hidden layer feed forward neural networks (SLFNs). However, unlike SLFNs, ELMs assign input weights and the bias randomly, without any iterative training. Consider the training set $(x_i, t_i) - x_i \in R^N$, I = 1,2, .., N. Here, x_i is an (n×1) input vector and t_i is a (m×1) target vector. The training process consists of (i) randomly assigning weights to the input neurons and hidden biases, and (ii) determination of output weights by inverse operation of the hidden layer biases, governed by the equation:

$$\sum_{i=1}^{L} \beta_i G\left(a_i, b_i, x_j\right) = t_j, \quad i = 1,2,...,N \tag{14}$$

where a_i is the input weight, b_i is the hidden layer bias, β_i is the output weight that connects the ith hidden node and the output node, and G is the activation function, L is the number of hidden neurons and N is the number of distinct inputs or outputs. It is equivalent to $H\beta = T$, where:

$$H = \begin{matrix} G\left(a_1, b_1, x_1\right) & \cdots & G\left(a_L, b_L, x_L\right) \\ \vdots & \vdots & \vdots \\ G\left(a_1, b_1, x_L\right) & \cdots & G\left(a_L, b_L, x_N\right) \end{matrix} \tag{15}$$

$$\beta = \begin{pmatrix} \beta_1^T \\ \cdot \\ \cdot \\ \cdot \\ \beta_L^T \end{pmatrix} \text{ and } T = \begin{pmatrix} T_1^T \\ \cdot \\ \cdot \\ \cdot \\ T_L^T \end{pmatrix} \tag{16}$$

where, H is the output matrix of the hidden layer. G(x) is the activation function and it must be assigned before carrying out the training. The sigmoid function has been used as the activation function:

$$G\left(a_i, b_i, x_j\right) = t_j \cdot \left(1 + e^{\left(a_i \cdot x_j + b_i\right)}\right), \quad i = 1, 2, \dots, N \tag{17}$$

Next, the output weight is computed using the formula, $\beta = H*T$, where H* is the *Moore-Penrose* generalized inverse or *pseudo-inverse* of H. The results obtained by using the ANN estimation model are displayed in Table 4. Although ANN performs better than MLR and QR in terms of MAPE and RMSE, it is found to perform poorly when execution time and energy efficiency are considered. Hence, other non-linear estimation algorithms, support vector regression and kernel ridge regression is investigated in the following paragraphs.

5.4. Support Vector Regression (SVR)

SVR is a statistical learning model which is based on structural risk minimization theory. SVR uses kernel functions to non-linearly map data into a high dimensional feature space, where linear regression is performed. The optimal approximation of indoor occupancy count Y using CO_2 concentration X is given as:

$$f(X, \alpha) = w \bullet \Phi(X) + T \tag{18}$$

where, Φ is the mapping function from the original data space of CO_2 concentration X to a high-dimensional feature space, is the parameter of the learning machine and T is the threshold. The kernel function is represented as:

$$K(X, Y) = \Phi(X) \bullet \Phi(Y) \tag{19}$$

The SVR problem is solved by maximizing:

$$W\left(\alpha^*, \alpha\right) = -\frac{1}{2} \sum_{i,j=1}^{l} \left(\alpha_i^* - \alpha_i\right)\left(\alpha_j^* - \alpha_j\right) K\left(X_i, X_j\right) - \varepsilon \sum_{i=1}^{l} \left(\alpha_i^* + \alpha_i\right) + \sum_{i=1}^{l} y_i \left(\alpha_i^* - \alpha_i\right) \tag{20}$$

subject to the condition:

$$\sum_{i=1}^{l} \left(\alpha_i^* - \alpha_i\right) = 0 \tag{21}$$

and:

$$0 \leq \alpha_i^*, \alpha_i \leq C \tag{22}$$

where l is the number of observations. Solving the above equations, Equation (20) is simplified as:

$$f(X) = \sum_{i=1}^{l} (\alpha_i^* - \alpha_i) K(X, X_i) + T \tag{23}$$

As seen in Table 4, although SVR has the least MAPE and RMSE among the 4 techniques discussed, it has a high execution time and poor energy efficiency as compared with other techniques. Hence, kernel ridge regression based estimation model is evaluated in the next sub-section.

5.5. Kernel Ridge Regression (KRR)

Ridge regression attempts to develop a linear function that models the dependencies between dependent variables x_i and response variables y_i such that the quadratic cost function C is minimum:

$$C(w) = \frac{1}{2} \sum_i \left(y_i - w^T x_i \right)^2 \tag{24}$$

where y_i is the actual occupancy count and $w^T x_i$ is the estimate. To avoid over-fitting, regularization is needed. Regularization is done by penalizing the norm of w, also known as "weight-decay". Hence, the total cost function to be minimized becomes:

$$C = \frac{1}{2} \sum_i \left(y_i - w^T x_i \right)^2 + \frac{1}{2} \lambda w^2 \tag{25}$$

where, λ is regularization parameter. Taking derivatives and equating them to zero gives:

$$\sum_i \left(y_i - w^T x_i \right) x_i = \lambda w \implies w = \sum_i \left(\lambda I + \sum x_i x_i^T \right)^{-1} \left(\sum_j y_j x_j \right) \tag{26}$$

Kernalization requires moving to high dimensional feature space, where x is replaced by $\Phi(x)$. The above equation hence becomes:

$$w = \left(\lambda I_d + \Phi \Phi^T \right)^{-1} \Phi y = \Phi (\Phi^T \Phi + \lambda I_n)^{-1} y \tag{27}$$

This equation can be re-written as:

$$w = \sum_{i} \alpha_i \Phi\left(x_i\right) \tag{28}$$

where:

$$\alpha = \left(\Phi^T \Phi + \lambda I_n\right)^{-1} y \tag{29}$$

Using Equation (29), Equation (27) can be written as:

$$y = w^T \phi\left(x\right) = y(\mid^{T}\mid + \lambda I_n)^{-1}\mid^{T}\mid \left(\text{x}\right) = y(K + \lambda I_n)^{-1}\kappa\left(x\right) \tag{30}$$

where the indoor occupancy now depends on K and κ instead of x. The values of K and κ are calculated using the transformation x→Φ(x):

$$K\left(bx_i, bx_j\right) = \Phi\left(x_i\right)^T \Phi\left(x_j\right) \tag{31}$$

$$k(x) = K(x_i, x) \tag{32}$$

Hence, indoor occupant count can be computed using dependent variables with the help of above equations.

6. PERFORMANCE EVALUATION OF OCCUPANCY ESTIMATION MODELS

In this section, we have evaluated the performance of the proposed occupancy estimation models. The parameters used for evaluation are discussed as follows:

1. **Speed:** The speed of the estimation model is calculated by running the estimation algorithm 100 times with the same data set, and then calculating the average time. Table 4 shows the speed of the estimation algorithms used in this work, in cloud as well as edge computing architecture. It is clearly visible that the execution time is far lower in an edge computing environment as compared with that of cloud based architecture.

As shown in Table 4, the average execution time is the least for quantile regression technique in both the platforms. Kernel ridge regression based estimation technique has the poorest execution speed in the cloud based platform, followed by support vector machines and artificial neural networks. The artificial neural network based estimation technique has the poorest execution speed in the edge-computing based architecture.

2. **Accuracy:** The accuracy score metric of each occupancy estimation algorithm is determined. It uses two variables: *total* and *count*, which are used to calculate the frequency at which predictions match the true value. This function simply divides the total by the count:

$$Accuracy = \frac{y_{predicted}}{y_{true}} \qquad (33)$$

Another metric to be used in this work to compute accuracy is the *coefficient of determination* (R^2). It is defined as:

$$R^2 = 1 - \frac{u}{v} \qquad (34)$$

where 'u' is the residual sum of squares and 'v' is the total sum of squares.
The best possible value is 1.

3. **Power consumption:** The power consumption of the Edge device (Raspberry Pi 3) for the time period while running the occupancy estimation algorithm is measured. This is achieved by measuring the algorithm's excess usage of power in comparison to when the device runs in idle mode. This is calculated in *Joules*:

$$P = V \times A \qquad (35)$$

where, P = power consumed in watts, V = voltage across the volts and A = current in Amperes. The power consumption (Watts) is measured using two digital multi-meters simultaneously, one of which is used to measure the current (Amperes) and the other is used to obtain the voltage (Volts) that is going from the socket to the device that is charging from it in real time. The power consumed is converted into Joules by multiplying the power consumed (P) with the execution time or speed of the algorithm (Table 4).

Table 4. Algorithm accuracy and coefficient of determination (R^2)

Estimation Algorithm	Accuracy	R^2	Execution Time(m)	Energy (J)	RMSE (Persons)	MAPE (%)
M.L.R.	0.94	0.88	0.024223	297	2.47	2.51
Q.R.	0.95	0.91	0.020164	295	2.25	2.47
S.V.R.	0.98	0.94	0.027968	583	1.92	1.57
A.N.N.	0.96	0.95	0.414823	911	0.56	1.80
K.R.R.	0.95	0.98	0.070117	462	1.08	1.01

4. **Root Mean Square Error (RMSE):** It is the square root of the second moment of the difference between actual and predicted indoor occupant counts. As errors are squared before averaging, RMSE is sensitive to outliers. RMSE is represented as:

$$RMSE = \sqrt{\frac{1}{N}\sum_{i=1}^{N}\left(y_i - f\left(x_i\right)\right)^2} \tag{36}$$

where:

- N is the number of observations;
- y_i is the occupancy count at time instant I;
- x_i is the input vector (time); and
- f is the estimation algorithm.

5. **Mean Absolute Percentage Error (MAPE):** MAPE is the measure of accuracy of an estimation algorithm. It is described by the equation below:

$$MAPE = \frac{1}{N}\sum_{i=0}^{N}\left|\frac{y_i - f\left(x_i\right)}{y_i}\right|*100 \tag{37}$$

where:

- N is the number of observations;
- y_i is the occupancy count at time instant I;
- x_i is the input vector (time); and
- f is the estimation algorithm.

Figure 8 shows the actual and predicted indoor occupancies for 37 test observations. The performance of the estimation algorithms is compared by means of root mean square error (RMSE), mean absolute percentage error (MAPE), execution speed, power consumption, coefficient of determination (R^2) and accuracy.

MAPE was the least for kernel ridge regression model, followed by support vector regression and artificial neural network techniques. It indicates that the estimates with the KRR are more accurate than any other technique. RMSE was the least for ANN, followed by KRR and SVR. As errors are squared before they are averaged in case of RMSE, it is more useful when large errors are particularly undesirable. The results of the Table 4 indicate that in comparison to the KRR and SVR, ANN performs fewer or lesser large errors.

Figure 8. Actual and estimated occupancy in classroom during 37 experimental observations

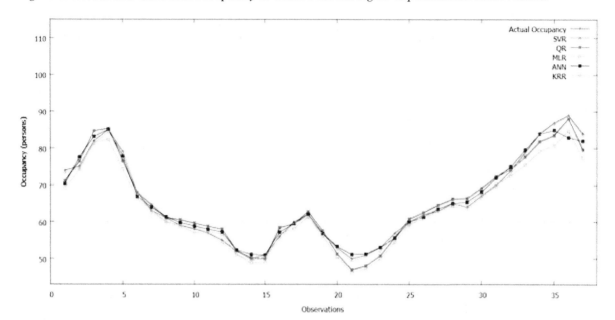

7. PERFORMANCE EVALUATION OF EDGE COMPUTING IOT FRAMEWORK

This section discusses the performance of edge computing framework and evaluates it against the cloud computing framework. The parameters used for evaluation are discussed below:

1. **Latency:** Latency is the time required to transmit the data packets across a network. The sensed data is uploaded to IoT cloud via smart edge device and occupancy estimates and other information is accessed by the end user. The time duration from sensing of the parameters to end user availability of occupancy estimates using those sensed values is calculated. The end-to-end delay is a sum of network delay, processing delay and buffering delay:

    a. **Network Delay:** The delay caused while the packets are travelling through the network is known as network delay. It is the sum of transmission delays from sensor node to smart edge, edge node to cloud server and cloud server to the Android application;

    b. **Processing Delay:** The delay experienced due to data processing tasks such as calibration at the sensor node and the running time of the occupancy estimation algorithms is termed as processing delay. The estimation algorithms are stored in form of a python code in the edge node;

    c. **Buffering delay:** When packets are transmitted from the host device, the packets that reach the destination early are buffered until all the packets arrive, so that they are ordered. This delay experienced due to the buffering of packets in the jitter buffer is known as buffering delay.

The end-to-end delay is computed in this work using a packet sniffing tool called *Wireshark*. Packet analysers or sniffers are computer programs that can intercept incoming and outgoing packets in a network. An ICMP packet is used to calculate the round trip time (RTT) between sensor node and end user device with the Android application. RTT measures the time spent in sending a packet from the sensor node to receiving the acknowledgment packet from the end user smartphone. RTT thus obtained (Table 5) is used to compute network delay. End-to-end delay is the sum of network delay (=RTT/2) and processing delay, which is the time required to execute the estimation algorithm (speed). Buffering delay is not considered while calculating the end-to-end delay as it is negligible as compared with other delays.

2. **Throughput:** It is defined as the quantity of data being sent/received by unit of time. The burst rate, which is the maximum number of packets sent in an interval of time, is high because data transmission from the edge device to the cloud is in the form of bursts, i.e. data transmission from the edge to the AWS cloud is not continuous and takes place only after aggregation, processing and application of estimation algorithms takes place;
3. **Network bandwidth:** Bandwidth is the amount of data that can be sent from one point to another in a certain period of time. The edge device has 1.2 GHz, 64-bit quad-core processor, 1 GB RAM and uses 4G LTE for communication, and hence the available network bandwidth is much higher than that provided by the sensor node.

Table 5 shows the improvement in performance by adopting edge computing architecture over cloud based architecture with the help of network parameters such as latency, bandwidth, round trip time, and throughput and burst rate.

Table 5. Comparison of performance for edge and cloud computing approaches

Parameter	Architecture	
	Cloud	Edge
Bandwidth(bits/sec)	75	1173
RTT (seconds)	00.931	00.685
Burst rate	00.050	00.390
Duration (bits tranfer in sec)	63.846	12.454
Throughput(MBps)	00.158	00.073

8. CONCLUSION AND FUTURE WORK

This work presented a novel edge-computing based IoT architecture for generating occupancy estimates of a university classroom. The edge based approach was found to perform better than the cloud approach in terms of latency and bandwidth. Occupancy estimation was performed using multiple linear, quantile, kernel ridge, support vector regression and artificial neural network techniques. A novel estimation method of kernel ridge regression was evaluated. Occupancy estimation models using these techniques were compared with the help of MAPE, RMSE, speed and power consumption. While KRR and ANN based estimation models proved to be more accurate with low MAPE and RMSE, they performed poorly when judged on power consumption and execution speed. As a future work, we propose to test our occupancy estimation system other indoor environments such as residential buildings, commercial and sports complexes and public facilities such as bus stations and airports to find the best performing estimation models.

REFERENCES

Adeogun, R., Rodriguez, I., Razzaghpour, M., Berardinelli, G., Christensen, P. H., & Mogensen, P. E. (2019). Indoor Occupancy Detection and Estimation using Machine Learning and Measurements from an IoT LoRa-based Monitoring System. 2019 Global IoT Summit (GIoTS), 1-5.

Akkaya, K., Guvenc, I., Aygun, R., Pala, N., & Kadri, A. (2015). IoT-based occupancy monitoring techniques for energy-efficient smart buildings. *2015 IEEE Wireless Communications and Networking Conference Workshops (WCNCW)*, 58-63. 10.1109/WCNCW.2015.7122529

Andrzej. (2016). Detection of occupancy profile based on carbon dioxide concentration pattern matching. *Measurement, 93*, 265-271.

Andrzej, S. (2017). Occupancy determination based on time series of CO_2 concentration, temperature and relative humidity. *Energy and Buildings, Elsevier, 147*, 142–154. doi:10.1016/j.enbuild.2017.04.080

Ansanay-Alex & Guillaume. (2013). *Estimating Occupancy Using Indoor Carbon Dioxide Concentrations Only in an Office Building: A Method and Qualitative Assessment.* CLIMA.

Bing, D. (2014). A real-time model predictive control for building heating and cooling systems based on the occupancy behavior pattern detection and local weather forecasting. *Building Simulation, 7*(1), 89–106. doi:10.100712273-013-0142-7

Brennan, Colin, Taylor, Graham, & Spachos. (2018). Designing Learned CO2-based Occupancy Estimation in Smart Buildings. *IET Wireless Sensor Systems, 8.* . doi:10.1049/iet-wss.2018.5027

Candanedo Luis, M., & ... . (2016). Accurate occupancy detection of an office room from light, temperature, humidity and CO_2 measurements using statistical learning models. *Energy and Building, 112*, 28–39. doi:10.1016/j.enbuild.2015.11.071

Chen, Z., Jiang, C., & Xie, L. (2018). Building occupancy estimation and detection: A review. *Energy and Buildings, 169*, 260-270.

Chiţu, C., Stamatescu, G., Stamatescu, I., & Sgârciu, V. (2017). Wireless system for occupancy modelling and prediction in smart buildings. *2017 25th Mediterranean Conference on Control and Automation (MED)*, 1094-1099. doi: 10.1109/MED.2017.7984264

Ciobotaru, A., Andronache, I., Dey, N., Petralli, M., Daneshvar, M. R. M., Wang, Q., Radulovic, M., & Pintilii, R.-D. (2019). Temperature-Humidity Index described by fractal Higuchi Dimension affects tourism activity in the urban environment of Focşani City (Romania). *Theoretical and Applied Climatology, 136*(3-4), 1009–1019. doi:10.100700704-018-2501-x

Curran, K., & Norrby, S. (2009). RFID-Enabled Location Determination Within Indoor Environments. *International Journal of Ambient Computing and Intelligence, 1*(4), 63–86. doi:10.4018/jaci.2009062205

Depatla, S., Muralidharan, A., & Mostofi, Y. (2015). Occupancy Estimation Using Only WiFi Power Measurements. *IEEE Journal on Selected Areas in Communications*, *33*(7), 1381–1393. doi:10.1109/JSAC.2015.2430272

Eedara, P., Janakiraman, H., Li, N., Tungala, N. R. A., Chamberland, J., & Huff, G. H. (2017). Occupancy Estimation With Wireless Monitoring Devices and Application-Specific Antennas. *IEEE Transactions on Signal Processing*, *65*(8), 2123-2135. doi:10.1109/TSP.2017.2649480

El-Sayed, H., Sankar, S., Prasad, M., Puthal, D., Gupta, A., Mohanty, M., & Lin, C.-T. (2018). Edge of Things: The Big Picture on the Integration of Edge. IoT and the Cloud in a Distributed Computing Environment. *IEEE Access: Practical Innovations, Open Solutions*, *6*, 1706–1717. doi:10.1109/AC-CESS.2017.2780087

Elham, D. (2017). The impact of occupants' behaviours on building energy analysis: A research review. *Renewable & Sustainable Energy Reviews*, *80*, 1061–1071. doi:10.1016/j.rser.2017.05.264

Esposito C., Castiglione A., Pop F., & Choo K. R. (2017). Challenges of Connecting Edge and Cloud Computing: A Security and Forensic Perspective. *IEEE Cloud Computing*, *4*(2), 13-17. doi:10.1109/MCC.2017.30

Han, Z., Gao, R. X., & Fan, Z. (2012). Occupancy and indoor environment quality sensing for smart buildings. *2012 IEEE International Instrumentation and Measurement Technology Conference Proceedings*, 882-887. 10.1109/I2MTC.2012.6229557

Hashimoto, K., Morinaka, K., Yoshiike, N., Kawaguchi, C., & Matsueda, S. (1997). People count system using multi-sensing application. *Proceedings of International Solid State Sensors and Actuators Conference (Transducers '97)*, 1291-1294.10.1109/SENSOR.1997.635472

Ho, R. S. (2016). Development of an occupancy prediction model using indoor environmental data based on machine learning techniques. *Building and Environment*, *107*, 1–9. doi:10.1016/j.buildenv.2016.06.039

Imahara, K. K., Kumazawa, T., & Hondo, Y. (2010). Counting People with a Motion Sensor Network for a Smart Phone. *International Conference onArtificial Intelligence and Applications*, 216-223. 10.2316/P.2010.674-138

Jiang, Masood, Soh, & Li. (2016). Indoor occupancy estimation from carbon dioxide concentration. *Energy and Buildings, 131*, 132-141.

Jiang, C., Masood, M. K., Soh, Y. C., & Li, H. (2016). Indoor occupan Grazcy estimation from carbon dioxide concentration. *Energy and Building*, *131*, 132–141. doi:10.1016/j.enbuild.2016.09.002

Jin, M., Bekiaris-Liberis, N., Weekly, K., Spanos, C. J., & Bayen, A. M. (2018). Occupancy Detection via Environmental Sensing. *IEEE Transactions on Automation Science and Engineering*, *15*(2), 443–455. doi:10.1109/TASE.2016.2619720

Kale, V. G., & Hemant, P. V. (2016). A Study of Vision based Human Motion Recognition and Analysis. *International Journal of Ambient Computing and Intelligence*, *7*(2), 75–92. doi:10.4018/IJACI.2016070104

Khan, M. A. A. H., Hossain, H. M. S., & Roy, N. (2015). SensePresence: Infrastructure-Less Occupancy Detection for Opportunistic Sensing Applications. *2015 16th IEEE International Conference on Mobile Data Management*, 56-61. doi: 10.1109/MDM.2015.41

Kim, J., Zhou, Y., Schiavon, S., Raftery, P., & Brager, G. (2018). Personal comfort models: Predicting individuals' thermal preference using occupant heating and cooling behavior and machine learning. *Building and Environment, 129*, 96–106. doi:10.1016/j.buildenv.2017.12.011

Linzmeier, D. (2004). Pedestrian detection with thermopiles using an occupancy grid. *Proceedings. The 7th International IEEE Conference on Intelligent Transportation Systems (IEEE Cat. No.04TH8749)*, 1063-1068.10.1109/ITSC.2004.1399054

McKenna, E., Krawczynski, M., & Thomson, M. (2015). Four-state domestic building occupancy model for energy demand simulations. *Energy and Building, 96*, 30–39. doi:10.1016/j.enbuild.2015.03.013

Mohottige, I. P., & Moors, T. (2018). Estimating Room Occupancy in a Smart Campus using WiFi Soft Sensors. *2018 IEEE 43rd Conference on Local Computer Networks (LCN)*, 191-199. doi: 10.1109/LCN.2018.8638098

Mukherjee, A., Dey, N., & De, D. (2020). EdgeDrone: QoS aware MQTT middleware for mobile edge computing in opportunistic Internet of Drone Things. *Computer Communications, 152*, 93-108. doi:10.1016/j.comcom.2020.01.039

Nan, L., & Gulben, C. (2012). Measuring and monitoring occupancy with an RFID based system for demand-driven HVAC operations. *Automation in Construction, 24*, 89–99. doi:10.1016/j.autcon.2012.02.013

Nirali, S., Chintan, B., & Divyesh, P. (2018). *IoT Gateway for Smart Devices, Internet of Things and Big Data Analytics Toward Next-Generation Intelligence. Sequence No. 7*. Springer International Publishing. doi:10.1007/978-3-319-60435-0_7

Pan, J., & McElhannon, J. (2018). Future Edge Cloud and Edge Computing for Internet of Things Applications. *IEEE Internet of Things Journal, 5*(1), 439–449. doi:10.1109/JIOT.2017.2767608

Rathore, P., Rao, A. S., Rajasegarar, S., Vanz, E., Gubbi, J., & Palaniswami, M. (2018). Real-Time Urban Microclimate Analysis Using Internet of Things. *IEEE Internet of Things Journal, 5*(2), 500–511. doi:10.1109/JIOT.2017.2731875

Ren, J., Yu, G., He, Y., & Li, G. Y. (2019). Collaborative Cloud and Edge Computing for Latency Minimization. *IEEE Transactions on Vehicular Technology, 68*(5), 5031–5044. doi:10.1109/TVT.2019.2904244

Sangogboye, F., Arendt, K., Singh, A., Veje, C. T., Kjærgaard, M. B., & Jørgensen, B. N. (2017). Performance comparison of occupancy count estimation and prediction with common versus dedicated sensors for building model predictive control. *Building Simulation, 10*(6), 1–15. doi:10.100712273-017-0397-5

Singh, A. P., Jain, V., Chaudhari, S., Kraemer, F. A., Werner, S., & Garg, V. (2018). *Machine Learning-Based Occupancy Estimation Using Multivariate Sensor Nodes. In 2018 IEEE Globecom Workshops*. GC Wkshps. doi:10.1109/GLOCOMW.2018.8644432

Timilehin, L. (2015). Occupancy measurement in commercial office buildings for demand-driven control applications—A survey and detection system evaluation. *Energy and Building*, *93*, 303–314. doi:10.1016/j.enbuild.2015.02.028

Timilehin, L., De Christel, B., Alexander, R., & Wim, Z. (2016). On the application of wireless sensors and actuators network in existing buildings for occupancy detection and occupancy-driven lighting control. *Energy and Building*, *127*, 75–83. doi:10.1016/j.enbuild.2016.05.077

Wahl, F., Milenkovic, M., & Amft, O. (2012). A Distributed PIR-based Approach for Estimating People Count in Office Environments. *2012 IEEE 15th International Conference on Computational Science and Engineering*, 640-647. doi: 10.1109/ICCSE.2012.92

Wang, W., Wang, J., Chen, J., Huang, G., & Guo, X. (2018). Multi-zone outdoor air coordination through Wi-Fi probe-based occupancy sensing. *Energy and Building*, *159*, 495–507. doi:10.1016/j.enbuild.2017.11.041

Yoshida, M., Kleisarchaki, S., Gtirgen, L., & Nishi, H. (2018). Indoor Occupancy Estimation via Location-Aware HMM: An IoT Approach. *2018 IEEE 19th International Symposium on, A World of Wireless, Mobile and Multimedia Networks (WoWMoM)*, 14-19. doi: 10.1109/WoWMoM.2018.8449765

Zhang, C., & Jia, Q. (2017). An occupancy distribution estimation method using the surveillance cameras in buildings. *2017 13th IEEE Conference on Automation Science and Engineering (CASE)*, 894-899. doi: 10.1109/COASE.2017.8256216

This research was previously published in the International Journal of Ambient Computing and Intelligence (IJACI), 11(4); pages 16-37, copyright year 2020 by IGI Publishing (an imprint of IGI Global).

Chapter 32
Challenges for Convergence of Cloud and IoT in Applications and Edge Computing

Rashmi S.
ⓘ https://orcid.org/0000-0002-6966-5647
Dayananda Sagar College of Engineering, India

Roopashree S.
ⓘ https://orcid.org/0000-0003-1327-1267
Dayananda Sagar University, India

Sathiyamoorthi V.
ⓘ https://orcid.org/0000-0002-7012-3941
Sona College of Technology, India

ABSTRACT

Cloud computing and internet of things (IoT) are two disparate technologies that can be united for a common purpose as in an operating profit. The technologies are integral parts of modern sophisticated human life. In the future, it is destined to proliferate boundlessly covering utmost spheres. This chapter describes the challenges faced in adopting the two technologies. Edge computing includes both computing and processing the information are carried at the edge of the IoT devices where vast information gathered instead of relying on the central location. Benefits include avoiding latency issues, improving the performance of the application, and cost effectiveness as it reduces the data volume to be processed in cloud/centralized location. In the advent of IoT devices, edge computing is a vital step in building any of its application which sends and receives enormous information to and from the cloud over the course of operations. Applications such as virtual reality and smart systems are benefited by edge computing as they expect higher rate of response and processing speed. A case study on video surveillance is done in this chapter.

DOI: 10.4018/978-1-6684-5700-9.ch032

INTRODUCTION

Cloud Computing and Internet of Things (IOT) are two disparate technologies that can be united for a common purpose as in an operating profit. The two technologies are integral parts of modern sophisticated human life. In future, it is destined to proliferate boundlessly covering utmost spheres. Edge computing for IoT enhances the deployments of IoT devices by processing the data closer to end devices. Non-IoT edge computing is much different when compared to IoT edge. IoT devices possess limited capability with respect to processing and storing the voluminous unstructured data generated by them. The edge environment will in-turn overcome the above limitations and also reduces the cost of the device as it can off-load the computation and storage to edge. Some of the industries that would benefit from edge computing are manufacturing, retail, oil and gas and healthcare. Some of consumer benefits would be in gaming, Augmented Reality / Virtual Reality and healthcare.

SIGNIFICANCE OF CLOUD IN IoT APPLICATIONS

IOT devices used in large scale industrial applications such as software actuators, sensors and other computer devices give rise to enormous data every second. Enterprises face problems is managing aforesaid data. Microsoft Azure and Amazon Web Services (AWS) are the most common platforms that provide a solution to applications by endowing themselves as a Cloud Backend for storage as well as for analysis and computation. This enhances the power of IOT and also simplifies interfacing with mobile and web apps.

COMPARISON BETWEEN IoT AND CLOUD

An inquiry of the essential characteristics of the Cloud and IOT gives an insight on the whole idea of integration (Atlam et al, 2017) as shown in Figure 1. To start with, in terms of Mobility, IOT refers to Pervasive computing (Low Mobility) whereas Cloud refers to ubiquitous Computing (High Mobility). Pervasive Computing includes devices that can be fit in any required place. Ubiquitous Computing can happen anywhere and everywhere irrespective of the location, device and format. IOT mainly uses real physical components such as sensors, RFID tag etc., Cloud is mainly dependent on virtual resources. Processing and storage capacities of IOT is either bounded or nil which conflicts with Cloud having boundless capacities with respect to processor and storage capacity. Internet plays a significant role in both domains, but Cloud uses it to deliver its services and IOT as a seamless point of connection. Though, both IOT and Cloud contributes to Big data but in a different way. IOT serves as a data generator for Big data applications. Cloud serves as one of the best platforms for handling the Big Data.

Figure 1. Comparison between IoT and cloud

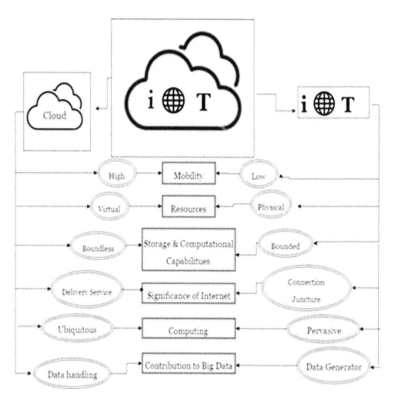

CHALLENGES AND ISSUES IN IoT AND CLOUD

IoT CHALLENGES

The skeleton of a sample IOT system consists of the following steps as shown in Figure 2. Another notion is a layered approach. Various researchers and experts have arrived at conventional architecture 3-layer, 4-layer and 5-layer architecture. Figure 3 shows a 5-layered approach (Said & Masud, 2013), (Liu et al, 2016). The lowermost Perception layer involves identifying the information in the real world and gather them using RFID, different sensors, GPS, IR, Actuators etc., Network layer is concerned with safe and authentic transmission of information across distributed networks. Support Layer deals mainly with Data Processing, Storage and Analytics. Application Layer refers to Industrial and consumer Applications. The topmost Layer, Business Layer, deals with system management and business models.

Figure 2. Sample IoT System

Security: Security (Vijayalakshmi & Arockiam, 2016), (Laeeq & Shamsi, 2015) is considered to be the most noteworthy challenge in most IoT applications. IoT basically is a galaxy of connected entities. Increase in connected space by addition of new nodes actually increases prospects for the hackers to enter into the system. Incompetent designs of the IoT based system gives way for the malicious users causing serious threats. As an example of Smart Healthcare, an Electronic Health Record is a convenient arrangement between the patient and the guardian or any well-wisher to keep a constant watch on the health condition using a connected device. If designed and used appropriately, it helps a medical practitioner on a clinical decision in case of an emergency. However, the health information may be used for a business purpose by an insurance agent breaching the confidentiality. Use of automated insulin pumps, drug infusion pumps that can be controlled remotely can also be misused.

In terms of the 5-layered IOT architecture shown in Figure 3, the Perception layer is prone to Denial of Service attack, malicious data/node attack, collusion attack, reply attacks, jammers etc., As the next layer is concerned with secure transmission, DOS attack and man-in-the-middle attack, computer viruses, eavesdropping, susceptible network servers, false routing etc., are the challenges to be faced. The support layer is also susceptible to DOS attack and malicious insider attack. Application layer faces challenges in dealing with mass data, cross site scripting which is an injection attack, malicious code attack and privacy protection. The Business layer is subject to business logic attack and zero day attack.

Figure 3. A 5-layered approach

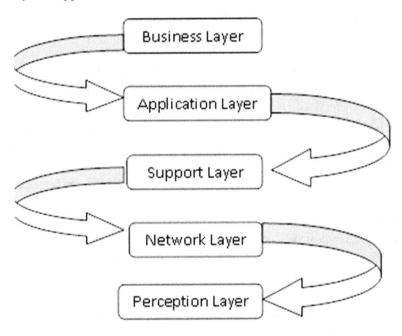

Privacy: Smart devices such as cell phones, smart watches, Smart TV, Smart Toaster etc., contribute majorly to compromise with private information. Technological changes have made possible to track location information of smart Phones although GPS services are not active. Some sensors and time zone information aid in this regard. It also helps to predict the lifestyle and pattern of the community. Such data may fall into wrong hands violating privacy law (Sun et al, 2017), (Salas-Vega et al, 2015).

Privacy issues can be classified as:

Location Privacy: Location based services play a vital role in the smart systems and social media. While the users are habituated with the conveniences provided by these services, it also has the threat of disclosing geo-localized history of users

Data Protection: As shown in the sample IOT system (Figure 2), the first step includes data collection which involves huge data. This data has to be protected from Data Falsification, Device manipulation, theft of identity, data and IP, cyber crime and network manipulation

Consumer Trust: Different challenges in IOT further dispirit the customers to procure smart devices. That disposes another challenge to keep up the true potential of IOT

Governing Laws: Smart systems based on IOT have customers distributed globally across the world. As the governing laws vary across regions, the data controllers in IOT system affected and expected to adapt to the regional laws accordingly.

Interoperability Issues: Many researchers and developers have felt a dearth of Interoperability Technology standards (Konduru & Bharamagoudra, 2017). Interoperability perks up the monetary benefit of the device/product in question in the market. The main concerns are dealing and handling with data while inter-switching between heterogeneous systems. Many organizations such as IETF, ITU, and IEEE are working towards the same. IT giants such as Microsoft, Apple, Google etc., have their share in this contribution. An interoperability framework needs to be designed at different levels.

Machine Level: In order to establish interconnectedness between different machines, compatibility in their software and hardware configurations has to be ensured

Data Level: Information from different IOT devices (sensors/actuators) is in different formats. When an application uses a collection of such devices, some conversion and computing is needed to arrive at a common data format.

Technology Level: IOT uses short, medium and large range communication technologies such as RFID, WiFi, QR code, Ethernet, GPS, Satellite etc., Interaction and communication between these technologies is a challenge.

Intelligent Analysis and Actions: A part of the IOT implementation is to mine information for testing and scrutiny. The technologies that assist in analysis of data collected from IOT devices are Computer Vision, Natural-Language processing and speech recognition. Oddity or insufficient data may lead to imprecise analysis causing false positives or false negatives. This limits the algorithmic efficiencies. IOT essentially deals with unstructured and real-time data. Some traditional applications use outdated former systems that are not well versed with data interaction in unstructured format. Managing real time dynamic data also becomes a challenge in such case.

Advanced analytics is the source of intelligent actions.IOT data demands instant action without which data becomes outdated. Rapid changes in data require new calibration and calculation in a continuous manner. This requires advanced machine serviceability. Some applications build machines that persuade human behaviour. Deep Learning tools are nowadays dominating the area. However, the impulsive behaviour of machines in unpredictable conditions is a challenge. This also affects the trust in application and as a consequence the acceptance rate decelerates.

CLOUD CHALLENGES

Cloud computing and cloud technologies are another giant in the new era that has spread its wings far and wide across domains. The sub-headings under the challenges in cloud are mostly similar to that IOT. Some of the common challenges are

Security: Various security risks and threats are discussed in (Shuijing, 2014), (Wadhwa & Gupta, S,2015), (Dooley et al, 2018). Distributed Denial-Of-Service (DDOS) attacks are common in a networked environment. Widely used yahoo website had suffered from DDOS attack in the year 2000. A Cloud Service Provider (CSP) needs to ensure availability, confidentiality and integrity. However, if a CSP is attacked by DDOS attack, it becomes hard to maintain availability. The different types of DOS and DDOS attacks on cloud can be Bandwidth attack, Amplification attack, ICMP Flood, DNS Flood, HTTP GET Flood, Reflector Attack etc., (Alotaibi, 2015) Man-in-the-middle (MITM)and playback attacks (**Amazon, 2015**). also contributes to IP Spoofing. CSP are threatened by attacks such as Guest-hopping, SQL injection, Side channel, malicious insider and data storage security (Turab, 2013). In addition to these, there are other security issues. Cloud users are given an opportunity to interact with CSP directly through Application Programming Interfaces (APIs). Security protocols must beamalgamated with APIs if not the interaction channel becomes unsafe. Simple registration procedures and interfaces may be misused by spammers to gain access to the services and stealthily discover passwords. This leads to hijacking of accounts and services. Data crash and unlawful access to confidential data is another threat.

Privacy (Liu et al, 2015), (Takabi et al, 2010), (Lar et al, 2011): Data Protection is one of the major fear factors that Cloud Service Users (CSU) faces. CSU panic to store confidential data away from their premises, the reason being loss and violation of data. In order to ensure that there is no loss of data, multiple copies of data had to be maintained by the CSP. This further increases the risk of data violation and breaches. As the security protocols are heterogeneous, the attackers now had to find the weakest link where one of the copies was available. Data synchronization among all the copies was an additional overhead. Most importantly, whenever there is a request to delete data, CSU must be sure that the corresponding CSP has completed deleted all of its copies. This requires an external auditing procedure. Data transmission in the distributed environment during proliferation is a concern. Data centres are geographically distributed and local laws and regulations may not be sufficient. As per the news stated in "The NewYork Times" in March 2010(Steve Lohr, 2010), Netflix cancelled its $1 Million contest over privacy concerns raised by Federal Trade Commission (FTC). The contest would help to enrich its business by building better ways for movie recommendations. However, it was blamed to disclose anonymous information of its clients that could be used to identify them.

Virtualization Issues (Han et al, 2015): Virtualization is the core of cloud environment that allows its computing resources such as memory, storage, operating systems, and networks to be virtualized. As it consists of multiple devices, both physical and virtual, privacy concerns arise as to whether all the diverse devices should be given equal privileges. User roles should be clearly defined and granular separation of roles and responsibilities has to be made to address this concern. A hypervisor controls multiple VMs. An attack on hypervisor would be hazardous to all VMs under it. All VMs creation and initiation procedures are stored in hypervisor. In addition, configuration files, status of all VMs (active or dormant) are also stored here. An attack to this location would break all VMs.

Interoperability (Mezgár & Rauschecker, 2014), (Rashidi et al, 2013): As known, CSPs are flexible in terms of usage but the process of integration and migration to cloud services has not been evolved at a greater extent. The organizations face difficulty in switching their services from one vendor to another vendor. There might exist some interoperability issues along with some system support uses during the migration to cloud platform. For example, applications developed on Linux Platform might not function properly on the Windows platform. The barriers involved in transition of an application from one cloud to another are:

i) Restructuring the application stack on the new cloud
ii) Establishing the network environment on the new cloud to provide uninterrupted services
iii) Set up security protocols similar to earlier cloud
iv) Management of applications in the new cloud
v) Encryption and decryption of data before and after transition between clouds

Furthermore, interoperability among heterogeneous data formats is difficult. To address the interoperability issue, different types of alliances can be formed by the CSPs. Federated clouds and Hybrid clouds are among them. Federated clouds are those in which the CSPs arrive at a mutual agreement and build a trust boundary that helps to scale and backup during a disaster. Hybrid Clouds allows applications to select resources/services from different clouds simultaneously by using crossed trust boundaries between CSPs.

Sky Computing (Keahey et al, 2009) is a secure way to access a remote resource by a user. It congregates a distributed trusted environment and enables users to manage remote resources. Multitier, e-commerce applications or databases swarmed on different clouds can benefit from sky computing. To facilitate Sky computing, a high-quality network connectivity is expected from CSP and CSU. Other issues include Performance and Service Level Agreements. To deal with these issues, a Virtual Network (ViNe) was used. ViNe router (VR) is the machine where ViNe software is installed. A virtual cluster is deployed with ViNe. VR is made available in every LAN section. APIs are put forward by the providers for virtual networking. In case ViNe services are unavailable, the VP can manage traffic across LAN sections. An association is established between IaaS providers, Application providers and Deployment orchestrators to uphold trust. However, the challenge of differentiated SLAs on varied infrastructure levels still exist.

With all the challenges taken to consideration, both IOT and Cloud computing has its own benefits and gains, and they are considered to be the future of Information and Communication Technology (ICT). The two main domains can be converged in two ways. IOT features and services can be brought into Cloud or Cloud services can be brought into IOT. Convergence of IOT and Cloud may give rise to a new set of challenges.

CHOICE OF COMMUNICATION PROTOCOLS FOR CONNECTING IoT AND CLOUD

The essence of IOT lies in its ability to connect and communicate with other devices/elements to deliver worthy business. One of the key factors to achieve this includes deploying an appropriate communication protocol. A communication protocol defines a set of rules for interaction between two or more elements of the system. It may include syntax, semantics, error recover methods, synchronization procedures etc., The requirements for IOT communication covers a broad spectrum. A possibility of all-in-one approach is fairy lesser. For instance, a smart home application requirement includes Wi-Fi, Ethernet or Bluetooth connections where as a smart farming or any remote application may require satellite network or mobile network. Consequently, the challenge here is to understand the requirements during the initial architectural and technological decisions. The communication protocols used in Application Layer in Figure 3 are MQTT, CoAP, AMQP and HTTP.

Message Queuing Telemetry Transport Protocol (MQTT): MQTT (Akbar et al, 2017) is Machine-to-Machine (M2M) communication protocol. It enables communication between low bandwidth networks over an unreliable network. It has a publish-subscribe method of communication. Its actors are broker, publisher and subscriber. The communication is initiated by the publisher by publishing the message with a specific Key-name. The broker is the intermediary that puts all such messages in queue. All subscribers for that Key-name gets the message with a push notification. Many IOT systems has used MQTT protocol in the area of robotics, medical, education, social media etc.,

Constrained Application Protocol (CoAP): The protocol has been designed by a working group called Constrained RESTful Environments (CoRE) in IETF. CoAP (Lerche et al, 2012) is apt for low bandwidth networks. It has compatibility with HTTP and can use its GET, POST, DELETE and PUT methods. However, it requires that the transport layer protocol to be UDP and not TCP.

CoAP has two layers: The upper Request/Response and the lower Messaging Layer. The Request/Response layer operates on resources using the earlier mentioned HTTP's methods. The messaging layer is responsible for ensuring reliability and also duplicate message detection. A message can be of four types:

1. Confirmable- A message where acknowledgment is needed
2. Non-Confirmable- A message for which no acknowledgment is needed
3. Acknowledgment- An acknowledgment message sent in response to Confirmable message
4. Reset- A message that could not be processed

CoAP has the following features as well:

1. Resource observation: it uses best effort mechanism by publish/subscribe method to track resources and its clients
2. Block Transfers: Data is transferred to and from the devices in blocks.
3. Multicast: A part of IP multicast feature is supported to enable group communication
4. Resource Discovery: CoRE Link format contains the resource information. CoAP identifies them through a URI

CoAP provides security using a transport layer protocol called Datagram Transport Layer Security (DTLS). The key features of DTLS are integrity, confidentiality, authentication, anti-replay protection and non-repudiation. It is a version of Transport Layer Security (TLS) that is meant for end-to-end communication securely using cryptography. CoAP has 4 modes of security (Dragomir et al, 2016):

1. NoSec: Security (DTLS) is disabled. Packet transmission takes place with UDP over IP
2. PreSharedKey: Security is enabled. Symmetric shared keys are used for either one-to-one or multicast communication.
3. RawPublicKey:Security is enabled. Asymmetric shared keys are used.
4. Certificates:Security is enabled. A X.5009 certificate is supplemented with a pair of asymmetric keys.

CoAP in combination with DTLS, uses Elliptic Curve cryptography (ECC) for RawPublicKey and Certificates. Elliptic Curve Digital Signature Algorithm (ECDSA) and Elliptic Curve Diffie-Hellman Algorithm (ECDHE) is also employed for authentication and key agreement techniques.

Advanced Message Queuing Protocol (AMQP): AMQP (Vinoski, 2006), (Fernandes et al, 2013) is a standard messaging protocol. AMQP supports a c convenient message transmission in different language/platform. It can transmit either using publish/subscribe model or point-to-point communication model. It uses a TCP connection ensuring at-least-once, at-most-once and exactly-once message delivery. Two kinds of messages bare and annotated are carried, the one sent and the one actually received. Similar to CoAP, AMQP also uses TLS over TCP. And hence implementation on IOT devices is intricate.

As Hyper Text Transfer Protocol (HTTP) is a much commonly used protocol, detailed discussion is not made here (Naik, 2017) gives a comparative study based on different parameters. Table 1 shows a comparison of the above discussed protocols based on different parameters.

The protocols, HTTP, AMQP and MQTT use TCP whereas CoAP use UDP. UDP transmits in datagrams and hence has a lower response time when compared to other protocols. Bandwidth utilization and latency is lowest is case of CoAP and then MQTT, AMQP and HTTP in increasing order. The HTTP offers highest levels of interoperability but lags behind in reliability. With respect to security, MQTT may rely on simplest username and password mechanism. COAP works with DTLS and IPSec that takes care of integrity, authentication and encryption. HTTP has HTTP Basic and HTTP Digest as authentication methods. AMQP has the robust security with single-port TLS, pure TLS and Tunnel TLS models.

CoAP has a set of extended services based on the IOT requirement. In order to build a more secure IOT system, a combination of these protocols can be used.

Table 1. (Naik, 2017). Comparison of Communication Protocols

Sl No	Characteristic	Lowest	Lower	Average	High
1	Message Overhead	CoAP	MQTT	AMQP	HTTP
2	Power Consumption	CoAP	MQTT	AMQP	HTTP
3	Resource Requirements	CoAP	MQTT	AMQP	HTTP
4	Latency	CoAP	MQTT	AMQP	HTTP
5	Interoperability	MQTT	AMQP	CoAP	HTTP
6	Reliability	HTTP	CoAP	AMQP	MQTT
7	Security	MQTT	CoAP	HTTP	AMQP
8	Standardisation	MQTT	AMQP	CoAP	HTTP
9	IOT usage/ M2M	HTTP	CoAP	AMQP	MQTT

IPv6 over Low Power Wireless Persona Area Networks (**6LowPAN**) (Sha et al, 2013): 6LowPAN operates in the network layer. It was introduced with an intention to support IPV6 in low power small embedded wireless devices. It is the most favourable method for enabling IOT based IP communication across smart devices. Specifically, it uses IEEE 802.15.4 of physical and MAC layers. It brings in a new layer between network and MAC layer called Adaptation Layer. This layer helps in interoperability with existing or obsolete networks. Some implementations of 6LowPAN work with a technique called

Low Power Listening (LPL) that are apt for noisy environments. The Table 1 and Figure 4 shows the protocols commonly used in each layer of the Internet model.

Figure 4. Protocols used in each layer of the Internet model

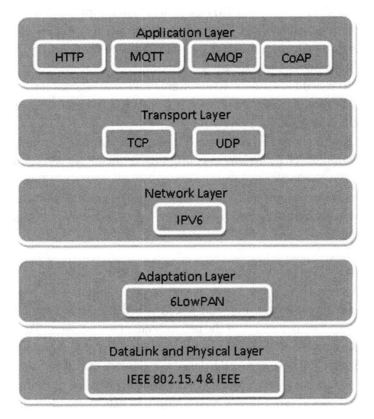

CLOUD_BASED IoT SYSTEMS

Until now, IOT and Cloud challenges were discussed separately. However, it need not be particularly emphasized that Cloud-based IOT combines challenges of both. Fusion of these two imperative domains has as much benefits as there are issues. IOT and Cloud can be brought together in two ways. Cloud –based IOT that incorporates IOT components into Cloud and IOT-based Cloud that fits in cloud modules into IOT system. Security, Privacy, Interoperability, Reliability concerns continue to exist on either way implemented.

For protection against security, fierce authentication techniques have to be chosen that provides protection against attacks such as DOS and MITM. CoAP, DTLS protocols mentioned above can be used when web transfers are involved in IOT system. IDS and firewalls can be used to detect desirous and malicious traffic based on rules and alert other nodes. This helps to prevent IP Spoofing.Encryption algorithms give individuals control over their confidential data to some extent. But the confusion is about who should take on the responsibility whether CSP or CSU. A CSP can take up the responsibility of encrypting and managing data as with one of the options available in Amazon S3 (Michael Wittig 2018), but the problem is the threat associated with malevolent insiders of CSP. A solution can be to involve a third party to verify whether the CSP abides by the SLA. The method is called Third Party Auditing. Tech giants such as Google are coming up with interoperability solutions with its recent release, Android Things platform. The Android Things Developer Preview 6 (DP6) enhances its IOT functionality by providing Android development tools and Google APIs to ease the potential of the developers. Below mentioned are a few frameworks (da Cruz et al, 2018), (Masek et al, 2016) for interoperability.

IOTivity – is a framework that facilitates direct connection among millions of devices. It is an open source platform supported by Open Connectivity Foundation (OCF). It uses CoAP block transfer and also provides secure connections using DTLS.

AllJoyn (Masek et al, 2016) is another software framework that enables interoperability among the software applications that runs on Linux, Windows, iOS, and Linux-based Android platforms. AllJoyn also works in collaboration with OCF.

Apple HomeKit -Though not as compatible as Google and Amazon's solution, it is growing at a faster rate. It is a framework which enables us to configure, communicate and control home automation accompaniments.

Google Weave- is a communication platform to single handily deal with IoT from Android and Google cloud. It provides features such as better security, internet agnostic and bug fixing.

EDGE COMPUTING

It is a new paradigm emerging to solve computing needs of IoT. Like cloud computing it migrates both storage or computation of data to the edge of the network near the end users. This ensures that the distributed nodes across the network offload the computation stress and reduce latency in exchange of message. In IoT, this distributed structure can well balance the network traffic and also reduce transmission latency between edge servers and the end users. This extends the lifetime of the individual nodes as the communication and computation are transferred from limited battery supply to nodes with significant power resources.

The IoT technologies such as smart city, smart health care impact the potential users, interests of US by 2025 (The national intelligence council sponsor workshop, 2008) by increasing billions of interconnected physical devices (The national intelligence council sponsor workshop, 2008), (Gubbi J. et.al., 2013), (Rose, K. et. al., 2015). Hence, IoT devices are main source for big data. The three communication models of IoT are machine to machine, machine to cloud and machine to gateway communication. In machine to machine communication, the devices communicate over different type of networks (not limited to Internet or IP networks) (Wortmann, F. & Flüchter, K. 2015) to achieve requirements of QOS. Applications include smart homes. Compatibility between various device communications is the issue of this model (Al-Fuqaha, et. al., 2015). In Machine to cloud, the different IoT devices seek cloud service for both application and storage (Jararweh, Y. et. al., 2016). The main limitations are on bandwidth and network resources. The Machine to gateway model consists of an intermediary gateway with protocol or data translation algorithm running between the cloud and IoT devices. Thus, increases flexibility and security and reduces power consumption of IoT devices. The sensors in IoT devices provide diverse types of measurement data. IoT gateways connect cloud servers and sensor network. The gateways collect and aggregate data from sensors to cloud servers and forward the processed results in cloud servers back to the end users. The cloud servers perform the data processing using its varied storage and computation capacity.

Figure 5. IoT applications and Edge Computing Architecture

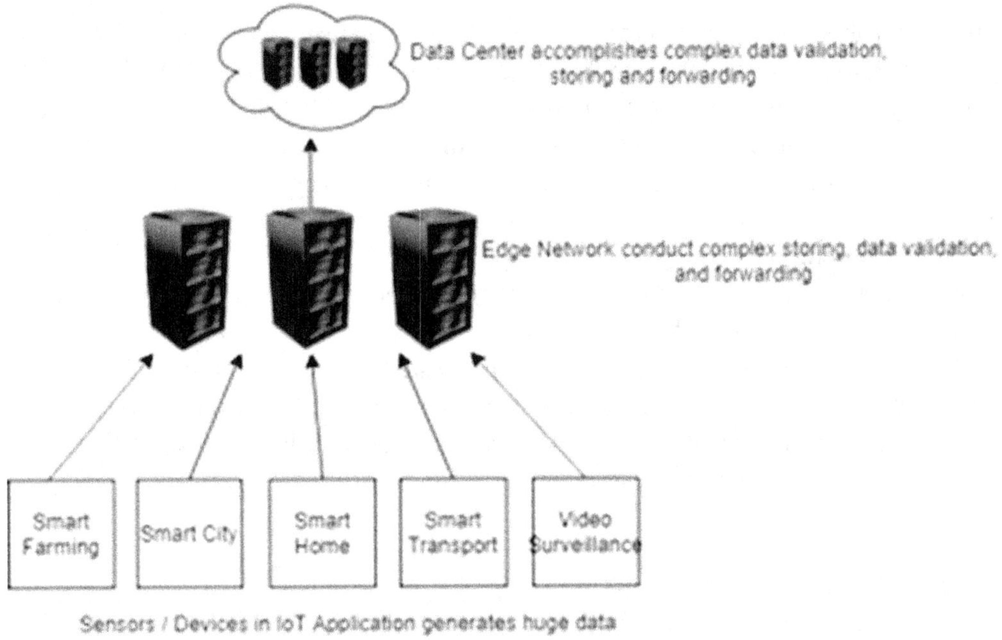

The Figure 5 illustrates the basic architecture between IoT and edge computing. Edge computing servers are closer to the end users than the cloud. Rapid increase in usage of mobile devices has made the cloud computing struggle for QoS whereas edge computing provides better Quality of Service to end users. The sensors / end devices provide good response to the end users than cloud. Most of the storage and data computation are computed in edge network. Deployed farthest to end devices are cloud servers provide massive storage and computation such as big data, machine learning etc.

Edge computing technology typically follow two types of models such as Hierarchical model and Software-defined model. Hierarchical model defines the functions built on distance and resources hence suitable to describe the edge computing network structure. (Jararweh, Y. et. al., 2016) propose a hierarchical model integrating cloudlet and edge computing servers. Software defined model would be an ideal solution to deal with complexity management of edge computing. (A. Ahmed and E. Ahmed, 2016) proposed a software defined model which reduces administration and management cost.

Comparing the characteristics of Cloud, IoT and edge computing is shown in Table 2.

Table 2. Features of Cloud, IoT and Edge computing

	Cloud	**IoT**	**Edge**
Components	Virtual Resources	Physical Devices	Edge Nodes
Storage	Unlimited	Small	Limited
Computation	Unlimited	Limited	Limited
Deployment	Centralised	Distributed	Distributed

CHALLENGES OF EDGE COMPUTING IN IoT

Edge computing is a heterogeneous system as it includes various network topologies, platforms and servers. The heterogeneous platform probes for challenges such as (Varghese, B., 2016), (Raychaudhuri, D., 2012) and (Zhang, L., 2010). The challenging issues are (Gennaro, R., 2010) is the discovery of edge nodes which runs the required server-side programs as the devices of IoT are unaware of the available platforms. Another challenge address on the data management as many storage servers run on different operating system platforms. The huge IoT devices generates and uploads data, the naming of the data resources is also a challenge to be faced. Yet another problem is regarding the security and privacy of the computational tasks to be uploaded. (Clemens, J., 2016) introduced verifiable computing, which enables the untrusted node to offload the tasks of computation. These computational nodes use and maintains the verifiable results to compare with the results of the trusted nodes of computation. As computation is moved from cloud to edge, a trust between IoT devices and edge servers without third party intervention in security must be maintained. (Schütze M, 2011) propose a solution to extend integrity of the end-devices under constrained operating systems.

VIDEO SURVEILLANCE – A CASE STUDY

Video surveillance is a process of observing the scenes/image frames for specific improper/illegal behaviours and revealing its existence or emergence in scenes. Video surveillance are mostly used in public areas such as Railway station, airports etc. and public events too. The whole procedure incorporates identifying the concerned area using groups of cameras where the output quality depends mainly on the quality of the captured image.

Surveillance used in health care is for deterrence in psychological conditions than on physical control. Many health organizations intend to use surveillance to keep intruders away from secured areas, monitoring critical areas ensuring the non-usage of dummy or non-working cameras. The recordings of the surveillance system are retained in the library for minimum of 10 days.

Common recommended areas for cameras in health-care environment are:

1. Entrance of waiting and emergency rooms
2. Reception / Admission area
3. Garages, parking lot and many more.

The higher the resolution of the camera, the images tend to be sharper. The cameras with IR (Infrared Technology) are best suited for a good night vision which is an important feature for outdoor security.

Many developed countries use video surveillance also known as Closed-circuit television for inpatient psychiatry (Vartiainen, H. & Hakola, P., 1994), (Olsen D. P., 1998), (Warr, J. et. al., 2005), (Stolovy, T. et. al., 2015), (Due, C. et. al., 2012), (Nolan, K. A., & Volavka, J., 2006) and (Desai, S., 2010) to increase in security for both patients and staff. A serious concern in psychiatric institutions is about the violence among patients, staffs or even between patients and staff. The surveillance would recognise, prevent and document sexual assaults, violence and any undesirable behaviours.

Disaster rescue can be benefited from camera captured images. But there are two limitations in this rescuing effort. They are the constraints on the bandwidth and increase in consumption of the energy.

During the disaster ECV's (Energy Communication Vehicle) provide communication services through satellites as the original communication would be congested or interrupted. The emergency communication in disaster areas are unstable and very poor (Manoj, B. S., & Baker, A. H., 2007).

Currently, IoT with its various sensors or mobile devices used in several applications such as detection of fire (Genovese, A., 2011) and in controlling industrial systems. Edge computing an emerging technology in which a bridge is constructed by edge servers between cloud and resource constrained mobile devices. Thus, forwarding the services to the edge network. MOCHA – Mobile Cloud Hybrid Architecture (Soyata, T., et. al., 2012) is a real-time face recognition using mobile-cloudlet cloud architecture. It distributes the load of computation among the cloud and cloudlets. In edge-based disaster rescue, ECV's are used edge servers by taking the advantage of storage capacity and large computing power.

Video surveillance are expected to grow widely in both developed and developing countries. This growth promotes for real-time video analytics, edge, public and private cloud / clusters in much demand. Added to the above, the huge need to increase in the computing power to analyse the security, traffic, and crime. An architecture of camera, edge and cloud is shown in Figure 6. A good solution will be a Geo-Distributed architecture for cloud, clusters, edge, and video cameras to meet the real-time constraints of video analytics, bandwidth, and latency.

Figure 6. Architecture for video surveillance in edge

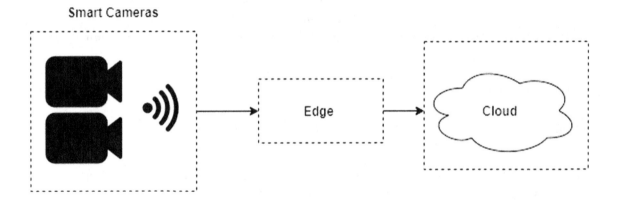

An example of a health care with IoT-edge-cloud based services where a variety of sensors are used to sense the human body, collect the information, and deliver to health broker for its authentication with hospital. The broker initiates a recommendation on family doctor, or any emergency as required. As noticed a lot of computation is involved. Hence, the usage of efficient edge devices will be able to perform the required computation much rapidly by minimizing the risk of user transmission of data. The author Uddin, M. Z. (2019) focuses on processing the health-related data on a fast edge device such as laptop (along with GPU). Some of the sensors incorporated in the experiment are accelerometer, gyroscope, electrocardiograph (ECG) and magnetometer. The Figure 7 depicts a schematic diagram of a health care system using IoT-edge-cloud services.

Some of the operational issues to be taken care are (1) Improvement in processing speed, production optimization and asset performance. (2) Reduction in security issues and latency issues.

Figure 7. A schematic diagram of a health-care smart system

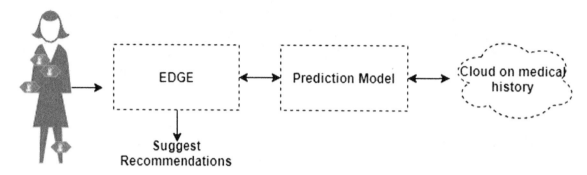

CONCLUSION

Internet of Things (IoT) and Cloud Computing are amongst the booming technologies that have become an indivisible part of our lives. The chapter ponders over the challenges and issues to be addressed while integrating IoT and Cloud. It also summarises on the choice of a communication protocol to be adopted. A significant potential gain to both consumers and industries are offered by IoT edge. Many verticals such as smart cities, intelligent transport system and smart factories can benefit from storage and data processing at edge. Deploy of IoT edge and cloud would create new opportunities with new services such as electric car linked to smart grid and intelligent public transport (bus) routed to stop with large group of people waiting for its service. Edge computing in IoT is gaining momentum as an exciting domain.

REFERENCES

Ahmed, A., & Ahmed, E. (2016, January). A survey on mobile edge computing. *Proc. 10th Int. Conf. Intell. Syst. Control (ISCO)*, 1-8.

Akbar, S. R., Amron, K., Mulya, H., & Hanifah, S. (2017, November). Message queue telemetry transport protocols implementation for wireless sensor networks communication—A performance review. In *2017 International Conference on Sustainable Information Engineering and Technology (SIET)* (pp. 107-112). IEEE. 10.1109/SIET.2017.8304118

Al-Fuqaha, A., Guizani, M., Mohammadi, M., Aledhari, M., & Ayyash, M. (2015). Internet of things: A survey on enabling technologies, protocols, and applications. *IEEE Communications Surveys and Tutorials*, *17*(4), 2347–2376. doi:10.1109/COMST.2015.2444095

Alotaibi, K. H. (2015). Threat in Cloud-Denial of Service (DoS) and Distributed Denial of Service (DDoS) Attack, and Security Measures. *Journal of Emerging Trends in Computing and Information Sciences*, *6*(5), 241–244.

Amazon, A. W. S. (2015). *Amazon Web Services Overview of Security Processes*. Author.

Atlam, H., Alenezi, A., Alharthi, A., Walters, R., & Wills, G. (2017). Integration of cloud computing with internet of things: challenges and open issues. Academic Press.

Clemens, J., Pal, R., & Philip, P. (2016, October). Extending trust and attestation to the edge. In *2016 IEEE/ACM Symposium on Edge Computing (SEC)* (pp. 101-102). IEEE. 10.1109/SEC.2016.29

da Cruz, M. A., Rodrigues, J. J. P., Al-Muhtadi, J., Korotaev, V. V., & de Albuquerque, V. H. C. (2018). A reference model for internet of things middleware. *IEEE Internet of Things Journal, 5*(2), 871–883. doi:10.1109/JIOT.2018.2796561

Desai, S. (2010). Violence and surveillance: Some unintended consequences of CCTV monitoring within mental health hospital wards. *Surveillance & Society, 8*(1), 84–92. doi:10.24908s.v8i1.3475

Dooley, R., Edmonds, A., Hancock, D. Y., Lowe, J. M., Skidmore, E., Adams, A. K., ... Knepper, R. (2018). *Security best practices for academic cloud service providers*. Academic Press.

Dragomir, D., Gheorghe, L., Costea, S., & Radovici, A. (2016, September). A survey on secure communication protocols for IoT systems. In *2016 International Workshop on Secure Internet of Things (SIoT)* (pp. 47-62). IEEE. 10.1109/SIoT.2016.012

Due, C., Connellan, K., & Riggs, D. (2012). *Surveillance, security and violence in a mental health ward: an ethnographic case-study of an Australian purpose-built unit*. Academic Press.

Fernandes, J. L., Lopes, I. C., Rodrigues, J. J., & Ullah, S. (2013, July). Performance evaluation of RESTful web services and AMQP protocol. In *2013 Fifth International Conference on Ubiquitous and Future Networks (ICUFN)* (pp. 810-815). IEEE. 10.1109/ICUFN.2013.6614932

Gennaro, R., Gentry, C., & Parno, B. (2010, August). Non-interactive verifiable computing: Outsourcing computation to untrusted workers. In *Annual Cryptology Conference* (pp. 465-482). Springer. 10.1007/978-3-642-14623-7_25

Genovese, A., Labati, R. D., Piuri, V., & Scotti, F. (2011, September). Wildfire smoke detection using computational intelligence techniques. In *2011 IEEE International Conference on Computational Intelligence for Measurement Systems and Applications (CIMSA) Proceedings* (pp. 1-6). IEEE. 10.1109/CIMSA.2011.6059930

Gubbi, J., Buyya, R., Marusic, S., & Palaniswami, M. (2013). Internet of Things (IoT): A vision, architectural elements, and future directions. *Future Generation Computer Systems, 29*(7), 1645–1660. doi:10.1016/j.future.2013.01.010

Han, B., Gopalakrishnan, V., Ji, L., & Lee, S. (2015). Network function virtualization: Challenges and opportunities for innovations. *IEEE Communications Magazine, 53*(2), 90–97. doi:10.1109/MCOM.2015.7045396

Jararweh, Y., Doulat, A., AlQudah, O., Ahmed, E., Al-Ayyoub, M., & Benkhelifa, E. (2016, May). The future of mobile cloud computing: integrating cloudlets and mobile edge computing. In *2016 23rd International conference on telecommunications (ICT)* (pp. 1-5). IEEE. 10.1109/ICT.2016.7500486

Jararweh, Y., Doulat, A., Darabseh, A., Alsmirat, M., Al-Ayyoub, M., & Benkhelifa, E. (2016, April). SDMEC: Software defined system for mobile edge computing. In *2016 IEEE International Conference on Cloud Engineering Workshop (IC2EW)* (pp. 88-93). IEEE.

Keahey, K., Tsugawa, M., Matsunaga, A., & Fortes, J. (2009). Sky computing. *IEEE Internet Computing*, *13*(5), 43–51. doi:10.1109/MIC.2009.94

Konduru, V. R., & Bharamagoudra, M. R. (2017, August). Challenges and solutions of interoperability on IoT: How far have we come in resolving the IoT interoperability issues. In *2017 International Conference On Smart Technologies For Smart Nation (SmartTechCon)* (pp. 572-576). IEEE. 10.1109/SmartTechCon.2017.8358436

Laeeq, K., & Shamsi, J. A. (2015). A study of security issues, vulnerabilities and challenges in internet of things. *Securing Cyber-Physical Systems, 10.*

Lar, S. U., Liao, X., & Abbas, S. A. (2011, August). Cloud computing privacy & security global issues, challenges, & mechanisms. In *2011 6th International ICST Conference on Communications and Networking in China (CHINACOM)* (pp. 1240-1245). IEEE.

Lerche, C., Hartke, K., & Kovatsch, M. (2012, September). Industry adoption of the Internet of Things: A constrained application protocol survey. In *Proceedings of 2012 IEEE 17th International Conference on Emerging Technologies & Factory Automation (ETFA 2012)* (pp. 1-6). IEEE. 10.1109/ETFA.2012.6489787

Liu, X., Lam, K. H., Zhu, K., Zheng, C., Li, X., Du, Y., . . . Pong, P. W. (2016). *Overview of spintronic sensors, Internet of Things, and smart living*. arXiv preprint arXiv:1611.00317

Liu, Y., Sun, Y. L., Ryoo, J., Rizvi, S., & Vasilakos, A. V. (2015). A survey of security and privacy challenges in cloud computing: Solutions and future directions. *Journal of Computing Science and Engineering: JCSE, 9*(3), 119–133. doi:10.5626/JCSE.2015.9.3.119

Manoj, B. S., & Baker, A. H. (2007). Communication challenges in emergency response. *Communications of the ACM, 50*(3), 51–53. doi:10.1145/1226736.1226765

Masek, P., Fujdiak, R., Zeman, K., Hosek, J., & Muthanna, A. (2016, April). Remote networking technology for IoT: Cloud-based access for AllJoyn-enabled devices. In *2016 18th Conference of Open Innovations Association and Seminar on Information Security and Protection of Information Technology (FRUCT-ISPIT)* (pp. 200-205). IEEE.

Mezgár, I., & Rauschecker, U. (2014). The challenge of networked enterprises for cloud computing interoperability. *Computers in Industry, 65*(4), 657–674. doi:10.1016/j.compind.2014.01.017

Michael Wittig. (2018). https://cloudonaut.io/encrypting-sensitive-data-stored-on-s3/

Naik, N. (2017, October). Choice of effective messaging protocols for IoT systems: MQTT, CoAP, AMQP and HTTP. In *2017 IEEE international systems engineering symposium (ISSE)* (pp. 1-7). IEEE.

Nolan, K. A., & Volavka, J. (2006). Video recording in the assessment of violent incidents in psychiatric hospitals. *Journal of Psychiatric Practice, 12*(1), 58–63. doi:10.1097/00131746-200601000-00010 PMID:16432448

Olsen, D. P. (1998). Ethical considerations of video monitoring psychiatric patients in seclusion and restraint. *Archives of Psychiatric Nursing, 12*(2), 90–94. doi:10.1016/S0883-9417(98)80058-7 PMID:9573636

Rashidi, B., Sharifi, M., & Jafari, T. (2013). A survey on interoperability in the cloud computing environments. *International Journal of Modern Education and Computer Science*, 5(6), 17–23. doi:10.5815/ijmecs.2013.06.03

Raychaudhuri, D., Nagaraja, K., & Venkataramani, A. (2012). Mobilityfirst: A robust and trustworthy mobility-centric architecture for the future internet. *Mobile Computing and Communications Review*, 16(3), 2–13. doi:10.1145/2412096.2412098

Rose, K., Eldridge, S., & Chapin, L. (2015). The internet of things: An overview. *The Internet Society (ISOC), 80.*

Said, O., & Masud, M. (2013). Towards internet of things: Survey and future vision. *International Journal of Computer Networks*, 5(1), 1–17.

Salas-Vega, S., Haimann, A., & Mossialos, E. (2015). Big data and health care: Challenges and opportunities for coordinated policy development in the EU. *Health Systems and Reform*, 1(4), 285–300. doi:10.1080/23288604.2015.1091538 PMID:31519092

Schütze, M. (2011). *Examination of the Attitudes of Mental Health Patients Towards Video Monitoring on a Secure Psychiatric Ward* (Doctoral dissertation). Bochum, Germany, Ruhr University Bochum Faculty of Medicine. http://www-brs.ub.ruhruni-bochum.de/netahtml/HSS/Diss/SchuetzeMorana/diss.pdf

Sha, M., Hackmann, G., & Lu, C. (2013, April). Energy-efficient low power listening for wireless sensor networks in noisy environments. In *Proceedings of the 12th international conference on Information processing in sensor networks* (pp. 277-288). 10.1145/2461381.2461415

Shuijing, H. (2014, January). Data security: the challenges of cloud computing. In *2014 Sixth International Conference on Measuring Technology and Mechatronics Automation* (pp. 203-206). IEEE. 10.1109/ICMTMA.2014.52

Soyata, T., Muraleedharan, R., Langdon, J., Funai, C., Ames, S., Kwon, M., & Heinzelman, W. (2012, May). COMBAT: mobile-Cloud-based cOmpute/coMmunications infrastructure for BATtlefield applications. In Modeling and Simulation for Defense Systems and Applications VII (Vol. 8403, p. 84030K). International Society for Optics and Photonics.

Steve Lohr. (2010). *The New York Times*. Retrieved from https://www.nytimes.com/2010/03/13/technology/13netflix.html

Stolovy, T., Melamed, Y., & Afek, A. (2015). Video surveillance in mental health facilities: Is it ethical? The Israel Medical Association journal. *The Israel Medical Association Journal*, 17(5), 274–276. PMID:26137651

Sun, G., Chang, V., Ramachandran, M., Sun, Z., Li, G., Yu, H., & Liao, D. (2017). Efficient location privacy algorithm for Internet of Things (IoT) services and applications. *Journal of Network and Computer Applications*, 89, 3–13. doi:10.1016/j.jnca.2016.10.011

Takabi, H., Joshi, J. B., & Ahn, G. J. (2010). Security and privacy challenges in cloud computing environments. *IEEE Security and Privacy*, 8(6), 24–31. doi:10.1109/MSP.2010.186

The national intelligence council sponsor workshop. (2008). *Intelligence, S. C. B., 2008. Disruptive Civil Technologies. Six Technologies with Potential Impacts on US Interests out to 2025.* Available: https://fas.org/irp/nic/disruptive.pdf

Turab, N. M., Taleb, A. A., & Masadeh, S. R. (2013). Cloud computing challenges and solutions. *International Journal of Computer Networks & Communications, 5*(5), 209–216. doi:10.5121/ijcnc.2013.5515

Uddin, M. Z. (2019). A wearable sensor-based activity prediction system to facilitate edge computing in smart healthcare system. *Journal of Parallel and Distributed Computing, 123*, 46–53. doi:10.1016/j.jpdc.2018.08.010

Varghese, B., Wang, N., Barbhuiya, S., Kilpatrick, P., & Nikolopoulos, D. S. (2016, November). Challenges and opportunities in edge computing. In *2016 IEEE International Conference on Smart Cloud (SmartCloud)* (pp. 20-26). IEEE. 10.1109/SmartCloud.2016.18

Vartiainen, H., & Hakola, P. (1994). The effects of TV monitoring on ward atmosphere in a security hospital. *International Journal of Law and Psychiatry, 17*(4), 443–449. doi:10.1016/0160-2527(94)90019-1 PMID:7890477

Vijayalakshmi, A. V., & Arockiam, L. (2016). A study on security issues and challenges in IoT. *International Journal of Engineering Sciences & Management Research, 3*(11), 1–9.

Vinoski, S. (2006). Advanced message queuing protocol. *IEEE Internet Computing, 10*(6), 87–89. doi:10.1109/MIC.2006.116

Wadhwa, A. V., & Gupta, S. (2015). Study of security issues in cloud computing. *International Journal of Computer Science and Mobile Computing IJCSMC, 4*(6), 230–234.

Warr, J., Page, M., & Crossen-White, H. (2005). *The appropriate use of CCTV observation in a secure unit.* Bournemouth University.

Wortmann, F., & Flüchter, K. (2015). Internet of things. *Business & Information Systems Engineering, 57*(3), 221–224. doi:10.100712599-015-0383-3

Zhang, L., Estrin, D., Burke, J., Jacobson, V., Thornton, J. D., Smetters, D. K., ... Papadopoulos, C. (2010). Named data networking (ndn) project. Relatório Técnico NDN-0001. *Xerox Palo Alto Research Center-PARC, 157*, 158.

This research was previously published in Challenges and Opportunities for the Convergence of IoT, Big Data, and Cloud Computing; pages 17-36, copyright year 2021 by Engineering Science Reference (an imprint of IGI Global).

Chapter 33
The Pivotal Role of Edge Computing With Machine Learning and Its Impact on Healthcare

Muthukumari S. M.
Bharathidasan University, India

George Dharma Prakash E. Raj
Bharathidasan University, India

ABSTRACT

The global market for IoT medical devices is expected to hit a peak of 500 billion by the year 2025, which could signal a significant paradigm shift in healthcare technology. This is possible due to the on-premises data centers or the cloud. Cloud computing and the internet of things (IoT) are the two technologies that have an explicit impact on our day-to-day living. These two technologies combined together are referred to as CloudIoT, which deals with several sectors including healthcare, agriculture, surveillance systems, etc. Therefore, the emergence of edge computing was required, which could reduce the network latency by pushing the computation to the "edge of the network." Several concerns such as power consumption, real-time responses, and bandwidth consumption cost could also be addressed by edge computing. In the present situation, patient health data could be regularly monitored by certain wearable devices known as the smart telehealth systems that send an enormous amount of data through the wireless sensor network (WSN).

INTRODUCTION

The large amount of generated healthcare data could be stored in the cloud environment maintaining their privacy that could be recommended to be viewed only by the concerned users. The physiological data could be obtained by the combined machine learning and signal processing modules in the

DOI: 10.4018/978-1-6684-5700-9.ch033

traditional telecare systems. Machine learning algorithms are designed to run on the powerful servers. The connectivity problem faced by the IoT devices could be answered by the edge computing thus maintaining its efficiency even though the connectivity is poor. Several benefits are impacted with the edge computing technology (Ali Hassan Sodhro et al. 2018). First, the workload could be reduced for the medical experts by prioritizing the important task at the top level thereby managing the collected data. The second will be enabling the healthcare facility all over the remote area, where these facilities falls behind. For instance, a truck outfitted with the edge computing devices could visit certain remote villages and promote healthcare facilities by connecting the patient to the telehealth services (*A. Tanaka et al.* 2016). The third advantage is to stimulate the advancement of medical technology. Opportunities will be more with the enormous collection of data. Edge computing involves in managing and labeling the data in an efficient and uniform way that makes the data to be shared securely making the process easier (Á. Alesanco and J. García, 2010). Mining of data could also be made simple for the researchers, which was said to the difficult task in the past era. The greatest impact of edge computing will be the treatment of chronic diseases by monitoring the collected data (A. Monteiro et al. 2016). Certain disorders such as diabetics and congestive heart problems could be monitored continously with the combination of 5G cellular networks along with the IoT by in-home monitoring of patients. This chapter presents the state-of-the-art edge computing and machine learning techniques, which can enhance the biomedical applications (Bellman R. 1957).

BACKGROUND

The development in the Internet of Things (IoT) and mobile usage has found a profound impact in the enhancement of cloud storage. Hyperscale data centers had been created due to the accelerated data center traffic that has been created by the increased usage of cloud computing environment (B. M. C. Silva et al. 2015). The data storage capacity should increase significantly due to the growth of IoT based application, which plays a major role in Smart city, Healthcare and Industries. According to the prediction done by the Cisco Global Cloud Index, the workload created by the cloud environment will be increased by 94% and the traditional data center will be just 6% by the year 2021(B. Mei et al. 2015). Certain impacts limit the blooming cloud infrastructure and reduce its flexibility that is as follows:

1. **Latency/Determinism:** The time delay created among the interaction of IoT devices and the cloud is known as latency. Certain industries like Electronics Health Records (EHR) and Telemedicine has a major concern with the latency requirements and this impact must be concerned essentially.
2. **Data/Bandwidth:** According to Statistics, the installation of IoT devices could increase by 31 billion worldwide by the year 2020. In generating the medical records, at least 15-20 devices should be connected at each patient's bed, which increases the data rate. This causes a limitation in the network bandwidth, overpowering the cloud and also increases data traffic.
3. **Privacy/Security:** According to IBM data breach study, the security and the privacy of each patient's data in the healthcare line could be affected due to the increased data breach cost, which will be about $480 per patient and this cost could be three times the data cost of other industries.

Edge computing is highly advantageous as the data could be processed and filtered, thereby sending only the useful data to the cloud (C. Orwat et al. 2008). This facility brings the cloud computing to the

EDGE of the network. The drawbacks mentioned above in the cloud infrastructure will be eradicated by the edge computing. According to a study conducted by Grand View Research, Inc., the global edge computing market size is estimated to reach USD 3.24 billion by the year 2025. CloudIoT makes cognitive healthcare framework possible along 5G (R. Dawson and P.W Lavori, 2004). This facility finds a major impact in the medical application, reaching human lives anywhere at the world. The development of Smart cities promotes cutting-edge technologies in the medical line and in fact emotion recognition module embedded into a framework is also made possible (Dr. S. Mohan Kumar and Darpan Majumdar, 2018).

EDGE COMPUTING IN SMART HEALTHCARE SYSTEMS

All IoT devices and wireless devices like Wearable Sensors, Hospital Monitors are connected to the edge nodes with low latency and some other devices directly connected to the cloud which leads high latency (E. Topol, 2013). Emergency Alert and medical Storage Files are connected to the Cloud and all these are comes under Edge of Network as shown in the above figure 1.

Figure 1. Edge Computing in Smart Healthcare Systems

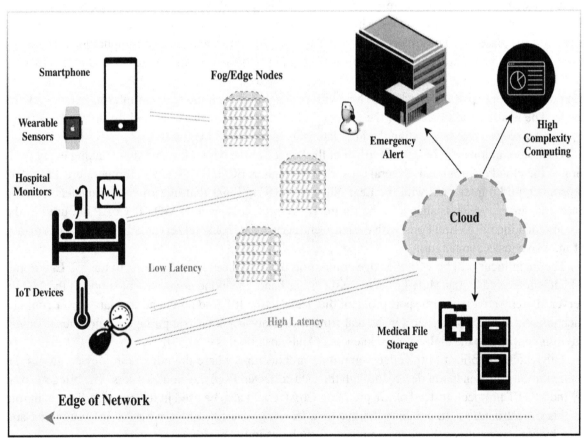

INTEGRATING EDGE COMPUTING AND MACHINE LEARNING FOR HEALTH CARE APPLICATION

In hospitals, a cloud infrastructure of Azure IoT Edge gateway (Linux server) could be registered with the Azure IoT Hub. Pipeline could be configured in the form of JSON file in the IoT Hub. For instance, the communication among the devices could be done with the data ingest container and the ML model shows the output (E. MacIntosh et al. 2016). The right container will be chosen from the container register that is handled by the edge devices, which is deployed by the JSON edge configuration file. Apple Company also introduces their version of AI integrated smart phone in iPhoneX with the new A11 Bionic chip (E. A. Oladimeji et al. 2011). Probably, many smart phones had been implemented with the AI technology, especially for the speech recognition, which enables digital assistants.

Moreover, this technology had been empowered by the cloud environment. In future, neural engine with several machine learning algorithms will be implemented in the smart phones and this heads the industries to the higher level (Frank Alexander Kraamer et al. 2017). Asserts leading to the misuse of cloud should be considered at the premature state. However, AI leads the way and has a real impact on everyday's life. Increase in the process tends to adapt the latest technology and this could also lead to cost savings with the role of edge technology with the decreased latency (G. J. Mandellos et al. 2009).

In healthcare application, a good IoT framework should intelligently prioritize and use the network resources with the trusted and secure channel. This could be possible by effectively preprocessing the input data retrieved from the sensor nodes. This could be done by connecting the leaf devices with the cloud servers at the back-end. These cloud servers has the capability to access heavy computational resources from which the incoming data could be prioritized and sends the information to the end point device.

The signatures could be extracted from the incoming data with the data mining and machine learning concepts applied at the back-end. Thus with the captured data, the medical interpretation could be made. The health condition data of the patient will be displayed at the front-end. In this concept, edge computing plays a role in avoiding the high latencies of decisions in cloud.

The computations will be done at IoT or at the "edge" of the network rather than making every decision at the cloud environment. Several sensor nodes such as ECG, EMG, EEG, Temperature and SPO2 sensors could be integrated with the Leaf Node or IoT End Point that in turn communicates with the back-end server, which is shown in the figure 1. IoT protocols such as MQTT, CoAP are used in the communication of IoT End Point with the back-end server. The backend server helps in the performance of intensive tasks computation.

The main focus will be with the edge computing that could send notifications to the IoT End Point, which is managed by the MQTT client. On the other hand, the cloud environment supports the MQTT server, thereby creating a transport protocol that leads to the IoT End point and the data server communication. As mentioned earlier, for the real-time data analysis, cloud computing will not the sufficient environment due to the high network latencies (Anagnostopoulos et al. 2015).

This extends the idea to the edge computing architecture, where the edge point device guides the computation of the endpoint device through the data collected from the cloud servers. The bill gets fixed by the MQTT protocol. Instead of IoT protocol, CoAP could also be used in this process. The main role of this infrastructure is to combine the machine learning concepts along with the IoT and cloud and thereby concentrating on the edge computing techniques in the healthcare domain.

Figure 2. IoT model for health care

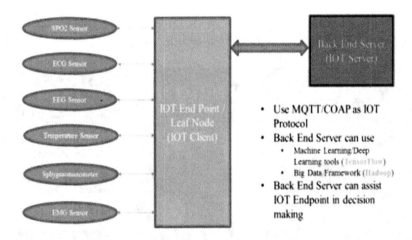

DEMYSTIFYING IMAGE PROCESSING IN HEALTHCARE

Image processing concept plays a major role in the healthcare industries. Strategies based on the Adaptive intervention had found its way in detecting breast cancer with the mammography screening test and also with the treatment of AIDS (J. Sametinger et al. 2015). But there is a scarcity of randomized trials that have employed dynamic treatment protocols, due to the historical lack of theory for the design and analysis of such a trial. The issues of sample size calculations with the randomization have been dealt recently with the better insights. The Bayesian framework discussed in deals with the multicenter design considerations and adaptive randomization of sequentially randomized trials (S.E Kahou et al. 2016). Sequentially randomized trials within the person mental illness and its theoretical innovations are dealt in and regarding cancer. With certain trials, these protocols are not considered to be sequential in nature but are rather considered to be a separate trial. Sequential decision problem are handled with the conventional backwards induction method, which is also known as Dynamic Programming (K. Wac et al. 2009). All the covariates of longitudinal distribution should be necessarily modeled in the dynamic regimes context. Treatment could be recommended incorrectly with the misspecification of the distribution due to the limited knowledge of this model. Methods do not have any such type of limitations. The time-varying covariates are adjusted with the optimal treatment discontinuation time through causal approaching. Analyzing sequentially randomized trials has been done in with the likelihood-based approach for the optimal regimes prostate cancer regions (K. Xu et al. 2016). Here the probabilities are taken from the information collected from the patient.

RECENT ADVANCEMENT IN MACHINE LEARNING

Figure 3. Applications of Machine Learning in Healthcare

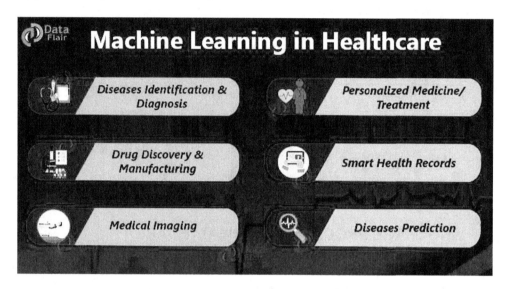

DISEASE IDENTIFICATION AND DIAGNOSIS

The major role played by the machine learning is to detect the disease through the image processing techniques, which could be very hard through the normal diagnosis. This disease could be anything like genetic disorders or cancers that is very difficult to be diagnosed at a very initial stage (K. Zhang et al. 2016).

Integration of cognitive computing with genome-based tumor sequencing done at IBM Watson Genomics is the very best example through which fastest diagnosis could be done. Therapeutic treatments are done with the AI based bio pharma followed by Berg in oncology (P.W Lavori, 2000). Moreover P1vital's PReDicT (Predicting Response to Depression Treatment) aims in promoting normal clinical conditions for the disease diagnosis and treatment.

DRUG DISCOVERY AND MANUFACTURING

Drug discovery process at the early-stage is one of the primary applications of machine learning. Precision medicine and Next-generation sequencing are certain R&D technologies included with this technique that could determine another alternative approach for the treatment of multiple diseases (L. M. Vaquero and L. Rodero-Merino, 2014). Unsupervised learning is a technique of machine learning that could identify patterns in the given data without providing any predicted output. Microsoft developed project Hanover that uses certain machine learning techniques with the AI technologies, which takes multiple initiatives in treating cancer as well as prescribing drugs for AML (Acute Myeloid Leukemia) (L. Catarinucci, 2016).

DIAGNOSING MEDICAL IMAGES

Computer vision is said to be a successful technology that works with the combination of Deep learning and machine learning. Image analysis had been done in Microsoft with the initiative technique called the Inner Eye mainly developed for the diagnosis of diseases with the images (S.A. Murphy, 2004). Due to the huge growth of medical data, machine learning plays its role in diagnosing the disease from the medical images with the role of AI.

SMART HEALTH RECORDS

Due to the update of technology, the maintenance of up-to-date medical reports could be highly possible with the special algorithms implemented for the data entry process. But still medical data entry takes time thereby increasing complexity (R. Bellman, 1957). This could be highly reduced with the machine learning techniques thereby producing high efficiency, saving cost, reducing computational time and effort.

The techniques such as ML-based OCR recognition and vector machines steps into the document classification methods and finds its place in machine learning-based handwriting recognition technology in MATLAB and Google's Cloud Vision API (G. Muhammad et al. 2014). MIT advances their development process to the next generation by stepping into the machine learning based tools that helps in the suggesting the clinical treatment with the diagnosis.

CROWD SOURCED DATA COLLECTION

In the healthcare field, crowd sourcing is found to be a rage due to the numerous amounts of medical data uploaded by the people and that helps the researchers and caretakers with the plenty of information. This type of real-time health data produces high consequences in such a way medicine will be apparent down the line (M. S. Hossain and G. Muhammad, 2015). Machine learning based face recognition had been developed in Apple's Research kit that helps with the treatment of Asperger's and Parkinson's disease.

IBM had made a partnership with the Medtronic for obtaining a real-time diabetes and insulin data with the crowd sourced information. Due to the development of IoT and mobile technologies, several researches had been carried out with the obtained crowd sourced data and also enhanced is done with the tough-to-diagnose cases data.

OUTBREAK PREDICTION

The combination of machine learning along with the AI based techniques had been implemented today for the epidemics prediction all around the world. Numerous data had been collected from the satellites, website information, social media etc, and researchers and scientist also have huge access to them all. From malaria till the impact of certain chronic disease identification and prediction could be done by the artificial neural networks through the obtained information.

This is extremely necessary for third-world countries that lacks with the medical and educational systems. ProMED-mail is the best example of this type, which is an reporting platform based n the internet that monitors the emerging diseases and the evolving ones and also promotes data at a real-time as shown in the figure 4.

Figure 4. Fog Computing in Healthcare IoT

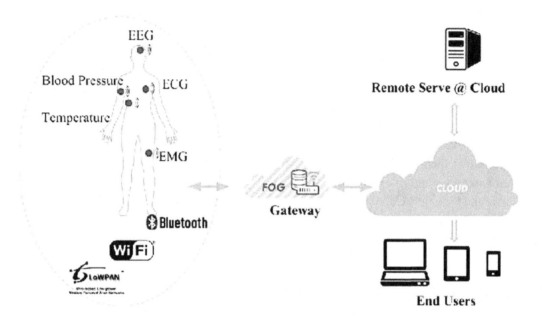

SMART e-HEALTH GATEWAYS AT THE EDGE OF HEALTHCARE MONITORING SYSTEMS

In Smart e-Health Gateways healthcare monitoring systems the Sensor Network monitor the patient body temperature, Blood pressure, Heart rate and monitor the sleep time of the patient. These sensed data's are sent to the gateway. The Gateway is then process the data and do data filtering and mining, give location notification of the patient and these processed data's are sent to Internet for data storage, data analytics, decision making and medical caregivers interface as shown in the figure

COMPONENTS OF IoT BASED HEALTHCARE MONITORING SYSYTEM

Here the Medical Devices and Hospital Rooms are monitored by Smart e-Health Gateways. And the Smart e-Health Gateways are fixed at each rooms by connecting sensors and formed Mesh-based Wireless Sensor Network which is used to sense the data and fetch information from the patients is shown in figure 6.

Figure 5. Smart e-Health Gateways at the Edge

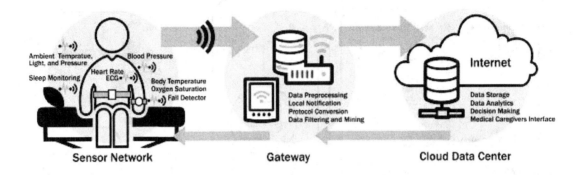

Table 1. Merits and Demerits of Edge Computing in Healthcare

Merits	Demerits
Provides telemedicine and Remote patient monitoring.	Need more security measurements to keep the patient health record safely.
Machine-to-machine communication or machine –to-human interaction.	Remote health monitoring only in smart cities.
It delivers applications and services to remote area by the use of data center locations.	Should increase the bandwidth capacity to the data center for fastest delivery of the medical services.
Smart sensors monitors the ill patients accurately.	Sometimes the range of the sensor for sensing the patient become collapsed due to long distance.
Virtualization technology brings the patients closer to the doctors.	Virtualization monitoring needs to bring more attention to the patient.
Telemedicine programs brought special care for the patients.	All suburban areas needs the telemedicine program.
Simple and Flexible to use	Limited number of services
It is powerful to use	Sometimes fails practically
Highly efficient and secure healthcare monitoring	Third party auditor requires for do operation
Very easy to use and secure	There are some challenges to secure healthcare monitoring
Data can be maintained privately	Not to resolve all issues
Easy Monitoring system	Sometimes it fails

EDGE COMPUTING BASED APPLICATION FOR HEALTHCARE IMAGE PROCESSING

The integration of several smart systems along with the smart healthcare falls into the category of smart cities. This successful endeavor is possible only with the combination of cloud computing along with the edge computing process. The resources and the process are assigned with the proposed healthcare system that comes out with the perfect workflow and pool of resources. The completion of the assigned task will be notified by its own edge nodes for every resource. Then the cloud environment plays a role in reassigning the resources with the scheduling algorithm. Rather than the regular client-server com-

Figure 6. IoT Based Healthcare Components

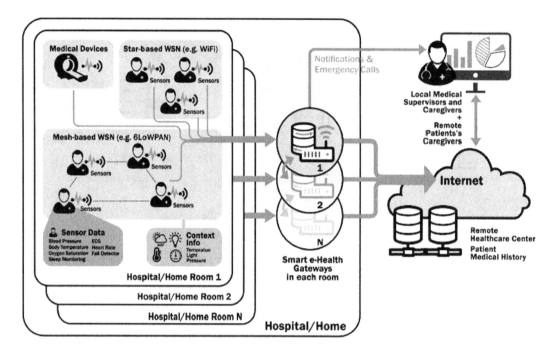

puting, cloud computing is found to be more effective, reliable and it is also said to be faster. Cloud also supports the fault tolerance policies and hence the workflow will also be ensured.

The cloud-fog based workflow system had been presented in figure 7. The software related to the workflow and the databases are stored in the cloud and on the other hand assigning the task with the completion of task notification will be send from the edge node to the cloud infrastructure. Tablet and cell phones acts on the edge node, which are said to be the resources of the smart devices. When the task assigned is accomplished by the resource then the respective notification will be send by the edge node to the cloud that the particular resource is available at the pool for it to be re-assigned.

The communication mode among the medical team and the cloud in the base station is shown in the above figure. This communication is said to be mobile and wireless. In this level, the edge and fog are found to be alike. The fog and the edge computing push the computing and processing capabilities closer to the originated place of the data. In the above framework, the data is found to be closer to the smart healthcare workflow. The resources are categorized as consumable and non-consumable according to the above framework. The resources is said to be consumable if it expires by time; else it is said to be non-consumable. Non-human resources such as equipments, machines etc, are said to be consumable resources. On the other hand, humans are the best example of non-consumable resources.

The process carried out in both the cloud and the edge mode is presented in figure 8. In the cloud mode, scheduling occurs and all the assignments in done at the edge mode.

Figure 7. Cloud-fog based workflow system

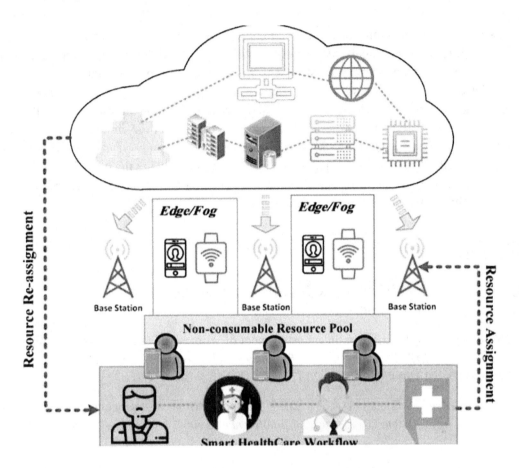

Figure 8. Combination of cloud and edge computing for task scheduling

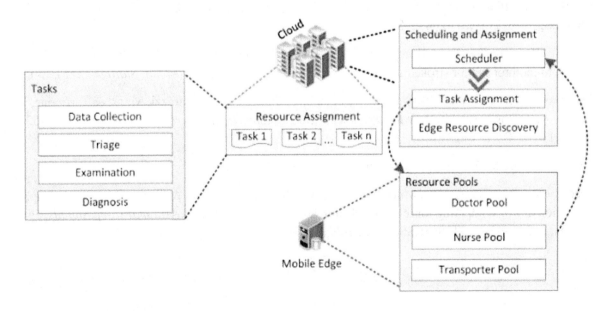

CONCLUSION

Fog severs as a new architecture for control, computing, storage and networking that brings the end users very closer to the technologies. Moreover, decentralization is also achieved at the edge of the network. Due to the increasing use of wearables (sensor devices), enormous amount of data is generated. The data related to healthcare could be in the form of numerical format or images. In case of images, the affected regions are identified and with the help of machine learning algorithms, classification and preprocessing is done based on the types of diseases. With the help of the clinical procedures, the data gets assisted by the cloud and the fog services. This large pool of data serves as a huge benefit for the IoT healthcare. Egde computing techniques could be involved in reducing the latencies produced by the cloud computing environment. Moreover, with the combination of these technologies, healthcare could be highly benefitted, thereby reaching people at every corner of the world.

REFERENCES

Alemdar, H., & Ersoy, C. (2010). Wireless sensor networks for healthcare: A survey. *Computer Networks*, *54*(15), 2688–2710. doi:10.1016/j.comnet.2010.05.003

Alesanco, Á., & García, J. (2010). Clinical assessment of wireless ECG transmission in real-time cardiac telemonitoring. *IEEE Transactions on Information Technology in Biomedicine*, *14*(5), 1144–1152. doi:10.1109/TITB.2010.2047650 PMID:20378476

Anagnostopoulos, C. N., & Giannoukos, T. I. (2015). Features and classifiers for emotion recognition from speech: A survey from 2000 to 2011. *Artificial Intelligence Review*, *43*(2), 155–177. doi:10.100710462-012-9368-5

Bellman, R. (1957). *Dynamic Programming*. Princeton University Press.

Bertini, M., Marcantoni, L., Toselli, T., & Ferrari, R. (2016). Remote monitoring of implantable devices: Should we continue to ignore it? *International Journal of Cardiology*, *202*, 368–377. doi:10.1016/j.ijcard.2015.09.033 PMID:26432486

Cao, Y., Chen, S., Hou, P., & Brown, D. (2015). FAST: A fog computing assisted distributed analytics system to monitor fall for stroke mitigation. *Proc. IEEE Int. Conf. Netw., Archit. Storage (NAS)*, 2–11.

Catarinucci, L., de Donno, D., Mainetti, L., Palano, L., Patrono, L., Stefanizzi, M. L., & Tarricone, L. (2016). An IoT-aware architecture for smart healthcare systems. *IEEE Internet Things J.*, *2*(6), 515–526. doi:10.1109/JIOT.2015.2417684

I. Corporation. (2016). *Bigger data for better healthcare*. Tech. Rep.

Craciunescu, R., Mihovska, A., Mihaylov, M., Kyriazakos, S., Prasad, R., & Halunga, S. (2015). Implementation of Fog computing for reliable E-health applications. *Proc. 49th Asilomar Conf. Signals, Syst. Comput.*, 459–463. 10.1109/ACSSC.2015.7421170

Dawson, R., & Lavori, P. W. (2004). Placebo-free designs for evaluating new mental health treatments: The use of adaptive treatment strategies. *Statistics in Medicine, 23*(21), 3249–3262. doi:10.1002im.1920 PMID:15490427

Digital Pills Make Their Way to Market. (2012). Available: http://blogs.nature.com/news/2012/07/digital-pills-make-their-wayto-market.html

(2018). Dr. S. Mohan Kumar and Darpan Majumdar (2018). Healthcare Solution Based on machine Learning Applications in IoT and Edge Computing. *International Journal of Pure and Applied Mathematics. Volume, 16*(119), 1473–1484.

Eide, R. (2016). *Low energy wireless ECG: An exploration of wireless electrocardiography and the utilization of low energy sensors for clinical ambulatory patient monitoring* (M.S. thesis). Dept. Comput. Inf. Sci., Norwegian Univ. Sci. Technol., Trondheim, Norway.

Farandos, N. M., Yetisen, A. K., Monteiro, M. J., Lowe, C. R., & Yun, S. H. (2015). Contact lens sensors in ocular diagnostics. *Advanced Healthcare Materials, 4*(6), 792–810. doi:10.1002/adhm.201400504 PMID:25400274

Gia, T. N., Jiang, M., Rahmani, A.-M., Westerlund, T., Liljeberg, P., & Tenhunen, H. (2015). Fog computing in healthcare Internet of Things: A case study on ECG feature extraction. *Proc. IEEE Int. Conf. Comput. Inf. Technol., Ubiquitous Comput. Commun., Dependable, Auto. Secur. Comput., Pervasive Intell. Comput. (CIT/IUCC/DASC/PICOM),* 356–363. 10.1109/CIT/IUCC/DASC/PICOM.2015.51

Hossain, M. S., & Muhammad, G. (2015). Cloud-assisted speech and face recognition framework for health monitoring. *Mobile Networks and Applications, 20*(3), 391–399. doi:10.100711036-015-0586-3

Hossain, M. S., & Muhammad, G. (2016). Cloud-assisted Industrial Internet of Things (IIoT) - enabled framework for health monitoring. *Computer Networks, 101,* 192–202. doi:10.1016/j.comnet.2016.01.009

Hossain, M. S., Muhammad, G., Al-Qurishi, M., Masud, M., Almogren, A., Abdul, W., & Alamri, A. (2017). Cloud-Oriented Emotion Feedback-based Exergames Framework. *Multimedia Tools and Applications.* Advance online publication. doi:10.100711042-017-4621-1

Hossain, M. S., Muhammad, G., Alhamid, M. F., Song, B., & Al-Mutib, K. (2016). Audio-Visual Emotion Recognition Using Big Data Towards 5G. *Mobile Networks and Applications, 221*(5), 753–763. doi:10.100711036-016-0685-9

Hosseini, M.-P., Hajisami, A., & Pompili, D. (2016). Real-time epileptic seizure detection from eeg signals via random subspace ensemble learning. *Proc. IEEE Int. Conf. Auto. Comput. (ICAC),* 209–218. 10.1109/ICAC.2016.57

Jenke, R., Peer, A., & Buss, M. (2014). Feature Extraction and Selection for Emotion Recognition from EEG. *IEEE Transactions on Affective Computing, 5*(3), 327–339. doi:10.1109/TAFFC.2014.2339834

Kahou, S. E., Bouthillier, X., Lamblin, P., Gulcehre, C., Michalski, V., Konda, K., Jean, S., Froumenty, P., Dauphin, Y., Boulanger-Lewandowski, N., Chandias Ferrari, R., Mirza, M., Warde-Farley, D., Courville, A., Vincent, P., Memisevic, R., Pal, C., & Bengio, Y. (2016, June). EmoNets: Multimodal deep learning approaches for emotion recognition in video. *Journal on Multimodal User Interfaces, 10*(2), 99–111. doi:10.100712193-015-0195-2

Khushaba, R. N., Kodagoda, S., Takruri, M., & Dissanayake, G. (2012). Toward improved control of prosthetic fingers using surface electromyogram (EMG) signals. *Expert Systems with Applications, 39*(12), 10731–10738. doi:10.1016/j.eswa.2012.02.192

Kim, Y., Lee, H., & Provost, E. M. (2013). Deep learning for robust feature generation in audiovisual emotion recognition. *2013 IEEE International Conference on Acoustics, Speech and Signal Processing*, 3687-3691. 10.1109/ICASSP.2013.6638346

Kraamer, B., Tamkittikhun, & Palma. (2017). Fog Computing in Healthcare – A Review and Discussion. *IEEE Access : Practical Innovations, Open Solutions*; Advance online publication. doi:10.1109/Access.2017.2704100

Lavori, P. W., & Dawson, R. (2000). A design for testing clinical strategies: Biased adaptive within-subject randomization. *Journal of the Royal Statistical Society. Series A (General), 163*(1), 29–38. doi:10.1111/1467-985X.00154

López, G., Custodio, V., & Moreno, J. I. (2016). LOBIN: E-textile and wirelesssensor-network-based platform for healthcare monitoring in future hospital environments. *IEEE Transactions on Information Technology in Biomedicine, 14*(6), 1446–1458. doi:10.1109/TITB.2010.2058812 PMID:20643610

MacIntosh, E., Rajakulendran, N., Khayat, Z., & Wise, A. (2016). *Transforming Health: Shifting From Reactive to Proactive and Predictive Care*. Available: https://www.marsdd.com/newsand-insights/transforming-health-shifting-from-reactive-to-proactive-andpredictive-care/

Mandellos, G. J., Koutelakis, G. V., Panagiotakopoulos, T. C., Koukias, M. N., & Lymberopoulos, D. K. (2009). Requirements and solutions for advanced telemedicine applications. In *Biomedical Engineering*. InTech.

Masip-Bruin, X., Marín-Tordera, E., Alonso, A., & Garcia, J. (2016). Fog-tocloud computing (F2C): The key technology enabler for dependable ehealth services deployment. *Proc. Medit. Ad Hoc Netw. Workshop (Med-Hoc-Net)*, 1–5.

Mei, B., Cheng, W., & Cheng, X. (2015). Fog computing based ultraviolet radiation measurement via smartphones. *Proc. 3rd IEEE Workshop Hot Topics Web Syst. Technol. (HotWeb)*, 79–84.

Monteiro, A., Dubey, H., Mahler, L., Yang, Q., & Mankodiya, K. (2016). Fit: A fog computing device for speech tele-treatments. *Proc. IEEE Int. Conf. Smart Computing*, 1–3. 10.1109/SMART-COMP.2016.7501692

Muhammad, G., Alsulaiman, M., Amin, S. U., Ghoneim, A., & Alhamid, M. (2017). A Facial-Expression Monitoring System for Improved Healthcare in Smart Cities. *IEEE Access: Practical Innovations, Open Solutions, 5*(1), 10871–10881. doi:10.1109/ACCESS.2017.2712788

Murphy, S. A. (2003). Optimal dynamic treatment regimes (with discussion). *Journal of the Royal Statistical Society. Series B. Methodological*, *65*(2), 331–366. doi:10.1111/1467-9868.00389

Murphy, S. A. (2004). An experimental design for the development of adaptive treatment strategies. *Statistics in Medicine*, *24*(10), 1455–1481. doi:10.1002im.2022 PMID:15586395

Nazir, Ali, Ullah, & Garcia-Magarino. (2019). Internet of Things for Healthcare Using Wireless Communications or Mobile Computing. *Wireless Communications and Mobile Computing*. Doi:10.1155/2019/5931315

Obermeyer, Z., & Emanuel, E. J. (2016). Predicting the future—Big data, machine learning, and clinical medicine. *The New England Journal of Medicine*, *375*(13), 1216–1219. doi:10.1056/NEJMp1606181 PMID:27682033

Oladimeji, E. A., Chung, L., Jung, H. T., & Kim, J. (2011). Managing security and privacy in ubiquitous ehealth information interchange. *Proc. 5th Int. Conf. Ubiquitous Inf. Manage. Commun. (ICUIMC)*, 26:1–26:10. Available: https://doi.acm.org/10.1145/1968613.1968645

Orwat, C., Graefe, A., & Faulwasser, T. (2008). Towards pervasive computing in health care—A literature review. *BMC Medical Informatics and Decision Making*, *8*(1), 26. doi:10.1186/1472-6947-8-26 PMID:18565221

Oueida, Kotb, Aloqaily, & Jararweh. (2018). An Edge Computing Based Smart Healthcare Framework For Resource Management. *Sensors, 18*(12), 4307.

Paksuniemi, M., Sorvoja, H., Alasaarela, E., & Myllyla, R. (2005). Wireless sensor and data transmission needs and technologies for patient monitoring in the operating room and intensive care unit. *Proc. 27th Annu. Int. Conf. Eng. Med. Biol. Soc. (IEEE-EMBS)*, 5182–5185. 10.1109/IEMBS.2005.1615645

Perera, C., Zaslavsky, A., Christen, P., & Georgakopoulos, D. (2014). Context aware computing for the internet of things: A survey. *IEEE Commun. Surveys Tuts.*, *16*(1), 414–454. doi:10.1109/SURV.2013.042313.00197

'Philips' Intelligent Pill Targets Drug Development and Treatment for Digestive Tract Diseases. (2008). Available: https://phys.org/news/2008-11-philips-intelligent-pill-drug-treatment.html

Robins, J. M. (1994). Correcting for non-compliance in randomized trials using structural nested mean models. *Communications in Statistics*, *23*(8), 2379–2412. doi:10.1080/03610929408831393

Sametinger, J., Rozenblit, J., Lysecky, R., & Ott, P. (2015). Security challenges for medical devices. *Communications of the ACM*, *58*(4), 74–82. doi:10.1145/2667218

Schneider, L. S., Tariot, P. N., Lyketsos, C. G., Dagerman, K. S., Davis, K. L., Davis, S., Hsiao, J. K., Jeste, D. V., Katz, I. R., Olin, J. T., Pollock, B. G., Rabins, P. V., Rosenheck, R. A., Small, G. W., Lebowitz, B., & Lieberman, J. A. (2001). National Institute of Mental Health Clinical Antipsychotic Trials of Intervention Effectiveness (CATIE): Alzheimer disease trial methodology. *American Journal of Geriatric Psychology*, *9*(4), 346–360. doi:10.1097/00019442-200111000-00004 PMID:11739062

Silva, B. M. C., Rodrigues, J. J. P. C., de la Torre Díez, I., López-Coronado, M., & Saleem, K. (2015). Mobile-health: A review of current state in 2015. *Journal of Biomedical Informatics*, *56*, 265–272. doi:10.1016/j.jbi.2015.06.003 PMID:26071682

Sodhro, Luo, & Arunkumar. (2018). Mobile Edge Computing Based QoS Optimization in Medical Healthcare Applications. *International Journal of Information Management*. DOI: .2018.08.004 doi:10.1016/j.ijinfomgt

Steele, R., & Lo, A. (2013). Telehealth and ubiquitous computing for bandwidthconstrained rural and remote areas. *Personal and Ubiquitous Computing, 17*(3), 533–543. doi:10.100700779-012-0506-5

Tanaka, A., Utsunomiya, F., & Douseki, T. (2016). Wearable self-powered diaper-shaped urinary-incontinence sensor suppressing response-time variation with 0.3 V start-up converter. *IEEE Sensors Journal, 16*(10), 3472–3479. doi:10.1109/JSEN.2015.2483900

Thall, P. F., Millikan, R. E., & Sung, H.-G. (2000). Evaluating multiple treatment courses in clinical trials. *Statistics in Medicine, 19*(8), 1011–1028. doi:10.1002/(SICI)1097-0258(20000430)19:8<1011::AID-SIM414>3.0.CO;2-M PMID:10790677

Thall, P. F., & Wathen, J. K. (2005). Covariate-adjusted adaptive randomization in a sarcoma trial with multistate treatments. *Statistics in Medicine, 24*(13), 1947–1964. doi:10.1002im.2077 PMID:15806621

The Cloud Standards Customer Council (CSCC). (2016). *Impact of cloud computing on healthcare*. Reference architecture, Version 1.0. Available: http://cloud-council.org

Topol, E. (2018). *The Creative Destruction of Medicine*. Basic Books.

Vaquero, L. M., & Rodero-Merino, L. (2014). Finding your way in the fog. *ACM SIGCOMM Comput. Commun. Rev., 44*(5), 27–32. doi:10.1145/2677046.2677052

Wac, K., Bargh, M. S., Beijnum, B. J. F. V., Bults, R. G. A., Pawar, P., & Peddemors, A. (2009). Power- and delay-awareness of health telemonitoring services: The mobihealth system case study. *IEEE Journal on Selected Areas in Communications, 27*(4), 525–536. doi:10.1109/JSAC.2009.090514

Xu, K., Li, Y., & Ren, F. (2016). An energy-efficient compressive sensing framework incorporating online dictionary learning for long-term wireless health monitoring. *Proc. IEEE Int. Conf. Acoust., Speech Signal Process*, 804–808. 10.1109/ICASSP.2016.7471786

Yin, Y., Zeng, Y., Chen, X., & Fan, Y. (2016). The Internet of Things in healthcare: An overview. *J. Ind. Inf. Integr., 1*, 3–13. doi:10.1016/j.jii.2016.03.004

Yogesh, H., Ngadiran, A., Yaacob, B., & Polat, K. (2017). A new hybrid PSO assisted biogeography-based optimization for emotion and stress recognition from speech signal. *Expert Systems with Applications, 69*, 149–158. doi:10.1016/j.eswa.2016.10.035

Zhang, K., Liang, X., Baura, M., Lu, R., & Shen, X. (2014). PHDA: A priority based health data aggregation with privacy preservation for cloud assisted WBANs. *Inf. Sci., 284*, 130–141. doi:10.1016/j.ins.2014.06.011

Zhang, R., Bernhart, S., & Amft, O. (2016). Diet eyeglasses: Recognising food chewing using emg and smart eyeglasses. *Proc. IEEE 13th Int. Conf. Wearable Implant. Body Sensor Netw.*, 7–12. 10.1109/BSN.2016.7516224

ADDITIONAL READING

Chen, H., & Liu, H. (2016). A remote electrocardiogram monitoring system with good swiftness and high reliablility. *Computers & Electrical Engineering, 53*, 191–202. doi:10.1016/j.compeleceng.2016.02.004

Chen, M., Li, W., Hao, Y., Qian, Y., & Humar, I. (2018). Edge cognitive computing based smart health-care system. *Journal of Future Generation Computer Systems, Elsevier, 86*, 403–411. doi:10.1016/j.future.2018.03.054

Huang, Y. M., Hsieh, M. Y., Chao, H. C., Hung, S. H., & Park, J. H. (2009). Pervasive, secure access to a hierarchical sensor-based healthcare monitoring architecture in wireless heterogeneous networks. *IEEE Journal on Selected Areas in Communications, 27*(4), 400–411. doi:10.1109/JSAC.2009.090505

Nejati, H., Pomponiu, V., Do, T.-T., Zhou, Y., Iravani, S., & Cheung, N.-M. (2016). Smartphone and mobile image processing for assisted living: Healthmonitoring apps powered by advanced mobile imaging algorithms. *IEEE Signal Processing Magazine, 33*(4), 30–48. doi:10.1109/MSP.2016.2549996

Øyri, K., Balasingham, I., Samset, E., Høgetveit, J. O., & Fosse, E. (2006). Wireless continuous arterial blood pressure monitoring during surgery: A pilot study. *Anesthesia and Analgesia, 102*(2), 478–483. doi:10.1213/01.ane.0000195232.11264.46 PMID:16428546

Pace, P., Aloi, G., & Caliciuri, G. (2018). *An edge-based architecture to support efficient applications for healthcare industry 4.0.* IEEE Transactions.

Sodhro, A. H., & Baik, S. W. (2019). Mobile edge computing based QoS optimization in medical healthcare applications. *International Journal of Information Management, Elsevier, 45*, 308–318. doi:10.1016/j.ijinfomgt.2018.08.004

Wang, H., Gong, J., & Zhuang, Y. (2017). Healthedge: Task scheduling for edge computing with health emergency and human behavior consideration in smart homes. *IEEE International Conference on Big Data.*

KEY TERMS AND DEFINITIONS

Cloud IoT: It integrates cloud computing and Internet of Things to alleviate the quality of service in healthcare organizations and improve the medical facilities in clinics. And do interaction among medical staff and general practitioners.

Edge Computing: Due to long distance causes number of risks factors. It may cause bandwidth congestion and network latency. To concern these things, foremost all healthcare organizations moves forward to edge computing, which analyze the data and send it to the nearby system situated at cloud.

Healthcare Applications: A good IoT framework should intelligently prioritize and use the network resources with the trusted and secure channel. This could be possible by effectively preprocessing the input data retrieved from the sensor nodes. This could be done by connecting the leaf devices with the cloud servers at the backend.

Image Processing: Image processing concept plays a major role in the healthcare industries. Strategies based on the Adaptive intervention had found its way in detecting breast cancer with the mammography screening test and also with the treatment of AIDS.

IoT Edge Gateway: It can generate and exchange data within single framework. It offered Remote patient monitoring system which reduces the time duration.

Machine Learning: The major role played by the machine learning is to detect the disease through the image processing techniques, which could be very hard through the normal diagnosis. This disease could be anything like genetic disorders or cancers that is very difficult to be diagnosed at a very initial stage.

Telehealth Service: For instance, a truck outfitted with the edge computing devices could visit certain remote villages and promote healthcare facilities by connecting the patient to the telehealth services.

This research was previously published in Deep Neural Networks for Multimodal Imaging and Biomedical Applications; pages 219-236, copyright year 2020 by Medical Information Science Reference (an imprint of IGI Global).

Chapter 34

A Constrained Static Scheduling Strategy in Edge Computing for Industrial Cloud Systems

Yuliang Ma
Northeastern University at Qinhuangdao, China

Yinghua Han
Northeastern University at Qinhuangdao, China

Jinkuan Wang
Northeastern University at Qinhuangdao, China

Qiang Zhao
Northeastern University at Qinhuangdao, China

ABSTRACT

With the development of industrial internet, attention has been paid for edge computing due to the low latency. However, some problems remain about the task scheduling and resource management. In this paper, an edge computing supported industrial cloud system is investigated. According to the system, a constrained static scheduling strategy is proposed to over the deficiency of dynamic scheduling. The strategy is divided into the following steps. Firstly, the queue theory is introduced to calculate the expectations of task completion time. Thereupon, the task scheduling and resource management problems are formulated and turned into an integer non-linear programming (INLP) problem. Then, tasks that can be scheduled statically are selected based on the expectation of task completion and constrains of various aspects of task. Finally, a multi-elites-based co-evolutionary genetic algorithm (MEB-CGA) is proposed to solve the INLP problem. Simulation result shows that the MEB-CGA significantly outperforms the scheduling quality of greedy algorithm.

DOI: 10.4018/978-1-6684-5700-9.ch034

INTRODUCTION

Nowadays, Information Technology and Internet affect everything from communication to industrial (Keshanchi, Souri, & Navimipour, 2017). As the emergence of recent exponentially growing technologies, such as big data (Mourtzis, Vlachou, & Milas, 2016), cloud computing (Varghese& Buyya, 2017), edge computing (Satyanarayanan, 2017), networking, artificial intelligence (Acemoglu & Restrepo, 2018), the Industrial Internet has attracted great interests.

The Industrial Internet is often understood as the application of the generic concept of Cyber Physical Systems (CPSs), within which the information from all industrial perspectives is closely collected, monitored from the physical space and synchronized with the cyber space (Li, Yu, Deng, Luo, Ming, & Yan, 2017). There are many successful applications for CPS in the industrial, especially with the emergence of Industrial Internet of Things (IIoT), it becomes possible to achieve real-time big data collect, storage, access, and processing in the cloud platform (Kaur, Garg, & Aujla, 2018). In IIoT, the data is generated by various sensors, which are distributed in the industrial sites. This data will be on the order of zettabytes in the near future (El-Sayed, Sankar, & Prasad, 2018). Therefore, uploading this massive data to the remote cloud platform for further processing will result in latency issues which affect the overall QoS (quality of service) for various applications in IIoT (Hoang & Dang, 2017; Song, Yau, & Yu, 2017). In addition, considering various types of IIoT devices, cloud computing cannot fully conform with delay-sensitive applications (Malik & Om, 2018). Also, the size of the cloud computing system is restricted due to high costs of communication. Fortunately, a novel computational paradigm called edge computing has emerged, which extends the cloud resources to the edge of network in a distributed way (Yang, Puthal, & Mohanty, 2017; Brogi & Forti, 2017). The emergence of edge computing makes it possible to perform the computations at the edge of network. The cooperation among cloud and edge devices can reduce latency and maintain the QoS for various applications in the Industrial Internet environment and improve the processing capability of system (Munir, Kansakar, & Khan, 2017; Yousefpour, Ishigaki, & Jue, 2017; Ning, Kong, & Xia, 2019). Since many tasks can be completed in edge, the resource management and task scheduling of edge computing have witnessed a boom of development in recent years (Fan, Cui, & Cao, 2019; Shao, Li, & Fu, 2019; La, Ngo, & Dinh, 2018).

This paper considers an edge computing supported industrial cloud system (EC-ICS). Edge computing nodes are usually distributed in the industrial site, so it can reduce latency by assigning the task to edge computing nodes (Shi, et al, 2016). However, the dynamic scheduling strategy is no longer suitable for system requirements. On the one hand, when using a dynamic scheduling strategy, the running time of scheduling algorithm increases as the number of tasks increases. On the other hand, dynamic scheduling strategy means that the same task may be processed on different nodes. So, the system needs to transfer data files frequently between different edge nodes which is obviously unrealistic due to the high costs of communication. In order to overcome the defect of dynamic scheduling and minimize task completion time, the authors introduce the queuing theory and genetic algorithm into task scheduling problem in edge computing and propose a constrained static scheduling strategy which assigns tasks to fixed nodes. The main contributions of this paper are summarized as follows:

- In order to accurately describe the task scheduling and resource management problem in industrial internet, a system model is proposed where the task requests are sent by clients and processed by edge side or cloud side.

- In this paper, the task completion time is described from the perspective of probability according to queuing theory. And the task completion time minimization problem is transformed into an integer non-liner programming problem.
- A multi-elites-based co-evolutionary genetic algorithm (MEB-CGA) is proposed in this paper for the task completion time minimization problem. Experiment results show that the scheduling scheme obtained by MEB-CGA is reasonable and effectively in reducing task completion time. In addition, the MEB-CGA can reasonably balance the task workload on both edge and cloud sides.

The remainder of this paper is organized as follows: first the literature review is presented. Then, the system model is proposed; next, the task classification and mathematical mode of task completion time minimization problem is formulated and the genetic algorithm is proposed to solve it. Finally, the results and future work are discussed.

LITERATURE REVIEW

There are a lot of researches on task scheduling and resource management in edge-cloud system (Li, You, & Jiang, 2019; Alkayal, Jennings, & Abulkhai, 2017; Yin, Luo, & Luo, 2018). Most of the approaches focus on dynamic scheduling, which are needed to meet the QoS requirements of tasks, such as deadline (Zhang & Zhou, 2017), makespan (Panda & Jana, 2015), cost, service profit (Chen & Chang, 2015), etc. This section describes baseline concepts of various task scheduling approaches such as heuristic algorithm-based approach, deep learning-based approach and other task scheduling approaches.

Heuristic Algorithm-Based Approach

Since the task scheduling problem of cloud computing is an NP-complete problem (Singh, Dutta & Aggarwal, 2017), various studies have been made to obtain near optimal solution of it (Madni, Latiff, Abdullahi & Usman, 2017). Genetic Algorithm (GA) is a popular type of evolutionary algorithm which is used to optimize complex problems (Favre, Robyr, Gonon & Niederh, 2018). Wang and Li (2016) propose a multi-population genetic algorithm (MPGA) to solve the problem of task scheduling and load balancing in Cloud Computing. In their research, the min-max algorithm and max-min algorithm are used for the population initialization to improve the search efficiency. And the metropolis criterion is used to screen the offspring to maintain the population diversity. Hamad and Omara (2016) propose a scheduling algorithm based on Genetic Algorithm for allocating and executing the tasks of application. Their algorithm aims to minimize the completion time and cost of tasks.

In addition to genetic algorithms, ant colony algorithm and particle swarm algorithm are also commonly used for task scheduling. Guo (2017) proposes a multi-objective optimization algorithm for Cloud Computing task scheduling based on improved ant colony algorithm. He improves the initialization of the pheromone and the pheromone update method to find the optimal resource allocation for each task which minimizes the makespan and costs of tasks. Alkayal, Jennings and Abulkhair (2017) propose a methodology to optimize task scheduling based on the multi-optimization and particle swarm optimization algorithm. Through this algorithm, the scheduler takes over the virtual machines and decides which is the best virtual machine for task execution.

Deep Learning-Based Approach

Recently, as novel machine learning algorithms are becoming increasingly versatile and powerful, the deep learning has received wide attention from scholars in various fields. There exists some recent study about Deep Learning-based task scheduling for edge computing networks.

A distributed deep learning-based offloading algorithm is proposed by Huang, Feng, Feng, Huang and Qian (2018). The algorithm uses multiple deep neural networks to generate offloading decisions and selects the best decisions as the training data to train and improve all deep neural networks. However, this method seems to be affected by the complexity of scheduling. As the number of tasks and nodes increases, the performance of this method becomes unsatisfactory. Wei, Pan, Liu, Wu and Meng (2018) propose an intelligent QoS-aware job scheduling framework using Deep Reinforcement Learning. In this framework, a reinforcement learning-based job scheduler is introduced to learn to make appropriate task allocation decisions for continuous task requests directly from its experience without any prior knowledge.

Other Task Scheduling Approach

A method is proposed to decide the offloading sequence and decision in mobile edge computing (MEC) by Tao, Ota and Dong (2017). However, it only considers the task scheduling in edge computing and does not take into account resource management of servers. Deng, Lu, and Lai (2016) focus on rummaging the optimal workload allocations between fog and cloud toward the minimal power consumption with the constrained service delay. However, it only considers costs and energy consumption. Zeng, Gu, and Guo (2016) apply an allocation strategy processing requests at local fog platforms. The response times of this method is much faster compared to handling the task at centralized clouds. But this method gets a scheduling tendency rather than an accurate scheduling scheme.

An algorithm of task scheduling and resource management based on Markov Decision Process (MDP) is proposed by Li and Huang (2017) to obtain tradeoff decisions between energy costs and QoS requirements. A two-step decision process is introduced by Kolomvatsos and Anagnostopoulos (2019) to select the tasks which are suitable to be executed locally and allocate them to appropriate node. A dynamic task scheduling algorithm based on weighted bi-graph model is proposed by Wang, Wei and Liang (2018) to improve the implementation effects for the tasks. An improved cache replacement strategy for online videos, which sets multi-level label indexes for the video contents in the cache list of the content delivery networks node, is discussed to reduce server load and latency (Miao, Chen, & Jin, 2017).

SYSTEM MODEL

The system model is shown as Figure 1, which has been divided into three parts. Client(I) is introduced to denote the clients which consist of various IIoT devices, such as monitoring devices and some industrial sensors. Edge(E) is introduced to denote the edge which refers to the IPC (Industrial Personal Computer) directly connected to the industrial IIoT devices, and Cloud(K) is introduced to denote the cloud which is consisted of servers with high performance.

The clients are usually distributed in the industrial production sites and they are inter-connected with edge and cloud. The transmission latency between two nodes, e.g., the client i and the cloud node k, is denoted as l_{lik}, and the other symbols are summarized in Table 1.

Figure 1. System model

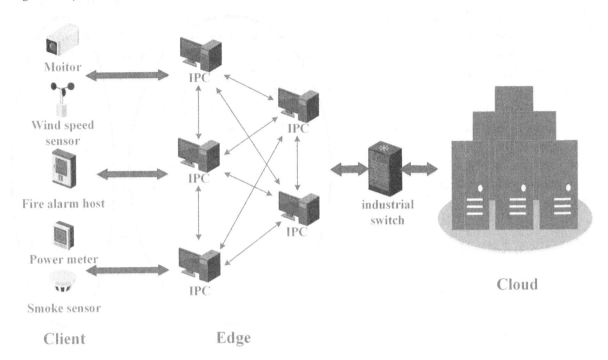

Table 1. Summary of notations

Symbol	Definition
K	The number of cloud nodes.
I	The number of clients.
E	The number of edge nodes.
T	The number of tasks.
μ_k^a	Service rate of edge node k.
μ_e^b	Service rate of cloud node e.
S_e	Storage resource of edge node e.
s_t	Data file size of task t
λ_t	Average request rate of task t.
l_{1ik}	Transmission latency between client i and cloud node k.
l_{2ie}	Transmission latency between client i and edge node e.
x_{glt}	Whether the task t have priority
c_{tk}^a	Whether the task t is processed in cloud node k
c_{te}^b	Whether the task t is processed in edge node e

In EC-ICS, task request is submitted by client and assigned to IPC (edge node) or cloud server (cloud node) for processing, and then the result is returned to the client. The total process is shown in Figure 2. As the outermost layer of the entire system, client will continuously submit task request over time. The system needs to assign the tasks to IPC or cloud servers. The processing of task in IPC and cloud server has different characteristic. Generally speaking, IPC has computation capabilities to execute the tasks. However, due to the limited computation capabilities to execute computation-complex tasks, the IPC can offload their tasks to the cloud servers (Zanzi, Giust, & Sciancalepore, 2018). The IPC usually lies in one-hop proximity to the IIoT sensors, so the transmission time will be lower if the task is processing in IPC. The cloud server has more computing and storage resource. Thus, the cloud servers have faster processing speed than IPC. But the cloud server tends to be geographically located away from the industrial scene. So, it will cause additional communication delays if the IPC offloading their tasks to cloud server.

Figure 2. Two types of task processing of system

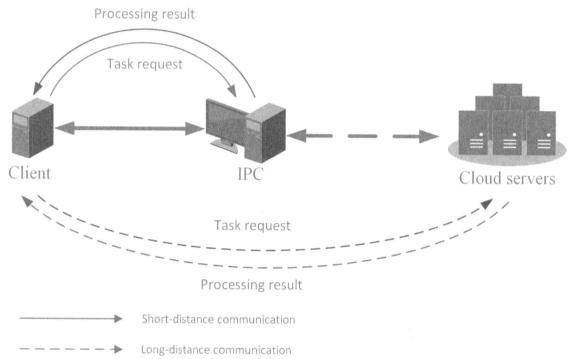

For those computation-complex tasks, it will take a long time to process the tasks on IPC. Cloud server with abundant storage and computing resource is naturally regarded as a good choice to reduce the execution time. Thus, the IPC should offload these tasks to the cloud server. But clients sometimes have requests which require low latency, examples are smart grid control applications and real time operational analytics of sensor data in energy generation and in the IIoT. In such cases, long latency between the cloud server and client is not desirable.

PROBLEM FORMULATION

In this section, a formal description of the problem about task scheduling and resource management is introduced and formulated into an integer non-liner programming problem.

Mathematical Expression of Task Scheduling Result

In order to translate the actual problem into a mathematical problem, two binary variables c_{tk}^a and c_{te}^b are introduced to denote the scheduling result, and they can be described as:

$$c_{tk}^a = \begin{cases} 1, & \text{if the task } t \text{ is proposed on cloud node } k \\ 0, & \text{others} \end{cases}$$

and:

$$c_{te}^b = \begin{cases} 1, & \text{if the task } t \text{ is proposed on edge node } e \\ 0, & \text{others} \end{cases}$$

In order to ensure the rationality of result, it is required that each task request must be assigned to a node for processing, whether it is a cloud node or an edge node. This leads to:

$$\sum_{k=1}^{K} c_{tk}^a + \sum_{e=1}^{E} c_{te}^b = 1, \ t = 1, 2, ..., T$$

Storage Resource Constraints

If a task is assigned to an edge node, the data files needed by this task must be placed on the corresponding edge node. For the edge node, it may store multiple data files for different tasks. But the storage resource of edge nodes is limited, so for each edge node, it must be ensured that:

$$\sum_{t=1}^{T} c_{te}^b s_t \leq S_e, e = 1, 2, ..., E$$

Analysis of Objective Function

The result of constrained static scheduling strategy is a scheduling scheme of task scheduling and resource management. Task completion time is the criterion to measure the performance of a scheduling scheme. The task completion time consists of two basic components, processing time and transmission time.

Analysis of Processing Time

The time between the task arriving at the computing node and the completion of the task is called processing time. It is consisted of two basic components, the time waiting in line for processing and the processing time.

The processing time of the task t depends on where the task processing takes place. For the cloud node, assuming that the task t is assigned to the cloud node k with the service rate μk the cloud node may be assigned more than one task. As the sum of multiple independent Poisson processes is still a Poisson process, the overall task arrival rate at cloud node k can be calculated as:

$$\Lambda_k = \sum_{t=1}^{T} c_{tk}^a \lambda_t, k = 1, 2, ..., K$$

According to the queuing theory, if the tasks arrival as the Poisson flow, the computation time is subject to an exponential distribution (Balla, Sheng, & Weipeng, 2018), so it can be regarded as a M/M/1 queue. The average computation time of all tasks at cloud node k can be thus calculated as:

$$\tau_k^{c1} = \cfrac{1}{\mu_k - \sum_{t=1}^{T} c_{tk}^a \lambda_t}, k = 1, 2, ..., K$$

The queuing becomes meaningless if the task arrival rate exceeds the service rate of service counter. Because in this case, the length of queue will increase without limit. In order to avoid this situation, it must be ensured that:

$$\mu_k > \sum_{t=1}^{T} c_{tk}^a \lambda_t, k = 1, 2, ..., K$$

Similarly, for the edge node e, the overall task arrival rate can be calculated as:

$$\Lambda_e = \sum_{t=1}^{T} c_{te}^b \lambda_t, e = 1, 2, ..., E$$

The average computation time of all tasks at cloud node e can be thus calculated as:

$$\tau_e^{c2} = \cfrac{1}{\mu_e - \sum_{t=1}^{T} c_{te}^b \cdot \lambda_t}, e = 1, 2, ..., E$$

and it must be ensured that:

$$\mu_e > \sum_{t=1}^{T} c_{te}^b \lambda_t, e = 1, 2, ..., E$$

This calculation method is only applicable when the tasks assigned on the node have the same priority. But in the actual production environment, this method is not suitable. In the actual production environment, some tasks require processing at high speed due to the importance of obtaining information in a timely manner, while other tasks require only good speed for processing. On the other hand, some tasks have stricter requirements for delays but others not. Just like the hospital will give priority to treating dying patients. Therefore, it is necessary to consider the case where some tasks have priority.

When the task with priority is assigned to the node, it can be queued to the front of the tasks without priority for processing. But it doesn't mean that the task with priority can always be processed first. According to the existing research, it will cause congestion in network if most tasks have priorities. In order to solve the queuing problem of multi-priority tasks, a non-preemptive limited-priority M/M/1 queuing system (Yewen, Hong, & Yuanshi, 2013) of task scheduling and resource management in EC-ICS is proposed to calculate the processing time when the node has tasks with different priorities.

Let the binary variable x_{g1t} indicating whether the task t have priority as:

$$x_{g1t} = \begin{cases} 1, & \text{if the task } t \text{ have priority} \\ 0, & \text{others} \end{cases}$$

The task with priority is called as first-level task and the task without priority as second-level task. Hence the overall task arrival rate of first-level and second-level tasks on cloud node k can be calculated as:

$$\Lambda_{k1} = \sum_{t=1}^{T} x_{g1t} c_{tk}^a \lambda_t, k = 1, 2, ..., K$$

$$\Lambda_{k2} = \sum_{t=1}^{T} \left(1 - x_{g1t}\right) c_{tk}^a \lambda_t, k = 1, 2, ..., K$$

The traffic intensity of tasks is expressed as:

$$\rho_{k1} = \frac{\Lambda_{k1}}{\mu_k}, k = 1, 2, ..., K$$

$$\rho_{k2} = \frac{\Lambda_{k2}}{\mu_k}, k = 1, 2, ..., K$$

where ρk_1 and $\rho k2$ represent the traffic intensity of first-level task and second-level task respectively. The overall traffic intensity on cloud node k can be calculated as:

$$\rho_k = \rho_{k1} + \rho_{k2} = \frac{\Lambda_{k1} + \Lambda_{k2}}{\mu_k}, k = 1, 2, \ldots, K$$

As the same, it must be ensured that:

$$\mu_k - \left(\sum_{t=1}^{T} x_{g1t} c_{tk}^a \lambda_t + \sum_{t=1}^{T} \left(1 - x_{g1t} \right) c_{tk}^a \lambda_t \right) > 0, k = 1, 2, \ldots, K$$

The W_{k1} is introduced to denote the processing time of first-level task and W_{k2} is introduced to denote the processing time of second-level task (Yewen, Hong, & Yuanshi, 2013). The following is a brief description of the formulas for W_{k1} and W_{k2} and the variables involved:

$$\begin{cases} W_{k1} = W_{q1} + \dfrac{1}{\mu} \\ W_{k2} = W_{q2} + \dfrac{1}{\mu} \end{cases}$$

where W_{q1} is the waiting time of first-level task and W_{q2} is the waiting time of second-level task. They can be calculated as:

$$\begin{cases} W_{q1} = W_{q1a1} P_{a1} + W_{q1a2} P_{a2} + W_{q1a3} P_{a3} \\ W_{q2} = W_{q2b1} P_{b1} + W_{q2b2} P_{b2} + W_{q2b3} P_{b3} \end{cases}$$

where:

$$\begin{cases} W_{q1a1} = \dfrac{\rho}{\mu(1 - \rho_1)} \\ W_{q1a2} = \dfrac{\rho}{\mu(1 - \rho_1 - \rho_2)} \\ W_{q1a3} = \dfrac{\rho}{\mu(1 - \rho_1 - \dfrac{\rho_1}{a})} - \dfrac{\rho_2(b + \rho)}{\mu(1 - \rho_2 - a\rho_2)(1 - \rho_1 - \dfrac{\rho_1}{a})} \end{cases}$$

$$\begin{cases} W_{q2b1} = \dfrac{b + \rho}{\mu(1 - \rho_2 - a\rho_2)} \\ W_{q2b2} = \dfrac{\rho_1 \rho}{\mu(1 - \rho_1)(1 - \rho_1 - \rho_2)} + \dfrac{\rho}{\mu(1 - \rho_1 - \rho_2)} \\ W_{q2b3} = \dfrac{b + \rho}{\mu(1 - \rho_2 - a\rho_2)} \end{cases}$$

where:

$$b = \sum_{i=1}^{a} (i-1)\rho_1^i + a\rho_2$$

where a is positive integer parameter which denotes the number of queues allowed to jump. When the task assigned to the node with different priority, the first-level task can be processed before they are queued to a second-level task, but each second-level task allows up to a first-level tasks to be queued before. The other variables involved are as follows:

$$P_{b1} = \frac{1-\rho_2}{1-\rho_1^a \rho_2}$$

$$P_{a1} = 1 - \frac{1-\rho_2}{1-\rho_1^a \rho_2}$$

$$P_{a2} = \begin{cases} \dfrac{1-\rho_2}{1-\rho_1^{\frac{a\rho_1}{\rho_1 - a\rho_2}}\rho_2}, & \text{if } \lambda_1 > a\lambda_2 \\ 0, & \text{others} \end{cases}$$

$$P_{a3} = 1 - P_{a1} - P_{a2}$$

$$P_{b2} = \begin{cases} 1 - \dfrac{1-\rho_2}{1-\rho_1^{a-\frac{\rho_1}{\rho_2}}\rho_2}, & \text{if } \lambda_1 < a\lambda_2 \\ 0, & \text{others} \end{cases}$$

$$P_{b3} = 1 - P_{b1} - P_{b2}$$

In order to minimize the processing time of first-level task, the τ_k^{c1} is proposed as the computation time of the cloud node k. Thus, the computation time of node k can be calculated as:

$$\tau_k^{c1} = W_{k1}, k = 1, 2, \ldots, K$$

Similarly, for the edge node e, if the tasks assigned on node e have same priority, the processing on edge node e can be also described as an M/M/1 queue. Hence the computation time of edge node e can be calculated as:

$$\tau_e^{c2} = \cfrac{1}{\mu_e - \sum\limits_{t=1}^{T} c_{te}^b \lambda_t}, e = 1,2,...,E$$

As same as cloud nodes, it must be guaranteed that the processing rate must be greater than total arrival rate of tasks. If the processing rate of edge node is lower than the arrival rate of task, this means that the queue length on the node will increase indefinitely over time. The queue system in this case is unstable. Therefore, it should be guaranteed that:

$$\mu_e > \sum_{t=1}^{T}\left(c_{te}^b \lambda_t\right), e = 1,2,...,E$$

If the task assigned on node e have different priority, the processing can be described as a non-preemptive limited-priority M/M/1 queue. Similarly, the tasks are divided into first-level tasks and second-level tasks. The overall task arrival rate of first-level and second-level tasks on edge node e can be calculated as:

$$\Lambda_{e1} = \sum_{t=1}^{T} x_{g1t} c_{te}^b \lambda_t, e = 1,2,...,E$$

$$\Lambda_{e2} = \sum_{t=1}^{T} (1 - x_{g1t}) c_{te}^b \lambda_t, e = 1,2,...,E$$

The overall traffic intensity on edge node e can be calculated as:

$$\rho_e = \frac{\Lambda_{e1} + \Lambda_{e2}}{\mu_e}, e = 1,2,...,E$$

and it must be ensured that:

$$\mu_e - \left(\sum_{t=1}^{T} x_{g1t} c_{te}^b \lambda_t + \sum_{t=1}^{T}\left(1 - x_{g1t}\right) c_{te}^b \lambda_t\right) > 0, e = 1,2,...,E$$

As same as the cloud node, the W_{e1} is introduced to denote the processing time of first-level tasks and W_{e2} is introduced to denote the processing time of second-level tasks, so:

$$W_{e1} = W_{q1} + \frac{1}{\mu}$$

$$W_{e2} = W_{q2} + \frac{1}{\mu}$$

where W_{q1} is the waiting time of first-level task and W_{q2} is the waiting time of second-level task. They can be calculated as (18). The processing time of node $k \in K$ can be calculated as:

$$\tau_e^{c2} = W_{e1}, e = 1,2,...,E$$

The queuing model should be determined first before a practical problem is solved as a queuing problem. Therefore, it is necessary to determine the distribution of customer arrival time intervals. Generally speaking, the task request arise randomly as a Poisson process from each client and the task completion time is exponentially distributed on a computation server. So, the system is regarded as multiple M/M/1 systems.

In some special scenarios, the system may have other distributions. In queuing theory, there are a lot of research on queuing models. For different scenarios (e.g., Kingman's approximation of the processing time), different queuing models can be used to calculate the task completion time (Baek, Lee, Ahn, & Bae, 2016; Yewen, Shenfen, Yongling, & Chunxia, 2016).

Analysis of Transmission Time

The task request is submitted by client and translated to the edge or cloud node for processing. The time spent in this process is called transmission time. The transmission time is determined by the transmission latency between client and edge or cloud node. The l_{ie} is introduced to denote the transmission latency between client i and edge node e, and use the l_{ik} to denote the transmission latency between client i and cloud node k. For example, the transmission time of task t on cloud node k is:

$$\tau_{tk}^a = \sum_{i=1}^{I} b_{ti} c_{tk}^a l_{ik}, t = 1,2,...,T, \ k = 1,2,...,K$$

where the b_{ti} is introduced to denote whether the task t is submitted by client i, it can be described as:

$$b_{ti} = \begin{cases} 1, & \text{if the task } t \in T \text{ is submitted by client } i \\ 0, & \text{the task } t \in T \text{ is not submitted by client } i \end{cases}$$

So, the average transmission time of the tasks assigned to cloud node k is:

$$\overline{\tau_k^a} = \frac{\sum_{t=1}^{T} \tau_{tk}^a}{\sum_{t=1}^{T} c_{tk}^a \lambda_t}, k = 1,2,...,K$$

Similarly, the transmission time of task t on cloud node e is:

$$\tau_{te}^{b} = \sum_{i=1}^{I} b_{ti} c_{te}^{b} l_{ie}, t = 1, 2, ..., T, \ e = 1, 2, ..., E$$

The average transmission time on edge node can be calculated as:

$$\overline{\tau_{e}^{b}} = \frac{\sum_{t=1}^{T} \tau_{te}^{b}}{T \sum_{t=1}^{T} c_{te}^{b} \lambda_{t}}, e = 1, 2, ..., E$$

Objective Function

The goal of this paper is to produce an optimal scheduling scheme. In other words, the goal of the article is to minimize the maximum average task completion time of all node. The p_k^a is introduced to denote the task completion time of cloud node k and p_e^a is introduced to denote the task completion time of edge node e as:

$$p_k^a = \tau_k^{c1} + \overline{\tau_k^a}, k = 1, 2, ..., K$$

$$p_e^b = \tau_e^{c2} + \overline{\tau_e^b}, e = 1, 2, ..., E$$

The variable t_{max} is introduced to denote the maximum time of all node and it can be calculated as:

$$t_{\max} = \max(p_1^a, p_2^a, ..., p_K^a, p_1^b, p_2^b, ... p_E^b)$$

Therefore, the aim is transferred into minimize the value of t_{max}.

Optimization Problem Formulation

From the discussed above, the calculation method of task completion time is obtained in EC-ICS. The problem of task scheduling and resource management can be solved by minimizing the t_{max}, and this can be regarded as an INLP called EC-ICS-INLP. The EC-ICS-INLP is described as shown follows:

EC-ICE-INLP:

$$\min : t_{\max}$$

$$\text{s.t.:} \sum_{k=1}^{K} c_{tk}^a + \sum_{e=1}^{E} c_{te}^b = 1, \ t = 1, 2, ..., T$$

$$\sum_{t=1}^{T} c_{te}^{b} s_{t} \leq S_{e}, e = 1, 2, \ldots, E$$

$$\mu_{k} > \sum_{t=1}^{T} c_{tk}^{a} \lambda_{t}, k = 1, 2, \ldots, K$$

$$\mu_{k} - \left(\sum_{t=1}^{T} x_{g1t} c_{tk}^{a} + \sum_{t=1}^{T} \left(1 - x_{g1t}\right) c_{tk}^{a} \lambda_{t} \right) > 0, k = 1, 2, \ldots, K$$

$$\mu_{e} > \sum_{t=1}^{T} \left(c_{te}^{b} \lambda_{t}\right), e = 1, 2, \ldots, E$$

$$\mu_{e} - \left(\sum_{t=1}^{T} x_{g1t} c_{te}^{b} + \sum_{t=1}^{T} \left(1 - x_{g1t}\right) c_{te}^{b} \lambda_{t} \right) > 0, e = 1, 2, \ldots, E$$

Task Screening Strategy

Not all the tasks are suitable for static task scheduling. A strategy is needed to select the right tasks from all. In order to achieve this goal, a task screening strategy is proposed in this paper. In this strategy, the tasks which are unsuitable for the static task scheduling can be eliminated. And the remaining tasks are suitable for the static scheduling. The strategy can be described as follows:

Step 1: Screening based on arrival rate of task.

According to the queuing theory, the queuing becomes meaningless if the arrival rate of task exceeds the service rate of compute node. Because in this case, the length of queue will increase without limit. Therefore, the arrival rate of the task should be detected. If the arrival rate of task exceeds the service rate of node, the task should be removed from task set. And these tasks can only be allocated by dynamic scheduling.

Step 2: Screening based on the size of data file.

The storage resource of edge nodes is limited. The size of the data file required by the task cannot exceed the storage capacity of the node. Hence the size of data file should be detected to remove the tasks whose data file size exceeds the node's storage capacity from task set. The data files of the removed task can only be placed on cloud. And these tasks can be processed in the cloud nodes by dynamic scheduling. Many scholars have put forward effective solutions to this problem such as Zhang and Zhou (2017) which will not be described in detail here.

Step 3: Screening based on the attribute of task.

There are two types of task, delay-tolerant task and delay-intolerant task. For a delay-intolerant task, once the task request is received, it must be immediately assigned to a node for processing. Therefore, it is obviously that the delay-intolerant task is unsuitable for static scheduling. The delay-intolerant tasks should be removed from task set and processed immediately after the task request appears.

Step 4: Screening based the deadline of task.

For each task, deadline is a hard constraint. The task must be processed and return the result before deadline. In other words, the completion time must be less than deadline. The n_t is introduced to denote the number of tasks. The number of cloud node is n_c and the number of edge node is n_e. A new variable s is introduced which can be calculate as:

$$s = \left\lceil \frac{n_t}{n_c + n_f} \right\rceil$$

The meaning of s is that at least s tasks are assigned to the same node. Firstly, the tasks are arranged from large to small according to the arrival rate. Then the first s tasks are assigned to each node. Finally, the completion time of each node is calculated and the maximum value is recorded as t_m. For a task, if the deadline of task is less than t_m, the task can be retained for static scheduling. If the deadline of task is larger than t_m, the task should be removed from task set.

Determination of Task Priority

There are two types of task in EC-ICS, the first-level task (task with priority) and the second-level task (task without priority), and the x_{glt} is introduced to denote the level of task. The x_{glt} is determined by the deadline and t_m. Let d_t to denote the deadline of task t. A new variable k is introduced which is called classification coefficient. Therefore, the x_{glt} can be described as:

$$x_{glt} = \begin{cases} 1, & \text{if } d_t < k \cdot t_{max} \\ 0, & \text{if } d_t > k \cdot t_{max} \end{cases}$$

MULTI-ELITES-BASED CO-EVOLUTIONARY GENETIC ALGORITHM

Since the EC-ICS-INLP is an NP-hard problem, it is difficult to solve it directly. So, the heuristic algorithms are used to find the optimum solution for the EC-ICS-INLP problem. In this paper, a multi-elites-based co-evolutionary genetic algorithm (MEB-CGA) is proposed to solve the EC-ICS-INLP.

Representation of Solutions

The most commonly used representation of solutions is an array of tasks for each node. For example, each task is represented by a number from 1, ..., N, where N is the total number of tasks in EC-ICS.

Due to the limitation of service rate and storage resource, the number of tasks that can be assigned to each node is different. In other words, the capacity of each node to hold tasks is different. Hence it is essential to know the capacity of each node.

The capacity of each node is determined by the service rate and the storage resource of node. Two new variables n_e and n_k are introduced to denote the capacity of edge node and cloud node. For the edge node, both service rate and storage resource are limited. Hence the n_e can be calculated as:

$$n_e = \max\left(\left\lfloor\frac{\mu_e}{\min\{\lambda_t\}}\right\rfloor, \left\lfloor\frac{S_e}{\min\{s_t\}}\right\rfloor\right)\Delta t = 1,2,...,T$$

where the n_e is the maximum number of tasks that can be assigned to the edge node e. For the cloud node k, the only constraint is service rate. Therefore, the n_k can be calculated as:

$$n_k = \max\left(\left\lfloor\frac{\mu_k}{\min\{\lambda_t\}}\right\rfloor\right), t = 1,2,...,T$$

where the n_k is the maximum number of tasks that can be assigned to the cloud node k. Therefore, the length of chromosome L can be calculated as:

$$L = \sum_{e=1}^{E} n_e + \sum_{k=1}^{K} n_k$$

Figure 3. Sample chromosome in EC-ICS-INLP

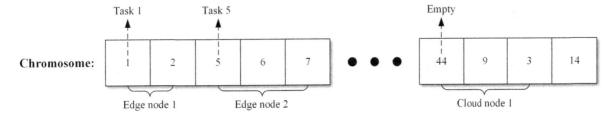

The L is must be more than N, hence the numbers 1, ..., N, can be used to denote the tasks and numbers N+1, ..., L, can be used to represent empty. The $\sum_{e=1}^{E} n_e$ bits denote edge nodes and the next $\sum_{k=1}^{K} n_k$ bits represent cloud nodes. For example, assuming the number of tasks N is 30, a sample encoding of a solution would be as in Figure 3.

This coding method can present the scheduling scheme efficiently and simply. A new individual can be obtained by changing the order of the numbers. The only thing should be noted is that the individual generated by this method may not meet the requirement of constraints. Every new individual should be checked for compliance with the constraints. Only individuals which satisfying constraints can be retained.

Fitness Function

In this paper, in order to maintain the diversity of population, two different fitness functions are proposed for evaluating individual in the population.

Fitness Function for Accelerating Convergence Speed

The first fitness function adopts the conventional strategy, that is, the fitness determined by the t_{max}. The smaller the value of t_{max}, the higher the fitness value is. The value of objective function t_{max} denotes the maximum task completion time of all nodes. But the goal is to minimize t_{max}, so the dynamic linear calibration method is used to transform t_{max} into fitness value. Let F denotes the fitness value of individual, f denotes the individual's value of objective function, $f_{\max}^k$ denotes the maximum objective function of the k generation population. The F can be calculated as:

$$F = -f + f_{\max}^k + \xi^k$$

where ξ^k is a constant greater than zero.

Fitness Function for Maintaining Population Diversity

Although the first fitness function can effectively evaluate individuals, it will dramatically reduce the diversity of algorithm, resulting in premature convergence of the algorithm. In this paper, a new variable $D(i, j)$ is introduced to denote the degree of discrepancy between individual a_i and a_j. $P = \{a_1, a_2, ..., a_n\}$ is the collection of individuals which are contained in a population. The $D(i, j)$ can be calculated as:

$$D(i, j) = \frac{1}{n_s} \sum_{l=1}^{n_s} (a_{li} - a_{lj}), \quad i, j = 1, 2, ..., n$$

where n_s is the length of chromosome and:

$$a_{li} - a_{lj} = \begin{cases} 0, a_{li} \neq a_{lj} \\ 1, a_{li} = a_{lj} \end{cases}$$

where a_{li}, a_{lj} represent the l-place values of individual i and j.

Therefore, the second fitness function F' can be described as:

$$F' = D(i, j) \times F$$

Double Elitist Preservation

In order to improve the global searching ability of MEB-CGA, two elites are set to ensure that the algorithm can find the best solution.

In this paper, two elites, *EliteA* and *EliteB* are set as evolutionary center. *EliteA* is the best individual from the elite set. *EliteB* is selected from the elite set using the roulette. And the *EliteB* must be different from *EliteA*. The algorithm sets up two different groups of evolutionary teams, *TeamA* and *TeamB*, to generate the next generation population. The selection criteria of members of two evolutionary teams are different. When selecting members of *TeamA*, the fitness values of population are calculated with the first fitness function. Assume the population size is N. Then the first $N/4$ individuals with higher fitness values are selected as members of *TeamA*. When selecting members of *TeamB*, the new fitness values of population are calculated with the second fitness function and the first $N/4$ individuals with higher fitness values are selected as members of *TeamB*.

In addition, the goals of the two evolutionary groups are different. The evolutionary group *TeamA*, which takes *EliteA* as core, aims to improve the convergence speed of algorithm. And the evolutionary group *TeamB*, which takes *EliteB* as core, aims to improve population diversity. The evolutionary model of *TeamA* is shown in Figure 4.

Figure 4. Evolutionary model of TeamA

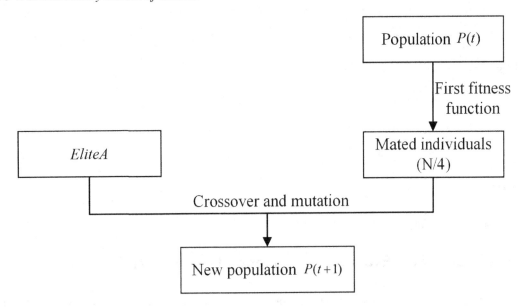

In order to maintain the diversity of the population and avoid premature convergence caused by selection pressure. The evolutionary group *TeamB*, which takes *EliteB* as core, uses the second fitness function. In addition, the random population is introduced to increase the diversity of the population. The evolutionary model of *TeamB* is shown in Figure 5 where the parameter r is used to adjust the size of random population.

Figure 5. Evolutionary model of TeamB

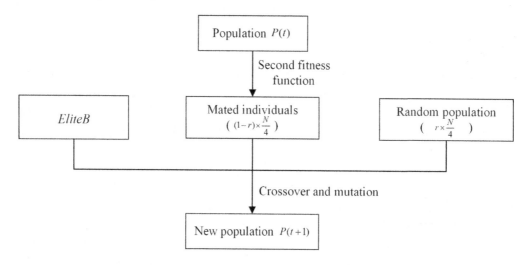

Let t to denote the evolution times, d to denote the adjustment step, *maxGen* to denote the maximum of evolutionary times. A new dynamic variable α is introduced as:

$$
\alpha = \begin{cases}
0, t \in [0, \dfrac{maxGen}{4}] \\[2mm]
1, t \in [\dfrac{maxGen}{4}, \dfrac{maxGen}{2}] \\[2mm]
2, t \in [\dfrac{maxGen}{2}, \dfrac{3 \cdot maxGen}{4}] \\[2mm]
3, t \in [\dfrac{3 \cdot maxGen}{4}, maxGen]
\end{cases}
$$

So, the r can be calculated as:

$$r = r_0 + \alpha \times d$$

where r_0 is a fixed parameter, d is step size.

Multi-Elites-Based Co-Evolutionary Genetic Algorithm (MEB-CGA)

The purpose of the algorithm proposed in this paper is to obtain the optimal solution of the mathematical of EC-ICS. From a practical point of view, the task scheduling and resource management are converted into decimal encoding. After the optimal solution is obtained by the algorithm, the final scheduling scheme is obtained by decoding. The whole process of genetic algorithm is shown as Figure 6.

Figure 6. The process of MEB-CGA

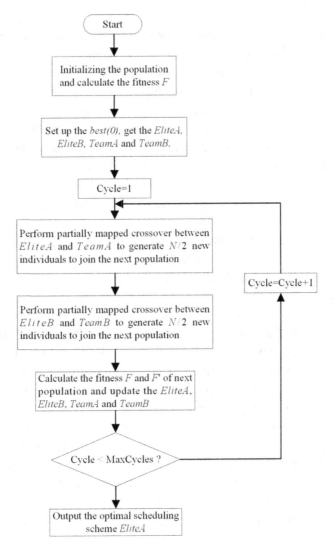

SIMULATION EXPERIMENTS

To evaluate the efficiency of the proposed Multi-elites-based co-evolutionary genetic algorithm (MEB-CGA), a simulator is strictly developed according to the system model defined in SYSTEM MODEL. In addition, in order to embody the superiority and rationality of the restricted static task scheduling policy proposed in this paper, two comparison objects are introduced, i.e., Cloud Greedy and Edge Greedy (Zeng, Gu, Guo, Cheng, &Yu, 2016) task scheduling policies. The Cloud Greedy policy first schedules tasks to cloud nodes until all the cloud node are fully loaded. The remaining tasks will be scheduled to the edge nodes. On the contrary, the Edge Greedy policy first scheduling the tasks to edge nodes until all the edge nodes are fully loaded. Both the two greedy policy assign the current task to the current optimal node during the running of algorithm.

Simulation Environment

According to the system model defined above. Three kinds of nodes are set in simulator. The first kind of node is client. The function of the client is to make a task request to the system. The number of three kinds of nodes is all set as 10. In the industrial production environment, the types of task requests are usually limited. During the operation of the system, these clients will submit certain task requests to the system from time to time. Thus, in the simulator, each client contains one or more task requests.

The other two nodes are edge nodes and cloud nodes. In the actual environment, the edge nodes are mostly composed of IPC, and the cloud nodes are generally composed of high-performance servers. Therefore, both the computing service and storage capacity of edge nodes are worse than cloud nodes. In order to make the simulation experiment closer to the real situation, the service rates of cloud nodes are set as 30 and the service rate of edge nodes are all set as 10. The storage of resources of edge nodes are all set as 40. But considering the actual situation, the edge nodes are also responsible for other works, such as data collection, thus the storage resource availability rate of each edge node is set within the range of [0.7, 1.0]. In other words, for an edge node, if the storage resource availability rate is 0.8, the actual available storage resource for this node is 32.

In the simulator, the data files needed by each task have different sizes which are randomly set within the range of [20, 36]. The reason for setting parameters like this is to ensure that the cloud node can take on more computing tasks than the edge node, and the processing time of the cloud node is lower than that of the edge node. The upper limit of the task arrival rate is set to 10. Because according to the constraints in the above, the arrival rate of the task cannot exceed the service rate of the node. In the subsequent simulations, the arrival rate of the task is set to different values to observe its effect on the scheduling result of the algorithm proposed in this paper.

Considering that the edge node is closer to the client, the transmission latencies between clients and edge nodes are randomly set in the range of [0.1, 0.4] and the transmission latencies between clients and cloud nodes are randomly set in the range of [0.4, 1.2]. The purpose of this setup is also to ensure that the simulation is closer to the real environment, that is, different tasks tend to be assigned to different nodes due to different task parameters. For a task, if the task arrival rate is higher, it is more suitable for the cloud node; if the task arrival rate is lower, it may be more suitable for the edge node.

Table 2. Setting values of experimental parameters

Item	Value
Population size N	200
The size of elite set M	5
r_0	0.1
Step size d	0.3
Maximum number of iterations	500
α	4

Parameter Setting of the Algorithm

In order to verify the feasibility and effectiveness of the algorithm, a data file was randomly generated for simulation experiments. The related parameters about the algorithm are set as Table 2.

On the Effect of Task Arrival Rate

In this set of simulation, the results of three algorithms, "Edge Greedy", "Cloud Greedy" and "MEB-CGA" are compared under different task arrival rates. The number of tasks is set as 18, and the tasks are randomly distributed among 10 clients. The service rate of edge nodes is set as 10 and the service rate of cloud nodes is set as 30. In general speaking, task arrival rate will affect the processing time of tasks assigned on node. When the arrival rate of the task approaches the service rate of the node, the processing time of the task on the node increases sharply. And the edge nodes are more susceptible to the task arrival rate due to their poor processing capacity. Therefore, two cases are considered for the experiment. In the first case, the task arrival rate starts at 5 and increases by 0.25 each time until it increases to 7.5. In the second case, the task arrival starts at 7.25 and increases by 0.25 each time until it increases to 9.5.

The experimental results in the first case are illustrated in Figure 7. It can be viewed that the performance of "MEB-CGA" is always better than the "Edge Greedy" and "Cloud Greedy" algorithm. For the "Cloud Greedy", the arrival rate of task is much lower than the service rate of cloud nodes. Even if two tasks are assigned to same cloud node, the total arrival rate of tasks on the cloud node is far lower than the service rate. The task completion time of cloud node is mainly affected by transmission delay. Therefore, the "Cloud Greedy" is insensitive to the change of task arrival rate. And the performance of "Edge Greedy" is better than "Cloud Greedy". For the "Edge Greedy", the task arrival rate is also lower than the service rate. However, with the increase of task arrival rate, the min-max task completion time of "Edge Greedy" is also increases gradually due to the lower computation capabilities. For the "MEB-CGA", when the task arrival rate is relatively small, tasks are reasonably assigned to edge nodes or cloud nodes. Thus, the min-max task completion time of "MEB-CGA" is lower than the other greedy algorithm.

The experimental results in the second case are illustrated in Figure 8. For "Edge greedy", as the task arrival rate increase, the min-max task completion time keeps increasing. The "Edge Greedy" reach the same performance as "Cloud Greedy" when the task arrival rate reach 7.75. The reason is that as the task arrival rate is getting closer to the service rate of the edge node, the processing time increases rapidly and becomes the main factor affecting the task completion time of edge nodes. This also explains why the min-max task completion time of "Edge Greedy" increases dramatically when the task arrival rate reaches around 9. When the task arrival rate around 7.75, the performance of "MEB-CGA" comes very close to "Edge Greedy". This is because in this situation, since the task arrival rate is close to the service rate of the edge node, the processing time of the task on the edge node becomes very long which causes the task completion time on the edge nodes exceed cloud nodes. Therefore, the "MEB-CGA" allocates almost all tasks to the cloud nodes. However, as the task arrival rate continues to increase, the min-max task completion time of "Cloud Greedy" also begins to increase. And the advantages of "MEB-CGA" are gradually revealed.

Figure 7. On the effect of task arrival rate in the first case

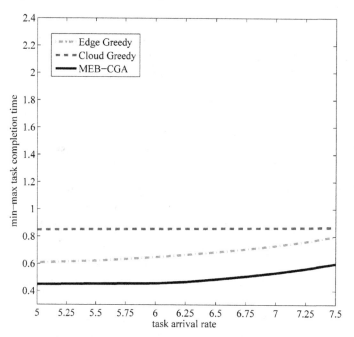

Figure 8. On the effect of task arrival rate in the second case

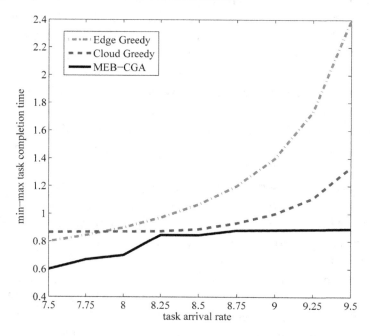

On the Effect of Service Rate of Edge Nodes

In this set of simulation, the results of three algorithms, "Edge Greedy", "Cloud Greedy" and "MEB-CGA" are compared under different service rates of edge nodes. In order to make the experiment as close as possible to the actual situation. The number of tasks is set as 18, and the tasks are randomly distributed among 10 clients. The task arrival rate is set as 7 and the service rate of cloud nodes is set as 30. In general speaking, the service rate of edge nodes will affect the processing time. In order to explore the influence of the change of edge node's service rate on the three algorithms. Two cases are considered for the experiment. In the first case, the task arrival rate starts at 8 and increases by 0.25 each time until it increases to 10.5. In the second case, the task arrival rate starts at 10.5 and increases by 0.25 each time until it increases to 13.

Figure 9 illustrates the min-max task completion time of "Edge Greedy", "Cloud Greedy" and "MEB-CGA" algorithms in the first case. Because the number of tasks does not reach the load limit of the cloud node. The tasks are all assigned to the cloud nodes in "Cloud Greedy". So, the performance of "Cloud Greedy" is not affected by the service rate of edge nodes. For the "Edge Greedy", it can be viewed from Figure 9 that when the service rate of edge node is below 9, the min-max task completion time is much higher than the other two algorithms. This is because the service rate of edge nodes is very close to the task arrival rate. So, the processing time in edge nodes is quite high. However, as the service rate of edge nodes increases, the advantages of edge nodes begin to emerge and the min-max task completion time drops rapidly. When the service rate of edge node exceeds 8, the min-max task completion time of "Edge Greedy" is lower than "Cloud Greedy". For the "MEB-CGA", when the service rate of edge nodes is under 9, the tasks are all assigned to the cloud nodes. Therefore, the change of service rate of edge node has no effect on the results of the algorithm. When the service rate of edge node exceeds 9, the advantages of edge nodes begin to manifest. The min-max task completion time of "MEB-CGA" decreases with the increase of service rate.

Figure 9. On the effect of edge nodes' service rate in the first case

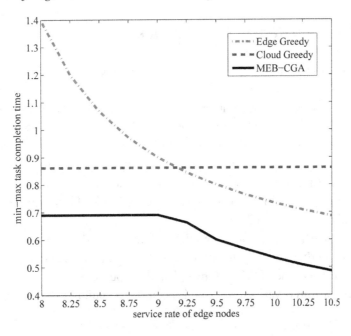

Figure 10 illustrates the min-max task completion time of "Edge Greedy", "Cloud Greedy" and "MEB-CGA" algorithm in the second case. It can be reviewed that with the increase of service rate of edge node, the min-max task completion time of "Edge Greedy" decreases continuously. However, the rate of decline in the second case is much lower than that in first case. Similarly, the min-max task completion time of "MEB-CGA" is also decreasing, and the rate of reduction is also much smaller than that in first case. What these two cases have in common is that the performance of "MEB-CGA" is always better than the other two greedy algorithms.

Figure 10. On the effect of edge nodes' service rate in the second case

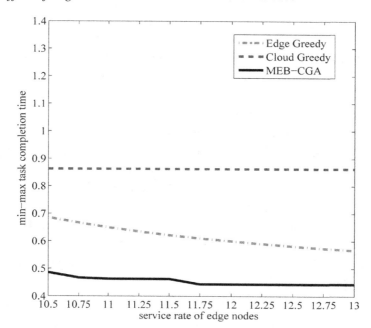

On the Effect of Service Rate of Cloud Nodes

In this set of simulation, the results of three algorithms, "Edge Greedy", "Cloud Greedy" and "MEB-CGA" are compared under different service rate of cloud nodes. In order to make the experiment as close as possible to the actual situation. The number of tasks is set as 18, and the tasks are randomly distributed among 10 clients. The task arrival rate is set as 7 and the service rate of edge nodes is set as 10. In general speaking, the service rate of cloud nodes will affect the processing time. In order to explore the influence of the change of cloud node's service rate on the three algorithms. Two cases are considered for the experiment. In the first case, the service rate of cloud nodes starts at 24.25 and increases by 0.25 each time until it increases to 27. In the second case, the task arrival rate starts at 27.25 and increases by 0.25 each time until it increases to 29.5.

Figure 11 illustrates the min-max task completion time of "Edge Greedy", "Cloud Greedy" and "MEB-CGA" algorithm in the first case. It can be seen that, as the service rate of cloud nodes increase, the min-max task completion time of "Edge Greedy" and "Cloud Greedy" are all declining and the performance of the two algorithm is very close. That is because the number of tasks exceeds the maximum load of edge nodes, so some task is assigned to cloud nodes in "Edge Greedy" algorithm. For the cloud nodes, the number of tasks is far from the full load of cloud nodes. In this case, although the computation time of tasks on edge nodes is relatively large, the task completion time of edge nodes is generally less than that of cloud nodes because of the small transmission time. In other words, the min-max task completion time is determined by the task completion time of cloud nodes. However, since "MEB-CGA" algorithm can always find a balance between cloud and edge, the change of service rate of cloud nodes has little effect on the results of "MEB-CGA". As the service rate of cloud nodes increases, the min-max task completion time of "Edge Greedy" and "Cloud Greedy" are both decrease.

Figure 11. On the effect of cloud nodes' service rate in first case

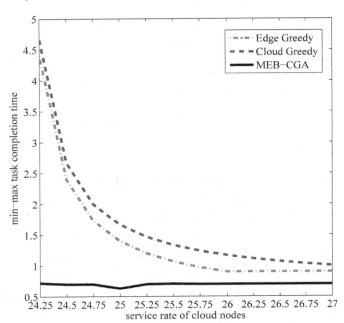

Figure 12 illustrates the min-max task completion time of "Edge Greedy", "Cloud Greedy" and "MEB-CGA" algorithm in the first case. It can be seen that, when the service rate of cloud node reaches 27.25. The performance of "MEB-CGA" is no longer changing. The reason is that the task completion time of cloud nodes is generally smaller than the edge nodes. For the "Cloud Greedy", with the increase of cloud nodes' service rate. The min-max task completion time is decreasing, but the decline rate is getting smaller and smaller. Although the change of "MEB-CGA" is not obvious, the performance of "MEB-CGA" is always better than the two greedy algorithms.

On the Effect of the Number of Tasks

In this set of simulation, the min-max task completion time of "MEB-CGA", "Edge Greedy" and "Cloud Greedy" algorithms is compared under different numbers of task. In order to make the experiment as close as possible to the actual situation. The task arrival rate is set as 7, the service rate of edge nodes is set as 10 and the service rate of cloud nodes is set as 30.

Figure 12. On the effect of cloud nodes' service rate in second case

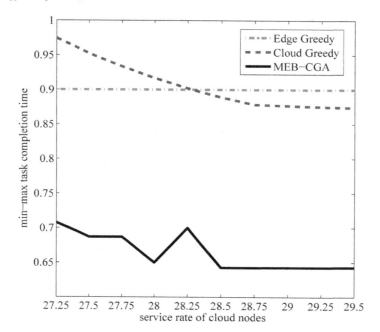

Performance results for this set of simulation are illustrated in Figure 13. It can be viewed that as the number of tasks increases, the min-max task completion time of the three algorithms is generally increased. However, no matter how the number of tasks changes, the performance of "MEB-CGA" is obviously better than that of two greedy algorithms. When the number of tasks is less than 14, the performance gap of the three algorithms is relatively small, especially the performance of the two greedy algorithms is almost the same. As the number of tasks continues to increase, the min-max completion time of Edge Greedy and Cloud Greedy algorithms begins to rise. But the "MEB-CGA" remains unchanged and the gap between the two greedy algorithms and "MEB-CGA" is gradually widens. When the number of tasks increase to 20, the min-max task completion time of the "MEB-CGA" begins to rise. After that, the gap between "Edge Greedy" and "MEB-CGA" remained at a relatively stable level. But there is a noticeable rise in cloud-greedy algorithm when the number of tasks rise to 27. The sudden rise may be due to the almost full load of cloud computing, so there are too few nodes to choose from for the tasks scheduled later.

Analysis of the Standard Deviation

For each group of simulation data in the previous, the task completion time of each point in the scheduling scheme obtained by the three algorithms are recorded. The change about standard deviation of task completion time in each scheduling scheme is showed in Figure 14.

It can be viewed from Figure 14 that when the number of tasks is under 12, the results of the three algorithms are small. As the number of tasks increase, the standard deviation of task completion time of the three algorithms becomes lager, especially the "Cloud Greedy" shows a significant increase. The value of "MEB-CGA" and "Edge Greedy" rise more smoothly. Obviously, the performance of "MEB-CGA" is the best in three algorithms. This fully demonstrates that the scheduling scheme obtained by "MEB-CGA" can achieve better load balancing.

Figure 13. On the effect of number of tasks

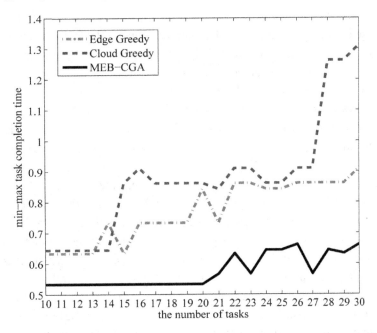

Figure 14. Standard deviation of task completion time

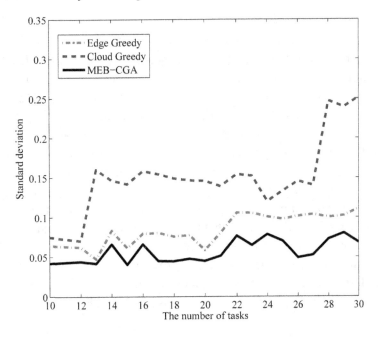

THE FUTURE WORK

The approach proposed in this paper is a part of the application of edge computing in industrial internet. This method effectively avoids the problem of data transmission between edge nodes through the form of static scheduling. The role of the edge computing node is fully utilized, which effectively enhances the processing power of the system and reduces the system delay.

The approach provides a new way to solve the problem of task scheduling of edge computing in the Industrial Internet and can map to more scenarios. For example, fog computing is a term created by Cisco which refers to extending computing to the edge of the network. In fog computing, the intermediate nodes (e.g., cloudlets) can host significant part of the workloads in addition to traditional clouds and edge devices. Similar to edge nodes and cloud nodes, these intermediate nodes can also be regarded as a compute node with certain computing and storage capabilities. As long as the relevant information of these nodes can be obtained, such as computing rate, storage capacity of nodes, transmission delay, the static task scheduling strategy proposed in this paper can also reasonably assign tasks to these nodes. Thus, the approach proposed in this paper can be easily mapped to fog computing and other similar scenarios.

The scheduling strategy proposed in this paper is a static scheduling strategy. According to the Task screening strategy mentioned above, some tasks are removed from the task set. In the future work, the proposed approach can add dynamic scheduling content to deal with these removed tasks. Moreover, more parameters can be added based on the requirements of actual production scenario.

CONCLUSION

In this paper, the main purpose is to come up with an optimal scheme of task scheduling and data files placement which can reduce the computation time for the submitted tasks and improve the utilization of computing resources in EC-ICS. In optimal placement of data files, the problem of data files transmission between edge nodes is avoided due to the static scheduling method. Thus, there is no need to keep much duplicate files and the utilization efficiency of storage resource is improved. In optimal scheduling of tasks, the queuing theory is introduced to calculate the expected value of task completion time and transform the optimization problem into an integer non-liner programming problem. And the multi-elites-based co-evolutionary genetic algorithm (MEB-CGA) is proposed to solve the non-liner programming problem. Finally, simulation experiments are conducted to demonstrate the performance of task scheduling strategy. The results show that the performance of proposed algorithm is better than the two greedy algorithms. And the validity and universal applicability of MEB-CGA has also proved by the simulation experiments. With the development of IIoT, edge computing will play a more and more important role in industrial internet. The model and solution proposed in this paper will provide new insight for solving the task scheduling and resource management problem in an edge cloud environment.

ACKNOWLEDGMENT

This work was supported by National Key Research and Development Program of China [2017YFB0304100]; Natural Science Foundation of Hebei Province of China [F2017501107]; Open Research Fund from the

State Key Laboratory of Rolling and Automation; Northeastern University [2017RALKFKT003] and Foundation of Northeastern University at Qinhuangdao [No. XNB201803].

REFERENCES

Acemoglu, D., & Restrepo, P. (2018). Artificial intelligence, automation and work (No. w24196). National Bureau of Economic Research.

Alkayal, E. S., Jennings, N. R., & Abulkhair, M. F. (2017, November). Survey of task scheduling in cloud computing based on particle swarm optimization. In *2017 International Conference on Electrical and Computing Technologies and Applications (ICECTA)* (pp. 1-6). IEEE. 10.1109/ICECTA.2017.8251985

Baek, J. W., Lee, H. W., Ahn, S., & Bae, Y. H. (2016). Exact time-dependent solutions for the M/D/1 queue. *Operations Research Letters*, *44*(5), 692–695. doi:10.1016/j.orl.2016.08.003

Balla, H. A., Sheng, C. G., & Weipeng, J. (2018, April). Reliability enhancement in cloud computing via optimized job scheduling implementing reinforcement learning algorithm and queuing theory. In *2018 1st International Conference on Data Intelligence and Security (ICDIS)* (pp. 127-130). IEEE. 10.1109/ICDIS.2018.00027

Brogi, A., & Forti, S. (2017). QoS-aware deployment of IoT applications through the fog. *IEEE Internet of Things Journal*, *4*(5), 1185–1192. doi:10.1109/JIOT.2017.2701408

Chen, Y. W., & Chang, J. M. (2015). EMaaS: Cloud-based energy management service for distributed renewable energy integration. *IEEE Transactions on Smart Grid*, *6*(6), 2816–2824. doi:10.1109/TSG.2015.2446980

Deng, R., Lu, R., Lai, C., Luan, T. H., & Liang, H. (2016). Optimal workload allocation in fog-cloud computing toward balanced delay and power consumption. *IEEE Internet of Things Journal*, *3*(6), 1171–1181. doi:10.1109/JIOT.2016.2565516

El-Sayed, H., Sankar, S., Prasad, M., Puthal, D., Gupta, A., Mohanty, M., & Lin, C. T. (2018). Edge of things: The big picture on the integration of edge, IoT and the cloud in a distributed computing environment. *IEEE Access: Practical Innovations, Open Solutions*, *6*, 1706–1717. doi:10.1109/ACCESS.2017.2780087

Fan, X., Cui, T., Cao, C., Chen, Q., & Kwak, K. S. (2019). Minimum-Cost Offloading for Collaborative Task Execution of MEC-Assisted Platooning. *Sensors (Basel)*, *19*(4), 847. doi:10.339019040847 PMID:30781710

Favre, L., Robyr, J. L., Gonon, F., & Niederh, E. L. (2018, April). Improvement of the environmental impact of the global energy management of buildings by genetic algorithm optimization. In *2018 5th International Conference on Electric Power and Energy Conversion Systems (EPECS)* (pp. 1-6). IEEE. 10.1109/EPECS.2018.8443522

Guo, Q. (2017). Task scheduling based on ant colony optimization in cloud environment. *International Conference on Computer-aided Design*. AIP Publishing LLC. 10.1063/1.4981635

Hamad, S. A., & Omara, F. A. (2016). Genetic-based task scheduling algorithm in cloud computing environment. *International Journal of Advanced computer Science and Applications, 7*(4), 550-556.

Hoang, D., & Dang, T. D. (2017, August). FBRC: Optimization of task scheduling in fog-based region and cloud. In 2017 IEEE Trustcom/BigDataSE/ICESS (pp. 1109-1114). IEEE.

Huang, L., Feng, X., Feng, A., Huang, Y., & Qian, L. P. (2018). Distributed Deep Learning-based Offloading for Mobile Edge Computing Networks. *Mobile Networks and Applications*, 1–8. doi:10.100711036-018-1177-x

Kaur, K., Garg, S., Aujla, G. S., Kumar, N., Rodrigues, J. J., & Guizani, M. (2018). Edge computing in the industrial internet of things environment: Software-defined-networks-based edge-cloud interplay. *IEEE Communications Magazine, 56*(2), 44–51. doi:10.1109/MCOM.2018.1700622

Keshanchi, B., Souri, A., & Navimipour, N. J. (2017). An improved genetic algorithm for task scheduling in the cloud environments using the priority queues: Formal verification, simulation, and statistical testing. *Journal of Systems and Software, 124*, 1–21. doi:10.1016/j.jss.2016.07.006

Kolomvatsos, K., & Anagnostopoulos, C. (2019). Multi-criteria optimal task allocation at the edge. *Future Generation Computer Systems, 93*, 358–372. doi:10.1016/j.future.2018.10.051

La, Q. D., Ngo, M. V., Dinh, T. Q., Quek, T. Q., & Shin, H. (2018). *Enabling intelligence in fog computing to achieve energy and latency reduction*. Digital Communications and Networks.

Li, J. Q., Yu, F. R., Deng, G., Luo, C., Ming, Z., & Yan, Q. (2017). Industrial internet: A survey on the enabling technologies, applications, and challenges. *IEEE Communications Surveys and Tutorials, 19*(3), 1504–1526. doi:10.1109/COMST.2017.2691349

Li, S., & Huang, J. (2017, December). Energy efficient resource management and task scheduling for IoT services in edge computing paradigm. In *2017 IEEE International Symposium on Parallel and Distributed Processing with Applications and 2017 IEEE International Conference on Ubiquitous Computing and Communications (ISPA/IUCC)* (pp. 846-851). IEEE. 10.1109/ISPA/IUCC.2017.00129

Li, W., You, X., Jiang, Y., Yang, J., & Hu, L. (2019). Opportunistic computing offloading in edge clouds. *Journal of Parallel and Distributed Computing, 123*, 69–76. doi:10.1016/j.jpdc.2018.09.006

Madni, S. H. H., Latiff, M. S. A., Abdullahi, M., & Usman, M. J. (2017). Performance comparison of heuristic algorithms for task scheduling in IaaS cloud computing environment. *PLoS One, 12*(5), e0176321. doi:10.1371/journal.pone.0176321 PMID:28467505

Malik, A., & Om, H. (2018). Cloud computing and internet of things integration: Architecture, applications, issues, and challenges. In *Sustainable Cloud and Energy Services* (pp. 1–24). Springer. doi:10.1007/978-3-319-62238-5_1

Miao, F., Chen, D., & Jin, L. (2017, December). Multi-level PLRU Cache Algorithm for Content Delivery Networks. In *2017 10th International Symposium on Computational Intelligence and Design (ISCID)* (Vol. 1, pp. 320-323). IEEE. 10.1109/ISCID.2017.45

Mourtzis, D., Vlachou, E., & Milas, N. (2016). Industrial Big Data as a result of IoT adoption in manufacturing. *Procedia CIRP, 55*, 290–295. doi:10.1016/j.procir.2016.07.038

Munir, A., Kansakar, P., & Khan, S. U. (2017). *IFCIoT: Integrated Fog Cloud IoT Architectural Paradigm for Future IoTs.* arXiv preprint arXiv:1701.08474

Ning, Z., Kong, X., Xia, F., Hou, W., & Wang, X. (2019). Green and sustainable cloud of things: Enabling collaborative edge computing. *IEEE Communications Magazine, 57*(1), 72–78. doi:10.1109/MCOM.2018.1700895

Panda, S. K., & Jana, P. K. (2015). Efficient task scheduling algorithms for heterogeneous multi-cloud environment. *The Journal of Supercomputing, 71*(4), 1505–1533. doi:10.100711227-014-1376-6

Satyanarayanan, M. (2017). The emergence of edge computing. *Computer, 50*(1), 30–39. doi:10.1109/MC.2017.9

Shao, Y., Li, C., Fu, Z., Jia, L., & Luo, Y. (2019). Cost-effective replication management and scheduling in edge computing. *Journal of Network and Computer Applications, 129*, 46–61. doi:10.1016/j.jnca.2019.01.001

Shi, W., Cao, J., Zhang, Q., Li, Y., & Xu, L. (2016). Edge computing: Vision and challenges. *IEEE Internet of Things Journal, 3*(5), 637–646. doi:10.1109/JIOT.2016.2579198

Singh, P., Dutta, M., & Aggarwal, N. (2017). A review of task scheduling based on meta-heuristics approach in cloud computing. *Knowledge and Information Systems, 52*(1), 1–51. doi:10.100710115-017-1044-2

Song, Y., Yau, S. S., Yu, R., Zhang, X., & Xue, G. (2017, June). An approach to QoS-based task distribution in edge computing networks for IoT applications. In *2017 IEEE International Conference on Edge Computing (EDGE)* (pp. 32-39). IEEE. 10.1109/IEEE.EDGE.2017.50

Tao, X., Ota, K., Dong, M., Qi, H., & Li, K. (2017). Performance guaranteed computation offloading for mobile-edge cloud computing. *IEEE Wireless Communications Letters, 6*(6), 774–777. doi:10.1109/LWC.2017.2740927

Varghese, B., & Buyya, R. (2017). Next generation cloud computing: New trends and research directions. *Future Generation Computer Systems.*

Wang, B., & Li, J. (2016, July). Load balancing task scheduling based on Multi-Population Genetic Algorithm in cloud computing. In *2016 35th Chinese Control Conference (CCC)* (pp. 5261-5266). IEEE. 10.1109/ChiCC.2016.7554174

Wang, T., Wei, X., Liang, T., & Fan, J. (2018). Dynamic tasks scheduling based on weighted bi-graph in Mobile Cloud Computing. *Sustainable Computing: Informatics and Systems, 19*, 214–222. doi:10.1016/j.suscom.2018.05.004

Wei, Y., Pan, L., Liu, S., Wu, L., & Meng, X. (2018). DRL-Scheduling: An Intelligent QoS-Aware Job Scheduling Framework for Applications in Clouds. *IEEE Access: Practical Innovations, Open Solutions, 6*, 55112–55125. doi:10.1109/ACCESS.2018.2872674

Yang, C., Puthal, D., Mohanty, S. P., & Kougianos, E. (2017). Big-sensing-data curation for the cloud is coming: A promise of scalable cloud-data-center mitigation for next-generation IoT and wireless sensor networks. *IEEE Consumer Electronics Magazine, 6*(4), 48–56. doi:10.1109/MCE.2017.2714695

Yang, L., Liu, B., Cao, J., Sahni, Y., & Wang, Z. (2019). Joint computation partitioning and resource allocation for latency sensitive applications in mobile edge clouds. *IEEE Transactions on Services Computing*, 1. doi:10.1109/TSC.2018.2890603

Yewen, H., Hong, W. U., & Yuanshi, W. (2013). *M/m/1 queuing model under non-preemptive limited-priority*. Computer Engineering and Applications.

Yewen, H., Shenfen, K., Yongling, Y., & Chunxia, Y. (2016). M/g/1 queuing model under non-preemptive limited-priority. *Jisuanji Yingyong*.

Yin, L., Luo, J., & Luo, H. (2018). Tasks scheduling and resource allocation in fog computing based on containers for smart manufacturing. *IEEE Transactions on Industrial Informatics*, *14*(10), 4712–4721. doi:10.1109/TII.2018.2851241

Yousefpour, A., Ishigaki, G., & Jue, J. P. (2017, June). Fog computing: Towards minimizing delay in the internet of things. In *2017 IEEE International Conference on Edge Computing (EDGE)* (pp. 17-24). IEEE. 10.1109/IEEE.EDGE.2017.12

Zanzi, L., Giust, F., & Sciancalepore, V. (2018, April). *M 2 EC: A multi-tenant resource orchestration in multi-access edge computing systems. In 2018 IEEE wireless communications and networking conference (wcnc)*. IEEE.

Zeng, D., Gu, L., Guo, S., Cheng, Z., & Yu, S. (2016). Joint optimization of task scheduling and image placement in fog computing supported software-defined embedded system. *IEEE Transactions on Computers*, *65*(12), 3702–3712. doi:10.1109/TC.2016.2536019

Zhang, P., & Zhou, M. (2018). Dynamic cloud task scheduling based on a two-stage strategy. *IEEE Transactions on Automation Science and Engineering*, *15*(2), 772–783. doi:10.1109/TASE.2017.2693688

This research was previously published in the International Journal of Information Technologies and Systems Approach (IJITSA), 14(1); pages 33-61, copyright year 2021 by IGI Publishing (an imprint of IGI Global).

Index

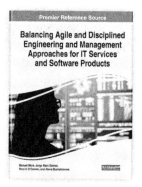

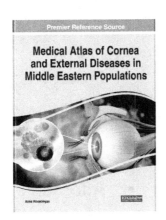
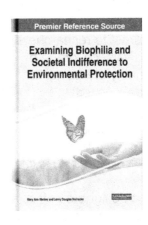
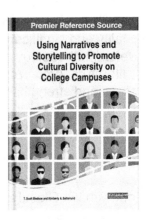

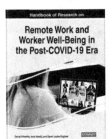
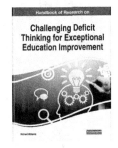

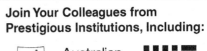

Printed in the United States
by Baker & Taylor Publisher Services